2009

RESTAURANT
GUIDE

This 16th edition published 2008
© Automobile Association Developments Limited 2008.

Please contact
Advertisement Sales: advertisingsales@theaa.com
Editorial Department: lifestyleguides@theaa.com

Cover photographs courtesy of F/C main AA/S Montgomery
F/C bl Orchid Restaurant - Torquay, Chocolate Fondant by Chef Marc Evans, photography by
www.antphoto.au F/C br Tom Aikens, London, photography by Andrew Twort
B/C l Orrery, London, B/C c Inverlochy Castle, Fort William, B/C r Fairlawns Hotel & Spa, Walsall,
photography by Graham Oakes
Photographs in the gazetteer provided by the establishments.
Typeset/Repro: Keenes, Andover
Printed by Trento Srl, Italy.
This directory is compiled by the AA Hotel Services Department; managed in the Librios Information
Management System and generated by the AA establishment database system.

Restaurant descriptions have been contributed by the following team of writers: Cathy Fitzgerald,
Sarah Gilbert, David Hancock, Lindsay Harriss, Felicity Jackson, Julia Hynard, Denise Laing,
Melissa Riley-Jones, Allen Stidwill, Mark Taylor and Andrew Turvil

Published by AA Publishing, a trading name of Automobile Association Developments Limited,
whose registered office is Fanum House, Basing View, Basingstoke, Hampshire RG21 4EA.
Registered number 1878835.
A CIP catalogue for this book is available from the British Library.
ISBN-13: 978-0-7495-5789-8
A03683

Maps prepared by the Mapping Services
Department of The Automobile Association.
Maps © Automobile Association
Developments Limited 2008.

 This product includes
mapping data licensed from
Ordnance Survey® with the permission of the
Controller of Her Majesty's Stationery Office.
© Crown copyright 2008. All rights reserved.
Licence number 100021153.

 This material is Crown Copyright and is
reproduced with the permission of Land
and Property Services under delegated
authority from the Controller of Her Majesty's
Stationery Office,© Crown copyright and database
rights LA59 © Crown copyright 2008.
Permit number 80035.

© Ordnance Survey Ireland/Government of Ireland.
Copyright Permit No. MP000108

Information on National Parks in England provided
by the Countryside Agency
(Natural England).
Information on National Parks in Scotland provided
by Scottish Natural Heritage.
Information on National Parks in Wales provided by
The Countryside Council for Wales.

Contents

How to Use the Guide

1 MAP REFERENCE

The atlas section at the back of the Guide. The map page number is followed by the National Grid Reference. To find a location, read the first figure horizontally and the second figure vertically within the lettered square. For Central London and Greater London, there is an 13-page map section starting on page 224.

2 PLACE NAME

Restaurants are listed in country and county order, then by town and then alphabetically within the town. There is an index by restaurant at the back of the book and a similar one for the Central & Greater London sections on pages 220-223.

3 RESTAURANT NAME

4 ⊚ THE AA ROSETTE AWARD

Main entries have been awarded one or more Rosettes, up to a maximum of five. See p6.

5 FOOD STYLE

Food style of the restaurant is followed by a short summary statement.

6 PHOTOGRAPHS

Restaurants are invited to enhance their entry with up to two photographs.

7 CHEF(S) AND OWNER(S)

The names of the chef(s) and owner(s) are as up-to-date as possible at the time of going to press, but changes in personnel often occur, and may affect both the style and quality of the restaurant.

8 PRICES

Prices are for fixed lunch (2 courses) and dinner (3 courses) and à la carte dishes. Service charge information (see also opposite). Note: Prices quoted are a guide only, and are subject to change.

---

2 | **MERSEYSIDE**
LIVERPOOL   MAP 3 F4 | **1**
See also **Wirral**
20
3 | **Harvey's Restaurant**
21
4 | ⊚ ⊚ Modern British V ♦ⁿ♨ 🐚 🖥 | **18**

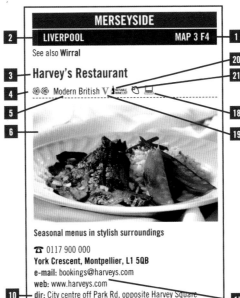

Seasonal menus in stylish surroundings

☎ 0117 900 000
York Crescent, Montpellier, L1 5QB
e-mail: bookings@harveys.com
web: www.harveys.com
10 | **dir:** City centre off Park Rd, opposite Harvey Square | **17**

An idyllic retreat, this Georgian property is set amid 16 acres of countryside, offering elegant accommodation, impressive leisure facilities and a popular bar serving informal meals. The serious dining takes place in the elegant restaurant, from a menu reflecting both British and European trends. Specialities include tempura of king prawns with aubergines, balanced by a robust main course of braised shoulder of lamb in a sauce of Oakham's beer with dauphinoise potatoes, or pan-fried monkfish with crab croquette, mussels and spinach. Finish with a trio of banana, including a pannacotta, crumble and tart, washed down with a recommended pudding wine. | **16**

7 | **Chef** Tom Smith **Owners** Davidson Partners
8 | **Times** 12-12/7/10, Closed Sun L Sat, 1 wk Feb, 2 wks Aug BHs **Prices** Fixed D £15, Starter £3.50-£5, Main
9 | £6.50-£12.50, Dessert £4.50-£6. Service added but optional **Wine** 10 bottles over £20, 5 bottles under £20, 8 by the glass (£5-£7) **Notes** Vegetarian menu | **15** | **14**
13 | **Seats** 60, Pr/dining room 40 **Children** Portions | **12**
11 | **Parking** NCP Park Road

9 NOTES

Additional information e.g. availability of vegetarian dishes, civil weddings, air conditioning etc.

10 DIRECTIONS

Directions are given if supplied.

---

11 PARKING DETAILS

12 CHILDREN

Menu, portions, age restrictions etc.

13 NUMBER OF SEATS

Number of seats in the restaurant, followed by private dining room (Pr/dining room).

14 NUMBER OF WINES

Number of wines under and over £20, and available by the glass.

15 DAILY OPENING AND CLOSING TIMES

Daily opening and closing times, the days of the week it is closed and seasonal closures. Note that opening times are liable to change without notice. It is wise to telephone in advance.

16 DESCRIPTION

Description of the restaurant and the food.

17 E-MAIL ADDRESS AND WEBSITE

18 🖥 TOPTABLE

Online Booking Service, see right.

19 VEGETARIAN MENU

V Indicates a vegetarian menu. Restaurants with some vegetarian dishes available are indicated under Notes.

20 NOTABLE WINE LIST

♦ⁿ♨ Indicates notable wine list (See p14-15).

21 LOCAL AND REGIONAL PRODUCE

🐚 Indicates the use of local and regional produce. More than 50% of the restaurant food ingredients are produced within a 50-mile radius. Suppliers are mentioned by name on the menu.

All establishments take major credit cards, except where we have specified otherwise.

All information is correct at the time of print but may change without notice. Details of opening times and prices may be omitted from an entry when the establishment has not supplied us with up-to-date information. This is indicated where the establishment name is shown in *italics*.

Service Charge

We ask restaurants the following questions about service charge: (their responses appear under Prices in each entry.)

- Is service included in the meal price, with no further charge added or expected?
- Is service optional – charge not automatically added to bill?
- Is service charge compulsory, and what percentage?

- Is there a service charge for larger groups, minimum number in group, and what percentage?

Many establishments automatically add service charge to the bill but tell the customer it is optional.

Smoking Regulations

From July 2007 smoking was banned in all public places in the United Kingdom and Ireland. A hotel or guest accommodation proprietor can designate one or more bedrooms with ventilation systems where the occupants can smoke, but communal areas must be smoke-free. Communal areas include the interior bars and restaurants in pubs and inns.

Facilities for Disabled Guests

The Disability Discrimination Act (access to Goods and Services) means that service providers may have to consider making adjustments to their premises. For further information see disability.gov. uk/dda. The establishments in this Guide

should all be aware of their responsibilities under the Act. Always phone in advance to ensure that the establishment you have chosen has appropriate facilities. See also holidaycare.org.uk.

Website Addresses

Where website addresses are included they have been supplied and specified by the respective establishment. Such websites are not under the control of The Automobile Association Developments Limited and as such The Automobile Association Developments Limited has no control over them and will not accept any responsibility or liability in respect of any and all matters whatsoever relating to such websites including access, content, material and functionality. By including the addresses of third-party websites the AA does not intend to solicit business or offer any security to any person in any country, directly or indirectly.

toptable.co.uk
free online restaurant & party booking

Online Restaurant Booking Service

We continue our relationship with toptable, Europe's largest online booking service. During 2008 they seated over 1.6 million diners. Readers of the AA Restaurant Guide will be able to take advantage of their experience and expertise with free online booking and hundreds of great offers. As you read through the Guide you'll see that some establishments feature the 'computer' symbol which indicates that they are bookable online.
All you have to do is log onto the AA website, www.theAA. com, and follow the links through to the restaurant pages. Enter the restaurant name, and, if it's bookable online, you'll see the BOOK NOW! button. Click on this and you'll be able to make bookings 24 hours a day, as well as using the unique features, including 360° images, to give you a real feel for the style of the place.

Register to use the service and you'll receive the very latest special offers by email.

Neighbourhood Restaurants

We've also included some neighbourhood restaurants which are bookable online. They have the computer symbol too, and you can find them in the same way as above or use the website address quoted in their entry.

Please note - it is possible that during the currency of the Guide more restaurants will sign up for the online booking service, and also that some, due to change of hands or other reasons, may withdraw.

How the AA Assesses for Rosette Awards

The AA's Rosette award scheme was the first nationwide scheme for assessing the quality of food served by restaurants and hotels. The Rosette scheme is an award, not a classification, and although there is necessarily an element of subjectivity when it comes to assessing taste, we aim for a consistent approach throughout the UK. Our awards are made solely on the basis of a meal visit or visits by one or more of our hotel and restaurant Inspectors, who have an unrivalled breadth and depth of experience in assessing quality. They award Rosettes annually on a rising scale of one to five.

So what makes a restaurant worthy of a Rosette Award?

For our Inspectors, the top and bottom line is the food. The taste of a dish is what counts, and whether it successfully delivers to the diner the promise of the menu. A restaurant is only as good as its worst meal. Although presentation and competent service should be appropriate to the style of the restaurant and the quality of the food, they cannot affect the Rosette assessment as such, either up or down. The summaries below indicate what our Inspectors look for, but are intended only as guidelines. The AA is constantly reviewing its award criteria, and competition usually results in an all-round improvement in standards, so it becomes increasingly difficult for restaurants to reach award level. For more detailed Rosette criteria, please visit www.theAA.com.

⍟ One Rosette

- Excellent restaurants that stand out in their local area
- Food prepared with care, understanding and skill
- Good quality ingredients

Around 50% of restaurants have one Rosette.

⍟⍟ Two Rosettes

- The best local restaurants
- Higher standards
- Better consistency
- Greater precision apparent in the cooking
- Obvious attention to the quality and selection of ingredients

About 40% of restaurants have two Rosettes.

⍟⍟⍟ Three Rosettes

- Outstanding restaurants demanding recognition well beyond local area
- Selection and sympathetic treatment of highest quality ingredients
- Timing, seasoning and judgement of flavour combinations consistent
- Excellent intelligent service and a well-chosen wine list

Around 10% of restaurants have three Rosettes.

⍟⍟⍟⍟ Four Rosettes

Dishes demonstrate:

- intense ambition
- a passion for excellence
- superb technical skills
- remarkable consistency
- appreciation of culinary traditions combined with desire for exploration and improvement
- Cooking demands national recognition

Twenty-six restaurants have four Rosettes.

⍟⍟⍟⍟⍟ Five Rosettes

- Cooking stands comparison with the best in the world
- Highly individual
- Breathtaking culinary skills
- Setting the standards to which others aspire
- Knowledgeable and distinctive wine list

Seven restaurants have five Rosettes.

AA Lifetime Achievement Award 2008–2009

Rick STEIN

Rick Stein's enduring passion for fresh, high-quality fish and seafood has been the driving force behind the thriving and exceptional businesses he has built over the past 33 years.

The Seafood Restaurant (page 82) in the small North Cornwall village of Padstow epitomises his philosophy.

Since opening in 1975, this 3-Rosette restaurant has grown from a simple seaside bistro into an award-winning internationally acclaimed restaurant with a reputation for imaginative cooking that draws on the very finest, freshest fish and seafood that comes straight from the day boats across the harbour to the kitchen door.

Over the years other equally inspirational and successful ventures have followed: St Petroc's Bistro (page 82), Rick Stein's Café and Stein's Fish & Chips, not to mention a delicatessen, patisserie, hotel, and a cookery school that covers every aspect of seafood cookery. As well as heightening the profile of Padstow and Cornwall, these businesses have also raised the profile of the West Country as a tourism and food destination. As a result, a number of other talented chefs have been encouraged to move to the area and have further enriched the region with the development of new high-quality restaurants.

Having made a number of TV cookery programmes focusing exclusively on fish and shellfish, in the first series of *Food Heroes* Rick Stein demonstrated that he is equally passionate about all produce by embarking on a gastronomic pilgrimage around the UK to seek out the very best food producers in Britain and Ireland. His more recent programmes have concentrated on food from Southern France and the Mediterranean. Alongside the TV series he has written a number of best-selling and award-winning cookery books, including *Fruits of the Sea*, *Seafood Odyssey*, and *Rick Stein's Seafood* which has become the acknowledged reference book on the subject. Highly accessible, they contain a number of recipes based on simple cooking that appeal to the way most of us cook.

It is hard to think of anyone who has done more to increase the popularity and understanding of fish and seafood, not only to the general public but to the hospitality industry as a whole. Rick Stein's outstanding contribution to widening the understanding and appreciation of excellent food and drink in Britain through his work as a chef, teacher, presenter and author has been recognised with numerous awards, including the Glenfiddich Trophy in 2001 and an OBE for services to West Country tourism in 2003. He has also cooked for numerous prime ministers and Queen Elizabeth and Prince Philip.

Rick Stein divides his time between Cornwall, London and Australia and is currently filming a TV series in Asia where he is exploring the cuisine of Vietnam, Cambodia and Malaysia.

'Nothing is more joyful or exhilarating than fresh fish simply cooked'.

AA Restaurants of the Year

Potential Restaurants of the Year are nominated by our team of full-time Inspectors based on their routine visits. In selecting a Restaurant of the Year, we look for somewhere that is exceptional in its chosen area of the market. Whilst the Rosette awards are based on the quality of the food alone, Restaurants of the Year takes into account all aspects of the experience.

ENGLAND

THE ROYAL OAK AT PALEY STREET
MAIDENHEAD, BERKSHIRE
PAGE 48 ◎ ◎

This whitewashed pub south of Maidenhead has celebrity connections, being owned by Nick Parkinson, son of famed TV presenter Michael Parkinson. There's an unstuffy, traditional feel to the interior though, with oak beams and timbers, polished-wood floors and a blazing log fire. The uncluttered dining area is an informal, white-linen-free zone, with well-styled contemporary furniture and original artwork, while hospitality and service is appropriately welcoming and attentive, headed up by Mo Gherras El Goum. With classical roots, head chef Dominic Chapman (previously at Heston Blumenthal's Hinds Head in Bray) creates modern twists to some well known dishes. Quality ingredients and seasonality drive his regularly-changing menu. The real strength of this property, apart from wonderful food, great service, warm hospitality and delightful relaxed surroundings, is the fact that it is accessible to everyone, providing good value for money.

LONDON

SCOTT'S
LONDON W1
PAGE 306 ◎ ◎

Dating back to 1851, this legendary fish restaurant - relaunched by Caprice Holdings (the people behind The Ivy, Le Caprice and J. Sheekey, see entries) - sees it return to its past glories in great style. The contemporary, fashionable remix of this classic oak-panelled restaurant comes inspired by its heyday, with rich burgundy-leather seating, an exquisite chandelier, specially commissioned modern art and a central crustacea bar in the style of a turn-of-the-century cruise liner. There's a doorman to greet, while table service is slick, attentive and polished. The kitchen uses top-notch ingredients in well-presented dishes, such as baked spider crab, skate wing with nut brown butter, or sautéed lamb sweetbreads with broad beans and mint. Scott's is many people's favourite London restaurant as the menu suits all pockets, the wine list is excellent and all the staff are friendly, helpful and knowledgeable.

SCOTLAND

THE KITCHIN
EDINBURGH
PAGE 498 ⊛⊛⊛

The Kitchin is home to Edinburgh-born chef-patron, Tom Kitchin, whose impressive CV includes stints in the lofty kitchens of the likes of Pierre Koffmann in London and Alain Ducasse and Guy Savoy in France (Tom also appeared on BBC Two's 'Great British Menu' TV series in 2008). Set on Leith's rejuvenated waterfront, The Kitchin was once a whisky distillery and has a fine outlook on to the smart maritime piazza and stylish waterfront houses. It's a delightful modern dining venue, with stylish grey décor, original stone pillars and high-quality furniture, together with a feature window offering views of the kitchen at work. Simple table appointments, soft lighting, highly comfortable leather seating and refreshingly informal but attentive and knowledgeable service complete the understated but upbeat package. Meanwhile, the slick, modern cooking from a dedicated team showcases a successful marriage of fresh, seasonal quality Scottish produce and classical French technique. From 'nature to plate' is Tom's strapline and cooking philosophy here. It's ambitious with impressive presentation to create a focal point on every plate.

WALES

WALNUT TREE INN
ABERGAVENNY, MONMOUTHSHIRE
PAGE 562 ⊛⊛⊛

The Walnut Tree forever has a place in the culinary lexicon. For nearly forty years Franco Taruschio's cooking represented the best of ingredient-led, seasonally-inspired, simple food. He's been gone for eight years and the restaurant has had its up-and-downs since then. Until now. Shaun Hill is a man with a big reputation, not based on ego or acts of culinary showmanship, but on being an excellent chef, and now he's back at the stoves, hands-on, getting down and dirty. The location among the Black Mountains doesn't change and is as beautiful as ever but the building itself has been smartened up and given a lick of cream paint. The bar provides a central focus and the dining room is simply and unpretentiously decorated in muted colours. The staff are well informed about the menu and their friendly and positive attitude creates confidence all round. Shaun's menu is based around superb produce and a sure hand is evident in the delivery. Scallop tartare with scallop wonton fritters sits alongside mussel and cockle pie among starters, while main-course saddle of rabbit includes the liver and kidneys. This restaurant genuinely suits all, with a relaxed atmosphere, enjoyable simple yet impressive food and very reasonable prices.

AA Chefs' Chef 2008-2009

This is the annual poll of all the chefs in The Restaurant Guide. Around 2,000 of the country's top chefs were asked to vote to recognise the achievements of one of their peers from a shortlist chosen by the AA's team of Inspectors.

Philip Howard

This year's AA Chefs' Chef Award goes to 41-year-old Philip Howard, head chef of modern French-style restaurant The Square in Mayfair, and also co-owner with Nigel Platts-Martin

The Square (page 308) first opened its doors in King Street, St James's in December 1991 and received four Rosettes in 1998 when the restaurant moved to Bruton Street. In addition, Philip Howard has amassed a host of awards and accolades over the years, including the prestigious Catey Award for Chef of the Year in 1999 and the Guild of Chefs' Chef of the Year award in 2005.

A quiet and thoughtful culinary professional, Philip first discovered his passion for cooking at the University of Kent where he studied microbiology. After spending a summer cooking in the Dordogne region of France, his career took a new direction when he returned to London to take up an apprenticeship at Roux Restaurants Ltd headed by Albert Roux OBE. He went on to spend a further year under Marco Pierre White at the legendary Harvey's, and was later under Simon Hopkinson at Bibendum.

Philip's distinctive style of classically-based modern French cuisine has evolved and progressed with experience, but his unique understanding of cooking, food chemistry and ingredients is instinctive. With exemplary attention to detail and a firm emphasis on simplicity and flavour, he uses the finest seasonal ingredients to create immaculately presented, elegant yet satisfying dishes that are perfectly portioned, timed and seasoned.

His exacting standards in the kitchen are complemented by an equally dedicated front-of-house team.

A firm believer in the importance of staff and professional development, Philip is a well respected mentor who has spent much of his career nurturing young chefs and encouraging them to experiment and think about different ways of cooking. An inspiration to young people in the industry, he remains

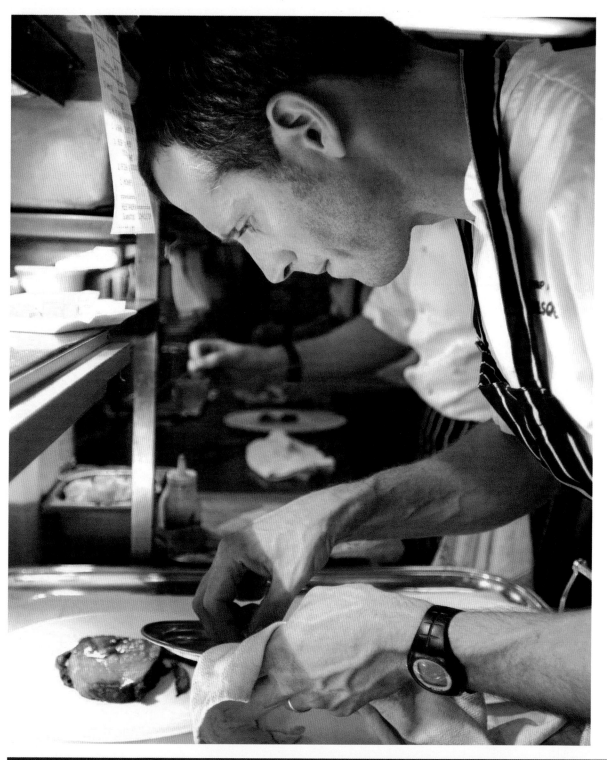

actively involved in culinary competitions and events. His second restaurant in partnership with Nigel Platts-Martin - The Ledbury (3 Rosettes, page 323) in Notting Hill - is a showcase for his protégé Brett Graham. The restaurant received its Rosettes within a year of opening in November 2005 and continues to go from strength to strength.

Philip attributes his success to creating an understated environment that is focused on providing sincere hospitality and a style of cooking that keeps people coming back for more. Characteristically self-effacing, he finds the AA Chefs' Chef award very humbling.

'I think it's fair to say that we chefs find intense scrutiny under the judgement of our peers.'

Menu

Roast Isles of Orkney scallops with morels, pea purée and white asparagus foam

Salad of smoked haddock, white asparagus, leek hearts and mousserons with a soft boiled egg and grain mustard

Steamed fillet of brill with pea and mint raviolis and an emulsion of asparagus and mousseron

Warm roasted pear with tiramisù, Dulce de Leche ice cream and salted caramel nougatine

'An award like this is a huge endorsement of what we do.'

Previous Winners

Michael Caines MBE
Gidlleigh Park, Chagford, Devon p122

Andrew Fairlie
Andrew Fairlie @ Gleneagles, Scotland p531

Germain Schwab
Winteringham Fields (former chef), Lincolnshire

Raymond Blanc
Le Manoir aux Quat' Saisons, Great Milton, Oxfordshire p363

Shaun Hill
Walnut Tree Inn, Abergavenny, Monmouthshire, Wales p562

Heston Blumenthal
The Fat Duck, Bray, Berkshire p44

Jean-Christophe Novelli
A Touch of Novelli at The White Horse, Harpenden, Hertfordshire p193

Gordon Ramsay
Restaurant Gordon Ramsay, London SW3 p271

Rick Stein
The Seafood Restaurant, Padstow, Cornwall p82

Marco Pierre White
Marco Pierre White's Yew Tree Inn, Highclere, Hampshire, p182

Kevin Viner

AA Wine Awards

The AA Wine Award

This year's AA Wine Awards sponsored by T&W wines attracted a very large response with over 1,000 entries. Three national winners were chosen – Ransome's Dock, London, England; The Strathearn, The Gleneagles Hotel, Scotland; and The Crown at Whitebrook, Wales. Ransome's Dock was the Overall Winner, and one of their wine team wins an all expenses paid trip to Willi Opitz's vineyards at Illmitz in Austria's Burgenland.

All 2,000 or so Rosetted restaurants in last year's Guide were invited to submit their wine lists. From these, the panel selected a shortlist of around 160 establishments who are highlighted in the Guide with the Notable Wine List symbol.

The shortlisted establishments were then asked to choose wines from their list (within a budget of £70 per bottle) to accompany a menu designed by Pierre Gagnaire; consultant master chef for Sketch (Lecture Room and Library), London, the 2008 England and Overall Winner.

The final judging panel included Simon Numphud, AA Hotel Services Manager, Frederick, head sommelier at Sketch (last year's winner), Fiona Sims, an independent wine journalist and Trevor Hughes, who is our wine sponsor. Judges comments on the three winning wine lists included the following. Ransome's Dock "a list full of passion and interest, both original and practical, great choices throughout that will appeal to all interested in wine", The Crown at Whitebrook "strong selections including a mix of classic and up-and-coming wines gets you moving around the list with great enthusiasm", The Strathearn at The Gleneagles Hotel "excellent presentation, good selections throughout and interesting choices by the glass".

Other lists that reached the final consideration and stood out included The Felin Fach Griffin in Brecon with an imaginative selection of wines, The Three Chimneys in Colbost, Skye for an all round great list, Old Bridge Hotel in Huntingdon for a list full of passion and great tasting notes and Perry's Restaurant in Weymouth for an unusual and exciting list.

Notable Wine Lists

So what makes a wine list notable? Clearly we want to see high-quality wines, with diversity/coverage across grapes and/or countries and style, and the best individual growers and vintages. The list should be well presented, ideally with some helpful notes and, to reflect the demand from diners, a good choice of wines by the glass. What upsets the judges are spelling errors, wines under incorrect regions, lack of vintage information, split vintages, lazy purchasing (all the wines from a country from just one grower or negociant) and confusing layout. Sadly, many restaurants still provide ill-considered wine lists.

To reach the final shortlist, we look for a real passion for wine, which should come across to the diner, a fair pricing policy (depending on the style of restaurant), an interesting coverage (not necessarily a large list), which might include a specialism, such as sherries or different-sized bottles.

The AA Wine Awards are sponsored by T&W Wines Ltd, 5 Station Way, Brandon Suffolk, IP27 0BH, Tel: 01842 814414 email: contact@tw-wines.com web: www.tw-wines.com

Ransome's Dock - Winning Wine Selection

Menu	Wine selection	Price
Canapés	Proseccodi Conegliano Valdobbiadene Extra-dry, Gianluca Frassinelli, NV	£20 per bottle
Appetiser – Eel and foie gras terrine, beetroot mustard, fresh figs and vinegar	Eitelsbacher Karthauserhofberg Feinherbspatlese 2004, Runer	£27 per bottle
Starter – Grilled and poached fillet of cod, glazed with an olive oil and honey dressing, roasted ceps, diced baby mackerel with cider and black olive jus	Neudorf 'Toms Block' Pinot Noir 2005, Nelson, NZ	£29.50 per bottle
Main course – Peppered fillet of deer and juniper, pear chutney, celeriac and horseradish cream, aloe vera sauce	Cornas 'Vieillesvignes' 1997, Alain Voge, Rhône	£45 per bottle
Cheese – Munster cheese with grape jelly with Vieux Marc, Ewe cheese ice cream parfait and fresh walnuts, salted crispy turnips	Jasnières Les Rosiers 2002, Domaine de Bellivière	£33 per bottle
Dessert – Mini Paris-Brest, a traditional French dessert with hazelnut paste, choux pastry and hazelnut	Vin de Constance 2001 Klein Constantia, S.A.	£46 per bottle
Coffee and Petits Fours	Digestif: Fernando de Castilla Solera Gran Reserva Brandy de Jerez	£5 per measure

WINNER FOR ENGLAND AND OVERALL WINNER

ⓐⓐ
Ransome's Dock
London SW11 Page 279

Ransome's Dock - located in a former ice cream factory overlooking the Thames close to Albert Bridge - has a loyal following and a reputation for serving good organic and seasonal food. With its cornflower blue walls and modern food-and-wine related artwork, this friendly, relaxed venue is unpretentious and informal, with snacks and coffees available in the bar area, while the outside terrace is the place to sit when the weather allows. The sourcing of quality, seasonal produce - much of it organic - is paramount to the kitchen's success, along with a spectacular wine list.

Judges' comments: A list full of passion and interest, both original and practical, great choices throughout that will appeal to all interested in wine.

WINNER FOR SCOTLAND

ⓐⓐ
The Strathearn, The Gleneagles Hotel
Auchterarder, Perth & Kinross Page 530

Residing in the world-renowned resort and conference hotel of Gleneagles, The Strathearn restaurant is a stronghold of sheer elegance and classic dining. The massive, grand ballroom-style room, complete with high ceilings, pillars and even a pianist playing, provides an impressively sophisticated setting. Classical dishes are given a contemporary slant on the seasonal menu, while service, by a whole brigade of staff, is formal but by no means stuffy and helps make the occasion memorable, especially with the showpiece carving and flambé trolleys and exceptional wine list.

Judges' comments: Excellent presentation, good selections throughout and interesting choices by the glass.

WINNER FOR WALES

ⓐⓐ
Crown at Whitebrook
Whitebrook, Monmouthshire Page 563

Situated in the heart of the Wye Valley Area of Outstanding Natural Beauty, the Crown at Whitebrook may be off the beaten track, but is well worth seeking out. This carefully renovated 17th-century drover's inn retains many original features, like old beams (although now whitewashed with lime ash), but the minimalist décor, elegantly dressed tables and original artwork create a fresh, contemporary feel. Service is attentive and friendly. The memorable menu, with bold interpretations of modern British ideas, is underpinned by a classical French theme, and the intelligent use of fresh, local ingredients produces some exhilarating results.

Judges' comments: Strong selections including a mix of classic and up-and-coming wines get you moving around the list with great enthusiasm.

Celebrity Chef Jean-Christophe Novelli

CELEBRITY
Gastro-Pubs
By Mark Taylor

It used to be retired sportsmen who ended up running pubs, but these days you are more likely to see the name of a well-known celebrity chef above the door than that of an ex-footballer or cricketer living off their memories and anecdotes.

In the past few years, the rise of the celebrity chef - by which I mean chefs who have gone on to successful careers beyond the kitchen - has coincided with the rise of the gastro-pub. A phenomenon which is widely regarded as starting in 1991 with Mike Belben and David Eyre's London pub The Eagle, there are now hundreds of pubs offering restaurant-quality food up and down the country.

Drink-driving and the smoking ban have conspired to make food the only serious option for many pubs in the country and a number of notable chefs - many of them from London - have spotted the potential by moving out to the provinces and turning run-down boozers into destination food pubs.

Celebrity chefs have also been quick to notice this growing trend of gastro-pubs and rather than opening restaurants, a number of the most high-profile chefs have turned their attention to pubs. Gordon Ramsay, Heston Blumenthal, Marco Pierre White, Antony Worrall Thompson and Jean-Christophe Novelli

are five of the biggest names in the chef world and they all have gastro-pubs of some note.

Ramsay opened The Narrow (page 239) in London's Lime house area in 2007 and followed it with The Devonshire (page 315) in Chiswick and The Warrington in Maida Vale. He plans to open more pubs in the future.

Heston Blumenthal has the highly acclaimed Hinds Head, just a few doors away from his world-famous The Fat Duck (page 45) restaurant, and Marco Pierre White's Yew Tree Inn (page 182) pub in Highclere, Hampshire, has built up a formidable reputation, with many of the chef's signature dishes on the menu.

Keith Floyd

But let us not forget that they have entered the pub world almost two decades after another well-known celebrity chef pipped them to the post. One only has to watch the re-runs of Keith Floyd's 1980s TV cookery shows to see that he was well ahead of the

game when it comes to being a celebrity chef. In many ways, he wrote the book. Not only did Floyd create the template for lively, informative and exciting food programmes, but he also opened a food-led pub in Devon as far back as 1988 - three years before so-called gastro-pubs were even 'invented'.

The Maltsers Arms - or 'Floyd's Inn (Sometimes)', as it was dubbed by the locals - was arguably the first ever gastro-pub, a fact that seems to have been overlooked by the celebrity chefs-turned-landlords of today. Looking back at it now, Floyd's pub bore a striking resemblance to the gastro-pubs of today. There was a snug where the locals could drink real ale and nibble on sandwiches, pork pies and pickled eggs, an open kitchen and a bistro-style restaurant. At The Maltsers Arms, there were no tablecloths, no bookings and a fixed-price menu of daily-changing dishes, mainly of Floyd's signature dishes - coq au vin, jugged hare, paella and so on.

Below: TV Chef Antony Worrall Thompson and one of his gastro-pubs Opposite: Mike Robinson outside The Pot Kiln.

"Having had a lot of experience in the restaurant business, I did not want the pub to be a restaurant per se," wrote Floyd in his colourful autobiography, *Out Of the Frying Pan.*

"I wanted a place where farmers and fishermen could walk in with their muddy boots and have a pint, eat a lovely fresh doorstep Dart salmon and mayonnaise sandwich or a hot, properly made British sausage at the bar with pickled eggs and pickled onions etc."

Although Floyd cooked for much of the time at The Maltsers Arms between filming commitments (unlike the celebrity chefs of today), he eventually employed a young, fresh-faced French chef by the name of Jean-Christophe Novelli. Novelli worked for Floyd as the chef-manager of the pub for a short time before opening his first restaurant, Provence, in Lymington, Hampshire.

Jean-Christophe Novelli

Since then, Novelli has become one of the most successful chefs in Britain, working at Four Seasons Hotel, Maison Novelli and Auberge du Lac at Brocket Hall. He now runs a very popular Cooking Academy, but also owns two gastro-pubs - the White Horse in Harpenden, Hertfordshire, and The French Horn in Steppingley, Bedfordshire. Novelli is one of a growing number of A-list celebrity chefs with an interest in pubs and the more relaxed, informal way of dining they offer. He also enjoys the flexibility of pubs as they are places where more rustic, less showy food can really shine.

"I think you are guaranteed to be more relaxed in a pub." he told a journalist when he took over The White Horse. "I'm doing a lot of things I would not have permitted myself before."
In Novelli's pubs, you can still order real ale at the bar, but in the restaurant, the food is more akin to a small French bistro with rustic dishes such as stuffed pigs' trotters or oxtail braised with liquorice.

Antony Worrall Thompson

Another celebrity chef who has a growing interest in village pubs is Antony Worrall Thompson. For him, it's as much about serving simple, "less poncy" food as it is saving community pubs. Worrall Thompson also has two pubs - The Lamb at Satwell and The Greyhound at Rotherfield Peppard, both in Oxfordshire. They both offer unpretentious, affordable food and local real ales. A typical menu could include Hungarian goulash, fillet steak au poivre and chocolate mousse.

"So many pubs are closing every month, that I think it's important us chefs save the demise of the local pub," says Worrall Thompson. "By making it a food-led operation, you still retain the drinking side which is really important. I don't like

it when food pubs take away the drinking side.

"It's important to retain the drinking side and keep your locals happy. I also think it's important to have some very normal food, like Marco has done at the Yew Tree and Heston has done at the Hinds Head. It may be slightly expensive normal food, but it's fantastic."

Pub Chef magazine

Jo Bruce is editor of the monthly pub trade magazine Pub Chef, which has charted the rise and rise of gastro-pubs over the past few years. She says that the arrival of celebrity chefs on the scene has been good for the pub industry. "Generally, it has been a positive thing, as it is a ringing endorsement of the improvement in quality in pub food in the last decade, especially now that the likes of Gordon Ramsay and Heston Blumenthal want to be part of the pub scene. Their pub food menus are more accessible to many consumers than their restaurant menus."

"The increasing involvement of celebrity chefs in the pub market has put pubs on people's agendas as good places to go out for all types of meal occasions, from a bar snack to fine dining, and they have increased consumer interest in eating out in pubs."

If there is a downside to big name chefs running local pubs, it is because too many people expect them to be cooking, or at least on the premises. With their busy schedules and other commitments, it may be unrealistic to expect your meal to be cooked by a TV chef, but Jo Bruce thinks they should sometimes be a little more hands-on than they are.

"Celebrity chefs are more advisors than actively involved in their pub businesses, which is to be expected, but it is a shame

that their involvement is so limited as their name is the reason people go there and some consumers will find it misleading that they aren't more actively involved."

"Wouldn't it be fantastic to see Gordon Ramsay behind the bar pulling a pint in one of his pubs!"

It's All About Saving Local Pubs

Antony Worrall Thompson can often be spotted in his two pubs, although he is well aware of the fact that some people are wary of celebrity chef landlords.

"When we were about to open The Lamb at Satwell, I read a few local websites and there were some comments like 'oh, we've got some flash git coming down from London and he'll do this and that to the pub'. I responded by telling them that we're doing real ales at competitive prices and we're doing some normal food. At the end of the day, I want to save local pubs and serve good food and local beer."

CELEBRITY CHEF PUBS

Gordon Ramsay:
The Narrow, Limehouse (page 239),
The Devonshire, Chiswick (page 315),
The Warrington, Maida Vale
Heston Blumenthal:
The Hinds Head, Bray, Berkshire
(page 45)
Marco Pierre White:
The Yew Tree Inn, Highclere,
Hampshire (page 182)
Antony Worrall Thompson:
The Greyhound, Rotherfield Peppard,
Oxon; The Lamb, Satwell, Oxon
Jean-Christophe Novelli:
A Touch of Novelli at The White
Horse, Harpenden, Hertfordshire
(page 193); The French Horn,
Steppingley, Bedfordshire
Mike Robinson:
The Pot Kiln, Frilsham, Yattendon,
Berkshire (page 47)

LOOK WHO'S COOKING

at the AA Centenary Awards 2008

By Andrew Turvil

In 1908 Robert Baden-Powell started the Boy Scout movement. In 1908 London held the IV Olympic Games, the one famous for the dramatic collapse of Italian marathon runner Dorando Pietri. In 1908 British eccentric Harry Bensley set off on a round-the-world trip pushing a pram and wearing a knight's helmet; the facts are a little sketchy as to whether he actually made it, but it seems unlikely. And 1908 saw the AA come to the rescue of the British public with the founding of AA Hotel Services, a unique and original idea to provide information for the increasingly mobile population on where to eat and sleep around the country, the details published in the AA Handbook.

The famous AA sign started to appear outside hotels in towns and villages across the country and weary travellers could pull in and expect a comfortable bed and good lunch (dinner wasn't a requirement at that time). The first AA Guide to Hotels and Restaurants was published in 1967, giving more detailed descriptions of the establishments.

One hundred years after those pioneering steps into hotel and restaurant assessments, the AA is an institution: a trusted source of knowledge and information through both its website and a comprehensive range of guide books. It inspects and recommends over 6,500 establishments across the country and its

classification criteria, in line with those of the tourist boards of England, Scotland and Wales, is respected in the industry and trusted by the traveller.

To celebrate the landmark 100 years, the AA Centenary Awards 2008 at the Grosvenor House Hotel will be an especially grand event. Five chefs who hold the coveted Five Rosettes in the 2009 AA Restaurant Guide will be cooking for their peers, producing a meal which will doubtless be expected to impress, to dazzle, to leave a lasting impression. No pressure then. The five chefs are Tom Aikens, Raymond Blanc, David Nicholls, Chris Staines and Marcus Wareing.

Raymond Blanc at work in the kitchen

TOM AIKENS opened his eponymous restaurant in Chelsea in 2003, and set about wowing the capital with his own brand of inventive and dynamic cooking. The presentation of his dishes is always impressive, often original, and Tom is a chef who is willing to swim against the tide. After a career in top London restaurants such as La Tante Claire and Pied à Terre, Tom is undoubtedly one of the top chefs cooking in the UK today. Roast scallops with crushed celeriac, poached chicken wings and celeriac horseradish soup is a dish from his Tasting Menu which shows his style – but will it make it onto the Centenary Awards Menu?

RAYMOND BLANC has been a major figure in the UK restaurant scene for twenty-five years. Le Manoir aux Quat' Saisons has been his passion since 1984 and it remains amongst the very top restaurants in the country. Le Manoir's menus are based around classical French cooking, the touch is light, flavour to the fore, and there's a wonderful children's menu for the next generation of gourmets. Raymond has been championing organic, seasonal and local food for decades and much of the vegetables, salad leaves, fruits and herbs that tantalise his customers with their freshness and flavour have been grown in the hotel's two-acre garden. Will the fruits of his garden be featuring at the Centenary Awards?

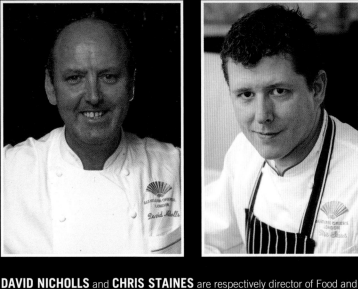

DAVID NICHOLLS and **CHRIS STAINES** are respectively director of Food and Beverage and head chef at Foliage, the chic and stylish restaurant at the Mandarin Oriental Hyde Park Hotel in central London. David is in charge of the Mandarin Oriental brand worldwide, so he is a man with a lot on his plate. Chris's domain is Foliage, where his menu descriptions can be short and to the point – 'scallops, cauliflower, ceps, sherry' – belying the complexity, intricacy and skill in the preparation. How will Chris choose to demonstrate his style of cooking at the Centenary dinner?

MARCUS WAREING began his career at The Savoy before moving on to Le Gavroche and in 1993 started his working partnership with Gordon Ramsay as sous-chef at Aubergine. Now, as chef-patron of Pétrus, Marcus has created one of the most consistent, elegant and refined dining experiences in the UK. His cooking is rooted in classicism but provides the 'wow' factor with modern interpretations and intelligent combinations in dishes such as roasted Cornish lamb with braised shoulder, caramelised shallots, confit tomato, saffron and lavender.

The Planning of the Menu

These five chefs are working together to produce a menu. Each chef wants to make an impression, give representation to their style, but do they have to compromise when it comes to such a large event, faced with having to reproduce the same dish 1,000 times on the night? Does something have to give?

David Nicholls takes a pragmatic approach, accepting that it is wise to go for something he feels comfortable with. So, the Centenary Awards is not the time for experimentation! Seasonality is the starting point for David with a bit of planning to avoid similarities between the ingredients and flavours throughout the menu. Some discussion between the chefs is enough to ensure the dishes are complementary and the meal has the same sort of balance of flavours the chefs would insist on in their own kitchens when devising menus or developing the pre-starters and pre-desserts that add a bit of 'wow' factor to the meal.

Tom Aikens is cooking the meat course, and as he says 'main courses are probably my favourite to prepare', it sounds like he's off to a good start. Tom puts the emphasis on the quality of the produce and he's opted for cutlet of Rhug Estate lamb, which he describes as 'exceptionally good.' The Rhug Estate is an organic farm covering 12,500 acres of Denbighshire countryside, and Tom's planning on serving their lamb with black olive mash and fig purée.

Raymond Blanc is cooking the dessert course and has chosen a dish from his ten course Tasting Menu. Ravioli of exotic fruits is part of a trio of desserts on that particular menu, but for the Centenary Dinner attempting three tasting desserts might be a little risky! Raymond has modified the ravioli dish slightly to enable it to be up-scaled to a solo dessert, and

one capable of impressing his peers. He knows the balance of flavours in the dish will work and it is a dish which can make an impact on the plate. The presentation is important too, and the change in scale will present a few issues regarding the way it looks – a few modifications will make all the difference.

Marcus Wareing is creating a classic starter of terrine of foie gras, cherries and dates, lapsang tea with spiced brioche. He says "For a banquet with a room full of foodies you can't go wrong with a nice foie gras terrine. It's also something you can serve to 1,000 people and still get close to how it would be served in a restaurant for just 6 covers".

Advance Preparation

Preparation is the key to success when catering for 1,000 people. Once the chefs have decided on the menu and sourced the produce, the headache is the planning and implementation on the day. Tom says, 'catering for this number is a tough task, but as long as you are 100% prepared and you follow a simple, straightforward system, service should be executed efficiently', and Raymond emphasis the importance of 'teamwork and preparing well', which is particularly important when working out of somebody else's kitchen. Marcus will send three of his chefs to join the Grosvenor House team and make the terrines two days in advance. Space will be at a premium, storage an issue, but these Five Rosette chefs will have considered every eventuality. Work on the actual dishes will begin a couple of days before the event.

On the Night

All that early planning will be a big help as the dishes are plated up on the night. This will be one of the most important periods of the long evening for each of

the chefs as it is critical to how the dishes will be perceived by the guests. Or as Tom puts it, 'the crucial few moments when the food can go from looking fantastic to looking disastrous'. Each chef wants the food to look wonderful, but doesn't want to present themselves with an impossible task.

Raymond wants a 'final flourish' but also to 'minimise risk.' Once the produce has been sourced, the food prepared and cooked, it is the final minutes before the food is whisked away to be taken to the hungry guests that will be the most stressful for the five chefs. And as there are 1,000 plates at each course to go through the pass, it will be a prolonged period of tension.

The Five Rosette, twenty-first century chefs have at their disposal some impressive technical kit and in the security of their own kitchens they can develop their dishes to perfection. They can move around almost with a sixth-sense which makes it much easier to deal with problems as they happen, from failures in the supply chain, staffing problems, and other unexpected occurrences. It is their domain, where they feel comfortable. But in the hot-house of a mass catering event, things are very different. The team at the Grosvenor House Hotel are there to help and, thankfully, they are well used to managing such large events. It is their job to offer the support the chefs need to make the event go smoothly.

The AA Centenary Awards Dinner will be a memorable event, especially for the winners on the night, but whatever happens the Five Rosette chefs cooking for their peers will be pulling out all the stops to make it a great night. As Tom Aikens says: 'It is a real honour to be able to give something back to the AA and be part of the Centenary Dinner.'

VEGETARIANS
Eating Out

By Alison Davison

Back in the 1970s, a request for a vegetarian meal in a restaurant would have been greeted with a blank stare. The waiter would probably have scratched his head for a few moments and suggested an omelette, or eating somewhere else.

That was the era when, as a highly ethical/bolshy teenager, I decided to drop meat and fish from my diet. People told me, in all seriousness, that I would die. Every meal then was meat-centred and even fish was seen as a bit namby-pamby.

Not only did I survive, I carried on with my strange ways and even ended up becoming a restaurant critic and food writer. How times have changed.

Eating out in the 70s wasn't the commonplace activity it is now, of course, and probably just as well for my egg consumption. Indian restaurants were the vegetarian's best friend – and are still great for flesh-phobics.

The 1980s
In the 80s, as the catering world grudgingly accepted that vegetarians weren't going away, a solitary meat-free option gradually appeared on menus. That in itself was a big step forward. Previously, vegetarians had to remember to mention it when booking – otherwise they'd get whatever the chef could think up on the hoof. Worst of all was being asked to suggest a dish ourselves.

"What would you like?" always made me feel like walking straight out. After all, we go to a restaurant partly to avoid having to think up a meal – not to do the chef's job for him.

There wasn't a great deal going on imaginatively for us in the 80s though. That single vegetarian option was inevitably vegetable lasagne.

The 1990s
In the 90s, when I started restaurant reviewing, lasagne became risotto. I've had more risottos than, well, hot dinners.

Some places offered more than one vegetarian option. Some even offered a vegetarian menu. Steady on now! This was often more clever marketing than anything - the two or three choices could just as easily have been included in the main menu. But what the hell; it made us feel special.

I was always pathetically grateful to be offered a choice. Grateful, and ever so slightly nonplussed, I wasn't used to actually choosing.

Ironically, as mainstream restaurants included vegetarian dishes on their menus, the dedicated vegetarian restaurant was pretty well killed off. Robbed of the reason for their existence, they are now as rare as hen's teeth.

But to the outrage of the sceptics, vegetarianism has taken off since then. Food scares and environmental worries left meat and fish considerably less attractive. Increasingly, we understood that it was actually healthier to eat less meat and more fruit, vegetables and pulses. It's estimated now that 45 per cent of people in Britain have reduced their meat consumption. Even at dinner parties with just one vegetarian guest, it has became OK to serve a non-meat dish to the entire group rather than stick something different on a single, lonely plate.

Vegetarian Food Arrives on the Menu

Perhaps the supreme vegetarian moment occurred in 2001. Legendary French chef Alain Passard announced at his renowned L'Arpege restaurant in Paris that he was dropping meat from his menu. This was doubly astonishing. It wasn't just that a restaurant had axed the stuff but that it was a restaurant in France, home of the world's most dedicated carnivores.

"I believe I have come far in the areas of poultry and meat based cuisine," he said at the time. "Today I aspire to another exploration based in vegetables. I voluntarily erase, without regret, 12 signature dishes of the house. I sense a fabulous adventure in exploring the depths of my passion."

He even threw open his two-hectare organic vegetable garden for good measure.

It was his love of the vegetable world's enormous variety and depth of flavour that had led to his decision rather than any ethical stance, of course.

But who cares? Vegetables were no longer the bit players on the restaurant plate. An increasing number of chefs joined the fan club. Pierre Gagnaire, Alice Waters and Charlie Trotter all created their own vegetarian cuisines.

The UK certainly wasn't left behind – indeed, if you've holidayed abroad, you'll know it's a damn sight easier for vegetarians to eat out well here than in most of the western world.

Rose Gray and Ruth Rogers of London's pioneering River Café (page 318), for instance, had been making waves with their interpretation of Italian country cooking since 1994. What they served up was the peasanty, veg-heavy side of the country's cuisine rarely seen in restaurants before. Forget the saltimbocca, this was more peperonata, caponata and vegetable carpaccio. And we loved it.

Now, even the carnivorous Hugh Fearnley-Whittingstall waxes lyrical about the glories of fine vegetables, as of course does Jamie Oliver.

Skye Gyngell, head chef of the award-winning Petersham Nurseries restaurant (page 335), declares proudly: "My kitchen is my garden. Every time I step outside, I am inspired."

The grow-your-own movement has worked wonders.

While Gordon Ramsay may pour scorn on vegetarianism, top London chef Paul Gayler of The Lanesborough (page 260) has come up with not just one book of vegetarian recipes but three. (The latest is *Pure Vegetarian*, Kyle Cathie, £14.99).

He looks both to the east and to Europe for inspiration and delivers such treats as black mushroom fideau or Swiss chard and sweetcorn crespelle.

"Even nowadays, it is not unusual for high-profile chefs to talk contemptuously about vegetarians, saying they don't appreciate good food," he says. "I believe chefs are missing a great opportunity when they neglect to cater imaginatively for vegetarians…I am still a meat-eater and as such I welcome the idea that everyone can enjoy vegetarian dishes … My greatest wish is that vegetarian cuisine will one day be on an equal footing with meat and fish cookery."

Another trail-blazer is Sat Bains of Nottingham's Restaurant Sat Bains with Rooms (page 357), which has the rare distinction of four AA Rosettes. He regularly puts together an entire vegan tasting menu but he's well aware of the challenge for chefs.

"I think vegetables are beautiful, they're my favourite things," he says. "But to cook them to a gastronomic level when someone else is having lobster, for example, you've got to really cook. That should be part of a chef's repertoire. You should be able to cook anything, not just protein."

Mind you, the vegetarian revolution hasn't spread everywhere. At a restaurant near Bolton recently, my mother asked if she could have something vegan. The waitress looked blank. "Do you eat chicken?" she asked.

Vegetarian readers will be pleased to know that every restaurant in the guide who told us they have a vegetarian menu shows the green V symbol.

Right: Skye Gyngell, Head Chef at Petersham Nurseries
Above left: Petersham Nurseries

"My kitchen is my garden. Every time I step outside, I am inspired."

ONE MAN'S Meat

By Simon Wright

I have writer's hands, strangely smooth and youthful for a man in his middle forties. This, I must be clear, is not because of a progressive attitude towards male skin care. No, the secret, and I'm happy to share it with you, is a lifetime's avoidance of manual labour.

When I entered the world of work it was at a leisurely pace. I joined local government in the planning department and in physical, or any other terms, this could not be described as taxing. When I left municipal employ I became a partner in a restaurant - undoubtedly a tougher challenge, long hours, late nights and much wine to be drunk, but little in the way of physical exertion. Then it got really demanding. I became a restaurant inspector, travelling the country eating out at someone else's expense and getting paid for it. Life can be cruel that way. I followed that up with a period as Editor of this very guide book - more food and usually of a better standard because I got to choose where I dined.

But somewhere towards the end of that journey I began to feel a little uneasy. Sitting in a restaurant on my ever-expanding rear end became a less comfortable experience. I thought of the place where all the real work was going on, in the heat of the kitchen, where some poor chef was working hard trying to please me, in the hope I might be good enough to jot down a few kind words in a restaurant guide. Sometimes it all seemed a bit pathetic on my part really, always being on the outside of the arena looking in, constructing nothing, deconstructing everything.

Moving On

So when I stopped doing the job I assuaged my guilt by writing a book about how very tough it is to be a top chef and how very easy it is to be a critic by comparison. This made me feel better. Then, *inter alia*, I went back to running a restaurant, helping to fix bad ones (I work as the 'Restaurant Consultant' on *Ramsay's Kitchen Nightmares*), with a little bit of writing and broadcasting thrown in. Things were okay for a while, I was working quite hard by my standards and most of the time I suppose I felt I was justifying my place in the world.

Finding Good Farmers and Suppliers

In the restaurant we were producing some really nice food which was rewarding. Nothing complicated; a sort of amalgam of French country and regional British dishes - honest, prepared with real care and, most importantly, based on top

quality produce. In fact, the most difficult part of the job was searching out those very ingredients. Finding farmers and producers who cared as much about the quality of their product as we did about ours – they were out there, not always easy to find and often much better at creating really good food than they were at marketing or distribution. What marked them out was the fact that they really had taken the time to think and learn about what goes in to producing good food. The other thing that distinguished them is that they all worked very hard – physically hard – proper work in other words. All of which made me question myself again. It seems that mid-life crises can be serial. There was I pontificating about great

food and the importance of fresh, non-intensive, local ingredients and the truth was all I knew about these things was that they tasted good.

Bright Ideas

So one morning I woke up and decided to become a gardener, grow my own and sell it in the restaurant. After breakfast, and about an hour's internet research, I abandoned the idea on the grounds that 1) there appeared to be rather too much attention to detail required for my liking, 2) I could see that it involved a huge amount of patience and a resilient attitude to failure and 3) I just didn't find plants very interesting. By lunchtime I had decided I would keep a few pigs

instead. By dinner that had expanded to include sheep. By the time I retired to bed the mental menagerie took in pigs, sheep, cattle, chickens, geese and ducks. I'd also arranged to rent the necessary land from my father-in-law. I called lots of people to tell them the good news, they laughed - and I laughed too - but made it clear I was really going to do this. I knew by saying that I was forcing myself into a corner and closing the gate behind me, I couldn't wimp out of it, there was no way back.

This soon became a worry. You see, I'm a stranger to the soil. Oddly, I've always lived in rural areas, almost without exception. If you couldn't see a farm from our house you could more than likely smell one. The processes of farming have always been around me, tractors have held me up, cows barred my progress. I have drinking buddies who are farmers, I went to school with farming children. The rhythms of agriculture have been with me all my life; the problem is, I wasn't listening.

All of which meant this escapade was going to be something of a challenge and others thought so too. A few days after deciding on this reckless course of action I mentioned it to a friend who has a television production company. Sensing the potential for disaster she offered to film it and sold the idea to BBC Wales. This being television, they wanted a bit more structure to it than just a half hour of me being rubbish at farming. "Why are you doing it?" they asked. "To see if I can produce really good meat for my restaurant table" I replied. "And how will you know if you've succeeded?" they wondered. "because I'm a food critic, I'll taste it." "Boring!" was their response. Apparently what I needed to do was to take some of my produce to a top restaurant, get them to cook a dish with it and also cook the same dish using their usual supplier. Then they'd feed me both and I would have to declare which was best not knowing which dish was mine. No pressure there then.

Choosing the Breeds

And so I embarked on my farming quest. My strategy was to work back from the knowledge I did have – mainly what I had found to taste best in my years of eating out for free. So, for instance, I chose middlewhite pigs on the basis of that rare breed of pork having been the best I'd ever tasted. I even conducted taste tests, comparing one species of chicken to another. A French breed came out on top so I bought a batch of day old

French chicks. For beef, I just had to go for Welsh Black cattle, I'd have been in trouble locally if I hadn't. Ducks were Muscovy and the geese were Embdens. Sheep were less straightforward. There's no shortage of the beasts in West Wales but sorting out a breed that would give me the best flavour was a challenge, largely because none of the sheep farmers I knew had a view on it. As is commonly known, sheep farming these days is a marginal existence and their concern, understandably, is which breed will put on the most weight quickest. I had a different agenda and eventually stumbled upon a type thought of as pathetically small by most of the local farming community. Balwens are a rare breed for that very reason but in all my enquiries just one farmer responded with real passion when questioned about which species had the best flavour. "You'll be wanting Balwens" he said "without a doubt." Funnily enough he just happened to be selling some.

Being an Animal Farmer

As I said, part of the motivation for embarking on this journey was to raise my self-esteem by, for once in my life, putting some real physical effort into a task. I wasn't disappointed. Almost before I knew it I was caught up in a whole new daily routine of feeding, cleaning, attending to minor ailments and chasing escaped animals. The truth is I loved every minute of it. The whole process was fascinating, from trying to keep tiny poultry alive in makeshift incubators to chasing Welsh Black steers around to get them TB tested and pulling a breach born lamb from inside its mother (I was well-prepared, I'd seen it done on *All Creatures Great and Small*).

I followed them to their end too. We've seen plenty of slaughterhouse scenes

on our screens in recent years but nothing really that prepares you for the otherworldliness of this strange room, peopled by gnarled slaughtermen and hard-hatted meat inspectors. A place where all sorts of life goes in, but only humans come out alive.

A Rewarding Experience

But that's what it's all about, meat. Meat in this case for our restaurant tables where, increasingly, we want to know where it comes from, what it ate and how it was treated both in life and death. I'd never make a real farmer, but for a year I played at being one and the main thing I got from it was a sense of respect. Respect for the dignity of the animals and respect for the farmers, especially those that strive to produce the best food they can as humanely as they can. And I guess I gained a little self-respect too.

Simon Wright's book *The Wright Stuff* with photographs by Julian Castaldi is published by Gomer. He is a partner in Y Polyn (page 551), a two-Rosetted restaurant in Carmarthenshire.

The Top Ten Per Cent

Each year all the restaurants in the AA Restaurant Guide are awarded a specially commissioned plate that marks their achievement in gaining one or more AA Rosettes. The plates represent a partnership between the AA and Villeroy & Boch two quality brands working together to recognise high standards in restaurant cooking.

Restaurants awarded three, four or five AA Rosettes represent the Top Ten Per Cent of the restaurants in this Guide. The pages that follow list those establishments that have attained this special status

ROSETTE AWARD

AA

AA Rosette Award for
Culinary Excellence

IN ASSOCIATION WITH

Villeroy & Boch
1748

2008-2009

Villeroy & Boch
1748

The Top Ten Per Cent

5 ROSETTES

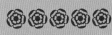

LONDON

Foliage
Mandarin Oriental Hyde Park
66 Knightsbridge, SW1
020 7235 2000

Pétrus
The Berkeley, Wilton Place,
Knightsbridge, SW1
020 7235 1200

Restaurant Gordon Ramsay
68 Royal Hospital Road,
SW3
020 7352 4441

Tom Aikens
43 Elystan Street, SW3
020 7584 2003

Sketch
(Lecture Room & Library)
9 Conduit Street, W1
0870 777 4488

ENGLAND
BERKSHIRE
The Fat Duck
High Street, BRAY,
SL6 2AQ
01628 580333

OXFORDSHIRE
Le Manoir aux Quat' Saisons
GREAT MILTON,
OX44 7PD
01844 278881

4 ROSETTES

LONDON

The Capital
Basil Street, SW3
020 7589 5171

Aubergine
11 Park Walk, SW10
020 7352 3449

The Greenhouse
27a Hay's Mews, W1
020 7499 3331

Locanda Locatelli
8 Seymour Street, W1
020 7935 9088

Maze
London Marriott Grosvenor
Hotel,10-13 Grosvenor
Square, W1
020 7107 0000

Pied à Terre
34 Charlotte Street, W1
020 7636 1178

The Square
6-10 Bruton Street, W1
020 7495 7100

LONDON, GREATER
Chapter One
Farnborough Common,
Locksbottom,
BROMLEY, BR6 8NF
01689 854848

ENGLAND
BERKSHIRE
Waterside Inn
Ferry Road, BRAY, SL6 2AT
01628 620691

The Vineyard at Stockcross
Stockcross, NEWBURY,
RG20 8JU
01635 528770

BUCKINGHAMSHIRE
Oak Room at Danesfield House
Henley Road,
MARLOW, SL7 2EY
01628 891010

CAMBRIDGESHIRE
Midsummer House
Midsummer Common,
CAMBRIDGE, CB4 1HA
01223 369299

CHESHIRE
Simon Radley at The Chester Grosvenor
Chester Grosvenor & Spa,
Eastgate, CHESTER,
CH1 1LT
01244 324024

CUMBRIA
L'Enclume
Cavendish Street, CARTMEL,
LA11 6PZ
01539 536362

DERBYSHIRE
Fischer's Baslow Hall
Calver Road, BASLOW,
DE45 1RR
01246 583259

DEVON
Gidleigh Park
CHAGFORD, TQ13 8HH
01647 432367

GLOUCESTERSHIRE
Le Champignon Sauvage
24 Suffolk Road,
CHELTENHAM, GL50 2AQ
01242 573449

NOTTINGHAMSHIRE
Restaurant Sat Bains with Rooms
Lenton Lane,
NOTTINGHAM, NG7 2SA
0115 986 6566

RUTLAND
Hambleton Hall
Hambleton, OAKHAM,
LE15 8TH
01572 756991

WILTSHIRE
Whatley Manor
Easton Grey, MALMESBURY,
SN16 0RB
01666 822888

JERSEY
Bohemia Restaurant
The Club Hotel & Spa,
Green Street, ST HELIER,
JE2 4UH
01534 880588

SCOTLAND
CITY OF EDINBURGH
Restaurant Martin Wishart
54 The Shore, Leith,
EDINBURGH, EH6 6RA
0131 553 3557

HIGHLAND
The Boath House
Auldearn, NAIRN, IV12 5TE
01667 454896

PERTH & KINROSS
Andrew Fairlie @ Gleneagles
AUCHTERARDER, PH3 1NF
01764 694267

NORTHERN IRELAND
CO BELFAST
Deanes Restaurant
36-40 Howard Street,
BELFAST, BT1 6PF
028 9033 1144

REPUBLIC OF IRELAND
DUBLIN
Restaurant Patrick Guilbaud
Merrion Hotel, 21 Upper
Merrion Street, DUBLIN
01 676 4192

3 ROSETTES

LONDON
EC1
Club Gascon
57 West Smithfield
020 7796 0600

EC2
1901 Restaurant
ANdAZ London
40 Liverpool Street
020 7618 7000

Rhodes Twenty Four
Tower 42, Old Broad Street
020 7877 7703

N7
Morgan M
489 Liverpool Road,
ISLINGTON
020 7609 3560

NW1
Odette's
130 Regent's Park Road
020 7586 8569

SE3
Chapters
43-45 Montpelier Vale,
Blackheath Village
020 8333 2666

SW1
Nahm
The Halkin Hotel,
Halkin Street
020 7333 1234

One–O–One
Sheraton Park Tower,
101 Knightsbridge
020 7290 7101

Zafferano
15 Lowndes Street
020 7235 5800

SW3
Rasoi Restaurant
10 Lincoln Street
020 7225 1881

SW4
Trinity Restaurant
4 The Polygon,
Clapham Old Town
020 7622 1199

SW17
Chez Bruce
2 Bellevue Road,
Wandsworth Common
020 8672 0114

W1
Alain Ducasse
The Dorchester,
53 Park Lane
020 7629 8866

Arbutus Restaurant
63-64 Frith Street
020 7734 4545

L'Autre Pied
5-7 Blandford Street
020 7486 9696

**L'Escargot –
The Picasso Room**
48 Greek Street
020 7439 7474

Le Gavroche Restaurant
43 Upper Brook Street
020 7408 0881

**Gordon Ramsay at
Claridge's**
Brook Street
020 7499 0099

**The Grill
(Dorchester Hotel)**
Park Lane
020 7629 8888

Hakkasan
No 8 Hanway Place
020 7927 7000

Hibiscus
29 Maddox Street
020 7629 2999

The Landau
The Langham London
Portland Place
020 7965 0165

Lindsay House Restaurant
21 Romilly Street
020 7439 0450

Rhodes W1 Restaurant
Great Cumberland Place,
020 7616 5930

Roka
37 Charlotte Street
020 7580 6464

Texture Restaurant
34 Portman Street
020 7224 0028

**Theo Randall,
InterContinental London**
1 Hamilton Place,
Hyde Park Corner
020 7318 8747

3 ROSETTES

CONTINUED

W1 continued
Umu
14-16 Bruton Place
020 7499 8881

W4
La Trompette
5-7 Devonshire Road,
CHISWICK
020 8747 1836

W6
The River Café
Thames Wharf,
Rainville Road
020 7386 4200

W11
The Ledbury
127 Ledbury Road,
NOTTING HILL
020 7792 9090

Notting Hill Brasserie
92 Kensington Park Road
020 7229 4481

WC1
Pearl Restaurant & Bar
Renaissance
Chancery Court,
252 High Holborn
020 7829 7000

WC2
L'Atelier de Joël Robuchon
13-15 West Street
020 7010 8600

Clos Maggiore
33 King Street,
COVENT GARDEN
020 7379 9696

LONDON, GREATER
The Glasshouse
14 Station Road,
KEW TW9 3PZ
020 8940 6777

ENGLAND
BERKSHIRE
Fredrick's Hotel,
Restaurant & Spa
Shoppenhangers Road,
MAIDENHEAD, SL6 2PZ
01628 581000

L'ortolan
Church Lane,
SHINFIELD, RG2 9BY
01189 888 500

BUCKINGHAMSHIRE
Hartwell House Hotel,
Restaurant & Spa
Oxford Road,
AYLESBURY, HP17 8NR
01296 747444

The Hand & Flowers
126 West Street,
MARLOW, SL7 2BP
01628 482277

Waldo's Restaurant,
Cliveden
Cliveden Estate,
TAPLOW, SL6 0JF
01628 668561

CAMBRIDGESHIRE
Restaurant Alimentum
152-154 Hills Road,
CAMBRIDGE, CB2 8PB
01223 413001

CORNWALL & ISLES OF
SCILLY
Restaurant Nathan Outlaw
Marina Villa Hotel
17 Esplanade,
FOWEY, PL23 1HY
01726 833315

Well House Hotel
St Keyne, LISKEARD,
PL14 4RN
01579 342001

The Seafood Restaurant
Riverside, PADSTOW,
PL28 8BY
01841 532700

Driftwood
Rosevine, PORTSCATHO,
TR2 5EW
01872 580644

Teän Restaurant @
St Martin's on the Isle
Lower Town, ST MARTIN'S,
TR25 0QW
01720 422092

Hotel Tresanton
Lower Castle Road,
ST MAWES, TR2 5DR
01326 270055

CUMBRIA
Hipping Hall
Cowan Bridge
KIRKBY LONSDALE,
LA6 2JJ
015242 71187

Macdonald Leeming House
Watermillock
PENRITH, CA11 0JJ
0870 400 8131

Rampsbeck
Country House Hotel
WATERMILLOCK, CA11 0LP
017684 86442

Gilpin Lodge Country House
Hotel & Restaurant
Crook Road,
WINDERMERE, LA23 3NE
015394 88818

Holbeck Ghyll Country
House Hotel
Holbeck Lane,
WINDERMERE, LA23 1LU
015394 32375

The Samling
Ambleside Road,
WINDERMERE, LA23 1LR
015394 31922

DERBYSHIRE
The Old Vicarage
Ridgeway Moor,
RIDGEWAY, S12 3XW
0114 247 5814

DEVON
The New Angel
2 South Embankment,
DARTMOUTH, TQ6 9BH
01803 839425

The Horn of Plenty
GULWORTHY, PL19 8JD
01822 832528

The Masons Arms
KNOWSTONE, EX36 4RY
01398 341231

Lewtrenchard Manor
LEWDON, EX20 4PN
01566 783222

The Mulberry
Bovey Castle,
MORETONHAMPSTEAD,
TQ13 8RE
01647 445000

Hotel Endsleigh
Milton Abbot,
TAVISTOCK, PL19 0PQ
01822 870000

**Corbyn Head Hotel &
Orchid Restaurant**
Sea Front, TORQUAY,
TQ2 6RH
01803 213611

**The Elephant Bar &
Restaurant**
3/4 Beacon Terrace,
TORQUAY TQ1 2BH
01803 200044

DORSET
Sienna Restaurant
36 High West Street,
DORCHESTER, DT1 1UP
01305 250022

**Summer Lodge Country
House Hotel,
Restaurant & Spa**
EVERSHOT, DT2 0JR
01935 482000

GLOUCESTERSHIRE
**Cotswold House,
Juliana's Restaurant**
The Square, CHIPPING
CAMPDEN, GL55 6AN
01386 840330

Lords of the Manor
UPPER SLAUGHTER,
Cheltenham, GL54 2JD
01451 820243

Lower Slaughter Manor
LOWER SLAUGHTER,
Cheltenham, GL54 2HP
01451 820456

5 North Street
5 North Street,
WINCHCOMBE GL54 5LH
01242 604566

HAMPSHIRE
**Le Poussin at
Whitley Ridge Hotel**
Beaulieu Road,
BROCKENHURST,
SO42 7QL
01590 622354

36 on the Quay
47 South Street,
EMSWORTH, PO10 7EG
01243 375592

Chewton Glen Hotel & Spa
Christchurch Road,
NEW MILTON, BH25 6QS
01425 275341

JSW
20 Dragon Street,
PETERSFIELD, GU31 4JJ
01730 262030

Avenue Restaurant
Lainston House Hotel,
Sparsholt, WINCHESTER,
SO21 2LT
01962 863588

HEREFORDSHIRE
Castle House
Castle Street, HEREFORD,
HR1 2NW
01432 356321

HERTFORDSHIRE
Colette's at the Grove
Chandler's Cross,
RICKMANSWORTH,
WD3 4TG
01923 296015

KENT
The West House
28 High Street,
BIDDENDEN, TN27 8AH
01580 291341

Apicius
23 Stone Street,
CRANBROOK, TN17 3HF
01580 714666

Rowhill Grange – Truffles
Rowhill Grange Hotel & Spa
DARTFORD, DA2 7QH
01322 615136

Read's Restaurant
Macknade Manor,
FAVERSHAM, ME13 8XE
01795 535344

Thackeray's
TUNBRIDGE WELLS,
TN1 1EA
01892 511921

LANCASHIRE
Northcote Manor
Northcote Road,
LANGHO, BB6 8BE
01254 240555

The Longridge Restaurant
104-106 Higher Road,
LONGRIDGE, PR3 3SY
01772 784969

LINCOLNSHIRE
Harry's Place
17 High Street,
Great Gonerby,
GRANTHAM, NG31 8JS
01476 561780

MERSEYSIDE
Fraiche
11 Rose Mount,
Oxton Village,
BIRKENHEAD, CH43 5SG
0151 652 2914

NORFOLK
Morston Hall
Morston, Holt,
BLAKENEY, NR25 7AA
01263 741041

3 ROSETTES

CONTINUED

NORFOLK continued
The Neptune Inn & Restaurant
85 Old Hunstanton Road,
HUNSTANTON, PE36 6HZ
01485 532122

NORTHAMPTONSHIRE
Equilibrium
Fawsley Hall, Fawsley,
DAVENTRY, NN11 3BA
01327 892000

SHROPSHIRE
Old Vicarage Hotel and Restaurant
BRIDGNORTH, WV15 5JZ
01746 716497

La Bécasse
17 Corve Street,
LUDLOW, SY8 1DA
01584 872325

SOMERSET
Bath Priory Hotel, Restaurant & Spa
Weston Road, BATH,
BA1 2XT
01225 331922

Little Barwick House
Barwick Village,
YEOVIL, BA22 9TD
01935 423902

SUFFOLK
The Bildeston Crown
104 High Street,
BILDESTON, IP7 7EB
01449 740510

SURREY
The Latymer
Pennyhill Park Hotel & Spa,
London Road,
BAGSHOT, GU19 5EU
01276 471774

Drake's Restaurant
The Clock House,
High Street, RIPLEY,
GU23 6AQ
01483 224777

SUSSEX, EAST
Newick Park Hotel & Country Estate
NEWICK, BN8 4SB
01825 723633

SUSSEX, WEST
Queens Room at Amberley Castle Hotel
AMBERLEY, BN18 9LT
01798 831992

West Stoke House
Downs Road, West Stoke,
CHICHESTER, PO18 9BN
01243 575226

Ockenden Manor
Ockenden Lane,
CUCKFIELD, RH17 5LD
01444 416111

Gravetye Manor Hotel
EAST GRINSTEAD,
RH19 4LJ
01342 810567

The Camellia Restaurant at South Lodge Hotel
Brighton Road, LOWER
BEEDING, RH13 6PS
01403 891711

WARWICKSHIRE
Mallory Court Hotel
Harbury Lane,
Bishop's Tachbrook,
ROYAL LEAMINGTON SPA,
CV33 9QB
01926 330214

WEST MIDLANDS
Simpsons
20 Highfield Road,
Edgbaston,
BIRMINGHAM, B15 3DU
0121 454 3434

WILTSHIRE
The Bybrook at the Manor
CASTLE COMBE, SN14 7HR
01249 782206

Lucknam Park
COLERNE, SN14 8AZ
01225 742777

The Harrow at Little Bedwyn
LITTLE BEDWYN, SN8 3JP
01672 870871

YORKSHIRE, NORTH
Black Swan Hotel
Market Place, HELMSLEY,
YO62 5BJ
01439 770466

Samuel's at Swinton Park
MASHAM, Ripon, HG4 4JH
01765 680900

Judges Country House Hotel
Kirklevington, YARM,
TS15 9LW
01642 789000

YORKSHIRE, WEST
Box Tree
35-37 Church Street,
ILKLEY, LS29 9DR
01943 608484

Anthony's Restaurant
19 Boar Lane,
LEEDS, LS1 6EA
0113 245 5922

JERSEY

Ocean Restaurant at the Atlantic Hotel
Le Mont de la Pulente,
ST BRELADE, JE3 8HE
01534 744101

Grand Jersey
The Esplanade,
ST HELIER, JE4 8WD
01534 722301

Longueville Manor Hotel
ST SAVIOUR, JE2 7WF
01534 725501

SCOTLAND

ABERDEENSHIRE
Darroch Learg Hotel
Braemar Road,
BALLATER, AB35 5UX
013397 55443

ARGYLL & BUTE
Isle of Eriska
ERISKA, PA37 1SD
01631 720371

Airds Hotel and Restaurant
PORT APPIN, PA38 4DF
01631 730236

DUMFRIES & GALLOWAY
Knockinaam Lodge
PORTPATRICK, DG9 9AD
01776 810471

EDINBURGH
The Kitchin
78 Commercial Quay, Leith,
EDINBURGH, EH6 6LX
0131 555 1755

Norton House Hotel
Ingliston, EDINBURGH,
EH28 8LX
0131 333 1275

**Number One,
The Balmoral Hotel**
Princes Street, EDINBURGH,
EH2 2EQ
0131 557 6727

Plumed Horse
50-54 Henderson Street,
Leith, EDINBURGH,
EH6 6DE
0131 554 5556

FIFE
Cellar Restaurant
24 East Green,
ANSTRUTHER, KY10 3AA
01333 310378

The Road Hole Grill
Old Course Hotel Golf Resort
& Spa, ST ANDREWS,
KY16 9SP
01334 474371

The Seafood Restaurant
The Scores, ST ANDREWS,
KY16 9AS
01334 479475

GLASGOW
**Hotel du Vin Bistro at
One Devonshire Gardens**
1 Devonshire Gardens
GLASGOW G12 0UX
0141 339 2001

HIGHLAND
The Three Chimneys
COLBOST, Isle of Skye
IV55 8ZT
01470 511258

Inverlochy Castle Hotel
Torlundy, FORT WILLIAM,
PH33 6SN
01397 702177

Abstract Restaurant
Glenmoriston Town House
Hotel
Ness Bank, INVERNESS,
IV2 4SF
01463 223777

The Cross at Kingussie
Tweed Mill Brae,
Ardbroilach Road,
KINGUSSIE, PH21 ILB
01540 661166

Ullinish Country Lodge
STRUAN, Isle of Skye
IV56 8FD
01470 572214

PERTH & KINROSS
Kinnaird
Kinnaird Estate, DUNKELD,
PH8 0LB
01796 482440

SCOTTISH BORDERS
The Horseshoe Inn
EDDLESTON, Peebles,
EH45 8QP
01721 730225

SOUTH AYRSHIRE
Glenapp Castle
BALLANTRAE, KA26 0NZ
01465 831212

Lochgreen House
Monktonhill Road,
Southwood
TROON, KA10 7EN
01292 313343

STIRLING
**Roman Camp Country
House Hotel**
CALLANDER, FK17 8BG
01877 330003

WEST DUNBARTONSHIRE
**De Vere Deluxe Cameron
House**
BALLOCH, G83 8QZ
01389 755565

WALES

CEREDIGION
Ynyshir Hall
EGLWYSFACH, Machynlleth,
SY20 8TA
01654 781209

CONWY
Tan-y-Foel Country House
Capel Garmon,
BETWS-Y-COED, LL26 0RE
01690 710507

Bodysgallen Hall and Spa
LLANDUDNO, LL30 1RS
01492 584466

MONMOUTHSHIRE
Walnut Tree Inn
Llandewi Skirrid
ABERGAVENNY NP7 8AW
01873 852797

POWYS
Carlton Riverside
Irfon Crescent,
LLANWRTYD WELLS,
LD5 4SP
01591 610248

REPUBLIC OF IRELAND

CO CORK
Longueville House
MALLOW
022 47156/47306

CO KILDARE
The Byerley Turk
The K Club
STRAFFAN
01 601 7200

CO MONAGHAN
Restaurant at Nuremore
CARRICKMACROSS
042 966 1438

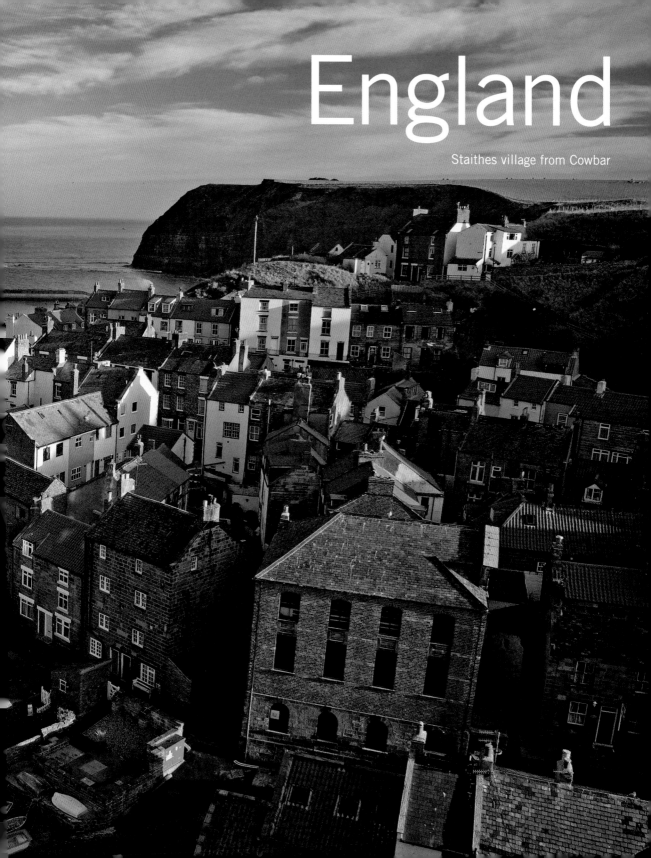

England

Staithes village from Cowbar

BEDFORDSHIRE

BEDFORD — Map 12 TL04

Knife & Cleaver Inn

◉ Modern Seafood

Modern cooking in historic inn

☎ 01234 740387
The Grove, Houghton Conquest MK45 3LA
e-mail: info@knifeandcleaver.com
dir: M1 junct 12-13 just off A6, 5m S of Bedford. Follow brown tourist signs from A6. Opposite church in village

This 17th-century inn, set in the heart of the village, has links to John Bunyan. The Jacobean panelling in the oak-beamed bar-lounge was acquired from nearby Houghton House - the model for House Beautiful in The Pilgrim's Progress. Light and airy with a buzzy atmosphere, the conservatory restaurant is the perfect place to enjoy simple British dishes with an emphasis on seasonality and local ingredients, especially fish and seafood. The weekly-changing menu includes the likes of pan-fried king scallops with caramelised red onion and potato cakes, followed by organic salmon fillet with teriyaki marinade and Japanese rice noodles, or perhaps try the hot and chilled seafood platter with lobster.

Chef Chris Bishopp **Owner** Mrs P & Mr D Loom
Times 12-2.30/7-9.30, Closed 27-30 Dec, Closed L Sat
Wines 35 bottles over £20, 21 bottles under £20, 20 by glass **Notes** 3 course seafood menu Saturday £26.95, Sunday L, Vegetarian available, Dress restrictions, Smart Casual, Air con **Seats** 80, Pr/dining room 12 **Children** Portions, Menu **Parking** 30

FLITWICK — Map 11 TL03

Menzies Flitwick Manor

◉ Modern British 💻 V

Enjoyable dining in a traditional manor house

☎ 0871 472 4016
Church Rd MK45 1AE
e-mail: flitwick@menzies-hotels.co.uk
dir: M1 junct 12, follow Flitwick after 1m turn left into Church Rd. Manor 200 yds on left.

In a picturesque setting, this imposing Georgian manor house is a grand place to dine. Retaining many of its original features and furnished throughout with antiques and fine art, it boasts a luxurious restaurant with white-clothed tables, rich drapes and elegant appointments, as well as some lovely views over parkland and manicured lawns. Modern British dishes form the backbone of the menu - expect ambitious fare from a kitchen that always aims to please. Hand-dived scallops are a typical starter, served with crispy ham, pea purée and mint oil, while mains might include steamed bream with crayfish and crab cannelloni, rocket purée and a chive emulsion.

Chef Oliver Jackson **Owner** Menzies Hotels plc
Times 12-2.30/7-9.30 **Prices** Fixed L 2 course £19.50, Fixed D 3 course £55, Service added but optional
Wines 50 bottles over £20, 4 bottles under £20, 8 by glass **Notes** Sunday L, Vegetarian menu, Dress restrictions, Smart casual, Civ Wed 50 **Seats** 50, Pr/dining room 40 **Children** Min 7 yrs, Portions, Menu **Parking** 30

LUTON — Map 6 TL02

Luton Hoo Hotel, Golf and Spa

◉◉ Modern European

Modern food in a quintessentially British stately home setting

☎ 01582 734437
The Mansion House LU1 3TQ
e-mail: reservations@lutonhoo.com
dir: Please telephone for directions

This stately home was re-born as a hotel, golf course and spa in 2007. It still looks stately in all respects, with 1000 acres of grounds including two large lakes, woodland and landscaped areas originally designed by 'Capability' Brown. The transformation into a hotel has not resulted in a reduction in grandeur as marble walls and sideboards, beautiful tapestries and grand chandeliers provide plenty to occupy the eye. The Wernher Restaurant, named after a former owner of the house, is a suitably grand space with exotic marble panelwork and richly coloured fabrics. The menu is broadly speaking modern European in direction, so salmon and langoustine tortellini is served in a rich shellfish bisque as a starter, and roast chump and braised leg of lamb comes with dauphinoise, cabbage and bacon and mint and caper dressing. Finish with a mango dessert of parfait, smoothie and salsa. Service throughout is well drilled and friendly. There are other dining options in the hotel, including a brasserie in the former stables.

Chef Ian Penn **Times** 12.30-2/7-10, Closed L Sat
Prices Food prices not confirmed for 2009. Please telephone for details.

MILTON ERNEST — Map 11 TL05

The Strawberry Tree

◉◉ Traditional British

Innovative cuisine using carefully-sourced produce in a lovely thatched cottage

☎ 01234 823633
3 Radwell Rd MK44 1RY
e-mail: strawberrytree_restaurant@yahoo.co.uk
dir: M1 junct 13, 4m N of Bedford on A6

A 17th-century thatched cottage which was originally divided into three, with a sweet shop at the front, laundry in the middle and cottage at the back. Run as a tea shop for ten years, the restaurant was then developed and refurbished, retaining original features like the bread oven, flagstone floors and inglenook fireplaces. Here you can enjoy carefully sourced local produce like Lincoln Red beef, Suffolk lamb and organic vegetables and herbs. Try a starter of celery and celeriac soup with a lasagne of wild mushrooms, followed by breast of local pheasant with smoked bacon, roast parsnips, pumpkin, bread sauce and cep mushroom sauce. Dessert might feature white chocolate and lime parfait with mascarpone sorbet and passionfruit.

Times 12-1.45/7-9, Closed 2 wks Jan & Sep, Closed Sun-Tue, Closed L Sat

WOBURN — Map 11 SP93

The Inn at Woburn

◉◉ Modern British 💻

Seamless blend of old and modern in lovely market town

☎ 01525 292292
George St MK17 9PX
e-mail: enquiries@theinnatwoburn.com
dir: 5 mins from M1 junct 13. Follow signs to Woburn. Inn in town centre at x-rds, parking to rear via Parm St

Just 8 miles from Milton Keynes, yet in the heart of the delightful Georgian market town, this original inn with courtyard-style extension is full of character, its sage-green paintwork and old stock brickwork set off by old-fashioned street lamps. Enjoy a drink in the beamed Tavistock bar before taking dinner in Olivier's restaurant. Named after the chef, it has a relaxed atmosphere and offers an interesting carte, a few specials and vegetarian options. Typical starters might include prawns in pomegranate and sherry dressing with celery and chicory leaves, while main courses feature the likes of seared fillet of sea bass on chorizo mash with baby spinach and chive butter sauce, with 'Canaletto's palette of Woburn ice creams' served with a tuile biscuit and chocolate pencil brush for dessert. Look out for gourmet evenings.

The Inn at Woburn

Times 12-2.30/6-10.15

Paris House Restaurant

@@ French V

Classical French cooking in a historic English park

☎ 01525 290692
Woburn Park MK17 9QP
e-mail: gail@parishouse.co.uk
web: www.parishouse.co.uk
dir: M1 junct 13. From Woburn take A4012 Hockliffe, 1m out of Woburn village on left

With its tree-lined avenues and graceful pastures, Woburn Park provides an idyllic setting for this fine-dining experience. The stunning black and white timbered house was built in 1878 for the Paris Exhibition and it was dismantled and rebuilt on the Woburn Estate by the 9th Duke of Bedford. In the early 1980s it was renovated and reopened in its present incarnation as a restaurant. Chef-patron Peter Chandler spent 12 years working for the Roux brothers and his classical French cookery is assured and well defined. A confit of crispy duck with orange salad could be followed by breast of corn-fed chicken with wild mushrooms and Madeira sauce. Hot raspberry soufflé is a classic way to end a meal. The carte and short menu du jour are supplemented by a gastronomic menu.

Chef Peter Chandler **Owner** Mr P Chandler
Times 12-2/7-10, Closed 26 Dec, 1-17 Jan, Closed Mon, Closed D Sun **Prices** Fixed L 2 course £20, Fixed D 3 course £25-£57, Service optional **Wines** 80 bottles over £20, 5 bottles under £20, 8 by glass **Notes** Sunday L, Vegetarian menu **Seats** 48, Pr/dining room 16 **Children** Portions, Menu **Parking** 24

BERKSHIRE

ASCOT
Map 6 SU96

Hyperion at Macdonald Berystede Hotel & Spa

@ British, International 🖥

Elegant dining room offering classical, seasonal cuisine

☎ 01344 623311 & 0844 8799 104
Bagshot Rd, Sunninghill SL5 9JH
e-mail: general.berystede@macdonald-hotels.co.uk
dir: M3 junct 3/A30, A322 then left onto B3020 to Ascot or M25 junct 13, follow signs for Bagshot. At Sunningdale turn right onto A330

Just a short canter from Ascot racecourse, the elegant Hyperion Restaurant (named after a famous racehorse) is part of the Macdonald Berystede, an impressive hotel in a large Victorian mansion. The hotel has state-of-the-art leisure facilities and the restaurant overlooks the roof terrace (perfect for fair-weather dining), the spa and manicured grounds. Modern British and international cuisine features on the menu: expect dishes such as fillet of pork, carrot dauphinoise, baby vegetables and morel jus, or halibut steak, vine tomatoes and truffle cream sauce, and apple tarte Tatin with vanilla ice cream to finish. Service is relaxed, friendly and attentive.

Chef Gordon Inglis **Owner** Macdonalds Hotels
Times 12.30-2/7-9.45, Closed L Sat **Prices** Food prices not confirmed for 2009. Please telephone for details. **Wines** 40 bottles over £20, 40 bottles under £20, 12 by glass **Notes** Sunday L, Vegetarian available, Civ Wed 150, Air con **Seats** 120, Pr/dining room 24 **Children** Portions, Menu **Parking** 120

BRACKNELL
Map 5 SU86

Rowans at Coppid Beech

@@ European, Pacific Rim 🖥 🖐

Modern Alpine-style hotel dining offering imaginative food

☎ 01344 303333
John Nike Way RG12 8TF
e-mail: welcome@coppidbeech.com
web: www.coppidbeech.com
dir: From M4 junct 10 follow A329(M) (Bracknell/Wokingham) to 1st exit. At rdbt take 1st exit to Binfield (B3408); hotel 200yds on right

This striking hotel was designed to resemble a Swiss chalet and stands beside a dry-ski slope, an ice rink and toboggan run, completing the Alpine picture. It has a choice of restaurants, including the basement Bier Keller with its brasserie-style menu. Rowans is the fine-dining option, a light-and-airy contemporary venue with a timber ceiling and crystal chandeliers. The imaginative, modern British carte with European influences is extensive enough to suit everyone. Typical choices might include scallop mousseline with light crab cream and chervil sauce to start, with pan-fried Cornish sea bass with pesto mash, lobster thermidor and salted spinach to follow, rounded off with apple tarte Tatin with Gewürztraminer ice cream.

Chef Nick Harris **Owner** Nike Group Hotels Ltd
Times 12-2.15/7-10.30 **Prices** Fixed L 2 course £19-£25, Fixed D 3 course £25-£40, Starter £6.25-£12, Main £14.25-£30, Dessert £5.50-£7.50, Service optional **Wines** 60 bottles over £20, 4 bottles under £20, 10 by glass **Notes** Sunday L, Vegetarian available, Dress restrictions, Smart casual, Civ Wed 300, Air con **Seats** 120, Pr/dining room 20 **Children** Portions, Menu **Parking** 350

The Fat Duck

BRAY Map 6 SU97

Modern British 🖥 V 🍷 NOTABLE WINE LIST

The epitome of contemporary dining

☎ 01628 580333
High St SL6 2AQ
dir: M4 junct 8/9 (Maidenhead) take A308 towards Windsor, turn left into Bray. Restaurant in centre of village on right

Who could have predicted that the well groomed Thames-side village of Bray would become home to British gastronomy. First with the Roux brothers at the Waterside Inn (see entry) bringing French classicism to Britain (and training a whole generation of big name chefs), and now Heston Blumenthal's Fat Duck, leading the way in innovative gastronomy. Two small cottages on the main village road seem an unassuming and unlikely international destination of culinary discovery and home to one of the world's best chefs, but The Fat Duck oozes understated quality and chic. Oak beams and low ceilings are complemented by modern art and coloured-glass screens, which combine effortlessly with the Tudor building. Comfortable chairs and white napery are backed by impeccable service (a real feature of The Fat Duck experience), which is professional, enthusiastic and friendly - with staff eager to share their knowledge without a hint of condescension. Blumenthal is a chef

par excellence as well as a true culinary pioneer, and a leading exponent of the scientific approach to cuisine. Whilst there's nothing bizarre about the ingredients he uses, it's this combination of flavours that sometimes raises eyebrows or catches the headlines. But it's not just the exciting combinations that are a hallmark of this stunning experience, it's Heston's absolute precision and clarity of flavour and balance that sets him apart. For the full-on show, look to the tasting menu with its eight or so courses (and dish names the likes of "Sound of the Sea", Mrs Marshall's Margaret cornet or parsnip cereal) and various head-turning tasters, though there is also a good-value lunch option and carte, which might deliver pot-roast loin of pork, braised belly and gratin of truffled macaroni, and perhaps a mango and Douglas fir purée dessert, served with bavarois of lychee and mango, blackcurrant sorbet and green peppercorn jelly. An extensive wine list rounds off the package in style. So just sit back and enjoy the multi-sensory journey with a culinary alchemist at the helm.

Chef Heston Blumenthal **Owner** Fat Duck Ltd **Times** 12-1.45/7-9.45, Closed 2 wks at Xmas, Closed Mon, Closed D Sun **Wines** 500 bottles over £20, 13 by glass **Notes** ALC 3 course £95, Vegetarian menu, Air con **Seats** 40 **Children** Portions **Parking** Two village car parks

BRAY

Map 6 SU97

The Fat Duck

ⓐⓐⓐⓐⓐ *see opposite*

Hinds Head Hotel

ⓐⓐ British 🖳

Authentic old English recipes in traditional pub setting

☎ 01628 626151
High St SL6 2AB
e-mail: info@hindsheadhotel.co.uk
dir: M4 junct 8/9, at rdbt take exit to Maidenhead Central, next rdbt take exit Bray & Windsor, after 0.5m take B3028 to Bray

Heston Blumenthal might have given this place new life when he opened it as an adjunct to the Fat Duck some years ago, but the Hinds Head has been a village pub for more than 400 years, and so it remains. Both outside and inside it looks the part, with its heavy oak beams, sturdy oak panelling, and wooden tables and leather chairs. A light and spacious restaurant creates a different atmosphere from the darker, more atmospheric bar, but the food is the same. The owners' trawl through historic recipes has yielded a variety of traditional Tudor dishes and seasonal British classics: oxtail and kidney pudding, Lancashire hotpot, Gloucestershire Old Spot pork chop with mustard mash and quaking pudding are authentic versions which still strike a chord today.

Chef Heston Blumenthal **Owner** Heston Blumenthal & James Lee **Times** 12-2.30/6.30-9.30, Closed 25-26 Dec, Closed D Sun **Prices** Starter £5.50-£9.50, Main £12-£18.50, Dessert fr £5.95, Service added but optional 12.5% **Wines** 64 bottles over £20, 10 bottles under £20, 15 by glass **Notes** Sunday L, Vegetarian available, Air con **Seats** 100, Pr/dining room 60 **Children** Portions **Parking** 40

The Riverside Brasserie

ⓐⓐ French

Brasserie dining beside Thames-side marina

☎ 01628 780553
Bray Marina SL6 2EB
e-mail: grrydws@aol.com
dir: Off A308, signed Bray Marina

Housed in a simple, café-like building in Bray marina, this contemporary, no-frills riverside eatery functions as a pit-stop for boats on the Thames, and draws the

summer crowds for leisurely alfresco lunches on the waterside decked terrace. Expect wooden floors, an open-to-view kitchen, a relaxed atmosphere, and unpretentious yet accomplished brasserie fare. Using top-notch ingredients, clean, well-presented dishes mix classics such as a starter of beetroot cured salmon with horseradish crème fraîche, followed by as roast chicken with fondant potato and jus gras, or slow-roasted lamb and potato rösti, as well as more innovative, Mediterranean-inspired ideas, for example pan-fried sea bass and caponata. Classic puddings include vanilla parfait with chocolate sauce, and coconut pannacotta with pineapple and chilli.

Times 12-3/6.30-10

Waterside Inn

ⓐⓐⓐⓐ *see page 46*

COOKHAM

Map 6 SU88

Malik's

ⓐⓐ Traditional Indian

Genuine Indian cooking in a very English setting

☎ 01628 520085
High St SL6 9SF
dir: M4 junct 7, take A4 towards Maidenhead, 2m

This award-winning Indian restaurant is located in the quintessentially English village of Cookham, in an ivy-covered former coaching inn near the River Thames. Wooden floors and white-clothed tables set the scene in the interior, each stylishly decorated with flowers and large church candles in black stands, and an open fire burns in winter. The extensive menu includes a good choice of tandoori, vegetarian and traditional dishes, from kormas to vindaloos, as well as seafood options such as calamari stuffed with minced prawn, chicken and herbs, Cox's Bazaar crab served on a bed of aromatic sauce, or gently steamed sea bass stuffed with fragrant herbs. Interesting desserts might include frini - an aromatic and creamy rice pudding with fresh coconut flavoured with saffron and cardamom.

Malik's

Chef Malik Ahmed, Shapon Miah **Owner** Malik Ahmed **Times** 12-2.30/6-11.00, Closed 25-26 Dec, Closed L Eid festival **Prices** Fixed D 3 course £25-£30, Starter £3.95-£7.95, Main £7.25-£15.95, Dessert £3.50-£6.95, Service added but optional 10% **Wines** 42 bottles over £20, 10 bottles under £20, 4 by glass **Notes** Sunday L, Vegetarian available, Dress restrictions, Smart dress **Seats** 70, Pr/dining room 30 **Children** Portions **Parking** 26

COOKHAM DEAN

Map 5 SU88

The Inn on The Green

ⓐⓐ Modern European 🖳

Modern classics at a stylish restaurant with rooms

☎ 01628 482638
The Old Cricket Common SL6 9NZ
e-mail: reception@theinnonthegreen.com
dir: From Marlow or Maidenhead follow Cookham Dean signs. In Cookham Dean turn into Hills Lane; into National Trust road by War Memorial

This charming inn nestles in a picturesque village in rural Berkshire, surrounded by the peace and tranquility of National Trust countryside. Its sophisticated décor and lavish furnishings - deep red velvet sofas sit beside enormous leather armchairs - combine to create a relaxed and intimate atmosphere. The stylish restaurant is comprised of three individually-styled dining areas: an airy conservatory leading on to a courtyard where alfresco dining is enjoyed in warm weather, the wood-panelled Stublie Room, and the Lamp Room, a modern creation with exposed brickwork and a magnificent chandelier. Expect imaginative modern European cooking with a twist of Japanese from a kitchen that doesn't disappoint. Try sea scallop céviche with Japanese fermented lemon dressing, or organic Loch Fyne smoked salmon with deep-fried oysters, with cranberry and walnut tart and blueberry ice cream to finish.

Chef Garry Hollihead **Owner** Andy Taylor, Mark Fuller & Garry Hollihead **Times** 1-4/7-10, Closed Mon, Closed L Tue-Sat, Closed D Sun **Prices** Fixed L 2 course £21.95, Fixed D 3 course £21.95, Starter £6-£17, Main £14-£20, Dessert £6.50, Service included **Wines** 40 bottles over £20, 4 bottles under £20, 10 by glass **Notes** Sunday L, Vegetarian available, Civ Wed 100, Air con **Seats** 60, Pr/dining room 35 **Children** Portions **Parking** 50

Waterside Inn

French 🖳

A gastronomic Thames-side legend delivering classic French cuisine

☎ 01628 620691
Ferry Rd SL6 2AT
e-mail: reservations@waterside-inn.co.uk
dir: M4 junct 8/9, A308(Windsor) then B3028 to Bray. Restaurant clearly signed

Though Bray may have become the epicentre of British gastronomy, this corner of the village will be forever France. Since 1972, the celebrated Waterside and the Roux family - a name synonymous with fine food - have been offering their special blend of classic-French-cuisine-meets-quintessential-English setting here. The Roux personnel may have changed, with son Alain having assumed the mantle of chef-patron from his father Michel in 2001, but standards at the Waterside never falter. Service here is impeccable and as good as it gets; traditional maybe, slick, polished, professional and knowledgeable, but unstuffy, friendly and genuine, and the valet parking adds just another touch of pampering. The lovely timbered building on the water's edge sports a classic, elegant dining room and, while most tables have a view of the river, the tiered terrace at the back is a magical setting

to sip champagne and nibble canapés on a warm summer day watching Thames life go by. Inside, the colour scheme is green and gold, with hand-painted frescoes of flowers and lots of mirrors giving an illusion of space. Large plate-glass windows offer diners those views over the Thames, while tables come clothed in heavy white linen set off by fresh orchids, and vases of fresh lilies further complement the room's garden theme. Like the service, the food still remains rooted in classical French, so expect impeccable ingredients, luxury, high skill and clear flavours to be delivered on a repertoire of fixed-price lunch, five-course menu Exceptionnel and a lengthy and appealing carte. Take a saddle of milk-fed lamb stuffed with morels and served with baby vegetables and a minted hollandaise sauce, and perhaps a warm rhubarb soufflé enhanced with raspberries to finish. The extensive and equally classy wine list stays as patriotically Gallic as the food, while peripherals like breads, amuse-bouche, pre-desserts and petits fours all hold form through to the end. (Note, due to major refurbishment of the kitchen, The Waterside is currently planned to close from Boxing Day 2008 to the middle of February 2009.)

Chef Michel Roux, Alain Roux
Owner Michel Roux & Alain Roux
Times 12-2/7-10, Closed 26 Dec-mid Feb (refurbishment), Closed Mon, Closed L Tue, Closed D Tue ex Jun-Aug
Wines 890 bottles over £20, 2 bottles under £20, 14 by glass **Notes** Fixed D 5 courses £93.50, Sunday L, Vegetarian available, Dress restrictions, Smart casual, Civ Wed 70, Air con **Seats** 75, Pr/dining room 8 **Children** Min 12 yrs, Menu **Parking** 20

FRILSHAM
Map 5 SU57

The Pot Kiln

Traditional British, European

Small gastro-pub serving country-style food

☎ 01635 201366
RG18 0XX
e-mail: info@potkiln.org
web: www.potkiln.org
dir: From Yattendon follow Frilsham signs, cross over motorway. Approx 0.25m pub on right

Hidden away down a narrow country lane, this small, charmingly unpretentious country pub is owned by TV chef and presenter Mike Robinson, who now has a game and wild food cookery school up the road. The L-shaped dining room off the tiny bar is decorated with hunting, shooting and fishing prints, and unclothed, rustic wooden tables add to the relaxed atmosphere. The menu takes a modern European approach and is meat and game focused. Most of the venison is shot by Mike, and many of the mushrooms are foraged by him and the chefs. Try home-made pheasant ravioli with leek tagliatelle, winter chanterelles and rosemary butter to start, then pavé of wild Berkshire fallow deer with pomme purée and peppercorn sauce.

Chef Mike Robinson **Owner** Mike Robinson
Times 12-2.30/7-9.30, Closed 25 Dec, Closed D Sun
Prices Starter £5.50-£8, Main £14-£18.50, Dessert £6.50, Service added but optional 10% **Wines** 51 bottles over £20, 8 bottles under £20, 6 by glass **Notes** Sunday L, Vegetarian available **Seats** 48, Pr/dining room 16 **Children** Portions **Parking** 70

HUNGERFORD
Map 5 SU36

The Bear Hotel

Modern British

Ambitious modern cooking in historic hotel with contemporary makeover

☎ 01488 682512
41 Charnham St RG17 0EL
e-mail: info@thebearhotelhungerford.co.uk
web: www.thebearhotelhungerford.co.uk
dir: M4 junct 14, follow A338/Hungerford signs. 3m to T-Junct turn right onto A4 over at 2 rdbts. Hotel 500yds on left

Dating back to the early 13th century, this hotel was once owned by King Henry VIII and visited by Queen Elizabeth I. Although it has retained its dark wooden beams, The Bear is now contemporary and stylish, with the restaurant's white walls featuring modern prints and tables set with crisp white linen. The kitchen deals in fresh, locally sourced produce and an accomplished, crowd-pleasing brasserie-style repertoire of intelligently simple dishes; from classics like beer-battered cod with chunky chips and mushy peas to more modern offerings like new season lamb served with roasted scallops and hot-pot potatoes, or to finish, perhaps a fine apple tart with orange marmalade ice cream and vanilla seed custard.

Chef Philip Wild **Owner** The Bear Hungerford Ltd
Times 12-2/7-9.30, Closed D Sun **Prices** Starter £4.95-£14.50, Main £10.50-£17.50, Dessert £5.95-£13.95, Service included **Wines** 24 bottles over £20, 26 bottles under £20, 8 by glass **Notes** Vegetarian available, Civ Wed 80 **Seats** 50, Pr/dining room 18 **Children** Portions **Parking** 68

HURLEY
Map 5 SU88

Black Boys Inn

Modern British

A corner of France in the English countryside

☎ 01628 824212
Henley Rd SL6 5NQ
e-mail: info@blackboysinn.co.uk
web: www.blackboysinn.co.uk
dir: M40 junct 4, A404 towards Henley, then A4130. Restaurant 3m from Henley-on-Thames

More a restaurant with rooms than a village pub, this family-run establishment is a popular local haunt and attracts an appreciative crowd even on mid-week evenings. Behind the traditional façade of the 16th-century inn, chic contemporary décor and polished wooden tables look well against the solid beams, original floorboards and wood-burning stove. The menu offers cuisine bourgeois, old-fashioned French country cooking but with a lighter modern touch. Recommended dishes are Landes foie gras with chutney and toasted brioche to start; then perhaps veal sweetbread petit choucroute with Meaux mustard sauce. Finish sweetly with chocolate sablé, bitter chocolate mousse and pistachio sauce. A particular feature is water drawn from the inn's own well.

Chef Simon Bonwick **Owner** Adrian & Helen Bannister
Times 12-2/7-9, Closed 2 wks Xmas, 2 wks Aug, BHs, Closed Mon, Closed D Sun **Prices** Starter £5.95-£9.50, Main £11.50-£19.50, Dessert £6.25, Service optional **Wines** 58 bottles over £20, 16 bottles under £20, 34 by glass **Notes** Sunday L, Vegetarian available **Seats** 45, Pr/dining room 12 **Children** Min 12yrs **Parking** 45

HURST
Map 5 SU77

The Castle Inn

Traditional British, French

Fine dining in an ancient building

☎ 0118 934 0034
Church Hill RG10 0SJ
e-mail: info@castlerestaurant.co.uk
dir: M4 junct 10, A329(M) towards Reading (E). Take first exit to Winnersh/Wokingham. Continue for 1m, at Sainsbury's turn left into Robin Hood Lane. Continue for 1.5m and go straight when approaching sharp left bend towards St Nicholas Church

This Grade II listed 16th-century inn sits in a quintessential English setting, just across from the village church and with views over the second oldest bowling green in Britain. Inside, the contemporary décor complements the wealth of original features, creating a fresh, minimalist feel. In the main dining room - the Oak Room - oak panels and wattle-and-daub plastering feature alongside chocolate brown chairs and wood floors, while the upstairs gallery room overlooks the tranquil countryside, and there's a lively bistro-style bar. Rustic French cuisine and classic British dishes form the backbone of the menu, with daily specials marked on the board. Hearty dishes feature the likes of moules frites, escargots with garlic butter, or côte de boeuf with dauphinoise potatoes and bourguignon sauce, as well as braised oxtail pie with horseradish mashed potato topping and pickled red cabbage.

Chef Jerome Leopold **Owner** Amanda Hill
Times 12-2/6.30-9.30 **Prices** Fixed L 2 course £10, Fixed D 3 course £15, Starter £4.50-£8.50, Main £10-£20, Dessert £5-£6, Service optional, Groups min 10 service 10% **Wines** 43 bottles over £20, 14 bottles under £20, 4 by glass **Notes** Early evening menu 6-7.30pm, Sunday L, Vegetarian available **Seats** 80, Pr/dining room 40 **Children** Portions **Parking** 43

The Hare Restaurant @ The Hare & Hounds

◎◎ Modern European

Assured cooking in stylishly converted pub

☎ 01488 71386
RG17 7SD
e-mail: cuisine@theharerestaurant.co.uk
dir: M4 junct 14, A338 towards Wantage, left onto B4000 towards Lambourn, restaurant 3m on left

This smartly painted former pub is located at a crossroads just outside the horse-racing village of Lambourn. Three separate rambling dining rooms sport a bright, modern and stylish décor, with slate floors, exposed beams, rustic wooden tables, and squashy leather sofas by the log fire. This is a relaxing and informal setting in which to sample some ambitious cooking that combines British with modern European influences. Sensibly compact menus (including a tasting option) are well balanced, using top-notch ingredients and interesting combinations to produce some adventurous dishes; perhaps sardine on a goat's cheese and tomato tart served with well-dressed rocket leaves, or roast quail with chorizo risotto and cauliflower purée. Finish with a classic lemon tart with lemon anglaise and fromage blanc granité. The lunch menu offers good value.

Chef Tom Snell **Owner** John Kirby **Times** 12-2/7-9.30, Closed 2 wks Jan, 2 wks summer, Tue after BH, Closed Mon, Closed D Sun **Prices** Fixed L 2 course £18, Fixed D 3 course £26, Starter £7.50-£9, Main £18-£20, Dessert £8-£8.50, Service optional, Groups min 10 service 10% **Wines** 70 bottles over £20, 6 bottles under £20, 6 by glass **Notes** Sunday L, Vegetarian available **Seats** 50, Pr/dining room 24 **Children** Portions **Parking** 30

Fredrick's Hotel, Restaurant & Spa

◎◎◎ *see opposite*

RESTAURANT OF THE YEAR

The Royal Oak at Paley Street

◎◎ British

Great food served in traditional-styled inn

☎ 01628 620541
Paley St, Littlefield Green SL6 3JN
e-mail: royaloakmail@aol.com
dir: M4 junct 8/9. Take A308 towards Maidenhead Central, then A330 to Ascot. After 2m, turn right onto B3024 to Twyford. Second pub on left

This whitewashed pub south of Maidenhead has celebrity connections, being owned by Nick Parkinson, son of famed TV presenter Michael Parkinson. There's an unstuffy, traditional feel to the interior though, with oak beams and timbers, polished-wood floors and a blazing log fire. The uncluttered dining area is an informal, white-linen-free zone, with well-styled contemporary furniture and original artwork, while hospitality and service is appropriately welcoming and attentive. With classical roots, head chef Dominic Chapman (previously at Heston Blumenthal's Hinds Head in Bray) creates modern twists to some well known dishes. Quality ingredients and seasonality drive his regularly-changing menu; take hare and trotter pie, or perhaps Gloucestershire Old Spot belly pork with mushy peas and braised onions, while baked Alaska might feature among homely desserts. **The Royal Oak at Paley Street is AA Restaurant of the Year for England.**

Chef Dominic Chapman **Owner** Nick Parkinson **Times** 12-3/6-12, Closed 1 Jan, Closed D Sun **Prices** Fixed L 2 course £16-£27, Fixed D 3 course £20-£32, Starter £6.50-£14, Main £9.50-£23.50, Dessert £5.95-£7, Service optional **Wines** 100 bottles over £20, 20 bottles under £20, 20 by glass **Notes** Sunday L, Vegetarian available, Air con **Seats** 50 **Children** Portions **Parking** 70

Red House

◎ British, French 🖥

Anglo-French dining in thatched restaurant

☎ 01635 582017
RG20 8LY
e-mail: enquiries@redhousemarshbenham.co.uk
dir: 400yds off A4, 3m from Newbury, 5m from Hungerford

Nestling in a small hamlet close to the Kennet and Avon canal, this well-presented 18th-century country dining pub started life long ago as a bakery. It has recently acquired a new thatched roof and bar, plus a new private room overlooking water meadows. Bookcases line the L-shaped dining room and tables are well spaced; the formal look balanced by friendly and efficient service. Expect generous modern European menus of unpretentious dishes with clear flavours and the occasional French and international accent. Pavé of halibut, braised fennel, grilled baby vegetables and celeriac purée is a fine example of the fare.

Chef Yves Girard **Owner** Tricrane Ltd
Times 11.30-2.30/7-9.45, Closed New Year **Prices** Fixed L 2 course £13.95-£17, Fixed D 3 course fr £17.95, Starter £5-£8.50, Main £9.95-£19.95, Dessert £5-£6.50, Service added but optional 10%, Groups min 6 service 10% **Wines** 33 bottles over £20, 19 bottles under £20, 11 by glass **Notes** Sunday L, Vegetarian available, Civ Wed 90 **Seats** 60, Pr/dining room 30 **Children** Portions, Menu **Parking** 60

Donnington Valley Hotel & Spa

◎◎ Modern British 🍷NOTABLE WINE LIST 🍴

Elegant wine-themed restaurant in a spa and golf hotel

☎ 01635 551199
Old Oxford Rd, Donnington RG14 3AG
e-mail: general@donningtonvalley.co.uk
dir: M4 junct 13, A34 towards Newbury. Take immediate left signed Donnington Hotel. At rdbt take right, at 3rd rdbt take left, follow road for 2m, hotel on right

A state-of-the-art spa, impressive conference facilities and an 18-hole golf course are among the facilities offered at this stylish modern hotel set amid lovely grounds. A raised gallery overlooks the central dining area of the informally styled Wine Press Restaurant, and the wine theme extends to a well-balanced wine list of some 300 bottles. When it comes to food, the emphasis is firmly on fresh produce, locally sourced and simply prepared. The head sommelier recommends some more unusual wines, suggesting the kinds of dishes they would complement. Expect mains such as rump of lamb with pease pudding, boulangère potatoes, spinach and yam, or pan-fried monkfish with curried mussels, okra and crushed new potatoes.

Chef Kelvin Johnson **Owner** Sir Peter Michael **Times** 12-2/7-10 **Prices** Fixed L 2 course fr £19, Fixed D 3 course fr £26, Starter £7-£11, Main £10-£27, Dessert £7-£9.50, Service optional **Wines** 190 bottles over £20, 34 bottles under £20, 30 by glass **Notes** Sunday L, Vegetarian available, Dress restrictions, Smart casual, Civ Wed 85, Air con **Seats** 120, Pr/dining room 130 **Children** Portions, Menu **Parking** 150

Fredrick's Hotel, Restaurant & Spa

MAIDENHEAD Map 6 SU88

Modern British, French 💻

Accomplished cooking at luxurious retreat

☎ 01628 581000
Shoppenhangers Rd SL6 2PZ
e-mail: eat@fredricks-hotel.co.uk
dir: From M4 junct 8/9 take A404(M), then turning (junct 9A) for Cox Green/ White Waltham. Left on to Shoppenhangers Rd, restaurant 400 mtrs on right

Just 30 minutes from London, this luxury hotel enjoys a peaceful location yet is within easy reach of the M4. This is a place where guests are pampered and the luxurious rooms and swanky spa are reason enough to visit, but the exquisite cuisine is another reason to stay and indulge. The elegant restaurant is traditionally styled in blues and golds with a backdrop of striking artwork and views over the terrace, patio and well-tended gardens. Enjoy aperitifs in the bar or on the patio in summer, and then take your seat for some accomplished cooking. Expect classic French and British dishes with a contemporary touch from a kitchen that likes to dot its menus with luxury ingredients and high quality produce. A selection of old favourites such as escalopes of veal Viennoise and warm lobster salad should suit those in the mood for familiar fare, while the more

adventurous might try pot pourri of sautéed rabbit, duck livers, girolles and asparagus, or grilled supreme of wild salmon trout with basil and garlic mayonnaise. Finish with strawberry parfait and lavender sorbet.

Times 12-2.30/7-10, Closed 25 Dec, 1 Jan, Closed L Sat

The Vineyard at Stockcross

Modern British V

Superb blend of innovation and tradition in the kitchen and setting

☎ 01635 528770
Stockcross RG20 8JU
e-mail: general@the-vineyard.co.uk
dir: M4 junct 13/A34 Newbury bypass southbound, take 3rd exit signed Hungerford/Bath road interchange. Take 2nd exit at 1st and 2nd rdbts signed Stockcross, 0.6 mile on right

Surprisingly, there's actually no vineyard here at Stockcross, instead it takes its name and inspiration from proprietor Sir Peter Michael's winery in California. But there's a dramatic steel 'grapevine' balustrade that wraps its way around the bright, stylish, split-level dining room, to offer a nod to this contemporary hotel's personality. And there are also two dazzling wine lists; one magnificent tome devoted appropriately to California, the other volume takes on the rest of the world. However, this little slice of California in the Berkshire countryside is nothing if not individual, mixing the contemporary with a dash of country-house décor and, its ultimate jewel in the crown, the platform for renowned chef John Campbell's inspired modern cuisine. Opulence reigns at this plush modern venue, though it's not over the top, with calming colours and a pleasing sense of space and light. Art and sculpture are another important facet of The Vineyard experience, as demonstrated by the contemporary 'Fire and Water' sculpture outside, which makes a dramatic statement, especially at night, with its flaming torches set on a large pond. Public areas provide the backdrop for a fine art collection, and there are two comfortable lounges for aperitifs or coffee. Service is expectedly slick and professional, like the food, but with a friendly touch, while dining tables are attractively set in homage to John Campbell's poised, contemporary and striking cooking. Campbell's inimitable style is based on the state-of-the-art scientific approach and takes itself seriously, delivering an exciting blend of flavours, textures and top-notch ingredients. So expect innovative and visually striking dishes to thrill the palate and senses on crisply-scripted menus; take turbot with pork belly, langoustines and lemongrass, or perhaps veal (cheeks, rump and sweetbreads) with spiced dates, and to finish, cucumber, lime, mango and yogurt.

Chef John Campbell, Peter Eaton **Owner** Sir Peter Michael **Times** 12-2/7-9.30 **Wines** 3000 bottles over £20, 22 bottles under £20, 23 by glass **Notes** ALC 2 courses £58, 3 courses £68, Sunday L, Vegetarian menu, Civ Wed 120, Air con **Seats** 86, Pr/dining room 120 **Children** Portions, Menu **Parking** 100

NEWBURY *Continued*

Newbury Manor Hotel

◎ Modern European

Good, honest food in idyllic riverside location

☎ 01635 528838
London Rd RG14 2BY
e-mail: enquiries@newbury-manor-hotel.co.uk

Hidden away on the edge of Newbury, surrounded by 9 acres of mature woodland and water meadows, this delightful Grade II listed watermill has recently been refurbished and returned to its former glory. A short stroll across herringbone brick paths and wooden bridges, through the herb gardens past the pond, brings you to the River Bar restaurant where full-length conservatory-style windows make the most of the views across the jetty and babbling River Kennett. Good honest cooking using quality ingredients prepared with skill and care is the draw here. Start with Devonshire king scallops with seared hot smoked salmon and pimento salsa, followed by a main course of fillet of beef with butter-braised pommes fondant, sun-dried tomatoes, braised shallots and wild mushrooms.

Times 12-2.30/7-9 **Prices** Food prices not confirmed for 2009. Please telephone for details.

Regency Park Hotel

◎ French, European 🖥

Imaginative cuisine with a contemporary, tranquil setting

☎ 01635 871555
Bowling Green Rd, Thatcham RG18 3RP
e-mail: info@regencyparkhotel.co.uk
dir: M4 junct 13, follow A339 to Newbury for 2m, then take the A4 (Reading), the hotel is signed

The pretty landscaped water gardens provide a tranquil backdrop at the Watermark Restaurant, set within this smart, stylish hotel within easy reach of the M4. It's an airy, modern Italian-influenced style restaurant, with large windows, crisp linen, and a brasserie-style menu of contemporary European with French-influenced dishes thoughtfully created to deliver uncomplicated, clean flavours. Using the freshest of seasonal ingredients, starters might include scallops with salsify purée and baby leeks perhaps, followed by rump of lamb Niçoise with rosemary and red wine jus, with apple frangipane tart with praline ice cream among the choice of desserts.

Chef Laurent Guyon **Owner** Pedersen Caterers **Times** 12.30-2/7-10, Closed L Sat **Prices** Fixed L 2 course £16.50-£21, Fixed D 3 course £25-£28.50, Starter £5.50-£6.75, Main £10.25-£17.50, Dessert £5.95-£8.50, Service optional **Wines** 24 bottles over £20, 26 bottles under £20, 12 by glass **Notes** Sunday L, Vegetarian available, Civ Wed 100 **Seats** 100, Pr/dining room 140 **Children** Portions, Menu **Parking** 210

The Vineyard at Stockcross

◎◎◎◎ **see opposite**

PANGBOURNE   Map 5 SU67

The Elephant at Pangbourne

◎ British, French 🌶

Modern food in a colonial setting

☎ 0118 984 2244 & 07770 268359
Church Rd RG8 7AR
e-mail: reception@elephanthotel.co.uk
dir: A4 Theale/Newbury, right at 2nd rdbt signed Pangbourne. Hotel on left

This is a rather elegant elephant, decorated in a way that is colonial in style without resorting to cliché. The dining room has views out over the garden to the church through large windows and service is unstuffy and friendly. Take a cocktail in the bar if you want to feel like Sir Stamford Raffles; BaBar has a bistro feel and serves simple dishes, while the main dining room delivers modern food with some international influences. A bowl of mussels as a starter is flavoured with Indian spices or there is the more traditional celeriac and artichoke soup. Main-course pigeon with foie gras and glazed chicory is a classic dish, while a dessert of carrot cake with carrot purée and a mascarpone sorbet demonstrates the kitchen's creative ambitions.

Chef Neil Dowson **Owner** Hillbrooke Hotels **Times** 12-2.30/7-9 **Prices** Fixed L 2 course £17, Fixed D 3 course £30, Starter £6.50, Main £17, Dessert £6.50, Service optional **Wines** 33 bottles over £20, 8 bottles under £20, 9 by glass **Notes** Vegetarian available, Civ Wed 70 **Seats** 65, Pr/dining room 40 **Children** Portions, Menu **Parking** 15

READING   Map 5 SU77

Cerise

◎ Modern British

☎ 08000 789789 & 0118 958 1234
Forbury Hotel, 26 The Forbury RG1 3EJ
e-mail: reservations@theforburyhotel.co.uk

This establishment was awarded its Rosette/s just as we went to press. Therefore we are unable to provide a description for it - visit www.theAA.com for the most up-to-date information.

Times 12-3/7-10 **Prices** Food prices not confirmed for 2009. Please telephone for details.

Forburys Restaurant

◎◎ French, European 🖥 🍷

Contemporary restaurant in the Forbury Square development

☎ 0118 957 4044 & 0118 956 9191
1 Forbury Square, The Forbury RG1 3BB
e-mail: forburys@btconnect.com
dir: M4 junct 11, 3m to town centre, opposite Forbury Gardens

With floor-to-ceiling windows overlooking Forbury Square and a terrace with heated umbrellas and delightful views over Forbury Gardens, this elegant, contemporary building was designed by the architect who created Canary Wharf. The sand-and-cream colour scheme is offset by chocolate brown leather seats, oak floors and crisp linen, and there's a private dining room and a contemporary-style wine bar in stainless steel and leather. Cooking is French British and, in addition to the seasonal carte, a good-value market menu is available at lunch and dinner, complemented by a great wine list and friendly, efficient service. Popular dishes include tian of Dorset crab with confit tomato and cucumber carpaccio, whole roasted Cornish cod with chorizo, squid and paprika risotto, with blackberry millefeuille, Chiboust cream and blackberry sorbet to finish.

Chef Gavin Young **Owner** Xavier Le-Bellego **Times** 12-2.15/6-10, Closed 26-28 Dec, 1-2 Jan, Closed Sun **Prices** Fixed L 2 course £13.95-£17.95, Fixed D 3 course £19.95-£22.95, Starter £7.25-£11, Main £12.50-£19.95, Dessert £6.50-£8.95, Service optional, Groups min 4 service 12.5% **Wines** 145 bottles over £20, 9 bottles under £20, 12 by glass **Notes** Tasting menu available, Vegetarian available, Air con **Seats** 80, Pr/dining room 16 **Children** Min 6 yrs, Portions **Parking** 40

Malmaison Brasserie

◎ Modern European 🌶

Contemporary brasserie dining in rejuvenated former Great Western Rail hotel

☎ 0118 956 2300 & 956 2302
18 - 20 Station Rd RG1 1JX
e-mail: reading@malmaison.com
web: www.malmaison.com
dir: Next to Reading station

This former Great Western Railway hotel has been transformed in typically chic Malmaison style, yet its past is not forgotten with numerous rail memorabilia and photographs adorning the walls. A central banquette with generous tables and high-backed chairs divides the long brasserie-style restaurant, stretching back to a glass wine wall, while exposed brickwork and black tiled flooring add to the funky feel. The cooking style is equally modern but classically based, allowing ingredients to take centre stage, and there's a firm emphasis on home-grown and local produce with suppliers extensively noted on the menu. Expect starters like celeriac velouté with truffle oil, with perhaps a main course of pan-fried sea

Continued

READING *Continued*

bass, pomme purée and braised oxtail, or maybe lobster and scallop shepherd's pie. An impressive wine list completes the upbeat package.

Chef Andrew Holmes **Owner** Malmaison H & V Group **Times** 12-2.30/6-11, Closed L Sat **Prices** Fixed L 2 course £9.95-£18, Fixed D 3 course fr £16.50, Starter £4.50-£7.50, Main £9.50-£23.50, Dessert £5.95-£7.50, Service added but optional 10% **Wines** 234 bottles over £20, 16 bottles under £20, 23 by glass **Notes** Sunday L, Vegetarian available, Air con **Seats** 64, Pr/dining room 14 **Children** Portions, Menu **Parking** NCP across road

Millennium Madejski Hotel Reading

◉◉ British, International ▢ V

Contemporary food in striking, modern stadium complex

☎ 0118 925 3500
Madejski Stadium RG2 0FL
e-mail: sales.reading@millenniumhotels.co.uk
dir: 1m N from M4 junct 11. 2m S from Reading town centre

Cilantro is the modern, fine dining restaurant in this stylish hotel that forms part of the impressive Madejski Stadium complex, home to both Reading FC and London Irish Rugby team. Have an aperitif in the lively Atrium bar before savouring some accomplished French-inspired cooking. Contemporary dishes include starters of foie gras with rhubarb and ginger confit, or poached lobster salad with pea coulis and liquorice. Main course might deliver monkfish with white beans, cherry tomatoes and fricassée of squid, or roast rib of lamb with sweetbreads, baby artichoke and aubergine confit, while chocolate fondant with Guinness ice cream makes a fitting finale. The buzzy atmosphere is made more enjoyable by the friendly and efficient service.

Chef Denzil Newton **Owner** Madejski Hotel Co
Times Closed 25 Dec, 1 Jan, BHs, Closed Sun, Closed L all

week **Prices** Fixed D 3 course fr £47.50, Tasting menu £49.50, Service optional **Wines** 64 bottles over £20, 36 bottles under £20, 12 by glass **Notes** Vegetarian menu, Dress restrictions, Smart casual, Air con **Seats** 55, Pr/dining room 12 **Children** Min 12 yrs, Portions **Parking** 100

Novotel Reading Centre

◉ Modern, International

New city-centre hotel with accomplished cooking

☎ 0118 952 2600
25b Friar St RG1 1DP
e-mail: h5432-fb@accor.com
dir: Within short distance of M4

Offering a stylish, relaxed vibe, innovative restaurant seating arrangements are offered at this stylish city-centre hotel, taking account of everyone from single diners to large groups. The open-plan bar area is furnished with high-backed leather seats, and in the airy, spacious restaurant large artworks catch the eye. The seasonal menu offers international cuisine and some dishes are offered in taster, starter and main course portions, so you can pick and mix between the likes of wild black bream with garlic mash and broad bean broth, Welsh rump of lamb with crushed peas and Anya potatoes, and wild mushroom ravioli.

Chef Miguel Oliveira **Owner** Novotel, Accor UK **Times** 12/mdnt **Prices** Fixed L 2 course £15, Starter £4.95-£7.50, Main £9.75-£20.50, Dessert £4-£6.95, Service optional **Wines** 8 bottles over £20, 15 bottles under £20, 19 by glass **Notes** Buffet L available Mon-Fri, Sunday L, Vegetarian available, Air con **Seats** 86, Pr/dining room 70 **Children** Portions, Menu **Parking** 18 **Parking** Also NCP

SHINFIELD Map 5 SU76

L'ortolan

◉◉◉ – *see opposite*

SLOUGH Map 6 SU97

The Pinewood Hotel

◉ Modern European ▢

Simple but appealing dining in a luxury small hotel

☎ 01753 896400
Wexham Park Ln, George Green SL3 6AP
e-mail: info@pinewoodhotel.co.uk
dir: Telephone for directions

Excellent design is at the forefront throughout this smart hotel on the outskirts of Slough. The contemporary and welcoming Eden Brasserie specialises in modern European style of cooking with North African influences, including dishes cooked in a wood-burning oven and stove. Start with roasted sardines in a North African marinade, followed by roasted Moroccan spiced rack of lamb with garlic and chilli aubergine and grilled herb polenta, or spinach and feta filo parcels with tomato and Greek kalamata olive sauce. Alfresco dining is available on the terrace in summer months. Service is relaxed and attentive.

Chef Phil Currie **Owner** Ravi & Bal Takhar **Times** 12-3/6-10 **Prices** Starter £5.95-£6.95, Main £9.95-£18.95, Dessert £5.95, Service added but optional 5% **Wines** 16 bottles over £20, 21 bottles under £20, 8 by glass **Notes** Sunday L, Vegetarian available, Civ Wed 100, Air con **Seats** 48, Pr/dining room 90 **Children** Portions, Menu **Parking** 100

SONNING Map 5 SU77

The French Horn

◉◉ Traditional French ▢

Classical dining on the Thames

☎ 0118 969 2204
RG4 6TN
e-mail: info@thefrenchhorn.co.uk
dir: From Reading take A4 E to Sonning. Follow B478 through village over bridge, hotel on right, car park on left

This long-established riverside restaurant nestles on the banks of a tranquil stretch of the Thames, and has a well deserved reputation for high quality cuisine. Take a drink in the cosy bar where a spit-roast duck turns above the fire, promising good things to come - or in summer sit out on the delightful terrace - before moving through to the elegant dining room which is almost entirely glass-fronted, making the most of the river views. Tables are well appointed, and a classical English and French menu with innovative touches suits the formal setting. Start with a tian of crab, or if you're hungry a whole lobster and Caesar salad, and then tuck into the likes of pan-fried halibut laced with a peppercorn sauce, Chateaubriand with béarnaise sauce, or a simply grilled whole Dover sole.

Times 12-1.45/7-9.15, Closed 26-30 Dec

STREATLEY Map 5 SU58

Cygnetures

◉◉ British, International ▢

Fine-dining hotel restaurant with a gorgeous Thames-side vista

☎ 01491 878800
The Swan at Streatley, High St RG8 9HR
e-mail: sales@swan-at-streatley.co.uk
dir: Follow A329 from Pangbourne, on entering Streatley turn right at lights. Hotel on left before bridge

This quintessentially English 17th-century inn was allegedly the site where Jerome K Jerome wrote Three Men in a Boat, and it's easy to see why he was so attracted to the beautiful Thames-side location. Diners at Cygnetures restaurant can enjoy the stunning riverside views and tranquil atmosphere, while sampling modern European dishes mixed in with traditional favourites. The chef maintains high standards on the daily-changing menu, drawing inspiration from the finest seasonal ingredients. Try a typical starter such as chargrilled Cornish scallops with English pea salsa and crisp air-dried Carmarthen

Continued

L'ortolan

French 🖥 V

Serious fine dining in stylish listed building

☎ 0118 988 8500
Church Ln RG2 9BY
e-mail: info@lortolan.com
web: www.lortolan.com
dir: From M4 junct 11 take A33 towards Basingstoke. At 1st rdbt turn left, after garage turn left, 1m turn right at Six Bells pub. Restaurant 1st left (follow tourist signs)

The red-brick vicarage in a pretty Berkshire village was built in the 17th century and has for the last few decades been a destination restaurant. Under the current ownership since 2001, its reputation as a fine dining venue continues. The interior is altogether modern, chic and sophisticated. The long dining room is enhanced by a small bar and conservatory, while private dining rooms, including a new 'Winecellars' room with opulent and lavish decoration, further completes the package. The cooking of Alan Murchison and his well established team is modern, creative, confident and French-focused, while underpinned by classical foundations. The kitchen uses high-quality seasonal produce to good effect, delivered via a long list of menus ranging from an appealing carte, excellent value lunch menu, seven-course gourmand, private dining menus and the new chef's table, which brings diners right into the heart of the action. Flavours are clear and refined throughout, combinations well considered and presentation another strong point. Start with pan fried scallops, sauce vièrge, gazpacho jelly and lemon purée before main-course stuffed saddle of rabbit served with carrots, peas and lettuce ravioli. Desserts include warm dark chocolate soufflé with salted white chocolate ice cream, while peripherals include excellent breads and interesting amuse-bouche. Service is suitably professional and friendly.

Chef Alan Murchison **Owner** Alan Murchison Restaurants Ltd
Times 11.45-2/7-10, Closed 2 wks Xmas/New Year, Closed Mon/Sun
Prices Food prices not confirmed for 2009. Please telephone for details.
Wines 350 bottles over £20, 5 bottles under £20, 10 by glass **Notes** Tasting menu 7 courses, Vegetarian menu, Dress restrictions, Smart casual, Civ Wed 60 **Seats** 64, Pr/dining room 20
Children Portions, Menu **Parking** 45

STREATLEY *Continued*

ham, followed by braised shoulder of beef, grain mustard mash and honey-roasted parsnips, with treacle tart and lavender milk ice cream to finish.

Owner John Nike Group **Times** 12.30-2/7-10 **Prices** Food prices not confirmed for 2009. Please telephone for details. **Wines** 89 bottles over £20, 31 bottles under £20, 18 by glass **Notes** Sunday L, Vegetarian available, Dress restrictions, Smart casual, Civ Wed 150 **Seats** 70, Pr/dining room 130 **Children** Portions, Menu **Parking** 130

WINDSOR Map 6 SU97

Mercure Castle Hotel

◉◉ Modern European 🖥

Fine dining in centrally-located hotel with castle views

☎ 0870 4008300 & 01753 851577
High St SL4 1LJ
dir: M25 junct 13 take A308 towards town centre then onto B470 to High St. M4 junct 6 towards A332, at rdbt first exit into Clarence Rd, left at lights to High St

Prominently situated opposite Sir Christopher Wren's Guildhall, this 16th-century former coaching inn is one of the oldest buildings in Windsor. Enjoying fine views of Windsor Castle, it's a popular venue for functions and weddings, from small dinners up to formal evening balls. The elegant contemporary-style restaurant is decorated in shades of aubergine and soft beige, and offers comprehensive modern international cuisine that makes the most of the finest seasonal produce, sourced from a range of suppliers countrywide. Cooking is thoughtful and innovative with a variety of classical dishes and modern interpretations on the seasonally-changing menus, complemented by an extensive wine list. Take a pan-fried fillet of red mullet, with oriental crab and sweet chilli dressing to start, and follow with lemon sole and lobster paupiette, served with a fricassée of baby vegetables and caviar.

Times 12-2.30/6.30-9.45

Oakley Court Hotel

◉ Modern, French

Modern cooking in Thames-side mansion hotel

☎ 01753 609988 & 609900
Windsor Rd, Water Oakley SL4 5UR
e-mail: reservations@oakleycourt.com
dir: M4 junct 6 to Windsor. At rdbt right onto A308. Hotel 2.5m on right.

Built in 1859, this splendid Victorian Gothic mansion - now country-house hotel - is set in extensive Thames-side grounds and, during the 1960s, provided the setting for the St Trinian's films and famous Hammer Horror productions like Dracula. Today though, there's nothing scary about the attractive, appropriately traditional setting of the Oakleaf Restaurant with its oak panels, well-spaced tables, pleasant views and attentive, professional service. The kitchen takes a classical

approach with modern twists on its ambitious carte; take pan-fried sea bass served on sweet pepper gnocchi with crispy chorizo, chargrilled artichokes and rocket pesto, and perhaps a glazed passionfruit tart with spun sugar to finish.

Chef Darran Kimber **Owner** Heuston Hospitality **Times** 12-2/7-9.30, Closed L Sat **Prices** Food prices not confirmed for 2009. Please telephone for details, Service optional **Wines** 60 bottles over £20, 4 bottles under £20, 6 by glass **Notes** Sunday L, Vegetarian available, Dress restrictions, Smart casual, Civ Wed 120, Air con **Seats** 110, Pr/dining room 25 **Children** Portions, Menu **Parking** 180

Sir Christopher Wren's House Hotel & Spa

◉◉ Modern British

Relaxed fine dining with unbeatable views

☎ 01753 861354
Thames St SL4 1PX
e-mail: reservations@windsor.wrensgroup.com
dir: Telephone for directions

Perched right beside the River Thames, this house was built by Wren, with meticulous attention to detail, to be his family home. Strok's restaurant enjoys wonderful views and guests today can watch the sun set behind the riverbank trees from the champagne terrace. Soft downlights, flickering candles, contemporary with a hint of traditional elegance is the style. The seasonally-changing menu takes a modern approach with classical influences. Quality ingredients meet skilful, balanced dishes with understated presentation. Perhaps choose ballotine of ham hock with roasted walnut brioche and apple vinaigrette, followed by breast of guinea fowl with a carrot and potato galette and butter onion cream, or best end of lamb with honey-glazed root vegetables and baby beetroot.

Chef Stephen Boucher **Owner** The Wrens Hotel Group **Times** 12.30-2.30/6.30-10 **Prices** Food prices not confirmed for 2009. Please telephone for details, Service optional **Wines** 60 bottles over £20, 8 bottles under £20, 6 by glass **Notes** 3 course jazz L 1st Sun each mth, Pre-theatre D available, Sunday L, Vegetarian available,

Dress restrictions, Smart casual preferred, Civ Wed 100, Air con **Seats** 65, Pr/dining room 100 **Children** Portions **Parking** 14 Plus parking at Riverside train station

YATTENDON Map 5 SU57

Royal Oak Hotel

◉ Modern European

Extensive menu and a setting to suit all occasions

☎ 01635 201325
The Square RG18 0UG
e-mail: info@royaloakyattendon.com
dir: M4 junct 12, follow signs to Pangbourne, left to Yattendon, or M4 junct 13 follow signs to Hermitage, after Post Office turn right to Yattendon

Standing on the square of a pretty Berkshire village, within easy reach of the M4, this 16th-century inn has been attracting diners since Oliver Cromwell reputedly ate here on the eve of the Battle of Newbury. There are three separate dining venues - the brasserie, the formal restaurant and the walled garden - each serving the same menu. There's a choice of hot and cold starters, and several speciality pasta and risotto dishes. Mains take in mozzarella and tomato ravioli with mushroom and cream sauce, or medallions of venison with port wine, cranberry and chestnut sauce.

Times 12-2.15/7-10, Closed 1 Jan

BRISTOL

BRISTOL Map 4 ST57

Bells Diner

◉◉ Modern European 🖥

Contemporary European cuisine in Bohemian surroundings

☎ 0117 924 0357
1-3 York Rd, Montpellier BS6 5QB
e-mail: info@bellsdiner.com
web: www.bellsdiner.com
dir: Telephone for further details

Set in a Bohemian quarter of Bristol, in a converted grocery shop, this eclectic restaurant continues to attract locals and gastronomes. The intimate, rustic restaurant retains some of the original shop fittings in the front dining room, with the rear dining area boasting more contemporary décor. Inventive European cooking remains the central focus with classic flavour combinations using modern and traditional techniques. Investment in cutting-edge equipment reflects the owner's commitment to developing and evolving the menu to the highest standard. With a tasting menu available, typical dishes might include a starter of macaroni cheese with black truffle, chives and white truffle oil. For a main course, try suckling pig with cauliflower purée, raisins, spinach, apple and coffee jus. Desserts include white chocolate pannacotta with coffee granita and praline ice cream.

Times 12-2.30/7-10.30, Closed 24-30 Dec, Closed Sun, Closed L Mon & Sat

Bordeaux Quay

◉ European 🖥

Enthusiastic seasonal cuisine in modern waterside warehouse restaurant

☎ 0117 906 5550
V-Shed, Cannons Rd BS1 5UH

Decked out over two floors and set around a wide central atrium (with ground-floor bar and deli, and smart first-floor restaurant), this modern warehouse restaurant overlooks the waterfront in the centre of the city. Light and airy, the high-ceilinged, open-plan restaurant cultivates the contemporary theme, with bags of elegant wood and a nod to industrial pipe work. The kitchen takes an equally modern, intelligently straightforward line, using carefully sourced regional produce. Think a tranche of halibut delivered with spinach, morels and a butter sauce, and perhaps treacle tart with vanilla ice cream to finish.

Times 12.30-3/6.30-10.30, Closed Sun

The Bowl Inn

◉ Modern British, International 🖐

Popular 16th-century inn serving skilfully prepared dishes

☎ 01454 612757
16 Church Rd, Lower Almondsbury BS32 4DT
e-mail: reception@thebowlinn.co.uk
dir: M5 junct 6 towards Thornbury, take 3rd left into Over Ln, then 1st right into Sundays Hill and next right into Church Rd

Overflowing with history and full of traditional character, this popular family-run 16th-century inn sits on the edge of the Severn Vale. Complete with exposed beams, country furniture and linen-clad tables, Lilies Restaurant offers a cosy and relaxed atmosphere, while a more informal menu and a range of cask ales is provided in the bar. Carefully prepared modern dishes, using quality free-range and local ingredients, include starters such as home-made game terrine with grape chutney and walnut bread, followed by main courses like Madgett Farm free-range chicken breast with pearl barley and fennel risotto and port reduction.

Chef Ricky Stephenson, David Jones **Owner** P Alley **Times** 12-2.30/6-9.30, Closed 25 Dec, Closed L Sat, Closed D Sun **Prices** Fixed D 3 course £20-£30, Starter £4.95-£5.95, Main £11.25-£21.50, Dessert £4.50-£5.45, Service optional **Wines** 5 bottles over £20, 27 bottles under £20, 9 by glass **Notes** Sunday L, Vegetarian available, Dress restrictions, Smart casual **Seats** 60, Pr/dining room 25 **Children** Portions, Menu **Parking** 60

The Bristol Marriott Royal

◉ Modern

Traditional and modern food in spectacular surroundings

☎ 0117 925 5100
College Green BS1 5TA
e-mail: bristol.royal@marriotthotels.co.uk
dir: Next to cathedral by College Green

This stunning hotel, established in 1863, occupies a prestigious city centre site overlooking the cathedral and the historic harbour. The dining room is truly spectacular with exceptionally high sandstone walls, classical statuary, balconies and an amazing stained glass wall. Tables are classically dressed with crisp white linen, silver cutlery and sparkling glassware. West Country produce is well to the fore in the choice of traditional and quintessentially British dishes with some modern twists, including Blue Vinney cheese tart with sun-blushed tomatoes, and pot-roasted Gloucestershire chicken with mini toffee apples and cider sauce. A less formal Terrace restaurant and champagne bar are also available.

Times 12-2.30/7-10, Closed Sun, Mon, BHs

Culinaria

◉◉ Mediterranean

Simple, Mediterranean cuisine to eat in or take away

☎ 0117 973 7999
1 Chandos Rd, Redland BS6 6PG

Culinaria's great idea is combining a busy and successful bistro/restaurant with a takeaway: eat in or choose something ready prepared by the chefs - either chilled or frozen - to eat at home. Whichever you choose, you'll get simple yet beautifully executed dishes. The dining room is light, bright and modern, the service relaxed and attentive. Mediterranean-style cooking sees crab bisque or aubergine fritters with tomato and basil sauce to start, with main courses such as whole grilled megrim sole with herb butter and spiced lamb served Moroccan-style with apricots. Desserts may include baked lime and ginger cheesecake. Both restaurant and takeaway menus change weekly and are updated on the restaurant website.

Chef Stephen Markwick **Owner** Stephen & Judy Markwick **Times** 12-2/6.30-9.30, Closed Xmas, New Year, BHs, 4 wks during year, Closed Sun-Wed **Prices** Fixed L 2 course £15.50, Starter £7-£7.75, Main £11.75-£16.75, Dessert £6-£6.75, Service optional **Wines** 13 bottles over £20, 20 bottles under £20, 4 by glass **Notes** Vegetarian available **Seats** 30 **Children** Portions **Parking** On street

Ellipse Bar & Restaurant

◉ Modern British

Stylish modern hotel dining on the riverside

☎ 0117 933 8200 & 929 1030
Mercure Brigstow Bristol, 5-7 Welsh Back BS1 4SP
e-mail: h6548@accor.com
dir: M32, follow signs for Bristol Temple Meads train station. At rdbt turn into Victoria St. Continue over Bristol bridge turn left and immediately left and then left again onto Welsh Back, hotel on left

With a prime position on the riverside at the heart of the old city, this handsome, modern, purpose-built hotel's smart Ellipse Restaurant opens directly onto the cobbled sidewalk of one of Bristol's more fashionable and popular areas. Inside, the lobby leads into the open-plan bar and restaurant, all stylishly appointed and comfortably furnished, and there's a mezzanine level too. The kitchen's modern approach suits the setting, with simplicity and flavour driven by fresh, high quality local ingredients from the West Country larder; take Cornish hake with gem batter, hand-cut chips and home-made tartare sauce, or confit of Sandridge Farm belly pork served with celeriac purée and a honey and sage sauce.

Chef Luke Trott **Owner** Accor Hotel **Times** 11-5/6-9.45, Closed 25 Dec **Prices** Fixed L 2 course £15-£25, Starter £5-£7, Main £10-£18.50, Dessert £5-£6.50, Service optional, Groups min 10 service 10% **Wines** 26 bottles over £20, 15 bottles under £20, 11 by glass **Notes** Sunday L, Vegetarian available, Civ Wed 70 **Seats** 65, Pr/dining room 50 **Children** Portions **Parking** NCP

BRISTOL *Continued*

Glass Boat Restaurant

⊛ British, European 💻

Accurate cooking in a unique riverside setting

☎ 0117 929 0704
Welsh Back BS1 4SB
e-mail: bookings@glassboat.co.uk
dir: Moored below Bristol Bridge in the old centre of
Bristol

Expect fabulous views from this recently refurbished
glass-topped 1920s boat, anchored in the historic docks
close to Bristol Bridge. Waterfront life provides the
perfect backdrop for an atmospheric lunch or candlelit
dinner. Original wooden floors, simple table settings and
nicely worn fixtures contribute to the effect. Cooking is
honest and appealing, with generous portions of British
and European fare prepared from fresh seasonal
ingredients. Recommendations include roast quail with
black pudding and caramelised apple, followed by halibut
fillet with salsify, chestnut and tarragon sauce; and
quince and cardamom filo parcel with fig syrup and
balsamic ice cream to finish.

Chef Neil Davis **Owner** Arne Ringer
Times 12-2.30/6.30-11, Closed 24-26 Dec, 1 Jan, Closed
L Sat, Closed D Sun **Prices** Fixed L 2 course £10-£16,
Fixed D 3 course fr £29.50, Starter £4.95-£9.95, Main
£9.95-£19.95, Dessert £5.25-£7.75, Service added but
optional 10% **Wines** 100 bottles over £20, 40 bottles
under £20, 8 by glass **Notes** Sunday L, Vegetarian
available, Civ Wed 120, Air con **Seats** 120, Pr/dining room
40 **Parking** NCP

Goldbrick House

⊛⊛ Modern British, European

**Stylish, modern city-centre dining with quality
ingredients and balanced flavours**

☎ 0117 945 1950
69 Park St BS1 5PB
e-mail: info@goldbrickhouse.co.uk
web: www.goldbrickhouse.co.uk
dir: M32, follow signs for city centre. Left side of Park St,
going up the hill towards museum

Converted from two Georgian townhouses and a Victorian
factory, Goldbrick House incorporates an informal café-
bar with upstairs champagne and cocktail bar,
restaurant and terrace. The fine-dining restaurant has a
stylish, contemporary simplicity to its design and period
features are treated with sensitivity, while table service
here is suitably relaxed and friendly but professional. The
kitchen's approach fits the surroundings, mixing British
and Mediterranean classics with a contemporary twist,
the intelligent straightforward approach driven by quality,
locally sourced produce and well-balanced flavours. Take
pan-fried squid with chorizo, sherry and garlic crisps, or
perhaps milk roast pork loin, creamed mash, crispy sage
and pear and ginger compôte, while dessert might
feature lemon tart with thyme and yogurt ice cream,
washed down with one of the recommended dessert
wines.

Chef Mark Stavrakakis **Owner** Dougal Templeton, Alex
Reilley, Mike Bennett **Times** 12-3/6-10.30, Closed 25-26
Dec, 1 Jan, Closed D Sun **Prices** Fixed L 2 course
£13.50, Fixed D 3 course £30, Starter £5-£9.75, Main
£13-£25.95, Dessert £6-£14, Service added but optional
10% **Wines** 36 bottles over £20, 18 bottles under £20,
12 by glass **Notes** Early evening D menu 6-7, Sunday L,
Vegetarian available, Civ Wed 100 **Seats** 180, Pr/dining
room 20 **Children** Portions, Menu **Parking** On street,
NCP

The Grand by Thistle

⊛⊛ Modern European

Modern cooking in relaxed hotel dining room

☎ 0117 930 3329 & 07764 943163
Broad St BS1 2EL
e-mail: alan.broadhurst@thistle.co.uk
dir: M32 follow signs to Gallerues Shopping Centre,
continue past shopping centre on left. As road bends to
left take 1st right onto Broad St

This centrally located hotel has an impressive and rather
grand façade and behind it, along with 182 bedrooms
and a health and leisure spa, is Tyrells Restaurant. The
light and bright room has smartly-set tables with fresh
flowers and modern artworks on the walls add splashes
of colour. A new head chef delivers an ambitious menu of
modern European food with the provenance of the
ingredients acknowledged when appropriate. Jerusalem
artichoke soup is enriched with truffle oil in a good,
simple first course, and main-course pan-roasted
Eversfield venison loin comes with spätzle, mushroom
ragout and a juniper jus. Dark chocolate fondant with
Grand Marnier sorbet is an enjoyable dessert. The kitchen
makes its own bread and provides an amuse bouche,
while the service is both enthusiastic and professional.

Times 12-2.30/7-10

Hotel du Vin & Bistro

⊛ French, European

Relaxed and friendly French bistro style

☎ 0117 925 5577
The Sugar House, Narrow Lewins Mead BS1 2NU
e-mail: info@bristol.hotelduvin.com
web: www.hotelduvin.com
dir: From M4 junct 19, M32 into Bristol. With Bentalls on
left take right lane at next lights. Turn right onto opposite
side of carriageway. Hotel 200yds in side road

This lively bistro-style restaurant is located in a Grade II
listed city-centre hotel converted from a 18th-century
sugar refinery. The restaurant has heavy wooden floors
and tables, hop garlands hang in the windows and
pictures of wine on the walls. The menu includes a good
selection of vegetarian choices and a 'simple classics'
selection offering favourites like coq au vin or
Chateaubriand for two. Good quality ingredients are used
and all the dishes show attention to detail with clear
flavours. Expect devilled kidneys with toasted brioche,
followed by roast breast of chicken with Savoy cabbage
and bacon. Finish with a memorable Calvados
cheesecake with blackberry granita. The wine list is a
highlight.

Times 12-2/6-10

The Restaurant @ Cadbury House

◉◉ Modern British ✪

Clean modern cooking in relaxed, stylish contemporary hotel

☎ 01934 834343
Frost Hill, Congresbury BS49 5AD
e-mail: info@cadburyhouse.com
dir: M5 junct 20, left at rdbt, turn onto B133 at next rdbt towards Congresbury. Continue through village of Yatton for 4m, hotel is on left after village

Externally, this newly developed hotel - complete with leisure club and spa - presents a blend of old and new, but inside its all resolutely stylish, contemporary, clean-lined good looks. The light-and-airy restaurant follows the theme - a modern relaxed affair with unclothed tables and comfortable upholstered chairs, while service is appropriately friendly. The cooking's clean-cut, straightforward modern approach blends with the surroundings and makes good use of seasonal local produce; take a fillet of beef served with watercress purée, fondant potato and a sautéed oyster mushroom sauce. And you can sip your pre-meal cocktails in the bar or on the terrace in fine weather.

Chef Richard Wilcox, Mark Veale **Owner** Nick Taplin **Times** Closed L all week **Prices** Fixed D 3 course £28, Starter £7-£10, Main £18-£24, Dessert £5-£7, Service optional **Wines** 24 bottles over £20, 12 bottles under £20, 10 by glass **Notes** Sunday L, Vegetarian available, Dress restrictions, Smart casual, Civ Wed 140, Air con **Seats** 80, Pr/dining room 80 **Children** Portions, Menu **Parking** 350

riverstation

◉ Modern European

Riverside dining location with a buzz

☎ 0117 914 4434
The Grove BS1 4RB
e-mail: relax@riverstation.co.uk
dir: On the dock side in central Bristol

Enjoying a popular riverside location on the new-look waterfront, this chic eatery was once a police station but now sports an arresting modern décor of glass, wood and steel. Downstairs there's a popular café/deli serving light meals and hot and cold snacks, while upstairs the airy restaurant caters to a smarter crowd lured by the buzzy ambience as much as the cooking. The modern menu offers good quality fresh food, simply prepared. Try Mediterranean fish soup with rouille to start perhaps, and

then tuck into braised shoulder noisette of lamb served with gratin dauphinoise and rosemary jus, or Cornish brill with purple kale and red wine jus.

Times 12-2.30/6-10.30, Closed Xmas, 1 Jan

Rodney Hotel

◉ British, French

Smart hotel restaurant offering a compact menu

☎ 0117 973 5422
4 Rodney Place, Clifton BS8 4HY
e-mail: rodney@cliftonhotels.com

This small hotel in the city's popular Clifton Village area boasts a smart bar and remodelled, stylish, modern restaurant. Think wooden floors, walls donned with local photographs and friendly and relaxed service. The short menu suits the surrounding, changing seasonally to reflect the best quality produce. Simple but carefully-prepared dishes are delivered from an equally small kitchen; take pork medallions served with a warm cabbage salad, broccoli, butternut squash purée and a sherry vinegar sauce, and to finish, perhaps a rich chocolate tart with red wine-poached pear.

BUCKINGHAMSHIRE

AMERSHAM Map 6 SU99

The Artichoke

◉◉ Modern French ▭

Smart high-street restaurant with refined cooking

☎ 01494 726611
9 Market Square, Old Amersham HP7 0DF
e-mail: info@theartichokerestaurant.co.uk
dir: M40 junct 2. 1m from Amersham New Town

This 16th-century house in old Amersham's pretty market square has all the expected features of ancient beams and a vast open fireplace, but the muted and subtle tones of a refined and civilised modern make-over reveal its 21st-century credentials as a serious dining venue. Modern art on the walls, Italian leather chairs and

smartly set tables set the tone, while the staff are a knowledgeable team who deliver a top-notch menu of modern French cuisine. High-quality ingredients, often local, are used in dishes that display skill in the matching of flavours and textures. Dorset crab and goat's cheese gnocchi comes with cucumber tagliatelle and warm fennel soup among starters, while hand-dived scallops from the Isle of Skye are partnered with slow-braised belly of pork, crisp pancetta, celery purée and thyme jus. Main-course fillet of Aberdeen Angus beef, kohlrabi, spinach, black truffle, foie gras, pommes purée, pickled walnuts and blue cheese foam is a dish which shows the confident and controlled hand in the kitchen.

Chef Laurie Gear **Owner** Laurie & Jacqueline Gear **Times** 12-2/6.45-10, Closed 1 wk Xmas, 2 wks Aug BH, 1 wk Apr, Closed Sun, Mon **Prices** Fixed L 2 course fr £18.50, Fixed D 3 course fr £38, Tasting menu fr £55, Starter fr £11, Main fr £20, Dessert fr £9, Service added but optional 12.5% **Wines** 76 bottles over £20, 5 bottles under £20, 8 by glass **Notes** Tasting menu 7 courses, Vegetarian available **Seats** 25 **Children** Portions **Parking** On street, nearby car park

AYLESBURY Map 11 SP81

Hartwell House Hotel, Restaurant & Spa

◉◉◉ – see page 58

BLETCHLEY Map 11 SP83

The Crooked Billet

◉ Modern British ▭ ✪

Popular village pub serious about its food

☎ 01908 373936
2 Westbrook End, Newton Longville MK17 0DF
e-mail: john@thebillet.co.uk
dir: M1 junct 14 follow A421 towards Buckingham. Turn left at Bottledump rdbt to Newton Longville. Restaurant on right as you enter the village

This traditional 17th-century oak-beamed, thatched village pub is located close to Bletchley Park, home to the wartime Enigma codebreakers. With seasonal produce arriving fresh each morning, there are sandwiches, wraps and burgers, plus traditional pub dishes on the lunchtime menu. In the evening the restaurant's offerings include wild mushroom and black truffle risotto with sherry butter, pan-fried sea bass, mash, mussel

Continued

BLETCHLEY *Continued*

butter and caramelised onions, with mango and passionfruit cheesecake and passionfruit sorbet, with a tasting menu to complete the package. The cheeseboard is particularly noteworthy, complemented by a fine wine list and an enormous selection of wines by the glass.

The Crooked Billet

Chef Emma Gilchrist **Owner** John & Emma Gilchrist **Times** 12.30-2.30/7-10, Closed 25 Dec, Closed L Mon-Sat, Closed D Sun **Prices** Tasting menu £60-£95, Starter £4.75-£10, Main £9-£19, Dessert £5-£7, Service optional **Wines** 300 bottles over £20, 20 bottles under £20, 300 by glass **Notes** Tasting Menu 8 courses, Sunday L, Vegetarian available **Seats** 50 **Children** Portions **Parking** 30

BUCKINGHAM   Map 11 SP63

Villiers Hotel Restaurant & Bar

◉◉ Modern British

Stylish brasserie-style restaurant serving appealing modern cuisine

☎ 01280 822444
3 Castle St MK18 1BS
e-mail: reservations@villiershotels.com
web: www.oxfordshire-hotels.co.uk
dir: Town centre - Castle Street is to the right of Town Hall near main square

A former coaching inn dating back to Cromwellian times, this hotel is steeped in history. With an atmospheric bar for drinks before dinner, the refurbished restaurant has a modern brasserie look and vibe. Simple modern cooking

---

to match provides some classics alongside new and interesting combinations, with pasta and rice options available as either starter or main course portions. Mains range from home-made venison burger with tomato chutney, seeded bun and home-cut chips, to fillet of sea bass with pak choi, creamed potatoes and rosemary jus. You might start with home-cured salmon, gravad lax, mustard dressing and wholemeal bread, and finish with warm sticky date pudding with gingerbread ice cream.

Villiers Hotel Restaurant & Bar

Chef Paul Stopps **Owner** Oxfordshire Hotels Ltd **Times** 12-2.30/6-9.30 **Prices** Starter £5.95-£9.95, Main £12.95-£21.95, Dessert £5.25-£6.95, Service optional, Groups min 6 service 10% **Notes** Sunday L, Vegetarian available, Civ Wed 150, Air con **Seats** 70, Pr/dining room 150 **Parking** 46

Hartwell House Hotel, Restaurant & Spa

AYLESBURY   Map 11 SP81

British ♦ NOTABLE WINE LIST 🍴

Luxurious dining in outstanding stately home

☎ 01296 747444
Oxford Rd HP17 8NR
e-mail: info@hartwell-house.com
dir: 2m SW of Aylesbury on A418 (Oxford road

This magnificent stately home with its Jacobean and Georgian façades and splendid public rooms stands in 94 acres of landscaped parkland, complete with serpentine walks, a picturesque lake and a ruined church. Home to Louis XVIII - exiled King of France - for 5 years from 1809, inside it features a dramatic Gothic hall and staircase with Jacobean carved figures, as well as individually styled, elegant day-rooms with outstanding decorative ceilings and oak panelling, fine paintings and antiques.

The high-ceilinged, neo-classical restaurant, with its wonderful views of the fantastic gardens, makes a graceful, understated backdrop for the talented kitchen's elaborate creations. This is thoughtful and imaginative cuisine with a classical foundation, distinguished by technical genius and quality ingredients. Pan-fried scallops with roasted celeriac purée, pea cress and coconut foam is a typical starter, followed by fillet of Sydenham Grange Farm beef with fondant potato, curly kale, confit shallot, braised oxtail and jus, or perhaps pan-fried sea bass with pumpkin gnocchi, spiced pumpkin purée and Chardonnay vinegar froth. To really do the place justice, try the six-course tasting menu. A luxurious spa completes the package, with light meals and snacks available in the Buttery.

Chef Daniel Richardson **Owner** Historic House Hotels **Times** 12.30-1.45/7.30-9.45 **Prices** Fixed L 2 course fr £22, Fixed D 3 course fr £38, Tasting menu £67.50, Service included **Wines** 300 bottles over £20, 11 bottles under £20, 10 by glass **Notes** Sunday L, Vegetarian available, Dress restrictions, Smart casual, No jeans, tracksuits/trainers, Civ Wed 60 **Seats** 56, Pr/dining room 30 **Children** Min 6 yrs, Portions **Parking** 50

BURNHAM
Map 6 SU98

Grays Restaurant

⚫ British, French

Elegant woodland setting for French-influenced classic cuisine

☎ 0844 736 8603 & 01628 600150
Burnham Beeches, Grove Rd SL1 8DP
e-mail: burnhambeeches@corushotels.com
web: www.corushotels.com
dir: off A355, via Farnham Royal roundabout

Originally built as a hunting lodge in 1727, Burnham Beeches is set in attractive mature gardens on the edge of ancient woodland. Recent refurbishment has restored the hotel to its original Georgian elegance. Gray's Restaurant, with its oak-panelled walls and sash windows, affords lovely views and provides attentive service from a courteous team. A typical selection of dishes from the seasonal British menu with French influences might be goats' cheese parfait to start, followed by roast rack of lamb with potatoes boulangère, gratin of vegetables and pan jus. To finish, perhaps blood peach charlotte with peach coulis or caramelised banana gâteau with chocolate toffee sauce.

Chef John Dickson Owner Corus Hotels
Times 12-2/7-9.30, Closed L Sat-Sun Prices Fixed D 3 course £26-£43.45, Starter £6-£9, Main £14-£26.95, Dessert £6-£7.50 Wines 19 bottles over £20, 5 bottles under £20, 6 by glass Notes Sunday L, Vegetarian available, Civ Wed 120 Seats 70, Pr/dining room 120 Children Portions, Menu Parking 200

The Grovefield House Hotel

⚫ Modern European

Country-house hotel with ambitious cooking

☎ 01628 603131
Taplow Common Rd SL1 8LP
e-mail: gm.grovefield@classiclodges.co.uk
dir: Telephone for directions

Grovefield House Hotel is undoubtedly a place with good connections: it is handy for the M4, M40 and Heathrow Airport. Set in 7 acres of grounds, the original parts of the building date from the Edwardian era and the hotel is undergoing major refurbishment as we go to press. The kitchen team will benefit from a spanking new dining room in which to present their brand of modern food.

Terrine of ox tongue, foie gras and corn-fed chicken is served with quince chutney and brioche in a typically ambitious starter, while main-course fillet of John Dory with crushed potatoes and butternut squash comes with pork belly in a fashionable partnership.

Chef I Blackwell Owner Classic Lodges Ltd
Times 12-2.30/7-9.30, Closed L Sat Prices Food prices not confirmed for 2009. Please telephone for details. Wines 37 bottles over £20, 28 bottles under £20, 4 by glass Notes Dress restrictions, No t-shirts, trainers, Civ Wed 150 Seats 60, Pr/dining room 50 Children Portions, Menu Parking 150

CHENIES
Map 6 TQ09

The Bedford Arms Hotel

⚫ Modern British

Popular hotel offering modern fare in relaxed surroundings

☎ 01923 283301
WD3 6EQ
dir: M25 junct 18/A404 towards Amersham, after 2m turn right & follow signs for hotel

This attractive, 19th-century country inn with rooms enjoys a peaceful rural setting in well-kept grounds. The cosy, wood-panelled restaurant currently has a traditional look (though there are plans afoot to give it a much lighter facelift), with its neatly clothed tables and smartly dressed, professional staff. Two bars, a lounge and traditionally-styled bedrooms - each named after a relation of the Duke of Bedford whose family has an historic association with the hotel - complete the package. The kitchen's modern approach comes driven by quality produce; take flame-grilled sirloin steak served with tomato, mushroom, watercress and a green peppercorn jus, and to finish, perhaps a moist lemon cake with passion fruit crème fraîche.

DINTON
Map 5 SP71

La Chouette

⚫ Belgian 💻

Quirky Belgian restaurant

☎ 01296 747422
Westlington Green HP17 8UW
dir: On A418 at Dinton

The setting is the delightful village of Dinton, and a former pub that stands on the green and retains a wealth of original 16th-century features including stone walls, wooden beams and a large inglenook fireplace. A choice of menus at this rustic Belgian restaurant offers an accomplished range of traditional dishes. Weekday lunchtimes you can have three courses in less than an hour from the prix d'ami (though you can take your time if you like!).Typical dishes are salad of red mullet, fillet of red deer in pepper sauce, and Belgian partridge in cabbage.

Chef Frederic Desmette Owner M F Desmette
Times 12-2/7-9, Closed Sun, Closed L Sat Wines 300 bottles over £20, 10 bottles under £20, 2 by glass Notes Menu degustation £39.50 Seats 35 Children Portions Parking 20

GREAT MISSENDEN
Map 6 SP80

Annie Baileys

⚫ Modern British

Ever-popular rural restaurant

☎ 01494 865625
Chesham Rd, Hyde End HP16 0QT
e-mail: david@anniebaileys.com
dir: Off A413 at Great Missenden. On B485 towards Chesham

Named after a local Victorian landlady, this popular rural restaurant is an informal and friendly place to take a relaxing meal or enjoy a drink at the bar or by the fire. The interior has a country-cottage feel, combined with a Mediterranean colour scheme. The Mediterranean theme fittingly extends to the food, presented on a crowd-pleasing brasserie-style menu. Take crispy pan-fried sea bass fillet served with red pepper and parmesan risotto and garlic-roasted potatoes, or perhaps confit duck leg with crispy pancetta and tomato and shallot haricot beans.

Chef Andrew Fairall Owner Open All Hours (UK) Ltd
Times 12-2.30/7-9.30, Closed D Sun Prices Fixed L 2 course £14.50, Fixed D 3 course £18.95-£23.95, Service optional Wines 10 bottles over £20, 20 bottles under £20, 16 by glass Notes Sunday L, Vegetarian available Seats 65 Children Portions Parking 40

HADDENHAM
Map 5 SP70

Green Dragon

⊛⊛ British 🖥

Quality food in a village inn atmosphere

☎ 01844 291403
8 Churchway HP17 8AA
e-mail: paul@eatatthedragon.co.uk
dir: From M40 take A329 towards Thame, then A418. Turn
1st right after entering Haddenham

Popular with TV and film crews, Haddenham is a
picturesque village with this 17th-century pub at the
heart of things, close to the church and duck pond.
Despite the focus on good, fresh food, customers who just
want a drink are welcome and the village beer is certainly
worth sampling. Produce is generally locally sourced and
the fresh fish in this land-locked county comes up from
Devon. Beautifully pink pigeon breast on a bed of sweet
red cabbage, some simply dressed rocket and a plum
dressing makes for a successful starter, and gilt head
bream with a good, crisp skin sitting on top of wilted
spinach with a scattering of wild mushrooms and a
subtle wild garlic cream is a typical main course.

Times 12-2/6.30-9.30, Closed 25 Dec, 1 Jan, Closed D
Sun

IVINGHOE
Map 11 SP91

The King's Head

⊛ Modern British, French V

**Charming inn with bags of character and traditional
dining**

☎ 01296 668388
LU7 9EB
e-mail: info@kingsheadivinghoe.co.uk
web: www.kingsheadivinghoe.co.uk
dir: From M25 junct 20 take A41 past Tring. Turn right
onto B488 (Ivinghoe), hotel at junct with B489

The ivy-clad frontage of this 17th-century former posting
house overlooks the village green and church in an
attractive English village. The interior in the bars and
dining room is as might be expected: large fireplaces, lots
of beams and antique furniture. The menu is a mix of

modern and classic French and English dishes, with
carving and flambé taking place at the table and
desserts selected from the sweet trolley. Pan-fried red
mullet is served on a bed of ratatouille in a successful
starter, and for main course there is roasted Aylesbury
duck carved in a piece of restaurant theatre, or a good
fillet of sea bass, with crisp, golden skin, served with
spinach and roasted shallots.

Chef Jonathan O'Keeffe **Owner** G.A.P.J. Ltd
Times 12-3/7-10, Closed 27-30 Dec, Closed D Sun
Prices Fixed L 3 course fr £19.50, Service added but
optional 12.5% **Wines** 80 bottles over £20, 8 bottles
under £20, 4 by glass **Notes** Sunday L, Vegetarian menu,
Dress restrictions, No jeans, trainers or shorts, Air con
Seats 55, Pr/dining room 40 **Children** Portions
Parking 20 **Parking** On street

LONG CRENDON
Map 5 SP60

The Angel Restaurant

⊛ Mediterranean, Pacific Rim

Gastro-pub with a friendly atmosphere

☎ 01844 208268
47 Bicester Rd HP18 9EE
e-mail: angelrestaurant@aol.com
dir: Beside B4011, 2m NW of Thame

Nestling in a picturesque village, The Angel is a 17th-

Dean Timpson at The Compleat Angler

⊛⊛⊛

MARLOW
Map 5 SU88

Modern British V

**Impressive cooking in fine-dining restaurant
overlooking the Thames**

☎ 0844 879 9128 & 01628 484444
Macdonald Compleat Angler, Marlow Bridge SL7 1RG
e-mail: compleatangler@macdonald-hotels.co.uk
dir: M4 junct 8/9 or M40 junct 4. A404 to rdbt, take
Bisham exit, 1m to Marlow Bridge, hotel on right

Idyllically situated on the banks of the River Thames, this
elegant Georgian hotel overlooks the rushing waters at
Marlow weir and was named after Izaak Walton's famous
book on angling. Whether enjoying a cosy fireside drink in
the 350-year-old cocktail bar in winter, perhaps a
champagne picnic aboard one of the hotel's private
boats, or aperitifs on the terrace on warm summer days,

the location is a cracker. Dean Timpson at The Compleat
Angler is an intimate, fine-dining restaurant (one of two
dining options here, the other being the more informal
Bowaters - see entry) and delivers modern British food in
a formal but friendly setting. The stylish décor here
combines a rich, vibrant colour scheme of purple, white
and silver with lush maple wood and polished oak
panels, offset with a clever use of fabrics and brocades
to create a sleek, sophisticated environment with a
luxurious feel that's still warm and welcoming. Dean
Timpson's accomplished cooking is delivered via a good-
value Market Menu at lunch, backed by a carte at both
lunch and dinner, and also his signature tasting option.
The philosophy of simplicity in style is reflected in clean
flavoured, attractively presented dishes based around
classical themes, featuring bags of technical skill and
focusing on local, seasonal ingredients with an emphasis
on quality. Take line-caught sea bass with pak choi and a
truffle butter sauce, or perhaps a saddle of rabbit served
with hipsy cabbage and English mustard oil, while coffee

and walnut cake accompanied by a coffee mousse,
walnut ice cream and coffee jelly might catch the eye at
dessert.

Chef Dean Timpson **Owner** Macdonald Hotels
Times 12-2.30/7-10, Closed 2 wks beg Jan, 2 wks Aug,
Closed Sun-Mon **Prices** Fixed L 2 course £20, Fixed D 3
course £45, Tasting menu £65, Service added but
optional 12.5% **Wines** 270 bottles over £20
Notes Vegetarian tasting menu, Vegetarian menu, Dress
restrictions, Smart casual, No jeans or trainers, Civ Wed
100, Air con **Seats** 40 **Children** Portions, Menu
Parking 100

century coaching inn, now operating as a friendly gastro-pub. Original wattle-and-daub walls, exposed beams and inglenook fireplaces set the scene, complemented by a bright-and-airy conservatory and a heated sun terrace for alfresco dining. Imaginative dishes prepared from local produce feature on the British menu with Mediterranean and Pacific Rim influences. Fish dishes are a speciality, with blackboard specials taking advantage of the latest catch. Recommendations include spicy fishcakes with lime and coriander mayonnaise, roast fillet of halibut on vegetable fettucine with mussel and saffron sauce, and for dessert who could resist 'chocolate fallen angel'. Excellent table service is managed by attentive, yet unobtrusive staff.

Chef Trevor Bosch **Owner** Trevor & Annie Bosch **Times** 12-2.30/7-9.30, Closed D Sun **Prices** Fixed L 2 course £14.95, Tasting menu £35, Starter £4.95-£7.95, Main £7.95-£26.50, Dessert £5.50, Service optional, Groups min 8 service 10% **Wines** 58 bottles over £20, 29 bottles under £20, 12 by glass **Notes** Tasting menu 5 courses Mon-Fri, Sunday L, Vegetarian available, Air con **Seats** 75, Pr/dining room 14 **Children** Portions **Parking** 30

MARLOW   Map 5 SU88

Bowaters

◉◉ Modern British

Modern British food served in traditional Thames-side setting

☎ 0844 879 9128 & 01628 484444
Macdonald The Compleat Angler, Marlow Bridge SL7 1RG
e-mail: compleatangler@macdonald-hotels.co.uk
dir: M4 junct 8/9 or M40 junct 4. A404 to rdbt, take Bisham exit, 1m to Marlow Bridge, hotel on right

You don't have to be an angling aficionado to delight in the views over the Thames and weir from the Bowaters restaurant in this elegant Georgian hotel, one of two dining options here, the other being Dean Timpson's restaurant (see entry). The historic Bowaters is a high quality, richly furnished affair, comfortably blending tradition with modernity. High-backed chairs, fine tableware and friendly, polished service add to the relaxed atmosphere ... and the best views in town! Menus change to reflect seasonal ingredients, the kitchen's modern approach using simple, precise, uncluttered, well-executed dishes that allow the main ingredient to shine. Think herb-crusted Atlantic cod served with roasted potato cake and red chard, and to finish, perhaps poached pear with cinnamon creamed rice and red wine glaze.

Chef Mark Constable **Owner** Macdonald Hotels **Times** 12.30-2/7-10 **Prices** Starter £6.50-£9.50, Main £16.50-£25, Dessert £7.50-£8.50, Service added but optional 12.5% **Wines** 115 bottles over £20, 5 bottles under £20, 13 by glass **Notes** Sunday L, Vegetarian available, Civ Wed 100 **Seats** 90, Pr/dining room 40 **Children** Portions, Menu **Parking** 100

Dean Timpson at The Compleat Angler

◉◉◉ – *see opposite*

The Hand & Flowers

◉◉◉ – *see page 62*

Oak Room at Danesfield House

◉◉◉◉ – *see page 63*

The Vanilla Pod

◉◉ Modern British, French 🖥 V

Historic house offering imaginative modern cuisine

☎ 01628 898101
31 West St SL7 2LS
e-mail: info@thevanillapod.co.uk
dir: From M4 junct 8/9 or M40 junct 4 take A404, A4155 to Marlow. From Henley take A4155

Once the home of poet and critic TS Eliot, this attractive house by the town centre has undergone a complete refurbishment in the elegant and luxurious dining room at the rear. Rich colours and clean lines complement the rustic room with its beamed walls and ceiling. The atmosphere is intimate and welcoming, with polite, professional and knowledgeable service. Modern cooking combines British style and French influences, with a deft touch and well-judged ingredients, in dishes of seared scallops with vanilla-poached pear purée and red wine shallots, followed by roasted venison with buttered beans, pear and chocolate oil, and maybe crème caramel with prunes in Armagnac or polenta cake with pineapple and lemon cream to finish.

Chef Michael Macdonald **Owner** Michael & Stephanie Macdonald **Times** 12-2.30/7-11, Closed 24 Dec-3 Jan, 25 May-3 Jun, 24 Aug-2 Sep, Closed Sun-Mon **Prices** Fixed L 2 course £15.50, Fixed D 3 course £40, Tasting menu £50, Service optional **Wines** 102 bottles over £20, 6 bottles under £20, 15 by glass **Notes** Tasting menu 8 courses, Vegetarian menu, Dress restrictions, Smart casual **Seats** 28, Pr/dining room 8 **Parking** On West Street

MILTON KEYNES   Map 11 SP83

Different Drummer Hotel

◉ British, Italian V

Contemporary-style dining in hotel wine bar

☎ 01908 564733
94 High St, Stoney Stratford MK11 1AH
e-mail: info@hoteldifferentdrummer.co.uk
dir: Please telephone for directions

Wooden floors, plain white walls dotted with artwork, high-backed leather-look chairs, wooden tables and windows overlooking the high street await at this contemporary wine bar adjacent to the hotel. There's a bar with a few high stools at the entrance and an open

fire creates a feature too, while service is suitably informal but professional. The kitchen takes an equally modern approach, driven by intelligent simplicity and quality fresh produce; take pork tenderloin with a light apple, sage and butter sauce served with a wholegrain mustard and leek potato stack and medley of fresh vegetables, and to finish, perhaps a baked Alaska with fruit coulis.

Owner Mr & Mrs Keswani **Prices** Food prices not confirmed for 2009. Please telephone for details. **Notes** Vegetarian menu, Dress restrictions, Smart, no jeans **Children** Portions **Parking** 8 **Parking** On street

TAPLOW   Map 6 SU98

Berry's at Taplow House Hotel

◉◉ Modern British 🖥

Skilful modern British cooking at a luxurious hotel

☎ 01628 670056
Berry Hill SL6 0DA
e-mail: reception@taplowhouse.com
dir: From Maidenhead follow A4 towards Slough, over Thames, 3m turn right at lights into Berry Hill, or M4 junct 7 towards Maidenhead, at lights follow signs to Berry Hill

This Georgian mansion combines period charm with country-house comfort and sits amid 6 acres of gardens. There's a champagne terrace for summer drinks, or a whisky bar if you'd rather sup a malt by the fire, while the elegant, high-ceilinged Berry's restaurant offers pretty views from well-spaced tables. The kitchen's modern British approach, underpinned by classical French themes, depends on prime local produce. Crayfish sausage served on saffron and pearl barley risotto with crayfish bisque is an appealing starter, followed by a robust saddle of Denham Estate venison served rare on braised red cabbage with venison pasty and fondant potato. For a sweet conclusion, try banana tart with coconut ice cream and caramel sauce.

Times 12-2/7-9.30, Closed L Sat

The Hand & Flowers

MARLOW **Map 5 SU88**

British, European

Unpretentious gastro-pub offering first-rate cooking

☎ 01628 482277
SL7 2BP
e-mail: theoffice@thehandandflowers.
co.uk
web: www.thehandandflowers.co.uk
dir: M40 junct 4/M4 junct 8/9 follow A404 to Marlow

Don't be fooled by first impressions, this unassuming whitewashed pub on the edge of town is a class act, and with chef-patron Tom Kerridge in the kitchen (ex Adlard's in Norwich and Monsieur Max at Hampton) it has a fine pedigree. Low wooden beams, flagstone flooring and exposed brick and stone walls help retain the country pub feel, with some modern art thrown in to add a contemporary twist. Plain, solid-wood tables (no cloths), a mix of individual chairs and banquette seating, subdued lighting and relaxed, friendly service from an enthusiastic young team (led by wife Beth), all help maintain the warm, unstuffy atmosphere. Tom's cooking is intelligently straightforward and elegant, with simplicity, flavour and skill top of his agenda. The style is modern-focused Anglo-French, with fresh, top quality produce of the utmost importance, while presentation is equally simple and true to each dish.

Expect dishes such as squab pigeon and foie gras en croûte with gem lettuce, and perhaps a rhubarb and ginger crumble tartlet served with vanilla ice cream to finish. At lunchtime, a three-dish bar menu is also offered, and there's a patio for summer alfresco dining.

Chef Tom Kerridge **Owner** Tom & Beth Kerridge **Times** 12-2.30/7-9.30, Closed 25-26 Dec, Closed D Sun **Prices** Starter £5.50-£9, Main £15.50-£23, Dessert £6.50, Service optional, Groups min 6 service 10% **Wines** 57 bottles over £20, 6 bottles under £20, 18 by glass **Notes** Sunday L, Vegetarian available **Seats** 50 **Children** Portions **Parking** 30

Oak Room at Danesfield House

MARLOW   Map 5 SU88

Modern British 🖥 🍷 NOTABLE WINE LIST

Stunning cuisine in fairytale surroundings overlooking the Thames

☎ 01628 891010
Henley Rd SL7 2EY
e-mail: adooley@danesfieldhouse.co.uk
web: www.danesfieldhouse.co.uk
dir: M4 junct 4/A404 to Marlow. Follow signs to Medmenham and Henley. Hotel is 3m outside Marlow

Set in the beautiful Chiltern Hills in 65 acres of magnificent grounds and formal gardens (complete with grand topiary and fountains), Danesfield is a country-house hotel on a grand scale. It's the third house to enjoy the magnificent view over the River Thames here since 1664, the present property was built in 1899 as a family home. Constructed of white stone with castellated towers, tall chimneys and raised terraces, it has all the hallmarks of a fairytale castle and oozes original features. The Oak Room Restaurant was redesigned with a light, airy feel in 2005 by Anouska Hempel - its bleached wood panelling, soft shades of fawn and latte and top-notch napery give a luxurious yet relaxing impression as you enter. Nothing prepares you, however, for the stunning culinary experience, where chef Adam Simmonds (ex Ynyshir Hall, see entry) shows off his fine kitchen pedigree. The modern approach is

underpinned by a classical theme to produce top quality, innovative cooking using top-notch seasonal produce and some serious technical skill. Clean flavours, textures and presentation allow each dish a unique taste experience; take roasted loin of venison served with butternut squash purée, chocolate polenta, braised snails and bohea lapsang jelly, and to finish, how about the chocolate marquise delivered with pumpkin ice cream, Tia Maria jelly, pumpkin purée and Tia Maria froth. Ancillaries, like amuse-bouche, breads, pre-desserts and petits fours hit top form too, while service, from a highly skilled team, delivers a friendly and attentive dining experience. Once you've eaten here, you'll certainly want to repeat the experience. (Afternoon teas in the spectacular lounge or on the terrace are also a delight.)

Chef Adam Simmonds
Times 12-2/7-9.30, Closed Xmas, New Year, BHs, Closed Sun-Mon, Closed L Tue **Wines** 390 bottles over £20, 20 by glass **Notes** ALC 3 courses fr £60, Dress restrictions, Smart casual, Civ Wed 100
Seats 30, Pr/dining room 14
Children Min 12 yrs, Portions
Parking 100

Waldo's Restaurant, Cliveden

TAPLOW — Map 6 SU98

Modern European 🖳 🍷 NOTABLE WINE LIST

Innovative new chef at historic and grand venue

☎ 01628 668561
Cliveden Estate SL6 0JF
e-mail: reservations@clivedenhouse.co.uk
dir: M4 junct 7, turn left onto A4, right at rdbt into Burnham, follow road to Cliveden

Cliveden is an impressive Italianate stately home and its list of former visitors is a veritable who's-who, including every British monarch since George I. It is a jewel in the National Trust crown. The discreet and luxurious Waldo's Restaurant, named after the sculptor of the famous Fountain of Love in the sweeping driveway, is staffed by a suitably professional and polished team. New chef Robert Thompson has arrived from Winteringham Fields to take charge of the kitchen and his menus, based around top quality produce, deliver highly crafted modern European food. Seared langoustine tails, quail eggs, marinated wild mushrooms and foie gras hollandaise is a tantalising combination in a starter, and main-course roasted Anjou squab pigeon, topped with pieces of liver, is served with a mini-tower of a roundel of beetroot, black pudding and orange. The dishes are evidently constructed with flavour in mind. A pre-dessert (passionfruit sabayon topped with caramelised apple foam) comes before the real deal, such as coconut and pineapple soufflé served with a cocktail glass containing a Piña Colada sundae. The wine list traverses the globe and the sommelier is on hand to help you through it.

Chef Robert Thompson **Owner** von Essen Hotels **Times** Closed Xmas, New Year, 2 wks Aug, Closed Sun & Mon, Closed L all wk **Prices** Fixed D 3 course fr £68, Service optional **Wines** All bottles over £20, 10 by glass **Notes** Vegetarian available, Dress restrictions, Jacket & tie, Civ Wed 120, Air con **Seats** 28, Pr/dining room 12 **Children** Min 12 yrs **Parking** 60

TAPLOW *Continued*

The Terrace Dining Room, Cliveden

◎◎ Mediterranean, French 🖥 📖NOTABLE WINE LIST

Fine dining in elegant surroundings

☎ 01628 668561
Cliveden Estate SL6 0JF
e-mail: reservations@clivedenhouse.co.uk
dir: M4 junct 7, turn left onto A4, right at next rdbt into Burnham, follow this road to Cliveden

Dining in one of England's finest country houses will always be a treat. Art meets nature in the Terrace Dining Room: fine portraits adorn the walls, while grand French windows overlook immaculate gardens to the Thames beyond. South-facing, the room catches the sun and with its chandeliers and wood panelling provides an elegant backdrop for the kitchen's imaginative interpretations of classic French cuisine. Try a smoked salmon pillow to start, served with marinated salmon and coriander, herbs and frisée lettuce, before moving onto something simple - steamed fillet of Dover sole with saffron risotto and red wine foam - or more involved, such as home-made venison tortellini with pumpkin purée, crispy rice and red chard salad.

Chef Carlos Martinez **Owner** von Essen Hotels
Times 12-2.30/7-9.30 **Prices** Fixed L 2 course fr £32, Fixed D 3 course fr £59, Service optional **Wines** All bottles over £20, 10 by glass **Notes** Sunday L, Vegetarian available, Dress restrictions, Smart casual L, Jacket & shirt D, Civ Wed 120 **Seats** 80, Pr/dining room 60
Children Portions, Menu **Parking** 60

Waldo's Restaurant, Cliveden

◎◎◎ – *see opposite*

◎◎◎ – *see opposite*

WOOBURN COMMON Map 6 SU98

Chequers Inn

◎ British, French 🖥

Cosy inn with simple style

☎ 01628 529575
Kiln Ln HP10 0JQ
e-mail: info@chequers-inn.com
dir: M40 junct 2, through Beaconsfield on A40 towards High Wycombe. Inn on left, turn into Broad lane. Hotel is 2.5m on left.

A haven of comfy sofas, quiet corners and open fires is provided at this 17th-century country inn with its old oak posts and beams and flagstone floors. There's an extensive bar menu or classier fare in the restaurant among the potted palms and greenery. Superb ingredients are simply handled by a confident kitchen. Ham hock and foie gras terrine with fruit chutney and figs makes a great starter; with Drambuie parfait and marinated strawberries for dessert. Mains range from seared scallops with prawn and crayfish risotto to lamb chump with dauphinoise potato and ratatouille.

Chef Michael Hazelton **Owner** PJ Roehrig
Times 12-2.30/7-9.30, Closed D 25 Dec, 1 Jan
Prices Fixed L 2 course fr £13.95, Fixed D 4 course £27.95-£29.95, Service optional **Wines** 36 bottles over £20, 25 bottles under £20, 11 by glass **Notes** Sunday L, Vegetarian available **Seats** 60, Pr/dining room 60
Children Portions **Parking** 50

CAMBRIDGESHIRE

BABRAHAM Map 12 TL55

The George Inn

◎ British, International 🕒

Flexible dining in lovingly restored coaching inn

☎ 01223 833800
High St CB22 3AG
e-mail: george@inter-mead.com
web: www.georgeinnbabraham.co.uk
dir: At junct of A11 & A1307 take A1307 towards Cambridge. Turn left after 200mtrs

A coaching inn since 1774, this smart gastro-pub was beautifully restored and extended after a fire in 2004, with original features complemented by contemporary furnishings. There is an additional new barn-style restaurant with antique furniture, and service is relaxed and professional. The cooking here is modern British with French and Asian influences. At lunch, choose from filled ciabattas or carte dishes such as spiced salmon fishcakes with sweet chilli dipping sauce. In the evening, pressed ham hock terrine with honey-roasted figs could be followed by roast fillet of venison with caramelised parsnips and bitter chocolate sauce. There is also a wonderful terrace for alfresco dining.

Continued

BABRAHAM *Continued*

Chef Mark Edgeley **Owner** G A Wortley
Times 11.30-3/5.30-11, Closed D Sun nights in winter
Prices Fixed L 2 course £17.95-£19.95, Starter
£5.95-£9.95, Main £14.95-£23.95, Dessert £6.95-£8.95,
Service optional, Groups min 10 service 10% **Wines** 17
bottles over £20, 21 bottles under £20, 8 by glass
Notes Sunday L, Civ Wed 40 **Seats** 115, Pr/dining room
40 **Children** Portions, Menu **Parking** 40

See advert on page 65

CAMBOURNE Map 12 TL35

The Cambridge Belfry

◉◉ Modern

Modern setting for classic European cuisine

☎ 01954 714995
Back St CB3 6BW
e-mail: cambridge@marstonhotels.com
dir: Telephone for directions

A modern hotel offering great views over the lake and
business park. Lighter meals are available in the brasserie,
but the Bridge restaurant is the real draw, a contemporary
space with sleek lines, polished tiles, and dramatic
splashes of deep red. Expect an eclectic menu rooted in
classic European cuisine and notable for good use of local
produce in season. Crab cakes are a typical starter, served
with soba noodles and a ginger and soy dressing, while
mains might include a tender piece of Gloucester Old Spot
pork belly with celeriac purée, Savoy cabbage, sauté
potatoes and roasted root vegetables. To finish, try the
pineapple up-side-down cake with cocoa citrus sorbet and
coconut foam. Service is relaxed but attentive.

Times 12.30-2.30/7.30-9, Closed L Sat

CAMBRIDGE Map 12 TL45

Best Western Cambridge Quy Mill Hotel

◉ Modern European

Listed property with a modern take on traditional fare

☎ 01223 293383
Newmarket Rd, Stow Cum Quy CB5 9AG
e-mail: cambridgequy@bestwestern.co.uk
dir: Turn off A14 at junct 35, E of Cambridge, onto B1102
for 50yds, hotel entrance opposite church

Set in open countryside, this 19th-century former
watermill and miller's house is convenient for Cambridge.

With dining options in the bars, conservatory and terrace,
the tastefully converted, traditional-style restaurant
occupies the dining room, kitchen and buttery of the old
house, and the private dining room features a waterwheel
behind glass. Expect an eclectic choice of modern British
dishes with Mediterranean touches like roast cod with a
cassoulet of borlotti beans, chorizo and black pudding,
and roast rack of lamb with herb brioche crust and
rosemary jus. Desserts range from espresso and Amaretto
brûlée to sticky toffee pudding.

Chef Juan Gomez **Owner** David Munro
Times 12-2.30/7-9.45, Closed 27-31 Dec **Prices** Fixed L 2
course £14.50, Fixed D 3 course £21.50, Starter £5-£6.50,
Main £11.50-£18.95, Dessert £5.50-£6, Service optional,
Groups min 8 service 10% **Wines** 23 bottles over £20, 11
bottles under £20, 11 by glass **Notes** Vegetarian
available, Dress restrictions, Smart dress/smart casual -
no shorts (men), Civ Wed 80 **Seats** 48, Pr/dining room 80
Children Portions, Menu **Parking** 90

Graffiti at Hotel Felix

◉◉ Modern British 🖥 ✎

Enjoyable brasserie dining in stylish hotel

☎ 01223 277977
Whitehouse Ln CB3 0LX
e-mail: help@hotelfelix.co.uk
web: www.hotelfelix.co.uk
dir: M11 junct 12. From A1 N take A14 turning onto
A1307. At City of Cambridge sign turn left into
Whitehouse Lane

The Hotel Felix - a beautiful Victorian mansion turned
sleek hotel set in 3 acres of landscaped gardens - artfully
combines original features with contemporary décor. The
Graffiti restaurant is a stylish place to dine and gives a
stunning first impression. With walls bedecked in modern
art, it has a terrace for alfresco summer dining and an
open fire for winter evenings. A brasserie-style menu
comprises modern British fare with a Mediterranean
twist. Expect starters such as potato and walnut gnocchi
with grilled butternut squash and sage, pickled walnuts
and wild rocket, while mains might include pan-roasted
wild sea bass with mussels Mouclade. Poached
pineapple, coconut sorbet, vanilla and star anise egg
custard and balsamic syrup would make a fine finale.

Graffiti at Hotel Felix

Chef Ian Morgan **Owner** Jeremy Cassel
Times 12-2/6.30-10 **Prices** Fixed L 2 course £12.95,
Starter £4.50-£10.75, Main £11-£21.50, Dessert £6.50-
£7.75, Service added but optional 10%, Groups min 10
service 10% **Wines** 37 bottles over £20, 14 bottles under
£20, 14 by glass **Notes** Sunday L, Vegetarian available,
Civ Wed 75 **Seats** 45, Pr/dining room 60 **Children** Portions
Parking 90

Hotel du Vin Cambridge

◉ French, European

French bistro-style dining in the heart of Cambridge

☎ 01223 227330
15-19 Trumpington St CB2 1QA
e-mail: info.cambridge@hotelduvin.com

Centrally located on Trumpington Street, this beautiful
building dates back in part to medieval times and has
been transformed into a luxury boutique hotel with
French-style bistro, while at the same time enhancing its
many quirky architectural features. Distressed yellow
walls with bistro-themed prints set the tone,
complemented by wooden floors, comfortable seating and
dried herbs adorning the windows. The first Hotel du Vin
to offer an open-style kitchen, it also boasts an unusual
cellar bar set in a labyrinth of vaulted rooms, library,
separate specialised wine tasting room, and private
dining room. Start with scallops and black pudding with
cauliflower purée and apple, and then take a main course
of roast rump of lamb with spinach and pommes
dauphinoise, with bitter chocolate tart and mango ice
cream to finish.

Prices Food prices not confirmed for 2009. Please
telephone for details.

Midsummer House Restaurant

◉◉◉◉ – *see opposite*

Restaurant Alimentum

◉◉◉ – *see page 68*

Midsummer House Restaurant

CAMBRIDGE   **Map 12 TL45**

French, Mediterranean 🖥 💧 NOTABLE WINE LIST

Seriously sophisticated, inspired cooking from a high-flyer

☎ 01223 369299
Midsummer Common CB4 1HA
e-mail: reservations@
midsummerhouse.co.uk
web: www.midsummerhouse.co.uk
dir: Park in Pretoria Rd, then walk across footbridge. Restaurant on left

Set in a handsome Victorian villa, on the romantically named Midsummer Common beside the River Cam, this delightful, high-flying restaurant is home to some seriously stylish food. The airy, elegant, conservatory-style dining room is stylishly decked out with white walls, Indian slate floors and large, well spaced tables dressed in crisp white linen with a single white lily. The atrium-style glass roof, windows and large mirrors deliver a feeling of light and space, while cream leather chairs follow the natural colour theme, with the room appropriately opening on to a pretty, secluded walled garden of fragrant herbs cultivated for the kitchen. Upstairs there's a private dining room, and a sophisticated bar and terrace for alfresco drinks with river views. Predominantly French service is polished and attentive, the team as enthusiastic about Daniel Clifford's innovative cooking as the chef himself

- his inspired cuisine has not only put Cambridge on the culinary map, it has made sure it stays there. Clifford's quest for culinary perfection has taken the restaurant to another level over the past few years; his is cooking at its best, modern-focused but underpinned by classical French technique, seriously sophisticated with dishes arriving dressed to thrill. Superb quality ingredients, advanced technique and technical prowess add wow factor to the carte and tasting menu, and allow flavours to shine, while unexpected texture contrasts and combinations hit the spot. This is a dedicated, committed and extremely talented kitchen. Take sautéed zander served with onion and cinnamon purée, wilted nettles, smoked eel and red wine, or perhaps slow-roast fillet of beef with shallots, celeriac, a bonbon of foie gras and essence of port, while dessert might surprise with a pear and fennel delice, marinated black olives, fennel cannelloni and olive oil ice cream. Excellent peripherals such as freshly baked breads, home-made chocolates, foams and shooters are all top drawer, duly complemented by a superb wine list.

Chef Daniel Clifford **Owner** Midsummer House Ltd **Times** 12-1.30/7-9.30, Closed 2 wks late Aug, 2 wks from 25 Dec, 1 wk Etr, Closed Sun & Mon, Closed L Tue **Prices** Food prices not confirmed for 2009. Please telephone for details. **Wines** 900 bottles over £20, 12 by glass **Notes** Vegetarian available **Seats** 54, Pr/dining room 16 **Children** Portions **Parking** On street

CAMBRIDGE *Continued*

22 Chesterton Road

◉ Modern British

Consistent and accomplished cooking in intimate setting

☎ 01223 351880
22 Chesterton Rd CB4 3AX
e-mail: aandstommaso@restaurant22.co.uk
dir: Telephone for directions

There may have been a change of owner, but the kitchen team remains the same at this relaxed, candlelit Victorian dining room. Tables are close together and there is an atmosphere of a private house, which is precisely what this once was. The kitchen's monthly-changing fixed-price modern British menu with French influences takes a modern approach. Sound skills and an emphasis on local ingredients and flavour ensure consistent results; think roast breast of pheasant with red cabbage, chestnuts and caramelised salsify, and perhaps a steamed Guinness and raisin pudding with liquorice ice cream to finish.

Chef Martin Cullum, Seb Mansfield **Owner** Mr A & Mrs S Tommaso **Times** Closed 25 Dec & New Year, Closed Sun-Mon, Closed L all wk **Prices** Fixed D 3 course £26.50, Service optional **Wines** 40 bottles over £20, 30 bottles under £20, 4 by glass **Notes** Vegetarian available, Air con **Seats** 26, Pr/dining room 12 **Children** Min 10 yrs, Portions **Parking** On street

---

DUXFORD   Map 12 TL44

Duxford Lodge Hotel

◉ British, European

Welcoming and historic surroundings for imaginative cuisine

☎ 01223 836444
Ickleton Rd CB22 4RT
e-mail: admin@duxfordlodgehotel.co.uk
web: www.duxfordlodgehotel.co.uk
dir: M11 junct 10, take A505 E, then 1st right at rdbt to Duxford; take right fork at T-junction, entrance 70 yds on left

An officers' mess during the First and Second World Wars, this attractive red-brick hotel is a good place for dinner after a day at the nearby Imperial War Museum, where Douglas Bader and Winston Churchill were former guests. The restaurant is an intimate room with neatly-clothed tables and large windows overlooking the garden. The menu offers intriguing combinations in dishes such as asparagus and oven-dried tomato with artichoke tortellini to start, and a main course of chargrilled rib-eye steak served with a bean casserole, fondant potato and beetroot jus. To finish, a decent crème brûlée is served with an unusual basil ice cream.

Times 12-2/7-9.30, Closed 26-30 Dec

ELY   Map 12 TL58

The Anchor Inn

◉ Modern British

Riverside inn serving imaginatively presented local produce

☎ 01353 778537
Sutton Gault, Sutton CB6 2BD
e-mail: anchorinn@popmail.bta.com
dir: Signed off B1381 in Sutton village, 7m W of Ely via A142

The Anchor was built in 1650, originally to provide shelter for workers digging the New Bedford River, as part of the mass draining of the Fens. Uneven tiled floors, antique pine furniture and roaring fires in winter welcome you to the historic inn. Food is an interesting mixture of traditional English dishes and those with European and

---

Restaurant Alimentum

CAMBRIDGE   Map 12 TL45

Modern European 💻

Trendy eatery with a relaxed atmosphere and polished service

☎ 01223 413001
152-154 Hills Rd CB2 8PB

Housed in a smart building opposite the city's Leisure Park, Cambridge's new landmark restaurant is making waves locally and nationally for its sleek and stylish design and its accomplished modern European cooking. The trendy, contemporary décor takes in floor-to-ceiling smoked glass, black lacquer surfaces, dark red seating, and blonde-wood parquet flooring, yet the atmosphere is relaxed and unpretentious, and the service is efficient and professional. Chef David Williams (formerly at Chapter One, see entry) produces an inventive weekly

menu that works with the seasons using top quality locally-sourced ingredients. High levels of skill and technique result in well-balanced dishes with good combinations of flavours and textures. Take an excellent lobster ravioli starter, served with a quenelle of smooth cauliflower purée and a full-flavoured Cognac and lobster sauce. Equally impressive is the slow-cooked Denham Estate lamb cooked three ways for main course - pink and succulent rump, tender braised neck and shoulder served as a pithivier, with swede purée and a lovely meaty jus. The well-balanced and finely constructed tiramisu to finish has a light texture, great espresso flavours and arrives with an espresso jelly and milk sorbet. Good quality breads, decent coffees and a reasonably priced wine list (10 by the glass) complete the promising picture.

Prices Food prices not confirmed for 2009. Please telephone for details.

international influences. Fine examples of the fare include tian of crayfish with guacamole in a lime-flavoured mayonnaise, followed by breast of Suffolk chicken stuffed with sun-dried tomato and mozzarella and wrapped in Parma ham. Finish with chocolate fondant served with peanut butter and chocolate ice cream.

Times 12-3.30/7-11

HUNTINGDON   Map 12 TL27

Old Bridge Hotel

◎◎ Modern British ◢NOTABLE

Charming hotel with high standards and versatile dining options

☎ 01480 424300
PE29 3TQ
e-mail: oldbridge@huntsbridge.co.uk
dir: Off A1 near junct with A1/M1 link and A604/M11

There's a choice of two dining venues at this 18th-century ivy-clad townhouse hotel, which stands guard over the old bridge into Huntingdon. The lively and informal Terrace restaurant serves a full menu, good-value lunches and snacks, and the smart Dining Room restaurant with its bold colour scheme, serves a full à la carte on Friday and Saturday evenings. The chef's love of traditional, rustic European cuisine is reflected in modern British dishes that speak with a strong French or Italian accent. Start with celeriac soup with hazelnut pesto, followed perhaps by fillet of halibut with parsley and garlic crust, mashed potato, spinach and lemon butter sauce. Black Forest trifle adds a welcome retro touch to puddings.

Chef Chris Tabbitt **Owner** J Hoskins
Times 12-2/6.30-9.30 **Prices** Fixed L 2 course fr £15, Starter £5.75-£9.95, Main £11.75-£25, Dessert £5.75-£8.95, Service optional **Wines** 350 bottles over £20, 50 bottles under £20, 16 by glass **Notes** Sunday L, Vegetarian available, Civ Wed 80, Air con **Seats** 100, Pr/dining room 40 **Children** Portions, Menu **Parking** 60

KEYSTON   Map 11 TL07

Pheasant Inn

◎ British, French

Gastronomic delights in a charming village inn

☎ 01832 710241
Village Loop Rd PE28 0RE
e-mail: info@thepheasant-keyston.co.uk
dir: 0.5m off A14, clearly signed, 10m W of Huntingdon, 14m E of Kettering

The Pheasant is a beautiful beamed and thatched village inn, dating from the 16th century, which backs on to its own vegetable garden. Situated in a sleepy village, old farming equipment is displayed as a decorative feature and the well-spaced, polished wooden tables and pine settles also have rustic appeal. Imaginative, no fuss traditional British and French cooking uses as much local produce as possible, with beef, lamb and pork all coming

from within a 10-mile radius. Try fish soup with rouille, gruyère and croûtes; rabbit with bubble-and-squeak, bacon and mustard sauce; and egg custard tart to finish. Excellent wine list available.

Chef Jay Scrimshaw/Liam Goodwill **Owner** Jay & Taffeta Scrimshaw **Times** 12-2.30/6-9.30, Closed Mon, Closed D Sun **Prices** Starter £5.50-£8.50, Main £13.50-£19.50, Dessert £5.50-£7.50, Service optional, Groups min 10 service 10% **Wines** 60 bottles over £20, 20 bottles under £20, 12 by glass **Notes** Sunday L, Vegetarian available **Seats** 80, Pr/dining room 30 **Children** Portions **Parking** 40

LITTLE WILBRAHAM   Map 12 TL55

Hole in the Wall

◎ Modern, British ⬡

Old inn serving imaginative food in the heart of horseracing community

☎ 01223 812282
2 High St CB21 5JY
dir: A14 junct 35. A11 exit at The Wilbrahams

As the name intimates, there was once a hole in the wall of the main bar - so local farmers could collect their ale (as only the gentry were allowed in the pub) - though nowadays, this fine old 15th-century timber-framed village inn welcomes all-comers. Inside, there are all the traditional country-pub trappings, such as exposed beams, hops, brass and roaring winter fires, while furnishings are suitably rustic in style with polished wood tables. The skilled kitchen comes with a modern British approach though, taking its cue from fresh seasonal local produce, with dishes intelligently not over-embellished to allow flavours to shine. Take slow-braised Lincolnshire pork cheeks with cider, onions and black pudding served with sauté potatoes and crispy sage.

Chef Christopher Leeton **Owner** Christopher Leeton, Jennifer Chapman, Stephen Bull **Times** 12-2/7-9, Closed 2 weeks in Jan & 2 weeks in Oct, Closed Mon (except L BH), Closed L 26 Dec & 1 Jan, Closed D Sun **Prices** Starter £3.50-£8, Main £9.50-£16, Dessert £5.50-£5.75, Service optional **Wines** 15 bottles over £20, 26 bottles under £20, 12 by glass **Notes** Sunday L, Vegetarian available **Seats** 65 **Children** Portions **Parking** 30

MADINGLEY   Map 12 TL36

Three Horseshoes Restaurant

◎ Italian

Modern Italian dining in village setting

☎ 01954 210221
High St CB3 8AB
e-mail: 3hs@btconnect.co.uk
dir: M11 junct 13, turn left, then next right and continue to end of road, and at mini-rdbt turn right

Despite its quintessentially English location - with a garden stretching down to the village cricket pitch - this

16th-century thatched gastro-pub has a decidedly relaxed, continental feel, complete with table service. Cooking is robust Italian with a cosmopolitan, gutsy edge to it. The daily-changing menu may include the likes of sea bass and cockle risotto, followed by a roast haunch of venison, served with parsnip purée, braised cavolo nero, Chianti and thyme. To finish, try the lemon tart with mandarin and vodka sorbet. The exciting, well-chosen wine list includes recommendations for dessert wines.

Chef Richard Stokes **Owner** Richard Stokes
Times 12-2/6.30-9.30, Closed 1-2 Jan **Prices** Starter £5.95-£8.95, Main £12.95-£24.95, Dessert £4.95-£7.95, Service optional, Groups min 8 service 10% **Wines** 70 bottles over £20, 15 bottles under £20, 14 by glass **Notes** Sunday L, Vegetarian available **Seats** 65 **Children** Portions **Parking** 50

PETERBOROUGH   Map 12 TL19

Best Western Orton Hall Hotel

◎ British

Impressive historic building serving modern cuisine

☎ 01733 391111
Orton Longueville PE2 7DN
e-mail: reception@ortonhall.co.uk
dir: Telephone for directions

The 17th-century former manor house is set in 20 acres of parkland in the conservation village of Orton Longueville, and was once home to the Marquis of Huntly. The elegant Huntly Restaurant retains many of its period features, including oak panelling and exquisite stained glass, and exudes an air of warmth and intimacy. The kitchen's approach, however, is firmly rooted in the present day with modern British dishes such as rabbit and Parma ham terrine with sweet pickled vegetables; and seared sea bass with saffron linguine and a basil and tomato butter sauce.

Chef Kevin Wood **Owner** Abacus Hotels
Times 12.30-2/7-9.30, Closed 25 Dec, Closed L Mon-Sat **Prices** Fixed L 2 course £13.50-£21.50, Fixed D 3 course £17.50-£29, Starter £5.75-£9.50, Main £14.50-£21.25, Dessert £5.50-£8.95, Service optional **Wines** 23 bottles over £20, 42 bottles under £20, 6 by glass **Notes** Sunday L, Civ Wed 150 **Seats** 34, Pr/dining room 40 **Parking** 200

The George Hotel & Brasserie

◉ Modern British

Stylish, busy brasserie in former coaching inn

☎ 01480 812300
High St, Buckden PE19 5XA
e-mail: mail@thegeorgebuckden.com
dir: Off A1, S of junct with A14

Set in the historic village of Buckden just a few minutes drive from the A1, this venerable coaching inn has served as a resting place for travellers for hundreds of years. A recent makeover has ensured it still looks good for its age and seen each of its twelve bedrooms converted into a chic homage to a famous George, including Orwell, Eliot and Best. Brown leather stools perch at a long metal bar in the ground-floor brasserie, while polished wooden tables gleam beneath sparkling glassware - it's a convivial setting that's perfectly complemented by a menu of modern British cuisine. Try Highland beef served with truffle oil mash, wild mushroom fricassée and horseradish butter, or teriyaki-marinated Old Spot pork belly with a warm noodle salad and Thai dressing.

Chef Ray Smikle **Owner** Richard & Anne Furbank
Times 12-2.30/7-9.30 **Prices** Food prices not confirmed for 2009. Please telephone for details. **Wines** 35 bottles over £20, 35 bottles under £20, 16 by glass
Notes Vegetarian available, Dress restrictions, Smart dress, Civ Wed 40 **Seats** 60, Pr/dining room 30
Children Portions **Parking** 25

Swynford Paddocks Hotel

◉ Traditional

Historic country-house hotel with reliable cooking

☎ 01638 570234
CB8 0UE
e-mail: info@swynfordpaddocks.com
dir: M11 junct 9, take A11 towards Newmarket, then onto A1304 to Newmarket, hotel is 0.75m on left

Overlooking the front lawn of this impressive hotel, the elegant and formal restaurant is named after Lord Byron who was a frequent visitor to this delightful country house. Set in 64 acres of parkland located close to the historic home of flat racing at Newmarket, the hotel has a long-standing association with the races. The food is modern British with Mediterranean influences, with an emphasis on satisfying, flavoursome fare created from the best of local produce. Expect starters such as spinach and chick pea soup, followed by fillet steak served with apple and sage boulangère potato and port sauce. Finish with white chocolate parfait with griottine cherries.

Chef Paul Buckley **Owner** Paul & Lucie Smith
Times 11.30-3/6.30-10, Closed Sat (if sole occupancy wedding) **Prices** Fixed L course £29.95, Fixed D 3 course £29.95, Starter £4.75-£6, Main £9.95-£59, Dessert £4.95-£6.95, Service optional **Wines** 34 bottles over £20, 28 bottles under £20, 10 by glass **Notes** Tasting menu 7 courses, Sunday L, Vegetarian available, Dress restrictions, No jeans/trainers at dinner, Civ Wed 220
Seats 30, Pr/dining room 50 **Children** Portions, Menu
Parking 100

Bell Inn Hotel

◉ British, French ✿

Charming inn with bags of character

☎ 01733 241066
Great North Rd PE7 3RA
e-mail: reception@thebellstilton.co.uk
web: www.thebellstilton.co.uk
dir: 1m N A1(M) junct 16 follow signs to Stilton. Hotel on High Street in centre of village

A wonderfully agreeable inn, steeped in history and possessed of numerous original features, the Bell is set in a delightful village on the outskirts of Peterborough. A consistently good standard of food is served in the atmospheric bar and bistro, and beamed first-floor Galleried Restaurant. You can also eat outside in the attractive courtyard, weather permitting. Imaginative British dishes with French influences are prepared from quality produce and might include confit of duck with cranberry and potato gratin and roast tangerines; and steamed loin of monkfish with roast pumpkins, sweet potato, buttered kale and pancetta with lemon butter sauce.

Chef Robin Devonshire **Owner** Mr L A McGivern
Times 12-2/7-9.30, Closed 25 Dec and New Years Eve, Closed L Sat, Closed D Sun **Prices** Fixed L 2 course £12.95, Fixed D 3 course £26.95, Starter £3.95-£7.95, Main £9.75-£17.95, Dessert £4.75, Service optional
Wines 30 bottles over £20, 30 bottles under £20, 8 by glass **Notes** Sunday L, Vegetarian available, Civ Wed 90, Air con **Seats** 60, Pr/dining room 20 **Children** Min 5 yrs
Parking 30

The Moorings

◉ Modern, Traditional

Contemporary brasserie-style restaurant with grill-inspired dining

☎ 01945 773391
Crown Lodge Hotel, Downham Rd, Outwell PE14 8SE
e-mail: office@thecrownlodgehotel.co.uk
dir: 5m SE of Wisbech on A1122, 1m from junct with A1101, towards Downham Market

Peacefully located on the banks of Welle Creek, this well-presented hotel was once a garage and transport café - the main building converted from the old car showroom. The open-plan brasserie-style restaurant has a warm, contemporary vibe, with modern paintings and objets d'art set against dark wood tables and floors, and screens to section off the large bar-lounge area. The kitchen's modern approach, showcasing a selection of grills, suits the surroundings and makes use of quality, locally-sourced produce, with dishes such as braised lamb shank with Puy lentils, flash-fried swordfish loin on a chick pea, chorizo and tomato stew, and pan-fried chicken breast with crushed potato cabbage cakes.

Chef Mick Castell **Owner** Mr W J Moore
Times 12-2.30/6-10, Closed 25-26 & 31 Dec, 1 Jan
Prices Starter £4.75-£6.95, Main £11.95-£19.95, Dessert £4.10-£6.95, Service optional **Wines** 13 bottles over £20, 44 bottles under £20, 9 by glass **Notes** Sunday L, Vegetarian available, Dress restrictions, Smart casual, Air con **Seats** 40, Pr/dining room 35 **Children** Portions
Parking 50

CHESHIRE

ALDERLEY EDGE   Map 16 SJ87

The Alderley Restaurant

◉◉ British 🖥 V 🕙

Inspired cuisine in a well-furnished country-house hotel

☎ 01625 583033
Alderley Edge Hotel, Macclesfield Rd SK9 7BJ
e-mail: sales@alderlyedgehotel.com
dir: A538 to Alderley Edge, then B5087 Macclesfield Rd

Modernised and extended to create a delightful hotel, this country house was originally built for one of the county's cotton merchants. The popular split-level conservatory restaurant, with its airy atmosphere, smartly appointed tables and high-backed leather chairs, has been known to play host to celebrity footballers from the Manchester United team. Little wonder that it attracts such stars when the food is so good. Innovative touches, creative use of flavours and locally-sourced ingredients feature in an imaginative menu, including a market menu, with mains such as tasting of Cheshire beef with glazed spring onions and Madeira, while sumptuous desserts could include warm apple and hazelnut cake with bay laurel ice cream and Cheshire apple caviar.

Chef Chris Holland **Owner** J W Lees (Brewers) Ltd
Times 12-2/7-10, Closed 1 Jan, Closed L 31 Dec, Closed D 25-26 Dec **Prices** Fixed L 2 course fr £13.95, Fixed D 3 course £29.50, Tasting menu £47.50-£65, Starter £7.50-£10.50, Main £22-£25.50, Dessert £6.95-£6.50, Service optional **Wines** 450+ bottles over £20, 30 bottles under £20, 7 by glass **Notes** Tasting menu 6 courses, Sunday L, Vegetarian menu, Dress restrictions, Smart casual, Civ Wed 150, Air con **Seats** 65, Pr/dining room 150 **Children** Portions, Menu **Parking** 82

ALSAGER   Map 15 SJ75

Best Western Manor House Hotel

◉ British V

Enjoyable dining in former farmhouse

☎ 01270 884000
Audley Rd ST7 2QQ
e-mail: mhres@compasshotels.co.uk
web: www.compasshotels.co.uk
dir: M6 junct 16, follow A500 towards Stoke on Trent. Leave A500 on 1st slip road, turn left & follow road for 3m. Hotel on left

Built around a 17th-century farmhouse, the hotel combines modern style and comfort with original features. Located in what was once the barn, The Ostler restaurant - with its vaulted ceiling, exposed oak beams and period fireplace - is the perfect setting for good quality British cooking, with flambé dishes a specialty. Choose between the daily fixed-price menu and seasonal carte of British and French dishes using locally-sourced produce. Start with sweet pepper and Shropshire Blue tartlet with cider vinaigrette, and follow with pan-seared medallions of beef with a red sauce of button onions, mushrooms and lardons, rounded off with delicious lemon torte for dessert.

Chef Ian Turner **Owner** Compass Hotels Ltd
Times 12-2/7.15-9.30, Closed 27-30 Dec, Closed L Sat, Closed D Sun **Prices** Fixed D 4 course £24.50-£26.50, Service optional **Wines** 5 by glass **Notes** Sunday L, Vegetarian menu, Dress restrictions, Smart casual, Civ Wed 200, Air con **Seats** 90, Pr/dining room 28 **Children** Portions, Menu **Parking** 150

CHESTER   Map 15 SJ46

La Brasserie at The Chester Grosvenor & Spa

◉ Modern International 🖥 🕙

Enjoyable brasserie dining in Chester's ancient heart

☎ 01244 324024
Eastgate CH1 1LT
e-mail: hotel@chestergrosvenor.co.uk
dir: 2m from M53, located in city centre

Set in a black and white timbered building in the heart of Chester, this chic, yet informal, restaurant evokes the bustling brasseries of Paris. Art deco mirrors hang above leather banquettes and sleek granite tabletops are smartly set with quality appointments. Brasserie classics such as moules marinière and lemon sole with shrimps and noisette butter form the mainstay of the menu, but there's also more imaginative fare on offer: blanc of cod with spiced squid, roast pork belly and chickpeas, for example. A range of lighter snacks is also available, including a classic omelette Arnold Bennett or open fillet steak sandwich with caramelised onions and fried egg.

Chef Simon Radley, Bradley Lean **Owner** Grosvenor - Duke of Westminster **Times** 12/10.30, Closed 25-26 Dec **Prices** Starter £5.95-£13.95, Main £13.95-£25.95,

Dessert £4.95-£6.50, Service optional, Groups min 8 service 12.5% **Wines** 40 bottles over £20, 5 bottles under £20, 11 by glass **Notes** Vegetarian available, Dress restrictions, Smart casual, Civ Wed 120, Air con **Seats** 80, Pr/dining room 250 **Children** Portions, Menu **Parking** 250; NCP attached to hotel

Rowton Hall Country House Hotel

◉◉ Traditional British

Magnificent Georgian country-house hotel with fine dining

☎ 01244 335262
Whitchurch Rd, Rowton CH3 6AD
e-mail: reception@rowtonhallhotelandspa.co.uk
dir: M56 junct 12 take A56 to Chester. At rdbt turn left on A41 to Whitchurch. Approx 1m and follow signs for hotel

History buffs might be interested to know that this cmfortable country-house hotel stands on the site of a major battle in the English Civil War, but these days you're more likely to encounter a jogger in the award-winning gardens than a cavalier, thanks to Rowton's impressive health facilities which include a beauty suite, pool and gym. Inside, surviving period features include an impressive Robert Adams fireplace, extensive oak panelling and a hand-carved, self-supporting fireplace. In the Langdale restaurant, choose from an extensive selection of complex dishes, which use local produce where possible. Try a starter of seared scallops with truffled celeriac purée and watercress foam, followed by assiette of duck, or steamed wild turbot, ox cheek, young vegetables and shallot jus.

Times 12-2/7-9.30

Simon Radley at The Chester Grosvenor

CHESTER — Map 15 SJ46

Modern French 🖥 V 🍷NOTABLE WINE LIST 🍸

Innovative and highly skilled cooking in top city hotel

☎ 01244 324024
Chester Grosvenor & Spa, Eastgate CH1 1LT
e-mail: hotel@chestergrosvenor.co.uk
dir: City centre (Eastgate St) adjacent to Eastgate Clock & Roman walls

The hotel dating back to 1865 is the jewel in Chester's crown and is situated right in the heart of the city. Behind the Grade II listed, black-and-white timbered façade is a hotel of considerable class and style. In fact, as we went to press, the restaurant was renamed after the chef who over the past 10 years has built up the reputation of the hotel as a destination for fine dining. Simon Radley at The Chester Grosvenor is the new name from summer 2008. There is a refurbishment planned as well, with the London-based designer Jane Goff creating a new look to the dining room. There is no doubt that Simon Radley has earned the right to have his name over the door. His cooking displays a high degree of technical skill, creativity and a light touch. This is complex cooking in the modern vein where combinations can catch the eye, but the top quality ingredients are not lost in the process. There is a Tasting Menu of 8 courses and the dishes are given names such as Duck Toast - sweet confit of rhubarb and ginger with Landaise duck crostini - and the chef shows his skills to good effect. On the carte, a starter of Spare Ribs is lusciously glazed meat, off the bone, with perfectly cooked scallops and an inspired soy foam, and main-course veal sweetbread is cooked sous-vide and comes with first class lobster and truffle lasagne. The creativity and innovation continues with desserts such as Lime Squash, which is warm vanilla and lime risotto enhanced with sugared nuts, a lemon froth and chocolate 'parmesan'. The extras - breads, canapés, amuse-bouche, pre-dessert - are exceptional, service a good balance between formality and friendliness, and the wine list runs to an impressive 1000 bins.

Chef Simon Radley, Ray Booker **Owner** Grosvenor - Duke of Westminster **Times** Closed 25-26 Dec, 1 wk Jan, Closed Sun-Mon, Closed L all week (except Dec) **Prices** Fixed D 3 course £59, Tasting menu £70, Service added but optional 12.5%, Groups service 12.5% **Wines** 600 bottles over £20, 5 bottles under £20, 15 by glass **Notes** Vegetarian menu, Dress restrictions, Smart dress, no jeans, shorts or sportswear, Civ Wed 120, Air con **Seats** 45, Pr/dining room 240 **Children** Min 12 yrs **Parking** 250 **Parking** NCP attached to hotel

CHESTER *Continued*

Simon Radley at The Chester Grosvenor

◎◎◎◎ – *see opposite*

CREWE　　　　　　　　　Map 15 SJ75

The Brasserie

◎ Modern European

Contemporary brasserie in modern wing of stately home

☎ 01270 253333
Crewe Hall, Weston Rd CW1 6UZ
e-mail: crewehall@qhotels.co.uk
dir: M6 junct 16, follow A500 to Crewe. Last exit at rdbt onto A5020. 1st exit next to Crewe. Crewe Hall 150 yds on right

Located in the modern wing of this stately Grade I listed Jacobean mansion, The Brasserie is linked to the main building by a glass walkway, and offers a thoroughly retro, modern dining experience with an impressive revolving bar, open kitchen, and a lively atmosphere. Grill and vegetarian options feature on an extensive menu of accomplished modern European cuisine, supplemented by daily specials. Cannelloni of crayfish and prawns with lobster sauce, or individual beef Wellington with Chantenay carrots and dauphinoise potatoes are fine examples of the fare, with perhaps summer fruit jelly terrine and lemon sherbet with lime crème fraîche for dessert.

Chef Russell Brown **Owner** Q Hotels **Times** all day, Closed Sun **Prices** Fixed L 2 course fr £11.50, Starter £3.50-£7.50, Main £11.50-£23.50, Dessert £5.90-£7.50, Service optional **Wines** 31 bottles over £20, 9 bottles under £20, 10 by glass **Notes** Vegetarian available, Civ Wed 280, Air con **Seats** 140 **Children** Portions, Menu **Parking** 500

Hunters Lodge Hotel

◎ Modern British

Seasonal menus in an 18th-century idyllic retreat

☎ 01270 539100
Sydney Rd, Sydney CW1 5LU
e-mail: info@hunterslodge.co.uk
dir: 1m from station, follow signs to Leighton Hospital

Impressive leisure facilities, elegant accommodation and a popular bar serving informal meals draw guests to this idyllic Georgian retreat, set in 16 acres of South Cheshire countryside. The serious dining takes place in the spacious, beamed restaurant, from a seasonal menu reflecting both British and European trends. Imaginative dishes range from confit duck leg with black pudding mash to starter too main courses like beef medallions with red wine jus, or grilled halibut with nut-brown butter. Desserts may include warm treacle tart with coconut parfait and sauce anglaise, washed down with a recommended pudding wine.

Times 12-2/7-9.30, Closed BHs, Closed D Sun

KNUTSFORD　　　　　　Map 15 SJ77

Mere Court Hotel & Conference Centre

◎ Modern British

Fine dining with fine views

☎ 01565 831000
Warrington Rd, Mere WA16 0RW
e-mail: sales@merecourt.co.uk
dir: M6 J19 and follow signs for A50

This smart hotel is set in extensive, well-tended gardens, with impressive conference facilities. There are views over the lake and parkland from the sophisticated, fine-dining Arboretum restaurant, an, elegant high-beamed room with open fire and crisp napery. The cooking here is modern British with well balanced flavours, using. locally sourced produce whenever possible. For starters, try risotto of Dublin Bay prawns with dill and feves and lobster sabayon, followed by thyme-roasted chicken breast with fondant potato, buttered spinach and sauce Albufiera, and lime and tequila parfait with apricot biscuit and orange syrup to finish.

Times 12-2/7-9.30, Closed L Sat

NANTWICH　　　　　　Map 15 SJ65

Rookery Hall

◎◎ Modern British 🍷 NOTABLE WINE LIST 🌿

Imaginative modern dining in Georgian splendour

☎ 01270 610016
Main Rd, Worleston CW5 6DQ
e-mail: rookeryhall@handpicked.co.uk
dir: On B5074 N of Nantwich, 1.5m on right towards Worleston

Set in 38 acres of gardens, wooded parkland and bordered by the River Weaver, this grand Georgian

mansion bears a striking resemblance to a French château. With its pale sandstone walls, polished wood panelling, ornamental ceilings, sumptuous leather sofas, rich brocades and stained glass, the place positively oozes style and charm. The elegant restaurant has views over the rolling Cheshire countryside and is the perfect setting for intimate candlelit dinners. Modern French-influenced British cooking delivers some imaginative flavour combinations in dishes such as seared scallops with braised pork belly, apple and vanilla purée to start, followed by seared sea bass, spring onion and herb couscous, roast peppers and courgettes and tomato dressing, with iced pear parfait with chocolate tart to finish. Smooth, efficient and unobtrusive service completes the picture.

Chef Gordon Campbell **Owner** Hand Picked Hotels/Julia Hands **Times** 12-2/7-9.30, Closed L Sat **Wines** 160 bottles over £20, 20 bottles under £20, 16 by glass **Notes** Gourmet evenings £85, Sunday L, Vegetarian available, Dress restrictions, Smart casual, no jeans or trainers, Civ Wed 200 **Seats** 90, Pr/dining room 60 **Children** Portions, Menu **Parking** 100

PRESTBURY　　　　　　Map 16 SJ87

White House Restaurant

◎◎ Modern British

Impressive cuisine in contemporary-styled former farmhouse

☎ 01625 829336
SK10 4DG
e-mail: enquiries@thewhitehouseinprestbury.com
dir: Village centre on A538 N of Macclesfield

Contemporary paintings, sculptures and etched glass screens rub shoulders with mullioned, leaded windows, stone fireplaces and limed oak beams in this chic dining room housed in a former farmhouse. A simple menu is available in the bar, but the dining room under the new chef offers more challenging fare. Classic and contemporary cooking styles take in French influences with occasional nods to Pan-Asian cuisine, with an emphasis on local produce. Start with king prawn dim sum and follow it with a more classic roast Goosnargh duck breast served with a confit of its leg and caramelised peaches. Apple and sultana tart with vanilla ice cream is one of several eye-catching desserts.

Chef James Roberts **Owner** Shade Down Ltd **Times** 12-2/6-9, Closed 25 Dec, 1 Jan, Closed Mon, Closed D Sun **Prices** Fixed D 3 course £18.95-£21.95, Starter £4.95-£14.50, Main £12.75-£22.75, Service optional **Wines** 12 by glass **Notes** Early bird offer Tue-Fri 6-7pm, Sunday L, Vegetarian available, Air con **Seats** 70, Pr/dining room 40 **Children** Portions, Menu **Parking** 11 **Parking** Car park adjoining

PUDDINGTON — Map 15 SJ37

Macdonald Craxton Wood

Modern

Stylish hotel for fine dining

☎ 0151 347 4000

Parkgate Rd, Ledsham CH66 9PB

e-mail: info@craxton.macdonald-hotels.co.uk

dir: From end of M56 W take A5117 Queensferry, right at 1st rdbt onto A540 (Hoylake). Hotel 200yds after next traffic lights

A smart establishment set in extensive grounds, the hotel offers excellent leisure facilities and an impressive conservatory, lounge and bar. The Garden Room restaurant is handsomely furnished and enjoys lovely garden views. The carte menu provides a wide choice of dishes prepared from excellent produce. A typical selection might include tournedos of Scottish beef with a pavé of mushroom and potato and truffle rarebit, or steamed red snapper with saffron and prawn risotto, seared scallop, and champagne and scallop roe beurre blanc. Vegetarian options feature the likes of open lasagne of ricotta cheese with peas and fresh mint.

Times 12.30-2/7-9.30, Closed L Sat

RAINOW — Map 16 SJ97

The Highwayman

British

Traditional inn with modern approach to food and service

☎ 01625 573245

Whaley Bridge Rd SK10 5UU

dir: Main road between Macclesfield & Whaley Bridge. Situated between Rainow and Kettleshulme

From the outside, The Highwayman looks like the stereotypical country inn, but inside it's a successful marriage of old-style pub and modern makeover. Here, character stone floors, open fires and low ceilings blend with leather sofas and, in the small dining room, wooden tables and leather chairs. Service takes a modern approach - attentive, knowledgeable and helpful - while the kitchen follows a traditional path with some interesting twists, driven by quality local produce and intelligent simplicity. Take Goosnargh duck breast served with a galette of Bury black pudding and celeriac, celeriac purée and blackberry jus, and perhaps home-made Eccles tart with sultana syrup and warm custard.

Chef Gareth Davies, Matthew Wray, Luke Jackson **Owner** Thwaites **Times** 12-2.30/5-9 **Prices** Starter £4.50-£6.95, Main £9.95-£20, Dessert £4.95, Service optional, Groups min 8 service 10% **Wines** 2 bottles over £20, 18 bottles under £20, 6 by glass **Notes** Sunday L, Vegetarian available **Seats** 50, Pr/dining room 24 **Children** Portions **Parking** 22

SANDIWAY — Map 15 SJ67

Nunsmere Hall Country House Hotel

British, European

Modern cuisine in a Victorian country house setting

☎ 01606 889100

Tarporley Rd CW8 2ES

e-mail: reservations@nunsmere.co.uk

dir: From M6 junct 19 take A56 for 9 miles. Turn left onto A49 towards Tarporley. Hotel is 1m on left

Historic Nunsmere Hall is a classic grand English country house, set in the heart of the Cheshire countryside and surrounded by acres of magnificent gardens and a beautiful lake. The Crystal restaurant, overlooking the south-facing terrace and sunken garden, offers an elegant and intimate dining experience. Accomplished modern British and European-style cooking is on offer, making good use of top quality ingredients. There's a tasting menu designed for the whole table, or try typical carte dishes like fillet of beef, roast Jerusalem artichokes, cannelloni of leek and trompette mushrooms and Madeira jus, or fillet of organic salmon, lobster crushed potatoes, braised baby bok choi and coconut broth, with perhaps a trio of chocolate to follow.

Chef Paul Robertson **Owner** Prima Hotels **Times** 12-2/7-10 **Prices** Fixed D 3 course £30, Tasting menu £55, Starter £6.50-£9.50, Main £16-£22, Dessert £6.50-£8, Service included, Groups service 5% **Wines** 140 bottles over £20, 12 bottles under £20, 8 by glass **Notes** Sunday L, Vegetarian available, Dress restrictions, No jeans, trainers or shorts, Civ Wed 100 **Seats** 60, Pr/dining room 45 **Children** Min 12 yrs, Portions **Parking** 80

TARPORLEY — Map 15 SJ56

Macdonald Portal Hotel

Modern British

Sophisticated country-club setting serving high-street restaurant food

☎ 0844 879 9082

Cobbiers Cross Ln CW6 0DJ

Set in the rolling Cheshire countryside, this luxurious new hotel boasts a championship golf course and academy in addition to a state-of-the-art health, fitness and beauty spa. Fine dining takes place in the spacious Ranulf Restaurant, named after the earl who built nearby Beeston Castle, and enjoys panoramic views over the surroundings. The mouthwatering menu features an ever-growing range of organic foods, from a kitchen that takes pride in sourcing only the best quality ingredients, including Scottish lamb and beef and Loch Fyne fish. Simple, precise combinations highlight the essence of the flavours. A ballotine of pink salmon with smoked haddock mousseline and red pepper syrup gets things off to a flying start, followed by an equally impressive main course of confit of cornfed chicken, served with creamed leeks and cep foam. And last but not least, chocolate millefeuille with vanilla pod sauce. Excellent breads and petits fours complete the package, complemented by friendly and knowledgeable service from smartly-dressed staff.

Prices Food prices not confirmed for 2009. Please telephone for details.

WILMSLOW — Map 16 SJ88

Stanneylands Hotel

Modern British

Country-house hotel dining close to Manchester airport

☎ 01625 525225

Stanneylands Rd SK9 4EY

e-mail: enquiries@stanneylandshotel.co.uk

dir: From M56 junct 5 follow signs for Cheadle. At lights turn right, through Styal, left at Handforth sign, follow into Stanneylands Rd

This traditional country-house hotel is set in 4 acres of beautifully maintained grounds and is within easy reach of Manchester airport and the city centre. The elegant panelled restaurant has well appointed tables, and is a popular venue for locals and visitors alike. Relax over a drink in one of the modern lounges before tucking into a starter of pan-fried foie gras with gingered plum purée, baby carrots, toasted pain d'épice and roasted carrot oil. Follow with poached monkfish tail, confit duck leg, sautéed cauliflower, borlotti beans, salsify and baby gem lettuce and toasted barley sauce. Desserts include some unusual choices, as in hazelnut and muscovado sugar tart with natural yogurt foam.

Chef Ernst Van Zyl **Owner** Mr L Walshe **Times** 12.30-2.30/7-9.30, Closed D Sun **Prices** Fixed L 2 course £14.50, Fixed D 4 course £30.50, Starter £5.50-£10, Main £14.50-£22.50, Dessert £7, Service optional **Wines** 108 bottles over £20, 31 bottles under £20, 6 by glass **Notes** Sunday L, Vegetarian available, Dress restrictions, Smart casual, Civ Wed 100 **Seats** 60, Pr/dining room 120 **Children** Portions, Menu **Parking** 110

CORNWALL & ISLES OF SCILLY

BODMIN   Map 2 SX06

Trehellas House Hotel & Restaurant

◉ Traditional British ✍

Welcoming setting for great local food

☎ 01208 72700
Washaway PL30 3AD
e-mail: enquiries@trehellashouse.co.uk
dir: 4m from Bodmin on A389 to Wadebridge, adjacent to Pencarrow

Both a farm and a courthouse in its time, this 18th-century inn retains many original features, and an interesting choice of dishes is offered in the impressive slate-floored restaurant. Cornish ingredients are to the fore, with fish and shellfish delivered from Fowey, Looe and Newlyn. Recommendations are seafood bouillabaisse, haunch of wild venison steak served with roasted sweet potato, butternut squash, and a port wine and juniper berry sauce, or whole wild sea bass with pink peppercorns, tarragon butter and new potatoes. A good selection of Cornish cheeses includes Yarg and St Endellion brie.

Chef Christopher Chappel **Owner** Alistair & Debra Hunter **Times** 12-2/7-9 **Prices** Fixed L 2 course £9.95-£49, Starter £5.95-£15.95, Main £14.95-£35, Dessert £4.95-£6.95, Service included **Wines** 7 bottles over £20, 24 bottles under £20, 6 by glass **Notes** Sunday L, Vegetarian available **Seats** 40 **Children** Portions, Menu **Parking** 25

BOSCASTLE   Map 2 SX09

The Bottreaux, Restaurant, Bar & Rooms

◉◉ Modern British

Local produce in a modernised 200-year-old building

☎ 01840 250231
PL35 0BG
e-mail: bottreaux@btconnect.com
dir: From Exeter take A30, take A395 to Camelford and B3263 to Boscastle

Within walking distance of the picturesque harbour, this historic 200-year old building combines a hotel, restaurant (the former village store) and slate-floored bar (once the stables) and is named after the founders of the village. The restaurant is contemporary in style, with modern leather chairs, wooden flooring and white and pale green décor. The daily-changing, imaginative menu focuses on fish and seafood dishes, with local Cornish produce the core ingredient. Expect starters such as steamed mussels in a creamy leek and cider broth, followed by oven-baked sea bass in a puff pastry lattice with sautéed greens on a glazed lemon hollandaise or Boscastle fillet of beef topped with a wild mushroom gratin with vegetable dauphinoise. Leave room for the tempting desserts, like mango and strawberry cheesecake and black cherry sauce.

Chef Terry Crockford **Owner** John Acornley **Times** Closed Xmas, Jan & Feb wkdays, Closed Sun-Mon (except BH wknds), Closed L all week **Prices** Starter £5.50-£8.50, Main £12-£18, Dessert £5.50-£8.50, Service optional **Wines** 4 bottles over £20, 15 bottles under £20, 6 by glass **Notes** Vegetarian available, Dress restrictions, no vests or T-shirts **Seats** 22 **Children** Min 8 yrs, Portions **Parking** 7

The Wellington Hotel

◉◉ Modern British

Imaginative cooking in quaint Cornish village

☎ 01840 250202
The Harbour PL35 0AQ
e-mail: info@boscastle-wellington.com
web: www.boscastle-wellington.com
dir: M5, A30, A39 to Camelford, then B3266 to Boscastle. Hotel is situated at the base of village by the harbour

Set in one of north Cornwall's most popular fishing villages, this 16th-century coaching inn sustained serious damage during the infamous Boscastle floods in 2004. Five years on - and with a little help from the BBC's 'Changing Rooms' team - it boasts a chic modern dining room, The Waterloo Restaurant, that's popular with locals and tourists alike. The menu changes daily and features imaginative dishes conjured from quality local produce: roast pork loin with carrot purée, rösti potato and cider jus perhaps, or roast duck suprême with braised red cabbage, roast parsnip purée and cranberry jus. Booking is essential as tables are limited, but if you're out of luck try the hotel bar - a friendly, beamed affair with a real log fire and a nice line in local specialities such as mackerel and eel.

Chef Scott Roberts **Owner** Paul Roberts **Times** Closed Thu **Prices** Food prices not confirmed for 2009. Please telephone for details. **Wines** 20 bottles over £20, 48 bottles under £20, 8 by glass **Seats** 35, Pr/dining room 28 **Children** Portions, Menu **Parking** 15

CALLINGTON   Map 3 SX36

Langmans Restaurant

◉◉ Modern British V ✍

Accomplished cuisine in a 16th-century former bakery

☎ 01579 384933
3 Church St PL17 7RE
e-mail: dine@langmansrestaurant.co.uk
web: www.langmansrestaurant.co.uk
dir: From the direction of Plymouth into town centre, left at lights and second right into Church St

A Grade II listed building tucked away off the main street, this former bakery has stylish modern sofas in the bar and crisply-clothed, candlelit tables in the relaxed dining room. Everything from bread rolls to petits fours is freshly prepared on the premises by the chef-owner. Local and organic produce is used wherever possible to produce dishes like scallop with cauliflower soup and truffle foam, or wild sea bass with salsify, Jerusalem artichoke and cep sauce. An irresistible banana and hazelnut praline parfait or passionfruit tart with coconut ice cream might prove your downfall at dessert. Staff are well trained and fully briefed on the menu and wine list.

Chef Anton Buttery **Owner** Anton & Gail Buttery **Times** Closed Sun-Wed, Closed L all week **Prices** Food prices not confirmed for 2009. Please telephone for details, Service optional **Wines** 37 bottles over £20, 50 bottles under £20, 11 by glass **Notes** Vegetarian menu, Dress restrictions, Smart casual preferred **Seats** 24 **Children** Min 12 yrs **Parking** Town centre car park

CONSTANTINE   Map 2 SW72

Trengilly Wartha Inn

◉ Traditional British, International ✍

Village inn serving good Cornish produce

☎ 01326 340332
Nancenoy TR11 5RP
e-mail: reception@trengilly.co.uk
web: www.trengilly.co.uk
dir: Between Falmouth and Helston off the former B3291 Penryn-Gweek road

Nestling in 6 acres of lovely gardens in a peaceful wooded valley near the Helford River, this is a traditional country pub with bags of character and an informal bistro attached. The kitchen specialises in home-made food prepared from fresh, locally sourced ingredients. It draws on influences from all over the world and typical dishes might include Thai crab soup made with local crab cooked with chilli, garlic, ginger, coriander and coconut, and pork belly slow-cooked in cider with fennel mash and white onion sauce, with a trio of miniature crème brûlées for dessert. The wine list is comprehensive and there's also an imaginative range of bar meals.

Chef Nick Tyler, Richard Penna **Owner** William & Lisa Lea **Times** 12-3/7-12, Closed 25 Dec **Prices** Starter £4-£9.50, Main £7.90-£26, Dessert £4.50, Service optional **Wines** 27 bottles over £20, 113 bottles under £20, 15 by glass **Notes** Sunday L, Vegetarian available **Seats** 25, Pr/dining room 16 **Children** Portions, Menu **Parking** 30

Falmouth Hotel

◉ Modern British V

Grand seaside hotel serving fresh seasonal fare

☎ 01326 312671 & 0800 44 888 44
Castle Beach TR11 4NZ
e-mail: reservations@falmouthhotel.com
dir: A39 Western Terrace, over rdbt onto Melvill Rd.
Continue to next rdbt, hotel on right

From its spectacular beachfront location, this graceful Victorian hotel ticks all the boxes, with its wonderful sea views, inviting lounges, leafy grounds, impressive leisure facilities and choice of dining options. The Trelawney Restaurant is full of period grandeur, complete with chandeliers. Appealing fixed-price menus make intelligent use of the abundant Cornish larder. Dishes are fresh, simply prepared and clean flavoured. Recommendations include pan-fried Gressingham duck breast with potato dauphinoise and lightly spiced black cherry sauce; and grilled fillet of salmon with crushed new potato salad, baby spinach and white wine and dill velouté.

Chef Paul Brennan **Owner** Richardson Hotels of Distinction **Times** 12.30-2/7-9.30, Closed L Sat **Prices** Fixed L 2 course £9.95-£15, Fixed D 3 course £25-£35, Service optional **Wines** 21 bottles over £20, 29 bottles under £20, 7 by glass **Notes** Sunday L, Vegetarian menu, Dress restrictions, Smart casual, no sportswear, Civ Wed 250 **Seats** 150, Pr/dining room 40 **Children** Portions, Menu

The Flying Fish Restaurant Bar

◉ Modern British

A great place to eat fresh fish by the sea

☎ 01326 312707
St Michael's Hotel and Spa, Gyllyngvase Beach, Seafront TR11 4NB
e-mail: info@stmichaelshotel.co.uk
dir: Please telephone for directions

This stylish hotel restaurant, recently refurbished in pastel shades, has a great atmosphere and buzz, and stunning views of Falmouth Bay and the Cornish coastline. The walls are hung with modern Cornish art, and the roof terrace is perfect for outdoor dining and a drink at sunset. Fresh local fish is the mainstay of the menu, though care is taken not to use species from depleted stocks. Try fillet of sea trout with Puy lentils, chorizo, purple sprouting broccoli and balsamic roasted cherry tomatoes; or prime Cornish rib-eye steak, grilled field mushrooms, pepper sauce and mixed leaf salad.

Chef Fiona Were **Owner** Nigel & Julie Carpenter **Times** 12-2/7-9 **Prices** Food prices not confirmed for 2009. Please telephone for details. **Wines** 13 bottles over £20, 19 bottles under £20, 12 by glass **Notes** Dress restrictions, Smart casual, Civ Wed 100 **Seats** 90, Pr/dining room 30 **Children** Portions, Menu **Parking** 30

Harbourside Restaurant

◉ Modern British

Contemporary-style restaurant with great harbour views

☎ 01326 312440
The Greenbank, Harbourside TR11 2SR
e-mail: sales@greenbank-hotel.co.uk
web: www.greenbank-hotel.co.uk
dir: Approaching Falmouth from Penryn, take left along North Parade. Follow sign to Falmouth Marina and Greenbank Hotel

Once a base for packet ship captains, this lovely old hotel still has its own private pier for guests arriving by boat. Its airy restaurant makes the most of the spectacular waterside views with its huge picture windows, and sustains the maritime theme. Accomplished cooking is the order of the day here: sea salt-roasted chump of lamb with a kidney skewer perhaps, served with hotpot potatoes, seasonal vegetables and red wine sauce, or spiced pollack fillet with Puy lentil and smoked bacon salsa, roast red pepper sauce, and an oyster and nettle emulsion. Desserts are creative and might include rhubarb and vanilla bavarois with deep-fried custard and roasted rhubarb, or apple jelly with parsnip ice cream and mint syrup.

Times 12-2/7-9.30, Closed L Sat

The Terrace Restaurant

◉◉ Modern International

Modern hotel dining with sea views

☎ 01326 313042
The Royal Duchy Hotel, Cliff Rd TR11 4NX
e-mail: info@royalduchy.co.uk
dir: At Pendennis Castle end of Promenade

Situated in a prime seafront location, with uninterrupted views across the bay and historic Pendennis Castle, the Royal Duchy is a relaxed, welcoming and well-maintained hotel. The comfortably-furnished dining room comes with traditional table settings and glamorous touches like chandeliers and a grand piano, while the cuisine focuses on top-quality local and seasonal ingredients using lots of fresh local seafood. Strong combinations and clarity of flavours demonstrate a passion for food and accurate cooking. International dishes feature starters like pan-roasted quail with beetroot, Savoy cabbage and quail broth, or crab lasagne with wild mushroom velouté, while mains might feature grilled Cornish plaice with spinach and shellfish bisque, or roast turbot with bouillabaisse, clams and tempura oyster. A range of sandwiches, focaccias, omelettes and jackets, as well as some traditional dishes like home-made steak pie, are also available.

Times 12.30-2/7-9, Closed L Mon-Sat

FOWEY — Map 2 SX15

The Fowey Hotel

◎◎ Modern European 🖥 V

Super views and elegant dining

☎ 01726 832551
The Esplanade PL23 1HX
e-mail: info@thefoweyhotel.co.uk
dir: From A390 take B3269 for approx 5m, follow signs for Fowey and continue along Pavillion Rd for 0.75m, 2nd right

A grand hotel perched on the slopes above the River Fowey estuary and enjoying marvellous marine views from many of the bedrooms and the public rooms, including the elegantly furnished restaurant where window tables are favourite. With a local reputation for accomplished cuisine and a commitment to locally sourced produce, expect plenty of local seafood on daily-changing dinner menus, perhaps dressed Cornish crab with carpaccio of melon, curried mango and Japanaise salad and sauce vièrge, and pan-fried curried monkfish with coconut-scented velouté. Alternatively, try the seared beef fillet with goats' cheese glaze and red wine reduction, or the honey-glazed duck breast with port jus, then finish with steamed plum sponge with crème anglaise and vanilla seed ice cream.

Chef Mark Griffiths **Owner** Keith Richardson
Times 12-3/6.30-9 **Wines** 14 bottles over £20, 29 bottles under £20, 7 by glass **Notes** Fixed D 5 courses £34, Sunday L, Vegetarian menu, Dress restrictions, Smart casual, No torn denim, trainers, shorts **Seats** 60 **Children** Portions, Menu **Parking** 13

Hansons

◎◎ British, French

Accomplished cuisine in ornate surroundings

☎ 01726 833866
Fowey Hall, Hanson Dr PL23 1ET
e-mail: info@foweyhall.com
dir: Into town centre, pass school on right, 400yds turn right onto Hanson Drive

This majestic property, with a grand château-inspired façade, was built in 1899 by the Lord Mayor of London in a prime hillside location overlooking the estuary across to Polruan. Public areas are rich in architectural detail, with Baroque plasterwork and vaulted ceilings. Hansons restaurant features oak panelling, gilt mirrors and floor-to-ceiling windows overlooking the croquet lawn, and at night it is particularly romantic by candlelight. Modern country-house style dishes are prepared from the best of local ingredients, such as crab and turbot fishcakes with salad and tartare sauce, and roast rack of West Country lamb with scallion potato purée, braised red cabbage, broad beans and baby carrots served with a Polonaise jus.

Times 12-2.15/7-10

The Old Quay House

◎◎ British, French 🍃

Fresh local produce served in waterfront location with views of Fowey estuary

☎ 01726 833302
28 Fore St PL23 1AQ
e-mail: info@theoldquayhouse.com
dir: From A390 through Lostwithiel, take left onto B3269 to Fowey town centre, on right next to Lloyds TSB bank

A beautifully restored building dating from 1859, this boutique hotel occupies an idyllic waterfront location. The terrace, on the old quay itself, juts out into the harbour and is a great place for drinks, as is the chic 'Q' Bar. The

architect-designed interior brings contemporary style to the historic setting, and views from the stylish restaurant are amazing. Accomplished cuisine relies on classic French technique but with some British and European influences. The emphasis is firmly on fresh, locally sourced produce, with seasonally-changing menus and regular specials. Try confit salmon with fennel and chickpea salad; and roast rump of lamb (for two) with tapenade, Parma ham, crushed potatoes and aubergine tian.

Chef Ben Bass **Owner** Jane & Roy Carson
Times 12.30-2.30/7-9, Closed L Mon to Fri (Oct to May) **Prices** Fixed D 3 course £35, Service optional **Wines** 15 bottles over £20, 15 bottles under £20, 5 by glass **Notes** Vegetarian available, Civ Wed 40 **Seats** 38 **Children** Min 12 yrs

Restaurant Nathan Outlaw

◎◎◎ — see page 78

GOLANT — Map 2 SX15

Cormorant Hotel and Riverview Restaurant

◎ Modern British

Fantastic views across the Fowey from dining room and alfresco terrace

☎ 01726 833426
PL23 1LL
e-mail: relax@cormoranthotel.co.uk
dir: From A390 take B3269 signed Fowey. Left to Golant, continue to harbour, then beside river. Hotel at end of road

Originally built back in 1920 as a private home, and designed so every room had views of the River Fowey below, this recently refurbished hotel's smart dining room maintains this delightful feature. The original Edwardian style blends well with a crisp modern look, with fresh clean tones, comfortable seating and many of the formally-laid tables enjoying those superb views over the river. The kitchen's modern approach is aptly driven by quality seasonal produce from the West Country larder, including Cornish seafood, meat, game and cheeses. Take Cornish scallops served with local black pudding, celeriac purée and rocket salad to start, and perhaps pan-fried fillet of Cornish beef partnered with horseradish butter, fondant potato, crushed swede and roasted shallots to follow.

Chef Martin Adams **Owner** Mrs Mary Tozer
Times 12.30-2.30/6.30-9.30, Closed L Mon, Tue (summer) **Prices** Fixed D 4 course £34-£45, Tasting menu £46-£70, Starter £6-£8, Main £11-£14, Dessert £6-£7, Service optional, Groups min 7 service 12% **Wines** 41 bottles over £20, 30 bottles under £20, 8 by glass **Notes** Tasting menu Sat only, Sunday L, Vegetarian available, Dress restrictions, Smart casual, no shorts **Seats** 30 **Children** Min 12 yrs D, Portions **Parking** 16 **Parking** Public car park

Restaurant Nathan Outlaw

FOWEY Map 2 SX15

European 🖥 V 🍷

Stunning views and Nathan Outlaw's imaginative cooking are a winning combination

☎ 01726 833315
Marina Villa Hotel, 17 Esplanade PL23 1HY
e-mail: enquiries@marinavillahotel.com
dir: Please telephone for directions

The jewel in the crown at the Marina Villa Hotel - set on the narrow streets of town and backing on to the River Fowey, with stunning views across the water to Polruan and out to sea - is this eponymous restaurant. The spacious hallway's stairs lead down to the lower-ground dining room, with its bar and lounge areas. Picture windows make the best of those views, while purple banquette seating or high-backed chairs provide the comforts, set to a backdrop of clothed tables, stylish cutlery and glassware and attentive, friendly service. Nathan, a Cornish phenomenon (previously at the Black Pig at Rock and St Ervan Manor, Padstow), opened his restaurant here in 2007 to showcase his fine pedigree. In competition with the views, the imaginative cuisine has eye appeal, too, the modern, intelligently simple approach delivering promised flavours and fine balance, driven by quality produce. Take a starter of ox tongue with anchovies, capers, tarragon and mint, with main courses like monkfish with ham, onion and lemon thyme, or venison with chervil root, orange, espresso and chicory, and for dessert, perhaps quince tart with stem ginger ice cream. Ancillaries like canapés, bread, amuse-bouche and pre-desserts all hit top form, too.

Chef Nathan Outlaw **Owner** Mr S Westwell
Times 12-2/7-9.30, Closed Mon (Tue out of season), Closed L Tue (in season) Wed-Fri & Sun **Prices** Fixed L 2 course £25-£30, Fixed D 3 course £40-£65, Starter £9-£15, Main £20-£35, Dessert £9-£15, Service optional, Groups min 6 service 10% **Wines** 65 bottles over £20, 15 bottles under £20, 10 by glass **Notes** Tasting menu available, Vegetarian menu, Civ Wed 45 **Seats** 40 **Children** Min 10 yrs **Parking** Car park

The Well House Hotel

LISKEARD Map 2 SX26

Modern European 🖥 V

Culinary hideaway in a tranquil valley

☎ 01579 342001
St Keyne PL14 4RN
e-mail: enquiries@wellhouse.co.uk
dir: A38 to Liskeard and A390 to town centre, then take B3254 to St Keyne 3m. In village take left fork at church signed St Keyne. Hotel 0.5m on left

Hidden away along a secluded country lane in a tranquil Cornish valley, this idyllic hotel is just 30 minutes from the Eden Project. Sitting in lovely grounds, it retains its country-house ambience, with modern additions such as all-weather tennis court, swimming pool and croquet lawn. Friendly staff provide attentive yet relaxed service, while the comfortable lounge offers deep-cushioned sofas and an open fire, and there's also an intimate bar for aperitifs. It's quite the perfect venue for a foodie getaway too; the spacious restaurant has a muted modern colour scheme with sculptures and fine art prints, and there are large bay windows offering views to the garden beyond. The cooking is assured and daily-printed menus are intelligently compact and driven by prime produce and seasonality. The well-balanced selection of modern-vogue British dishes are cooked with skill, care and accuracy, and come dotted with interest yet deliver without unnecessary fuss or confusion, showcasing clean, clear flavours and well-judged sauces. Expect main courses like a fillet of Cornish beef served with celeriac and white truffle purée, caramelised onion and a white port sauce, while a chocolate brownie with honeycomb ice cream and chocolate sauce makes a fitting finale.

Chef Tom Hunter **Owner** Richard Farrow
Times 12-3/6.30-10 **Prices** Fixed L 2 course £18.50, Fixed D 3 course £32.50-£37.50, Tasting menu £42.50, Service optional **Wines** 68 bottles over £20, 52 bottles under £20, 5 by glass **Notes** Tasting menu 6 courses, Sunday L, Vegetarian menu, Dress restrictions, Smart casual, Civ Wed 25 **Seats** 34 **Children** Menu **Parking** 30

HELSTON
Map 2 SW62

New Yard Restaurant

◉◉ Modern British 🍷

Fresh local food in an 18th-century stable yard

☎ 01326 221595
Trelowarren, Mawgan TR12 6AF
e-mail: info@trelowarren.com
dir: 5m from Helston

A medieval manor house on the Trelowarren Estate provides the backdrop for this restaurant, which occupies a delightful carriage house in the stable yard next to a gallery, pottery and weaving studio. The estate is at the centre of the Lizard peninsula, a nature reserve and a designated Area of Outstanding Natural Beauty. Most of the ingredients are sourced from within a 10-mile radius, and there is an emphasis on local fish and shellfish, plus game, herbs and fruit supplied by the estate. The menu lists favourite suppliers with typical dishes including Falmouth Bay spider crab and smoked sea trout timbale with spring salad shoots, and sautéed venison with organic spring vegetables, prune and thyme sauce.

Chef Greg Laskey **Owner** Sir Ferrers Vyvyan **Times** 12-2/7-9.30, Closed Mon (mid Sep-Whitsun), Closed D Sun **Prices** Fixed L 3 course fr £15, Fixed D 3 course £22.50-£24, Starter £4.95-£10.95, Main £12-£28, Dessert £4.95-£8, Service optional **Wines** 29 bottles over £20, 28 bottles under £20, 4 by glass **Notes** Sunday L, Vegetarian available, Dress restrictions, Smart dress, smart casual **Seats** 45 **Children** Portions, Menu **Parking** 20

LISKEARD
Map 2 SX26

The Well House Hotel

◉◉◉ – **see opposite**

LOOE
Map 2 SX25

Trelaske Hotel & Restaurant

◉ Modern, Traditional British 🍷

Tranquil Cornish hideaway championing local produce

☎ 01503 262159
Polperro Rd PL13 2JS
e-mail: info@trelaske.co.uk
dir: Over Looe bridge signed Polperro. After 1.9m signed on right.

This small, friendly hotel is situated between the fishing villages of Looe and Polperro, set in 4 acres of beautiful landscaped grounds with lovely views over the gardens and rolling Cornish countryside. Fish and seafood are prominent, and there's an emphasis on local, seasonal produce with particular attention to animal welfare and the environment. Honest and unpretentious cooking sees modern British dishes appear alongside some old favourites. Relax over a drink in the bar before going through to the light-and-airy dining room, where you can expect to enjoy pan-fried scallops with chorizo and Trelaske tomato chutney, followed by Tregonning flat mushroom and goats' cheese stack with chive gratin or slow-cooked rabbit in cider, and warm lemon tart with black pepper ice cream and confit strawberries for dessert.

Chef Ross Lewin **Owner** Ross Lewin & Hazel Billington **Times** 12-2/7-9 **Prices** Food prices not confirmed for 2009. Please telephone for details. **Wines** 11 bottles over £20, 23 bottles under £20, 32 by glass **Notes** Sunday L, Vegetarian available, Dress restrictions, Smart casual **Seats** 70 **Children** Portions, Menu **Parking** 60

MARAZION
Map 2 SW53

Mount Haven Hotel

◉ Modern British

Enjoyable dining in stylish surroundings with lovely views

☎ 01736 710249
Turnpike Rd TR17 0DQ
e-mail: reception@mounthaven.co.uk
dir: From centre of Marazion, up hill E, hotel 400yds on right

There are fabulous views out across St Michael's Mount from this stylish hotel: sunsets are particularly splendid, enjoyed from the terrace over a drink. White walls, tables and crockery create a light, airy atmosphere in the dining room which overlooks the garden. Seafood dominates the menu, unsurprisingly given the location, and modern dishes are both interesting and uncomplicated: Helford mussels with cuttlefish and laksa noodles; and roast monkfish tail with Cajun spices, saffron and bay pilaff rice, and red pepper and zhug dressing. Finish with walnut tart accompanied by espresso syrup and Roddas crème fraîche.

Chef Julie Manley **Owner** Orange & Mike Trevillion **Times** 12-2.30/6.45-9.30, Closed last wk Dec-end Jan **Prices** Starter £5.50-£8.75, Main £14.95-£18.50, Dessert £6.50-£7.95, Service optional, Groups min 8 service 10% **Wines** 22 bottles over £20, 29 bottles under £20, 7 by glass **Notes** Sunday L, Vegetarian available, Dress restrictions, Smart casual **Seats** 50 **Children** Portions **Parking** 30

MAWGAN PORTH
Map 2 SW86

Bedruthan Steps Hotel

◉ Modern British

Atlantic views and full-flavoured food with visual impact

☎ 01637 860555
TR8 4BU
e-mail: office@bedruthan.com

Stunning views of Mawgan Porth Bay and out to the Atlantic are a big draw of the spacious Indigo Bay restaurant in this smart family hotel between Newquay and Padstow. Enjoy alfresco summer drinks on the grassed terraces before dining in the cool and contemporary restaurant, with white linen, candles and orchids, where you can watch the setting sun while savouring some accomplished cooking. Appealing menus use fresh local produce and dishes are well presented, perhaps taking in Falmouth Bay scallops, Cornish hog's pudding, girolles and mousseline potatoes, followed by Cornish cassoulet of local duck, bacon, sausage and haricot beans.

Times 12-2/7.30-9.30, Closed Xmas

MAWNAN SMITH Map 2 SW72

Budock Vean - The Hotel on the River

@ Traditional British **V**

Creative Cornish cuisine in a peaceful hotel location

☎ 01326 252100 & 250288
TR11 5LG
e-mail: relax@budockvean.co.uk
dir: Telephone for directions

Sitting in 65 acres of attractive grounds, this tranquil hotel offers an impressive range of facilities. Its candlelit, high-ceilinged traditional restaurant, complete with beams and minstrels' gallery, enjoys live music from local musicians every night. The British menu features the finest fresh Cornish produce in uncomplicated dishes, creatively prepared and presented, and served by friendly staff. Enjoy starters such as locally-smoked duck with a fresh fig, orange and mixed leaf salad, followed by mains like pan-roasted supreme of locally landed John Dory with crab and chive mash, leeks and a basil butter sauce, and for dessert why not try dark chocolate and hazelnut brownie served with fresh strawberries and Cornish clotted cream?

Chef Darren Kelly **Owner** Barlow Family
Times 12-2.30/7.30-9, Closed 3 wks Jan, Closed L Mon-Sat **Wines** 52 bottles over £20, 42 bottles under £20, 7 by glass **Notes** Fixed D 5 courses £32.50, Sunday L, Vegetarian menu, Dress restrictions, Jacket & tie, Civ Wed 60, Air con **Seats** 100, Pr/dining room 40 **Children** Min 7 yrs, Portions, Menu **Parking** 100

Meudon Hotel

@ Traditional British 🍃

Accomplished cooking at a friendly Cornish hotel by the sea

☎ 01326 250541
TR11 5HT
e-mail: wecare@meudon.co.uk
dir: From Truro take A39 towards Falmouth. At Hill Head rdbt turn left. Hotel is 4m on left

This charming Victorian mansion incorporates two 300-year old coastguard cottages and has been in the same family for five generations. Dine beneath an exotic fruiting vine in the conservatory restaurant, with spectacular views down the 8-acre garden to the private beach. The accent here is on locally sourced West Country

ingredients and seafood, with deliveries coming daily from Newlyn, oysters from Helford and cheese from a farm two miles away. Classic English dishes on the fixed-price menu might include harvest of local seafood terrine, poached fillet of Falmouth Market lemon sole with leek, crab meat and whisky reduction and citrus tart served with Cornish clotted cream.

Chef Alan Webb **Owner** Mr Pilgrim **Times** 12.30-2/7.30-9, Closed Jan **Prices** Fixed L 2 course £14.95-£21, Fixed D 3 course £31-£35, Service optional **Wines** 80 bottles over £20, 39 bottles under £20, 5 by glass **Notes** Sunday L, Vegetarian available, Dress restrictions, Smart dress **Seats** 60 **Children** Portions, Menu **Parking** 30

Trelawne Hotel

@ Modern British

Imaginative British cooking and magnificent views

☎ 01326 250226
TR11 5HS
e-mail: info@trelawnehotel.co.uk
dir: From Truro take A39 towards Falmouth. Right at Hillhead rdbt, take exit signed Maenporth. After 3m, past Maenporth Beach, hotel at top of hill

Situated in a designated Area of Outstanding Natural Beauty, this small, family-run hotel is surrounded by attractive gardens and enjoys superb views over Falmouth Bay. Imaginative modern British menus, priced from two to four courses, are served in the spacious restaurant, with dishes such as sliced smoked haunch of venison with Parma ham and pine nuts to start, and steamed fillet of sea bass with smoked salmon and dill dressing as a main course. Quality local produce features, organic where possible, and all the meats and vegetables come from local farms.

Times Closed 30 Nov-20 Feb, Closed L all week

MOUSEHOLE Map 2 SW42

The Cornish Range Restaurant with Rooms

@@ Modern British 🛏️

Vibrant restaurant serving the best local seafood

☎ 01736 731488
6 Chapel St TR19 6SB
e-mail: info@cornishrange.co.uk
dir: Mousehole is 3m S from Penzance, via Newlyn. Follow road to far side of harbour

As you would expect from a restaurant with rooms housed in a former pilchard processing factory, fish and seafood play a prominent part on the menu here, with the freshest produce landed locally at nearby Newlyn and delivered daily. Interiors are decorated with earthy tones, with sturdy chairs and tables, soft lighting, flowers and local contemporary artwork giving a rustic, almost Mediterranean feel to the dining room. The accomplished kitchen's modern approach delivers consistency, interest and diner appeal; take pan-fried fillet of brill with pomme purée, pan-fried salsify and merlot butter sauce, or perhaps roast fillet of cod with garlic potato purée, asparagus and wild mushroom sauce. Alfresco dining is also available in the sub-tropical garden.

Chef Keith Terry **Owner** Richard O'Shea, Chad James & Keith Terry **Times** 10.45-2.15/6-9.30 **Prices** Food prices not confirmed for 2009. Please telephone for details. **Wines** 13 bottles over £20, 19 bottles under £20, 4 by glass **Notes** Vegetarian available **Seats** 60 **Children** Portions **Parking** Harbour car park

The Old Coastguard Hotel

@ @ Modern British 🖥 🖐

Popular summer alfresco destination with stunning sea views

☎ 01736 731222
The Parade TR19 6PR
e-mail: bookings@oldcoastguardhotel.co.uk
web: www.oldcoastguardhotel.co.uk
dir: A30 to Penzance. From Penzance take coast road through Newlyn to Mousehole. Inn 1st large building on left on entering village, after car park

As the name might suggest, this commanding hotel and restaurant overlooks the sea - but what the name doesn't reveal is how splendid those sea views are and just how quaint and absorbingly lovely the location is, situated in what Dylan Thomas described as 'the most beautiful village in England'. The simple, clean-lined, contemporarily styled décor inside provides a suitably unobtrusive backdrop to enjoy those views over Mount's Bay and the accomplished cuisine. Fish - most from nearby Newlyn - features heavily on a modern menu that might include dishes such as linguine of clams or mussels, Old Coastguard fishcakes, or Newlyn crab, celeriac ravioli and tomato consommé. Assiette of tropical fruits - banana Tatin, pineapple chilli soup, mango kaffir lime pannacotta - makes a fitting finale.

Chef Barnaby Mason, Darren Stephens, Kate McMaster **Owner** A W Treloar **Times** 12-2.30/6-9.30, Closed 25 Dec **Prices** Fixed L 2 course £14.95, Starter £8.50-£10.50, Main £17.95-£25.95, Dessert £6-£11.95, Service optional **Wines** 52 bottles over £20, 20 bottles under £20, 20 by glass **Notes** Sunday L, Vegetarian available, Dress restrictions, Smart casual preferred **Seats** 80 **Children** Portions, Menu **Parking** 15, Car park adjacent to building

---

NEWQUAY **Map 2 SW86**

Headland Grill

@ Modern British 🖐

Elegant dining with wonderful sea views

☎ 01637 872211
Headland Hotel, Fistral Beach TR7 1EW
e-mail: office@headlandhotel.co.uk
web: www.headlandhotel.co.uk
dir: A30 onto A392 towards Newquay, follow signs to Fistral Beach, hotel is adjacent

Views over Fistral beach and the stunning coastal scenery are the perfect backdrop for this imposing Victorian hotel, set on a rocky headland well away from the bustling town. Both the relaxing, sleek, period feel of Sand Brasserie and the more formal restaurant make the most of the stunning views. Using the freshest of local ingredients, modern British fixed-price menus focus on local fish and shellfish so expect the likes of seared scallops and pan-fried monkfish to start, followed perhaps by pan-fried medallions of Cornish beef, and tiramisu with a coffee and amaretti biscuit for dessert.

Chef Chris Wyburn-Ridsdale **Owner** John & Carolyn Armstrong **Times** 12.30-2/6-9.45, Closed 25-26 Dec, Closed L Mon-Sat **Prices** Fixed L course £17.95, Fixed D 3 course fr £30, Starter £4-£11, Main £9.95-£24, Dessert £6-£8, Service included **Wines** 79 bottles over £20, 51 bottles under £20, 13 by glass **Notes** Sunday L, Vegetarian available, Dress restrictions, Smart casual, Civ Wed 200 **Seats** 250, Pr/dining room 40 **Children** Min 3 yrs, Portions, Menu **Parking** 200

PADSTOW **Map 2 SW97**

Margot's

@ British

Friendly family-run bistro serving good fresh food

☎ 01841 533441
11 Duke St PL28 8AB
e-mail: enquiries@margots.co.uk
dir: Please telephone for directions

There are just nine tables in this cheerful little shop-fronted bistro, with the genial chef-proprietor combining serving and cooking, a formula that's proven both efficient and popular. The restaurant walls are hung with paintings by local artists, most of them for sale. The menu changes constantly according to the local produce available, and includes fish fresh from the harbour. Cooking is accurate and straightforward, delivering

---

dishes like baked ray wing with anchovies, garlic and parsley served with a herb mash, or perhaps sirloin of Cornish beef accompanied by sautéed potatoes, mixed mushrooms and a thyme sauce.

Chef Adrian Oliver, Lewis Cole, Claire Drake **Owner** Adrian & Julie Oliver **Times** 12-2/7-9, Closed Nov, Jan, Closed Sun-Mon **Prices** Fixed D 3 course fr £25.95, Tasting menu £36, Starter £4.95-£8.95, Main £11.50-£19.95, Dessert £4.50-£6.95, Service optional **Wines** 10 bottles over £20, 16 bottles under £20, 5 by glass **Notes** Tasting menu 6 courses **Seats** 22 **Children** Portions

The Metropole

@ Modern British 🖥

Enjoyable British dining in an elegant hotel

☎ 01841 532486
Station Rd PL28 8DB
e-mail: info@the-metropole.co.uk
dir: M5/A30 past Launceston, follow signs for Wadebridge and N Cornwall. Then take A39 and follow signs for Padstow

A favourite haunt of the Prince of Wales in the 1930s, this grand old hotel retains the elegance and sophistication of a bygone era. Lighter snacks are available in the café bar, but to get the full measure of the place you should eat in the restaurant with its wonderful views over the Camel estuary. Modern British dishes take in crab and brown shrimp tian with boiled egg and caper salad, and pan-roasted cannon and braised shoulder of lamb with fondant potato, Puy lentils, pepper stew and basil jus.

Times Closed L Mon-Sat

No. 6

@ @ Modern British V 🖐

Contemporary surroundings meet ambitious modern cuisine

☎ 01841 532093
Middle St PL28 8AP
e-mail: enquiries@number6inpadstow.co.uk
dir: A30 follow signs for Wadebridge then sign to Padstow

No. 6 is certainly a worthy addition to Padstow's culinary heritage. This Georgian townhouse, once known as a smugglers' den, has been stylishly refurbished in contemporary vogue, with polished-wood tables, smart cutlery and glassware and white linen napkins. Service is friendly and unstuffy, the atmosphere relaxed and

Continued

PADSTOW *Continued*

informal. Paul Ainsworth (who previously worked at London high-flyer Pétrus, see entry) shows his pedigree in accomplished, attractively presented modern dishes that use top-notch ingredients. Expect poached and sautéed sirloin of veal with garlic, veal marrow and Lyonnaise potatoes, or perhaps confit halibut served with chicken wings, cannellini blanquette, cauliflower and tarragon.

Chef Paul Ainsworth, David Boulton **Owner** Paul Ainsworth, David Boulton, Chris Mapp, Molly Haslett **Times** Closed Jan, Closed 23-27 Dec, Closed L all week, Closed D Sun, Mon **Prices** Fixed D 3 course £45, Service added but optional 10% **Wines** 53 bottles over £20, 8 bottles under £20, 17 by glass **Notes** Tasting menu 8 courses, Vegetarian menu, Dress restrictions, Smart casual **Seats** 40, Pr/dining room 24 **Children** Portions

St Petroc's Bistro

◉ French, Mediterranean

Rick Stein's bustling seafood bistro

☎ 01841 532700
4 New St PL28 8EA
e-mail: reservations@rickstein.com
dir: Follow one-way around harbour, 1st left, situated 100 yds on right

One of the oldest buildings in town, just up the hill from the picturesque harbour, houses Rick Stein's renowned bistro. The interior design of this large brasserie-style room is thoroughly modern with clean white walls hung with modern paintings. The open fire is a big draw in winter, while in summer you can eat outside under a huge canopy. Cooking has a fresh, local focus with an emphasis on fish, with friendly service from an enthusiastic team. Minty pea and ham soup to start, followed by top quality grilled haddock accompanied by beer bacon and Savoy cabbage, with sticky toffee pudding to finish shows the style.

Chef David Sharland, Paul Harwood **Owner** R & J Stein **Times** 12-2/7-10, Closed 25-26 Dec, 1 May, Closed D 24 Dec **Prices** Starter £6.50-£8.25, Main £13.50-£19.95, Dessert £4.50-£6, Service optional **Wines** 22 bottles over £20, 13 bottles under £20, 11 by glass **Notes** Vegetarian available, Air con **Seats** 54 **Children** Portions, Menu **Parking** Car park

The Seafood Restaurant

◉◉◉ – *see below*

Treglos Hotel

◉ Modern British **V**

Seaside hotel with bay views and fish on the menu

☎ 01841 520727
PL28 8JH
e-mail: stay@treglos-hotel.com
dir: Take B3276 (Constantine Bay). At village stores turn right, hotel 50yds on left

Owned by the Barlow family since 1965, this traditional country-house hotel maintains high standards and enjoys wonderful views over Constantine Bay. Dinner is served in the recently refurbished restaurant and the conservatory extension, with modern fabrics and furnishings, which retains a stylish period feel. The menu includes classic dishes prepared from locally grown produce, including vegetables from the garden. Dishes might include salmon fishcake with parsley sauce to start, followed by monkfish with tarragon butter, or beef tenderloin on black pudding farce with horseradish cream. Finish with sticky toffee pudding with butterscotch sauce and clotted cream, or a plate of West Country cheeses.

Chef Paul Becker **Owner** Mr & Mrs J Barlow **Times** Closed Jan-Feb, Closed all week except by arrangement **Prices** Fixed D 4 course fr £29, Main £13-£26, Service optional **Wines** 44 bottles over £20, 25 bottles under £20, 3 by glass **Notes** Sunday L, Vegetarian menu, Dress restrictions, Jacket or tie **Seats** 90 **Children** Min 7 yrs, Menu **Parking** 40

The Seafood Restaurant

| **PADSTOW** | Map 2 SW97 |

International Seafood

Rick Stein's famous restaurant

☎ 01841 532700
Riverside PL28 8BY
e-mail: reservations@rickstein.com
dir: Follow signs for town centre. Restaurant on riverside

Finding good seafood restaurants beside the harbours of Cornish towns is easier than it was a couple of decades ago, and Rick Stein can take some of the credit for that. His Seafood Restaurant is now the stuff of legend and is deservedly popular all year round. The faintly designer edge of the conservatory entrance gives a clue to the contemporary interior, which belies the simple rusticity of the quayside setting. The room is a large and open space with bright canvases of modern art adding splashes of colour. The tables are smartly laid with linen cloths, but the menu at the flagship of the group (also in the town are the Stein-owned bistro, fish and chip restaurant, deli, pâtisserie, gift shop and cookery school) remains unselfconsciously straightforward with the emphasis firmly placed on the superb quality of the local seafood. That is not to say it is boring: starters such as four large scallops served in the shell with coriander and hazelnuts, or nigiri sushi of salmon, tuna and sea bass might make choosing difficult. Main-course monkfish comes wrapped in Parma ham with sauerkraut, or as a vindaloo with pilau rice and naan bread, and the skill in the making of chocolate fondant shows the kitchen is strong all round. Service is by a smartly turned out and well-drilled team.

Chef Stephane Delourme, David Sharland **Owner** R & J Stein **Times** 12-2/7-10, Closed 25-26 Dec, 1 May, Closed D 24 Dec **Prices** Food prices not confirmed for 2009. Please telephone for details. **Wines** 162 bottles over £20, 6 bottles under £20, 13 by glass **Notes** Vegetarian available, Air con **Seats** 120 **Children** Min 3 yrs, Portions, Menu **Parking** Pay & display opposite

PENZANCE
Map 2 SW43

The Abbey Restaurant

⍟⍟ Modern French 🍷

Skilful cooking in a modern setting with harbour views

☎ 01736 330680
Abbey St TR18 4AR
e-mail: abbeyrestaurant@btinternet.com
web: www.abbeyrestaurant.com
dir: In centre of Penzance turn into Chapel Street opposite Lloyds TSB Bank, 500 yds & turn left at Admiral Benbow public house, onto Abbey St

The bar at the Abbey - Moroccan-themed and bright red - pays homage to its former incarnation as a 1960s nightclub. The upstairs dining room is more elegantly subdued, with white walls, modern sculpture and lovely views of St Michael's Mount and the harbour. Expect classic French cooking underpinned by top quality British ingredients sourced from local suppliers, with the emphasis firmly on seasonality, simplicity and flavour. The ethos of the kitchen is exemplified in starters such as monkfish with juniper, cauliflower purée and caramel, followed by roast roe deer with Baileys sauce, fine cabbage leaves, runner beans and walnut and olive crunch. For dessert, try the chocolate torte with orange jelly, lemon and pepper sorbet and banana purée.

Chef Michael Riemenschneider **Owner** Michael Riemenschneider/Arthur W Treloar
Times 12-2.30/6.30-9.30, Closed Jan, Closed Sun-Mon **Prices** Fixed D 3 course £45, Tasting menu £89, Starter £8.50-£10, Main £19-£23, Dessert £6-£9.50, Service optional, Groups min 6 service 10% **Wines** 140 bottles over £20, 16 bottles under £20, 46 by glass
Notes Tasting menu 12 courses, menu surprise 7 courses, Vegetarian available, Dress restrictions, No trainers or ripped jeans, Air con **Seats** 24
Children Portions **Parking** On street

The Bay Restaurant

⍟⍟ Modern British 💻 🍷

Contemporary restaurant with fabulous views

☎ 01736 366890
Hotel Penzance, Britons Hill TR18 3AE
e-mail: table@bay-penzance.co.uk
web: www.bay-penzance.co.uk
dir: Approaching Penzance from A30, at 'Tesco' rdbt take first exit towards town centre. Britons Hill is third turning on right

Panoramic views over Penzance harbour and Mounts Bay are a feature of this stylishly redesigned Edwardian property, which also incorporates a café and art gallery exhibiting the work of local artists. The aptly-named Bay Restaurant has a light-and-airy feel, with contemporary décor, polished wooden tables and an outdoor terrace for alfresco dining in warmer weather. The focus on style is also apparent in the award-winning cuisine based on fresh Cornish produce. Dishes offered from the sea, land and garden might include pan-fried Cornish fishcake with tomato and smoked garlic dressing, followed by grilled fillet of Newlyn pollack with watercress, cockles and deep-fried tempura courgettes, or perhaps a platter of day-fresh fruits de mer with lobster. For those with a sweet tooth, an assortment of miniature desserts will not disappoint, or choose from the interesting selection of local cheeses.

Chef Ben Reeve, Katie Semmens, Roger Hoskin
Owner Yvonne & Stephen Hill **Times** 11-2/6.15-11, Closed L Sat & Sun **Prices** Fixed L 2 course fr £11, Fixed D 3 course fr £27, Tasting menu £47.50-£79.50, Service optional, Groups min 8 service 10% **Wines** 15 bottles over £20, 16 bottles under £20, 10 by glass
Notes Tasting menu available 7 courses, Vegetarian available, Dress restrictions, Smart casual, no shorts, Air con **Seats** 60, Pr/dining room 12 **Children** Portions, Menu **Parking** 13 **Parking** On street

Harris's Restaurant

⍟ Modern European

Simple, freshly cooked food in a charming little restaurant

☎ 01736 364408
46 New St TR18 2LZ
e-mail: contact@harrissrestaurant.co.uk
dir: Located down narrow cobbled street opposite Lloyds TSB

Harris's has been in the food industry since 1860. The attractive restaurant is located on the ground floor, and has a fine pressed metal ceiling and a decorative spiral staircase leading to the upstairs bar, where lighter lunches are also served. Service, like the atmosphere, is friendly, relaxed but efficient. The modern European menu changes seasonally, offering more fish and shellfish during the summer. Best quality local produce is simply cooked with good sauces and no over-embellishment. Recommended dishes include line-caught sea bass, crab Florentine, and medallions of venison with beetroot, caraway seeds and glazed pear.

Chef Roger Harris **Owner** Roger & Anne Harris
Times 12-2/7-9.30, Closed 3 wks winter, 25-26 Dec, 1 Jan, Closed Sun, Mon (winter), Closed L Mon **Wines** 27 bottles over £20, 17 bottles under £20, 6 by glass
Notes Light L & D menu £8.50-£14.95, Vegetarian available, Dress restrictions, Smart casual **Seats** 40, Pr/dining room 20 **Children** Min 5 yrs **Parking** On street, local car park

The Navy Inn

⍟ Modern British 🍷

Penzance local with an ambitious kitchen

☎ 01736 333232
Lower Queen St TR18 4DE
e-mail: keir@navyinn.co.uk
dir: In town centre, follow Chapel St for 50 yds, turn right into Queen St and follow to the bottom of road

Decked out in shabby-chic style with wooden floors, open fires, candle-topped wooden tables and an array of marine artefacts, the brightly coloured Navy Inn enjoys stunning views across Mounts Bay and is a short walk from Penzance promenade. Working with the best of local Cornish ingredients, notably fresh fish from Newlyn, the Navy's accomplished kitchen conjures an eclectic mix of dishes ranging from typical pub grub to more ambitious fare like grilled fish on Jerusalem artichoke purée with herb dressing, and slow-cooked shoulder of lamb in red wine and cinnamon sauce with lemon and parsley risotto.

Chef Keir Meikle **Owner** Keir Meikle **Times** 12-10, Closed D 25 Dec **Prices** Starter £4.95-£7.50, Main £8.95-£18.95, Dessert £4.95-£6.95, Service optional **Wines** 5 bottles over £20, 14 bottles under £20, 12 by glass **Notes** Sunday L, Vegetarian available **Seats** 54 **Children** Portions, Menu **Parking** Free parking on promenade

The Summer House

⍟⍟ Mediterranean 🍷

Mediterranean style and Cornish produce a stone's throw from the sea

☎ 01736 363744
Cornwall Ter TR18 4HL
e-mail: reception@summerhouse-cornwall.com
web: www.summerhouse-cornwall.com
dir: Into Penzance on A30. Along harbour past open-air bathing pool onto the Promenade at Queens Hotel. Turn right immediately after hotel, restaurant 30mtrs on left

Continued

PENZANCE *Continued*

This Grade II listed Regency house is situated near the seafront and harbour and was once home to two of Cornwall's renowned artists. Sympathetically converted with a Mediterranean theme, today it's a stylish boutique hotel with a delightful restaurant that spills out into a tropical walled garden, where dinner and drinks are served on summer evenings. The philosophy is simple - great food, beautiful surroundings and an informal, happy atmosphere. After years spent managing some of London's famous hotel restaurants, chef-patron Ciro Zaino has found true inspiration in Cornwall's fine larder, providing a daily-changing menu that includes a wide range of fish and seafood. Main courses like Newlyn cod cooked in traditional Italian style with tomatoes, black olives, capers, basil and garlic might feature alongside seared king scallops with a light ginger and saffron sauce, or perhaps a simple dish of sea bass pan-fried with pernod.

Chef Ciro Zaino **Owner** Ciro & Linda Zaino **Times** Closed Nov-Feb, Closed Mon-Wed, Closed L all week **Prices** Fixed D 3 course £31.50, Service added 10% **Wines** 42 bottles over £20, 12 bottles under £20, 6 by glass **Notes** Vegetarian available **Seats** 22 **Children** Min 8 yrs **Parking** 5

PERRANUTHNOE   **Map 2 SW52**

The Victoria Inn

⊚ Modern British ✪

Simply great food served in a friendly village inn

☎ 01736 710309
TR20 9NP
e-mail: enquiries@victoriainn-penzance.co.uk
dir: A30 to Penzance, A394 to Helston. After 2m turn right into village of Perranuthnoe, pub is on right as you enter

Popular with visitors and locals alike and just a stone's throw from the beach, this cosy village pub is reputed to be one of the oldest in Cornwall. Top-notch local produce is handled with care and reverence by a chef with a good pedigree, his confident cooking style producing rustic, punchy dishes at lunch and dinner. Daily specials, locally-baked breads and excellent fish and seafood are among the highlights, with meals served in the bar, dining room and gardens - weather permitting. Try a starter of cappuccino of pumpkin and sweet potato with smoked bacon and Welsh rarebit, and for mains look out for Tregothnan Estate pheasant with crispy potato cake, caramelised parsnip and apple and bacon. Finish with a selection of West Country artisan cheeses.

Chef Stewart Eddy **Owner** Stewart & Anna Eddy **Times** 12-2.30/6.30-9, Closed 25 Dec, 1st wk Jan, 26 Jan, Closed Mon (off season), Closed D Sun **Prices** Starter £4.50-£6.50, Main £9.50-£16.95, Dessert £5, Service optional **Wines** 4 bottles over £20, 23 bottles under £20, 6 by glass **Notes** Sunday L, Vegetarian available **Seats** 60 **Children** Portions, Menu **Parking** 10

PORTHLEVEN   **Map 2 SW62**

Kota Restaurant with Rooms

⊚ British, Pacific Rim

Modern British and Asian cooking by the sea

☎ 01326 562407
Harbour Head TR13 9JA
e-mail: kota@btconnect.com
dir: Take B3304 from Helston to Porthleven, restaurant situated on harbour head opposite slipway

Housed in an 18th-century former corn mill, Kota restaurant with rooms overlooks Harbour Head in an idyllic Cornish coastal village. The modern French bistro-style décor creates a relaxed atmosphere, though the cooking is modern British with Asian influences. Produce is locally sourced, organic where possible, and there's plenty of fish on the menu (Kota being Maori for shellfish). Dishes like Kota fishcakes with home fries or pan-fried John Dory with Tuscan potatoes, mussels, cockles and cider, sit alongside roast five-spiced pork belly with champ potatoes, braised Savoy cabbage, spiced apple and pear chutney, and star anise jus.

Chef Jude Kereama **Owner** Jude & Jane Kereama **Times** 12-2/6-9.30, Closed 25 Dec, Jan, Closed Sun (off season), Closed L Mon-Wed (off season) **Prices** Fixed L 2 course £14, Fixed D 3 course £18, Starter £3.95-£8.95, Main £10.50-£17.95, Dessert £5.50, Service optional, Groups min 6 service 10% **Wines** 30 bottles over £20, 23 bottles under £20, 13 by glass **Notes** Tasting menu available, Sun L Summer & BHs, Vegetarian available **Seats** 40 **Children** Portions, Menu **Parking** On street

---

PORTLOE   **Map 2 SW93**

The Lugger Hotel

⊚ Modern European

Fresh, well prepared Cornish fare with stunning harbour views

☎ 01872 501322 & 501238
TR2 5RD
e-mail: office@luggerhotel.com
dir: M5, exit onto A30. Take A390 St Austell to Truro road onto the B3287 to Tregony. Then A3078 St Mawes road, in 2m fork left for Veryan/Portloe, turn left at T-junct for Portloe

Originally a 16th-century inn, said to have been frequented by smugglers, The Lugger sits on the water's edge in this classic Cornish fishing village and derives its name from a small ship with lugsails. The modern restaurant offers superb harbour views and in warmer weather a sun terrace proves particularly popular. Carefully prepared fresh local produce is the order of the day here, with seafood delivered direct from the boat. Subject to availability you may find Portloe lobster or Helford oysters on offer, alternatively try dishes such as grilled baby Dover sole with melted parsley butter, tartare sauce, new potatoes and steamed broccoli.

Chef Franz Hornegger **Owner** Oxford Hotels **Times** 12-2.30/7-9.30 **Prices** Food prices not confirmed for 2009. Please telephone for details. **Wines** 80 bottles over £20, 10 bottles under £20, 6 by glass **Seats** 54 **Children** Min 12 yrs **Parking** 24

PORTSCATHO   **Map 2 SW83**

Driftwood

⊚⊚⊚ – *see opposite*

PORTWRINKLE   **Map 3 SX35**

Whitsand Bay Hotel & Golf Club

⊚ Modern British ✪

Luxurious setting to dine in style

☎ 01503 230276
PL11 3BU
e-mail: whitsandbayhotel@btconnect.com
dir: M4/M5 onto A38 for Plymouth, continue over Tamar Bridge into Cornwall. At Trerulefoot rdbt turn left to Polbathic. After 2m turn right towards Crafthole, Portwrinkle Hotel on right

This imposing Victorian stone hotel, resplendent with oak panelling, stained-glass windows and a sweeping staircase, was moved brick by brick from Torpoint and retains many original features. Facilities include an 18-hole cliff-top golf course. The elegant dining room has comfortable high-backed leather chairs and a subtle cream and brown décor gives a restrained air of luxury. The modern British menu focuses on the best of Cornish local produce including excellent fish from Looe. A typical meal might begin with farmhouse terrine with plum chutney, with main course options like roast pork tenderloin with braised red cabbage and Calvados sauce, or roast skate wing with lemon and parsley butter.

Chef Tony Farmer **Owner** Chris, Jennifer, John, Tracey & Paul Phillips **Times** 12-3/7-9 **Wines** 20 bottles over £20, 28 bottles under £20, 5 by glass **Notes** ALC fixed menu £26.95, Dress restrictions, Smart dress, no jeans, T-shirts, Air con **Seats** 70 **Children** Min 12 yrs, Portions, Menu

ROCK
Map 2 SW97

The St Enodoc Hotel Restaurant

Modern British, European

Contemporary cooking in bright modern hotel

☎ 01208 863394
The St Enodoc Hotel PL27 6LA
e-mail: info@enodoc-hotel.co.uk
dir: M5/A30/A39 to Wadebridge. B3314 to Rock

Set in the fashionable village of Rock, this contemporary, relaxed hotel boasts spectacular views across the Camel estuary to Padstow. Housed in a conservatory-style extension, the bright and airy bar and split-level restaurant, with its large windows and patio doors and collection of local art, open out on to a panoramic terrace. The daily-changing menu highlights well-loved classics with a modern twist and great emphasis is placed on local seasonal produce, notably seafood, meat and vegetables. Starters might include hand-picked Cornish crab and herb linguine with crab oil and parmesan, with a main of grilled whole Newquay sole with herb-crushed new potatoes, crisp proscuitto and black butter with capers and perhaps a vanilla pannacotta with chocolate terrine for dessert.

The St Enodoc Hotel Restaurant

Chef Ian Carter **Owner** Linedegree Ltd
Times 12.30-2.30/7-10, Closed 2 mths (late Dec - early Feb) **Prices** Fixed D 4 course £30, Starter £6.25-£8.95, Main £16.25-£20.95, Dessert £6.45-£8.45, Service added but optional 12.5% **Wines** 35 bottles over £20, 15 bottles under £20, 10 by glass **Notes** Sunday L, Vegetarian available, Dress restrictions, Smart casual, Air con
Seats 55, Pr/dining room 30 **Children** Portions, Menu
Parking 60

RUAN HIGH LANES
Map 2 SW93

Fish in the Fountain

British, Mediterranean

Charming country-house dining offering the best of local produce

☎ 01872 501336
The Hundred House Hotel TR2 5JR
e-mail: enquiries@hundredhousehotel.co.uk
dir: On A3078 towards St Mawes, hotel 4m after Tregony on right, just before Ruan High Lanes

Wonderfully evocative of summers of a bygone era, with its three acres of immaculate gardens including croquet lawn, this handsome Georgian gentleman's residence, and former court house, is beautifully located on the Roseland Peninsula. With its romantic touches, the elegant Fish in the Fountain Restaurant offers British cuisine with strong Mediterranean influences, with daily menus making the very best use of seasonal and home grown produce. Start with lightly spiced roast cherry tomato and aubergine soup, follow with rack of Cornish lamb with redcurrant, mint and garlic dressing, and finish with individual blackberry and strawberry cheesecake made with Cornish goats' cheese. Service is friendly, efficient and attentive.

Chef Richard Maior-Barron **Owner** Richard Maior-Barron
Times Closed Jan-Feb, Closed L all week **Prices** Fixed D 4 course £30, Service optional **Wines** 7 bottles over £20, 33 bottles under £20, 4 by glass **Notes** Vegetarian available, Dress restrictions, Smart casual **Seats** 24 **Children** Min 14 yrs, Portions **Parking** 15

Driftwood

PORTSCATHO
Map 2 SW83

Modern European

Unique, relaxing location for exquisite cuisine

☎ 01872 580644
Rosevine TR2 5EW
e-mail: info@driftwoodhotel.co.uk
dir: 5m from St Mawes off the A3078, signposted Rosevine

Perched on the side of a cliff overlooking the English Channel and the Atlantic beyond, Driftwood does minimalism with soul, awash with chic modern décor in harmony with those stunning blue-horizon views. And you can hear the waves from the garden as you enjoy an alfresco aperitif from the decked area. Contemporary New England is the hotel's style, with neutral colours and a relaxed feel. The smart dining room continues the theme; bright and airy with plenty of windows to take in those views of the bay. Expect highly accomplished cooking with an equally light, contemporary tone, driven by prime quality produce from the abundant local larder (unsurprisingly featuring fresh fish and shellfish from local waters). Quality and consistency are the kitchen bywords, from clean flavours to presentation and clever combinations that surprise and delight the palate throughout, including peripheries like amuse-bouche, breads and petits fours. So expect a threesome like John Dory with St Mawes Bay prawns served with parmesan gnocchi and shellfish sauce, followed by loin and belly of pork perhaps accompanied by butternut squash, pickled apple purée and coco beans with wild mushrooms, and to finish, maybe a pineapple tart Tatin with lemon-grass rice pudding cannelloni and home-made gingerbread ice cream to round of a memorable meal.

Chef Christopher Eden **Owner** Paul & Fiona Robinson
Times Closed Mid Dec-Mid Jan, Closed L all week
Prices Fixed D 3 course fr £40, Service optional **Wines** 50 bottles over £20, 7 bottles under £20, 6 by glass

Notes Vegetarian available **Seats** 34 **Children** Min 6 yrs **Parking** 20

Valley Restaurant

◉ Traditional British

Carefully-cooked and presented cuisine in relaxed surroundings

☎ 01872 562202
Rose-in-Vale Country House Hotel, Mithian TR5 0QD
e-mail: reception@rose-in-vale-hotel.co.uk
web: www.rose-in-vale-hotel.co.uk
dir: A30 S. At Chiverton Cross rdbt take 3rd exit and at the next rdbt take 3rd exit signed B3277 towards St Agnes. After 0.3m follow brown tourist info signs to Rose-in-Vale

It's all in the name really, a lovely Georgian country manor-house hotel delightfully hidden away in a wooded valley bathed in peace and tranquillity. The spacious Valley Restaurant follows the theme, with relaxed, informal yet efficient service, linen-dressed tables and sweeping bay windows overlooking the gardens. The compact, fixed-price imaginative modern menus change daily to make the best of the abundant local larder - meat and vegetables from local farms, fish landed at nearby harbours - and deliver carefully cooked, well-presented dishes, allowing the main ingredient to shine through.

Chef Colin Hankins, Simon Hawkins **Owner** James & Sara Evans **Times** 12-2/7-9, Closed L Mon-Wed (winter) **Prices** Food prices not confirmed for 2009. Please telephone for details. **Wines** 10 bottles over £20, 25 bottles under £20, 5 by glass **Notes** Vegetarian available, Dress restrictions, Smart dress, Civ Wed 100 **Seats** 80, Pr/dining room 12 **Children** Min 7 yrs, Portions **Parking** 50

Austell's

◉◉ Modern, British ✿

Solid, seasonal cooking in chic surroundings

☎ 01726 813888
10 Beach Rd PL25 3PH
e-mail: brett@austells.net
web: www.austells.net
dir: From A390 towards Par, 0.5m after Charlestown rdbt at 2nd lights turn right. Left at rdbt. Restaurant 600yds on right

Set in tranquil Carlyon Bay on the approach road to the beach, Austell's is close to six golf courses and just 20 minutes from the Eden Project. The chic, modern dining area is raised and allows a view of the chefs in the open kitchen. Chef Brett trained at The Ivy in London and also worked with Jean-Christophe Novelli and this pedigree shines through in his seasonal, uncomplicated British food. Local produce is a cornerstone of the kitchen and the frequently-changing menu could start with a confit of local pork belly with black pudding mousse and Granny Smith purée and be followed by an assiette of Cornish lamb (rack, rump and braised shoulder) with dauphinoise potatoes and vièrge dressing.

Chef Brett Camborne-Paynter **Owner** J & S Camborne-Paynter **Times** Closed 25, 26 Dec & 1 Jan, Closed Mon (Tue Jan-Mar), Closed L Sun **Prices** Starter £5.95-£8.50, Main £14.50-£24, Dessert £5-£10, Service optional **Wines** 16 bottles over £20, 13 bottles under £20, 5 by glass **Notes** Vegetarian available **Seats** 48 **Children** Portions **Parking** 30

Carlyon Bay Hotel

◉ Modern, Traditional

Sweeping sea views and a fine-dining menu

☎ 01726 812304
Sea Rd, Carlyon Bay PL25 3RD
e-mail: info@carlyonbay.co.uk
web: www.carlyonbay.com
dir: A390 towards St Austell; from town follow Charlestown then Carlyon Bay/Crinnis. Hotel at end of Sea Rd near Cornwall Coliseum. Hotel at end of Sea Rd

Built in 1929, this impressive art deco hotel has a fantastic cliff-top location and 250 acres of grounds, including a championship golf course. Sea views are afforded from the restaurant, which has recently been refurbished in a bright modern style with bold artwork and comfortable new high-backed leather chairs. Modern British cuisine is inspired by quality West Country produce, including fish and shellfish from the Cornish coast, and dishes such as pork and apple terrine, local rack of lamb, and grapefruit bavarois with apple sorbet. Formal table service is delivered by friendly, professional staff.

Times 12-2/7-9.30

Wreckers

◉ International

Fresh, exciting cooking in historic Charlestown Harbour

☎ 01726 879053
Charlestown Harbour PL25 3NJ
e-mail: mail@wreckers.me.uk
dir: Follow signs for Charlestown from St Austell bypass, restaurant on right, next to square rig ships

Contemporary style blends with interesting old features at this white-painted building (a former sail and rope store) set alongside the port. The terrace is a great place for fair-weather aperitifs, while inside is light and airy, with burgundy chairs, white tablecloths and attentive service delivering the comforts. Punchy flavours, quality ingredients and a confident kitchen impress, alongside a deserved reputation for fresh fish and seafood. Lunch is a lighter affair (with a more café-bar buzz), while dinner cranks up a gear and transforms things to a restaurant vibe. Think a starter of goat's cheese on toasted ciabatta with red onion marmalade, and mains such as West Country pheasant with Calvados sauce.

Times 10-2.45/6.30-10, Closed Mon, Closed D Sun

Alba Restaurant

◉ Modern European 🖥 V

Dining in a former lifeboat house with sea views and fresh local produce

☎ 01736 797222
Old Lifeboat House, Wharf Rd TR26 1LF
e-mail: julia.stevens@tiscali.co.uk
web: www.thealbarestaurant.com
dir: First building on St Ives harbour front, opposite the new Lifeboat House

Huge picture windows make the most of the splendid views at this former lifeboat house located on the harbourside.

Bright modern art, suede chairs and banquette seating complement the warm décor in the contemporary interior. The kitchen's equally modern approach is intelligently straightforward, showcasing fresh local and seasonal produce on the modern British menu. Fittingly fish is the order of the day, with organic meat and vegetarian options also available. A fixed-price menu is available at lunch and dinner (before 7pm) to bolster the cartes, while specials and home-made breads add to the appealing repertoire. Provençale fish soup with rouille, parmesan and garlic croutons, and Cornish crab and pea risotto show the style, with perhaps a selection of Neal's Yard cheeses to close.

Chef Grant Nethercott **Owner** Harbour Kitchen Co Ltd **Times** 11.30-2/5-9.45, Closed 25-26 Dec **Prices** Fixed L 2 course £13.50, Fixed D 3 course £16.50, Starter £5.95-£8.95, Main £12.95-£19.95, Dessert £4.95-£6.95, Service optional, Groups min 6 service 10% **Wines** 26 bottles over £20, 38 bottles under £20, 33 by glass **Notes** Fixed price menus before 7.30 in season or 7 rest of yr, Vegetarian menu, Air con **Seats** 60 **Children** Portions, Menu

Garrack Hotel & Restaurant

◉ Modern British ✋

Relaxed hotel dining with great fish choices

☎ 01736 796199 & 792910
Burthallan Ln, Higher Ayr TR26 3AA
e-mail: aarest@garrack.com
dir: From Tate Gallery & Porthmeor Beach car park follow road uphill to top. Burthallan Lane & Garrack Rd signs on right

There are fine views across the harbour and Porthmeor Beach from the peaceful, elevated position of this well-established hotel. Public rooms include a cosy bar, comfortable lounge and airy, attractive L-shaped restaurant which blends traditional and contemporary style. A wide range of dishes is offered from the modern British carte, including fresh lobster priced by live weight per kilo. Expect good fish portions, perhaps pan-fried local mackerel fillet with wilted kale and roast pine nut, lemon and horseradish pesto, or seared fillet of red mullet with herb aïoli, shellfish and sea fish chowder and fresh gnocchi dumpling.

Chef Neil O'Brien **Owner** Kilby family
Times 12.30-2/6.30-9, Closed L Mon-Sat **Prices** Fixed D 3 course £28, Starter £7-£11, Main £14-£24, Dessert £4.95-£7.95, Service optional **Wines** 21 bottles over £20, 56 bottles under £20, 8 by glass **Notes** Sunday L, Vegetarian available, Dress restrictions, Smart casual **Seats** 40 **Children** Portions, Menu **Parking** 36

Porthminster Beach Restaurant

◉ Modern International V

Global cooking right on the beach

☎ 01736 795352
Porthminster TR26 2EB
e-mail: pminster@btconnect.com
dir: On Porthminster Beach, beneath the St Ives Railway Station

An original art deco building, formerly a tea room, this beachside restaurant has a distinctly Mediterranean feel, with terracotta tiles, unclothed wooden tables and great artwork from Anthony Frost, plus a relaxed, informal vibe. Window tables are understandably popular, and there is a sunny patio with heating when needed. Locally caught seafood - the freshest possible - dominates the menus. Dishes are exciting and modern, prepared in any style from Italian to Thai, including the likes of Indonesian-style monkfish curry; scallops with chorizo, konbu (edible kelp) and grilled wasabi mayo; and chocolate brûlée with affrogato.

Chef M Smith, Isaac Anderson **Owner** Jim Woolcock, David Fox, Roger & Tim Symons, M Smith
Times 12-3.30/6, Closed 25 Dec, Closed Mon (Winter) **Prices** Starter £5-£10, Main £15-£22, Dessert £4-£6.50, Service optional **Wines** 13 bottles over £20, 15 bottles under £20, 9 by glass **Notes** Sunday L, Vegetarian menu **Seats** 60 **Children** Portions **Parking** 300yds (railway station)

Sands Restaurant

◉ Traditional Mediterranean

Traditional beachside hotel with enjoyable dining

☎ 01736 795311
Carbis Bay Hotel, Carbis Bay TR26 2NP
e-mail: carbisbayhotel@btconnect.com
dir: A3074 to Carbis Bay, turn right along Porthrepta Rd to the sea. The restaurant is on Carbis Bay beach

Savour the views across Carbis Bay from this comfortable hotel, built in 1894 by Cornish architect Sylvanus Trevail, set back from its own private white sand beach. The spacious restaurant offers a traditional, no nonsense European menu with contemporary touches, and an emphasis on flavour and seasonality. With dishes based on the best of local produce, expect the likes of asparagus with Parma ham and a lemon and coriander dressing, beef fillet with a mushroom duxelle in puff pastry and sherry sauce, and chocolate roulade with fresh raspberries. Service is friendly and attentive.

Times 12-3/6-9, Closed 3 wks Jan

The Wave Restaurant

◉ Modern Mediterranean ✋

Stylish St. Ives dining close to the harbour

☎ 01736 796661
17 St Andrews St TR26 1AH
dir: Located just outside the town centre, 100yds from the parish church

Situated in a quaint St. Ives street close to the harbour, this popular, stylish restaurant has a distinctly Mediterranean feel to it. Bright, modern and with clean lines, the two separate dining areas feature an array of local artwork. Service is friendly and relaxed. In keeping with the feel of the place, the menu offers modern Mediterranean fare, as well as a scattering of Asian-influenced food. Good use is made of local, seasonal produce, including lots of locally-caught fish, in dishes such as local crab gnocchi with star anise beurre blanc, red pesto roasted cod with saffron mash, or pan-fried line-caught sea bass with lemon risotto cake.

Chef S M Pellow **Owner** Mr & Mrs Cowling, Mr & Mrs Pellow **Times** Closed end Nov-beg Mar, Closed Sun, Closed L all week **Prices** Starter £4.95-£7.95, Main £13.95-£18.95, Dessert £5.50-£6.95, Service optional **Wines** 4 bottles over £20, 20 bottles under £20, 8 by glass **Notes** Fixed D 6-7.15pm, Vegetarian available, Dress restrictions, Smart casual, no swimwear or bare chests **Seats** 50 **Children** Portions, Menu **Parking** Station car park

ST MAWES	Map 2 SW83

Hotel Tresanton

◉◉◉ – *see page 88*

ST MAWES *Continued*

Idle Rocks Hotel

◉◉ Modern European

Innovative cooking at the water's edge

☎ 01326 270771
Harbour Side TR2 5AN
e-mail: reception@idlerocks.co.uk
dir: From St Austell take A390 towards Truro, turn left onto B3287 signed Tregony, through Tregony, left at T-junct onto A3078, hotel is on left on waterfront

This hotel has splendid sea views overlooking the attractive and well-heeled fishing port of St Mawes. Set on the edge of the harbour wall, the aptly-named, modern split-level Water's Edge restaurant echoes the surroundings, decked out in shades of blue, gold and sand with lightwood floor and picture windows that allow all diners a view. And summer dining on the terrace is just perfect. The talented kitchen takes a modern approach - underpinned by classic techniques - and features top-notch local produce and clean flavours on the appealing, daily-changing menus. Take roast foie gras Lyonnaise tart with sauce soubise and pickled wild mushrooms to start, followed by braised lamb and kidneys with turnip purée and young vegetables. Close with Cox's tarte Tatin with Granny Smith sorbet and vanilla ice cream.

Times 12-3/6.30-9

SCILLY, ISLES OF

BRYHER Map 2 SV81

Hell Bay

◉◉ Modern British

Stunning location, stunning food

☎ 01720 422947
TR23 0PR
e-mail: contactus@hellbay.co.uk
web: www.hellbay.co.uk
dir: Helicopter from Penzance to Tresco, St Mary's. Plane from Southampton, Bristol, Exeter, Newquay or Land's End

The cool ocean blue and green décor of this smart hotel located on the smallest of the Scilly Isles evokes the constantly changing Atlantic seascape outside, while Lloyd Loom furniture and Malabar fabrics create a relaxed vibe. Given the setting, it's no surprise that fresh local seafood is a highlight, but the concise menu offers other options too: slow-roast pork belly for example, served with buttered Bryher spinach, rösti potato, and warm apple and pine nut chutney. Menus change daily and are conjured from first-rate ingredients in a pleasingly simple and uncluttered style. Start with roast butternut squash and ginger soup perhaps, and then tuck into pan-friend black bream with a mussel and fresh herb nage.

Chef Glenn Gatland **Owner** Tresco Estate
Times 12-3/6.30-9.30 **Prices** Fixed D 3 course £35, Service optional **Wines** 32 bottles over £20, 17 bottles under £20 **Notes** Vegetarian available, Dress restrictions, No jeans, T-shirts in eve **Seats** 75, Pr/dining room 20 **Children** Portions, Menu

---

ST MARTIN'S Map 2 SV91

Teän Restaurant@St Martin's on the Isle

◉◉◉ – *see opposite*

ST MARY'S Map 2 SV91

St Mary's Hall Hotel

◉ International

Stunning modern restaurant offering international dishes

☎ 01720 422316
Church St, Hugh Town TR21 0JR
e-mail: recp@stmaryshallhotel.co.uk

This elegant townhouse was originally built by Count Leon de Ferrari. The restaurant (Café de Ferrari) has been named after him and given an appropriately Metropolitan feel using leather, glass, granite and natural wood, supplemented by a brasserie and modern bar. There is a very hands-on approach to service from the family who own the hotel, and their friendly staff. The menu takes you on a tour of international cuisine featuring a range of dishes which might include steak as easily as sushi, while still representing a feel for local produce in the use of seafood and shellfish.

Times 12-2/6-8, Closed Xmas, Closed Sun (exc residents)

Hotel Tresanton

ST MAWES Map 2 SW83

Modern British, Mediterranean ✆

Chic boutique hotel reinventing seaside dining

☎ 01326 270055
Lower Castle Rd TR2 5DR
e-mail: info@tresanton.com
dir: On the waterfront in town centre

Once a yachtsman's club, this fashionable hillside hotel was renovated in 1998 by interior designer Olga Polizzi (sister of Sir Rocco Forte) in her much admired urban-retro design. Perched just above the sea, it is an idyllic place to dine or stay, with magical views over the bay to the Roseland Peninsula and St Anthony's Lighthouse. The dining room comes appropriately surrounded by glass to make the best of those views and has a two-tiered decked terrace - the perfect spot for pre-dinner aperitifs, or

watching the sun go down. Like the hotel, the restaurant is design-led and very stylish with a calm, cool Mediterranean air, fine mosaic floor and nautical blue-and-white themed décor. An impeccable team of front-of-house staff, both in appearance and skill, fit the bill perfectly too. The accomplished kitchen's approach majors on cracking, high-quality ingredients - sourced locally wherever possible - simply cooked with integrity to maximise freshness and flavour, with the fruits of the sea an obvious strength. Take a starter of langoustine tails with saffron risotto and carpaccio of fennel, and perhaps follow with Calenick beef fillet served with chervil root, crispy potatoes, confit shallots and 'hedgehog' mushrooms.

Chef Paul Wadham **Owner** Olga Polizzi
Times 12-2.30/7-9.30 **Prices** Fixed L 2 course £23, Fixed D 3 course £40, Service optional **Wines** 79 bottles over £20, 5 bottles under £20, 7 by glass **Notes** Sat brunch, Sunday L, Vegetarian available, Civ Wed 50 **Seats** 50, Pr/dining room 40 **Children** Min 6 yrs D, Menu **Parking** 30

Teän Restaurant@St Martin's on the Isle

ST MARTIN'S Map 2 SV91

Modern British V

Highly accomplished cooking in idyllic island paradise

☎ 01720 422092
Lower Town TR25 0QW
e-mail: stay@stmartinshotel.co.uk
dir: By helicopter or boat from Penzance to St Mary's - flights from Bristol, Exeter, Southampton, Newquay or Land's End. Then 20 min launch transfer to St Martin's

Nestling into the hillside, this attractive waterfront hotel - the only one on the island - was built to resemble a cluster of granite fishermen's cottages. It enjoys an idyllic position overlooking Teän sound and the uninhabited islands beyond, and comes with its own quay and powder white beach. More informal dining is available in the Round Island Bar and Bistro, while the first-floor fine-dining Teän Restaurant - decked out in natural tones to reflect the surroundings - has a split-level lounge where guests and diners can also enjoy those stunning views. Well-spaced tables come simply but stylishly appointed, set with seasonal flower displays. A highly accomplished kitchen team provides Mediterranean-influenced modern British cuisine to match the impressive location, with daily-changing menus driven by the abundance of the local larder, particularly fish and seafood, where freshness, quality and seasonality are showcased. Expect a light modern touch that allows intense, clean flavours to shine in dishes like sautéed Falmouth Bay scallops with cannelloni of local crab and apple and carrot salad, or braised local pollack with risotto of lobster and lobster sauce.

Chef Kenny Atkinson **Owner** Peter Sykes **Times** 12.30-2/7-10, Closed Nov-Feb inc., Closed L all week **Prices** Fixed D 3 course £47.50, Service included **Wines** 50 bottles over £20, 25 bottles under £20, 20 by glass **Notes** Sunday L, Vegetarian menu, Dress restrictions, Smart casual, Civ Wed 100 **Seats** 60 **Children** Min 9 yrs, Portions, Menu

TRESCO — Map 2 SV81

Island Hotel

◉◉ British

Refined cuisine in wonderful location

☎ 01720 422883
TR24 0PU
e-mail: islandhotel@tresco.co.uk
web: www.islandhotel.co.uk
dir: 20 minutes from Penzance by helicopter

Uniquely situated on its own private island, this delightful colonial-style hotel is a truly memorable seaside location. Furnished in contemporary style, the light-and-airy restaurant enjoys stunning sea views and forms an elegant backdrop for displays of original art. Carefully prepared, imaginative modern British cuisine is the order of the day, drawing inspiration from international sources and local ingredients, particularly seafood. Fish-lovers will not be able to resist grilled whole lemon sole with nut brown butter and vegetables, perhaps preceded by potted wild mushrooms and warm croûton fingers, with rich chocolate tart and clotted cream for dessert, or maybe a refreshing citrus brûlée.

Chef Peter Marshall **Owner** Mr R Dorrien-Smith **Times** 12-2.30/7-9, Closed 2 Nov-1 Mar, Closed L all week **Prices** Food prices not confirmed for 2009. Please telephone for details. **Notes** May-Sep Sun D buffet, Dress restrictions, Smart casual, no jeans or T-shirts **Seats** 150, Pr/dining room 25 **Children** Portions, Menu **Parking** No cars on island

New Inn

◉ British

Traditional coaching inn with a contemporary restaurant

☎ 01720 422844
TR24 0QQ
e-mail: newinn@tresco.co.uk
web: www.tresco.co.uk
dir: 250yds from harbour (private island, contact hotel for details)

Steeped in history, The New Inn has plenty of old-world character, although the restaurant has a modern New England style - light and airy, with stained-wood floors, panelled walls, artwork from around the islands and brightly-coloured table settings. The same menu and daily specials are offered in the elegant restaurant, the Driftwood Bar, the Pavilion and for eating outside, of course. The cooking relies on quality local produce - especially seafood - with the accomplished dishes boasting simple flavours. Take crisp fried devilled whitebait and tartare sauce followed by scallops in their shells with garlic butter and a rocket salad or oven-roasted St Mary's monkfish and steamed mussels with home-made tarragon tagliatelle.

Chef Pete Hingston, Nick Kittle **Owner** Mr R Dorrien-Smith **Times** 12-2.30/6-9, Closed L all week **Prices** Starter £4.50-£8, Main £9-£25, Dessert £5-£8, Service optional **Wines** 10 bottles over £20, 27 bottles under £20, 13 by glass **Notes** Sunday L, Vegetarian available **Seats** 40 **Children** Portions, Menu

TALLAND BAY — Map 2 SX25

Terrace Restaurant at Talland Bay Hotel

◉◉ Modern British

Wonderful location and refined cuisine

☎ 01503 272667
PL13 2JB
e-mail: reception@tallandbayhotel.co.uk
dir: Signed from x-rds on A387 between Looe and Polperro

Spectacular sea views and direct access to the coastal path from the end of the garden are just some of the attractions at this friendly, family-run hotel. The refined dining room, characterised by oak panelling, glowing log fire in winter and soft evening candlelight, has beautiful views over the sub-tropical gardens to the sea. Modern British dishes utilise top-notch local and seasonal produce, and both the cooking and presentation are simple and unfussy, allowing the main ingredient to shine through. Typically, tuck into slow-cooked pork belly with pickled red cabbage, follow with Cornish rib-eye steak with wilted spinach and a red wine reduction, and finish with caramelised pineapple with pecan brittle.

Owner Mr & Mrs G Granville **Times** 12.30-2/7-9, Closed L Mon-Sat (Oct-mid Apr) **Prices** Fixed D 3 course £32.50, Service optional **Wines** 50 bottles over £20, 20 bottles under £20, 12 by glass **Notes** Sunday L, Vegetarian available, Dress restrictions, Smart casual minimum **Seats** 40 **Children** Min 12 yrs **Parking** 20

TRURO — Map 2 SW84

Alverton Manor

◉◉ Traditional British

Inspired Cornish cooking in a converted convent

☎ 01872 276633
Tregolls Rd TR1 1ZQ
e-mail: reception@alvertonmanor.co.uk
web: www.alvertonmanor.co.uk
dir: From Truro bypass take A39 to St Austell. Just past the church on left

A Grade II listed former convent, with gothic windows and ornate wooden staircases, has been converted into a modern hotel set in six acres of gardens in an elevated position close to the city centre. The dining room is elegant, and the service

thoughtful and attentive. Innovative modern cooking is driven by quality produce from local suppliers, allotments and small growers. They rear their own Devon Red Cattle, keep their own bees, and have sourced free-range eggs, lamb, chicken and pork. Dishes to impress include crab and ginger ravioli served on bok choy with a langoustine and ginger sauce; and poached beef sirloin with braised shoulder, potato cake and rosemary jus.

Owner Mr M Sagin **Times** 11.45-1.45/7-9.15, Closed L Mon-Sat **Prices** Food prices not confirmed for 2009. Please telephone for details. **Wines** 80 bottles over £20, 40 bottles under £20, 15 by glass **Notes** Vegetarian available, Dress restrictions, Smart casual, Civ Wed 80 **Seats** 30, Pr/dining room 80 **Children** Min 12 yrs, Portions, Menu **Parking** 80

Probus Lamplighter Restaurant

◉◉ Modern British ⌨

Local favourite with a sound reputation

☎ 01726 882453
Fore St, Probus TR2 4JL
e-mail: maireadvogel@aol.com
dir: 5m from Truro on A390 towards St Austell

With a reputation for top-notch cooking, this veteran establishment has welcomed locals and tourists alike since the 1950s. Elegantly decked out in white and blue, with log fires, linen-clad tables and comfy sofas, the cosy 300-year-old oak-beamed restaurant is run by a husband-and-wife team who ensure relaxed and friendly service. There are two candlelit dining areas - a harmonious mix of old and new. Modern British dishes predominate on the fixed-price repertoire that includes home-made breads, canapés and amuse-bouche. The emphasis is on fresh local produce from land and sea, with straightforward presentation allowing the ingredients to speak for themselves. Tempting combinations include the likes of steamed fillet of brill served on crushed potatoes with a smoked salmon beurre blanc, with rich chocolate tart and bourbon ice cream to finish. Cookery classes are also on offer.

Chef Robert Vogel **Owner** Robert & Mairead Vogel **Times** Closed Sun-Mon, Closed L all wk **Prices** Fixed D 3 course £28.90 **Wines** 16 bottles over £20, 17 bottles under £20, 6 by glass **Notes** Vegetarian available, Dress restrictions, Smart casual **Seats** 32, Pr/dining room 8 **Children** Portions **Parking** On street & car park

Tabb's

◉◉ Modern British ⌨ ✆

Contemporary dining in former pub championing local produce

☎ 01872 262110
85 Kenwyn St TR1 3BZ
dir: Down hill past train station, right at mini rdbt, 200yds on left

Located in a one-time corner pub on the edge of the city centre, the building has been completely refurbished to create a chic modern restaurant. Black slate floors and lilac walls, complemented by high-backed leather chairs in cream and lilac and white linen-clothed tables, create a stylish, contemporary vibe. The cooking similarly takes an exciting modern approach, with everything from the bread, to ice cream and petits fours being produced on the premises. The appealing menu has an emphasis on quality local produce - mostly game and fish - with suppliers duly credited. Expect a beautifully presented warm goats' cheese salad with roast onions, bean shoots and red onion chutney, followed by a main course of pan-fried pigeon breast, with girolles, confit garlic, couscous and dry sherry reduction. For dessert, try delicious tonka bean pannacotta with poached pear.

Chef Nigel Tabb **Owner** Nigel & Melanie Tabb **Times** 12-2.30/6.30-9.30, Closed 25 Dec, 1 Jan, 1 wk Jan, Closed Sun, Mon, Closed L Sat **Prices** Starter £4.95-£8.50, Main £12.95-£21.75, Dessert £6.50-£6.95, Service optional **Wines** 17 bottles over £20, 20 bottles under £20, 6 by glass **Notes** Pre-theatre 5.30-6.30, Vegetarian available **Seats** 30 **Children** Portions **Parking** Parking 200yds

TYWARDREATH   Map 2 SX05

Trenython Manor

◎ Modern British

Imaginative cuisine in Palladian setting

☎ 01726 814797
Castle Dore Rd PL24 2TS
e-mail: enquiries@trenython.co.uk
dir: From Exeter join A30 towards Cornwall, then B3269 to Lostwithiel. Take A390 St Austell/Fowey, follow Fowey signs for approx 4m. The hotel is then signed

Dating from the 1800s, there is something distinctly different about Trenython, a classic English manor house designed by an Italian architect. The impressive dining room with carved oak panelling looks out across the gardens towards St Austell Bay. Modern British cooking is the order of the day with a fixed-price dinner menu rich in appeal. Think sea bass with a pine nut crust served with parsnip purée and crushed potato and chives, or perhaps a stem ginger and cinnamon sponge pudding to finish, served with crème anglaise. There's a more relaxed bistro for lunch.

Times 12-2.30/7-9.30

VERYAN   Map 2 SW93

Nare Hotel

◎ Traditional British

Traditional dining experience in a seaside hotel with great views

☎ 01872 501279
Carne Beach TR2 5PF
e-mail: office@narehotel.co.uk
dir: Through Veryan village passing New Inn on left, continue 1 mile to the sea

A delightful hotel on the popular Roseland Peninsula, the Nare offers a relaxed, country-house atmosphere in a

spectacular coastal setting. The terraces, lawns, lounges, bar and restaurants all have wonderful views across Gerran's Bay. The nautically-themed Quarterdeck restaurant has a teak inlaid deck and Class J yachting prints, while the dining room is more formal in style. Both serve traditional fare with an emphasis on locally-landed fish and seafood. Make your selection from the hors d'oeuvre trolley to start, then treat yourself to fresh local Portloe lobster, Cornish beef from the carving trolley, or Heligan lamb fricassée with minted polenta ratatouille.

Chef Malcolm Sparks **Owner** T G H Ashworth **Times** 12.30-2.30/7.30-10, Closed L Mon-Sat **Wines** 300 bottles over £20, 200 bottles under £20, 18 by glass **Notes** Fixed D 5 courses £45, Nare Oyster Boat £72 for 2 people, Sunday L, Vegetarian available, Dress restrictions, Jacket and tie, Air con **Seats** 75 **Children** Min 7 yrs, Portions, Menu **Parking** 70

WATERGATE BAY   Map 2 SW86

The Brasserie

◎ Modern European

Dine in comfort with superb views after a day on the beach

☎ 01637 860543
Watergate Bay Hotel, The Hotel and Extreme Academy TR8 4AA
e-mail: life@watergatebay.co.uk
dir: 2nd right off A30 after The Victoria Inn onto A3059 straight across rdbt following airport signs. Turn right after 1.5m at B3276 T-junct, turn left to bay

You can enjoy fantastic beach and sea views from the spacious decking of the bar and lounge of this modern, stylish hotel or from The Brasserie restaurant. The private beach is home to the Extreme Academy hosting sports competitions and lessons in beach and watersports. The imaginative modern menu is changed daily offering modern British and European dishes, including some traditional favourites. Terrine of ham hock and quail with tomato chutney, followed by roast salmon fillet with citrus-braised fennel, chunky chips and tarragon velouté, and tonka and vanilla bean pannacotta to finish show the style.

Times Closed L all week

Fifteen Cornwall

◎ Modern British, Italian 🖥 🕐

Italian-influenced dishes in a relaxed atmosphere at an incredible location

☎ 01637 861000
On The Beach TR8 4AA
e-mail: restaurant@fifteencornwall.co.uk
dir: M5 to Exeter & join A30 westbound. Exit Highate Hill junct, following signs to airport and at T-junct after airport, turn left & follow road to Watergate Bay.

Exploiting the contrasts between fine dining and beach hut, this much-heralded restaurant translates the original Fifteen urban look into something more relevant

to its coastal location. Accessed via a decked area, the contemporary new-build beachside restaurant is a relaxed open-plan affair with wood floors and stylish décor. At first-floor level above the 2-mile beach, window tables enjoy superb views across the bay and the surfers. Like Jamie Oliver's blueprint London outlet, Fifteen Cornwall supports disadvantaged youngsters as they build a career in the industry. The sunny Mediterranean-style cooking is rooted in Italy, driven by simplicity and quality seasonal produce. Cornish fillet of John Dory with Charlotte potatoes, cockles, and rock samphire in a crab brodo shows the style.

Chef Neil Haydock **Owner** Cornwall Foundation of Promise **Times** 12-2.30/6.15-9.15 **Prices** Fixed L course £24.50, Tasting menu £50, Starter £6.50-£9, Main £11-£19, Dessert £6, Service optional **Wines** 90 bottles over £20, 3 bottles under £20, 10 by glass **Notes** Tasting menu only served evenings, Vegetarian available, Air con **Seats** 100, Pr/dining room 12 **Children** Portions, Menu **Parking** Nearby

ZENNOR   Map 2 SW43

The Gurnard's Head

◎◎ British 🖥

Honest modern cooking in relaxed, friendly inn

☎ 01736 796928
Treen TR26 3DE
e-mail: enquiries@gurnardshead.co.uk
dir: 6m W of St Ives by B3306

Located on the winding coast road and close to the cliffs, this substantial inn combines a country atmosphere - log fires, solid wood floors and tables - with modern cooking. The inn has long been a refuelling stop for walkers, but these days it is the food that is attracting attention. Service is suitably relaxed and friendly, while the kitchen makes good use of the abundant local larder on a sensibly compact daily-changing menu. Traditional British classics sit comfortably alongside ideas from the European mainland, mostly France and Spain. Expect simply presented, clean and vibrant cooking in dishes like jellied pork and sage terrine or shin of beef braised in ale with mashed potato and thyme dumplings. Lemon posset is a typical dessert, or finish with a plate of three West Country cheeses served with soda bread and apple jelly.

Chef Robert Wright **Owner** Charles & Edmund Inkin **Times** 12-2.30/6.30-9.30, Closed 24-25 Dec **Prices** Starter £4.50-£9, Main £10-£16.50, Dessert £4.50-£5.50, Service optional **Wines** 27 bottles over £20, 16 bottles under £20, 8 by glass **Notes** Sunday L, Vegetarian available **Seats** 50 **Children** Portions **Parking** 40

CUMBRIA

ALSTON — Map 18 NY74

Lovelady Shield House

◉◉ Modern British

Family-run country-house hotel with innovative cuisine

☎ 01434 381203
CA9 3LF
e-mail: enquiries@lovelady.co.uk
web: www.lovelady.co.uk
dir: 2m E of Alston, signed off A689 at junct with B6294

Hidden away along a tree-lined drive in the heart of the Pennines, this delightful country-house hotel boasts a cosy bar with an impressive array of fine malts, as well as several comfortable lounges. Take an aperitif by the fire, before moving through to the restaurant, an elegant room decorated with antiques and paintings. There you'll find a daily-changing menu of modern British and classical French dishes, including starters such as twice-baked lobster soufflé with brandied bisque, or mains of slow-braised haunch and rare roasted loin of venison with prune purée, roasted root vegetables, and beer and juniper jus. Round things off with crème caramel with glazed banana and praline wafer.

Times 12-2/7-8.30, Closed L Mon-Sat

AMBLESIDE — Map 18 NY30

Drunken Duck Inn

◉◉ Modern British, European 🔖 NOTABLE WINE LIST 🌿

Great local produce in a fantastic Lakeland setting

☎ 015394 36347
Barngates LA22 0NG
e-mail: info@drunkenduckinn.co.uk
dir: Take A592 from Kendal, follow signs for Hawkshead (from Ambleside), in 2.5m sign for inn on right, 1m up hill

Set on a crossroads, high above Lake Windermere, this characterful coaching inn is 400 years old. Run by the same family for more than thirty years, it's an unstuffy mix of old and new teaming wide oak floorboards with open fires, leather club chairs and a slate-top bar. Real ales come courtesy of the inn's very own brewery, Barngates, which draws its water supply from the nearby fells, while the restaurant plunders the local larder for the best in seasonal produce. Take your seat for some accomplished cooking: braised ham hock terrine to start perhaps, served with piccalilli and herb salad; followed by roasted Cumbrian beef fillet with Whinow blue cheese rarebit, fondant potato and forestière garnish, or roasted monkfish in pancetta with fresh pea risotto, wilted spinach and red wine butter.

Drunken Duck Inn

Chef Marcus Hall **Owner** Stephanie Barton
Times 12-2.30/6-9.30 **Prices** Fixed L 2 course fr £18, Starter £5.50-£12.95, Main £14.25-£24.95, Dessert £6.50-£8.25, Service optional **Wines** 155 bottles over £20, 25 bottles under £20, 17 by glass **Notes** Sunday L, Vegetarian available **Seats** 60 **Children** Portions **Parking** 40

The Log House

◉ Modern Mediterranean

Norwegian log-house restaurant with flavour-driven modern fare

☎ 015394 31077
Lake Rd LA22 0DN
e-mail: nicola@loghouse.co.uk
dir: M6 junct 36. Situated on A591 on left, just beyond garden centre

An eye-catching Norwegian construction, the Log House was imported in the late 19th century by the artist Alfred Heaton Cooper to be both his family home and studio. These days it is a popular split-level restaurant and bar, decked out with lightwood floors, terracotta walls, wooden chairs and clothed tables creating a modern feel. The kitchen adapts classic techniques for its modern day cooking with a colourful nod to the Mediterranean. Using as much fresh and local seasonal produce as possible, expect dishes like braised roulade of Gloucester Old Spot pork belly, roasted loin of Vale of Lune lamb with crushed new potatoes and asparagus and salsa verde, and sea bass with hand-cut chips and gherkin salsa.

Chef Heath Calman **Owner** Nicola & Heath Calman
Times 12-3/6-10, Closed 7 Jan-7 Feb, Closed Mon
Prices Fixed L 2 course £15-£17.50, Fixed D 3 course £17.50-£19.50, Starter £4.95-£8.95, Main

£13.95-£21.95, Dessert £5.50-£6.95, Service optional **Wines** 32 bottles over £20, 31 bottles under £20, 5 by glass **Notes** Chef's choice menu available, Sunday L, Vegetarian available **Seats** 40 **Children** Portions, Menu **Parking** 3 **Parking** Pay & Display opposite

Regent Hotel

◉ British

Long-established hotel championing organic produce

☎ 015394 32254
Waterhead Bay LA22 0ES
e-mail: info@regentlakes.co.uk
dir: 1m S of Ambleside at Waterhead Bay

This attractive hotel, known for its award-winning display of summer flowers, is located close to Waterhead Bay on the shores of Lake Windermere. The contemporary restaurant overlooks a pretty Italianate courtyard and the walls are hung with modern art. The brasserie-style menu showcases organic Cumbrian produce, allowing the quality of the ingredients to shine through. Expect dishes like Mansergh Hall lamb cutlets with dauphinoise potatoes and vegetable casserole with balsamic jus; Lowther Park chicken breast on creamy pearl barley and celeriac risotto; and Esthwaite Hawkshead trout baked with a horseradish and dill crust on wilted baby spinach with lemon butter sauce.

Chef John Mathen **Owner** Vogue Leisure Ltd.
Times 12-2/6.30-8, Closed Xmas wk **Prices** Fixed D 3 course £25-£35 **Wines** 6 bottles over £20, 20 bottles under £20, 12 by glass **Seats** 60 **Children** Portions, Menu **Parking** 35

Rothay Manor

◉ Traditional British 🌿

Fine dining in the Lakes

☎ 015394 33605
Rothay Bridge LA22 0EH
e-mail: hotel@rothaymanor.co.uk
web: www.rothaymanor.co.uk
dir: From Ambleside, follow signs for Coniston (A593). Hotel is 0.25 mile SW from the centre of Ambleside opposite the rugby club

Built as a summer residence for a prosperous Liverpool merchant in 1825, this elegant country-house hotel has a Grade II listed Regency façade and has been in the current owner's family for some 40 years. The interior retains many original features and is furnished in a classical, elegant style with antiques and floral displays, while outside a revolving summer house is a feature of the pretty garden. The friendly, family-run concern offers a mainly traditional British menu, taking in the likes of terrine of guinea fowl, pork and wood pigeon, followed by roast loin of venison on red cabbage baked with red wine and herbs. Finish off on a light note perhaps with lemon posset with raspberries and mint. A separate children's menu is available.

Chef Jane Binns **Owner** Nigel Nixon
Times 12.30-1.45/7.15-9, Closed 3-23 Jan, Closed D 25 Dec **Prices** Fixed D 3 course £39, Starter £3.80-£5, Main £7.50-£10.50, Dessert £4.50, Service optional **Wines** 111 bottles over £20, 42 bottles under £20, 8 by glass **Notes** ALC L only, Sunday L, Vegetarian available, Dress restrictions, Smart casual, Air con **Seats** 65, Pr/dining room 34 **Children** Min 7 yrs D, Portions, Menu **Parking** 35

APPLEBY-IN-WESTMORLAND   Map 18 NY62

Appleby Manor Country House Hotel

◉ Modern British

Accomplished cuisine in relaxed country-house hotel

☎ 017683 51571
Roman Rd CA16 6JB
e-mail: reception@applebymanor.co.uk
dir: M6 junct 40 take A66 for Scotch Corner for 12m, take turn for Appleby. Manor 1.5m on right

Two very different styles distinguish the separate parts of this restaurant, one featuring wood panelling and the original fireplace, and the other a light-and-airy conservatory. Both share views over the manor-house gardens and the surrounding fells. The accomplished food comes in interesting combinations featuring regional produce, as in confit of Cumbrian belly pork with a cabbage, apple and black pudding timbale, butternut squash purée, champ potatoes and a home-made faggot; and Appleby Manor hot-smoked supreme of sea trout fillet on buttered asparagus, sautéed new potatoes and slow-roast vine tomatoes, topped with horseradish hollandaise sauce.

Times 12-2/7-9, Closed 24-26 Dec

BARROW-IN-FURNESS   Map 18 SD26

Clarence House Country Hotel & Restaurant

◉◉ British, International

Enjoyable dining in comfortable conservatory surroundings

☎ 01229 462508
Skelgate LA15 8BQ
e-mail: info@clarencehouse-hotel.co.uk
dir: Telephone for directions

This cosy country-house hotel likes to feed its guests well. Kick off the day with a hearty English breakfast, while away the hours over a genteel afternoon tea, and then round things off with a delicious meal in the airy orangery-style restaurant. Long windows make the most of pretty views over St Thomas' valley, and there's a terrace for alfresco dining in the summer. There's a good mixture of straightforward local dishes as well as British and European items on the menu. Expect starters such as goat's cheese pannacotta, followed by beef fillet with peppercorn sauce, carrots and potato fondant. Treat yourself to a delicious trio of desserts: mini chocolate brûlée, chocolate torte and praline mousse to finish.

Times 12-2/7-9, Closed 25-26 Dec, Closed D Sun

BASSENTHWAITE   Map 18 NY23

The Pheasant

◉ Modern British

Good honest food in traditional inn

☎ 017687 76234
CA13 9YE
e-mail: info@the-pheasant.co.uk
dir: M6 junct 40, take A66 (Keswick and North Lakes). Continue past Keswick and head for Cockermouth. Signed from A66

Standing in lovely gardens, this cosy old coaching inn dates back to the 16th century and has a picture-postcard setting beside Bassenthwaite Lake. There are comfy lounges for afternoon tea and an oak-panelled bar with log fires and a great selection of malts, but it's the dining room that's the real draw, where you can sample an accomplished menu of modern British dishes conjured from the freshest local ingredients. Tea-smoked breast of Gressingham duck is a typical starter, served with caramelised pear purée , roasted hazelnuts and Earl Grey syrup, while mains might include seared loin of local wild venison with confit haunch, red cabbage, purée potatoes and a port and chocolate sauce, or roast cannon of Lakeland lamb.

Chef Malcolm Ennis **Owner** Trustees of Lord Inglewood
Times 12-1.30/7-9, Closed 25 Dec **Prices** Fixed L 2 course fr £21.95, Fixed D 3 course fr £31.95, Service optional, Groups min 8 service 10% **Wines** 60 bottles over £20, 19 bottles under £20, 12 by glass **Notes** Sunday L, Vegetarian available, Dress restrictions, Smart casual, No jeans, T-shirts, trainers **Seats** 45, Pr/dining room 12 **Children** Min 8 yrs D **Parking** 40

BORROWDALE   Map 18 NY21

Borrowdale Gates Country House Hotel

◉ Modern British Ⅴ ◔

Ambitious cuisine in a peaceful Cumbrian setting

☎ 017687 77204
CA12 5UQ
e-mail: hotel@borrowdale-gates.co.uk
dir: B5289 from Keswick, after 4m turn right over bridge to Grange. Hotel 400yds on right

Built as a private residence in 1860, the hotel is set in wooded gardens in the Borrowdale Valley. Windows running the length of the dining room afford magnificent views of dramatic Lakeland scenery (book ahead for a window table). Traditional British cooking with a modern French twist utilises the best local produce in dishes such as Cartmel Valley smoked salmon, pan-fried Harryman's reared fillet steak, with Pont-Neuf potatoes, red onion marmalade and wild mushroom cappuccino, or roast Yew Tree farmed lamb cutlets, served pink, with Lyonnaise potatoes, parsnip purée and rosemary jus.

Chef Shaun Dixon **Owner** Green Symbol Ltd
Times 12-2/6.30-8.45, Closed L open on request
Prices Fixed L 2 course £20-£25, Starter £9-£12, Main £19-£28.75, Dessert £9-£12.50, Service optional
Wines 58 bottles over £20, 15 bottles under £20, 6 by glass **Notes** Sunday L, Vegetarian menu, Dress restrictions, Smart casual, Civ Wed 60 **Seats** 53 **Children** Portions **Parking** 25

BORROWDALE *Continued*

Hazel Bank Country House

◉ British, European

Elegant Victorian house with Lakeland views and honest food

☎ 017687 77248
Rosthwaite CA12 5XB
e-mail: enquiries@hazelbankhotel.co.uk
web: www.hazelbankhotel.co.uk
dir: From M6 junct 40, leave the A66 and take the B5289 to Borrowdale. Just before Rosthwaite turn left over hump-back bridge

This traditional Victorian Lakeland residence offers magnificent views over Borrowdale and fine fell walking across Langdale Pikes. With views of mountain peaks and the lush gardens sweeping down towards Rosthwaite village, the elegant dining room has a friendly, informal house-party atmosphere with all guests taking their place for dinner at 7pm. Traditional British dishes with European influences feature local ingredients, and may include a gratin of Cumbrian smoked haddock or a tenderloin of pork with Shrewsbury sauce and dauphinoise potatoes. Puddings are to die for and may include apricot and almond tart with apricot brandy ice cream.

Chef Brenda Davies **Owner** Glen & Brenda Davies
Times Closed 25-26 Dec, Closed L all wk **Prices** Fixed D 4 course £32.50, Service optional **Wines** 6 bottles over £20, 45 bottles under £20, 7 by glass **Notes** Vegetarian available, Dress restrictions, Smart casual, No shorts or jeans **Seats** 22 **Children** Min 12 yrs **Parking** 12

Leathes Head Hotel

◉ Modern British

Solid cooking in restaurant with fabulous views

☎ 017687 77247
CA12 5UY
e-mail: enq@leatheshead.co.uk
dir: 3.75m S of Keswick on B5289, set back on the left

Once an Edwardian gentleman's residence, this family-run hotel is a haven of peace and tranquillity. It's located in pretty gardens in one of the most beautiful areas of England - the picturesque Borrowdale Valley. There are comfy lounges for pre-dinner drinks, plus an elegant restaurant that makes the most of the stunning fell views. Take your seat for some flavourful, unpretentious cuisine using well-sourced ingredients. Baked fillet of

Scottish salmon with a cucumber and lime cream sauce, or grilled Ullswater lamb cutlets with cured Cumberland sausage and a rich port wine jus are fine examples of the fare. Round things off with hot date and walnut pudding with dairy ice and maple syrup.

Times Closed mid Nov-mid Feb

The Cottage in the Wood

◉ Modern British

Good food and service in marvellous, tranquil surroundings

☎ 017687 78409
Whinlatter Pass CA12 5TW
e-mail: relax@thecottageinthewood.co.uk
dir: M6 junct 40. take A66 signed Keswick, 1m after Keswick take B5292 signed Braithwaite, hotel 2m from Braithwaite

Set in the tranquil heart of Whinlatter Forest, this former 17th-century coaching inn is now a charming hotel with stunning views down the valley to the mountains of Skiddaw. The elegant, light-and-airy restaurant offers a daily-changing, fixed no-choice menu (three courses during the week, four at the weekend) utilising the best seasonal ingredients from local farmers. The modern British cooking is underpinned with European and Mediterranean influences. Expect dishes such as sauté of forest ceps with creamy scrambled free-range eggs on sourdough toast to start, followed by slow-roasted belly and caramelised fillet of Cumbrian saddleback pork with blackcurrant-glazed baby beetroot to follow, rounded off with Jane Grigson's English trifle.

Chef Liam Berney **Owner** Liam & Kath Berney
Times 12-2.30/6-9.30, Closed Jan, Closed Mon
Prices Starter £5.50-£7.50, Main £12-£18, Dessert £5.25-£6.25, Service optional, Groups min 8 service 10% **Wines** 14 bottles over £20, 26 bottles under £20, 10 by glass **Notes** Sunday L, Vegetarian available **Seats** 36 **Children** Min 7yrs D, Portions **Parking** 15

Farlam Hall Hotel

◉◉ Modern British **V** ♨

Elegant dining in a traditional setting

☎ 016977 46234
Hallbankgate CA8 2NG
e-mail: farlam@relaischateaux.com
dir: On A689, 2.5m SE of Brampton (not in Farlam village)

This beautiful Victorian country house with earlier origins boasts landscaped gardens including an ornamental lake and stream. The fine furnishings and fabrics of the interior recall an earlier age when the house was home to a large family, who frequently entertained guests. The classic dining room - with huge bay windows - has lovely garden views and makes a fine setting for the traditional English china, crystal glasses and silver cutlery. English country-house cooking is the style, using quality ingredients on the compact dinner menu. Expect a medallion of local beef fillet with horseradish potato galette and pink peppercorn sauce, while to finish, perhaps a toffee, banana and walnut flan with caramel sauce and banana ice cream.

Chef Barry Quinion **Owner** Quinion & Stevenson Families
Times Closed 25-30 Dec, Closed L all wk **Prices** Fixed D 4 course £42.50-£45, Service optional **Wines** 43 bottles over £20, 10 bottles under £20, 11 by glass **Notes** Vegetarian menu, Dress restrictions, Smart dress, No shorts **Seats** 40, Pr/dining room 20 **Children** Min 5 yrs, Portions **Parking** 25

Aynsome Manor Hotel

◉ British ♨

Country-house hotel with traditional cuisine and ambience

☎ 015395 36653
LA11 6HH
e-mail: aynsomemanor@btconnect.com
dir: Leave A590 signed Cartmel. Take left at junctions. Hotel on right 0.5m before reaching Cartmel village

Dating back to the 16th century, this handsome manor house has stunning views over the fells and nearby priory. In the elegant dining room gentlemen are required to wear a jacket and tie, tables are set with a well-rehearsed formality and soup is served in tureens. That

Continued

L'Enclume

Modern French 🍷 NOTABLE WINE LIST

Exhilarating, innovative cuisine to stir a quiet Lakeland village

☎ 015395 36362
Cavendish St LA11 6PZ
e-mail: info@lenclume.co.uk
dir: 10m from M6 junct 36 follow signs for A590 W, turn left for Cartmel before Newby Bridge

The setting is Lakeland sure enough, everything else exceeds expectations. The former blacksmith's forge dating back to the 13th century is now, some 800 years later, a unique restaurant with rooms. Traces of the past are still visible in the light and bright dining room as modernisation has respected the history of the building. The tones are mellow, the floors laid with Lakeland stone and the art on the walls is the work of the chef-patron, Simon Rogan. Well-spaced tables, crisp white linen and bold flowers help create a smart but unpretentious setting for what follows. And what follows is something extraordinary, dazzling even. The cooking is based around local produce, the very best of it, and Simon also likes to include unusual herbs and flowers, bringing them back into the fold often after centuries of neglect, and to explore flavour combinations. It is important before looking at the menu to realise the playfulness of the chef and appreciate

the integrity of what he does. The food may be complex, but it is not heavy or rich; flavours are given room to breathe. The Introduction and Tour menus allow the chef to show his skills in a parade of magnificently creative dishes, the descriptions sometimes intriguing (Re-hydration, De-hydration), mischievous (Sticky Tacky Pudding) or just appealing (foie gras, figs, corn, sweet bracken). The skill displayed in the composition of flavours and textures is extraordinary, each dish there for a reason and exceeding expectations. LA11 venison (the prefix is the postcode from whence it came) with pine nuts, banana and yuzu is a dish which delivers the wow factor in spades, as is 'Hot Pot', a mutton broth with little parcels delivering the flavours of red cabbage and potato, while that sticky tacky pudding is a clever and amusing take on the famous dessert. The staff show genuine enthusiasm for the menu and are on hand with explanations when required (which is quite often), and the atmosphere is genuinely relaxed.

Simon Rogan has recently opened his second, more informal restaurant called Rogan & Company. Spread over two floors of a traditional cottage in the heart of Cartmel, the sophisticated, welcoming interior has a large lounge bar area and dining room on the ground floor with three main dining areas on the first floor offering seasonally-changing, more rustic modern European dishes.

Chef Simon Rogan **Owner** Simon Rogan, Penny Tapsell **Times** 12-1.30/7-9.30, Closed 1st wk Jan, Closed Mon, Closed L Tue-Fri **Prices** Fixed L 2 course £18, Fixed D 3 course £39, Tasting menu £50-£70, Service optional **Wines** 156 bottles over £20, 7 bottles under £20, 10 by glass **Notes** Tasting menu 10 & 15 courses **Seats** 40, Pr/dining room 8 **Children** Min 10yrs D **Parking** 7

CARTMEL *Continued*

said, the candlelit Georgian dining room enjoys a relaxed, house-party atmosphere when the hotel is full - at other times there's never any sense of stuffiness. The food likewise follows traditional lines and uses good, locally sourced produce; take chargrilled tenderloin of Cumbrian pork marinated in honey, balsamic vinegar and olive oil served on creamed potatoes with a full flavoured mustard cream sauce.

Chef Gordon Topp **Owner** P A Varley **Times** 1/7-8.30, Closed 25-26 Dec, 2-28 Jan, Closed L Mon-Sat, Closed D Sun (ex residents) **Prices** Fixed D 3 course £25, Service optional **Wines** 25 bottles over £20, 60 bottles under £20, 6 by glass **Notes** Sunday L, Vegetarian available, Dress restrictions, Smart dress **Seats** 28 **Children** Min 5 yrs, Portions, Menu **Parking** 20

L'Enclume

◉◉◉◉ — *see page 95*

COCKERMOUTH — Map 18 NY13

The Trout Hotel

◉ International

Classic dishes in a lovely riverside setting

☎ 01900 823591
Crown St CA13 0EJ
e-mail: enquiries@trouthotel.co.uk
dir: M6 junct 40, follow A66 to Cockermouth, hotel situated next to Wordsworth's House

Ideally situated on the River Derwent, next door to Wordsworth's House, the hotel dates in parts from 1670 and many period features have been retained. The Derwent Restaurant has recently been refurbished in classical style and there are separate lounges for pre-dinner drinks and coffee. Local produce is a feature of the menu, which includes venison, lamb and Dovenby pheasant. Start with tiger prawns in garlic butter with braised rice, followed by Cumbrian fell-bred fillet of beef served with Byron potatoes and peppercorn sauce, or for a lighter alternative try steamed lemon sole. The Terrace Bar and Bistro serves food all day and has a sheltered patio area.

Times 12-2/7-9.30, Closed L Mon-Sat

CROSTHWAITE — Map 18 SD49

The Punchbowl Inn at Crosthwaite

◉ Modern, Traditional 💻

Historic, elegantly refurbished inn with refined cooking

☎ 015395 68237
Lyth Valley LA8 8HR
e-mail: info@the-punchbowl.co.uk
dir: 6m from Kendal

Located in the stunning Lyth Valley beside the ancient village church, this historic inn (sibling to The Drunken Duck, Ambleside, see entry) has been sympathetically and stylishly remodelled, retaining bags of character. Dine in the bar, with its slate floors, cosy sofas and wood-burning stove, or more formally in the chic restaurant, where oak beams and an open fireplace complement a minimalist décor of polished wood boards, white linen and brown leather high-backed chairs. Service is professional and well informed, while the kitchen shows pedigree, too, its accomplished modern approach making the most of local ingredients. Braised pig's trotter with seared scallops and a quail egg makes a hearty starter, while mains might include braised daube of beef with garlic mash and pot-roast seasonal vegetables.

Chef Jonathon Watson **Owner** Paul Spencer, Steph Barton, Richard Rose, Amanda Robinson **Times** 12-6/6-9.30 **Prices** Starter £4.25-£8.50, Main £10.95-£18.95, Dessert £2.95-£5.95, Service optional, Groups min 10 service 10% **Wines** 58 bottles over £20, 15 bottles under £20, 14 by glass **Notes** Sunday L, Vegetarian available, Civ Wed 45 **Seats** 30 **Children** Portions **Parking** 40

ELTERWATER — Map 18 NY30

Purdeys

◉ Modern, Traditional British

Enjoyable dining in a mill-styled restaurant

☎ 015394 37302 & 38080
Langdale Hotel & Country Club LA22 9JD
e-mail: purdeys@langdale.co.uk
web: www.langdale.co.uk
dir: M6 junct 36, A591 or M6 junct 40, A66, B5322, A591

This modern hotel, set in 35 acres of woodland and waterways, was founded on the site of a 19th-century gunpowder works and still has the original cannon used to test gunpowder. The main restaurant, Purdeys, is designed in the style of an old mill with oak floors, local stone and water features creating an interesting and unique atmosphere. Mainly British fare is cooked and presented with care, utilising fresh, local produce. Crayfish cocktail with celeriac remoulade and mango salsa, daube of fell-bred beef with sweet carrots, horseradish potato and bordelaise sauce, and champagne and rhubarb cheesecake show the style.

Chef John Adler-Connor **Owner** Langdale Leisure **Times** Closed L Group L booking essential **Prices** Fixed D 3 course fr £27.50, Service optional **Wines** 22 bottles over £20, 40 bottles under £20, 9 by glass **Notes** Vegetarian available, Dress restrictions, Smart casual, Civ Wed 60 **Seats** 80, Pr/dining room 40 **Children** Portions, Menu **Parking** 50

GLENRIDDING — Map 18 NY31

The Inn on the Lake

◉ Modern European V 🐾

Lakeside setting for traditional-style dining experience

☎ 017684 82444
Lake Ullswater CA11 0PE
e-mail: info@innonthelakeullswater.co.uk
dir: M6 junct 40, A66 Keswick, A592 Windermere

This restored grand Victorian hotel comes complete with its own traditional pub in the grounds called the Ramblers Bar, and enjoys one of the most spectacular settings in the Lake District, sitting in 15 acres with lawns sweeping to the shores of Ullswater. The restaurant is in the traditional mould, with clothed tables, full-length curtains, upholstered chairs and coordinated patterned carpet and, of course, fabulous views over the water. In line with the surroundings, service strikes a traditional note, while the kitchen follows suit, dealing in well-executed fare utilising quality local ingredients. Take crab consommé with spring onions, chives and crab and fraîche tortellini, with 'textures of local beef' (shin, brisket and oxtail and mint steak-and-kidney pudding) for main course, and hot chocolate fondant with chocolate sauce and toasted hazelnut and chocolate ice cream to close.

Chef Nick O'Mahoney **Owner** Charles & Kit Graves **Times** 12.30-2/7-9, Closed L Sat **Prices** Fixed L 2 course £9.95-£17.95, Fixed D 3 course £21.95-£29.95, Starter £3.50-£8.95, Main £11.95-£22.95, Dessert £3.95-£6.95, Service optional **Wines** 27 bottles over £20, 28 bottles under £20, 8 by glass **Notes** Sunday L, Vegetarian menu, Dress restrictions, Smart casual, Civ Wed 110 **Seats** 100, Pr/dining room 40 **Children** Portions, Menu **Parking** 100

GRANGE-OVER-SANDS   Map 18 SD47

Clare House

◉ Modern British ◌

Satisfying country-house cooking in relaxing surroundings with great views

☎ 015395 33026 & 34253
Park Rd LA11 7HQ
e-mail: info@clarehousehotel.co.uk
dir: From M6 take A590, then B5277 to Grange-over-Sands. Park Road follows the shore line. Hotel on left next to swimming pool

Comfortable, family-run country house hotel set in lovely, well-tended gardens with panoramic views out over Morecambe Bay. Retaining a wealth of period features throughout, the elegant dining room has high ceilings, open fireplaces, deep yellow walls, polished mahogany furniture and traditional settings. The dinner menu lists simple, effective traditional and modern dishes, such as slow-roast lamb shoulder with rosemary gravy and apple and mint jelly, and perhaps baked ginger parkin with rhubarb ripple ice cream or interesting cheese menu to finish. Service is friendly and efficient.

Chef Andrew Read, Mark Johnston **Owner** Mr & Mrs D S Read **Times** Closed Dec-Apr, Closed L all wk **Prices** Fixed D 4 course £30, Service optional **Wines** 7 bottles over £20, 30 bottles under £20, 2 by glass **Notes** Vegetarian available **Seats** 32 **Children** Portions, Menu **Parking** 16

GRASMERE   Map 18 NY30

Grasmere Hotel

◉ Traditional European

Traditional country-house hotel with good food

☎ 015394 35277
Broadgate LA22 9TA
e-mail: enquiries@grasmerehotel.co.uk
dir: Off A591 close to village centre

The River Rothay runs through the grounds of this Victorian, stone-built hotel, and the views over the formal garden and water can be enjoyed from the dining room. The traditionally decorated mansion house retains many original features including wood panelling in the lounge areas, a wonderful staircase and a stunning acanthus chandelier in the dining room. The dining experience is traditional and formal, with diners congregating in the lounge for drinks before being ushered through to eat at one sitting. Cooking is very much in the country-house vein with a daily-changing menu: cheese soufflé with nicely dressed leaves precedes leg of Kentmere lamb served traditionally, before lime cheesecake to finish.

Chef Mr P Hetherington **Owner** Stuart & Janet Cardwell **Times** Closed Jan-early Feb, Closed L all week **Prices** Food prices not confirmed for 2009. Please telephone for details. **Wines** 10 bottles over £20, 40 bottles under £20, 8 by glass **Notes** Fixed D 4 courses, Vegetarian available, Dress restrictions, Smart casual, no jeans or shorts **Seats** 28 **Children** Min 10 yrs **Parking** 14

Rothay Garden Hotel & Restaurant

◉◉ Modern European V

Delightful hotel with stunning scenery and fine dining

☎ 015394 35334
Broadgate LA22 9RJ
e-mail: stay@rothaygarden.com
dir: From N M6 junct 40, A66 to Keswick, then S on A591 to Grasmere. From S M6 junct 36 take A591 through Windermere/Ambleside to Grasmere. At N end of village adjacent to park

Situated on the outskirts of Grasmere village, and set amidst large riverside gardens with spectacular views across the fells, this delightful Lakeland hotel offers a choice of relaxing lounges, a cosy bar with inglenook fireplace and a light-and-airy conservatory restaurant for fine dining which takes advantage of those views. Service is relaxed and professional, from long-serving, friendly staff. The daily-changing seasonal menu offers a variety of modern British dishes, including some more traditional fare. Try for example chicken and ham terrine with piccalilli, followed by Lakeland beef fillet with red wine jus, pea tartlet and château potatoes, or grilled halibut with herb fondue. Round things off with mango soufflé with passionfruit ice cream.

Chef Andrew Burton **Owner** Chris Carss **Times** 12-1.45/7-9.30, Closed L 24, 25, 31 Dec, 1 Jan **Prices** Fixed L 2 course £13.95, Fixed D 4 course £37.50, Service optional **Wines** 113 bottles over £20, 30 bottles under £20, 22 by glass **Notes** Sunday L, Vegetarian menu, Dress restrictions, Smart casual, No jeans or T-shirts **Seats** 60 **Children** Min 5 yrs, Portions **Parking** 35

GRASMERE *Continued*

Wordsworth Hotel

◉◉ Modern British

Honest food in elegant hotel

☎ 015394 35592
LA22 9SW
e-mail: enquiry@thewordsworthhotel.co.uk
web: www.thewordsworthhotel.co.uk
dir: From Ambleside follow A591 N to Grasmere. Hotel in town centre next to church

This traditional Victorian hotel, a former hunting lodge, is set in fine gardens and located next to the churchyard where the famous poet Wordsworth is buried. With the backdrop of towering fells, guests and diners alike can enjoy a pleasant haven away from the tourist throngs and enjoy some fine British cooking. The bar has been refurbished and there is a new conservatory. In the light, airy traditional-styled Prelude Restaurant, the interesting fixed price menu offers quality, local produce throughout with some interesting ingredient combinations. Expect good flavours and textures, and first class presentation. Start with leek and potato soup, then move on to an accurately cooked beef fillet with Madeira truffle jus, and finish with chocolate tart and crème anglaise.

Chef Lee Woodend **Owner** Mr Gifford
Times 12.30-2/7-9.30 **Prices** Fixed L 2 course £12.50, Fixed D 4 course £39.50, Service optional **Wines** 50 bottles over £20, 22 bottles under £20, 10 by glass **Notes** Sunday L, Vegetarian available, Dress restrictions, Smart casual, jacket preferred, Civ Wed 100, Air con **Seats** 65, Pr/dining room 18 **Children** Min 8 yrs, Portions, Menu **Parking** 50

HAWKSHEAD   **Map 18 SD39**

Queen's Head Hotel

◉ British, International

Charming old-world inn serving honest fare

☎ 015394 36271 & 0800 137263
Main St LA22 0NS
e-mail: enquiries@queensheadhotel.co.uk
web: www.queensheadhotel.co.uk
dir: Village centre

Dating back to the 16th century, this one-time coaching inn has bags of character, from the open fire that greets you when you enter, to flagstone floors, low ceilings and a wood-panelled bar. Generous, uncomplicated meals are served in the bar and pretty dining room. Good use is made of quality local ingredients in a lengthy menu bolstered by daily specials. Try game terrine to start perhaps, wrapped in Cumbrian air-dried ham and served with Hawkshead relish tomato chutney and olive bread; followed by lamb King Henry - slow-roasted shoulder of lamb coated in an orange demi-glace, or a venison casserole, slow-braised with shallots.

Chef Michelle Stevens **Owner** Anthony Merrick
Times 12-2.30/6.15-9.30 **Prices** Fixed L course £21, Starter £3.95-£6.75, Main £10.25-£22.50, Dessert £5.25, Service optional **Wines** 8 bottles over £20, 40 bottles under £20, 14 by glass **Notes** Sunday L, Vegetarian available, Dress restrictions, Smart casual, Air con **Seats** 38, Pr/dining room 20 **Children** Portions, Menu **Parking** NCP permits issued

---

West Vale Country House & Restaurant

◉◉ Modern ✪

Fine dining in a classic country house

☎ 01539 442817
Far Sawrey LA22 0LQ
e-mail: dee.pennington@btconnect.com
dir: Please telephone for directions

Overlooking Grizedale Forest and The Old Man of Coniston, this delightful Lakeland stone-built house sits in the heart of Beatrix Potter country, on the edge of the beautiful village of Far Sawrey. Built in the 1890s as a Victorian gentleman's residence, it has been refurbished in traditional country-house style combining character and elegance with outstanding service and hospitality. The restaurant continues the theme with stunning views, well-spaced tables, white linen and quality tableware. Dishes are classical with a modern twist, the daily-changing menu featuring the best of local and seasonal produce. Take a main course of local Graythwaite venison with braised cabbage, smoked bacon and cranberry sauce, or perhaps seared yellowfin tuna in Cajun spices with sour cream and chive dressing, and a lemon and lime charlotte finale.

Chef Glynn Pennington **Owner** Dee & Glynn Pennington
Times 12-2/7-8, Closed Jan, Closed Mon **Prices** Fixed D 4 course £36-£39.75, Service included **Wines** 8 bottles over £20, 6 bottles under £20, 4 by glass **Notes** Vegetarian available, Dress restrictions, Smart casual **Seats** 24 **Children** Min 12 yrs, Portions **Parking** 7

HOWTOWN · Map 18 NY41

Sharrow Bay Country House Hotel

British, International V

Country-house dining in a beautiful Lakeland setting

☎ 017684 86301
Sharrow Bay CA10 2LZ
e-mail: info@sharrowbay.co.uk
dir: M6 junct 40. From Pooley Bridge fork right by church towards Howtown. At x-rds turn right and follow lakeside road for 2m

Often described as the first country-house hotel, Sharrow Bay is idyllically located on the shores of Lake Ullswater amid its own extensive grounds. Opulently furnished public areas, brimful with antiques, soft furnishings and fresh flowers, include a choice of lounges and two dining rooms. The kitchen takes up the theme with classic country-house cooking, exemplified by dressed crab, sautéed scallop and rosette of local smoked salmon to start, followed by lamb rolled in a fresh herb brioche crust and served with pea purée, dauphinoise potato and tomato and rosemary sauce. Desserts include a honey pannacotta with spicy fruits stewed in rum. Gourmet wine dinners are a regular feature.

Chef Colin Akrigg, Mark Teasdale **Owner** Sharrow Bay Hotels Ltd **Times** 1/8 **Wines** 708 bottles over £20, 38 bottles under £20, 19 by glass **Notes** Fixed L 5 courses fr £39.50, Fixed D 6 courses fr £55, Sunday L, Vegetarian menu, Dress restrictions, Smart casual, Civ Wed 35, Air con **Seats** 55, Pr/dining room 40 **Children** Min 13 yrs **Parking** 30

IREBY · Map 18 NY23

Overwater Hall

Modern British

☎ 017687 76566
CA7 1HH
e-mail: welcome@overwaterhall.co.uk

This establishment was awarded its Rosette/s just as we went to press. Therefore we are unable to provide a description for it - visit www.theAA.com for the most up-to-date information.

Times 7–8.30 **Prices** Food prices not confirmed for 2009. Please telephone for details. **Seats** 30

KENDAL · Map 18 SD59

Best Western Castle Green Hotel in Kendal

Modern British, European

Modern restaurant with the kitchen on view

☎ 01539 734000
Castle Green Ln LA9 6BH
e-mail: reception@castlegreen.co.uk
web: www.castlegreen.co.uk
dir: From Kendal High St, take A684 towards Sedbergh, hotel is last on left leaving Kendal

Enjoying stunning views over the fells and castle ruins, this smart, modern hotel offers a relaxed stay in a peaceful Lakeland setting, while also being conveniently situated for both the town centre and M6. The bright-and-airy Greenhouse restaurant is decorated in muted shades that provide a perfect foil for the dramatic scenery outside the large plate-glass windows. By night, candlelight and stars create a warm, intimate atmosphere, complemented by friendly and unhurried service. The ambitious cooking is showcased on the modern British menu, using local produce wherever possible. Daily specials complement the good-value carte, offering starters like succulent scallops with maple pork belly, spiced onion purée and pickled apples, followed by an impressive tasting of Cumbrian lamb with roast loin and confit shoulder, baked goats' cheese, basil and roast garlic mash. Finish with baked custard, damson relish and bay leaf ice cream. Diners can watch the chefs at work through a window into the state-of-the art theatre kitchen.

Chef Justin Woods **Owner** James & Catherine Alexander **Times** 12-2/6-10 **Wines** 23 bottles over £20, 27 bottles under £20, 12 by glass **Notes** ALC £23.95 2 courses, £27.95 3 courses, Vegetarian available, Dress restrictions, Smart casual, Civ Wed 100, Air con **Seats** 80, Pr/dining room 200 **Children** Portions, Menu **Parking** 200

KESWICK · Map 18 NY22

Dale Head Hall Lakeside Hotel

Modern British

Country house dining in a beautiful location

☎ 017687 72478
Lake Thirlmere CA12 4TN
e-mail: onthelakeside@daleheadhall.co.uk
dir: 5m from Keswick on A591

Set in attractive grounds on the shores of Lake Thirlmere with Helvellyn as a backdrop, this lakeside residence dates from the 16th century. Inviting public areas include a choice of lounges and an atmospheric beamed restaurant. The menu changes daily, two dishes at each of four courses. A typical selection might include country-style pork terrine wrapped in Parma ham served with raisin dressing, and pan-fried fillet of Borrowdale trout with hongroise potatoes and prawn paella sauce. Choose between cheese or dessert to finish (maybe treacle and pecan tart with nutmeg cream).

Times Closed Jan

Highfield Hotel & Restaurant

Modern European

Ambitious cooking in friendly Lakeland hotel with marvellous views

☎ 017687 72508
The Heads CA12 5ER
e-mail: info@highfieldkeswick.co.uk
dir: M6 junct 40, follow signs for Keswick, approaching Keswick, ignore first sign. Continue on A66, at Peach rdbt turn left. At next T-junct turn left, and continue to mini-rdbt and take right exit then third right onto The Heads

This lovely country-house hotel has won plaudits for both its food and stunning Lakeland views. Built at the end of the nineteenth century, it still retains many original features, including turrets, bay windows and a veranda, and is handily located just a few minutes' walk from the centre of Keswick, not far from the town's famous 'Theatre by the Lake'. But while traditional may sum up the setting, the cooking takes a modern approach - classical in style but with contemporary twists. The imaginative, daily-changing, dinner-only menu comes peppered with quality Cumbrian produce in the form of roast fillet of Cumbrian beef with colcannon potato, sautéed wild mushrooms and bay leaf jus, or pan-seared collop of Cumbrian-farmed venison with a pot-roast of root vegetables.

Chef Gus Cleghorn **Owner** Howard & Caroline Speck **Times** Closed Jan-Early Feb, Closed L all week **Prices** Fixed D 4 course £37.50-£42, Service optional **Wines** 22 bottles over £20, 41 bottles under £20, 7 by glass **Notes** Vegetarian available, Dress restrictions, Smart casual, Air con **Seats** 40 **Children** Min 8 yrs, Portions **Parking** 23

KESWICK *Continued*

Lyzzick Hall Country House Hotel

◉ European

Quality cooking accompanied by Lakeland views

☎ 017687 72277
Under Skiddaw CA12 4PY
e-mail: info@lyzzickhall.co.uk
dir: Leave Keswick towards Carlisle, at main rdbt take 2nd exit signed A591 Carlisle, Lyzzick Hall 1.5m on right

Perched in the foothills of Skiddaw overlooking Keswick, this cosy Lakeland hotel boasts beautiful views all year round. The restaurant has a classical décor with quality table settings and fresh flowers. Nothing is too much trouble for its friendly staff, while the kitchen team conjure a menu of accomplished fare from the finest ingredients Cumbria has to offer. Dishes are modern British in style, and feature the odd nod to the Mediterranean and beyond - you might start with spinach and white butterbean soup perhaps, and move on to baked cod fillet wrapped in Lakeland pancetta served with buttered leeks and saffron and chive sauce.

Times 12-2/7-9, Closed Jan

Swinside Lodge

◉◉ British, European V ☺

Delightful country house with indulgent food and friendly service

☎ 017687 72948
Grange Rd, Newlands CA12 5UE
e-mail: info@swinsidelodge-hotel.co.uk
web: www.swinsidelodge.com
dir: M6 junct 40 take A66 to Cockermouth, ignore exits to Keswick, next left to Portinscale. Follow country road for 2m (do not leave this road). Hotel on right

No visit to the Lake District is complete without a stay at this delightful Georgian country house, just five minutes' stroll from the shores of Derwentwater. The intimate dining room is decked out in red with fresh flowers, candles and clothed tables. Take your seat for a four-course, dinner-only menu of modern British dishes that make the most of quality produce from local farmers and the kitchen garden. The daily-changing set menu lets you know you're in safe hands; the cooking here is creative, skilful and great value for money. Kick off with warm terrine of Cumbrian lamb with spices, mint and pistachio nuts, and then tuck into roast breast of Swinside pheasant wrapped in cured ham, butternut squash, caramelised apple and red wine jus.

Chef Clive Imber **Owner** Eric & Irene Fell **Times** Closed 25 Dec, Closed L all wk **Prices** Fixed D 4 course £40, Service optional **Wines** 10 bottles over £20, 8 bottles under £20,

4 by glass **Notes** Vegetarian menu **Seats** 18 **Children** Min 12 yrs, Portions **Parking** 12

Hipping Hall

◉◉◉ – *see below*

The Sun Inn

◉ Modern British ☺

17th-century inn with contemporary restaurant in historic market town

☎ 015242 71965
6 Market St LA6 2AU
e-mail: email@sun-inn.info
web: www.sun-inn.info
dir: M6 junct 36 onto A65 to Kirkby Lonsdale. Take 1st turning to Kirkby Lonsdale, straight ahead at junct Sun Inn at bottom of hill

Backing on to St Mary's churchyard and overlooking the church in this ancient little market town, the tastefully refurbished Sun Inn oozes 17th-century charm and character. Quaff local ales and decent wines by the log fire in the beamed and wood-floored bar before tucking into some hearty modern British dishes in the surprisingly contemporary rear dining room, decorated with colourful local artwork. With an emphasis on using quality local

Hipping Hall

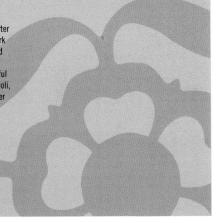

British

Accomplished cooking in Tudor splendour

☎ 015242 71187
Cowan Bridge LA6 2JJ
e-mail: info@hippinghall.com
dir: 8.5m E of M6 J36 on A65

Steeped in history, wisteria-clad Hipping Hall is a four-square 17th-century house with its dining room in a 15th-century banqueting hall, where high-vaulted ceilings with oak beams from old ships, tapestries and a minstrels' gallery make for an atmospheric backdrop to the classy cooking. And it is all set in landscaped parkland surrounded by beautiful English countryside. The building has been restored with care and attention to detail and the furnishings are a mix of old and new - it

cuts quite a dash. Good use is made of local produce - especially the high quality meats - in a menu of modern and creative dishes. Attention to detail is evident from the amuse-bouche to the petits fours, and flavour and balance are given due consideration throughout. A starter of confit belly of Kitridding Gloucestershire Old Spot pork comes with roasted langoustine and a fennel purée and is topped with a langoustine-flavoured foam, while main-course saddle of Holker Hall venison has wonderful flavour in a well balanced dish with black pudding ravioli, parsnip purée, creamed cabbage, beetroot and a juniper jus.

Times Closed 24 Dec-10 Jan, Closed Mon-Tue

ingredients, the menu takes in slow-roast duck leg with apple purée and red wine syrup, or seafood chowder to start, followed by roast rump and confit shoulder of lamb with mint sauce, and baked chocolate and orange cheesecake for dessert. Service is friendly and professional.

Chef Sam Carter **Owner** Lucy & Mark Fuller **Times** 12-2.3/7-9 **Prices** Starter £3.95-£7.95, Main £9.95-£22.50, Dessert £4.50, Service optional **Wines** 7 bottles over £20, 22 bottles under £20, 7 by glass **Notes** Sunday L **Seats** 34 **Children** Portions, Menu **Parking** On street & nearby car park

---

NEAR SAWREY   Map 18 SD39

Ees Wyke Country House

⚜ British, French

Glorious country-house setting for fine local fare

☎ 015394 36393
LA22 0JZ
e-mail: mail@eeswyke.co.uk
dir: On B5285 between Hawkshead and the Windermere Ferry

A former holiday home of Beatrix Potter, this Georgian country house nestles into the hillside, offering stunning views over Esthwaite Water and the surrounding countryside. Cosy day rooms are warmed by log fires in the colder months, and period features have been preserved in the spacious dining room, which looks towards the lake. British dishes with European influences feature on an interesting and varied menu, including noisettes of local lamb with wine jus, mint and garlic, or salmon baked in puff pastry with mint, cucumber and shallot stuffing, and a creamy saffron sauce.

Chef Richard Lee **Owner** Richard & Margaret Lee **Prices** Food prices not confirmed for 2009. Please telephone for details. **Wines** 29 bottles over £20, 36 bottles under £20, 5 by glass **Notes** Fixed D 5 courses **Seats** 16 **Children** Min 12 yrs **Parking** 12

NEWBY BRIDGE   Map 18 SD38

Lakeside Hotel

⚜⚜ Modern British

Relaxed, traditional hotel dining in picturesque Lakeland shore setting

☎ 015395 30001
Lakeside, Lake Windermere LA12 8AT
e-mail: sales@lakesidehotel.co.uk
dir: M6 junct 36 follow A590 to Newby Bridge, straight over rdbt, right over bridge. Hotel within 1m

Set on the peaceful southern shore of Lake Windermere, this is an impressive, family-run hotel where guests and diners can expect high standards of service. Dinner is served in the elegant, oak-panelled Lakeview restaurant, with its fresh flowers, floor-length tablecloths and sparkling glassware, but more informal meals can be enjoyed in the contemporary John Ruskin's brasserie. Cooking is accomplished, with traditional British and European dishes prepared and presented with flair and expertise - classical dishes with a modern twist. Take seared scallops with prune purée and citrus velouté, followed by Cumbrian beef fillet with fondant potato and red wine jus, and to finish, perhaps a lavender crème caramel with honey ice cream. Staff are professional and highly skilled.

Chef Richard Booth **Owner** Mr N Talbot **Times** 12.30-2.30/6.45-9.30, Closed 23 Dec-10 Jan **Prices** Food prices not confirmed for 2009. Please telephone for details. **Wines** 190 bottles over £20, 15

bottles under £20, 12 by glass **Notes** Dress restrictions, Smart casual, no jeans, Civ Wed 80, Air con **Seats** 70, Pr/dining room 30 **Children** Portions, Menu **Parking** 200

Roland

⚜ Modern British

Stylish modern restaurant in idyllic riverside location

☎ 015395 31681
Swan Hotel LA12 8NB
e-mail: enquiries@swanhotel.com
dir: M6 junct 36, at rdbt take 1st exit. A590 to Barrow for approx 16m, then follow signs for Newby Bridge

Set beside the river Leven at the southern end of Lake Windermere, this 17th-century coaching inn boasts a choice of dining areas. The restaurant area is split over two floors. The more formal option is the completely refurbished, modern-styled restaurant called Roland, where the vaulted ceiling, painted white beams, exposed stone work and funky décor give it a loft-style feel. Here diners can expect attentive service and well-presented, modern British dishes. Starters include pressing of hock ham and black pudding, herb salad and mustard dressing, followed by seared Goosnargh duck breast, celeriac purée and caramelised pear. Desserts include iced banana parfait with butterscotch sauce. The informal River Room on the ground floor serves pizzas and pasta.

Times 12-2.30/7-10, Closed D Sun
See advert below

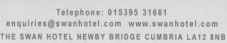

Edenhall Country Hotel

◉ Modern British

Formal dining in a friendly village hotel

☎ 01768 881454
Edenhall CA11 8SX
e-mail: info@edenhallhotel.co.uk
dir: M6 junct 40, take A66 towards Scotch Corner. At rdbt follow signs to Alston (A686). Edenhall is 3m on right

A cosy retreat, popular with fishermen from the nearby River Eden and walkers from the Lakes, Edenhall is set in its own pretty grounds. The large, attractive dining room is blessed with huge windows and overlooks the garden and surrounding countryside. The modern menu is inspired by the best of Cumbrian produce. Start with grilled fillet of smoked mackerel, served with plum tomato stew and drizzled with pesto dressing, followed by roast rump of Lakeland lamb with roasted thyme vegetables and redcurrant and thyme jus. Finish with traditional sticky toffee pudding with home-made vanilla ice cream and butterscotch sauce.

Chef Steve Kerr, Adam Cartwright **Owner** Wayne Williams & Paula Williams **Times** Closed L all week (bar meals only) **Prices** Food prices not confirmed for 2009. Please telephone for details. **Wines** 3 bottles over £20, 22 bottles under £20, 4 by glass **Notes** Civ Wed 60 **Seats** 60, Pr/dining room 25 **Children** Portions, Menu **Parking** 60

The Martindale Restaurant

◉ Traditional British

Fine regional ingredients at modern hunting lodge-style hotel

☎ 01768 868111
North Lakes Hotel & Spa, Ullswater Rd CA11 8QT
e-mail: nlakes@shirehotels.com
dir: M6 just off junct 40

Striking interior design, featuring timber beams, traditional Lakeland stone, wooden floors and impressive fireplaces, catches the eye at this contemporary hunting lodge-styled hotel with excellent leisure facilities. The Martindale Restaurant is where the main dining action takes place, the accomplished kitchen's straightforward, ingredient-led approach making fine use of quality local produce. The Cumbrian starter table (buffet selection of hors d'oeuvre) proves a highlight, while mains might feature slow-cooked Stainton belly pork and confit of duck, with Bramley apple mash, Savoy cabbage and cider sauce, and traditional-style desserts could include the ubiquitous sticky toffee pudding.

Times 12.15-1.45/7-9.15, Closed L Sat, Sun

The Pennington Hotel

◉ British

Great British food by the sea

☎ 01229 717222 & 717626
CA18 1SD

A converted 16th-century coaching house, The Pennington is a charming beachfront hotel in the village of Ravenglass. The restaurant is a light-and-airy space with blue- and cream-coloured chairs and décor and attractive flower displays. The cooking style is hearty, so tuck into a starter of cognac crêpes filled with fresh crab, lemon and dill mayonnaise, served with a chilli cucumber salad, followed by a main course of locally sourced rack of lamb with a garlic and Marsala jus on a bed of sautéed fine beans with dauphinoise potatoes. Finish with an excellent selection of local cheeses.

Times 12-2.30/7-9

Cumbrian Lodge

◉ British, Mediterranean ⊗

Homely restaurant with wonderful speciality dishes

☎ 019467 27309
Gosforth Rd CA20 1JG
e-mail: cumbrianlodge@btconnect.com
dir: From A595 onto B5344, hotel on left after 2m

Expect a relaxing, contemporary interior design at this sensitively refurbished building, built in 1874 and now a stylish restaurant with rooms. The comfortable dining room sports a modern, minimalist décor, with modern art lining the walls and crisp linen-clothed tables, and offers a quality bistro-style menu listing a mix of traditional British dishes with European and Asian influences. Take moules marinière, Thai-style chicken and the house speciality Geschnetzeltes Schweinefleisch - thinly sliced pork fillet sautéed in butter, wine and cream. On warm summer evenings dine alfresco in one of the impressive new thatched garden buildings.

Chef R Hickson & A Carnall **Owner** David J Morgan **Times** 12-2/6.30-9.30, Closed Xmas, New Year, BHs, Closed Sun, Closed L Mon & Sat **Prices** Starter £5.95, Main £11.95-£18.95, Dessert £4.95-£6.95, Service optional **Wines** 17 bottles over £20, 19 bottles under £20, 15 by glass **Notes** Vegetarian available **Seats** 32 **Parking** 17

Westmorland Hotel & Restaurant

◉ Modern British

Friendly modern hotel overlooking rugged moorland

☎ 015396 24351
Near Orton CA10 3SB
e-mail: reservations@westmorlandhotel.com
web: www.westmorlandhotel.com
dir: Accessed from the Westmorland Motorway Services M6 between junct 38 & 39, N & S bound

This modern hotel has picture-postcard views of the Howgill fells and uses natural materials - wood and stone - to reflect its setting. The split-level Bretherdale restaurant offers a scenic outlook and there's a cascading water feature right outside. The kitchen has close ties with the local farming community; lamb and beef come from the hotel's own farm three miles away, and a farm shop is part of the complex. Imaginative modern cooking delivers the likes of slow-roasted partridge leg and smoked duck, farm's seared lamb's liver, and twice-baked Blengale Blue cheese soufflé.

Chef Bryan Parsons **Owner** Westmorland Ltd **Prices** Starter £4.95-£5.95, Main £12.95-£18.50, Service optional **Wines** 4 bottles over £20, 32 bottles under £20, 8 by glass **Notes** Set menus can be provided for pre-booked groups, Vegetarian available, Dress restrictions, Smart casual, No jeans or T-shirts, Civ Wed 120, Air con **Seats** 100, Pr/dining room 40 **Children** Portions, Menu **Parking** 60

Temple Sowerby House Hotel & Restaurant

◉◉ Modern British ⊗

Intimate setting for ambitious cooking

☎ 017683 61578
CA10 1RZ
e-mail: stay@templesowerby.com
web: www.templesowerby.com
dir: M6, junct 40 travel E on A66, take 1st exit off Temple Sowerby bypass & follow signs for hotel. Situated centre of village opposite green

A peaceful haven in the heart of the Eden Valley, this Grade II listed country-house hotel makes a great touring base for the northern Lake District. Its bright and pretty restaurant has large picture windows that overlook a lovely walled garden that provides many of the herbs, fruit and vegetables you'll find on your plate. Expect innovative techniques and a bold mix of modern British and classic French cooking. Using the best of local produce, butter-roasted fillet of pork with a caramelised apple, cider velouté and beetroot dauphinoise, or feather beef slow-cooked in red wine and served with creamed potato and celeriac are fine examples of the fare. In fine weather, the terrace is a splendid spot for pre-dinner drinks.

Chef Ashley Whittaker **Owner** Paul & Julie Evans
Times Closed 8 days Xmas, Closed L all wk **Prices** Starter
£6.50-£8.25, Main £15.95-£19.95, Dessert £6.50-£7.95,
Service optional **Wines** 30 bottles over £20, 10 bottles
under £20, 7 by glass **Notes** Vegetarian available, Dress
restrictions, Smart casual preferred, Civ Wed 40
Seats 24, Pr/dining room 24 **Children** Min 12 yrs
Parking 20

WATERMILLOCK	Map 18 NY42

Macdonald Leeming House

🌸🌸🌸 — *see below*

Rampsbeck Country House Hotel

🌸🌸🌸 — *see page 104*

— *see page 104*

WINDERMERE	Map 18 SD49

Best Western Burn How Garden House Hotel

🌸 Modern British

Formal dining overlooking pretty gardens

☎ 015394 46226
Back Belsfield Rd, Bowness LA23 3HH
e-mail: info@burnhow.co.uk
dir: 7m from M6. Follow A590 to A591 (Windermere to Bowness)

This delightful Victorian hotel is set in leafy grounds, just a few minutes' walk from Lake Windermere and the centre of Bowness. Its airy restaurant is a genteel affair with polished wooden tables and large windows overlooking the gardens. Take a seat and choose from a menu of hearty British fare with the odd nod to further-flung climes. Starters might include a feta, basil and tomato tart with wild rocket and balsamic reduction, while mains are along the lines of baked cod in pancetta with asparagus and ratatouille, or turkey escalope on a bed of potato rösti with a rosemary sauce.

Chef Jane Kimani **Owner** Michael Robinson **Times** Closed Xmas, Closed L all wk **Prices** Food prices not confirmed for 2009. Please telephone for details. **Seats** 40 **Children** Min 5 yrs, Portions, Menu **Parking** 28

Burlington's Restaurant

🌸🌸 British, French 💻 🍴

Fine dining in a stylish lakeside setting

☎ 015394 42137
The Beech Hill Hotel, Newby Bridge Rd LA23 3LR
e-mail: reservations@beechhillhotel.co.uk
web: www.beechhillhotel.co.uk
dir: M6 junct 36, take A591 to Windermere, left onto A592 to Newby Bridge, hotel 4m on right

This stylish terraced hotel boasts breathtaking views over Lake Windermere that are hard to resist. The dining room's oak panelling and rich furnishings also make an elegant statement. Take drinks on the terrace in fine weather or by the log fire in the lounge in cooler months, then order from the popular Simple Taste of the Lakes or five-course Gourmet menu. The skilfully cooked and presented modern dishes make full use of fresh

Continued

Macdonald Leeming House

WATERMILLOCK	Map 18 NY42

Modern British

A taste of Cumbria in sumptuous country house with a view

☎ 0870 4008131
CA11 0JJ
e-mail: leeminghouse@macdonald-hotels.co.uk
dir: M6 junct 40, continue on A66 signed Keswick. At rdbt follow A592 towards Ullswater, at T-junct turn right, hotel 3m on left

Set in a stunning location amid 20 acres of landscaped grounds and mature woodland on the shores of Ullswater, the hotel dates from the 1800s and retains many original features. Beautiful views over the lake and its backdrop of rugged mountain fells enhance the ornate but informal surroundings in the Regency-style restaurant. Well

presented classical dishes are given a modern, lighter twist, revealing imagination and flair, all driven by the best seasonal Cumbrian produce and an intelligent simplicity that allows flavours to shine. Think a ham hock and foie gras terrine served with sautéed langoustine, apple and mache salad, perhaps followed by fillets of wild brill teamed with a morel risotto, salsify, chicken wings and white asparagus, while a coffee pannacotta 'foam' served with hazelnut cristaliant, poached pears and mascarpone ice cream might catch the eye at dessert. Ancillaries like amuse-bouche, bread, pre-dessert and petits fours continue the upbeat form, while three sumptuous lounges, a cosy bar and library complete the pampering.

Times 12-2/6.30-9

Rampsbeck Country House Hotel

WATERMILLOCK Map 18 NY42

Modern British, French

Innovative modern cooking in lakeside hotel

☎ 017684 86442
CA11 0LP
e-mail: enquiries@rampsbeck.co.uk
web: www.rampsbeck.co.uk
dir: M6 junct 40, A592 to Ullswater, T-junct turn right at lake's edge. Hotel 1.25m

This elegant 18th-century country house stands in 18 acres of parkland and gardens on the shores of Lake Ullswater, enjoying spectacular views over the Lake and Fells. With its extensive lake frontage it is rightly regarded as one of the most beautifully situated hotels in England, and boasts many original features - including marble fireplaces and ornate ceilings - as well as period and antique pieces. There are three delightful and comfortable lounges plus a small traditional bar (that opens out on to a terrace on warm summer days), as well as the newly refurbished restaurant decked out in neutral shades with red floral silk panels creating a dramatic effect. Its large windows make the best of those views, while tables are well spaced and service nicely traditional, though appropriately friendly and attentive. The modern British and French cooking proves a real highlight thanks to the kitchen's

innovative, modern approach, using fresh, top-quality produce in thoughtful, well-judged combinations. Expect clean flavours and interesting textures in complex dishes like pan-fried turbot with langoustine tortellini and cider emulsion, or braised belly pork with oxtail ravioli, puréed potatoes and braising jus, while hot plum soufflé with nutmeg ice cream might feature at dessert.

Chef Andrew McGeorge
Owner Blackshaw Hotels Ltd
Times 12-1.15/7-8.30, Closed 5 Jan-9 Feb, L booking only **Prices** Fixed L 2 course £20-£25, Fixed D 3 course £43, Service optional **Wines** 44 bottles over £20, 59 bottles under £20, 6 by glass **Notes** Sunday L, Vegetarian available, Dress restrictions, Smart casual, no jeans or shorts, Civ Wed 65 **Seats** 40, Pr/dining room 15 **Children** Min 7 yrs, Portions **Parking** 30

WINDERMERE *Continued*

Cumbrian produce. Start with terrine of ham shank, black pudding and Longridge corn-fed chicken, followed by tasting of Barley Bridge lamb, cutlet and kidney, salsa verde and lamb jus, or fillet of fell-bred beef with horseradish béarnaise.

Chef Christopher Davies **Owner** Mr & Mrs E K Richardson **Times** Closed L all week **Prices** Fixed D 3 course £25-£35, Service optional **Wines** 11 bottles over £20, 29 bottles under £20, 11 by glass **Notes** Dress restrictions, Smart casual, no denim or trainers, Civ Wed 130 **Seats** 130, Pr/dining room 90 **Children** Portions, Menu **Parking** 60

Cedar Manor Hotel & Restaurant

◉ Modern British

Charming country retreat for relaxed atmosphere and dining

☎ 015394 43192 & 015394 445970
Ambleside Rd LA23 1AX
e-mail: info@cedarmanor.co.uk
web: www.cedarmanor.co.uk
dir: A591 to Windermere, hotel is located on main road next to St Mary's church

Built in 1854 as a gentleman's residence and set in a peaceful location, this Gothic-style manor house retains many period features and takes its name from a 200-year-old Indian cedar tree in the mature garden. The restaurant is cosy and romantic in a modern country-house style with white linen, crystal glassware and silver cutlery. As much locally sourced produce as possible is used in classic British dishes with a hint of European influence, such as chicken liver and Madeira parfait, calves' liver with creamed potatoes, curly kale, beer-battered onion rings and crispy pancetta, and chocolate and almond brownie dessert with Cointreau-poached clementine.

Chef Alan Dalton **Owner** Caroline & Jonathan Kaye **Times** Closed 6-25 Jan, Closed L all week **Prices** Fixed D 3 course £24.95-£29.95, Starter £4.95-£8.95, Main £11.95-£19.95, Dessert £5.25-£7.25, Service optional **Wines** 4 bottles over £20, 14 bottles under £20, 4 by glass **Notes** Vegetarian available, Dress restrictions, Smart casual, no mountain wear **Seats** 22 **Children** Portions **Parking** 12

Fayrer Garden Hotel

◉◉ Modern British, Traditional

Country-house dining with lake views

☎ 015394 88195
Lyth Valley Rd, Bowness on Windermere LA23 3JP
e-mail: lakescene@fayrergarden.com
dir: M6 junct 36, onto A591. Past Kendal, at rdbt turn left onto B5284 (signposted Crook Bowness & Ferry) and continue for 8m, then turn left onto A5074 for 400yds

Sitting in 5 acres of gardens and grounds in the heart of the Lake District, this elegant hotel enjoys panoramic lake views. Originally an Edwardian gentleman's residence, today it still retains the feel of a private country house with stylish lounges, sumptuous fabrics and drapes, a relaxed atmosphere, and an air of understated luxury. The lounges and bar have recently been refurbished to give a more contemporary feel, while the Terrace Restaurant is decked out in opulent blue wallpaper complemented by well-appointed tables and stylish seating. Generously priced, five-course, daily-changing menus use local, seasonal ingredients that keep locals and visitors returning. The traditional British approach comes with a few modern twists. Take chicken liver parfait with fruit chutney, Melba toast and Cumberland sauce, and breast of guinea fowl with a tart of woodland mushrooms and cep velouté.

Times Closed 1st 2wks Jan, Closed L all week

Gilpin Lodge Country House Hotel & Restaurant

◉◉◉ *– see page 106*

Holbeck Ghyll Country House Hotel

◉◉◉ *– see page 107*

Langdale Chase Hotel

◉ European

Enjoyable dining with stunning lakeside views

☎ 015394 32201
Langdale Chase LA23 1LW
e-mail: sales@langdalechase.co.uk
dir: 2m S of Ambleside & 3m N of Windermere

With its unrivalled views of Lake Windermere, this late Victorian mansion has plenty to please the discerning guest, including splendid terraced gardens leading down to the lake and oak-panelled public areas with carved fireplaces. (The BBC filmed here for a couple of episodes of Poirot.) Picture windows in the dining room take full advantage of stunning westerly views to the distant fells. Here, an interesting daily fixed-price menu is offered at lunch and dinner and may include confit of duckling to start, followed by fennel-rubbed organic pork, with the Langdale Chase hot chocolate gâteau to finish.

Chef Daniel Hopkins **Owner** Mr TG Noblett **Times** 12-2/7-9 **Prices** Fixed L 2 course £15, Fixed D 3 course £29, Starter £3.95-£10, Main £9.95-£20, Dessert £3.95-£10, Service optional **Wines** 24 bottles over £20, 14 bottles under £20, 7 by glass **Notes** Sunday L, Dress restrictions, Smart casual, Civ Wed 120, Air con **Seats** 80, Pr/dining room 36 **Children** Portions, Menu **Parking** 60

Lindeth Fell Country House Hotel

◉ Modern British ✤

Enjoyable dining in a tranquil haven in the Lakes

☎ 015394 43286 & 44287
Lyth Valley Rd, Bowness-on-Windermere LA23 3JP
e-mail: kennedy@lindethfell.co.uk
dir: 1m S of Bowness-on-Windermere on A5074

This elegant, family-run Edwardian country-house hotel, complete with log fires and oak panelling, is perched on the wooded slopes above Windermere in 7 acres of gardens full of colourful rhododendrons and azaleas. There are three interconnecting dining rooms, one the original with period features and two more modern rooms with large windows taking advantage of the views. A traditional dinner menu with canapés is served, showcasing Cumbrian produce in dishes like Flookburgh brown shrimps with home-made brioche bun, followed by medallions of Cartmel venison with Lyth Valley damson sauce; and Westmoreland tart with Cumberland rum butter to finish.

Chef Philip Taylor, Harry Coates **Owner** Pat & Diana Kennedy **Times** 12.30-1.45/7.30-9, Closed 3 wks in Jan **Wines** 41 bottles over £20, 47 bottles under £20, 5 by glass **Notes** Fixed D 5 courses £33, Sunday L, Vegetarian available, Dress restrictions, Smart casual preferred, Air con **Seats** 50, Pr/dining room 30 **Children** Min 7 yrs D, Portions, Menu **Parking** 20

Gilpin Lodge Country House Hotel & Restaurant

WINDERMERE Map 18 SD49

Modern British V NOTABLE WINE LIST

Elegant restaurant with food to match

☎ 015394 88818
Crook Rd LA23 3NE
e-mail: hotel@gilpinlodge.co.uk
web: www.gilpinlodge.co.uk
dir: M6 junct 36 & A590, then B5284 for 5m

Built in 1901, this luxurious family-run hotel is situated in the beautiful rural setting of the Lake District. Set in 20 acres of woodland, moors and award-winning gardens, it has a relaxed, friendly atmosphere redolent of an elegant private country house. Each of the 14 bedrooms is immaculately decorated in chic contemporary style, and an ongoing programme of refurbishment has seen the addition of an extension to the lounge encompassing a champagne bar and walk-in wine cellars, as well as additional terraces and patio areas. Dinner - the highlight of any stay - is served in four intimate dining rooms, at tables elegantly dressed with fresh flowers, gleaming silver and crisp white linen. The modern British food is bold, imaginative, and technically daring, yet firmly rooted in classical cuisine. Gilpin Lodge consistently impresses, handling the best and freshest of local ingredients with deft simplicity to ensure intense flavours on the plate.

Expect an imaginative selection of dishes, as in roasted hand-dived scallops with crispy pork belly, apple salad and five-spice sauce, or South Coast turbot lightly poached in red wine with creamed leeks and crispy vegetables. Round things off in style with carpaccio of black figs with orange and pepper powder, aged balsamic ice cream and a spiced cake.

Chef Chris Meredith **Owner** The Cunliffe Family **Times** 12-2/6.45-9 **Wines** 230 bottles over £20, 1 bottle under £20, 14 by glass **Notes** Fixed D 5 courses £47, Tasting menu with wine, Sunday L, Vegetarian menu, Dress restrictions, Smart Casual **Seats** 60, Pr/dining room 20 **Children** Min 7 yrs **Parking** 40

Holbeck Ghyll Country House Hotel

WINDERMERE   Map 18 SD49

Modern British V   ◊ NOTABLE WINE LIST

Classical cuisine in former hunting lodge

☎ 015394 32375
Holbeck Ln LA23 1LU
e-mail: stay@holbeckghyll.com
dir: 3m N of Windermere on A591. Past Brockhole Visitor Centre. Turn right into Holbeck Lane. Hotel is 0.5m on left

Built in the 19th century as a hunting lodge and set in pretty gardens on a hillside above Lake Windermere, breathtaking views over the Lake and the Langdale Fells are just two of the many attractions of this sumptuous hotel and restaurant. The rooms come appropriately decorated in luxurious country-house style with deep sofas and antiques, while a brace of elegant, classically-styled dining rooms (one oak-panelled, the other with French doors leading on to the terrace) take full advantage of the scenery. The terrace provides opportunities for alfresco drinks, lunches or early evening meals on warm summer days. The professionalism and attentiveness of the staff are exemplary, and the kitchen's modern approach is underpinned by a classical theme, in harmony with the surroundings, delivering a repertoire of fixed-price, compact menus (bolstered by a gourmet option on Fridays and Saturdays) that

aren't short on appeal or imagination. An intelligent simplicity allows the high quality produce to shine in well presented, clear-flavoured dishes; take roasted wild turbot served with crisp boneless oxtail and beetroot foam, while to finish, maybe a millefeuille of rhubarb, oat and vanilla. An extensive wine list, with a good range of half bottles, and a fine selection of cheeses make this a class act.

Chef David McLaughlin **Owner** David & Patricia Nicholson
Times 12.30-2/7-9.30 **Wines** 264 bottles over £20, 19 bottles under £20, 14 by glass **Notes** Gourmet menu £70, Sunday L, Vegetarian menu, Dress restrictions, Smart casual, No jeans or T-shirts, Civ Wed 65 **Seats** 50, Pr/dining room 20 **Children** Min 8 yrs, Portions, Menu **Parking** 34

WINDERMERE *Continued*

Lindeth Howe Country House Hotel

◉◉ Modern British

Accomplished food in the former home of a famous author

☎ 015394 45759
Lindeth Dr, Longtail Hill LA23 3JF
e-mail: hotel@lindeth-howe.co.uk
web: www.lindeth-howe.co.uk
dir: 1m S of Bowness onto B5284, signed Kendal and Lancaster. Hotel 2nd driveway on right

The views from this charming country-house hotel set on a wooded hillside are across the valley to Lake Windermere and the distant fells: a perfect Lake District vista. The house is a former family home of Beatrix Potter, which enhances further its status within the region. The bright, conservatory-style restaurant overlooks the secluded gardens and provides a traditional setting in which to enjoy well-presented modern cooking. Dinner is a traditional five-course affair starting with canapés and aperitifs in the lounge or on the terrace while perusing the menu. Locally-reared ham hock and foie gras terrine is a well executed starter with apple and celeriac salad, toasted brioche and hazelnut vinaigrette demonstrating the ambition and skill in the kitchen. Main-course loin of Holker Hall venison is tender and full of flavour and comes with red cabbage marmalade, roasted root vegetables and a red wine jus.

Times 12-2.30/7-9

Linthwaite House Hotel

◉◉ Modern British 🖳 V 🐾

Modern cooking in stunning Lakeland setting

☎ 015394 88600
Crook Rd LA23 3JA
e-mail: stay@linthwaite.com
web: www.linthwaite.com
dir: Take 1st left off A591 at rdbt NW of Kendal (B5284). Follow for 6m, hotel is 1m after Windermere Golf Club on left

The setting on a hillside amongst 14 acres of gardens and woods with spectacular views over Lake Windermere and the hills and crags beyond is second to none. The house itself, built in 1901, is an elegant creeper-covered country house, positioned to make the best of the views from inside and out, including from the weather-defying conservatory. The décor is a refined combination of period chic with a clean, modern colour scheme and plenty of natural light flooding the dining room. The new chef's menus show modern British sensibilities, with the focus on local produce, and plenty of appealing ideas and interesting flavour combinations. Start with roasted cod cheek in a contemporary partnership with fellbred oxtail, Puy lentils and shimeji mushrooms before main-course slow-braised fellbred feather beef with onion tarte Tatin, calves' sweetbreads and truffle jus.

Chef Paul Peters **Owner** Mike Bevans **Times** 12.30-2/7-9.30, Closed Xmas (ex residents) **Prices** Fixed L 2 course £14.95, Fixed D 4 course £50, Service optional **Wines** 100 bottles over £20, 10 bottles under £20, 13 by glass **Notes** Sunday L, Vegetarian menu, Dress restrictions, Smart casual, Civ Wed 64 **Seats** 60, Pr/dining room 16 **Children** Min 7yrs D, Portions, Menu **Parking** 40

Miller Howe Hotel

◉◉ Modern British 🖳 V 🍷

Regency hotel with sweeping views

☎ 015394 42536
Rayrigg Rd LA23 1EY
e-mail: lakeview@millerhowe.com
dir: M6 junct 36. Follow the A591 bypass for Kendal. Enter Windermere, continue to mini rdbt, take left onto A592. Miller Howe is 0.25m on right

This impressive Edwardian country house stands well above Lake Windermere, with probably the grandest and most stunning views of any hotel in the Lake District. The interiors have a traditional feel with many period features, the refurbished two-tiered dining room has an understated Edwardian elegance featuring polished wood panelling and floors, and magnificent views of the Langdale Pikes. The food is described as modern British with a twist, but there are influences from all over Europe, especially France, incorporated in sophisticated and accomplished cooking. Innovative dishes at dinner might include roast quail breasts with Jerusalem artichoke risotto and hazelnut foam to start, a main of braised Cumbrian beef with grain mustard dumpling and hotpot vegetables, with Black Forest soufflé with cherry anglaise for dessert.

Chef Andrew Beaton **Owner** Martin & Helen Ainscough **Times** 12.30-1.45/6.45-8.45 **Wines** 100 bottles over £20, 10 bottles under £20, 8 by glass **Notes** Gourmet D 5 courses £45, Sunday L, Vegetarian menu, Dress restrictions, Smart casual, Civ Wed 64, Air con **Seats** 64, Pr/dining room 30 **Children** Portions **Parking** 40

The Samling

◉◉◉ – **see opposite**

Storrs Hall Hotel

◉◉ Modern British V

Accomplished, imaginative cuisine in luxurious country surroundings

☎ 015394 47111
Storrs Park LA23 3LG
e-mail: storrshall@elhmail.co.uk
web: www.elh.co.uk/hotels/storrshall
dir: On A592, 2m S of Bowness on the Newby Bridge Road

On the shores of Lake Windermere, this elegant Georgian house stands in beautifully landscaped grounds and commands views across the lake and surrounding fells. Sumptuous furnishings and period antiques create an air of traditional elegance throughout the comfortable lounges and the Terrace Restaurant - book a window table and savour the fine lake views. The food is bold and imaginative, using quality seasonal ingredients, with dishes like wild rabbit and foie gras terrine with pickled carrots, or wild crayfish bisque to start, followed by local wood pigeon with bread sauce, braised red cabbage and Puy lentils. To finish, try the rhubarb crumble, served with hot rhubarb soufflé and vanilla crumble ice cream.

Chef Will Jones **Owner** English Lakes Hotels **Times** 12.30-2/7-9 **Prices** Fixed D 3 course £39.50, Service included **Wines** 167 bottles over £20, 26 bottles under £20, 6 by glass **Notes** Tasting menu and themed eves available, Sunday L, Vegetarian menu, Dress restrictions, Smart casual, no jeans or trainers, Civ Wed 90 **Seats** 64, Pr/dining room 40 **Children** Min 12 yrs, Portions **Parking** 50

The Samling

WINDERMERE · Map 18 SD49

Modern British V

Impressive dining in Lakeland hillside retreat

☎ 015394 31922
Ambleside Rd LA23 1LR
e-mail: info@thesamling.com
dir: On A591 towards Ambleside. 1st on right after Low Wood Hotel. 2m from Windermere

The white-painted building is charming without perhaps leaving a lasting impression, but the setting on a wooded hillside with views down to Lake Windermere and the indefatigably tasteful interior are certainly memorable. The 18th-century house is part of a 67 acres estate, while inside the hotel's emphasis is firmly on rest and relaxation - the stylishly furnished bedrooms, comfortable drawing room and small library make it ideal for those in search of a bit of first-class peace and quiet. Staff are enthusiastic, clearly happy to be on duty, and knowledgeable about the food. The two small dining areas are kitted out with quality glassware and crockery and provide a stylish backdrop to the lively, creative cooking. High quality seasonal produce, much of it local, is used to good effect from the canapés right through to the accomplished petits fours. There's a menu gourmand with wine suggestions and a carte of well executed modern British dishes. Start with red mullet in a well considered dish with crushed ratte potatoes, minestrone and basil, and follow on with roast duck breast, confit of the gizzard, foie gras, morels and wild garlic foam. This is modern food with flavours that ring true and displaying an eye for presentation.

Chef Nigel Mendham **Owner** Tom Maxfield
Times 12.30-2/7-10, Closed L Mon-Sun (ex bookings)
Prices Food prices not confirmed for 2009. Please telephone for details. **Wines** 97 bottles over £20, 15 by glass **Notes** Gourmand tasting menu, Vegetarian menu, Civ Wed 20 **Seats** 22 **Children** Min 12 yrs, Portions, Menu **Parking** 15

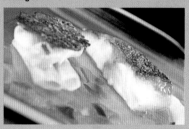

The Macdonald Old England Hotel & Spa
Windermere, Cumbria, England

The Old England Hotel sits proudly on the shores of Windermere surrounded by rolling hills and the gentle beauty of the Lake District. The award winning 2 AA Rosettes Vinand Restaurant, headed by Executive Head Chef, Mark Walker has an unrivaled location with views over the garden and lake, serving classical English cuisine with modern, international overtones. Following a £10 million investment the Old England has been transformed into one of the leading hotels in the north of England with 106 bedrooms and suites, a luxury spa including pool, gym and treatment rooms. The restaurant and public areas including the terrace and lounge which also serve light meals and afternnon teas have all been refurbished with contemporary decor to create a relaxing ambience.

Tel: 0844 879 9144   email: groups.oldengland@macdonald-hotel.co.uk   www.macdonaldhotels.co.uk/oldengland

WINDERMERE *Continued*

Vinand Restaurant at the Old England

◉◉ Classic British, International

Stylish modern dining with stunning lake views

☎ 0870 400 8130
Macdonald Old England Hotel & Spa
Church St, Bowness LA23 3DF
e-mail: general.oldengland@macdonald-hotels.co.uk
dir: Towards the lake and Bowness, straight over mini-rdbt, hotel behind church on right

Located right on the shore of Lake Windermere, The Old England combines Victorian elegance with contemporary facilities. The stylish, modern Vinand Restaurant is decked out with white walls, white linen, patterned carpet and upholstered chairs, their neutral, contemporary tones offering the perfect backdrop for the stunning lake views through its large windows. The kitchen follows the theme, its equally modern approach delivering carefully presented, intelligently uncomplicated dishes of balance and flavour. Take a starter of oxtail with cauliflower, scone and soup, followed by Dover sole with langoustine, fennel and pak choi, finishing with a dessert of a tasting of blood orange or assiette of chocolate.

Chef Mark Walker **Owner** Macdonald Hotels **Times** Closed L all week **Prices** Starter £7.50-£14.50, Main £16.50-£22.95, Dessert £6.95-£8.50, Service optional **Wines** 69 bottles over £20, 15 bottles under £20, 13 by glass **Notes** Vegetarian available, Dress restrictions, Smart casual Jacket prefered No denim/vests, Civ Wed 150, Air con **Seats** 170, Pr/dining room 12 **Children** Min 4yrs, Portions, Menu **Parking** 100

See advert on page 109

WORKINGTON　　　　　**Map 18 NY02**

Washington Central Hotel

◉ Modern British V

Relaxing dining in comfortable surroundings

☎ 01900 65772
Washington St CA14 3AY
e-mail: kawildwchotel@aol.com
dir: M6 junct 40, follow A66 to Workington. At bottom of Ramsay Brow turn right, hotel 100mtrs on right

The red-brick Washington Central was built in the 1980s and is popular with visitors to the Lake District and with locals who frequent the Carlton Restaurant. Hospitality is a key factor in the appeal and the traditionally furnished dining room is both comfortable and calm, with pastel shades of green and cream décor providing a contemporary feel. A meal starts with canapés before moving on to starters such as pan-fried breast of mallard with celeriac remoulade, creamed potatoes with wholegrain mustard and thyme jus. Mainland Europe is also the inspiration for main courses such as oven-baked salmon wrapped in Parma ham with warm Niçoise salad, garlic confit and sauce vièrge. For special occasions, ask about dining in the clock tower.

Chef Michael Buckley **Owner** William Dobie
Times 12-2/7-9.30, Closed 25 Dec, Closed L BHs, Closed D 31 Dec **Prices** Fixed L course £18.50, Fixed D 3 course £24, Service included **Wines** 17 bottles over £20, 40 bottles under £20, 10 by glass **Notes** Sunday L, Vegetarian menu, Dress restrictions, Smart casual, No jeans or trainers, Civ Wed 350 **Seats** 45, Pr/dining room 40 **Children** Portions, Menu **Parking** 10; multistorey car park 150mtrs

---

DERBYSHIRE

ASHBOURNE　　　　　**Map 10 SK14**

Bramhall's of Ashbourne

◉ Modern British ▭

Imaginative cooking in a relaxed bistro setting

☎ 01335 346158
6 Buxton Rd DE6 1EX
e-mail: info@bramhalls.co.uk
dir: From Ashbourne Market Square take Buxton road N. Restaurant 30yds on left

Located in the heart of historic Ashbourne, this charming restaurant with rooms occupies a conversion of Georgian and Edwardian buildings, with parts dating back 250 years. Refurbished under new owners, it remains the hub of local gastronomy with a reputation for imaginative cooking, attentive service and good value for money. The cooking is bright and simple - the ingredients are market-fresh, and brought together in simple combinations on modern, regularly-changing menus. Try confit duck and fig terrine with balsamic pickled shallots, baked organic salmon with pea and cherry tomato risotto, or Derbyshire steak with thyme potato cake and shallot jus.

Chef Richard Light **Owner** Tim & Sharon Cross
Times 12-2.30/6.30-9.30, Closed 25-26 Dec, 1 Jan, Closed L Mon-Thu, Closed D Sun **Prices** Fixed L 2 course £12-£20, Fixed D 3 course £16-£25, Starter £4.50-£6.95, Main £12.95-£18.45, Dessert £4.75-£6.50, Service optional **Wines** 15 bottles over £20, 20 bottles under £20, 8 by glass **Notes** Sunday L, Vegetarian available, Dress restrictions, Smart casual **Seats** 60, Pr/dining room 10 **Children** Portions, Menu **Parking** 5 **Parking** On street, free car park

Callow Hall

◎◎ Modern British, French

Family-run country house overlooking the Dove Valley

☎ 01335 300900
Mappleton Rd DE6 2AA
e-mail: reservations@callowhall.co.uk
dir: A515 through Ashbourne in Buxton direction, left at
Bowling Green Pub, 1st right Mappleton Rd

Situated at the gateway to the Peak National Park, this
creeper-clad Victorian mansion stands in 44 acres of
woods and garden overlooking the Dove Valley. Five
minutes drive from the centre of Ashbourne, this family-
run operation makes an ideal retreat. Period features
abound throughout, most notably in the William Morris
dining room with its warm red décor. The kitchen relies
heavily on local produce and fresh fish when preparing
the traditional British menus. The result is honest, full-
flavoured dishes, such as oak-smoked and cured organic
Scottish salmon with oyster fritters and chilled
horseradish soufflé, followed by fillet of monkfish with
fennel, dry-cured bacon and Pernod-scented fish fumé,
and hot chocolate fondant cake with warm chocolate
sauce, berries and home-made ice cream to finish. The
traditional Sunday lunches are excellent.

Chef David & Anthony Spencer **Owner** David, Dorothy,
Anthony & Emma Spencer **Times** 12.30-1.30/7.30-9,
Closed 25-26 Dec, Closed L Mon-Sat, Closed D Sun (ex
residents) **Wines** 138 bottles over £20, 45 bottles under
£20, 26 by glass **Notes** Fixed D 5 courses £42, Sunday L,
Vegetarian available, Dress restrictions, Smart casual
Seats 70, Pr/dining room 40 **Children** Portions
Parking 30

The Dining Room

◎◎ Modern British 🍃

**Ambitious modern cuisine in intimate, characterful
surroundings**

☎ 01335 300666
33 St John St DE6 1GP
dir: On A52 Derby to Leek road

One of the oldest buildings in the town, The Dining Room
dates back to 1604 and is full of character, with low-
beamed ceilings, original cast-iron range and wood-
burning stove. The intimate, six-table restaurant is chic
with muted tones, serving up modern British cuisine with
some global influences using locally-sourced, organic
seasonal produce (suppliers listed on the back of the
menu). A starter of home-smoked organic salmon makes
way for a main course like local beef served '2 ways' with
triple-cooked chips and home-made ketchup. Desserts
need to be ordered with the other courses, and might
include Victoria plum tart with vanilla ice cream and
plum jam brandy jelly. There is also an impressive
17-course tasting menu on Saturday evenings and an
award-winning cheese board.

Chef Peter Dale **Owner** Peter & Laura Dale
Times 12.30/7.30, Closed 2 wks 26 Dec, 1 wk Sep, 1 wk
Mar, Closed Sun-Mon **Prices** Fixed D 3 course fr £36,
Tasting menu fr £40, Starter £8-£10, Main £16-£20,
Dessert £6-£7, Service optional **Wines** 35 bottles over
£20, 10 bottles under £20, 3 by glass **Notes** Tasting
menu 12 courses, Dress restrictions, Smart casual
Seats 16 **Children** Min 12yrs, Portions **Parking** Opposite
restaurant (evening)

ASHFORD-IN-THE-WATER Map 16 SK16

Riverside House Hotel

◎◎ Modern French

Fine dining in opulent surroundings on the Wye

☎ 01629 814275
Fennel St DE45 1QF
e-mail: riversidehouse@enta.net
dir: M1 junct 29 take A619 and continue to Bakewell. 2m
from the centre of Bakewell on A6 towards Buxton. In
Ashford village located on Fennel St

A former shooting lodge, this gracious Georgian country
house is set in its own grounds on the banks of the River
Wye in the lovely Peak District village of Ashford-in-the-
Water. The property is full of character and diners can
relax in luxurious comfort surrounded by exquisite

fabrics, beautiful artwork and chic antique tables and
chairs in the Riverside Room restaurant. An imaginative
choice of intelligently straightforward dishes might
include terrine of confit organic chicken with baby
artichoke, piquillo peppers and girolle mushroom salad,
followed by pan-roasted fillet of Derbyshire beef, macaire
potatoes, creamed leeks and shallots. Finish with
Valrhona chocolate and raspberry tian with raspberry
sorbet. Lighter food is also served in the Conservatory
Room restaurant.

Times 12-2.30/7-9.30

BAKEWELL Map 16 SK26

Piedaniel's

◎ French, European

Elegant restaurant in the town centre

☎ 01629 812687
Bath St DE45 1BX
dir: From Bakewell rdbt in town centre take A6 Buxton
exit. 1st right into Bath St (one-way)

This recently renamed and refurbished restaurant
occupies a comfortable stone-built townhouse in the
centre of Bakewell. There are painted stone walls and
ceiling beams and a separate bar area. Three eating
options are available: the full menu, changed monthly
and priced for three courses with some supplements; a
good-value set menu from Tuesday to Thursday evening;
and a lunchtime Bistro serving traditional French dishes
with a European twist. The main menu includes snail
profiteroles with garlic butter sauce, monkfish fillet
wrapped in salmon mousse served with lentil and saffron
sauce, with pear and almond steamed sponge pudding to
finish.

Chef E Piedaniel, J Gibbard **Owner** E & C Piedaniel
Times 12-2/7-10, Closed Xmas & New Year, 2 wks Jan,
2 wks Aug, Closed Mon, Closed D Sun **Prices** Fixed L 2
course £10, Fixed D 3 course £22-£27, Starter £5, Main
£12-£17, Dessert £5, Service included **Wines** 6 bottles
over £20, 23 bottles under £20, 10 by glass **Notes** Sunday
L, Vegetarian available **Seats** 50, Pr/dining room 16
Children Portions **Parking** Town centre

Fischer's Baslow Hall

BASLOW Map 16 SK27

Modern European 🖥

Sophisticated cuisine in memorable setting

☎ 01246 583259
Calver Rd DE45 1RR
e-mail: reservations@fischers-baslowhall.co.uk
dir: From Baslow on A623 towards Calver. Hotel on right

Dating from the early part of the 20th century, Baslow Hall was built in the style of a 17th-century manor house and approaching down the chestnut lined driveway it makes quite an impression on the 21st-century visitor. Located on the edge of the Chatsworth Estate, the handsome, stone-built house is set in 5 acres of beautiful gardens with hidden corners and potagers. Max and Susan Fischer have been in residence for a little over 20 years and have created a charming and elegant environment. The house is filled with well chosen antiques, pictures and fine fabrics, log fires flicker and comfortable sofas invite relaxation, while the dining room with its stylish classical appeal, complemented by fine china, cutlery and glassware, proves the real heart of the house. Max has developed a strong team in the kitchen - led by head chef Rupert Rowley - and he seeks out the best produce - if it isn't grown in the grounds - and together they apply their

undoubted technical skills to provide outstanding food on the plate. The style is modern European, but underpinned by classical French technique, and results are precise and sophisticated. There is a tasting menu alongside the fixed-price carte and menu du jour. The peripheral elements from wonderful bread to amuse-bouche and pre-dessert are all part of the experience, perfectly judged, and devoured with gusto. Skill in the balancing of flavours is to the fore in a starter of terrine of foie gras with Yorkshire forced rhubarb and toasted brioche as well as main-course roast loin of veal with linguine, asparagus and finished with a rosemary cream and veal jus. Desserts such as lemon chiboust with bay leaf ice cream and lemon jelly maintain the standard to the end. Service is polished and formal, but friendly with it.

Chef Max Fischer/Rupert Rowley
Owner Mr & Mrs M Fischer
Times 12-2/7-9.30, Closed 24-26 Dec, 31 Dec, Closed L Mon, Closed D Sun (ex residents) **Prices** Fixed L 2 course £24, Gourmet D £68, Prestige Tasting menu £63 **Wines** 117 bottles over £20, 4 bottles under £20, 6 by glass
Notes Gourmet D £68, Sunday L, Vegetarian available, Dress restrictions, Smart casual, no jeans, sweatshirts, trainers, Civ Wed 40 **Seats** 38, Pr/dining room 20 **Children** Min 12 yrs D, Portions **Parking** 38

BAKEWELL Continued

The Prospect

Modern British

Town-centre restaurant with a good atmosphere

☎ 01629 810077
Theme Court, Bridge St DE45 1DS
e-mail: theprospect@btinternet.com
dir: From A6 (Matlock to Buxton road), follow signs for
Baslow. Theme Court is opposite The Queens Arms pub

Reclaimed antique oak panelling mixes well with
polished tabletops and modern place settings at this
former forge, and a brand new bar and lounge area
create the perfect setting for pre- or post-dinner drinks.
The kitchen's no-nonsense approach uses the freshest
local ingredients, delivering dishes that are modern in
style with Mediterranean and Asian influences, yet firmly
rooted in the British tradition. You might start with
smoked mackerel, salmon and sorrel fishcakes with aïoli
and lemon dressing, and then follow with Elton estate
venison Wellington with sweet potato purée, braised red
cabbage and Cumberland sauce, with a delicious bread-
and-butter pudding and apricot coulis to finish.

Times 12-2.30/6.30-12, Closed 25-26 Dec, 1 Jan, Easter
Sun, Closed Mon

Rutland Arms Hotel

Traditional, British

Enjoyable dining in welcoming, traditional hotel

☎ 01629 812812
The Square DE45 1BT
e-mail: rutland@bakewell.demon.co.uk
web: www.bakewell.demon.co.uk
dir: On A6 in Bakewell centre opposite war memorial.
Parking opposite side entrance

This imposing 19th-century stone-built hotel - in whose
kitchens the Bakewell pudding was invented - is a local
landmark at the heart of town. Its Four Seasons
restaurant is classically traditional in style, with polished
granite fireplace, lofty ceilings, chandeliers and several
clocks, evoking an endearing air of a bygone era. By
contrast, the accomplished cooking is up-to-date,
showcasing Peak District fare - sirloin steak served with
country-fried potatoes and a creamy mushroom and
brandy sauce, or honey-roasted lamb shank served on
grain mustard mash and a red wine jus and, of course,
traditional Bakewell pudding served with clotted cream
and fresh berry compôte to finish.

Times 12-2/7-9

BASLOW   Map 16 SK27

Cavendish Hotel

Modern British 🍃

Luxurious surroundings for sumptuous cooking

☎ 01246 582311
Church Ln DE45 1SP
e-mail: info@cavendish-hotel.net
dir: M1 junct 29 follow signs for Chesterfield. From
Chesterfield take A619 to Bakewell, Chatsworth & Baslow

This stylish 18th-century property is delightfully situated
on the edge of the Chatsworth Estate. There's a real
sense of luxury here - the antiques and original artworks
a reminder that the Duke and Duchess of Devonshire had
a hand in the design. Guests can dine in the more
informal conservatory Garden Room or in the smart and
contemporary Gallery Restaurant. The cooking style
balances technique and flavour well and presentation is
minimalist with some precise garnishing and restrained
artistry. Expect a modern menu with some interesting
twists on classic dishes, accompanied by excellent
service that combines friendliness with helpful advice. A
starter of confit mackerel and brown shrimp rillettes with
a sour cream and chive dressing, and pan-roasted
halibut steak with roast stuffed baby squid, chorizo,
chickpeas and roasted red pepper butter show the style.

Chef Chris Allison **Owner** Eric Marsh
Times 12.30-2.30/6.30-10 **Prices** Fixed L 2 course
£29.50, Fixed D 3 course £38.50, Service added 5%
Wines 39 bottles over £20, 13 bottles under £20, 8 by
glass **Notes** Sunday L, Vegetarian available, Dress
restrictions, No trainers, T-shirts **Seats** 50, Pr/dining
room 16 **Children** Portions **Parking** 40

Fischer's Baslow Hall

— *see opposite*

Rowley's Restaurant & Bar

Modern British

**Contemporary setting for fine local produce and quality
cuisine**

☎ 01246 583880
Church Ln DE45 1RY
e-mail: info@rowleysrestaurant.co.uk
dir: A619/A623 signed Chatsworth, Baslow edge of
Chatsworth estate.

Next door to the village's pretty church, this old pub has
been turned into a modern bar and restaurant by the

---

team behind nearby Fischer's Baslow Hall. This sibling
venue offers an informal mix of stone-flagged bar area
alongside the chic, more contemporary feel of its three
dining areas upstairs. With mainly aubergine-coloured
walls, contemporary local art, banquette seating and
modern lightwood furniture complete the picture. At
lunch, the ground floor and bar are also used, while the
food is an appealing mix of modern and traditional
British, with emphasis on high-quality local produce
presented with style. Lunch ranges from light bites to
prime steaks, while dinner could deliver slow-braised
belly pork with apple fondant and black pudding, roast
cod with basil pesto dressing, or pan-fried sesame-
crusted calves' liver.

Chef James Grant **Owner** Susan & Max Fischer, Rupert
Rowley **Times** 12-2.30/6-10, Closed 1-4 Jan, Closed D
Sun **Prices** Food prices not confirmed for 2009. Please
telephone for details. **Wines** 7 bottles over £20, 15
bottles under £20, 6 by glass **Notes** Vegetarian available
Seats 64, Pr/dining room 18 **Children** Portions, Menu
Parking 17 **Parking** On street

BELPER   Map 11 SK34

The Orangery at Shottle Hall

Modern British 🍃

Country-house setting for quality modern cooking

☎ 01773 550577
Shottle Hall, White Ln, Shottle DE56 2EB
e-mail: info@shottlehall.co.uk
dir: 0.3m from A517, 2m from Belper

This delightfully refurbished family-owned hotel stands
in extensive grounds on the famous Chatsworth Estate,
with views over the rolling Derbyshire countryside. Stylish
modern décor and furnishings combine with fine art to
create a sense of informal country-house luxury. Unwind
over a drink in the Gallery Bar before going through to the
contemporary Orangery restaurant, complete with floor-
to-ceiling windows and starlight roof. The kitchen's
seasonal menus showcase quality local ingredients,
including Chatsworth venison and locally-grown organic
vegetables. The approach is modern with some classical
spin. Roasted fillet of beef served with red pepper
piperade and Hartington stilton and girolle gratin show
the style, with hot chocolate and praline fondant to
finish.

Chef Dean Crews **Owner** Joanne & Steve Nicol
Times 12-2/7-9, Closed D Sun **Prices** Fixed L 2 course
£14.95, Starter £4.95-£6.75, Main £16.75-£23, Dessert
£4.75-£6.50 **Wines** 36 bottles over £20, 19 bottles under
£20, 8 by glass **Notes** Sunday L, Vegetarian available,
Dress restrictions, Smart casual, no jeans, Civ Wed 90
Seats 60, Pr/dining room 20 **Children** Portions
Parking 60

HATHERSAGE *Continued*

pollack with marsh samphire and cockle beurre blanc, or venison medallions with beetroot jus, and for dessert orange and crème brûlée with home-made shortbread.

Chef Robert Navarro **Owner** Robert & Cynthia Emery **Times** 11.30-2.30/6.30-9.30, Closed 25 Dec **Prices** Fixed L 2 course £16.25-£17.95, Starter £5-£8.95, Main £10.95-£19.95, Dessert £4.50-£7.95, Service optional **Wines** 10 bottles over £20, 28 bottles under £20, 16 by glass **Notes** Sunday L, Vegetarian available, Dress restrictions, Smart Casual, Air con **Seats** 40, Pr/dining room 24 **Children** Portions **Parking** 40

HIGHAM   Map 16 SK35

Santo's Higham Farm Hotel

⊛ Modern ✪

Modern cuisine in a romantic setting

☎ 01773 833812
Main Rd DE55 6EH
e-mail: reception@santoshighamfarm.demon.co.uk
dir: M1 junct 28, A38 towards Derby, then A61 to Higham, left onto B6013

A conversion of a 15th-century farmhouse and crook barn, this delightful hotel has panoramic views over the Amber Valley. Guiseppe's restaurant has deep red padded suede chairs and crisp white table linen, and exposed stonework and oil-filled candles to add to the relaxed atmosphere. With strong emphasis on local produce, a

starter of ham hock terrine with home-made chutney, with salmon escalope served with fresh green pea risotto and smoked Italian ham to follow, and a trio of apples - crisp mini strudel, a refreshing apple sorbet and a pleasantly tart apple jelly - for dessert shows the style.

Chef Raymond Moody **Owner** Santo Cusimano **Times** 12-2/7-9.30, Closed L Mon-Sat, Closed D Sun **Prices** Fixed D 3 course £21-£25, Starter £6-£8, Main £15-£25, Dessert £6-£8, Service added but optional 5% **Wines** 26 bottles over £20, 23 bottles under £20, 3 by glass **Notes** Sunday L, Dress restrictions, Smart casual, Civ Wed 70 **Seats** 50, Pr/dining room 34 **Children** Portions **Parking** 100

See advert below

MARSTON MONTGOMERY   Map 10 SK13

The Crown Inn

⊛ British, European

Modern brasserie in a converted Georgian farmhouse

☎ 01889 590541
Riggs Ln DE6 2FF
e-mail: info@thecrowninn-derbyshire.co.uk
dir: From Ashbourne take A515 towards Lichfield, after 5m turn right at Cubley x-rds then follow signs to Marston Montgomery for 1m, take left into Marston Montgomery. The Crown Inn is in centre of village

Georgian farmhouse features, including beamed ceilings and original fireplaces, combine with contemporary furnishings and décor at this modern brasserie. Local

painters' work hung on earthy coloured walls complements sumptuous leather sofas and armchairs. The menu offers traditional dishes with European influences prepared and presented with imaginative flair. Locally-sourced produce is used wherever possible and the specials menu delivers interesting and unusual dishes. Typically, start with ham hock and black pudding terrine with farmhouse chutney, with maybe pan-fried sea bass with caper sauce vièrge, or rack of lamb with spring green ragout to follow, and glazed citrus tart for dessert.

Chef Richard Bloomfield **Owner** Janice & Craig Southway **Times** 12-2.30/6-9.30, Closed 25 Dec, 1 Jan, Closed D Sun **Prices** Fixed L 2 course £10, Starter £4.25-£7.50, Main £11.95-£18, Dessert £4.25-£6, Service optional **Wines** 11 bottles over £20, 25 bottles under £20, 7 by glass **Notes** Sunday L, Vegetarian available **Seats** 40, Pr/dining room 12 **Children** Portions, Menu **Parking** 16

See advert opposite

MATLOCK   Map 16 SK35

The Red House Country Hotel

⊛ Traditional British ✪

Simple, flavoursome cooking in friendly, relaxed country-house hotel

☎ 01629 734854
Old Rd, Darley Dale DE4 2ER
e-mail: enquiries@theredhousecountryhotel.co.uk
web: www.theredhousecountryhotel.co.uk
dir: M1 junct 28 travelling N & junct 29 travelling S, follow signs to Matlock then A6 to Bakewell

Built in 1891 for a Manchester architect, this peaceful, privately-owned country-house hotel is set in delightful Victorian, lawned gardens with superb views of the Derwent Valley. The same view can be seen from the attractive dining room, which is situated within the elegant former drawing room with its oak floor, smart, formal table settings and attentive service. The regularly-

changing menu moves with the seasons and the uncomplicated dishes could include king prawns sautéed with butter, diced tomato, shallots, garlic and Cognac, followed by baked duck breast with pomegranate and walnut sauce.

Chef Alan Perkins **Owner** David & Kate Gardiner **Times** Closed 26-29 Dec, 1st 2 wks Jan, Closed L all wk **Prices** Fixed D 4 course £27-£30, Service optional **Wines** 13 bottles over £20, 16 bottles under £20, 6 by glass **Notes** Dress restrictions, Smart casual **Seats** 30 **Children** Min 12yrs **Parking** 15

Riber Hall

◎◎ European

Atmospheric hotel with imaginative food

☎ 01629 582795
DE4 5JU
e-mail: info@riber-hall.co.uk
dir: Off A615 at Tansley, 1m up Alders Lane & Carr Lane

Riber Hall dates back to Elizabethan times and, although the building has been extended and expanded over the centuries, it still looks like a grand old house. There are attractive grounds to explore, including a walled garden and old orchard, and it stands surrounded by beautiful, peaceful countryside. The rooms are decorated in traditional style in keeping with the antiquity of the house, including the dining room with its pink walls and formal table settings. The fixed-price menus deliver pan-European dishes from traditional home-made gravad lax with shallot and caper salad to the more modern goat's cheese with mulled pear and walnut froth. Main-course venison fillet is served with pommes Maxime, Savoy cabbage and brandy-braised prunes, and supreme of chicken comes with black pudding and vanilla mash.

Times 12-1.30/7-9.30, Closed 25 Dec

The Bay Tree

◎ Modern British

Imaginative cuisine in contemporary village setting

☎ 01332 863358
4 Potter St DE73 8HW
e-mail: enquiries@baytreerestaurant.co.uk
dir: Telephone for directions

Expect robust modern brasserie-style cuisine at this smart but unpretentious village centre eatery. The 17th-century building has been extended to create a new bar. The spacious, informal dining room is smartly decorated in warm yellow with timber floors and modern artwork on the walls. Dishes have a rustic style and attention is given to presentation, depth of flavour and use of good-quality produce. Dishes include Thai fishcakes with plum and spring onion garnish, and crispy Lunesdale duckling with Saint Clements sauce. For a special treat, try the champagne breakfast.

Times 10.30-3/6.30-10.30

The Morley Hayes Hotel - Dovecote Restaurant

◎ Modern British

Converted 17th-century farmhouse serving creative modern cooking

☎ 01332 780480
Main Rd DE7 6DG
e-mail: enquiries@morleyhayes.com
dir: Please telephone for directions

This charming 18th-century former farmstead is now a friendly hotel complete with an 18-hole championship golf course, so there's no excuse for arriving without a hearty appetite. Taking its name from the converted dovecote which it occupies, the brightly lit dining room oozes character from its vaulted ceiling and exposed beams to its original brickwork walls. After a pre-dinner drink in the piano bar, guests have a choice of menus to peruse: one leans towards the luxurious, while the other is more simply conceived and cooked. Smoked salmon terrine with a confit lemon and herb salad is a typical starter, followed by Derbyshire fillet of beef with beetroot, caramelised shallots and horseradish mash.

Times 12-2/7-9.30, Closed 1 Jan, Closed L Sat

The Old Vicarage

◎◎◎ – **see page 118**

see page 118

The Old Vicarage

Modern British NOTABLE WINE LIST

Memorable dining in striking house and gardens

☎ 0114 247 5814
Ridgeway Moor S12 3XW
e-mail: eat@theoldvicarage.co.uk
dir: Please telephone for directions

This charming country house, built in 1846 by a celebrated Victorian horticulturalist, is approached by a sweeping gravel drive and set in rolling lawns with fine specimen trees, a woodland and a wild flower copse. The welcome is warm and friendly, the décor pleasingly unfussy with clean modern lines accentuating the period details of the architecture. The main dining room comes in soft pastel shades with modern artwork bringing the room to life. Bright and sunny in summer and warm and cosy in winter with log fires and candlelight, it's decked out with parquet flooring and crisp white linen tablecloths. The conservatory dining area opens out on to the terrace, which comes into its own in summer, and has lovely views. The kitchen's modern focus is admirably inspired by top-quality, seasonal produce from local and specialist suppliers, as well as the kitchen garden itself. The precision cooking produces some unusual flavour combinations, while not being tied to fashion or gimmicks. Sound

combinations, accomplished skills and clear flavours abound in dishes like roasted wild sea bass and lobster tortellini on braised leeks with passionfruit butter sauce and Sévruga caviar, or roasted local partridge wrapped in pancetta with vanilla fondant potato and broccoli with prunes and pine nuts. Rhubarb jelly and fool with sorbet and frangipane with rhubarb and vanilla compôte makes a fine choice for dessert.

Chef T Bramley, N Smith **Owner** Tessa Bramley **Times** 12.30-2.30/6.30-10, Closed 10 days Xmas/New Year, 2 wks Aug & BHs, Closed Sun & Mon, Closed L Sat **Prices** Fixed L 2 course £30, Fixed D 4 course £60, Tasting menu £65, Service optional **Wines** 24 bottles under £20 **Notes** Tasting menu 7 courses, Vegetarian available, Civ Wed 50 **Seats** 40, Pr/dining room 22 **Children** Portions **Parking** 18

RISLEY
Map 11 SK43

Risley Hall

🏵 European

Fine dining in charming manor house

☎ 0115 939 9000
Derby Rd DE72 3SS
e-mail: enquiries@risleyhallhotel.co.uk
dir: From M1 junct 25 take Sandiacre exit, left at T-junct, 0.5 miles on left

Set in 17 acres of landscaped grounds, this 11th-century manor house is now a popular hotel and spa. The formal fine-dining restaurant offers superb views across the manicured gardens through large picture windows. Friendly and attentive service complements some imaginative cuisine where modern British dishes are underpinned by classical French technique. Start with ham hock and duck liver, perhaps followed by pan-fried turbot set on pomme matière with aromatic thyme and a demi-glace of chicken, and rhubarb crème brûlée to finish.

Times 12-6.30/7-10.30

ROWSLEY
Map 16 SK26

East Lodge Hotel

🏵🏵 Modern British

Country-house hotel dining in romantic setting

☎ 01629 734474
DE4 2EF
e-mail: info@eastlodge.com
web: www.eastlodge.com
dir: On A6, 5m from Matlock & 3m from Bakewell, at junct with B6012

This hotel enjoys a delightfully tranquil, romantic setting in 10 acres of picturesque landscaped grounds. The conservatory lounge area overlooks the gardens and is just the place to study the menu before entering the modern, country-look restaurant. With generous portions, the emphasis is on good quality local produce, with clear flavours, mainly straightforward combinations and no unnecessary embellishment. A starter of pressed ham hock and parsley terrine with home-made chutney is served with slices of walnut bread, followed by pavé of turbot with quartered artichokes, salsify purée and wild mushrooms. Desserts are a highlight, as in orange and Grand Marnier crème brûlée with a millefeuille of griottine cherries, or honeycomb parfait with banana tart and chocolate sorbet.

Times 12-2/7-9.30

The Peacock at Rowsley

🏵 Modern British V

Ambitious cooking at a chic hotel

☎ 01629 733518
Bakewell Rd DE4 2EB
e-mail: reception@thepeacockatrowsley.com
web: www.thepeacockatrowsley.com
dir: M1 junct 29 (Chesterfield), 20 mins to Rowsley

Under the ownership of the Haddon Hall estate, this chic little establishment (the former dower house) has undergone a contemporary makeover - a clever fusion of ancient manor with ultra-modern boutique-hotel styling. The mix is easy on the eye, its cool interiors enriched with original features and period furnishings. The dining room follows the theme, backed by well-drilled, hospitable service and garden views. Highly accomplished, flavourful dishes come dressed to thrill and testify to the kitchen's ambition and technical skill. The enticing repertoire takes a modern approach, and making a decision can be tricky; perhaps crab tian with pickled carrot, fennel salad and crab beignet, or local lamb cutlet with rosemary polenta, confit lamb shoulder, marinated courgettes and feta cheese.

Chef Daniel Smith **Owner** Rutland Hotels **Times** 12-2/7-9, Closed D 24-26 Dec **Prices** Fixed L 2 course fr £20.50, Fixed D 3 course fr £45, Starter £3.95-£9.75, Main £14.75-£27.50, Dessert £5.75-£7.95, Service optional **Wines** 35 bottles over £20, 20 bottles under £20, 15 by glass **Notes** Sunday L, Vegetarian menu, Civ Wed 20 **Seats** 40, Pr/dining room 20 **Children** Min 10 yrs, Portions, Menu **Parking** 25

STRETTON
Map 16 SK36

The White Bear

🏵 British, French

Accomplished modern cooking at a friendly gastro-pub

☎ 01246 863274
Main Rd DE55 6ET
dir: 15 min from M1 junct 29. On A61 between Clay Cross and Shirland

Locals beat a path to this unassuming roadside pub-restaurant that has been serving customers for over 200 years. Inside you'll find stone floors, stone and roughcast walls, leaded windows and wooden tables set with candles. Chef-patron Jason Wardill, who has worked in many top northern restaurants, shows his pedigree in an appealing modern British repertoire with French

influences, and wife Stephanie provides warm and friendly service. Seasonal dishes are prepared from as much local produce as possible: goat's cheese and caramelised onion tart, fillet of beef with oxtail cottage pie, roast shallots and red wine sauce, and chocolate espresso mousse with almond shortbread.

Chef Jason Wardill **Owner** Jason Wardill **Times** 12-2/5.30-9.30, Closed 1 wk Jan, 2 wks Oct, Closed Mon-Tue, Closed L Sat **Prices** Starter £5-£6.50, Main £12-£19.50, Dessert £5-£6, Service optional **Wines** 6 bottles over £20, 19 bottles under £20, 7 by glass **Notes** Sunday L, Vegetarian available **Seats** 40 **Children** Portions **Parking** 30

THORPE
Map 16 SK15

Izaak Walton Hotel

🏵🏵 Modern European

Contemporary cooking in a fisherman's paradise

☎ 01335 350555
Dovedale DE6 2AY
e-mail: reception@izaakwaltonhotel.com
dir: Telephone for directions

Nestled within the Derbyshire Peaks, this converted 17th-century farmhouse was named after the famous author of The Compleat Angler and has its own two-mile stretch of the River Dove for excellent fishing and views of the Dovedale Valley. The restaurant is traditionally decorated and offers outstanding views of Thorpe Cloud in the Peak District National Park. Modern cooking is exemplified in dishes like carpaccio of beetroot with pears, Dovedale blue and dressed leaves, and pressed belly pork with celeriac mash, buttered greens and Calvados jus, followed by a chocolate pavé with praline mousse, rice pudding fritter and hazelnut tuile. The bar features fishing memorabilia and pictures, and bar meals are served here.

Chef James Harrison **Owner** Mrs Bridget Day **Times** 12.30-2.30/7-9 **Prices** Food prices not confirmed for 2009. Please telephone for details. **Wines** 40 bottles over £20, 25 bottles under £20, 4 by glass **Notes** Sunday L, Vegetarian available, Dress restrictions, Smart casual, Civ Wed 80 **Seats** 100, Pr/dining room 20 **Children** Portions, Menu **Parking** 80

DEVON

ASHBURTON
Map 3 SX77

Agaric

Modern British

Honest cooking in an inviting setting

☎ 01364 654478
30 North St TQ13 7QD
e-mail: eat@agaricrestaurant.co.uk
dir: Opposite town hall. Ashburton off A38 between Exeter & Plymouth

Located in a Georgian listed building in the ancient stannary town of Ashburton - famous for its antique shops - is this cosy restaurant with rooms, complete with open fireplace, granite wall and beautiful courtyard garden. A large carved wooden mushroom pays deference to the restaurant's name, while the wood-fired oven delivers great pizzas and bread, doubling as a smoker for fish and meat. The daily-changing menu matches the unpretentious setting, using local meat and fish, and wild ingredients like samphire, mushrooms and laver which are picked locally. Expect straightforward, honest dishes such as pan-fried sea bass with grilled fennel and orange hollandaise, or lightly spiced steamed and crispy duck leg with spinach and spiced plum sauce.

Chef Nick Coiley **Owner** Mr N Coiley & Mrs S-Coiley **Times** 12-2/7-9.30, Closed 2 wks Aug, Xmas, 1 wk Jan, Closed Mon-Tue, Closed L Sat, Closed D Sun **Prices** Fixed L 2 course £12.95-£14.95, Starter £4.95-£8.95, Main £14.95-£17.95, Dessert £5.95-£6.95, Service optional **Wines** 16 bottles over £20, 9 bottles under £20, 2 by glass **Notes** Sunday L, Vegetarian available **Seats** 30 **Children** Portions **Parking** Car park opposite

ASHWATER
Map 3 SX39

Blagdon Manor Hotel & Restaurant

Traditional British V

Confident cooking in delightful Devon retreat

☎ 01409 211224
EX21 5DF
e-mail: stay@blagdon.com
dir: From A388 towards Holsworthy, 2m N of Chapman's Well take 2nd right towards Ashwater. Next right by Blagdon Lodge. Hotel 2nd on right

Set within 20 acres, this Grade II listed Devon longhouse is now a relaxed country-house hotel. Dating back to the

16th century, the hotel retains many original features, including heavy oak beams, slate flagstones and a freshwater well. Service is formal but friendly and the atmosphere is relaxed. Popular with locals, the main restaurant is candlelit and cosy, and leads through to the light and airy conservatory extension. The traditional British cuisine makes the most of high-quality local produce, as in a chilled celeriac mousse with pan-fried scallops, followed by pan-fried fillet of cod with oxtail and corned beef faggots and a rich red wine reduction. Tempting desserts include mixed spice and pear soufflé.

Chef Stephen Morey **Owner** Stephen & Liz Morey **Times** 12-2/7-9, Closed 2 wks Oct, 2 wks Jan, Closed Mon (ex residents), Closed L Tue, Closed D Sun **Prices** Fixed L 2 course £17, Fixed D 3 course £35, Service optional **Wines** 20 bottles over £20, 10 bottles under £20, 6 by glass **Notes** Sunday L, Vegetarian menu, Dress restrictions, Smart casual **Seats** 24, Pr/dining room 16 **Children** Min 12 yrs **Parking** 12

AXMINSTER
Map 4 SY29

Fairwater Head Country House Hotel

British, European

Relaxing country-house hotel dining with stunning views

☎ 01297 678349
Hawkchurch EX13 5TX
e-mail: info@fairwaterheadhotel.co.uk
dir: A358 into Broom Lane at Tytherleigh, follow signs to Hawkchurch & hotel

Set in two acres of gardens and surrounded by beautiful countryside, this enchanting Edwardian country-house hotel offers a peaceful and tranquil setting. Features in the cosy public rooms include the reception area fireplace with its inscription: 'East or West home is best', dating from 1900. The elegant Garden restaurant, with its large picture windows overlooking the Axe Valley, provides a menu of modern and traditional British and European cuisine employing excellent local produce, prepared with care and expertise. Expect braised neck of Devonshire lamb with creamed potatoes, minted vegetables and red wine sauce, followed by garden apple and lavender crème brûlée with home-made ginger ice cream.

Chef Andre Moore, Anthony Muir **Owner** Adam & Carrie Southwell **Times** 12-2/7-9, Closed Jan, Closed L Mon & Tue **Prices** Fixed D 4 course £27.50, Service optional **Wines** 33 bottles over £20, 27 bottles under £20, 6 by glass **Notes** Sunday L, Vegetarian available, Dress restrictions, Smart casual **Seats** 60, Pr/dining room 18 **Children** Portions, Menu **Parking** 40

BEER
Map 4 SY28

Steamers Restaurant

Modern, Seafood

Popular village restaurant offering local seafood

☎ 01297 22922
New Cut, Fore St EX12 3JH
e-mail: info@steamersrestaurant.co.uk
dir: Just off A3052 between Sidmouth and Lyme Regis

Situated at the heart of a beautiful fishing village, this one-time chandlery and village bakery has been skilfully converted into an informal, characterful restaurant with modern décor and interconnecting wine bar. As you might expect, fish and seafood take centre stage on the menu with their own daily-changing selection, while meat-lovers are also well catered for with a good selection of locally-sourced chicken, lamb, beef and duck dishes available. Main courses might range from grilled fillet of local brill topped with smoked salmon and onion marmalade, to a classic home-made steak-and-kidney pudding, preceded by a starter of River Teign mussels in garlic and white wine.

Chef Andy Williams **Owner** Steamers Ltd **Times** 12-2/7-9.30, Closed 25 & 26 Dec, Closed Sun-Mon **Prices** Starter £4.50-£7, Main £6-£16, Dessert fr £5, Service optional **Wines** 5 bottles over £20, 22 bottles under £20, 12 by glass **Notes** Vegetarian available, Air con **Seats** 65 **Children** Portions, Menu **Parking** On street & council car park 150mtrs

BIDEFORD
Map 3 SS42

Yeoldon Country House Hotel

British

Modern cooking in traditional country-house setting

☎ 01237 474400
Durrant Ln, Northam EX39 2RL
e-mail: yeoldonhouse@aol.com
web: www.yeoldonhousehotel.co.uk
dir: A361 to Bideford. Go over Torridge Bridge and at rdbt turn right. Take 3rd right into Durrant Lane. Hotel 0.25m

A charming Victorian country house in a peaceful location, offering superb views over the River Torridge. The ground floor restaurant has an air of casual elegance, making the most of the views with large windows. There's an intelligent simplicity to the cooking style, the accomplished kitchen delivering well-executed, honest, unpretentious British dishes using fresh, local produce. On the daily-changing menu you might spot salmon, cod and caper fishcake with tomato and basil salsa, rump of West Country lamb with parsnip and horseradish mash, and a summer pudding with clotted cream.

Chef Brian Steele **Owner** Brian & Jennifer Steele **Times** Closed Xmas, Closed Sun, Closed L all wk **Prices** Fixed D 3 course £32.50, Service included **Wines** 7 bottles over £20, 32 bottles under £20, 3 by glass **Notes** Vegetarian available, Civ Wed 60 **Seats** 30 **Children** Portions **Parking** 30

The Masons Arms

Traditional British

Popular village inn with bags of character and a wonderful beach nearby

☎ 01297 680300

EX12 3DJ

e-mail: reception@masonsarms.co.uk
web: www.masonsarms.co.uk
dir: Village off A3052 between Sidmouth and Seaton

Dating back to 1360, The Masons Arms started life as a humble cider house with one tiny bar. Six centuries later and it has taken over any number of nearby cottages and is now a destination gastro-pub with bags of rustic old-world charm. There are hearty open fires in winter, while summer sees the extensive outdoor seating, busy bar and restaurant areas packed with happy diners enjoying dishes such as grilled fillets of sea bass with lemon and garlic risotto and mustard-glazed baby fennel, or grilled West Country lamb cutlets with crushed new potatoes, asparagus and a tomato and basil jus. After dinner take a stroll to nearby Branscombe Beach - it's one of the loveliest in Devon.

Chef S Garland, A Deam **Owner** Mr & Mrs C Slaney
Times 12-2/7-9 **Prices** Fixed D 3 course £27.50, Service optional **Wines** 15 bottles over £20, 34 bottles under £20, 12 by glass **Notes** Sunday L, Vegetarian available, Dress restrictions, No shorts or jeans **Seats** 70, Pr/dining room 20 **Children** Min 14 yrs **Parking** 45

Drewe Arms

Modern, Seafood

Classic seafood dining pub

☎ 01404 841267

EX14 3NF

dir: M5 junct 28, take A373 Cullompton to Honiton. Follow signs for 5.2m

This Grade II listed inn dates from 1228 and is set in an attractive, sleepy thatched village. An abundance of appealing features includes a lovely garden for summer, oak beams, open winter fires and a welcoming atmosphere. The straightforward food majors on fish and seafood, with the focus on simplicity, seasonality and freshness. The quality of the fish shines through in dishes such as brill with a slice of grilled pancetta and herb butter sauce. A typical starter might include pheasant and partridge terrine with fruit chutney, with toffee apple brûlée for dessert.

Times 12-2/7-9, Closed 25 Dec, Closed D Sun

Northcote Manor

Modern British V

Accomplished cooking in historic country house

☎ 01769 560501

EX37 9LZ

e-mail: rest@northcotemanor.co.uk
web: www.northcotemanor.co.uk
dir: M5 junct 27 towards Barnstaple. Left at rdbt to South Molton. Do not enter Burrington village. Follow A377, right at T-junct to Barnstaple. Entrance after 3m, opp Portsmouth Arms railway station and pub

An idyllic setting, impressive grounds and the warmth and natural friendliness of the staff make this lovely gabled manor house a delightful place to visit. Built in 1716, the house has a long and varied history, dating back to its origins as a Benedictine monastery, and bright murals adorn the comfortable, refurbished dining room. Good sourcing of quality, local seasonal produce highlights the daily fixed-price dinner menus. Cooking is mature and unfussy and dishes are well executed, simply presented and show good combinations of natural flavours. So expect the likes of fillet of line-caught halibut with herb risotto, confit fennel and fish velouté, or breast of local duckling with red wine sauce, and for dessert, perhaps an iced lemon parfait with poached berries.

Chef Richie Herkes **Owner** J Pierre Mifsud **Times** 12-2/7-9 **Prices** Fixed L 3 course £15-£25.50, Fixed D 3 course £38.50, Service optional **Wines** 40 bottles over £20, 6 bottles under £20, 9 by glass **Notes** Sunday L, Vegetarian menu, Dress restrictions, Smart casual preferred, Civ Wed 80 **Seats** 34, Pr/dining room 14 **Children** Portions, Menu **Parking** 30

Gidleigh Park ⬡⬡⬡⬡ – *see page 122*

Mill End

Modern French

A watermill with terrific food in a quiet Dartmoor hideaway

☎ 01647 432282

TQ13 8JN

e-mail: info@millendhotel.com
dir: From A30 turn on to A382. Establishment on right before Chagford turning

Tucked away on the banks of the River Teign, this 18th-century former flour mill - once the home of Sir Frank Whittle, inventor of the jet engine - is more like a family home than a hotel, with guests encouraged to relax and enjoy the surroundings. The restored water wheel churns away delightfully just outside the dining room, which boasts olive-green walls, large comfortable chairs and well-appointed tables, with original artwork, subdued lighting and candles creating an air of understated elegance. The cooking style is modern French, the menu showcasing the best locally sourced produce and featuring many classic dishes with attention to detail in presentation. Take a starter of grilled Capricorn goat's cheese with confit red peppers and aubergine caviar, followed by a main course of Cornish sea bass with beetroot purée and asparagus velouté.

Times 12-2/7-9, Closed L (open by appoint) (open Sun L)

---

22 Mill Street Restaurant & Rooms

Modern European V

New owners and a modern menu

☎ 01647 432244

22 Mill St TQ13 8AW

e-mail: info@22millst.com
dir: Please telephone for directions

Now under the same ownership as Browns Hotel in Tavistock, 22 Mill Street has been refurbished. The new look is very contemporary, with wooden floorboards, high-backed leather chairs and bright works of modern art combining with elegantly-set tables to create a smart but unfussy dining room with an informal air. With friendly and polite service, the monthly-changing modern European menu lists local ingredients when they feature, which is often, so grilled breast of Creedy Carver duck is served with fig tarte Tatin and Savoy cabbage with pancetta in a main course. Falmouth Bay scallops come as a starter with cauliflower pannacotta and fennel caramel, or sautéed breast of wood pigeon with Puy lentils, parsnips, honey and Madeira. Desserts can be as equally creative, as in a dish featuring new season English rhubarb, crème fraîche sorbet, ginger snap and sugared doughnuts.

Chef John Hooker **Owner** Helena King **Times** 12-4/6.3-10, Closed Mon, Closed D Sun **Prices** Fixed L 2 course £30-£40, Fixed D 3 course £42-£50, Service optional **Wines** 50 bottles over £20, 10 bottles under £20, 4 by glass **Notes** Sunday L, Vegetarian menu **Seats** 28, Pr/dining room 14 **Children** Min 5yrs, Portions **Parking** On street

Gidleigh Park

Modern European 🖥 V ▲NOTABLE WINE LIST

The epitome of modern, luxury country-house fine dining

☎ 01647 432367
TQ13 8HH
e-mail: gidleighpark@gidleigh.co.uk
web: www.gidleigh.com
dir: From Chagford Sq turn right at Lloyds TSB into Mill St, after 150yds right fork, across x-rds into Holy St. Restaurant 1.5m

The twisting, one-and-a-half-mile drive along a private lane to this globally acclaimed, black-and-white mock-Tudor Dartmoor retreat is so worth the effort - magically set in extensive gardens traversed by the tumbling River Teign, it's nothing short of idyllic! And, though Gidleigh was stylishly transformed and rejuvenated by a multi-million pound, 11-month refurbishment programme back in 2006 (and is now in the secure hands of Andrew Brownsword, chef Michael Caines' business partner in the Abode group), it has cleverly lost none of its timeless charm and homely atmosphere ... a quite stunning achievement! There are now three dining rooms all with a different style - the more contemporary room comes with a glass wine wall and oak floor, while the 'Teign' is a light room with access out on to the garden terrace and the 'Meldon' is oak panelled and traditional

in style. And, a pre- or post-meal stroll in the 45 acres of grounds is still a Gidleigh requisite, sauntering among delightful terraced gardens and beech woods, on manicured lawns and beside the riverbank, while the views from the interior and terraces over the peerless Dartmoor setting are unforgettable. The name Michael Caines alone draws people from far and wide to experience the exquisite, modern, classically-inspired seasonal cuisine. The imaginative cooking showcases fresh, tip-top quality local ingredients, brimful of luxury and intricate presentation, offered as fixed-price lunch, dinner and tasting options. Think braised turbot and scallops served with wild mushrooms and a chive butter sauce, or slow-roast Hatherleigh venison served with braised pork belly and red cabbage and fig and chestnut purées, and perhaps a hot pistachio soufflé and pistachio ice cream to finish. The cheeseboard is a cracking feature, the wine list superb, while peripherals like canapés, breads, amuse-bouche and petits fours all hit top form too. The rejuvenated Gidleigh is a must-visit destination.

Chef Michael Caines MBE
Owner Andrew and Christina Brownsword **Times** 12-2/7-9.45
Prices Fixed L 2 course £33-£35, Fixed D 3 course £85-£95, Tasting menu £95, Service added but optional 10%
Wines 750 bottles over £20, 9 by glass

Notes Vegetarian menu, Dress restrictions, Shirt with collar, no jeans or sportswear, Civ Wed 52 **Seats** 52, Pr/dining room 20 **Children** Min 8 yrs D, Portions, Menu **Parking** 30

Swallows Eaves

Ⓢ Traditional

Classical cuisine in a traditional environment

☎ 01297 553184
Swan Hill Rd EX24 6QJ
e-mail: swallows_eaves@hotmail.com
dir: In village centre on A3052 opposite village shop

Swallows Eaves is an Edwardian hotel located a short distance from the coast. Traditional values are upheld in the genuinely warm welcome, the immaculate presentation of the property and the homely décor, with china ornaments, oil paintings and prints inside and lovingly tended gardens outside. Similarly, the daily menu has a traditional feel with dishes like chicken liver and sherry pâté; fresh halibut with lemon parsley butter, and whisky and raspberry posset with honey and oatmeal. The cooking has flair and quality local ingredients are allowed to take centre stage.

Times Closed Nov-Feb, Closed L Mon-Sun

Jan and Freddies Brasserie

Ⓢ Modern British 🍸

Enjoyable brasserie dining in a relaxed atmosphere

☎ 01803 832491
10 Fairfax Place TQ6 9AD
e-mail: info@janandfreddiesbrasserie.co.uk
web: www.janandfreddiesbrasserie.co.uk
dir: Fairfax Place runs parallel to S Embankment. Restaurant faces Hawley Rd

Located in the heart of Dartmouth, this stylish brasserie with contemporary yet comfortable décor, polished wood tables, smart lighting and lots of mirrors is just a stone's throw from the River Dart. The informal atmosphere is complemented by relaxed and friendly service, and there's a lively bar area at the rear. Unfussy modern British dishes are prepared with an emphasis on top-quality local ingredients and a focus on flavour. Begin with a light bavarois with Devon Blue cheese and pear and walnut salad, or maybe a fresh bisque of local crab with saffron oil, followed by halibut poached in red wine with roasted beetroot, cauliflower purée and a light fish sauce. Enticing desserts include the likes of a superb hot chocolate fondant accompanied by vanilla parfait, roasted hazelnuts and an espresso caramel.

Chef Richard Hilson **Owner** Jan & Freddie Clarke **Times** 12.30-2/6.30-9, Closed Xmas, Closed Sun, Closed L Mon **Prices** Fixed D 3 course fr £23.95, Starter £4.95-£7.50, Main £13.95-£19.50, Dessert £5.95-£7.50, Service optional **Wines** 8 bottles over £20, 22 bottles under £20, 10 by glass **Notes** Vegetarian available **Seats** 40 **Children** Min 5 yrs **Parking** On street

---

The New Angel Restaurant & Rooms

Ⓢ Ⓢ Ⓢ – see page 124

River Restaurant

Ⓢ Ⓢ Modern British 💻

Riverside restaurant serving accomplished cuisine

☎ 01803 832580
The Dart Marina Hotel, Sandquay Rd TQ6 9PH
e-mail: info@dartmarinahotel.com
dir: A3122 from Totnes to Dartmouth. Follow road which becomes College Way, before Higher Ferry. Hotel sharp left in Sandquay Rd

This superb waterfront development is attracting high profile guests not only to the dramatically revamped hotel but also to the two restaurants. The main River Restaurant offers diners superb views across the busy river and the chance to dine alfresco in summer. It retains much of the traditional style, although presented in a more modern look. The skilled kitchen delivers accomplished cuisine, using carefully sourced, top-notch ingredients. Expect starters like Dartmouth smoked haddock and celeriac soup, followed by the harmonious flavours of assiette of pork - braised belly, herb-crusted loin, cannelloni of cheek. Lemon and galangal rice pudding with caramel ice cream is a dessert to come back for. The Wildfire Bistro offers an alternative, informal eating option.

Chef Mark Streeter **Owner** Richard Seton **Times** 12-2/6-9 **Prices** Fixed D 3 course £32.50, Service optional **Notes** Sunday L, Vegetarian available, Dress restrictions, Smart casual, Air con **Seats** 80 **Children** Portions

---

Barton Cross Hotel

Ⓢ British, French Ⅴ

Quality cooking in engaging 17th-century thatched property

☎ 01392 841245
Huxham, Stoke Canon EX5 4EJ
e-mail: bartonxhuxham@aol.com
dir: 0.5m off A396 at Stoke Canon, 3m N of Exeter

This converted 17th-century thatched longhouse is in a pretty rural setting just five miles from Exeter. The restaurant is an impressive room with a huge inglenook fireplace and a minstrels' gallery, and looks fabulous by candlelight. Cob walls and low beams remind guests of the building's age, while the food is more modern: expect assured cuisine from a kitchen that makes good use of local produce. Begin with venison carpaccio with apricot chutney perhaps, and then tuck into rump of lamb with mint rösti and redcurrant sauce, or pan-fried monkfish with sun-blushed tomato mash, red pepper sauce and pesto, followed by dark chocolate truffle cake with caramel sauce.

Chef Paul Bending **Owner** Brian Hamilton **Times** Closed Sun, Closed L Mon **Prices** Fixed D 3 course £23.50, Starter £4.50-£6.50, Main £14.50-£18, Dessert £4.50-£6.50, Service optional **Wines** 49 bottles over £20, 42 bottles under £20, 10 by glass **Notes** Vegetarian menu, Dress restrictions, Smart casual **Seats** 50, Pr/dining room 26 **Children** Portions, Menu **Parking** 50

The New Angel Restaurant & Rooms

French

Revitalised harbour-side eatery and one of England's master chefs

☎ 01803 839425
2 South Embankment TQ6 9BH
e-mail: info@thenewangel.co.uk
web: www.thenewangel.co.uk
dir: Dartmouth centre, on the water's edge

Refurbished and revitalised once again, the new New Angel is still in the capable hands of John Burton Race. The TV work goes on, but Mr Burton Race has found the time to inject further impetus into this elegant waterfront restaurant. The half-timbered Tudor building, with its large windows overlooking the busy river Dart estuary, is painted a sophisticated dark grey and the new interior is refined without being overbearing. Tables are now clothed in white linen and smartly set. The ground-floor dining room with its open-plan kitchen buzzes with life, while the upstairs cocktail lounge is intended to be the more mellow space. The food is a little more straightforward in presentation, local produce gets star billing and the flavours hit the mark. Fricassée of snails, tender and delicious, cooked in red wine fill a puff pastry tartlet with the addition of an onion cream in an impressive starter, while main-course braised pig's trotter, foie gras, potato purée and fine beans

further confirms the French sensibilities of the chef. Chocolate fondant with pistachio ice cream is a divine dessert, and service throughout is on the ball.

Chef John Burton Race & Robert Spencer **Owner** Clive Jacobs
Times 12-2.30/6.30-10, Closed Jan
Prices Fixed L 2 course £24.50, Starter £8-£14, Main £19-£26, Dessert £8.50, Service optional, Groups min 10 service 12.5% **Wines** 150 bottles over £20, 32 bottles under £20, 8 by glass
Notes Sunday L, Vegetarian available, Dress restrictions, Smart casual, Air con
Seats 80, Pr/dining room 6
Children Portions **Parking** 6
Parking Dartmouth central car park

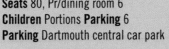

EXETER *Continued*

Best Western Lord Haldon Country House Hotel

◎◎ Modern European

Stylish country-house dining near Exeter

☎ 01392 832483
Dunchideock EX6 7YF
e-mail: enquiries@lordhaldonhotel.co.uk
dir: From M5 junct 31 or A30 follow signs to Ide, continue through village for 2.5m, left after red phone box, 0.5m, pass under stone bridge, left

Just four miles from Exeter and affording glorious views over the Exe Valley, this historic country house stands hidden away amidst rural tranquillity. The light-and-airy Courtyard Restaurant is a popular dining venue and makes full use of the views of the courtyard and 'Capability' Brown landscape. The cooking combines classics with European influences, with the daily-changing menus featuring skilfully conceived and executed dishes using locally-sourced West Country produce. A typical meal may take in a terrine of rabbit, pigeon, guinea fowl and wild boar with red onion marmalade to start, followed by chump of lamb with garlic mash and a balsamic and redcurrant reduction. Knowledgeable service from uniformed staff.

Chef Fred Gallow **Owner** Pullman Premier Leisure **Times** 12-2.30/7.15-9.30, Closed L Mon-Sat **Prices** Food prices not confirmed for 2009. Please telephone for details. **Wines** 3 bottles over £20, 40 bottles under £20, 7 by glass **Notes** Sunday L, Vegetarian available, Dress restrictions, Smart casual, Civ Wed 120 **Seats** 60, Pr/dining room 25 **Children** Portions, Menu **Parking** 120

Michael Caines at Abode Exeter

◎◎ Modern European 🖥 V 🕯

Innovative modern cooking overlooking the cathedral

☎ 01392 223638
Cathedral Yard EX1 1HD
e-mail: tablesexeter@michaelcaines.com
web: www.michaelcaines.com
dir: Town centre, opposite Cathedral

Enjoying stunning views over the cathedral, this intimate and stylish restaurant is located in a veteran Exeter hotel - the first of a chain of boutique hotels that were rolled out in historic towns and key city centres across the UK. Fashionable art decks the walls in the modern dining room, with its subtle lighting, darkwood floor and crisp white linen setting the scene for some tempting contemporary cuisine. The kitchen shows a strong commitment to local produce and seasonality, backed by innovative, highly accomplished cooking. Brixham scallops with grilled leek, lemon purée, crème fraîche and bacon lardons, followed by line-caught sea bass with cauliflower purée, shiitake mushrooms, braised sweet chard and red wine butter are fine examples of the fare. A small champagne and cocktail bar rounds off an upbeat, cosmopolitan package.

Chef Ross Melling **Owner** Michael Caines & Andrew Brownsword **Times** 12-2.30/7-10, Closed Sun, Closed D Xmas **Prices** Fixed L 2 course fr £14.50, Tasting menu £62, Starter £8.50-£14.95, Main £21.50-£24.50, Dessert £8.50, Service added but optional 11%, Groups min 10 service 12.5% **Wines** 158 bottles over £20, 8 bottles under £20, 8 by glass **Notes** Vegetarian menu, Dress restrictions, Smart casual, Civ Wed 50, Air con **Seats** 70, Pr/dining room 80 **Children** Portions, Menu **Parking** Mary Arches St car park

No 21

◎ Modern European

Relaxed, contemporary bistro dining overlooking the cathedral

☎ 01392 210303
21a Cathedral Yard EX1 1HB
e-mail: restaurant@21cathedralyard-exeter.co.uk
dir: Opposite Cathedral

No 21 is set amongst a row of attractive shops, restaurants and bars overlooking the cathedral. Inside, the chunky oak tables, chairs and floor deliver traditional bistro styling, while the décor and artwork have a more contemporary edge. During the day there's a servery offering a quick-snack café format, while in the evenings there is full table service. Accomplished modern European cooking, using good quality local produce, results in dishes such as risotto cake of Mediterranean vegetables with red wine dressing, pan-seared venison and pigeon pie, and pavé of cod with parsley crust.

Chef Andrew Shortman **Owner** Andrew Shortman **Times** 9-5/6-9.30, Closed 25 Dec, 1 Jan, Closed D Sun, Mon **Prices** Starter £3.95-£6.50, Main £12.95-£16.50,

Dessert £4.75-£5.95, Service optional **Wines** 6 bottles over £20, 20 bottles under £20, 4 by glass **Notes** Sunday L, Vegetarian available, Air con **Seats** 56, Pr/dining room 18 **Children** Portions

The Rougemont by Thistle

◎ British

☎ 0871 376 9018
Queen St EX4 3SP

This establishment was awarded its Rosette/s just as we went to press. Therefore we are unable to provide a description for it - visit www.theAA.com for the most up-to-date information.

Times 7-10 **Prices** Food prices not confirmed for 2009. Please telephone for details.

GULWORTHY	Map 3 SX47

The Horn of Plenty

◎◎◎ – *see page 126*

HAYTOR VALE	Map 3 SX77

Rock Inn

◎ British

Beautifully located country inn serving accomplished British food

☎ 01364 661305
TQ13 9XP
e-mail: reservations@rockinn.co.uk
dir: From A38 at Drum Bridges, join the A382 to Bovey Tracey. After 2m join B3387 towards Haytor and continue for 3.5m, follow brown signs

Popular old-world country inn with beams and flagstone floors, dating from the 1750s and set below the Haytor Rocks just inside the Dartmoor National Park. It's a family-run establishment, traditional in style, with classic fare such as rib-eye steak with a peppercorn sauce and home-cut chunky chips, or perhaps oven-baked fillets of gilthead bream with herb and orange served with braised fennel and fine beans on the dinner carte. Dishes are based on quality local ingredients, while Devon cheeses are a feature and wines include the county's own Dart Valley Reserve from the Sharpham Vineyard.

Chef Sue Beaumont Graves **Owner** Mr C Graves **Times** 12-2.15/6.30-9, Closed 25-26 Dec **Prices** Food prices not confirmed for 2009. Please telephone for details. **Notes** Dress restrictions, No jeans **Seats** 75 **Children** Portions, Menu **Parking** 25

The Horn of Plenty

GULWORTHY Map 3 SX47

Modern International 🖥️ ✋

Serious cuisine in stunning countryside location

☎ 01822 832528
PL19 8JD
e-mail: enquiries@thehornofplenty.co.uk
web: www.thehornofplenty.co.uk
dir: 3m from Tavistock on A390. Turn right at Gulworthy Cross, follow signpost

Nestling in the heart of the Tamar Valley, this creeper-clad, archetypal country-house hotel was built in 1870 for the Mine Captain of the Great Devon Consol and stands in 5 acres of wonderful gardens with mature trees, walled gardens and wild orchards. The chic, light-and-airy restaurant is simply decorated and all eyes are drawn to the windows, which afford panoramic views across the breathtaking scenery. The mood is romantic at night, when the room is lit by table lanterns. In the kitchen, a well-established team led by Peter Gorton produces modern British cuisine with international influences, drawing on fine seasonal ingredients - many from the kitchen's own organic fruit and vegetable garden. Clever combinations produce complementary flavours and textures; sample a starter of sautéed scallops and king prawns wrapped in prosciutto on coriander lentils and an oriental dressing. A

perfectly executed main course choice would be lightly-spiced venison with celeriac purée, red wine shallots and Cassis-flavoured sauce, rounded off with a decadent trio of chocolate. The wine list is equally well constructed, offering an extensive selection plus a good range of ports and digestifs.

Chef Peter Gorton **Owner** Mr & Mrs P Roston, Peter Gorton **Times** 12-4/7-12, Closed 24-26 Dec **Prices** Fixed L course £26.50, Fixed D 3 course £45, Service included, Groups min 10 service 10% **Wines** 115 bottles over £20, 20 bottles under £20, 11 by glass **Notes** Sunday L, Vegetarian available, Dress restrictions, Smart casual, Civ Wed 150, Air con **Seats** 60, Pr/dining room 12 **Children** Portions, Menu **Parking** 20

HOLBETON   Map 3 SX65

The Dartmoor Union Inn

◉ International

Stylish restaurant in a village setting

☎ 01752 830288
Fore St PL8 1NE
e-mail: sue.constantine@dartmoorunion.co.uk

Set in the very heart of the picture-postcard village of Holbeton, this award-winning establishment is all clean lines with lots of wood and a log fire surrounded by deep sofas and comfortable seating. The long bar has shelves at the back displaying a large selection of wines, while the small restaurant area has separate tables and good quality high-backed leather chairs. The appealing modern menu includes starters like cappuccino of white onion and rosemary with truffle oil, or maybe a tian of spiced Brixham crab with citrus truffle mayonnaise and avocado purée, with locally-caught pheasant breast in Parma ham and sage with fondant potato and red wine jus for mains.

Times 12-2.30/5.30-11

HOLSWORTHY   Map 3 SS30

Rydon Inn & Restaurant

◉ British ❦

Traditional pub-atmosphere dining with accomplished, careful cooking

☎ 01409 259444
EX22 7HU
e-mail: info@rydon-inn.com
web: www.rydon-inn.com
dir: 1m outside Holsworthy on A3072

A 300-year-old converted Devon longhouse, the Rydon Inn is decked out with pine-topped tables, benches and chairs, and has a restaurant with a vaulted pine ceiling and a handsome conservatory overlooking the lake and two-acre garden. The kitchen is committed to serving fresh, locally sourced food in a variety of dishes from a modern menu, ranging through salmon teriyaki with Thai vegetables and noodles, local pork and leek sausages with chive mash and cider sauce, or Red Ruby Devon sirloin steak with chips, salad, onion rings and pepper sauce.

Chef Mark Warren **Owner** Dennis & Janice Harper **Times** 11.30-3/6-11, Closed 3 wks in Jan, Closed Mon Mid-Sep-Jun (ex BHs) **Prices** Starter £4.50-£6.50, Main £9.95-£17.50, Dessert £5.50-£7.50, Service optional **Wines** 4 bottles over £20, 23 bottles under £20, 7 by glass **Notes** Sunday L, Vegetarian available, Civ Wed 50 **Seats** 80, Pr/dining room 30 **Children** Portions, Menu **Parking** 80

HONITON   Map 4 ST10

Combe House

◉◉ Modern British Ⅴ ▮ᴺᴼᵀᴬᴮᴸᴱ ᵂᴵᴺᴱ ᴸᴵˢᵀ ❦

Fine-dining experience in stunning Elizabethan manor

☎ 01404 540400
Gittisham EX14 3AD
e-mail: stay@thishotel.com
web: www.thishotel.com
dir: M5 junct 28/29, A373 to Honiton. Right in High St and follow signs for Sidmouth A375, then brown tourist signs for Combe House

Set in 3,500 acres of Devonshire parkland grazed by Arabian horses, this stunning Elizabethan mansion house - now a luxurious country-house hotel - is approached via a winding mile-long drive. The interior is hugely atmospheric, with ornate ceilings, mullioned windows, ancestral portraits, fine antiques, fresh flowers and blazing log fires throughout the panelled public rooms. Dining is equally impressive, with a skilled kitchen using the best of local, seasonal and home-grown produce to underpin contemporary British dishes with French influences. There's a good choice for vegetarians (goat's cheese and roasted onion tart with Jerusalem artichoke vinaigrette), and vegans are willingly catered for. Brixham fish, bought daily at auction, might include sweet pickled red mullet with provençal vegetables, or gilthead bream with crushed ratte potatoes, smoked eel and tomato and caper butter.

Combe House

Chef Hadleigh Barrett, Stuart Brown **Owner** Ken & Ruth Hunt **Times** 12-2/7-9.30, Closed 2 wks end Jan **Prices** Fixed L 2 course fr £22, Tasting menu £59, Service optional **Wines** 78 bottles over £20, 11 bottles under £20, 8 by glass **Notes** Tasting menu 6 courses, Sunday L, Vegetarian menu, Dress restrictions, Smart casual, Civ Wed 100 **Seats** 60, Pr/dining room 48 **Children** Portions, Menu **Parking** 35

Home Farm Restaurant & Hotel

◉ Modern British

Former farmhouse hotel offering refined cuisine

☎ 01404 831278
Wilmington EX14 9JR
e-mail: info@thatchedhotel.co.uk

This thatched former farmhouse is set in well-tended gardens complete with original cobbled courtyard, and has been transformed into a comfortable hotel. Refurbished in contemporary style, the restaurant retains many original features, and in keeping with the hotel's name diners are made to feel really at home. The chef makes good use of herbs, delicate flavours and fine ingredients, offering a balanced choice of simple British dishes with a modern twist. You might start with caramelised red onion and Somerset brie tartlet, and follow with a main course of pan-fried brill topped with crab butter and tarragon sauce. Traditional desserts like Trinity burnt cream or steamed syrup pudding round things off nicely.

Times 12-2/7-9

HORNS CROSS
Map 3 SS32

The Hoops Inn & Country Hotel

British, Mediterranean

Gastro-pub fare at an ancient inn

☎ 01237 451222
EX39 5DL
e-mail: sales@hoopsinn.co.uk
dir: Follow A39 from Bideford towards Clovelly/Bude, through Fairy Cross and Horns Cross, restaurant on the right

Surrounded by natural gardens, stream and ponds close to Devon's north coast, this 13th-century thatched longhouse is worth seeking out. Dine in the bar or in the oak-panelled dining room with its open fire, red-tiled floor and an eclectic mix of furnishings. Locally sourced produce is at the heart of the operation and a mature approach to cooking results in honest, unfussy dishes cooked with care and accuracy. The modern British menu has some French and Italian influences, and may take in shellfish and seafood soup, followed by wild sea bass on wilted spinach with beurre blanc, or the popular half shoulder of local lamb slow-cooked in red wine and garlic, with Eton Mess to finish.

Chef M Somerville & Jo Winter **Owner** Gerry & Dee Goodwin **Times** 12-4/6-11 **Prices** Starter £5-£8, Main £10-£20, Dessert £4.50-£8.50, Service included **Wines** 98 bottles over £20, 132 bottles under £20, 15 by glass **Notes** Sunday L, Vegetarian available, Dress restrictions, Smart casual **Seats** 90, Pr/dining room 16 **Children** Portions, Menu **Parking** 100

ILFRACOMBE
Map 3 SS54

The Quay

Modern British

Exciting food in an 'upturned boat'

☎ 01271 868090 & 868091
11 The Quay EX34 9EQ
e-mail: info@11thequay.com
dir: Follow signs for harbour and pier car park. Restaurant on left before car park

There is inevitably an air of expectation when visiting a restaurant owned by artist Damien Hirst and The Quay doesn't disappoint - his artworks and sculptures adorn the premises and the first-floor dining room is in the shape of a fish, but with the appearance of an upturned boat! With large windows overlooking the sea, the white-painted boards, clothed tables, banquette seating and chairs are all pretty straightforward however, as is the traditional British cooking, albeit with a modern emphasis. Start with scallops with black pudding, mash potato, capers and salsify purée, followed by pan-roasted partridge breast served with confit leg, fondant potato and game jus. A Taste Menu comes with the option of selected wines.

Chef Lawrence Hill-Wickham **Owner** Simon Browne & Damien Hirst **Times** 10-3/6-9.30, Closed 25-26 Dec, 2-25 Jan **Prices** Food prices not confirmed for 2009. Please telephone for details. **Wines** 50 bottles over £20, 30 bottles under £20, 29 by glass **Notes** Sunday L, Vegetarian available **Seats** 32, Pr/dining room 26 **Children** Portions, Menu **Parking** Pier car park 100yds

ILSINGTON
Map 3 SX77

Ilsington Country House Hotel

Modern European

Traditional dining in Dartmoor country-house hotel

☎ 01364 661452
Ilsington Village TQ13 9RR
e-mail: hotel@ilsington.co.uk
web: www.ilsington.co.uk
dir: A38 to Plymouth, exit at Bovey Tracey turn, then 3rd exit from rdbt to Ilsington, then 1st right and hotel 5m after Post Office

This friendly, family-owned country-house hotel offers tranquillity and far-reaching views from its elevated position on the southern slopes of Dartmoor. The new restaurant has been specifically designed to capture the impressive views across the moor and the Haytor Rocks, and the walls are hung with moor views by local painters. The kitchen takes care in its sourcing of top quality ingredients and skilful preparation produces mostly French dishes full of flavour. Try a starter of pan-fried loin of yellow fin tuna with beetroot tartare, beetroot sorbet and balsamic reduction, followed perhaps by a main course of breast of duck with braised red cabbage, dauphinoise potatoes and rosemary jus. Desserts include a warm treacle tart with cinnamon ice cream and toffee sauce.

Chef Mike O'Donnell **Owner** Hassell Family **Times** 12-2/6.30-9 **Prices** Fixed L 2 course £14.50-£15.95, Fixed D 3 course £33.95-£35, Service included **Wines** 31 bottles over £20, 40 bottles under £20, 12 by glass **Notes** Sunday L, Vegetarian available, Dress restrictions, Shirt with a collar (smart casual) no shorts, Air con **Seats** 75, Pr/dining room 70 **Children** Portions **Parking** 60

INSTOW
Map 3 SS43

Decks Restaurant

◎ Modern British

Hearty modern cooking at a renowned Devon seafront restaurant

☎ 01271 860671

Hatton Croft House, Marine Pde EX39 4JJ

e-mail: decks@instow.net

dir: From Barnstaple follow A38 to Bideford. Following signs for Instow, restaurant situated at far end of sea front

Stunning views of the estuary make this two-floored beachside restaurant a very appealing spot - eat alfresco or at a window table on the first floor to make the most of the view. Expect carefully prepared hearty, contemporary cuisine with good combinations that work well and attractive presentation. Try dishes like seared West Country beef with japonaise dressing, or baked fillet of hake with mashed potato, button onions, and bacon and red wine jus, and to finish, perhaps a nougat parfait with roasted plums. Lighter fare is available at lunchtime. There's also a fixed-price option running alongside the carte, and there's a downstairs bar.

Times 12-2.30/7-9.30, Closed 25-26 Dec, 1 Jan, Closed Sun-Mon

KINGSBRIDGE
Map 3 SX74

Buckland-Tout-Saints

◎◎ Modern British, French V 🕙

Quality dining in an elegant Queen Anne manor house

☎ 01548 853055

Goveton TQ7 2DS

e-mail: buckland@tout-saints.co.uk

dir: 3m NE of Kingsbridge off A381. Through hamlet to Goveton, 500 yds past church

Hidden away down winding country lanes, this elegant country-house hotel dates back some 300 years and nestles in its own valley in Devon's stunning South Hams, in extensive, beautifully tended gardens and woodland. Striking Russian pine panelling, antiques and open fires are features of the luxurious interior, with the restaurant, bar and lounge lovingly restored to their original grandeur. The elegant restaurant has quality table appointments and comfortable high-backed chairs, and showcases the best of the county's abundant produce on the concise, seasonal, modern-focused menu. Smoked fish tortellini with pea shoots and horseradish sauce, best end of lamb, mini shepherd's pie and vegetable gratin, or pan-fried fillet of black bream with champ and broad beans are fine examples of the fare.

Chef Callum Kier **Owner** Sir Peter Rigby
Times 12-2/7-9.30 **Prices** Fixed L 2 course £15-£21, Fixed D 3 course £34.50-£40, Starter £7.50-£9, Main £15-£20, Dessert £7.50-£9.50, Service optional **Wines** 71 bottles over £20, 24 bottles under £20, 7 by glass **Notes** Sunday L, Vegetarian menu, Dress restrictions, Smart casual, no shorts, Civ Wed 120 **Seats** 40, Pr/dining room 18 **Children** Portions, Menu **Parking** 40

KNOWSTONE
Map 3 SS82

The Masons Arms

◎◎◎ — *see page 130*

LEWDOWN
Map 3 SX48

Lewtrenchard Manor

◎◎◎ — *see page 131*

LIFTON
Map 3 SX38

Arundell Arms

◎◎ Modern British V 🕙

A celebration of local produce at an 18th-century coaching inn

☎ 01566 784666

PL16 0AA

e-mail: reservations@arundellarms.com

web: www.arundellarms.com

dir: Just off A30 in village of Lifton, 3m E of Launceston

Located on the edge of Dartmoor near the River Tamar, this carefully renovated 18th-century coaching inn sits in the heart of a peaceful Devon village. Public rooms full of character provide a relaxed atmosphere with an open log fire for chilly evenings, and the elegant, well lit restaurant offers accomplished modern British cooking and friendly service. The confidently created cuisine is a celebration of local produce, with major suppliers mostly from Devon and Cornwall listed on the menu. Expect starters like boned and stuffed quail with shallots, garlic and herbs, and choose from mains such as casserole of sea bass, halibut and monkfish with saffron and chives, or mignon of Devon beef with roasted artichokes, Savoy cabbage and a peppercorn sauce.

Chef Steven Pidgeon **Owner** Anne Voss-Bark
Times 12.30-2.30/7.30-10, Closed 24-25 Dec **Wines** 37 bottles over £20, 7 by glass **Notes** Fixed D 5 courses £40, Sunday L, Vegetarian menu, Dress restrictions, Smart casual **Seats** 70, Pr/dining room 24 **Children** Portions, Menu **Parking** 70

LIFTON *Continued*

Tinhay Mill Guest House and Restaurant

British, French V

Cottage-style restaurant serving locally-sourced food

☎ 01566 784201
Tinhay PL16 0AJ
e-mail: tinhay.mill@talk21.com
dir: From M5 take A30 towards Okehampton/Launceston. Lifton off A30 on left. Follow brown tourist signs. Restaurant at bottom of village near river

Two 15th-century mill cottages were converted to provide this delightful restaurant with rooms. The interior is traditional with thick whitewashed walls, beamed ceilings, a log fire and a separate lounge bar with the comfort of leather sofas. Chef proprietor and cookery writer Margaret Wilson has long been a champion of local produce, used to good effect in dishes such as pan-fried scallops with sweet chilli and lime sauce; and local venison fillet with poached plums and thyme and port wine sauce. Home-made breads, sorbets, ice creams and truffles also feature.

Chef Margaret Wilson Owner Mr P & Mrs M Wilson
Times Closed 2 wks Xmas & New Year, 3 wks Feb & Mar, Closed Sun & Mon (ex residents), Closed L all wk
Prices Fixed D 3 course £22.75-£28.50, Starter £5.25-£8.75, Main £13.25-£19.50, Dessert £5.25-£7.50, Service optional, Groups min 8 service 10% Wines 14 bottles over £20, 16 bottles under £20, 4 by glass Notes Vegetarian menu, Dress restrictions, Smart casual, no jeans, T-shirts or trainers Seats 24, Pr/dining room 24 Children Min 12 yrs Parking 10

LYDFORD
Map 3 SX58

Dartmoor Inn

Modern British

Stylish, rural gastro-pub

☎ 01822 820221
EX20 4AY
e-mail: info@dartmoorinn.co.uk
dir: On A386, Tavistock to Okehampton road

This attractive country inn is a mixture of old-fashioned charm and a contemporary style strongly influenced by both Sweden and New England. There's a tiny bar with a log fire and real ales, while the restaurant comprises a series of small dining rooms with well-spaced tables and upholstered chairs. Dishes are sensitively balanced to stress the main element and menus are tightly aligned to seasonal and locally sourced produce - beef is a particular strength. A set menu is offered alongside a simpler carte of perennial favourites (fish and chips, or oxtail and Madeira). Impressive dishes include fillet of red mullet with crab, leek and potato broth, and rump of lamb with Indian spices and a piquant saffron sauce, or mignon of beef fillet with chanterelle mushrooms and roasted artichokes. Look out for the special supper nights.

Times 12-2.15/6.30-9.30, Closed Mon, Closed D Sun

The Masons Arms

KNOWSTONE
Map 3 SS82

Modern British, French

Stunning food in the relaxed setting of a charming inn

☎ 01398 341231
EX36 4RY
e-mail: dodsonmasonsarms@aol.com
dir: Signed from A361, turn right once in Knowstone

This 13th-century thatched village inn (albeit nowadays more a destination restaurant) oozes rustic character and charm, and a pleasing lack of pretension. The beamed bar has a huge fireplace and very low doorway, with steps to the restaurant in its more modern rear extension with stunning views of the Exmoor countryside. Hand-painted murals adorn the apex ceiling here, offering a complete contrast to the bar areas of the original inn. Mark Dodson's cooking has fine pedigree (for many years he was head chef at The Waterside Inn in Bray - see entry), his style here is full of maturity and confidence, delivering refreshingly uncluttered, clean-cut dishes that use top-notch ingredients. And his modern take on British and French classics has justifiably created a stir in this sleepy mid-Devon hideaway. Take a starter duo of chicken liver and ham hock terrine served with vegetables à la Grecque and brioche toast, and to follow, perhaps monkfish loin wrapped in prosciutto ham and accompanied by potato purée and an orange and balsamic vinegar sauce. It's deservedly busy so book well in advance, especially for weekends.

Chef Mark Dodson Owner Mark & Sarah Dodson
Times 12-2/7-9, Closed 1st 2 wks Jan, Closed Mon, Closed D Sun Prices Starter £8.50-£14, Main £14-£19.50, Dessert £7.50-£8.50, Service optional Wines 30 bottles over £20, 12 bottles under £20, 9 by glass Notes Sunday L, Vegetarian available Seats 24 Children Portions Parking 10

Lewtrenchard Manor

Modern British

Fine food in Jacobean splendour in a secret valley

☎ 01566 783222
EX20 4PN
e-mail: info@lewtrenchard.co.uk
dir: Take A30 signed Okehampton from M5 junct 31. Continue for 25m and exit at Sourton Cross. Follow signs to Lewdown, then Lewtrenchard

Hidden away in a quiet valley on the fringe of Dartmoor and surrounded by idyllic gardens and peaceful parkland, this magnificent Jacobean manor house was once the home of the celebrated hymn writer and novelist Reverend Sabine Baring-Gould of 'Onward Christian Soldiers' fame. Seemingly untouched by time, the interior oozes understated charm and wonderful period detail, complete with oak panelling, beautifully ornate ceilings, stained-glass windows, large fireplaces, period furnishings and family portraits. The candlelit, panelled dining room continues the theme - it's a relatively intimate affair overlooking the pretty colonnaded courtyard, bedecked with flowers in summer and providing the perfect setting for alfresco dining. The kitchen takes a modern approach with the focus on top quality fresh local produce and seasonality, including Devon game, fish from the quayside at

Looe, and herbs and vegetables from the hotel's own walled garden. Deceptively and intelligently simple themed dishes conceal a flair and confidence to allow clear, clean flavours to shine, with the main ingredient taking centre stage. Take roast loin of venison served with celeriac, quince and braised cabbage, or perhaps sea bass with a squid and chorizo ragout, black olive tapenade and basil, while a warm honey parfait with fig tarte Tatin and raspberry sorbet might catch the eye at dessert. Service is formal, but with a friendly yet professional approach, while a good value wine list bolsters the package.

Chef Jason Hornbuckle, Andrew Carter
Owner von Essen Hotels
Times 12-1.30/7-9, Closed L Mon
Prices Fixed L 2 course £15, Fixed D 3 course £45, Service optional **Wines** 234 bottles over £20, 5 bottles under £20, 13 by glass **Notes** The Chef's Table £95, Sunday L, Vegetarian available, Dress restrictions, L smart casual, D no jeans or T-shirts, Civ Wed 100 **Seats** 45, Pr/ dining room 22 **Children** Min 8 yrs, Portions, Menu **Parking** 40

LYNMOUTH   Map 3 SS74

Rising Sun Hotel

◉ British, French

Harbourside dining in former smugglers' inn

☎ 01598 753223
Harbourside EX35 6EG
e-mail: risingsunlynmouth@easynet.co.uk
dir: M5 junct 23 (Minehead). Take A39 to Lynmouth.
Opposite the harbour

Overlooking Lynmouth Bay, this delightful thatched inn on the harbour front was once the haunt of smugglers. The building is full of character and has a fascinating history dating from the 14th century. R D Blackmore wrote several chapters of Lorna Doone here, and Shelley purportedly honeymooned here. The oak-panelled dining room, candlelit at night, serves quality local produce cooked with care, in dishes such as terrine of smoked salmon and trout, pan-fried sea bass with roasted baby fennel, saffron and dill potato rösti, or honey-roast duck with grain mustard and red wine sauce.

Times Closed L all week

Tors Hotel

◉ Modern, Traditional European ♥

Enjoyable dining in relaxed surroundings overlooking the sea

☎ 01598 753236
EX35 6NA
e-mail: torshotel@torslynmouth.co.uk
dir: M5 junct 23 (Bridgwater). Continue 40m on A39 through Minehead. Hotel at base of Countisbury Hill on left

On a hill overlooking the Exmoor coastline, this friendly hotel sits in 5 acres of woodland, with wonderful views of the harbour and sea. The recently refurbished, smartly decorated restaurant has a colonial feel and makes a spacious and welcoming venue for modern European and Thai cuisine. The best of Devon seafood, game and meat are delivered to the table without over-working them, allowing the flavour of ingredients to shine through. Expect starters like Thai salmon fishcakes served with salad garnish, and lime and sweet chilli dipping sauce, or pan-seared pigeon breast with black pudding and red onion marmalade, while mains might include pan-fried escalope of veal with a Madeira, pancetta and cep sauce.

Chef Andy Collier **Owner** Mrs Braunton, Mrs Dalgarno **Times** Closed 3 Jan-4 Feb (wknds only in Feb), Closed L all week **Prices** Fixed L 3 course £15-£30, Fixed D 3 course £30-£42, Service included **Wines** 11 bottles over £20, 39 bottles under £20, 3 by glass **Notes** Vegetarian available, Civ Wed 80 **Seats** 50 **Children** Portions, Menu **Parking** 40

LYNTON   Map 3 SS74

Lynton Cottage Hotel

◉◉ Modern British V ♥

Stunning views and skillfully cooked food

☎ 01598 752342
North Walk EX35 6ED
e-mail: enquiries@lynton-cottage.co.uk
dir: M5 junct 27, follow A361 towards Barnstaple. Follow signs to Lynton A39. In Lynton turn right at church. Hotel on right

Spectacular views across Lynmouth Bay can be enjoyed from this country-house hotel, perched on the hillside 500 feet above the pounding waves. The spacious but intimate restaurant has a fresh and vibrant feel with colourful local artworks, and makes the best of the magnificent outlook. The short carte is well balanced, with local, organic and seasonal produce making their own positive statement. Expect modern presentations and careful cooking that shows maturity and a deft touch. Start with pan-fried scallops with chorizo and spicy tomato dressing, follow with a Taste of Exmoor - steak pie, beef sirloin and lamb breast served with mustard cream - and round off with chocolate terrine with vanilla bean ice cream.

Chef Allan Earl **Owner** Allan Earl, Heather Biancardi **Times** 12-2.30/7-9.30, Closed Dec & Jan **Prices** Food prices not confirmed for 2009. Please telephone for details. **Wines** 8 bottles under £20, 4 by glass **Notes** Fixed D 4 courses, Vegetarian menu **Seats** 40 **Children** Portions **Parking** 18

MORETONHAMPSTEAD   Map 3 SX78

The Mulberry

◉◉◉ – *see opposite*

The White Hart Hotel

◉ British

One-time coaching inn serving traditional and modern cuisine

☎ 01647 441340
The Square TQ13 8NF
e-mail: enquiries@whitehartdartmoor.co.uk

Dating back to the 1700s, this former coaching inn is located on the edge of Dartmoor and comes with a more contemporary styled restaurant. There's a relaxed and friendly atmosphere, with young staff providing friendly, attentive service. The kitchen delivers quality local produce in a range of traditional and modern styles; take king prawn cocktail, chicken supreme or tournedos Rossini alongside the likes of chargrilled John Dory fillets with a mango, avocado, prawn and chilli salsa. Desserts follow the theme, perhaps a strawberry and kiwi millefeuille vying for attention alongside the ubiquitous bread-and-butter pudding and custard. A good selection of bar food is also available.

Times 12-2, 6-9 **Prices** Food prices not confirmed for 2009. Please telephone for details.

NEWTON ABBOT   Map 3 SX87

Sampsons Farm & Restaurant

◉ British ▭

Fresh local produce in a charming farmhouse hotel

☎ 01626 354913
Preston TQ12 3PP
e-mail: info@sampsonsfarm.com
dir: M5/A380/B3195 signed Kingsteignton. Pass Ten Tors Inn on left & take 2nd rd signed B3193 to Chudleigh. At rdbt 3rd exit, left after 1m

A family-run, medieval thatched farmhouse, this place is Devon through and through. The food has impeccable local credentials and service is genuine under the proprietor's enthusiastic leadership; it has been in the same family for over 30 years. The cosy interior with low beams, subdued lighting and crackling log fires is all very reassuring and romantic, and artwork by Devon-based artist Sarah Bell is a feature. The menu is modern, offering Exmouth mussels cooked in a garlic-smoked bacon and white wine cream sauce, and caramelised breast of Crediton duck with confit croquette of the leg and a honey and anise sauce.

Chef Daniel Dennis **Owner** Nigel Bell **Times** 12-2/7-9, Closed 25-26 Dec **Prices** Food prices not confirmed for 2009. Please telephone for details. **Notes** Dress restrictions, No jeans **Seats** 36, Pr/dining room 20 **Children** Portions, Menu **Parking** 20

NEWTON POPPLEFORD
Map 3 SY08

Moore's Restaurant & Rooms

Modern British

Stylish village restaurant serving imaginative dishes

☎ 01395 568100
6 Greenbank, High St EX10 0EB
e-mail: mooresrestaurant@aol.com
dir: Located on A3052, close to M5 junct 30

Located in the centre of pretty Newton Poppleford, this friendly restaurant is run by the Moores, a husband-and-wife team. Formerly two cottages, one of which doubled as a grocer's store, it boasts several bedrooms as well as an intimate dining room with wide windows that overlook the village and a neutral décor that's easy on the eye. Dishes are imaginative and full of flavour, making use of good quality, locally sourced ingredients wherever possible, including Mr Moore's very own catch of the day. Seared scallops are a typical starter, served with pea purée, with roast chump of Gatcombe Farm lamb to follow, accompanied by sea salt baked Pink Fir potatoes and wild mushroom sauce. Round off with Baileys bread-and-butter pudding with Devonshire clotted cream.

Chef Jonathan Moore **Owner** Jonathan & Kate Moore **Times** 12-1.30/7-9.30, Closed 25-26 Dec, 1st 2 wks in Jan, Closed Mon, Closed D Sun **Prices** Fixed L 2 course £12.50-£13.95, Fixed D 3 course £19.50-£29.50, Service optional **Wines** 19 bottles over £20, 12 bottles under £20, 6 by glass **Notes** Sunday L, Vegetarian available

Seats 32, Pr/dining room 12 **Children** Portions **Parking** 2 **Parking** On street & free car park behind church

PLYMOUTH
Map 3 SX45

Artillery Tower Restaurant

British

Accomplished cooking in a unique setting at Plymouth's waterside

☎ 01752 257610
Firestone Bay PL1 3QR
dir: 1m from city centre and train station

One of the oldest military buildings in Plymouth and once part of the strategic sea defences, this restaurant faces the sea in a historic circular 16th-century stone-built tower looking out across Plymouth Sound towards Drakes Island. The restaurant is simply furnished with wooden tables set against stone walls in a round room. As a champion of local produce, the kitchen offers unfussy dishes prepared with respect for the excellent quality of the ingredients. Try an impressive starter of scallops grilled with garlic butter, followed by a sirloin of Gulworthy beef with horseradish mash and red wine sauce, and apricot and Amaretto trifle for dessert.

Chef Peter Constable **Owner** Peter Constable **Times** 12-2.15/7-9.30, Closed Xmas & New Year, Closed Sun-Mon, Closed L Sat **Prices** Fixed D 3 course £28.50 **Wines** 60 bottles over £20, 30 bottles under £20, 6 by glass **Seats** 40, Pr/dining room 16 **Children** Portions **Parking** 20 (Evening only)

Barbican Kitchen

Modern British

The Tanner Brothers' stylish brasserie serving contemporary food

☎ 01752 604448
Plymouth Gin Distillery, 60 Southside St PL1 2LQ
e-mail: info@barbicankitchen.com
dir: On Barbican, 5 mins walk from Bretonside bus station

The contemporary Barbican Kitchen is housed in the Plymouth Gin distillery, the oldest surviving industrial building in Plymouth, which is still fully operational. The open-plan kitchen and vibrant brasserie fuse old and new with striking interior design. Come for lunch, a pre-theatre meal, dinner or Sunday roast. Dishes are simple and well-executed and the flexible menu offers the likes of Dart smoked salmon with capers, red onion and horseradish; and marinated chicken breast with potato and pea korma.

Chef Lee Holland **Owner** Christopher & James Tanner **Times** 12-3/5-10, Closed 25-26 & 31 Dec **Wines** 16 bottles over £20, 22 bottles under £20, 13 by glass **Notes** Pre-theatre menu 2 courses £9.95, 3 courses £13.95, Sunday L, Vegetarian available, Air con **Seats** 80 **Children** Portions, Menu **Parking** Drakes Circus, Guildhall

The Mulberry

MORETONHAMPSTEAD
Map 3 SX78

Modern European V

Elegant dining in opulent surroundings

☎ 01647 445000
Bovey Castle TQ13 8RE
e-mail: enquiries@boveycastle.com
dir: A30/A382 to Moretonhampstead, onto B3212 signed Postbridge. Hotel 2m outside Moretonhampstead on left

Delightfully located in immaculately maintained grounds, this magnificent house turned five-star hotel was built in 1907 and has been restored to its former glory with architecture typical of the extravagance of the era. The entrance is set with smart shrubs, while a liveried doorman greets and ushers you inside. Beautiful public rooms include the Cathedral Room (with wood panelling and a minstrels' gallery), the snooker room and the

library. Artwork - in keeping with the 20s theme - is also a feature, while lounges offer deep comfort. The Edwardian Dining Room restaurant is a spacious and traditional setting, its style continuing the theme, with restful hand-painted silk wallpaper, and, most evenings, a pianist plays, while the smaller Mulberry Restaurant is the hotel's fine-dining option offering a chic, contemporary dining experience. Service is appropriately skilled and friendly, and the talented kitchen delivers exciting, well considered and well constructed modern dishes, with great emphasis placed on quality produce and the successful combinations of flavour and texture. Kick off with sweet spiced langoustines with fennel bavarois and shellfish bisque, and follow with a main course of South Devon beef with consommé of new season vegetables, broad beans and Devon asparagus. Informal dining and light lunches are also served in the refurbished bistro.

Chef Darron Bunn **Owner** Hilwood Resorts & Hotels **Times** Closed Sun, Closed L all week **Prices** Fixed D 3 course £38.50-£58.50, Tasting menu £65, Service optional **Wines** 75 bottles over £20, 11 by glass **Notes** Vegetarian menu, Dress restrictions, Smart casual, Civ Wed 130 **Seats** 40, Pr/dining room 20 **Children** Min 16 yrs **Parking** 100

PLYMOUTH *Continued*

Best Western Duke of Cornwall Hotel

◎ British, European **V**

☎ 01752 275850
Millbay Rd PL1 3LG
e-mail: chutereservations@hotmail.com
dir: City centre, follow signs 'Pavilions', hotel road is opposite

This establishment was awarded its Rosette/s just as we went to press. Therefore we are unable to provide a description for it - visit www.theAA.com for the most up-to-date information.

Chef Darren Kester **Owner** W Combstock, J Morcom **Times** Closed 26-31 Dec, Closed L all wk **Prices** Starter £4.95-£6.95, Main £13.95-£17.50, Dessert £3.95-£5.50 **Wines** 50% bottles over £20, 50% bottles under £20, 6 by glass **Notes** Vegetarian menu, Civ Wed 300 **Seats** 80, Pr/dining room 30 **Children** Portions, Menu **Parking** 40

Bistro Bacchanalia

◎ Traditional British

Relaxed, friendly atmosphere in refurbished harbourside bistro

☎ 01752 254879
Dolphin House, Sutton Harbour, The Barbican PL4 0DW
e-mail: bb@suttonharbour.net
dir: From A38 follow signs at Marsh Mill to City Centre, then to Barbican. Left to Sutton Wharf and Barbican

This stunning waterside restaurant in the heart of the city's historic Sutton Harbour has recently been refurbished. Modern high-backed raffia chairs and striking banquette seating, lightwood tables and seafood-themed prints create a fresh, simple décor. Ideally situated to offer the catch of the day, the unpretentious menu makes excellent use of local produce in some novel combinations - haddock in cider and parsley batter perhaps, served with minted garden peas and crisp chips, or pan-fried squid rings with sautéed potatoes, tomato and pepper jam and prosciutto. A generous helping of sticky toffee pudding with caramel sauce and local ice cream can't fail to please for dessert. Plenty of wines by the glass available.

Chef Chris Whitehead **Owner** Bruce & Lesley Brunning **Times** 12-2/7-9.30, Closed 25 Dec, 1 Jan, Closed Sun, Mon **Prices** Fixed L 2 course £11, Starter £5-£9, Main £8-£18, Dessert £5, Service optional **Wines** 25 bottles over £20, 23 bottles under £20, 16 by glass **Notes** Vegetarian available **Seats** 90 **Parking** 200 yds

Langdon Court Hotel

◎ Traditional British **V** 🕙

Wonderful produce and creative cuisine in Tudor surroundings

☎ 01752 862358
Down Thomas, Wembury PL9 0DY
e-mail: enquiries@langdoncourt.com
dir: From A379 at Elburton, follow brown tourist signs

This magnificent Grade II listed Tudor manor house has an impressive history, with royal connections to Henry VIII and Elizabeth I. Its location is hard to beat as well; set in acres of lush countryside, including a formal garden, with direct access to the beach and coastal footpaths. The bar has a simple menu, while the brasserie-style restaurant menu offers classic dishes with clarity of flavour. Fresh local seafood is a speciality but organically-reared meat and game is also on offer. Perhaps try the tian of Brixham crab and pepper salsa to start, followed by the seared fillet of Devonshire beef, fondant potato, buttered spring green beans and a rich jus.

Chef Carl Smith **Owner** Emma & Geoffrey Ede **Times** 12-2.30/6.30-9.30 **Prices** Fixed L 2 course £15.95-£25.95, Fixed D 3 course £25, Starter £6.25-£7.25, Main £12.95-£21.95, Dessert £6.25-£7.95, Service optional **Wines** 10 bottles over £20, 36 bottles under £20, 8 by glass **Notes** Sunday L, Vegetarian menu, Dress restrictions, Smart casual, Civ Wed 100 **Seats** 60, Pr/dining room 60 **Children** Portions **Parking** 80

Tanners Restaurant

◎◎ Modern British **V** 🕙

Exciting, modern cuisine in medieval West Country setting

☎ 01752 252001
Prysten House, Finewell St PL1 2AE
e-mail: tannerbros@aol.com
dir: Town centre. Behind St Andrews Church on Royal Parade

The building dates back to the 1490s, which makes it Plymouth's oldest by all accounts. It was there when Drake saw the Armada and the Pilgrim Fathers headed for the New World. Now it is a restaurant, run for the last nine years by the Tanner brothers, two young men very much based in the present. Flagstone walls hung with oil canvases, slate floors and beams may be a reminder of the past, but the food is contemporary with British and European ideas on a seasonally changing menu. Cream of Jerusalem artichoke soup or ravioli of confit duck with white bean and truffle velouté are typical starters, followed by roast wild sea bass with crushed potatoes and a mussel and herb nage. Lemon curd and crème fraîche is a suitably indulgent dessert. The success of the restaurant has lead to TV appearances for James Tanner, and the brothers have a second venue in the city - the Barbican Kitchen (see entry) - a lively brasserie.

Chef Christopher & James Tanner, J Barker Jones **Owner** Christopher & James Tanner **Times** 12-2.30/7-9.30, Closed 25, 31 Dec, 1st wk Jan, Closed Sun & Mon **Prices** Fixed L 2 course £14.50, Fixed D 3 course £32, Service optional **Wines** 40 bottles over £20, 20 bottles under £20, 8 by glass **Notes** Tasting menu available, Vegetarian menu, Dress restrictions, Smart casual preferred, no trainers **Seats** 45, Pr/dining room 26 **Children** Portions **Parking** On street, car parks

The Jack In The Green

◎◎ Modern British 🕙

An informal setting for some serious cooking

☎ 01404 822240
EX5 2EE
e-mail: info@jackinthegreen.uk.com
dir: 3m E of M5 junct 29 on old A30

The Jack In The Green Inn offers a choice of contemporary and relaxed areas in which to dine with soft leather chairs and dark wood tables, or the Otter room with its traditional pub feel. The emphasis is on using fresh local produce delivered daily by trusted local suppliers, and menus change regularly to make best use of seasonal fare. The British cooking is underpinned by French influences, as in a starter of grilled goat's cheese with roasted beetroot salad, a main course of Creedy Carver duck breast with potato fondant, apples and Calvados, and a dessert of chocolate mousse and black cherry sorbet. There is also a tasting menu, an impressive choice of bar meals and private rooms are available for celebrating special occasions.

Chef Matthew Mason, Craig Sampson **Owner** Paul Parnell **Times** 12-2/6-9.30, Closed 25 Dec-28 Feb **Prices** Fixed L 2 course £19, Fixed D 3 course £25, Starter £4.95-£8.50,

Main £16.50-£23.50, Dessert £5.75, Service optional **Wines** 40 bottles over £20, 60 bottles under £20, 12 by glass **Notes** Tasting menu available Mon-Sat (pm), Sunday L, Dress restrictions, Smart casual, Air con **Seats** 80, Pr/dining room 60 **Children** Portions, Menu **Parking** 120

SALCOMBE Map 3 SX73

Restaurant 42

◎◎ Modern British

Classy cooking in an idyllic setting

☎ 01548 843408
Fore St TQ8 8JG
e-mail: jane@restaurant42.demon.co.uk
dir: 15m from A38 Exeter to Plymouth

Restaurant 42 takes its name from Douglas Adams' answer to 'Life, the Universe and Everything'. Ten metres from the sea, it enjoys spectacular views of the beaches and estuary from its lovely terrace. You can also relax in the lounge on great squashy leather sofas. The restaurant capitalises on its splendid location by offering sensible, serious food with ingenious touches. The format has recently been extended to offer a wine bar, brasserie and restaurant, and not-to-be-missed dishes include Salcombe crab, Bigbury Bay oysters, and chargrilled fillet of Aune Valley Aberdeen Angus beef, served with slow-roasted plum tomato, field mushroom, balsamic onions and chunky chip potatoes.

Times Closed Sun (Sep-May), Mon (except Jul-Aug), Closed L winter

Soar Mill Cove Hotel

◎◎ Modern British ♨

Stunning coastal views and superb local ingredients

☎ 01548 561566
Soar Mill Cove, Marlborough TQ7 3DS
e-mail: info@soarmillcove.co.uk
dir: A381 to Salcombe, through village follow signs to sea

Set amid spectacular Devon countryside with dramatic sea views, this family-owned hotel's elegant restaurant and lounge make the most of their location above the lovely tranquil cove. Glorious sunsets are just one of the benefits, and the comfortable Serendipity restaurant has a relaxing neutral-themed décor with polished wood tables, and local artists' paintings on display. The outside terrace is also perfect for alfresco dining and the new Champagne Bar is an impressive addition. The

cooking is ingredient-led, with an emphasis on quality West Country produce and suppliers. The accomplished kitchen's approach is via a seasonal fixed-price menu and tasting option, with fresh fish and seafood a speciality. Take wild sea bass with Salcombe scallops, pancetta and wilted spinach, or locally-caught lobster cooked with garlic and herbs.

Chef I Macdonald **Owner** Mr & Mrs K Makepeace & family **Times** Closed Jan, Closed L all week **Prices** Fixed D 3 course £29, Service optional **Wines** 67 bottles over £20, 11 bottles under £20, 4 by glass **Notes** Vegetarian available **Seats** 60 **Children** Portions, Menu **Parking** 25

Tides Reach Hotel

◎ Modern British

Holiday hotel dining in splendid beach location

☎ 01548 843466
South Sands TQ8 8LJ
e-mail: enquire@tidesreach.com
dir: Take cliff road towards sea and Bolt Head

Snugly situated in the valley immediately behind South Sands beach, with beautiful views over Salcombe estuary, this personally-run holiday hotel has a modern yet timeless feel throughout elegant public areas. Competition for the window tables is brisk in the conservatory-style Garden Room restaurant. Cooking breathes a contemporary feel into a traditional British menu, which specialises in local fish and seafood. Daily fixed-price menus may list local mussels steamed in white wine with garlic, parsley and cream, followed by roast monkfish on a bed of olives and peppers with capers and mint.

Chef Finn Ibsen **Owner** Edwards Family **Times** Closed Dec-Jan, Closed L all week **Prices** Food prices not confirmed for 2009. Please telephone for details. **Wines** 90 bottles over £20, 14 bottles under £20, 6 by glass **Notes** Dress restrictions, Smart casual, no jeans or T-shirts **Seats** 80 **Children** Min 8 yrs **Parking** 80

SHALDON Map 3 SX97

ODE true food

◎ Modern British ♨

Global cuisine conjured from local and organic produce

☎ 01626 873977
21 Fore St TQ14 0DE
e-mail: info@odetruefood.co.uk
dir: Cross bridge from Teignmouth then first left into Fore St

Set in a three-storey Georgian townhouse in the picturesque coastal village of Shaldon, the owners of ODE true food are passionate advocates of organic produce and local sourcing. Even the interior has been created with environmentally-friendly reclaimed woods, recycled glass and the use of local craftsmen. The food has strong global influences, but the dishes are well defined with clear flavours and a lightness of touch. Start with

Paignton brown crab blini with poached Hafod farm egg, followed by day boat red mullet with black olive tapenade, white bean cassoulet, or organic chump of lamb with smoked eggplant and tahini.

Chef Tim Bouget **Owner** Tim & Clare Bouget **Times** 11-2/7-11, Closed 25 Dec, BHs, Closed Mon, Closed L Winter Tue-Fri, Closed D Sun **Prices** Fixed L 2 course £14.95-£19.95, Starter £6-£12.50, Main £15.50-£24.50, Dessert £6.50-£9.50, Groups min 6 service 10% **Wines** 67 bottles over £20, 8 bottles under £20, 5 by glass **Notes** Sunday L, Vegetarian available **Seats** 24 **Parking** Car park 3 mins walk

SIDMOUTH Map 3 SY18

Riviera Hotel

◎◎ Modern British

Fine dining in Regency splendour

☎ 01395 515201
The Esplanade EX10 8AY
e-mail: enquiries@hotelriviera.co.uk
web: www.hotelriviera.co.uk
dir: From M5 junct 30 take A3052 to Sidmouth. Situated in centre of Esplanade

This family-run hotel is a fine example of Regency architecture and occupies a prime position on Sidmouth's historic Esplanade, with splendid views over Lyme Bay. The restaurant epitomises traditional standards of comfort and elegance, with bay windows offering panoramic coastal vistas and a terrace perfect for alfresco dining. The kitchen offers a daily-changing menu of innovative dishes alongside more traditional fare, with fixed-priced menus bolstered by carte and dedicated vegetarian options. Expect starters such as crab and saffron tart with hollandaise and watercress salad, followed by a main course of lamb braised shoulder, roast rack and mini shepherd's pie. Leave room for a dessert such as mango soufflé with marshmallow ice cream.

Chef Matthew Weaver **Owner** Peter Wharton **Times** 12.30-2/7-9 **Prices** Fixed L 2 course £26, Fixed D 3 course £37, Starter £8.50-£12, Main £20.50-£29, Dessert £6-£6.95 **Wines** 45 bottles over £20, 30 bottles under £20, 4 by glass **Notes** Fixed L 5 courses, Fixed D 6 courses, Vegetarian available, Air con **Seats** 85, Pr/dining room 65 **Children** Portions, Menu **Parking** 26

SIDMOUTH *Continued*

The Salty Monk

⊛ ⊛ Modern British

Talented and stylish cooking in an old ecclesiastical building

☎ 01395 513174
Church St, Sidford EX10 9QP
e-mail: saltymonk@btconnect.com
web: www.saltymonk.co.uk
dir: From M5 junct 30 take A3052 to Sidmouth, or from Honiton take A375 to Sidmouth, left at lights in Sidford, 200yds on right

This attractive restaurant with rooms was originally a salt house used by Benedictine monks, dating from the 16th century. The lounge and bar are full of original character while the L-shaped restaurant at the rear has a more contemporary feel. It is a light and airy room with views over the award-winning gardens. Tables are well spaced and West Country artists' work adorns the walls. The two owners both cook, using fresh local produce (suppliers listed on the menu) to create accomplished dishes with robust flavours, such as chargrilled Devon Ruby Red sirloin steak served with dauphinoise potatoes on a three-herb mustard sauce; or pan-fried fillets of brill scattered with sautéed girolles, and black truffled potatoes.

Chef Annette & Andy Witheridge **Owner** Annette & Andy Witheridge **Times** 12-1.30/7-9, Closed 3 wks Jan, 2 wks Nov, Closed L Sun-Wed **Prices** Fixed L 2 course fr £24, Fixed D 3 course fr £34.50, Service optional, Groups min 15 service 10% **Wines** 24 bottles over £20, 56 bottles under £20, 6 by glass **Notes** Mineral water complimentary, Vegetarian available **Seats** 55, Pr/dining room 14 **Children** Portions **Parking** 18

Victoria Hotel

⊛ Traditional

Victorian splendour, friendly service and appetising dishes

☎ 01395 512651
The Esplanade EX10 8RY
e-mail: info@victoriahotel.co.uk
dir: At the western end of The Esplanade

The Victoria is a smart hotel in an elevated position at the end of the promenade, set in well tended gardens overlooking the bay. The interior retains its period character and the restaurant is a large room with high ceilings and ornate plaster moulding. The décor is restful and dividers with plantings break up the well spaced tables. The menu offers traditional-style dishes with modern influences - grilled salmon fillet with mustard sauce, roast loin of pork with apple sauce, Exmoor venison casserole or grilled lobster with lemon butter, prawns and saffron rice - notable for quality, freshness and flavour.

Times 1-2/7-9

SOUTH BRENT	**Map 3 SX66**

Glazebrook House Hotel & Restaurant

⊛ British ⊙

Relaxed country-house dining in a tranquil setting

☎ 01364 73322
TQ10 9JE
e-mail: enquiries@glazebrookhouse.com
dir: From A38, between Ivybridge and Buckfastleigh turn off at South Brent and follow hotel signs

Set in 4 acres of pretty gardens on the edge of Dartmoor National Park, this former 18th-century gentleman's residence now makes a welcoming country-house hotel. Beautifully maintained and classic in style, it's a relaxing place to eat and has a log fire you won't want to move away from in winter. Local produce is selected for quality,

Hotel Endsleigh

⊛ ⊛ ⊛

TAVISTOCK	**Map 3 SX47**

Modern British ▢

Memorable setting, stunning surroundings, accomplished cooking

☎ 01822 870000
Milton Abbot PL19 0PQ
e-mail: mail@hotelendsleigh.com
dir: Follow Tavistock signs for B3362, continue through Milton Abbot. On brow of hill, next to school, turn right for hotel. At top of drive turn right at lodge

The location is breathtaking, set in 108 acres of lush, green, rolling Devon countryside, woodlands and gardens, and with the Tamar River as a natural boundary. The house was built in 1812 as a lodge for the Duke of Bedford who used it with his family only once a year, but these days, under the stewardship Olga Polizzi (see entry for Hotel Tresanton, St Mawes), it is a stylish hotel. The building is rather grand and the impeccably tasteful blend of traditional and more contemporary styling, plus well chosen furniture and sensitive restoration of original features, has resulted in the creation of a truly beautiful and quietly luxurious hotel. The panelled dining room is elegant and comfortable, with tables laid with crisp white linen and enjoying fine views, not least from the terrace - the place to eat if the weather allows. In the evening, this magnificent room is entirely lit by candlelight. The menu is based around first-rate produce, much of it local, and takes a modern approach and displays a distinctly English flavour alongside modern European influences and ideas. The new head chef is displaying fine technique in dishes such as wild mushroom risotto, given a rich creaminess with the addition of truffled Cornish brie and finished with a saffron velouté. Sound combinations and creative touches are also evident in main courses such as loin of saddleback pork served with a crisp piece of crackling, the cheek cooked slowly until tender, and butternut squash purée, wild garlic and grain mustard emulsion. Presentation is impressive right through to a dessert of chocolate fondant with a white chocolate pannacotta and butterscotch ice cream. The uniformed staff are professional and suitably friendly.

Chef Nick Fisher **Owner** Olga Polizzi
Times 12.30-2.30/7-10 **Prices** Fixed D 3 course £39, Service optional **Wines** 108 bottles over £20, 27 bottles under £20, 15 by glass **Notes** Tasting menu available, Sunday L, Vegetarian available, Civ Wed 100 **Seats** 50, Pr/dining room 40 **Children** Portions, Menu

and dishes are cooked to order and quite simply presented. Recommendations include West Country scallops with orange and cardamom; noisette of South Devon lamb with celeriac gratin and port wine sauce; and warm dark chocolate sponge with local clotted cream.

Chef David Merriman **Owner** Dave & Caroline Cashmore **Times** Closed 2 wks Jan, 1 wk Aug, Closed Sun, Closed L all week **Prices** Fixed D 3 course £15-£22.50, Starter £4.50-£6.50, Main £16.50-£20.50, Dessert £3.50-£4.95, Service optional **Wines** 17 bottles over £20, 19 bottles under £20, 6 by glass **Notes** Vegetarian available, Civ Wed 80 **Seats** 60, Pr/dining room 12 **Children** Portions **Parking** 40

STRETE — Map 3 SX84

The Kings Arms

⊛ 🖥 Modern British

Fine sea views and an emphasis on fresh local fish

☎ 01803 770377
Dartmouth Rd TQ6 0RW
e-mail: kingsarms_devon_fish@hotmail.com

From the outside this looks like a traditional pub, but inside the style is contemporary, with a small bar area and the main restaurant at the back with many tables enjoying fine views of Start Bay. Fresh fish is the order of the day here, simply prepared but with some twists. A main course of wonderfully fresh sea bream with braised fennel, crispy pancetta and apple and vanilla syrup might be preceded by seared peppered tuna with Szechuan pickled mushrooms and cucumber ribbons, or maybe seared local scallops with aubergine caviar and carrot and star anise syrup. Coffee liqueur crème brûlée with three mini cinnamon doughnuts makes a great dessert.

Times 12-2/6.30-9 Closed Mon, Closed D Sun

TAVISTOCK — Map 3 SX47

Bedford Hotel

⊛ British, European

Best of local produce served in a landmark hotel

☎ 01822 613221
1 Plymouth Rd PL19 8BB
e-mail: enquiries@bedford-hotel.co.uk
dir: Leave M5 J31, take (Okehampton) A30. Take A386 (Tavistock). On entering Tavistock follow signs for town centre. Hotel opposite church.

An impressive castellated building, this charming hotel is the oldest in the town, built on the site of a Benedictine abbey. The elegant Woburn Restaurant offers a formal dining experience in refined surroundings. Using the best of local produce, the seasonal menu provides modern British fare with a nod towards the traditional. Chicken, wild mushroom and spinach terrine, served with piccalilli and mustard dressing, makes a colourful starter. While great tasting rack of lamb - local, from the moor - served with rosti and mushroom ragout, also hits the spot, and to finish, raspberry parfait is cleverly balanced with a slightly tart wild berry compote.

Times 12-2.30/7-9.30, Closed L Mon-Sat

Hotel Endsleigh

⊛⊛⊛ — *see opposite*

THURLESTONE — Map 3 SX64

Thurlestone Hotel

⊛ Modern, Traditional British 🍴

Simple, enjoyable food in long-established seaside hotel

☎ 01548 560382
TQ7 3NN
e-mail: enquiries@thurlestone.co.uk
web: www.thurlestone.co.uk
dir: At Buckfastleigh on A38, take A384 into Totnes and then A381 (Kingsbridge). Continue for 10m then turn right at mini rdbt onto A379 towards Churchstow, turn left at rdbt onto B3197, then turn right into lane signed Thurlestone

In the same family ownership since 1896, this elegant seaside hotel doesn't rest on its laurels, with an extensive selection of leisure facilities added over the years, including indoor and outdoor pools, a beauty salon and a golf course. The restaurant benefits from floor-to-ceiling windows overlooking the bay. The menu changes daily and acknowledges its seaside location, with plenty of local fish and seafood taking starring roles in dishes like skate wing served with crushed scallion potatoes, king prawns and a lemon hollandaise, or perhaps roast rump of Penhalvean lamb teamed with creamed potatoes, basil pesto and black olives.

Chef H Miller **Owner** Grose Family **Times** 12.30-2.30/7.30-9, Closed L Mon-Sat **Prices** Fixed D 4 course £35, Service optional **Wines** 113 bottles over £20, 40 bottles under £20, 8 by glass **Notes** Fish tasting menu, Sunday L, Vegetarian available, Dress restrictions, Jacket, Civ Wed 150, Air con **Seats** 150, Pr/dining room 150 **Children** Portions, Menu **Parking** 120

TORQUAY — Map 3 SX96

Corbyn Head Hotel & Orchid Restaurant

⊛⊛⊛ — *see page 138*

The Elephant Bar & Restaurant

⊛⊛⊛ — *see page 139*

Orestone Manor Hotel & Restaurant

⊛ Modern British V 🍷 🍴

Beguiling country house serving West Country produce

☎ 01803 328098
Rockhouse Ln, Maidencombe TQ1 4SX
e-mail: info@orestonemanor.com
dir: From Teignmouth take A379, through Shaldon towards Torquay. 3m take sharp left into Rockhouse Lane. Hotel signed

Orestone is a delightful colonial-style country-house hotel set in a tranquil wooded valley well away from the town, with glorious views of the coast and Lyme Bay from the stylish lounges and sun-trap terrace. The elegant restaurant, decorated in bold colours, offers an imaginative menu that takes full advantage of wonderful seasonal, local produce, plus herbs, fruits and vegetables from the kitchen garden. A typical meal may take in Start Bay crab with mustard cress, fillet of South Devon beef with horseradish fondant potato and locally-farmed snail tortellini, and zabaglione with vanilla biscotti. A Terrace menu is available in the summer months.

Chef Chris May **Owner** Jean & Alan May **Times** 12-2/7-9, Closed 2-26 Jan **Prices** Fixed L 2 course £15, Fixed D 3 course £39.50, Service optional **Wines** 124 bottles over £20, 44 bottles under £20, 15 by glass **Notes** Sunday L, Vegetarian menu, Dress restrictions, L smart casual, D smart dress, Civ Wed 75 **Seats** 65, Pr/dining room 20 **Children** Portions, Menu **Parking** 40

TOTNES — Map 3 SX86

The Normandy Arms

⊛ British, Mediterranean

Revitalised village pub serving seriously good food

☎ 01803 712884
Chapel St, Blackawton TQ9 7BN
e-mail: peter.alcroft@btconnect.com
dir: From Totnes follow A3188 for 9m and continue onto the A3122 (Dartmouth Rd) and turn right into the village of Blackawton

A recently refurbished village local, named to commemorate the Normandy landings, this place takes a serious approach to food while staying true to its pub roots by retaining a small bar. The open-plan interior has a simple, uncluttered feel, with tiled floors and solid-wood tables. The accomplished kitchen's sensibly compact menus fit the bill perfectly, offering classic food with a Mediterranean twist. With careful but unfussy presentation and bold flavours, typical dishes include fillet of beef carpaccio with celeriac and three-flavoured vinegar, sea bream fillet with pak choi, saffron and ginger potato chutney, and chocolate fondant with pistachio ice cream.

Chef Peter Alcroft **Owner** Peter Alcroft, Sharon Murdoch **Times** 12-2/6.30-11, Closed 25-26 Dec, 2 wks winter period, Closed Mon, Closed L Tue-Thu, Closed D Sun in winter **Prices** Starter £4.50-£7.95, Main £9.95-£18.95, Dessert £4.95-£5.95, Service optional **Wines** 12 bottles over £20, 26 bottles under £20, 6 by glass **Notes** Sunday L, Vegetarian available **Seats** 42 **Children** Portions, Menu **Parking** 4, On street

Corbyn Head Hotel & Orchid Restaurant

Modern British ✍

Superb views combine with superlative cooking

☎ 01803 296366 & 213611
Sea Front TQ2 6RH
e-mail: dine@orchidrestaurant.net
web: www.orchidrestaurant.net
dir: Follow signs to Torquay seafront, turn right, hotel on right on the edge of Cockington Valley, on seafront

The hotel is English Riviera to a tee, enjoying an enviable position looking out across the bay. Its showpiece restaurant, Orchid, is up on the first floor, where those views can be enjoyed through large, curved picture windows. The dining room is smartly decorated in neutral cream, comfortably furnished, while the tables, laid with crisp white linen cloths, have plenty of space between them. Service is similarly formal and mainly French, while the food is modern and imaginative. There's a confidence to the cooking that impresses and top-notch local produce is used to good effect. Start with tian of crab and avocado, red pepper gazpacho and avocado sorbet, before moving on to pavé of turbot, herb risotto, confit fennel and vanilla foam. Finish with dessert such as warm banana cake with caramelised bananas and cookie ice cream, or Devon Blue cheese with spiced tomato chutney. Ancillaries like canapés, bread and petits fours show attention to detail and run through from start to finish.

Chef Daniel Kay, Marc Evans
Owner Rew Hotels Ltd
Times 12.30-2.30/7-9.30, Closed 2 wks Jan, 2 wks Nov, 1 wk Apr, Closed Sun-Mon, Closed L Tue **Prices** Fixed L 2 course £20.95, Fixed D 3 course £37.95, Service optional **Wines** 47 bottles over £20, 65 bottles under £20, 11 by glass **Notes** Vegetarian available, Air con **Seats** 26 **Children** Min 6 yrs, Portions, Menu **Parking** 50

TWO BRIDGES | Map 3 SX67

Prince Hall Hotel

◉ British, European ◍

Devon dining with sweeping views of Dartmoor

☎ 01822 890403
PL20 6SA
e-mail: info@princehall.co.uk
dir: Located on B3357 (Ashburton to Tavistock road), 1m E of Two Bridges junct with B3212

A traditional country-house hotel set in the midst of Dartmoor National Park, Prince Hall was originally built as a private residence in 1787. Recently refurbished, the stylish, intimate restaurant is hung with paintings from local artists, combines contemporary décor with country-house character and provides superb views over the moor and river. The kitchen impresses with well prepared, skilfully presented dishes using carefully sourced local produce. To start perhaps try tian of white crabmeat with smoked salmon and citrus juice, followed by pan-fried fillet of Dartmoor venison, caramelised red onions and wild berry jus, and to finish enjoy chocolate and brandy torte with chocolate sauce and Devonshire clotted cream.

Chef Leslie Pratt **Owner** Fi & Chris Daly **Times** 12-3/7-9 **Prices** Fixed L 3 course £25-£35, Fixed D 3 course £35, Service optional, Groups min 10 service 10% **Wines** 15 bottles over £20, 20 bottles under £20, 6 by glass **Notes** Vegetarian available, Dress restrictions, Smart casual **Seats** 24 **Children** Min 8 yrs, Portions **Parking** 12

Two Bridges Hotel

◉ British

Quality dining in moorland setting

☎ 01822 890581
PL20 6SW
e-mail: enquiries@twobridges.co.uk
dir: 8m from Tavistock on B3357, hotel at junct with B3312.

Occupying a beautiful riverside location in the heart of the Dartmoor National Park, this relaxing hotel is a wonderful place to get away from it all. There is a choice of lounges and the fine-dining restaurant has a traditional feel with lots of oak, linen table cloths and great views. A young, enthusiastic team provides attentive service that is formal but friendly at the same time. The concise menu changes frequently depending on the seasons and what's available locally, with game being a speciality. Fillet of beef with oxtail and black truffle jus, onion confit and parsnip mash could, perhaps, be followed by vanilla and goat's milk pannacotta served with baked rhubarb and ginger brandy snap.

Times 12-2/7-9.30

WOODBURY | Map 3 SY08

The Atrium

◉ British 🍽 ◍

Modern hotel with straightforward cooking and good leisure facilities

☎ 01395 233382 & 234735
Woodbury Park Hotel, Golf & Country Club, Woodbury Castle EX5 1JJ
e-mail: enquiries@woodburypark.co.uk
web: www.woodburypark.co.uk
dir: M5 junct 30, take A376/A3052 towards Sidmouth, turn right opposite Halfway Inn onto B3180 towards Budleigh Salterton to Woodbury Common, hotel signed on right

Now under ambitious new owners, this modern hotel is set in 500 acres of grounds and has good leisure facilities including golf. The Atrium is contemporary in style and has a welcoming atmosphere, with staff striking just the right balance between formality and

Continued

The Elephant Bar & Restaurant

TORQUAY | Map 3 SX96

Modern British 🍽 ◍

Contemporary harbourside restaurant with fresh, vibrant food

☎ 01803 200044
3/4 Beacon Ter TQ1 2BH
e-mail: info@elephantrestaurant.co.uk
dir: Follow signs for Living Coast, restaurant opposite

The Elephant's refurbished fine-dining restaurant and brasserie are housed in two stylishly converted Georgian houses overlooking the bustling harbour. Downstairs, the Elephant Brasserie offers a more informal setting, open for lunch and dinner and serving good quality, simple brasserie dishes at affordable prices. The fine-dining restaurant - The Room - is located on the first floor with spectacular bay views, the showcase for the award-winning cuisine of Simon Hulstone and his accomplished team. At the stove is a chef with a strong culinary pedigree, whose growing reputation for precise, confident and accomplished cooking sees the popularity of this establishment continue to blossom. Quality West Country ingredients and vibrant flavours shine through well-constructed dishes, and a six-course tasting menu is available alongside the carte; perhaps fillet of Torbay brill on parsnip purée with spring onion and verjus butter sauce, or aged fillet of Ruby Red beef on the bone with fondant potato and snail and wild garlic butter sauce might jostle for your attention. To finish, perhaps gingerbread tansy pudding with pumpkin and vanilla ice cream with pumpkin seed tuile.

Chef Simon Hulstone **Owner** Peter Morgan, Simon Hulstone **Times** Closed Jan, Closed Sun-Mon, Closed L all wk **Prices** Fixed D 3 course fr £39.50, Tasting menu fr £55, Service optional, Groups min 8 service 10% **Wines** 36 bottles over £20, 15 bottles under £20, 9 by glass **Notes** Vegetarian available, Air con **Seats** 24 **Children** Min 12 yrs **Parking** Opposite restaurant

WOODBURY *Continued*

friendliness. Menus comprise simple, modern British dishes with the occasional Mediterranean accent and a focus on West Country ingredients. Typical examples include pan-fried Budleigh scallops with a truffle-infused balsamic vinegar, followed by roast rump of lamb on a warm asparagus, baby leek and watercress salad. Try saffron poached pear with vanilla rice pudding for dessert.

Chef Matthew Pickett **Owner** Sue & Robin Hawkins **Times** 12-2.30/6.30-9.30, Closed L Mon-Sat **Prices** Starter £4.95-£9, Main £10.50-£19.50, Dessert £4.50-£6, Service optional **Wines** 17 bottles over £20, 26 bottles under £20, 12 by glass **Notes** Sunday L, Vegetarian available, Dress restrictions, Prefer smart casual, Civ Wed 180, Air con **Seats** 120, Pr/dining room 180 **Children** Portions **Parking** 350

WOOLACOMBE   Map 3 SS44

Watersmeet Hotel

◉ European **V**

Fine dining with a dramatic backdrop

☎ 01271 870333
Mortehoe EX34 7EB
e-mail: info@watersmeethotel.co.uk
dir: M5 junct 27. Follow A361 to Woolacombe, right at beach car park, 300yds on right

Nestled on the rugged north Atlantic coastline, the elegant Watersmeet country-house hotel offers dining with magnificent views, with steps leading directly to the beach. The panoramic windows of the relaxed, tiered Pavilion restaurant take full advantage of the stunning vista across the waters of Woolacombe Bay, past Hartland Point to Lundy Island. The kitchen draws on quality local produce, particularly fresh fish, to deliver honest and well-balanced dishes such as confit duck leg accompanied by herb polenta cake and raspberry vinaigrette, and fillets of John Dory served with tarragon velouté, smoked bacon, peas and onions. Save space for a dessert such as toffee pannacotta with caramelised pineapple.

Chef John Prince **Owner** Mr & Mrs James **Times** 12-2/7-8.30 **Notes** Fixed D 5 courses £38, Sunday L, Vegetarian menu, Dress restrictions, Jacket & tie preferred, Civ Wed 65, Air con **Seats** 50, Pr/dining room 22 **Children** Min 8 yrs, Portions, Menu **Parking** 40

YEALMPTON   Map 3 SX55

The Rose & Crown

◉ Modern British, Pacific Rim

Village gastro-pub

☎ 01752 880223
Market St PL8 2EB
e-mail: info@theroseandcrown.co.uk
web: www.theroseandcrown.co.uk
dir: A379 8m from Plymouth. A38 from Exeter, take A3121 through Ermington, turn right onto A379 towards Plymouth

Part of the Wykeham Inns growing empire of gastro-pubs (which includes the Dartmoor Union at Holbeton), this ordinary village local has been transformed into a stylish modern eatery with large, comfortable sofas, an enticing log fire and an open-plan bar. While there's an international bistro feel to this informal menu, local produce is very much in evidence in dishes such as seared local pigeon with beetroot tarte Tatin, cannon of Totnes lamb with Mediterranean vegetable tart and mushroom and thyme sauce, and pan-fried sea bass with basil mash, mussels and beurre blanc.

Chef Laur Gales **Owner** Wykeham Inns Ltd **Times** 12-2/6.30-9.30 **Prices** Fixed L 2 course £9.95, Tasting menu £35, Starter £3.95-£8.95, Main £8.95-£18.95, Dessert £3.95-£6.50, Service optional **Wines** 3 bottles over £20, 15 bottles under £20, 12 by glass **Seats** 38, Pr/dining room 8 **Children** Min 12 yrs, Portions **Parking** 70

The Seafood Restaurant

◉◉ Seafood ♨

Vibrantly fresh fish in a nautical setting

☎ 01752 880502
Market St PL8 2EB
e-mail: enquiries@theseafood-restaurant.co.uk
web: www.theseafood-restaurant.co.uk
dir: A379 8m from Plymouth. A38 from Exeter, take A3121 through Ermington, turn right onto A379 towards Plymouth

Oak floorboards and whitewashed wood-panelled walls give the impression of a fisherman's shanty at this thoroughly modern seafood restaurant, with well-spaced, white-clothed tables, huge white plates and an open kitchen giving diners a feeling of involvement. Photographs of local fishing boats and fisherman complete the décor, while the formal table service delivers accomplished modern British seafood dishes, using the freshest local produce. Kick off with a starter of lobster tortellini with smoked belly pork and pea fritters, moving on to pan-fried fillet of pollack with garlic-scented mash, braised baby gem, chorizo and chicken reduction. Alternatively, try herb-stuffed saddle of Loddiswell lamb with boulangère potato, lamb shank tart and rosemary jus.

Chef Daniel Gillard **Owner** Wykeham Inns Ltd **Times** 12-2/6.30-9.30, Closed Sun & Mon **Prices** Fixed L 2 course fr £9.95, Fixed D 3 course fr £12.95, Tasting menu £35, Starter £3.95-£8.95, Main £8.95-£18.95, Dessert £3.95-£6.50, Service optional **Wines** 3 bottles over £20, 15 bottles under £20, 12 by glass **Seats** 40 **Children** Min 12 yrs, Portions **Parking** 70

YELVERTON   Map 3 SX56

Moorland Links Hotel

◉ Traditional British

Classic cooking in hotel with views

☎ 01822 852245
PL20 6DA
e-mail: moorland.links@forestdale.com
dir: Please telephone for directions

Set in 9 acres of well-tended grounds in Dartmoor National Park, this long-established hotel overlooks spectacular moorland scenery and the Tamar Valley. Understandably, it's a popular venue for weddings. The restaurant is formal but relaxed and friendly, and has a good local following. The classical décor of the room is matched by British cuisine with French influences (think coquilles St Jacques, or suprême of chicken with mushrooms, shallots, and bacon in red wine sauce). Light meals are served in the Gun Room Bar and afternoon tea can be enjoyed in the lounge.

Times 12.30-2/7.30-10

DORSET

BEAMINSTER   Map 4 ST40

BridgeHouse

◉ Modern British 🏮

Good food, locally sourced, in Beaminster's oldest building

☎ 01308 862200
3 Prout Bridge DT8 3AY
e-mail: enquiries@bridge-house.co.uk
dir: From A303 take A356 towards Dorchester. Turn right onto A3066, 200mtrs down hill from town centre

The heart of this striking period property is 13th century and oozes charm and character, with thick stone walls, beamed ceilings, mullioned windows and inglenook fireplaces testifying to its great age. The attractive Georgian panelled dining room has a soothing, modern décor and an Adam fireplace, and opens into a conservatory which looks over the pretty walled garden. The kitchen makes good use of local produce on an appealing modern menu, the fixed-price repertoire offering a versatile choice that might include Lyme Bay scallops with red pesto butter, rack of Wyld Meadow lamb with dauphinoise potatoes and redcurrant sauce, and perhaps a chocolate rum mousse to finish.

Chef Mrs Linda Paget **Owner** Mark and Joanna Donovan **Times** 12-2/7-9 **Prices** Fixed L 2 course fr £10, Fixed D 3 course fr £37, Service added but optional 10%, Groups min 10 service 10% **Wines** 39 bottles over £20, 22 bottles under £20, 7 by glass **Notes** Sunday L, Vegetarian available, Civ Wed 50 **Seats** 36, Pr/dining room 30 **Children** Portions, Menu **Parking** 20

BOURNEMOUTH   Map 5 SZ09

Blakes @ Best Western The Connaught Hotel

◉ Modern British

Friendly, relaxed hotel restaurant serving imaginative cuisine

☎ 01202 298020
30 West Hill Rd, West Cliff BH2 5PH
e-mail: dining@theconnaught.co.uk
dir: Please telephone for directions

Built in 1901 as a gentleman's residence, The Connaught stands on the West Cliff in its own acre of grounds, close to the beaches and town centre. With a relaxed and friendly atmosphere and well-trained staff, the restaurant, Blakes@The Connaught, offers simply cooked dishes prepared from quality local produce. A typical selection might begin with local steamed mussels and Thai spiced sauce, or duck confit and pickled beetroot. Main courses take in goats' cheese frittata with red onion and rocket; or rump of lamb with roast carrot and pea risotto. Finish with chocolate St Emilion and orange salad.

Chef Paul James, Iaman Santos **Owner** Franklyn Hotels Ltd **Times** Closed L Mon-Sat **Prices** Fixed D 3 course £19.95-£25.95, Service optional **Wines** 6 bottles over £20, 24 bottles under £20, 9 by glass **Notes** Sunday L, Vegetarian available, Dress restrictions, Smart casual, no jeans or T-shirts, Civ Wed 150, Air con **Seats** 80, Pr/dining room 16 **Children** Menu **Parking** 66

Chine Hotel

◉ Modern British, European

Seaside hotel with views from spacious restaurant

☎ 01202 396234
Boscombe Spa Rd BH5 1AX
e-mail: reservations@chinehotel.co.uk
dir: From M27, A31 and A338 follow signs to Boscombe Pier, Boscombe Spa Rd is off Christchurch Rd near Boscombe Gardens

This former 19th-century school turned popular hotel stands in 3 acres of delightful gardens and boasts stunning views across Poole Bay. The Seaview Restaurant lives up to its name, with picture windows looking out to sea and private access to the beach. Expect modern British cooking with Mediterranean influences, making good use of quality ingredients. The set three-course menu offers dishes such as sweetcorn bavarois with a spring onion salsa to start, followed by poached salmon and dill potato cake with poached egg and vermouth cream sauce and rum baba with crème Chantilly and poached pineapple to finish.

Chef Carl Munroe **Owner** Brownsea Haven Properties Ltd **Times** 12.30-2/7-9, Closed L Sat **Prices** Fixed L 2 course £12.50, Fixed D 3 course £25.95, Service optional **Wines** 21 bottles over £20, 8 bottles under £20, 20 by glass **Notes** Sunday L, Vegetarian available, Dress restrictions, No jeans, T-shirts or trainers at D, Civ Wed 120, Air con **Seats** 180, Pr/dining room 120 **Children** Portions, Menu **Parking** 67

BOURNEMOUTH *Continued*

Hermitage Hotel

◉ British

Honest cooking in a central location

☎ 01202 557363
Exeter Rd BH2 5AH
e-mail: info@hermitage-hotel.co.uk
dir: Follow A338 Ringwood-Bournemouth & signs to pier, beach & BIC. Hotel directly opposite

This smart hotel has an enviable position close to the seafront, opposite the pier, Pavilion and International Conference Centre. The wood-panelled lounge is suitably grand and the well-appointed dining room offers a regularly-changing menu featuring plenty of local produce. Among starters, local oysters and mussels come respectively with shallot vinegar and lemon and white wine, garlic and cream. Dishes can be a simple trio of seasonal melon with fruit coulis or as imaginative as roast loin of Dorchester pork with leek mash, rhubarb compôte and tarragon and orange jus. The menu is sensibly concise - six or so dishes at each course - and hot chocolate fondant with pistachio ice cream is an indulgent finish.

Chef Paul Groves **Owner** Mr P D Oram
Times 12.30-2/6.15-9, Closed L Mon-Sat **Prices** Fixed L 2 course £12-£25, Fixed D 3 course £18-£35, Starter £4.50-£7, Main £11.50-£22, Dessert £4.50-£7, Service optional **Wines** 12 bottles over £20, 40 bottles under £20, 8 by glass **Notes** Sunday L, Vegetarian available, Dress restrictions, No T-shirts or shorts, Air con **Children** Portions, Menu **Parking** 69

Langtry Restaurant

◉ Modern

Contemporary cuisine in an Edwardian setting

☎ 01202 553887
Langtry Manor, 26 Derby Rd, East Cliff BH1 3QB
e-mail: lillie@langtrymanor.com
dir: On the East Cliff, at corner of Derby & Knyveton Roads

This splendid Edwardian manor was built by Edward VII in 1877 for Lillie Langtry as a 'love nest' for their illicit affair. The unique restaurant, where Edwardian banquets were once held, is full of character, complete with minstrels' gallery, tapestries, elaborate velvet chairs and elegant, linen-draped tables. The fixed-price menu

reflects the seasons, offering an interesting choice of dishes, perhaps pea and mint soup with crisp pancetta or tian of crab, followed by New Forest venison fillet with a chocolate and raspberry vinegar sauce, or monkfish with mussel and chorizo fricassée, and rhubarb bavarois with ginger cream to finish.

Chef Matthew Clements **Owner** Mrs P Hamilton-Howard **Times** 12-2/7-9, Closed L all week **Prices** Fixed D 3 course £32-£40, Service optional **Notes** Vegetarian available, Dress restrictions, Smart casual, Civ Wed 100 **Seats** 60, Pr/dining room 16 **Children** Portions, Menu **Parking** 20

'Oscars' at the De Vere Royal Bath Hotel

◉ Modern British

Seafront views from hotel restaurant with a fine reputation

☎ 01202 555555
Bath Rd BH1 2EW
dir: A338 follow signs for pier and beaches. Hotel is in Bath Rd, just before the Bournemouth International Centre

Once the haunt of Oscar Wilde, Oscars is the fine dining option at this historic Victorian hotel with panoramic views across Bournemouth seafront. Attentive staff add to the formal yet friendly atmosphere that pervades the stylishly retro-themed dining rooms. The menu consists largely of classic British dishes with an imaginative twist, using the freshest locally sourced ingredients. Start with warm plum tomato tart with rocket pesto, then progress on to rack of pork with sage and onion dressing, or wild sea bass with spinach bubble-and-squeak and fennel broth, with burnt Cambridge cream to finish.

Chef Paul Muddiman **Owner** De Vere - AHG **Times** 12.30-1.45/7-9.45 **Prices** Fixed L course £16.95, Fixed D 3 course £30, Starter £7.50-£12.95, Main £15.95-£22.95, Dessert £5.95, Service optional **Wines** 40 bottles over £20, 20 bottles under £20, 10 by glass **Notes** Vegetarian available, Dress restrictions, Smart dress, Civ Wed 400 **Seats** 80, Pr/dining room 240 **Children** Portions, Menu **Parking** 70; NCP

The Print Room & Ink Bar & Brasserie

◉ Classic Brasserie

Eye-catching, buzzy, town-centre all-day brasserie and bar

☎ 01202 789669
The Print Room & Ink Bar, & Brasserie, Richmond Hill BH2 6HH
e-mail: info@theprintroom-bournemouth.co.uk
dir: Town centre - located in landmark art deco listed Daily Echo newspaper building

The South Coast's answer to London's Wolseley, this brasserie-style grand café and bar bursts with art deco good looks. Set in the former Daily Echo building's press room, the brasserie is a bright, double-height space with vast windows, white wall tiles, mirrors, chequerboard-tiled floor and spectacular Swarovski chandeliers. Throw in dining booths, brown-leather seating and a long zinc-topped bar and the place takes shape, though there's still a marble-topped charcuterie bar, partially open kitchen and pâtisserie counter to catch the eye. The menu is a lengthy, crowd-pleasing affair serving breakfast and afternoon tea, while the main menu kicks off at noon and runs until late. Expect classics like steak and frites to pan-fried halibut served with garlic green beans and sauce hollandaise.

Chef Simon Trepess **Owner** Andy Price **Times** 12/mdnt **Prices** Fixed L 2 course fr £12.50, Fixed D 3 course fr £20, Starter £4.50-£8.50, Main £8-£28, Dessert £5-£7.50, Service optional **Wines** 80 bottles over £20, 40 bottles under £20, 14 by glass **Notes** Sunday L, Vegetarian available **Seats** 145, Pr/dining room 14 **Children** Portions, Menu **Parking** NCP - 100yds

West Beach

◉◉ Modern ▱ ✋

Buzzy, modern, relaxed beachfront restaurant

☎ 01202 587785
Pier Approach BH2 5AA
e-mail: enquiry@west-beach.co.uk
web: www.west-beach.co.uk
dir: 100yds W of the pier

Situated on the promenade, just yards from beach and pier, with panoramic views across Poole Bay, this contemporary, relaxed brasserie delivers a simple, modern menu with a focus on seafood. Light colours and pale wood create a light and airy modern vibe and floor-to-ceiling windows allow uninterrupted sea views. Chefs in the open-to-view kitchen make good use of fresh seasonal ingredients to produce uncomplicated dishes with balanced flavours. Start with tiger prawn Caesar salad, follow with whole local crab on crushed ice with tarragon mayonnaise and fries, or whole Mudeford line-caught sea bass with caramelised baby onions, spinach and oyster mushrooms. Super decked terrace is available for summer alfresco dining.

Chef Lee Bishop **Owner** Andrew Price
Times 12-3.30/6-10, Closed 25 Dec, Closed D 26 Dec, 1 Jan **Prices** Fixed L 3 course £20-£50, Fixed D 3 course £20-£50, Starter £4.50-£8.50, Main £10.50-£40, Dessert £5.50, Service optional, Groups min 10 service 10% **Wines** 23 bottles over £20, 16 bottles under £20, 17 by glass **Notes** Pre-theatre meal offer available, Vegetarian available, Dress restrictions, No bare feet or bikinis, Air con **Seats** 90 **Children** Portions, Menu **Parking** NCP 2 mins

---

Riverside Restaurant

◉ Seafood, International ✋

Seaside location for celebrated 1970s architecture and local seafood

☎ 01308 422011
West Bay DT6 4EZ
e-mail: artwattfish@hotmail.com
web: thefishrestaurant-westbay.co.uk
dir: A35 Bridport ring road, turn to West Bay at Crown rdbt

It was in 1976 that well-known architect Piers Gough re-constructed this restaurant which is uniquely located on an 'island' overlooking the West Bay fishing port. A recent extension has provided a further dining area. The business has been in the same family for some 44 years, with the emphasis today unsurprisingly based around fresh fish and shellfish - mostly from local waters - alongside an intelligent, simply-cooked approach. There is shellfish (when available of course) such as crab salad (whole or dressed), or local Channel lobster served in a number of ways. The daily specials are worth checking out, such as fillets of sea bass with slow-roasted belly of pork. Meat and vegetarian options are also offered on the daily specials list.

Chef N Larcombe, G Marsh, A Shaw **Owner** Mr & Mrs A Watson **Times** 12-2.30/6.30-9, Closed 30 Nov-14 Feb, Closed Mon (ex BHs), Closed D Sun **Prices** Fixed L 2 course £16.50, Starter £4.75-£9.50, Main £11.95-£19.50, Dessert £4.50-£6.50, Service optional, Groups min 6 service 10% **Wines** 23 bottles over £20, 35 bottles under £20, 10 by glass **Notes** Sunday L, Vegetarian available **Seats** 70, Pr/dining room 30 **Children** Portions, Menu **Parking** Public car park close by

---

Captain's Club Hotel

◉◉ Modern International ✋

Contemporary riverside restaurant focusing on locally-sourced ingredients

☎ 01202 475111
Wick Ferry, Wick Ln BH23 1HU
e-mail: enquiries@captainsclubhotel.com
web: www.captainsclubhotel.com
dir: Hotel just off Christchurch High St, towards Christchurch Quay

This hotel is a stunning piece of modern architecture on the edge of the River Stour with a luxurious contemporary interior. Tides Restaurant is furnished with wooden tables, fabric-covered chairs and carpeted floors, and has large patio windows overlooking the river. Friendly and professional service is provided by staff in long black aprons. The kitchen sources high quality local ingredients and delivers flavoursome, attractively presented dishes from a seasonal menu supported by daily specials. Recommendations are hand-dived sea scallops with crisp pork belly and pea purée, roast rump of Dorset lamb with crushed peas and marjoram, roast potatoes and natural jus, and pineapple carpaccio with coconut mousse and coconut brittle.

Chef Andrew Gault **Owner** Platinum One Hotels Ltd **Times** 12-2.30/7-10 **Prices** Fixed L 2 course £16, Fixed D 3 course £25, Starter £6-£9, Main £14-£24, Dessert £6-£9, Service optional **Wines** 90 bottles over £20, 35 bottles under £20, 14 by glass **Notes** Sunday L, Vegetarian available, Civ Wed 100, Air con **Seats** 72, Pr/dining room 44 **Children** Portions, Menu **Parking** 41

CHRISTCHURCH *Continued*

Christchurch Harbour Hotel Restaurant

Traditional

Refurbished hotel restaurant offering innovative cuisine

☎ 01202 483434
95 Mudeford BH23 3NT
e-mail: info@theavonmouth.co.uk
dir: M27 junct 1/A31/A338/A35 to Christchurch & then Mudeford

Major refurbishment in 2008 has restored this elegant hotel to its former splendour. The Grade II listed property, once a gentleman's residence, is ideally located overlooking Mudeford Quay and Christchurch Harbour, and now features a new version of the Quays Restaurant offering predominantly seafood cuisine and a second waterside restaurant, Muddys. From the Quays' carte come a starter of chicken liver parfait with red onion chutney and toasted brioche; and a main course of pan-fried fillet of sea bream with tarragon cream sauce. For dessert, try warm caramel and walnut tartlet with clotted cream.

Chef Kevin Hartley, Phil Clark **Owner** Christchurch Hotels Ltd **Times** 12-2/7-9.30 **Prices** Fixed L 2 course £18-£30, Fixed D 3 course £39-£45, Service optional **Wines** 40 bottles over £20, 10 bottles under £20, 12 by glass **Notes** Afternoon tea available, Sunday L, Vegetarian available, Dress restrictions, Smart casual, Civ Wed 120 **Seats** 100, Pr/dining room 100 **Children** Portions, Menu **Parking** 70

Crooked Beam Restaurant

Modern British

Neighbourhood restaurant full of old world charm

☎ 01202 499362
Jumpers Corner, 2 The Grove BH23 2HA
e-mail: info@crookedbeam.co.uk
dir: Situated on corner of Barrack Road A35 and The Grove

The Crooked Beam brims with history and crooked beams, as parts of the building date back three hundred years. It is a family-run place, full of old world charm where the service is hospitable and friendly (genuine service with a smile). The cooking is equally as straightforward and honest with everything possible made on the premises, including walnut bread, which is served with unsalted butter. The menu avoids current fads and fashions to

deliver lobster bisque and duck and pistachio parfait among starters, and main courses such as pan-fried sea bass, the skin crisp and the flesh succulent, served with a crab risotto and a delicate lemon cream sauce.

Chef Simon Hallam **Owner** Simon & Vicki Hallam **Times** 12-2/7-11, Closed Mon, Closed L Sat, Closed D Sun **Prices** Fixed L 2 course fr £12.95, Fixed D 3 course fr £21.95, Starter £4.75-£7.50, Main £13.95-£17.95, Dessert £4.95, Service optional, Groups min 10 service 10% **Wines** 4 bottles over £20, 28 bottles under £20, 6 by glass **Notes** Sunday L, Vegetarian available, Dress restrictions, Smart casual, Air con **Seats** 80, Pr/dining room 20 **Children** Portions **Parking** 10 **Parking** On street

The Lord Bute Restaurant

British, European

Fine dining in historic surroundings

☎ 01425 278884
170-181 Lymington Rd, Highcliffe-on-Sea BH23 4JS
e-mail: mail@lordbute.co.uk
web: www.lordbute.co.uk
dir: Follow A337 to Lymington, opposite St Mark's churchyard in Highcliffe

This elegant hotel and restaurant stands directly behind the original entrance lodges of Highcliffe Castle, close to the beach and historic town of Christchurch. The entrance hall displays pictures of former resident and Prime Minister Lord Bute, as well as famous visitors to the castle. Diners can enjoy drinks in the orangery or patio area before dining in the smart restaurant. Well prepared modern British food is on offer here, making good use of quality produce, sourced locally where possible. Expect main courses like braised shank of Romsey lamb set on a bed of herb mash with a silky redcurrant and mint glaze, or whole Dorset plaice with rock salt, served with a saffron butter sauce and a fresh lime crown.

Times 12-2/7-9.30, Closed Mon, Closed L Sat, Closed D Sun

The Ship In Distress

Modern British, Seafood

Friendly, nautical-themed restaurant

☎ 01202 485123
66 Stanpit BH23 3NA
dir: A35, Stoney Ln rdbt, Stanpit

A former 300-year-old smugglers' pub close to Mudeford Quay specialising in fish and seafood caught by local fishermen. Lively and popular, the traditional restaurant has a strong nautical theme, with contemporary marine paintings adorning the walls. Service is relaxed and friendly from young, local staff. Fresh, top quality local produce is simply cooked and presented allowing the subtle flavours of the fish to shine through. Expect seared scallops with carrot purée and pancetta crisps or skewered crevettes served with fruity mango and cucumber chutney to start. Move on to roast cod with tomato beurre blanc or grilled sea bass with a honey and sesame seed glaze, and finish with a vanilla and pistachio crème brûlée. Alfresco dining is available during the warmer weather.

Chef Phil Etheridge **Owner** Maggie Wheeler **Times** 12-2.30/6.30-9.30, Closed 25 Dec, 1 Jan, Closed D 26 Dec **Prices** Starter £4.50-£10, Main £12.50-£20, Dessert £4.50-£5.50, Service optional, Groups min 8 service 10% **Wines** 8 bottles over £20, 20 bottles under £20 **Notes** Vegetarian available **Seats** 70 **Children** Portions **Parking** 25

Splinters Restaurant

British, International

Family-run restaurant in listed building

☎ 01202 483454
12 Church St BH23 1BW
e-mail: eating@splinters.uk.com
dir: Directly in front of Priory gates

The prettiest in a row of quaint buildings leading up to the old priory, this Christchurch institution oozes character with its winding corridor, old wooden staircase, cosy booths and various nooks and crannies. The main focus is the bar-lounge from which five dining areas lead. With relaxed and friendly table service, begin with salmon and prawn terrine with chive and mustard, wrapped in smoked salmon with a beetroot chutney, and then move on to roast rump of lamb with mint and herb crust and a mixed bean and vegetable cassoulet. Desserts also delight: try the orange and Grand Marnier vanilla pannacotta or pecan and toffee tartlet with pineapple iced parfait. The cooking, like the service and setting, is consistently pleasing.

Chef Paul Putt **Owner** Paul & Agnes Putt
Times 11-2/7-10, Closed 26 Dec, 1-10 Jan, Closed Sun-Mon **Prices** Fixed L 2 course fr £10.95, Fixed D 3 course fr £25.95, Main £30.50-£37.50, Service included, Groups min 8 service 10% **Wines** 105 bottles over £20, 37 bottles under £20, 5 by glass **Notes** ALC 2-3 courses, Vegetarian available, Dress restrictions, Smart casual **Seats** 42, Pr/dining room 30 **Children** Portions

---

CORFE CASTLE — Map 4 SY98

Mortons House Hotel

◉◉ Traditional British

Notable dining in Elizabethan surroundings

☎ 01929 480988
East St BH20 5EE
e-mail: stay@mortonshouse.co.uk
web: www.mortonshouse.co.uk
dir: In centre of village on A351

With the ruins of Corfe Castle as a backdrop and set in delightful gardens and grounds, this impressive Tudor house was built in an 'E' shape to honour Queen Elizabeth I. Beautifully updated and stylishly furnished, it retains a timeless feel. The serene oak-panelled dining room may have formal table settings, but service is friendly and knowledgeable. Classical in style, the cooking is skilful and accomplished, with well-executed dishes utilising produce of high quality, sourced locally whenever possible. Take roast loin of venison served with braised cabbage, mushroom casserole and dauphinoise potatoes, or perhaps a fillet of halibut accompanied by plum tomato, chorizo and piquillo pepper purée, ricotta and olive tortellini and salsa verde.

Chef Ed Firth **Owner** Mr & Mrs Hageman, Mr & Mrs Clayton **Times** 12-1.45/7-9 **Prices** Starter £6-£12, Main £17-£25, Dessert £6-£9, Service optional, Groups min 20 service 10% **Wines** 55 bottles over £20, 8 bottles under £20, 4 by glass **Notes** Sunday L, Vegetarian available, Dress restrictions, Smart casual, Civ Wed 60 **Seats** 50, Pr/dining room 22 **Children** Min 5 yrs, Portions, Menu **Parking** 40

CORFE MULLEN — Map 4 SY99

The Coventry Arms

◉ Modern British

Local delicacies in popular country pub

☎ 01258 857284
Mill St BH21 3RH
dir: A31 2m from Wimborne

This popular village pub - a converted 15th-century watermill - is idyllically situated by the river and positively oozes rustic, old-world charm with its original flagstone floors, large open fireplace, low ceilings and exposed beams. There's a choice of six distinctive drinking and dining areas, and the fishing paraphernalia reflects the interests of the proprietor, who supplies the menu with local rod-caught trout. Local produce also includes a variety of game when in season and venison, pigeon and pheasant are sourced from local estates. The modern British menu includes starters like fillet of red gurnard with red onion and tomato salsa, followed by main courses such as rump steak, Guinness and smoked oyster puff-pastry pie with caramelised onion mash.

Times 12-2.30/6-9.30

CRANBORNE — Map 5 SU01

La Fosse at Cranborne

◉ Modern British

Accomplished cuisine in long established friendly village restaurant

☎ 01725 517604
London House, The Square BH21 5PR
e-mail: mac@la-fosse.com
dir: M3, M27 W to A31 to Ringwood. Turn left to B3081 to Verwood, then Cranborne (5 m)

This large Victorian house was developed from a 16th-century farmhouse, complete with low ceilings, beams and an inglenook fireplace. Mac La Fosse and his wife Sue have run this charming restaurant with rooms for over twenty years now, and have a well-earned local reputation for hospitality and fine food. They deliver a varied and interesting menu of dishes, ranging from old favourites such as half lobster and scallop thermidor or slow-roast rare breeds pork with apple sauce, to more imaginative fare: New Forest game soup, for example, or supreme of salmon with a ginger crumb and champagne sauce.

Times 12-2/7-9.30, Closed Mon-Tue, Closed D Sun

DORCHESTER — Map 4 SY69

Sienna

◉◉◉ – *see page 146*

Yalbury Cottage & Restaurant

◉◉ Modern British

Country cottage serving seasonal local produce

☎ 01305 262382
Lower Bockhampton DT2 8PZ
e-mail: yalburyemails@aol.com
dir: 2m E of Dorchester, off A35

This 300-year-old thatched cottage is now under the new ownership of Jamie and Ariane Jones. It is full of character and is set in the hamlet fictionalised by Thomas Hardy as the village of Mellstock in Under the Greenwood Tree. Steeped in tradition, the dining room comes replete with wood burner, oak beams and wooden floors. Jamie aims to offer creative but classical menus using the best of locally available produce in dishes such as Lyme Bay scallops on smoked haddock ravioli, with leek purée and garlic foam, and best end of Tolpuddle lamb with herb crust and white bean cassoulet. The menu changes daily and is priced for two or three courses, and on Sunday there's a speciality three-course Farmers' Market lunch.

Times Closed 2 wks Jan, Closed L all week

EVERSHOT — Map 4 ST50

The Acorn Inn

◉ Modern, Traditional

Picturesque village inn of literary legend and local fare

☎ 01935 83228
DT2 0JW
e-mail: stay@acorn-inn.co.uk
dir: 2m off A37, between Dorchester and Yeovil. In village centre

This delightful stone-built village inn - called 'The Sow and Acorn' from Thomas Hardy's Tess of the D'Urbervilles - dates from the 16th century and nestles among the rolling hills in the heart of Hardy country. Inside, historic features abound with exposed beams, flagstone floors, oak panelling and open fires. A good choice of food ranges from a popular bar menu to more formal fare in

Continued

EVERSHOT *Continued*

the cosy restaurant. Quality local produce figures strongly in well presented dishes, bolstered by blackboard specials. Take deep-fried breaded Somerset brie with sweet orange and cranberry sauce, or perhaps pan-fried fillets of Brixham plaice with lemon, garlic and herb butter. A generous helping of chocolate and hazelnut roulade will not disappoint for dessert.

Times 12-2/6.45-9.30

Summer Lodge Country House Hotel

◉◉◉ – *see opposite*

The Museum Inn

◉◉ Modern British

Great gastro-pub with accomplished cooking and contemporary spin

☎ 01725 516261
DT11 8DE
e-mail: enquiries@museuminn.co.uk
dir: 12m S of Salisbury, 7m N of Blandford Forum on A354

This red-brick and thatched inn stands in an idyllic village setting and makes a charming statement. Sympathetic refurbishment has retained original flagstones and fireplaces, but pastel tones, a light-and-airy feel and stylish country furnishings add a modern, upmarket vibe, albeit with a relaxed, friendly atmosphere. Eat from the same menu in a variety of comfortable bar rooms or in the more formal Shed restaurant at weekends. Driven by judiciously sourced quality produce (meats are fully traceable and traditionally reared, many other ingredients are organic or free range, while fish is delivered daily from the south coast), the accomplished kitchen takes a modern British line; think slow-roast belly pork with cider apple sauce, spinach and colcannon potatoes. There's also a sunny terrace.

Times 12-2/7-9.30, Closed 25 & 31 Dec

Stock Hill Country House Hotel & Restaurant

◉◉ Austrian, European

Classic cuisine with an Austrian twist in elegant country house

☎ 01747 823626 & 822741
Stock Hill SP8 5NR
e-mail: reception@stockhillhouse.co.uk
dir: 3m E on B3081, off A303

Set in 11 acres of mature grounds, Stock Hill is a handsome Victorian country house which has been restored and maintained by Peter and Nita Hauser for over 20 years. The period décor throughout the house is entirely in keeping with the building and helps create an atmosphere of comfort and refinement. The dining room, with its formally laid tables, interesting bronze statues and genteel atmosphere, benefits from views out over the manicured lawns. Service by a smartly turned out team lead by Mrs Hauser is suitably formal and friendly. There are distinct Austrian touches to the menu which is otherwise firmly rooted in classical French cookery with locally sourced produce to the fore. Poached Brixham crab quenelles are served with julienne of root vegetables among starters, and main-course Aga-roasted breast of Gressingham duckling comes with rösti potatoes, buttered Savoy cabbage and Madeira jus.

Times 12.30-1.45/7.30-8.45, Closed L Sat & Mon

Sienna

Modern British 🍃

Small but beautifully formed restaurant of real class

☎ 01305 250022
36 High West St DT1 1UP
e-mail: browns@siennarestaurant.co.uk
dir: Near top of town rdbt in Dorchester

This unassuming, shop-fronted restaurant at the top of the high street - run by delightful husband-and-wife team, Russell and Elena Brown - may come on an endearingly bijou scale, but the cooking is beautifully formed. With just 15 covers (booking is essential) there's an obvious intimacy, the décor suitably understated, with a restful 'sienna' colour scheme, unclothed wooden-topped tables and modern artwork all lending a contemporary feel. Elena delivers a charming front-of-

house presence, ensuring diners experience a real treat, with graceful, unhurried and professional service. Russell struts his stuff behind the scenes at the stove with equal aplomb; his elegant and well-conceived cooking parades with deft touches, beautifully balanced combinations, clear flavours and accurate seasoning. Underpinned by high quality produce, the confident cooking intelligently flourishes without over embellishment or empty bravado. Take a roast loin of Dorset lamb served with shepherd's pie, 'carrot and peas' and a lamb jus, while Russell's pastry is sublime too, so don't miss the likes of a pear tarte Tatin with clotted cream ice cream and ginger syrup. Sit back and enjoy a highly personal and memorable experience.

Chef Russell Brown **Owner** Russell & Elena Brown **Times** 12-2/7-9, Closed 2 wks Feb/Mar, 2 wks Sep/Oct, Closed Sun-Mon **Prices** Fixed L 2 course £18.50, Fixed D 3 course £36, Service optional **Wines** 20 bottles over £20, 15 bottles under £20, 7 by glass **Notes** Vegetarian available, Air con **Seats** 15 **Children** Min 10 yrs **Parking** Top of town car park, on street

LYME REGIS
Map 4 SY39

Hotel Alexandra & Restaurant

🌼 Modern British, International V 🐾

Attractively presented food in an elegant setting

☎ 01297 442010
Pound St DT7 3HZ
e-mail: enquiries@hotelalexandra.co.uk
dir: From Bridport take A35 to Lyme Regis, through Chideock, Marcombe Lake, past Charmouth, turn left at Charmouth rdbt, follow for 2m

The plethora of model sailing ships, and marine and local pictures around this Grade II listed hotel leave you in no doubt that this elegant restaurant is by the sea, even if you miss the amazing view over Lyme Bay. Using modern and traditional cooking styles resulting in simply presented dishes, the good-value menu also leans towards the sea, perhaps offering Lyme Bay scallops with cauliflower purée and white truffle oil and baked grey mullet with herb risotto, while meat-lovers might opt for calves' liver with bubble-and-squeak and red wine jus. Leave room for vanilla and hazelnut mousse or a plate of West Country cheeses.

Chef Ian Grant **Owner** Kathryn Richards
Times 12-2/7-8.30, Closed last Sun before Xmas-end Jan **Prices** Food prices not confirmed for 2009. Please telephone for details. **Wines** 29 bottles over £20, 29 bottles under £20, 5 by glass **Notes** Vegetarian menu, Dress restrictions, Smart casual, Civ Wed 70, Air con

Seats 60, Pr/dining room 24 **Children** Min 10 yrs, Portions, Menu **Parking** 26

Rumours

🌼 Modern 🐾

Friendly seaside restaurant featuring fresh local fish

☎ 01297 444740
14-15 Monmouth St DT7 3PX
e-mail: fish@rumoursrestaurant.eclipse.co.uk
dir: Please telephone for directions

A husband-and-wife-run restaurant, Rumours is located in the old part of town just a few minutes from the seafront. The dining room is contemporary in style with an original black-and-white tiled floor. The repertoire is awash with the fruits of the sea, locally-caught where possible, and locally reared Dorset meat. Try tian of Lyme Bay crab and prawns on avocado, followed by pan-roasted sea bass with scallions and ginger. There are plenty of non-fish options too - perhaps rack of rosemary roasted Dorset lamb with redcurrant and Marsala jus - and all the desserts are home made.

Chef Lynda Skelton **Owner** Lynda & Ron Skelton **Times** Closed Dec-Feb, Closed Sun & Wed (open Sun BHs), Closed L all week **Prices** Starter £4.25-£7.50, Main £9.75-£20, Dessert £4.75-£5.50, Service optional **Wines** 1 bottles over £20, 21 bottles under £20, 4 by glass **Notes** Vegetarian available **Seats** 26 **Children** Min 14 yrs **Parking** On street 25 yds

MAIDEN NEWTON
Map 4 SY59

Le Petit Canard

🌼 Modern British, French

Pretty village restaurant; delicious dining

☎ 01300 320536
Dorchester Rd DT2 0BE
e-mail: craigs@le-petit-canard.co.uk
web: www.le-petit-canard.co.uk
dir: In centre of Maiden Newton, 8m W of Dorchester

This former coaching inn, dating back over 300 years, has been divided up into several individual properties. Among its neighbours in this attractive conservation area is Le Petit Canard, a restaurant with a small but charming dining room featuring exposed brickwork and old beams highlighted by sensitive décor, candlelit at

Continued

Summer Lodge Country House Hotel

EVERSHOT
Map 4 ST50

Modern British 🏅

Idyllic, intimate retreat meets refined cooking

☎ 01935 482000
DT2 0JR
e-mail: summer@relaischateaux.com
web: www.summerlodgehotel.com
dir: 1.5m off A37 between Yeovil and Dorchester

Nestling in the Dorset Downs in delightful grounds (designed in part by local architect and celebrated chronicler, Thomas Hardy, no less), this former dower house turned intimate, quintessential country-house hotel is a true hideaway, blessed with a picture-postcard village setting. There's an air of luxury and high quality about the interior, decked out in classically elegant, chintzy country-house style. Service is predictably on the

formal side (with cheese trolley, dessert wine trolley and roast trolleys for Sunday lunch), but appropriately friendly too, while the sommelier brings serious expertise to the classy wine list. With walls covered in sumptuous fabrics, plus a log fire, the spacious, split-level restaurant is as cosy in winter as it is refreshing in summer. The recently added conservatory enjoys views of the 4-acre walled garden, while the adjoining patio creates a relaxed dining area with sweeping views over the lawns and borders. The accomplished kitchen's modern focus, underpinned by a classical theme, suits the surroundings perfectly, focusing on prime local produce, its refined treatment displaying high skill, clean, clear flavours, balance and modern presentation. Try chargrilled local scallops with chicory and walnut salad, perhaps followed by a main course of pot-roasted breast of guinea fowl with Sauternes, white beans and winter vegetables. There's a tasting menu option available too.

Chef Steven Titman **Owner** Red Carnation Hotels
Times 12-2.30/7-9.30 **Prices** Tasting menu £65-£125,
Starter £11.50-£16.95, Main £19.95-£26.95, Dessert £8.95-£12.50, Service included, Groups min 12 service 12.5% **Wines** 1400 bottles over £20, 6 bottles under £20, 11 by glass **Notes** Sunday L, Vegetarian available, Dress restrictions, No shorts, T-shirts or sandals, jackets pref, Civ Wed 30, Air con **Seats** 48, Pr/dining room 12 **Children** Portions, Menu **Parking** 60

MAIDEN NEWTON *Continued*

night. Just about everything is made on the premises by the chef-proprietor and his wife. Modern British dishes with French and occasional oriental influences reflect seasonal ingredients and might include fresh Dorset crab linguine, loin of local venison with red wine and redcurrants and sticky toffee pudding with caramel sauce.

Chef Gerry Craig **Owner** Mr & Mrs G Craig
Times 12-2/7-9, Closed Mon, Closed L all week (ex 1st & 3rd Sun in month), Closed D Sun **Prices** Fixed D 3 course £31-£33.75, Service optional **Wines** 18 bottles over £20, 14 bottles under £20, 6 by glass **Notes** Vegetarian available, Dress restrictions, Smart casual preferred **Seats** 28 **Children** Min 12 yrs **Parking** On street/village car park

POOLE
Map 4 SZ09

Harbour Heights Hotel

 Modern British, French

Contemporary bistro commanding the best views across Poole Harbour

☎ 01202 707272
73 Haven Rd, Sandbanks BH13 7LW
e-mail: enquiries@harbourheights.net
dir: From A338 follow signs to Sandbanks, restaurant on left past Canford Cliffs

From the hotel's sun terrace, a spectacular vista of sea and sky greets visitors who come to sip champagne and while away the hours watching the cross-channel ferries slip slowly in and out of Poole Harbour. Floor-to-ceiling picture windows ensure diners at the hotel's contemporary brasserie don't miss out - it's a smart open-plan affair decked out with polished-wood tables and matching chairs in brown leather upholstery. Expect skilfully prepared dishes conjured from quality local ingredients: fresh caught lobster salad served with crushed potatoes, sea beans and a shellfish reduction to start, perhaps followed by pork in Parma ham with Dorset Blue Vinney mash, cabbage, Pommery mustard and a cider vinegar cream sauce, or West Country beef with braised oxtail, horseradish beetroot and a port wine sauce.

Harbour Heights Hotel

Chef Stephane Jouan **Owner** FJB Hotels
Times 12-2.30/7-9.30 **Prices** Fixed L 2 course fr £17, Tasting menu £95, Starter £7-£14, Main £18.50-£22.50, Dessert £7.85, Service optional **Wines** 155 bottles over £20, 6 bottles under £20, 28 by glass **Notes** Sunday L, Vegetarian available, Dress restrictions, Smart casual, Civ Wed 120, Air con **Seats** 90, Pr/dining room 120 **Children** Portions, Menu **Parking** 80

Haven Hotel

 Modern British

Fine dining with stunning sea views

☎ 01202 707333
Banks Rd, Sandbanks BH13 7QL
e-mail: reservations@havenhotel.co.uk
dir: Follow signs to Sandbanks Peninsula; hotel next to Swanage ferry departure point

The former home of radio pioneer Marconi is now a well established hotel overlooking the mouth of Poole Harbour. La Roche restaurant, with its chic modern décor, formal table service and relaxed atmosphere, enjoys stunning views across the bay, while the lounge terrace is perfect for outdoor dining in summer. The menu offers locally sourced seasonal produce in British dishes with an emphasis on fish and seafood, including fresh lobster or catch of the day. Typical options include a starter of crayfish tails with Portland crab meat, fennel pannacotta and blood orange and cardamom dressing, and a main course of roast monkfish with crispy Parma ham served with steamed lemon rice and tomato coulis.

Haven Hotel

Times 12-2/7-9, Closed Xmas, Closed Mon (winter), Closed D Sun (winter)

H V Restaurant

 Modern, Pacific Rim

Modern hotel restaurant with harbour views and fresh fish

☎ 01202 666800 & 0870 333 9143
Thistle Hotel Poole, The Quay BH15 1HD
e-mail: poole@thistle.co.uk
web: www.thistlehotels.com/poole
dir: Follow signs to Poole port (A350) & Poole Pottery signs. Hotel on waterfront

Situated on the quayside overlooking Poole harbour, this modern hotel's first-floor Harbour View Restaurant delivers stunning views. Dream away your lottery millions on the yachts and speedboats moored alongside, or watch the day's catches being landed from the windows. The room is smart and modern with formally set tables, and there's a small fish counter where you can choose your fish for the chef to cook. Otherwise, the menu's straightforward modern approach (including some meat options) might take in sardines marinated in soy and ginger; or whole chargrilled lemon sole with sea salt, lemon and oregano.

Times 12-2/7-9.45

Sandbanks Hotel

◎ Traditional European V

Vibrant beachside brasserie

☎ 01202 707377
15 Banks Rd, Sandbanks BH13 7PS
e-mail: reservations@sandbankshotel.co.uk
dir: From Poole or Bournemouth, follow signs to
Sandbanks Peninsula. Hotel on left

This popular hotel enjoys an enviable location, set as it is
on the delightful Sandbanks peninsula with direct access
to a blue flag beach. Dinner in the Seaview Restaurant is
a pleasant affair, but it's the more formal Sands
brasserie that's the real draw, not least for its stunning
waterside position. It's a modern, minimalist space, with
glass walls, 180 degree sea views and a contemporary
carte. Expect modern variations on classical themes: a
starter of seared scallops, chick peas, chorizo and lime
foam for example, followed by crispy duck leg with roast
beetroot, curly kale and grain mustard mash.

Chef Paul Harper **Owner** Mr J Butterworth
Times 12-3/6-10, Closed Mon-Tue, Closed D Sun
Prices Starter £7-£11, Main £14-£20.50, Dessert
£6.50-£7, Service optional **Wines** 73 bottles over £20, 10
bottles under £20, 17 by glass **Notes** Sunday L,
Vegetarian menu, Dress restrictions, No jeans, smart
casual, Civ Wed 40, Air con **Seats** 65, Pr/dining room 40
Children Portions, Menu **Parking** 130

The Bluefish Restaurant

◎ Modern European

Relaxed dining in simple surroundings

☎ 01305 822991
15-17a Chiswell DT5 1AN
e-mail: thebluefish@tesco.net
dir: Take A354 by Chesil Bank, off Victoria Square in
Portland, over rdbt towards Chesil Beach, next to 72hr
free car park

This simple yet stylish restaurant is housed at the top of
a 400-year-old Portland stone building. You can dine
alfresco in fine weather, or sit in one of the two
interconnecting dining rooms under starry lights, but
wherever you choose, service is warm, friendly and
relaxed. And don't be mislead by the restaurant name,
you'll find meat and vegetarian choices as well as fish on
the modern European menu based around fresh, quality
ingredients. Think sea bream served with potato gnocchi,
artichokes, peas and chorizo cream and aubergine
caviar, or perhaps 70-hour braised beef bourguignon
with olive oil mash.

Chef Luciano Da Silva **Owner** Jo & Luciano Da Silva
Times 12-3/6.45-10, Closed Mon, Tue-Wed (winter),
Closed L Tue-Fri **Prices** Starter £4.50-£9.50, Main
£10.50-£19.50, Dessert £4.50-£6.50, Groups min 8
service 10% **Wines** 3 bottles over £20, 15 bottles under
£20, 6 by glass **Notes** Sunday L, Vegetarian available
Seats 35 **Children** Portions **Parking** 72-hr free car park,
on street

Best Western Royal Chase Hotel

◎ Modern British

Imaginative cooking in friendly surroundings

☎ 01747 853355
Royal Chase Roundabout SP7 8DB
e-mail: royalchasehotel@btinternet.com
dir: On rdbt at A350 & A30 junction (avoid town centre)

This one-time monastery and local landmark in pretty
Shaftesbury is now a friendly hotel located not far from
Gold Hill, a picture-perfect street that has graced the
cover of countless chocolate boxes. The elegant Byzant
Restaurant is an intimate affair, presided over by a team
who strike just the right note of friendliness and
formality. Expect modern British cooking that might take
in the likes of goats' cheese charlotte with watercress
pesto, confit cod and seared scallops with tomato and
basil vinaigrette, or lamb shoulder stuffed with wild
mushrooms with a provençale sauce, with desserts like
rhubarb cheesecake.

Chef Stuart Robbins **Owner** Travel West Inns
Times 12-2/7-9.30 **Prices** Starter £4.95-£5.75, Main
£11.50-£14.75, Dessert £4.95-£5.75, Service optional
Wines 11 bottles over £20, 39 bottles under £20, 5 by
glass **Notes** Sunday L, Vegetarian available, Civ Wed 78
Seats 65, Pr/dining room 120 **Children** Portions, Menu
Parking 100

La Fleur de Lys Restaurant with Rooms

◎◎ French, European

Smart restaurant with rooms to suit all tastes

☎ 01747 853717
Bleke St SP7 8AW
e-mail: info@fleurdelys.co.uk
web: www.lafleurdelys.co.uk
dir: Junct A350/A30

This light and airy restaurant with rooms is just a few
minutes' walk from Shaftesbury's famous Gold Hill. The
elegant, L-shaped dining room with its conservatory
extension has a relaxed and friendly atmosphere, and
there is a comfortable lounge for pre-dinner drinks. The
kitchen's approach is modern, underpinned by classical
French techniques. Quality seasonal ingredients are used
in the accomplished, confidently presented dishes,
sometimes in imaginative combinations, as in white crab
mousse topped with fresh crab set on samphire and
avocado with fennel cream; and chargrilled saddle of
seka venison served with prunes, apples and shallots in
an Armagnac sauce. Finish with hot William pear soufflé,
raspberry sorbet and clove sauce anglaise.

Times 12-2.30/7-10.30, Closed 3 wks Jan, Closed L Mon
& Tue, Closed D Sun

CO DURHAM

BEAMISH   Map 19 NZ25

Beamish Park Hotel

◎◎ Modern International 💻

International bistro dining in modern surroundings

☎ 01207 230666
Beamish Burn Rd NE16 5EG
e-mail: reception@beamish-park-hotel.co.uk
web: www.beamish-park-hotel.co.uk
dir: A1(M) turn off onto A692, continue for 2m into
Sunniside. At traffic lights take A6076 signposted
Beamish Museum & Tanfield Railway. Hotel is situated
behind Causey Arch Inn

The Conservatory Bistro, reached through the welcoming
lounge of this stylish hotel, is effortlessly relaxed. Modern
and chic, with a contemporary colour scheme, artistic
lighting and distinctive fabrics, it boasts a host of
individual design features. Like the ambience, the
restaurant's regularly-changing menu is modern in style
and includes a selection of British dishes with a
smattering of international influences - all making good
use of local, seasonal produce. Try the pressed ham hock
terrine with home-made pease pudding to start, followed
by a main course of slow-cooked organic beef blade with
two celeries and rich gravy, making room for a dessert of
warm lemon polenta cake, lime syrup and mascarpone.

Chef Christopher Walker **Owner** William Walker
Times 12-2.30/7-10.30 **Prices** Fixed L 2 course £12.50,
Starter £4.25-£8, Main £9.95-£18, Dessert £4.95-£6.95,
Service optional **Wines** 7 bottles over £20, 15 bottles
under £20, 7 by glass **Notes** Sunday L, Vegetarian
available, Dress restrictions, Smart casual preferred, Air
con **Seats** 70, Pr/dining room 150 **Children** Portions
Parking 100

DARLINGTON   Map 19 NZ21

Headlam Hall

◎ British, French

Interesting modern dishes served in a Jacobean hall

☎ 01325 730238
Headlam, Gainford DL2 3HA
e-mail: admin@headlamhall.co.uk
dir: 8m W of Darlington off A67

Retaining many of its original Jacobean features, this
impressive manor house stands in beautiful walled
gardens, surrounded by rolling farmland and its own nine-
hole golf course. The restaurant occupies a conservatory
and two stately rooms, one panelled and one Victorian-style
with deep green walls, gilt mirrors and elegant pictures.
This time-honoured style is echoed in the menu, which
blends French and British classics with more innovative
modern dishes. Expect beef fillet with fondant potato and
Madeira sauce, or grilled fillet of Scottish salmon with
butter-poached lobster, fennel and shellfish velouté,
followed by lemon tart with mango coulis.

Chef Austen Shaw **Owner** JH Robinson
Times 12-2.30/7-9.30, Closed 25-26 Dec **Prices** Food
prices not confirmed for 2009. Please telephone for
details. **Wines** 25 bottles over £20, 30 bottles under £20,
10 by glass **Notes** Dress restrictions, No sportswear or
shorts, Civ Wed 150 **Seats** 70, Pr/dining room 30
Children Portions, Menu **Parking** 70

DURHAM   Map 19 NZ24

Bistro 21

◎ Modern British, European V 🐾

Stylish bistro offering popular cuisine

☎ 0191 384 4354
Aykley Heads House, Aykley Heads DH1 5TS
e-mail: admin@bistrotwentyone.co.uk
web: www.bistrotwentyone.co.uk
dir: Off B6532 from Durham centre, pass County Hall on
right and Dryburn Hospital on left. Turn right at double
rdbt into Aykley Heads

Seaham Hall Hotel - The White Room Restaurant

Rosettes not confirmed at time of going to press

SEAHAM   Map 19 NZ44

Modern, Traditional British, European V 🔖NOTABLE WINE LIST

Exciting dining in contemporary, luxury spa hotel

☎ 0191 516 1400
Lord Byron's Walk SR7 7AG
e-mail: reservations@seaham-hall.com
dir: A19 at 1st exit signed B1404 Seaham and follow
signs to Seaham Hall

In 1815 Lord Byron married Annabella Milbanke here, and
stayed on for their honeymoon, no doubt, benefiting from
the bracing North Sea coastal ozone. This imposing,
listed hotel with its 19th-century façade, stylish, modern
interiors and lavish spa facilities continues to attract
visitors from far and wide. The contemporary theme
continues in the dining room with wooden floors, neutral
colours and quality furnishings creating a calm and
comfortable ambience. Fully draped tables have
expensive settings, and service is formal and discreet.
Adventurous and skilfully executed combinations
characterise unashamedly modern dishes that make full
use of best quality ingredients. In between the numerous
appetisers, amuses and extras, fit a starter of crab salad
with confit salmon, avocado ice cream, passionfruit
vinaigrette and caviar or a main course of Balmoral
Estate venison loin with pumpkin purée, chestnuts and
crosnes, bitter chocolate sauce and scallop. Cheese and
desserts come with wine pairings.

As we went to press we understand there was a change of
ownership and chef taking place.

Times 12-2.30/7-10 **Wines** 100% bottles over £20, 9 by
glass **Notes** Tasting menu 10 courses, Market menu 8
courses £55, Sunday L, Vegetarian menu, Dress
restrictions, Smart casual, Civ Wed 112, Air con **Seats** 55,
Pr/dining room 20 **Children** Portions **Parking** 150

A modern business park has sprung up around this 18th-century former farmhouse. Original features include white-painted stone walls, wooden and stone floors, an inner courtyard and a vaulted bar. These, combined with the rustic chic décor, create the feel of a French country bistro. The bistro-style dishes are simple and effective with clean, clear flavours, demonstrated in crisp langoustine fritters with fennel salad and lemon mayonnaise, or perhaps venison pâté with apple, chicory and watercress salad, followed by pan-roasted halibut with asparagus, tomato confit and sage, and profiteroles with pistachio ice cream and hot chocolate sauce to finish.

Bistro 21

Chef Tom Jackson **Owner** Terence Laybourne **Times** 12-2/7-10.25, Closed 25 Dec, 1 Jan, BHs, Closed Sun **Prices** Fixed L 2 course £14, Fixed D 3 course £16.50, Starter £6.50-£10.50, Main £14-£22.50, Dessert £5-£8, Service added but optional 10% **Wines** 20 bottles over £20, 20 bottles under £20, 6 by glass **Notes** Early evening menu available, Vegetarian menu **Seats** 55, Pr/dining room 20 **Children** Portions **Parking** 11

ROMALDKIRK   Map 19 NY92

Rose & Crown Hotel

◉◉ Traditional British

Cosy country inn with a quintessentially English setting

☎ 01833 650213
DL12 9EB
e-mail: hotel@rose-and-crown.co.uk
dir: 6m NW of Barnard Castle on B6277

The oak panelled restaurant, with its starched white linen, silvery cutlery and candlelight, is very much in keeping with the atmosphere of this 18th-century coaching inn. The Rose & Crown is set in a picture-postcard Teesdale village, on the village green next to the Saxon church and opposite the old stocks and water pump. You can also dine in the cosy bar, complete with crackling fire, carriage lamps, old settle and prints. The

kitchen showcases well-executed, clear-flavoured classic British fare with modern and regional influences. Start with baked local Cotherstone cheese soufflé, moving onto roast pink fillet of lamb, woodland mushroom and kidney casserole with Madeira wine and béarnaise sauce, and finishing with warm apple and spice brown Betty.

Chef Chris Davy, Andrew Lee **Owner** Mr & Mrs C Davy **Times** 12-1.30/7.30-9, Closed Xmas, Closed L Mon-Sat **Prices** Fixed L 3 course £17.25-£19.75, Fixed D 4 course £30-£34, Service optional **Wines** 46 bottles over £20, 20 bottles under £20, 14 by glass **Notes** Sunday L, Vegetarian available **Seats** 24 **Children** Min 6 yrs, Portions **Parking** 24

SEAHAM   Map 19 NZ44

Seaham Hall Hotel - The White Room Restaurant

See opposite

ESSEX

BRENTWOOD   Map 6 TQ59

Marygreen Manor

◉◉ Modern European **V**

Exciting dining in baronial setting

☎ 01277 225252
London Rd CM14 4NR
e-mail: info@marygreenmanor.co.uk
web: www.marygreenmanor.co.uk
dir: 1m from Brentwood town centre, 0.5m from M25 junct 28

Back in the 16th century this striking house was owned by one Robert Wright, a local nobleman who named it the 'Manor of Mary Green' after his young bride. The title has survived to this day, along with many of the property's period features, including the baronial hall, now the hotel's Tudors restaurant. It is decorated in grand style with barley-twist columns, high beamed ceiling and coats of arms, and is the perfect setting for a special occasion. Modern European dishes are the order of the day: choose from the carte or a tasting menu and expect confident classics based on quality seasonal produce. Caramelised scallops on a bed of roasted cauliflower purée is a typical starter, while mains might include pan-fried fillet of veal with salsify, spinach, veal sweetbreads, ceps and truffle jus.

Marygreen Manor

Chef Majid Bourote **Owner** Mr S Bhattessa **Times** 12.30-2.30/7.15-10.15, Closed D Sun **Prices** Fixed L 2 course £19.95, Fixed D 3 course fr £42.50, Tasting menu £45.50, Service added but optional 12% **Wines** 80 bottles over £20, 21 bottles under £20, 7 by glass **Notes** Tasting menu 6 courses, Sunday L, Vegetarian menu, Dress restrictions, No jeans or trainers, Civ Wed 60, Air con **Seats** 80, Pr/dining room 85 **Children** Portions **Parking** 100

CHELMSFORD   Map 6 TL70

New Street Brasserie

◉ Modern, International

Brasserie dining in modern town-centre hotel

☎ 01245 268179
Best Western Atlantic Hotel, New St CM1 1PP
e-mail: info@atlantichotel.co.uk
dir: 5-minute walk from High Street

Situated in a purpose-built modern hotel, this refurbished brasserie has a contemporary look, with white leather and rich dark woods complemented by aubergine and fuchsia décor. Using good quality produce, the kitchen delivers well-executed dishes, including the fresh fish catch of the day displayed in the fish cabinet in the conservatory. Expect Scottish rope-grown mussels in white wine and garlic cream sauce with fresh parsley, followed by roasted lamb rump with mint and date crust, hand-cut chips, mushrooms and béarnaise sauce, or poached wing of skate with a sauce of bacon and capers and new potatoes. Service is professional yet relaxed from uniformed staff.

Times 12-3/6-10.30, Closed 27-30 Dec, Closed L Sat-Sun

CHELMSFORD *Continued*

Russells

◉ Modern English, French

Innovative cuisine in an ancient barn

☎ 01245 478484
Bell St, Great Baddow CM2 7JR
e-mail: russellsrestaurant@hotmail.com
dir: Please telephone for directions

A Grade II listed conversion of a 14th-century barn, Russells comprises a lounge, bar and restaurant divided into four areas. The place is traditionally decorated and very smart with formal service, and the cooking has both French and English influences. Expect dishes like fillets of sea bass served with a baby gem and fennel compôte and dill velouté, or perhaps slow-roasted belly of pork teamed with black pudding mash, apple compôte and a sage and apple infused jus, while a white chocolate pannacotta with fresh strawberries and shortbread biscuits might head-up desserts.

Chef Barry Warren-Watson **Owner** Mr B J Warren-Watson
Times 12-2.30/7-11.30, Closed 2 wks from 2 Jan, Closed Mon, Closed L Sat, Closed D Sun **Prices** Fixed L 2 course £11.95-£13.95, Fixed D 3 course £15.90-£17.90, Starter £5.50-£10.50, Main £13.95-£20.95, Dessert £3.95-£7.95, Service added but optional 10%, Groups min 10 service 15% **Wines** 42 bottles over £20, 30 bottles under £20, 8 by glass **Notes** Sunday L, Vegetarian available, Dress restrictions, No jeans, Air con **Seats** 70, Pr/dining room 36 **Children** Portions, Menu **Parking** 40

COGGESHALL	Map 7 TL82

Baumann's Brasserie

◉ British, French ▣

Buzzy brasserie in historic building

☎ 01376 561453
4-6 Stoneham St CO6 1TT
e-mail: food@baumannsbrasserie.co.uk
dir: A12 from Chelmsford, turn off at Kelvedon into Coggleshall, restaurant is in centre opposite the Clock Tower

This busy brasserie occupies a historic hall house in the heart of town. Clothed tables and antique chairs contrast with stripped floors and whitewashed walls hung with colourful artwork. The seasonally-changing menu is gutsy and interesting, offering traditional French and British cuisine with a few twists. Try forest mushroom tart with

chimi churri foam, followed by noisettes of venison with haricot beans and Cumberland sauce. Desserts include the house speciality Mars Bar cheesecake with whipped cream. Check out 'The Billingsgate Best' for daily fresh fish, and the light lunch for great value.

Baumann's Brasserie

Chef Mark Baumann, C Jeanneau **Owner** Baumann's Brasserie Ltd **Times** 12-2/7-9.30, Closed 2 wks Jan, Closed Mon-Tue **Prices** Fixed L 2 course £14, Fixed D 3 course £21.50, Starter £5.50-£8.50, Main £15-£19.50, Dessert £6.50, Service optional **Wines** 20 bottles over £20, 24 bottles under £20, 11 by glass **Notes** Sunday L, Vegetarian available **Seats** 80 **Children** Portions **Parking** Opposite

White Hart Hotel

◉ Modern European

Modern food in market town hotel

☎ 01378 561654
Market End CO6 1NH
e-mail: 6529@greeneking.co.uk
web: www.oldenglish.co.uk

Located in the bustling market town of Coggeshall stands this delightful hotel which dates back to the 15th century. Inside, there is oodles of charm and character with original beams still featuring. A snug bar serves good wines and beers, as well as a more traditional style of food, whilst in the restaurant there's a more refined approach, with the cooking being more classical. A starter of fresh salmon lasagne could be followed by fillet of beef with foie gras, potato rosti and red wine jus. Leave room for the chocolate truffle cake with vanilla ice cream.

COLCHESTER	Map 13 TL92

Best Western Rose & Crown Hotel

◉◉ Traditional, International

Contemporary dining in a traditional Tudor building

☎ 01206 866677
East St CO1 2TZ
e-mail: info@rose-and-crown.com
dir: From A12 take exit to Colchester North onto the A1232

A black and white 14th-century posting inn, situated in the oldest recorded town in England, the Rose & Crown retains much of its original character, with a wealth of exposed beams and timbered walls. Inside, furnishings and colours surprise with a contemporary look that

blends well with the historic setting. There is a choice of dining, either in the bar with its more relaxed menu or the East Street Grill restaurant, recently refurbished in a modern style, with smart rosewood tables, darkwood floor and contemporary prints. Using the best of local produce and with some international influences, wild mushroom soup with a quenelle of sour cream, tender lamb curry with basmati rice and fresh mango chutney and Baileys white chocolate mousse are fine examples of the fare.

Chef Venu Mahankali **Owner** Bremwell Limited
Times 12-2/7-9.45, Closed 27-30 Dec, Closed D Sun
Prices Starter £3.95-£6.95, Main £7.95-£16.25, Dessert £3.95-£6.25, Service optional, Groups min 5 service 10% **Wines** 12 bottles over £20, 19 bottles under £20, 6 by glass **Notes** Sunday L, Vegetarian available, Civ Wed 150 **Seats** 80, Pr/dining room 50 **Children** Portions **Parking** 60

Clarice House

◉ Modern British ▣

Health spa with an orangery-style restaurant

☎ 01206 734301
Kingsford Park, Layer Rd CO2 0HS
e-mail: colchester@claricehouse.co.uk
web: www.claricehouse.co.uk
dir: SW of town centre on B1026 towards Layer

An imposing building, Kingsford Park, houses a luxurious Clarice House health spa, providing an extensive range of treatments, leisure facilities and great food. Snacks are available in the trendy bar and lounge, but the serious food is served in the light-and-airy orangery-style restaurant with its bamboo chairs, magnolia colour scheme and conservatory roof. Menus offer modern British food with provincial touches, more refined than the homely descriptions might lead you to believe. Start with gin and tonic cured salmon with fine capers, shallots, pickled cucumber and potato blinis; moving on to steak and wild mushroom pudding. Finish with dark chocolate and banana parfait.

Chef Paul Boorman **Owner** Clarice House (Colchester) Ltd
Times 12-2.30/7-9, Closed 25-26 Dec, 1 Jan, Closed D Sun-Wed **Prices** Fixed L 2 course £16, Fixed D 3 course £25-£27, Service optional **Wines** 14 bottles over £20, 19 bottles under £20, 10 by glass **Notes** Monthly pudding club, Sunday L, Vegetarian available, Dress restrictions, Smart casual, Civ Wed 75, Air con **Seats** 60 **Parking** 100

DEDHAM
Map 13 TM03

milsoms

@@ International 🖐

Fun and informal dining experience in the Dedham Vale

☎ 01206 322795
Stratford Rd CO7 6HN
e-mail: milsoms@milsomhotels.com
web: www.milsomhotels.com
dir: 7m N of Colchester, just off A12

This split-level restaurant utilises natural fabrics, stone, wood and leather to create a relaxed, contemporary feel. The terrace comes with new lighting and heating, enabling diners to eat alfresco for most of the year. Informality is the order of the day - there is a no-booking policy and diners write up their own orders on the notepads provided - and it's loved by locals of all ages. The well-travelled chef has brought a variety of global influences to bear on the crowd-pleasing, brasserie-style menu, which includes the likes of Asian, Greek and British favourites. Take the griddled king prawns with Asian slaw to start, and perhaps roast Suffolk pork belly, black pudding mash, sauerkraut and rich jus to follow.

Chef Stas Anastasiades, Sarah Norman **Owner** Paul Milsom **Times** 12-9.30 **Prices** Starter £5-£7.50, Main £8.75-£18.50, Dessert £5.50, Service optional **Wines** 34 bottles over £20, 16 bottles under £20, 11 by glass **Notes** Air con **Seats** 80, Pr/dining room 16 **Children** Portions, Menu **Parking** 60

Le Talbooth Restaurant

@@ Modern British 🍷 🖐

Traditional quality in a picture-postcard setting

☎ 01206 323150
CO7 6HP
e-mail: talbooth@milsomhotels.com
web: www.milsomhotels.com
dir: 6m from Colchester: follow signs from A12 to Stratford St Mary, restaurant on left before village

A riverside setting, immaculate lawns, a picturesque bridge, leaded windows and a timber frame - no wonder Constable painted this magnificent property. Inside it boasts old beams, leather chairs, striking artwork and smart table settings, and you'd need a vivid imagination to picture it as the weaver's cottage and toll booth it once was. There's a terrace for all-weather alfresco dining beside the river, complete with sail canopy and heaters. The food matches the setting, with its emphasis on superior seasonal ingredients, local whenever possible, revealed on a balanced carte with modern undertones. Think lobster tail and monkfish cooked in a vermouth and rosemary sauce and served with basmati rice, and perhaps a delice of lemon with raspberry and thyme sorbet and lemon-grass jelly to finish.

Chef Ian Rhodes, Tom Bushell **Owner** Paul Milsom **Times** 12-2/7-9, Closed D Sun (Oct-Apr) **Prices** Fixed L 2 course £22, Starter £6.50-£14.95, Main £15.95-£28, Dessert £7.50-£8.25, Service included **Wines** 560 bottles over £20, 38 bottles under £20, 10 by glass **Notes** Sunday L, Dress restrictions, Smart casual, No jeans, Civ Wed 50 **Seats** 75, Pr/dining room 34 **Children** Portions **Parking** 50

FELSTED
Map 6 TL62

Reeves Restaurant

@ Modern British

Seasonal produce in charming setting

☎ 01371 820996
Rumbles Cottage, Braintree Rd CM6 3DJ
e-mail: reevesrestaurant@tiscali.co.uk
dir: A120 E from Braintree, B1417 to Felsted

Housed in a 16th-century cottage, this intimate oak-beamed restaurant is full of character with large windows, starched linen and plenty of fresh flowers. The cosy lounge is a lovely place for after-dinner drinks. The menus offer a range of interesting dishes inspired by the head chef's worldwide travel with the McLaren racing team. Starters might feature griddled summer quail, tarragon dressing and fried celery leaves. Main courses include the likes of rump of new season lamb with gratin potatoes, Puy lentils and Cumberland sauce; the elderflower crème brûlée might be a good choice to finish on.

Times 12-2/7, Closed Mon-Wed

GREAT CHESTERFORD
Map 12 TL54

The Crown House

@ British

Refreshing cooking in a peaceful village setting

☎ 01799 530515
CB10 1NY
e-mail: stay@thecrownhouseonetel.net

Much of the original character has been retained at this sympathetically restored Georgian coaching inn. Public rooms include an attractive lounge bar, oak-panelled restaurant and a conservatory. Terrace dining is an option in the summer months, between the main house and the walled garden. Sound cooking from good-quality produce delivers simple dishes with excellent flavours. Expect the likes of Crown House fishcake (crab and salmon) with mixed salad and sweet chilli sauce, followed by tender noisette of new season lamb, with minted caramelised pears, dauphinoise potatoes and thyme and port gravy. Finish with a chocolate brownie with a quenelle of Chantilly cream.

Times 12-2/7-9.15

GREAT YELDHAM　　　　Map 13 TL73

White Hart

◉ British, European ♨

Historic inn with good, honest cooking

☎ 01787 237250
CO9 4HJ
e-mail: mjwmason@yahoo.co.uk
dir: On A1017, between Halstead and Haverhill

This heavily-timbered 500-year old inn is full of character and sits on the banks of the River Colne in landscaped grounds. It has had several intriguing incarnations: from a tiny highwaymen's prison, to a private dining room that served as a communications centre in World War II. Today, it offers an extensive selection of crowd-pleasing dishes, making the most of local, seasonal ingredients. Expect dishes such as Colne Valley rack of lamb with fondant potato, swede and carrot purée and mint jus, or Tilbury Meadow Hereford rib-eye steak with tarragon potato rosti and feta cheese salad. More informal brasserie dining is also available.

Chef Kevin White & Wu Zhenjiang **Owner** Matthew Mason **Times** 12-3/6-9.30, Closed D 25-26 Dec **Prices** Fixed L 2 course £16.95-£19.95, Fixed D 3 course £16.95-£19.95, Starter £4.50-£9.95, Main £13.50-£24.95, Dessert £3.95-£5.50, Service optional, Groups min 7 service 10% **Wines** 45 bottles over £20, 35 bottles under £20, 7 by

glass **Notes** Sunday L, Vegetarian available, Dress restrictions, Smart casual, Civ Wed 80 **Seats** 60, Pr/dining room 36 **Children** Portions, Menu **Parking** 40

HARWICH　　　　Map 13 TM23

The Pier at Harwich

◉◉ British

Stylish quayside hotel restaurant with wide-ranging seafood menu

☎ 01255 241212
The Quay CO12 3HH
e-mail: pier@milsomhotels.com
web: www.milsomhotels.com
dir: A12 to Colchester then A120 to Harwich Quay

Perched on the quay overlooking the Stour and Orwell estuaries, The Pier is the perfect destination for seafood lovers. The first-floor Harbourside Restaurant, housed in this small contemporary hotel, provides a stylish setting complete with leather armchairs, a chrome cocktail bar, an open-plan dining area and impressive views. Service is relaxed but professional and the extensive menu includes a generous selection of dishes which can be enjoyed as starters or mains. Fresh fruits of the sea are in plentiful supply, featuring locally-caught and locally-smoked produce, in dishes such as smoked haddock fish cakes on leaf spinach with poached egg and hollandaise sauce, walnut and herb-crusted sea bass with parsnip

purée, or perhaps grilled Harwich lobster. For informal bistro-style food, try the Ha'penny downstairs.

The Pier at Harwich

Chef Chris Oakley **Owner** Paul Milsom **Times** 12-2/6-9, Closed D 25 Dec **Prices** Fixed L 2 course £18.50, Starter £6.25-£9, Main £12.75-£31.50, Dessert £5.95-£6.95, Service added 10% **Wines** 82 bottles over £20, 25 bottles under £20, 6 by glass **Notes** Sunday L, Vegetarian available, Dress restrictions, Smart casual, Civ Wed 50, Air con **Seats** 80, Pr/dining room 16 **Children** Portions, Menu **Parking** 20 **Parking** On street, pay & display

INGATESTONE　　　　Map 6 TQ69

The Woolpack

◉◉ Modern British

Modern dining in a traditional inn

☎ 01277 352189
Mill Green Rd, Fryerning CM4 0HS
e-mail: thewoolpack@aol.com
dir: M25 junct A12, between Brentwood & Chelmsford

There has been a Woolpack Inn on this site since the 1100s, but the current building is around 135 years old. A contemporary interior features polished oak floors, oak beams, ivory-coloured half panelling and luxurious leather seating. Smoked glass, wooden blinds and 1950s fashion photographs complete the look. The kitchen

brigade delivers accomplished modern British cooking offering clean, clear flavours from excellent produce. House favourites include pan-roasted Loch Duart salmon with tomato risotto and spinach sauce, braised belly of pork with butterbean and bacon cassoulet and pork and thyme dumpling, or pan-fried Goosnargh chicken, herb gnocchi and sherry gravy. Look out for the value weekday lunches and the family gourmet Sunday lunches.

Chef Daniel Holland-Robinson **Owner** John & Lisa Hood **Times** 12-4/7-12.30, Closed 1 wk in Aug, 2 wks after Xmas, Closed Mon & Tue, Closed L Sat, Closed D Sun **Prices** Fixed L 2 course fr £13.95, Starter £4.95-£8.95, Main £13.95-£21.95, Dessert £5.95-£7.95, Service optional, Groups min 6 service 10% **Wines** 36 bottles over £20, 12 bottles under £20, 5 by glass **Notes** Sunday L, Vegetarian available, Dress restrictions, Smart casual, No headgear, Air con **Seats** 50 **Children** Min 12 yrs **Parking** 20

MANNINGTREE — Map 13 TM13

The Mistley Thorn

◉◉ International 🖐

Delightful inn serving bistro-style quality, locally-sourced produce

☎ 01206 392821
High St, Mistley CO11 1HE
e-mail: info@mistleythorn.co.uk
web: www.mistleythorn.co.uk
dir: From A12 take A137 for Manningtree and Mistley

A setting beside the River Stour is part of the appeal of this bustling Georgian inn, built on what was once the site of some of Matthew Hopkins' infamous Witchfinder trials. Inside the bistro-style restaurant has an air of American New England about it - light and airy with terracotta-tiled floors, high-quality furnishings, exposed beams and tongue-and-groove walls. The simple approach to cooking suits the venue, with the abundant local, seasonal produce, in particular fresh fish, ensuring good, clean flavours. Think potted shrimps, Mersea Island rock oysters with spinach and Pernod, seared bass with samphire and sauce vièrge, chargrilled local lamb steak with mint vinaigrette and roasted balsamic tomatoes, and perhaps hazelnut chocolate cake for dessert. Cookery lessons are available.

Chef Sherri Singleton, Chris Pritchard **Owner** Sherri Singleton, David McKay **Times** 12-2.30/6.30-9.30, Closed 25 Dec **Prices** Fixed L 2 course £11.95, Starter £4.25-£7.95, Main £8.95-£16.95, Dessert £4.50-£6.95, Service optional, Groups min 8 service 10% **Wines** 22 bottles over £20, 19 bottles under £20, 17 by glass **Notes** Sunday L, Vegetarian available **Seats** 75, Pr/dining room 28 **Children** Portions, Menu **Parking** 7

SAFFRON WALDEN — Map 12 TL53

The Cricketers' Arms

◉ Modern European 🖥

Imaginative, modern menu in refurbished village inn

☎ 01799 543210
Rickling Green CB11 3YG
e-mail: reservations@cricketers.demon.co.uk
dir: M11 junct 8, A120 to Bishops Stortford then B1383 and follow signs to Rickling

Once the cricket pavilion for the local team, The Cricketers' Arms overlooks Rickling village green and parts of this fully refurbished inn date back to the 16th century. Inside this gastro-pub, exposed beams and fireplaces are among the many retained original character features, while contemporary restyling has added a smart, modern minimalist touch to the décor. The kitchen delivers skilfully presented, imaginative modern British cuisine with lovely flavours, making good use of local and seasonal produce. Expect portobello mushrooms stuffed with goat's cheese or crayfish risotto, followed by roast belly of pork and caramelised apple mash with a cider sauce and, to finish, enjoy dark Belgian chocolate mousse with chocolate shavings.

Chef Eamon Moore **Owner** Spice Inns Ltd **Times** 12-2.30/6-9.30 **Prices** Fixed L 2 course £12.50, Starter £5-£9.50, Main £10.50-£19, Dessert £5-£6, Service optional **Wines** 9 bottles over £20, 16 bottles under £20, 9 by glass **Notes** Sunday L, Vegetarian available, Air con **Seats** 60, Pr/dining room 12 **Children** Menu **Parking** 40

SHENFIELD — Map 6 TQ69

Lot 67

◉ Modern European

Lively and informal town-centre brasserie

☎ 01277 212213
67 Hutton Rd CM15 8JD

This stylish, informal brasserie has an uncluttered, contemporary feel. With oak flooring, dark wood tables and matching wood and cream leather chairs, modern art provides splashes of colour on the neutral walls. Service is relaxed but professional and, in warm weather, you can dine alfresco on the terrace. Typical dishes on the seasonally-changing menu include garlic mushroom with goat's cheese on bruschetta and salsa verde to start, and chicken teriyaki with stir-fried vegetables and bok choy to follow. Leave room for the chocolate brownie with vanilla ice cream and hot chocolate fudge sauce.

SOUTHEND-ON-SEA — Map 7 TQ88

Fleur de Provence

◉ French

Modern French cooking in resort restaurant

☎ 01702 352987
52-54 Alexander St SS1 1BJ
e-mail: mancel@fleurdeprovence.co.uk

A stone's throw from the town centre, the frosted glass, high-street frontage of this French restaurant may look unassuming, but inside the stylish, intimate and cosy interior has soft colours and lighting to create a genuinely romantic setting, while service is friendly but discreet. Modern meets classical in the menu; take rib-eye of beef with a bourguignon sauce, or lamb cannon coated in minted breadcrumbs with a garlic-scented jus, and to finish, perhaps an assiette of chocolate or trio of crème brûlées.

Times 12-2/7-10, Closed 1st 2 wks Jan, BHs, Closed Sun, Closed L Sat

TOLLESHUNT KNIGHTS — Map 7 TL91

The Camelot Restaurant at Five Lakes

◉◉ Modern British 🖐

Fine dining restaurant in a resort hotel

☎ 01621 868888
Five Lakes Hotel, Colchester Road CM9 8HX
e-mail: enquiries@fivelakes.co.uk
web: www.fivelakes.co.uk
dir: M25 junct 28, then on A12. At Kelvedon take B1024 then B1023 to Tolleshunt Knights, clearly marked by brown tourist signs

This resort hotel boasts two golf courses and extensive health, leisure and sporting facilities set within 320 acres of open countryside. The split-level Camelot restaurant is themed around the legend of King Arthur. Close attention to detail keeps the modern British and European food to a high standard. Start with partridge and girolle mushroom tartlet with Madeira cream sauce, followed perhaps by lemon poached seafood medley with fresh lasagne and chive cream sauce, or meat-eaters might opt for classic tournedos rossini with goat's cheese mash, baby beetroot and bordelaise sauce. Finish with apricot bread-and-butter pudding with cinnamon and ginger cream, or choose from a selection of home-made ice creams and sorbets.

Continued

TOLLESHUNT KNIGHTS *Continued*

Chef Mark Joyce **Owner** Mr A Bejerano **Times** Closed 26, 31 Dec, 1 Jan, Closed Sun-Mon **Prices** Fixed D 3 course £33.50, Starter £6-£7.95, Main £14.50-£25, Dessert £6-£7.25, Service optional **Wines** 63 bottles over £20, 18 bottles under £20, 7 by glass **Notes** Sunday L, Vegetarian available, Dress restrictions, Smart casual, no trainers, T-shirts or jeans, Civ Wed 300, Air con **Seats** 80 **Children** Portions, Menu **Parking** 550

See advert on page 156

GLOUCESTERSHIRE

ALMONDSBURY   Map 4 ST68

Quarterjacks Restaurant

Modern British

Relaxed, brasserie-style dining in modern Nordic-style hotel

☎ 01454 201090
Aztec Hotel & Spa, Aztec West Business Park BS32 4TS
e-mail: aztec@shirehotels.co.uk
dir: Telephone for directions

Built in the Nordic style, this modern hotel north of Bristol features timber beams, vaulted ceilings, contemporary artwork, stone-flagged floors and log fires. The Quarterjacks Restaurant, re-launched in April 2008, has a relaxed brasserie vibe and looks out across the terrace - perfect for alfresco summer dining - and gardens to the rear. Typical dishes include rustic fish soup, gruyère cheese, rouille and sourdough croûtons to start, followed by new season roasted lamb rump, colcannon mash and garlic crisps. Finish with rhubarb and pistachio syllabub and ginger shortbread.

Times 12.30-2/7-10, Closed 26 Dec, Closed L Sat & Sun

ARLINGHAM   Map 4 SO71

The Old Passage Inn

Seafood

Seafood restaurant with river and forest views

☎ 01452 740547
Passage Rd GL2 7JR
e-mail: oldpassage@ukonline.co.uk
web: www.fishattheoldpassageinn.co.uk
dir: M5 junct 13/A38 towards Bristol, 2nd right to Frampton-on-Severn, over canal & bear left follow road to river bank

Formerly a ferry station for services crossing the river, this charming early 19th-century inn stands on the banks of the tidal Severn. The large dining room is open and airy, and there's a garden terrace for summer meals outside with views of the river and the Forest of Dean. For private parties there's a second intimate dining room. The food is almost exclusively fish and shellfish, and the restaurant has two seawater tanks - one for lobster and the other for oysters and shellfish. Dishes are imaginatively presented, with intelligently simple

treatment of sea-fresh produce. Among the recommended dishes are scallops thermidor with buttered spinach and creamy sherry mustard sauce, lobster naturel with hand-cut chips, and sea bass on crab risotto.

The Old Passage Inn

Chef Mark Redwood, Raoul Moore **Owner** Sally & David Pearce **Times** 12-2/6.30-9.30, Closed 25 Dec, Closed Mon, Closed D Sun **Prices** Starter £6-£10, Main £14-£35, Dessert £6-£8.50, Service optional **Wines** 53 bottles over £20, 36 bottles under £20, 15 by glass **Notes** Sunday L, Vegetarian available, Air con **Seats** 60, Pr/dining room 14 **Children** Portions **Parking** 40

BARNSLEY   Map 5 SP00

The Village Pub

Modern British

Cotswold inn dining with understated class

☎ 01285 740421
GL7 5EF
e-mail: info@thevillagepub.co.uk
dir: 4m from Cirencester, on B4425 to Bibury

A warm welcome awaits within at this enduringly popular Cotswold inn, complete with open winter fires, exposed beams, flagstones and floorboards. Five dining areas, situated around a central bar, provide plenty of space at this far from average village pub and the garden patio supplies a setting for summer alfresco dining. There is a contemporary touch to the cooking and excellent local produce is prepared with great skill to maximum effect. This is unpretentious food that allows the main ingredient to shine through. Starters might include potted rabbit with toasted sourdough, celeriac and mustard, followed by main courses like roasted halibut with artichokes, potatoes and steamed cockles, and enjoyable desserts such as chocolate and espresso tart.

Times 11-2.30/7-9.30

BIBURY   Map 5 SP10

Bibury Court

British

Comfortable and relaxing formal dining in Tudor manor

☎ 01285 740337 & 740324
GL7 5NT
e-mail: info@biburycourt.com
web: www.biburycourt.com
dir: On B4425 between Cirencester & Burford; hotel behind church

Dating back to 1633, this grand country-house hotel in 6 acres of grounds is tucked away behind a beautiful Cotswold village in a picture-postcard spot on the River Coln. With traditional wood panelling, log fires, comfy sofas and antique furniture, it oozes historic charm and character while offering an oasis of calm in a relaxed and informal atmosphere. For such a grand and elegant setting the cooking is refreshingly unfussy, unpretentious and understated. A confident kitchen uses fine seasonal ingredients to create modern, classically-based dishes with excellent flavour combinations. There's a strong emphasis on local produce, with suppliers duly noted on the menu. Hearty dishes might include the likes of citrus- and dill-cured salmon with pickled Cheltenham beetroot, mustard leaves, horseradish and Avruga caviar or oxtail linguini, followed by a main course of caramelised sea bream, olive oil mashed potatoes, balsamic-roasted onions, cep mushrooms and red wine. Dine in the more informal conservatory at lunch and the formal restaurant at dinner.

Chef Antony Ely **Owner** Robert Johnston **Times** 12-2/7-9 **Prices** Fixed L 2 course £12.50-£19.50, Fixed D 3 course £35-£39, Service optional, Groups min 6 service 10% **Wines** 117 bottles over £20, 24 bottles under £20, 8 by glass **Notes** Tasting menu available, Sunday L, Vegetarian available, Civ Wed 32 **Seats** 65, Pr/dining room 30 **Children** Portions, Menu **Parking** 100

Swan Hotel

◉ International

Relaxed dining in peaceful, picturesque surroundings

☎ 01285 740695

GL7 5NW

e-mail: info@swanhotel.co.uk

dir: On B4425 between Cirencester (7 miles) and Burford (9 miles). Beside bridge in centre of Bibury

The creeper-covered Swan is a classic Cotswold-stone building located right on the river bank and with views that would satisfy any chocolate box maker. The village is awash with tourists and this former coaching inn provides any number of refuelling options from bar, café and Gallery restaurant. The traditional dining room is furnished with quality fabrics and crisp linen, and the walls adorned with animal-themed original artwork. The menu makes good use of local produce including smoked Bibury trout from literally over the road, while seafood comes up from Cornwall. That smoked trout comes with garlic and thyme pannacotta and crisp Parma ham as a starter, while main course sea bass is served with Carmargue rice, pak choi and saffron cream.

Chef Chris Hutchings **Owner** Pamela & Michael Horton **Times** Closed L Mon-Sun **Prices** Food prices not confirmed for 2009. Please telephone for details. **Notes** Civ Wed 90 **Seats** 60, Pr/dining room 30

BUCKLAND Map 10 SP03

Buckland Manor

◉◉ Traditional British, French ⬩NOTABLE WINE LIST

Accomplished cuisine in medieval manor

☎ 01386 852626

WR12 7LY

e-mail: info@bucklandmanor.com

web: www.bucklandmanor.com

dir: 2m SW of Broadway. Take B4632 signed Cheltenham, then take turn for Buckland. Hotel through village on right

The setting for this quintessential 13th-century, mellow-stone manor house is glorious, tucked away on a hillside within extensive and impeccably maintained grounds. Inside has more a feeling of traditional country home than luxury country-house hotel, with roaring open fires, stone floors, tapestries and comfortable sitting rooms, while the atmosphere is one of calm and tranquillity. The equally traditional restaurant has unusual white-painted wood panelling, portraits and lovely views, backed by

skilled, attentive service. The kitchen's accomplished approach is underpinned by a classical theme and showcases quality fresh local produce. Take roast fillet of Cotswold venison with gratin dauphinoise and beetroot purée, and to finish, hot chocolate fondant with ginger ice cream.

Buckland Manor

Chef Matt Hodgkinson **Owner** Buckland Manor Country House Hotel Ltd **Times** 12.30-1.45/7.30-9 **Prices** Fixed L 2 course £19.50, Starter £7.95-£13.95, Main £23.50-£32.50, Dessert £9, Service optional **Wines** 574 bottles over £20, 7 bottles under £20, 35 by glass **Notes** Pre-theatre D available, Sunday L, Vegetarian available, Dress restrictions, Jacket & tie **Seats** 40 **Children** Min 8 yrs **Parking** 30

CHARINGWORTH Map 10 SP13

The John Greville Restaurant

◉◉ Modern International

Modern cuisine in an ancient manor

☎ 01386 593555

Charingworth Manor GL55 6NS

e-mail: charingworthmanor@classiclodges.co.uk

dir: M40 exit at signs for A429 Stow. Follow signs for Moreton in the Marsh. From Chipping Camden follow signs for Charingworth Manor

Set in glorious Cotswold countryside, within a 55-acre estate, the ancient manor of Charingworth dates back to the early 14th century, with beams showing original medieval decoration. The small, traditional restaurant has beamed ceilings and a warm décor of red rag-rolled walls with tables divided into separate areas. The cuisine is modern and global with the accent on really fresh ingredients and straightforward presentation. Daily-changing menus are sensibly compact and might feature crisp filo tartlet of mussels in a saffron, brie, bacon and cream sauce, followed by oven-roasted rump of Lighthorne lamb, pancetta and thyme mash, balsamic roasted shallots and wild mushroom and truffle jus.

Finish with a shiny vanilla pannacotta, poached pears in pear consommé with a tuile biscuit.

Times 12-2/7-9.30

See advert on page 160

CHELTENHAM Map 10 SO92

Le Champignon Sauvage

◉◉◉◉ – *see page 161*

The Greenway

◉◉ Modern British, European 🅥

Accomplished cooking at an Elizabethan manor

☎ 01242 862352

Shurdington GL51 4UG

e-mail: info@thegreenway.co.uk

dir: 3m S of Cheltenham on A46 (Stroud), pass through the village of Shurdington

Set on the outskirts of Cheltenham, this Elizabethan country manor house makes a handy touring base for the Cotswolds. Inside, period features are teamed with comfy sofas and open fires to create a timeless quality of understated relaxed charm and elegance, which extends to the conservatory restaurant, a bright, elegant room with views over a pretty sunken garden. The accomplished kitchen's flair ensures innovative combinations: pavé of beef with sweet potato purée and braised snails perhaps, or fillets of wild Irish sea bass with soft-poached oyster, butternut gnocchi, artichoke and sauce piquant. A melting dark chocolate fondant with strawberry and tarragon sorbet and roasted hazelnuts might catch the eye at dessert.

Chef Luke Richards **Owner** von Essen Hotels **Times** 12-2.30/7-9.30 **Wines** All bottles over £20, 10 by glass **Notes** ALC 3 courses £48.50, Tasting menu 6 courses, Sunday L, Vegetarian menu, Dress restrictions, Smart casual, No jeans, T-shirts or trainers, Civ Wed 45 **Seats** 50, Pr/dining room 30 **Children** Portions **Parking** 50

CHELTENHAM *Continued*

Hotel du Vin Cheltenham

British, European

☎ 01242 588450
Parabola Rd GL50 3AQ
e-mail: info.cheltenham@hotelduvin.com
web: www.hotelduvin.com
dir: Please telephone for directions

This establishment was awarded its Rosette/s just as we went to press. Therefore we are unable to provide a description for it - visit www.theAA.com for the most up-to-date information.

Chef Michael Wilson **Owner** MWB **Times** 12-2/6.30-10.30, Closed L 31 Dec **Prices** Fixed L 2 course fr £15, Starter £4.50-£6.95, Main £13.50-£18.50, Dessert fr £6.75, Service added but optional 10% **Wines** 450 bottles over £20, 20 bottles under £20, 20 by glass **Notes** Sunday L, Vegetarian available, Air con **Seats** 92, Pr/dining room 22 **Parking** 23

Lumière

Modern

Bold modern cooking at a chic town-centre haunt

☎ 01242 222200
Clarence Pde GL50 3PA
e-mail: dinner@lumiere.cc
dir: Town centre, near bus station

Don't be put off by the modest, understated exterior. This stylish and comfortable dining room may be tucked away behind an unassuming etched-glass frontage but it conceals one of the town centre's shining culinary lights. Modern abstract artworks, white tablecloths, elegant chairs and mirror-lined banquette seating all add to the warm contemporary edge, while service is run with plenty of charm and vitality by Lin Chapman, who's equally informed and passionate about husband Geoff's cooking and the well-chosen wine list. His dishes are bold,

generous, clean-cut and highly personal, with the sensibly compact, fixed-price menus certainly standing out from the crowd. Expect seared wild sea bass with tiger prawn coleslaw and spicy shrimp salsa, or perhaps slow roasted Barbary duck leg confit on braised sweet chilli bok choy from this dinner-only affair.

Chef Geoff Chapman **Owner** Lin & Geoff Chapman **Times** Closed 2 wks Jan, 2 wks summer, Closed Sun-Tue, Closed L all wk, Closed D 25 Dec **Wines** 75 bottles over £20, 2 bottles under £20, 4 by glass **Notes** Pre-theatre 2 courses & bag of truffles to go £38, Air con **Seats** 30 **Children** Min 8 yrs **Parking** On street, nearby car parks

Mercure Queen's Hotel

International

Fashionable Regency hotel with assured cooking

☎ 01242 514754
The Promenade GL50 1NN
e-mail: H6632@accor.com
dir: M5 junct 11, Queens Hotel is at the junct of the Promenade and Imperial Square

This landmark Regency hotel is located at the top of the historic spa town's main promenade and has a contemporary neo-colonial feel. Smart public rooms include the popular Gold Cup bar - perfect for snacks and pre-dinner drinks - and the refurbished conservatory-style Napier restaurant, where sleek wooden floors, high ceilings, unclothed tables, high-backed chairs, eye-catching planters and superb natural light are complemented by friendly and attentive service. The kitchen's well-balanced, well-executed modern approach offers the best of traditional and contemporary cuisine using quality seasonal produce. Take a starter of coconut-coated prawns with mango and coriander salsa, followed by sirloin of Hereford beef with oxtail rösti, girolles and red wine jus, with perhaps white chocolate cheesecake and caramel sauce for dessert.

Chef Robin Dudley **Owner** Moorefields
Times 12.30-2/7-9.30 **Prices** Fixed L 2 course £16.95,

Fixed D 3 course £25, Starter £4.95-£9.50, Main £14.50-£19.50, Dessert £6, Service optional **Wines** 16 bottles over £20, 15 bottles under £20, 11 by glass **Notes** Sunday L, Vegetarian available, Civ Wed 60, Air con **Seats** , Pr/dining room 70 **Children** Portions **Parking** 60

Monty's Brasserie

Modern International

Confident cooking in stylish, contemporary setting

☎ 01242 227678
George Hotel, 41 St Georges Rd GL50 3DZ
e-mail: info@montysbraz.co.uk
dir: M5 junct 11, follow signs to town centre. At lights (TGI Fridays) turn left onto Gloucester Road. Straight on, traffic lights turn right, Monty's 0.75m on left

One of Cheltenham's finest Regency hotels, just a few minutes walk from the tree-lined promenades and elegant terraces in the town centre, the George has been stylish refurbished. The lively Monty's Brasserie continues the contemporary vibe with luxurious leather seating and a warm décor, and attentive but relaxed service. The confident, innovative, elegant modern cooking fits the bill, and reflects skilled treatment of quality produce, with the clear flavours of the main ingredients allowed to shine through. Presentation is eye-catching, as seen in an accurately cooked salmon and smoked haddock fishcake with beurre blanc and herb salad, and a well-judged rack of Cotswold lamb served with butternut squash purée, wilted spinach and lamb jus. Equally impressive desserts may include a creamy vanilla crème brûlée with ginger biscuits.

Chef Rob Owen **Owner** Jeremy Shaw **Times** 12-2/6-10, Closed 25-26 Dec **Prices** Starter £5.95-£8.95, Main £11.95-£19.95, Dessert £5.95-£7.95, Service added but optional 10% **Wines** 25 bottles over £20, 16 bottles under £20, 10 by glass **Notes** ALC D, Sunday L, Vegetarian available, Air con **Seats** 40, Pr/dining room 26 **Children** Portions, Menu **Parking** 30

Le Champignon Sauvage

Modern 💻

Serious French cooking, attentive service and modern, stylish environment

☎ 01242 573449
24 Suffolk Rd GL50 2AQ
e-mail: mail@lechampignonsauvage.co.uk
dir: S of the town centre, on A40, near Cheltenham College

Strolling past this unassuming terrace building in the Montpelier part of the town there is nothing to suggest what culinary stirrings lie within. The décor is smart and erring on the traditional side - an unpretentious, sunny yellow-painted dining room with modern art on the walls and well-spaced tables neatly clothed in white linen. It is the food that leaves the lasting impression. David Everitt-Matthias is a chef dedicated to his craft, always to be found in the kitchen and never standing still. Luckily he found the time to write his first book, 'essence', in 2007. His cooking is innovative though not distracted by flights of fancy, precise without being precious, and at its core is a feeling for the produce itself from the humble to the refined. France, both old and modern, is the inspiration for many of the preparations and ideas but much of the produce is local. An amuse-bouche consisting of a shot glass of Moroccan-spiced split pea soup is topped with a coconut foam, while breads - bacon and onion brioche among them - set the bar at a high level. Presentation skills are highly developed as seen in a starter of seared squid partnered with Gloucestershire Old Spot pork, the meat placed on a creamy mousseline, with crisp toasted hazelnuts and a deliciously light hazelnut foam - a first-class first course. Flavours combine to maximum effect in a main course of Dexter beef with salted orange, aubergine and pine nut 'tapenade' and in a fish dish of zander with a ceps casserole, duck hearts and red wine emulsion. Warm cherry tart exhibits considerable skill in the making and comes with lemon verbena ice cream and cherry compôte and the creativity of the kitchen carries on to the very end with elegant petits fours. Service, headed up by Helen Everitt-Matthias, is both friendly and knowledgeable of the menu.

Chef David Everitt-Matthias
Times 12.30-1.30/7.30-9, Closed 10 days Xmas, 3 wks Jun, Closed Sun-Mon

CHELTENHAM *Continued*

Thistle Cheltenham

◉ Modern British

Hotel dining room with a creative kitchen team

☎ 0870 333 91 31
Gloucester Rd GL51 0TS
e-mail: cheltenham@thistle.co.uk

Situated on the edge of town, the Thistle may lack the charm of the historic buildings in the centre of Cheltenham, but it has great facilities including a health and leisure club. It also has a good, traditional-styled restaurant called the Burford. The menu combines quality produce in excellent flavour combinations, extending to the modern partnership of scallops with black pudding and to making a pastilla of the leg meat to go with breast of Gressingham duck. Gloucestershire pork loin and braised belly is served with pommes Anna, Savoy cabbage and a light Granny Smith jus. Efficient service is on the formal side.

Times 12.30-2/7-10 **Prices** Food prices not confirmed for 2009. Please telephone for details.

CHIPPING CAMPDEN	Map 10 SP13

Cotswold House, Juliana's Restaurant

◉◉◉ — *see below*

Hicks' Brasserie and Bar

◉ Modern British 🖥 🖐

Relaxed, modern brasserie-style dining in contemporary surroundings

☎ 01386 840330
Cotswold House, The Square GL55 6AN
e-mail: reception@cotswold.com
dir: 1m N of A44 between Moreton-in-Marsh & Broadway on B4081

With its sweeping marble-topped bar, chic contemporary design and modern artwork, this contemporary hotel's more relaxed dining option cannot fail to impress. Ivory or burgundy-coloured walls, banquettes or cool chairs and polished-wood tables are all colour-coordinated and suitably fashionable, while the youthful service is unstuffy and friendly. The kitchen's equally modern approach to brasserie fare takes a straightforward but highly accomplished line, playing to the gallery with old favourites delivered with a modern twist. A satisfying starter of fishcakes with green bean relish and caper balsamic dressing might be followed by the likes of pan-fried sea bass with sautéed potatoes, parsnip purée, curly kale and leeks, or maybe grilled Gloucestershire pork cutlet with black pudding mash.

Chef Steve Love **Owner** Concorde Hotels
Times 12-3/6-9.45 **Prices** Fixed L 2 course £14.95-£16.50, Fixed D 3 course fr £19.50, Starter £4.95-£6.95, Main £10.75-£24.50, Dessert £4.50-£6.25,

Service optional, Groups min 8 service 10% **Wines** 22 bottles over £20, 13 bottles under £20, 12 by glass **Notes** Sunday L, Vegetarian available, Air con **Seats** 50, Pr/dining room 14 **Children** Portions, Menu **Parking** 26

The Kings

◉ Traditional British V

Friendly, contemporary restaurant in a Cotswold inn

☎ 01386 840256 & 841056
The Square GL55 6AW
e-mail: info@kingscampden.co.uk
dir: Please telephone for directions

This Grade II listed Georgian inn with traditional Cotswold stone exterior is popular with locals and visitors alike and is situated in the town's historic centre. In the restaurant, old and new come together with well-spaced candlelit tables and modern art contrasting with original features like an inglenook fireplace. Friendly staff contribute to the convivial buzz, and there's something for everyone on the extensive menu, with an emphasis on quality produce, carefully prepared, including a good selection of fish from Brixham. You might start with a well presented trio of smoked fish served with whisky and horseradish cream, and maybe follow with lemon sole fillets in provençal sauce. The Kings Plate - a mixture of mini desserts - is not to be missed. There's also a good selection of wines available by the glass.

Times 12-3/6.30-10, Closed 25 Dec

Cotswold House, Juliana's Restaurant

CHIPPING CAMPDEN	Map 10 SP13

Modern British 🖥 V 🏅NOTABLE WINE LIST

Attractive Georgian hotel with a first-class restaurant

☎ 01386 840330
Cotswold House, The Square GL55 6AN
e-mail: reception@cotswoldhouse.com
dir: 1m N of A44 between Moreton-in-Marsh & Broadway on B4081

The pretty town of Chipping Campden is resplendent with Georgian character and brings forth images of Jane Austen's characters; it's easy to imagine them walking past the former Regency wool merchant's house. Once through the front door though a different kind of impression is perceived. This is a truly contemporary hotel, one that successfully blends the old and the new to create elegant and engaging spaces. Stunning features

such as the circular staircase have been retained and joined by a clever mix of old and new furniture, antique and retro. There are two dining options at the hotel: Hicks Brasserie (see above) for lighter options and informality, and the main dining room, Juliana's, which has views over the garden through arched French doors. New chef Steve Love delivers a modern menu based around top-quality produce and his interpretation of classical techniques. A starter of meli-melo of salmon offers layers of the fish, both smoked and warmed, with an oyster beignet and light chive butter sauce, and attention to detail is demonstrated in 63°c coddled free-range egg with wild mushrooms, duck leg, pancetta and cep sauce. Main-course sea bass is cooked slowly and flavoured with lemon grass in a winning combination with salt-cod croquettes, chicken wings (pressed squares of the meat) and a blood orange curd. The level of invention continues into the dessert stage with an apple crumble, the fruit nicely caramelised, and presented with a rosemary ice cream and a shot-glass of vanilla milkshake.

Chef Steve Love **Owner** Concorde Hotel
Times 12-2.30/7-10, Closed L Mon-Sat **Prices** Fixed L course £27.50, Fixed D 3 course £49.50, Service optional, Groups min 8 service 10% **Wines** 150 bottles over £20, 10 by glass **Notes** Sunday L, Vegetarian menu, Civ Wed 80, Air con **Seats** 40, Pr/dining room 96 **Children** Portions **Parking** 25

Three Ways House

◉ Modern, Traditional British

Cotswold home of the famous Pudding Club

☎ 01386 438429
Mickleton GL55 6SB
e-mail: reception@puddingclub.com
web: www.puddingclub.com
dir: On B4632, in village centre

Dating from 1870, this welcoming Cotswold hotel has plenty of period charm, though the restaurant is more contemporary in style, with cool blue décor, armchair seating and crisp linen. The focus is on local seasonal produce in uncomplicated dishes, using braising and chargrilling to highlight natural flavours - try trio of Severn and Wye smoked fish; or braised estate pheasant. Don't miss the traditional puddings, all served with lashings of custard - spotted Dick, bread-and-butter, syrup sponge - for this is the home of the famous Pudding Club, founded in 1985, where even the bedrooms have pudding themes.

Chef Mark Rowlandson **Owner** Simon Coombe & Peter Henderson **Times** 12-2.30/7-9.30, Closed L Mon-Sat **Prices** Fixed L 2 course £19-£20, Fixed D 3 course £33-£38, Service optional **Wines** 30 bottles over £20, 20 bottles under £20, 15 by glass **Notes** Sunday L, Vegetarian available, Civ Wed 80, Air con **Seats** 80, Pr/dining room 70 **Children** Portions, Menu **Parking** 37 **Parking** On street parking

Hare & Hounds

◉ Traditional, International

Satisfying food in a charming Cotswold inn

☎ 01285 720288
Fosse-Cross GL54 4NN
e-mail: stay@thehareandhoundsinn.com
dir: On A429 Stow road 6m from Cirencester

This typical Cotswold inn, parts of which date back to the 14th century, is bursting with character with open fires, stone and wood floors and cosy, candlelit nooks and crannies for intimate dining. Expect a mix of traditional and international cooking, which shows great efforts to incorporate local produce. You could expect a starter of North Cerney goat's cheese soufflé, or seared scallops with whisky cream sauce followed by medallions of pork fillet on braised fennel with lemon and sage jus. The

dessert list is heavy on robust favourites such as sticky toffee pudding. There is alfresco dining available in the warmer months.

Times 12-3/6-10, Closed Xmas, New Yr, BHs

Tudor Farmhouse Hotel & Restaurant

◉◉ Modern British ☕

Hearty fare at romantic converted farm

☎ 01594 833046
GL16 8JS
e-mail: info@tudorfarmhousehotel.co.uk
dir: Leave Monmouth to Chepstow road at Redbrook, follow signs Clearwell, turn left at village cross. Hotel on left

This 13th-century, Grade II listed converted farm is in the heart of the Forest of Dean and within walking distance of Clearwell Castle. It retains a host of original features, including exposed stonework, oak beams, wall panelling, wonderful inglenook fireplaces and, more unusually, wooden spiral staircases. With a growing reputation in the area, the creative menus offer quality cuisine served in the intimate, candlelit restaurant. Local ingredients are duly celebrated in generous, full-flavoured dishes like braised shin of Herefordshire beef served with horseradish creamed potato, spinach, parsnip purée and Madeira sauce, or pan-fried breast of Madgetts Farm duck with braised Puy lentils, carrot purée, wild mushrooms and a liquorice-scented sauce. For dessert, try Bramley and Pink Lady apple cheesecake with cranberry ice cream.

Chef Stephen Frost **Owner** Owen & Eirwen Evans **Times** 12-2.30/7-9, Closed 24-27 Dec **Prices** Starter £5.25-£8.95, Main £14.95-£21.55, Dessert £5.95-£8.25, Service optional **Wines** 9 bottles over £20, 26 bottles under £20, 8 by glass **Notes** Sunday L, Vegetarian available **Seats** 30, Pr/dining room 22 **Children** Portions, Menu **Parking** 24

The Wyndham Arms Hotel

◉ Modern British ☕

Ancient hostelry serving up modern gastro-pub fare

☎ 01594 833666
GL16 8JT
e-mail: stay@thewyndhamhotel.co.uk
dir: Please telephone for directions or check website

With a history that can be traced back over 600 years, this traditional village inn is filled with oak beams, flagstones, exposed original red brick and open log fires, one in an impressive inglenook fireplace. Expect a cosy, relaxed atmosphere, an extensive bar menu and a modern British carte, the latter served in the Old Spot Country Restaurant. Produce is locally sourced and free-range where possible. Try ham hock and grain mustard terrine, follow with rump of Welsh lamb with parsnip mash, ratatouille and red wine sauce, and finish with sticky toffee and date pudding with caramel sauce.

Chef Mark Belford **Owner** Nigel Stanley **Times** 12-2/6.30-9, Closed 1st wk Jan **Prices** Starter £4.50-£7.50, Main £8.50-£17.50, Dessert £4.50-£6.50, Service optional, Groups min 8 service 10% **Wines** 6 bottles over £20, 24 bottles under £20, 12 by glass **Notes** Sunday L, Vegetarian available, Civ Wed 80 **Seats** 50, Pr/dining room 24 **Children** Portions, Menu **Parking** 30

The New Inn at Coln

◉◉ Modern European

Contemporary food in sensitively modernised village inn

☎ 01285 750651
GL7 5AN

This creeper-covered inn presents a traditional face to the world but, once over the threshold you will find it has been revitalised and refurbished. A sensitive make-over has created light, bright and welcoming spaces using natural colours and smart contemporary furniture while maintaining the heart and soul of the building. Eat in the bar, the three small rooms making up the dining area or out on the terrace, and choose from a modern menu that focuses on high quality produce, much of it local. Thus Cerney goat's cheese and potato roulade is a simple and well judged starter, while glazed belly of Kelmscott pork, tender and full of flavour, comes with creamy herb mash and is finished with a red wine jus. There is a tasting menu available, bread is home-made and service is both friendly and efficient.

Times 12-2/7-9 **Prices** Food prices not confirmed for 2009. Please telephone for details.

CORSE LAWN
Map 10 SO83

Corse Lawn House Hotel

British, French

Attractive Queen Anne house with dining of long-standing reputation

☎ 01452 780771
GL19 4LZ
e-mail: enquiries@corselawn.com
dir: 5m SW of Tewkesbury on B4211, in village centre

Laid back from the road and village green, behind it's own ornamental pond (originally a coach wash from its days as a coaching inn), this sympathetically extended Queen Anne house has been the home of the Hine family since 1978 and maintains high standards of service and cuisine. The light-and-airy, elegant restaurant has a soothing warm terracotta colour scheme with French windows into the gardens. Everything from the bread to the chocolates served with coffee is made in the kitchen, using only the best of local seasonal ingredients. Classic and modern, French and English culinary influences blend seamlessly on an extensive menu that features plenty of fish and game in season. Cooking is precise, delivering clarity of flavours in dishes of roast saddle of venison with celeriac purée and red cabbage, or roast best end of neck of lamb with ratatouille and pesto.

Chef Andrew Poole **Owner** Hine Family
Times 12-2/7-9.30, Closed 24-26 Dec **Prices** Fixed L 2

course £21.95, Fixed D 3 course £31.50, Starter £4.95-£10.95, Main £14.95-£20.95, Dessert £5.95-£6.95, Service optional **Wines** 400 bottles over £20, 39 bottles under £20 **Notes** Sunday L, Civ Wed 80 **Seats** 50, Pr/dining room 28 **Children** Portions, Menu **Parking** 60

FRAMPTON MANSELL
Map 4 SO90

The White Horse

Modern British

Colourful foodie pub

☎ 01285 760960
Cirencester Rd GL6 8HZ
e-mail: emmawhitehorse@aol.com
dir: 6m from Cirencester on the A419 towards Stroud

A relaxed dining-pub vibe can be found at this roadside pub on the A419. Outwardly unassuming, the remodelled interior has pastel-coloured walls, seagrass carpeting, high-backed chairs and colourful artwork in the

restaurant, where a large bow window overlooks a garden that is ideal for alfresco dining in the summer. There's a separate bar area, too. The modern British menu offers honest food, making good use of quality produce presented in a simple, unpretentious style. A potted Cornish crab and salmon with lemon and granary bread starter might be followed by breast of pheasant with parsnip mash and blueberry sauce. Crowd-pleasing desserts - like lemon and lime cheesecake with fresh raspberries - provide the finale.

Times 11-3/6-11, Closed 24-26 Dec, 1 Jan, Closed D Sun

GLOUCESTER
Map 10 SO81

Carrington's Restaurant

Modern European

European cuisine in a country-house hotel

☎ 01452 617412
Hatton Court Hotel, Upton Hill, Upton St Leonards
GL4 8DE
e-mail: res@hatton-court.co.uk
dir: On B4017 between Gloucester and Painswick

Carrington's Restaurant is part of Hatton Court Hotel, where there's an emphasis on traditional style and service and waiting staff delight diners with a daily dish flambéed at the table. That continental touch continues throughout the attractive à la carte menu with dishes such as confit duck leg with braised red cabbage and fondant potato, or seared sea bass with spaghetti and

---

Lower Slaughter Manor

LOWER SLAUGHTER
Map 10 SP12

Modern

Accomplished cooking in elegant and sumptuous country-house hotel

☎ 01451 820456
GL54 2HP
e-mail: info@lowerslaughter.co.uk
dir: Off A429, signposted The Slaughters. 0.5m into village on right

Located in ample grounds on the edge of the charming Cotswolds village of Lower Slaughter, a manor house has stood on this site since AD 1004. Used as a convent in the 15th century, it was rebuilt as a house in 1658 and is today an elegant country house full of style and sophistication. Refurbished throughout, the restaurant is decked out with chocolate brown silk walls, Murano

crystal and ocean blue chandeliers which create a stylish, intimate atmosphere. The original chapel is used for private dining parties. Accomplished modern British cuisine includes the likes of home-smoked quail with soft poached quail's egg, shiitake mushrooms, crisp pancetta and celeriac remoulade, or pan-fried king scallops with Gloucestershire Old Spot belly pork, artichoke purée and apple dressing. Main courses make use of wonderful produce and might include fillet of brill with bacon and leek tartlet and tarragon butter sauce. Finish with Granny Smith apple soufflé pancake, caramelised apple and cider syrup or warm pineapple and rice pudding cannelloni with rum and coconut milk ice cream.

Chef David Kelman **Owner** von Essen Collection
Times 12-2.30/7-9.30 **Prices** Fixed L 2 course £19.50, Starter £9.50-£13.75, Main £19.50-£30, Dessert £8.50-£10.50, Service optional **Wines** All bottles over £20, 6 by glass **Notes** Sunday L, Vegetarian menu, Dress

restrictions, Smart, no jeans or trainers, Civ Wed 70 **Seats** 55, Pr/dining room 20 **Children** Portions, Menu **Parking** 30

mixed bean and herb cassoulet, with perhaps an Amaretto and white chocolate-filled chocolate cup with coffee cream for dessert. Delightful views over the surrounding countryside and the thoughtful arrangement of outdoor seating make this a wonderful place to enjoy in summer.

Times 12.30-2/7-9.30

LOWER SLAUGHTER Map 10 SP12

Lower Slaughter Manor

◎◎◎ – *see opposite*

Washbourne Court Hotel

◎◎ Modern British, French V

Fine dining in a riverside setting

☎ 01451 822143
GL54 2HS
e-mail: info@washbournecourt.co.uk
dir: Off A429, village centre by river

This charming 17th-century building is set in riverside gardens in the quintessential Cotswold village of Lower Slaughter. Beamed ceilings, log fires and flagstone floors abound throughout, while the elegant and stylish dining room, replete with chandeliers and gold wall lights, provides a fairly formal setting for enjoying some competent modern cooking. Seasonal menus draw on quality seasonal ingredients, and dishes display clear flavours and some interesting combinations. Start with pan-fried scallops with apple, and then tuck into cannon of Cotswold lamb and round off with warm apple tarte Tatin with rosemary ice cream. A sunny terrace proves an added bonus for summer drinks and light lunches. Service is friendly and unstuffy.

Owner von Essen Hotels **Times** 12.30-2.30/7-9.30 **Prices** Fixed L 2 course £21.95, Fixed D 3 course £45, Starter £5.50-£13.50, Main £10.50-£27, Dessert £6.50-£10.50, Service optional **Wines** 60 bottles over £20, 10 bottles under £20, 8 by glass **Notes** Sunday L, Vegetarian menu, Dress restrictions, Smart casual, No trainers or T-shirts, Civ Wed 60 **Seats** 60, Pr/dining room 25 **Children** Min 12 yrs, Portions, Menu **Parking** 40

MORETON-IN-MARSH Map 10 SP23

Mulberry Restaurant

◎◎ Modern British 🍃

Contemporary dining in Cotswold manor house

☎ 01608 650501
Manor House Hotel, High St GL56 0LJ
e-mail: info@manorhousehotel.info
web: www.cotswold-inns-hotels.co.uk/manor
dir: Off A429 at south end of town

Dating back to the 16th century, this charming former coaching inn combines an original Cotswold stone exterior with a stylish, modern interior. Old beams, stone walls and impressive fireplaces add to the country-house atmosphere, while the Mulberry Restaurant has been given a contemporary makeover, with high-backed chairs, leather banquettes and modern artwork. The cooking is equally contemporary, with an ambitious kitchen delivering well-composed, clean-flavoured and elegantly presented dishes. The set and tasting menus offer a modern British approach with French influences, with dishes such as velouté of broccoli, walnuts and Cerney goat's cheese to start, followed by poached pavé of turbot, oxtail and cockles, fennel Barigoule, grain mustard emulsion and parsley coulis, and rounded off with a dark chocolate fondant.

Chef Jonathan Harvey-Barnes **Owner** Michael & Pamela Horton **Times** 12-2.30/7-9.30 **Prices** Fixed D 3 course £35, Service added but optional 10% **Wines** 53 bottles over £20, 26 bottles under £20, 8 by glass **Notes** Tasting menu 7 courses, Dress restrictions, Smart casual, no jeans, shorts or trainers, Civ Wed 120 **Seats** 65, Pr/dining room 120 **Children** Min 8 yrs, Portions **Parking** 32

Redesdale Arms

◎ British

Relaxed dining in bar, restaurant or courtyard of historic Cotswold inn

☎ 01608 650308
High St GL56 0AW
e-mail: info@redesdalearms.co.uk

This fine old Cotswold inn has played a central role in bustling Moreton for centuries and offers a relaxed

blend of traditional features and modern comforts, where food can be taken in either bar or conservatory restaurant and, in fairweather, its courtyard garden. The dining room has a light, airy feel with large windows, while varnished oak tables offer an unstuffy, white-linen-free zone. Walls are hung with modern art and mix harmoniously with wood panelling and oak floorboards, while the lengthy menu is a crowd-pleasing seasonal affair. The focus is on local produce and flavour, with the straightforward approach successfully delivering traditional favourites (Hook Norton beer-battered haddock served with home-cut chips and tartare sauce) alongside more modern ideas (Asian-style Gloucestershire Old Spot belly pork with wok-fried greens and sweet potato).

NAILSWORTH Map 4 ST89

The Wild Garlic Restaurant

◎◎ British, French

Chef-patron delivering impressive food in Cotswold setting

☎ 01453 832615
3 Cossack Square GL6 0DB
e-mail: mafindlay@waitrose.com
dir: M5 junct 13. A419 to Stroud and then A46 to Nailsworth. Take a right at rdbt and then an immediate left, restaurant is located opposite Britannia Pub

The new chef-patron of this restaurant with rooms (Heavens Above is the upstairs business providing comfortable accommodation) has experience working for top chefs in London and around the world. He has settled in this attractive Cotswold town and opened his own place, a stylish restaurant with the emphasis on friendly service and fresh, intelligently assembled dishes. The reasonably-priced menus are sensibly short - four choices for each course - and care is taken in the sourcing of produce. Chicken liver parfait comes with a glass of fig compôte with blossom honey to pour and a home-made brioche in a first-class starter, followed by a main course rump of Daylesford beef, marinated in cracked pepper and ginger and served with pumpkin purée and winter greens. Fish (sea bass with mussel and garlic broth) and vegetarian dishes (pan-fried chestnut gnocchi, wild mushrooms, ricotta and sage) also feature on the menu, while the high standards and creativity carry on into desserts such as toasted banana cake with iced banana parfait.

Times 12.30-2/7.30-9, Closed end Jan-early Feb, 1st wk Jun, 1st 2 wks Aug, Closed Mon-Tue, Closed D Sun-Tue

Three Choirs Vineyards

◉◉ Modern British

Tuscan-style vineyard views and summer terrace dining

☎ 01531 890223
GL18 1LS
e-mail: ts@threechoirs.com
dir: 2m N of Newent on B4215, follow brown tourist signs

This thriving vineyard is a wonderful place to eat or to stay, not least because of its idyllic setting. The light-and-airy Vineyard Restaurant, with its leather-backed chairs and large picture windows, has stunning views across the vineyard's 100-acre estate. Wine lovers will delight in the vineyard's produce and foodies will be impressed with the well-executed dishes that make full use of fresh local ingredients. Expect modern, French-influenced cuisine in starters such as pressed ham hock and locally grown spring onion terrine, and perhaps seared fillet of English bream with wilted baby spinach, crispy potato and light parmesan velouté to follow. Leave room for the rich chocolate mousse with raspberries steeped in brandy and bitter chocolate sorbet.

Chef Darren Leonard **Owner** Three Choirs Vineyards Ltd **Times** 12-2/7-9, Closed Xmas, New Year **Prices** Starter £4.50-£9.50, Main £10.50-£21, Dessert £5.50-£7.50, Service optional, Groups min 10 service 10% **Wines** 20 bottles over £20, 34 bottles under £20, 12 by glass **Notes** Sunday L, Vegetarian available **Seats** 50, Pr/dining room 20 **Children** Portions, Menu **Parking** 50

The Puesdown Inn

◉◉◉ Modern British V

Stylish coaching inn offering skilfully cooked local produce

☎ 01451 860262
Compton Abdale GL54 4DN
e-mail: inn4food@btopenworld.com
dir: On A40 (Cheltenham-Oxford), 7m from Cheltenham, 3m from Northleach

A friendly welcome is assured at this privately owned, traditional Cotswold coaching inn. Said to date back to 1236, it has been lovingly refurbished by its hands-on owners. The warm colours, cosy sofas and log fires create a welcoming, relaxed atmosphere, while chic Italian chairs and a personal collection of paintings and

photographs are stylish additions. The daily-changing menu reflects market and seasonal variations, with quality produce carefully sourced from local producers. Typical dishes might include seared scallops with black pudding, pancetta, celeriac purée and pea foam to start, followed by fillet of wild sea bass with saffron mash, julienne vegetables and sauce vierge, and perhaps a warm chocolate fondant with white chocolate ice cream and red berries to finish.

The Puesdown Inn

Chef John Armstrong **Owner** John & Maggie Armstrong **Times** 10-3/6-11, Closed 1 wk Jan, Closed D Sun-Mon **Prices** Fixed L 2 course £12.50-£18.75, Fixed D 3 course £23.50-£28.50, Starter £5-£9, Main £10-£19, Dessert £5.50-£6.25, Service optional, Groups min 10 service 10% **Wines** 13 bottles over £20, 18 bottles under £20, 15 by glass **Notes** Sunday L, Vegetarian menu **Seats** 48, Pr/dining room 28 **Children** Portions **Parking** 80

Churchill Arms

◉ Modern British

Confident cooking in a charming Cotswold pub

☎ 01386 594000
GL55 6XH
e-mail: mail@thechurchillarms.com
dir: Situated 2m E of Chipping Campden

With its inglenook fireplace, beams, oak flooring and flagstones, the Churchill Arms is an endearingly unpretentious Cotswold stone pub, so the clean-cut, modern-focused cooking may come as a bit of a surprise. Although the space has been opened up, the pub still has plenty of rustic charm and relaxed informality, with an assortment of wooden furniture, a collection of prints, and chalkboards for both food and wine. Food is ordered at the bar in the traditional fashion. Expect attractively presented, modern dishes that might include smoked haddock rarebit, halibut with parmesan and herb crust and maple and mascarpone cheesecake.

Chef D Toon & S Brooke-Little **Owner** Sonya & Leo Brooke-Little **Times** 12-2.30/7-9.30, Closed 25 Dec **Prices** Starter £4.50-£8.50, Main £9-£18, Dessert £4-£6.50, Service optional **Wines** 12 bottles over £20, 24 bottles under £20, 8 by glass **Notes** Sunday L, Vegetarian available **Seats** 60 **Children** Portions **Parking** On street

The Swan at Southrop

◉◉ British, European

Accomplished modern cooking in peaceful, gastro-pub style surroundings

☎ 01367 850205
GL7 3NU

Set on the edge of the green in a sleepy Cotswold village, the Swan still maintains its pub roots with a public bar and skittle alley, though the real focus these days is on its accomplished cuisine. The dining room retains a rustic vibe, with ceiling beams and low-beamed doorways, while walls are hung with artwork and old pub photographs. Solid-wood tables (some desks), fresh flowers and efficient yet relaxed and friendly service suit the surroundings too. The kitchen's modern approach makes use of fresh local produce, with dishes pleasingly not overworked. Flavours come clean cut in well-presented, brasserie-style dishes like escargots de Bourgogne, or grilled entrecôte with béarnaise sauce, pommes frites and green salad, and a pumpkin tarte Tatin with star anise ice cream.

Times 12-2.30/7-9.30

Stonehouse Court

◉◉ British, Mediterranean

Imaginative cuisine in historic manor house

☎ 0871 8713240
Bristol Rd GL10 3RA
e-mail: info@stonehousecourt.co.uk
dir: M5 junct 13/A419 (Stroud). Straight on at 2 rdbts, under rail bridge. Hotel 100yds on right.

Set in 6 acres of secluded gardens, this Grade II listed manor house dates back to 1601. Henry's restaurant offers a mixture of traditional and contemporary style, providing a relaxing atmosphere in which to enjoy modern British dishes with some mediterranean and Asian influences. Excellent use is made of fresh, local produce with suppliers listed on the seasonally-changing carte. Imaginative dishes could include the likes of pressed terrine of Gloucestershire Old Spot pork with caramelised apple juice and apple pearls, followed by a main course of monkfish tail coated with Japanese breadcrumbs and served with creamed Jersey Royal potatoes, warm tartare sauce and lemon-dressed leaves. In warmer weather, afternoon tea is served on the terrace.

Times 12-3/7-10, Closed L Sat

STOW-ON-THE-WOLD   Map 11 SP12

The Conservatory Restaurant

◉◉ British, French

Fine dining in a romantic setting

☎ 01451 830344
Grapevine Hotel, Sheep St GL54 1AU
e-mail: enquiries@vines.co.uk
dir: Take A436 towards Chipping Norton; 150yds on right facing green

Situated in the heart of this unique market town, the Grapevine is a delightful 17th-century hotel full of charm and character. The Conservatory Restaurant has an ancient Black Hamburg vine as a canopy, making an enchanting setting for candlelit dining in the evenings. The youthful staff ensure that service is unstuffy but there's just enough formality to make it a special occasion. Well-chosen flavour combinations abound on the ambitious and competently cooked menu. Try seared scallops, cauliflower purée, lemon confit and peanut brittle to start, perhaps followed by roast fillet of Gloucestershire Old Spot pork, with fondant potato, black pudding and apple sauce, with white chocolate and thyme pannacotta and strawberry soup to finish.

Chef Matthew Warburton **Owner** Mark & Janine Vance
Times 12-2.30/7-9.30 **Prices** Food prices not confirmed for 2009. Please telephone for details. **Wines** 24 bottles over £20, 15 bottles under £20, 8 by glass **Notes** Civ Wed 80 **Seats** 40, Pr/dining room 20 **Children** Portions, Menu **Parking** 25

Fosse Manor

◉◉ Modern British

Imaginative cuisine in country-house setting

☎ 01451 830354
GL54 1JX
e-mail: enquiries@fossemanor.co.uk
dir: From Stow-on-the-Wold take A429 S for 1m

Set back from the A429 (originally the Fosse Way), this stylish and comfortable country-house hotel stands in five acres of tranquil grounds. Formerly a rectory, the mellow stone exterior belies an interior that nicely balances a contemporary and traditional décor. Modern British cuisine is very much rooted in classical techniques here, using lots of interesting local ingredients. Try a starter of pressed local ham and parsley terrine served with spiced pear chutney. With a main course menu offering grills, pasta and risotto, and meat and fish, pheasant breast with Savoy cabbage and bacon, fondant potato and port sauce, or pumpkin and parmesan risotto with poached Broadway Blue Legbar egg are fine examples of the fare. Alfresco dining is available on the patio terrace.

Chef Mark Coleman **Owner** Fosse Manor Hotel Ltd
Times 12-2/7-9 **Prices** Starter £4.50-£8.25, Main £9.50-£19.50, Dessert £4.50-£6.50, Service optional **Wines** 96 bottles over £20, 14 bottles under £20, 10 by glass **Notes** Sunday L, Vegetarian available **Seats** 80 **Children** Portions, Menu **Parking** 40

The Kings Head Inn

◉ Traditional British

Charming village-green inn serving accomplished traditional food

☎ 01608 658365
The Green, Bledington OX7 6XQ
e-mail: kingshead@orr-ewing.com
dir: On B4450, 4m from Stow-on-the-Wold

With its delightful village-green setting near the river, this classic country pub dates back to the 16th century and comes complete with open fires, uneven floors and plenty of beams - plus a dozen bedrooms in contemporary style. The comfortable restaurant offers excellent dining and friendly and professional service. Expect homely and traditional dishes, simply presented and underpinned by quality local produce: local venison steak with Savoy cabbage, bubble-and-squeak and redcurrant jus for example, or smoked haddock and crayfish pie. Round things off with cappuccino crème brûlée with home-made shortbread or bread-and-butter pudding with custard.

Chef Charlie Loader **Owner** Archie & Nicola Orr-Ewing
Times 12-2/7-9.30, Closed 25-26 Dec **Prices** Starter £4.50-£6.95, Main £9.95-£18.95, Dessert fr £5.50, Service optional, Groups min 8 service 10% **Wines** 17 bottles over £20, 28 bottles under £20, 8 by glass **Notes** Sunday L, Vegetarian available **Seats** 32 **Children** Portions **Parking** 20

The Old Butcher's

◉ Modern 🍃

Relaxed, contemporary dining in attractive Cotswold town

☎ 01451 831700
Park St GL54 1AQ
e-mail: info@theoldbutchers.com

A one-time butcher's shop, and now a contemporary, brasserie-styled eatery, the Old Butcher's stands out from the crowd in attractive, bustling Stow, with its modern glass frontage, awnings, signboard and sprinkling of terrace tables at the front. The modern theme continues inside with polished wood tables, comfortable chairs or banquette seating, white linen napkins, a stylish bar area and friendly, relaxed but professional service. The kitchen follows the modern approach too, utilising fresh, quality local produce - some home grown - in refreshingly uncomplicated, clean-cut, well-presented modern dishes on regularly-changing menus. Think breaded veal, prosciutto and parmesan, and perhaps pistachio Pavlova, rhubarb and vanilla cream to finish.

Chef Peter Robinson **Owner** Louise & Peter Robinson
Times 12-2.30/6-9.30 **Prices** Starter £5-£8.50, Main £10.50-£16, Dessert £5.25-£6.75, Service optional **Wines** 55 bottles over £20, 19 bottles under £20, 14 by glass **Notes** Sunday L, Vegetarian available, Air con **Seats** 45 **Children** Portions **Parking** On street

The Royalist Hotel

◉◉ Modern European

Assured cooking in a historic hostelry

☎ 01451 830670
Digbeth St GL54 1BN
e-mail: info@theroyalisthotel.com
dir: Please telephone for directions

The UK has many old inns, but The Royalist is the oldest inn in Britain. Dating from an incredible 947AD it has a delightful Jacobean façade and the historical details include 1,000-year-old timbers and a leper hole. The restaurant has a contemporary styling, which blends in very well and does not jar, but it also has a rather grand fireplace featuring the markings of a witch. Cooking is accomplished, with well-judged combinations and quality ingredients. Expect good flavours from the off in starters such as seared Atlantic scallops with squid ink risotto and cauliflower purée, followed by confident main courses like fillet of mackerel with baby leeks, clams and shellfish bisque. Desserts are a highlight: take toasted almond and chocolate fondant served with pistachio ice cream.

Times 12-2.30/7-9.30

STOW-ON-THE-WOLD *Continued*

The Unicorn Hotel

◉ Traditional British

Robust, vibrant cooking in a relaxed former coaching inn

☎ 01451 830257
Sheep St GL54 1HQ
e-mail: reception@birchhotels.co.uk
dir: Junct A40 (Fosse Way) & Sheep St

A 17th-century coaching inn, set on the edge of this popular Cotswold village, the Unicorn has an inviting bar with original oak beams, flagstone floors and rare Spit Jack fireplace. In contrast, the restaurant has a smart contemporary look with maple furniture and leather upholstered seating. With menus changing monthly, the food is honest and straightforward, using top quality seasonal produce. The emphasis is on hearty old-fashioned dishes such as haunch of venison with Savoy cabbage, chestnuts and bacon, or saddle of rabbit stuffed with Gloucester Old Spot pork, with wild mushrooms and thyme.

Chef Stuart Wiggins **Owner** Brian Shepherd
Times 12-2/7-9 **Prices** Starter £5.25-£5.95, Main £9.95-£17.95, Dessert £5.50, Service optional **Wines** 4 bottles over £20, 22 bottles under £20, 5 by glass
Notes Sunday L, Vegetarian available, Civ Wed 0
Seats 40, Pr/dining room 25 **Parking** 50

| STROUD | Map 4 SO80 |

Burleigh Court Hotel

◉◉ British, European

Classical country-house style

☎ 01453 883804
Burleigh, Minchinhampton GL5 2PF
e-mail: info@burleighcourthotel.co.uk
web: www.burleighcourthotel.co.uk
dir: 2.5m SE of Stroud, off A419

Nestling into the hillside with stunning views over the Golden Valley, this Grade II listed Cotswold-stone manor house dates back to the 18th century and is set in 3.5 acres of beautifully maintained terraced gardens designed by Clough Williams-Ellis. Once a gentleman's residence, the hotel remains true to its classical country-house roots with its oak-panelled bar and the elegant restaurant which provides a suitably formal setting for enjoyable modern British cuisine. The seasonally-

changing menu is extensive at lunch and dinner and makes the most of the freshest local produce, with many herbs and vegetables home grown. Typical starters include warm Cornish crab and dill ravioli with spaghetti of vegetables and caviar cream sauce, followed by a main course of pan-roasted Angus beef fillet with creamed leeks, cocotte potato, haggis and whisky reduction.

Burleigh Court Hotel

Chef Adrian Jarrad **Owner** Louise Noble **Times** 12-2/7-9, Closed 24-26 Dec **Prices** Starter £4.95-£9.95, Main £14.50-£22.50, Dessert £6.50-£7.95 **Wines** 50 bottles over £20, 15 bottles under £20, 7 by glass **Notes** Sunday L, Vegetarian available, Civ Wed 50 **Seats** 34, Pr/dining room 18 **Children** Portions, Menu **Parking** 28

| TETBURY | Map 4 ST89 |

Calcot Manor

◉◉ Modern British ⬛NOTABLE WINE LIST

Charming 14th-century Cotswold retreat with vibrant modern cuisine

☎ 01666 890391
Calcot GL8 8YJ
e-mail: reception@calcotmanor.co.uk
dir: M4 junct 18, take A46 towards Stroud and at x-roads with A4135 turn right and then 1st left

This lovely English farmhouse, hotel and restaurant, built in the 14th century by Cistercian monks, offers all the contemporary creature comforts of a 21st-century retreat - beautifully decorated bedrooms, a superb health spa and fabulous facilities for children. The Conservatory Restaurant, with its light-and-airy atmosphere, linen-clad tables and subtle elegance makes a perfect setting for an intimate meal or group celebration. Service is friendly as well as efficient in this stylish restaurant. The modern British menu offers up-to-the-minute, uncomplicated dishes, making full use of the freshest seasonal ingredients. Why not try roast wild duck with

cinnamon poached quince, glazed turnips and beetroot and dauphine potatoes, perhaps followed by Kirsch cherry and almond clafoutis with clotted cream ice cream.

Calcot Manor

Chef Michael Croft **Owner** Richard Ball (MD)
Times 12-2/7-9.30 **Prices** Fixed L 2 course £19, Starter £7.95-£12.50, Main £17.50-£19, Dessert £7.50, Service included **Wines** 6 bottles under £20, 12 by glass
Notes Sunday L, Vegetarian available, Civ Wed 100, Air con **Seats** 100, Pr/dining room 16 **Children** Portions, Menu **Parking** 150

The Trouble House

◉◉ Traditional French

Exquisite, innovative food with a relaxed atmosphere that favours drinkers as well as diners

☎ 01666 502206
Cirencester Rd GL8 8SG
e-mail: enquiries@troublehouse.co.uk
dir: 1.5m outside Tetbury on A433 towards Cirencester

At first glance, this unassuming roadside inn looks no different from any other Cotswold stone pub. Step inside and it's a different matter - it's usually bustling with both drinkers and diners who flock here for this next-generation gastro-pub food. Interiors have been sensitively upgraded to a contemporary style with white walls, bare wood unclothed tables and wood floors. On the menu, simple, rustic and honest dishes (shin of beef braised in red wine with spicy couscous or jugged hare in Yorkshire puddings) rub shoulders with more adventurous offerings (roast squid stuffed with sun-dried tomatoes and mozzarella with chilli lentils) that betray the chef's background at high-end establishments such as Le Manoir and City Rhodes.

Times 12-2/7-9.30, Closed Xmas to New Year & BHs, Closed Mon, Closed D Sun

THORNBURY — Map 4 ST69

Thornbury Castle

Modern British

Modern cuisine in a fairytale castle setting

☎ 01454 281182
Castle St BS35 1HH
e-mail: info@thornburycastle.co.uk
dir: M5 junct 16. N on A38. Continue for 4m to lights and turn left. Following brown Historic Castle signs. Restaurant located behind St Mary's Parish Church

Henry VIII and Anne Boleyn stayed in this grand castle in Tudor times. Today, impressive baronial public rooms, featuring magnificent fireplaces, high mullioned windows, tapestries, grand portraits and suits of armour, combine historic atmosphere with present-day comforts. Candlelit wood-panelled dining rooms make a memorable setting for a leisurely meal. Straightforward British-based menus are enhanced with international influences. A competent kitchen demonstrates good technical skills and makes excellent use of quality seasonal ingredients, including home-grown herbs and vegetables. Choices include seared scallops with pea mousse, celeriac purée, pancetta and lie de vin sauce, followed by loin of Exmoor venison, textures of cauliflower, red cabbage and juniper-scented sauce, and a dessert selection including milk Valrhona chocolate mousse with raspberry and tarragon sorbet and brandy snap. Excellent wine list available.

Chef Lee Heptinstall **Owner** von Essen **Times** 11.45-2/7-9 **Wines** 278 bottles over £20, 2 bottles under £20, 7 by glass **Notes** Mon-Fri rapid L 3 course £18 Jan-Nov, Sunday L, Vegetarian available, Dress restrictions, Smart casual, No jeans, trainers, T-shirts, Civ Wed 50 **Seats** 72, Pr/dining room 22 **Children** Portions, Menu **Parking** 50

UPPER SLAUGHTER — Map 10 SP12

Lords of the Manor

— *see below*

WICK — Map 4 ST77

Oakwood

Modern British

Resort hotel dining with quality produce and straightforward approach

☎ 0117 937 1800
The Park, Bath Rd BS30 5RN
e-mail: info@ppresort.com
dir: Just off A420 in Wick

Oakwood is in an old Masonic lodge, part of the The Park Hotel resort, which consists of a fine Georgian

Continued

Lords of the Manor

UPPER SLAUGHTER — Map 10 SP12

Modern British

Relaxed and welcoming country-house dining

☎ 01451 820243
GL54 2JD
e-mail: enquiries@lordsofthemanor.com
dir: Follow signs towards The Slaughters 2m W of A429. Hotel on right in centre of Upper Slaughter

A 17th-century former rectory of mellow Cotswold stone, this welcoming hotel - with Victorian-era additions - sits in 8 acres of gardens and parkland that deliver an idyllic, picture-postcard setting. Beautifully updated in early 2008, the new look interior cleverly combines the traditional country-house feel, with antiques and open fires dotted around its warren of rooms, with a stylish, contemporary look using modern fabrics and furnishings that evoke the glorious countryside surrounding the hotel. The smart, classic dining room continues the theme, with brightly striped Provençal drapes, big and bold modern artwork on cream walls, comfortable high-backed chairs and eye-catching flower displays, while service is professional, discreet and informed. New chef Matt Weedon (formerly at Glenapp Castle, see entry) displays a modern approach, underpinned by a classical theme, and he makes good use of well-sourced, high quality local ingredients to produce balanced dishes with interesting combinations and wonderful simple flavours and textures. Attention to detail and consistency characterise the style, with plentiful skill and passion parading alongside some innovative elements on a repertoire of fixed-price menus that includes a tasting option. Think scallops with pancetta, cauliflower and curry oil to start, perhaps followed by roasted loin and braised shoulder of Lighthorne Farm lamb with wild garlic, caramelised sweetbreads and rosemary jus, and to finish, perhaps a praline mousse with Pedro Ximenez jelly and prune ice cream, or a choice from the first-class cheeseboard. Alfresco summer dining completes the accomplished package.

Chef Matt Weedon **Owner** Empire Ventures **Times** 12-2.30/7-9 **Prices** Fixed D 4 course £49, Tasting menu £59, Service added but optional 10% **Wines** 246 bottles over £20, 4 bottles under £20, 12 by glass **Notes** Tasting menu 7 courses, Sunday L, Vegetarian available, Dress restrictions, Smart casual, no trainers or jeans, Civ Wed 50 **Seats** 50, Pr/dining room 30 **Children** Min 7 yrs, Portions, Menu **Parking** 40

WICK *Continued*

mansion surrounded by two championship golf courses. Impressive stone work and high vaulted ceilings set the scene in the dining room, while the open-plan kitchen brings a touch of the modernity to the setting. A large woodstone oven is used to good effect roasting meat, fish and game, and breads are all home-baked. The cooking's straightforward approach is driven by high-quality, seasonal produce, simply presented allowing the main ingredient to shine without over-complication. Mackerel is presented boneless with marinated vegetables, star anis and saffron as a starter, followed by a slow-roasted shoulder of lamb with a mustard and caper sauce. Finish with iced toffee parfait with milk chocolate sauce.

Chef Mark Treasure **Times** Closed L all week **Prices** Fixed D 3 course £30, Service added but optional 12.5% **Notes** Vegetarian available **Children** Portions

WINCHCOMBE	Map 10 SP02

5 North Street

◉◉◉ — *see below*

Wesley House

◉◉ Modern Mediterranean

Stylish restaurant in a bustling Cotswold town

☎ 01242 602366
High St GL54 5LJ
e-mail: enquiries@wesleyhouse.co.uk
web: www.wesleyhouse.co.uk
dir: In centre of Winchcombe

A 15th-century, half-timbered property named after John Wesley, who stayed here in the 18th century, this black and white former merchant's house has beamed ceilings and open stone fireplaces which sit comfortably with modern aspects like a glass atrium over the terrace, and effective modern lighting. Seasonal variations ring the changes on the modern British menus with Mediterranean influences, and look out for special offers at lunch. Start with roast Cotswold wood pigeon, roast beetroot, baby

spinach and aged Spanish vinegar sauce and follow it perhaps with fillet of Scottish beef, potato purée, ceps, foie gras and Madeira jus. Finish with Medjool date, walnut and maple syrup strudel and Amaretto custard.

Wesley House

Chef Martin Dunn **Owner** Matthew Brown **Times** 12-2/7-9, Closed D Sun **Prices** Fixed L 2 course fr £19.50, Fixed D 3 course fr £38, Service optional **Wines** 65 bottles over £20, 20 bottles under £20, 15 by glass **Notes** Sunday L, Vegetarian available, Civ Wed 60, Air con **Seats** 70, Pr/ dining room 24 **Children** Portions **Parking** In the square

5 North Street

WINCHCOMBE	Map 10 SP02

Modern European 🖥 V

Unpretentious cooking makes this a gourmet gem

☎ 01242 604566
5 North St GL54 5LH
e-mail: marcusashenford@yahoo.co.uk
dir: 7m from Cheltenham

Tucked away behind a mellow-stone shop-front, this understated little eatery in the heart of Winchcombe is one of the Cotswolds' gourmet gems. There is an intimate, split-level interior, simple and pared back, with wooden beams and bare tables, and packed with rustic charm. The friendly service creates a relaxed atmosphere. Marcus Ashenford's cooking is clean-cut in style and delightfully simple, delivering wonderful flavours without pretension. Focusing on quality ingredients and high

skill, combinations are interesting, seasonality is well respected and flavours are prominent. Expect a modern approach underpinned by a classical French foundation, the sensibly compact, fixed-price menus bolstered by a seven-course gourmet menu. Begin with roasted scallops served with Gloucestershire Old Spot belly pork, sweet onion, creamed artichoke and sesame dressing, before moving on to roasted sea bass with Salcombe crab mousse, braised lettuce, carrot purée and lightly spiced sauce. Round things off with caramel and parkin mousse with passionfruit sorbet.

Chef Marcus Ashenford **Owner** Marcus & Kate Ashenford **Times** 12.30-1.30/7-9, Closed 1st 2 wks Jan, 1 wk Aug, Closed Mon, Closed L Tue, Closed D Sun **Wines** 60 bottles over £20, 12 bottles under £20, 6 by glass **Notes** Gourmet menu 7 courses £55, Tasting menu 10 courses, Sunday L, Vegetarian menu **Seats** 26 **Children** Portions, Menu **Parking** On street, pay & display

GREATER MANCHESTER

HORWICH   Map 15 SD61

De Vere Whites

◎◎ Modern British, French

Football fans' dream restaurant

☎ 01204 667788
De Havilland Way BL6 6SF
e-mail: whites@devere-hotels.com
dir: Off M61 junct 6

This classy restaurant is part of the Reebok stadium, home to Bolton Wanderers. Situated on the second floor, Reflections restaurant is accessed via a wooden illuminated walkway and offers a bird's eye view of the football pitch. Booths in front of a plate glass window that overhangs the pitch offer the best seats in the house. The restaurant has its own cocktail-style bar, well-spaced tables, classic white linen and fresh flowers. Service is relatively formal with cloched dishes, reflecting the classical feel of the French-influenced menu which offers the likes of John Dory on potato rösti, with an étuvée of leek and sauce lie de vin. You can dine here Wednesday to Saturday evenings, although on a match night it might be difficult to keep your eye on the ball and enjoy the fine cuisine at the same time.

Times Closed 25 Dec, Closed Sun-Tues, Closed L all week

MANCHESTER   Map 16 SJ89

Abode Manchester

◎◎ Modern British

☎ 0161 247 7744
107 Piccadilly M1 2DB
e-mail: reservationsmanchester@abodehotels.co.uk
dir: Located in city centre 2min walk from Piccadilly station

This establishment was awarded its Rosette/s just as we went to press. Therefore we are unable to provide a description for it - visit www.theAA.com for the most up-to-date information.

Chef Ian Matfin **Owner** Andrew Brownsword, Michael Caines **Times** 12-2.30/6-10, Closed 1 Jan, Closed Sun **Wines** 150 bottles over £20, 10 bottles under £20, 15 by glass **Notes** Grazing menu £30, Vegetarian available, Dress restrictions, Smart casual, Air con **Seats** 56, Pr/dining room 24 **Children** Portions **Parking** Opposite hotel 20% discount

Brasserie Blanc

◎ French

Authentic French cooking at a slick, city-centre brasserie

☎ 0161 832 1000
55 King St M2 4LQ
e-mail: manchester@brasserieblanc.co.uk
dir: King St, city centre

The former National Westminster headquarters for the northwest is a modern listed building, overlooking Chapel Walks, and now houses a funky brasserie (part of an established small chain). It provides comfort and crowd appeal with black leather booth seating, upholstered chairs, wooden tables, feature artworks and a bar. Two private dining rooms are also available. The imaginative menu offers 'real French food, close to home', conjured from quality, fresh, seasonal British produce. The confident kitchen offers dishes with clear and vibrant flavours; take goat's cheese parcel and tomato chutney, crab and salmon fishcake with butter sauce, and classic crème brûlée.

Chef Ravi Pothula **Owner** Raymond Blanc, Brasserie Blanc Ltd **Times** 12-2.45/5.30-10.30, Closed 25-26 Dec, 1 Jan **Wines** 20 bottles over £20, 12 bottles under £20, 12 by glass **Notes** Fixed menu 5.30-6.30, 2 courses £11.50, 3 courses £15, Sunday L, Vegetarian available, Air con **Seats** 110, Pr/dining room **Children** Portions, Menu **Parking** NCP Deansgate

Choice Bar & Restaurant

◎ Modern British 🖥

Friendly waterside dining

☎ 0161 833 3400
Castle Quay, Castlefield M15 4NT
e-mail: book@choicebarandrestaurant.co.uk
web: www.choicebarandrestaurant.co.uk
dir: A5067 & A56 x-rds, off Bridgewater viaduct

This 1830s spice warehouse overlooking the canal has been converted into a chic, modern restaurant with exposed brickwork, low ceilings and cream furnishings. In the evening candlelight creates an intimate ambience, as does the romantic piano bar, whilst there's live music on Saturday nights and alfresco dining in fine weather. The menu's roots are in the north west, focusing on local produce and regional recipes with a contemporary twist. Take a starter of tempura battered haddock, sweet potato chips and wasabi mushy peas, then move on to beef fillet three ways (steak and chips with béarnaise sauce, steak-and-kidney pie on smashed peas, and mini cottage pie), and round off with peach and pomegranate crumble and custard.

Times 11/11, Closed 25-30 Dec

The Dining Rooms @ Worsley Park

◎ British

Modern food in country club setting

☎ 0161 975 2000
Walkden Rd, Worsley M28 2QT
e-mail: anna.colloer@marriotthotels.com
dir: Just off M60 junct 13, take A575. Hotel is signed

Once the Duke of Bridgwater's estate, this hotel and country club is set in over 200 acres of delightful parkland complete with championship golf course. Brindley's, the hotel's fine-dining option, is light and airy, with contemporary décor, beams and well-spaced tables, offering good views of the courtyard and surrounding area. The menu is modern British with a European twist, allowing the main ingredients to speak for themselves, with dishes simply yet attractively presented. For a starter, try the organic salmon gravad lax, then follow with a traditional Lancashire hotpot, or opt for the Goosnargh duck, rounding off with a melting chocolate fondant.

Chef Sean Kelly **Owner** Marriott Hotels **Times** 1-3/5-10, Closed L Mon-Sat **Wines** 40 bottles over £20, 27 bottles under £20, 20 by glass **Notes** Fixed L 4 course fr £18.95, Sunday L, Vegetarian available, Dress restrictions, Smart casual, Civ Wed 200, Air con **Seats** 140, Pr/dining room 14 **Children** Portions, Menu **Parking** 250

The French

◎◎ French 🖥

Imposing Edwardian hotel for an opulent dining experience

☎ 0161 236 3333
The Midland Hotel, Peter St M60 2DS
e-mail: midlandsales@qhotels.co.uk
dir: Telephone for directions

One of Manchester's most popular hotels, and an historic landmark, this Grade II listed property was purpose-built for the Midland Railway in 1903 to accommodate the discerning traveller. It still attracts plenty of VIPs today. The restaurant is magnificent, with high ceilings, chandeliers, and a colour scheme of pale pinks and golds. Staff are superb and a long-standing crowd of regulars flock here to enjoy the excellent service as well as the food. The menu is more modern French these days, with traditional elements. Expect tarte fine of forest mushrooms, fried quail eggs, pea shoots and white truffle oil, followed by cutlet, saddle, rillette of Cumbrian fell-bred lamb, buttered leeks and confit potatoes. Finish, perhaps, with custard tart, nutmeg ice cream and Eccles cake.

Chef Paul Beckley **Owner** QHotels **Times** Closed BHs, Closed Sun-Mon, Closed L all wk **Prices** Fixed D 3 course £35, Starter £7.95-£14.95, Main £19.95-£28.95, Dessert £7.50, Service optional **Wines** 56 bottles over £20, 6 bottles under £20, 18 by glass **Notes** Dress restrictions, Smart casual, No sportswear, Civ Wed 500, Air con **Seats** 55 **Children** Portions **Parking** NCP behind hotel

MANCHESTER *Continued*

Greens

◉ Modern Vegetarian **V**

Well-established vegetarian restaurant

☎ 0161 434 4259
43 Lapwing Ln, Didsbury M20 2NT
e-mail: simoncgreens@aol.com
dir: Telephone for directions, or see website

Serving up classy vegetarian food for over ten years, Greens is something of an institution, which goes some way to explaining the permanently bustling atmosphere. The split-level restaurant is minimal in design, with unclothed tables and friendly, relaxed service. Rather peculiarly for a vegetarian restaurant, chef Simon Rimmer is actually a meat-eater - a fact that can only be impacting on the food in a good way, as the menu here is both eclectic and exciting. Think griddled aubergine and pumpkin curry with jasmine coconut rice, or perhaps butter and cannellini beans in a smoky tomato sauce with wild mushroom and vegetarian black pudding served with toasted brioche.

Chef Simon Connolly & Simon Rimmer **Owner** Simon Connolly & Simon Rimmer **Times** 12-2/5.30-10.30, Closed BHs, Closed L Mon & Sat **Prices** Starter £3.25-£5.95, Main £10.95, Dessert £5, Service optional, Groups min 6 service 10% **Wines** 6 bottles over £20, 10 bottles under £20, 5 by glass **Notes** Sunday L, Vegetarian menu **Seats** 48 **Children** Portions, Menu **Parking** On street

Harvey Nichols Second Floor Restaurant

◉ Modern European 🖵 🍷

Trendy dining for designer shoppers, overlooking Exchange Square

☎ 0161 828 8898
21 New Cathedral St M1 1AD
e-mail: secondfloor.reservations@harveynichols.com
web: www.harveynichols.com
dir: Just off Deansgate, town centre. 5 min walk from Victoria Station, on Exchange Sq

A place to meet as well as eat, this stylish restaurant shares the trendy department store's second floor with an upmarket food hall, a brasserie and bar. The black and white colour scheme makes a bold statement and the floor-to-ceiling windows offer expansive views over the Manchester skyline. Lunch, afternoon tea and dinner are served. The fresh

modern European menu is constantly evolving, and could offer fillet of red mullet with baby squid, chorizo and red peppers, followed by breast and loin of Cheshire lamb with spiced aubergine, potato purée and rosemary jus. As an added benefit, anything that catches your eye on the global wine list can be purchased from the food hall.

Harvey Nichols Second Floor Restaurant

Chef Alison Seagrave **Owner** Harvey Nichols **Times** 12-3/6-10.30, Closed 25-26 Dec, 1 Jan, Etr Sun, Closed D Sun-Mon **Prices** Fixed L 2 course fr £30, Fixed D 3 course fr £40, Tasting menu £50, Service added but optional 10% **Wines** 100+ bottles over £20, 30 bottles under £20, 20 by glass **Notes** Tasting menu 6 courses, Sunday L, Vegetarian available, Air con **Seats** 50 **Children** Portions, Menu **Parking** Under store, across road

Lowry Hotel, The River Restaurant

◉ Modern British 🖵

Stylish dining in a sophisticated, contemporary setting

☎ 0161 827 4000 & 827 4041
50 Dearmans Place, Chapel Wharf, Salford M3 5LH
e-mail: hostess@roccofortehotels.com
dir: Telephone for directions

Situated in the modern, city-centre setting of the Lowry Hotel, this stylish dining destination overlooks the River Irwell and trendy new apartment blocks. The spacious restaurant, with its designer chairs, leather banquettes, crisp, white linen-clad tables, plain wooden flooring, and pleasant artwork adorning the walls, exudes an air of sophistication, while service is supplied by friendly and obliging staff. The creative kitchen comes up trumps with skilfully prepared, modern brasserie fare, presented without over-embellishment. To start perhaps try black pudding and potato muffin with peas, followed by a main course of poached halibut with red wine syrup and candied hazelnut, and to complete the occasion, why not enjoy Earl Grey scented crème brûlée with mini Eccles cakes?

Times 12-2.30/6-10.30

Macdonald Manchester Hotel

◉ Modern British

Brand new city centre hotel with restaurant with views

☎ 0844 879 9088 & 0161 272 3200
London Rd M1 2PG
e-mail: general.manchester@macdonald-hotels.co.uk

Opened in 2007, the Manchester Macdonald is a smart new hotel opposite Piccadilly Station. The mezzanine

restaurant is set high above the bustling streets and has views over the urban skyline. The restaurant, away from the hubbub below, delivers modern British cooking with a Scottish theme from an open kitchen, which adds a bit of theatre to the room. Watercress soup comes with slivers of smoked salmon as a starter, before main-course loin of pork roasted with garlic and thyme and served with Calvados and apple jus, and desserts include passionfruit cheesecake.

Prices Food prices not confirmed for 2009. Please telephone for details.

Malmaison Brasserie

◉ British, French 🍷

Contemporary dining in buzzing yet relaxed atmosphere

☎ 0161 278 1000
1-3 Piccadilly M1 1LZ
e-mail: manchester@malmaison.com
dir: From M56 follow signs to Manchester, then to Piccadilly

This city-centre offering from the Malmaison boutique hotel group - situated in a striking converted warehouse - exudes French style. The restaurant marries art deco with booth-style seating, while the bar-lounge comes with an impressive cocktail range and there's an on-display wine cellar. The accomplished brasserie-style cooking suits the surroundings, majoring on flavour rather than fussy presentation, its seasonally-changing carte offering a grill selection as well as a Homegrown & Local menu. Tuck into a hearty starter of seared baby squid and chorizo, and for mains why not try whole baked rainbow trout with haricot vert, sultanas and almonds. Desserts are equally robust - take steamed blueberry sponge with crème fraîche.

Chef Kevin Whiteford **Owner** Malmaison Limited **Times** 12-3/6-11 **Prices** Fixed D 3 course £16.50, Starter £4.95-£8.95, Main £9-£25, Dessert £5.95-£8, Service added but optional 10% **Wines** 173 bottles over £20, 19 bottles under £20, 21 by glass **Notes** Vegetarian available, Air con **Seats** 85, Pr/dining room 10 **Children** Portions **Parking** NCP 100 mtrs

Moss Nook

◉ Modern British, French

Classical food in a formal setting

☎ 0161 437 4778
Ringway Rd, Moss Nook M22 5WD
e-mail: enquiries@mossnookrest.co.uk
dir: 1m from airport at junction of Ringway with B5166

A daily menu surprise (by table only) and a seasonal à la carte are served at this spacious open-plan restaurant. The traditionally-styled room has well-spaced tables laid with crisp linen and quality tableware, befitting the formal but friendly cloche service. Cuisine is classical French with some modern interpretations of traditional dishes. Start with lobster and smoked salmon salad, then choose between fresh fish of the day, or a traditional main course like local lamb with red cabbage and caraway. A medley of chocolate desserts is recommended to finish. There is a stunning outside terrace for the summer months.

Chef Kevin Lofthouse **Owner** P & D Harrison **Times** 12-1.30/7-9.30, Closed 2 wks Xmas, Closed Sun & Mon, Closed L Sat **Wines** 100 bottles over £20, 18 bottles under £20, 5 by glass **Notes** Fixed L 5 courses £19.50, Fixed D 7 courses £37, Vegetarian available, Dress restrictions, No jeans, trainers, Air con **Seats** 65 **Children** Min 12 yrs **Parking** 30

Palmiro

◉ Modern Italian

Contemporary Italian dining in up-and-coming area of Manchester

☎ 0161 860 7330
197 Upper Chorlton Rd M16 0BH
e-mail: bookings@palmiro.net
dir: Please telephone for directions

This sleek modern Italian is tucked away in a small row of shops in Manchester's up-and-coming Chorlton district. A recent expansion has seen additions including a bar area and an outside terrace that's perfect for pre-meal drinks or dining in warmer weather. Inside, the décor is rustic and cheerful - fashionably distressed floors and grey walls, enlivened by bright splashes of red. As for the food: expect rustic Italian cooking rooted in the northern regions and based on well-sourced fresh ingredients, some direct from Italy. Begin with lentils and truffle ravioli with sage butter and then tuck into swordfish steak with mash, or herb-stuffed chicken supreme before rounding things off with pear and polenta cake or forest fruit parfait.

Chef Martin Matiasko **Owner** Stefano Bagnoli **Times** 12-5/4-10.30, Closed 25-30 Dec, 1-4 Jan, Closed L Mon-Fri **Prices** Fixed L 3 course fr £11.50, Starter £4.95-£6.25, Main £10.75-£15.25, Dessert £4.45-£4.95, Service optional, Groups min 8 service 10% **Wines** 20 bottles over £20, 41 bottles under £20, 16 by glass **Notes** Sunday L, Vegetarian available, Civ Wed 120, Air con **Seats** 80 **Children** Portions **Parking** On street

Simply Heathcotes

◉ British

Bold British brasserie cuisine in stylish setting

☎ 0161 835 3536
Jacksons Row, Deansgate M2 5WD
e-mail: manchester@heathcotes.co.uk
dir: M62 junct 17. Restaurant at top end of Deansgate

This buzzy, spacious, first-floor restaurant is accessed via a sweeping staircase in Manchester's old registry office building. The interior is cool, modern and minimalist, with high ceilings, big mirrors, natural surfaces, Philippe Starck bucket chairs and smiley, knowledgeable staff. Its lengthy menu plays to the gallery and deals in modern brasserie staples that embrace regional British cooking. Take seared king scallops and

black pudding with Bramley apple and mustard dressing to start, perhaps roast breast of Goosnargh duck, mulled red wine pear and celeriac, and to close, maybe the famous Heathcotes bread-and-butter pudding with apricot compôte and clotted cream.

Chef Laurance Tottingham **Owner** Mr P Heathcote **Times** 12-2.30/5.30-10, Closed 25-26 Dec, 1-3 Jan, BHs **Prices** Food prices not confirmed for 2009. Please telephone for details. **Wines** 49 bottles over £20, 19 bottles under £20, 10 by glass **Notes** Civ Wed 60, Air con **Seats** 170, Pr/dining room 60 **Children** Portions, Menu **Parking** On street

Yang Sing Restaurant

◉ Chinese ▯ V

Famous Chinese restaurant and banqueting rooms

☎ 0161 236 2200 & 236 9438
34 Princess St M1 4JY
e-mail: info@yang-sing.com
dir: Located in city centre on Princess St, which runs from Albert Square

Established in Manchester's China Town since 1977, Yang Sing is as popular as ever. Current décor is on a '30s Shanghai theme - grey and white décor with murals of ladies in a city setting, plus brown leather chairs, polished wooden tables, stylish black chopsticks - all quite sophisticated and formal. The famous banquets for two or more are the best way to experience the food here. Examples are on the menu, but in practice staff design a tailor-made menu for each group after a brief discussion. This way, leanings towards vegetarian, seafood or meat options are easily catered for.

Chef Harry Yeung **Owner** Harry & Gerry Yeung **Times** 12-11.30, Closed 25 Dec **Prices** Food prices not confirmed for 2009. Please telephone for details. **Wines** 91 bottles over £20, 15 bottles under £20, 3 by glass **Notes** Sunday L, Vegetarian menu, Air con **Seats** 260, Pr/dining room 220 **Children** Portions **Parking** Public car park adjacent

Label

▯

☎ 0161 833 1878
78 Deansgate M3 2FW
web: http://www.theaa.com/travel/index.jsp

In a prime spot on Manchester's Deansgate. The British/Med menu is a happy-go-lucky mix of nibbles, sharing plates, salads, mains, sandwiches and great desserts.

Prices Food prices not confirmed for 2009. Please telephone for details.

Samsi

▯

☎ 0161 279 0022
36-38 Whitworth St M1 3NR
web: http://www.theaa.com/travel/index.jsp

The basement is home to Samsi Express (casual eating in a modern space) and a colourful Japanese supermarket. Upstairs, things are slightly more formal. The exciting menu lists a huge range of dishes from every corner of Japan.

Prices Food prices not confirmed for 2009. Please telephone for details.

Shimla Pinks Manchester

▯

☎ 0161 831 7099
16 Leftbank, Spinningfields M3 3AN
web: http://www.theaa.com/travel/index.jsp

One of a chain of very funky, modern Indian eateries. Traditional and lesser known dishes on offer.

Prices Food prices not confirmed for 2009. Please telephone for details.

MANCHESTER *Continued*

Stock

🖥

☎ 0161 839 6644
The Stock Exchange, 4 Norfolk St M2 1DW
web: http://www.theaa.com/travel/index.jsp

Stunning location in the old Stock Exchange building.
Hearty and inventive Southern Italian dishes.

Prices Food prices not confirmed for 2009. Please
telephone for details.

Etrop Grange Hotel

◉ Modern, Traditional British

Country-house elegance handy for the airport

☎ 0161 499 0500
Thorley Ln M90 4EG
e-mail: etropgrange@foliohotels.com
dir: Off M56 junct 5. Follow signs to Terminal 2, take 1st
left (Thorley Ln), 200yds on right

Given its proximity to the airport, it might be surprising
that the Georgian Etrop Grange still manages to attain an
ambience more akin to a rural country house than a
heaving international thoroughfare. The stylish Coach
House restaurant is a modern affair with a classical twist
and oozes style and sophistication, while the creative,
fixed-priced menus follow the décor's theme. Take slow
braised lamb with duck confit and glazed vegetables, or
perhaps saddle of rabbit with Koffman cabbage and
thyme jus. Desserts may include tiramisù and pistachio
parfait with coffee cream.

Chef Marc Mattocks, Patrick Mansel **Owner** Folio Hotels
Ltd **Times** 12-2/6.30-10, Closed L Sat **Prices** Fixed L 2
course fr £10.95, Fixed D 3 course fr £38, Starter
£4.95-£7.95, Main £17.95-£25, Dessert £4.50-£6.50
Wines 5 bottles under £20, 14 by glass **Notes** Sunday L,
Civ Wed 80, Air con **Seats** 60, Pr/dining room 90
Children Portions **Parking** 80

Clough Manor

◉ Modern British

Quality cooking in contemporary setting

☎ 01457 871040
Rochdale Rd, Denshaw OL3 5UE

Under ambitious new ownership, this recently refurbished
hotel is set in the moors near Oldham and offers views
across the valley. The contemporary restaurant is run by
pleasant, friendly staff who complement the
accomplished and confident food being created in the
kitchen. The menu is well thought out and flavours come
to the fore in dishes such as chicken and black pudding
terrine with spiced apple chutney or spring chicken
served with petits pois and its own velouté. Finish with a
decadent chocolate tart with coconut ice cream and
caramelised rum banana.

Prices Food prices not confirmed for 2009. Please
telephone for details.

White Hart Inn

◉◉ Modern British, European

Great food in a restored inn with bags of character

☎ 01457 872566
51 Stockport Rd, Lydgate OL4 4JJ
e-mail: bookings@thewhitehart.co.uk
dir: M62 junct 20, take A627 and continue to the end of
bypass, then take the A669 to Saddleworth. Enter Lydgate
turn right onto Stockport road, White Hart In is 50yds on
left

This 200-year-old coaching inn was built to provide a
warm welcome to travellers crossing the windswept
Pennines above Oldham. It still offers the same
hospitality today, along with a range of dining options.
Choose from the rustic brasserie, with its beams,
brickwork and open fire, or the stylish décor of the
contemporary restaurant. The constant is the bold and
imaginative cooking, with a focus on clean, simple
flavours. The European-influenced menu typically offers
monkfish tail with sticky rare breed ribs and smoked
garlic to start, followed by fillet of Lakeland beef with
griddled tiger prawns, angels on horseback and bubble-
and-squeak. Finish with an excellent rum Baba with
cherries and clotted cream and perhaps a platter of local
cheeses.

Chef John Rudden **Owner** Mr C Brierley & J Rudden
Times 12-2.30/6-9.30, Closed Mon-Tue (brasserie open
Mon-Sun), Closed L Wed-Sat, Closed D Sun **Prices** Starter
£5.50-£7.25, Main £12-£22, Dessert £5, Service optional
Wines 150 bottles over £20, 40 bottles under £20, 18 by
glass **Notes** Sunday L, Civ Wed 85, Air con **Seats** 50, Pr/
dining room 38 **Children** Portions **Parking** 75

The Crimble Restaurant

◉ Modern British 🍷

Enjoyable dining in relaxed setting

☎ 01706 368591
The Peacock Room, Crimble Ln, Bamford OL11 4AD
e-mail: crimble@thedeckersgroup.com
dir: M62 junct 20 onto A627M. Along Roch Valley Way, left
at lights (B6222) & again at pub.

Originally a 17th-century farmhouse, with an additional
coach house built in 1863, the dining room here was
inspired by 1930s ocean liners and it retains a decadent
art deco theme with its mirrored ceiling and attractive
drapes. There's also a small ornate bar with mullioned
glass windows for drinks. The kitchen delivers modern
British cuisine, based on classical French techniques,
using quality seasonal, regional ingredients. Start with
pan-seared diver scallops with spiced butternut squash
and green lentil dressing, followed by local stuffed pork
fillet with Bury black pudding and truffled macaroni
cheese. Apple and blackberry Eve's pudding with
cinnamon custard makes a comforting finale.

Chef Daniel Richardson **Owner** Deckers Restaurants Ltd
Times 12-2.30/6.30-10, Closed Mon, Closed L Sat
Prices Fixed L 2 course fr £12.45, Fixed D 3 course
£17.95, Starter £5-£10, Main £12-£21, Dessert £5-£7.50,
Service optional **Wines** 22 bottles over £20, 10 bottles
under £20, 6 by glass **Notes** Sunday L, Vegetarian
available, Dress restrictions, No jeans or trainers, Air con
Seats 80 **Children** Portions **Parking** 150

Nutters

◉◉ Modern British **V** 🍷

Ambitious cooking in dramatic surroundings

☎ 01706 650167
Edenfield Road (A680), Norden OL12 7TT
e-mail: enquiries@nuttersrestaurant.com
dir: From Rochdale take A680 signed Blackburn. Nutters is
situated on Edenfield Rd and is on right when leaving Norden

Housed in a 19th-century manor in over six acres of
groomed parkland, this high-ceilinged restaurant has
superb Gothic arches that add a sense of theatre to the
overall dining experience. Overlooking Ashworth Moor, the
restaurant offers formal dining but with a relaxed feel.
Impressive, top-notch modern British cuisine is served,
conjured from the finest local and regional produce. Ham
hock and foie gras roulade is served with brioche crisps

to start, while mains range from caramelised Goosnargh duck breast with ginger and garlic roasted sweet potato with pak choi, to seared sea bass with a basil and flat leaf mousse with potato splinters and lemon and tomato butter. Gourmet menu and afternoon teas also available.

Nutters

Chef Andrew Nutter **Owner** Mr A Nutter, Mr R Nutter, Mrs K J Nutter **Times** 12-2/6.30-9.30, Closed 1-2 days after Xmas and New Year, Closed Mon **Wines** 128 bottles over £20, 29 bottles under £20, 9 by glass **Notes** Gourmet menu 6 courses £35, afternoon tea specials Tue-Sat, Vegetarian menu, Dress restrictions, Smart casual, Civ Wed 120, Air con **Seats** 143, Pr/dining room 30 **Children** Portions, Menu **Parking** 100

WIGAN   Map 15 SD50

Laureate Restaurant

◉ Modern British

Contemporary food served in stunning location with good motorway links

☎ 01257 472100
Macdonald Kilhey Court, Chorley Rd, Standish WN1 2XN
e-mail: general.kilheycourt@macdonald-hotels.co.uk
dir: M6 junct 27, through village of Standish. Take B5239, left onto A5106, hotel on right

With good links for the M6 and M61, Kilhey Court is a useful address in the Manchester area. The Victorian-style building has impressive grounds with views over the Worthington Lakes as well as leisure and business facilities. The split-level Laureate Restaurant is in a large and airy conservatory with its own water feature, and benefits from the views. The seasonal menu features some modern ideas and combinations: creamy celery soup comes with Stilton rarebit crostini and crème fraîche, and foie gras and chicken parfait with morels, fig jam and warm brioche. A main course slow-roast belly of pork is served with a fondant potato and well-timed vegetables, and bitter chocolate pudding with pistachio ice cream.

Chef Colin Cannon **Owner** Macdonald Hotels **Times** 12.30-2.30/7-9.30, Closed L Sat **Prices** Starter £5-£9.50, Main £16-£24, Dessert £5-£7, Service optional **Wines** 24 bottles over £20, 16 bottles under £20, 13 by glass **Notes** Vegetarian available, Civ Wed 0 **Seats** 80, Pr/dining room 22 **Children** Portions, Menu **Parking** 300

HAMPSHIRE

ALTON   Map 5 SU73

Alton Grange Hotel

◉◉ Modern European

Contemporary cuisine in a country hotel

☎ 01420 86565
London Rd GU34 4EG
e-mail: info@altongrange.co.uk
web: www.altongrange.co.uk
dir: 300yds from A31 on A339

A friendly, family-run hotel, Alton Grange is set in two acres of lovingly tended gardens on the outskirts of this market town. The hotel offers a choice of dining venues: lighter meals in Muffins brasserie, or the main Truffles restaurant, where oriental objets d'art, lush green plants and a host of Tiffany lamps create an intimate ambience inside, or you can dine alfresco on the fragrant sun terrace. Modern European dishes draw on the best quality seasonal ingredients to offer the likes of black pudding on a cassoulet of haricot beans and tomatoes to start, with pan-roasted loin of venison, braised red cabbage and celeriac gratin to follow, rounded off with roasted almond pannacotta with marinated prunes and pear sorbet.

Chef David Heath **Owner** Andrea & David Levene **Times** 12-2.30/7-9.30, Closed 24 Dec-3 Jan, ex 31 Dec **Prices** Starter £4.95-£8.95, Main £10.95-£16.95, Dessert £5.95-£6.50, Service added but optional 10% **Wines** 122 bottles over £20, 18 bottles under £20, 12 by glass **Notes** 7 course Gourmet menu also available, Sunday L, Vegetarian available, Dress restrictions, No shorts or jeans, Civ Wed 100 **Seats** 45, Pr/dining room 18 **Children** Min 5 yrs, Portions **Parking** 40

The Anchor Inn

◉◉ British

Atmospheric gem of a gastro-pub serving modern English classics

☎ 01420 23261
GU34 4NA

This new venture and second gastro-pub with rooms from the duo behind The Peat Spade Inn (see entry) at Longstock is yet another English country gem. Cosy snug and saloon bars come brimful of atmosphere, as does the main dining room in the sympathetically remodelled interior, which retains bags of original features while

period furnishings and eclectic prints hint at a bygone era. Take a mix of polished-wood tables decked out with big candlesticks, floorboards and green-painted ceilings and wood panelling to conjure a dark, romantic atmosphere in the dining room. Andy Clark's classic seasonal English menu (bolstered by daily specials) comes driven by modern presentation and quality local produce and blends intelligent simplicity with skill. Take calves' liver, bacon and mash or Donald Russell rib-eye with hand-cut chips and béarnaise.

Prices Food prices not confirmed for 2009. Please telephone for details.

ANDOVER   Map 5 SU34

Esseborne Manor

◉ Modern British V

Contemporary cooking in timeless country-house setting

☎ 01264 736444
Hurstbourne Tarrant SP11 0ER
e-mail: info@esseborne-manor.co.uk
web: www.esseborne-manor.co.UK
dir: On A343, halfway between Andover and Newbury

This charming Victorian country house is set high above the Bourne Valley, enjoying delightful views over the well-kept gardens and rolling countryside from its smart restaurant's windows. Still retaining the feel of a private residence, the coral red dining room is adorned with rich fabric-lined walls, floor-to-ceiling curtains and an open log fire, while canapés are taken in the adjoining bar. The kitchen's modern approach is reflected in a range of menus, with the carte a typically more ambitious, innovative experience, displaying high technique, quality produce and clear flavours. A starter of scallops served with pea purée and crispy pancetta shows the style, perhaps followed by sliced fillet of Angus beef with home-made crisps, baby vegetables and red wine jus.

Chef Anton Babarovic **Owner** Ian Hamilton **Times** 12-2/7-9.30 **Prices** Fixed L 2 course £12, Fixed D 3 course £22, Starter £5-£14, Main £16-£28, Dessert £7.50-£8.50, Service optional **Wines** 90 bottles over £20, 42 bottles under £20, 11 by glass **Notes** Sunday L, Vegetarian menu, Dress restrictions, Smart dress, Civ Wed 100 **Seats** 35, Pr/dining room 80 **Children** Portions **Parking** 40

BARTON-ON-SEA   Map 5 SZ29

Pebble Beach

◉ French, Mediterranean

Cliff-top restaurant serving fresh ingredients simply prepared, especially fish

☎ 01425 627777
Marine Dr BH25 7DZ
e-mail: mail@pebblebeach-uk.com
dir: Follow A35 from Southampton onto A337 to New Milton, turn left down Barton Court Ave to clifftop

The full-length windows at this seaside restaurant make the most of superb views of The Needles, Hurst Castle and the Isle of Wight coast. There is also a fabulous summer terrace for alfresco dining. The open kitchen, which makes riveting viewing, delivers a versatile menu with French influences. Plenty of fresh local seafood is available - well presented and perfectly grilled whole melt-in-the-mouth Dover sole - alongside meat options such as cassoulet of confit duck with pork belly and home-made sausages. An apple tarte Tatin served with Calvados crème fraîche makes a fine finale.

Chef Pierre Chevillard **Owner** Mike Caddy
Times 11-2.30/6-11, Closed D 25 Dec & 1 Jan
Prices Food prices not confirmed for 2009. Please telephone for details. **Wines** 52 bottles over £20, 26 bottles under £20, 11 by glass **Notes** Vegetarian available, Dress restrictions, Smart casual, no beachwear, Air con **Seats** 70 **Children** Portions **Parking** 20

BASINGSTOKE   Map 5 SU65

Audleys Wood

◉◉ European

☎ 01256 817555
Alton Rd RG25 2JT
e-mail: audleys.wood@thistle.co.uk
dir: 2 miles from M3 J6 and Basingstoke town centre

This establishment was awarded its Rosette/s just as we went to press. Therefore we are unable to provide a description for it - visit www.theAA.com for the most up-to-date information.

Times 12.30-2/7-9.45, Closed L Sat, BHs (booking only)

The Hampshire Court Hotel

◉ Modern British

Imaginative cooking in a smart, modern hotel restaurant

☎ 01256 319700
Centre Dr, Chineham RG24 8FY
e-mail: hampshirecourt@qhotels.co.uk
dir: M3 junct 6 take A33 towards Reading. Right at Chineham centre rdbt onto Great Binfields Rd. Hotel is 400m on left

This impressive modern hotel is conveniently located for business and leisure guests. Overlooking a terrace and the centrecourt, the smart, contemporary restaurant has traditional white linen dressed tables and friendly service. An extensive monthly-changing menu offers traditional British dishes with a contemporary twist. Ambitious cooking sees starters like carpaccio of beef with rocket, dressed with olive oil and dolcelatte cream. Mains might feature delicious combinations like slow-roast Gloucester Old Spot pork belly with fondant potato, apple purée, pancetta and sage jus. The bittersweet marquise of chocolate clotted cream and salt caramel sugar-dipped almonds might prove irresistible for dessert.

Times 12-2/7-9.30, Closed L Sat

Vespers

◉ International 🖥

Elegant hotel dining

☎ 01256 796700
Apollo Hotel, Aldermaston Roundabout RG24 9NU
e-mail: admin@apollo-hotels.co.uk
dir: From M3 junct 6 follow ring road N & signs for Aldermaston/Newbury. Follow signs for A340 (Aldermaston) & on rdbt take 5th exit onto Popley Way. Hotel entrance 1st left

This well-appointed hotel boasts a business centre and leisure club, as well as a choice of two eateries. A brasserie serves more informal fare, while the fine-dining restaurant, Vespers, is an intimate room where the tables are dressed with crisp white napery, unusual glassware and fresh flowers. It's only open for dinner and serves a modern menu of well-balanced dishes; your choice might include salmon tournedos with a smoked salmon and leek risotto, or breast of duck with pear chutney and vanilla parsnip purée, followed by steamed orange pudding with marmalade ice cream, or deep-fried rice pudding with raspberry coulis. Book in advance.

Times 12-2/7-10, Closed Xmas, New Year, Closed Sun, Closed L Sat

BAUGHURST   Map 5 SU56

The Wellington Arms

◉◉ Modern British 🍃

Impressive cooking in small, cosy pub

☎ 0118 982 0110
Baughurst Rd RG26 5LP
e-mail: info@thewellingtonarms.com
dir: M4 junct 12/A4 towards Newbury. At rdbt turn left to Aldermaston, from next rdbt at top of hill take 2nd exit & left at t-junct. 1m on left

Set in the heart of the Hampshire countryside, this charming Grade II listed whitewashed building was once a hunting lodge to the Duke of Wellington. The intimate dining room boasts a wood-burning stove and terracotta floor, complemented by large oak tables and simple antique chairs, original art and beeswax candles, and immaculate table settings. The daily-changing menu is listed on the blackboard and offers a good range of modern British dishes. Dishes are honestly and simply presented with lots of attention to detail, using predominantly organic, home-produced ingredients, including free-range eggs, honey, preserves, herbs and vegetables, as well as home-made bread. Typical starters include line-caught local trout with dill, lemon zest and chilli, or perhaps hand-dived scallops in pancetta with crushed peas, mint and brown butter, while for mains you might tuck into a generous rack of free-range pork, slow-cooked with red cabbage and apple sauce.

Chef Jason King **Owner** Simon Page & Jason King
Times 12-2.30/6.30-9.30, Closed Mon, Closed L Tue, Closed D Sun **Prices** Fixed L 2 course fr £15, Starter £5.50-£9, Main £10.50-£17.50, Dessert fr £5.50, Service added but optional 10% **Wines** 38 bottles over £20, 19 bottles under £20, 9 by glass **Notes** Vegetarian available **Seats** 30 **Children** Portions **Parking** 25

BEAULIEU   Map 5 SU30

Beaulieu Hotel

◉ Modern British, European

Classic country-house cuisine

☎ 023 8029 3344
Beaulieu Rd SO42 7YQ
e-mail: beaulieu@newforesthotels.co.uk
dir: On B3056 between Lyndhurst & Beaulieu. Near Beaulieu Rd railway station

This lovely country-house hotel, set in open heathland with stunning panoramic views of the New Forest, is the perfect place to explore this beautiful area. Its traditional country-house cooking is popular with locals and guests alike. Starters might feature fresh tian of prawn in a chive mayonnaise or oak-smoked salmon fishcakes with a lemon salad and chilli sauce, followed by the likes of chargrilled corn-fed chicken breast glazed with a pink peppercorn café crème sauce. Irresistible desserts include warm black cherry and Belgian dark chocolate tart, or crisp brandy snap basket with fresh fruit salad in a pool of raspberry coulis.

The Montagu Arms Hotel

◉◉ British, European ✦

Old-world charm meets modern cuisine

☎ 01590 612324
Palace Ln SO42 7ZL
e-mail: reservations@montaguarmshotel.co.uk
dir: From M27 junct 2 take A326 & B3054 for Beaulieu

Nestling at the heart of this famous, picturesque village, in sight of the river and Palace House, this traditional country-house hotel is brimful of original features. The oak-panelled Terrace Restaurant overlooks a rear courtyard with well-kept gardens, while high-backed seating, smartly dressed tables and knowledgeable, formally turned out staff complete the fine-dining experience. The accomplished cooking - from a talented and ambitious kitchen - takes on a surprisingly modern, simple and unfussy approach, letting local, seasonal and organic ingredients do the talking. Take plate of Romsey lamb - braised shoulder, rack and sweetbreads - with olive potato cake, or perhaps pan-fried bass with Lyonnaise potatoes and garlic foam, while a pear and rice pudding dessert might be finished off with a mulled wine foam.

Chef Rogerio Calhau **Owner** Greenclose Ltd, Mr Leach **Times** 12-2.30/7-9.30 **Prices** Food prices not confirmed for 2009. Please telephone for details. **Wines** 200+ bottles over £20, 9 bottles under £20, 12 by glass **Notes** Sunday L, Dress restrictions, Smart casual, Civ Wed 60 **Seats** 60, Pr/dining room 32 **Children** Min 8 yrs, Portions **Parking** 45

BOTLEY Map 5 SU51

Macdonald Botley Park, Golf & Country Club

◉ British, European 🖥 ✦

Relaxed dining in elegant surroundings

☎ 01489 780888 & 0870 194 2132
Winchester Rd, Boorley Green SO32 2UA
e-mail: botleypark@macdonald-hotels.co.uk
dir: M27 junct 7 take A334 to Botley. At rdbt take 1st exit and continue straight over next 5 mini rdbts, at 6th mini rdbt turn right, continue for 0.5m, hotel on left

Set in 176 acres of landscaped gardens with an 18-hole parkland golf course, this large country hotel is a short drive from the New Forest, the Solent coast and the cathedral city of Winchester. There is a traditional feel to the restaurant here, with formal yet friendly service. The light-and-airy dining room is contemporary in style with wood panelling and decorated mirrors. It all creates a comfortable setting for the simple and honest cooking. A starter of diver-caught scallops with herb spaghetti could be followed by a seared fillet of Scottish beef with braised oxtail Charlotte and asparagus.

Chef Matt Wallace **Owner** Macdonalds Hotel Group **Times** 12.30-2.30/7-9.45, Closed L Sat **Prices** Fixed L 2 course £12.50-£16.50, Fixed D 3 course £21-£27.50, Starter fr £5.50, Main £16.50-£23, Dessert £6.50-£8.50, Service added but optional 12.5% **Wines** 48 bottles over £20, 20 bottles under £20, 14 by glass **Notes** Sunday L, Vegetarian available, Civ Wed 200, Air con **Seats** 70, Pr/dining room 250 **Children** Portions, Menu **Parking** 200

BRANSGORE Map 5 SZ19

The Three Tuns

◉◉ British, European

A traditional village inn serving classic pub grub alongside more sophisticated fare

☎ 01425 672232 & 07850 713406
Ringwood Rd BH23 8JH
e-mail: threetunsinn@btconnect.com
dir: On A35 at the junct for Walkford/Highcliffe follow Bransgore signs, stay on this country road for 1.5m, the "Tuns" is on the left

A popular, traditional country pub with plenty of character and charm, a buzzing atmosphere and a cosy, relaxed feel. Between the carte and the regularly changing blackboard specials, there's something on the menu to suit all tastes and appetites. A simple ploughman's lunch, classic pub grub like fish and chips, and more sophisticated restaurant-style dishes (minus any sense of formality) are all on offer here. If you're after the latter, you could start with tempura soft shell crab or moules marinière, followed by fillet of beef with grape pickers potato and wild mushrooms with a red wine and thyme jus, or roasted halibut with polenta and a fricassée of artichoke, salsify, olives and baby squid.

Save room - depending on the season - for the honey-roasted quince with tonka bean pannacotta.

Chef Colin Nash **Owner** Peter Jenkins & Nigel Glenister **Times** 12-2.15/6.30-9.15, Closed 25 Dec **Prices** Starter £5.50-£7.95, Main £6.95-£18.95, Dessert £6, Service optional **Wines** 2 bottles over £20, 21 bottles under £20, 11 by glass **Notes** Sunday L, Vegetarian available, Dress restrictions, Smart casual, Air con **Seats** 60, Pr/dining room 50 **Children** Portions **Parking** 50

BROCKENHURST Map 5 SU30

Balmer Lawn Hotel

◉ Modern British

Fine dining at a grand New Forest hotel

☎ 01590 623116 & 625725
Lyndhurst Rd SO42 7ZB
e-mail: info@balmerlawnhotel.com
web: www.balmerlawnhotel.com
dir: Take A337 towards Brockenhurst, hotel on left after 'Welcome to Brockenhurst' sign

A serene New Forest setting close to Brockenhurst for this imposing former hunting lodge, now a comfortable and friendly hotel popular with both leisure and business visitors. The Beresfords restaurant, with its leather seating, rich decorations and understated contemporary style, offers a relaxing atmosphere and modern British menu that makes good use of local ingredients. Follow seared scallops with pear confit and crayfish oil, with rib-eye steak with Café de Paris butter, or whole plaice meunière with beurre noisette. To finish, try the vanilla toffee brûlée or a plate of interesting local cheeses. There is an alfresco dining area for the warmer months.

Chef Gavin Barnes **Owner** Mr C Wilson **Times** 12.30-2.30/7-9.30 **Prices** Fixed L 2 course £15.95, Starter £4.95-£8, Main £14.50-£18.95, Dessert £5.95-£6.95, Service optional, Groups min 10 service 12.5% **Wines** 26 bottles over £20, 24 bottles under £20, 18 by glass **Notes** Sunday L, Vegetarian available, Dress restrictions, Smart casual, no jeans or trainers, Civ Wed 120, Air con **Seats** 80, Pr/dining room 100 **Children** Portions, Menu **Parking** 100

BROCKENHURST *Continued*

Carey's Manor Hotel

◉◉ Modern British

Great local produce in elegant manor house surroundings

☎ 01590 623551
SO42 7RH
e-mail: stay@careysmanor.com
dir: M27 junct 2, follow signs for Fawley A326. Continue over 3 rdbts, at 4th rdbt take right lane signposted Lyndhurst A35. Follow A337 Lymington/Brockenhurst

Carey's Manor provides quite a range of eating and relaxation options. Blaireau's French bistro and bar is found in the grounds, and the fabulous Thai style Sen Spa has its own Zen Garden Restaurant. The Manor Restaurant in the main hotel offers traditional hotel dining in formal surroundings. The cooking style is British, with French and European influences, and service is attentive, professional and friendly. The chef takes care to source quality products; as far as possible these are local, free-range and organic. Expect starters such as sautéed breast of pigeon with lentil and cumin samosa and rocket and pear salad. Follow this with pan-roasted organic sea trout on Savoy cabbage with spiced fondant potato and cauliflower and cumin velouté.

Times 12-2/7-10, Closed L Mon-Sat

New Park Manor Hotel & Spa

◉◉ Modern

Honest cuisine in historic country setting

☎ 01590 623467
Lyndhurst Rd SO42 7QH
e-mail: info@newparkmanorhotel.co.uk
dir: On A337, 8m S of M27 junct 1

In the heart of the New Forest, this well presented hotel and spa is set in picturesque surroundings. It was once the favoured hunting lodge of King Charles II and has its own equestrian centre, croquet lawn and spa. With sofas and log fires, the public areas are very comfortable. The restaurant is split into two rooms, with high ceilings and original features - some of which date back to the 15th century, but it's refreshingly informal and large windows provide views of the parkland and forest. The food is predominantly modern British with some French influences, based on quality seasonal produce and good

technical skills. Take chicken and leek terrine with shallot and bacon dressing, followed by seared sea bass on balsamic crushed new potatoes, with banana tarte Tatin and vanilla mascarpone to finish. Lighter meals are served in the Polo Bar.

Times 12-2/7-9

Le Poussin at Whitley Ridge Hotel

◉◉◉ – *see below*

Rhinefield House

◉◉ Modern British ☘

Imaginative cooking in stylish hotel with stunning grounds

☎ 01590 622922
Rhinefield Rd SO42 7QB
e-mail: info@rhinefieldhousehotel.co.uk
web: www.rhinefieldhousehotel.co.uk
dir: From M27 junct 1 take A337 to Lyndhurst, follow A35 W towards Christchurch. 3.5m from Lyndhurst, turn left into the Forest at sign for Rhinefield House. Hotel 1.5m on right

This stunning baronial-style hotel is set in 40 acres, with Italianate ponds and ornamental gardens that complement the Alhambra and Parliament - inspired décor. The elegant Armada Restaurant is richly furnished and features a huge Elizabethan-style carved fireplace,

Le Poussin at Whitley Ridge Hotel

BROCKENHURST	**Map 5 SU30**

Modern British, French ⭐NOTABLE WINE LIST

Fine dining, a tranquil setting and some of the best food in the New Forest

☎ 01590 622354
Beaulieu Rd SO42 7QL
e-mail: info@whitleyridge.co.uk
web: www.whitleyridge.com
dir: From Brockenhurst, 1m along Beaulieu Rd

This 18th-century former royal hunting lodge is set in 14 acres of secluded grounds in the heart of the New Forest - a delightful country-house setting for Alex Aitken's renowned restaurant. The hotel has recently been refurbished, with a lounge extension and the addition of a new picture window, as well as terraces and lakes in the grounds, and a walled vegetable garden. The small but elegant dining room has large linen-clothed tables, a

high ceiling, and beautiful mirrors and chandelier to give that luxury feel, while large bay windows offer views over the grounds. Alex has always been at the forefront of New Forest gastronomy, and continues to go from strength to strength. His modern approach is underpinned by a classical theme, enhanced by the abundant New Forest larder. High quality reigns supreme throughout, from breads to petits fours or the tasting menu, with exquisite dishes displaying accomplished skill and fine professionalism. Take a starter of feuilleté of roasted scallop and cep with a light butter sauce, and follow with poached breast of pheasant on a potato galette and casserole of root vegetables, with 'Autumn Fruits' - five individual desserts including blackberry and apple crumble, and pear charlotte infused with Poire William - to finish. (See also Simply Poussin Restaurant in Brockenhurst village. The Aitkens have also been busy at their other ventures, with the imminent opening of a luxury spa hotel at nearby Lyndhurst.)

Chef Alex Aitken, Neil Duffet **Owner** A & C Aitken **Times** 12-2/6.30-9.30 **Wines** 300 bottles over £20, 30 bottles under £20, 30 by glass **Notes** Tasting menu 8 courses, ALC 3 courses £45, Sunday L, Vegetarian available, Dress restrictions, Smart casual, Civ Wed 45 **Seats** 50, Pr/dining room 24 **Children** Portions **Parking** 30

which took several years to complete. Imaginative modern British and European dishes range from New Forest fur and feather game pie to Poole scallops with white Dorset crab tian, vichyssoise frappé and avocado jelly to start. Main courses include loin of Hampshire venison, confit venison boulangère, cranberry and chestnut, or pan-seared fillet of turbot with lobster ravioli. Yogurt tonka bean pannacotta with vanilla crumble, mandarin orange sorbet and strawberry marshmallows makes an intriguing dessert. There is also a relaxed brasserie and a delightful terrace for alfresco dining. An excellent wine list is available.

Rhinefield House

Chef Kevin Clark **Owner** Hand Picked Hotels Ltd **Times** 12.30-2/7-9.30 **Prices** Fixed L 2 course £15.95, Fixed D 3 course £37.45, Service optional **Wines** 100+ bottles over £20, 15 by glass **Notes** Dress restrictions, Smart casual preferred, Civ Wed 130 **Seats** 58, Pr/dining room 12 **Children** Portions, Menu **Parking** 150

Simply Poussin

◎◎ Modern

Pretty village dining destination with an emphasis on quality

☎ 01590 623063
The Courtyard, Brookley Rd SO42 7RB
e-mail: info@simplypoussin.co.uk
dir: Village centre through an archway between two shops on the High St

A former stable block, tucked away behind Brockenhurst's high street, has been converted to create this courtyard eatery, the sister restaurant to Le Poussin at Whitley Ridge Hotel (see entry). Simply Poussin features a conservatory dining area with York stone flooring and Lloyd Loom furniture. Tables and chairs are also provided outdoors in summer. A typical choice of dishes might include curry salted scallops served with apple purée to start; followed by a hearty duo of venison as a main course - rare haunch and braised shoulder served with fondant potato, swede purée and caramelised walnut. Finish with a hot passionfruit soufflé and passionfruit sauce, served with passionfruit sorbet.

Chef Martin Dawkins **Owner** Alex & Caroline Aitken **Times** 12-2/6.30-9.45, Closed Sun-Mon **Prices** Food prices not confirmed for 2009. Please telephone for details. **Wines** 14 bottles over £20, 6 bottles under £20, 10 by glass **Seats** 36 **Children** Portions **Parking** 4

Briscoe's

◎◎ Modern English

New Forest haven with a tempting menu

☎ 023 8081 2214
Bell Inn SO43 7HE
e-mail: bell@bramshaw.co.uk
web: www.bellinnbramshaw.co.uk
dir: M27 junct 1 (Cadnam) 3rd exit onto B3079, signed Brook, follow for 1m on right

Set in the heart of the New Forest National Park in the pretty hamlet of Bramshaw, this 18th-century inn offers a range of popular golfing breaks for those who want to take advantage of three nearby 18-hole courses. A recent refurbishment freshened up the restaurant without sweeping away its old-fashioned charm and the result is a tasteful blend of chic modern colours and period features. The menu follows suit, taking a modern approach to traditional dishes and offering the likes of warm quail pudding with crispy pancetta and sage to start, followed by New Forest fillet of beef with sultanas, black pepper and jabron potatoes, or honey-glazed duck with poached quince and Savoy cabbage. Ingredients are locally sourced wherever possible.

Chef Scott Foy **Owner** Crosthwaite Eyre Family **Times** 12-2.30/7-9.30, Closed L Mon-Sat **Prices** Fixed D 3 course £29.50, Service optional **Wines** 77 bottles over £20, 25 bottles under £20, 10 by glass **Notes** Sunday L, Dress restrictions, No jeans, T-shirts, trainers or shorts **Seats** 50, Pr/dining room 40 **Children** Portions, Menu **Parking** 40

Master Builders House Hotel

◎◎ Modern European

Contemporary cooking in historic maritime setting

☎ 01590 616253
SO42 7XB
e-mail: res@themasterbuilders.co.uk
dir: From M27 junct 2 follow signs to Beaulieu. Turn left onto B3056, then 1st left, hotel in 2m

During the great age of sail, this 18th-century building was home to master shipbuilder Henry Adams, who oversaw construction of the navy's fleet. The house stands in a famous shipbuilding village, with grounds running down to the Beaulieu River. Heavy beams and maritime memorabilia set the scene in the Yachtsman's Bar, while the Riverside Restaurant has a light contemporary feel and tranquil river views. In summer, guests can dine on the terrace under the stars. The modern menu combines excellent local ingredients, innovative ideas and sound cooking skills to produce honest and uncomplicated dishes, such as sea bass with crushed potatoes and saffron sauce, or pan-fried chicken stuffed with tarragon mousse.

Chef Denis Rhoden **Owner** Jeremy Willcock, John Illsley **Times** 12-3/7-10 **Prices** Fixed L 2 course £16.50, Starter £5.50-£8.50, Main £13.90-£19.85, Dessert £5.95-£7.25, Service included **Wines** 37 bottles over £20, 27 bottles under £20, 64 by glass **Notes** Sunday L, Vegetarian available, Dress restrictions, Smart casual, Civ Wed 60 **Seats** 80, Pr/dining room 40 **Children** Portions **Parking** 60

Moorhill House

◎ Modern British

Enjoyable New Forest hotel dining

☎ 01425 403285
BH24 4AG
e-mail: moorhill@newforesthotels.co.uk

Situated in the New Forest on the edge of a pretty village, this hotel was built as a grand gentleman's residence. The hotel's Burley Restaurant overlooks the extensive grounds and opens on to a patio area. The fixed-price, three-course dinner menu, available to non-residents, offers modern British dishes with some European influences, based on local produce. Expect chargrilled marlin steak served with Niçoise salad and basil pesto, or crisp duck leg confit set on egg noodles and coated in Thai-style sauce. Finish with iced fruits of the forest parfait with fruit coulis, or traditional crème brûlée.

Times 12-2/7-9, Closed L Mon-Sat

CADNAM
Map 5 SZ21

Bartley Lodge

Traditional British

Former hunting lodge with food that hits the spot

☎ 023 8081 2248
Lyndhurst Rd SO40 2NR
e-mail: reservations@newforesthotels.co.uk
dir: M27 junct 1, A337 and follow signs for Lyndhurst. Hotel on left

This fine 18th-century listed building was once the hunting lodge for the founder of the New Forest Hounds. Today it's a comfortable and friendly hotel and is quietly situated in picturesque grounds despite being only minutes from the M27. A host of charming period features include hand-crafted oak panelling, a minstrels' gallery and a magnificent fireplace. Wonderful views over the garden can be enjoyed from the Crystal Restaurant, which offers a traditionally based menu with influences from France, the Mediterranean and Asia. Kick off with a light starter of poached salmon and tarragon hollandaise sauce served with roasted pimento salad, followed by roasted pork loin with apple and cinnamon compôte and red wine jus.

Chef John Lightfoot **Owner** New Forest Hotels plc **Times** 12.30-2.30/7-9, Closed L Mon-Sat **Prices** Fixed D 3 course £21.50-£30, Service optional **Wines** 16 bottles over £20, 25 bottles under £20, 2 by glass **Notes** Sunday L, Vegetarian available, Civ Wed 80 **Seats** 60 **Children** Portions, Menu **Parking** 60

DENMEAD
Map 5 SU61

Barnard's Restaurant

Modern British

Accomplished cooking in friendly neighbourhood restaurant

☎ 023 9225 7788
Hambledon Rd PO7 6NU
e-mail: mail@barnardsrestaurant.co.uk
dir: A3M junct 3, B1250 into Denmead. Opposite church

Exposed brick walls, a warm yellow décor and bright prints enliven this small, homely, family-run country restaurant tucked away in a row of shops in sleepy Denmead. Expect relaxed and informal service, an upbeat atmosphere and consistent modern cooking using fresh local produce. Accomplished, straightforward dishes are vibrantly presented and deliver clean, clear flavours. Take

goat's cheese soufflé on crispy bacon and baby leaf salad, followed by perhaps braised pheasant with red wine sauce and game chips. Leave room for a dessert like pear brûlée with cinnamon shortbread or chocolate brownie with vanilla sauce.

Chef David & Sandie Barnard **Owner** Mr & Mrs D Barnard **Times** 12-1.30/7-9.30, Closed 25-26 Dec, New Year, Closed Sun-Mon, Closed L Sat **Prices** Fixed L 2 course £9.50, Fixed D 3 course £20, Starter £5.30-£8.50, Main £11.50-£19.95, Dessert £5.30-£7.15, Service optional **Wines** 8 bottles over £20, 20 bottles under £20, 8 by glass **Notes** Vegetarian available **Seats** 40, Pr/dining room 34 **Children** Portions **Parking** 3 **Parking** Car park opposite

DOGMERSFIELD
Map 5 SU75

Seasons

French, European V

Elegant dining with superb views

☎ 01252 853000
Four Seasons Hotel Hampshire, Dogmersfield Park, Chalky Lane RG27 8TD
e-mail: reservations.ham@fourseasons.com
dir: M3 junct 5, take A287 towards Farnham for approx 3m, turn left onto Chalky Ln continue 1m, hotel drive on left

A Georgian manor house surrounded by acres of rolling countryside and heritage-listed gardens is the impressive setting for this elegant restaurant. The stylish interior takes full advantage of the abundant natural light cascading through the French windows, framing the beautiful grounds of Dogmersfield Park. The French/European menu is executed with contemporary style, and features the likes of local mapleleaf watercress soup with Portland crabmeat spring roll, followed by seared sea bass with warm potato and chorizo pavé and baby spinach in cockle vinaigrette. Milk chocolate cheesecake and espresso crème anglaise might appeal for dessert, or choose from the extensive selection of local and British cheeses. Service is slick and attentive.

Chef Cyrille Pannier **Owner** Four Seasons Hotels and Resorts **Times** 12.3-2.3/6-10.3 **Prices** Food prices not confirmed for 2009. Please telephone for details. **Wines** 167 bottles over £20, 17 by glass **Notes** Tasting menu weekdays, Sunday L, Vegetarian menu, Dress restrictions, Smart casual, Civ Wed 250, Air con **Seats** 100, Pr/dining room 24 **Children** Min 8yrs D, Portions **Parking** 100

EAST TYTHERLEY
Map 5 SU22

The Star Inn Tytherley

Modern British

Traditional country inn with well-presented modern cooking

☎ 01794 340225
SO51 0LW
e-mail: info@starinn.co.uk
dir: Romsey A3057 N, left onto B3084, then left to Awbridge, Kents Oak, through Lockerley on right

This 16th-century one-time coaching inn with rooms comes delightfully hidden away in the Test Valley. There's a real air of English country inn about the place, with its courtyard garden and views over the village cricket green. Inside the cosy atmosphere's more country restaurant than local hostelry though, with warm colours, exposed beams, log fires, tub chairs and leather Chesterfields. The light and comfortable dining room follows the theme, its pine-clad walls adorned with country prints, while lightwood tables offer a relaxed, white-linen-free zone. The kitchen's approach adds modern twists to traditional themes using quality seasonal produce, with clean-cut dishes creatively presented. Take supreme of guinea fowl and confit leg served with roast butternut squash risotto, roasted shallots and thyme jus, and to finish, perhaps a panettone bread-and-butter pudding with apricot coulis.

Chef Justin Newitt **Owner** Alan & Lesley Newitt **Times** 11-2.30/6-11, Closed Mon, Closed D Sun **Prices** Fixed L 2 course £12, Starter £4.25-£7.50, Main £8.50-£17.25, Dessert £5.50-£5.50, Service optional **Wines** 15 bottles over £20, 15 bottles under £20, 9 by glass **Notes** Sunday L, Vegetarian available, Dress restrictions, Smart casual **Seats** 36, Pr/dining room 12 **Children** Portions, Menu **Parking** 60

EMSWORTH
Map 5 SU70

Fat Olives

British, Mediterranean

Friendly brasserie by the sea

☎ 01243 377914
30 South St PO10 7EH
e-mail: info@fatolives.co.uk
dir: In town centre, 1st right after Emsworth Square, 100yds towards the Quay. Restaurant on left with public car park opposite

You can almost smell the sea air from this cosy, traditional fisherman's cottage just up from the quayside. Stripped floorboards and plain wooden tables strike a pleasing contemporary note and service is attentive yet unobtrusive. 'Fresh' is the kitchen's keyword, with the punchy, exciting and reassuringly simple menu making good use of the adjacent sea as well as local game and meats, and producing wonderful honest flavours. Cooking is modern British with Mediterranean influences and dishes may include smoked eel with horseradish cream or scallops with pea velouté and pancetta to start, followed by tender and pink venison loin with braised red cabbage, creamy dauphinoise and a port wine jus. Desserts may take in a memorable upside down pineapple ginger sponge with fizzy ginger beer jelly.

Chef Lawrence Murphy **Owner** Lawrence & Julia Murphy **Times** 12-1.45/7-9.15, Closed 2 wks Xmas, 2 wks Jun, Closed Sun-Mon & Tue after a BH **Prices** Fixed L 2 course £15.95-£16.50, Starter £5.50-£8.50, Main £14.50-£26, Dessert £5.75-£6.75, Service optional, Groups min 10 service 10% **Wines** 35 bottles over £20, 11 bottles under £20, 6 by glass **Notes** Vegetarian available **Seats** 28 **Children** Min 8 yrs **Parking** Opposite restaurant

Spencers Restaurant & Brasserie

◉ Modern British, Mediterranean

A popular venue in restaurant-rich Emsworth

☎ 01243 372744 & 379017
36 North St PO10 7DG
dir: Off A259, in town centre

Fish in imaginative guises dominate the menu at this inviting restaurant and brasserie in this attractive coastal village. Opt for a more casual style of dining in the brasserie, or climb the rustic staircase to dine in one of the booths or alcoves, where the tables are white-clothed and well spaced. Wherever you choose, the excellent menu is the same and may include fish soup or fresh crab salad to start, followed by roast rack of lamb with a minted lamb jus, or whole Dover sole with lemon and tarragon butter.

Chef Carey McClean **Owner** Carey and David McClean **Times** 12-2/6-10, Closed 25-26 Dec, BHs, Closed Sun,

Mon, Closed D (Brasserie Mon-Sat 12-2, 6-10)
Prices Fixed L 2 course £9.95, Fixed D 3 course £13.50, Starter £3.95-£6.50, Main £13.95-£18.50, Dessert £4.50-£6.50, Service optional **Wines** 14 bottles over £20, 18 bottles under £20, 6 by glass **Notes** Fixed price menu only avail 6-7pm, Vegetarian available, Air con **Seats** 64, Pr/dining room 8 **Children** Portions

36 on the Quay

◉◉◉ – **see below**

EVERSLEY Map 5 SU76

The New Mill

◉◉ Modern European

Innovative cooking in historic, peaceful surroundings

☎ 0118 973 2277
New Mill Rd RG27 0RA
e-mail: info@thenewmill.co.uk
web: www.thenewmill.co.uk
dir: Off A327 2m S of Arborfield Cross. N of village and follow brown signs. Approach from New Mill Rd

The location by the River Blackwater is idyllic and the 400-year-old converted mill sits in attractive gardens and still has a working waterwheel. The place positively oozes character on the inside, too, with low ceilings, old beams, grand fireplaces and flagstone floors. The menu is modern European in focus with a few global influences

and skill is evident in the delivery. A tian of crabmeat and smoked salmon is served with a chunky guacamole and some Avruga caviar for a simply presented and vibrant starter, or there is pan-fried foie gras with apple tarte Tatin with Muscat syrup. Main course saddle of New Forest venison is served pink with crisp rösti, caramelised roasted chestnuts and juniper juices, while herb-roasted monkfish is partnered with sauerkraut, spring vegetables and red wine jus.

The New Mill

Chef Colin Robson-Wright **Owner** Sean Valentine & John Duffield **Times** 12-2/7-10, Closed 1-2 Jan **Prices** Fixed L 2 course £16.50, Fixed D 3 course £27.50, Starter £7.75-£11.95, Main £15.50-£25.50, Dessert £7.75-£17.50, Service optional, Groups min 8 service 10% **Wines** 80 bottles over £20, 20 bottles under £20, 10 by glass **Notes** Sunday L, Vegetarian available, Dress restrictions, Smart casual, Civ Wed 150, Air con **Seats** 80, Pr/dining room 32 **Children** Portions **Parking** 60

36 on the Quay

EMSWORTH Map 5 SU70

Modern French 🖥 📖

Exciting modern food by the waterfront

☎ 01243 375592 & 372257
47 South St PO10 7EG
e-mail: info@36onthequay.com

Occupying a prime position on the quayside with far-reaching views over the picturesque fishing village and estuary, this pristine 17th-century house takes in all the sights and sounds of the sea. The elegant restaurant occupies centre stage, its peaceful neutral shades punctuated with brightly coloured artwork creating a contemporary vibe. Tables are well spaced, service is polished and friendly, and the mood relaxed. There's a cosy bar for aperitifs and canapés, while the small terrace comes into its own in summer. Home to some of

the best cuisine on the South Coast, the kitchen's modern approach is delivered via a fixed-price repertoire that includes a good-value lunch, impressive carte and eleven-course tasting option. Quality ingredients, flawless execution and memorable flavours distinguish the complex cooking style. Expect starters like pan-fried fillets of John Dory in hazelnut oil with griddled asparagus, baby leeks and pancetta finished with tomato cream sauce, perhaps followed by medallion of beef fillet on Jerusalem artichoke velouté, with a ravioli of mushrooms and rich morel sauce. Impressive desserts include the 36 speciality - a presentation of banana and caramel in five miniature desserts. Good home-made breads, amuse bouche, pre-desserts and petits fours, together with an impressive wine list and four ensuite bedrooms, complete the comprehensive package.

Chef Ramon Farthing **Owner** Ramon & Karen Farthing **Times** 12-2/7-10, Closed 1 wk end Oct, 25-26 Dec, 1st 3 wks Jan, 1 wk May, Closed Sun, Mon **Prices** Fixed L 2 course fr £19.95, Fixed D 3 course fr £46.95, Service optional **Wines** 15 bottles over £20, 10 bottles under £20, 7 by glass **Notes** Dress restrictions, Smart casual, no shorts **Seats** 45, Pr/dining room 12 **Children** Portions **Parking** 6 **Parking** Residents only, car park near by

FAREHAM — Map 5 SU50

The Richmond Restaurant

◉ Modern European ☕

Elegant surroundings for fine European-style cuisine

☎ 01329 822622
Lysses House Hotel, 51 High St PO16 7BQ
e-mail: lysses@lysses.co.uk
dir: M27 junct 11, follow signs for Fareham. Stay in left lane to rdbt, 3rd exit into East St - road veers to right onto High St. Hotel on left opposite junction with Civic Way

Housed in a later addition to the main building of the elegant Grade II listed Lysses House Hotel, The Richmond Restaurant offers a calm, relaxing atmosphere with a soft décor in delicate shades. As part of Hampshire Fare, the hotel is committed to using local suppliers, and fresh herbs come from the hotel's garden. Typical dishes cooked to order include medallion of Blackmoor venison and pan-fried shallots finished with a Gales damson wine sauce, or crispy cod fillet set on a base of creamy Savoy cabbage served with pan-fried chorizo sausage and white wine sauce.

Chef Clive Wright **Owner** Dr Colin Mercer
Times 12-1.45/7-9.45, Closed 24 Dec-2 Jan, BHs, Closed Sun, Closed L Sat **Prices** Fixed L 2 course fr £10.50, Fixed D 3 course fr £21, Starter £4.25-£6.25, Main £12.75-£17.50, Dessert £4.95-£7.25, Service optional **Wines** 8 bottles over £20, 19 bottles under £20, 8 by glass **Notes** Vegetarian available, Civ Wed 95 **Seats** 60, Pr/dining room 10 **Children** Portions **Parking** 30

Terrace Restaurant at The Solent Hotel

◉ British, European

Modern cuisine in stylish setting

☎ 01489 880000
Rookery Av, Whiteley PO15 7AJ
e-mail: solent@shirehotels.com
dir: From M27 junct 9 follow signs to Solent Business Park & Whiteley. At rdbt take 1st left, then right at mini rdbt

Nestled in woods and meadowland just off the M27, this smart, purpose-built hotel enjoys a peaceful location. The refurbished Terrace Restaurant, Bar & Grill includes a Mediterranean-style alfresco terrace and grill overlooking the water meadow for summer dining. Vivid modern artwork complements the light-beige décor, while chrome and wicker chairs and glass shelves housing wine bottles add to the stylish ambience. The kitchen delivers simple, well-executed, colourful dishes using quality local produce, with daily specials and barbecue dishes bolstering the varied carte. You might start by sampling the South Coast fish and shellfish from the hors d'oeuvre table, before tucking into a hearty daube of beef, slow-cooked in ale with herbs and vegetables and served with parsnip mash.

Chef Peter Williams **Owner** Shire Hotels
Times 12.15-2/7-9.30, Closed L Sat **Prices** Fixed L 2

course fr £12.50, Starter £6.50-£9, Main £14.50-£21, Dessert fr £6.50, Service optional **Wines** 44 bottles over £20, 17 bottles under £20, 15 by glass **Notes** Sunday L, Vegetarian available, Dress restrictions, No T-shirts, Civ Wed 160, Air con **Seats** 130, Pr/dining room 40 **Children** Portions, Menu **Parking** 200

FLEET — Map 5 SU85

The Gurkha Square

◉ Nepalese

Subtle Nepalese specialities in traditional surroundings

☎ 01252 810286 & 811588
327 Fleet Rd GU51 3BU
e-mail: gurkhasquare@hotmail.com
dir: Please telephone for directions

Nepalese pictures, woodcarvings and artefacts transport diners to the Himalayan Kingdom at this intimate little restaurant, set in a parade of shops. The interior is highly traditional, with its white-textured walls lined with wooden roof awnings, red carpet, clothed tables and cane chairs. Friendly uniformed waiters guide diners through the extensive menu of authentic Nepalese specialities, such as sandheko khasi, a delicious combination of rich spices with boneless lamb cooked over charcoal, and bhuteko saag - fresh vibrant spinach, simply presented in a light sauce with mild herbs and spices.

Chef Pradip Basnet **Owner** Bishnu & Imansingh Ghale
Times 12-2.30/6-11, Closed 25-26 Dec, Nepalese festivals **Prices** Fixed L 2 course fr £16.99, Starter £3.50-£9, Main £6.25-£10.99, Dessert £1.95-£3.75 **Wines** All bottles under £20, 2 by glass **Notes** Sunday L, Air con **Seats** 44 **Parking** Gurkha Square public car park

FORDINGBRIDGE — Map 5 SU11

Hour Glass

◉ Modern British

Rustic charm blended with modern design and food

☎ 01425 652348 & 07788 132114
Burgate SP6 1LX
e-mail: hglassrestaurant@aol.com
dir: 1m from Fordingbridge on A338 towards Salisbury

Lovingly restored and converted into a modern dining pub, this traditional thatched country inn has a welcoming bar with large leather sofas around a wood-burning stove and informal tables to attract casual diners. The bar area leads into a warren of beamed alcoves that show the building's 16th-century origins. A huge inglenook fireplace is an impressive feature of the dining room where tables are set in a myriad of nooks and crannies around it. A young team offer tantalising, unfussy dishes using locally sourced ingredients. Expect starters such as confit of pork belly and rich bean cassoulet, while mains might include lightly grilled sea bass fillet, sautéed potatoes and sauce vierge.

Times 12-2/7-10, Closed 25 Dec, 1 Jan, Mon (incl BHs), Closed D Sun

HIGHCLERE — Map 5 SU45

Marco Pierre White's Yew Tree Inn

◉◉ British, French

Stylish dining pub close to Highclere Castle

☎ 01635 253360
Hollington Cross, Andover Rd RG20 9SE
e-mail: info@theyewtree.net
dir: M4 junct 13, A34 S, 4th junct on left signed Highclere/Wash Common, turn right towards Andover A343, Yew Tree Inn on right

MPW is generally recognised by the use of the single name, Marco, these days, which is a sign not only of his position as an important figure in the restaurant industry, but as a 'celebrity' in a broader sense. His sympathetically remodelled white-washed, 17th-century inn retains bags of character, its low-beamed ceilings and log fires blending sympathetically with a contemporary finish. While the bar area has dining tables, there's a more formal restaurant laid with white linen off to one side. The Anglo-French cooking takes a brasserie approach that's steeped in the classics and stamped with Marco's influence. The menu - split into sections like hors d'oeuvre, soups and potages, egg dishes, fish and seafood, and roasts and grills - delivers accomplished, well-presented, intelligently straightforward dishes driven by quality ingredients. Croustade of quail eggs Maintenon starter might be followed by succulent honey-roast belly pork served with apple sauce, crackling, butter beans and the roasting juices.

Times 12-3/6-10

Stanwell House

◉ Modern European

A choice of eating styles in a stylish setting

☎ 01590 677123
14-15 High St SO41 9AA
e-mail: enquiries@stanwellhouse.com
web: www.stanwellhouse.com
dir: M27 junct 1, follow signs for Lyndhurst/Brockenhurst, A337 and Lymington. Head into the main high street for hotel

Eat in either the bistro or the new seafood restaurant at this Georgian former coaching inn on the High Street. The recently refurbished bistro, overlooking the terrace, strikes a contemporary note in black and white with huge ornate mirrors, plus lighting and music to set the mood. The seafood restaurant takes full advantage of local resources, while the bistro offers a choice between the fixed-price Simply Bistro menu or the Fine Bistro carte. Options from the latter include pan-fried scallops with black pudding, apple and mustard to start, followed by venison loin with crisp potato, blackberry compôte and celeriac fondant.

Chef Mr Stuart White **Owner** Mrs V Crowe, Mr R Milton **Times** 12-2/7-9.30 **Prices** Fixed L 2 course fr £10, Fixed D 3 course fr £24.95, Starter £5-£8.95, Main £15-£19.95, Dessert £5-£6.45, Service included **Wines** 55 bottles over £20, 18 bottles under £20, 8 by glass **Notes** Sunday L, Vegetarian available, Civ Wed 90 **Seats** 70, Pr/dining room 18 **Children** Portions **Parking** Public car park or on street

The Glasshouse

◉◉ Modern

Modern fine dining in the New Forest

☎ 023 8028 3677 & 023 8028 6129
Best Western Forest Lodge, Pikes Hill, Romsey Road SO43 7AS
e-mail: forest@newforesthotels.co.uk
web: www.newforesthotels.co.uk
dir: M27 junct 1 signed Lyndhurst A337, after 3m turn right into Pikes Hill

Set on the edge of town, this traditional Georgian town-house hotel sports the stylish, contemporary, fine-dining Glasshouse restaurant. Black tableclothts paired with

white undercloths, a modern central chandelier and a darkwood floor help deliver that up-to-the-minute edge, while a large print of the domed ceiling of a Victorian glasshouse echoes the restaurant's name. Service is professional but relaxed, while the kitchen's modern approach - underpinned by a classical theme - suits the surroundings and showcases quality fresh local and seasonal ingredients. Think accurate flavours and clean-cut well-presented dishes with some adventurous tweaks; perhaps crispy duck confit served with leek and pancetta lasagne, pea croquettes and slow-roasted tomato essence, and to finish, a chocolate and thyme fondant with avocado ice cream.

Chef Richard Turner **Owner** New Forest Hotels **Times** 12-2.30/7, Closed Mon, Closed D Sun **Prices** Fixed L 2 course £18-£22, Fixed D 3 course £30, Service optional **Wines** 31 bottles over £20, 10 bottles under £20, 8 by glass **Notes** Sunday L, Dress restrictions, Smart dress, Civ Wed 90, Air con **Seats** 40, Pr/dining room 10 **Parking** 60

Westover Hall

◉◉ Modern British V 🍴

Fine dining in magnificent Victorian mansion with stunning sea views

☎ 01590 643044
Park Ln SO41 0PT
e-mail: info@westoverhallhotel.com
dir: From M27 junct 1 take A337 then B3058. Hotel just outside centre of Milford, towards clifftop

A Grade II listed Victorian seaside mansion with superb sea views overlooking the Needles and the Isle of Wight, this hotel is packed with stained-glass windows, oak panelling and decorative ceiling friezes. Service is friendly and professional, and the intimate, stylish restaurant also boasts contemporary art, parquet flooring and direct sea views. The kitchen delivers modern interpretations of classics alongside some dishes with innovative twists. Expect eye-catching presentation and quality seasonal produce - sourced from local suppliers - in dishes like Hampshire beef fillet served with dauphinoise potatoes, oxtail cone, seasonal vegetables and a Madeira jus, and to finish, perhaps lemon tart with lemon soufflé and basil ice cream. (Try for a window seat.)

Westover Hall

Chef Richard Whiting **Owner** David & Christine Smith **Times** 12-2/7-9 **Prices** Fixed L 2 course £15-£20, Fixed D 3 course £42-£51.50, Starter £11-£15, Main £21.50-£27, Dessert £9.50, Service optional **Wines** 60 bottles over £20, 11 bottles under £20, 11 by glass **Notes** Gourmet menu available, Sunday L, Vegetarian menu, Civ Wed 50 **Seats** 40, Pr/dining room 10 **Children** Min 12 yrs, Portions **Parking** 60

Chewton Glen Hotel & Spa

◉◉◉ *– see page 184*

The Dew Pond Restaurant

◉ Modern British, French

Country restaurant with fine views and modern cooking

☎ 01635 278408
RG20 9LH
dir: Telephone for details

This 16th-century country-house restaurant may be conveniently close to the A34, but it feels miles from anywhere, set on a narrow lane and enjoying fine views over rural Hampshire. Inside there are a duo of snug lounges and a pair of interlinking dining rooms, with original oak beams and decked out in pastel shades with colourful artwork (for sale). Pleasant, uniformed staff provide unassuming service at white-clothed tables, while black leather chairs provide the comforts. The food is modern British in style, taking its cue from local seasonal produce with simple, yet flavourful, well presented dishes on a fixed-price, dinner-only repertoire. Think pan-fried sea bass with a saffron and vermouth sauce, salmon fishcake, confit fennel and vine tomatoes. There's a delightful decked terrace for pre-prandial summer drinks, too.

Times Closed 2 wks Xmas & New Year, 2 wks Aug, Closed Sun-Mon, Closed L (by appointment only)

Chewton Glen Hotel & Spa

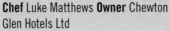

Traditional British V

Fine dining in impeccable, Palladian-style country-house hotel

☎ 01425 275341
Christchurch Rd BH25 6QS
e-mail: reservations@chewtonglen.com
web: www.chewtonglen.com
dir: Off A35 (Lyndhurst) turn right through Walkford, 4th left into Chewton Farm Rd

It's a very English setting down to the croquet hoops set out on the immaculately cut lawn, and as soon as you pull through the iron gates in your car you know this is somewhere special and exclusive. Set in its own landscaped grounds, this outstanding, internationally renowned country-house hotel is a haven of luxury and tranquillity. Impeccable service throughout confirms this is a very well run establishment, and warming log fires, afternoon teas and traditional country-house furnishings combine with fine views from the lounges and bar to further enhance the setting. The equally renowned and stylish restaurant, also focused around garden views, has an elegant feel, while the chic conservatory has an impressive tented ceiling. The menu follows the seasons and uses good local ingredients alongside produce from further afield, but all of it carefully sourced, and with the

suppliers name-checked at the back of the menu. Classical dishes form the backbone, with the accomplished, refined cooking delivering clear, clean and well-balanced flavours on an appealing repertoire of fixed-priced options and five-course Menu Gourmand. Among starters Scottish scallops and langoustines are served with a carrot and Sauternes velouté and vegetable macédoine, while main-course loin of veal is rolled in trompette mushrooms and comes with tomato and garlic confit, baby leeks, Jerusalem artichoke purée and a truffle sauce. The impressive wine list has more than 500 bins.

Chef Luke Matthews **Owner** Chewton Glen Hotels Ltd
Times 12.30-1.45/7.30-9.30
Prices Fixed L 3 course fr £24.50, Fixed D 3 course fr £65, Tasting menu £77.50, Starter £8-£15, Main £20-£35, Dessert £10-£20, Service included **Wines** 750 bottles over £20, 13 bottles under £20, 18 by glass **Notes** Tasting menu 5 courses, Sunday L, Vegetarian menu, Dress restrictions, Jackets preferred, no denim, Civ Wed 60, Air con **Seats** 120, Pr/dining room 120 **Children** Portions, Menu **Parking** 150

PETERSFIELD · Map 5 SU72

Annie Jones Restaurant

◉◉ Modern European

Confident cooking amongst beams and church pews

☎ 01730 262728
10 Lavant St GU32 3EW
e-mail: stevenranson@hotmail.com
dir: A3 town centre, head towards Winchester. Restaurant situated in Lavant St (road which leads to railway station)

Full of character and interest, this little restaurant is just a few hundred yards from Petersfield's marketplace and main shopping streets. Once a private cottage and still cosy and inviting, Annie Jones is full of nooks and crannies where stacked logs and curios are crammed, and wooden tables are comfortably shoehorned. Pews covered in cushions and high-backed leather chairs add to the old-world atmosphere. The food makes a bold statement in this small space, with confident dishes from southern Europe offering a wide appeal. An early bird menu brings a tiny taster of the main menu's choices: fillet of sea bass with a spiced cassoulet of baby squid perhaps, or breast of guinea fowl with truffle risotto. Alfresco dining is available in the summer months.

Chef Steven Ranson **Owner** Steven Ranson, Jon Blake
Times 12-2/6-late, Closed 4 wks per yr, Closed Mon, Closed L Tue, Closed D Sun **Prices** Fixed L 2 course fr £14.95, Tasting menu fr £30, Starter £5.95-£8.95, Main £12.50-£21.95, Dessert £5.95-£6.25, Service added but optional 10% **Wines** 6 bottles over £20, 26 bottles under £20, 4 by glass **Notes** Tasting menu 7 courses, early bird Tue-Thu 6-7.30pm, Sunday L, Vegetarian available **Seats** 32 **Children** Portions **Parking** On street or Swan Street car park

Frederick's Restaurant, Langrish House

◉◉ Modern International

Historic setting for accomplished cooking

☎ 01730 266941
Langrish House, Langrish GU32 1RN
e-mail: frontdesk@langrishhouse.co.uk
dir: From Petersfield A272 towards Winchester, turn left into Langrish & follow hotel signs

Built by Royalist prisoners taken at the Battle of Cheriton, Langrish House has, since 1842, been home to seven generations of the Talbot-Ponsonby family. It is set in beautiful gardens surrounded by rolling countryside just outside Petersfield. The intimate restaurant, Frederick's, has garden views and a cosy log fire in winter. Good use is made of quality, seasonal ingredients in a modern

Continued

JSW

PETERSFIELD · Map 5 SU72

Modern British V ⓦ

Quality and élan are the bywords of this restaurant with exceptional food and wines

☎ 01730 262030
20 Dragon St GU31 4JJ
e-mail: jsw.restaurant@btconnect.com
dir: A3 to town centre, follow one-way system to College St which will turn into Dragon St, restaurant on left

Jake Watkins is now well and truly settled in this sympathetically restored 17th-century former coaching inn just around the corner from the original premises, and the addition this year of three B&B rooms shows how the business is constantly evolving. With large oak beams and generously sized, linen-clad tables, the dining room is an attractive space, smart yet unpretentious, and the walls are dotted with original artworks (by the chef-proprietor's sisters). Service is by a professional, well trained team who display good knowledge of the menu. Everything about JSW is understated - this is not a loud restaurant in any sense and it doesn't preach or try to win over the customer with gimmicks or over-elaborate presentation. There is a sense that you are in safe hands. The food is based on quality produce, the chef so hands-on he might even have caught the pike that turns up in a risotto with bacon and peas. The presentation of dishes allows the food to speak for itself, but technique is good and the balance of flavours paramount: fricassée of monkfish with samphire and ceps is a starter full of vibrancy and tastes of the earth and sea. Main-course fillet and shin of beef is top quality meat and turbot as fresh as it gets and cooked perfectly, is served with asparagus and a sorrel and lobster vinaigrette. Finish with well crafted desserts such as flat apple tart with burnt butter ice cream, or English cheeses with home-made biscuits.

Chef Jake Watkins **Owner** Jake Watkins
Times 12-1.30/7-9.30, Closed 2 wks Jan & summer, Closed Sun-Mon **Prices** Fixed L 2 course £19.50-£26.50, Fixed D 3 course £44, Tasting menu £45, Service optional, Groups min 10 service 10% **Wines** 556 bottles over £20, 14 bottles under £20, 10 by glass **Notes** Tasting menu 8 courses, Vegetarian menu **Seats** 44, Pr/dining room 18 **Children** Min 7 yrs **Parking** 19

PETERSFIELD *Continued*

menu with international influences, offering the likes of seared scallops with piperade, scallop cracker and shellfish foam; and roast rump of lamb with leek fondue, pancetta, and braised eggplant spring roll.

Chef Peter Buckman **Owner** Mr & Mrs Talbot-Ponsonby **Times** 12-2/7-9.30 **Prices** Food prices not confirmed for 2009. Please telephone for details. **Wines** 15 bottles over £20, 13 bottles under £20, 2 by glass **Notes** Vegetarian available, Dress restrictions, Smart casual, Civ Wed 60 **Seats** 24, Pr/dining room 20 **Children** Portions **Parking** 100

JSW

◉◉◉ – *see page 185*

PORTSMOUTH & SOUTHSEA   Map 5 SU60

8 Kings Road

◉ Modern French, European ▱

Classic French cooking in stunning Victorian building

☎ 08451 303234 & 02392 851 698
8 Kings Rd, Southsea PO5 3AH
e-mail: info@8kingsroad.co.uk
dir: M27 junct 12/M275/A3 left at rdbt onto Kings Road

Only a stone's throw from Southsea's seafront and town centre, 8 Kings Road is housed in a classic Victorian former bank, complete with wood panelling and tall, narrow windows. The two seven-tiered chandeliers hanging from the high ceiling create an instant wow factor on entering this grand building. The modern French cooking is classical and freshness of ingredients is evident, especially in the locally caught fish. You could start with crab and avocado with mango and chilli, before moving onto honey-glazed pork with bubble-and-squeak and cinnamon apples. Finish with a decadent chocolate marquise with rum and raisin anglaise and Valrhona chocolate sauce.

Chef Karl Byron **Owner** Keven Hollands, Todd Hyatt **Times** 12-2.30/7-9.30, Closed 26-27 Dec, 1-3 Jan, Closed Mon, Closed D Sun **Wines** 135 bottles over £20, 15 bottles under £20, 10 by glass **Notes** Live music menu 3 courses £29.50, Sunday L, Vegetarian available, Dress restrictions, Smart casual, Air con **Seats** 80, Pr/dining room 32 **Children** Portions, Menu **Parking** On street

---

ROTHERWICK   Map 5 SU75

Tylney Hall

◉◉ Modern British ▱ 🌱

Smart formal dining in opulent country-house surroundings

☎ 01256 764881
RG27 9AZ
e-mail: sales@tylneyhall.com
dir: M3 junct 5 take A287 (Newnham). From M4 junct 11 take B3349 (Hook), at sharp bend left (Rotherwick), left again & left in village (Newnham) 1m on right

This grand red-brick Victorian country house is set in 66 acres of beautiful parkland and gardens designed by Gertrude Jekyll, complete with cascading waterfalls, ornamental lakes and woodland walks. The interior is no less impressive with its oak panelling and ornate plasterwork - the ceiling in the Italian lounge came from a Florentine palace. The glass-domed Oak Room restaurant overlooks the gardens, and a sense of grandeur and old-fashioned service pervades throughout. The modern cooking focuses on quality British produce, including some luxury items, with dishes displaying a refreshing simplicity, based on classical roots with an innovative modern twist. A main course of pan-fried skate with mango, avocado and chilli might be preceded by a salad of goat's cheese, paw paw and spring onions with sesame dressing.

Chef Stephen Hine **Owner** Elite Hotels **Times** 12.30-2/7-10 **Prices** Fixed L 2 course fr £18, Fixed D 3 course fr £37.50, Starter fr £12.50, Main fr £25, Dessert fr £10, Service included **Wines** 350 bottles over £20, 2 bottles under £20, 10 by glass **Notes** Sunday L, Vegetarian available, Dress restrictions, Jacket & tie at D, no jeans, Civ Wed 100 **Seats** 80, Pr/dining room 100 **Children** Portions, Menu **Parking** 150

SHEDFIELD   Map 5 SU51

Marriott Meon Valley Hotel & Country Club

◉ Modern British 🌱

Enjoyable dining in smart surrounding with golf course views

☎ 01329 833455
Sandy Ln SO32 2HQ
e-mail: gareth.bowen@marriotthotels.co.uk
dir: Please telephone for directions

This classy hotel has its own golfing academy as well as two championship courses. Other facilities include tennis courts, a health and beauty spa, and two places to eat: the Long Weekend Café Bar for casual meals, and the split-level Treetops Restaurant for fine dining. Treetops has a warm, contemporary yet rustic feel and fabulous golf course views. The menu majors on quality ingredients such as wild New Forest mushrooms, Rother Valley organic beef, and Hampshire cheeses. Try country pâté with artisan bread; rack of lamb with broad beans and fresh mint jelly, with hot pear charlotte to finish.

Chef Gareth Bowen & Mark Grieverson **Owner** Whitbread **Times** 1-2/7-9.45, Closed L Mon-Sat **Prices** Food prices not confirmed for 2009. Please telephone for details. **Wines** 28 bottles over £20, 24 bottles under £20, 17 by glass **Notes** Sunday L, Vegetarian available, Dress restrictions, Smart casual, Civ Wed 80, Air con **Seats** 90, Pr/dining room 20 **Children** Menu **Parking** 200

SOUTHAMPTON   Map 5 SU41

De Vere Grand Harbour Hotel

◉◉ European

Eclectic fine dining at Southampton's premier hotel

☎ 023 8063 3033
West Quay Rd SO15 1AG
e-mail: grandharbour@devere-hotels.com
dir: M3 junct 13/M27 junct 3, follow Waterfront signs to West Quay Rd

You can't help but feel inspired by the bold modern architecture of this soaring glass structure on Southampton's waterfront. It is the city's only five-star hotel and with fabulous leisure facilities and a choice of three dining options it certainly exerts a pull on the local affluent set. Through large windows, Allertons looks across at the old fortified walls of the town and almost has the feel of a luxury ocean liner. Take your seat and tuck into a dish of seared scallops with cauliflower purée, pancetta and balsamic, followed by an eye-catching concoction of curried monkfish, couscous, and mussels in a leek and tomato ragout, and a zesty lemon tart with raspberry sorbet.

Times Closed Mon, Closed L private parties for L only

Avenue Restaurant

Modern British V ▮NOTABLE WINE LIST 🐦

Elegant country-house restaurant serving creative food

☎ 01962 776088
Lainston House Hotel, Sparsholt SO21 2LT
e-mail: enquiries@lainstonhouse.com
dir: 2.5m NW off A272, road to Stockbridge, signed

This fine William and Mary country house sits at the end of a long winding drive, amidst 63 acres of beautifully maintained gardens and majestic Hampshire parkland. Inside, historic charm and contemporary elegance blend seamlessly, with expansive lounges looking out over a magnificent avenue of lime trees, and a clubby bar made entirely from a single cedar that fell in the grounds in the 1930s. The elegant panelled restaurant (one of two rooms) is reminiscent of an English manor house dining room and is complemented by a terrace for alfresco dining or to enjoy one of the house cocktails. Service is polished and professional, and the cooking in these fine surroundings more than lives up to expectations, offering a classical menu with some tried-and-tested combinations, with great technical skills and a range of modern cooking styles in evidence. Locally-sourced produce, flair, imagination and clean

flavours all come together in well-executed dishes like Portland crab ravioli with pak choi, grapefruit and vanilla dressing, or Stockbridge organic wild mushroom orzo with winter truffle and cep foam. For dessert, chocolate-lovers will not be able to resist the 'world chocolate compilation' assiette (crème brûlée, ice cream, mousse and hot chocolate shot). Excellent home-made breads and amuse bouche complete the upbeat package, and there's a vegetarian tasting menu with recommended wines.

Chef Andre Mackenzie **Owner** Exclusive Hotels **Times** 12-2/7-10 **Prices** Fixed L 2 course £21.50, Fixed D 3 course £43.50, Tasting menu £65, Starter £9.50-£15.90, Main £25-£27, Dessert £9.50, Service optional **Wines** 200 bottles over £20, 200 by glass **Notes** Sunday L, Vegetarian menu, Dress restrictions, Smart dress, Civ Wed 200 **Seats** 60, Pr/dining room 120 **Children** Portions, Menu **Parking** 200

SOUTHAMPTON *Continued*

Legacy Botleigh Grange Hotel

◉ Modern European

Country-house hotel offering a formal dining experience

☎ 01489 787700
Hedge End, Grange Rd SO30 2GA
e-mail: enquiries@botleighgrangehotel.co.uk
dir: On A334, 1m from M27 junct 7

Botleigh Grange is an impressive mansion set in extensive grounds with two lakes close to the M27. The spacious restaurant, flooded with sunlight from a domed glass ceiling and wide windows, overlooks the terrace and well tended garden. Popular with locals and residents alike, it delivers a tempting menu of modern European dishes conjured from the freshest ingredients. Typical dishes are seared scallops with cauliflower purée and balsamic reduction, and best end of lamb with fondant potato, fine ratatouille and rosemary jus. Finish with iced chocolate parfait, chocolate sauce and chocolate ice cream.

Times 12.30-2.30/7-9.45, Closed L Sat

| STOCKBRIDGE | Map 5 SU33 |

The Greyhound

◉◉ Modern British

Popular gastro-pub on the River Test

☎ 01264 810833
High St SO20 6EY
e-mail: enquiries@thegreyhound.info
dir: 9m NW of Winchester, 8m S of Andover

Located in the heart of the Test Valley, between the cathedral cities of Winchester and Salisbury, this popular gastro-pub makes good use of its back garden riverside setting. Inside it has a relaxed, informal character but with a modern edge. Old beams and timbers, floorboards and inglenook fireplaces meet with stripped wooden tables and high-backed leather chairs. The kitchen's modern approach sits well, delivering high quality 'city' food without pretension, based around fresh seasonal produce. Start with a classic fishcake with poached egg and chive beurre blanc. For mains, expect the likes of roast loin of free-range Greenfield pork, black pudding hash cake, sauerkraut and apple, and perhaps apple crumble crème brûlée to finish.

Chef Jonathan Howe **Owner** Tim Fiducia **Times** 12-2/7-9, Closed 25-26 Dec, 1 Jan, 1 wk Jan, Closed D Sun **Prices** Fixed L 2 course fr £18.25, Starter £6-£10, Main £15-£22, Dessert £6-£9 **Wines** 100 bottles over £20, 40 bottles under £20, 12 by glass **Notes** Sunday L **Seats** 52 **Children** Portions **Parking** 20

Peat Spade Inn

◉ British

Gem of a dining pub in fly-fishing country

☎ 01264 810612
Longstock SO20 6DR
dir: 1.5m N on A3057

Tucked away in a pretty Test Valley village at the heart of fly-fishing country, the Peat Spade is a cracking dining pub with bedrooms. The modishly remodelled interior is spot on; typically relaxed and brimming with charm and character. Aubergine-coloured walls and ceilings, polished floorboards and scrubbed-wood tables find a place alongside an eclectic mix of chairs and old photographs. There's a patio area for summer dining, too, while service is notably friendly and attentive. The kitchen's intelligently simple modern British approach utilises seasonal produce from the abundant local larder. Accomplished, clean-flavoured, lightly portioned dishes hit the mark; take rainbow trout with samphire and shrimps, and familiar desserts like baked cherry cheesecake.

Times 12-2/6.30-9.30 Closed 3 wks Feb/Mar & 25-26 Dec, Closed D Sun

| WICKHAM | Map 5 SU51 |

Old House Hotel & Restaurant

◉◉ Modern International 🍷

Georgian splendour and impressive cuisine

☎ 01329 833049
The Square PO17 5JG
e-mail: enquiries@oldhousehotel.co.uk
web: www.oldhousehotel.co.uk
dir: In centre of Wickham, 2m N of Fareham at junct of A32 & B2177

Handsome, creeper-clad Grade II listed early Georgian townhouse occupying a prime position on the village square. Its three separate dining areas - with one room set at the front - have a contemporary look and can easily be adapted for private dining. Expect a brasserie-style vibe and a modern, seasonally-changing menu that features British and continental dishes, with sound use of local produce. Take a starter of seared Black Moor Farm pigeon with chestnut purée, followed perhaps by fillet of red mullet with scallop ravioli and chive butter sauce, and to finish, a trio of lemon desserts - lemon tart, mousse and sorbet. Staff are dressed smartly and service is efficient and attentive.

Chef James Parsons **Owner** Mr J R Guess
Times 12-2.30/7-9.30, Closed D Sun **Prices** Fixed L

course £15.95, Starter £5.95-£10.95, Main £15.50-£24.95, Dessert £5.95-£8.95, Service optional, Groups min 8 service 10% **Wines** 72 bottles over £20, 24 bottles under £20, 12 by glass **Notes** Sunday L, Vegetarian available, Dress restrictions, Smart casual, Civ Wed 70, Air con **Seats** 85, Pr/dining room 34 **Children** Portions **Parking** 12 **Parking** Street parking

| WINCHESTER | Map 5 SU42 |

Avenue Restaurant

◉◉◉ – *see page 187*

The Black Rat

◉ Modern British

Relaxed, unbuttoned dining in character-packed surroundings

☎ 01962 844465
88 Chesil St SO23 0HX

A white-painted one-time pub, The Black Rat (and don't be put off by the name!) has been sympathetically remodelled and oozes old world, rustic charm and character. Think original beams and timbers, exposed brickwork, wide floorboards and an inglenook fireplace, while walls are lined with an eclectic mix of prints, drawings and old oils. Solid-wood tables come partnered by old church chairs, while upstairs there's a small red-walled bar and sitting room decked out in striking period flock wallpaper (there's also a private dining room). Service is friendly and informal, while the kitchen is driven by locally sourced, seasonal produce and shows its pedigree via a modern British approach delivering generosity, flavour and consistency; take grilled halibut with baked fennel, basil and a bisque sauce, for example.

Times 12-2.30/7-9.30, Closed L Mon-Fri **Prices** Food prices not confirmed for 2009. Please telephone for details.

The Chesil Rectory

◉◉ Modern French

Quality cooking in atmospheric medieval surroundings

☎ 01962 851555
1 Chesil St SO23 0HU
e-mail: info@chesilrectory.co.uk
dir: S from King Alfred's statue at bottom of The Broadway, cross small bridge, turn right, restaurant on left, just off mini rdbt

The beautiful, oak framed Chesil Rectory is reputed to be the oldest house in the historic city of Winchester, dating from 1425. Original timbers, low ceilings, white walls and an inglenook fireplace create a warm, uncluttered setting for dining. Everything from bread to petits fours is made in-house, and the accomplished kitchen's modern French output is studded with extravagant ingredients and boosted by quality local produce, including superbly fresh fish. Line-caught sea bass with creamy parsnip purée, braised baby fennels, mussels and oyster sauce, or fillet of Hampshire beef topped with spiced foie gras and served with pomme purée, shallot marmalade and truffle sauce, are fine examples of the fare.

Chef Mr R Quehan **Owner** Mr & Mrs Carl Reeve
Times 12-2/7-9.30, Closed 2 wks Xmas-New Year, 2 wks Aug, Closed Sun-Mon, Closed L Tue **Prices** Fixed L 2 course £19, Fixed D 3 course £49, Tasting menu £59, Service optional, Groups min 7 service 12.5% **Wines** 90 bottles over £20, 4 bottles under £20, 6 by glass **Notes** Vegetarian available, Civ Wed 30 **Seats** 42, Pr/dining room 15 **Parking** NCP Chesil Street

Hotel du Vin & Bistro

◉◉ Traditional, International 🖳 ⓘNOTABLE WINE LIST

Busy bistro in popular, city-centre, boutique-chain hotel

☎ 01962 841414
14 Southgate St SO23 9EF
e-mail: info@winchester.hotelduvin.co.uk
web: www.hotelduvin.co.uk
dir: M3 junct 11, follow signs to Winchester town centre, located on left

The original Hotel du Vin occupies an early 18th-century townhouse in a city-centre location and, as its name suggests, wine is the dominant theme. The charming interior has a relaxed elegance, shown to best effect in the bustling, French-style bistro and bar. Here, bare boards, an eclectic mix of polished tables and chairs, and wine memorabilia crowding the walls, form the backdrop for a modern, Mediterranean-influenced menu that utilises locally sourced produce. Look out for the Land Sea Local menu. Expect simple, light, clean-cut, well-presented classics with imaginative twists: chicken liver and foie gras parfait with red onion marmalade perhaps, or roast duck with celeriac gratin and beetroot jus. Finish with caramelised rice pudding with strawberry jam. Knowledgeable staff apply Gallic commitment, and the wine list is a delight.

Chef Matthew Sussex **Owner** MWB **Times** 12-1.45/7-10 **Prices** Fixed L 2 course £15.50, Service added but optional 10%, Groups service 10% **Wines** 90% bottles over £20, 10% bottles under £20, 10 by glass **Notes** Sunday L, Vegetarian available, Dress restrictions, Smart casual, Civ Wed 60 **Seats** 65, Pr/dining room 48 **Children** Portions, Menu **Parking** 40; NCP Tower St

Hutton's Brasserie & Bar

◉ Modern European 🖳

Accomplished brasserie dining in sophisticated surroundings

☎ 01962 709988
The Winchester Hotel, Worthy Ln SO23 7AB
e-mail: info.winchester@pedersenhotels.com
dir: M3 junct 9, at rdbt take 3rd exit (A34 Newbury). Continue for 0.5m and bear right follow signs for A33 Basingstoke. Take 1st left onto B3047 to Winchester, Hotel is 2m on right

Situated just a few minutes walk from the city centre, this stylish contemporary brasserie and bar in a smartly appointed refurbished hotel boasts walnut floors, leather banquette seating, and a stunning feature wall. Contemporary European cuisine is the order of the day, accompanied by efficient, friendly service. Start with salmon and beetroot gravad lax with watercress and beetroot salsa, and for main course try fillet of English beef with beer rarebit, roast root vegetables, wilted spinach and red wine jus, or perhaps roast fillet of red mullet with sweet potato curry, baby spinach and rocket salad. Finish with an interesting dessert of Earl Grey crème brûlée and vanilla shortbread.

Chef Paul Bentley **Owner** Pederson Hotels
Times 12.30-2/7-9.30 **Prices** Fixed L 2 course £15.95, Starter £5-£10, Main £12-£21, Dessert £4-£8, Service optional **Wines** 15 bottles over £20, 25 bottles under £20, 9 by glass **Notes** Sunday L, Vegetarian available, Dress restrictions, Smart casual, Civ Wed 180, Air con **Seats** 80, Pr/dining room 40 **Children** Portions, Menu **Parking** 70

The Running Horse

◉◉ Modern International

Seasonal fare in an up-market pub restaurant

☎ 01962 880218
88 Main Rd, Littleton SO22 6QS
e-mail: runninghorseinn@btconnect.com
dir: 3m from city centre, 2m off A34

Local atmosphere combines with high quality cuisine at this village gastro-pub on the western outskirts of Winchester. Warm colours, clean lines, tiled floors, leather sofas and a marble-topped bar characterise the interior, and you can choose your meal from the restaurant, bar or blackboard menus, though in fine weather you might prefer to dine out on either the front or the rear terrace. A varied choice of accomplished dishes might include pan-seared black tiger prawns on braised couscous with garlic and parsley butter, or braised lamb shank with dauphinoise potatoes, sweet red cabbage and five bean and bacon jus. Locally brewed beers and a comprehensive wine list complete the package.

Owner Light Post Ltd **Times** 11-3/5.30-11, Closed 25 Dec **Prices** Food prices not confirmed for 2009. Please telephone for details. **Wines** 9 bottles over £20, 17 bottles under £20, 10 by glass **Notes** Vegetarian available **Seats** 48 **Children** Portions, Menu **Parking** 42

The Winchester Royal

◉ Traditional

Well-designed menu offering something for everyone in Winchester's historic centre

☎ 01962 840840
St Peter St SO23 8BS
e-mail: winchester.royal@forestdale.com
dir: Take one-way system through Winchester, turn right off St George's Street into St Peter Street. Hotel on right

This historic town-centre hotel provides a delightful backdrop for the Conservatory Restaurant, which is set in a bright room overlooking the garden. The food is stylishly presented and makes good use of quality produce, providing some interesting food combinations. A starter of pressed beetroot and goat's cheese gâteau with walnut and parsley pesto, or a roasted vine tomato tartlet with buffalo mozzarella and basil oil show the style. For mains, expect the likes of pan-fried fillet of sea bass on a bed of steamed pak choi, served with a liquorice and garlic dressing.

Times 12/7

HEREFORDSHIRE

HEREFORD   Map 10 SO53

Castle House

◉◉◉ – see page 190

KINGTON   Map 9 SO25

The Stagg Inn and Restaurant

◉◉ Modern British ⓒ

Friendly, quality-driven gastro-pub

☎ 01544 230221
Titley HR5 3RL
e-mail: reservations@thestagg.co.uk
dir: Between Kington and Presteigne on B4335

The Stagg is a rambling old pub with three separate dining rooms on different levels, the largest in a medieval barn. Farmhouse tables and open fires make for a relaxed, rustic atmosphere. All the dining rooms connect to the bar, where friendly locals enjoy a drink and a chat. The kitchen prides itself on its straightforward modern approach and makes admirable use of quality seasonal and local produce. Recommended dishes include scallops on cauliflower purée with black pepper oil, fillet of Herefordshire beef with celeriac, red wine sauce and potato dauphinoise, with a dessert of three crèmes brûlées - vanilla, elderflower and coffee - to finish. An extensive range of regional cheeses enhances the repertoire.

Chef S Reynolds, M Handley **Owner** Steve & Nicola Reynolds **Times** 12-3/6.30-9.30, Closed Mon, Closed D Sun **Prices** Starter £4-£9, Main £14-£18, Dessert £6-£8, Service included **Wines** 8 by glass **Notes** Sunday L, Vegetarian available **Seats** 70, Pr/dining room 30 **Children** Portions **Parking** 22

Castle House

Modern British

Adventurous cooking in contemporary luxury

☎ 01432 356321
Castle St HR1 2NW
e-mail: info@castlehse.co.uk
dir: City centre, follow signs to Castle House Hotel

This rather handsome Georgian townhouse hotel is located beside the old Hereford Castle moat. The Grade II listed property has been sensitively maintained and everything from its lovingly landscaped gardens to the sumptuously furnished bar with its bold lamps, silver-framed pictures and coats of arms is done with some style. The chic restaurant has a topiary theme and enjoys views over the garden, or better still, weather permitting, guests can eat on the terrace. Tables are smartly set with good quality settings of silver and crystal. The menu delivers lively combinations underpinned by classical good sense. Presentation is a strength in eye-catching dishes such as starters of seared scallops with confit potatoes, local asparagus and lemon dressing, or Asian-spiced pressing of duck with gooseberry and chilli jam and bean sprouts salad. Local meat is used to good effect in a main-course fillet of Hereford beef with ceps, sautéed new potatoes and watercress purée, and

artfully created desserts include caramel pannacotta with ginger-poached rhubarb and grenadine syrup.

Chef Claire Nicholls **Owner** David Watkins **Times** 12.30-2/7-10 **Prices** Fixed L 2 course £10-£19, Tasting menu £49, Starter £5-£10, Main £10-£18, Dessert £6-£7, Service optional **Wines** 6 by glass **Notes** Tasting menu 7 courses, Vegetarian available, Air con **Seats** 30 **Children** Portions **Parking** 12

Feathers Hotel

◉ Modern British 🌜

Popular and well established 500 year old inn serving modern food

☎ 01531 635266
High St HR8 1DS
e-mail: mary@feathers-ledbury.co.uk
web: www.feathers-ledbury.co.uk
dir: M50 junct 2, Ledbury is on A449/A438/A417, hotel is on main street

This impressive black and white coaching inn has dominated historic Ledbury's main street since Elizabethan times. Full of charm, it combines all the characteristics of a town-centre hostelry with the comforts of a modern hotel. Dinner is served in the elegant Quills Restaurant at weekends or in the bustling Fuggles brasserie with adjoining bar on weekdays. The cooking style is modern British and features local Herefordshire beef and lamb, and a good range of fresh fish dishes. For starters, try sautéed scallops, lentils, chervil and sultana beurre blanc with pancetta, followed by a main course of roast cannon of local lamb with white bean and smoked bacon cassoulet.

Chef Steve Rimmer **Owner** David Elliston **Times** 12-2/7-9.30 **Prices** Starter £5-£10, Main £11-£22.50, Dessert £5.25-£7.25, Service added but optional 10% **Wines** 45 bottles over £20, 57 bottles under £20, 10 by glass **Notes** Sunday L, Civ Wed 100, Air con **Seats** 55, Pr/dining room 60 **Children** Portions **Parking** 30

Verzon House Bar, Brasserie & Hotel

◉◉ Modern British, European

Quality local produce in a modern, stylish environment

☎ 01531 670381
Hereford Rd, Trumpet HR8 2PZ
e-mail: info@theverzon.com
dir: M5 junct 8, M50 junct 2 (signposted Ledbury A417). Follow signs for Hereford (A438) hotel on right

Far-reaching views of the Malvern Hills can be enjoyed from the extensive grounds of this large Georgian country house. The restaurant is modish in appearance with stylish fixtures and fittings and colours chosen from contemporary natural tones. Service is formal but friendly. The accomplished kitchen seeks out high quality, locally-sourced produce and delivers modern British food. Thus a crisp leg of Madgetts Farm duck with an apple and hazelnut salad sits alongside hand-picked Cornish crab with roast tomato and avocado among starters. Main course spring lamb is cooked three ways - rack, braised shoulder and deep-fried, breaded tongue - with ratatouille celeriac fondant and marjoram-scented sauce in a rather complicated main course. First-class puff pastry is filled with vanilla parfait and served with warm blueberries in a well judged dessert.

Chef François Gardillou **Owner** Audrey and Peter Marks **Times** 12-2/7-9.30 **Prices** Fixed L 2 course £16.95, Starter £7-£12.50, Main £16.50-£23, Dessert £7.50-£10, Service optional **Wines** 50 bottles over £20, 12 bottles under £20, 12 by glass **Notes** Sunday L, Vegetarian available **Seats** 50, Pr/dining room 70 **Children** Min 8 yrs, Portions **Parking** 80

The Scrumpy House Restaurant & Bar

◉ Traditional British 🌜

Quality local produce in an authentic scrumpy house

☎ 01531 660626
The Bounds HR8 2NQ
e-mail: matt@scrumpyhouse.co.uk
dir: On A417 between Ross-on-Wye & Ledbury. At village shop follow signs to Cider Mill

Part of the Weston's cider estate, this rustic restaurant is housed in a converted 17th-century barn and oozes character, with thick beams, a stone floor and a wealth of cider memorabilia. The light lunch menu includes simple but good quality basics such as cider-braised ham, free-range eggs and home-made chunky chips, while from the main daily menu you can tuck into roast belly pork with black pudding mash, calves' liver and bacon with onion gravy, and a traditional dessert, perhaps sticky toffee pudding. With an award-winning garden, enjoy a tour of the cider-making process before lunch.

Chef Ula Pruchlinska **Owner** Matthew & Annalisa Slocombe **Times** 12-3/6.30-11, Closed Tue (Winter), Closed D Sun-Tue **Prices** Fixed L 2 course £16-£20, Fixed D 3 course £20-£25, Starter £4-£8, Main £7-£15, Dessert £5-£6, Service optional, Groups min 10 service 10% **Wines** 8 bottles over £20, 13 bottles under £20, 5 by glass **Notes** Sunday L, Vegetarian available, Dress restrictions, Smart casual preferred, Air con **Seats** 45 **Children** Portions **Parking** 100

The Bridge at Wilton

◉◉ Modern British, French 🌜

Accomplished cooking on the banks of the Wye

☎ 01989 562655
Wilton HR9 6AA
e-mail: info@bridge-house-hotel.com
web: www.bridge-house-hotel.com
dir: A49 3rd rdbt and left into Ross. 150yds on left before river bridge

Just a stroll across a pretty medieval bridge from the town of Ross-on-Wye, this small boutique hotel is set in a walled garden so close to the water's edge you can watch the trout jump as you sip your drink. Inside, period features are teamed with a display of contemporary paintings by a local artist, and gnarled oak floorboards creak underfoot. Local produce, including vegetables and herbs from the hotel's own garden, forms the mainstay of the menu, with key ingredients treated with a confident simplicity that allows their quality to shine through. Start with Hereford hop soufflé served with a rhubarb compôte and beetroot vinaigrette, and then tuck into the likes of roast wild sea bass with fennel fondant and shellfish cappuccino.

Chef James Arbourne **Owner** Mike & Jane Pritchard **Times** 12-2/7-9 **Prices** Starter £6.50-£10, Main £14-£24, Dessert £6.50-£10, Service optional **Wines** 27 bottles over £20, 27 bottles under £20, 4 by glass **Notes** Dress restrictions, Smart casual **Seats** 40, Pr/dining room 26 **Children** Min 14 yrs **Parking** 40

Glewstone Court

◉ Modern British, French 🌜

Local produce lovingly prepared in fine surroundings

☎ 01989 770367
Glewstone HR9 6AW
e-mail: glewstone@aol.com
dir: From Ross Market Place take A40/A49 (Monmouth/Hereford) over Wilton Bridge. At rdbt left onto A40 (Monmouth/S Wales), after 1m turn right for Glewstone. Hotel 0.5m on left

Overlooking the Wye Valley and set in an Area of Outstanding Natural Beauty amid orchards, this listed Georgian country house retains many original features. Perhaps the most spectacular is the carved oak staircase that curves elegantly up to a galleried and porticoed

Continued

ROSS-ON-WYE *Continued*

landing. The restaurant is decorated in a contemporary style - local artists exhibit on the walls - while the cooking is traditionally based. The French-influenced menu features the best of local produce, including the double pear (Conference and avocado) platter with Ledbury Blue cheese and sautéed breast of Gloucestershire maize-fed chicken with mushrooms and Madeira. Leave room for the brioche bread-and-butter pudding served with rich clotted cream.

Glewstone Court

Chef Christine Reeve-Tucker, Richard Jefferey, Tom Piper **Owner** C & W Reeve-Tucker **Times** 12-2/7-10, Closed 25-27 Dec **Prices** Fixed L 2 course £14.95, Starter £4.50-£8.95, Main £13-£20, Dessert £5.75-£6, Service optional, Groups min 8 service 10% **Wines** 20 bottles over £20, 22 bottles under £20, 6 by glass **Notes** Sunday L, Vegetarian available, Dress restrictions, No baseball caps or mobile phones **Seats** 36, Pr/dining room 36 **Children** Portions, Menu **Parking** 28

Harry's

◉ Modern European

Ambitious cuisine in an elegant Georgian hotel

☎ 01989 763161
Chase Hotel, Gloucester Rd HR9 5LH
e-mail: res@chasehotel.co.uk
dir: M50 junct 4 A449, A440 towards Ross-on-Wye

The Chase Hotel is an attractive Georgian mansion set in its own landscaped grounds a short walk from the town centre. The restaurant, Harry's, retains its period features, with high ceilings and ornate plaster cornices, but has a crisp, contemporary feel with leather seats and pale silk curtains. There is a choice of fixed-price and carte menus offering a great choice of dishes such as seared king scallops with pea purée, black pudding and red wine reduction; and roast loin of venison with fondant potato and spiced pear jus.

Chef Malcolm Rollings **Owner** Camanoe Estates Ltd **Times** 12-2/7-10, Closed 24-27 Dec **Prices** Fixed L 2 course £9.95-£16, Fixed D 3 course £17.95-£25, Starter £5.50-£9.95, Main £12.25-£23, Dessert £5.25-£7.95, Service included **Wines** 19 bottles over £20, 23 bottles under £20, 11 by glass **Notes** Sunday L, Vegetarian available, Civ Wed 300 **Seats** 70, Pr/dining room 300 **Children** Portions **Parking** 150

The Lough Pool Inn at Sellack

◉◉ British, International **V** ◉

Top-notch food in a charming, rustic pub setting

☎ 01989 730236
Sellack HR9 6LX
e-mail: enquiries@loughpool.co.uk
web: www.loughpool.co.uk
dir: 4m NW of Ross-on-Wye. 2m off the A49 Hereford Road, follow signs for Sellack

Full of rustic charm, with inglenook fireplaces, flagstone floors and beams, this popular Herefordshire pub is situated in a tranquil setting just outside Ross-on-Wye. Diners can enjoy food in the bar or in the adjacent bistro-style restaurant, with its solid wood furniture and walls adorned with the artwork of local artists. Good use is made of fresh, locally sourced ingredients, including home-grown herbs, which are skilfully cooked and well presented. The menu of modern British cuisine with international influences might include starters such as ham hock terrine with lime pepper jelly, rocket and mustard leaf salad, followed by mains like roasted saddle of Weobley lamb with sweet and sour peppers, Ragstone goat's cheese mash and wilted greens. To finish, perhaps try rhubarb posset with olive oil and gingerbread crust.

Chef Lee Jones **Owner** David & Janice Birch **Times** 12-2.30/6.30-9.30, Closed 25 Dec, Closed Mon (Nov, Jan-mid Mar), Closed D Sun (Nov, Jan-mid Mar) **Prices** Starter £4.95-£7.95, Main £10.95-£18, Dessert fr £5.25, Service optional **Wines** 5 bottles over £20, 28 bottles under £20, 10 by glass **Notes** Sunday L, Vegetarian menu, Dress restrictions, Smart casual **Seats** 35 **Children** Portions, Menu **Parking** 50

Mulberry Restaurant

◉◉ British, German ◉

Charming, riverside period property with great food

☎ 01989 562569
Wilton Court Hotel, Wilton Ln HR9 6AQ
e-mail: info@wiltoncourthotel.com
web: www.wiltoncourthotel.com
dir: M50 junct 4 follow signs to Ross, turn into Ross at rdbt at junct of A40 and A49. Take 1st right after 100yds, hotel opposite river

With a glorious riverside location on the banks of the River Wye and embracing its 16th-century origins, this country-house hotel offers a relaxed and unhurried atmosphere in the light-and-airy Mulberry Restaurant. With mullion windows, original oak beams and Lloyd Loom-style chairs and tables, there are delightful views from the restaurant over the terrace and walled garden. Simple, accomplished modern British cooking uses quality, locally-sourced ingredients and delivers clean and vibrant flavours. You might kick off with a light and full-flavoured red onion tartlet with Ragstone goat's cheese and dressed rocket, followed by rack of Welsh spring lamb with braised cabbage and a well-judged summer truffle sauce. Round off with a creamy vanilla pannacotta with passionfruit sauce. Service is friendly and efficient.

Chef Hans-Peter Hulsmann **Owner** Roger and Helen Wynn **Times** 12-2.30/7-9.30, Closed L Mon-Sat, Closed D Sun **Prices** Fixed L 2 course fr £10, Starter £5.45-£7.95, Main £13.45-£18.95, Dessert £5.50-£6.95, Service optional **Wines** 11 bottles over £20, 23 bottles under £20, 7 by glass **Notes** Sunday L, Vegetarian available, Dress restrictions, Smart casual preferred, Civ Wed 50 **Seats** 40, Pr/dining room 12 **Children** Portions, Menu **Parking** 25

ULLINGSWICK
Map 10 SO54

Three Crowns Inn

◉ British, French ✿

Relaxed dining in a charming village inn

☎ 01432 820279
HR1 3JQ
e-mail: info@threecrownsinn.com
dir: Please telephone for directions

This converted, half-timbered 16th-century farmhouse and former cider house is now a charming village inn with dark oak beams, brick fireplaces and log fires. The restaurant, with its décor of cream washed walls, timber pillars and eclectic mix of wooden furniture including church pews, provides a welcoming and relaxed setting. The finest quality seasonal produce from local suppliers features well on the menu of accomplished British-style cuisine with a hint of French influence. Starters might include Jerusalem artichoke soup with morels, followed by mains like Madgett's Farm chicken with sweet-and-sour beets and, to finish, perhaps try rhubarb, saffron and cardamom brûlée.

Chef Brent Castle **Owner** Brent Castle & Rachel Baker **Times** 12-3/7-10, Closed 25 Dec, 1 Jan, Closed Mon **Prices** Fixed L 2 course £12.95, Starter £6.50, Main £14.50, Dessert £5, Service optional **Wines** 14 bottles over £20, 12 bottles under £20, 7 by glass **Notes** Sunday L, Vegetarian available **Seats** 75, Pr/dining room 36 **Children** Portions **Parking** 30

WEOBLEY
Map 9 SO45

The Salutation Inn

◉ British

Popular country inn serving good local produce

☎ 01544 318443
Market Pitch HR4 8SJ
dir: On A4112, just off Leominster-Hereford road

Combining a former ale and cider house and an adjoining timbered cottage, this 500-year-old inn stands in the heart of medieval Weobley. Beams, sloping floors and low doors abound, and there's a fine inglenook fireplace in the cosy Oak Room restaurant. More than a hint of French influence is evident in the cuisine, and the emphasis is on local produce with traditional sauces. Dishes may include baked mint camembert, then pan-fried fillet of Hereford beef, with crunchy Seville bread-and-butter pudding with Weobley clotted cream to finish. Good bar meals are also offered.

Times 12-2/7-9.30, Closed 25 Dec, Closed D Sun (bar meals served all week)

HERTFORDSHIRE

BISHOP'S STORTFORD
Map 6 TL42

Ibbetson's Restaurant

◉◉ Modern British

Stylish dining in imposing country-house hotel

☎ 01279 732100 & 01279 731441
Down Hall Country House Hotel, Matching Rd, Hatfield Heath CM22 7AS
e-mail: info@downhall.co.uk
web: www.downhall.co.uk
dir: Take A414 towards Harlow. At 4th rdbt follow B183 towards Hatfield Heath, keep left and follow hotel sign

The imposing Victorian country house of Down Hall is surrounded by 100 acres of grounds and was built by Sir Henry Selwin Ibbetson in 1873. The beautifully presented public areas, including the Ibbetson's dining room, are impressive - full of Victorian design excess and open fires. Seasonal availability of local ingredients dictates a menu of accomplished modern dishes of exacting flavours, which come underpinned by a classical theme. Take a starter of crab bisque with poached oyster, or perhaps rock lobster cocktail, followed by fillet of beef with wild mushroom gratin, Chantenay carrots, and Madeira and truffle jus. Finish with 'the four seasons of chocolate' (hot soufflé, dark chocolate mousse, chocolate and orange sorbet and white chocolate ganache).

Chef Mark Jones **Owner** Veladail Collection **Times** Closed Xmas, New Year, Closed Sun-Mon, Closed L all week **Prices** Starter £6.75-£11.50, Main £18.50-£29, Dessert £7.50-£12, Service added but optional 10% **Wines** 65 bottles over £20, 9 by glass **Notes** Vegetarian available, Dress restrictions, Smart casual, Civ Wed 130, Air con **Seats** 30 **Parking** 100

HARPENDEN
Map 6 TL11

A Touch of Novelli at the White Horse

◉ British, French ▭

Glamorous gastro-pub

☎ 01582 713428
Hatching Green AL5 2JP
e-mail: info@atouchofnovelli.com
dir: Telephone for directions

The white-painted, part-boarded building looks like a typical, smart country pub. But this White Horse has been given the gastro-treatment by no less than Jean-Christophe Novelli. This means a few modern touches in the décor, while keeping the heart and soul of the place, and putting the focus firmly on good, fresh food. There is a bar which helps maintain the pub atmosphere, but the restaurant is the real draw. Potted Morecambe Bay shrimps with Armagnac butter and cider bread aptly reflects the dual nationalities at work here. Chicken liver parfait is enlivened with prunes marinated in Armagnac, while a main course Cornish skate wing is accurately cooked and comes with baby fennel, salsify marinated in port and a herby Montpellier butter. Novelli is famous for his desserts, so check out the pear and almond tart. The Terrace is an alfresco eating area, open from May to September weather permitting, complete with its own menu.

Times 12.30-3/6-10, Closed 25 & 26 Dec

The Silver Cup

◉ Modern British

Traditional inn serving local produce in exciting combinations

☎ 01582 713095
5 St Albans Rd AL5 2JF
e-mail: info@silvercup.co.uk
dir: Please telephone for directions

Idyllically situated overlooking Harpenden Common, this recently refurbished, traditional coaching inn dates back to the 1800s and is named after a horse race that once took place on the Common. With its warm, cosy décor, wooden tables, comfortable leather seats and copper fittings, it retains much of its original character and charm. The kitchen serves a lengthy, crowd-pleasing repertoire of imaginative modern dishes - with a nod to the Mediterranean - driven by fine local produce. Portions are hearty, and bar snacks and light meals are also available. Typical dishes may include pan-fried aniseed-infused duck breast with butternut squash purée, raspberry and balsamic dressing with crispy onion, or saffron-poached lemon sole fillets and mussels with steamed fennel and sweet potato in herb broth. A good selection of wines is available by the glass.

Chef Jonathan Harding **Owner** Liz Gaire **Times** 12-3/6-9.30 **Prices** Food prices not confirmed for 2009. Please telephone for details. **Wines** 31 bottles over £20, 20 bottles under £20, 16 by glass **Notes** Sunday L, Vegetarian available **Seats** 40 **Children** Portions **Parking** 6

Kiplings at Bush Hall

◉◉ Modern British ♥

Modern cooking at an elegant hotel

☎ 01707 271251
Mill Green AL9 5NT
e-mail: enquiries@bush-hall.com
dir: From A1 (M) follow signs for A414 (Hereford/Welwyn Garden City). Take slip road onto A1000 (signs for Hatfield Hse). Left at lights, immediately left into hotel drive

Standing amid 120 acres of attractive parkland, Bush Hall is a popular wedding and conference venue. Riverside terraces and a lake garden make the most of the Lea as it meanders through the grounds, while a host of outdoor activities are available for those who feel like more than a post- or pre-meal stroll. Dinner is served in the Kiplings restaurant, a cosy room with green and gold décor and oak panelling, and there's a comfortable lounge for aperitifs or late-night tipples. Expect an accomplished modern British approach; duo of smoked haddock and salmon mousse with cucumber relish perhaps, or crisp breast of Barbary duck with dauphinoise potatoes, sautéed leaf spinach, pancetta crisp and port sauce.

Chef Scott McKenzie **Owner** Kiplings **Times** 12-2/7-10, Closed D 25 Dec-early Jan, Closed L Sat-Sun **Prices** Starter £4.95-£11.25, Main £11.45-£24.95, Dessert £5.75-£8.95, Service added but optional 12.5% **Wines** 93 bottles over £20, 40 bottles under £20, 8 by glass **Notes** Vegetarian available, Dress restrictions, Smart casual, Civ Wed 150, Air con **Seats** 38, Pr/dining room 22 **Children** Min 8 yrs, Portions **Parking** 100

Outsidein at Beales Hotel

◉◉ Modern British ♥

Enjoyable dining in contemporary surroundings

☎ 01707 288500
Comet Way AL10 9NG
e-mail: outsidein@bealeshotels.co.uk
dir: Please telephone for directions

This hotel was completely rebuilt in 2004 and is now a stunning contemporary property, with a striking exterior incorporating giant glass panels and cedar wood slats. With a relaxed atmosphere, the modern restaurant has darkwood tables, light wood floors, hanging glass effect curtains and modern art on the walls. Smartly uniformed staff offer professional service. With a strong focus on local produce, the regularly-changing menu offers daily specials. For starters, try chicken liver parfait with toasted brioche, followed by Hertfordshire fillet of beef with wild mushroom fricassée, potato rosti and Madeira jus. Leave room for chocolate and toffee fondant with pistachio ice cream.

Chef Wayne Turner **Owner** Beales Ltd **Times** 10-10 **Wines** 60 bottles over £20, 26 bottles under £20, 14 by glass **Notes** Pre-concert D £35 incl tickets, Sunday L, Vegetarian available, Civ Wed 300, Air con **Seats** 80, Pr/dining room 300 **Children** Portions, Menu **Parking** 126

Redcoats Farmhouse Hotel

◉ Traditional European

Family-run hotel with a busy restaurant

☎ 01438 729500
Redcoats Green SG4 7JR
e-mail: sales@redcoats.co.uk
dir: Telephone for directions

This delightful 14th-century farmhouse, with original features like exposed brickwork, oak beams and open fireplaces, is set in 4 acres of landscaped grounds close to the A1. Restored over the years, the building now has an attractive Victorian red-brick frontage. The main dining area at the thriving restaurant is a conservatory with views over the garden. Good quality local produce is used to produce enduring classics cooked with precision. Expect moules marinière, wild Cornish sea bass fillet with a light tomato and saffron and coriander sauce, and perhaps a lemon and lime crème brûlée with an almond tuile to finish.

Redcoats Farmhouse Hotel

Times 12/6.30, Closed 1 wk after Xmas, BH Mons, Closed L Sat, Closed D Sun

Ponsbourne Park Hotel

◉◉ Modern International ▭

Stately manor with a contemporary flavour

☎ 01707 876191 & 879277
SG13 8QT
e-mail: reservations@ponsbournepark.co.uk
web: www.ponsbournepark.co.uk
dir: Telephone or see website for directions

Set in 200 acres of peaceful countryside, this grand 17th-century house makes an imposing first impression. Inside, by contrast, it's a restrained, contemporary affair with bold colours and clean lines. There's a choice of two dining venues: an informal bistro and the more formal fine-dining restaurant which delivers a comprehensive menu of modern dishes firmly rooted in classic French cuisine with some oriental influences. You might start with an assiette of shellfish to include scallop parfait, creamed lobster broth and Thai crab, and follow with roast rump of lamb with a duo of white and black pudding, winter greens and redcurrant and cinnamon jus. Pistachio and chocolate mousse in a dark chocolate tower and toffee sauce might prove a fitting finale.

Chef Sushmito Roy **Owner** Tesco **Times** 12-4/6.30-11, Closed 1 Jan, Closed D Sun **Prices** Fixed L 3 course fr £21.95, Fixed D 3 course fr £31.95, Service optional **Wines** 10 bottles over £20, 20 bottles under £20, 3 by glass **Notes** Sunday L, Vegetarian available, Dress restrictions, Smart casual, Civ Wed 86, Air con **Seats** 60, Pr/dining room 90 **Children** Portions, Menu **Parking** 80

| RICKMANSWORTH | Map 6 TQ09 |

Colette's at The Grove

⊛⊛⊛ – **see below**

| ROYSTON | Map 12 TL34 |

The Cabinet at Reed

⊛ Modern British, European

Impressive food in a charming village inn

☎ 01763 848366
High St, Reed SG8 8AH
e-mail: thecabinet@btconnect.com
dir: Just off A10 between Buntingford and Royston

With its low ceilings, original beams and open fire, this charming, contemporary-styled 16th-century inn is located in the village of Reed. The restaurant promises a relaxed dining experience with a team of highly skilled chefs presenting seasonal menus using locally sourced ingredients. With Mediterranean and global influences, expect dishes like carpaccio of beef with aged balsamic, rocket and parmesan, followed by pan-seared sea bass, pickled tomatoes, bok choy and lime. Desserts include chocolate and cardamom mousse or a selection of some of the finest English cheeses available. Snacks and light bites are also available in the bar.

The Cabinet at Reed

Times 12-2.30/7-9, Closed 1 Jan, Closed Mon (some in winter), Closed D Sun

---

| ST ALBANS | Map 6 TL10 |

The Noke by Thistle

⊛ Modern European V

Interesting menus in a popular hotel restaurant

☎ 01727 854252 & 0870 3339144
Thistle St Albans, Watford Rd AL2 3DS
e-mail: stalbans@thistle.co.uk
dir: M25 junct 21A, A405 to St Albans, at rdbt take first exit into hotel

Conveniently located close to St Albans, this Thistle Hotel - set in its own grounds - has fed and watered travellers since Victorian times. Retaining period features, the recently refurbished, bright and airy, conservatory-style Noke Restaurant has an attractive traditional décor, and offers modern European menus that make good use of local and seasonal produce. Flambé dishes are very popular, or you could try seared scallops with cauliflower purée, roast sweetbreads and garlic foam for starters, following with beef fillet with snail ravioli, sauce soubise and parsley purée, or milk poached pork with apple purée and mustard dressing.

Chef Darren Jory **Owner** CIT **Times** 12-2/7-9.30, Closed L Sat, Closed D Sun **Prices** Fixed L 2 course fr £17, Fixed D 3 course fr £26.95, Starter £7.50-£10, Main £19.50-£24.50, Dessert £7, Service included **Wines** 50 bottles over £20, 15 bottles under £20, 15 by glass **Notes** Sunday L, Vegetarian menu, Dress restrictions, Smart casual, Civ Wed, Air con **Seats** 75, Pr/dining room 250 **Children** Portions, Menu **Parking** 120

Colette's at The Grove

| RICKMANSWORTH | Map 6 TQ09 |

Modern British V

Fine dining in smart, contemporary, relaxed setting of 'London's country estate'

☎ 01923 296015 & 296010
Chandler's Cross WD3 4TG
e-mail: restaurants@thegrove.co.uk
dir: M25 junct 19, follow signs to Watford. At first large rdbt take 3rd exit. Continue on 0.5m entrance on right

The Grove may be within the M25, but it certainly doesn't feel that way when you're there. The 300 acre grounds of this grand 18th-century stately residence are now home to a championship golf course and fine formal gardens, each enjoying beautiful views over Charlotte's Vale. The house itself has been transformed into a world-class, contemporary hotel, which successfully combines historic character with cutting-edge modern design. There is a smart spa, a relaxing bar and lounge, and a choice of three restaurants. Colette's is the fine dining, evening-only option, with its own separate entrance and stylish lounge and bar. The dining room is smart and slick with cream leather chairs, darkwood floor and the walls painted a dignified mustard-yellow. With service on the formal side, dinner includes all the extras from canapés in the bar through to pre-dessert and petits fours, and quality remains high throughout. The cooking is in the contemporary vein, with lots of clever ideas and presentations, displaying the acute technical abilities of the kitchen team. Jerusalem artichoke risotto is a vibrant starter, with wine-braised oxtail and truffle-scented cream, while slow-roasted Aylesbury duck with 'peas & carrots' and a pastilla of Morteau sausage is a creative and well-crafted main course.

Chef Chris Warwick **Owner** Ralph Trustees Ltd **Times** Closed Sun & Mon except BHs, Closed L all week **Prices** Fixed D 3 course fr £54, Tasting menu £58-£65, Service optional **Wines** 250 bottles over £20, 10 by glass **Notes** Tasting menu 4 & 6 courses, Vegetarian menu, Civ Wed 450, Air con **Seats** 45 **Children** Portions **Parking** 500

ST ALBANS *Continued*

St Michael's Manor

◎◎ Modern British

Accomplished cooking in a luxury hotel

☎ 01727 864444
Fishpool St AL3 4RY
e-mail: reservations@stmichaelsmanor.com
dir: At the Tudor Tavern in High St turn into George St. After abbey & school on left, road continues onto Fishpool St. Hotel is 1m on left

Only a 5-minute walk into the centre of St Albans, St Michael's Manor is a hidden gem. The building dates back 500 years and is now a luxurious country-house hotel in 6 acres of beautifully landscaped grounds including a lake. The airy dining room benefits from an elegant conservatory to make the best of the garden view in all weathers. The room is light and bright, painted in calm and soothing pastel shades, and the tables decorated with fresh flowers. There is a sun terrace too, so pre-dinner drinks can be taken outside when the weather allows. The menu is focused on local produce and wine recommendations are made for each starter and main course on the carte. The modern British food shows attention to detail and understanding of flavours and textures. Confit rabbit and foie gras ballantine come with quince purée and Melba toast as a starter, followed by gilt head bream with tarragon-crushed potatoes and panzanella salad. Service is by a professional team of smartly uniformed staff.

Chef Haydn Lailow **Owner** David & Sheila Newling-Ward
Times 12-2.30/7-9.30, Closed L 31 Dec, Closed D 25 Dec
Prices Fixed L 2 course £14.95, Fixed D 3 course £24.95, Starter £6.25-£8.95, Main £13.75-£19.50, Dessert £6.50-£7.95, Service added but optional 12.5% **Wines** 86 bottles over £20, 7 bottles under £20, 32 by glass
Notes Sunday L, Vegetarian available, Dress restrictions, Smart casual, Civ Wed 90 **Seats** 95, Pr/dining room 24
Children Portions, Menu **Parking** 75

Sopwell House

◎ Modern British, European

Sophisticated dining in an elegant country-house hotel

☎ 01727 864477
Cottonmill Ln, Sopwell AL1 2HQ
e-mail: enquiries@sopwellhouse.co.uk
dir: On London road from St Albans follow signs to Sopwell, under railway bridge, over mini-rdbt, hotel 0.25m on left

The stunning centrepiece of this Georgian country house, the former home of Lord Mountbatten, is the contemporary but elegant restaurant, with its wooden floors, mirrors, New England shutters and lovely garden views. The modern British menu with European influences makes excellent use of seasonal local produce in dishes that are imaginatively conceived and simply presented. A recommended selection includes seared hand-dived scallops on apple ginger purée with a red wine reduction and apple crisp, calves' liver and bacon set with onion confit, shallots and red wine jus, and strawberry and black pepper soufflé with white chocolate ice cream.

Chef James Chapman **Owner** Abraham Bejerano
Times 12-3/7-10, Closed L Sat, Mon **Prices** Food prices not confirmed for 2009. Please telephone for details.
Notes Sunday L, Vegetarian available, Dress restrictions, Prefer no jeans or trainers, Civ Wed 250, Air con
Seats 100, Pr/dining room 12 **Children** Portions, Menu **Parking** 350

TRING	Map 6 SP91

Pendley Manor

◎ Modern

Fine dining in an imposing manor house

☎ 01442 891891
Cow Ln HP23 5QY
e-mail: sales@pendley-manor.co.uk
dir: M25 junct 20. Take A41 and Tring exit, follow signs for Berkhamsted. 1st left, right after rugby club

A grand Tudor-style manor house built in 1872, this impressive hotel is set in 35 acres of wooded parkland. Public rooms include a cosy bar and conservatory lounge, as well as The Oak Room, a panelled restaurant with high ceilings, large bay windows and heavy drapes. The chef favours modern English cooking, making good use of local and seasonal produce. Impressive dishes include smoked duck with watercress salad and blackberry and orange compôte, roast Ashridge venison with hotpot potato and red wine jus, and, best of all, coffee pannacotta with cappuccino foam.

Chef Simon Green **Owner** Craydawn Pendley Manor
Times 12.30-2.30/7-9.30 **Prices** Fixed L 2 course £21, Fixed D 3 course £31, Service optional **Wines** 34 bottles over £20, 22 bottles under £20, 1 by glass **Notes** Sunday L, Vegetarian available, Dress restrictions, Smart casual, Civ Wed 225 **Seats** 75, Pr/dining room 200
Children Portions **Parking** 150

WARE	Map 6 TL31

Marriott Hanbury Manor Hotel

◎◎ French, European

Impressive cuisine in elegant surroundings

☎ 01920 487722
SG12 0SD
e-mail: david.ali@marriotthotels.co.uk
dir: From M25 junct 25, take A10 towards Cambridge, for 12m. Leave A10 Wadesmill/Thundridge/Ware. Right at rdbt, hotel on left

An impressive Jacobean-style mansion surrounded by 200 acres of grounds and wonderful gardens, with a popular health and leisure club and championship golf course. The seasonal cooking, with French and European influences, is savoured in the opulent Zodiac restaurant, with intricate carved walls and signs of the zodiac on the painted ceiling, huge chandeliers and richly coloured drapery, and shows good technical skill, with some imaginative ingredient combinations. Classic dishes are simply presented with modern and exotic twists. Start with poached lobster with parsley aïoli, follow with rack of lamb with potato soufflé and rosemary jus, or roast veal with fennel nage and artichoke, and finish with iced green apple soufflé with spiced bread.

Chef Carsten Kypke **Owner** Marriott Hotels
Times 12-2/7.30-9.30, Closed BHs, 1-9 Jan, Closed Mon, Closed L Sat, Closed D Sun **Prices** Fixed L 2 course fr £16.50, Tasting menu £75, Starter £9-£17, Main £18.50-£27.50, Dessert fr £9, Service optional **Wines** 300 bottles over £20 **Notes** Tasting menu 7 courses, Sunday L, Dress restrictions, Smart casual, jacket preferred for men, Civ Wed 120 **Seats** 50, Pr/dining room 20
Children Min 12 yrs, Portions **Parking** 200

WELWYN | Map 6 TL21

Auberge du Lac

◉◉ French, European 🖳 ◈ NOTABLE WINE LIST

Sophisticated restaurant in fabulous location

☎ 01707 368888
Brocket Hall Estate AL8 7XG
e-mail: auberge@brocket-hall.co.uk
web: www.brocket-hall.co.uk
dir: A1(M) junct 4, B653 to Wheathampstead. In Brocket Ln take 2nd gate entry to Brocket Hall

Set in the magnificent 543-acre parkland of the stately Brocket Hall Estate, this beautifully restored, former 18th-century hunting lodge sits, as its name suggests, beside a tranquil lake - the perfect spot for sophisticated alfresco dining in the summer months. A wealth of original features include exquisite fireplaces, exposed brickwork and beams, while the airy and elegant restaurant boasts large windows and fabulous flower arrangements, presided over by an attentive serving team. The kitchen's focus is on a modern French approach, delivering well-presented dishes distinguished by tried-and-tested combinations as well as more unusual flavours. High quality produce and impressive skills shine throughout, as in caramelised hand-dived scallops with prune-rolled confit belly pork and white onion purée, or poached Kilmelford halibut with braised oxtail dumpling, roast winter root vegetables and horseradish velouté.

Chef Phil Thompson **Owner** CCA International
Times 12-3/7-10, Closed Mon, Closed D Sun **Prices** Fixed L 3 course £29.50-£55, Fixed D 3 course fr £55, Tasting menu £65, Service added but optional 10% **Wines** 750 bottles over £20, 14 by glass **Notes** Tasting menu 6 courses, Sunday L, Vegetarian available, Dress restrictions, Jackets required, no jeans or trainers, Civ Wed 60 **Seats** 70, Pr/dining room 24 **Children** Portions, Menu **Parking** 50

See advert below

The Restaurant at Tewin Bury Farm

◉ British

Fine cuisine in an impressive converted barn setting

☎ 01438 717793
AL6 0JB
e-mail: kim.correia@tewinbury.co.uk
web: www.tewinbury.co.uk
dir: on B1000

Set in the grounds of a working farm in beautiful Hertfordshire countryside, this 17th-century barn has been turned into an enchanting country-house hotel. The traditional rustic-style restaurant - classically decorated with solid oak tables and chairs, and oak beams - prepares traditional English dishes infused with Mediterranean influences, using the best of seasonal and regional produce. The food is presented simply, allowing

Continued

Auberge du Lac

A former 18th Century hunting lodge with many period features, exquisite furnishings and stunning views beyond its own peaceful riverside setting to the splendour of Brocket Hall stately home. Auberge du Lac offers immaculate service and the finest cuisine by Phil Thompson, Executive Chef.

Auberge du Lac is Hertfordshire's most acclaimed restaurant, set within the magnificent parkland of the private Brocket Hall Estate. The restaurant promises to uphold the finest culinary standards.

WELWYN *Continued*

the imaginative flavours to speak for themselves. Try the smoked duck and orange tian served with young sprouts and girolle cherry compôte to start, followed by slow confit Suffolk pork with boudin noir, or Tewin Bury Farm-caught rainbow trout with toasted fennel and mustard seed crust.

Times 12-2.30/6.30-9.30 **Prices** Food prices not confirmed for 2009. Please telephone for details.

WILLIAN **Map 12 TL23**

The Fox

Modern British

Relaxed gastro-pub in a peaceful village setting

☎ 01462 480233
SG6 2AE
e-mail: info@foxatwillian.co.uk
dir: A1M junct 9 towards Letchworth, 1st left to Willian village, The Fox is 0.5m on left

Set in a pretty village, this stylish, chic gastro-pub is sister to the popular White Horse at Brancaster Staithe in Norfolk (see entry). With original art work on soft grey walls, sage-painted woodwork, glazed atrium ceiling and fashionable furniture and table settings, the bar and restaurant have an air of contemporary comfort. The cooking is accurate with clear flavours and well executed, using carefully sourced, top quality local ingredients. For starters, take spiced fish and crab cakes with mixed leaves and saffron mayonnaise, followed by fillet of cod on a coconut and lime linguini, or The Fox Slate to share - chilli and lime squid, whitebait, smoked salmon bruschetta, chorizo, houmous, olive and spare ribs.

Chef Hari Kodagoda **Owner** Clifford Nye
Times 12-2/6.45-9.15, Closed D Sun **Prices** Starter £4.75-£8.35, Main £11.50-£18.85, Dessert £6.25, Service added but optional 10% **Wines** 33 bottles over £20, 25 bottles under £20, 14 by glass **Notes** Sunday L, Vegetarian available, Air con **Seats** 70 **Children** Portions **Parking** 40

KENT

ASHFORD **Map 7 TR04**

Eastwell Manor

English, French

Creative, classical cooking in a grand manor house setting

☎ 01233 213000
Eastwell Park, Boughton Lees TN25 4HR
e-mail: enquiries@eastwellmanor.co.uk
dir: From M20 junct 9 take 1st left (Trinity Rd). Through 4 rdbts to lights. Take left filter onto A251 signed Faversham. 0.5m to sign for Boughton Aluph, then 200yds to hotel

Dating back to the Norman Conquest, this magnificent manor-house hotel sits in 62 acres of landscaped grounds and boasts a wealth of period features, with impressive baronial fireplaces and carved-wood-panelled rooms. The high-ceilinged restaurant, with its stylish table appointments, contemporary artwork, fresh flowers and views of the garden, exudes elegance, while service is fittingly formal and professional. The creative menus offer classical cooking with a modern twist, employing top quality local and seasonal produce. The kitchen delivers well-defined, clean flavours in dishes such as dill-marinated smoked salmon with oyster beignet and citrus butter sauce, followed by cannon of lamb on crushed new potatoes with sweet bread, kidneys and broad beans. To finish, why not indulge in nougatine parfait with raspberry tuile and raspberry sorbet?

Chef Neil Wiggins **Owner** Turrloo Parrett
Times 12-2.30/7-10 **Prices** Fixed L 2 course fr £12, Fixed D 3 course fr £37.50, Service optional **Wines** 231 bottles over £20, 19 bottles under £20, 20 by glass **Notes** Tasting menu available, Vegetarian available, Dress restrictions, Jacket and tie at D, no jeans or sportswear, Civ Wed 250 **Seats** 80, Pr/dining room 80 **Children** Portions, Menu **Parking** 120

AYLESFORD **Map 6 TQ75**

Hengist Restaurant

Modern French V

Contemporary interior design and modern French cuisine in historic building

☎ 01622 719273
7-9 High St ME20 7AX
e-mail: the.hengist@btconnect.com
dir: M20 junct 5 & 6, follow signs to Aylesford village

Hengist and his brother Horsa led the invasion that landed in Aylesford in 449 AD and named themselves the first kings of Kent. An elegant contemporary interior with quirky individual touches is striking within a timbered building that dates from 1560 and retains original oak beams and stonework. The cooking takes an accomplished modern French approach and makes fine use of excellent local produce. Take braised shoulder of Romney Marsh lamb with lavender and pea risotto and lamb and mint jus, and to finish, perhaps an apple tarte Tatin with almond parfait and apricot and Szechuan pepper sauce. Private dining is available in the elegant and romantic Crystal Room or dramatic Japanese Room.

Chef R Phillips & Jean-Marc Zanetti **Owner** Richard Phillips, Paul Smith & Kevin James **Times** 12/6.30, Closed 26 Dec & 1 Jan, Closed Mon, Closed D Sun **Prices** Fixed L 2 course £6.95-£10.95, Starter £6.95-£8.95, Main £15.25-£19.25, Dessert £6.95-£16.95, Service added but optional 11% **Wines** 24 bottles over £20, 12 bottles under £20, 11 by glass **Notes** Fixed L Tue-Sun, Fixed D Tue-Thu, Sunday L, Vegetarian menu, Dress restrictions, Smart casual, Air con **Seats** 70, Pr/dining room 18 **Children** Portions **Parking** Free car park nearby

BEARSTED — Map 7 TQ85

Soufflé Restaurant

Modern European

Understated, cosy and relaxed village setting

☎ 01622 737065

31 The Green ME14 4DN

dir: Please telephone for directions

The restaurant, once the village bakery, is housed in a charming 16th-century cottage overlooking the historic village green. The front terrace is perfect for summer dining, while the interior is full of period character with exposed brickwork, low beams, timbers and an inglenook fireplace. Seated on high-backed chairs at white-clothed tables, guests tuck into classic cookery with a modern twist. Try pan-fried scallops with black pudding, parsley sauce and creamed potato or loin of venison with red onion tarte Tatin, beetroot and red wine sauce. Soufflé for pudding is a must - maybe hot pistachio with vanilla ice cream.

Soufflé Restaurant

Chef Nick Evenden **Owner** Nick & Karen Evenden **Times** 12-2.30/7-10, Closed Mon, Closed L Sat, Closed D Sun **Prices** Fixed L 2 course fr £13.50, Fixed D 3 course fr £25, Starter £7.50-£8.50, Main £17-£19, Dessert £7.50, Service added but optional 10% **Wines** 38 bottles over £20, 25 bottles under £20, 6 by glass **Notes** Sunday L, Vegetarian available **Seats** 40, Pr/dining room 23 **Children** Portions **Parking** 15

BIDDENDEN — Map 7 TQ83

The West House

 – *see below*

BRANDS HATCH — Map 6 TQ56

Brandshatch Place Hotel & Spa

Modern British V

Manor house dining near the racing circuit

☎ 01474 875000

Brands Hatch Rd, Fawkham DA3 8NQ

e-mail: brandshatchplace@handpicked.co.uk

dir: From M25/M20 follow signs for Brands Hatch Circuit onto A20. Follow signs to Paddock entrance, hotel is located on Brands Hatch Rd

A red-brick Georgian manor house, the hotel stands close to the entrance of Brands Hatch racing circuit in 12 acres of tranquil gardens. Elegant public rooms, leisure and spa facilities make this a great place to unwind after a day at the track. The dining room has a smart contemporary look with mirrors, objets d'art and gleaming glassware on linen-clothed tables. First rate ingredients are used in dishes such as escabèche of mackerel with herb salad and braised belly of Kentish pork with caramelised apple, sautéed winter vegetables

Continued

The West House

BIDDENDEN — Map 7 TQ83

Modern European

Assured modern cooking in picturesque village setting

☎ 01580 291341

28 High St TN27 8AH

e-mail: thewesthouse@btconnect.com

dir: Junct of A262 & A274. 14m S of Maidstone

At the heart of the tiny Wealden village with its charming ancient houses and shops, the family-run West House is full of character, charm and confidence. Grade II listed former weavers' cottages, it dates back to the late 1500s, so think old beams and timbers, white walls and an inglenook with log-burning stove, teamed with fashionable high-backed cream leather chairs, polished-wood tables, colourful artwork and modern floorboards. A relaxed, friendly atmosphere completes the smart but unstuffy, rustic-chic setting. Chef-patron Graham Garrett's pedigree shines through in the kitchen's confident modern approach - underpinned by a classical theme - that perfectly fits the bill here, delivering self-assured, highly accomplished, clear-flavoured and balanced dishes that 'just leave you wanting more'. The fixed-price menu offers a continually changing repertoire driven by top-notch local seasonal produce, intelligent simplicity, flair and an eye for detail. Take an eye-catching threesome of West Mersea oysters with apple jelly and horseradish crème fraîche ice cream, followed by grilled fillet of hake served with white bean, cabbage and chestnut casserole, and a warm chocolate and Kirsch pudding with sour cherry ice cream to finish.

Chef Graham Garrett **Owner** Jackie Hewitt & Graham Garrett **Times** 12-2/7-9.30, Closed 25 Dec-1 Jan, Closed Mon, Closed L Sat, Closed D Sun **Prices** Food prices not confirmed for 2009. Please telephone for details. **Wines** 46 bottles over £20, 20 bottles under £20, 6 by glass **Seats** 32 **Children** Portions **Parking** 7

BRANDS HATCH *Continued*

and cider jus, or roasted rump of South Downs lamb with sweet potato purée, roasted chestnuts and smoked bacon.

Chef Stephen Redpath **Owner** Hand Picked Hotels **Times** 12-2/7-9.30, Closed L Sat **Prices** Starter £6.50-£11, Main £16-£25, Dessert £8, Service optional **Wines** 64 bottles over £20, 2 bottles under £20, 6 by glass **Notes** Sunday L, Vegetarian menu, Civ Wed 110, Air con **Seats** 60, Pr/dining room 110 **Children** Portions, Menu **Parking** 100

Thistle Brands Hatch - Genevieve's Restaurant

◉◉ Modern British

Trackside hotel serving accomplished cuisine

☎ 0870 333 9128
DA3 8PE
e-mail: BrandsHatch@Thistle.co.uk
dir: M25 junct 3 follow signs for A20 Brands Hatch. At Brands Hatch main gates turn left off slip road

In a unique location, overlooking Brands Hatch race track, this purpose-built hotel has open-plan public areas including a choice of bars, a large lounge and an award-winning restaurant. The restaurant is classically decorated in warm, neutral shades with neatly laid, well-spaced tables. A courtyard is available for outdoor dining in summer. Seasonal local produce is used wherever possible in the creation of simply presented modern British dishes, which are based on quality ingredients. Favourites include pan-fried Orkney scallops with artichoke à la Greque, black pudding and sauce nero, and best end of Cornish lamb with provençale vegetables, boulangère potatoes and thyme jus. Friendly, professional service enhances an impressive dining experience.

Chef William Lamotte **Owner** Thistle Hotels Ltd **Times** 12.30-2.30/7-9.45 **Prices** Fixed L 2 course fr £18, Fixed D 3 course fr £23, Starter £6.50-£9, Main £16-£20, Dessert £6-£9.50, Service optional **Wines** 52 bottles over £20, 31 bottles under £20, 17 by glass **Notes** Sunday L, Vegetarian available, Dress restrictions, Smart casual, Civ Wed 120, Air con **Seats** 80, Pr/dining room 40 **Children** Portions, Menu **Parking** 180

CANTERBURY Map 7 TR15

Augustine's Restaurant

◉ Modern European

Impressive food in popular modern restaurant

☎ 01227 453063
1 & 2 Longport CT1 1PE
e-mail: info@augustinesrestaurant.co.uk
dir: Follow signs to St Augustine's Abbey, facing entrance to Abbey turn left, restaurant is ahead

An elegant Georgian townhouse with grand windows overlooking the street is the stylish setting for this intimate dining experience. Dark wood tables, high-backed chairs and subdued lighting add to the overall ambience. Traditional French and British cuisine with a European twist combine with top quality produce, organic whenever possible. The cooking has clarity of flavour with colourful, vibrant presentation. Try the creamed celeriac soup with hazelnut oil and chives to start, perhaps followed by the roasted loin of Moroccan-spiced Kentish lamb with fondant potatoes, crushed chickpeas, spinach, yogurt and red wine sauce, rounded off with the poached Kentish pear with blackberry and port compôte, almond nougatine and mascarpone ice cream.

Chef Ben Williams, Simon Corke **Owner** Nigel Willis & Lesley Stephens **Times** 12-2/6.30-9.30, Closed 2 wks Xmas, Closed Sun-Mon **Wines** 30 bottles over £20, 15 bottles under £20, 6 by glass **Notes** Pre-theatre set menu 2 or 3 courses £17/£20, Vegetarian available **Seats** 38, Pr/dining room 18 **Parking** On street & car park nearby

The Dove Inn

◉ French

A touch of French farmhouse style in deepest Kent

☎ 01227 751360
Plumpudding Ln, Dargate ME13 9HB
e-mail: nigel@thedoveinn.fsnet.co.uk
dir: 5m NW of Canterbury. Telephone for directions

This vine-clad, family-run gastro-pub has an abundance of rustic charm with log fire and oak beams combined with light décor and scrubbed wooden tables and chairs to make it cosy and inviting. The chef has a talent for producing country cooking with a strong French influence. Local gamekeepers provide much of the meat and game, which is evident in starters like terrine of wild rabbit wrapped in prosciutto served with a garnish of wild rocket and crusty sour dough toast, followed by fillet of sea bass with brown shrimp and confit of red peppers.

Times 12-2/7-9, Closed Mon, Closed D Sun, Tue

The Goods Shed

◉ British

Delicious, rustic food in converted Victorian railway shed

☎ 01227 459153
Station Road West CT2 8AN

A quirky Victorian former railway shed turned farmers' market and restaurant serving rustic, unfussy British dishes with a Mediterranean influence. Rustic reclaimed wood and exposed brickwork are abundant, complemented by simple furniture to create a warm, welcoming feel. Specials are marked on the blackboard twice daily to reflect the pick of the crop (mostly organic) from the farmers' market. Solid cooking skills are in evidence in the unfussy but imaginatively prepared dishes, accompanied by a well-chosen wine list and superb rustic bread from the market's Italian baker. A simple dish of mussels in local cider with fresh tarragon, cream and garlic might appear alongside braised mallard with pears served with kale and crispy roast potatoes, with apple cake and ice cream to finish. Booking is highly recommended.

Times 12-2.30/6-mdnt, Closed Mon, Closed D Sun

Michael Caines Abode Canterbury

◉◉ Modern British 💻

Classy modern cooking in the heart of the city

☎ 01227 766266
High St CT1 2RX
e-mail: reservationscanterbury@abodehotels.co.uk

Dating back to the 12th century, this hotel has undergone a total makeover to bring it under the Abode banner - a blossoming boutique hotel chain that delivers smart, modern and comfortable styling alongside classy food. The Michael Caines Restaurant follows the theme, its cream walls hung with modern art and smart black-and-white photos, while tables are white-linen clad and leather chairs come in cream or dark-brown. The kitchen delivers some exciting, sophisticated modern food, assured and well timed, impressing with its presentation, balanced flavours and focus on high-quality ingredients. Take line-caught sea bass with braised fennel, fennel cream and a red wine sauce, and perhaps a passionfruit soufflé finish, served with banana ice cream. There's a chef's table overlooking the kitchen, as well as a champagne bar and informal Tavern.

Times 12-2.30/7-10, Closed D Sun

The White Horse Inn

⊛ Traditional British

Sophisticated dining in country inn setting

☎ 01227 832814

High St, Bridge CT4 5LA
dir: 3m S of Canterbury on Dover road, A2 signed for Bridge

Historic inn turned upmarket gastro-pub within easy reach of Canterbury. The smart restaurant has one half traditionally styled, the other half modern and bright with doors into the garden. The list of local suppliers on the concise menu suggests a passion for quality, reflected in seasonal English traditional cooking with modern flair. Typical dishes include spiced fishcakes with sweet chilli dressing or duck pâté to start, followed by roast rack of lamb with butternut squash and lamb jus, or traditional beer-battered fish and chips, with lemon tart and raspberry coulis to finish.

Times 12-3/7-11, Closed 25 Dec, 1 Jan

CHATHAM	Map 7 TQ76

Bridgewood Manor

⊛⊛ Modern British

Fine dining in modern purpose-built hotel

☎ 01634 201333
Bridgewood Roundabout, Walderslade Woods ME5 9AX
e-mail: bridgewoodmanor@qhotels.co.uk
dir: From M2 junct 3 or M20 junct 6 follow A229 towards Chatham. At Bridgewood rdbt take 3rd exit (Walderslade). Hotel 50yds on left

There's a subtle Gothic theme to the décor at this modern, purpose-built hotel, with warm, deep colours creating an inviting ambience in the restaurant areas. Dine in the informal Terrace Bistro, or - if you're in a celebratory mood - choose the more formal Squires restaurant. Staff are smartly dressed, friendly and attentive, while the food on the reasonably-priced modern British menu, with international influences, relies on classical principles and an emphasis on quality produce, and is accurately cooked and well presented. Expect beef fillet with wild mushroom jus, or pan-fried sea bass with warm Niçoise salad and poached quails' eggs, and perhaps a chocolate fondant with raspberry sorbet to finish.

Chef Nigel Stringer **Owner** QHotels
Times 12.30-2.30/7-9.45, Closed 24-27 Dec (ex

---

residents), Closed L Sat **Prices** Food prices not confirmed for 2009. Please telephone for details. **Wines** 30 bottles over £20, 25 bottles under £20, 10 by glass **Notes** Sunday L, Dress restrictions, Smart casual, no denim or trainers, Civ Wed 150, Air con **Seats** 120, Pr/dining room 30 **Children** Portions, Menu **Parking** 170

CRANBROOK	Map 7 TQ73

Apicius

⊛⊛⊛ – see below

DARTFORD	Map 6 TQ57

Rowhill Grange - Truffles

⊛⊛⊛ – see page 202

Apicius

CRANBROOK	Map 7 TQ73

Modern European 🍽 🕮

Serious cuisine in pretty town setting

☎ 01580 714666
23 Stone St TN17 3HF
dir: In town centre, opposite Barclays Bank, 50yds from church

This small restaurant is named after a famous Roman gastronomic text, a choice which perhaps demonstrates the owners', all-encompassing passion for food. Tucked away in the narrow streets of this pretty Kent town, Apicius delivers first-class cooking in a glass-fronted, timber-clad building dating back to 1530. Low-beamed ceilings and old timbers are teamed with high-backed chairs, lightwood floorboards and crisp white tablecloths to make an intimate and relaxed setting for some truly

accomplished cuisine. In the kitchen, with a support team of one, Timothy Johnson creates dishes that are led by quality seasonal ingredients in clear-flavoured, refined and well-presented dishes that reflect high skill, meticulous workmanship and plenty of creativity. The compact, fixed-price menus take a modern approach to classic combinations at unexpectedly reasonable prices. A starter of baked mackerel fillet has succulent flesh and is served with beetroot and mozzarella and quenelles of balsamic ice cream, and a main course fillet of brill is deftly combined with roasted artichokes, Savoy cabbage, roasted tomatoes, oven-dried tomatoes and a white onion purée. Apple Tatin is a modern interpretation of a classic dish, with cider cream served in a glass and a delicate green apple sorbet accompanying the deconstructed tart. Service, led by Faith Hawkins, is personal, friendly and attentive.

Chef Timothy Johnson **Owner** Timothy Johnson, Faith Hawkins **Times** 12-2/7-9, Closed 2 wks Xmas/New Year, Etr, 2 wks summer, Closed Mon, Closed L Tue, Sat, Closed D Sun **Prices** Fixed L 2 course fr £22, Fixed D 3 course fr £31, Service added but optional 12.5% **Wines** 26 bottles over £20, 5 bottles under £20, 7 by glass **Notes** Vegetarian available **Seats** 24 **Children** Min 8 yrs **Parking** Public car park at rear premises

DEAL — Map 7 TR35

Dunkerleys Hotel

◉◉ Modern British

Fresh seafood on the seafront

☎ 01304 375016
19 Beach St CT14 7AH
e-mail: ddunkerley@btconnect.com
dir: Turn off A2 onto A258 to Deal - situated 100yds before Deal Pier

Situated in the heart of Deal, just a stone's throw from the beach, this friendly hotel has been refurbished to provide guests with even greater levels of comfort. Pre-dinner drinks are served in the small bar where you can relax on a comfy sofa before going through to dinner in the bistro-style restaurant. As you'd expect, seafood is the order of the day here, with some of the freshest produce around given simple but skilful treatment in the kitchen. The seasonal carte is complemented by a set menu. Start with local mackerel fillet with roast new season rhubarb, ginger and lime velouté, and follow with seared Scottish salmon accompanied by a fricassée of lobster and cep and puréed potato.

Times 12-2.30/7-9.30, Closed L Mon

DOVER — Map 7 TR34

Oakley & Harvey at Wallett's Court

◉◉ Modern British ✿

Creative cooking in historic manor

☎ 01304 852424
Wallett's Court, West Cliffe, St Margarets-at-Cliffe CT15 6EW
e-mail: dine@wallettscourt.com
dir: M2/A2 or M20/A20, follow signs for Deal (A258), 1st right for St Margaret's at Cliffe. Restaurant 1m on right

Set in pretty gardens in a peaceful location on the outskirts of town, this country-house hotel is based around a lovely Jacobean manor. The restaurant - a dinner-only affair - is formally laid with white linen and high-backed chairs, set to a backdrop of oak beams, inglenook fireplaces and evening candlelight. Walls are hung with original art, and there are carved pillars dating back to 1627. But there's nothing remotely historic about the cooking. The accomplished modern British repertoire - driven by a commitment to quality local seasonal produce, including ingredients from the hotel's kitchen garden - comes fashionably dotted with European influences. Try breast of pheasant with parsnip mash and a port, chestnut and cranberry jus, or fillet of Miller's 30-day matured Aberdeen Angus, served with blue cheese butter, roasted pumpkin, a bacon wafer and crushed mustard seeds.

Chef Stephen Harvey **Owner** Gavin Oakley
Times 12-2/7-9, Closed 25-26 Dec, Closed L Mon-Sat **Prices** Fixed L course £25, Fixed D 3 course £40, Service added but optional 10% **Wines** 60 bottles over £20, 20 bottles under £20, 17 by glass **Notes** Sunday L, Vegetarian available **Seats** 60, Pr/dining room 40 **Children** Portions, Menu **Parking** 50

EDENBRIDGE — Map 6 TQ44

Haxted Mill & Riverside Brasserie

◉ Modern British ▣ ✿

Quality ingredients and classic-inspired cooking in rustic, riverside setting

☎ 01732 862914
Haxted Rd TN8 6PU
e-mail: david@haxtedmill.co.uk
dir: M25 junct 6, A22 towards East Grinstead. Through Blindley Heath and after Texaco garage left at lights, 1m take 1st left after Red Barn PH. 2m to Haxted Mill

A working watermill in a tranquil setting with a country-style restaurant in the 500-year-old converted stables.

Rowhill Grange - Truffles

DARTFORD — Map 6 TQ57

Modern European ▣ V

Classy country setting for a formal conservatory restaurant

☎ 01322 615136
Rowhill Grange Hotel & Spa DA2 7QH
e-mail: admin@rowhillgrange.com
dir: M25 junct 3, take B2173 towards Swanley, then B258 towards Hextable. Straight on at 3 rdbts. Hotel 1.5m on left

Set amid 9 acres of mature woodland, complete with a lake and Victorian walled garden, this 19th-century country house enjoys a tranquil setting with views over the Kent countryside. The main culinary attraction here is the refurbished Truffles Restaurant, which boasts its own Victorian conservatory with views across the gardens. Alternatively, make the most of the idyllic setting and dine out on the terrace when weather permits. Truffles is stylishly furnished with a relaxed, unimposing atmosphere and minimalist, modern-chic style complete with high-backed leather chairs and crisp linen, and it's especially romantic at night with subdued lighting and candles. Service is appropriately relaxed yet professional, while the accomplished kitchen's ambitious international and modern European cooking comes driven by quality seasonal produce in well-executed, cleverly presented dishes of clean, clear flavours. Take guinea fowl (poached breast and roasted leg) served with celeriac purée and Puy lentils, and to finish, perhaps a hot chocolate fondant teamed with cumin caramel and gingerbread ice cream. (A modern range of lighter, bistro-style dishes is available in the hotel's more casual Elements brasserie.)

Chef Richard Cameron **Owner** Utopia Leisure
Times 12-2.30/7-9.30, Closed L Sat **Prices** Tasting menu £50, Starter £8-£11, Main £19-£25, Dessert £8, Service added but optional 12.5% **Wines** 38 bottles over £20, 11 bottles under £20, 12 by glass **Notes** Sunday L, Vegetarian menu, Dress restrictions, No shorts, T-shirts, trainers, Civ Wed 120, Air con **Seats** 90, Pr/dining room 160 **Children** Min 16 yrs D, Menu **Parking** 200

The millstream races beneath the windows of the ground-floor bar and the beamed upstairs restaurant features photos and angling memorabilia, while a terrace overlooks the millpond, ideal for summer dining. An evolving list of mainly fish and game dishes is offered from a carte of classically-inspired modern cooking; the emphasis is on quality ingredients, sympathetic handling and unfussy presentation. Take roast venison loin with game sauce, casserole of mixed fish with Jerusalem artichokes, or roast duck with a rich Bigarade sauce.

Haxted Mill & Riverside Brasserie

Chef David Peek, Olivier Betremieux **Owner** David & Linda Peek **Times** 12-2/7-9, Closed 23 Dec-6 Jan, Closed Mon, Closed D Sun **Prices** Fixed L 2 course £16.95, Fixed D 3 course £27.95, Starter £5.95-£13.95, Main £10.95-£25, Dessert £6, Service added but optional 10% **Wines** 45 bottles over £20, 9 bottles under £20, 6 by glass **Notes** Sunday L, Vegetarian available, Dress restrictions, Smart casual **Seats** 52 **Parking** 100

FAVERSHAM   Map 7 TR06

Read's Restaurant

❀❀❀ — **see below**

LENHAM   Map 7 TQ85

Chilston Park Hotel

❀❀ Modern British

Stylish cooking in splendid Georgian mansion

☎ 01622 859803

Sandway ME17 2BE

e-mail: chilstonpark@handpicked.co.uk

dir: Telephone for directions.

This elegant Georgian country house is set in acres of immaculately landscaped gardens and parkland and dates back to at least 1100. An impressive collection of paintings and antiques creates a unique environment and the sunken Venetian-style restaurant boasts a grand fireplace and elegant crystal chandeliers. Expect careful use of top quality ingredients and clarity of flavour, with many interesting and unusual combinations to choose from. The French influenced modern British menu also offers thoughtful wine recommendations for many of the dishes. Try ham hock ravioli, parsley velouté and smoked leeks to start, perhaps followed by aged Scotch beef fillet, beef and mushroom pudding and port jus, with pecan soufflé with maple syrup and honeycomb ice cream to finish.

Chef Gareth Brown **Owner** Hand Picked Hotels **Times** 12-1.30/7-9.30, Closed L Sat **Prices** Fixed L 2 course £11-£14, Fixed D 3 course £29-£39, Starter £5-£7.50, Main £19-£28, Dessert £5.50-£7.50, Service added but optional **Wines** 90 bottles over £20, 1 bottle under £20, 6 by glass **Notes** Sunday L, Vegetarian available, Dress restrictions, Smart casual, Civ Wed 90 **Seats** 54, Pr/dining room 8 **Children** Portions, Menu **Parking** 100

Read's Restaurant

FAVERSHAM   Map 7 TR06

Modern British 🏆

Distinctive cuisine in an elegant Georgian manor house

☎ 01795 535344

Macknade Manor, Canterbury Rd ME13 8XE

e-mail: enquiries@reads.com

dir: From M2 junct 6 follow A251 towards Faversham. At T-junct with A2 (Canterbury road) turn right. Hotel 0.5m on right

Set in an elegant Georgian manor house, surrounded by 4 acres of tranquil gardens and grounds and its own walled kitchen garden, Read's Restaurant (with rooms) boasts six individually designed bedrooms tastefully furnished in period style, complemented by an elegant drawing room and the grand, spacious restaurant. Here you will find distinctive cooking of passion and simplicity using home-grown herbs and vegetables in dishes that make fine use of local game and fish fresh from the quayside at nearby Whitstable and Hythe. Modern British cuisine is the order of the day, with dinner a grander affair than lunch. The menu offers an impressive choice of dishes with detailed descriptions and little gems of quotations to accompany them, like the immortal words of Miss Piggy ... 'Never eat more than you can lift'. With that in mind, you could try the seven-course tasting menu, or order from the appealing carte. Expect the likes of hot mature Montgomery cheddar soufflé set on glazed smoked haddock in cream sauce, or fillet of Scottish beef with sweetheart cabbage, roasted salsify and shallot jus, while white peach soufflé with vanilla ice cream, raspberry coulis and home-made shortbread might feature at dessert. The equally accomplished wine list has an extensive choice (over 250 wines) with many heavyweights and a good selection by the glass, too.

Chef David Pitchford & Ricky Martin **Owner** David & Rona Pitchford **Times** 12-2.30/7-10, Closed BHs, Closed Sun, Mon **Prices** Fixed L 3 course fr £24, Tasting menu £52, Main £52, Service optional **Wines** 250 bottles over £20, 12 bottles under £20 **Notes** ALC 3 courses, Tasting menu 7 courses, Vegetarian available, Dress restrictions, Smart casual, Civ Wed 60 **Seats** 40, Pr/dining room 30 **Children** Portions **Parking** 30

ROCHESTER Map 6 TQ76

Topes Restaurant

◉◉ Modern British

Creative modern cooking in an historic building

☎ 01634 845270
60 High St ME1 1JY
e-mail: julie.small@btconnect.com
dir: M2 junct 1, through Strood High Street over Medway
Bridge, turn right at Northgate onto Rochester High Street

Just a couple of minutes away from the cathedral, this
part-boarded building has additions from the 16th and
17th centuries added on to the 15th century original.
There is a lot of history in Rochester and this house
featured in Charles Dickens' novel The Mystery of Edwin
Drood. The 21st-century incarnation has kept much of the
character of the building, including wooden beams and a
narrow staircase leading to the kitchen and a further
dining room, while updating the rooms with sensitivity.
The seasonally-changing menu is bolstered by daily
specials and there is good use of local and regional
produce on the modern British menu. Crab, brown shrimp
and mussel risotto is abundant with shellfish in an
impressive starter, and main-course pot-roasted Norfolk
pheasant delivers good gamey flavour and sits on chunky
root vegetables, roasted to perfection, and the addition of
chopped chorizo on the Savoy cabbage shows a creative
kitchen on the up. Service is as charming as the venue
itself and there is a terrace for alfresco dining.

Chef Chris Small **Owner** Chris and Julie Small
Times 12-2.30/6.30-9, Closed 1 wk Jan, Closed Mon-Tue,
Closed D Sun **Prices** Fixed L 2 course £13.50-£17.50, Fixed
D 3 course £17.50, Starter £6, Main £15, Dessert £5.50,
Service optional **Wines** 15 bottles over £20, 25 bottles
under £20, 6 by glass **Notes** Sunday L **Seats** 55, Pr/dining
room 16 **Children** Portions, Menu **Parking** Public car park

SEVENOAKS Map 6 TQ55

Greggs Restaurant

◉◉ Modern British, European

Popular high street restaurant with hands-on owners

☎ 01732 456373
28-30 High St TN13 1HX
dir: 1m from Sevenoaks train station. 500yds from top of
town centre towards Tonbridge on left

Greggs is a distinctive Grade II listed property, with a
triple-bay window frontage and black-and-white

paintwork, located at the top of town near the entrance to
the National Trust's Knole House. Inside, the original
features of the 16th-century building - dark wood beams
and timbers - set off light floors, high-backed black
leather chairs and white tablecloths. The kitchen takes a
modern approach with imaginative dishes skilfully cooked
and creatively presented. Good examples include slow
cooked duck leg, smoked duck spring roll and sesame
seed brittle, and roasted halibut with parmesan mash,
spiced cauliflower and pancetta. Finish with roasted
pineapple five spice with passionfruit and coconut cream
and liquorice caramel.

Chef Andrew Wilson **Owner** Gavin & Lucinda Gregg
Times 12-2/6.30-9.30, Closed Mon, Closed D Sun
Prices Fixed L 2 course £14-£17, Fixed D 3 course
£22.50-£25, Tasting menu £42.50-£55, Starter £6-£9,
Main £15-£22, Dessert £7-£10.50, Service added 10%
Wines 34 bottles over £20, 16 bottles under £20, 9 by
glass **Notes** Tasting menu 7 courses Fri-Sat evenings,
Sunday L, Vegetarian available, Air con **Seats** 50, Pr/
dining room 32 **Children** Portions **Parking** Town centre

SISSINGHURST Map 7 TQ73

Rankins

◉ Modern British

Bistro-style cuisine in rustic surroundings

☎ 01580 713964
The Street TN17 2JH
e-mail: rankins@btconnect.com
dir: Village centre, on A262

This intimate restaurant is housed in a timber-framed
building dating from 1898, which has in its time been a
saddler's and general store. The beamed interior has
the feel of a cottage, but with well-spaced tables. The
British bistro-style cooking places an emphasis on
quality ingredients and simple but attractive
presentation. Try Rankins' smokie - a pot of naturally
smoked haddock baked in a creamy lemon sauce with
cheddar glaze to start, followed by pan-fried lamb
noisettes with cauliflower and garlic cream and
rosemary gravy. Finish with golden syrup lemon sponge
with vanilla ice cream.

Chef Hugh Rankin **Owner** Hugh & Leonora Rankin
Times 12.30-2/7.30-9, Closed BHs, Closed Mon, Tue,
Closed L Wed-Sat, Closed D Sun **Prices** Fixed L 2 course
£23.50, Fixed D 3 course £32.50, Service optional
Wines 17 bottles over £20, 11 bottles under £20, 2 by
glass **Notes** Sunday L, Vegetarian available, Dress
restrictions, Smart casual minimum **Seats** 25
Children Portions **Parking** On street

SITTINGBOURNE Map 7 TQ96

Lakes Restaurant

◉ British, French

Conservatory restaurant serving imaginative cuisine

☎ 01795 428020
**Hempstead House Country Hotel, London Rd, Bapchild
ME9 9PP**
e-mail: lakes@hempsteadhouse.co.uk
dir: On A2 1.5m E of Sittingbourne

Built in 1850 by Robert Lake, Hempstead House is a
charming, traditional country hotel set in 4 acres of
landscaped grounds. Fine dining is offered in the tastefully
furnished Lakes Restaurant and the relaxed atmosphere of
an elegant conservatory extension. Cooking is ambitious,
with interesting ideas skilfully executed on a British menu
with French influences. The quality produce is full of flavour
in dishes such as pork, apricot and pistachio terrine with
piccalilli, followed by rabbit loin with cider sauce, and
chocolate truffle tart with Horlicks ice cream.

Chef John Cosgrove, Liam McClay **Owner** Mr & Mrs A J
Holdstock **Times** 12-2.30/7-10, Closed D Sun to non
residents **Prices** Fixed L 2 course fr £12.50, Fixed D 3
course fr £24.50, Starter £5.50-£6.50, Main £14.75-£21,
Dessert £6.50-£7.50, Service optional **Wines** 30 bottles
over £20, 25 bottles under £20, 4 by glass **Notes** Sunday
L, Vegetarian available, Dress restrictions, Smart casual,
Civ Wed 150 **Seats** 70, Pr/dining room 30
Children Portions **Parking** 100

TUNBRIDGE WELLS (ROYAL) Map 6 TQ53

Hotel du Vin & Bistro

◉ British, French 💻 ⌖

Elegant bistro in stylish townhouse

☎ 01892 526455
Crescent Rd TN1 2LY
e-mail: reception.tunbridgewells@hotelduvin.com
web: www.hotelduvin.com
dir: Please telephone for directions

This imposing 18th-century building has been transformed
into a contemporary boutique hotel by the hugely respected
Hotel du Vin chain, with stylish, comfortable
accommodation and a tastefully designed bar and bistro.
The latter draws discerning diners with its inspired
contemporary menu, which successfully balances modern
dishes with simple classics. Using the very best, carefully

Continued on page 206

Thackeray's

Modern French 🖥 V ⚑ NOTABLE WINE LIST

Inventive, contemporary cuisine in chic surroundings

☎ 01892 511921
85 London Road TN1 1EA
e-mail: reservations@
thackeraysrestaurant.co.uk
web: www.thackerays-restaurant.co.uk
dir: A21/A26, towards Tunbridge Wells.
On left 500yds after the Kent & Sussex Hospital

This fashionable restaurant occupies celebrated novelist William Makepeace Thackeray's former home, a wide-fronted property that has the distinction of being the oldest building in Tunbridge Wells and comes covered in original, whitewashed Kent peg tiles. The stylish interior combines period architecture with modern touches such as chocolate suede banquettes, cream tub chairs, wooden floors and glass panels. There's also a Japanese terrace for alfresco dining, and a choice of chic candlelit bars, as well as a private dining area with deep red leather-textured walls and a table decorated with old-fashioned fish bowls (complete with goldfish). Service is formal and attentive but delivered in a friendly and relaxed style. The kitchen's modern approach - underpinned by a classical theme - sits perfectly with its sleek surroundings and exudes confidence

and ambition. High quality luxury ingredients (with an ethos for sourcing local produce), modern presentation (with food a work of art on stylish plates), flair, precision, high technical skill and flavour all deliver on a repertoire of value fixed-price lunch and dinner menus, plus tasting option and an enticing carte. Take medallions of roasted monkfish served with cured ham, butternut squash and sage risotto and spiced red wine dressing, while an assiette of mango and passionfruit (mango delice, passionfruit Bellini, mango and mascarpone terrine, mango Pavlova and a tropical fruit sorbet) might catch the eye at dessert.

Chef Richard Phillips, Christopher Bower **Owner** Richard Phillips
Times 12-2.30/6.30-10.30, Closed Mon, Closed D Sun **Prices** Fixed L 2 course fr £15.95, Fixed D 3 course fr £28.50, Tasting menu £58-£88, Service included **Wines** 160 bottles over £20, 8 bottles under £20, 21 by glass **Notes** Sunday L, Vegetarian menu, Air con **Seats** 54, Pr/dining room 16 **Children** Portions **Parking** NCP, on street in evening

TUNBRIDGE WELLS (ROYAL) *Continued*

selected local produce, you might begin with potted shrimps with balsamic croûton or salmon and haddock fishcake with chilli butter, and then move on to pot-roasted guinea fowl with herb mash, or confit pork belly with cabbage fondue and caramelised apple jus. Desserts take in a classic apple tarte Tatin with clotted cream and a more ambitious thyme mousse with roasted plums. Excellent wine list.

Chef Paul Nixon **Owner** Hotel du Vin Ltd **Times** 12-2/7-10.30, Closed L 31 Dec **Prices** Fixed L 2 course fr £15.50, Starter £4.50-£7.25, Main £10.50-£18.75, Dessert £6.75-£8.75, Service added but optional 10% **Wines** 700 bottles over £20, 50 bottles under £20, 16 by glass **Notes** Pre-theatre meal offer on selected nights, Sunday L, Vegetarian available, Civ Wed 84 **Seats** 80, Pr/dining room 84 **Children** Portions, Menu **Parking** 30; NCP

The Spa Hotel

◉ Modern, Traditional British ◐

Enjoyable dining in a grand setting

☎ 01892 520331
Mount Ephraim TN4 8XJ
e-mail: info@spahotel.co.uk
web: www.spahotel.co.uk
dir: On A264 leaving Tunbridge Wells towards East Grinstead

Set in 14 acres of picturesque grounds, this imposing 18th-century country-house hotel has undergone an

impressive refurbishment. The Chandelier Restaurant offers an elegant dining experience, with high ceilings, stunning chandeliers, ornate flower arrangements and quality tableware the order of the day, complemented by suitably formal table service. The menu offers a range of modern British dishes utilising traditional techniques and seasonal local produce. Try the roasted Jerusalem artichoke and truffle soup to start, perhaps followed by roasted South Downs lamb rack, stuffed with mild capers and onions, or locally-reared pheasant en crepinette with Mediterranean vegetables and rosemary potato cake.

Chef Steve Cole **Owner** Scragg Hotels Ltd **Times** 12.30-2/7-9.30, Closed L Sat **Prices** Fixed L 2 course £13-£15, Fixed D 3 course £29.50-£35.50, Starter £5.50-£12, Main £14.50-£20, Dessert £5.50-£7.50, Service included **Wines** 69 bottles over £20, 29 bottles under £20, 8 by glass **Notes** Sunday L, Vegetarian available, Dress restrictions, Smart casual, No jeans or T-shirts, Civ Wed 200 **Seats** 80, Pr/dining room 200 **Children** Portions, Menu **Parking** 140

Thackeray's

◉◉◉ – *see page 205*

WESTERHAM **Map 6 TQ45**

Rendezvous Café

◉ French, Mediterranean ◐

Popular modern brasserie serving French cuisine

☎ 01959 561408 & 561387
26 Market Square TN16 1AR
e-mail: info@rendezvous-brasserie.co.uk
web: www.rendezvous-brasserie.co.uk
dir: M25 junct 5 towards Westerham. M25 junct 6 take A22, then A25 towards Oxted/Westerham

This stylish high-street brasserie is a great place to people-watch. The décor is modern with muted colours, while service is attentive and knowledgeable. Grab a

table near the huge front windows, choose from the extensive all-day menu, and then sit back and let village life unfold in front of you. The cuisine is largely French and uses a combination of freshly imported French and local produce. Quail stuffed with foie gras and grapes makes a decadent starter, with best end of lamb to follow, served with an olive crust, aubergine caviar and provençale ratatouille, or perhaps calves' liver with sage mash, mange-tout and Lyonnaise sauce.

Rendezvous Café

Chef A Mourdi **Owner** A Mourdi, Mr Chaib-Doukkali, Mr Otman **Times** 8.30am-10 **Prices** Fixed L 2 course £11.50-£14.50, Fixed D 3 course £14.50-£18.50, Starter £5.75-£8.95, Main £8.95-£17.95, Dessert £4.50-£5.50, Service added but optional 10% **Wines** 20 bottles over £20, 20 bottles under £20, 13 by glass **Notes** Sunday L, Vegetarian available, Dress restrictions, Smart casual, Air con **Seats** 50 **Children** Portions, Menu **Parking** 25 spaces available evenings & wknds

See advert below

WEST MALLING   Map 6 TQ65

The Swan

⊚ Traditional British ☙

Brasserie cooking in the lively setting of a transformed pub

☎ 01732 521910
35 Swan St ME19 6JU
e-mail: info@theswanwestmalling.co.uk
dir: M20 junct 4 follow signs for West Malling

At this radically converted 15th-century coaching inn, wood, granite and stainless steel are softened by neutral tones, banquette seating, modern artwork and mirrors. Lively and vibrant, The Swan trades over three floors, including two steak bars and three private dining rooms. There is also a paved and shaded terrace outdoors. British classics are prepared from quality ingredients supplied by local farms and growers. These include Scottish loin of venison with cauliflower purée, roast port onions and red cabbage, and roast cod with Kent Down mushrooms and braised chicory. Swan About provides an outside catering service.

Chef S Goss **Owner** Fishbone Ltd **Times** 12-2.45/6-10.45, Closed 26 Dec, 1 Jan, Closed L 27 Dec, 2 Jan **Prices** Starter £5-£8, Main £11-£17, Dessert £5-£9, Service added but optional 12.5% **Wines** 57 bottles over £20, 10 bottles under £20, 12 by glass **Notes** Sunday L, Vegetarian available, Dress restrictions, Smart dress, Civ Wed 100, Air con **Seats** 90, Pr/dining room 20 **Children** Portions, Menu **Parking** Long-stay car park

WHITSTABLE   Map 7 TR16

Crab & Winkle Seafood Restaurant

⊚ British Seafood ☐ ☙

Buzzy harbour restaurant serving the freshest of fish

☎ 01227 779377
South Quay, The Harbour CT5 1AB
e-mail: info@seafood-restaurant-uk.com
web: www.seafood-restaurant-uk.com
dir: Please telephone for directions

This popular modern restaurant has a light-and-airy feel, and is ideally situated above the town's fish market on the quay overlooking the harbour. Fittingly, it's decked out with maritime art, complemented by polished lightwood tables and chairs. In summer the decked balcony is a great place for alfresco dining, while on less clement days the views of the harbour and fishing fleet

more than compensate. Not surprisingly given its location, the daily-changing modern menus come awash with fish and seafood, straight from the boats and simply cooked. Take steamed oak-smoked haddock, served with root vegetable rösti, warm leek and wild mushroom salad with grain mustard cream, or shellfish (scallops, mussels, oysters, crevettes and cockles), red onion, fennel and saffron broth with lemon mash.

Chef Ben Walton **Owner** Andrew & Victoria Bennett **Times** 11.30-9.30, Closed 25 Dec, Closed D 26 Dec, 1 Jan **Prices** Fixed L 2 course £14.50, Fixed D 3 course fr £25, Starter £6-£10, Main £10-£26, Dessert £5-£9, Service added but optional 12.5%, Groups min 8 service 12.5% **Wines** 12 bottles over £20, 25 bottles under £20, 10 by glass **Notes** Vegetarian available, Air con **Seats** 72 **Children** Portions **Parking** Gorrel Tank Car Park

The Sportsman

⊚⊚ Modern British ☙

Passionate cooking in unpretentious surroundings

☎ 01227 273370
Faversham Rd, Seasalter CT5 4BP
dir: 3.5m W of Whitstable

Situated along the old coastal road from Seasalter to Faversham, The Sportsman is a culinary haven situated in an area of unique food production - land, estuary and sea. Stripped wooden floorboards, reclaimed timber tables and local art provide the low-key, shabby-chic setting for some fabulous food conjured from the finest ingredients, delivered on the day from nearby farms. The chef makes his own fleur de sel (sea salt) from the marshes and cures his own hams. Try the eight-course tasting menu to really get the measure of the place and sample the likes of pigeon risotto, braised brill with deep-fried oyster and Avruga caviar sauce, roast Seasalter marsh lamb, and warm chocolate mousse with salted caramel and soured ice cream.

Chef Stephen Harris **Owner** Stephen & Philip Harris **Times** 12-2/7-9, Closed 25-26 Dec, Closed Mon, Closed D Sun **Prices** Tasting menu £55, Starter £5.95-£9.95, Main £13.95-£19.95, Dessert £5.95, Service optional, Groups min 6 service 10% **Wines** 21 bottles over £20, 30 bottles under £20, 7 by glass **Notes** Sunday L, Vegetarian available, Air con **Seats** 60 **Children** Portions **Parking** 20

LANCASHIRE

ACCRINGTON   Map 18 SD72

Mercure Dunkenhalgh Hotel & Spa

⊚ British, International

Traditional hotel dining in splendid surroundings

☎ 01254 398021
Blackburn Rd, Clayton-le-Moors BB5 5JP
e-mail: H6617@accor.com

This impressive, castellated mansion dates back 700 years and is set in 17 acres of delightful, well-tended grounds. The hotel has excellent conference facilities and

is very popular for weddings. The attractive, elegant Cameo Restaurant has recently undergone refurbishment and is a charming place to enjoy the British food with international influences on offer. An excellent selection of breads kicks things off, and you could start with smoked mackerel rillette, garnished with cockles, perhaps, followed by sautéed lamb cutlets served on a bed of haggis mash. Finish with vanilla crème brûlée.

Times 7-9.30 **Prices** Food prices not confirmed for 2009. Please telephone for details.

BARTON   Map 18 SD53

Healey's @ Barton Grange Hotel

⊚ Modern ☙

Stylish hotel restaurant offering innovative modern British and European dishes

☎ 01772 862551
Garstang Rd PR3 5AA
e-mail: stay@bartongrangehotel.com
dir: M6 junct 32, travel N A6 Garstang. Barton Grange is 2.5m on right

Built in 1900 as a country residence, this stylish modern hotel has much to offer, including an award-winning garden centre and leisure facilities. The Walled Garden restaurant is open for all-day eating, while Healey's restaurant has a lively, cosmopolitan feel, with a seasonally-changing menu based firmly on local produce. Dishes are full of imagination and creative flair as in cod and king prawn cannelloni with braised chicory and fish sauce, and Lancastrian rack of lamb with lamb and chilli sausage, kale, tomato and black olive tapenade and corned beef fritter. To finish, you might try chocolate tart with parsnip ice cream and white chocolate mascarpone.

Chef Andrew Nash, John Riding **Owner** The Topping Family **Times** Closed 25 Dec- 2 Jan, Closed Sun-Mon, Closed L all week **Prices** Fixed D 3 course £20-£29, Tasting menu £39, Starter £5.95-£7.50, Main £14.95-£21.95, Dessert £5.95-£7.95, Service optional **Wines** 12 bottles over £20, 19 bottles under £20 **Notes** Tasting menu 6 courses, Vegetarian available, Dress restrictions, No jeans or T-shirts, Civ Wed 300, Air con **Seats** 35, Pr/dining room 20 **Children** Min 11 yrs **Parking** 240

Northcote Manor

LANGHO	Map 18 SD73

Modern British V NOTABLE WINE LIST

A powerhouse of regional British gastronomy

☎ 01254 240555
Northcote Rd BB6 8BE
e-mail: sales@northcotemanor.com
web: www.northcotemanor.com
dir: M6 junct 31 take A59, follow signs for Clitheroe. Left at 1st traffic light, onto Skipton/Clitheroe Rd for 9m. Left into Northcote Rd, hotel on right

Built in the 1870s for a wealthy Victorian textile mill owner, today Northcote Manor is a gastronomic haven that continues to go from strength to strength, its famous kitchen twice producing the Young Chef of the Year. Contemporary in style with a modern minimalist feel, high quality lighting and eye-catching local modern art, the restaurant is a light-and-airy, spacious affair with a conservatory front that enjoys excellent views of chef-patron Nigel Haworth's organic garden and the distant hills of the Ribble Valley through its bay windows. Crisp white linen, a wine list of some 450 bins and service with a formal air of professionalism all play their part at this foodie destination. Nigel creates an enticing repertoire which has its roots firmly in Lancashire, making the most of the North West's abundant local larder to create dishes of true terroir. The cooking is

intelligently simple and exudes high technique. Roast halibut with Shorrocks cheese fondue, tempura cauliflower and bacon makes a fine starter, followed by a superb main course of breast of corn-fed Goosnargh chicken with Périgord truffles, Jerusalem artichoke, puréed spinach and white leek fritter.

Chef Nigel Haworth/Lisa Allen
Owner Nigel Haworth, Craig Bancroft
Times 12-2/7-9.30, Closed 25 Dec, 1 Jan **Wines** 285 bottles over £20, 22 bottles under £20, 6 by glass
Notes Fixed D 5 courses £50, Sunday L, Vegetarian menu, Dress restrictions, No jeans, Civ Wed 40 **Seats** 80, Pr/dining room 40 **Children** Portions, Menu
Parking 60

BLACKBURN
Map 18 SD62

The Millstone at Mellor

@@ Modern British

Classic fare in a traditional setting

☎ 01254 813333
Church Ln, Mellor BB2 7JR
e-mail: info@millstonehotel.co.uk
dir: 4m from M6 junct 31 follow signs for Blackburn.
Mellor is on right 1m after 1st set of lights

The Millstone is a former coaching inn that has retained
all its charm and character. Along with a traditional bar,
its sensitively refurbished, elegant restaurant boasts
wood-panelled walls, a beamed ceiling, an antique
grandfather clock and framed prints of the countryside;
setting the scene for tables adorned with white linen,
quality glassware and fresh flowers. The wide-ranging
menu is served in both the bar and the restaurant.
Classic dishes are presented in a simple, straightforward
manner, utilising the best local, seasonal ingredients.
Typical starters feature king prawn, anchovy and scampi
tail fritters, pea purée and parsley sauce, followed by a
main course of grilled sirloin of Bowland beef,
horseradish mash, baby Yorkshire pudding and roast root
vegetables. Leave room for dessert, such as cinder toffee
cheesecake with ginger biscuit crumb.

Chef Anson Bolton **Owner** Shire Hotels Ltd
Times 12-2.15/6.30-9.30 **Prices** Fixed D 3 course £29.95,
Starter £3.50-£7.50, Main £12.95-£18.95, Dessert
£4.95-£5.95 **Wines** 55 bottles over £20, 30 bottles under
£20, 8 by glass **Notes** Sunday L, Vegetarian available,
Dress restrictions, Smart casual, Civ Wed 60 **Seats** 62,
Pr/dining room 20 **Children** Portions, Menu **Parking** 45;
also on street

BLACKPOOL
Map 18 SD33

Kwizeen

@ Modern

**Serious cooking in an area normally renowned for its
fast food**

☎ 01253 290045
47-49 Kings St FY1 3EJ
e-mail: info@kwizeen.co.uk
web: www.kwizeenrestaurant.co.uk
dir: From front of Blackpool Winter Gardens, 100yds to
King St, and as road forks restaurant 30yds on left

The oriental façade of this chic modern restaurant looks
right at home amid the joke shops, pubs, nightclubs and

kitsch close to the famous Tower, but the exterior belies
the cool, contemporary, minimalist décor of the interior
with its wood floors, chrome furniture and subtle lighting.
The appealing, good-value menus take an equally
modern approach, using fresh local produce: think
Pugh's suckling pig, chicken tournedos and fondant
potatoes, or perhaps Lancashire lamb fillet, wild
mushroom risotto and parsnip crisps. For dessert, try
farmhouse blueberry and apple pie with vanilla bean
custard.

Chef Marco Calle-Calatayud **Owner** Marco Calle-
Calatayud, Antony Beswick **Times** 12-1.45/6, Closed 21
Feb-10 Mar, last wk Aug, Closed Sun, Closed L Sat
Prices Fixed L 2 course fr £8.50, Fixed D 3 course fr
£15.95, Starter £5.50-£7.50, Main £13-£15.95, Dessert
£4.95-£10, Service included **Wines** 6 by glass
Notes Dress restrictions, Smart casual **Seats** 40
Parking On street

GARSTANG
Map 18 SD44

Crofters Hotel & Tavern

@ British

Imaginative cooking in hotel brasserie

☎ 01995 604128
New Rd, A6 Cabus PR3 1PH

An attractive hotel on the edge of the charming market
town of Garstang, the Crofters commands an impressive
roadside position. Inside, the popular refurbished
brasserie has an attractive, well-coordinated modern
style, with the cooking befitting the surroundings and
offering a choice of imaginatively presented dishes with
the emphasis on local seasonal ingredients. Think roast
loin of Cumbrian lamb served with boulangère potatoes
and a rosemary-infused jus, while a baked strawberry
crème brûlée - accompanied by shortbread and ice cream
- might catch the eye at dessert.

Times noon-9.30 **Prices** Food prices not confirmed for
2009. Please telephone for details.

LANCASTER
Map 18 SD46

Lancaster House Hotel

@ Traditional British

Smart hotel restaurant offering local produce

☎ 01524 844822
Green Ln, Ellel LA1 4GJ
e-mail: lancaster@elhmail.co.uk
dir: 3m from Lancaster city centre. From S M6 junct 33,
head towards Lancaster. Continue through Galgate
village, and turn left up Green Ln just before Lancaster
University

The restaurant at this modern country-house hotel has
been recently refurbished and now has a smart new décor
to go with its new name: The Foodworks. The interior
combines dark wood with an easy-on-the-eye colour
scheme of beige, brown and cream, while influences of
Lancashire are evident in an outline mural of working

men. A new chef has introduced a more pared-down
modern cooking style and sets stock by his Lancashire
roots, sourcing ingredients locally where possible and
dotting the menu with regional favourites such as home-
made black pudding with caramelised apple and
mustard, or lamb hotpot with carrot and swede
dauphinoise and pickled red cabbage.

Chef Alistair Tasker **Owner** English Lakes Hotels
Times 12.30-3/7-9.30 **Prices** Fixed L 2 course £11.25,
Starter £4.25-£6.95, Main £10.25-£17.95, Dessert
£1.95-£5.95, Service optional **Wines** 45 bottles over £20,
35 bottles under £20, 12 by glass **Notes** Special occasion
menus throughout the year, Sunday L, Vegetarian
available, Dress restrictions, Smart casual, no jeans or
sportswear, Civ Wed 100, Air con **Seats** 95, Pr/dining
room 190 **Children** Portions, Menu **Parking** 140

LANGHO
Map 18 SD73

Northcote Manor

@@@ – see opposite

LONGRIDGE
Map 18 SD63

The Longridge Restaurant

@@@ – see page 210

LYTHAM ST ANNES
Map 18 SD32

Chicory

@ Modern International

Eclectic cooking in a lively ambience

☎ 01253 737111
5 Henry St FY8 5LE
web: www.chicorygroup.co.uk
dir: In town centre, behind Clifton Arms Hotel

This contemporary restaurant and cocktail bar was
renovated in November 2007 and the comfortable and
cosy interior boasts brown leather armchairs and suede
banquettes, with local artists' work displayed on the
walls. Well-drilled staff serve dishes from a generous,
eclectic menu, where dishes like classic Caesar salad sit
alongside duck wontons with lemongrass, chilli and
ginger broth. Among the main courses, a roast venison
loin with beetroot and barley risotto vies for attention
with tagine of monkfish and lobster with light chilli
tabbouleh. Finish with dark chocolate and rum fondant
with hazelnut ice cream.

Continued

The Longridge Restaurant

LONGRIDGE   Map 18 SD63

Modern British 🖳

Chic setting for first-rate British cuisine

☎ 01772 784969
104-106 Higher Rd PR3 3SY
e-mail: longridge@heathcotes.co.uk
web: www.heathcotes.co.uk/collection/
longridge/index.php
dir: Follow signs for Golf Club & Jeffrey
Hill. Higher Rd is beside White Bull Pub
in Longridge

An illicit drinking venue in the 1880s
and then a cyclists' café and Indian
restaurant in more recent times, this
chic eatery is now the flagship of Paul
Heathcote's culinary empire. A lounge
- with soft pale grey walls, silver framed
pictures and a glass cabinet displaying
awards and cookbooks - leads the way
to the interconnected dining areas with
light grey décor and tablecloths and
crisp white linen slip cloths, while
discreet windows onto the kitchen let
diners in on all the culinary action. Its
brigade consistently impresses,
handling high-quality ingredients with
confident simplicity to deliver an
appealing, seasonally-influenced,
bistro-style carte - complemented by
daily specials - of straightforward
modern British fare. Take Lancashire
cheese hash brown with black pudding,
crisp bacon and poached hen egg, or
honey-glazed Goosnargh duck with

green peppercorns, fondant potato and
glazed beetroot, while a classic glazed
lemon tart with crème fraîche, or more
adventurous hot passionfruit soufflé
with passionfruit sorbet might catch the
eye at dessert. Treat yourself to the
seven-course tasting menu to really do
the place justice, or a day course at the
cookery school, many of which are
hosted by Paul Heathcote himself.

Chef James Holah, Paul Heathcote
Owner Paul Heathcote
Times 12-2.30/6-10, Closed 1 Jan,
Closed Mon, Closed L Sat **Prices** Food
prices not confirmed for 2009. Please
telephone for details. **Wines** 22 bottles
under £20, 10 by glass **Notes** Sunday L
Seats 70, Pr/dining room 18
Children Portions **Parking** 10; on street

LYTHAM ST ANNES *Continued*

Chicory

Chef Steven Shepherd **Owner** F Santoni & R Martin **Times** 12-2/6-9.30, Closed 25 Dec, 1 Jan **Prices** Fixed L 2 course £13-£19, Fixed D 3 course fr £18.95, Starter £4.25-£8.50, Main £11.25-£18.95, Dessert £5.95-£7.20, Service optional **Wines** 20 bottles over £20, 19 bottles under £20, 17 by glass **Notes** Sunday L, Vegetarian available, Dress restrictions, Smart Casual, Air con **Seats** 70 **Children** Portions, Menu **Parking** On street

Greens Bistro

◎ Modern British ☘

Imaginative modern cooking in an intimate atmosphere

☎ 01253 789990
3-9 St Andrews Road South, St Annes-on-Sea FY8 1SX
e-mail: info@greensbistro.co.uk
dir: Just off St Annes Sq

Hidden among the shops and residences in the heart of town, the stairs down to this romantic cellar restaurant create an immediate sense of expectation, even, perhaps, a little theatre. Inside, the subtle décor and lighting - with tables discreetly hidden in nooks and crannies - and smart uniformed staff conspire to create an ideal atmosphere for a special night out. The food is modern British and punches above its weight with great ingredients ticking the requisite local and seasonal

boxes. Expect honey-glazed breast of Goosnargh duck served with Granny Smith purée and duck gravy, or perhaps roasted monkfish with bacon and sage risotto and a saffron vinaigrette.

Chef Paul Webster **Owner** Paul Webster **Times** Closed 25 Dec, BHs, 2 wks Jan, 1 wk summer, Closed Sun-Mon, Closed L all week **Prices** Fixed D 3 course £15.95, Service optional, Groups min 8 service 10% **Wines** 7 bottles over £20, 15 bottles under £20, 7 by glass **Notes** Vegetarian available **Seats** 38 **Children** Portions **Parking** On street

The West Beach Restaurant

◎ Modern British

Stylish hotel restaurant offering fine dining

☎ 01253 739898
Clifton Arms Hotel, West Beach FY8 5QJ
e-mail: welcome@cliftonarms-lytham.com
web: www.cliftonarms-lytham.com
dir: M55 junct 4, first left onto A583 (Preston), take right hand lane. At lights turn right onto Peel Rd. Turn right at t-junct into Ballam Rd. Continue onto Lytham town centre. Turn right and then left into Queen St

Occupying a prime position on the seafront overlooking the Ribble estuary is the traditional Clifton Arms Hotel, with its elegant West Beach Restaurant offering views of Lytham Green. Enjoy candlelit dining in a unique setting with an intimate ambience. Choose from an imaginative menu showcasing modern British cuisine, complemented

by fine wines. Expect starters such as Lytham Bay shrimps with mace and Melba toast, or mains like cannon of heather-fed lamb, asparagus with mint, dauphinoise potatoes, buttered cabbage and lamb jus. Desserts include dark chocolate sponge with white chocolate ice cream.

Times 12-2.30/7-9.30

See advert below

PRESTON   **Map 18 SD52**

Pines Hotel

◎ Traditional British

Traditional fare in comfortable surroundings

☎ 01772 338551
570 Preston Rd, Clayton Le-Woods PR6 7ED
e-mail: mail@thepineshotel.co.uk
web: www.thepineshotel.co.uk
dir: M6 junct 28/29 off A6 & S of B5256

Originally a cotton mill owner's house, set in 4 acres of landscaped gardens and mature woodlands, this friendly, late Victorian hotel has been extended over the years and the function suite is a renowned cabaret venue. Haworths Bar and grill serves quality local produce in traditional style with a modern twist on a seasonally-changing menu. Expect old favourites like Chateaubriand steak and chips as well as classier dishes - seared venison

Continued

PRESTON *Continued*

with smoked bacon rösti, for example, served with wilted spinach, roast chestnuts and a Muscat jus - so there's plenty to tempt. Not least at dessert, when your choice might include anything from sticky toffee pudding to Pimm's poached pears.

Chef Ryan Greene, Sarah Lowe, Paul Dugdale **Owner** Betty Duffin **Times** 12-2.30/6-9.30, Closed 28 Dec **Prices** Fixed D 3 course fr £15, Starter £4.50-£6.95, Main £12.50-£48, Dessert £4.95-£6, Service optional **Wines** 16 bottles over £20, 28 bottles under £20, 8 by glass **Notes** Sunday L, Vegetarian available, Dress restrictions, No jeans, T-shirts or trainers, Civ Wed 200 **Seats** 95, Pr/dining room 46 **Children** Portions **Parking** 150

Winckley Square Chop House and Bar

◉ Modern British 🖥

Classic town-centre brasserie dining

☎ 01772 252732
23 Winckley Square PR1 3JJ
e-mail: preston@heathcotes.co.uk
dir: City centre, on Winckley Sq, near train station

Right in the town centre, this former convent school has been converted into one of celebrity chef, Paul Heathcote's chain of brasseries. The interior boasts an impressive bar space and eclectic décor, with lots of marble and hardwood surfaces and a mixture of contemporary and antique furniture. The menu is a crowd-pleaser, mixing classic hand-made dishes like steak and chips with local produce such as honey and ginger-spiced pork belly with spring vegetable broth and pak choi. Puddings include a melting chocolate tart with lime sorbet, or try the delicious home-made ice creams.

Times 12-2.30/6-10, Closed 1-2 Jan, BHs, Closed L 3 Jan

Twelve Restaurant and Lounge Bar

◉◉ Modern British 🍃

Modern food in an intriguing architectural setting

☎ 01253 821212
Marsh Mill Village, Marsh Mill-in-Wyre FY5 4JZ
e-mail: info@twelve-restaurant.co.uk
web: www.twelve-restaurant.co.uk
dir: A585 follow signs for Marsh Mill Complex. Turn right into Victoria Rd East, entrance 0.5m on left

Housed in a former dance studio situated just feet away from the oldest working windmill in Europe, this buzzy

contemporary restaurant is minimalist in design with a sculptural, city-chic feel and an industrial theme. Exposed brickwork, steel girders and aluminium fencing on the mezzanine floor set the scene, while the bar's glazed roof and wall offers stunning views of the 18th-century 60-ft Marsh Mill - a unique spot to enjoy a pre-dinner cocktail. The seasonally-changing modern British menu uses local produce wherever possible, offering traditional dishes with a modern twist. Potted sea trout and watercress with soused vegetables and melba toast might be followed by Bowland Forest aged beef fillet with mushroom gratin. Banana 'butty' will not disappoint for dessert - banana bread, crème brûlée, ice cream and milk shake.

Chef Paul Moss **Owner** Paul Moss & Caroline Upton **Times** 12-3/6.30-12, Closed 1st 2 wks Jan, Closed Mon, Closed L Tue-Sat **Prices** Fixed L 2 course £16.95, Fixed D 3 course £18.95-£25.50, Starter £5.95-£9.50, Main £14.95-£24, Dessert £5.95-£8.50, Service optional **Wines** 49 bottles over £20, 37 bottles under £20, 12 by glass **Notes** Sunday L, Vegetarian available, Air con **Seats** 90 **Children** Portions **Parking** 150

The Three Fishes at Mitton

◉ Traditional British 🏆 NOTABLE WINE LIST 🍃

Vintage inn where local suppliers are championed

☎ 01254 826888
Mitton Rd, Mitton BB7 9PQ
e-mail: enquiries@thethreefishes.com
dir: M6 junct 31, A59 to Clitheroe. Follow signs for Whalley, take B6246 and continue for 2m

You are assured an informal and relaxing dining environment at this friendly 400-year-old inn, where a sensitive refurbishment by the team behind Northcote Manor (see entry) has kept the traditional features and feel - craggy stone floors and warm solid wood furniture. With a well-deserved reputation for great gastro-pub style cooking, the menu focuses on traditional, regional specialities and British classics, based around a staunch commitment to named local and regional suppliers. Typical dishes on the seasonally-changing menu might include Winnie Swarbrick's corn-fed Goosnargh chicken liver pâté with Cumberland sauce, and Three Fishes pie - Fleetwood fish and seawater prawns baked with mashed potato and sprinkled with Mrs Kirkham's Lancashire cheese. The inn operates a no-reservation policy, so make sure you arrive early. A great children's menu completes the package.

Chef Richard Upton **Owner** Craig Bancroft & Nigel Haworth **Times** 12-2/6-9, Closed 25 Dec **Prices** Starter £5-£7.50, Main £8.50-£16.95, Dessert £4.50-£5, Service optional **Wines** 22 bottles over £20, 24 bottles under £20, 10 by glass **Notes** Sunday L, Vegetarian available **Seats** 140 **Children** Portions, Menu **Parking** 60

The Inn at Whitewell

◉ Modern British

Confident cooking in historic inn with views

☎ 01200 448222
Forest of Bowland, Clitheroe BB7 3AT
e-mail: reception@innatwhitewell.com

With some fantastic views over the River Hodder, this former deer keeper's cottage dates back to the 14th century. Set within the Forest of Bowland, this period inn has immense charm with rustic furniture, antiques and memorabilia throughout adding to its character. The informative menu is written with a sense of humour and dishes are modern British in style with an obvious Mediterranean influence - potted confit of Goosnargh duck leg with caramelised oranges, for example, or roast loin of Bowland lamb with cassoulet of beans and root vegetables and potato purée. Market fish of the day also available.

Chef Jamie Cadman **Owner** The Inn at Whitewell Ltd **Times** 12-2/7.30-9.30, Closed L all week **Prices** Food prices not confirmed for 2009. Please telephone for details. **Wines** 120 bottles over £20, 60 bottles under £20, 20 by glass **Notes** Vegetarian available, Civ Wed 80 **Seats** 60, Pr/dining room 20 **Children** Portions **Parking** 70

The Mulberry Tree

◉◉ Modern British

Ambitious cooking in Lancashire village gastro-pub

☎ 01257 451400
Wrightington Bar WN6 9SE
dir: 4m from Wigan. From M6 junct 27 towards Parbold, right after motorway exit, by BP garage into Mossy Lea Rd. On right after 2m

Located in a quiet Lancashire village, but close to the M6, this bright, modern gastro-pub and fine dining restaurant is popular with the locals who enjoy its imaginative dishes. Simple table settings and personable service add to the attraction. The bar menu has a large choice of food, while the restaurant offers more refined dishes. Cooking is accomplished modern British with European influences, so expect the likes of steamed Delmaine mussels with a well-balanced white wine, shallot, garlic and parsley sauce, or roast fillet of wild sea bass with broccoli, French beans and asparagus with a prawn beurre blanc and golden potatoes. Finish with blackberry cheesecake served with blackcurrant sorbet.

Times 12-2.30/6-9.30, Closed 26 Dec, 1 Jan

LEICESTERSHIRE

BELTON
Map 11 SK42

The Queen's Head

◎◎ Modern European

Modern gastro-pub operation with food to match

☎ 01530 222359
2 Long St LE12 9TP
e-mail: enquiries@thequeenshead.org
dir: Located just off B5324 between Loughborough and Ashby de la Zouch

A former coaching inn, the Queen's Head is now a contemporary gastro-pub, with a stylish, minimalist décor. The large open-plan bar, once the local alehouse, comes with blondwood flooring that continues into its two dining rooms. Here, cream walls, modern pictures and quality table appointments maintain the theme, while service is appropriately relaxed, friendly and helpful. The fashionable, modern European cooking fits the bill too, dealing in quality local produce, good flavours and balance. Take a warm crab and basil tart with rocket salad and lemon vinaigrette to start, follow with crispy duck confit with sweet-and-sour cabbage and oriental sauce, or sea bream with basil mash, sautéed squid, chorizo and courgettes.

Chef Marc Billings **Owner** Henry & Ali Weldon **Times** 12-2.30/7-9.30, Closed 25-26 Dec, 1 Jan, Closed D Sun **Prices** Fixed L 2 course £13, Fixed D 3 course £17, Starter £5.95-£9.50, Main £12.50-£19.50, Dessert £5-£7, Service added 10% **Wines** 49 bottles over £20, 25 bottles under £20, 13 by glass **Notes** Sunday L, Vegetarian available, Civ Wed 40 **Seats** 70, Pr/dining room 40 **Children** Portions, Menu **Parking** 20

BUCKMINSTER
Map 11 SK82

The Tollemache Arms

◎◎ Modern British V ✎

Vibrant restaurant and sharp modern cooking

☎ 01476 860007
48 Main St NG33 5SA
e-mail: enquiries@thetollemachearms.com

This 18th-century grey stone roadside inn on the Tollemache estate has been revamped as a restaurant with rooms, though locals can still prop up the bar and chat to visitors. The smart interior has a minimalist décor of neutral colours, oak floors, bold pictures, brown leather chairs, white tablecloths and fresh flowers. The kitchen takes a modern approach with dishes simply prepared from fresh quality produce. There is an emphasis on game supplied daily from the estate, with dishes such as peppered hare loin with grilled goat's cheese, or roasted partridge breasts with shallot tarte Tatin. For dessert, try house speciality Tollemache apple and stilton tart.

Chef Mark Gough **Owner** Mark Gough **Times** 12-3.30/5.30-12, Closed Mon, Closed D Sun **Prices** Fixed L 2 course £11.50, Fixed D 3 course £15.50, Starter £4.50-£10, Main £9.50-£18, Dessert £5-£8.50, Service optional, Groups min 8 service 10% **Wines** 15 bottles over £20, 10 bottles under £20, 6 by glass **Notes** Sunday L, Vegetarian menu **Seats** 50, Pr/dining room 20 **Children** Portions, Menu **Parking** 15

CASTLE DONINGTON

FOR RESTAURANT DETAILS SEE EAST MIDLANDS AIRPORT

EAST MIDLANDS AIRPORT
Map 11 SK42

Best Western Premier Yew Lodge Hotel

◎ Traditional

Imaginative cooking in relaxed surroundings

☎ 01509 672518
Packington Hill, Kegworth DE74 2DF
e-mail: info@yewlodgehotel.co.uk
dir: M1 junct 24, follow signs for Loughborough & Kegworth on A6. At bottom of hill take 1st right onto Packington Hill. Hotel 400yds on right

This smart family-owned hotel is in a peaceful location yet is close to both the motorway and East Midlands Airport. It has a well-equipped spa and leisure centre, and is a popular venue for conferences and weddings. The library bar overlooks the Orchard Restaurant and is a good place for a drink before moving downstairs where large windows let in lots of natural light, and diners are seated at smartly appointed tables, presided over by friendly and attentive staff. The cuisine offers tempting modern interpretations of traditional dishes, such as scallops with cauliflower purée and light curry sauce, or breast of guinea fowl, Puy lentils and port jus, followed by pear tarte Tatin with honey and whisky ice cream.

Times 12-2.30/6.30-10, Closed L Sat

Donington Manor Hotel

◎ Modern British

Accomplished modern cooking in traditional surroundings

☎ 01332 810253
High St, Castle Donington DE74 2PP
e-mail: enquiries@doningtonmanorhotel.co.uk
web: www.doningtonmanorhotel.co.uk

Donington Manor is a gracious Georgian property close to the village centre. Original features have been pleasingly preserved and a programme of refurbishment has maintained the hotel's high standards. The elegant Adam-styled dining room is particularly appealing, with its traditional feel and attentive service. The kitchen takes a modern approach, underpinned by classical influences. Quality ingredients are sympathetically handled in dishes such as seared red mullet with chargrilled fennel and lemon dressing to start, and a main course of free-range sautéed chicken breast with blue cheese sauce and crispy bacon.

Times 12-2.30/7-9.30, Closed Xmas

The Priest House on the River

◎◎ Modern British V

Unique location for fine dining

☎ 01332 810649
Kings Mills, Castle Donington DE74 2RR
e-mail: thepriesthouse@handpicked.co.uk
dir: Northbound: M1 junct 23A to airport. After 1.5m turn right to Castle Donington. Left at 1st lights, 2m. Southbound: M1 junct 24A onto A50. Take 1st sliproad signed Long Eaton/Castle Donington. Turn right at lights in Castle Donington

Perched on the banks of the River Trent amid 54 acres of mature woodland, the original watermills on the site of the Priest House were mentioned in the Domesday Book. Nowadays modern comforts are found throughout the hotel, which includes conference rooms, a modern brasserie and a fine-dining restaurant. The cooking style is modern, and the menus are both seasonal and regional, focusing on local speciality ingredients and dishes. Everything is home-made, including the olive oil from the hotel's villa in Italy. Starters may include fig and quail salad with truffle dressing and fried egg, followed by braised blade of Scottish beef with fondant potato and lentil sauce. Finish with an apple tarte Tatin with rosemary ice cream.

Continued

EAST MIDLANDS AIRPORT *Continued*

Chef Mark Fletcher **Owner** Hand Picked Hotels
Times 12-3/7-10, Closed L Sat, Closed D Sun
Prices Fixed L 2 course fr £15.25, Fixed D 3 course fr £30,
Starter £7.95-£12.95, Main £16-£24, Dessert
£7.95-£8.95, Service included **Wines** 75 bottles over £20,
2 bottles under £20, 8 by glass **Notes** Sunday L,
Vegetarian menu, Civ Wed 90 **Seats** 38, Pr/dining room
100 **Children** Portions, Menu **Parking** 200

HINCKLEY Map 11 SP49

Sketchley Grange Hotel

British, European

Modern hotel with its finger on the culinary pulse

☎ 01455 251133
Sketchley Ln, Burbage LE10 3HU
e-mail: reservations@sketchleygrange.co.uk
web: www.sketchleygrange.co.uk
dir: From M69 junct 1 take B4109 (Hinckley). Straight on
1st rdbt, left at 2nd rdbt & immediately right into
Sketchley Lane. Hotel at end of lane

Conveniently situated for the motorway, this elegant
modern hotel is set in its own landscaped grounds and
enjoys peaceful open country views. Ongoing
refurbishment and an extensive range of facilities -
including a health and leisure complex, choice of bars,
and two eateries - make it a popular destination. Light
meals are served in the brasserie, while the Willow
Restaurant is the fine-dining option - a spacious venue
that overlooks pretty gardens. Candlelit by night, it's
staffed by a well-trained and enthusiastic kitchen
brigade who incorporate the best of culinary fashion in an
ambitious modern menu of dishes. Start with lobster
ravioli with braised baby fennel and saffron
bouillabaisse, followed by mains such as wild sea bass
served with basil oil and parmesan mash, provençale
vegetables, plum tomato dressing, wilted chives and
black olive purée.

Chef Stewart Westwater **Owner** Nigel Downes
Times Closed Mon, Closed L Tue-Sat, Closed D Sun
Prices Food prices not confirmed for 2009. Please
telephone for details. **Wines** 32 bottles over £20, 36
bottles under £20, 4 by glass **Notes** Dress restrictions,
Smart casual, Civ Wed 250, Air con **Seats** 80, Pr/dining
room 40 **Children** Portions **Parking** 200

KEGWORTH

FOR RESTAURANT DETAILS SEE EAST MIDLANDS AIRPORT

KNIPTON Map 11 SK83

The Manners Arms

Modern British

**Former hunting lodge with rooms serving imaginative
food**

☎ 01476 879222
Croxton Rd NG32 1RH
e-mail: info@mannersarms.com
dir: From Grantham take A607 (Melton road), after
approx. 4m turn right at Croxton Kerrial

Part of the Rutland Estate, this former hunting lodge -
built for the 6th Duke of Rutland in the 1880s - has been
redesigned with a relaxed country feel by the current 11th
Duchess. Period features abound, and the restaurant
boasts high corniced ceilings, wooden floors, polished
wooden furniture, and heavy drapes matching the
banquette seating. Expect dishes like Belvoir Estate
partridge cooked three ways (roasted breast, confit leg
and ballotine) served with fondant potato, creamed Savoy
and a juniper reduction, or perhaps poached salmon
teamed with a smoked haddock brandade and shellfish
essence.

Chef Paul Hoad **Owner** Duke of Rutland
Times 12.30-3/7-9, Closed D Sun (after 8pm), 25 Dec
Prices Fixed L 2 course £9.95-£12.95, Fixed D 3 course
£18.95, Starter £5-£10, Main £12.50-£22, Dessert
£6-£6.95, Service optional **Wines** 15 bottles over £20, 15
bottles under £20, 8 by glass **Notes** Sunday L, Vegetarian
available, Civ Wed 50 **Seats** 50, Pr/dining room 20
Children Portions, Menu **Parking** 80

LEICESTER Map 11 SK50

Watsons Restaurant & Bar

Modern European V

**Modern brasserie-style cooking in one of Leicester's
most popular eateries**

☎ 0116 222 7770
5-9 Upper Brown St LE1 5TE
e-mail: watsons.restaurant@virgin.net
dir: City centre, next to Phoenix Arts Theatre

This well-established restaurant is set in an 18th-century
former cotton mill and is entered via a discreet courtyard.

Inside, there's a contemporary feel to the stylish décor -
exposed brickwork, polished-wood floors and subtle
halogen lighting combine with generously spaced tables,
crisp linen and background jazz to create a relaxing
atmosphere. Service is relaxed, friendly and professional.
As for the food - classic French and Mediterranean
influences run throughout the menu and there's a high
level of skill and obvious attention to detail in the
cooking, alongside the use of quality ingredients. You
might start with pan-fried scallops with Vietnamese
cabbage salad, and ginger and soy dressing, and
perhaps follow with oven-roasted Scottish salmon with
crab and crayfish risotto, with chocolate fondant and
vanilla ice cream to finish. There's a strong regular
clientele, so booking is advisable, even at lunchtime.

Chef Graeme Watson, Scott Mills **Owner** Graeme Watson
Times 12-2.30/7-10.30, Closed BHs, 10 days at Xmas,
Closed Sun **Prices** Fixed L 2 course fr £10.95, Fixed D 3
course fr £16.95, Starter £5-£7, Main £9.95-£19.50,
Dessert fr £5.50, Service added but optional 10%
Wines 12 bottles over £20, 18+ bottles under £20, 10 by
glass **Notes** Fixed D available Mon-Fri, Vegetarian menu,
Air con **Seats** 80 **Children** Portions

MEDBOURNE Map 11 SP89

The Horse & Trumpet

Modern British

Culinary adventures in a sleepy village

☎ 01858 565000
Old Green LE16 8DX
e-mail: info@horseandtrumpet.com
dir: Between Market Harborough and Uppingham on B664

Tucked away behind the village bowling green, this
carefully restored, thatched former farmhouse is now a
restaurant with rooms and offers fine dining in three
intimate areas, or alfresco in summer. Imaginative food
comes courtesy of an accomplished kitchen team, who
deliver accurate and skilful cooking without over-
embellishment. The creative menu of modern dishes is
distinguished by quality ingredients, fresh flavours and
clever combinations. Start with guinea fowl and confit
chicken mosaic with chicory marmalade and herb
mascarpone and then tuck into wild sea bass with
langoustine broth, or venison saddle with grain mustard
sauce, followed by strawberry and caramel pannacotta, or
- better still - treat yourself to the imaginative tasting
menu.

Chef G Magnani **Owner** Horse & Trumpet Ltd
Times 12-1.45/7-9.30, Closed 1st week Jan, Closed Mon,
Closed D Sun **Prices** Fixed L 2 course £16, Fixed D 3
course £25, Starter £7-£10, Main £18-£22, Dessert £7,
Service optional, Groups min 16 service 10% **Wines** 40
bottles over £20, 6 bottles under £20, 8 by glass
Notes Fixed D Tue-Thu only, Sunday L, Vegetarian
available, Dress restrictions, Smart casual, no trainers or
baseball caps **Seats** 50, Pr/dining room 32 **Children** Min
12 yrs **Parking** On street parking

MELTON MOWBRAY — Map 11 SK71

Stapleford Park

◉◉ Modern French

Fine dining amid the splendour of 'Capability' Brown parkland

☎ 01572 787000
Stapleford LE14 2EF
e-mail: reservations@stapleford.co.uk
web: www.staplefordpark.com
dir: A1 to Colsterworth rdbt. left onto B676, signed Melton Mowbray.In approx 9m turn left to Stapleford

A former stately home set in 500 acres of Capability Brown-designed parkland, Stapleford Park dates back to the 14th century and makes a stunning country-house hotel. The impressive, fine-dining restaurant is the Grinling Gibbons, a magnificent room featuring Grinling Gibbons carvings, inspired by the Spanish Riding School in Vienna. Dishes are studded with luxury items and make good use of local produce. Examples include tortellinis of Cornish crab with pea purée and Ibérico ham; and fillet of beef with truffle mash, garden vegetables and red wine jus. A less formal dining experience is provided in the Pavilion Restaurant, the golf club house, and the Old Kitchen, with private dining available in the Harborough Room, the Grand Hall and the Billiard Room.

Times 12.30-2.30/7-9.30, Closed L Mon-Sat

NORTH KILWORTH — Map 11 SP68

Kilworth House Hotel

◉◉ Modern British

Country-house hotel offering comfortable elegance and opulent fine dining

☎ 01858 880058
Lutterworth Rd LE17 6JE
e-mail: info@kilworthhouse.co.uk
dir: Located on A4304, 4m E of M1 junct 20 towards Market Harborough

Set amid 38 acres of parkland and gardens, this sympathetically restored Victorian country house captures the spirit of a bygone age, its gracious public rooms featuring period pieces, sumptuous fabrics and original artworks. There's a choice of dining venues: the more informal Orangery, offering a lighter menu and fine views, or the opulent, fine-dining Wordsworth Restaurant - its gloriously ornate vaulted ceiling, glittering chandeliers and high-domed fireplace instantly raising the spirits. The menu here reads almost lyrically with an emphasis on using the finest local produce in an imaginative and innovative way. A starter of lobster consommé shows the style, with vegetable pearls and truffle dumplings, perhaps followed by prime fillet of beef with potato and crab pancake, provençale vegetables and balsamic jus.

Times 12-3/7-9.30

STATHERN — Map 11 SK73

Red Lion Inn

◉ Modern British **V** 🐾

Gutsy bistro food in a friendly village inn

☎ 01949 860868
2 Red Lion St LE14 4HS
e-mail: info@theredlioninn.co.uk
dir: From A1 take A52 towards Nottingham signed Belvoir Castle, take turn to Stathern on left

This is a comfortable British pub in the best possible sense, with furniture, fittings and food that create a homely atmosphere. Set in a lovely village nestling under Belvoir Scarp, it has a traditional feel without being overbearingly olde-worlde. With open beams, flagstone floors and wood-burning stove, the kitchen provides modern-focused food that is rustic and well done, using local produce throughout. The daily-changing menu might include local hare terrine with quince compôte, or roast monkfish with bean cassoulet and crispy bacon, and to finish, perhaps a treacle tart with clotted cream. Also on site is Red Lion Foods, offering everything from takeaway bread, dressings and marinades to hampers.

Chef Sean Hope **Owner** Ben Jones, Sean Hope **Times** 12-2/7-9.30, Closed 1 Jan, Closed Mon, Closed D Sun **Prices** Fixed L 2 course £13, Starter £4.50-£6.50, Main £10.50-£16.50, Dessert £5.75-£6.25, Service optional, Groups min 11 service 10% **Wines** 9 bottles over £20, 21 bottles under £20, 8 by glass **Notes** Sunday L, Vegetarian menu **Seats** 50 **Children** Portions, Menu **Parking** 20

WOODHOUSE EAVES — Map 11 SK51

The Woodhouse

◉◉ Modern British 🐾

Modern neighbourhood restaurant with friendly, helpful service

☎ 01509 890318
43 Maplewell Rd, Woodhouse Eaves LE12 8RG
e-mail: info@thewoodhouse.co.uk
dir: M1 junct 23 towards Loughborough, right into Nanpantan Rd, left into Beacon Rd, right in Main St & again into Maplewell Rd

A low, whitewashed cottage exterior conceals this vibrant modern restaurant. Inside, there's a contemporary edge, with a separate bar-lounge for pre-meal drinks and canapés, while the dining area (a few steps down) is decked out with dark-blue upholstered high-backed chairs and formally set tables. Contrasting wall colours are adorned with modern art, while floral displays and friendly, relaxed but efficient service hit just the right note. The kitchen's modern approach delivers contemporary classics driven by fresh, carefully sourced prime local ingredients sympathetically balanced and attractively presented. Take belly and fillet of local rare breed pork served with sweet potato purée, pak choi and oriental jus, while an apple pannacotta with apple sorbet and cinnamon syrup might catch the eye at dessert.

Chef Paul Leary **Owner** Paul Leary **Times** 12-3/6.30-12, Closed BHs, Closed Mon, Closed L Sat, Closed D Sun

Prices Fixed L 2 course £14.95, Fixed D 3 course £16.95, Tasting menu fr £45, Starter £6.50-£10.95, Main £15.50-£22.50, Dessert £6.50-£8.95, Service optional **Wines** 100 bottles over £20, 20 bottles under £20, 8 by glass **Notes** Sunday L, Vegetarian available **Seats** 50, Pr/dining room 40 **Children** Portions **Parking** 15

LINCOLNSHIRE

CLEETHORPES — Map 17 TA30

Kingsway Hotel

◉ Traditional British **V**

Traditional dining by the sea

☎ 01472 601122
Kingsway DN35 0AE
e-mail: reception@kingsway-hotel.com
dir: At junction of A1098 and seafront

An authentic British seaside experience is offered by this long-established hotel, run by four generations of the Harris family and their loyal staff. The dining room, with its superb view over the Humber estuary, is decorated in traditional style and the tables are set with white linen and silver cutlery. It is a popular venue for business lunches and family gatherings, delivering an extensive menu of straightforward dishes. A house favourite is roast rump of Aberdeen Angus beef, well hung and tender, with freshly made Yorkshire puddings and horseradish sauce.

Chef Guy Stevens **Owner** Mr J Harris **Times** 12.30-1.45/7-9, Closed 26-27 Dec, Closed D 25 Dec **Prices** Fixed L 2 course fr £17, Fixed D 3 course fr £27.95, Starter £4.95-£8.95, Main £12.95-£22.95, Dessert £5.95, Service optional **Wines** 36 bottles over £20, 38 bottles under £20, 6 by glass **Notes** Sunday L, Vegetarian menu **Seats** 85, Pr/dining room 24 **Children** Min 5 yrs, Portions **Parking** 50

GRANTHAM — Map 11 SK93

Angel & Royal Hotel

◉ Traditional British

Dining in the historic haunt of kings

☎ 01476 565816
High St NG31 6PN
e-mail: enquiries@angelandroyal.co.uk
web: www.angelandroyal.co.uk
dir: Grantham exit off A1 and follow signs to the town centre

Dating back to the 14th century, this is reputedly one of the oldest coaching inns in Britain. A host of original features remain, including fine plaster ceilings, elaborate stone oriel windows and a huge log fire. A high standard of cooking is offered in both the modern ground-floor bistro bar, Simply Berties, and in the baronial first-floor King's Room, which is open for lunch and dinner at weekends. Fixed-price menus include starters such as tomato and brie tartlet, or mains of roast pork belly, pepper mash and red wine jus, with lemon tart to finish.

Times 12-2.30/7-9.30, Closed L Mon-Sat, Closed D Sun-Thu

GRANTHAM *Continued*

Harry's Place

@@@ – *see below*

HORNCASTLE   Map 17 TF26

Magpies Restaurant

@@ British, European V

Imaginative cuisine in a cosy setting

☎ 01507 527004
71-75 East St LN9 6AA
dir: 0.5 miles from town centre on A158 toward Skegness

This small family-run restaurant, set in a charming row of 200-year-old black- and-white terraced cottages just a short walk from the town centre, is quite a gem. Inside, the honey and russet colour scheme and wood-burning stove contribute to the warm, cosy environment, or during summer months, enjoy the small alfresco courtyard. The L-shaped dining room, with its silver candlesticks, linen cloths and fresh flowers, provides a menu of predominantly British cuisine with international influences. Top-quality seasonal produce rules here with an emphasis on impressive presentation. To start, try partridge breast marinated in tamarind and orange with oriental-style noodles and caramelised pecans, followed by baked halibut on Grimsby crab risotto with vanilla bisque, and to finish macadamia nut chocolate cake with coconut ice cream and dark chocolate sauce.

Chef Andrew Gilbert **Owner** Caroline Ingall
Times 12-2/7-9.30, Closed 27-30 Dec, Closed Mon-Tues, Closed L Sat **Prices** Fixed L 2 course £21, Fixed D 3 course £25, Service optional **Wines** 62 bottles over £20, 50 bottles under £20, 4 by glass **Notes** Sunday L, Vegetarian menu, Dress restrictions, Smart casual, Air con **Seats** 34 **Children** Portions **Parking** On street

HOUGH-ON-THE-HILL   Map 11 SK94

The Brownlow Arms

@ British

Popular village inn with something to suit everyone

☎ 01400 250234
High Rd NG32 2AZ
e-mail: paulandlorraine@thebrownlowarms.com

This cosy inn dates from the 17th century and is tucked away in a pretty Lincolnshire village. Hand-pumped prize-winning ales are served in the bar, and the country-house-style restaurant is often booked up weeks in advance. A landscaped terrace provides the perfect place for summer dining. The kitchen makes good use of local produce, including game from nearby estates and fish from Brixham. Daily specials supplement an imaginative menu with dishes such as crab, prawn and salmon timbale with horseradish cream; roast breast of chicken with Portobello mushroom and stilton sauce; and chocolate tart with raspberry Pavlova ice cream.

Chef Paul Vidic **Owner** Paul & Lorraine Willoughby
Times 12-3/6.30-9.30, Closed 25-26 Dec, 1-23 Jan, 1 wk

Sep, Closed Mon, Closed L Tues-Sat, Closed D Sun **Prices** Starter £4.95-£9.95, Main £13.95-£22.95, Dessert £5.95-£7.95, Service optional **Wines** 28 bottles over £20, 18 bottles under £20, 5 by glass **Notes** Sunday L, Vegetarian available, Air con **Seats** 80, Pr/dining room 26 **Children** Min 14 yrs **Parking** 26; on street

LINCOLN   Map 17 SK97

Lakeside Restaurant

@@ Modern International

Contemporary food in Victorian country-house splendour

☎ 01522 793305
Branston Hall Hotel, Branston Park, Branston LN4 1PD
e-mail: jon@branstonhall.com
web: www.branstonhall.com
dir: On B1188, 3m S of Lincoln. In village, hotel drive opposite village hall

Harry's Place

GRANTHAM   Map 11 SK93

Modern French

Small restaurant, big heart

☎ 01476 561780
17 High St, Great Gonerby NG31 8JS
dir: 1.5m NW of Grantham on B1174

To describe Harry and Caroline Hallam simply as 'hands on' doesn't seem descriptive enough. There are no other hands at Harry's Place. They run it alone, completely, entirely, all by themselves. This leads to a special kind of experience, something perhaps unique among UK restaurants. It all takes place in a charming listed Georgian building, where the dining room takes ten people at any given time on three tables. Antique furniture and fresh flowers make for a civilised and unpretentious space in which to relax and let Harry cook

for you while Caroline serves with just the right balance of informed professionalism and genuine friendliness. The hand-written menu lists two choices at each course based around the very best of local and seasonal produce. French cuisine provides the template for Harry's cooking, while exceptional technical skills and a keen eye for the balance of flavours are very much in evidence throughout. Filey lobster with green leaves, herbs, avocado, truffle oil and a relish of mango, lime, ginger and basil is a starter of lively and well-judged flavours, or there is the comfort of a soup of locally grown celeriac. Main-course fillet of wild Scottish turbot is lightly seared and comes with crispy lardons and a red wine sauce with sage and thyme, and to finish there is apricot ice cream with Amaretto syrup.

Chef Harry Hallam **Owner** Harry & Caroline Hallam
Times 12.30-2/7-8.30, Closed 1 wk from 25 Dec, Closed Sun & Mon **Prices** Starter £9.50-£19.50, Main fr £35, Dessert £7, Service optional **Wines** All bottles over £20, 4 by glass **Seats** 10 **Children** Min 5 yrs, Portions **Parking** 4

Dating back to 1885, this imposing country-house hotel is set in 88 acres of wooded parkland and lakes. The elegant Lakeside Restaurant comes suitably decked out with chandeliers, paintings, Italian-style chairs and plenty of original features. The ambitious carte and fixed-price menus take a distinctly modern approach, with fine regional produce, imagination and interest, culinary skill and careful service all coming together with style. Well-balanced dishes are executed with precision and combine some unusual ingredients, as seen in slow-cooked pork belly with Cornish scallops starter, followed by monkfish with braised oxtail, potato cream, clams in red wine and persillade, with Charlotte of rhubarb and ginger biscuits with strawberry sorbet to finish.

Lakeside Restaurant

Chef Miles Collins **Owner** Southsprings Ltd **Times** 12-2/7-9.30, Closed 1 Jan **Prices** Food prices not confirmed for 2009. Please telephone for details. **Wines** 17 bottles over £20, 36 bottles under £20, 14 by glass **Notes** Dress restrictions, Smart casual, no jeans or T-shirts, Civ Wed 120 **Seats** 75, Pr/dining room 28 **Children** Min 12 yrs, Portions **Parking** 75

The Old Bakery

◉◉ International 🖥 🐾

Accomplished cooking in former bakery using quality local produce

☎ 01522 576057
26/28 Burton Rd LN1 3LB
e-mail: enquiries@theold-bakery.co.uk
web: www.theold-bakery.co.uk
dir: From A46 follow directions for Lincoln North & follow brown signs for The Historic Centre

As the name suggests, this restaurant with rooms was once a bakery (1837-1945) and still retains many of the original features, including the quarry-tiled floor and ovens still in the walls. Consisting of two well-furnished rooms and a new garden room, the restaurant's atmosphere is rustic, homely and full of character, a theme not lost on the attentive staff either, who are fittingly friendly and polite. The skilled Italian chef-patron is passionate about the food, delivering clear flavours and using local, seasonal Lincolnshire produce. The approach is modern underpinned by a classical base; think tournedos of beef with Lincoln Blue cheese and wrapped in Parma ham, or hay slow-roasted baby pig, and do save room for the home-made breads and impressive cheese selection.

The Old Bakery

Chef Ivano de Serio **Owner** Alan & Lynn Ritson, Tracey & Ivano de Serio **Times** 12-2.30/7-9.30, Closed Mon **Prices** Fixed L 2 course £15-£19, Fixed D 3 course £21-£27, Tasting menu fr £49.95, Starter £4.50-£9.95, Main £14.50-£21.95, Dessert £5.25-£5.95, Service optional, Groups min 5 service 5% **Wines** 37 bottles over £20, 38 bottles under £20, 9 by glass **Notes** Sunday L, Vegetarian available, Dress restrictions, Smart casual, Air con **Seats** 85, Pr/dining room 15 **Children** Portions **Parking** On street, public car park 20mtrs

---

Wig & Mitre

◉ Modern British, International

A shrine to good eating on the old pilgrim trail

☎ 01522 535190
32 Steep Hill LN2 1LU
e-mail: email@wigandmitre.com
dir: At the top of Steep Hill, adjacent to Lincoln Cathedral and Lincoln Castle car parks

Located at the top of the aptly-named Steep Hill, this old inn is an interesting mixture of 14th-century, 16th-century and new build. The main restaurant is both cosy and airy, with skylight ventilation and lovely views of the cathedral towers and castle walls. It is open from early to late, offering comfort and good food throughout the day. The British food with international influences is imaginative, clean and uncomplicated, listed on a carte and blackboard. Typical dishes might include cheese soufflé with Stilton, celery and walnuts, followed by Aberdeen Angus fillet steak with anchovy butter and coffee crème brûlée to finish.

Chef Valerie Hope **Owner** Hope family **Times** 8/11 **Prices** Fixed L 2 course £11, Fixed D 3 course £19.95, Main £10.95-£22.95, Dessert £4.95-£5.25, Service

optional **Wines** 47 bottles over £20, 17 bottles under £20, 25 by glass **Notes** Sunday L, Vegetarian available **Seats** 65, Pr/dining room 20 **Children** Portions, Menu **Parking** Public car park adjacent

---

LOUTH Map 17 TF38

Brackenborough Hotel

◉ Modern European

☎ 01507 609169
Cordeaux Dorner, Brackenborogh LN11 0SZ
e-mail: aridgard@oakridgehotels.co.uk
web: www.oakridgehotels.co.uk

This establishment was awarded its Rosette/s just as we went to press. Therefore we are unable to provide a description for it - visit www.theAA.com for the most up-to-date information.

Prices Food prices not confirmed for 2009. Please telephone for details.

SPALDING Map 12 TF22

Cley Hall Hotel

◉ British, International

A fine Georgian hotel overlooking the river

☎ 01775 725157
22 High St PE11 1TX
e-mail: cleyhall@enterprise.net
dir: Telephone for directions

This attractive Georgian house overlooks the River Welland and has landscaped gardens at the rear. The Grade II listed property continues to be lovingly restored, having been rescued from near dereliction in the 1960s. The popular brasserie restaurant, which forms an integral part of the ground floor area, is divided in two and has a pleasant atmosphere. The straightforward use of quality ingredients results in a consistently good menu with plenty to interest even the most jaded palate. Expect dishes like beef Wellington served with spring greens and fondant potato, and egg custard tart served with creamy, smooth praline ice cream.

Times 12-2/6.30-9.30, Closed D 25-26 Dec

The George of Stamford

Traditional British 🖳 🍷 NOTABLE WINE LIST

Coaching inn popular for its old-fashioned charm and food

☎ 01780 750750
71 St Martins PE9 2LB
e-mail: reservations@georgehotelofstamford.com
dir: From A1(N of Peterborough) take rdbt signed B1081. Follow road to 1st set of lights, hotel on left

This stunning, old coaching inn is steeped in history with its medieval crypt, pillars and archways standing testimony to its colourful past as a hostelry to the great and the good as they travelled the length of England. Meals are served in the magnificent oak-panelled restaurant, the Garden Lounge or in the ivy-clad courtyard. Ingredients are locally sourced, and cooking is careful and accurate with much traditionally based fare on offer - think dessert, cheese and carving trolleys. For mains, expect the likes of steamed fillet of red bream with sautéed baby leeks, wild mushrooms and a herb butter sauce, or perhaps more adventurous whole roasted local partridge with haggis, crushed swede and whisky sauce. Excellent wine list available.

Chef Chris Pitman, Paul Reseigh **Owner** Lawrence Hoskins **Times** 12.30-2.30/7.30-10.30 **Prices** Fixed L 2 course £19.45, Starter £6-£14.75, Main £16.20-£32.50, Dessert £6.25, Service optional **Wines** 115 bottles over £20, 47 bottles under £20, 14 by glass **Notes** Sunday L, Vegetarian available, Dress restrictions, Jacket & tie, no jeans or sportswear, Civ Wed 50 **Seats** 90, Pr/dining room 40 **Children** Min 10 yrs, Portions **Parking** 110

Jim's Yard

Traditional French

Relaxed contemporary dining in secluded courtyard

☎ 01780 756080
3 Ironmonger St PE9 1PL
dir: Please telephone for directions

This stone building, as the name suggests, is set in a courtyard and comes with something of a conservatory feel on the ground floor, with windows overlooking the alfresco dining area, while upstairs has a more loft-house vibe. Brick walls, black-and-white pictures and tables simply laid with crisp white napkins conform to a traditional French theme, while service is suitably relaxed and friendly. The kitchen follows suit with an

accomplished traditional approach with French influences on daily-changing menus. Take diver-caught scallops with cauliflower purée and crisp bacon for openers, with a fillet of salmon main course served with parmesan risotto and roasted beetroot, while a classic apple tarte Tatin with vanilla ice cream might provide the finish.

Chef James Ramsay **Owner** James & Sharon Trevor **Times** 11.30-2.30/6.30-9.30, Closed 24 Dec 2 wks, last wk Jul-1st wk Aug, Closed Sun-Mon **Prices** Fixed L 2 course £13.50, Starter £4.50-£7.95, Main £8.95-£17.50, Dessert £4.95-£6.50, Service optional **Wines** 30 bottles over £20, 18 bottles under £20, 12 by glass **Notes** Vegetarian available, Air con **Seats** 50, Pr/dining room 14 **Children** Portions **Parking** Broad St

Grange & Links Hotel

Traditional, International V

A beautiful setting for freshly cooked fare

☎ 01507 441334
Sea Ln, Sandilands LN12 2RA
e-mail: grangeandlinkshotel@btconnect.com
dir: A1111 to Sutton-on-Sea, follow signs to Sandilands

This friendly family-run hotel stands in 5 acres of grounds close to the beach and has its own 18-hole links golf course. Flavoursome food is carefully prepared, including fish from Grimsby, Lincolnshire Red beef and local vegetables, with lobster a house speciality. The comprehensive European menu with international influences offers dishes such as chicken con pori - mouth-sized pieces of chicken breast in a cream sherry sauce with sautéed leeks, stilton cheese and herbs - and pan-fried duck breast with spinach and a home-made compôte of rhubarb, whisky and honey. Choose home-made sweets from the trolley or a selection of cheeses to finish.

Chef Ann Askew **Owner** Ann Askew **Times** 12-2/7-9 **Prices** Starter £4-£6.80, Main £11.50-£16, Dessert £4.50 **Wines** 10 bottles over £20, 20 bottles under £20, 5 by glass **Notes** Sunday L, Vegetarian menu, Dress restrictions, Smart dress, Civ Wed 150 **Seats** 60, Pr/dining room 100 **Children** Portions, Menu **Parking** 60

Winteringham Fields

Modern French, European 🍷 NOTABLE WINE LIST

Luxurious restaurant with rooms

☎ 01724 733096
DN15 9PF
e-mail: wintfields@aol.com
dir: Village centre, off A1077, 4m S of Humber Bridge

This 16th-century former manor house is a jewel in the north-eastern crown, where The Humber Bridge can be glimpsed from the grounds. Owner Colin McGurran has overseen sensitive refurbishment while maintaining the spirit and reputation of this renowned restaurant with

rooms. Log fires, original beams, antiques, rich soft furnishings and period features help maintain a traditional feel. The dining room is traditionally decorated with flowing curtains and polished stone floor, while well spaced tables are smartly set. High quality produce is to the fore and technical skill is evident in the delivery of modern European food. A first course of crab salad with pink grapefruit jelly and langoustine ravioli might be followed by braised pork belly with chick peas, paprika-flaked cod and squid fritter.

Chef Colin McGurran **Owner** Colin McGurran **Times** 12-1.30/7-9.30, Closed 2 wks Xmas, last wk Apr, last 2 wks Aug, Closed Sun-Mon **Wines** 200 bottles over £20, 20 by glass **Notes** Menu Surprise 7 courses £79, Dress restrictions, Smart dress preferred **Seats** 60, Pr/dining room 12 **Children** Portions **Parking** 20

The Chequers Inn

Modern British

Coaching inn turned gastro-pub

☎ 01476 870701
Main St NG32 1LU
e-mail: justinnabar@yahoo.co.uk
dir: From A1exit A607 towards Melton Mowbray follow heritage signs for Belvoir Castle

The Chequers is a 17th-century inn set in the lee of Belvoir Castle, by the village cricket pitch, and has its own petanque lawn. Inside you'll find a cosy warren of dining rooms furnished with dark wood tables and high-backed leather chairs, looking quite contemporary set against the beams and exposed brickwork. Options range through steaks from the grill, pub classics (sausage and mash with onion gravy) and fine dining dishes such as fillet of sea bass, wild mushrooms, crushed new potatoes, red wine and shallot sauce. There's also a good choice of real beers.

Chef Derek Peart **Owner** Justin & Joanne Chad **Times** 12-3/5.30-11, Closed D 25-26 Dec, 1 Jan **Prices** Fixed L 2 course fr £11.50, Fixed D 3 course fr £15, Starter £4.50-£8.50, Main £9-£19.95, Dessert £5.50-£6.50, Service optional **Wines** 25 bottles over £20, 29 bottles under £20, 29 by glass **Notes** Sunday L, Vegetarian available **Seats** 70, Pr/dining room 14 **Children** Portions, Menu **Parking** 35

London

St Paul's from Millennium Bridge

Index of London Restaurants

This index shows rosetted restaurants in London in alphabetical order, followed by their postcodes and map references. Page numbers precede each entry.

London Plan 1

6

0   1   2 miles
0   1   2   3 kilometres

Northwood Hills

Eastbury

Grims Dyke Hotel

Hatch End

Harrow Weald

Harrow Weald

Edgware

Pinner Green

Belmont

Burnt Oak

Hendon Hall

Church End

Finchley

Pinner ● Friends Restaurant

Wealdstone

Queensbury

Eastcote Village

North Harrow

HARROW

Kenton

Kingsbury

Colindale

West Hendon

Hendon

5

Eastcote

Rayners Lane

Incanto Restaurant

Harrow on the Hill

Preston

North Wembley

Neasden

Golders Green

● Hawtrey's Restaurant at the Barn Hotel

South Harrow

North Wembley

Cricklewood

Ickenham

South Ruislip

Sudbury

WEMBLEY

Willesden

Kensal Green

Kilburn

Northolt Aerodrome

Northolt

Perivale

Alperton

Stonebridge

Harlesden

North Hillingdon

Park Royal

Kensal Green

4

Hillingdon

Hayes End

Greenford

North Acton

North Kensington

Lonsdale

Yiewsley

Wood End

Momo

EALING

East Acton

E & O

The Ledbury

Hayes

Southall

Hanwell

Acton

Notting Hill Brasserie

Notting Hill

West Drayton

Shepherds Bush

Edera

Chez Kristof

Snows-on-the-Green

Cibo

Kensington

3

Sipson

Harlington

Norwood Green

Heston Services

Osterley Park

Heston

Brentford

Kew

Anglesea Arms

High Road Brasserie

Agni

The Brackenbury

Sagar

Timo

Sam's Brasserie & Bar

La Trompette

Devonshire House

The Devonshire

HAMMERSMITH

The Gate

Ma

Sonny's Restaurant

The River Café

Blue Elephant

Cranford

Kew

FULHAM

Dee

Saran Rom

Yi Ban Chelsea

HEATHROW AIRPORT

Hatton

HOUNSLOW

Isleworth

GARDENS

The Glasshouse

Barnes

Mortlake

The Depot

Waterfront Brasserie

Redmond's

Spencer Arms

Wyndham Gran

Harbour Hotel (Aquasia)

Enoteca Turi

West Bedfont

East Bedfont

Whitton

Crane Park

La Brasserie McClements

Twickenham

Bingham Hotel, Restaurant & Bar

Brula

Restaurant at the Petersham

Petersham Nurseries

RICHMOND

La Buvette

Richmond Hill Hotel

Gates on the Park (Richmond Gate Hotel)

East Sheen

Talad Thai

Putney

Roehampton

RICHMOND

2

Feltham

Lower Feltham

Hanworth

Hampton Hill

Teddington

Ham

PARK

WIMBLEDON COMMON

WIMBLEDON

Ashford

Felthamhill

Hampton

Hampton Wick

BUSHY PARK

Ayudhya Thai Restaurant

Common

The Light House Restaurant

Charlton

Sunbury

Hampton

HAMPTON COURT PARK

Frère Jacques

KINGSTON UPON THAMES

Norbiton

New Malden

Raynes Park

Morden

1

Central London Congestion Charging Zone

Upper Halliford

West Molesey

East Molesey

Thames Ditton

The French Table

Surb

Berrylands

Motspur Park

Shepperton

Walton-on-Thames

Island Barn Reservoir

Queen Elizabeth II Reservoir

A   **B**   **C**   **D**

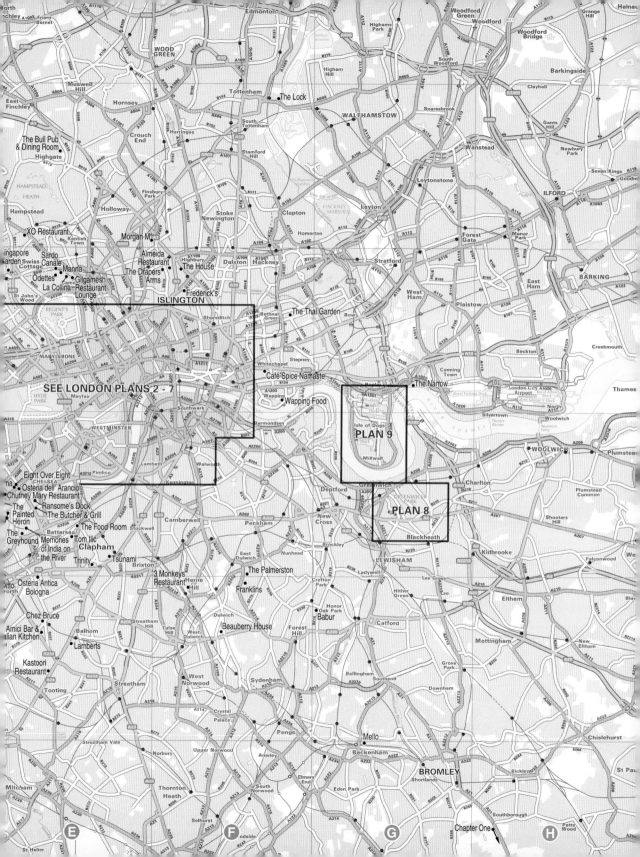

The Bull Pub
& Dining Room
Highgate

XO Restaurant
Morgan M
Singapore
Garden   Swiss
Cottage
Sardo
Canale
Odettes
Manna
Camo
Gilgamesh
La Collina   Restaurant
Lounge
St John's
Wood

Almeida
Restaurant
The Drapers
Arms
The House
Frederick's

ISLINGTON

Café Spice Namaste

Wapping Food

The Thai Garden

The Narrow

PLAN 9

SEE LONDON PLANS 2 - 7

Eight Over Eight
Osteria dell' Arancio
Chutney Mary Restaurant
The
Painted
Heron
Ransome's Dock
The Butcher & Grill
The
Greyhound
Memories
of India on
the River
The Food Room
Tom Ilic
Trinity
Tsunami

PLAN 8

Ditto
Osteria Antica
Bologna

3 Monkeys
Restaurant
Franklins

The Palmerston

Chez Bruce

Amici Bar &
Italian Kitchen
Lamberts

Beauberry House

Babur

Kastoori
Restaurant

Mello

Chapter One

BROMLEY

E   F   G   H

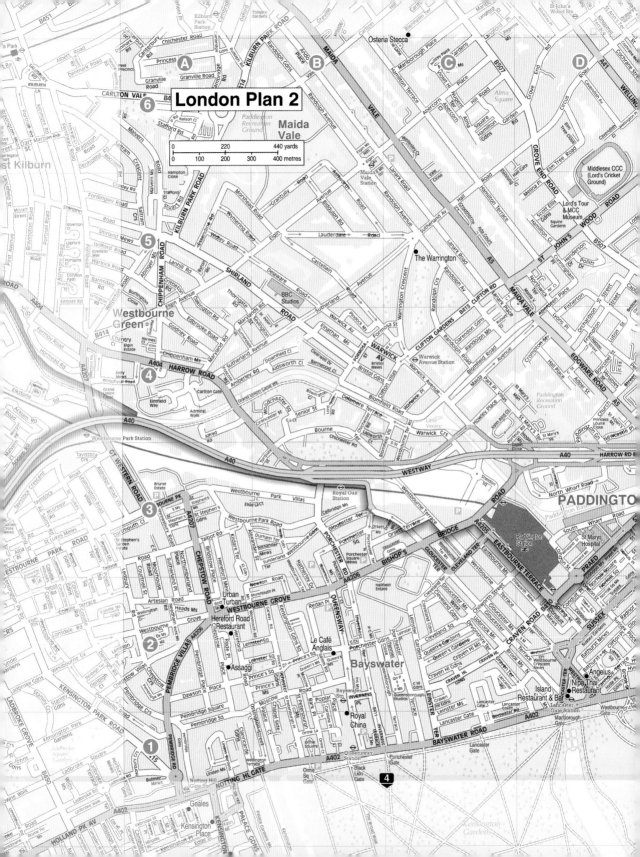

London Plan 2

Maida Vale

Scale: 0 100 200 300 400 metres / 0 220 440 yards

London Plan 3

Regent's Park

Somers Town

St Pancras

King's Cross Station

St Pancras Station

British Library

Mirrors - Novotel London St Pancras

Megaro

Acorn House Restaurant

Euston Station

University Coll Hosp

University College London

Bloomsbury

British Museum

The Montague on the Gardens

National Hosp for Sick Children (Great Ormond St)

Coram's Fields Playground

Russell Square Station

The Landau

Orrery

Villandry

Archipelago

Salt Yard

Fino
Roka
Pied à Terre
Passione
Camerino
Rasa Samudra
Bam-Bou
Latium
Ozer
Hakkasan

Birkbeck Coll

Uni of London

Holborn Station

Pearl Restaurant & Bar

Jurys Great Russell Street

Goodge St Station

Tottenham Court Road Stn

St Giles

32 Great Queen Street

Oxford Circus

Vasco & Piero's Pavilion Restaurant

The Red Fort
Quo Vadis
Arbutus
L'Escargot
Mon Plaisir

La Trouvaille
Yauatcha
Barrafina
Alastair Little
Incognico

L'Atelier de Joel Robuchon

Bond Street Stn

Ristorante Semplice

Sketch (Lecture Room & Library)
Dehesa
Hibiscus

Soho

Lindsay House
Y Ming
Bar Shu

The Ivy

Royal Opera House

Covent Garden Station

Orso
Christophers

Axis at One Aldwych & Indigo

Maze Grill
La Petite Maison
Gordon Ramsay at Claridge's
Cipriani
Umu
Wild Honey
Via Condotti
Sartoria
The Westbury Hotel

China Town

Imperial China

Maggiore's

Strand

The Admiralty Restaurant

Millennium Hotel Mayfair
Berkeley Square Café
The Square
Nicole's
Embassy
Cecconi's
So Restaurant

J. Sheekey

Sumosan
Bellamy's
Veeraswamy Restaurant
Le Meridien Piccadilly
The Terrace
Cocoon

The Savoy

The Strand Terrace

Scotts
Benares

Mayfair

The Grill (Brown's)
Bentley's Oyster Bar & Grill
Aslan

Mitsukoshi
St Alban

The Portrait Restaurant

Automat
Alloro
Mosaico

Nobu Berkeley

Royal Academy of Arts

Al Duca
Brasserie Roux

National Gallery

Trafalgar Square

Kai Mayfair
The Only Running Footman
Butlers
The Greenhouse
Mirabelle

Benares

The Wolseley
The Ritz Restaurant
Quaglino's
Sake No: Hana
Green Le Caprice
Just St James

Mint Leaf
Albannach

One Twenty

Queen El Golden Jub Bridge

EUSTON ROAD

MARYLEBONE ROAD

PENTONVILLE ROAD

OXFORD ST

PICCADILLY

PALL MALL

STRAND

CHARING CROSS RD

SHAFTESBURY AV

REGENT STREET

GRAY'S INN RD

TOTTENHAM COURT RD

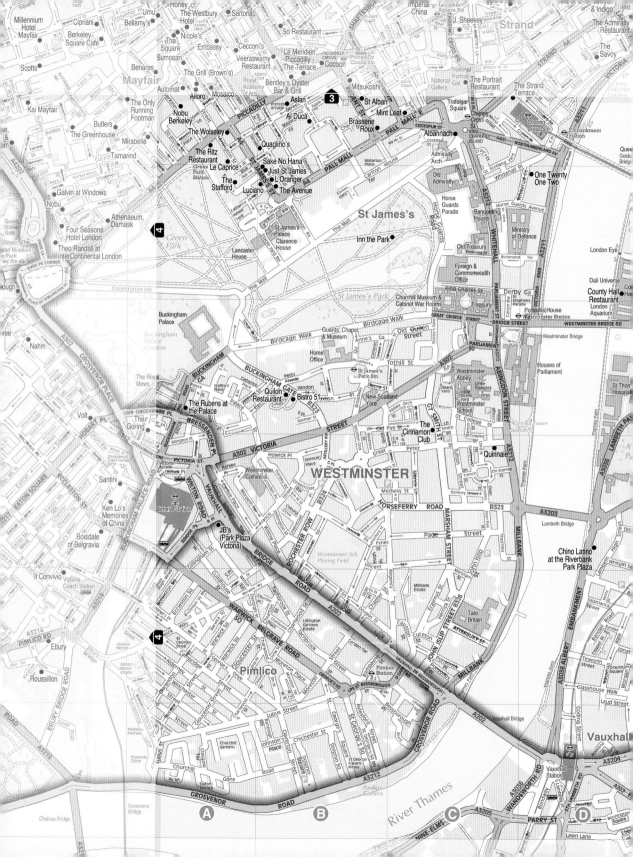

London Plan 6

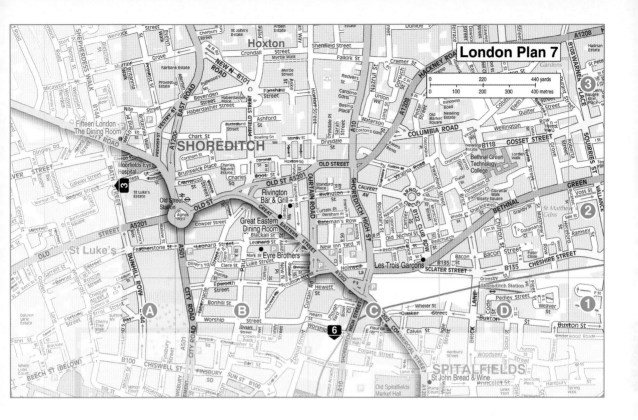

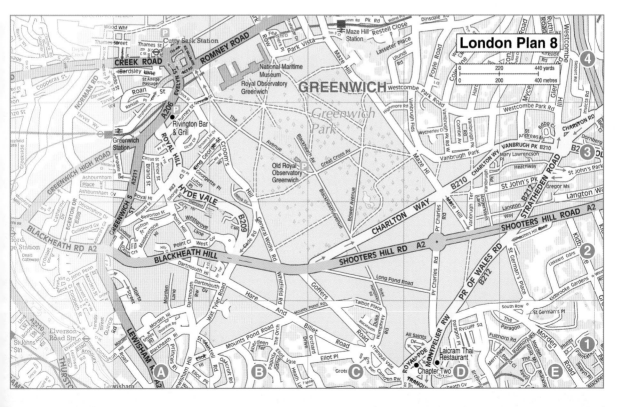

LONDON

LONDON

Greater London Plans 1-9, pages 224-236. (Small scale maps 6 & 7 at back of Guide.) Restaurants are listed below in postal district order, commencing East, then North, South and West, with a brief indication of the area covered. Detailed plans 2-9 show the locations of restaurants with AA Rosette Awards within the Central London postal districts. If you do not know the postal district of the restaurant you want, please refer to the index preceding the street plans for the entry and map pages. The plan reference for each restaurant also appears within its directory entry.

LONDON E1

Café Spice Namasté

Indian Plan 1 F4

Authentic Indian café dining

☎ 020 7488 9242
16 Prescot St E1 8AZ
e-mail: binay@cafespice.co.uk
dir: Nearest station: Tower Gateway (DLR), Aldgate, Tower Hill Walking distance from Tower Hill

'Namasté' means 'gracious hello' in Hindi and you're certainly guaranteed of a genuinely warm welcome as you walk through the doors of this listed building that began life in the 18th century as a magistrate's court. Now it is a bright, colourful and vibrant restaurant, focusing on the regional foods of India with the occasional influence from elsewhere in Asia. Bhael poori flies the flag for Bombay among starters, or there is squid dynamite (squid rings marinated in a fiery Goan peri-peri sauce). Main-course badak kay tikkay is breast of Barbary duck marinated in extract of garlic and ginger with yoghurt, chilli and spices, and monkfish chettinad uses fish from Falmouth.

Chef Cyrus Todiwala, Angelo Collaco **Owner** Cyrus & Pervin Todiwala **Times** 12-3/6.15-10.30, Closed Xmas, BHs, Closed Sun, Closed L Sat **Prices** Fixed L 3 course £25-£35, Fixed D 3 course fr £30, Starter £4.75-£6.95, Main £14.25-£16.50, Dessert £3.25-£5.75, Service added but optional 12.5% **Wines** 20 bottles over £20, 20 bottles under £20, 10 by glass **Notes** Tasting menu available, Dress restrictions, Smart casual, Air con **Seats** 120 **Children** Portions **Parking** On street; NCP

Canteen

Modern British Plan 6 D6

All-day eatery in Spitalfields

☎ 0845 686 1122
2 Crispin Place, Spitalfields E1 6DW
e-mail: spitalfields@canteen.co.uk
dir: Nearest station: Spitalfields, Liverpool Street Overlooking Spitalfields Market

This unpretentious eatery is situated in Spitalfields Market. Featuring materials like oak, cork, leather and marble, the restaurant is glass-walled on three sides,

with retro booth seating and long shared tables. High-quality cuisine prepared from British produce is offered at reasonable prices. A lengthy all-day menu includes breakfast, designated 'fast service' dishes, as well as a daily roast, home-made pies (with meat and vegetable versions), stews, bakes and fish options. Expect British classics conjured from the finest ingredients - a starter of smoked mackerel and potato salad, followed by roast chicken with chips and garlic mayonnaise. Treacle tart is a favourite dessert and there's a popular cake counter.

Chef Cass Titcombe **Owner** Cass Titcombe, Patrick Clayton-Malone, Dominic Lake **Times** 8/11 **Prices** Starter £4.50-£8, Main £7-£11.50, Dessert £5, Service added but optional 12.5% **Wines** 29 bottles over £20, 11 bottles under £20, 40 by glass **Notes** Vegetarian available, Air con **Seats** 160 **Children** Portions

Lanes Restaurant & Bar

Modern European Plan 6 C5

Modern city brasserie with cooking to match

☎ 020 7247 5050
109-117 Middlesex St E1 7JF
e-mail: info@lanesrestaurant.co.uk
web: www.lanesrestaurant.co.uk
dir: Nearest station: Liverpool Street

Tucked away off Bishopsgate, just a short stroll from Liverpool Street station, this modern and relaxed basement restaurant and lounge bar is popular with City types, but, unusually for this area, it also opens on Saturday evenings attracting a different crowd. The split-level space has burgundy leather banquettes and chairs, polished-wood floors and large contemporary artworks on the part-panelled walls. Leather tub chairs and matching bar stools populate the bar area, while service is suitably youthful and attentive. The cooking fits with the contemporary styling, its modern-European brasserie repertoire driven by quality ingredients and a carefully presented, clean-cut, accomplished approach. Start with Jerusalem artichoke and truffle soup before parmesan-crusted pork cutlet with caramelised apple salad, finishing with crème brûlée.

Chef Halim Harrache **Owner** James & Rachael Robertson, Liam Cooper, Caroline Judd **Times** 12-3/5.30-10, Closed BHs, 25 Dec, 1 Jan, Closed Sun, Closed L Sat **Prices** Fixed D 3 course £27.50, Starter £6.50-£12.50, Main £12.50-£25, Dessert £6.50-£8.50, Service added but optional 12.5% **Wines** 60 bottles over £20, 6 bottles under £20, 14 by glass **Notes** Vegetarian available, Air con **Seats** 70, Pr/dining room 28 **Children** Min 7 yrs L, Portions **Parking** On street after 6.30 pm

St John Bread & Wine

British Plan 6 D6

Unpretentious all-day restaurant, bakery and wine shop in Spitalfields

☎ 020 7251 0848
94-96 Commercial St E1 6LZ
e-mail: reservations@stjohnbreadandwine.com
dir: Nearest station: Liverpool Street

Hidden away behind the old Spitalfields Market, this no-frills spin-off to big brother St John (see entry) is a resoundingly British affair. Whitewashed walls lined with clothes pegs, parquet flooring, simple wooden furniture and an open-to-view kitchen set a wonderfully utilitarian, buzzy, canteen-like edge. The trademark British food is flavour-driven and equally unfussy, using quality seasonal produce to deliver some robust dishes using humble, lesser-used ingredients; take pig's cheek, chicory and shallots, or salted middlewhite pork and lentils, and perhaps Eccles cake with Lancashire cheese. The menu eschews the formal three-course format and service is friendly and well informed, while wines - like the great in-house breads - are on sale to take out.

Chef James Lowe **Owner** Trevor Gulliver & Fergus Henderson **Times** 9/11, Closed 25 Dec-1 Jan, BHs **Prices** Food prices not confirmed for 2009. Please telephone for details. **Wines** 31 bottles over £20, 15 bottles under £20, 25 by glass **Notes** Vegetarian available, Air con **Seats** 60 **Parking** on street

Les Trois Garçons

Modern French Plan 7 C2

Quirky ex-pub with authentic French menus

☎ 020 7613 1924
1 Club Row E1 6JX
e-mail: info@lestroisgarcons.com
dir: Nearest station: Liverpool Street 10mins walk from station, at the end of Brick Ln

Although the cooking here is classically French with flavours from across Europe, you might wonder at the setting - a cross between an exotic Eastern bazaar and a Victorian antique shop. Outrageously garish stuffed animals hang from the walls, while giant crystals cast a seductive glow on the tables below. It's a surreal background to the serious dining, and an amusing conversation piece. There's nothing funny about the menu, though, where pan-seared foie gras with apple compôte and foie gras caramel sauce makes an elegant prelude to, say, braised shoulder of Farmer Sharp's pink veal with creamed parsnips, chanterelle mushrooms and home-made saffron linguini. Tarte Tatin is a suitably Gallic dessert. Great care is taken to source the freshest, seasonal local produce.

Chef Jérôme Henry **Owner** Stefan Karlson, Hussan Abdullah, Michel Lasserre **Times** Closed Xmas & New Year, Closed Sun **Prices** Fixed D 3 course fr £29, Starter £8.50-£15, Main £18.50-£33, Dessert £6.50-£8.50, Service added but optional 12.5% **Wines** 130-150 bottles over £20, 20 by glass **Notes** Fixed D Mon-Wed, Vegetarian available, Dress restrictions, Smart casual, Air con **Seats** 80, Pr/dining room 12 **Children** Min 12 yrs **Parking** On street after 7pm

LONDON E1 *Continued*

Wapping Food

◉ Modern International   Plan 1 F4

Inspired cooking meets industrial heritage at the Wapping Project

☎ 020 7680 2080
Wapping Hydraulic, Power Station, Wapping Wall E1W 3SG
dir: Nearest station: Shadwell DLR Between Wapping Wall & King Edward VII Memorial Park, parallel to the river

If a former hydraulic pumping station in the East End is not a conventional place to eat, then long live unconventionality. This part art gallery, part restaurant manages to team old machinery, tiles and girders from its industrial days with dangling chandeliers, designer furniture and flickering candles to create a chic urban space. Importantly, the food manages to live up to the setting. A menu of inspired international dishes is distinguished by high-quality ingredients and imaginative combinations. Starters such as potted shrimps or smoked eel and trout rillette precede robust main courses like chargrilled veal chop, Jerusalem artichoke and lemon butter.

Chef Cameron Emirali **Owner** Womens Playhouse Trust **Times** 12-3/6.30-11, Closed 24 Dec-3 Jan, BHs, Closed D Sun **Prices** Fixed L course £45, Fixed D 3 course £45, Starter £5.50-£15, Main £13-£20, Dessert £5.50-£8.25, Service added but optional 12.5% **Wines** 132 bottles over £20, 8 bottles under £20, 27 by glass **Notes** Brunch at wknds, Sunday L, Vegetarian available **Seats** 150 **Children** Portions **Parking** 20

LONDON E2

The Thai Garden

◉ Thai V   Plan 1 F4

Authentic vegetarian and seafood Thai restaurant

☎ 020 8981 5748
249 Globe Rd E2 0JD
e-mail: thaigarden@hotmail.com
dir: Nearest station: Bethnal Green 2nd left off Roman Rd (one-way street). Near London Buddhist Centre

This Thai vegetarian and seafood restaurant is the real deal, despite its unlikely setting in Bethnal Green. The unpretentious shop-front bistro gives way to a small dining room with 20 seats. The authentic cooking is fragrant with some serious chillies, so be warned or go

for the gentler herb options. The menu is in Thai and English and offers a wide choice of dishes, such as gaeng phed (Thai aubergines and mixed vegetable curry with coconut cream), and goong pahd king (fried prawns with eggs, wine sauce, ginger, spring onions, dry mushrooms and red chilli).

Chef Napathorn Duff **Owner** S & J Hufton **Times** 12-2.30/6-11, Closed BHs, Closed L Sat & Sun **Prices** Food prices not confirmed for 2009. Please telephone for details. **Notes** Vegetarian menu **Seats** 32, Pr/dining room 12 **Children** Portions **Parking** on street

Hanoi Café

💻

☎ 020 7729 5610
98 Kingsland Rd E2 8DP
web: http://www.theaa.com/travel/index.jsp

Choose from over 100 freshly home-made Vietnamese dishes in a buzzy atmosphere.

Prices Food prices not confirmed for 2009. Please telephone for details.

LONDON E14

Curve Restaurant & Bar

◉ Fish & Seafood   Plan 9 B6

Relaxed Docklands dining with fabulous views

☎ 020 7517 2808 & 7517 2806
London Marriott W India Quay, 22 Hertsmere Rd, Canary Wharf E14 4ED
e-mail: mhrs.loncw.restaurant.supervisor@ marriotthotels.com
dir: Nearest station: Canary Wharf/West India Quay DLR Telephone for directions

Located in a spectacular skyscraper, this new-build hotel overlooks West India Quay in the heart of Docklands. The Curve restaurant takes its name from the curved glass façade of the building. The full-length windows overlook the water and the pretty terrace is the perfect location for dining alfresco. The emphasis is on fresh fish from nearby Billingsgate Fish Market, with a wide selection of simply

cooked modern dishes that rely on the quality of the fish. Typical options are starters such as juicy king prawns grilled with mustard seeds and coriander and served with rocket salad, and mains including pan-fried salmon fillet with beurre blanc, sautéed spinach and fries.

Times 12-2.30/5-10.30

Four Seasons Hotel Canary Wharf

◉◉ Italian   Plan 9 A6

Simple Italian fare in chic surroundings

☎ 020 7510 1999
Westferry Circus, Canary Wharf E14 8RS
dir: Nearest station: Canary Wharf Just off Westbury Circus rdbt

Quadrato is a sophisticated Thames-side eatery set in a modern Docklands hotel with superb views over the London skyline. Here you can tuck into a versatile range of modern Italian dishes, or some classic regional specialities, strong on fresh, seasonal ingredients and packed with flavour. The food is prepared with great accuracy in full view of diners in the open-to-view theatre kitchen. Simple flavoursome combinations might include a starter of seared scallops with home-made pasta, served with herb and tomato sauce, followed by an impressive main course of roast duck breast with Jerusalem artichoke flan, served with sautéed spinach and asparagus. The predominantly Italian staff are friendly and enthusiastic.

Times 12-3/6-10.30

The Gun

◉ British 💻   Plan 9 D5

Smart Docklands gastro-pub serving modern British food

☎ 020 7515 5222
27 Coldharbour, Docklands E14 9NS
e-mail: info@thegundocklands.com
dir: Nearest station: South Quay DLR, Canary Wharf From South Quay DLR, E down Marsh Wall to mini rdbt, turn left, over bridge then take 1st right

A fabulous Thames-side location with a stunning terrace affording great views of the Millennium Dome and the river are among the attractions at this beautifully restored 18th-century dockers' pub. No longer spit-and-sawdust, expect oak timber floors, Georgian-style fireplaces, crisp linen-clothed tables in smart dining rooms, and an inviting bar. Competent modern British cooking results in versatile menus that include the likes of mussel, fennel and saffron broth, or sirloin steak with garlic butter and fat chips, alongside pan-fried John Dory with shellfish velouté. The Gun is also a great spot for Sunday brunch and summer barbecues.

Times 12-3/6-10.30, Closed 25-26 Dec

The Narrow

◉ British 🖳   Plan 1 G4

Gordon Ramsay's waterside pub serving classic British dishes

☎ 020 7592 7950
44 Narrow St E14 8DP
e-mail: thenarrow@gordonramsay.com
dir: Nearest station: Limehouse

This Grade II listed former dockmaster's house dates back 100 years and has been part of the Gordon Ramsay empire since 2007. Set on the edge of the Thames, there are great views across the water and bags of character in both the pub's ground floor bar area and separate dining room. Half-wall panelling, fireplaces and black-and-white vintage photographs and prints help create informal but civilised spaces. Bar snacks include pickled cockles and whelks, and there is a full menu based around classic British dishes such as a starter of pork pie with home-made piccalilli or soft herring roes on toast. The focus is genuinely placed on traditional foods including a main-course whole rainbow trout with samphire and peas. 'The Captain's Table' private dining room is on the first floor.

Times 11.30/10.30

Plateau

◉◉ Modern French V 🖳 ⬧NOTABLE WINE LIST   Plan 9 B6

Sophisticated, contemporary fine dining in futuristic landscape

☎ 020 7715 7100
Canada Place, Canada Square, Canary Wharf E14 5ER
e-mail: plateauR@DandDLondon.com
dir: Nearest station: Canary Wharf Facing Canary Wharf Tower and Canada Square Park

Boasting dramatic views over Canada Square and the rooftops of Canary Wharf, this modern glass-and-steel restaurant is the epitome of contemporary style, bringing a touch of Manhattan glamour to the heart of Docklands. The stunning complex has floor-to-ceiling glass frontage and two dining areas divided by a semi-open kitchen, each side with its own outside terrace and bar, and the bustling Bar & Grill which offers a simpler menu. The restaurant has a calm atmosphere, the futuristic design mixing classic 1950s style with warm, restrained colours and contemporary spin, including white 'tulip' swivel chairs, marble-topped tables, swirling banquettes and huge floor-standing arching lamps. The modern French menu follows the theme, with highly accomplished, clean-cut modern dishes driven by high-quality ingredients and delivered dressed to thrill. Expect starters like lobster and celeriac cannelloni with herb salad and tarragon oil, and for mains, organic Shetland cod with braised lettuce, and courgette and shallot chutney. Service is slick and professional. (The restaurant is accessed via a lift from Canada Place shopping mall.)

Chef Tim Tolley **Owner** D & D London
Times 12-3/6-10.30, Closed 25-26 Dec, 1 Jan, BHs, Closed Sun, Closed L Sat **Prices** Fixed D 3 course fr £26.50, Tasting menu £52-£83, Starter £8.50-£15, Main

£22-£28, Dessert £7.50-£9, Service added but optional 12.5% **Wines** All bottles over £20, 13 by glass **Notes** Tasting menu 5 courses, Sun L bar & grill only, Sunday L, Vegetarian menu, Dress restrictions, Smart casual, Civ Wed 180, Air con **Seats** 124, Pr/dining room 24 **Children** Portions **Parking** 200

Royal China

◉ Traditional Chinese   Plan 9 A6

Accomplished Chinese food with wonderful views of the river

☎ 020 7719 0888
Canary Wharf Riverside, 30 Westferry Circus E14 8RR
e-mail: info@royalchinagroup.co.uk
dir: Nearest station: Canary Wharf

An impressive glass-fronted building on the river's edge at Canary Wharf is the setting for this popular Chinese restaurant. The interior features lots of black and gold lacquering and crisp white linen. Head outside in summer for fantastic views and savour the wholesome, traditional Cantonese cooking, which makes the most of good ingredients. Dishes range from set meals and gourmet seafood including lobster to dim sum, cold appetisers, plenty of seafood, meat dishes, vegetables and bean curd. There's also a good selection of rice and noodle dishes.

Times Noon/11, Closed 23-25 Dec

Ubon by Nobu

◉◉ Japanese, American 🖳   Plan 9 A6

Swish celebrity hangout with an impeccable Japanese dining experience

☎ 020 7719 7800
34 Westferry Circus, Canary Wharf E14 8RR
e-mail: ubon@noburestaurants.com
dir: Nearest station: Westferry, Canary Wharf Follow signs to Canary Wharf, then Canary Riverside. Restaurant behind Four Seasons Hotel

Nobu is one of the hottest names in restaurant dining in the world, renowned for stylish design, flawless service and innovative food. This chic Docklands restaurant, with a stunning Thames-side location, maintains this exceptional fusion and has a panoramic view with floor-to-ceiling glass walls on three sides of the dining room. You can sample some truly cutting-edge cuisine that takes classic Japanese and adds a liberal sprinkling of South American tastes and textures with oodles of contemporary panache and intricate presentation.

Indulge your palate with dishes such as black cod with miso, perhaps scallops with wasabi pepper sauce, lobster salad with spicy lemon dressing, rock shrimp tempura with ponzu, or anti-cucho Peruvian-style spicy rib-eye steak. Leave room for the chocolate Bento box.

Chef Nobuyuki Matsuhisa **Owner** Nobuyuki Matsuhisa **Times** 12-2/6-10, Closed BHs, Closed Sun, Closed L Sat **Prices** Starter £5-£15, Main £10-£40, Dessert £5-£10, Service added 15% **Wines** 60 bottles over £20, 7 by glass **Notes** Promotional menu 5 signature dishes available on request, Vegetarian available, Air con **Seats** 120 **Parking** Riverside car park

LONDON EC1

Ambassador

◉◉ European   Plan 3 F5

Relaxed, super-friendly Clerkenwell dining

☎ 020 7837 0009
55 Exmouth Market EC1R 4QL
e-mail: clive@theambassadorcafe.co.uk
dir: Nearest station: Farringdon Take 1st right off Roseberry Av, heading N from Farringdon Rd junct. Turn right into Exmouth Market

With glass doors opening out on to the pavement and outside tables filling up with the Exmouth Market crowd, The Ambassador is a local café-cum-restaurant that has something for everyone. Open for breakfast, brunch, lunch and dinner, there are cocktails, too, served at the long, cool bar. The friendliest of service and good food at reasonable prices help to make it a local gem. Plainly decorated in magnolia, offset by the odd print or mirror, the long room comes decked out with dark green tables, simple wooden seating and crimson banquettes. The kitchen's modern approach is assured and accomplished, whether it's sweet-cured bacon with waffles for breakfast or red pepper omelette for lunch. Dinner might start with venison carpaccio with truffled celeriac remoulade before moving on to slow-cooked Herdwick mutton with creamed parsnips.

Times 12-3/6.30-12, Closed 1 wk Xmas, Closed D Sun

The Bleeding Heart

◉ Modern French 🖳 ⬧NOTABLE WINE LIST   Plan 3 F4

Discreet and romantic Hatton Garden French restaurant

☎ 020 7242 2056
Bleeding Heart Yard, off Greville St EC1N 8SJ
e-mail: bookings@bleedingheart.co.uk
dir: Nearest station: Farringdon Turn right out of Farringdon Station onto Cowcross St, continue up Greville St for 50mtrs. Turn left into Bleeding Heart Yard

Located in a historic cobbled courtyard where society beauty Lady Elizabeth Hatton was found murdered in the 17th century, this establishment comprises a tavern, bistro, and romantic restaurant - the latter exuding atmosphere, with wooden floors and beams, intimate lighting and smartly dressed tables. The place buzzes with gallic charm,

Continued

LONDON EC1 *Continued*

slick service and robust modern French cuisine using top notch ingredients. Papillote of sea bass with crab and ginger farci, baby fennel croquante and vanilla jus shows the style, or meat-lovers might opt for grilled tournedos of South Devon beef with five-peppercorn crust, sautéed spinach and truffled croquettes. Classic desserts feature the likes of tarte au citron with raspberries, or prune and Armagnac parfait with Earl Grey syrup.

Chef Peter Reffell **Owner** Robert & Robyn Wilson **Times** 12-3.15/6-11, Closed Xmas & New Year (10 days), Closed Sat-Sun **Prices** Starter £6.50-£10.50, Main £12.95-£23.95, Dessert £6.45-£7.25, Service added but optional 12.5% **Wines** 270 bottles over £20, 8 bottles under £20, 20 by glass **Notes** Dress restrictions, Smart casual, Air con **Seats** 110, Pr/dining room 40 **Children** Min 7 yrs **Parking** 20 evening only, NCP nearby

Le Café du Marché

◉ French　　　　　　　　　　　　　　Plan 3 G4

Welcoming French brasserie

☎ 020 7608 1609
Charterhouse Mews, Charterhouse Square EC1M 6AH
dir: Nearest station: Barbican Telephone for directions (or see website)

Tucked away down a cobbled mews a short hop from several major markets is this truly welcoming little brasserie. Friendly French staff add their bit to the

authentic atmosphere, which comes undiluted from provincial France. Exposed bricks and beams, and closely-packed tables, lend a cosy touch, and though it's usually packed with business people it doesn't feel overcrowded. The pick of the markets finds its way on to the fixed price menus, where the freshest of fish, perhaps pan-fried marlin, and the hottest cuts of meat, such as côte de boeuf with sauce bearnaise, are well matched by the day's soups, starters and desserts.

Chef Simon Cottard **Owner** Anna Graham-Wood **Times** 12-2.30/6-10, Closed Xmas, New Year, Etr, BHs, Closed Sun, Closed L Sat **Prices** Fixed D 3 course £31.50, Service added but optional 15% **Notes** Air con **Seats** 120, Pr/dining room 65 **Children** Portions **Parking** Next door (small charge)

The Clerkenwell Dining Room & Bar

◉◉　Modern European　　　　　　　　　Plan 3 G4

Relaxed fine dining in trendy Clerkenwell

☎ 020 7253 9000
69-73 St. John St EC1 4AN
e-mail: restaurant@theclerkenwell.com
dir: Nearest station: Farringdon, Barbican From Farringdon station, continue 60mtrs up Farringdon Rd, left into Cowcross St, left into Peters Ln, left into St John St

Behind a blue and terracotta-red frontage, The Clerkenwell's interior surprises with its clean, warm tones and contemporary lines. White-clothed tables, black leather chairs and cream leather banquettes provide the

comforts, while parquet floors, modern artwork and flamboyant flower displays catch the eye, combining with slick and professional service to create an upbeat mood and style. The ambition of the kitchen echoes the surroundings, its creatively presented, cultured and confident modern approach driven by quality produce; take lamb saddle served with tagliolini, mint, sweet pea emulsion and pea shoots, or perhaps halibut accompanied by baby squid with lemon and parsley, white coco bean purée and tomato and light curry sauce. (Also see sister restaurant, The Chancery, EC4.)

Times 12-3/6-11, Closed Xmas, BHs, Closed Sun, Closed L Sat

Club Gascon

◉◉◉ – *see below*

Club Gascon

LONDON EC1	Plan 3 G3

Modern French ▭ 〈NOTABLE WINE LIST〉

With the cuisine of Gascony as its bedrock, this Smithfield stalwart has a huge following

☎ 020 7796 0600
57 West Smithfield EC1A 9DS
e-mail: info@clubgascon.com
dir: Nearest station: Barbican or Farringdon Telephone for directions

The premises, a former Lyons Teahouse, may be steeped in history - St Bart's hospital and the main entrance to Smithfield's market are just across the way - but it is now every inch the sophisticated, modern dining venue. A favourite spot for the fabled 'long lunch' of the City, you can expect to be greeted on arrival by stunning flower arrangements created by the chef himself, then drink in

the marble-clad walls and old oak flooring in this small bustling dining room. Advance booking is essential - as is confirming the booking - and service from the smart, black-tied waiting staff is unhurried. The dishes are served in small portions (tasting plates) and the restaurant has its roots in the French provincial cooking of Gascony - think foie gras. 'Le Marche' is a seasonal menu for the whole table, or chose from over 20 enticingly creative dishes. All the ingredients are of the very best quality, painstakingly sourced from South West France, but the menu contains imaginatively compelling combinations; so expect the likes of confit of organic salmon, violet tea and citrus chutney alongside foie gras popcorn or cappuccino of black pudding and lobster. To finish, 'Gold Sensation' - vanilla foie gras, candied chestnuts and sweet mango - is hard to resist. The extensive French wine list specialises in the South and South West of France.

Chef Pascal Aussignac **Owner** P Aussignac & V Labeyrie **Times** 12-2/7-10, Closed Xmas, New Year, BHs, Closed Sun, Closed L Sat **Prices** Fixed L course £28, Service added but optional 12.5% **Wines** 101 bottles over £20, 3 bottles under £20, 9 by glass **Notes** Monthly 5 course tasting menu, Vegetarian available, Air con **Seats** 45 **Children** Portions **Parking** NCP opposite restaurant

Le Comptoir Gascon

◉ Traditional French 🖥 Plan 3 F4

Bistro/deli serving classic French dishes

☎ 020 7608 0851
61-63 Charterhouse St EC1M 6HJ
e-mail: info@comptoirgascon.com
web: www.comptoirgascon.com
dir: Nearest station: Farringdon, Barbican, St Paul's,
Chancery Ln Telephone for directions, or see website

Part of the Club Gascon (see entry) collection, this small
establishment opposite Smithfield Market comprises a
bistro-style restaurant with around a dozen small tables
and a deli serving quality takeaway items in the same
room. The aim is to provide generous portions of
traditional French food inspired by the South West of
France in a setting that recreates easy-going country chic
in the City. Many items are sourced directly from France;
think cassoulet Toulousain, perhaps beef onglet served
with sauce bordelaise, or perhaps chargrilled baby squid
with peppers and rouille. Booking is highly advisable.

Chef Julien Carlon **Owner** Vincent Labeyrie, Pascal
Aussignac **Times** 12-2/7-11, Closed 25 Dec, 1 Jan,
Closed Sun & Mon **Prices** Starter £4-£10, Main
£10.50-£14.50, Dessert £3.50-£6, Service added but
optional 12.5% **Wines** 14 bottles over £20, 3 bottles
under £20, 8 by glass **Notes** Air con **Seats** 32

Malmaison Charterhouse Square

◉◉ Modern British, French 🖥 ☁ Plan 3 G4

Boutique hotel with accessible, easy-going brasserie

☎ 020 7012 3700
18-21 Charterhouse Square, Clerkenwell EC1M 6AH
e-mail: london@malmaison.com
dir: Nearest station: Barbican

Once a nurses' residence for St Bart's Hospital, this
attractive red-brick Victorian building is set in a cobbled
courtyard just off Charterhouse Square and shares the
same high production values upheld by other
establishments in the Malmaison chain. In the chic,
buzzing brasserie-style restaurant with its mood-
enhancing lighting, tables are set on two levels, some in

brick-backed alcoves. The menu offers mainly French
cuisine prepared from the quality produce of named
suppliers, and delivered with simplicity and skill. Expect
the likes of Maldon oysters to start, then naturally reared,
grass-fed entrecote steak, dry aged on the bone and
served with a choice of classic sauces. Finish with a
Malmaison vanilla crème brûlée.

Chef John Woodward **Owner** Malmaison Hotels
Times 12-2.30/6-10.30, Closed 23-28 Dec, Closed L Sat
Prices Fixed L 2 course £15.50, Fixed D 3 course £17.50,
Starter £5.50-£7.95, Main £13.95-£21.95, Dessert
£5.95-£9.25, Service added but optional 12.5%
Wines 200 bottles over £20, 6 bottles under £20, 21 by
glass **Notes** Brunch style menu Sun, Vegetarian
available, Air con **Seats** 70, Pr/dining room 12
Children Portions **Parking** Smithfield Market 200m

Moro

◉◉ Islamic, Mediterranean 🖥 Plan 3 F5

Exotic fare from an open kitchen in the City

☎ 020 7833 8336
34/36 Exmouth Market EC1R 4QE
e-mail: info@moro.co.uk
dir: Nearest station: Farringdon or Angel 5 mins walk
from Sadler's Wells theatre, between Farringdon Road
and Rosebery Ave

An understated and simple style of high ceilings, round
pillars and unclothed tables makes for a relaxed
atmosphere in this lively Clerkenwell restaurant, with its
striking long zinc bar and open kitchen. Tapas is served
all day at the bar, and the kitchen's unpretentious
approach suits the surroundings, with food cooked on the
charcoal grill or wood-burning oven. Dishes generally
explore something less familiar, with the robust flavours
of Spain and the exotic spices of North Africa and the
Middle East. So expect the likes of seared pork fillet with
jamon and goat's horn pepper on toast, wood roasted
chicken with spiced pumpkin, chickpeas and tahini, and
perhaps yogurt cake with pistachios to finish.

Chef Samuel & Samantha Clark **Owner** Mr & Mrs S Clark
& Mark Sainsbury **Times** 12.30-2.30/7-10.30, Closed
Xmas, New Year, BHs, Closed Sun **Prices** Fixed L 2 course
£20.50-£27, Fixed D 3 course £26-£34.50, Starter £6-£8,
Main £14.50-£19, Dessert £5.50-£6, Groups min 6
service 12.5% **Wines** 45 bottles over £20, 11 bottles
under £20, 11 by glass **Notes** Tapas available
12.30-10.30pm, Air con **Seats** 90, Pr/dining room 14
Children Portions **Parking** NCP Farringdon Rd

St John

◉◉ British 🖥 Plan 3 G4

The best of British nose-to-tail cooking

☎ 020 7251 0848
26 St John St EC1M 4AY
e-mail: reservations@stjohnrestaurant.com
dir: Nearest station: Farringdon 100yds from Smithfield
Market, northside

Once a smokehouse for ham and bacon, this popular
restaurant is just across the road from Smithfield Market.
Rescued from disrepair by Fergus Henderson and Trevor
Gulliver, the utilitarian-styled restaurant, above the
bustling bar and bakery, has high ceilings, coat-hook-
lined white walls, white-painted floorboards, white
paper-clothed tables and wooden café-style chairs, set in
serried ranks that echo the rows of industrial-style lights
above. The kitchen's open to view, staff are
knowledgeable, friendly and relaxed, in tune with the
robust, honest, simplistic, bold-flavoured British food
that uses the whole animal. Menus change twice daily.
Think chitterlings and dandelion, smoked eel and
beetroot, or roast middlewhite pork and chicory, followed
by Eccles cake and Lancashire cheese, or hot chocolate
pudding and milk toffee ice cream. (See also Spitalfields
spin-off, St John Bread & Wine.)

Chef Christopher Gillard **Owner** T Gulliver & F Henderson
Times 12-3/6-11, Closed Xmas, New Year, Etr BH, Closed
Sun, Closed L Sat **Prices** Food prices not confirmed for
2009. Please telephone for details. **Wines** 72 bottles over
£20, 14 bottles under £20, 34 by glass **Notes** Vegetarian
available, Air con **Seats** 100, Pr/dining room 18
Parking Meters in street

Smiths of Smithfield

◉◉ Modern British Plan 3 F4

**Impressive warehouse conversion in Smithfield Meat
Market**

☎ 020 7251 7950
(Top Floor), 67-77 Charterhouse St EC1M 6HJ
e-mail: reservations@smithsofsmithfield.co.uk
dir: Nearest station: Farringdon, Barbican, Chancery Lane
Opposite Smithfield Meat Market

Boasting views over the City and St Paul's Cathedral, this
Grade II listed four-floor restaurant is situated in
London's Smithfield Meat Market. The building was empty
for over 40 years before being converted by the Smiths
team and is now a popular and stylish dining venue.
Original brick walls, reclaimed timber and steel all add to
the ambience, with each floor having its own individual
style. This also extends to the food, which offers
something to suit every pocket and occasion. The menu in
the Top Floor restaurant includes luxury ingredients like
Irish rock oysters and caviar, as well as the best aged
steaks. For mains, try venison Wellington with spinach
and juniper sauce.

Times 12-3.30/6.30-12, Closed 25-26 Dec, 1 Jan,
Closed L Sat

LONDON EC2

Boisdale of Bishopsgate

◉ Traditional 🖥 Plan 7 C5

A great taste of Scotland in the heart of the City

☎ 020 7283 1763
Swedeland Court, 202 Bishopsgate EC2M 4NR
e-mail: katie@boisdale-city.co.uk
dir: Nearest station: Liverpool Street Opposite Liverpool St station

Set down a narrow Dickensian alley off Bishopsgate, Boisdale oozes character. Like its Belgravia sister venture, it comes decked out in patriotic Scottish style with a buzzy, clubby atmosphere. The ground floor is a traditional champagne and oyster bar, while the restaurant and piano bar are in the cellar downstairs. Vibrant red-painted brick walls laden with pictures and mirrors, tartan carpet or dark floorboards, leather banquettes and tartan or leather chairs all create a moody, upbeat atmosphere. The Caledonian menu supports the theme, the kitchen's approach driven by traditional, high-quality north-of-the-border produce. Think Speyside Angus beef steaks, Macsween haggis, Lochcarnan hot-smoked salmon or Shetland Isle scallops.

Times 11-3/6-12, Closed Xmas, 31 Dec, BHs, Closed Sat & Sun

Bonds

◉◉ Modern French 🖥 Plan 6 B4

A grand setting for some slick modern cooking

☎ 020 7657 8088 & 7657 8090
Threadneedles, 5 Threadneedle St EC2R 8AY
e-mail: bonds@theetongroup.com
dir: Nearest station: Bank

Built to imperious Victorian specifications, this grand dining room retains many features recognisable from its days as a financial institution. The client base is strictly city business folk with generous expense accounts, and the menu is succinctly scripted, studded with luxury produce and shows clear aspiration from a talented kitchen. A good-value lighter lunch is offered, while the carte lifts quality, technique and pricing accordingly. Try ravioli of lobster with Armagnac bisque, or Dorset crab with smoked salmon, crème fraîche and Oscietra caviar, followed by roast duck with caramelised red onion tart Tatin, fondue of gem lettuce and Madeira jus, or roast cod, scallops and octopus daube, confit celeriac and potato purée, with banana and caramel parfait and passionfruit sorbet to finish.

Times 12-2.30/6-10, Closed 2 wks Xmas, 4 days Etr & BHs, Closed Sat, Sun

Catch Restaurant

◉◉ Seafood, Modern European 🖥 Plan 6 C5

Enjoyable seafood dining in a city hotel

☎ 020 7618 7200
ANdAZ London, 40 Liverpool St EC2M 7QN
e-mail: london.restres@andaz.com
dir: Nearest station: Liverpool Street Please telephone for directions

The display of fresh shellfish sums up what this restaurant in the former Great Eastern Hotel is all about and diners can watch as the chefs prepare the crustacea for service. The elegantly marble-clad room is the setting for a wide selection of fresh and saltwater fish, backed up with an award-winning wine list. There is a Champagne Bar, dominated by a mosaic-covered horseshoe bar, which has an extensive list of Champagnes, including some rare vintages, and the food on offer includes oysters and caviar. In the main dining room, expect those oysters, a good selection (when available) including Colchester, Falmouth Bay natives and Loch Fyne, plus potted shrimps and South Devon dressed crab. (Catch is committed to the use of sustainable seafood and supporting small business fishermen.) Main-course grey mullet steamed in a banana leaf with coconut juice and pak choi shows the style.

Chef Stuart Lyall **Owner** Hyatt Int **Times** 12-2.30/6-10, Closed Xmas, New Year, BHs, Closed Sat-Sun **Prices** Starter fr £10, Main £15-£32, Dessert £7.50, Service added but optional 12.5% **Wines** 95% bottles over £20, 5% bottles under £20, 9 by glass **Notes** Vegetarian available, Air con **Seats** 96 **Parking** NCP London Wall St

Eyre Brothers

◉◉ Spanish, Portuguese 🖥 Plan 7 B2

Lively, relaxed Iberian dining in trendy Shoreditch

☎ 020 7613 5346
70 Leonard St EC2A 4QX
e-mail: eyrebros@btconnect.com
dir: Nearest station: Old Street Exit 4

Tucked away down a long street of reclaimed Shoreditch loft buildings, this gem is just a short hike from Old Street and Liverpool Street stations. The plate glass windows and smart sign offer a hint of what is inside, but the sharp metropolitan blend of dark wood, cool leather and long trendy bar are still a welcome surprise. Authentic Portuguese regional cooking and classic Spanish cuisine combine effortlessly to achieve bold rustic dishes with big flavours and lively colours: seafood, potato, sweet pepper and saffron stew and wild rabbit rice with red wine, chorizo, broad beans and globe artichokes fit the bill nicely. Attentive staff encourage the mood.

Chef Dave Eyre, Joao Cleto **Owner** Eyre Bros Restaurants Ltd **Times** 12-3/6.30-11, Closed Xmas-New Year, BHs, Closed Sun, Closed L Sat **Prices** Starter £6-£16, Main £12-£25, Dessert £5-£7, Service optional **Wines** 40 bottles over £20, 13 bottles under £20, 6 by glass **Notes** Vegetarian available, Air con **Seats** 100 **Parking** On street, 2 car parks on Leonard St

Great Eastern Dining Room

◉ Pan Asian 🖥 Plan 7 B2

High-octane Asian-style eatery

☎ 020 7613 4545
54 Great Eastern St EC2A 3QR
e-mail: martyn@thediningrooms.com
dir: Nearest station: Liverpool St

A trendy, buzzy, contemporary bar-restaurant in the vibrant, gritty, up-and-coming City extremities. It gets packed even on mid-week evenings, so don't expect much space at your paper-clad table. Service is relaxed with knowledgeable staff, while darkwood walls and floors, leather seating and funky chandeliers reign alongside high decibels. A well-executed Pan-Asian menu - based on the grazing concept and ideal for sharing - delivers on presentation and flavour. From dim sum to sashimi, curries to barbecues and roasts or house specials; think black cod with sweet miso, perhaps an aubergine and lychee green curry, or coconut and pandon pannacotta dessert.

Times 12-3/6-10.30, Closed Xmas & Etr, Closed Sun, Closed L Sat

Mehek

◉ Indian 🖥 Plan 7 B5

Modern Indian dining with innovative and classic dishes in stylish surroundings

☎ 020 7588 5043 & 7588 5044
45 London Wall, Moorgate EC2M 5TE
e-mail: info@mehek.co.uk
web: www.mehek.co.uk
dir: Nearest station: Moorgate/Liverpool St Close to junct of Moorgate and London Wall

Situated on historic London Wall, this popular Indian unfolds like the Tardis into a number of stylish eating areas with a stunning décor courtesy of a well-known Bollywood designer. A long bar draws local city types for after-work drinks, while discreet lighting, smartly dressed tables and genuinely interested waiters make it easy to linger over a meal. The food is a modern take on Northern Indian traditional dishes, though the creative kitchen team bring in classics from other parts of the subcontinent as well. You'll find all the old favourites (korma, dhansak, madras, vindaloo), plus some more unusual treats: guinea fowl in traditional Bengal herbs, or Goan fish curry.

Continued on page 244

1901 Restaurant

LONDON EC2 Plan 6 C5

Modern European 🖥

Modern cooking with flair in a dramatic setting

☎ 020 7618 7000
ANdAZ London, 40 Liverpool St EC2M 7QN
e-mail: london.restres@andaz.com
dir: Nearest station: Liverpool Street Please telephone for directions

Set within the chic, designer City hotel adjacent to Liverpool Street station, '1901' (formerly the Aurora) is a stunning, palatial Victorian dining room dominated by a majestic stained-glass dome, while ceilings also reach lofty cathedral height and there are pillars and high-arched windows. Billowing voiles in deep red and grey and enormous, striking funky chandeliers keep things contemporary while making the most of the original architecture. A stylish, brushed-steel bar lines one side of the room, while service is knowledgeable, slick and professional. The kitchen's modern European approach - underpinned by a classical theme - is delivered via an appealing range of menus that make the best of tip-top seasonal produce. Exciting dishes of flair, imagination and flavour deliver with elegant simplicity and clean presentation to fit the fine-dining City bill; take Pyrenees milk-fed lamb served with peas, broad beans, morels and garlic, or perhaps steamed Cornish brill with spring vegetables and lemon thyme, while a rhubarb vanilla pannacotta with poached rhubarb foam and purée might catch the eye at dessert. There's the addition of a daily lunchtime carving trolley - of imposing dimensions - serving more traditional roasts, plus a seven-course dégustation option, excellent breakfasts - for early-morning business meetings - and a big-hitting wine list to complete the slick package.

Chef Dominic Teague **Owner** Hyatt
Times 12-2.30/6.45-10, Closed Xmas, New Year, BHs, Closed Sat-Sun **Prices** Fixed L 2 course £25, Tasting menu £55-£85, Starter £10.25-£13.15, Main £18.50-£28, Dessert £8.50, Service added but optional 12.5%
Wines 11 bottles under £20, 12 by glass **Notes** Tasting menu 7 courses, Vegetarian available, Civ Wed 160, Air con **Seats** 100 **Parking** NCP London Wall

Rhodes Twenty Four

LONDON EC2 Plan 6 C5

Modern British

Truly classic Rhodes cuisine overlooking the City

☎ 020 7877 7703
Tower 42, Old Broad St EC2N 1HQ
dir: Nearest station: Bank/Liverpool Street Telephone for directions, see website

The old Nat West building may not be the hottest tower in town anymore, but as a location for a restaurant the 24th floor takes some beating. And it has views right across to the 'Gherkin', so you can enjoy gazing at cutting-edge architecture while you eat. The sophisticated operation has its own bar (with seats naturally facing away from it to take in those views), while the dining room comes dressed in its best white linen with stylish appointments and all tables benefiting from the spectacular panoramas. Service is slick and friendly, with good attention paid to wine, while the cuisine is Gary's hallmark modern British with a twist. Impeccable ingredients, crystal-clear flavours, perfect balance and sharp presentation parade on exciting dishes. Clearly defined menus might feature seared scallops with shallot mustard sauce and mashed potato followed by pan-fried sea bream with globe artichoke and tomato casserole. Finish with baked egg custard tart with rhubarb sorbet. Leave time for security check-in at this landmark tower block. (Rhodes W1 Restaurant - and sister Rhodes Brasserie (see entries) - are Gary Rhodes-run ventures at the Cumberland Hotel, Marble Arch.)

Chef Gary Rhodes **Times** 12-2.30/6-9, Closed BHs, Xmas, Closed Sat-Sun

LONDON EC2 *Continued*

Chef A Matlib **Owner** Salim B Rashid **Times** 11.30-3/5.30-11, Closed Xmas, New Year, BHs, Closed Sat-Sun **Wines** 26 bottles over £20, 9 bottles under £20, 9 by glass **Notes** Fixed L 5 courses fr£11.95, Fixed D 8 courses fr £24.95, Vegetarian available, Dress restrictions, Smart casual, Air con **Seats** 120 **Parking** On street, NCP

1901 Restaurant

⊛⊛⊛ – *see page 243*

Rhodes Twenty Four

⊛⊛⊛ – *see page 243*

Rivington Bar & Grill

⊛ British 🖥 Plan 7 B2

Straightforward, best of British classics in buzzy setting

☎ 020 7729 7053
28-30 Rivington St EC2A 3DZ
e-mail: shoreditch@rivingtongrill.co.uk
dir: Nearest station: Old St/Liverpool St Telephone for directions

A combined restaurant, bar and deli, this buzzy place is tucked away down a narrow side street in fashionable Hoxton. White walls and wooden floors make for a suitably relaxed backdrop to a parade of simple, confident, seasonal, no-frills modern British cooking using top-notch produce. Think roast Lancashire suckling pig with greens and quince sauce, or fish fingers and chips with mushy peas, while comforting desserts might feature Bakewell tart with vanilla ice cream. Nice touches include chips served in little buckets and your own small loaf of bread. (Also sibling establishment in Greenwich, see entry.)

Times 12-3/6.30-11, Closed Xmas & New Year, Closed L Sat

Tatsuso Restaurant

⊛ Japanese Plan 6 C5

Authentic City oriental

☎ 020 7638 5863
32 Broadgate Circle EC2M 2QS
dir: Nearest station: Liverpool Street. Ground floor of Broadgate Circle

Situated on the lower level of Broadgate Circle, this slick, glass-fronted, two-tier City Japanese comes brimming with professional service and clean modern lines. Lightwood furniture and screens set the scene with waitresses in traditional Japanese dress. On the ground floor there's the theatre of the teppan-yaki grill to enjoy, while in the basement, a lengthy, authentic carte and sushi menu reign in a more relaxed atmosphere. You will find quality ingredients, plentiful set-menu options and

City prices. Try seaweed su - a refreshing, chilled soup-like dish with seaweed and ginger, served with crispy lotus root, or perhaps vegetable tempura with beef fillet butter-yaki. Less wallet-friendly choices are Kobe beef, or the most expensive Ran menu featuring half a lobster and turbot.

Times 11.45-2.45/6.30-10.15, Closed Xmas, New Year, BHs, Closed Sat-Sun

LONDON EC3

Addendum

⊛⊛ Modern European Plan 6 C4

Skilled and concise cooking in slick, boutique hotel

☎ 020 7977 9500 & 7702 2020
Apex City of London Hotel, No 1 Seething Ln EC3N 4AX
e-mail: reservations@addendumrestaurant.co.uk
dir: Nearest station: Tower Hill, Fenchurch Street Follow Lower Thames St, left onto Trinity Square, left onto Muscovy St, right onto Seething Ln, opposite Seething Ln gardens

Situated close to Tower Bridge, this modern, elegant restaurant contributes to the overall cutting-edge design at this City hotel. Think dark chocolate-coloured fixtures and fittings, amber lighting, clever use of mirrors, leather seats and booths, and tables turned out in their crispest whites, while service is slick from a friendly team of equally impeccably presented staff. Skilled, passionate cooking focusing on stunning ingredients, seasonality and crisp, clear flavours is the kitchen's style. Menus offer real value and quality, with classic dishes benefiting from modern twists, and there's plenty of luxury too. Start perhaps with smoked venison loin with quince and pickled walnuts and follow it with baked hake, pumpkin ravioli, braised lettuce and celeriac.

Chef Darren Thomas **Owner** Norman Springford **Times** 12-2.30/6-9.30, Closed 23 Dec-3 Jan, BHs, Closed Sat-Sun **Prices** Fixed L 2 course fr £21.95, Starter £6.95-£10.50, Main £15.75-£25, Dessert £7.50-£10, Service added but optional 12.5% **Wines** 78 bottles over £20, 2 bottles under £20, 11 by glass **Notes** Vegetarian available, Dress restrictions, Smart casual, Air con **Seats** 65, Pr/dining room 50 **Parking** Car park in Lower Thames St

Chamberlains Restaurant

⊛⊛ Modern British, Seafood 🖥 Plan 6 C4

Market-fresh fish beloved of city slickers

☎ 020 7648 8690
23/25 Leadenhall Market EC3V 1LR
e-mail: info@chamberlains.org
dir: Nearest station: Bank and Monument Telephone for directions

Leadenhall Market, thronging with City workers at midday and early evening, makes a relaxed setting for this seafood restaurant. It sits beneath the restored Victorian glass roof of the old market, alongside the cobbled walkway, with excellent views of the exquisite

architecture from the first floor and mezzanine dining areas. You can also eat more casually in the basement wine bar, or bag a table outside on warmer days. Fish from owners Chamberlain and Thelwell (suppliers to the trade) guarantees freshness. Try a starter of smoked eel fillets with horseradish potato and beetroot dressing, followed by pan-fried red mullet with aubergine purée and semi-dried tomato. Plenty of non-fish alternatives are also available.

Chef Matthew Marshall **Owner** Chamberlain & Thelwell **Times** 12/9.30, Closed Xmas, New Year & BHs, Closed Sat & Sun **Prices** Starter £7.50-£14.95, Main £18.95-£32, Dessert £6.50-£8.50, Service optional **Wines** 60 bottles over £20, 10 bottles under £20, 8 by glass **Notes** Vegetarian available, Air con **Seats** 150, Pr/dining room 65 **Children** Portions

Prism Restaurant and Bar

⊛⊛ Modern International 🖥 Plan 6 C4

Eclectic dining opposite Leadenhall Market

☎ 020 7256 3888
147 Leadenhall St EC3V 4QT
e-mail: belinda.jarman@harveynichols.com
web: www.harveynichols.com
dir: Nearest station: Bank and Monument Take exit 4 from Bank tube station, 5 mins walk

City bankers and brokers can use this stylish restaurant as the firm's canteen, so central is it to the financial action. Red braces are a not uncommon sight as the money men relax in the impressive surroundings of this former Bank of New York, though the bar downstairs is the place to let your hair down when the champagne corks fly. Smartly laid tables are far enough apart to keep market tips private, and well-versed staff offer a discreet presence. Stunning presentations on oversized white crockery create instant interest, and the food itself - a modish take on international staples - doesn't disappoint. Hand-dived scallops with herb crushed frogs' legs is a typically stylish dish. An excellent wine list is available.

Chef Richard Robinson **Owner** Harvey Nichols **Times** 11.30-3/6-10, Closed 25 Dec, BHs, Closed Sat & Sun **Prices** Starter £9.50-£16.50, Main £18-£26.50, Dessert fr £6.50, Service added but optional 12.5% **Wines** 412 bottles over £20, 4 bottles under £20, 20 by glass **Notes** Vegetarian available, Air con **Seats** 150, Pr/dining room 55 **Children** Portions **Parking** On street & NCP

Restaurant Sauterelle

◉◉ French 🖥 Plan 6 B4

Stylish French cuisine inside the Royal Exchange building

☎ 020 7618 2483
The Royal Exchange EC3V 3LR
web: www.restaurantsauterelle.com
dir: Nearest station: Bank In heart of business centre. Bank tube station exit 3

Taking its inspiration from the bourgeois traditions of French cooking, this restaurant on the first-floor mezzanine of the Royal Exchange overlooks the bustling courtyard interior, where the Grand Café and many world-famous jewellers and retailers ply their trade. The atmosphere is fittingly chic, while service is correspondingly efficient, welcoming and professional. The carefully prepared, straightforward but classy, classic regional French cuisine uses the freshest produce from the markets and sits well with the surroundings. Typically, start with diver-caught scallops, herb purée, caramelised baby onions, Alsace bacon and sauce nero, follow with braised featherblade of Longhorn beef, apple compôte and caramelised carrots and sauce bordelaise, or perhaps roast pollack, Puy lentils with quince, smoked eel and sauce bouillabaisse, and finish with cinnamon millefeuille with Calvados apple compote.

Chef Darren Kerley **Owner** D & D London
Times 12-2.30/6-10, Closed BHs, Closed Sat & Sun
Prices Fixed D 3 course £19.95, Starter £6.50-£14, Main £12.50-£19.50, Dessert £6, Service added but optional 12.5% **Wines** 61 bottles over £20, 9 bottles under £20, 13 by glass **Notes** Vegetarian available, Air con **Seats** 66, Pr/dining room 20 **Children** Portions

---

LONDON EC4

The Chancery

◉◉ Modern British, French 🖥 Plan 3 E3

Enjoyable brasserie-style dining in legal land

☎ 020 7831 4000
9 Cursitor St EC4A 1LL
e-mail: reservations@thechancery.co.uk
dir: Nearest station: Chancery Lane Situated between High Holborn and Fleet St, just off Chancery Ln

Secreted away in the narrow streets and historic buildings of the law community, this modern, glass-fronted restaurant lies close to Lincoln's Inn and Chancery Lane. The black and white décor is contemporary - black leather chairs and white linen blend seamlessly with polished mahogany floors and black woodwork. Mirrors and modern abstract art hang on the white walls. There's a bar downstairs, while the dining space - split into two sections with arched openings - is also crisp and modern. In keeping with the surroundings, the well-executed cooking is confident, clean-cut and well presented. Roulade of foie gras and guinea fowl with prune and sherry vinegar chutney, followed by line-caught sea bass, spider crab and crushed new potatoes in a shellfish bouillabaisse sauce feature on the value, fixed-price menus. (Sibling to the Clerkenwell Dining Room, see entry).

Chef Steve Carss **Owner** Zak Jones & Andrew Thompson
Times 12-2.30/6-10.30, Closed Xmas, Closed Sat-Sun
Wines 12 bottles over £20, 5 bottles under £20, 3 by glass **Notes** ALC £34, Air con **Seats** 50 **Children** Portions **Parking** On street

---

Refettorio

◉◉ Italian Plan 3 F2

☎ 020 7438 8052
Crowne Plaza London - The City, 19 New Bridge St EC4V 6DB
e-mail: loncy.refettorio@ihg.com

Sleek, stylish and contemporary, Refettorio blends comfortably with the swish modernism of its Crowne Plaza Hotel setting. The L-shaped room has a long bar, tall windows hung with Venetian blinds and polished wood floors and tables accompanied by smart brown leather chairs. There's booth-style seating along one side, a long row of tables down the centre and a white-linen zone at the back, all attended by smartly attired, suitably attentive Italian staff. Authentic Italian food, including excellent breads, impeccably-sourced regional cheeses, hams and salamis (offered on a 'to share' section heading the menu), fine home-made pasta and an all-Italian wine list, provide an impressive backdrop to an appealing carte of straightforward but accomplished and well presented dishes. Think linguine with crab, or perhaps pan-fried venison served with celeriac purée and chargrilled radicchio.

Times 12-2.30/6-10.30 **Prices** Food prices not confirmed for 2009. Please telephone for details.

The White Swan Pub & Dining Room

◉ Modern, Traditional British 🖥 Plan 3 F3

Busy, upmarket gastro-pub with a smart dining room

☎ 020 7242 9696
108 Fetter Ln EC4A 1ES
e-mail: info@thewhiteswanlondon.com
dir: Nearest station: Chancery Lane Tube Station Fetter Lane runs parallel with Chancery Lane in the City of London and it joins Fleet St with Holborn

The White Swan has a ground floor pub bar, a tastefully restored first floor dining room, and a mezzanine area - available for drinks parties - over the pub. It has a stylish feel with its white-clothed tables, handsome wooden floors, contemporary chairs, banquettes and mirrored ceiling. Friendly, attentive and relaxed French service adds to the experience. The menu combines classics alongside more esoteric dishes; think smoked black pudding salad with quails' eggs set on a tarragon and mustard purée, or Gloucestershire Old Spot pork belly, celeriac purée, and cider and Calvados jus. Desserts might feature Baileys cheesecake served with fresh raspberries and a drizzle of vanilla pod syrup, while daily specials provide additional interest.

Times 12-3/6-10, Closed 25 Dec, 1 Jan and BHs, Closed Sat-Sun (except private parties)

Paternoster Chop House

☎ 020 7029 9400
Warwick Court EC4M 7DX

A modern, white-walled restaurant in a new development in Paternoster Square, offering simple, excellently sourced British produce.

Prices Food prices not confirmed for 2009. Please telephone for details.

LONDON EC4 *Continued*

Vivat Bacchus

☎ 020 7353 2648
47 Farringdon St, Holborn EC4A 4LL

Classic French and international dishes and three wine cellars to choose wine from, plus a cheese cellar.

Prices Food prices not confirmed for 2009. Please telephone for details.

LONDON N1

Almeida Restaurant

◉◉ French   Plan 1 F4

French-inspired dishes in a modern setting

☎ 020 7354 4777
30 Almeida St, Islington N1 1TD

e-mail: almeida-reservations@conran-restaurants.co.uk
dir: Nearest station: Angel/Islington/Highbury Turn right from station, along Upper St, past church

Almeida has undergone a face-lift and is now every inch a contemporary space replete with muted shades of white and brown. There is a wine bar to the front and a more formal dining area to the rear, where things smarten up further with the addition of white, crisp tablecloths. The menu has its heart in France but successfully avoids cliché. Thus Bouchot mussel and saffron soup sits alongside steak tartare with Poilâne toast among starters, and steamed halibut comes with curly kale and hollandaise sauce as a main course. Pyrenean lamb shoulder with a cassoulet of beans and artichoke and a thyme jus is a creative interpretation of a classic dish, and desserts can be as British as rhubarb crumble with crème anglaise or as bold as Guanaja chocolate soufflé with chilli ice cream.

Times 12-2.30/5.30-11, Closed 25-26 Dec, 1 Jan, Good Fri, Closed 17 Apr

The Drapers Arms

◉ Modern British   Plan 1 F4

Convivial gastro-pub in trendy Islington

☎ 020 7619 0348
44 Barnsbury St N1 1ER

e-mail: info@thedrapersarms.co.uk
dir: Nearest station: Highbury & Islington/Angel Just off Upper St, situated between Angel/Highbury & Islington tube stations, opposite town hall

Gastro-pub in a smart residential area of Islington; a lovely building with wooden floors, comfy sofas and large bay windows overlooking a lush green square. A central door opens into the bar area with long wide spaces on either side for tables. The place is packed Sunday lunchtime with young families, older couples and groups of friends. The restaurant upstairs occupies the same large space with a fireplace at either end. Cooking is classic and modern English with influences from around the world. Try chicken liver and foie gras parfait followed by double pork chop, braised cabbage, pancetta and grilled Braeburn apple. Desserts include the likes of banoffee and white chocolate cheesecake with butterscotch sauce.

Chef Mark Emberton **Owner** Mark Emberton
Times 12-3/7-10.30, Closed 24-27 Dec, 1-2 Jan, Closed L Mon-Sat, Closed D Sun **Prices** Starter £5.50-£8, Main £12.50-£16, Dessert £5.50-£6.50, Service added but optional 12.5% **Wines** 43 bottles over £20, 16 bottles under £20, 18 by glass **Notes** Vegetarian available **Seats** 60, Pr/dining room 45 **Children** Portions **Parking** On street

Fifteen London - The Dining Room

◉ Italian, Mediterranean 🖥   Plan 3 H6

Funky, informal, unpretentious not-for-profit outfit

☎ 0871 330 1515
13 Westland Place N1 7LP

dir: Nearest station: Old Street Exit 1 from Old St tube station, walk up City road, opposite Moorfields Eye Hospital

Now into its sixth year, Jamie Oliver's pioneering culinary venture into youth training is still going strong. There are offshoots in Cornwall (see entry), Amsterdam and Melbourne, and Jamie's profile remains as high as ever thanks to his books and TV programmes. This unpretentious, funky warehouse-style joint still pulls in the crowds and tourists. On the ground floor the buzzy trattoria is the place for lighter meals, while the main restaurant is in the basement. The open-plan kitchen, graffiti-esque murals and brown leather banquettes and chairs make for a lively and informal space. The cooking's approach is Italian-Mediterranean, driven by an insistence on quality fresh and seasonal ingredients. Straightforward simplicity is the name of the game on the daily-changing menu, from wonderfully light potato gnocchi with tomato sauce, basil and olives in a classic combination to pan-fried breast of Telmara duck with beetroot, Swiss chard and a salmoriglio sauce made with marjoram.

Chef Andrew Parkinson **Owner** Fifteen Foundation
Times 12-2.45/6.30-9.30, Closed Xmas, New Year
Wines 200+ bottles over £20, 12 by glass **Notes** Fixed D

5 courses, Tasting menu 6 courses, Vegetarian £50, Sunday L, Dress restrictions, Smart casual, Air con **Seats** 68 **Children** Portions **Parking** On street & NCP

Frederick's Restaurant

◉ Modern European 🖥   Plan 1 F4

Fashionable food in contemporary setting

☎ 020 7359 2888
Camden Passage, Islington N1 8EG

e-mail: eat@fredericks.co.uk
web: www.fredericks.co.uk
dir: Nearest station: Angel From underground 2 mins walk to Camden Passage. Restaurant among the antique shops

Located in Islington's popular antiques quarter, the Victorian façade of this well-established restaurant opens up into a smart restaurant and a large conservatory and alfresco dining area with painted and plain brick walls, clothed tables and suede chairs. Modern art on the walls and clever lighting add to the stylish ambience. The fashionable menu offers a wide choice and includes some traditional dishes with a modern twist, as well as vegetarian options. For mains, try stone black bass, asparagus, wild rocket and hollandaise, or cured shank of lamb with crushed new potatoes, roasted onions and minted peas, and raspberry crème brûlée to finish. Set lunch and pre-theatre menu also available.

Times 12-2.30/5.45-11.30, Closed Xmas, New Year, Closed Sun (ex functions)

The House

◉ British 🖥 ☺   Plan 1 F4

Enjoyable, simple cooking in a gastro-pub style environment

☎ 020 7704 7410 & 020 7354 8143
63-69 Canonbury Rd N1 2DG

e-mail: info@inthehouse.biz
dir: Nearest station: Highbury & Islington tube Behind town hall on Upper St Islington. Between Highbury Corner and Essex Rd

This cosy neighbourhood restaurant with its maroon awning and redbrick façade has quite a local following. Wooden floors, whitewashed walls and simple artwork give the dining room a light and airy feel during the day. In the evening, locals gather around the comfortable bar sofas and well-spaced dining tables. Simple, honest dishes prove very satisfying in this setting, using organic produce wherever possible. Try delicious Dorset crab spring rolls with ginger, spring onions and balsamic to start, then for main course maybe tarragon crayfish and Pernod risotto, or baked cod with Mallorca potatoes and lemon crème fraîche. Everything from the breads to ice creams is home made.

Chef Richard Robb **Owner** Barnaby Meredith
Times 12-3.30/6-10.30, Closed L Mon **Prices** Fixed L 2 course £14.95, Fixed D 3 course £30-£125, Service added but optional 12.5% **Wines** 40 bottles over £20, 12 bottles under £20, 12 by glass **Notes** Sunday L, Vegetarian available **Seats** 80 **Children** Portions, Menu **Parking** Meter parking on street

Cru

📠

☎ 020 7729 5252
2-4 Rufus St, Hoxton N1 6PE
web: http://www.theaa.com/travel/index.jsp

European dishes with some global additions, served in a relaxing friendly environment.

Prices Food prices not confirmed for 2009. Please telephone for details.

The Bull Pub & Dining Room

🌸 British, French   Plan 1 E5

Lively modern gastro-pub offering confident cooking

☎ 0845 456 5033
13 North Hill N6 4AB
e-mail: info@inthebull.biz
dir: Nearest station: Highgate 5 min walk from Highgate tube station

This contemporary, informal gastro-pub (sister to The House at Islington, see entry), situated in a two-storey Grade II listed building, has a buzzy central bar and smart dining area with an open hatch to the kitchen. (Upstairs are private function facilities and a games room.) Polished wood floors, leather banquettes and modern art create a relaxed, upbeat vibe, while at the front there's a terrace for fair-weather dining. Confident modern British cuisine is the thing here, with the emphasis on simplicity, freshness and quality produce. The carte comes supplemented by blackboard specials and includes an express lunch option, so there's something for everyone; try prawn and cockle linguine with basil, tomato and crème fraîche, followed by whole roast lemon sole with brown shrimp, dill and cucumber butter.

Times 12-3.30/6-10.30, Closed L Mon, Closed D 25 Dec

Morgan M

🌸🌸🌸 – **see below**

The Lock

🌸🌸 Modern British 📠   Plan 1 F5

Chic eatery offering good honest food

☎ 020 8885 2829
Heron House, Hale Wharf, Ferry Lane N17 9NF
e-mail: thelock06@btconnect.com
dir: Nearest station: Tottenham Hale, Black Horse Station Telephone for directions

Described by one restaurant critic as "a big yellow building in the middle of nowhere", this chic eatery is just a few minutes walk from Tottenham Hale station. With its North African furnishings, dark wooden tables, leather-backed chairs, chocolate leather sofas and works of art by local painters, there is the feel of a New York loft house here. An open-plan kitchen delivers a menu of modern British dishes with influences from around the world. Starters might include the likes of steamed lasagne of Cornish crab with shellfish bisque sauce, or pressed game and foie gras terrine, followed by 28 day-hung forerib of steak with bubble-and-squeak and roasted Mediterranean vegetables. Finish with lemongrass and vanilla crème brûlée.

Chef Adebola Adeshina **Owner** Adebola Adeshina, Fabrizio Russo **Times** 12-2/6.30-10, Closed Mon, Closed L Sat (except match days), Closed D Sun **Prices** Fixed L 2 course £11-£19.50, Starter £3.95-£9, Main £9.95-£17.95, Dessert £4-£7, Service added but optional 10% **Wines** 10 bottles over £20, 15 bottles under £20, 12 by glass **Notes** Tasting menu available on request, Sunday L, Dress restrictions, Smart casual, no hats/caps, Air con **Seats** 60, Pr/dining room 18 **Children** Portions, Menu **Parking** 20

Morgan M

Modern French 📠 V

Authentic, top-notch French cooking in intimate surroundings

☎ 020 7609 3560
489 Liverpool Rd, Islington N7 8NS
dir: Nearest station: Highbury and Islington

The green-painted exterior may be reminiscent of a British pub, but Morgan M is a Gallic affair; a personal, individual and intimate restaurant. The single room is not large, but that is a good thing: Morgan Meunier is a chef who wants to make a connection with his customers via his food. The room is handsomely decorated to look rather like a French parlour, albeit a stylish one, with walls clad in elegant wooden panels, covered in floral wallpaper and painted a rich burgundy. It is a successful mix of old and new, classy and unpretentious. Service from the French team is professional yet relaxed and the chef-patron circulates at the end of service, his enthusiasm and passion is on show but not obtrusive. The seasonally-changing menu is based around French classical cooking with modern ideas and techniques used with restraint and displaying a sure hand. Ravioli of snails in Chablis, poached garlic and red wine jus is a starter of refinement and simplicity, while main-course grilled Anjou squab pigeon comes with the liver of the bird in ravioli, plus glazed baby turnips, poêlée of runner beans and sweet potato purée. There is a six-course tasting menu, plus another vegetarian version, while the wine list is not surprisingly French focused. Imaginative amuse-bouche, good breads and pre-dessert are all well considered and desserts such as apricot soufflé with a coulis of the same fruit and rosemary ice cream completes the picture.

Chef M Meunier & S Soulard **Owner** Morgan Meunier **Times** 12-2.30/7-10.30, Closed 24 Dec-30 Dec, Closed Mon, Closed L Tues, Sat, Closed D Sun **Wines** 140 bottles over £20, 3 bottles under £20, 6 by glass **Notes** Tasting menu £45 (vegetarian £39), Sunday L, Vegetarian menu, Dress restrictions, Smart casual, Air con **Seats** 48, Pr/dining room 12 **Children** Portions **Parking** On Liverpool Rd

LONDON NW1

La Collina

◉ Italian   Plan 1 E4

Authentic, vibrant Italian cooking in swanky Primrose Hill

☎ 020 7483 0192
17 Princess Rd, Chalk Farm NW1 8JR

It's a rare London eatery that manages to capture all the flavour and authenticity of Italian cooking back home. La Collina is a period-style building close to picturesque Primrose Hill, with white-washed walls, linen-clothed tables, wooden chairs and stripped wooden floorboards. Dine upstairs and watch the well-heeled passers-by, or downstairs, where an open kitchen lets you in on the culinary action. Friendly, attentive staff create a warm informal environment. The kitchen delivers fresh, vibrant mainly Northern dishes with Piedmontese influences that are homely and full of flavour. Tuck into the likes of chestnut noodles with wild boar ragu, or grilled tuna with stewed peppers.

Times 12-2.30/6-11, Closed Xmas wk, Closed L Mon-Fri

Dorset Square Hotel

◉ Modern British   Plan 2 F4

Relaxed bar-restaurant with cricketing roots

☎ 020 7723 7874
39-40 Dorset Square NW1 6QN
e-mail: info@dorsetsquare.co.uk
dir: Nearest station: Baker St/Marylebone Telephone for directions

Standing on the original site of Lords cricket ground, this smart Regency townhouse hotel is home to the popular lower-ground floor Potting Shed Restaurant and Bar - a split-level affair with skylights and a warm, sunny feel. The gardening theme is developed with an array of terracotta pots and seed boxes across one wall, while a cricketing mural adorns another wall. The cooking is predominantly British with contemporary twists. The seasonal menu is kept simple and wholesome, focusing on accurate flavours. Tuck into a wild mushroom and artichoke tart, served warm with freshly dressed leaves, or roast Barbary duck breast with braised red cabbage and Calvados jus, followed by white chocolate cheesecake with blackcurrant compote.

Times 12-3/6-10.30, Closed 25 Dec, BHs, Closed L Sat, Closed D Sun

Gilgamesh

◉ Pan-Asian 🖵   Plan 1 E4

Eclectic range of dishes in mega-lavish surroundings

☎ 020 7482 5757
Camden Stables Market, Chalk Farm Rd NW1 8AH

This £12m, Babylonian-inspired mega-lavish, elaborately decorated, restaurant/bar/tearoom/private lounge offers more of a 'food theatre' experience than out-and-out restaurant with its fantastic atmosphere - and all this in Camden! Imagine a huge bar of lapis stone, constantly-changing lighting and a vast retractable roof, while seating is a mix of high bar stools, banquettes and foot stalls that come paired with matching-height solid-wood tables. The menu is classic Ian Pengelley and just so fits the bill, with Pan-Asian cuisine swiftly served by knowledgeable and friendly staff. The eclectic mix takes in the likes of sashimi, sushi, tempura, dim sum and Gilgamesh signature dishes like beef Penaeng or best end of Asian spiced lamb.

Times 12-2.30/6, Closed L Mon-Thu, Closed D Fri-Sun

Odette's

LONDON NW1   Plan 1 E4

Modern European V

Refined modern cooking in stylish Primrose Hill favourite

☎ 020 7586 8569
130 Regent's Park Rd NW1 8XL
e-mail: odettes@vpmg.net
dir: Nearest station: Chalk Farm. By Primrose Hill. Telephone for directions

The partnership of Vince Power, music promoter and nightclub owner, and Bryn Williams, chef and Welshman, has revitalised the sleeping giant that is Odette's. Just what Primrose Hill needed. The décor by designer Shaun Clarkson has a stylish 'boudoir' vibe going on, which means floral wallpaper, yellow leather chairs, exposed brick and numerous little artistic touches, plus there's a slick bar and a conservatory where the combination of skylights and mirrors creates a light-and-airy space. Service is efficient and effective but relaxed, while the kitchen shows its pedigree with Williams' technically assured, light, well-balanced modern cooking. Unfussy presentation, clear flavours and a focus on quality seasonal ingredients - including produce from his native Wales - make this more than just a neighbourhood restaurant. Fixed-price menus include a six-course tasting option (one for vegetarians as well) and a good value, mid-week, early-evening set menu. Pan-fried hand-dived scallops come as a starter with butternut squash purée, chestnut and apple, while main-course pan-fried line-caught turbot is served with braised oxtail and cockles. Finish with pear and almond crumble with star anise ice cream and port reduction.

Chef Bryn Williams **Owner** Vince Power
Times 12-2.30/6.30-10.30, Closed 25 Dec -1 Jan, Closed Mon (incl BH's), Closed D Sun **Prices** Fixed L 2 course fr £14.95, Fixed D 3 course fr £23.95, Tasting menu £60-£95, Starter fr £12.50, Main fr £25, Dessert fr £8, Service added but optional 12.5% **Wines** 134 bottles over £20, 3 bottles under £20, 20 by glass **Notes** Tasting menu 7 courses, Sunday L, Vegetarian menu, Air con **Seats** 75, Pr/dining room 25 **Children** Portions **Parking** On street

Megaro

⊚ Modern British   Plan 3 C6

Contemporary cuisine and décor in smart hotel restaurant

☎ 020 7843 2221
23 /27 Euston Rd, St Pancras NW1 2SD

This stylish new hotel opposite King's Cross and St Pancras stations boasts the equally smart Megaro Restaurant. It's a basement affair with a separate entrance, the staircase tiled with Italian granite and smooth Welsh slate. Contemporary and cool is the theme here, with smart red leather-style chairs and high quality beech-topped tables, while service is upbeat and professional. The kitchen's ambitious modern cuisine and menu fit the surroundings, the emphasis on prime ingredients, skill and attractive presentation; take roast chump of lamb served with basil and sun-dried tomatoes, and perhaps a lemon tart with raspberry sorbet.

Prices Food prices not confirmed for 2009. Please telephone for details.

Mirrors

⊚ Modern European   Plan 3 C5

Sleek modern hotel restaurant with a wide-ranging carte

☎ 020 7666 9080
Novotel London St Pancras, 100-110 Euston Rd NW1 2AJ
e-mail: h5309-fb@accor.com
dir: Nearest station: King's Cross/Euston/St Pancras International 5 mins walk between King's Cross and Euston underground station. 3 min walk from St Pancras International (Eurostar). The hotel is adjacent to the British Library

Centrally located, this modern, purpose-built hotel is situated adjacent to the British Library. Designed around a carvery and open kitchen area, its ground-floor restaurant and bar, Mirrors, is a bustling space; all glass and neutral woods with a bright modern range of comfy maroon sofas and purple leather chairs, with high windows that look out onto the busy streets. Modern European dishes form the backbone of the menu: chicken liver and foie gras parfait to start, for example, served with red onion marmalade and brioche, followed by roast rump of lamb with boulangère potato, confit garlic and marjoram jus, with date and toffee pudding with clotted cream ice cream to finish.

Chef Rees Smith **Owner** Accor UK Business & Leisure **Times** 12-2.30/6-10.30, Closed L Sat, Sun, BHs **Wines** 10 bottles over £20, 13 bottles under £20, 17 by glass **Notes** Buffet L £18.50, D £23.50, Vegetarian available, Air con **Seats** 89, Pr/dining room 250 **Children** Portions, Menu **Parking** Ibis Euston

Odette's

⊚ ⊚ ⊚ – **see opposite**

Sardo Canale

⊚ Italian 🖳   Plan 1 E4

Authentic Italian cuisine in an unusual setting

☎ 020 7722 2800
42 Gloucester Av NW1 8JD
e-mail: info@sardocanale.com
dir: Nearest station: Chalk Farm/Camden Town Please telephone for directions

This unusual restaurant is located in a new building, designed around an old tunnel and tower dating back to 1850. The original brick tunnel with cobbled stones was used by horses pulling barges in the nearby Grand Union Canal. It's certainly a novel place to find a modern Italian restaurant, serving up regional Italian cooking using fresh ingredients and authentic Sardinian recipes. Service is formal, but the atmosphere is relaxed and friendly, so take some time to peruse the extensive Italian menu, complete with English subtitles. Try spada alla griglia con olio all'arancio - grilled swordfish with orange-infused oil served with asparagus, and for dessert frozen panettone cream with dark chocolate sauce.

Times 12-3/6-11, Closed 25-26 Dec, BHs, Closed L Mon

The Winter Garden

⊚ ⊚ Modern British 🖳   Plan 2 F4

Stunning atrium restaurant at Marylebone hotel

☎ 020 7631 8000
The Landmark London, 222 Marylebone Rd NW1 6JQ
e-mail: restaurants.reservation@thelandmark.co.uk
dir: Nearest station: Marylebone M25 turn on to the A40 and continue 16m following signs for West End. Continue along Marylbone Rd for 300 mtrs. Restaurant on left

Former headquarters of British Rail, The Landmark was once one of the last truly grand railway hotels. The Winter Garden is a stunning open-plan, naturally lit main restaurant situated at the base of a magnificent eight-storey atrium complete with palm trees, which also houses the sophisticated Mirror Bar. There's a real alfresco feeling to dining here, a great place to see and be seen, while at night, it's a more intimate affair. The appealing menu takes a modern British approach driven by fresh quality produce. Take roasted John Dory served with purple sprouting broccoli and sauce vièrge, while a Valrhona chocolate tart with caramel sauce might catch the eye at dessert.

Chef Gary Klaner **Owner** Jatuporn Sihanatkathakul **Times** 11.30-3/6-11.30 **Prices** Fixed L 2 course £30, Starter £9-£14, Main £25-£31, Dessert £8-£9, Service optional **Wines** 38 bottles over £20, 15 by glass **Notes** Sunday L, Vegetarian available, Civ Wed 280, Air con **Seats** 80, Pr/dining room 360 **Children** Portions, Menu **Parking** 75

King Sitric

☎ 020 8452 4175
142-152 Cricklewood Broadway NW2 3ED

A fusion of modern Irish and international dishes in modern, art deco influenced surroundings.

Prices Food prices not confirmed for 2009. Please telephone for details.

Philpotts Mezzaluna

☎ 020 7794 0455
424 Finchley Rd NW2 2HY

Italian restaurant with modern interior. Clothed tables, red walls and modern art set the scene for enjoying inventive dishes.

Prices Food prices not confirmed for 2009. Please telephone for details.

LONDON NW3

Manna

⊛ International Vegetarian V   Plan 1 E4

Charming, fun and informal vegetarian restaurant

☎ 020 7722 8028
4 Erskine Rd, Primrose Hill NW3 3AJ
e-mail: yourhost@manna-veg.com
dir: Nearest station: Chalk Farm Telephone for directions

Manna was founded in the 1960s to bring a gourmet experience to vegetarians and vegans. Top-quality organic ingredients are used in uncomplicated but imaginative dishes that take their inspiration from around the world. Examples are Thai tempeh falafel balls flavoured with lemongrass and galangal served on shaved pickled green papaya salad with a sweet chill dipping sauce; and Creole sweet potato galette baked with Monterey Jack cheese topped with black bean, red pepper and sweetcorn hotpot and fried okra served with grilled plantain, avocado and lime purée and coconut and habenero salsa.

Chef Marlin Janicki **Owner** S Hague, R Swallow, M Kay **Times** 12–3/6.30–11, Closed 25 Dec–1 Jan (open New Year's Eve), Etr Sun, Closed L Mon **Prices** Food prices not confirmed for 2009. Please telephone for details. **Wines** 10 bottles over £20, 20 bottles under £20, 4 by glass **Notes** Vegetarian menu, Air con **Seats** 50 **Children** Portions **Parking** On street

XO

⊛ Pan Asian ▭   Plan 1 E5

Stylish Pan-Asian dining at trendy Belsize Park venue

☎ 020 7433 0888
29 Belsize Ln NW3 5AS
dir: Nearest station: Swiss Cottage/Belsize Park From Havistock Hill turn right into Ornan Road (Before BP garage), restaurant on right

Taking its name from the term meaning 'highly desirable' (and also a beloved Hong Kong chilli sauce), XO is a suitably trendy venue in London's fashionable area of Belsize Park. Part of the Will Ricker restaurant group, it is similar in style to sister establishments such as Notting Hill's E&O (see entry). The bustling low-lit bar leads through to a chic colonial-style restaurant with white linen-clad tables, dark wood floor and panelling and grey leather banquette seating. Offering attractive plates of fusion food, dim sum and sashimi rub shoulders on a Pan-Asian menu, which also includes the likes of rock shrimp tempura and red braised barramundi. The occasional Western influence shows itself in desserts like raspberry and white chocolate cheesecake.

Chef John Higgonson **Owner** Will Ricker **Times** 12–3/6–11, Closed 25–26 Dec **Prices** Starter £5.50–£8, Main £8.50–£21, Dessert £5.50–£6.50, Service added but optional 12.5% **Wines** 60 bottles over £20, 12 bottles under £20, 14 by glass **Notes** Sunday L, Vegetarian available, Air con **Seats** 92, Pr/dining room 22 **Children** Portions, Menu **Parking** on street

LONDON NW4

See LONDON SECTION plan 1 D5

Hendon Hall Hotel

⊛ Modern European

Theatrical setting for modern bistro fare

☎ 020 8203 3341 & 020 8457 2502
Ashley Ln, Hendon NW4 1HF
dir: M1 junct 2. A406. Right at lights onto Parson St. Next right into Ashley Lane, Hendon Hall is on right

Hendon Hall is an impressive historic property with a dramatic, theatrical Gothic dining room. Set against a rich décor of deep reds, there are grand columns, high-backed seating, polished wooden tables and crisp white napery. The walls are hung with modern paintings which are available for sale. Service is delightful, while the crowd-pleasing menu offers old favourites with a modern twist driven by quality, locally sourced produce. Twice baked blue cheese soufflé, sautéed calves' liver with Pommery mustard mash, crispy pancetta and red wine sauce, and warm chocolate fondant with milk chocolate ice cream are fine examples of the fare.

Times 12–2.30/7–10

The Gallery

☎ 020 8202 4000
407-411 Hendon Way NW4 3LH

Art gallery highlighting the talents of young British and French artists. English cuisine with French influences.

Prices Food prices not confirmed for 2009. Please telephone for details.

LONDON NW6

Singapore Garden Restaurant

⊛ Singaporean, Malaysian ▭   Plan 1 E4

Well-established oriental restaurant with authentic flavours

☎ 020 7328 5314 & 7624 8233
83-83a Fairfax Rd, West Hampstead NW6 4DY
dir: Nearest station: Swiss Cottage, Finchley Road Off Finchley Rd, on right before Belsize Rd rdbt

A modern restaurant with a contemporary décor of red, gold and beige and sophisticated appeal, the Singapore Garden is situated in a parade of upmarket shops close to Finchley Road tube station. The menu incorporates a variety of authentic dishes inspired by Chinese, Malay and Singaporean cuisine. Quality fresh ingredients are used, and no allowance is made for the Western palate in the spicing - the food tastes just at it would 'back home'. Recommendations include kuay pie tee (crispy pastry cups filled with shredded bamboo shoots, chicken and prawns), black pepper and butter crab, and ho jien (oyster omelette).

Chef Kok Sum Toh **Owner** Hibiscus Restaurants Ltd **Times** 12-2.45/6-10.45, Closed 4 days at Xmas **Prices** Fixed D 3 course fr £28, Starter £5-£7.50, Main £7.20-£29, Dessert fr £6, Service added but optional 12.5% **Wines** 39 bottles over £20, 4 bottles under £20, 6 by glass **Notes** Sunday L, Vegetarian available, Air con **Seats** 85 **Parking** Meters on street

LONDON NW8

Osteria Stecca

⊛ Italian   Plan 2 C5

Contemporary Italian cuisine in elegant surroundings

☎ 020 7328 5014
1 Blenheim Ter NW8 0EH
e-mail: rosmarinonw8@hotmail.com
dir: Nearest station: St John's Wood, Maida Vale Off Abbey Rd

Located in an upmarket residential area, this split-level eatery has understated whitewashed décor and wooden tables simply dressed with white linen and top-notch glassware and cutlery. Darkwood floors, mirrors and lilac banquette seating along one wall complete the elegant look. The glass conservatory area opens out on to an attractive front courtyard full of colourful potted plants. Simple contemporary Italian cooking using high quality ingredients delivers starters like perfectly cooked pan-fried scallops with mushroom cream and wild leaves, or crab ravioli with mixed pepper sauce, with perhaps pan-fried sea bass in caper sauce with braised fennel for mains.

Times 12-2.30/6.30-10.30, Closed 25-26 Dec, 1 Jan, Etr, Closed L Mon

Sofra - St John's Wood

▭

☎ 020 7240 4411
11 Circus Rd NW8 6NX
web: http://www.theaa.com/travel/index.jsp

Traditional Turkish restaurant with modern approach. Menu includes healthy eating choices.

Prices Food prices not confirmed for 2009. Please telephone for details.

LONDON SE1

The Anchor & Hope

◎◎ British Plan 5 F5

Hectic gastro-pub with deft cooking

☎ 020 7928 9898
36 The Cut SE1 8LP
e-mail: anchorandhope@btconnect.com
dir: Nearest station: Southwark/Waterloo Telephone for directions

The popularity of this flourishing gastro-pub makes for a great atmosphere - lively yet relaxed. It is packed as soon as the doors open and, as there's no booking, it's a case of showing up and waiting your turn. Wooden floors, bare walls and an open kitchen characterise the interior, with a heavy curtain separating the bar from the restaurant area. Tables are set sociably close together and you may have to share. The menu changes with every meal and really good ingredients arrive daily from carefully selected suppliers. Typically robust, rustic fare includes duck hearts on toast, seven-hour mutton with butter beans and kale, and pistachio cake with quince and crème fraîche.

Chef Jonathon Jones **Owner** Robert Shaw, Mike Belben, Jonathon Jones, Harry Lester **Times** 12-2.30/6-10.30, Closed BHs, 25 Dec-1 Jan, Closed L Mon, Closed D Sun **Prices** Starter £5-£10, Main £10-£22, Dessert £2.20-£5.80, Service optional **Wines** 25 bottles over £20, 26 bottles under £20, 13 by glass **Notes** Sunday L, Vegetarian available **Seats** 58 **Parking** On street

Baltic

◎ Eastern European Plan 5 F5

Authentic Eastern European cooking with stylish surroundings

☎ 020 7928 1111
74 Blackfriars Rd SE1 8HA
e-mail: info@balticrestaurant.co.uk
dir: Nearest station: Southwark Opposite Southwark station, 5 mins walk from Waterloo

Popular with politicians from nearby Westminster, this minimalist, open-plan restaurant is dominated by a striking chandelier made of shards of amber. Light pours in through the roof windows, while beams give a rustic feel to the stylish space. Vodka cocktails, jazz and an extensive Eastern European menu appeal to a trendy, friendly crowd. Start with blini and caviar, smoked eel and bacon salad, or Polish black sausage with pickled cabbage. Mains take in roast saddle of wild boar and cranberries, weiner schnitzel with beetroot and shallot salad, and pan-fried sea bass with fennel and tomatoes. Nalesniki (crêpes stuffed with sweet cheese, almonds and raisins) is an appealingly authentic way to finish.

Chef Peter Resinski **Owner** Jan Woroniecki **Times** 12-3/6-11, Closed Xmas, 1 Jan, BHs **Wines** 30 bottles over £20, 20 bottles under £20, 15 by glass **Notes** Pre-theatre 6-7pm 2 courses £14.50, 3 courses £17.50, Civ Wed 300, Air con **Seats** 100, Pr/dining room 30 **Children** Portions, Menu **Parking** Meters on The Cut

Bincho Yakitori

◎ Japanese Plan 5 F6

Japanese tapas overlooking the Thames and St Paul's

☎ 020 7803 0858 & 7803 0888
2nd Floor, Oxo Tower Wharf, Bargehouse Street SE1 9PH
e-mail: miki@bincho.co.uk
dir: Nearest station: Waterloo/Blackfriars From Waterloo Station head for River Thames, turn right along the Thames path to the OXO Tower

On the second floor of the Oxo Tower, Bincho Yakitori is a fun, vibrant, modern restaurant offering Japanese tapas alongside views over the Thames and chefs at work at the charcoal grills of the open-kitchen. Relaxed and informal, the long, glass-sided room comes with polished darkwood furniture and floors, lantern-style lighting, plus a wood-clad sake bar and pillars. Tapas-style dishes are the thing, generally threaded on mini-bamboo skewers and cooked over the charcoal grills (Yakitori is a specialist cuisine from the Japanese Izakaya-style eatery found in Tokyo). Think chicken breast with shishito peppers, or duck with spring onion and wasabi. It's great for sharing; just order a couple of inexpensive dishes at a time, then keep on ordering. It's such fun!

Chef Hideori Ohata **Owner** Dominic Ford, Ronnie Truss, David Miney **Times** 12-3/5-11.30, Closed 24-26 Dec **Prices** Fixed L 2 course £15-£20, Fixed D 4 course £25-£35, Service optional 12.5% **Wines** 13 bottles over £20, 5 bottles under £20, 11 by glass **Notes** Vegetarian available, Air con **Seats** 150 **Children** Portions **Parking** NCP 100yds

Cantina del Ponte

◎ Italian Plan 6 D2

Trendy riverside Italian

☎ 020 7403 5403
The Butlers Wharf Building, 36c Shad Thames SE1 2YE
e-mail: cantinareservations@danddlondon.co.uk
dir: Nearest station: Tower Hill, London Bridge. SE side of Tower Bridge, on river front

A corner of Italian sunshine in Butlers Wharf, Cantina del Ponte offers the influences, flavours and atmosphere of Italy. Outside, a huge canopy covers a heated terrace with views of Tower Bridge and the Thames. Inside, the restaurant offers a modern twist on the traditional trattoria with clean lines and contemporary furnishings, and a huge mural depicts a busy Italian market scene. The food is robust and full of flavour, from warming bowls of pasta and freshly baked pizzas out of the traditional pizza oven to veal Milanese and some great seafood.

Chef Brian Fantoni **Owner** D and D London Company **Times** 12-3/6-11, Closed 24-26 Dec **Prices** Fixed L 2 course fr £10, Fixed D 3 course fr £17.99, Starter £3-£8, Main £6.50-£14.50, Dessert £4.50-£7.50, Service added but optional 12.5% **Wines** 33 bottles over £20, 11 bottles under £20, 10 by glass **Notes** Sunday L, Vegetarian available **Seats** 110 **Children** Portions **Parking** NCP Gainsford St

Cantina Vinopolis

◎◎ Mediterranean Plan 6 A3

Vaulted open-plan restaurant with a smart cocktail lounge

☎ 020 7940 8333
1 Bank End SE1 9BU
e-mail: info@cantinavinopolis.com
dir: Nearest station: London Bridge 5 min walk from London Bridge on Bankside between Southwark Cathedral & Shakespeare's Globe Theatre

An impressive location under the railway arches means massive vaulted ceilings and the background rumble of passing overhead trains. The latter might cause consternation in the first time visitor, but the exposed stretches of brickwork create a stunning atmosphere for dining, as well as a home for this restaurant's other business, that of renowned wine merchant. You can watch the chefs in the open-plan kitchen create carefully prepared and accurately cooked Mediterranean specials like Spanish black pudding, chorizo and potato salad, and cured pork loin with rocket salad and celeriac remoulade, each dish coming with a recommended wine. Nearby Borough Market is the source of many of the ingredients.

Times 12-3/6-10.30, Closed BHs, Closed D Sun

Champor Champor

◎ Modern Malay-Asian Plan 6 B2

Creative Malay-Asian fusion cooking in a quirky ethnic setting

☎ 020 7403 4600
62-64 Weston St SE1 3QJ
e-mail: mail@champor-champor.com
dir: Nearest station: London Bridge Joiner St exit. Left onto Saint Thomas St & 1st right into Weston St, restaurant 100yds on left

A magical little restaurant tucked away beyond London Bridge and Guy's Hospital. A feast for the eyes as well as the stomach awaits inside, with barely a space left uncovered by tribal masks, Buddhist statues, brightly coloured wall paintings and intricate carvings. Gracious waiters trailing the scent of incense bring tiny appetisers, delicious canapés and exotic breads, while the short set modern Malay-Asian menu offers both subtle and intense flavours from all over South East Asia. Each dish has several components designed to thrill and surprise: Balinese-style baked sea bream in banana leaf, fennel somtam and coconut rice, or wild mushroom parcels in masala spinach purée and three-ways salad.

Chef Adu Amran Hassan **Owner** Champor-Champor Ltd **Times** 12-2/6-10, Closed Xmas-New Year (7 days), Etr (5 days), BHs, Closed Sun, Closed L Mon **Prices** Fixed L 2 course fr £19.90, Fixed D 3 course fr £29.50, Tasting menu fr £44, Service added but optional 15% **Wines** 19 bottles over £20, 22 bottles under £20, 4 by glass **Notes** Tasting menu 7 courses, Vegetarian available, Air con **Seats** 38, Pr/dining room 8 **Parking** On street, Snowsfields multi-storey

LONDON SE1 *Continued*

Chino Latino @ The Riverbank Park Plaza

◉ Pan-Asian   Plan 5 D3

Modern Pan-Asian food in a lively setting

☎ 020 7958 8000 & 020 7769 2500
The Riverbank Park Plaza, Albert Embankment SE1 7SP
e-mail: rppres@pphe.com
dir: Nearest station: Vauxhall Please telephone for directions

Located five minutes from Westminster Palace on the banks of the River Thames and set in a de-luxe hotel, this buzzy, modern eaterie is all dark wood tables, padded leather chairs, back-lit glass panels and generous use of black and red. Lively use of fresh quality ingredients in a modern Pan-Asian style incorporates flavours from Japan, China and Thailand. Sushi - bass, salmon, tuna, yellow tail and prawn with seaweed - arrives with classic accompaniments, whilst oyster tempura is dressed with fiery curry sauce studded with pink peppercorns. Seared marble beef is unmissable. Guests are encouraged to share dishes by keen, friendly staff.

Chef Antony Sousa Tam, Patrick Sousa Tam **Owner** Park Plaza Hotels **Times** 12-2.30/6-10.30, Closed 25-27 Dec, 1 Jan, Closed L Sun **Prices** Fixed D 3 course £32, Starter £3.50-£14, Main £17-£25, Dessert £6-£12, Service added but optional 12.5% **Wines** 45 bottles over £20, 9 bottles under £20, 8 by glass **Notes** Vegetarian available, Dress restrictions, No sportswear, Air con **Seats** 75 **Children** Portions **Parking** 60

The County Hall Restaurant

◉ British 🖥   Plan 5 D5

Stunning Thames-side dining in the heart of Westminster

☎ 020 7902 8000 & 0207 928 5200
London Marriott Hotel, Westminster Bridge Rd SE1 7PB
dir: Nearest station: Waterloo, Westminster Situated next to Westminster Bridge on the South Bank. Opposite side to Houses of Parliament.

With an enviable position on the south bank of the Thames, adjacent to the London Eye, this Grade I listed building dates back to 1909. The crescent-shaped restaurant, with its oak panels and high ceiling, was once the members' reading room of County Hall and offers outstanding views of Big Ben and Westminster. The formal atmosphere is reflected in professional, informed but friendly service, and the kitchen creates modern British dishes with European influences. Perhaps try chargrilled fillet of Angus beef with Parma ham wrap, sage and onion polenta, cannelloni of oxtail and red wine reduction, followed by honey-roasted figs with sultana chutney and Amaretto ice.

Chef Christopher Basten **Owner** Marriott International **Times** 12.30-3/5.30-10.30, Closed 26 Dec **Wines** 107 bottles over £20, 14 by glass **Notes** Jazz menu £25, Sunday L, Vegetarian available, Dress restrictions, Smart casual, Civ Wed 100, Air con **Seats** 90, Pr/dining room 80 **Children** Portions, Menu **Parking** Valet parking

Fire Station

◉ Modern European   Plan 5 E5

Bustling gastro-pub appealing to all ages

☎ 020 7620 2226
150 Waterloo Rd SE1 8SB
e-mail: firestation.waterloo@pathfinderpubs.co.uk
dir: Nearest station: Waterloo Adjacent to Waterloo station

A tasteful refurbishment has softened some of the sharp edges from this large converted fire station, handily placed near Waterloo Station and the Old Vic. Huge fabric lampshades help to soak up the noise, and padded banquettes and chairs enhance the dining experience still further. You can lunch cheaply from set gastro-pub favourites like collar of ham, mint and pea risotto, or vegetable curry with rice, though the carte offers more sophisticated fare - perhaps crispy pancetta and rabbit with rocket, and pork belly with garlic mash. The place can get very busy, but the competent, smiling staff cover the ground with impressive speed.

Times 12-3/5.30-11

Magdalen

◉◉ European   Plan 6 C2

Classy restaurant offering quirky English dishes with French influence

☎ 020 7403 1342
152 Tooley St SE1 2TU
e-mail: info@magdalenrestaurant.co.uk
web: www.magdalenrestaurant.co.uk
dir: Nearest station: London Bridge 5 min walk from London Bridge end of Tooley Street. Restaurant opposite Unicorn Theatre

There's a deceptively French feel to this popular two-storey restaurant, with its warm burgundy décor, bentwood chairs, mirrors and chandeliers, and impressive fresh flower displays. The food, however, has a British foundation with European influences, and the daily-changing menu is fiercely seasonal, with much of the produce sourced from nearby Borough Market. Try a starter of potted Devon crab or watercress, potato and oyster soup, and follow with a gutsy main course of roast pheasant with braised red cabbage, bacon and chestnuts. Rum baba with a quenelle of vanilla mascarpone will not disappoint for dessert. A notable, French-heavy wine list includes many by the carafe.

Chef James Faulks, Emma Faulks, David Abbott **Owner** Roger Faulks & James Faulks

Times 12-2.30/6.30-10.30, Closed Xmas, BHs, 2wks Aug, Closed Sun, Closed L Sat **Prices** Food prices not confirmed for 2009. Please telephone for details. **Wines** 66 bottles over £20, 12 bottles under £20, 14 by glass **Notes** Vegetarian available, Air con **Seats** 90 **Parking** On street

The Oxo Tower Restaurant

◉◉ Modern European V ⭐NOTABLE WINE LIST   Plan 3 F1

Stylish venue with a 'top of the world' feel

☎ 020 7803 3888
8th Floor, Oxo Tower Wharf, Barge House Street SE1 9PH
e-mail: oxo.reservations@harveynichols.co.uk
web: www.harveynichols.com
dir: Nearest station: Blackfriars/Waterloo Between Blackfriars & Waterloo Bridge on the South Bank

This landmark art deco building echoes the design of a 1930s ocean liner and the elegant modern restaurant is beautiful in its simplicity. Situated on the eighth floor with glass down both sides, there is a long open terrace enabling diners to take full advantage of the stunning views over the Thames and St Paul's, and leather-clad bars, slate tables and original art all add to the luxurious feel. The innovative modern European menu features a series of classics with a twist, as well as a sprinkling of dishes combining Mediterranean/Pacific Rim and French/Asian ingredients. Tempting descriptions highlight each dish's many component parts, as in a starter of king scallops with curried parsnip and apple, or roast fillet of beef with cep purée, oxtail and truffle cream bon bon.

Chef Jeremy Bloor **Owner** Harvey Nichols & Co Ltd **Times** 12-2.30/6-11, Closed 25-26 Dec, Closed D 24 Dec **Prices** Fixed L course £33, Starter £9.50-£14.50, Main £20-£40, Dessert £7.25-£9.50, Service added but optional 12.5% **Wines** 660 bottles over £20, 19 bottles under £20, 23 by glass **Notes** Sunday L, Vegetarian menu, Civ Wed 120, Air con **Seats** 250 **Children** Portions, Menu **Parking** On street, NCP

Le Pont de la Tour

◎◎ Traditional French 💻   Plan 6 D2

Wharfside restaurant, stylish destination dining and unbeatable views

☎ 020 7403 8403

The Butlers Wharf Building, 36d Shad Thames SE1 2YE
dir: Nearest station: Tower Hill, London Bridge SE of Tower Bridge

The views of Tower Bridge are especially memorable at night when it is floodlit, but even by day the vista over the Thames is impressive from this wharfside restaurant. The terrace is not surprisingly popular in summer as diners flock to watch the world go by on the river, while inside this elegant restaurant you step into a luxury world reminiscient of a cruise liner. Smart table settings, clean lines and well-dressed staff set the tone for some serious cooking. The French menu offers an extensive choice of dishes, drawing on traditional ingredients like celeriac soup with garlic croûtons to start. There's lots of fresh fish, crustacea or caviars, while meat options might include Label Anglais chicken, braised cabbage and morel sauce. There's an impressive and extensive wine list, too.

Times 12-3/6-11

Roast

◎ British 💻 📓NOTABLE WINE LIST 👐   Plan 6 B3

Vibrant, buzzy restaurant perched above Borough Market

☎ 020 7940 1300

The Floral Hall, Borough Market, Stoney Street SE1 1TL
e-mail: info@roast-restaurant.com
dir: Nearest station: London Bridge Please telephone for directions

The floral portico featured in the dining room of Roast was bought from Covent Garden by Borough Market trustees and the market provides the atmospheric setting for this first-floor establishment. From the bar, there are views of the hubbub below and St Paul's Cathedral is visible from the dining room - a split level room with white décor, chocolate brown carpet, dark wood tables and brown leather chairs. With an open kitchen, the restaurant is dedicated to British seasonal produce and the best of British cooking. Think roast rack of lamb with garlic, onions and thyme, Suffolk pork chop with Cox's apple and Shropshire blue cheese salad or steamed gamekeepers' pudding with cabbage and boar bacon. Breakfast and afternoon tea are served, and there's a superb cocktail list.

Roast

Chef Lawrence Keogh **Owner** Iqbal Wahhab
Times 12-3/5.30-11, Closed D Sun **Prices** Starter £6-£13, Main £12-£25, Dessert £6.50, Service added but optional **Wines** 100 bottles over £20, 6 bottles under £20, 10 by glass **Notes** Sunday L, Vegetarian available, Air con **Seats** 110 **Children** Portions, Menu

RSJ, The Restaurant on the South Bank

◎ Modern British   Plan 5 F6

Perfect pre-theatre dining

☎ 020 7928 4554

33 Coin St SE1 9NR
e-mail: sally.webber@rsj.uk.com
dir: Nearest station: Waterloo Telephone for directions

Long-established, simple, modern restaurant, popular with media types and theatre- or concert-goers from the adjacent South Bank. Friendly staff keep everything moving efficiently with an eye on performance times. The menu changes monthly or more frequently, reflecting a passion for fresh seasonal produce. With Loire Valley wines a speciality, there are wine events from time to time. The cuisine makes good use of fine quality ingredients to deliver carefully prepared, attractively presented dishes, like wild halibut served with truffled wild mushroom coquiette, and perhaps a raspberry crème brûlée to finish.

Times 12-2/5.30-11, Closed Xmas, 1 Jan, Closed Sun, Closed L Sat

Georgetown

💻

☎ 020 7357 7359
10 London Bridge St SE1 9SG
web: http://www.theaa.com/travel/index.jsp

Authentic Malay plus Indian Malaysian and Chinese Malaysian dishes. Décor is colonial with wicker chairs and lots of plants.

Prices Food prices not confirmed for 2009. Please telephone for details.

LONDON SE3

Chapters

◎◎◎ – see page 254

Laicram Thai Restaurant

◎ Thai   Plan 8 D1

Authentic Thai in a cosy setting

☎ 020 8852 4710

1 Blackheath Grove, Blackheath SE3 0DD
dir: Nearest station: Blackheath Off main shopping street, in a side road near the Post Office. Opposite station, near library

This Thai restaurant of long-standing is in the centre of Blackheath village, enjoying a fine reputation in the area for good food and being easy on the wallet. The décor has a homely feel, with understated Thai touches such as prints of the Thai royal family on the walls and typically welcoming and friendly service from the staff. The menu consists largely of mainstream Thai dishes such as green curry, prawn satay, fishcakes, phat Thai noodles goong pau (grilled prawns in a spicy sauce), and pla neung (steamed sea bass with lime sauce and fresh chilli).

Times 12-2.30/6-11, Closed Xmas & BHs, Closed Mon

LONDON SE10

Rivington Bar & Grill - Greenwich

◎ British, European 💻   Plan 8 A3

Buzzy surroundings for simple British food

☎ 020 8293 9270

178 Greenwich High Rd, Greenwich SE10 8NN
e-mail: greenwich@rivingtongrill.co.uk
dir: Nearest station: Greenwich (DLR)

Right next to the Greenwich Picture House, this converted pub - sibling to the sister establishment of the same name in Shoreditch (see entry) - delivers the blueprint buzzy, informal brasserie act. It's decked out in informal style, with dark wooden floors, white-washed walls and white paper-clothed tables, which offer the perfect backdrop for the kitchen's simple, seasonal, modern British cooking. With a vegetarian menu available, quality raw materials shine in dishes like Wetherall's Blackface mutton and turnip pie, or perhaps Glen Fyne steak and chips, and a Bakewell tart finish. There's a small alfresco terrace and a mezzanine level above the ground floor.

Times 12-3/6:30-11

LONDON SE10 *Continued*

North Pole Piano Restaurant

☎ 020 8853 3020
131 Greenwich High Rd, Greenwich SE10 8JA
web: http://www.theaa.com/travel/index.jsp

Elegant restaurant serving European dishes. Roast Sunday lunch a good deal and live jazz Sunday evenings.

Prices Food prices not confirmed for 2009. Please telephone for details.

Beauberry House

🏵🏵 French, Japanese 💻 | Plan 1 F2

Contemporary French meets oriental fusion food in Georgian splendour

☎ 020 8299 9788
Gallery Rd SE21 7AB
dir: Nearest station: West Dulwich Telephone for directions

Pure white décor - with tables all turned out in their best whites and set against a juicy orange floor and chairs - provides the stylish setting for this French meets East Asian fusion restaurant. The beautiful Georgian mansion (formerly Belair House) is set in leafy parkland near Dulwich village, its revamped interiors respecting the classical features while adding bags of contemporary pizzazz. Outdoor terraces abound for alfresco dining with views over gardens and lawns, while service is attentive and informed. The kitchen's fittingly contemporary approach delivers French cuisine with oriental influences using top-quality ingredients; take lobster tempura served with ponzu and wasabi mayonnaise, or flash-fried wagyu beef fillet with black truffles.

Times 12-3/6-11, Closed Xmas, 1 Jan, Closed Mon, Closed D Sun

---

Franklins

🏵 British | Plan 1 F2

Smart restaurant and popular pub operation

☎ 020 8299 9598
157 Lordship Ln SE22 8HX
e-mail: info@franklinsrestaurant.com
dir: Nearest station: East Dulwich 0.5m S from East Dulwich Station travel along Dog Kennel Hill and Lordship Ln

A traditional pub on the outside, Franklins opens off Lordship Lane into a popular, open-all-day, local pub. A few paces beyond this atmospheric space is a bright bistro-style restaurant where diners can glimpse the kitchen operation through a wide hatch. The menu features authentic British dishes, prepared with the minimum of fuss, with a real emphasis on local seasonal produce and traditional cuts of meat and cooking methods. Expect dishes like oxtail soup, veal kidneys with chard and mustard, calf's tongue with radish, hare with red cabbage and bacon, alongside Colchester rock oysters, and rich custardy bread-and-butter pudding. The daily-changing set lunch menu offers excellent value for money.

Chef Tim Sheehan, P Greene **Owner** Tim Sheehan & Rodney Franklin **Times** 12/12, Closed 25-26, 31 Dec, 1 Jan **Prices** Fixed L 2 course fr £11.50, Starter £5-£9, Main £11-£19.50, Dessert £5.25, Service optional, Groups min 6 service 10% **Wines** 7 bottles over £20, 5 bottles under

---

Chapters

Modern European 💻

Refurbished and re-launched Blackheath favourite

☎ 020 8333 2666
43-45 Montpelier Vale, Blackheath Village SE3 0TJ
e-mail: info@chaptersrestaurants.co.uk
dir: Nearest station: Blackheath 5 mins from Blackheath Village train station

Chapter Two - sibling to big brother Chapter One (see entry) - will be refurbished and re-branded as Chapters. Covering two floors, the new premises is a mix of café, bar and brasserie, open all day from breakfast to dinner. The stylish make-over will create informal and comfortable rooms, while the pleasant village location will remain the same. The new menu will take in both the serious upscale restaurant food as before - pan-fried sea

trout with tortellino and ginger velouté - alongside brasserie classics such as French onion soup. Start with chicken liver and foie gras parfait with grape chutney and toasted sourdough bread and follow on with roast rib of beef with gratin potatoes, or simply pop in for a snack or a drink. There will be a plat du jour menu and daily specials board, and carefully sourced, good quality produce are always used throughout.

Chef Trevor Tobin **Owner** Selective Restaurants Group **Times** 12-2.30/6.30-10.30, Closed 2-4 Jan **Prices** Fixed L 2 course fr £15.95, Starter fr £5.50, Main fr £12.95, Dessert fr £5.50, Service added but optional 12.5% **Wines** 65 bottles over £20, 10 bottles under £20, 6 by glass **Notes** Sunday L, Vegetarian available, Dress restrictions, Smart casual, no shorts or trainers, Air con **Seats** 70 **Children** Portions **Parking** Car park by station

£20, 6 by glass **Notes** Sunday L, Vegetarian available, Air con **Seats** 42, **Pr/dining room** 24 **Children** Portions **Parking** Bawdale Road

The Palmerston

Modern British   Plan 1 F3

Good, honest food in a popular, traditional pub

☎ 020 8693 1629
91 Lordship Ln, East Dulwich SE22 8EP
e-mail: info@thepalmerston.net
dir: Nearest station: East Dulwich 2m from Clapham, 0.5m from Dulwich Village, 10min walk from East Dulwich station

Located on Lordship Lane, close to Dulwich village, The Palmerston has successfully reinvented itself into a popular gastro-pub. Inside, the high-ceilinged, wood-panelled long bar and separate dining area each have a warming real fire in winter, and a welcoming, friendly atmosphere awaits. However, the food is the real star of the show, with quality, fresh ingredients adeptly prepared to provide good, honest fare. Expect rabbit rillette with apple chutney and cornichons, followed by grilled free-range Aberdeen Angus rib-eye steak en persillade with red wine sauce, and to finish, perhaps almond, sherry and quince tart with Chantilly cream. There is also a great-value set lunch.

Chef Jamie Younger **Owner** Jamie Younger, Paul Rigby, Remi Olajoyegbe **Times** 12-2.30/7-midnight, Closed 25-26 Dec, 1 Jan **Prices** Fixed L 2 course fr £11, Starter £5-£8.50, Main £11-£18.50, Dessert £4.75-£6.50, Service added but optional 10% **Wines** 34 bottles over £20, 22 bottles under £20, 17 by glass **Notes** Sunday L, Vegetarian available, Air con **Seats** 70 **Children** Portions **Parking** On street

LONDON SE23

Babur

Indian   Plan 1 G2

Contemporary Indian cuisine

☎ 020 8291 2400 & 8291 4881
119 Brockley Rise, Forest Hill SE23 1JP
e-mail: mail@babur.info
web: www.babur.info
dir: Nearest station: Honor Oak 5 mins walk from Honor Oak Station, where parking is available

Easily identified by the life-size, prowling Bengal tiger on its roof, this popular brasserie has been serving southeast London for over 20 years. The décor is stylish and modern with a contemporary ethnic feel, eye-catching artwork and exposed Victorian brickwork adding to the ambience. The

menu includes unusual options such as ostrich and kangaroo and is dotted with tiger heads to indicate the intensity of the chilli heat expected. One head equals hot and two means roaring hot! Start perhaps with beetroot and potato cakes coated in sago, then follow with Old Delhi-style curried rabbit in aromatic spices, or pan-fried Barbary duck breast glazed with honey and coriander. The selection of home-made chutneys is exquisite.

Chef Enam Rahman & Jiwan Lal **Owner** Babur 1998 Ltd **Times** 12.30-2.30/6-11.30, Closed 25-26 Dec **Prices** Fixed L 2 course £9.95, Starter £4.95-£6.95, Main £8.95-£13.50, Dessert £3.95-£5.95, Service optional **Wines** 13 bottles over £20, 26 bottles under £20, 13 by glass **Notes** Sunday L, Vegetarian available, Air con **Seats** 72 **Parking** 15 **Parking** On street

LONDON SE24

3 Monkeys Restaurant

Indian V   Plan 1 F2

Contemporary neighbourhood Indian restaurant

☎ 020 7738 5500
136-140 Herne Hill SE24 9QH
e-mail: info@3monkeysrestaurant.com
dir: Nearest station: Herne Hill, Brixton Adjacent to Herne Hill Station

Not your run of the mill curry house, this elegant restaurant is arranged over two levels with stripped wooden floors, white walls hung with modern artwork and furniture draped in white cotton. The menu offers a delightful cross-section of authentic regional Indian cuisine, and there's an open grill as a central feature. Fresh mussels are tossed with garlic, spring onion and tomato, and flavoured with curry leaves and lemongrass in a starter called mussel hara masala, and main-course tandoori chicken Amritsari, with an exotic marinade, is cooked on the bhatti (grill).

Chef Rajiv Guilati **Owner** Kuldeep Singh **Times** 12-2.30/5.30-11, Closed Xmas **Prices** Fixed L 2 course £7.95-£17.95, Starter £3.95-£6.95, Main £5.95-£14.95, Dessert £2.95-£3.25, Service added but optional 12.5% **Wines** 20% bottles over £20, 80% bottles under £20, 9 by glass **Notes** Sunday L, Vegetarian menu, Air con **Seats** 90 **Children** Portions, Menu **Parking** On street, Carver Rd

LONDON SW1

Al Duca

Modern Italian   Plan 5 B6

Straightforward Italian cooking just off Piccadilly

☎ 020 7839 3090
4-5 Duke of York St SW1Y 6LA
e-mail: info@alduca-restaurant.co.uk
dir: Nearest station: Piccadilly 5 mins walk from station towards Piccadilly. Right into St James, left into Jermyn St. Duke of York St halfway along on right

This smart, modern St James's Italian draws the crowds with its affordable pricing, contemporary good looks and

buzzy atmosphere. Etched glass, neutral tones, modern seating and closely-packed tables cut a stylish but relaxed edge, while feature wine racks set into the wall catch the eye and patio-style windows fold back for an alfresco summer vibe. Straightforward, unpretentious, clean-cut modern Italian cooking fits the bill, driven by fresh, quality seasonal ingredients. Think chargrilled calves' liver served with sautéed spinach and a marsala, raisin and pine-nut sauce, and to finish, perhaps a pistachio and cherry semi-fredo might catch the attention. All-Italian wine list.

Chef Michele Franzolin **Owner** Cuisine Collection **Times** 12-2.30/6-11, Closed Xmas, New Year, BHs, Closed Sun **Wines** 84 bottles over £20, 5 bottles under £20, 16 by glass **Notes** Pre & Post theatre menu 2-4 courses £15.50-£20.50, Vegetarian available, Dress restrictions, Smart casual, no shorts, Air con **Seats** 56 **Children** Portions **Parking** Jermyn St, Duke St

Amaya

Indian   Plan 4 G4

Entertaining kitchen theatre with enticing South Asian food

☎ 020 7823 1166
Halkin Arcade, Motcomb St SW1X 8JT
e-mail: amaya@realindianfood.com
dir: Nearest station: Knightsbridge Please telephone for directions

Amaya cuts quite a dash with its pink sandstone panels, hardwood floors and rosewood furniture, and light floods into the room via a glass atrium. It is a smart, contemporary space and the vibrant ambience is added to by the presence of the open-plan theatre kitchen where chefs marinate meats or labour over tandoors or sigris - charcoal grills. Dishes are mostly North Western in style but regional dishes also figure, with the emphasis on clean, clear flavours and combinations and modern presentation. Many dishes are offered in small or mains sizes - there are no conventional starters or main courses - so you might start with griddled diver-caught king scallops or venison before tandoori monkfish tikka or grilled lamb chops.

Continued

LONDON SW1 *Continued*

Chef Karunesh Khanna **Owner** R Mathrani, N Panjabi **Times** 12-2.30/6-11.15, Closed 25 Dec **Wines** 70 bottles over £20, 2 bottles under £20, 26 by glass **Notes** Fixed D 2 courses, Vegetarian tasting menu £35.50, Vegetarian available, Air con **Seats** 90, Pr/dining room 14 **Parking** NCP

The Avenue

◉ European 🖳 Plan 5 B5

Buzzy, contemporary bar and restaurant

☎ 020 7321 2111
7-9 St James's St SW1A 1EE
e-mail: avenue@egami.co.uk
dir: Nearest station: Green Park Turn right past The Ritz, 2nd turning into St James's St. Telephone for further details

This large, cavernous, starkly minimalist brasserie makes an ever-popular St James's destination, and reverberates with a buzzy atmosphere. High ceilings come decked out with recessed spots, plain white walls donned with large colourful modern art and floors clad in limestone. There's a long bar up front, while trendy dining chairs come in white or grey and tables clothed in white linen. The lengthy brasserie-format menu offers a straightforward, uncomplicated modern approach, blending the more contemporary alongside classics. Take halibut served with crayfish mash and leek frittata, or goujons of cod with tartare sauce.

Times 12-3/5.45-11.30, Closed 25-26 Dec, 1 Jan, Closed Sun, Closed L Sat

Bank Westminster

◉ Modern, International Plan 5 B4

Ultra-modern brasserie-style dining

☎ 020 7630 6644 & 7630 6630
45 Buckingham Gate SW1E 6BS
e-mail: westminster.reservations@bankrestaurants.com
dir: Nearest station: St James Park Facing Buckingham Palace, left to Buckingham Gate, after 100mtrs hotel on right

The Crowne Plaza is an elegant Victorian hotel close to Buckingham Palace in the heart of Westminster and the prestigious St James's area. Its Bank restaurant, accessed via the street or hotel lobby, is ultra modern and conservatory-styled, with glass windows and one side overlooking a delightful courtyard complete with fountain, where meals are served in warmer weather. The cooking is modern and global, almost gastro pub-style with a mix of European and Asian dishes, such as Szechuan peppered tuna with wok-fried Asian greens, or roast halibut with crab and herb crumb and shellfish pavé. The adjacent stylish Zander cocktail bar was once the longest bar in the UK.

Times 12-3/5.30-10.30, Closed 25 & 26 Dec, 1 Jan, BHs, Closed Sun, Closed L Sat

Boisdale of Belgravia

◉ British 🖳 Plan 4 H3

Traditional, clubby but fun Scottish restaurant

☎ 020 7730 6922
15 Eccleston St SW1W 9LX
e-mail: info@boisdale.co.uk
dir: Nearest station: Victoria Turn left along Buckingham Palace Rd heading W, Eccleston St is 1st on right

A resolutely Scottish experience is delivered at this Belgravia restaurant-cum-whisky and cigar bar (sister City venue at Bishopsgate, see entry), with its deep reds and greens, tartan, dark floorboards and panelled, picture-laden walls. There is an endearingly clubby atmosphere to its labyrinth of dining areas and bars, and live jazz adds to the upbeat vibe in the evenings. The patriotic Caledonian menu further supports the theme, showcasing quality Scottish produce; expect potted hand-picked Hebridean crabmeat with toasted sour-dough bread and spiced avocado, daily offal, game and fish dishes, or 21-day matured Scottish beef served with a variety of sauces and accompaniments.

Chef Colin Wint **Owner** Mr R Macdonald **Times** 12-2.30/7-11.15, Closed Xmas, New Year, Etr, BHs, Closed Sun, Closed L Sat **Prices** Fixed L 2 course £18.70, Fixed D 3 course £18.70, Starter £7.50-£17.50, Main £14-£65, Dessert £6.50-£7.95, Service added but optional 12.5% **Wines** 150 bottles over £20, 8 bottles under £20, 30 by glass **Notes** Vegetarian available, Air con **Seats** 100, Pr/dining room 22 **Parking** On street, Belgrave Sq

Boxwood Café

◉◉ British 🖳 V Plan 4 G4

Classy brasserie in high-class hotel

☎ 020 7235 1010
The Berkeley Hotel, Wilton Place, Knightsbridge SW1X 7RL
e-mail: boxwoodcafe@gordonramsay.com
dir: Nearest station: Knightsbridge Please telephone for directions or check website

Located on one corner of The Berkeley Hotel with its own street entrance on Knightsbridge, this upmarket Gordon Ramsay-owned establishment is an interpretation of a New York-style café. The elegant dining room is a stylish, split-level basement affair, with a bar and smart table settings. Natural earthy tones parade alongside golds and bronzes and lashings of darkwood and leather, while service is youthful, slick but relaxed, and there's a vibrant metropolitan buzz. The accomplished kitchen's upmarket brasserie repertoire hits the spot, utilising high quality seasonal ingredients with the emphasis on flavour, innovative combinations and stylish presentation; think ceviche of organic salmon and Cornish crab with chilli, lime, coriander and grapefruit, followed by grilled Black Angus rib-eye chop with beef marrowbone and port wine braised shallots.

Chef Stuart Gillies **Owner** Gordon Ramsay Holdings Ltd **Times** 12-3/6-1am **Wines** 100 bottles over £20, 2 bottles under £20, 10 by glass **Notes** Taste of Boxwood £55,

Sunday L, Vegetarian menu, Air con **Seats** 140, Pr/dining room 16 **Children** Portions, Menu **Parking** On street

Brasserie Roux

◉ French Plan 5 B6

Stylish brasserie serving rustic French cuisine

☎ 020 7968 2900 & 747 2200
Sofitel St James London, 6 Waterloo Place SW1Y 4AN
e-mail: h3144-fb8@accor.com
dir: Nearest station: Piccadilly Circus Please telephone for directions

This classic French brasserie comes with an elegant Pierre Yves Rochon design. Set within the imposing Sofitel St James hotel, the cockerel is its main decorative theme which is, of course, the symbol of France. High ceilings, enormous lampshades, yellow walls, contemporary furniture upholstered in dark green and red and wooden tables all add to the chic and vibrant atmosphere, backed by friendly and relaxed but unobtrusive service. The traditional, unfussy French regional cuisine offers flavoursome classics utilising quality ingredients, including quenelle of pike 'a la Lyonnaise', Glendale organic smoked salmon tartare with horseradish and pot au feu 'jarret et queue de boeuf'.

Chef Paul Danabie **Owner** Accor UK **Times** 12-3/5.30-11 **Prices** Fixed L 3 course fr £20, Fixed D 3 course fr £20, Service added but optional 12.5% **Wines** 21 by glass **Notes** Pre-theatre menu 5.30-7pm, Vegetarian available, Civ Wed 150, Air con **Seats** 100, Pr/dining room 130 **Children** Portions, Menu **Parking** NCP at Piccadilly

Le Caprice Restaurant

◉◉ Modern European V Plan 5 A6

Quality cooking in a restaurant that brings out the stars

☎ 020 7629 2239
Arlington House, Arlington St SW1A 1RT
dir: Nearest station: Green Park Arlington St runs beside The Ritz. Restaurant is at end

Still teeming with devoted fans, this classy, fashionable outfit has been the darling of the celebrity circuit for years. Secreted away behind the Ritz, this St James's institution sports a retro-chic brasserie look; think revolving front door, black and white décor and eye-catching David Bailey photographs. Comfortable seating, closely set tables and a relaxed, unbuttoned but vibrant and unashamedly glamorous atmosphere comes supported by seamless service. Tables maybe turned and moneyed heads may swivel looking for the celebrity count, but the crowd-pleasing menu keeps everyone happy. The wide-ranging repertoire of European comfort food is driven by high quality seasonal produce and uncomplicated, clean-cut flavours and presentation. Take deep-fried haddock with minted pea purée, chips and tartare, and to close, perhaps gooseberry meringue pie.

Chef Paul Brown **Owner** Caprice Holdings Ltd
Times 12-3/5.30-12, Closed 25-26 Dec, 1 Jan, Aug BH, Closed D 24 Dec **Prices** Starter £6.50-£15.75, Main £8.75-£26.50, Dessert £3.50-£9.50, Service optional **Wines** 120 bottles over £20, 5 bottles under £20, 22 by glass **Notes** Vegetarian menu, Air con **Seats** 80 **Children** Portions **Parking** On street, NCP

Le Cercle

◎◎ Modern French 🖳　　　　　Plan 4 F3

Discreet basement restaurant offering modern French grazing food

☎ 020 7901 9999
1 Wilbraham Place SW1X 9AE
e-mail: info@lecercle.co.uk
web: www.clubgascon.com/lc_intro.php
dir: Nearest station: Sloane Square Just off Sloane St

Close to Sloane Square, this discreet basement restaurant continues to guarantee a memorable night out. The dining areas combine a sense of refined intimacy with a surprising spaciousness, accentuated by the high ceilings, neutral colour scheme and artful lighting. The glass-fronted wine cave and cheese room provide suitable stages to highlight two French passions celebrated here, while the menu offers a good overview of the rest of Gallic gastronomy. Dishes such as venison saddle with parsnip purée and red berry sauce, roast sea bass with julienne of vegetables and liquorice sauce, and chocolate fondant with pistachio ice cream are cooked with aplomb, with small but perfectly-formed portions, refined presentation and clear flavours.

Chef Thierry Beyris **Owner** Vincent Labeyrie & Pascal Aussignac **Times** 12-3/6-11, Closed Xmas & New Year, Closed Sun, Mon **Prices** Fixed D 3 course £15, Starter £4.50-£35, Main £5-£16, Dessert £5-£6, Service added 12.5% **Wines** 200 bottles over £20, 15 by glass **Notes** Vegetarian available, Air con **Seats** 60, Pr/dining room 12 **Children** Menu **Parking** Outside after 6pm, NCP in Cadogan Sq

The Cinnamon Club

◎◎ Indian 🖳　　　　　Plan 5 C4

Sophisticated Indian dining in former library

☎ 020 7222 2555
The Old Westminster Library, Great Smith St SW1P 3BU
e-mail: info@cinnamonclub.com
dir: Nearest station: Westminster Take exit 6, across Parliament Sq, then pass Westminster Abbey on left. Take 1st left into Great Smith St

This impressive Grade II listed building - the old Westminster Library - is a truly unique setting for a contemporary Indian restaurant. Still with books lining the walls, the restaurant's high-vaulted ceilings and domed skylights, polished parquet floors and dark wood lend it an air of old-world grandeur and elegance that perfectly complements its outstanding cuisine, set off by high-backed suede chairs and white linen-clad tables to create a clubby feel. Peruse the menu over a Bellini, and then enjoy the traditional Indian cuisine which is based around fine ingredients and well-judged spicing. Breakfast, lunch, pre- and post-theatre and carte menus offer a wide selection of dishes. Try stir-fried crab with roasted coconut and spices, or perhaps pan-seared black cod with tomato lemon sauce.

Times 12-3/6-11, Closed Xmas, Etr, BHs, Closed Sun, Closed L Sat

David Britton at The Cavendish

◎ Modern British 🖳　　　　　Plan 5 B6

Accomplished cooking in stylish location

☎ 020 7930 2111
The Cavendish London, 81 Jermyn St SW1Y 6JF
e-mail: info@thecavendishlondon.com
web: www.thecavendishlondon.com
dir: Nearest station: Green Park, Piccadilly Situated directly behind Fortnum & Mason Department Store

Once owned and run by Rosa Lewis - 'the Duchess of Duke Street' - the Cavendish Hotel enjoys an enviable location in the prestigious St James's area of central

London. The recently re-branded restaurant is situated on the first floor, with large plate-glass windows that take full advantage of the views of the exclusive galleries and boutiques below. Despite its glamorous location, the style here is relaxed, with no dress code and linen napkins decorating tables rather than table cloths. The menu is traditional British with contemporary twists. You might start with roast scallops with bubble-and-squeak and lemon dressing and follow it with chargrilled Gloucestershire sirloin steak with sautéed potatoes, curly kale and red wine sauce. Lunch and pre-theatre set menus are terrific value.

David Britton at The Cavendish

Chef David Britton **Owner** Ellerman Investments Ltd **Times** 12-2.30/5.30-10.30, Closed 25-26 Dec, 1 Jan, Closed L Sat-Sun & BH Mon **Wines** 20 bottles over £20, 10 bottles under £20, 10 by glass **Notes** Pre-theatre menu available 2 courses £14.95, Vegetarian available, Air con **Seats** 80, Pr/dining room 70 **Children** Portions, Menu **Parking** 60 **Parking** secure on-site valet parking

Drones

◎◎ Traditional French 🖳　　　　　Plan 4 G3

Classy Belgravia venue with experience factor

☎ 020 7235 9555
1 Pont St SW1X 9EJ
e-mail: sales@whitestarline.org.uk
dir: Nearest station: Knightsbridge

This classic from the Marco Pierre White stable oozes style, glamour and confidence. Walls are lined with black and white photographs of show-biz legends - think David Niven and Audrey Hepburn - while floors are polished parquet, there's leather banquette seating, tables are white clothed and service is slick and attentive. The discreet glass frontage is hung with Venetian blinds, while there's an eye-catching bar and art-deco style wall lighting. The crisply scripted, lengthy menu parades a repertoire of classic French dishes using quality ingredients and an assured, intelligent, straightforward style. Expect parfait de foie gras en gelée, or perhaps Dover sole à la meunière. Desserts like Drones rice pudding with compôte of red fruits or prune and Armagnac tart with crème anglaise catch the eye too, while the fixed-price lunch is great value.

Times 12-2.30/6-11, Closed 26 Dec, 1 Jan, Closed L Sat, Closed D Sun

LONDON SW1 *Continued*

Ebury

◉◉ British, French 🖥 Plan 4 G2

Fashionable, buzzy Pimlico eatery serving highly accomplished modern cuisine

☎ 020 7730 6784

11 Pimlico Rd SW1W 8NA
e-mail: info@theebury.co.uk
dir: Nearest station: Sloane Sq/Victoria From Sloane Sq Tube left into Holbein Place, then left at intersection with Pimlico Rd. The Ebury is on right on corner of Pimlico Rd & Ranelagh Grove. From Victoria, left down Buckingham Palace Rd, then right onto Pimlico Rd

This large, smart, contemporary bar-brasserie-restaurant certainly stands out from the crowd. On the ground floor there's a lively bar, crustacea counter and stylish, low-slung brown leather seating for more relaxed dining, while the upstairs restaurant has a more formal, romantic edge. An equally modern confection, it comes decked out in white linen with cream leather seating, stunning chandeliers and photographs of jazz legends. A glass window allows glimpses into the kitchen, while service is slick, professional and friendly. The refined, modern brasserie-style repertoire is underpinned by a classical French theme, driven by quality ingredients, clear flavours and creative presentation. Take roast rump of lamb served with boulangère potatoes and caramelised onion purée, or hot chocolate fondant with peanut ice cream and honeycomb.

Times 12-3.30/6-10.30, Closed 24-30 Dec

Fifth Floor Restaurant

◉◉ French, European 🖥 Plan 4 F4

Fashionable dining at landmark London store

☎ 020 7235 5250 & 7235 5000

Harvey Nichols, 109-125 Knightsbridge SW1X 7RJ
e-mail: reception@harveynichols.com
web: www.harveynichols.com
dir: Nearest station: Knightsbridge, Hyde Park Corner Entrance on Sloane Street

Five floors up above the Knightsbridge traffic, Harvey Nichols contemporary food hall - with restaurant, bar, café, wine shop and sushi bar - remains achingly fashionable and as popular as ever. The flagship restaurant is a light, bright oval-shaped space as stylish as it is comfortable, with space-age-like fibre-optic lighting, glass-domed ceiling and white leather tubular chairs casting an upbeat glow. The kitchen's clean-cut, well-presented, modern-European brasserie repertoire hits the right note too, driven by prime seasonal ingredients, accurate simplicity and flavour; take home-smoked Atlantic halibut with creamed coco beans, courgettes and a red wine jus. And, though the popular adjoining bar cranks up the decibels, the wine list soothes with a corking choice and plenty by glass.

Times 12-3/6-11, Closed Xmas, Closed D Sun

Foliage

◉◉◉◉◉ – *see opposite*

The Goring

◉◉ Traditional British 🖥 Plan 4 H4

Sumptuous hotel serving British classics

☎ 020 7396 9000

Beeston Place SW1W 0JW
e-mail: reception@goringhotel.co.uk
dir: Nearest station: Victoria From Victoria St turn left into Grosvenor Gdns, cross Buckingham Palace Rd, 75yds turn right into Beeston Place

This family-owned property may be traditional in style but it's anything but stuffy with staff providing friendly and efficient service. A sumptuous and elaborate hotel done out in the grand style, as befits a traditional property in its central London location just behind Buckingham Palace. David Linley's design offers a lighter, modern touch to the grand Victorian dining room, with its plush silks and contemporary centrepiece 'Blossom' chandeliers. Menus are a celebration of all things British: accomplished classics using prime quality, fresh produce. Think roast leg of Holker Estate salt marsh lamb with boulangère potatoes and a rosemary jus, or poached baby chicken with a vegetable and wild celery broth, while there are British cheeses from the trolley and puddings like a classic custard tart to finish.

Chef Derek Quelch **Owner** Goring Family
Times 12.30-2.30/6-10, Closed L Sat **Prices** Fixed L 3 course fr £34, Fixed D 3 course fr £46.20, Service added but optional 12.5% **Wines** 100+ bottles over £20, 10 by glass **Notes** Pre-theatre D available, Vegetarian available, Dress restrictions, Smart dress, Civ Wed 50, Air con **Seats** 70, Pr/dining room 50 **Children** Portions, Menu **Parking** 5

Foliage

Modern European 🖥

Intricate cooking in one of the capital's most fashionable addresses

☎ 020 7235 2000
**Mandarin Oriental Hyde Park,
66 Knightsbridge SW1X 7LA**
e-mail: molon-reservations@mohg.com
web: www.mandarinoriental.com/london
dir: Nearest station: Knightsbridge In Knightsbridge with Harrods on right, hotel is 0.5m on left, opposite Harvey Nichols

Backing on to Hyde Park, this imposing luxury Knightsbridge hotel fairly bristles with class. To the uninitiated, its liveried doorman and fluttering flags outside might give the impression of a grand Edwardian edifice in the old tradition, yet it's anything but. Smiling greeting staff are contemporarily dressed, as are the equally fashionable bar and glass-fronted wine-store entrance to Foliage, the fine-dining restaurant. Chic, stylish and intimate, the restaurant's theme is all in the name, with giant glass wall panels enclosing thousands of white silk leaves that come alive with lighting and change colour to echo the seasons. A split-level floor affords views of park life too, and striking flower displays and luxury fabrics and furnishings add to the sophisticated modern tone. These fine details support the dining room's

reputation as one of London's finest under chef's David Nicholls' and Chris Staines' sublime cooking. Their approach is via an enticing repertoire of fixed-price menu options that take in a great value lunch jour, carte and tasting dinner offering. Luxury ingredients grace the intricate cooking, showcasing the kitchen's silky technical skills, with well-conceived, strikingly presented, thoroughly modern dishes to match the setting. Expect smoked beef, soubise, confit garlic and roast vegetables, or perhaps sea bass with broccoli, lobster and mushroom, while the supporting service is superbly friendly, knowledgeable and nothing short of world class. (Foliage's Adam Tihany's design is currently planned for refurbishment during 2009.)

Chef Chris Staines **Owner** Mandarin Oriental Hyde Park
Times 12-2.30/7-10.30, Closed 26 Dec, 1 Jan **Wines** 400 bottles over £20, 15 by glass **Notes** Fixed L 4 courses £29, Sunday L, Vegetarian available, Dress restrictions, Smart casual, Civ Wed 250, Air con **Seats** 46 **Parking** Valet parking, NCP

LONDON SW1 *Continued*

Il Convivio

◉◉ Modern Italian ▭ Plan 4 H2

Stylish Italian dining in upmarket Belgravia

☎ 020 7730 4099
143 Ebury St SW1W 9QN
e-mail: comments@etruscarestaurants.com
dir: Nearest station: Victoria 7 min walk from Victoria
Station - corner of Ebury St and Elizabeth St

The combination of the quiet residential street in smart
Belgravia and the handsomeness of the converted
Georgian house makes for an alluring and chic location.
The split-level premises has a few sought-after tables at
street level, with the main restaurant on the lower level. A
conservatory-style room has a sliding roof so the space
magically becomes alfresco when the weather allows.
Deep red walls hung with stone slabs inscribed with
quotes from Dante's Il Convivio are set off by modern
wooden-backed chairs and cream leather cushions. The
upmarket Italian cuisine includes a few unconventional
touches that show the kitchen has confidence. Wild
pollack carpaccio risotto comes with a fig and anchovy
pesto, and veal shank ravioli is served in a creamy wild
mushroom sauce. A wide-ranging choice is supplemented
by daily specials and an extensive wine list.

Chef Lukas Pfaff **Owner** Piero & Enzo Quaradeghini
Times 12-2.45/7-10.45, Closed Xmas, New Year, BHs,
Closed Sun **Prices** Fixed L 2 course £17.50, Starter
£7.50-£12.50, Main £16.50-£22, Dessert £5.50-£9.50,
Service added but optional 12.5% **Wines** 156 bottles over
£20, 12 bottles under £20, 10 by glass **Notes** Vegetarian
available, Dress restrictions, Smart casual, Air con
Seats 65, Pr/dining room 14 **Parking** On street

Inn the Park

◉ British Plan 5 C5

All-day eatery in park setting

☎ 020 7451 9999
St James's Park SW1A 1AA
e-mail: info@innthepark.co.uk
dir: Nearest station: St James's Park, Charing Cross 200
metres down The Mall towards Buckingham Palace

The long, grass-roofed, Scandinavian-style building
blends invisibly into the rolling landscape of St James's
Park. The cleverly named all-day eatery looks out across
the lake to Duck Island and beyond to the London Eye. A
café by day, with a counter for quick snacks, it becomes a

restaurant at night offering simple, full-flavoured,
brasserie-style dishes using quality produce from small
suppliers. Expect the likes of ham hock terrine, broad
beans, pea shoots and spring onion followed by roasted
belly of pork, quince jam and parsnip purée. There is a
super decked area for summer alfresco dining.

Times 12-3/6-10.45, Closed D Sun-Mon (winter)

JB's

◉ Modern French Plan 5 A3

Modern hotel brasserie dining

☎ 020 7769 9772 & 020 7769 9999
Park Plaza Victoria, 239 Vauxhall Bridge Rd SW1V 1EQ
e-mail: gfernando@pphe.com
web: www.parkplaza.com
dir: 2 min walk from Apollo Victoria Theatre

A smart modern hotel conveniently close to Victoria
station, the Park Plaza boasts airy, stylish public areas
that include an elegant bar and restaurant as well as a
popular coffee bar. The restaurant itself (JB's) follows the
contemporary theme, and has large windows and a
lengthy, crowd-pleasing menu that offers something for
everyone in its medley of modern and classics. Think
simple, good-looking, well-executed dishes using quality
produce like pan-fried fillet of John Dory served with
braised fennel and a chive beurre blanc, or perhaps
English lamb rack with a date glaze and truffle mash.
Puddings strike a homely note, maybe a strawberry
Pavlova or steamed dark chocolate pudding might catch
the eye.

Chef Paul Keninson **Owner** Park Plaza Hotels
Times 12-2/6-10, Closed BHs, Closed Sun, Closed L Sat
Wines 26 bottles over £20, 11 bottles under £20, 15 by
glass **Notes** Pre-theatre D available from 6-7pm 2
courses £18, Vegetarian available, Dress restrictions,
Smart casual, Civ Wed 300, Air con **Seats** 99
Children Portions **Parking** 32

Just St James

◉ Modern British ▭ V Plan 5 B5

Dining in high style in old St James's

☎ 020 7976 2222
12 St James's St SW1A 1ER
e-mail: bookings@juststjames.com
dir: Nearest station: Green Park Turn right on Piccadilly
towards Piccadilly Circus, then right into St James's St.
Restaurant on corner of St James's St & King St

One of the most expensive grand banking halls ever built,
back in the late 1800s, this former Lloyd's makes for a
lavish restaurant. Italian marble columns, a sweeping
glass and wooden staircase and a central glass lift lead
up to a semi-private mezzanine floor, which affords great
views over the bar and restaurant below. Dishes offer a
new perspective on British bistro-style classics using the
finest of British produce. Western Isles scallops with
black pudding and pancetta; and medallions of venison
with roast baby vegetables, straw potatoes and Madeira
jus are fine examples of the fare.

Chef Peter Gladwin, Debi Van Zyl **Owner** Peter Gladwin
Times 12-3/6-11, Closed 25-26 Dec, 1 Jan, Closed Sun,
Closed L Sat **Prices** Fixed L 3 course £30-£35, Fixed D 3
course £35-£48, Starter £5.75-£14.50, Main £12-£24.50,
Dessert £5.50-£7.50, Service added but optional 12.5%
Wines 55 bottles over £20, 10 bottles under £20, 13 by
glass **Notes** Vegetarian menu, Civ Wed 0, Air con
Seats 120, Pr/dining room 140 **Children** Portions
Parking St James Square - meters

Ken Lo's Memories of China

◉◉ Chinese ▭ Plan 4 H3

Refined Chinese cooking close to Victoria

☎ 020 7730 7734
65-69 Ebury St SW1W 0NZ
e-mail: memoriesofchina@btconnect.com
dir: Nearest station: Victoria At junction of Ebury Street &
Eccleston St.

This legendary Pimlico restaurant with an enviable
reputation for high quality, authentic Chinese cuisine has
a refined, upmarket feel. Quality abounds from the stylish
table settings, starched linen and chopsticks, to the
subtle Chinese décor which has a contemporary edge. A
lengthy carte showcases the classic Chinese food, backed
up by a set menu that offers excellent value for money
from the same quality produce and refined presentations.
Accurate flavours reflect the skilful handling of good raw
ingredients, yielding the likes of siu mau (steamed
chicken and prawn dumplings), crispy soft-shell crab,
iron-plate sizzled mixed seafood (scallops, prawns and
squid) in black bean sauce, or kuo ta egg-battered
chicken. Service is speedy and efficient.

Times 12-2.30/7-11, Closed BHs, Closed L Sun

The Lanesborough

◉◉ Italian Plan 4 G5

Accomplished Italian cuisine in stylish hotel restaurant

☎ 020 7259 5599
Hyde Park Corner SW1X 7TA
e-mail: info@lanesborough.com
dir: Nearest station: Hyde Park Corner On Hyde Park
corner

It's all change at the Lanesborough, where the newly
renamed and refurbished restaurant of this grand hotel
on Hyde Park Corner has taken on an Italian flavour in
recent months. You can still expect world-class luxury,
stunning service and an aperitif in the swanky cocktail
bar, before moving through to the glass-roofed
conservatory restaurant, Apsleys, where you take a seat
among exotic palms and trickling fountains, at a table
set with the finest crystal and china. Quality ingredients
are to the fore on the wide-ranging modern Italian menu,
and there's no shortage of skill. Kick off with sea urchins
with bigoli pasta and sweet chilli perhaps, followed by
veal sweetbreads with peas, broad beans and morels, or
scallops saltimbocca with pea mash, samphire and
sauce vierge.

Times 12-2.30/6-11.30

Luciano

◉◉ Italian 💻 Plan 5 B5

Classy St James's Italian with a touch of 'Marco' magic

☎ 020 7408 1440
72-73 St James's St SW1A 1PH
e-mail: info@lucianorestaurant.co.uk
dir: Nearest station: Green Park Tube Please telephone for directions

The St James's collaboration between Marco Pierre White and the Forte group, Luciano's comes brimful of class and glamour. There's a large chic bar at the front with a mosaic-tiled floor and large windows overlooking St James's Street - just the place for a pre-meal Bellini. The atmospheric restaurant - down a few steps beyond the bar - oozes style and glamour, with provocative photograph-lined walls, slate pillars, polished wood floors, burgundy leather banquettes and matching chairs, and mood lighting. Smartly attired mainly Italian staff and an Italian-dominated wine list are impressive too. Cooking is classic Italian using top-notch produce, delivering straightforward, full-flavoured dishes. Take whole sea bass with tardivo clam and barolo, or fillet of brill with lentils and salsa verde.

Chef Marco Corsica **Owner** Marco Pierre White
Times 12-3/6-11, Closed Xmas, 1 Jan, Etr day, BHs, Closed D 24 Dec **Prices** Starter £6.50-£12.50, Main £16-£28, Dessert £6.50-£8.50, Service added but optional 12.5% **Wines** 150 bottles over £20, 5 bottles under £20, 12 by glass **Notes** Vegetarian available, Air con **Seats** 130, Pr/dining room 22 **Children** Portions

Mango Tree

◉ Thai **V** Plan 4 G4

Authentic Thai food in a stylish setting

☎ 020 7823 1888
46 Grosvenor Place, Belgravia SW1X 7EQ
e-mail: reservations@mangotree.org.uk
dir: Nearest station: Victoria Please telephone for directions

A fine-dining Thai restaurant in Belgravia, the Mango Tree is the sister restaurant to Awana, a Malaysian restaurant in Chelsea (see entry). The spacious dining room has a sleek, modern feel, with materials sourced directly from Thailand to create a beautiful, authentic setting. Traditional Thai food takes in dishes such as steamed fresh prawns in tom yum sauce; green chicken curry; and pad Thai chicken and prawn. Festivals and events are held on a regular basis, with themed food, processions and local music. Tasting menus and banquets are also available.

Chef Mark Read **Owner** Eddie Lim **Times** 12-3/6-11, Closed Xmas, New Year **Prices** Fixed L 2 course £17-£30, Fixed D 3 course £25-£45, Starter £5.50-£10, Main £9.80-£18, Dessert £5.50-£12, Service added but optional 12.5% **Wines** 15 bottles over £20, 2 bottles under £20, 16 by glass **Notes** Sunday L, Vegetarian menu, Air con **Seats** 160 **Children** Portions, Menu **Parking** On Wilton St

Mint Leaf

◉ Modern Indian 💻 Plan 5 C3

Trendy, subterranean, nightclub-styled modern Indian

☎ 020 7930 9020
Suffolk Place, Haymarket SW1Y 4HX
e-mail: reservations@mintleafrestaurant.com
web: www.mintleafrestaurant.com
dir: Nearest station: Piccadilly/Charing Cross At end of Haymarket, on corner of Pall Mall and Suffolk Place. Opposite Her Majesty's Theatre, 100m from Trafalgar Square

With a long, striking cocktail bar and large dining area divided into intimate areas by walnut louvres and designer wire mesh, Mint Leaf immediately cuts trendy, nightclubby good looks. Throw in a central raised catwalk, darkwood, modern seating, low lighting and a backing track of contemporary music, and you have cool, hard-surfaced designer-led styling. The kitchen fits the bill, dealing in relatively straightforward but equally modern Pan-Indian cooking using quality ingredients, colourful presentation and polite spicing to run alongside a buzzy vibe and black-clad staff. Try fillet of wild sea bass poached in a fenugreek-scented curry, or paneer braised with guntoor chilli and coconut tempered with asafoetida.

Chef A Jay Chopra **Owner** Out of Africa Investments
Times 12-3/5.30-11, Closed 25-26 Dec, 1 Jan, Closed L Sat, Sun **Prices** Fixed L 2 course £15, Starter £5-£12.50, Main £11-£21.50, Dessert £5.50-£7, Service added but optional 12.5% **Wines** 140 bottles over £20, 4 bottles under £20, 12 by glass **Notes** Vegetarian available, Dress restrictions, Smart casual, no scruffy jeans or trainers, Civ Wed 100, Air con **Seats** 144, Pr/dining room 66 **Children** Portions **Parking** NCP, on street

Mitsukoshi

◉ Japanese 💻 Plan 3 B1

Authentic Japanese cooking in a department store restaurant

☎ 020 7930 0317
Dorland House, 14-20 Lower Regent St SW1Y 4PH
e-mail: lonrest@mitsukoshi.co.jp
web: www.mitsukoshi-restaurant.co.uk
dir: Nearest station: Piccadilly Circus

Set in the basement of its namesake Japanese department store just off Piccadilly Circus, Mitsukoshi is very much a traditional-styled Japanese. Descend the stairs to the popular sushi bar, or down a further tier to the main dining room, decked out in simple, light, neutral tones with booth-style areas set with dark lacquered tables. The kitchen deals in fresh, quality ingredients and a broad selection of authentic Japanese cuisine. Sushi, sukiyaki and shabu-shabu are the main specialities, with plenty of set-meal options on offer too. Otherwise expect grilled beef fillet with teriyaki sauce or perhaps deep-fried prawns with tempura sauce.

Mitsukoshi

Times 12-2/6-10, Closed 25, 26 Dec, 1 Jan, Etr

MU at Millennium Knightsbridge

◉ Modern International 💻 Plan 4 F4

Reliable dining in the heart of Knightsbridge

☎ 020 7201 6330
17 Sloane St, Knightsbridge SW1X 9NU
web: www.millenniumhotels.com/knightsbridge
dir: Nearest station: Knightsbridge/Victoria 200yds from Knightsbridge Stn/near Harrods

Occupying a curvaceous space on the first floor of the fashionable Millennium Hotel in the prestigious shopping area of Knightsbridge, MU combines contemporary design and urban chic with classic colours, imaginative lighting and artwork to dramatic effect without losing a sense of warmth and intimacy. The kitchen focuses on successful combinations of ingredients to create full-flavoured and skilfully presented dishes. Start perhaps with poached squab and foie gras mousse with truffle dressing, followed by roast monkfish and baby squid with sun-dried tomato couscous and Reisling nage.

Chef Paul Knight **Owner** Millennium & Copthorne Hotels
Times 12-2.30/6-10.30, Closed BH's, Closed Sun
Prices Fixed L 2 course £18.50, Fixed D 3 course £31.50, Tasting menu £50, Starter £7-£12, Main £16-£22, Dessert £6-£7, Service added but optional 12.5% **Wines** 310 bottles over £20, 4 bottles under £20, 30 by glass **Notes** Air con **Seats** 110, Pr/dining room 50 **Children** Portions **Parking** 8 **Parking** NCP Pavilion Rd

Nahm

LONDON SW1   **Plan 4 G4**

Thai 🍴

Top-notch traditional Thai in chic hotel

☎ 020 7333 1234
The Halkin Hotel, Halkin St, Belgravia SW1X 7DJ
e-mail: res@nahm.como.bz
dir: Nearest station: Hyde Park Corner Halkin Street just
off Hyde Park Corner

A taste of Bangkok is brought to Georgian Belgravia at
Nahm, a Thai restaurant located in the chic Halkin Hotel,
a luxurious bolthole for the well-heeled. Based on
traditional Thai recipes, the restaurant creates the Nahm
Arharn banquet-style menu, an excellent way to sample
this sophisticated and very often extraordinary cuisine -
in the evening Nahm echoes with the appreciative sounds
of diners enjoying the unforgettable flavours of what

many consider the world's best Thai food. Slatted wooden
panelling creates intimate spaces within a large, bright
room, while gold and russet colours add to the minimalist
furnishings. This unassuming décor allows the food to do
the talking - backed up by assured and knowledgeable
service with its emphasis on explaining how the menu
works to create a Thai banquet. Tickle the palate with
kanom krok bpuu (coconut cup cakes with a red curry of
crab and Thai basil), then sample dishes such as lon
dtow jiaw (yellow beans simmered in coconut cream with
ginger and shallots served with star fruit and betel
leaves) or geng prik thai sai neua gwarng (green
peppercorn curry of venison with holy basil and kaffir lime
leaves). If the prices leave you a little breathless, you can
content yourself with the knowledge that it's cheaper
than flying to Bangkok.

Chef David Thompson, Matthew Albert **Owner** Halkin
Hotel Ltd **Times** 12-2.30/7-11, Closed 25 Dec & BHs,
Closed L Sat-Sun **Wines** 190 bottles over £20, 12 by glass
Notes Traditional Nahm Arharn menu £55, Vegetarian
available, Dress restrictions, No jeans, Air con **Seats** 78,
Pr/dining room 36 **Children** Portions **Parking** On street

One-O-One

LONDON SW1   **Plan 4 F4**

French, Seafood **V**

First-rate seafood restaurant

☎ 020 7290 7101
Sheraton Park Tower, 101 Knightsbridge SW1X 7RN
e-mail: darren.neilan@luxurycollection.com
dir: Nearest station: Knightsbridge E from station, just
after Harvey Nichols.

With stunning views over the city, The Sheraton Park
Tower houses its flagship seafood restaurant, One-O-One,
which has had a complete make-over and has emerged
as a venue worthy of the cooking of chef Pascal Proyart.
The room is now more in line with today's fashion for
mellow, natural tones, with atmospheric new lighting and
a huge central illuminated glass-topped table. There is
also a stylish bar and private dining room. Service

remains friendly and efficient, while the restaurant has
taken a new direction and is now based around the
grazing-style of dining, although the traditional three-
course format is still available. The 4 sections of the
menu are given names like 'Low tide and wonderful
discovery' and 'The goodness of the sea and earth' and
feature the chef's French-inspired food, cooked with
considerable flair and creativity using top rate produce.
Thus red tuna tartar comes with soft-shell crab in
beautifully cooked tempura batter, and a stunning
wasabi sorbet, with the waiter dramatically injecting soy
sauce into some sushi rice at the table. Another dish sees
grilled pavé of wild brill combined with squid ink
pappardelle, a tian of fondant vegetables and sauce
Provençal. (There are a few meat dishes on the menu.)

Chef Pascal Proyart **Owner** Starwood Hotels & Resorts
Times 12-2.30/6.30-10 **Prices** Fixed L 2 course £15-£46,
Tasting menu £50, Starter £8-£18, Main £13-£28,
Dessert £6, Service optional **Wines** 101 bottles over £20,
12 by glass **Notes** Tasting menu 5 courses, Sunday L,
Vegetarian menu, Dress restrictions, Smart casual
preferred, Air con **Seats** 50, Pr/dining room 10
Children Portions **Parking** 60

LONDON SW1 *Continued*

Nahm

◉◉◉ – *see opposite*

One-O-One

◉◉◉ – *see opposite*

One Twenty One Two

◉ International   Plan 5 D5

Hotel fine dining in the heart of Whitehall

☎ 020 7451 9333
Royal Horseguards Hotel, 2 Whitehall Court SW1A 2EJ
e-mail: f&broyalhorseguards@guoman.co.uk
dir: Nearest station: Embankment, Charing Cross From
Trafalgar Sq take exit to Whitehall. Turn into Whitehall
Place then into Whitehall Court

A Grade I listed building on the banks of the Thames, this
landmark hotel in the heart of Whitehall is the epitome of
grand Victorian design. Inside modern refinement and
comfort are seamlessly woven into the architectural
elegance. Paying tribute to its former neighbour, Scotland
Yard, the restaurant is named after the Yard's once
universally famous telephone number, Whitehall 1212.
One Twenty One Two offers contemporary dining in
sophisticated but relaxed surroundings, with an inviting
piano bar, delightful outside terrace and unrivalled views
of the London Eye and city skyline. The kitchen offers a
repertoire blending modern with traditional, and a focus
on fresh quality produce. Take a starter of seared king
scallops with fine herb salad and ginger relish, followed
by pan-seared wild sea bass on fennel confit with
seafood risotto.

Chef Michael Birmingham **Times** 12-3/5.30-10, Closed L
Sun **Prices** Fixed L 2 course £19.95-£30, Fixed D 3 course
£45-£60, Starter £9.95-£13.95, Main £15.95-£30,
Dessert £6.95-£7.95, Service added but optional 12.5%
Notes Vegetarian available, Dress restrictions, Smart
casual, Civ Wed 250, Air con **Seats** 40, Pr/dining room 30
Children Portions **Parking** NCP Trafalgar Square

L'Oranger

◉◉ Modern French 🖥   Plan 5 B5

**Classic French cuisine at impeccably elegant
restaurant**

☎ 020 7839 3774
5 St James's St SW1A 1EF
e-mail: loranger@londonfinediningroup.com
dir: Nearest station: Green Park Access by car via Pall
Mall

A short walk from St James's Palace and the park is one
of London's most beautiful restaurants, L'Oranger. Flower
displays and antique mirrors decorate the long panelled
room and a domed glass ceiling lets in the light. There's
a pretty courtyard as well for alfresco dining in summer.
Fish is a speciality, but the wide-ranging French menu
covers all the bases, featuring a selection of classics
enlivened by the odd modern twist, and the food is rich
and flavours robust and bold. Try creamy aubergine soup
with poached quail's eggs and green apple, tuna on toast
and spicy olive oil to start, with mains such as roast wild
sea bass, purée of celeriac, mushrooms and chestnut
emulsion, or fillet of beef en croûte with bone marrow and
fourme d'Ambert cheese and vegetables cooked with
rosemary 'barbajuans' beignets.

Chef L Michel, D Pierre **Owner** A to Z Restaurants Ltd
Times 12-2.45/6.30-10.45, Closed Xmas, Etr, BHs, last
wk Aug, Closed Sun, Closed L Sat **Wines** 290 bottles over
£20, 4 bottles under £20, 12 by glass **Notes** Menu
Degustation £75, Vegetarian available, Dress restrictions,
Smart casual, Air con **Seats** 70, Pr/dining room 40
Children Portions **Parking** On street or NCP

Pétrus

◉◉◉◉◉ – *see page 264*

Quaglino's

◉ French Brasserie 🖥   Plan 5 B6

St James's buzzy, glamorous basement brasserie

☎ 020 7930 6767
16 Bury St, St James's SW1Y 6AJ
e-mail: saschak@danddlondon.com
dir: Nearest station: Green Park/Piccadilly Circus Bury St
is off Jermyn St

Built on the site of the original society restaurant, this
ex-Conran contemporary incarnation still offers bags of
glamour too. A dramatic marble staircase sweeps down

from a mezzanine bar to a cavernous dining room with
high glass ceiling, colourful supporting columns, serried
ranks of tables and huge flower displays in true ocean-
liner style. Modern chairs and banquette seating, mirrors,
a crustacea bar and live music all add to the bustling,
animated atmosphere. Straightforward, clean-cut,
crowd-pleasing dishes come driven by quality seasonal
ingredients on an extensive brasserie-style repertoire;
take poached halibut with spinach and a saffron and
mussel broth. A fixed-price menu option - lunch, early or
late evening - adds to the upbeat package.

Chef Craig James **Owner** D & D London
Times 12-3/5.30-mdnt, Closed 24-25 Dec, 1 Jan, Closed
L 31 Dec **Prices** Fixed L 2 course fr £14.50, Fixed D 3
course fr £19, Starter £7-£16, Main £10.50-£28.50,
Dessert £6-£8, Service added but optional 12.5%
Wines 85 bottles over £20, 15 bottles under £20, 14 by
glass **Notes** Fixed D pre & post theatre 5.30-6.30pm &
10.30pm onwards, Vegetarian available, Dress
restrictions, Smart casual, Air con **Seats** 267, Pr/dining
room 44 **Children** Portions, Menu **Parking** Arlington
Street NCP

The Quilon

◉◉ Indian   Plan 5 B4

**Smart, haute-cuisine southern Indian with helpful,
friendly service**

☎ 020 7821 1899
41 Buckingham Gate SW1E 6AF
e-mail: info@quilonrestaurant.co.uk
dir: Nearest station: St James's Park Next to Crowne
Plaza Hotel St James

Rubbing shoulders with the best address in town - just
down the road from Buckingham Palace - this posh
Indian comes with a separate street entrance at the
Crowne Plaza hotel. It's a stylish, modern affair, decked
out with yellow banquettes, blond-wood floor and sunny
blue and yellow paintwork, while carpet and big wall
murals bring a slightly more dated feel elsewhere. Chef
Sriram Aylur's cooking specialises in South Indian's
coastal cuisine, with a blend of authentic and
progressive dishes driven by quality ingredients. Mild,
subtle and refined are bywords, with attractively
presented, colourful dishes delivered via a great value
fixed-price lunch menu or lengthy carte; expect roasted
tilapia fish in plantain leaf, or perhaps koondapur fish,
pistachio lamb or mango curries.

Chef Sriram Aylur **Owner** Taj International Hotels Limited
Times 12-2.30/6-11, Closed 25-26 Dec, Closed L Sat
Prices Fixed L 2 course fr £17.50, Starter £6.50-£12.50,
Main £18-£25, Dessert £5.50, Service added but optional
12.5% **Wines** 80 bottles over £20, 1 bottles under £20,
13 by glass **Notes** Sunday L, Vegetarian available, Dress
restrictions, Smart casual, Air con **Seats** 90
Children Portions **Parking** On street, NCP

Pétrus

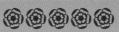

Modern European 🖥 V 🍷NOTABLE WINE LIST

Top-of-the-range dining in an opulent Knightsbridge hotel

☎ 020 7235 1200
The Berkeley, Wilton Place, Knightsbridge SW1X 7RL
e-mail: petrus@marcuswareing.com
dir: Nearest station: Knightsbridge, Hyde Park Corner Please telephone for directions or check website

Oozing sophistication and opulence, Pétrus comes discreetly located off the foyer and beyond the stylish Caramel Room lounge-bar at the luxury Berkeley Hotel - the unobtrusive name on the handles of its tinted-glass doors lets you know you've arrived. As soon as you enter you're cosseted by slick and attentive staff, consummate professionals, though not at all stuffy. Rich, vivid and sexy, the interior is the work of design guru David Collins, the sensual claret colours and textures reflecting that of the world-renowned wine that lends the restaurant its name, plus inspiration from Château Pétrus. Eye-catching features grab the attention - two giant abacuses complete with blown-glass beads act as a screen for the wine chillers, fantastic chandeliers, stunning French blinds, chairs of soft burgundy leather and red velvety walls all seduce. Trolleys for cheeses, liqueurs and, most

importantly, the bonbons, with its wonderful selection of sweetmeats, all circle the floor in style and add a sense of theatre to the occasion. There's also a small lounge area for aperitifs and a chef's table in the heart of the kitchen for up to eight guests. It's all a bold and striking complement to the impeccable cooking that makes Pétrus a dining magnet on the international culinary map. Marcus Wareing's modern approach is classically based, has great integrity and owes much to the insistence on the absolute best in raw ingredients. The elegant, richly detailed cuisine oozes technical wizardry, precision, balance, texture contrast, clear flavours and wow factor ... this is skill of the highest order, world-class cooking at its best. Take a roasted entrecôte of veal served with green asparagus, courgette flower salad and veal vinaigrette, or perhaps braised halibut with buffalo ricotta tortellini, confit egg yolk and nasturtium flower sauce, while dessert might showcase an almond pannacotta with glazed apricots, amaretti biscuits and tonka bean ice cream. A serious wine list, with a good selection by glass, naturally includes offerings from that namesake château, while set-price lunch continues to offer great value at this level.

Chef Marcus Wareing **Owner** Marcus Wareing at the Berkeley Ltd **Times** 12-2.30/6-11, Closed 1 wk Xmas, Closed Sun, Closed L Sat **Prices** Fixed L course £30, Fixed D 3 course £65, Tasting menu £80, Main £65, Service added but optional 12.5% **Wines** 1000 bottles over £20, 4 bottles under £20, 10 by glass **Notes** ALC 3 courses, Vegetarian menu, Dress restrictions, Smart-jacket preferred, No jeans/ trainers, Air con **Seats** 70, Pr/dining room 16 **Children** Portions **Parking** NCP and on street

LONDON SW1 *Continued*

Quirinale

◎◎ Italian 💻 Plan 5 C3

High-end Italian a stone's throw from Parliament

☎ 020 7222 7080
North Court, 1 Great Peter St SW1P 3LL
e-mail: info@quirinale.co.uk
dir: Nearest station: Westminster From Parliament Sq to Lambeth Bridge take 2nd left into Great Peter St, restaurant on left

A smart, modern interior from design guru David Collins sets the scene at this intimate, upmarket, basement Italian, discreetly tucked away on a pleasant street in the lee of the Houses of Parliament. Bevelled mirrors, blond-wood floor, pastel shades and a large below-pavement window create a light, airy space, while white linen and elegant cream leather chairs and central banquette seating provide the comforts. The cooking is unashamedly Italian, a mixture of classic and modern, the presentation and flavours as clean cut and stylish as the surroundings or prime ingredients. Expect intelligent simplicity but with flair; perhaps tortelli filled with radicchio and chestnut with quail ragu, or roasted fillet of veal served with a parmesan crust, creamed spinach and black truffle.The carte comes bolstered by daily specials and a fine selection of Italian wines.

Chef Stefano Savio **Owner** Nadine Gourgey
Times 12-3/6-12, Closed Xmas & New Year, 2 wks Aug, Closed Sat -Sun **Prices** Starter £8-£12.50, Main £9-£24, Dessert £6.50, Service added but optional 12.5%
Wines 98 bottles over £20, 4 bottles under £20, 13 by glass **Notes** Vegetarian available, Air con **Seats** 50
Children Portions **Parking** Street parking available, NCP

The Rib Room

◎◎ British 💻 Plan 4 F4

Robust British cooking in the heart of Knightsbridge

☎ 020 7858 7250
Jumeirah Carlton Tower Hotel, Cadogan Place SW1X 9PY
e-mail: JCTinfo@jumeirah.com
dir: Nearest station: Knightsbridge From major roads follow signs for City Centre, towards Knightsbridge/Hyde Park/Sloane Sq, then into Sloane St/Cadogan Place

This sophisticated restaurant is housed on the ground floor of the towering Jumeirah Carlton Tower Hotel in an enviable central Knightsbridge location. Its moody club-like atmosphere - with acres of wood panelling, stunning floral displays, seductive lighting, Feliks Topolski artwork and crisp napery - is enhanced in the evenings by live piano music, while tantalising aromas waft from the large open 'theatre' kitchen. The repertoire here is pure British gastronomy driven by the best home-reared produce and the successful blend of traditional and more contemporary style, with service gently balancing British etiquette with friendliness. Start with a salad of honey- and mustard-roasted quail with Irish black pudding and Suffolk bacon, followed by perfectly baked halibut with

mussel chowder and sautéed spinach, or maybe Scottish lobster, crab and prawn thermidor.

Chef Simon Young **Times** 12.30-2.45/7-10.45
Prices Fixed L 2 course fr £34, Starter fr £8.50, Main fr £16.50, Dessert fr £8.50, Service added but optional 12.5% **Notes** Sunday L, Dress restrictions, Smart casual, Civ Wed 400, Air con **Seats** 84, Pr/dining room 16
Children Portions, Menu **Parking** 70

Roussillon

◎◎ Modern French 💻 V 📖 Plan 4 G2

Discreet French restaurant focused on the seasons

☎ 020 7730 5550
16 St Barnabas St SW1W 8PE
e-mail: michael@roussillon.co.uk
dir: Nearest station: Sloane Square Telephone for directions

There is no doubting the serious aspirations of this Pimlico restaurant with its large curved bay window: a formal and professional French team complete with sommelier matches the fine-dining menus and sophisticated modern ambience. With cream and brown décor and low lighting, the generously-sized, spacious tables are ideal for business lunches or evening get-togethers. A short lunch menu, carte and several specialist menus present classical French dishes based on luxury seasonal ingredients. The cooking is accurate and very imaginative, and there's a rustic style to the presentation. Typical dishes include classic foie gras terrine with walnut and artichoke salad to start, followed by lobster and sautéed girolle, oven-roasted pigeon with creamed morels, or Highland venison chasseur, with perhaps pineapple delice with caramel ice cream and white chocolate to finish.

Chef A Gauthier, Gerard Virolle **Owner** J & A Palmer, A Gauthier **Times** 12-2.30/6.30-11, Closed 24 Dec-5 Jan, Closed Sun, Closed L Sat **Prices** Fixed L 3 course fr £35, Fixed D 3 course fr £55, Tasting menu £70, Service added 12.5% **Wines** 560 bottles over £20, 20 bottles under £20, 20 by glass **Notes** Tasting menu 6 courses, Vegetarian menu, Dress restrictions, No shorts or flip flops, Air con **Seats** 50, Pr/dining room 28 **Children** Min 8 yrs, Portions, Menu **Parking** NCP

The Rubens at the Palace

◎ British, Mediterranean Plan 5 A4

Quintessentially British hotel overlooking Buckingham Palace

☎ 020 7834 6600
39 Buckingham Palace Rd SW1W 0PS
e-mail: bookrb@rchmail.com
dir: Nearest station: Victoria From station head towards Buckingham Palace

Once the headquarters of the commander in chief of the Polish forces in World War II, this hotel is situated opposite Buckingham Palace and is a tourist favourite. The Library restaurant's décor has the intimate feel of a gentleman's club, with rich embroidered fabrics and

large comfortable armchairs. There's an unobtrusive formality to the service, with traditional flourishes, such as smoked salmon being carved at the table. The cuisine is mainly European, quite classic with some modern interpretations, epitomised by dishes like rump of lamb, seared scallops or a signature dish of Dover sole with chive and butter sauce.

Chef Daniel Collins **Owner** Red Carnation Hotels
Times Closed Xmas week, Closed L all week **Prices** Fixed D 3 course £35-£45, Starter £8-£16, Main £20-£31, Dessert £7.50-£10.50, Service added but optional 12.5% **Wines** 4 bottles over £20, 8 bottles under £20, 12 by glass **Notes** Vegetarian available, Dress restrictions, No shorts or track suits, Air con **Seats** 30, Pr/dining room 50 **Children** Menu **Parking** NCP at Victoria Coach Station

St Alban

◎ Modern Mediterranean 💻 📖 ♨ Plan 5 B6

Celebrity hotspot serving Mediterranean food

☎ 020 7499 8558
4-12 Lower Regent St SW1Y 4PE
dir: Nearest station: Piccadilly Circus From Piccadilly Circus tube station into Regent Street. Carlton Street 2nd left

The Wolseley's sibling restaurant in St James's continues to wow the celebrity crowd with its Mediterranean-inspired menu. It's a smart modern affair, from the bright seating to the contemporary graphic murals of household objects lining the frosted glass windows and grey walls. Service is spot on, while the kitchen's modern, simply presented approach is inspired by the flavours of Italy as well as Spain and Portugal; expect Tuscan vegetable soup, Sardinian fish stew, braised lamb with chilli and chick peas, slow-roast Norfolk pork belly with pumpkin and cavalo nero, and perhaps a pistachio ice cream zabaglione to finish. Booking ahead is essential.

Chef Dale Osborne **Owner** Chris Corbin & Jeremy King
Times 12-3/5.30-mdnt, Closed 25-26 Dec, 1 Jan, Aug BH, Closed D 24 & 31 Dec **Prices** Starter £6.25-£15.75, Main £7.75-£29.25, Dessert £6.25-£8.50, Service added 12.5% **Wines** 133 bottles over £20, 15 bottles under £20, 24 by glass **Notes** Sunday L, Vegetarian available, Civ Wed, Air con **Seats** 140

Sake No Hana

◎ Japanese Plan 5 B5

Modern Japanese restaurant in the heart of St James's

☎ 020 7925 8988
23 St James St SW1 1HA

This latest offering from acclaimed restaurateur Alan Yau (creator of Wagamama) has a discreet entrance complete with doorman. Located on the first floor, accessed via two narrow escalators, upstairs the restaurant is spacious and chic, decked out in a striking lattice of blond wood and bamboo, with traditional low tables flanking the floor-to-ceiling windows. A legion of knowledgeable Japanese staff is on hand to navigate the extensive menu

Continued

LONDON SW1 *Continued*

and advise on choices, most of which are ideal for sharing. Japanese classics grouped under cooking methods feature alongside luxuries like Wagyu beef and white truffle rice. A starter of kani no umeshu - a delicate sweet-and-sour dish of crab in plum jelly studded with red salmon roe eggs - is an excellent choice, with tori netsuke - chicken marinated in sake and soy sauce, and zucchini and asparagus tempura to follow.

Prices Food prices not confirmed for 2009. Please telephone for details.

Salloos Restaurant

⊛ Pakistani   Plan 4 G4

Romantic mews restaurant with a Pakistani menu

☎ 020 7235 4444
62-64 Kinnerton St SW1X 8ER
dir: Nearest station: Knightsbridge Kinnerton St is opposite Berkeley Hotel on Wilton Place

In a mews setting, this long established, professional and well run restaurant deserves its undeniable status. It's a real family business, with a touch of luxury and glamour to the interior. Chicken shish kebab is an excellent all-round dish, delivered to the table on a large skewer with peppers and onions, the meat having a great tandoor flavour. Specialities include king prawn karahi, chicken jalfrezi and raan masala - slow roasted whole leg of lamb marinated in mild spices. Soups, tandoori dishes and interesting vegetable dishes, perhaps chana (chick peas cooked in tomatoes, onions and spices) complete the picture.

Chef Abdul Aziz **Owner** Mr & Mrs M Salahuddin **Times** 12-3/7-11.45, Closed Xmas, Closed Sun **Prices** Starter £6.45-£11.95, Main £14.50-£17.50, Dessert £5.50, Service added but optional 12.5% **Wines** 2 by glass **Notes** Air con **Seats** 65 **Children** Min 8 yrs **Parking** Meters & car park Kinnerton St

Santini

⊛⊛ Italian ▭   Plan 4 H3

Sophisticated, family-run Italian restaurant

☎ 020 7730 4094 & 7730 8275
29 Ebury St SW1W 0NZ
e-mail: info@santini-restaurant.com
web: www.santini-restaurant.com
dir: Nearest station: Victoria Take Lower Belgrave St off Buckingham Palace Rd. Restaurant on 1st corner on left opposite Grosvenor Hotel

A long-established, refined Belgravia Italian restaurant with alfresco terrace dining in summer. Inside, large windows, slatted blinds, light marble floors, pastel walls, suede banquettes and tub-style chairs cut an elegant, modern edge. The carte offers a typically lengthy choice of authentic, seasonally inspired, regional Italian dishes with a strong Venetian accent and emphasis on simplicity, flavour and quality ingredients. Expect home-made pasta ribbons with tomato, olives, capers and basil, and classics like grilled calves' liver served with baby spinach and crisp pancetta. Attentive, professional service and good wines ooze Italian appeal too.

Santini

Chef Luca Lamari **Owner** Mr G Santin **Times** 12-3/6-11, Closed Xmas, 1 Jan, Etr Sun & Mon, Closed L Sat & Sun **Prices** Fixed D 3 course £25, Service added but optional 12.5% **Wines** all bottles over £20, 7 by glass **Notes** Vegetarian available, Dress restrictions, Smart casual, Air con **Seats** 65, Pr/dining room 30 **Children** Portions **Parking** Meters (no charge after 6.30pm)

Zafferano

LONDON SW1   Plan 4 F4

Italian ⚑

Chic and popular Knightsbridge Italian

☎ 020 7235 5800
15 Lowndes St SW1X 9EY
e-mail: info@zafferanorestaurant.com
web: www.zafferanorestaurant.com
dir: Nearest station: Knightsbridge Located off Sloane St, behind Carlton Tower Hotel

This stylish and deservedly popular Italian may look somewhat understated from the outside, but when judged by the difficulty in securing a table, it's clear that this is somewhere special. Drawing an adoring crowd, the suave, upmarket surroundings include a chic cocktail bar/lounge and private dining room, and there's a relaxed, friendly vibe and vibrant see-and-be-seen atmosphere throughout. Darkwood, glass, exposed brick and tiled floors deliver a sophisticated modern edge, punctuated by flower displays, crisp white linen and elegant chairs and banquettes, and all supported by friendly, professional service. Andrew Needham's drawcard cooking makes certain this Italian is packed for all the right reasons. Intelligently simple, authentic and accomplished dishes allow the freshest, top-notch seasonal ingredients to shine. Flawless execution, clear flavours and clean, colourful presentation feature on the appealing fixed-price menus (with a few supplements), while a well-constructed, patriotic Italian wine list and fabulous bread selection rounds things off in style. Expect to be seduced by the likes of pheasant ravioli with rosemary, perhaps roasted halibut served with a potato crust, caramelised endive, red onions and thyme, and maybe a warm pine nut and orange tart with Cointreau ice cream. (Zafferano Delicatessen is located adjacent to the restaurant and comes brimful of food sourced from Italy.)

Chef Andrew Needham **Owner** A-Z Restaurants **Times** 12-2.30/7-11, Closed 1 wk Xmas & New Year, Closed BHs **Prices** Fixed L 2 course £29.50, Fixed D 3 course £44.50, Service added 13.5%, Groups min 8 service 15% **Wines** 400 bottles over £20, 2 bottles under £20, 6 by glass **Notes** Seasonal truffle menu available, Sunday L, Vegetarian available, Dress restrictions, Smart casual, Air con **Seats** 85, Pr/dining room 20 **Children** Portions **Parking** NCP behind Restaurant

The Stafford Hotel

◉◉ British 🖥 Plan 5 A5

Luxurious hotel dining in an exclusive location

☎ 020 7493 0111
16-18 St James's Place SW1A 1NJ
e-mail: information@thestaffordhotel.co.uk
dir: Nearest station: Green Park 5 mins St James's Palace

Quietly tucked away in the heart of St James's, this genteel hotel has the feel of a luxurious country house. Public areas are comfortable with an understated opulence. The world-famous American bar, known for mixing a mean martini, displays an eccentric collection of club ties, sporting mementoes and signed celebrity photographs. A simpler menu is offered at lunchtime with a daily special from the trolley Sunday to Friday, generally a roast, and fish on Friday. Quality ingredients are to the fore on the extensive carte: starters might include a simple but satisfying steak tartare (prepared at the table), while mains range from cannon of lamb with beetroot Tatin to Chateaubriand, with wild strawberry cheesecake among the choice of desserts. There is an excellent wine list.

Times 12.30-2.30/6-10.30, Closed L Sat

Volt

◉◉ Italian 🖥 Plan 4 H4

Trendy Belgravia restaurant with Italian-inspired cuisine

☎ 020 7235 9696
17 Hobart Place SW1W 0HH
e-mail: info@voltlounge.com
dir: Nearest station: Victoria Behind Buckingham Palace, off Eaton Square and Grosvenor Gardens

An elegantly curved dining room radiates around the funky central bar of this cool Belgravia restaurant. Contemporary chairs, leather banquettes and smartly dressed tables shout style, while three equally chic, intimate dining areas, fringing the main room, can be booked for more intimate private dining. The cooking complements the surroundings, its modern Mediterranean approach oozing Italian influence, while excellent home-made breads and petits fours add further appeal. A mezze-style antipasti selection will appeal to those who wish to sample a little bit of everything on the menu. Dishes are clean-cut, clear-flavoured and elegantly presented and use top quality produce; think lobster pasta served with cherry tomatoes, garlic and basil, or perhaps lamb cutlets marinated in thyme and garlic served with wild mushrooms and potato purée.

Chef Giovanni Andolfi **Owner** Bou Antoun **Times** 12-3/6-11, Closed Xmas, last 2 wks Aug, BHs, Closed Sun, Closed L Sat **Prices** Fixed L 2 course fr £15, Fixed D 3 course fr £34, Starter £6-£16, Main £12-£20, Dessert £6.50-£8.50, Service optional, Groups service 12.5% **Wines** 90 bottles over £20, 7 bottles under £20, 8 by glass **Notes** Vegetarian available, Dress restrictions, Smart casual, Air con **Seats** 120, Pr/dining room 45 **Children** Portions

Zafferano

◉◉◉ – *see opposite*

Greens Restaurant and Oyster Bar

🖥

☎ 020 7930 4566
36 Duke St, St James's SW1Y 6DF
web: http://www.theaa.com/travel/index.jsp

Clubby atmosphere and an emphasis on fish, which is perfectly cooked. Classic nursery puddings round things off.

Prices Food prices not confirmed for 2009. Please telephone for details.

LONDON SW3

Awana

◉ Traditional Malaysian 🖥 V Plan 4 E2

Authentic Malaysian restaurant and satay bar

☎ 020 7584 8880
85 Sloane Av SW3 3DX
e-mail: info@awana.co.uk
dir: Nearest station: South Kensington Left out of South Kensington station onto Penam Rd. Continue past Fulham Rd and this will lead onto Sloane Av

Awana, which means 'in the clouds' in Malay, is the sister restaurant of The Mango Tree in Belgravia. The dining room is inspired by traditional Malaysian teak houses; think lush silk panels, delicate glass screens and burgundy leather seating to highlight the darkwood interior. Modern style is given to authentic Malaysian cuisine too, featuring satay, skewered dishes, starters, soups, curry, grills and stir-fries. Typical dishes include assorted seafood from the satay bar (where you can watch the chefs at work), and favourites such as beef rendang, chicken sati and nasi lemak.

Chef Mark Read **Owner** Eddie Lim **Times** 12-3/6-11, Closed 25-26 Dec, 1 Jan, Closed D 24 Dec **Prices** Fixed L 2 course fr £12.50, Tasting menu £36, Starter £5-£10.50, Main £7.50-£25, Dessert £5.50-£7.50, Service added 12.5% **Wines** All bottles over £20, 12 by glass **Notes** Sunday L, Vegetarian menu, Dress restrictions, Smart casual, Air con **Seats** 110 **Children** Portions **Parking** Car park

Bibendum

◉◉ European 🖥 V ♨ NOTABLE WINE LIST Plan 4 E3

Modern classics at a landmark West London restaurant

☎ 020 7581 5817
Michelin House, 81 Fulham Rd SW3 6RD
e-mail: reservations@bibendum.co.uk
web: www.bibendum.co.uk
dir: Nearest station: South Kensington Left out of South Kensington underground station on to Pelham Street and walk as far as the traffic lights, the Michelin Building is opposite.

The Art Deco Michelin building at the top of Fulham Road needs no introduction: the iconic Michelin man Bibendum strikes a variety of highly visible poses in blue stained glass around what has been called the most French-looking building in London. This landmark hosts a variety of eating options that includes a crustacean counter, an all-day coffee house and an oyster bar in addition to the stylish upstairs restaurant which has a light and airy feel. You can spot the celebrities while browsing the French menus with strong British influences, where classic sauces are matched to top notch ingredients: grilled onglet (a French cut of beef) with baby turnips and bordelaise sauce, and poached chicken breast with crêpe Parmentier and foie gras sauce, plus several fish choices.

Chef Matthew Harris **Owner** Sir Terence Conran, Simon Hopkinson, Michael Hamlyn **Times** 12-2.30/7-11.30, Closed 25 & 26 Dec, 1 Jan, Closed D 24 Dec **Prices** Fixed L 2 course fr £25, Starter £8.50-£24.50, Main £16.50-£26.50, Dessert £7-£9.50, Service added but optional 12.5% **Wines** 530 bottles over £20, 20 bottles under £20, 10 by glass **Notes** Sunday L, Vegetarian menu, Air con **Seats** 80 **Children** Portions **Parking** On street

The Capital

◉◉◉◉ – *see page 268*

The Capital

Modern French

Inspired cooking and impeccable service at Knightsbridge landmark

☎ 020 7589 5171
Basil St, Knightsbridge SW3 1AT
e-mail: reservations@capitalhotel.co.uk
web: www.capitalhotel.co.uk
dir: Nearest station: Knightsbridge Off Sloane St, beside Harrods

The Knightsbridge address - Harrods is just around the corner - and elegantly refined interior make this townhouse hotel one of the best in London. And then there is the restaurant, the domain of Eric Chavot, which elevates The Capital to world class status. It is a discreet and eminently tasteful place, the furnishings are chic without being overly contrived, and the restaurant is equally civilised and understated. It isn't a large dining room, but the high ceiling, big windows, light-wood panelling and pale blue velvet curtains and chairs help keep it light and inject just the right amount of luxury. There is a bar with an equally appealing demeanour. Service is flawless, attentive to just the right degree, and the wine list is an exceptional piece of work, as lengthy as any encyclopaedia, and, although France is the focus, it does not ignore the rest of the world. The cooking is inspired by Eric's homeland - he hails from south-western

France - and a strong classical French grounding is evident in the menu. This is not the whole story. First-class produce is skilfully and precisely transformed with a lightness of touch and a sensitivity to flavour into dishes with a modern soul and an eye for presentation. There is a Menu Dégustation or a fixed-price carte (particularly good value at lunch). A starter of pan-fried langoustine - perfectly fresh and beautifully cooked - and slow-cooked belly pork of outstanding flavour is topped with a potato espuma by the waiter in a piece of theatre, while main-course fillet of lamb with cumin juice and spicy couscous is both eye-catching and full of flavour. A light touch is evident at dessert stage too, with a coffee, chocolate and caramel 'melting pot' with Baileys ice cream, strong on technique but not overly rich in the eating.

Chef Eric Chavot **Owner** Mr D Levin **Times** 12-2.30/6.45-11 **Prices** Fixed L 2 course £29.50, Fixed D 3 course fr £58, Tasting menu £48-£58, Service added but optional 12.5% **Wines** All bottles over £20, 37 by glass **Notes** Sunday L, Vegetarian available, Dress restrictions, Smart casual, Air con **Seats** 35, Pr/ dining room 24 **Children** Min 12 yrs **Parking** 10

LONDON SW3 *Continued*

Le Colombier

◉ French 🖳   Plan 4 D2

Popular French brasserie in the middle of Chelsea

☎ 020 7351 1155
145 Dovehouse St SW3 6LB
e-mail: lecolombier1998@aol.com
dir: Nearest station: South Kensington Please telephone for directions

Le Colombier is a traditional-style French brasserie just off the Fulham Road in the lee of the Royal Marsden Hospital. Brimful with Gallic charm and atmosphere, it has a distinctive blue and cream colour scheme, polished floorboards and white linen, while a glass-covered terrace up front offers all-year-round alfresco dining. Straightforward French brasserie fare is prepared with a light touch from quality ingredients. Try poached eggs in red wine sauce with bacon and baby onions, followed by pan-fried veal kidneys with Dijonnaise cream sauce and crêpes Suzette or tarte bourdalou to finish.

Chef Philippe Tamet **Owner** Didier Garnier
Times 12-3/6.30-10.30 **Prices** Fixed L 2 course £17.50-£19, Starter £5.80-£12.50, Main £13.50-£25.80, Dessert £5.90-£6.50, Service added but optional 12.5% **Wines** 150 bottles over £20, 12 bottles under £20, 10 by glass **Notes** Sunday L, Vegetarian available, Dress restrictions, Smart casual **Seats** 70, Pr/dining room 30 **Children** Min 10 yrs **Parking** Metered parking

Eight Over Eight

◉ Pan-Asian 🖳   Plan 1 E3

Pan-Asian cooking with real attitude

☎ 020 7349 9934
392 King's Rd SW3 5UZ
e-mail: richard@rickerrestaurants.com
dir: Nearest station: Sloane Sq Telephone for directions

The bright red Eight Over Eight logo (it means 'lucky forever' in China) stands out over the pale grey walls of this corner bar/restaurant, divided inside by Japanese-style mock ironwork. The contemporary brown-and-beige look is minimal and stylish, with beautiful low-hanging oriental lampshades. The menu takes in the standard Pan-Asian cooking styles, with sushi/sashimi, curries, dim sum, salads, tempura and roasts, but there are modern twists and good use of seasonal fish combined with exotic spices. Expect specials like crispy garlic duck with hoisin pâté, perhaps monkfish with shiso and ginger, or lamb cutlets with Korean spices.

Chef Grant Brunsden **Owner** Will Ricker **Times** 12-3/6-11, Closed 24-29 Dec, Closed L Sun **Prices** Fixed L 2 course fr £15, Fixed D 3 course fr £45, Starter £6-£11, Main £11.50-£21.50, Dessert £5.50-£6.50, Service added but optional 12.5% **Wines** 80 bottles over £20, 5 bottles under £20, 13 by glass **Notes** Vegetarian available, Air con **Seats** 95, Pr/dining room 14

Foxtrot Oscar

◉ Modern British   Plan 4 F1

Gordon Ramsay's revamped neighbourhood bistro

☎ 020 7349 9595
79 Royal Hospital Rd SW3 4HN
e-mail: foxtrotoscar@gordonramsay.com
dir: Nearest station: Sloane Square Please telephone for directions

Fine dining, pubs, brasseries and now...the bistro. Gordon Ramsay has taken over this long-running Chelsea favourite and kept hold of the principles of providing good, simple food in an unpretentious environment. The muted natural tones, well-designed wood tables and slate floor give it a bit more style and edge than many a traditional bistro, while the menu is an appealing mix of classic and modern. Crab cakes come with a good home-made mayonnaise, there is Dublin Bay prawn cocktail, and pâté made with wild boar and chestnut. Main courses deliver stunning lemon sole with shrimp butter, pies such as braised beef in red wine, and blanquette of lamb with well judged spicing.

Chef Mark Sargeant **Owner** Gordon Ramsay
Times 12-2.30/6-10.30 **Prices** Food prices not confirmed for 2009. Please telephone for details. **Notes** Vegetarian available **Seats** 46, Pr/dining room 20 **Children** Portions **Parking** On street

Frankie's Italian Bar & Grill

◉ Italian 🖳   Plan 4 E3

Glitzy basement restaurant serving simple Italian food

☎ 020 7590 9999
3 Yeoman's Row, Brompton Rd SW3 2AL
e-mail: infofrankies@btconnect.com
dir: Nearest station: South Kensington/Knightsbridge Near The Oratory on Brompton Rd, close to Harrods

Frankie's Italian restaurant is the result of a collaboration between chef Marco Pierre White and jockey Frankie Dettori. Tucked away in a quiet Knightsbridge side street, the entrance at ground level doesn't prepare you for the shimmering basement interior - the glitzy décor oozes Marco class, from mirror-lined walls and huge revolving disco balls to good-sized tables, leather seating and attentive, informed staff. A chequered mosaic-style floor and small bar complete a sparkling line up, served up to a 1950s backing track and buzzy atmosphere. No fuss, simple Italian food, accurately cooked from fresh ingredients on a straightforward menu of one-price salads, antipasti, pasta, burgers, fish and meat, including Frankie's steak tartare americano - hits the appropriate note.

Times 12-3/6-11, Closed 26 Dec, Closed D 25 Dec

Manicomio

◉ Italian   Plan 4 F2

Buzzy, modern, informal Italian in stylish surroundings

☎ 020 7730 3366
85 Duke of York Square, Chelsea SW3 4LY
e-mail: manicomio@btconnect.com
dir: Nearest station: Sloane Square Duke of York Sq 100mtrs along King's Rd from Sloane Sq

A prime drawcard for this bustling Italian - with adjoining deli/café - is its large, outdoor terrace, smartly decked out with contemporary glass roof and screens, potted plants and trees. It's an inviting spot to sample the authentic fair while taking in a spot of people-watching. Inside it's rustic chic, with a bar and exposed brickwork finding their place alongside oak tables, darkwood floors, red leather seating and abstract artwork. Simple, seasonal, regional Italian cuisine is the attraction on the plate, with many ingredients sourced direct from Italy. Take tagliatelli served with hare and cotechino ragù, or perhaps roasted tarragon-stuffed pheasant wrapped in Parma ham with al forno potatoes and spinach.

Chef Tom Salt **Owner** Ninai & Andrew Zarach
Times noon-3/6.30-10.30, Closed Xmas & New Year **Prices** Starter £8.50-£10.50, Main £9.50-£24, Dessert £6.50-£9, Service added but optional 12.5% **Wines** 64 bottles over £20, 9 bottles under £20, 20 by glass **Notes** Sunday L, Vegetarian available, Air con **Seats** 70, Pr/dining room 30 **Children** Portions **Parking** on street

Nozomi

◉◉ Japanese   Plan 4 E4

Luxury Japanese cuisine in chic Knightsbridge

☎ 020 7838 1500 & 7838 0181
14 - 15 Beauchamp Place, Knightsbridge SW3 1NQ
e-mail: info@nozomi.co.uk
web: www.nozomi.co.uk
dir: Nearest station: Knightsbridge Telephone fo directions

The front bar of this popular Japanese restaurant heaves with after work drinkers once the doors open at 6.30. The chic surroundings of silver leather seating and black granite bar make this a favourite haunt for upmarket locals, though the real pull is the two dining rooms which exude a Zen-like calm. Muted colour schemes, dimmed lighting and softly-spoken waiters combine to create a

Continued

LONDON SW3 *Continued*

soothing space in which to enjoy the traditional Japanese cooking. The menu is long but clearly defined, with its lists of yakitori, tempura, seafood, poultry and meat. There are some distinct stars: seared wagyu beef salad with lotus root and ginger dressing, or crab salad with white asparagus and black truffle.

Times 12-3/6.30-11.30

Racine

◉ French ▣ ♨   Plan 4 E3

Authentic neighbourhood French bistro serving classic fare

☎ 020 7584 4477
239 Brompton Rd SW3 2EP
dir: Nearest station: Knightsbridge, South Kensington Restaurant opposite Brompton Oratory

A genuinely local French restaurant, popular with Knightsbridge shoppers and foodies alike, Racine stands across the road from the Brompton Oratory. It is a clean cut bistro with a curtained entrance, brown leather banquettes, wooden floors and mirrored walls, where waiters in formal attire provide discreet and knowledgeable service. The menu takes in rustic fare, including some quite substantial dishes, and classic favourites such as soupe de poisson with rouille, gruyère and croûtons; fillet steak au poivre; and clafoutis aux

griottines with crème anglaise, with an option of flaming with Kirsch.

Chef Henrick Zetnick **Owner** Eric Garnier
Times 12-3/6-10.30, Closed 25 Dec **Prices** Fixed L 2 course fr £17.50, Fixed D 3 course fr £19.50, Starter £5.90-£12, Main £14-£22, Dessert £5.90-£6.50, Service added but optional 14.5% **Wines** 55 bottles over £20, 13 bottles under £20, 16 by glass **Notes** Fixed D up to 7.30 only, Sunday L, Vegetarian available, Air con **Seats** 75, Pr/dining room 16 **Children** Portions

Rasoi Restaurant

◉◉◉ – *see below*

Restaurant Gordon Ramsay

◉◉◉◉◉ – *see opposite*

Tom Aikens

◉◉◉◉◉ – *see page 272*

Tom's Kitchen

◉◉ British, French ▣   Plan 4 E2

Posh comfort food served in a trendy Chelsea diner

☎ 020 7349 0202
27 Cale St SW3 3QP
e-mail: info@tomskitchen.co.uk
dir: Nearest station: South Kensington Cale St (Parallel to Kings Rd), midway between Chelsea Green and St Lukes Church

This trendy see-and-be-seen brasserie-style diner near the King's Road is the latest addition to the Tom Aikens empire, located in a quiet area of Chelsea. Housed in a period-style building with large windows, the brasserie has an informal, upbeat vibe, with light wooden tables and coloured and black-and-white canvasses on whitewashed walls adding to the atmosphere. You can relax with a cocktail in the first-floor bar and games room, and there's also a private dining room with its own lounge. The cooking style is based on English and French brasserie dishes, delivered in style from an accomplished team. You might start with butternut squash, sage and honey soup, or maybe wild mushroom risotto with sage and pine kernels, and follow with baked fillet of sea bass with red pepper relish, wilted spinach and olive oil mash. Open every day for dinner, and for breakfast and lunch from 7am Monday to Friday, there's also a brunch menu at weekends.

Times 12-3/6-12, Closed 24-27 Dec, Closed L 28 Dec

Rasoi Restaurant

LONDON SW3   Plan 4 F2

Modern Indian V

Elegant and intimate townhouse Indian restaurant - simply one of the best

☎ 020 7225 1881
10 Lincoln St SW3 2TS
e-mail: info@rasoirestaurant.co.uk
dir: Nearest station: Sloane Square Near Peter Jones and Duke of York Sq

Discreetly hidden away down a side street off the King's Road close to Sloane Square, this elegant Chelsea townhouse (where you have to ring the doorbell to gain entry) is home to the much-lauded Vineet Bhatia's Rasoi (kitchen). Bhatia's modern, progressive attitude to Indian cuisine is echoed in the restrained décor, though it is rich in vibrant Eastern styling to set the scene for a truly

intimate, but relaxed and sophisticated experience. Sandy beige and chocolate brown tones, silk cushions, woodcarvings and a bewitching array of tribal masks create an exotic atmosphere, alongside specially sourced contemporary cutlery and crockery, crisp white linen and highly knowledgeable front-of-house service. There's a snug front room overlooking the street, while the back room comes bathed in daylight from a conservatory-style skylight. Vineet Bhatia's contemporary, thoroughly evolved cuisine redefines the concept of Indian food and dining, and makes a visit here a real experience. There's an elegance to the kitchen's technical skill, with fine clarity and balance to vibrant flavours and textures, while presentation is refined, cultured and eye-catching. Luxury ingredients parade on an enticing range of menu options that include stunning gourmand tasting offerings. The carte is equally tantalising, perhaps delivering tandoori black-spice chicken breast served with tomato and cashew nut chutney, chilli khichdi, creamy yellow lentils, mooli and carrot relish and pure gold leaves, while

desserts are anything but ordinary, take crispy marble chocolate-almond samosa with Madras coffee-walnut mousse and Baileys ice cream. Ancillaries and an upmarket wine list are impressive too. This is a 'must visit' for lovers of modern Indian cuisine!

Chef Vineet Bhatia **Owner** Vineet & Rashima Bhatia
Times 12-2.30/6.30-10.30, Closed Xmas, New Year, BHs, Closed Sun, Closed L Sat **Prices** Fixed L 2 course fr £21, Tasting menu £75, Starter £12-£19, Main £15-£42, Dessert £9-£12, Service added but optional 12.5% **Wines** 250 bottles over £20, 4 bottles under £20, 10 by glass **Notes** Tasting menu 7 courses, Vegetarian menu, Dress restrictions, Smart casual, Air con **Seats** 35, Pr/dining room 20 **Parking** On street

Restaurant Gordon Ramsay

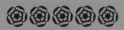

LONDON SW3 Plan 4 F1

French 🖥 V 🔖NOTABLE WINE LIST

London's finest and Britain's most celebrated chef

☎ 020 7352 4441

68 Royal Hospital Rd SW3 4HP

dir: Nearest station: Sloane Square At junct of Royal Hospital Road & Swan Walk

While his face is rarely off our TV screens and the Ramsay restaurant empire continues its expansion both globally and on home soil, this Chelsea temple of gastronomy - opened back in 1998 - still remains the treasured mothership of his London operations. A slick black and white frontage discreetly marks out the restaurant's entrance, while the intimate dining room - remodelled by design guru David Collins - is wonderfully stylish and sophisticated, the clean lines cleverly allowing the food to take centre stage. The cream interior also delivers the contemporarily elegant platform for unparalleled front-of-house service - this is as good as it gets. Slick, professional and polished, charmingly orchestrated by maître d' Jean-Claude Breton, whose unique, magical management style makes you feel like you're the only diners in the room. Enthusiastic explanations of dishes increase anticipation, while there's plenty of help navigating the fabulous wine list, too. Classical dishes with contemporary spin grace the kitchen's tantalising fixed-price repertoire of lunch, carte and seven-course Menu Prestige, which come studded with luxury. Simplicity, integrity and lightness of touch are hallmarks of the approach, coupled with innovation, flair, stunning ingredients, precision and depth of flavour. The superlatives may roll on, but the skills on display are exceptional, with consistency and execution nigh faultless. So expect to be wowed by the likes of pan-fried fillets of John Dory served with Cromer crab, caviar, crushed new potatoes and a basil vinaigrette, or perhaps roasted Barbary duck breast with creamed Savoy cabbage, quince, chestnuts and Madeira, while marinated pineapple ravioli with mango and raspberries might catch the eye at dessert. Royal Hospital Road remains as popular as ever, with bookings now taken two months in advance (previously just one month), so be ready to hang on the end of the telephone to secure that table. You certainly won't be disappointed, this is one of life's musts!

Chef Gordon Ramsay, Mark Askew **Owner** Gordon Ramsay Holdings Ltd **Times** 12-2.30/6.30-11, Closed 1 wk Xmas, Closed Sat & Sun **Wines** 100+ bottles over £20, 2 bottles under £20, 18 by glass **Notes** ALC 3 courses, Menu prestige £110, Vegetarian menu, Dress restrictions, Smart dress, no jeans or trainers, Air con **Seats** 70 **Children** Portions

Tom Aikens

Modern French V NOTABLE WINE LIST

Gastronomic big-hitter of supreme class and distinction

☎ 020 7584 2003
43 Elystan St SW3 3NT
e-mail: info@tomaikens.co.uk
dir: Nearest station: South Kensington
Off Fulham Rd (Brompton Rd end)

Tucked away in a quiet residential street, this eponymous, much-heralded Chelsea temple to the serious foodie just gets better, and has deservedly put Tom Aikens up there among the pinnacle of top London kitchens. It's an understated, discreet setting for a premier leaguer, a one-time pub transformed by Anouska Hempel's design into a dining room dedicated to the theatre of fine dining. Dark wooden floors and window shutters, black leather chairs and white walls dotted with modern artwork set the interior's minimalist, self-confident lines. Bamboo screens, table lamps set high into window frames and sumptuous flower displays further distinguish the room, alongside the crockery, cutlery and slate serving plates and well-directed, professional and knowledgeable service. The presentation of Aikens' fixed-priced menu repertoire (lunch, dinner and tasting option) follows the theme of the clean-lined surroundings, with dishes eye-catchingly laid out under their main ingredient; take 'foie gras', which translates as poached and seared foie gras served with jabugo ham, haricot beans and Sauternes sauce. But it's the successful marriage of classical roots, modern interpretation, first-class ingredients and flamboyant presentation that makes Aikens' food sexy and stand out from the crowd. Attention to detail dominates every aspect with its sheer quality, with ancillaries like breads, amuse-bouche, pre-dessert and breathtaking petits fours (of afternoon-tea proportions) hitting top form. Technical skill and intricate design and presentation pepper inventive, generous-portioned, vibrant dishes, their innovative combinations showering the senses with visual and flavour sensations. Expect starters like roasted scallops with braised oxtail, black pudding, parsnip purée, oxtail chicken boudin and red wine sauce, and perhaps roast salt marsh lamb served with sheep's cheese tart, quince purée and braised shallot to follow, while the suitably extensive, French-themed wine list certainly befits the cuisine. This is zenith-class cooking from one of the country's greatest culinary talents - so do make this Chelsea pilgrimage.

Chef Tom Aikens **Owner** Tom Aikens
Times 12-2.30/6.45-11, Closed 2 wks Xmas & N Year, Etr, BHs & last 2 wks Aug, Closed Sat & Sun **Prices** , Fixed L course £29, Fixed D 3 course £65, Tasting menu £80-£100, Service added but optional 12.5% **Wines** 590 bottles over £20, 10 bottles under £20, 12 by glass **Notes** Tasting menu 6 courses. Tom Aikens classic menu 7 courses, Vegetarian menu, Dress restrictions, Smart dress, no trainers/sportswear/T-shirts, Air con **Seats** 60, Pr/dining room 10 **Children** Min 7 yrs, Portions **Parking** Parking meters outside

LONDON SW3 *Continued*

Tom's Place

◉ Seafood   Plan 4 E2

Sustainable fish and chips in the heart of Chelsea

☎ 020 7351 1806
1A Cale St, Chelsea SW3 3QT

A stone's throw from Sloane Square, this small, unassuming property looks like an upmarket fish-and-chip shop from the outside. Inside, the theme is retro and cool with a relaxed, fun atmosphere - the realisation of Tom Aikens' greatest food passions in the form of an eco-friendly restaurant that promotes and teaches about sustainability while at the same time featuring sustainable fish resources on the menu. High quality ingredients are sourced with sustainability in mind, with fish mostly line-caught from approved sources. Traditional fish and chips are offered alongside more contemporary takes on classic fish dishes, both to eat in and take away. Start with a classic dish of moules marinière, and follow with a perfectly timed grilled megrim sole served with lemon and caper butter sauce.

Times 11am-11pm **Prices** Food prices not confirmed for 2009. Please telephone for details.

Toto's

◉ Traditional Italian   Plan 4 F3

Popular, friendly Italian restaurant

☎ 0871 332 7293 & 020 7589 0075
Walton House, Walton St SW3 2JH
dir: Nearest station: Knightsbridge

Tucked away at the back of Knightsbridge, this lovely white-painted corner property has a patio/courtyard area where you can lunch alfresco. Inside a mezzanine overlooks the main dining room, taking in the sunny yellow walls, clothed tables, huge wooden fireplace and fronds of greenery, while a Venetian chandelier makes a striking centrepiece. The friendly service and great Italian cooking make this a very popular destination, packed with locals and those lucky enough to get a table by chance. The extensive menu offers modern Italian cuisine with classical undertones. Expect home-made black spaghetti with baby squid and clams, or veal cutlet Milanese style with marinated tomatoes and rocket.

Times 12.15-3/7-11.30, Closed 25-27 Dec

Brasserie St Quentin

💻

☎ 020 7589 8005
243 Brompton Rd SW3 2EP
web: http://www.theaa.com/travel/index.jsp

Good value French inspired dishes (and wines) in stylish brasserie dining room.

Prices Food prices not confirmed for 2009. Please telephone for details.

The Collection

💻

☎ 020 7225 1212
264 Brompton Rd SW3 2AS
web: http://www.theaa.com/travel/index.jsp

Buzzy, vibrant and fashion conscious bar-restaurant.

Prices Food prices not confirmed for 2009. Please telephone for details.

Haandi

☎ 020 7823 7373
136 Brompton Rd SW3 1HY

Northern Frontier Indian cuisine often served in haandis (narrow necked cooking pots). The chefs can be seen hard at work.

Prices Food prices not confirmed for 2009. Please telephone for details.

Shikara

💻

☎ 020 7581 6555
87 Sloane Av SW3 3DX
web: http://www.theaa.com/travel/index.jsp

Wholesome Indian fare with the tandoor put to good use.

Prices Food prices not confirmed for 2009. Please telephone for details.

LONDON SW4

Trinity Restaurant

◉◉◉ – **see page 274**

Tsunami

◉ Japanese   Plan 1 E3

Vibrant, informal, contemporary neighbourhood Japanese

☎ 020 7978 1610
5-7 Voltaire Rd SW4 6DQ
dir: Nearest station: Clapham North Off Clapham High Street

This buzzy, stylish, new-wave Japanese is a honey pot for a cool crowd - and wouldn't look out of place in the West End rather than its side-street location by Clapham High Street station. Inside the fashionable minimalist décor comes with contemporary good looks; think leather seating, darkwood tables, mirrors, modern artwork and a big funky lampshade. Throw in an open-to-view kitchen and stone floor, and you have a relaxed, vibrant, high-decibel platform for modern Japanese fusion cooking. Tempura, sashimi, sushi and weekly specials all find a place on the lengthy menu driven by tip-top ingredients, skill and imaginative presentation, with dishes designed for sharing. Take Scottish beef fillet with teriyaki sauce or steamed sea bass served with sake and soy.

Times 12.30-4/6-11, Closed 25 Dec-4 Jan, Closed L Mon-Fri

LONDON SW5

Cambio De Tercio

◉ Spanish   Plan 4 C2

Modern Spanish cuisine, bold décor and buzzy atmosphere

☎ 020 7244 8970
163 Old Brompton Rd SW5 0LJ
dir: Nearest station: Gloucester Road Close to junction with Drayton Gardens

What appears to be a small inconsequential restaurant in a parade of shops on the fringes of South Kensington, is in fact, a real find. Its flamboyant interior is as vibrant and lively as its friendly neighbourhood atmosphere. There's a black slate floor, bold paintwork (deep red, terracotta, pink and yellow) and equally audacious, eye-catching artwork, while white-clothed tables come with black undercloths and banquettes or round-backed chairs in black leather. You can follow three-course convention or, with all dishes also offered tapas style, go the grazing route instead. Expect quality ingredients, clear flavours and attractive modern presentation; perhaps a supreme of hake Basque style with garlic, chilli and sherry vinegar vinaigrette, potato and sea asparagus.

Times 12-2.30/7-11.30, Closed 2 wks at Xmas, New Year

Strada

💻

☎ 020 7835 1180
237 Earls Court Rd SW5 9AH
web: http://www.theaa.com/travel/index.jsp

Superior pizza from quality ingredients cooked in wood-fired ovens.

Prices Food prices not confirmed for 2009. Please telephone for details.

LONDON SW6

Blue Elephant

◉ Traditional Thai 🖥   Plan 1 D3

Truly extravagant Fulham Thai

☎ 020 7385 6595
4-6 Fulham Rd SW6 1AA
e-mail: london@blueelephant.com
dir: Nearest station: Fulham Broadway Please telephone for directions

From bustling Fulham Broadway, this extravagant Thai restaurant instantly transports you to another world - the experience is almost like dining in a tropical rainforest. Think lush plants, trickling fountains, bridges spanning koi carp-filled ponds, and truly welcoming Thai staff. Candles twinkle, while the scent of tropical flowers mingles with the heady aroma of exotic herbs and spices flown in fresh to service an equally flamboyant, lengthy menu. 'Pearls of the Blue Elephant' is a selection of starters enabling you sample a number of classic dishes, including a wonderful filo-wrapped prawn with peanut stuffing. For mains, expect homok talay (a spicy fish stew), or perhaps chiang rai (a very spicy stir-fried pork with chillies, garlic and green peppercorns). Vegetarian dishes are plentiful.

Times 12-2.30/7-12, Closed Xmas, Closed L Sat

Deep

◉◉ Seafood   Plan 1 E3

Contemporary Thames-side surroundings for impressive seafood

☎ 020 7736 3337
The Boulevard, Imperial Wharf SW6 2UB
e-mail: info@deeplondon.co.uk
dir: Nearest station: Fulham Broadway From underground station take Harwood Rd then Imperial Rd

The name and stunning Thames-side location may hint at Deep's fish and seafood orientation, though it doesn't prepare you for its classy, ultra-minimalist good looks. Set in the upmarket waterside development of Imperial Wharf, Deep comes with floor-to-ceiling windows, crisp clean lines and two terraces; one for alfresco drinks, the other for fair-weather dining. Stainless steel, backlit panels, pastel shades and fashionable suede seating all catch the eye in both bar and dining area, as does the on-view kitchen. The cooking's impressive modern presentation suits the backdrop, with carefully-sourced produce skilfully delivered in interesting combinations with a nod to its Scandinavian owner's roots. Expect a seafood platter to open perhaps, while mains might feature steamed halibut served with egg, prawns and horseradish in warm butter. (Sushi and meat options are also part of the upbeat package.)

Chef Mr C Sandefeldt & Mr F Bolin **Owner** Christian & Kerstin Sandefeldt **Times** 12-3/7-11, Closed Mon, Closed

L Sat, Closed D Sun **Prices** Tasting menu £42, Starter £7-£12.50, Main £12-£24, Dessert £5-£5.50, Service added but optional 12.5% **Wines** 60 bottles over £20, 9 bottles under £20, 9 by glass **Notes** Tasting menu 7 courses, Vegetarian available, Dress restrictions, Smart casual, Air con **Seats** 120 **Parking** Public car park, street parking after 5.30pm

Marco

◉◉ Modern European 🖥   Plan 1 D3

Stylish modern brasserie at Chelsea FC

☎ 020 7915 2929
M&C Hotels At Chelsea FC, Stamford Bridge, Fulham Road SW6 1HS
e-mail: reservations.chelsea@mill-cop.com

Set in the Chelsea Football Club complex at Stamford Bridge, Marco - a collaboration between restaurateur Marco Pierre White and club owner Roman Abramovich - is as classy as the multi-million-pound football team. Located on the ground floor of the complex's Copthorne Hotel, it's unsurprisingly elegant and very Marco Pierre White, with subtle black hues, low lighting, plush curved leather banquettes and a striking golden pillar of Swarovski crystal. Throw in white linen-clad tables, terrazzo-style flooring, wooden Venetian blinds and a sleek long bar, and you've premier-league style and comfort. The equally classy and typically Pierre White brasserie repertoire - driven by quality ingredients,

Trinity Restaurant

LONDON SW4   Plan 1 E3

British, French 🖥

Stylish, relaxed local restaurant of pedigree and class

☎ 020 7622 1199
4 The Polygon, Clapham Old Town SW4 0JG
dir: Nearest station: Clapham Common Please telephone for directions

Situated in the heart of Clapham Old Town adjacent to leafy Clapham Common, Trinity opened its doors in November 2006 with chef-restaurateur Adam Byatt returning to his Clapham roots after a sojourn among the bright lights of WC2 (ex Thyme and Origin at Covent Garden's Hospital media complex, and originally of the much-acclaimed Thyme in Clapham Park Road). Set well back from the road, it's an exciting, buzzy, neighbourhood venture which catches the eye and the light with its

smart exterior and large window frontage. Inside there's a sophisticated, friendly atmosphere, the room decked out with white-clothed tables, elegant cream and chocolate-coloured walls, comfortable cane-backed chairs and soft lighting, all providing a contemporary backdrop to the polished, modern cooking. There are also distant glimpses of the kitchen, plus a large private-dining 'kitchen table' that offers a closer window on all the action. Service is relaxed and friendly, yet suitably professional and knowledgeable. Adam's appealing menus feature interesting and adventurous combinations alongside some simpler dishes (including a Joint of the Day) on a repertoire that includes his hallmark tasting options. High technique, clear flavours, creative presentation and tip-top produce add to the wow-factor. Kick off with lasagne of crisp sardines, basil pesto and red pepper pipinard with crab velouté, and follow with braised beef short rib and onion cottage pie with bone marrow and organic carrots.

Chef Adam Byatt **Owner** Angus Jones & Adam Byatt **Times** 12.30-2.30/6.30-10.30, Closed 24-26 Dec, Closed L Mon **Wines** 80 bottles over £20, 9 bottles under £20, 10 by glass **Notes** Fixed D 5 courses £25, Tasting menu available, Sunday L, Vegetarian available, Air con **Seats** 63, Pr/dining room 12 **Children** Portions **Parking** On street

flavour and skill - proves a winner too; take grilled halibut with porcini and young leeks or Aberdeen Angus rib-eye with sauce béarnaise.

Times 12-2.30/6-10.30, Closed Sun,Mon

Memories of India on the River

Indian 🖥 🕭 Plan 1 E3

Stylish modern Indian amid luxury riverside apartments

☎ 020 7736 0077
7 The Boulevard, Imperial Wharf, Townmead Rd, Chelsea SW6 2UB
dir: Nearest station: Fulham Broadway Close to Chelsea Harbour

The name offers a nod to its location, set in the plush Thames-side development of Imperial Wharf, but the sophisticated, contemporary interior owes nought to Indian restaurants of old. Think stylish tan leather banquettes or elegant chairs, white linen, modern wooden screens, interesting objects d'art and feature lighting. Add a centrepiece palm tree, polished-wood floors, and vibrant splashes of colour from artworks and paintwork, and you have an upmarket eatery befitting its luxury setting. The lengthy menu remains true to classic regional recipes but reflects a modern vogue that echoes the décor. Expect a Goan fish curry or perhaps lamb chops adraki (chargrilled with ginger and spinach).

Chef Rajdip Bhattacharya **Owner** Mr Belal Ali & Mr Abdul Jalil **Times** 12-3/5.30-11.30, Closed 25-Dec **Prices** Fixed L 2 course £10.95-£15.95, Fixed D 3 course £19.95-£25.95, Starter £7.95-£12.95, Main £10.95-£29.95, Dessert £4.50-£7.95, Service added but optional 12.5% **Wines** 25 bottles over £20, 20 bottles under £20, 6 by glass **Notes** Sun brunch inc. 5 course menu, Vegetarian available, Air con **Seats** 100, Pr/dining room 30 **Children** Portions, Menu **Parking** 50

Saran Rom

Thai 🖥 Plan 1 E3

Luxury riverside Thai restaurant specialising in authentic cuisine

☎ 020 7751 3111 & 7751 3110
Imperial Wharf, The Boulevard, Townmead Road SW6 2UB
e-mail: info@saranrom.com
dir: Nearest station: Fulham Broadway 1.5m from Stamford Bridge/Fulham Broadway tube station

This chic eatery brings a touch of eastern glamour to west London, its sumptuous décor paying homage to Thailand's royal palaces. No expense was spared in its creation and visitors dine amid a luxurious hotch-potch of silk hangings, 19th-century antiques and teak carvings. Add a ground floor bar, an outside terrace and riverside views, and it all adds up to a fantastic location to enjoy some traditional Thai hospitality. Main courses might include meaty fare such as panang beef or smoked duck curry, while vegetarians are well catered for too: a

separate menu features the likes of sweet-and-sour tofu, tom yam hed - the famous hot and spicy Thai soup - and som tom je - papaya salad with carrots and peanuts flavoured with lemon and chilli.

Times 12-3/5-midnight, Closed 25 Dec, 1-4 Jan

Yi-Ban Chelsea

Japanese, Chinese Plan 1 E3

Stylish modern oriental dining in Thames-side development

☎ 020 7731 6606
No 5 The Boulevard, Imperial Wharf, Imperial Road SW6 2UB
e-mail: michael@yi-ban.co.uk
dir: Nearest station: Fulham Broadway Please telephone for directions

This stylish, contemporary oriental outfit's design matches its location in the impressive new riverside development at Imperial Wharf. The dark, moody, minimalist-styled dining room is located beyond a trendy front bar and adjacent teppan-yaki counter, where darkwood, grey voile curtain dividers and dangling contemporary-style red lanterns create an upbeat but relaxed mood. Polished-wood tables, black-lacquered chairs with leather seating and matching wall banquettes create the comforts, while youthful staff clad in long aprons provide slick, attentive service. The modern, attractively presented oriental cuisine marries with the surroundings, encompassing Chinese food and teppan-yaki, the latter cooked at the counter where diners can watch the chef in action. Otherwise, expect sizzling black pepper beef fillet, black cod, or Szechuan prawns.

Times Closed 1 wk from 22 Dec, Closed Sun, Closed L all week

Strada

🖥

☎ 020 7731 6404
175 New Kings Rd, Parsons Green SW6 4SW
web: http://www.theaa.com/travel/index.jsp

Superior pizza from quality ingredients cooked in wood-fired oven.

Prices Food prices not confirmed for 2009. Please telephone for details.

The Bentley Hotel

French, European Plan 4 C2

Fine-dining experience in ornate restaurant

☎ 020 7244 5555
27-33 Harrington Gardens SW7 4JX
e-mail: info@thebentley-hotel.com
dir: Nearest station: Gloucester Road Off A4 Cromwell Rd, opposite Gloucester Hotel

This luxurious townhouse hotel is discreetly set in the heart of residential Kensington. Originally four grand private residences, it has been magnificently and sympathetically restored behind the original façades and positively oozes lavish opulence, the yellows and golds and wall-to-wall marble adding an almost Louis XV edge to proceedings. On the hotel's lower-ground floor, and accessed by the sweeping circular staircase, is the Malachite Bar, replete with jade-green marble counter and leopard-skin furnishings. The fine-dining restaurant is called 1880 (the date of the building) - a palatial affair offering a real sense of occasion. Think elaborate ceilings, crystal chandeliers, silk wall panels and richly-coloured furnishings. The sophisticated and contemporary cooking is notable for its grazing-concept menus, all miniature versions of dishes on the carte. Expect ballotine of foie gras with pear and saffron, or Angus beef fillet with cavolo nero and bordelaise sauce.

Times 12-2.30/6-10, Closed Easter & Xmas, Closed BHs, Sun-Mon

Brunello

Italian 🖥 Plan 4 C4

An opulent setting for classy Italian cuisine

☎ 020 7368 5900 & 7368 5700
Baglioni Hotel, 60 Hyde Park Gate, Kensington Road SW7 5BB
e-mail: brunellolondon@baglionihotels.com
dir: Nearest station: Kensington High Street Hotel entrance on Hyde Park Gate facing park & Kensington Palace.

The Baglioni, a sophisticated Italian-owned hotel overlooking Hyde Park and Kensington Gardens, is home to the fashionable and achingly chic Brunello Restaurant. The restaurant oozes luxury and style, its huge mirrors, black silk curtains and ornate black Murano glass chandeliers - together with burnished gold velvet seating

Continued

LONDON SW7 *Continued*

and large gilded napkin rings - creating an opulent, almost regal, setting. The restaurant's carte is divided into antipasti, soups, pasta and risotto, with interpretations of classic regional Italian dishes, and the fish and meat dishes include seafood and meat from the grill. Seasonal favourites include starters like scallop gratin, mixed fried prawns and squid, while for main course choose from roast turbot with spinach, pine nuts and bacon, or pan-fried duck with glazed apricots and puntarelle.

Chef Andrea Vercelli **Owner** Baglioni Hotels **Times** 12-3/5.30-11 **Prices** Fixed L 2 course £20-£22, Starter £8-£13.50, Main £16-£24, Dessert £6.50-£8.50, Service added but optional 12.5% **Wines** 250 bottles over £20, 5 bottles under £20, 12 by glass **Notes** Vegetarian available, Civ Wed, Air con **Seats** 70, Pr/dining room 60 **Children** Portions **Parking** NCP (Young St)

L'Etranger

◉ French, Japanese 🖳 🖹NOTABLE WINE LIST   Plan 4 C4

Chic and sophisticated setting for classy fusion cuisine

☎ 020 7584 1118
36 Gloucester Rd SW7 4QT
e-mail: axelle@circagroupltd.co.uk
dir: Nearest station: Gloucester Rd 5 mins walk from Gloucester Rd tube station at junct of Queens Gate Terrace and Gloucester Rd

Chic, sophisticated and elegant L'Etranger is part of a complex including an adjacent wine shop and basement cocktail bar. The richly decorated restaurant with a floor mosaic and design by Andy Martin, features fresh orchid displays, leather chairs and white linen. The food is French with Japanese influences and the French head chef's passion for fresh Eastern ingredients results in dishes such as tuna spring rolls with coriander and mint leaves and tamarind dipping sauce, miso-roasted duck breast with coriander butter asparagus, and ginger cheesecake with toffee sauce. Service is professional, attentive and gallic.

Chef Jerome Tauvron **Owner** Ibi Issolah **Times** 12-3/6-11, Closed 25 Dec, 1 Jan, Closed L Sat **Prices** Fixed L 2 course £16.50, Fixed D 3 course fr £19.50, Starter £7.50-£15.50, Main £18-£49, Dessert £7.50-£9, Service added but optional 12.5% **Wines** 750 bottles over £20, 9 bottles under £20, 14 by glass **Notes** Sunday L, Vegetarian available, Dress restrictions, Smart casual, no T-shirts, Air con **Seats** 75, Pr/dining room 20 **Children** Portions **Parking** NCP

Swag and Tails

◉ Modern International   Plan 4 E4

Upmarket Knightsbridge village gastro-pub

☎ 020 7584 6926
10-11 Fairholt St SW7 1EG
e-mail: theswag@swagandtails.com
dir: Nearest station: Knightsbridge From Harrods off Brompton Rd turn onto Montpelier St. 1st left onto Cheval Place, 2nd right onto Montpelier Walk, 1st left

Discreetly hidden away just across the road from Harrods, this convivial, well-heeled, flower-festooned Knightsbridge mews pub is predictably well groomed. There's stripped floorboards, winter fire, swagged-and-tailed curtains and newspapers to peruse in the bustling bar, while the small, quieter restaurant behind parades a lighter, more contemporary edge. Here, cream walls come adorned with attractive prints, while service is attentive and friendly. The same crowd-pleasing, bistro-style menu is served throughout; expect smoked haddock terrine to start, followed by roast pork fillet with sun-dried tomato mash, buttered spinach and balsamic jus, or skate wing with caper mash and shrimp beurre noisette.

Chef Alan Jenkins **Owner** Annemaria & Stuart Boomer-Davies **Times** 12-3/6-10, Closed Xmas, New Year, BHs, Closed Sat-Sun **Prices** Starter £8.25-£10.95, Main £11.25-£15.50, Dessert £5.50-£6.50, Service added but optional 10% **Wines** 17 bottles over £20, 16 bottles under £20, 11 by glass **Notes** Vegetarian available **Seats** 34 **Parking** On street

---

Zuma

◉◉ Modern Japanese 🖳   Plan 4 F4

Stylish, cutting-edge Japanese cuisine

☎ 020 7584 1010
5 Raphael St SW7 1DL
e-mail: info@zumarestaurant.com
dir: Nearest station: Knightsbridge Telephone for directions

The impossibly glamorous Zuma is a temple to good design with stone, wood, glass, lighting and carefully placed plants combining to create a space of cutting-edge modernity. Only a stone's throw from Harrods and Harvey Nichols in the heart of Knightsbridge, it is an ideal setting for innovative and sophisticated Japanese cuisine. Ultra fresh produce is at the heart of the repertoire of vibrant, beautifully-presented dishes served from the main kitchen, the sushi bar or the robata grill. This parade of dishes is ideal for sharing. Nigiri sushi sees scintillatingly fresh salmon and tuna, the rice just-so, and there are maki rolls and excellent sashimi. From the robata grill there is suzuki no shioyaki (salted sea bass with burnt tomato and ginger relish), or yakitori-negima yaki (chicken skewers with baby leek).

Times 12-2.30/6-10, Closed 25-26 Dec, 1 Jan, Closed D 24 Dec

The Delhi Brasserie

☎ 020 7370 7617
134 Cromwell Rd SW7 4HA

Elegant, authentic Indian restaurant. The menu includes slightly more unusual dishes as well as old favourites.

Prices Food prices not confirmed for 2009. Please telephone for details.

LONDON SW8

Tom Ilic

◉◉ Modern European   Plan 1 E3

Battersea newcomer delivering good value French-focused food

☎ 020 7622 0555
123 Queenstown Rd SW8 3RH

The eponymous Mr Ilic is a chef who has previously proved himself in the tough London restaurant scene and now he has his name above the door of this shop-front eatery. And he has created a restaurant delivering a lively atmosphere, fair value, and good French-focused food. Warm colours of terracotta and soft pink with red wood moulded seats set the tone for this informal place, where music plays and the staff smile. The two- or three-course lunch is great value and even the evening carte is fairly priced. The food is not over-worked or contrived, but neither is it dull. Honey-glazed pork belly with black pudding and apple and parsnip purée is a starter showing great balance and depth of flavour, while main-course roast rump of lamb with spinach and gratin potatoes is a lesson in simplicity. Finish with pear tarte Tatin with cinnamon ice cream.

Times 12-2.30/6-10.30, Closed L Mon-Tue & Sat
Prices Food prices not confirmed for 2009. Please telephone for details.

LONDON SW10

Aubergine

◉◉◉◉ – **see page 278**

Chutney Mary Restaurant

◉◉ Indian ▭   Plan 1 E3

Seductive, modern Indian offering refined cuisine

☎ 020 7351 3113
535 King's Rd, Chelsea SW10 0SZ
e-mail: chutneymary@realindianfood.com
dir: Nearest station: Fulham Broadway On corner of King's Rd and Lots Rd; 2 mins from Chelsea Harbour

This highly acclaimed, stylish Chelsea restaurant has been luring lovers of Indian cooking for almost 20 years now and has a well-deserved reputation for a refined and creative approach (part of the Masala World group with sister restaurants Veeraswamy and Amaya). A ground-level reception leads down to the classy, split-level

basement where antique etchings are teamed with mirrors and moody lighting - including bags of candles - to create a romantic but contemporary setting. There's also a conservatory ringed by leafy plants too. The kitchen's refined regional cuisine remains true to classical recipes while reflecting modern-day trends. Clean-cut, balanced dishes use prime ingredients and come attractively presented; take Goa green curry or Tawa masala lamb chops, while the tasting menu comes with the option of specially paired wines.

Chef Siddharth Krishna **Owner** R Mathrani, N Panjabi **Times** 12.30-3/6.30-11.30, Closed L Mon-Fri, Closed D 25 Dec **Prices** Fixed L course £22, Service added but optional 12.5% **Wines** 100 bottles over £20, 4 bottles under £20, 30 by glass **Notes** Sunday L, Vegetarian available, Civ Wed 100, Air con **Seats** 110, Pr/dining room 24 **Parking** Parking meters outside

Osteria dell'Arancio

◉ Modern Italian ▭   Plan 1 E3

Great Italian regional food and wine in a lively Chelsea setting

☎ 020 7349 8111
383 King's Rd SW10 0LP
e-mail: info@osteriadellarancio.co.uk
dir: Nearest station: Sloane Square Situated next to Moravian Church in Chelsea's World's End

A green-and-white striped awning and a few fair-weather pavement tables distinguish this authentic, vibrant little Italian osteria, right on the corner of Milman's Street. Its individual style, colourful, eye-catching paintings by well-known artist Vittoria Facchini, and an eclectic collection of tables all help to capture the Mediterranean mood, and service is equally warm and relaxed. The rustic home cooking of the Marche region is driven by quality ingredients and simplicity. Look out for linguine with clams, langoustine and squid, Irish Angus beef tagliata with rocket, crispy parmesan and balsamic reduction, or traditional aubergine Parmigiana.

Chef Giuseppe De Gregorio **Owner** Rachel & Harry Hampson **Times** 12-3/6.30-11, Closed 25 Dec-1 Jan, Closed L Mon **Prices** Fixed L 2 course £20, Starter £8-£13, Main £14-£20, Dessert £6-£8, Service added but optional 12.5% **Wines** 16 by glass **Notes** Vegetarian available, Air con **Seats** 75, Pr/dining room 30 **Children** Portions **Parking** On street

The Painted Heron

◉◉ Modern Indian ▭   Plan 1 E3

Stylish, upmarket and impressive modern Indian venue and cuisine

☎ 020 7351 5232
112 Cheyne Walk SW10 0DJ
e-mail: thepaintedheron@btinternet.com
dir: Nearest station: South Kensington Telephone for directions

A blue awning and glass frontage picks out this modern Chelsea Indian close to Battersea Bridge. Minimalist

décor with black lacquered leather-upholstered chairs, dark slatted blinds and plain white walls adorned with striking modern art deliver a stylish, contemporary edge to this deceptively roomy, split-level restaurant. There's just a hint of the nautical reflecting its Thames-side location, with blond-wood floors and black metal handrails lining steps, together with a small bar, and an alfresco courtyard at the back. High-quality modern Indian cooking, with traditional dishes given contemporary spin and presentation, focuses on fresh ingredients and intelligently subtle spicing. Take black tiger prawns and queen scallops in a hot and sour Goan curry, and perhaps a honey and cinnamon pudding with cardamom ice cream to finish.

Times 12-3/6.30-11, Closed Xmas & Etr, Closed L Sat

Vama

◉◉ Indian ▭   Plan 1 E3

Upmarket modern Indian on the King's Road

☎ 020 7565 8500 & 7351 4118
438 King's Rd SW10 0LJ
e-mail: manager@vama.co.uk
dir: Nearest station: Sloane Square About 20 mins walk down King's Rd

An awning and glass frontage - hedged in by potted plants - picks out this modern Indian close to World's End. Stylishly decorated in warm colours, with large floor tiles, elegant handcrafted wooden chairs with cushioned seats and rich ochre walls (one side flanked with drapes) hung with huge, eye-catching old oils, combining to create a comfortable, well-groomed modern feel. There's a small atrium-style roof at the rear of the long narrow room, while tables come dressed in white linen, staff are smartly attired, and there's a vibrant buzz of conversation. Classical North West Indian cuisine, mainly Punjabi, is Vama's thing, using traditional recipes and cooked in a clay oven with authentic marinades. Typical dishes include a machlin curry (tandoori salmon sautéed with herbs and spices and simmered in a light mustard and coconut curry sauce), and perhaps a gajjerella finish (delicate carrot and milk halva served with cardamom ice cream and fine saffron sauce).

Chef Andy Varma **Owner** Andy Varma, Arjun Varma **Times** 12-4/6.30-12, Closed 25-26 Dec, 1 Jan **Prices** Fixed L 2 course fr £8.99, Fixed D 3 course fr £16.99, Starter £5.95-£13.95, Main £6.95-£18.95, Dessert £5-£6.50, Service added 12.5%, Groups min 6 service 12.5% **Wines** 26 bottles over £20, 9 bottles under £20, 12 by glass **Notes** Sunday L, Dress restrictions, Smart casual, Air con **Seats** 120, Pr/dining room 35 **Parking** 25 **Parking** Edith Grove, NCP

Aubergine

LONDON SW10   Plan 4 C1

French

Accomplished and refined cooking from eminent Chelsea eatery

☎ 020 7352 3449
11 Park Walk, Chelsea SW10 0AJ
e-mail: info@auberginerestaurant.co.uk
dir: Nearest station: South Kensington, Fulham Broadway W along Fulham Rd, close to Chelsea and Westminster Hospital

The eponymous fruit figures large - technically aubergine is a fruit although it is used as a vegetable in cooking terms and might look out of place in your fruit bowl next to the apples - from the colour of the front canopy, the shape of the door handles, the pictures on the plates and as a motif on the cutlery, although it does not seem overly contrived or in your face. An impressive floral display at the entrance, oak floors, abstract art and generously sized tables laid with crisp white linen help create a calm and civilised dining room, where formal and attentive staff move smoothly between the tables. William Drabble has been head chef since 1998 and his modern French cooking continues to be based around high quality produce and shows regard for the seasons. Bread is a fine selection, including excellent black pudding, before the usual array of extras from amuse-bouche through to the stack of petits fours with the coffee. There is a menu gourmand, set lunch and a carte with around seven choices per course. First-course pithivier of crab is a stunning looking dish with an accompanying marinated carrot and tarragon salad, while main-course pan-fried halibut is served with smoked salmon velouté, wilted greens and a creamy sauce. Clementine soufflé is served with hot dark chocolate sauce which is poured at the table, and you can choose a selection of French and British cheeses from the trolley.

Chef William Drabble **Owner** A-Z Restaurants **Times** 12-2.30/7-11, Closed Xmas, Etr, BHs, Closed Sun, Closed L Sat **Wines** 500 bottles over £20, 1 bottles under £20 **Notes** Menu gourmand 7 courses £77-£132, Dress restrictions, Smart casual preferred, Air con **Seats** 60 **Parking** Local parking available

LONDON SW10 *Continued*

Wyndham Grand Hotel

⊛ International   Plan 1 E3

Sophisticated waterside dining

☎ 020 7300 8443
Chelsea Harbour SW10 0XG
web: www.wyndham.com

Set against the picturesque backdrop of fashionable Chelsea Harbour's small marina, the luxurious Wyndham Grand attracts an equally stylish, well-heeled crowd. Peruse the menu over a relaxing drink in the glamorous Aquasia Bar, or head straight for the fine-dining Aquasia Restaurant with its stylish contemporary décor and stunning harbour-side views. On warm summer days the restaurant's floor-to-ceiling glass panels open to allow guests a unique alfresco dining experience; by evening the mood changes subtly, exuding warmth and intimacy. An array of flavours parade on the mouthwatering, seasonally-changing, modern menu: a main course of plump, perfectly cooked scallops with red mullet, chicory, braised fennel and butter sauce might be preceded by chicken liver terrine with toasted brioche and chutney, with pear strudel and ice cream for dessert.

Times all day

LONDON SW11

The Butcher & Grill

⊛ Modern, Traditional 🖳   Plan 1 E3

A carnivore's delight in warehouse-style surroundings

☎ 020 7924 3999
39-41 Parkgate Rd, Battersea SW11 4NP
e-mail: info@thebutcherandgrill.com
dir: Nearest station: Clapham Junction, Battersea

Entry through a stylish butcher's and deli/food emporium helps make a connection between the produce and what appears on the plate. The warehouse-style Grill restaurant, with its bare red-brick walls, whitewashed ceilings and wooden tables, chairs and floors, has a bustling, lively atmosphere. Service is friendly and informative and in keeping with the setting. The food fits the surroundings, with its straightforward and honest approach. Top-notch raw materials are prepared with skill and meat is what it is all about: the grills are the star attraction. Start with smoked salmon or charcuterie before Highfields lamb burger or T-bone or rib-eye and add the sauce of your choice (onion gravy, red wine etc.).

Chef Siaka Touray **Owner** Paul Grout, Dominic Ford, Simon Tindall **Times** 12-3.30/6-11, Closed 25-27 Dec, Closed D Sun **Prices** Fixed L 2 course £12.50-£29, Fixed D 3 course £20-£35, Starter £4.95-£12.50, Main fr £7.50, Dessert £5-£7.50, Service added but optional 12.5% **Wines** 52 bottles over £20, 16 bottles under £20, 13 by glass **Notes** Sunday L, Vegetarian available, Air con **Seats** 131 **Children** Portions, Menu **Parking** On street

The Greyhound at Battersea

⊛⊛ Modern European 🖳   Plan 1 D3

Trendy, stylish gastro-pub with top-notch cuisine and wines

☎ 020 7978 7021
136 Battersea High St SW11 3JR
e-mail: eat@thegreyhoundatbattersea.co.uk
web: www.thegreyhoundatbattersea.co.uk
dir: Nearest station: Clapham Junct Located near Battersea Bridge and Clapham Junction

The transformation of an old down-at-heel pub on bustling Battersea High Street to chic, trendy local and dining room presses all the right buttons. Large flash bar, leather seating, polished-wood floors, with crystal glasses and expensive table appointments place it a cut above your average gastro-pub. Service is attentive, friendly and relaxed, and product knowledge is excellent. Great quality, serious skill and some innovative dishes show the kitchen's fine pedigree and prove a match for the fabulous wine list. Clear flavours, fine presentation, seasoning and balance all hit a high note. Expect a starter of grilled octopus, carrot salad, ginger and white wine sauce and main dishes such as slow-roasted pork belly, Savoy cabbage and potato purée.

Times 12-3/7-10, Closed 23 Dec-3 Jan, Closed Mon, Closed D Sun

WINE AWARD WINNER

Ransome's Dock

⊛⊛ Modern British   Plan 1 E3

Simple seasonal cooking in waterside setting

☎ 020 7223 1611 & 7924 2462
35-37 Parkgate Rd, Battersea SW11 4NP
e-mail: chef@ransomesdock.co.uk
dir: Nearest station: Sloane Square/Clapham Junction Between Albert Bridge & Battersea Bridge

Ransome's Dock - located in a former ice cream factory overlooking the Thames close to Albert Bridge - has a loyal following and a reputation for serving good organic and seasonal food. With its cornflower blue walls and modern food-and-wine related artwork, this friendly, relaxed venue is unpretentious and informal, with snacks and coffees available in the bar area, while the outside terrace is the place to sit when the weather allows. The sourcing of quality, seasonal produce - much of it organic - is paramount to the kitchen's success. Start with Jerusalem artichoke soup or Ummera organic Irish smoked salmon before pot-roasted red leg partridge with Cumbrian bacon, cavolo nero, mashed potato and port sauce, before a finish of ginger crème caramel with gingerbread and glazed pears. The exceptional wine list is worth exploring.
Ransome's Dock is AA Wine Award Winner for England and Overall Winner

Chef Martin Lam, Vanessa Lam **Owner** Mr & Mrs M Lam **Times** 12/6-11, Closed Xmas, Closed D Sun **Prices** Fixed

L 2 course fr £15.50, Starter £5.50-£12.50, Main £10.50-£22.50, Dessert £5.50-£7.50, Service added but optional 12.5% **Wines** 360 bottles over £20, 22 bottles under £20, 10 by glass **Notes** Brunch menu Sat & Sun, Sunday L, Vegetarian available **Seats** 55 **Children** Portions **Parking** 20 **Parking** spaces at evenings & wknds only

LONDON SW12

Lamberts

⊛⊛ Modern British 🌱   Plan 1 E2

Relaxed, modern fine dining with impressive cooking

☎ 0208 675 2233
2 Station Pde, Balham High Rd SW12 9AZ
e-mail: bookings@lambertsrestaurant.com
dir: Nearest station: Balham Just S of Balham station on Balham High Rd

Balham's Lamberts is a cool, minimalist-vogue modern venue and, whilst styling itself as a fine-dining restaurant, the atmosphere's relaxed and comfortable. It's a deservedly popular venue too, with a growing reputation for its fresh and vibrant food. No surprise then that the kitchen prides itself on using the freshest seasonal British ingredients, including organic produce, with the majority of meat sourced direct from farms and fish comes straight from day boats. The impressive, well-presented cooking takes a modern approach that suits the surroundings, with old favourites sitting comfortably alongside contemporary interpretations of classics; think British saddleback loin, belly and trotter served with kale, mash and apple, and a marmalade sponge pudding with vanilla custard.

Chef Chas Tapaneyasastr **Owner** Mr Joe Lambert **Times** 12-3/7-10.30, Closed 25 Dec, 1 Jan, BH's (except Good Fri) **Prices** Fixed L 2 course £17-£20, Starter £6.50-£9.50, Main £15-£18, Dessert £6, Service added but optional 12.5% **Wines** 65 bottles over £20, 15 bottles under £20, 12 by glass **Notes** Sunday L, Vegetarian available, Air con **Seats** 50 **Children** Portions, Menu **Parking** On street

LONDON SW13

Sonny's Restaurant

⊛⊛ Modern 🖳   Plan 1 D3

Imaginative cooking in modern surroundings

☎ 020 8748 0393
94 Church Rd, Barnes SW13 0DQ
e-mail: barnes@sonnys.co.uk
dir: Nearest station: Barnes/Hammersmith From Castelnau end of Church Rd on left by shops

Tucked away in a parade of shops behind a glass frontage, this smart, long-standing neighbourhood favourite is bigger than it looks from the street. The interior is light and airy, with a pale blue and white colour scheme, striking contemporary artwork, and an open fire set into a wall of opaque glass bricks at the far

Continued

LONDON SW13 *Continued*

end. White tablecloths, a black floor and modern chairs hit the spot too, while the atmosphere's buzzy and upbeat and service friendly and efficient. The accomplished kitchen's modern European brasserie approach is a skilful, clean-cut affair that delivers quality ingredients, clear flavours and colourful presentation; think salad of red and yellow beetroot with lardons, walnuts and quail eggs, or double baked cheese soufflé with creamed leeks, with tarte Tatin and Calvados ice cream to finish. Sonny's Food Shop and café is next door.

Times 12.30-2.30/7.30-11, Closed BHs, Closed D Sun

LONDON SW14

The Depot Waterfront Brasserie

🌐 Modern British   Plan 1 D3

Popular, informal riverside brasserie

☎ 020 8878 9462
Tideway Yard, Mortlake High St SW14 8SN
e-mail: info@depotbrasserie.co.uk
dir: Nearest station: Barnes Bridge Between Barnes Bridge & Mortlake stations

With a Thames-side location, situated in what used to be a stable block, this brasserie successfully blends rusticity with contemporary styling giving the place both character and style. Think striped-top banquette seating and modern bar meets scrubbed-wood tables, café-style chairs, exposed brick and parquet flooring, with views over the Thames to the rear and courtyard alfresco tables out front a big drawcard. The crowd-pleasing menu delivers a good selection of simply constructed, modern brasserie-style dishes; take Cumberland sausages with mash and onion gravy, or pan-fried royal bream with scallops and crayfish served with a tarragon and baby spinach risotto, and puddings like Eton Mess or crème brûlée.

Times 12-3.30/6-12, Closed 24-26 Dec

Redmond's

🌐🌐 Modern British   Plan 1 D3

Well-executed cooking in a sophisticated setting

☎ 020 8878 1922
170 Upper Richmond Road West SW14 8AW
e-mail: pippa@redmonds.org.uk
dir: Nearest station: Mortlake Located halfway between Putney and Richmond. On the South Circular Road at the Barnes end of Sheen

A big blue awning and white-painted frontage distinguish this high-street restaurant in Sheen. It's a fitting setting for chef-patron Redmond Hayward, and wife Pippa leading front of house. The chic, understated dining room is hung with modern artwork, while simple glassware gleams in the mood lighting, and tables are clad in crisp white linen. Top-notch raw materials are competently handled; cooking is sound, and presentation stylish. There are some classic combinations like roast partridge

with roast root vegetables, pommes Anna and game port jus, and dishes with a more modern twist like fillets of plaice wrapped in smoked salmon with braised leeks and basil sauce.

Times 12-2.30/7-10, Closed 4 days Xmas, BH Mons, Closed L Mon-Sat, Closed D Sun

LONDON SW15

Enoteca Turi

🌐🌐 Italian 🖥 ♦︎NOTABLE WINE LIST   Plan 1 D3

Seasonal, regional Italian cooking in Putney

☎ 020 8785 4449
28 Putney High Street SW15 1SQ
e-mail: enoteca@tiscali.co.uk
dir: Nearest station: Putney Bridge Opposite Odeon Cinema near bridge

Tucked amongst the shops at the bottom end of Putney High Street, just a stone's throw from the river, this family-run restaurant is both contemporary and cosy, with its three interconnecting rooms, warm, rustic Tuscan colours, black and white pictures of Italy, wooden floors and wine racks. Traditional dishes from the central Italian regions of Marche, Umbria and Lazio take on a modern twist; flavours are bold, ingredients seasonal and dishes well presented. A great set lunch menu is available, while the carte includes dishes such as baked asparagus cannoli with parmesan-coated deep-fried egg, and move on to a colourful dish of ravioli filled with roasted beetroot and ricotta, with a butter and poppyseed sauce. Every wine-producing region of Italy is represented on the extensive list, while suggested wines for each dish are available by the glass.

Chef Mr R Serjent **Owner** Mr G & Mrs P Turi
Times 12-2.30/7-11, Closed 25-26 Dec, 1 Jan, Closed Sun, Closed L BHs **Prices** Fixed L 2 course fr £14.50, Starter £7.50-£11.50, Main £11.50-£21.50, Dessert £5.50-£8.50, Service added but optional 12.5%
Wines 300 bottles over £20, 16 bottles under £20, 9 by glass **Notes** Vegetarian available, Dress restrictions, Smart casual, Air con **Seats** 85, Pr/dining room 18
Children Portions **Parking** Putney Exchange car park

Talad Thai

🌐 Thai   Plan 1 D3

Authentic cooking at a popular Thai restaurant

☎ 020 8789 8084
320 Upper Richmond Rd, Putney SW15 6TL
e-mail: info@taladthai.co.uk
dir: Nearest station: Putney/East Putney Please telephone for directions

The people of Putney are lucky to have this small Thai restaurant, which is a few doors down from a Thai supermarket under the same ownership, on their doorstep. The restaurant has a very homely air, with its informal wooden tables packed closely together, and a relaxed and buzzing atmosphere. With a skilled team working in the kitchen, the traditional menu is fairly long and split into sections like starters, salads, soups, curries, stir-fries and noodle dishes. Out front, the friendly waiting staff work hard to make you feel at home. Expect the likes of chicken satay, lamb massaman curry with roti, pad Thai noodles, or stir-fried prawns with chilli and Thai basil.

Times 11.30-3/5.30-11, Closed 25 Dec, 1 Jan

Louhannah

🖥

☎ 020 8780 5252
30 Putney High St, Putney SW15 1SQ
web: http://www.theaa.com/travel/index.jsp

Popular with shoppers and cinema goers this eatery has a modern continental menu and laid-back atmosphere.

Prices Food prices not confirmed for 2009. Please telephone for details.

LONDON SW17

Amici Bar & Italian Kitchen

🌐 Italian   Plan 1 E3

Authentic Italian dining in a relaxed setting

☎ 020 8672 5888
35 Belleuve Rd, Wandsworth Common SW17 7EF
e-mail: info@amiciitalian.co.uk
dir: Nearest station: Wandsworth A214, situated on corner of Bellevue Rd

Overlooking Wandsworth Common, this stylish eatery is already a local favourite. Behind the commanding frontage, a contemporary bar replete with comfy sofas leads seamlessly into the dining area, where the chefs serve up classic, unfussy dishes from the busy open kitchen. Wood panelling inset with coloured glass, Venetian blinds and a stone bath doubling as a bread station all add to the informal atmosphere. Try fritto misto con verdure (fried shrimp, calamari, sea bass and red mullet), followed by risotto with radicchio, gorgonzola and Chianti, and make sure you try the excellent fresh bread. Carte, lunch, Sunday brunch and children's menus are all on offer and in summer you can dine alfresco on the shady terrace.

Times 12-3/6-10.30, Closed 24-26 Dec

Chez Bruce

◎◎◎ – *see below*

Kastoori

◎ Indian **V**   Plan 1 E2

Fresh vegetarian Indian dishes made daily from scratch

☎ 020 8767 7027
188 Upper Tooting Rd SW17 7EJ
dir: Nearest station: Tooting Bec & Tooting Broadway. Situated between two stations.

Worth the trek to Tooting from further into London or the suburbs if you're not a local, this welcoming vegetarian Indian restaurant presents a cheery face with its bright, closely-packed tables and relaxing colour scheme of yellow, white, grey and blue. A delightful choice of Gujarati dishes is threaded with East African flavours in main dishes like special tomato curry - a hot and spicy traditional dish from the family's roots in exotic Katia Wahd, or kasodi (sweetcorn in coconut milk with a ground peanut sauce). Remember to ask for the chef's choices and daily specials.

Chef Manoj Thanki **Owner** Mr D Thanki **Times** 12.30-2.30/6-10.30, Closed 25-26 Dec, Closed L Mon & Tue **Prices** Food prices not confirmed for 2009. Please telephone for details. **Wines** 1 bottles over £20, 19 bottles under £20, 2 by glass **Notes** Sunday L, Vegetarian menu, Air con **Seats** 82 **Children** Portions **Parking** On street

---

Ditto Bar & Restaurant

◎ Modern European   Plan 1 D3

Informal local offering bags of choice

☎ 020 8877 0110
55-57 East Hill SW18 2QE
e-mail: info@doditto.co.uk
dir: Nearest station: Wandsworth Town, Clapham Junction

Popular with locals, this relaxed bar-restaurant is conveniently set on the high street just off Wandsworth Common. The front windows open on to the street - great on hot days or to watch the world go by - and the walls are hung with paintings by local artists. There's rugged wooden and leather furniture in the bar area, and polished wooden tables, suede and leather chairs in the restaurant section. The menu offers a good choice of simple, well presented modern dishes such as confit pork belly with braised red cabbage and red wine sauce; or pan-fried gnocchi with braised rabbit, wild mushrooms and parmesan crackling.

Chef Jean Chaib **Owner** George Herodotou **Times** 12-3/6.30-11, Closed 25 Dec, 1 Jan, Closed D Sun **Prices** Starter £5.50-£8.95, Main £12.50-£17.50, Dessert £5.50-£8.50, Service added but optional 12.5% **Wines** 21 bottles over £20, 15 bottles under £20, 12 by glass **Notes** Sunday L, Vegetarian available, Air con **Seats** 75, Pr/dining room 24 **Children** Portions, Menu **Parking** On street

---

Common

◎◎ Modern European ◐   Plan 1 D2

Country-house style hotel with views and imaginative cooking

☎ 020 8879 1464
Cannizaro House, West Side, Wimbledon Common SW19 4UE
e-mail: info@cannizarohouse.com
dir: Nearest station: Wimbledon From A3 (London Rd) Tibbets Corner, take A219 (Parkside) right into Cannizaro Rd, then right into West Side.

This elegant 18th-century house, with a long tradition of hosting London society, is peacefully set overlooking Cannizaro Park, its former grounds, a few miles from the city centre. The country-house vibe extends to the

Continued

Chez Bruce

Modern British, French 🖳 🔖

Memorable dining at Wandsworth big-hitter

☎ 020 8672 0114
2 Bellevue Rd, Wandsworth Common SW17 7EG
e-mail: enquiries@chezbruce.co.uk
dir: Nearest station: Wandsworth Common/Balham Near Wandsworth Common station

The position overlooking Wandsworth Common is nice enough, the location on a parade of shops is perfectly pleasant with planters full to bursting with vegetation. But nothing is ordinary about Chez Bruce: Bruce Poole has created a restaurant of conviction and confidence. The ground-floor is an uncluttered room where the neutral tones on the walls, dark-wood floor, tables clad in white linen, soft lighting and collection of simple prints on the walls create an unpretentious and comfortable space. The room is not the star. Diners go straight to table - there is no space for a bar area - and the service is informed, attentive and relaxed. The menu is equally to the point - no tasting menus or flame throwers at the tables here - just a fixed-price carte of a sensible length. The foundation is classical and provincial French cooking where humble ingredients are not ignored, the seasons are duly followed, but inspiration also comes from farther a field. Skill is evident when it comes to giving the fine produce room to breathe, balancing flavours, and in the sheer technical ability of the team. Start with warm smoked eel with crab mayonnaise, potato pancake, beetroot remoulade and herbs, before main-course glazed and stuffed pig's trotter with creamed potatoes and Madeira. Desserts are equally well made and can be as simple as crème brûlée or lemon tart, while the cheeseboard is a treat worth saving room for.

Chef Bruce Poole, James Lawrence **Owner** Bruce Poole, Nigel Platts-Martin **Times** 12-2/6.30-10.30, Closed 24-26 Dec, 1 Jan, Closed L 27,31 Dec & 2nd Jan **Prices** Fixed L 2 course £18.50-£27.50, Fixed D 3 course £37.50, Service added but optional 12.5% **Wines** 500 bottles over £20, 9 bottles under £20, 15 by glass **Notes** Sunday L, Vegetarian available, Dress restrictions, Smart casual, Air con **Seats** 75, Pr/dining room 16 **Children** Min L only, Portions, Menu **Parking** On street, station car park

LONDON SW19 *Continued*

Common dining room, with its comfortably upholstered chairs, while fine art, murals and stunning fireplaces feature throughout. Focusing on seasonal produce, classic French techniques are used to create a menu of fresh, vibrant colours and textures. Dishes are simply presented with no accompaniments overstated or redundant, as in a stunningly light pressé of marinated plum tomatoes, with parmesan foam, parmesan crisp and basil garnish; and crispy skinned sea bass with dandelion leaf salad and Roscoff onion tarte Tatin.

Chef Christian George **Owner** Bridgehouse Hotels **Times** 12-3/7-10 **Prices** Fixed L 2 course fr £19, Fixed D 3 course fr £27, Starter £6.50-£10.50, Main £16.95-£23.95, Dessert £6.50-£9.25, Service optional **Wines** 110 bottles over £20, 20 bottles under £20, 14 by glass **Notes** Sunday L, Vegetarian available, Dress restrictions, No shorts, Civ Wed 60 **Seats** 46, Pr/dining room 120 **Children** Portions, Menu **Parking** 55

The Light House Restaurant

◉ Modern International 🖵 Plan 1 D2

Simple modern cooking in upmarket suburbia

☎ 020 8944 6338
75-77 Ridgway, Wimbledon SW19 4ST
e-mail: info@lighthousewimbledon.com
dir: Nearest station: Wimbledon From station turn right up Wimbledon Hill then left at mini-rdbt onto Ridgway, restaurant on left

Set in a small row of shops in Wimbledon's upmarket village, this relaxed, upbeat restaurant stands out from the crowd, with its potted trees either side of the entrance and contemporary good looks. Inside continues the fashionable theme, with light walls and pale woods; think blond-wood floors, tables and high-backed slated chairs with brown leather upholstery. There's a bar off to one side and a semi-open kitchen towards the back, opposite a small alfresco inner courtyard. Clad in black, the staff are friendly and knowledgeable. The kitchen's modern approach comes with a tilt to Europe and beyond. Take confit of duck leg with baked swede, caramelised salsify and cavolo nero, and a buttermilk pannacotta with Armagnac prunes.

Chef Chris Casey **Owner** Mr Finch & Mr Taylor **Times** 12-2.30/6.30-10.30, Closed 24-26 Dec, 1 Jan, Etr Sun & Mon, Closed D Sun **Prices** Fixed L 2 course £14.50, Fixed D 3 course £18.50, Starter £5-£11.50, Main £11.50-£16.50, Dessert £5.50, Service added but optional 12.5% **Wines** 56 bottles over £20, 14 bottles under £20, 12 by glass **Notes** Fixed D Mon-Thu order before 7.30pm, Sunday L, Vegetarian available **Seats** 80 **Children** Portions, Menu

LONDON W1

Alain Ducasse

◉◉◉ – *see opposite*

Alastair Little Restaurant

◉ European Plan 3 B2

Simple seasonal cooking and harmonious flavours at informal Soho fixture

☎ 020 7734 5183
49 Frith St W1V 5TE
dir: Nearest station: Tottenham Court Rd/Leicester Square Near Ronnie Scott's Jazz Club

This small blue-painted shop-front restaurant - unassumingly tucked away in the heart of Soho - is easily missed. Although Alastair Little is no longer associated with the enterprise, his influence remains, reflected in the admirably uncomplicated style of the cuisine. The décor follows suit, with blond-wood floors, simple blue chairs and white-clothed tables, while bold artwork adds colour and the wacky, dated ceiling lighting a talking point. It's relaxed and friendly, with the kitchen's straightforward, colourful modern cooking delivering clear, balanced flavours and quality seasonal produce to a daily-changing, three-course fixed-price menu format. Organic salmon served with seaweed, shrimps and a caviar butter sauce shows the style.

Times 12-3/5.30-11.30, Closed Xmas, BHs, Closed Sun, Closed L Sat

Albemarle

◉◉ British 🖵 Plan 3 A1

Elegant, traditional British dining in landmark London hotel

☎ 020 7518 4060
Brown's Hotel, Albemarle St W1S 4BP
e-mail: reservations.brownshotel@roccofortehotels.com
dir: Nearest station: Green Park Off Piccadilly between Green Park tube station and Bond Street

This remodelled landmark Mayfair hotel still retains an air of its original charm with the successful marriage of traditional and contemporary styling. The Albemarle restaurant (formerly The Grill) follows this theme too; modern and stylish, it comes with beautiful oak panelling, green leather banquettes and some thought-provoking artwork, while service is highly professional.

The kitchen - now under Mark Hix (ex Caprice Holdings - think Le Caprice, The Ivy, J. Sheekey, Scott's, etc) and exec-chef Lee Streeton - takes a classic British approach driven by high quality seasonal ingredients; think Blackface mutton and turnip pie, Aberdeenshire fillet steak or whole Dover crab, and, at lunch, the serving trolley also offers traditional roasts like Brymore veal. Brown's renowned afternoon teas are served in the lounge, while the fashionable Donavon Bar is the place for aperitifs.

Times 12.30-2.30/7-10.30

Alloro

◉ Italian 🖵 Plan 3 A1

A taste of Italy in the heart of Mayfair

☎ 020 7495 4768
20 Dover St W1S 4LU
e-mail: alloro@hotmail.co.uk
dir: Nearest station: Green Park From Green Park station continue towards Piccadilly, Dover St is 2nd on left

A blue awning and glass frontage picks out this smart, discreet and contemporary Mayfair Italian. Banquettes and leather chairs, polished dark-and-lightwood, chessboard-like flooring, pastel tones, sculptured laurel-leaf-themed artwork (alloro means laurel) and smartly attired staff all set a classy tone at this popular, sleek and stylish restaurant with interconnecting bar dining area. The modern Italian cooking delivers simplicity, quality ingredients, clean flavours and a light touch on its fixed-price repertoire (with a few supplements) and separate bar menu. Think pan-fried turbot served with lettuce ravioli and braised leeks, and perhaps a traditional cocoa and rum Piedmonte dessert to finish, all accompanied by an all-Italian wine list.

Chef Daniele Camera **Owner** A-Z Restaurant Ltd **Times** 12-2.30/7-10.30, Closed Xmas, 4 days Etr & BHs, Closed Sun, Closed L Sat **Prices** Fixed L 2 course fr £27, Fixed D 3 course fr £35, Service added but optional 12.5% **Wines** 200 bottles over £20, 2 bottles under £20, 16 by glass **Notes** Vegetarian available, Dress restrictions, No shorts or sandals, Air con **Seats** 60, Pr/dining room 16 **Children** Portions **Parking** On street

Arbutus Restaurant

◉◉◉ – *see page 284*

Alain Ducasse

Modern French

Culinary legend comes to London

☎ 020 7629 8866 & 7629 8888
The Dorchester, 53 Park Ln W1K 1QA
e-mail: alainducasse@thedorchester.
com
dir: Nearest station: Hyde Park Corner/
Marble Arch Please telephone for
directions

This signature restaurant from
legendary French chef and restaurateur
Alain Ducasse - with over 25
restaurants across the globe to his
name - sits well in its landmark hotel
setting. The large Patrick Jouin-
designed dining room presents a very
modern face (certainly compared with
the rest of The Dorchester), with two
design features catching the eye; a
huge leather screen greets arrivals near
the entrance and, at the other end, a
private table comes surrounded by a
giant sparkling curtain of lights. Décor
is a soothing mix of neutral shades,
predominantly creams and coffees,
while the floor blends carpeting with
wood. Tables are predictably large and
immaculately set and come teamed with
comfortable leather chairs, while service
from a legion of staff is professional
and knowledgeable. The Ducasse
signature food is deeply rooted in the
classics with modern presentation and
technique on a menu peppered with

luxury ingredients. Think rack and
saddle of lamb served with truffled early
vegetables, or perhaps braised halibut
with spicy lemon condiment and
sautéed cereals. It all comes at a price,
of course, like the accompanying
heavyweight wine list that oozes quality.

Chef Jocelyn Herland, Bruno Riou,
Angelo Ercdono **Owner** The Dorchester
Collection **Times** 12-2/6.30-9.45, Closed
26-30 Dec, 1-5 Jan, Etr, Aug, Closed
Mon-Sun, Closed L Sat **Prices** Fixed L 3
course fr £35, Fixed D 3 course £75,
Tasting menu £115, Service added but
optional 12.5% **Wines** 600 bottles over
£20, 4 by glass **Notes** Tasting menu 7
courses. Fixed price ALC L & D,
Vegetarian available, Dress restrictions,
Smart casual L, smart D, Air con
Seats 82, Pr/dining room 24
Children Min 10 yrs **Parking** 20

LONDON W1 *Continued*

Archipelago

◉◉ Modern, International ▭ Plan 3 B3

Unique, exotic and adventurous dining experience

☎ 020 7383 3346
110 Whitfield St W1T 5ED
e-mail: info@archipelago-restaurant.co.uk
dir: Nearest station: Warren Street From underground
south along Tottenham Court Rd. 1st right into Grafton
Way. 1st left into Whitfield St

Set on an unremarkable side street not far from the
Telecom Tower, this tiny, offbeat restaurant exceeds all
expectations. A treasure trove of peacock feathers, golden
Buddhas, primitive carvings, bird cages and colourful
fabrics and seating are among the riot of exotic
memorabilia that fill every inch of the green and red
walls; it's dark, romantic and atmospheric. Even the

menu is unusual, a ribbon-bound scroll with an ancient
map on the back reveals the treasures in store; an equally
idiosyncratic safari of accomplished, exotic-named
dishes that might include crocodile, peacock, zebra or
even chocolate-covered scorpions - perhaps peanut-
crusted wildebeest rump with sour green mango soba
noodles. Service is knowledgeable, relaxed and friendly.

Chef Daniel Creedon **Owner** Bruce Alexander
Times 12-2.30/6-11, Closed Xmas, BHs, Closed Sun,
Closed L Sat **Prices** Fixed D 3 course £31.50-£38.50,
Starter £7-£10.50, Main £13.50-£20.50, Dessert £6-£8,
Service added but optional 12.5% **Wines** 42 bottles over
£20, 7 bottles under £20, 3 by glass **Notes** Tasting menu
L Mon-Fri, Vegetarian available, Air con **Seats** 32
Parking NCP, on street

The Athenaeum, Damask

◉ Modern British Plan 4 H5

Skilful cooking in refined surroundings

☎ 020 7499 3464
116 Piccadilly W1J 7BJ
e-mail: info@athenaeumhotel.com
web: www.athenaeumhotel.com
dir: Nearest station: Hyde Park Corner, Green Park
Telephone for directions

Sumptuous, exclusive and discreet, the Edwardian
Athenaeum exudes contemporary style. The Damask
Restaurant is a sophisticated yet relaxed space, with rich

colours and glamorous soft furnishings. The kitchen
sources raw ingredients of exceptional quality for the
seasonal menu. Classic and modern British dishes are
mixed with some more individual items. Try chicken foie
gras terrine with red onion marmalade, line-caught wild
Dorset sea bass seared with chive butter and wild
mushrooms; and warm chocolate and lavender pudding
with Regent's Park honey ice cream. Service from smartly
attired staff is of the highest level.

The Athenaeum, Damask

Chef David Marshall **Owner** Ralph Trustees Ltd
Times 12.30-2.30/5.30-10.30 **Prices** Fixed L 2 course fr
£18, Fixed D 3 course fr £26, Starter £8.50-£12.50, Main
£12-£29, Dessert £8, Service optional **Wines** 44 bottles
over £20, 15 by glass **Notes** All-day dining menu 11am-
11pm, Vegetarian available, Civ Wed 55, Air con
Seats 46, Pr/dining room 44 **Children** Portions, Menu
Parking Close car park

Arbutus Restaurant

LONDON W1	Plan 3 B2

Modern French ▭

Stunning but simple, affordable food and wine from
Soho gem

☎ 020 7734 4545
63-64 Frith St W1D 3JW
e-mail: info@arbutusrestaurant.co.uk
dir: Nearest station: Tottenham Court Road Exit
Tottenham Court Road tube station, turn left into Oxford
St. Left onto Soho St, cross over or continue around Soho
Sq, restaurant is on Frith St 25mtrs on right

Since opening to universal acclaim in 2006, with the aim
of offering great quality, value-for-money dining in
relaxed and informal surroundings, this high-achieving
brainchild of ex-Putney Bridge restaurant duo Anthony
Demetre and Will Smith has gone from strength to

strength. Located at the Soho Square end of bustling
Frith Street, its unassuming dark-grey frontage conceals
an equally understated interior that is cool and calm,
with a smart, simple décor dominated by creams and
dark browns. In the style of the bistro moderne, white
tablecloths and formal service have been put aside in
favour of a relaxed atmosphere in smart yet unpretentious
surroundings. Service (with Will Smith out front) is
friendly but slick and polished, and bar-seating is also
available in the U-shaped dining room. Anthony
Demetre's impressive modern bistro cooking displays
obvious pedigree, the style intelligently simple, highly
skilled, imaginative and innovative, with a shopping list
of more humble ingredients also helping to elevate it
above the crowd. Flavours are clear and confident and
combinations well judged, as in a vibrant starter of squid
and mackerel 'burger' served with parsley emulsion, pea
shoots, razor clams and finely sliced baby squid. For main
course, take perfectly cooked line-caught Cornish pollack
with macaroni, chorizo and octopus, or perhaps bavette

of Scottish beef with dauphinoise potatoes.

Chef Anthony Demetre **Owner** Anthony Demetre, Will
Smith **Times** 12-2.30/5-10.30, Closed 25-26 Dec, Closed
1 Jan **Prices** Fixed L 3 course fr £15.50, Starter
£5.95-£9.95, Main £12.95-£18.95, Dessert £5.95-£6.95,
Service added but optional 12.5% **Wines** 40 bottles over
£20, 10 bottles under £20, 50 by glass **Notes** Pre-theatre
D 5-7pm 2 courses, Sunday L, Vegetarian available, Air
con **Seats** 75 **Children** Portions

Automat

⊚ American 🖥   Plan 3 A1

Stylish dining in American-style brasserie

☎ 020 7499 3033
33 Dover St W1S 4NF
e-mail: info@automat-london.com
web: www.automat-london.com
dir: Nearest station: Green Park Dover St is off Piccadilly

This elegant diner-themed restaurant delivers American-style comfort food to Mayfair. Up front there's a café edge, in the middle an upmarket diner vibe with leather banquette-style booth seating, subdued lighting and lots of wood veneer, while at the back there's a brighter, buzzier space with an open kitchen, white-tiled walls and tables set on different levels. The food is uncomplicated but accomplished, featuring some stereotypical Stateside diner favourites, though dishes benefit from modern interpretation and presentation, and quality ingredients.

Take a Manhattan clam chowder, perhaps an Automat burger or New York strip-loin steak, and a Mississippi mud pie finish.

Times 12-3/6-11, Closed Xmas, New Year, Closed L Sun

L'Autre Pied

⊚⊚⊚ – **see below**

Bam-Bou

⊚ South East Asian 🖥 V   Plan 3 B3

Lively restaurant inspired by Indo-China

☎ 020 7323 9130
1 Percy St W1T 1DB
e-mail: managers@bam-bou.co.uk
dir: Nearest station: Tottenham Court Rd/Goodge St 1 min from Tottenham Court Rd underground station at the bottom of Charlotte St

Located in a Georgian townhouse smack bang in the middle of Fitzrovia, Bam-Bou is a discreet Asian-style restaurant with a French colonial feel. Intimate rooms with authentic artefacts, wood floors, retro lighting and jazzy music provide the setting for a vibrant ethnic menu that draws on Thai, Vietnamese and Chinese cuisine with a strong Western influence. Sound cooking results in full-flavoured dishes, along the lines of slow-cooked duck leg with pickled plum relish, lemongrass red snapper with mango and ginger, or Vietnamese country-style vegetable curry. Service is informal, friendly and helpful.

Chef Michelle Makaew **Owner** Caprice Holdings **Times** 12-3/6-11, Closed 25-26 Dec, Aug BH, Closed Sun, Closed L Sat **Prices** Starter £2.95-£6.95, Main £9.25-£14.50, Dessert £3.75-£5.50, Service added but optional 12.5% **Wines** 60 bottles over £20, 5 bottles under £20, 10 by glass **Notes** Vegetarian menu, Air con **Seats** 80, Pr/dining room 20 **Children** Portions **Parking** On street parking

Barrafina

⊚ Spanish 🖥   Plan 3 B2

Barcelona-style tapas in the heart of Soho

☎ 020 7813 8016
54 Frith St, Soho W1D 4SL
dir: Nearest station: Tottenham Court Rd

This is as authentic as it gets, a simple and traditionally casual tapas bar in the heart of Soho, inspired by the iconic Cal Pep tapas bar in Barcelona. With no booking policy, arrive early or be prepared to queue in this long, narrow room for the high stools that run around the L-shaped, marble-topped counter where the food is cooked and handed over to you. With food ideal for sharing, sip on a glass of fino or manzanilla as you wait for plates of charcuterie, perhaps cured jabugo ham, or well-cooked authentic hot and cold tapas such as tuna tartare, chorizo with potato and watercress, grilled lamb cutlets and prawn and piquillo pepper tortilla. Staff are lively and friendly.

Continued

L'Autre Pied

LONDON W1   Plan 2 G3

Modern European 🖥 V

Classy modern cooking and relaxed ambience in Marylebone village

☎ 020 7486 9696
5-7 Blandford St W1U 3DB
e-mail: info@lautrepied.co.uk
dir: Nearest station: Bond St Please telephone for directions.

New sibling to David Moore and Shane Osborn's well-established and much revered Mayfair big brother, Pied à Terre, L'Autre Pied is its less-formal offshoot situated just off Marylebone High Street. At the helm in the kitchen is Osborn protégé Marcus Eaves, whilst joining him is Eaves' brother Jason - formerly sous chef at Cheltenham's Le Champignon Sauvage. As you'd expect,

this is no run-of-the-mill brasserie with a generic menu, but a highly classy affair with an ambience of relaxed, unbuttoned formality. There's a small bar at the front and bespoke furnishings; lovely touches include hand-painted artwork depicting flowers and spices on backlit glass screens (with an oriental nod), silk wallpapers and opulently grained wood tables with inbuilt placemats. The modern European cooking is an equally classy affair. Superbly executed, well balanced, refined dishes of flavour are delivered via a seasonal repertoire of both humble (think braised pork belly, braised cheeks and aromatic cooking jus) and luxury ingredients (ballotine of foie gras with quince purée and wild rocket, or haunch of venison served with pumpkin and orange purée and a port sauce) on a winter carte, with perhaps apple bavarois with blackberry sorbet and cinnamon crème fraîche to finish. The repertoire also offers a value fixed-price lunch/pre-theatre option and five-course surprise tasting affair. Our advice: eat here before the secret gets out.

Chef Marcus Eaves **Owner** Marcus Eaves, Shane Osborn, David Moore **Times** 12-3/6-11, Closed 4 days Xmas, 1 Jan **Prices** Fixed L 2 course fr £16.50, Tasting menu £49.50-£59.50, Starter £5.75-£15, Main £12.50-£23, Dessert £5.50-£7.50, Service added but optional 12.5% **Wines** 10 by glass **Notes** Vegetarian menu, Air con **Seats** 53, Pr/dining room 15

LONDON W1 *Continued*

Chef Nieves Barragan **Owner** Sam & Eddie Hart
Times 12-3/5-11, Closed BHs, Closed Sun **Prices** Starter
£2-£12.50, Main £6-£17, Dessert £4-£6.50, Service
added but optional 12.5% **Wines** 18 bottles over £20, 8
bottles under £20, 20 by glass **Notes** Vegetarian
available, Air con **Seats** 23 **Children** Portions

Bar Shu

◉ Chinese   Plan 3 C2

One of the capital's 'hottest' Chinese restaurants
offering Sichuanese cuisine

☎ 020 7287 6688
28 Frith St W1D 5LF

Clean-lined and contemporary, this glass-fronted Soho
restaurant is just over the road from Chinatown.
Traditional touches have their place though, with red
lanterns, authentic wooden furniture and objets d'art. Bar
Shu is dedicated to the food of the Sichuan province of
Southwest China, famous for the fiery spiciness that
comes from its liberal use of chillies and lip-tingling
Sichuan peppercorns. Recommendations include boiled
sea bass with sizzling chilli oil, braised chicken with
chestnuts and Chinese dates, or Chinese tea-tree
mushrooms. Formal table service is provided by helpful
and knowledgeable staff.

Chef Wen Hong Fu **Owner** Wei Shao **Times** 12/11.30,
Closed 24-25 Dec **Prices** Starter £6.80-£13.50, Main
£8.50-£31.50, Dessert £3.40-£9.60, Service added but
optional 12.5% **Wines** 41 bottles over £20, 4 bottles
under £20, 3 by glass **Notes** Vegetarian available, Air con
Seats 100, Pr/dining room 16 **Children** Portions
Parking On street, car park

Bellamy's

◉ French   Plan 2 H2

Classy French brasserie tucked away in quiet mews

☎ 020 7491 2727
18-18a Bruton Place W1J 6LY
e-mail: gavin@bellamysrestaurant.co.uk
dir: Nearest station: Green Park/Bond St Off Berkeley Sq,
parallel with Bruton St

There's a buzz to this popular Mayfair-mews French
brasserie-cum-deli that's highly appealing. Dark-green
leather banquettes and matching chairs ride stylishly
alongside polished-wood floors and white linen, while
pale yellow walls lined with French prints and posters

add to the upmarket but relaxed vibe. Accessed via the
adjoining deli/shop and Oyster Bar, the restaurant's
cuisine is unashamedly classic French brasserie, simply
but competently prepared from top-notch ingredients and
delivered by professional but friendly Gallic staff. Expect
carte offerings such as John Dory à la planche with
tomato and tarragon, or perhaps favourites like a terrine
of foie gras or sliced entrecôte of beef and pommes frites
to ride alongside luxury items like caviar, oysters and
lobster.

Chef Stephane Pacoud **Owner** Gavin Rankin and
Syndicate **Times** 12-3/7-10.30, Closed Xmas, New Year,
BHs, Closed Sun, Closed L Sat **Prices** Fixed L 2 course
£24, Fixed D 3 course £28.50, Starter £6.50-£15.50, Main
£18.50-£28, Dessert £6.50, Service added but optional
12.5% **Wines** 54 bottles over £20, 20 by glass
Notes Vegetarian available, Air con **Seats** 70
Children Portions **Parking** On street, NCP

Benares

◉◉ Indian   Plan 2 H1

Fine-dining Indian with striking design and cutting-
edge cooking

☎ 020 7629 8886
12 Berkeley Square W1J 6BS
e-mail: reservations@benaresrestaurant.com
web: www.benaresrestaurant.com
dir: Nearest station: Green Park E along Piccadilly
towards Regent St. Turn left into Berkeley St and continue
straight to Berkeley Square

Discreetly set on Berkeley Square, Benares puts on a
classy Mayfair performance with its striking contemporary
design. A wide staircase sweeps up to a cool, funky bar
with a series of water-filled ponds decorated with brightly
coloured floating flowers. The slick dining room is decked
out with limestone flooring, dark leather banquettes and
ebony-coloured chairs with creamy white upholstery. The
modern Indian cuisine is as sophisticated as the
surroundings. Highly lauded chef-patron Atul Kochhar
(previously at Tamarind) produces eye-catching food,
utilising tip-top, luxury European-style produce. Vibrant
cooking, subtle spicing and authenticity triumphantly
fuse East and West. Expect dishes such as sea bass
poached in a coconut and tamarind sauce and served
with coconut rice, or perhaps grilled lamb chops
marinated with cardamom and fennel and served with
pomegranate, dates, green beans, feta cheese and mint
salad.

Times 12-2.30/5.30-11, Closed 23-26 Dec, Closed L
27-31 Dec, Sat

Bentley's Oyster Bar & Grill

◉◉ British, European   Plan 3 B1

Classic seafood powerhouse

☎ 020 7734 4756
11/15 Swallow St W1B 4DG
e-mail: reservations@bentleys.org
dir: Nearest station: Piccadilly Circus 2nd right after
Piccadilly Circus

Now over ninety years young, Bentley's was rejuvenated
by Richard Corrigan in 2005 and the arts and crafts
interior is a reminder of the glory days of old, while the
sensitivity of the refurbishment has kept the heart and
soul of the place. The oyster bar is on the ground floor
where you can sit at leather booths or along the counter,
while upstairs is the more formal series of rooms that
make up the Grill restaurant. Corrigan draws on his Irish
roots to deliver a menu of accomplished dishes, firmly
focusing on the freshness of Bentley's fish, meat and
game, and allowing the main ingredients to shine
through. If it seems rude not to try the oysters, they are
available by the half-dozen, nine or dozen, or the boat
can be pushed out for a shellfish platter, which adds a
dressed crab, half a lobster and langoustines to a
selection of the bivalves. Tartare of mackerel is flavoured
with soy and mirin among starters, or there is a pot of
wild Cornish mussels. Main course fish dishes are
presented in a straightforward manner and there is a
good range of meat dishes such as Elwy Valley lamb with
lettuce, mint and peas. Black-clad staff provide
professional service.

Chef Brendan Fyldes **Owner** Richard Corrigan
Times 12/11.30 **Prices** Food prices not confirmed for
2009. Please telephone for details. **Wines** 100 bottles
over £20, 40 bottles under £20, 7 by glass **Notes** Dress
restrictions, Smart casual **Seats** 90, Pr/dining room 14
Children Portions **Parking** 10 yds away

Brian Turner Mayfair

◎ Modern British Plan 2 G1

Back-to-basics British cooking in upmarket hotel

☎ 020 7596 3444
Millennium Hotel, 44 Grosvenor Square, Mayfair W1K 2HN
e-mail: annie.mckale@mill-cop.com
web: www.brianturneronline.co.uk/mayfair.asp
dir: Nearest station: Bond Street, Green Park Close to Oxford St, Bond St and Park Ln

In contrast to the other smart eateries in this swanky Mayfair hotel, Brian Turner's split-level restaurant - which makes the most of the views across Grosvenor Square - boasts understated retro-chic, decked out in contemporary shades and natural materials. Famed for his interest in traditional British comfort food, cooking is based on simple, wholesome and satisfying British classics, yet dishes are given a light and modern touch. Think spit-roast duck on butternut purée with crisp potato, broad beans and bacon, or Finnebrogue venison loin with potato and parsnip terrine, while a soft-centred chocolate pudding with Jaffa Cake ice cream might catch the eye at dessert.
As we went to press we understand Brian Turner was leaving this restaurant.

Times 12.30-2.30/6.30-10.30, Closed BHs, Closed Sun, Closed L Sat

Butler's

◎ Traditional British 🖳 Plan 4 H6

Traditional dining in elegant Mayfair retreat

☎ 020 7491 2622
Chesterfield Mayfair Hotel, 35 Charles St, Mayfair W1J 5EB
e-mail: fandbch@rchmail.com
dir: Nearest station: Green Park From N side exit tube station turn left and then first left into Berkeley St. Continue down to Berkeley Sq and then left heading towards Charles St

Step through the door of this exclusive hotel and you'll find a luxurious Georgian interior appropriate to its prestigious Mayfair address. A clubby feel pervades the public spaces thanks to high quality antiques, leather chairs, and heavy fabrics, and the elegance continues into Butler's restaurant, a sumptuous room with a strong red and brown décor and a subtle African theme. Dine here, or in the light and airy Conservatory, where a

traditional British menu offers a good range of straightforward dishes based on high-quality ingredients. Kick things off with tea-smoked Barbary duck with caramelised mandarins, before tucking into the likes of chicken pie served in a copper pot, or Casterbridge rib-eye steak with garlic mushrooms, roasted tomatoes and béarnaise sauce.

Times 12.30-2.30/5.30-10.30

Camerino

◎ Modern Italian 🖳 Plan 3 B3

Friendly Italian restaurant stamped with originality

☎ 020 7637 9900
16 Percy St W1T 1DT
e-mail: info@camerinorestaurant.com
dir: Nearest station: Tottenham Court Rd, Goodge St Please telephone for directions

Camerino means 'theatre changing room' and this smart restaurant off Tottenham Court Road certainly has a theatrical feel to it with its striking fuschia-coloured wall drapes painted white with black swirls and patterns. There's a warm Italian welcome and you can eat modestly from the set menus or pre-theatre choice, or more extravagantly from the carte - the market-fresh produce is the same, and so is the expert handling from a forward-looking kitchen team. The well-presented dishes look and taste good. Try smoked salmon with rocket and lemon and oil dressing, and mains such as chicken breast filled with black truffle and sautéed spinach. Desserts like lemon cake, sorbets and ice cream are another strength.

Chef Valerio Daros **Owner** Paolo Boschi **Times** 12-3/6-11, Closed 1 wk Xmas, 1st Jan, Etr Day, most BHs, Closed Sun, Closed L Sat **Prices** Fixed L 2 course £18.50-£30, Fixed D 3 course fr £20.50, Service added but optional 12.5%, Groups min 8 service 12.5% **Wines** 95 bottles over £20, 6 bottles under £20, 8 by glass **Notes** Vegetarian available, Dress restrictions, Smart casual preferred, Air con **Seats** 70 **Children** Portions **Parking** Goodge St

Cecconi's

◎◎ Traditional Italian Plan 3 A1

All-day Italian cuisine, swish design and buzzy atmosphere

☎ 020 7434 1500
5a Burlington Gardens W1X 1LE
dir: Nearest station: Piccadilly Circus/Oxford Circus Burlington Gdns between New Bond St and Savile Row

In keeping with its Mayfair location behind the Royal Academy, Cecconi's is a chic, stylish modern affair from the Nick Jones (Soho House) stable and attracts a trendy, moneyed crowd. The Venetian-inspired brasserie comes with a big glass frontage and large bar, white-clothed tables and eye-catching modern seating, while service is suitably slick and Italian. The crowd-pleasing all-day menu means you can come in at any time for a great range of straightforward, clean-cut classic dishes driven by prime ingredients, including cichetti (Italian tapas). The show kicks off at 7am in the week for breakfast, while at weekends there's brunch from 12 until 5 too. Enjoy pot-roast monkfish with porcini and saffron, or perhaps veal Milanese served up in a fashionable see-and-be-seen atmosphere.

Times 12/midnight, Closed Xmas, New Year

China Tang

◎◎ Chinese ⚜ Plan 4 G6

Sophisticated Chinese set in luxurious surroundings

☎ 020 7629 9988
The Dorchester, Park Ln W1A 2HJ
e-mail: reservations@chinatanglondon.co.uk
dir: Nearest station: Hyde Park Corner Please telephone for directions

Lavish, opulent and stunning are just a few words to describe this glittering, ultra-deluxe Chinese, situated in the basement of The Dorchester, where no expense has been spared. With a swish cocktail bar and spacious dining room, the décor is an eclectic mix of art deco and 1960s Hong Kong - a sumptuous take on the style of colonial Shanghai. Think mirrored pillars, stunning glass-fronted fish-themed artworks, tables with marble-insert tops laid with heavy silver chopsticks, hand-carved chairs and deep banquette seating - it's unashamedly decadent with prices to match. The classic Cantonese cooking, utilising top-notch produce, offers dim sum and carte menus that come dotted with luxuries. Take China Tang braised prawns, stir-fried lobster in black bean sauce or braised beef in oyster sauce, and classic Peking duck.

Chef Ringo Chow **Owner** David Tang **Times** 11am/midnight, Closed 25 Dec **Prices** Fixed L 2 course £15, Starter £5-£22, Main £15-£42, Dessert £8-£50, Service added but optional 12.5% **Wines** 512 bottles over £20, 5 bottles under £20, 12 by glass **Notes** Sunday L, Vegetarian available, Dress restrictions, Smart casual, Air con **Seats** 120, Pr/dining room 80 **Children** Portions

LONDON W1 *Continued*

Cipriani

ⓜⓜ Italian   Plan 2 H2

A dazzling piece of Venice in Mayfair

☎ 020 7399 0500
25 Davies St W1E 3DE
dir: Nearest station: Bond Street Please telephone for directions

Arrigo Cipriani's first venture outside Venice - the people behind Harry's Bar - is the haunt of the fashionable, rich and famous and comes ideally located just off Berkeley Square. The modern glass-fronted exterior leads to a large, stylish dining room, where impeccable art deco style meets beautiful Murano chandeliers, and white-jacketed staff offer slick, attentive service. Low, leather-upholstered seating and magnolia tablecloths provide added comfort, while the atmosphere fairly buzzes in line with its see-and-be-seen status. Classic, accurate, straightforward Italian cooking - with lots of Cipriani touches, authentic prime quality ingredients and unfussy presentation - hits the mark in dishes such as veal ravioli alla Piemontese, or swordfish with cherry tomatoes and black olives, and do save room for the dessert selection of cakes.

Times 12-3/6-11.45, Closed 25 Dec

Cocoon

ⓜ Pan-Asian 🖳   Plan 3 B1

Happening Pan-Asian restaurant and bar

☎ 020 7494 7600
65 Regents St W1B 4EA
e-mail: reservations@cocoon-restaurants.com
dir: Nearest station: Piccadilly Circus 1 min walk from Piccadilly Circus

Overlooking Regent Street, Cocoon has a highly fashionable, trendy, nightclub vibe that proves unreservedly popular, particularly in the evenings. The eye-catching, curvaceous minimalism of the long first-floor room makes quite an impact, with its liberal use of retro-like orange and green, contemporary lighting, centrepiece circular bar and loud music. Seating is either funky swivelling bucket chairs or semi-circular banquettes in green leather, while round glass tables encase colourful rose petals. Dine at the sushi bar or choose from a crowd-pleasing, fashionable Pan-Asian menu, with the likes of dim sum, tempura and sashimi all finding their place alongside mains like wasabi lamb with grilled asparagus. Clean-cut, creatively presented dishes come driven by prime ingredients and flavour, and are ideal for plate sharing.

Chef Azman Said, Joan Ming Pang **Owner** Matt Hermer, Paul Deeming, Ignite Group **Times** 12-3/5.30-mdnt, Closed 25-26 Dec, 1 Jan, Closed Sat **Wines** 100% bottles over £20, 14 by glass **Notes** Pre-theatre Bento Box offer £20, Vegetarian available, Dress restrictions, Smart casual, Air con **Seats** 180, Pr/dining room 14 **Parking** NCP Brewer St

The Cumberland - Rhodes Brasserie

ⓜ Modern British   Plan 2 F2

Exciting concept in Marble Arch

☎ 0870 333 9280
Great Cumberland Place W1A 4RF
e-mail: enquiries@thecumberland.co.uk
dir: Telephone for directions

A genuinely exciting dining venture within the landmark Cumberland Hotel in a prime location at Marble Arch. The high-ceilinged restaurant is a cool, elegant dining space, with unclothed wood tables, crimson upholstered chairs and banquette seating, and provides an impressive backdrop for some simply and well prepared modern dishes, influenced with Gary's distinctly British approach. The menu offers crowd-pleasing classics like bread-and-butter pudding alongside more contemporary dishes. Enjoy a pre-prandial drink in the smart, new and trendy Carbon bar.

Times 12-2.30/6-10.15

Dehesa

ⓜ Spanish, Italian   Plan 3 A2

Walk-in tapas restaurant near Carnaby Street

☎ 020 7494 4170
25 Ganton St W1F 9BP
e-mail: info@dehesa.co.uk

This popular walk-in tapas restaurant is tucked away a short walk from Carnaby Street. With its sleek black awnings, copper-fronted bar, high bench tables and tall, leather-cushioned stools it's reminiscent of a New York diner, and also has a canopied seating area outside. The food is a successful mix of Spanish tapas and Italian charcuterie, with rustic, unfussy food relying on freshness and flavour rather than fussy presentation. Try confit Gloucestershire Old Spot pork belly with rosemary-scented cannellini beans, or salmon with castelluccio lentils, peppers and black olives. No bookings are taken, so arrive early to avoid disappointment, especially in the evenings. Same owners as Salt Yard, see entry.

Times 12/11 **Prices** Food prices not confirmed for 2009. Please telephone for details.

Embassy London

ⓜⓜ Modern European 🖳   Plan 3 A1

Modern, sophisticated Mayfair restaurant and club

☎ 020 7851 0956
29 Old Burlington St W1S 3AN
e-mail: embassy@embassylondon.com
dir: Nearest station: Green Park, Piccadilly Circus Just off Burlington Gardens, running between Bond and Regent St

Set behind a modern glass frontage in the heart of the West End, this Mayfair restaurant is as stylish and sophisticated as its address. The ground-floor dining room is a smart, contemporary affair, sandwiched between a large, less formal bar area along the back and floor-to-ceiling windows and a pavement-style alfresco terrace up front. Soothing creams and browns, mirrored walls, linen-clad tables and contemporary white leather chairs cut an understated, upmarket, romantic edge. Attentive black-clad staff and enticing, skilful modern European cooking hit a high note, too. So expect clear, clean-cut flavours and neat presentation, balanced combinations and tip-top produce to deliver a class act; think monkfish tail served with piquillo peppers and blushed tomatoes, and perhaps an apricot soufflé and walnut ice cream finish. Dine before descending to the basement nightclub in the evening, while lunch is an altogether quieter affair.

Chef Garry Hollihead **Owner** Mark Fuller & Garry Hollihead **Times** 12-3/6-11.30, Closed 25-26 Dec, 1 Jan, Good Fri, Closed Sun-Mon, Closed L Sat **Prices** Fixed L course £29.50, Fixed D 3 course £39.50, Starter £6-£14, Main £12-£24, Dessert £7-£9, Service added but optional 12.5%, Groups min 10 service 15% **Wines** 63 bottles over £20, 2 bottles under £20, 7 by glass **Notes** Vegetarian available, Dress restrictions, Smart casual, no trainers, smart jeans only, Air con **Seats** 120 **Parking** NCP opposite restaurant

L'Escargot - The Ground Floor Restaurant

ⓜⓜ French 🖳 ⚜NOTABLE WINE LIST   Plan 3 C2

Soho institution combining stunning artwork with classic French cuisine

☎ 020 7439 7474
48 Greek St W1D 4EF
e-mail: sales@whitestarline.org.uk
web: www.lescargotrestaurant.co.uk
dir: Nearest station: Tottenham Court Rd, Leicester Square Telephone for directions

Once a private residence to the Duke of Portland, the art collection on the walls of this Soho grandee is worth a visit in its own right, with Warhol, Hockney and Matisse all represented. The accomplished French cuisine more than lives up to the artwork and classic bistro fare is the order of the day, whisked up from quality seasonal produce and delivered to the table by an obliging serving team who handle the crowds with aplomb. Start with ballotine of guinea fowl and foie gras with pickled celeriac and brioche, and then plump for braised shoulder of Elwy Valley lamb, pommes boulangère and sautéed curly kale, or seared diver-caught scallops with tarragon and tomato risotto. There's a full carte at lunch and dinner, and a good-value menu du jour for lunch and pre-theatre dinner.

L'Escargot – The Ground Floor

Chef Michael Awoyemi **Owner** Jimmy Lahoud
Times 12-2.30/6-11.30, Closed 25-26 Dec, 1 Jan, Closed Sun, Closed L Sat **Prices** Fixed L 2 course fr £15, Fixed D 3 course fr £18, Starter £8.50, Main £12.95-£14.95, Dessert £6.95, Service added but optional 12.5%, Groups service 15% **Wines** 281 bottles over £20, 6 bottles under

£20, 8 by glass **Notes** Pre-theatre menu available, Vegetarian available, Air con **Seats** 70, Pr/dining room 60 **Children** Portions **Parking** NCP Chinatown, on street parking

L'Escargot - The Picasso Room

@@@ – *see below*

Fino

@@ Spanish 📖 🍷NOTABLE WINE LIST   Plan 3 B3

Fashionable tapas with an authentic range and good service

☎ 020 7813 8010
33 Charlotte St W1T 1RR
e-mail: info@finorestaurant.com
dir: Nearest station: Goodge St/Tottenham Court Rd Entrance on Rathbone St

An upmarket and lively Spanish restaurant hidden away in a surprisingly bright and airy basement off chic Charlotte Street. High ceilings, pale wood floors, red leather chairs and a contemporary mezzanine bar set the stylish scene for sampling some skilfully cooked tapas. Great for grazing and groups' dining from a daily menu that lists both classic and contemporary offerings, and watch them being prepared in the open-to-view kitchen. Expect robust, gutsy dishes and flavours, such as clams with sherry and ham, chickpeas, chorizo and spinach, or

tuna with sun-dried tomatoes. Extremely helpful, well-drilled service.

Chef Jean Philippe Patruno **Owner** Sam & Eddie Hart **Times** 12-2.30/6-10.30, Closed Xmas & BH, Closed Sun, Closed L Sat **Prices** Starter £4-£12, Main £8-£24, Dessert £5-£7, Service added but optional 12.5% **Wines** 118 bottles over £20, 7 bottles under £20, 9 by glass **Notes** Vegetarian available, Air con **Seats** 90 **Children** Portions

Four Seasons Hotel London

Modern European, Asian   Plan 4 G5

Relaxed, contemporary dining with views of Hyde Park and Park Lane

☎ 020 7499 0888
Hamilton Place, Park Ln W1A 1AZ
e-mail: fsh.london@fourseasons.com
dir: Nearest station: Green Park/Hyde Park Corner Hamilton Place, just off Hyde Park Corner end of Park Lane

Sophisticated dining just a stone's throw from Hyde Park is provided at the well-known Lanes Restaurant at the Four Seasons Hotel. The dining room has a lovely dark, clubby feel, all understated luxury (stained glass, wood panelling and marble), and service is seamless yet unpretentious with obvious attention to detail. The cosmopolitan menu has some Asian influences, with a

Continued

L'Escargot - The Picasso Room

LONDON W1   Plan 3 C2

Modern French 📖 🍷NOTABLE WINE LIST

Accomplished French cuisine in an intimate dining room

☎ 020 7439 7474
48 Greek St W1D 4EF
e-mail: sales@whitestarline.org.uk
dir: Nearest station: Tottenham Court Rd, Leicester Square Telephone for directions

This elegant dining room above the famous Ground Floor restaurant is dedicated to Picasso and boasts a collection of original ceramics (plates, vases and jugs) by the artist as well as a number of prints. Comfortable leather seating and quality table settings are provided, with service both formal and discreet. Starters featuring snails, frogs' legs and smoked foie gras set the tone for a

predominantly classic French dining experience, but if that doesn't appeal you might kick off with seared loin of yellowfin tuna with tropical grapefruit, pomegranate and coriander. Mains are simply and skilfully prepared and showcase lots of top British produce and might include fillet of John Dory with garlic purée, lasagne of chanterelles and celery and truffle velouté, or a perfectly timed assiette of rabbit - roasted loin, braised leg and confit shoulder with crisp belly and livers. Desserts stick to the Gallic theme with the likes of nougat and vanilla parfait with nut clusters and almond custard. An extensive wine list, dominated by the main French regions, echoes the quality of the food.

Chef Toby Stuart **Owner** Jimmy Lahoud
Times 12-2.15/7-11, Closed 2 wks from 24 Dec (excluding New Year), Aug, Closed Sun-Mon, Closed L Sat **Prices** Fixed L 2 course fr £20, Fixed D 3 course £42, Service added but optional 15% **Wines** 281 bottles over £20, 6 bottles under £20, 8 by glass **Notes** Tasting menu available, Vegetarian available, Dress restrictions, Smart casual, Air con **Seats** 30 **Children** Min 8 yrs **Parking** NCP or street parking

LONDON W1 *Continued*

starter of pan-fried crab cake with cucumber salad, teriyaki and tobikko, and a main course of grilled tandoori chicken satay with minted sticky rice, alongside classics like Dover sole with chive sauce, and roast beef with Yorkshire pudding.

Chef Bernhard Mayer **Owner** Four Seasons Hotels & Resorts **Times** 12-3/6-11 **Prices** Food prices not confirmed for 2009. Please telephone for details. **Wines** 14 by glass **Notes** Fixed L 3 courses, Civ Wed 300, Air con **Seats** 90, Pr/dining room 300 **Children** Portions, Menu **Parking** 50

Galvin at Windows

◎◎ Modern French 🖥   Plan 4 G5

Exciting restaurant in the heart of Mayfair with magnificent views

☎ 020 7208 4021
London Hilton on Park Ln, 22 Park Ln W1K 1BE
e-mail: reservations@galvinatwindows.com
dir: Nearest station: Green Park, Hyde Park Corner On Park Lane, opposite Hyde Park

Perched on the 28th-floor of the London Hilton on Park Lane, this destination restaurant boasts unrivalled 360-degree views over the capital's skyline. Chef-patron Chris Galvin (see also Galvin Bistrot de Luxe) oversees André Garrett (ex-Orrery) in the kitchens of this slick modern French affair. It's glamorous, swish and contemporary, with leather seating, crisp linen and an eye-catching golden-ribbon feature suspended from the ceiling, while the raised central area allows all a view. The spacious bar enjoys the panorama, too, while the confident, skilful modern French approach is driven by tip-top seasonal ingredients and clean-cut flavours and presentation; take a fillet of Speyside beef Rossini with truffle pomme purée and mushroom and caramelised pear tarte Tatin with Calvados crème fraiche and caramel sauce.

Chef Chris Galvin/André Garrett **Owner** Hilton International **Times** 12-2.30/7-11, Closed L Sat, Closed D Sun **Wines** 200 bottles over £20, 1 bottles under £20, 14 by glass **Notes** D 6 courses £150 with wine, Sunday L, Vegetarian available, Dress restrictions, Smart casual, Air con **Seats** 108, Pr/dining room 24 **Parking** NCP

Galvin Bistrot de Luxe

◎◎ French   Plan 2 G3

Traditional, seasonal French cuisine at a classy bistro

☎ 020 7935 4007
66 Baker St W1U 7DJ
e-mail: info@galvinuk.com
dir: Nearest station: Baker Street Please telephone for directions

Bistro deluxe is the perfect name for this place as it excels in serving French classics in a stylish environment. The brothers Galvin worked in some of London's top kitchens before going it alone in order to create this classy bistro with a Parisian feel. Mahogany panelled walls, slate floors, black leather banquettes and crisp white linen set the tone, while fans whirl overhead, mirrors adorn the walls, and tantalizing glimpses are offered of the kitchen. Fittingly, the highly accomplished cooking is unmistakeably Gallic, with great ingredients and superb flavours at value-for-money prices. Pressed Pyrenees lamb with black olives, anchovies and anchoiade dressing is a typical starter, while mains are rooted in traditional cuisine: daube of beef with bourguignon garnish and pommes mousseline, for example, with blueberry soufflé and vanilla ice cream to finish. The newly-opened Le Bar downstairs is an ideal way to enjoy pre-meal drinks.

Galvin Bistrot de Luxe

Chef Chris & Jeff Galvin, Sian Rees **Owner** Chris & Jeff Galvin **Times** 12-2.30/6-11, Closed 25-26 Dec, 1 Jan, Closed D 24 Dec **Prices** Fixed L course £15.50, Fixed D 3 course £17.50, Starter £6-£14.50, Main £10.50-£17,

---

Le Gavroche Restaurant

❀❀❀

LONDON W1   **Plan 2 G1**

French 🖥

Mayfair's bastion of French tradition

☎ 020 7408 0881 & 7499 1826
43 Upper Brook St W1K 7QR
e-mail: bookings@le-gavroche.com
dir: Nearest station: Marble Arch From Park Lane into Upper Brook St, restaurant on right

The list of chefs who have passed through the kitchen since the restaurant opened in 1967 is a who's-who of talent, and the legacy of the Roux brothers' is the impact that many have gone on to make in UK restaurants. Le Gavroche itself has remained a bastion of a certain kind of French classical cooking, one of luxury, refinement and quality. It matters not that this is a basement restaurant - somehow that adds to the sense of exclusivity. The bar and dining room are elegant and comfortable in a traditional kind of way, the tables set to the nearest degree with crystal and silver, and the service, headed by Silvano Giraldin, is impeccably formal and almost telepathic - they seem to know what you want before you do. The cooking of Michel Roux Jnr, who took over way back in 1991, is true to the values of yesteryear but is not stuck in the past. The bilingual menu still has old favourites such as soufflé Suissesse, but a lighter touch can be seen in roasted fillets of John Dory in a light broth with fennel, mussels and garlic croûton. There is a Menu Exceptionnel with matching wines or a carte, where artichoke filled with foie gras, truffles and chicken mousse precedes stuffed pig's trotter with roasted vegetable salad, fried celery and parsley leaf. Finish with hot passionfruit soufflé with white chocolate ice cream.

Chef Michel Roux Jnr **Times** 12-2/6.30-11, Closed Xmas, New Year, BHs, Closed Sun, Closed L Sat

Dessert £5-£6.50, Service added but optional 12.5%
Wines 121 bottles over £20, 10 bottles under £20, 16 by
glass **Notes** Sunday L, Vegetarian available, Air con
Seats 95, Pr/dining room 22 **Children** Portions
Parking On street & NCP

Le Gavroche Restaurant

◉◉◉ – *see opposite*

Gordon Ramsay at Claridge's

◉◉◉ – *see below*

The Greenhouse

◉◉◉◉ – *see page 292*

The Grill (Dorchester Hotel)

◉◉◉ – *see page 293*

Hakkasan

◉◉◉ – *see page 294*

Hibiscus

◉◉◉ – *see page 295*

Kai Mayfair

◉ Chinese 🖥   Plan 4 G6

Luxurious venue for authentic Chinese cooking

☎ 020 7493 8988
65 South Audley St W1K 2QU
e-mail: kai@kaimayfair.co.uk
dir: Nearest station: Marble Arch Please telephone for
directions, or see website

A setting of comfortable opulence is de rigueur at this
smart, sophisticated and contemporary two-tier Chinese
in exclusive Mayfair. Rich reds and muted golds and
silvers lead the way, backed by glass pillars, granite
flooring and modern lighting, while banquette seating,
high-backed chairs and white linen extend the luxury
oriental accent. Service is predictably professional, while
the kitchen offers bags of choice and top-notch
ingredients in classy renditions of regional favourites and

more innovative interpretations and specialities. Creative
dish titles might include 'The Drunken Phoenix on the
Scented Tree' (roast whole chicken marinated with a
light, fragrant infusion of cinnamon bark and Chinese
wine), while tea comes with chocolates theatrically
steaming above dry ice.

Chef Alex Chow **Owner** Bernard Yeoh
Times 12-2.15/6.30-11, Closed 25-26 Dec, New Year
Prices Fixed L 2 course £25-£100, Fixed D 3 course
£40-£100, Starter £11-£21, Main £12-£108, Dessert
£7-£10, Service added but optional 12.5% **Wines** 115
bottles over £20, 8 by glass **Notes** Sunday L, Vegetarian
available, Air con **Seats** 110, Pr/dining room 12
Parking Directly outside

See advert on page 296

The Landau

◉◉◉ – *see page 295*

Gordon Ramsay at Claridge's

LONDON W1   Plan 2 H2

European **V** 🍷

**Elegant dining and gastronomic flair in stunning art
deco surroundings**

☎ 020 7499 0099
Brook St W1K 4HR
e-mail: claridges@gordonramsay.com
dir: Nearest station: Bond Street At the corner of Brook &
Davies St

Once renowned as the resort of kings and princes,
Claridge's today continues to set the standards by which
other hotels are judged, while its marriage with Gordon
Ramsay has elevated it to one of London's most popular
dining venues. The restaurant defines glamour and
exudes 1930s sophistication, from its dramatic three-
tiered light shades to its delicate etched-glass panels.

The elegant, high-ceilinged room - restored to its lavish
former art deco glory by designer and architect Thierry
Despont - is all very grand. Service is expectedly slick and
professional and tables elegantly appointed, while there's
an intimate bar area, and, for the ultimate experience, a
chef's table in the heart of the kitchen. Chef Mark
Sargeant's highly accomplished, modern haute-European
cuisine focuses around top class seasonal ingredients,
the fixed-price repertoire of lunch, carte and six-course
tasting option dotted with luxury, the cooking fitting
perfectly under the Ramsay stable umbrella. There's an
intelligent simplicity and integrity that allows main
ingredients to shine in clean-flavoured dishes; perhaps
braised Pacific halibut served with roasted scallop,
caramelised onions and kale, crispy bacon and civet
sauce, and maybe a rum-and-raisin chocolate fondant
with feuillantine and milk ice cream to close. Save room
for all the extra touches (tasters, petits fours), while a
galaxy of stars populate the serious wine list.

Chef Mark Sargeant **Owner** Gordon Ramsay Holdings Ltd
Times 12-2.45/5.45-11 **Wines** 800 bottles over £20, 3
bottles under £20, 10 by glass **Notes** ALC 3 courses,
Prestige menu 6 courses £75, Sunday L, Vegetarian
menu, Dress restrictions, Smart, jacket preferred, no
jeans/trainers, Air con **Seats** 100, Pr/dining room 60
Children Portions **Parking** On street

The Greenhouse

LONDON W1   Plan 4 H6

Modern European V NOTABLE WINE LIST

Fine dining at a discreet Mayfair address

☎ 020 7499 3331
27a Hay's Mews W1J 5NY
e-mail: reservations@
greenhouserestaurant.co.uk
dir: Nearest station: Green Park, Hyde Park, Bond St Behind Dorchester Hotel just off Hill St

The approach via a delightful urban garden with decking and potted plants sets the tone for this eminently civilised and sophisticated Mayfair mews restaurant. Given both the name of the establishment and the garden it shouldn't be too much of a surprise to find the décor alludes to things botanical. But this is no theme park. The recently refurbished chic dining room exudes serenity with neutral colours and the use of natural textures extending to a feature wall artfully arranged with twigs and branches. Leather chairs and banquettes are in varying tones of green and a glass wall etched with vines separates off a private dining area. Tables are expensively laid and the service is formal without being aloof. Chef Antonin Bonnet's (formerly of Morton's, London) menus fizz with ideas and deliver sophisticated and intelligent modern European food with creative

interpretations of French and Mediterranean classics, all based around the highest quality produce from the markets. Duck foie gras terrine with pistachio vinaigrette, cocoa jelly and a warm brioche is technically impressive and superb to eat. Main-courses like Scottish lobster with roasted artichokes, green cardamom and fromage blanc gnocchi, or milk-fed veal rump with bitter praline, parsnip Chantilly and fresh morels are as equally refined. Carré Dubuffet with chocolate biscuit and pralinée makes a fitting finale. Meals include the full range of extras, including outstanding breads (fig and hazelnut among them), canapés and petits fours, plus the team of excellent sommeliers is around to help with the monumental wine list.

Chef Antonin Bonnet **Owner** Marlon Abela Restaurant Corporation
Times 12-2.30/6.45-11, Closed 23 Dec-5 Jan, Etr, Closed Sun, Closed L Sat
Wines 3200 bottles over £20, 19 bottles under £20, 27 by glass **Notes** Tasting menu £75 Vegetarian menu £65, Vegetarian menu, Air con **Seats** 65, Pr/dining room 10 **Children** Portions
Parking NCP, Meter Parking

The Grill (Dorchester Hotel)

LONDON W1 Plan 4 G6

Modern British 🖳 V

Refined and ambitious food in opulent surroundings

☎ 020 7629 8888
The Dorchester, 53 Park Ln W1K 1QA
e-mail: reservations@thedorchester.com
dir: Nearest station: Hyde Park Corner On Park Ln, overlooking Hyde Park

Arriving at the Dorchester is an event in itself as liveried doormen usher you through the doors into this iconic building. Once inside, a vast flower arrangement confirms that all is as grand and lavish as you might hope. The Grill has a decidedly traditional feel with a Highland theme: large murals of kilted lairds gaze down from burnished gold walls, oversized lampshades and colourful tartan chairs, delivering a striking statement. The formal setting is matched by copious professional and polite staff. Expectation is high and chef Aiden Byrne delivers a menu of flair and imagination right from the off, with amuse-bouche of onion and parmesan soup and foie gras parfait served on a stick. A modern pairing of roast crayfish and ballotine of rabbit is the centre point of an impressive starter, with the leg meat presented in a cannelloni. Main-course pan-fried John Dory is perfectly cooked and comes with braised snails inside little lettuce parcels; lettuce is also introduced as an emulsion and finished with some smoked bacon - a complex and intricate dish. Roasted figs with smoked honey ice cream and almond cake is an equally creative dessert. There is a 7-course tasting menu with the option of a wine selection for five of the courses.

Chef Aiden Byrne **Owner** The Dorchester Collection **Times** 12.30-2.30/6.30-10.30 **Prices** Fixed L 2 course £25, Fixed D 3 course £27.50, Tasting menu £70, Starter £15-£22, Main £19.50-£42, Dessert £10.50-£15.50, Service added but optional 12.5% **Wines** 400 bottles over £20, 2 bottles under £20, 19 by glass **Notes** Tasting menu 7 courses, Sunday L, Vegetarian menu, Dress restrictions, Smart casual, Air con **Seats** 75 **Children** Menu **Parking** 20

Hakkasan

LONDON W1 Plan 3 B3

Modern Chinese NOTABLE WINE LIST

Exotic Chinese dining in central London

☎ 020 7927 7000
No 8 Hanway Place W1T 1HD
e-mail: reservation@hakkasan.com
dir: Nearest station: Tottenham Court Rd From station take exit 2, then 1st left, 1st right, restaurant straight ahead

This incredibly popular restaurant and bar is fashionably tucked away in a back street off Tottenham Court Road. Housed in a dramatic basement at the bottom of an Indian slate stairwell, it's presided over by a doorman and attracts an adoring crowd with its dark, club-like atmosphere. The dazzling modern interior reflects the wealth of Chinese culture, with lots of black lacquer and red calligraphy, and delicate Balinese latticework used to divide up seating areas lit by low-slung spotlights. Add close-set, darkwood-polished tables and leather banquette seating, club-style music, a long bar and attentive, knowledgeable staff and the backdrop's set for some exceptional Chinese cuisine. The lengthy menu is built on Cantonese foundations, with influences from other regions, and includes a dim sum selection (available lunchtime only) as well as a range of 'small eat' snacks, and a handful of specials requiring 24-hour notice, such as braised

supreme dried whole Japanese abalone with morels and sea cucumber, or whole Peking duck with Royal Beluga caviar and baby cucumber. There are old favourites too, often with a twist, and distinguished by first-class ingredients, dazzling technique and plenty of flair. And if all that weren't enough, the cocktail list is great too: an enticing array of tipples that includes Jasmine FonFon, The Long Dragon, and the intriguingly named Green Destiny. Not to be missed.

Chef C Tong Chee Hwee **Owner** Alan Yau **Times** 12-2.45/6-12.30, Closed 24-25 Dec, Closed L 26 Dec, 1 Jan **Prices** Fixed L 3 course £40-£100, Fixed D 3 course £55-£100, Starter £5.50-£18.50, Main £9.50-£58, Dessert £6.50-£13.50, Service added but optional 13% **Wines** 301 bottles over £20, 10 by glass **Notes** Wine flights available, Vegetarian available, Dress restrictions, No jeans, shorts, trainers, caps or vests, Air con **Seats** 225 **Parking** Valet parking (dinner only), NCP

Hibiscus

LONDON W1   Plan 3 A2

French

Innovative French cooking moved from Ludlow to London

☎ 020 7629 2999
29 Maddox St W1S 2PA

Claude and Claire Bosi made a mark in Ludlow with their restaurant of the same name, playing a part in making the town a mecca for foodies over the last decade. They still own a pub in the Herefordshire countryside, but it is their new Mayfair restaurant where Claude is showcasing his considerable talents. It is a smart and civilised space with light-oak panelling, slate, natural colours and immaculately laid tables. This Lyon-born chef has not forgotten his roots and the classical cooking of France is evident in his menus, but this is a chef with a creative mind and bold and exciting ideas. Take pig's head terrine, for example, which is certainly traditional, although here it is caramelised and joined by iced goat's cheese, passion fruit and pickled beetroot in an imaginative starter. Main-course roast Cornish cod is a stunning piece of fish, perfectly cooked, with glazed broccoli, toasted pine nuts and an anchovy jus, while a dessert of champagne rhubarb cheesecake, a subdued Szechuan pepper ice cream and rhubarb compôte shows strong technical skills. Service is charmingly unaffected yet efficient and professional.

Chef Claude Bosi **Times** 12-2.30/6.30-10 **Prices** Food prices not confirmed for 2009. Please telephone for details.

The Landau

LONDON W1   Plan 2 H4

Modern European 🖵 V

Refined and ambitious cooking in a stunningly opulent dining room

☎ 020 7965 0165 & 020 7636 1000
The Langham London, Portland Place W1B 1JA
e-mail: reservations@thelandau.com
dir: Nearest station: Oxford Circus On N end of Regent St, by Oxford Circus

The Langham Hotel, a gloriously imposing Victorian building opposite the BBC in Portland Place, made quite a splash when it opened in 1865 and now, with its newly revamped and refurbished restaurant, The Landau, it looks set to do so again. The renowned designer David Collins has created a chic and gilded interior in the restaurant with panelled walls, three giant brass light fittings and a pale gold, jade green and pastel blue contemporary décor. The equally plush Artesian Bar invokes thoughts of Oscar Wilde and Jules Verne and a visit starts here before diners are walked through the vaulted wine cellar to the dining room. It takes a chef with confidence and ability to complement such a setting and Andrew Turner's menu is suitably refined and ambitious. The seasonally-changing carte is bolstered with daily specials and much is made of the provenance of the produce such as Castle Mey beef from the Prince of Wales' estate. A first course of carpaccio of milk-fed veal, Iberico ham, hazelnuts and a parmesan biscuit is an impressive start, followed by a main-course fillet of Welsh lamb with a confit mini suet pudding alongside some braised shoulder, deeply rich jus and a lemon purée. The complexity continues into desserts such as toffee cheesecake with pineapple and coconut ice cream. Service is as formal as the setting demands.

Chef Andrew Turner **Owner** Langham Hotels International **Times** 12.30-2.30/5.30-11 **Prices** Fixed L 2 course £30-£40, Fixed D 3 course £30-£35, Starter £9.50-£17, Main £19-£30, Dessert £8, Service added but optional 12.5% **Wines** 135 bottles over £20, 20 by glass **Notes** Theatre menu 2-3 courses, Grazing menu 5-8 courses, Sunday L, Vegetarian menu, Dress restrictions, Smart casual, Civ Wed 220, Air con **Seats** 100, Pr/dining room 16 **Children** Portions, Menu **Parking** On street & NCP

Kai Mayfair
foods of china

Best Chinese Restaurant in London
Zagat Guide 2005, 2004 & 2003
Harden's London Restaurant Guide 2002

Best Oriental Restaurant in Britain
Carlsberg Best in Britain Awards 2005 & 2007

Best Kitchen Finalist
Tatler Magazine Restaurant Awards 2006

Best Chinese Chef
Westminster Chinese Masterchef Awards 2005

65 South Audley Street, London WIK 2QU   Tel:020 74938988   www.kaimayfair.co.uk

LONDON W1 *Continued*

Latium

◉◉ Italian   Plan 3 B3

Fresh, authentic Italian cooking with service to match

☎ 020 7323 9123
21 Berners St W1T 3LP
e-mail: info@latiumrestaurant.com
dir: Nearest station: Goodge St & Oxford Circus Please
telephone for directions

Given the Latin name for the chef-patron's home town
(Latina), this smart, intimate restaurant (one of the
Capital's best kept secrets) provides such authentic
tastes and atmosphere, you'll feel as though you are in
Italy. The restaurant is bright and contemporary with
modern art on the walls. Maurizio Morelli's unique
passion for Italian cuisine has created a great seasonal
menu with a strong commitment to sourcing fine Italian
produce and delivering authentic flavours with flair and
panache. Ravioli is a particular speciality, in dishes like
selection of fish ravioli with sea bass bottarga. Try
poached guinea fowl with winterblack truffle, and
pastiera Napoletana with orange sauce to finish.

Chef Maurizio Morelli **Owner** Maurizio Morelli, Claudio
Pulze **Times** 12-3/6-10.30, Closed BHs, Closed Sun,
Closed L Sat **Prices** Fixed L 2 course £15.50, Fixed D 3
course £28.50, Service added but optional 12.5%
Wines 97 bottles over £20, 5 bottles under £20, 7 by
glass **Notes** Air con **Seats** 50 **Children** Portions

Levant

◉ Lebanese, Middle Eastern   Plan 2 G3

**Vivid colours, scents and flavours in an atmospheric
basement restaurant**

☎ 020 7224 1111
Jason Court, 76 Wigmore St W1H 9DQ
e-mail: info@levant.co.uk
dir: Nearest station: Bond Street From Bond St station,
walk through St Christopher's Place, reach Wigmore St,
restaurant across road

Leave the sobriety of Wigmore Street behind when you
descend the stone stairs of Levant into a scene from the
Arabian Nights. Lanterns light the way into an exotic
basement where colours are rich, fabrics sumptuous, and
the atmosphere seductive and beguiling. A long
banquette and separate tables dominate the centre of
the room, while cosy private areas offer floor cushions for
lounging over the Lebanese cooking. The Middle Eastern
spices bring an authentic flavour to hot and cold mezzes,
and special treats like slow-roasted whole shoulder of
lamb served with a nut pilaf.

Times 12/midnight, Closed 25-26 Dec

Lindsay House

◉◉◉ – *see below*

Locanda Locatelli

◉◉◉◉ – *see page 298*

Maze

◉◉◉◉ – *see page 299*

Maze Grill

◉◉ Grill, British 🖵   Plan 2 G2

Unique, high-quality modern grill of class

☎ 020 7495 2211
London Marriott, 10-13 Grosvenor Square W1K 6JP

Sitting alongside its sister restaurant Maze in the
Marriott Grosvenor Square, this is another Jason Atherton
and Gordon Ramsay stable combo, though it's sibling in
name and chef-patron only, as this venture comes
modelled on the New York grill-style restaurants. A smart,
modern, white-linen-free zone, the Grill features a
butcher's block table - made from a single piece of
English oak - that overlooks the kitchen action and acts
as chef's table seating 12. The quality of raw ingredients
is outstanding and the cooking (on coals then under a
special 'unique-to-Europe' grill) is spot on. Expect to
choose from the likes of Hereford grass-fed 25-day-aged
or perhaps Creekstone prime U.S.D.A corn-fed 35-day-
aged beef steaks, while knowledgeable staff bring the
raw cuts to the table when ordering to explain the
varieties.

Times 12-2.30/5.45-10 **Prices** Food prices not confirmed
for 2009. Please telephone for details.

Lindsay House Restaurant

LONDON W1   Plan 3 C2

Modern British, European 🖵 V

**Vibrant flavours and top-notch ingredients in a Soho
townhouse**

☎ 020 7439 0450
21 Romilly St W1D 5AF
e-mail: richardcorrigan@lindsayhouse.co.uk
dir: Nearest station: Leicester Square Just off Shaftesbury
Avenue, off Dean Street

A traditional 18th-century townhouse set over four floors is
the elegant setting for this popular Soho restaurant, its
discreet doorbell rung by a loyal band of regulars and
foodies year after year. The warren of dining rooms with
open fires and comfortable, stylish furnishings and décor
make this a favourite for those looking for discreet yet
homely dining. On the ground and first floors, elegant

traditional-style dining rooms are cosy and inviting, while
on the second floor the Chef's Library provides an intimate
setting for private parties. Diners can choose from an array
of menus, including a seasonal lunchtime market menu,
garden (vegetarian), tasting option and carte to suit the
occasion, waistband or wallet. Richard Corrigan's cooking
style relies on marrying top quality, quintessentially British
and Irish ingredients with French cooking techniques to
create robust, simple flavours. It's hard to choose from all
the delights, but clever combinations and excellent
presentation might deliver a starter of white gazpacho with
organic yogurt, Muscat grapes and warm potted crab, or a
main course of fillet of hake in almond milk with
langoustine ravioli and spiced carrot, while for dessert a
dreamy chocolate mousse filled with orange parfait and
served with rich dark chocolate sauce really hits the spot.
Breads, amuse-bouche and petits fours are all top notch.

Chef Richard Corrigan **Owner** Richard Corrigan
Times 12-2/6-11, Closed Xmas, New Year, Closed Sun,
Closed L Sat **Wines** 16 by glass **Notes** Pre-theatre meal

£27, Vegetarian menu, Dress restrictions, Smart casual,
Air con **Seats** 50, Pr/dining room 30 **Parking** NCP

Locanda Locatelli

Italian 🖥 🍷NOTABLE WINE LIST

Inspired Italian cuisine in chic contemporary setting that attracts a celebrity crowd

☎ 020 7935 9088
8 Seymour St W1H 7JZ
e-mail: info@locandalocatelli.com
dir: Nearest station: Marble Arch
Opposite Marylebone police station

From the grissini to the espresso, Giorgio Locatelli's restaurant a couple of blocks behind Selfridges is effortlessly confident. Everything produced by the kitchen suggests a restaurant firing on all cylinders and it is hard to envisage a better Italian restaurant in the United Kingdom. The outside of the building is all straight lines and clean edges, with blinds keeping the privacy of those within. The David Collins' designed décor is smart, slick in places - glass dividers allow a bit of personal space - yet comfortable in a retro sort of way. Cream banquette seating, concave mirrors and modern art on the grained wood walls add a touch of glamour as do the clientele, who head to this part of town for the Northern Italian cooking. The menu is structured in the Italian way, so pasta comes between antipasti and main course, although sticking to three courses is not frowned upon, and the use of top quality produce is evident throughout. Start with broad bean and

ewe's cheese salad or another of pan-fried scallops with saffron vinaigrette before the pasta course, oxtail ravioli, perhaps, or gnocchi with goat's cheese and black truffle. The ideas are based on trusted combinations, the flavours allowed to shine, and the craftsmanship considerable. Next up is the fish or meat course, so roasted turbot with cherry tomatoes and green olives competes with confit rabbit legs with polenta and radicchio trevisano. The kitchen is not so rarefied as to ignore a classic such as tiramisù at dessert, or else there is carnaroli rice and lemon soufflé or a selection of Italian cheeses. The excellent wine list is particularly strong on Tuscany and Piedmont, while service is memorably charming, efficient and passionate.

Chef Giorgio Locatelli **Owner** Plaxy & Giorgio Locatelli **Times** 12-3/7-11, Closed Xmas, BHs **Prices** Food prices not confirmed for 2009. Please telephone for details. **Wines** 2 bottles under £20, 24 by glass **Notes** Sunday L, Vegetarian available, Air con **Seats** 70 **Children** Portions **Parking** NCP adjacent, parking meters

Maze

Modern French, Pacific Rim — NOTABLE WINE LIST

Grazing in elegance at the heart of Mayfair

☎ 020 7107 0000
London Marriott Grosvenor Hotel
10-13 Grosvenor Square W1K 6JP
e-mail: maze@gordonramsay.com
dir: Nearest station: Bond Street Entrance off Grosvenor Sq

Part of the Gordon Ramsay stable, Maze isn't so difficult to find, with entrances from the imposing London Marriott Hotel Grosvenor Square or directly off the square itself. Contemporary and bright, the extensive dining area follows the maze theme, decked out in split levels with the lowest at the centre, surrounded by a glass screen featuring the restaurant's maze motif. Tables are simply laid, while service exudes style and panache, from its professional demeanour to its knowledge. (There is also a chef's table overlooking the main pass.) And, though the name on the menus maybe Gordon Ramsay, the cutting-edge cooking (highly accomplished, confident and clever) is from talented executive chef Jason Atherton's - formerly of Ramsay's Dubai venture, Verre, and a Brit with an amazing pedigree. His cooking delivers a modern French approach with Asian influences, via a fashionable, grazing-style menu featuring an impressive and appealing array of innovative and complex tapas-style dishes that come dressed to thrill and showcase the best seasonal ingredients. There's also a traditional carte, plus a Sunday roast offering. Expect the likes of beef tongue 'n' cheek with casper raisin and ginger carrots, or monkfish with dehydrated black olives, bouillabaisse and fennel pollen, while the 'flights of wines' innovation, offering three glasses based on a country or grape variety, ideally suits the grazing concept. (Maze Grill, see entry — another Atherton-Ramsay combination — across the hotel corridor, opened in 2008, coinciding with the launch of Atherton's first recipe book, 'maze, the cookbook'.)

Chef Jason Atherton **Owner** Gordon Ramsay Maze Ltd
Times 12-2.30/6-10.30 **Wines** 600 bottles over £20, 2 bottles under £20
Notes Fixed L 4 & 6 courses £28.50-£42.50, Vegetarian available, Dress restrictions, Smart casual, no sportswear, Air con **Seats** 110, Pr/dining room 10 **Children** Portions

LONDON W1 *Continued*

Mews of Mayfair

◉◉ Modern ▯ Plan 2 H2

Chic place to see and be seen with cooking to match

☎ 020 7518 9395 & 7518 9388
10-11 Lancashire Court W1S 1EY
e-mail: info@mewsofmayfair.com
dir: Nearest station: Bond Street Between Brook St &
Maddox St. Opposite Dolce & Gabbana

This contemporary restaurant stands in a lovely mews just
off Bond Street close to the exclusive Mayfair shops.
There's a bar and terraced tables on the ground floor, while
upstairs the main restaurant has a more sophisticated
edge with striking black-and-white décor. There has been a
slight change in the kitchen's approach under new chef
Oliver Clark, who has worked with Philip Howard, Gordon
Ramsay and Richard Corrigan. Though the menu is still
dictated by quality seasonal produce, it is now influenced
by both French and British cuisine, delivering dishes such
as ragoût of braised rabbit with morels, tarragon and
mustard dumplings, and braised skate ballotine with
smoked garlic mash, cucumber and white asparagus.

Times 12-3/6-11, Closed 25-26 Dec, New Year, Etr Mon,
Closed D Sun

Mirabelle

◉◉ Traditional French Plan 4 H6

Classic French cuisine with Mayfair glamour

☎ 020 7499 4636
56 Curzon St W1J 8PA
e-mail: sales@whitestarline.org.uk
dir: Nearest station: Green Park Telephone for directions.

Step through the low-key lobby of this Mayfair grandee and
you'll find a glamorous bar and restaurant, complete with
art deco mirrors, bold artworks and a resident pianist. Part
of the Marco Pierre White empire, it lures a well-heeled
crowd with its easy cosmopolitan ambience and classic
French dishes. Expect unfussy, flavourful cooking that
belies the grand surroundings and has an authentic Gallic
feel: sole à la provençale, for example, or braised pig's
trotters with morels, pomme purée and sauce Périgueux.
Desserts might include prune and Armagnac soufflé or
lemon tart, and there's an extensive wine list. Private
dining rooms are available with a separate menu and there
are great-value set lunches. At the time of going to press
we understand a refurbishment was taking place.

Times 12-2.30/6-11.30, Closed 26 Dec & 1 Jan

Mosaico

◉◉ Italian Plan 3 A1

Slick, stylish and modern Mayfair Italian

☎ 020 7409 1011
13 Albermarle St W1S 4HJ
e-mail: mosaico-restaurant.co.uk
dir: Telephone for further details

With its Mayfair location beneath the DKNY store
opposite Brown's Hotel, with The Ritz just round the
corner, this smart Italian restaurant is suitably
sophisticated and well groomed. The big news is the
arrival of a new chef, Francesco Furriello, who has
joined after running One Paston Place in Brighton. The
carte has been reduced in size and showcases the
chef's modern Italian cooking. The format is traditional
enough and Italian regional influences are evident
throughout. Diners sit on red leather banquettes or
stylish chairs, tables are dressed in their best whites
and limestone floors give it a clean, contemporary edge.
Cream walls, prints of Italian scenes and a mirrored
frieze keeps things light, while service is slick, attentive
and Latin. Expect a pasta dish such as lobster ravioli
with courgette and Norcia black truffle. Main-course
oven-baked fillet of beef comes with wilted spinach and
wild mushrooms.

Times 12-2.30/6.30-10.45, Closed Sun, Closed L Sat,
Sun, Xmas, Etr, BHs

Nicole's

◉ Modern Mediterranean Plan 3 A1

Fashionable lunchtime retreat for the chic and well-
heeled

☎ 020 7499 8408
158 New Bond St W1S 2UB
e-mail: nicoles@nicolefarhi.com
dir: Nearest station: Green Park, Bond St Between Hermés
& Asprey

A wide stone staircase leads down to the bright, split-
level restaurant below Nicole Farhi's fashion store on
exclusive Bond Street, so expect a stylish, contemporary
edge to match that designer label. A small upper level
has a steel and glass bar with more informal tables,
while oak floors, brown leather and white linen
distinguish the main dining area a few steps down. The
cooking takes an assured modern approach, based
around simplicity and quality seasonal ingredients.
Typically, start with smoked haddock chowder, follow with
grilled calves' liver with mash, bacon and onions, and
finish with rhubarb tart with ginger ice cream.

Chef Annie Wayte **Owner** Stephen Marks **Times** 12-3.30/,
Closed BHs, Closed Sun, Closed D all week **Prices** Starter
£6-£10.25, Main £19.95-£24, Dessert £7, Service added
but optional 15% **Wines** 4 bottles over £20, 4 bottles
under £20, 16 by glass **Notes** Air con **Seats** 65, Pr/dining
room 80

Nobu

◉◉ Japanese Plan 4 G5

Stylish, minimalist, upmarket Japanese

☎ 020 7447 4747
The Metropolitan, Old Park Ln W1K 1LB
e-mail: london@noburestaurants.com
dir: Nearest station: Hyde Park Corner/Green Park Located
on 1st floor of Metropolitan Hotel

Nobu has managed to remain a 'cool' destination for the
glitterati for over a decade. Nobuyuki Matsuhisa has
subsequently opened two other restaurants in London
(see entry for Nobu Berkeley Street, also in W1, and Ubon
by Nobu, E14), and his style is now much copied. Taking
up the whole of the first floor of the Metropolitan Hotel,
the interior is minimalist, with clean lines accentuated by
stylish neutral colours, stark tiled floors, leather
banquettes and chairs, while huge windows give
fantastic views over Park Lane and Hyde Park. The staff
are upbeat when guiding the uninitiated through the
lengthy, flexible-styled menu, predominantly aimed at
grazing and sharing. The style of Japanese dishes with
the occasional South American twist continues to deliver
dishes like tuna tataki with ponzu - fresh and zingy, sea
urchin tempura in light batter and beef tenderloin tataki.

Chef Mark Edwards **Owner** Nobuyuki Matsuhisa
Times 12-2.15/6-10.15 **Wines** 8 by glass **Notes** Chef
choice Omakase menu L (6 course), D (7 course) £50-£90,
Vegetarian available, Dress restrictions, Smart casual,
Air con **Seats** 160, Pr/dining room 40 **Parking** Car Park
nearby

Nobu Berkeley Street

◉◉ Japanese ▯ Plan 5 A6

Fun modern Japanese restaurant with a serious
approach to food

☎ 020 7290 9222
15 Berkeley St W1J 8DY
e-mail: berkeley@noburestaurants.com
dir: Nearest station: Green Park Telephone for directions

Very much a place to see and be seen, the sister of the
famous Nobu restaurant off Park Lane (see entry), is one
of the West End's most stylish eateries. Downstairs a
spacious bar serves drinks until the early hours, while the
upstairs restaurant is open for dinner only and features a
sushi restaurant with an open kitchen, a wood-burning oven and
a 12-seater hibachi table where guests can cook their
own food with a chef's assistance. The waiters know their
stuff and are happy to guide you through the menu;
alternatively plump for the six-course tasting menu to
really do the place justice. Black cod den miso is a hit, as
is Chinese cabbage steak with matsuhisa dressing.

Chef Mark Edwards **Owner** Nobu Hatsuhisa, Robert de
Niro **Times** 12-2.15/6-1am, Closed 25 & 26 Dec, Closed L
Sat & Sun **Prices** Tasting menu fr £60, Starter £8-£26,
Main £10.50-£32, Dessert £7-£9, Service added but
optional 15% **Wines** 10 by glass **Notes** Tasting menu
called Omakase, Vegetarian available, Air con **Seats** 120
Parking Mayfair NCP

The Only Running Footman

⦿ Modern British 🖥   Plan 4 H6

Mayfair townhouse gastro-pub with fine-dining, chef's table and cookery school

☎ 020 7499 2988
5 Charles St, Mayfair W1J 5DF

Occupying four floors of an elegant former Mayfair townhouse, The Only Running Footman (sister to The House in Islington and The Bull in Highgate) is a contemporary gastro-pub dining concept that pushes all the right buttons. The smart ground-floor pub offers breakfast, coffee and an all-day menu, while the first-floor cranks up the ante with a stylish fine-dining room, complete with leather banquettes, white-clothed tables and apron-clad staff. (On the second floor there's a private dining room, while the top floor has a chef's table and small cookery school). The straightforward modern British cooking fits the bill, driven by quality ingredients and flavour; take Gloucestershire Old Spot slow-roast pork served with apple sauce and marjoram jus, and a Bakewell tart and vanilla ice cream finish.

Times 12-2.3/5.3-10.30

Orrery

See below

Ozer

⦿⦿ Turkish, Middle Eastern 🖥   Plan 3 A3

A bustling Turkish delight just a stone's throw from Oxford Circus

☎ 020 7323 0505
5 Langham Place, Regent St W1B 3DG
e-mail: info@sofra.co.uk
dir: Nearest station: Oxford Circus 2 min walk towards Upper Regent Street.

Ozer's fairly narrow street frontage belies its spacious interior, with a buzzy bar area at the front, stretching back into the large restaurant beyond. The walls are sumptuous red, with floaty white curtains draped along one side, contemporary ceiling lighting, white tablecloths, leather chairs, and friendly, hard-working staff. The atmosphere is electric, but the accomplished, authentic Turkish cuisine is the real star of the show. An array of menu options offers a wide range of traditional dishes. Kick things off with complimentary olives, bread and hummus, then take your pick from an excellent, keenly-priced selection of meze, and move on to some well made kofte chicken (grilled chicken patties), lamb tagine or a Turkish pizza with an ultra-thin flatbread base.

Times Noon/mdnt

Passione

⦿⦿ Italian   Plan 3 B3

Wonderful flavours from an intimate, lively Italian

☎ 020 7636 2833
10 Charlotte St W1T 2LT
dir: Nearest station: Goodge Street 5 min walk from underground station

Its pinkish-terracotta and glass frontage seem somewhat unremarkable for a widely esteemed Italian, though the name on the awning perfectly sums up this small but big-hearted restaurant, epitomising chef-patron Gennaro Contaldo's love affair with great food. Green walls are hung with food photographs, while blond-wood floors and chairs add a modern edge to close-set tables and a lively, informal atmosphere; there's an endearing neighbourhood local vibe here. It's not difficult to see why Gennaro is a Jamie Oliver mentor, his regional Italian cooking driven by fresh, high-quality seasonal produce, herbs and simple, clean-flavoured style. Perhaps try tagliatelle with summer truffle sauce, or wild sea bass served with sauté peas and broad beans and marinated samphire.

Times 12.30-2.15/7-10.15, Closed 1 wk Xmas, BHs, Closed Sun, Closed L Sat

Orrery

Rosettes not confirmed at time of going to press

LONDON W1   **Plan 2 G4**

Modern European 🖥

Stunning food and service in equal measures in prestigious dining venue

☎ 020 7616 8000
55-57 Marylebone High St W1U 5RB
e-mail: oliviere@conran-restaurants.co.uk
dir: Nearest station: Baker St, Regent's Park At north end of Marylebone High St

Perched above the Conran shop, this first-floor restaurant is all cool, clean lines and sophisticated simplicity, with an etched glass screen at the far end depicting the namesake orrery - a mechanical model of the solar system. One of London's most prestigious dining venues, it is set on the High Street in Marylebone village in what was once the site of Henry VIII's hunting lodge. The pedigree of Terence Conran design is unmistakable; contemporary, streamline and typically understated, it comes flooded by light from large arched windows and skylights. Two long rows of tables lined with banquettes and chairs fill the narrow, bright room, where service is as stylish as the surroundings, while there's a small, intimate lounge bar for pre-meal drinks. The cooking style is suitably innovative and creative, intricate, light and contemporary, its roots firmly in the classics. Meticulous presentation, highly accomplished technical skills and top-notch produce pepper the repertoire.
As we went to press we understand there was a change of chef taking place here.

Times 12-2.30/6.30-10.30, Closed 25-26 Dec, New Year, Good Friday, Closed D 24 Dec

LONDON W1 *Continued*

Patterson's

◉◉ Modern European 🖳   Plan 3 A2

Elegant cuisine in a stylish setting

☎ 020 7499 1308
4 Mill St, Mayfair W1S 2AX
e-mail: info@pattersonsrestaurant.co.uk
dir: Nearest station: Oxford Circus Located off Conduit St opposite Savile Row entrance

Tucked away in a tiny Mayfair street at the top end of Savile Row, glass-fronted, family-run Patterson's provides an elegant, popular setting for fine dining, complemented by slick, professional service. The bar area and longish dining room come complete with fish and lobster tanks, herringbone wood flooring, high-backed leather chairs and matching banquettes and colourful artwork. In the kitchen, father-and-son team Raymond and Tom produce dishes that surprise and delight with flavour, presentation and ambition, their modern approach driven by carefully-sourced, prime local and organic produce on a fixed-price repertoire sprinkled with luxury. Take Scottish beef three ways - seared fillet paired with smoked foie gras, oxtail cannelloni with baby spinach, and consommé with bone marrow and button onion petals.

Chef Raymond & Thomas Patterson **Owner** Raymond & Thomas Patterson **Times** 12-3/6-11, Closed 25-26 Dec, 1 Jan, Good Fri & Etr Mon, Closed Sun, Closed L Sat **Prices** Food prices not confirmed for 2009. Please telephone for details. **Wines** 92 bottles over £20, 4 bottles under £20, 9 by glass **Notes** Vegetarian available, Air con **Seats** 70, Pr/dining room 20 **Children** Portions, Menu **Parking** Savile Row

La Petite Maison

◉◉ French, Mediterranean   Plan 2 H2

Refined French cuisine in authentic surroundings

☎ 020 7495 4774
54 Brooks Mews W1K 4EG

This London version of the original Nice restaurant, frequented by the rich and famous, was opened by Arjun Waney, co-owner of the now renowned Japanese restaurants Zuma and Roka (see entries). This La Petite Maison is tucked away behind Claridge's on the site of an earlier restaurant, Teca. It offers a similar style of Niçoise, Mediterranean and Ligurian food to its illustrious

sister. The high-ceilinged restaurant is a diamond-shaped open room with light cream walls, large windows and an open kitchen. Start with your selection from an extensive choice of help-yourself hors d'oeuvres, including artichoke salad, carpaccio of scallops and French beans with foie gras. Main courses, with some up-market price tags, are along the lines of turbot with artichoke, white wine and olive oil, and grilled marinated lamb cutlets with aubergine caviar.

Times 12-2.30/7-10.45, Closed Sun

Pied à Terre

◉◉◉◉ – *see opposite*

The Providores

◉◉ Fusion ⬧NOTABLE WINE LIST   Plan 2 G3

Complex-flavoured fusion food in contemporary surroundings

☎ 020 7935 6175
109 Marylebone High St W1U 4RX
e-mail: anyone@theprovidores.co.uk
dir: Nearest station: Bond St, Baker St, Regent's Park From Bond St station cross Oxford St, down James St, into Thayer St then Marylebone High St

Once a Victorian pub, The Providores - smack at the heart of Marylebone High Street - delivers a buzzy, contemporary, relaxed all-day café, wine/tapas-bar operation downstairs and fine-dining restaurant upstairs. Enjoy breakfast, brunch, coffee and a fascinating menu of tapas-inspired fare below, and an eye-catching choice of highly accomplished fusion food in the dining room proper above. Both menus change frequently according to produce and inspiration, but chef Peter Gordon's New Zealand roots shine through with the use of unfamiliar ingredients (from the global larder) and combinations in innovative, exciting, well-executed and presented dishes. Take line-caught wild sea bass on a som tam green papaya and chilli salad with fried peanuts, crispy shallots and a tapioca shrimp crisp.

Chef Peter Gordon **Owner** P Gordon, M McGrath, J Leeming **Times** 12-2.30/6-10.30, Closed 24 Dec-3 Jan, Etr Mon **Prices** Starter £7.80-£15, Main £18-£25.50, Dessert £9.20, Service added but optional 12.5% **Wines** 89 bottles over £20, 5 bottles under £20, 31 by glass **Notes** Vegetarian available, Air con **Seats** 38 **Children** Portions

Quo Vadis

◉◉ Grill   Plan 3 B2

Soho dining landmark rejuvenated as a classic grill

☎ 020 7437 9585
26-29 Dean St W1D 3LL
e-mail: info@quovadissoho.co.uk
dir: Nearest station: Tottenham Court Road/Leicester Square Please telephone for directions

Sam and Eddie Hart, the duo behind Spanish restaurants Fino and Barrafino (see entries) have bought this iconic Soho Italian - once the home of Karl Marx and more recently part of the Marco Pierre White restaurant portfolio. After restoring the landmark building to its former glory, it launched in May 2008 as a grill restaurant (on the ground floor) and private member's club on the top two floors. A classic grill room, inspired by the all but extinct grills of the great London hotels, its interior is sympathetic to the building's original features - many of which date back to the 1840s - while displaying a selection of contemporary artworks from young British artists. Chef Jean Philippe Patruno (ex Fino) fronts up the kitchen, with dishes driven by well-sourced prime produce and simplicity.

Chef Jean Philippe Patruno **Owner** Sam & Eddie Hart **Times** 12-2.30/5.30-11, Closed 24-25 Dec, 1 Jan, BHs, Closed Sun **Prices** Starter £7-£14, Main £12-£25, Dessert £6-£9, Service added but optional 12.5% **Wines** 80 bottles over £20, 6 bottles under £20 **Notes** Vegetarian available, Air con **Seats** 80, Pr/dining room 25 **Parking** On street or NCP

Rasa Samudra

◉◉ Indian   Plan 3 B3

Bright, friendly and authentic Keralan restaurant

☎ 020 7637 0222
5 Charlotte St W1T 1RE
e-mail: dasrasa@hotmail.com
dir: Nearest station: Tottenham Court Road, Goodge Street Telephone for directions

Part of the popular Rasa group of Indian restaurants, this colourful venue on Charlotte Street specialises in authentic Keralan cooking and is noted for its fish and seafood. Beyond the bold pink exterior, you'll find several rooms decorated in traditional style, with exotic Indian art, bright silks and richly coloured oils. Courteous and attentive staff deliver delicious poppadoms and pickles to the table while you select from the range of soups, dosas and main meals, the latter now offering a range of meat dishes. Try a peppery lentil broth laced with garlic, tomato and tamarind to start, then rasa kayi, a spicy vegetable curry with garlic, ginger and fennel sauce, and finish with a banana dosa - tiny pancakes made from bananas, plain flour and cardamom.

Times 12-3/6-11, Closed 2 wks Dec, Closed L Sun

Pied à Terre

Modern French 🖥 V ⚜ NOTABLE WINE LIST

Outstanding, highly refined, modern cooking in contemporary, understated luxury surroundings

☎ 020 7636 1178 & 7419 9788
34 Charlotte St W1T 2NH
e-mail: info@pied-a-terre.co.uk
web: www.pied-a-terre.co.uk
dir: Nearest station: Goodge Street S of BT Tower and Goodge St

One of London's best, this class act continues to run on top form with some superlative and exciting cooking. Its frontage is intimate and unassuming, while the sleek interior is fittingly stylish and glamorous. The décor is contemporary and oozes understated luxury, with cream suede and rosewood furniture and architectural glass combining harmoniously. There's also a bar upstairs to relax pre and post meal, featuring leather seats and art by Hamilton, Blake and Hodgkin. Service is as impeccable as ever, led by excellent host David Moore. Oz-born chef Shane Osborn continues to deliver his brand of stylish and creative modern French cuisine; it is sophisticated, refined and brimful of class and emphatic flavours, using top-notch luxury ingredients and innovation - technically superb, it ticks all the boxes. The tantalising fixed-price repertoire of lunch, carte and tasting menu (with the option of accompanying

wines or champagne) promotes an agony of choice, delivering top-drawer dishes. Maybe pan-fried John Dory served with braised leeks, basil oil, squid tagliatelle, pea shoots and a red wine jus, or perhaps roasted rib of veal with garlic gnocchi, creamed morels, roasted garlic and a sage jus, while dessert might feature a baked apple pudding with apple foam, hazelnut crumble and a fromage frais and anise sorbet. A stunning range of ancillaries (canapés, amuse-bouche, breads, pre-desserts and petits fours) burst with flavour and attention to detail like everything else here, while an impressive wine list rounds off this high-flyer in style.

Chef Shane Osborn **Owner** David Moore & Shane Osborn **Times** 12-2.45/6.15-11, Closed 2 wks Xmas & New Year, Closed Sun, Closed L Sat **Prices** Fixed L 2 course £24.50-£52.50, Fixed D 3 course £65, Tasting menu £80, Service added but optional 12.5% **Wines** 620 bottles over £20, 11 bottles under £20, 15 by glass **Notes** Tasting menu 9 courses, Vegetarian menu, Air con **Seats** 40, Pr/ dining room 12 **Parking** Cleveland St

LONDON W1 *Continued*

The Red Fort

◉◉ Traditional Indian ▣   Plan 3 B2

Stylish, elegant and contemporary Soho Indian

☎ 020 7437 2525 & 7437 2115
77 Dean St W1D 3SH
e-mail: info@redfort.co.uk
dir: Nearest station: Leicester Square Walk north on
Charing Cross Rd. At Cambridge Circus turn left into
Shaftesbury Ave. Dean St is 2nd rd on right

The red-painted, carved-timber façade of this Soho
Indian might initially suggest it is lost in a time warp,
but don't be fooled as this is a cool, stylish,
contemporary, upmarket affair. The entrance leads either
to its subterranean Akbar Bar or long ground-floor dining
room, where restful neutral tones set the scene alongside
walls adorned with Mughal arches inlaid with authentic
artefacts. At the back, there's a sleek water feature and
open kitchen. Banquettes line walls, tables are laid with
white linen and staff are smartly attired. The menu
embodies the theme, while dishes are primarily Mughal
Court/North Western in style and utilise quality
ingredients; think Scottish lamb chops from the grill in
star anise and pomegranate jus.

Chef Iqbal Ahamad **Owner** Amin Ali
Times 12-2.15/5.45-11.15, Closed 25 Dec, Closed L Sat &
Sun **Prices** Fixed L 2 course £12, Fixed D 3 course £16,
Starter £6.50-£9.95, Main £14-£33, Dessert £7-£8,

Service added but optional 12.5% **Wines** 70 bottles over
£20, 15 bottles under £20, 7 by glass **Notes** Air con
Seats 84

Rhodes W1 Restaurant

◉◉◉ – *see below*

Ristorante Semplice

◉◉ Italian ▣   Plan 2 H2

Classy Italian with a passion for authenticity

☎ 020 7495 1509
10 Blenheim St W1S 1LJ

Semplice means simple in Italian and that's the mantra
of this Mayfair eatery, formerly two small restaurants,
with highly polished ebony walls carved in gold, leather
seating in brown and cream, and an impressive Murano
chandelier. Top-notch ingredients form the foundation
of the menu, either garnered from the best British
producers, or flown in from home - mozzarella arrives
daily and free-range Italian meat features prominently.
A variety of regional Italian dishes is delivered with an
emphasis on flavour. Take, for example, squid ink
stracci di pasta with cuttlefish, clams and parsley
sauce, and roasted and pan-fried Italian rabbit with
spinach, polenta and Scottish mushrooms. Service is
slick and very Italian.

Times 12-2.30/7-10.30, Closed BHs, Closed Sun

The Ritz London Restaurant

◉◉ British, French ▣ ⚜NOTABLE WINE LIST   Plan 5 A6

Luxurious dining in a magical setting

☎ 020 7493 8181 & 7300 2370
150 Piccadilly W1J 9BR
e-mail: enquire@theritzlondon.com
dir: Nearest station: Green Park 10-minute walk from
Piccadilly Circus or Hyde Park Corner

As the song 'puttin' on the Ritz' suggests, glad rags are all
the rage at this top London venue, so dress up and make
the most of the occasion by booking ahead for a table with
a view of the patio and park. The impressively opulent
dining room, justly renowned as one of the most beautiful
in Europe, displays an abundance of palatial marble, Louis
XVI furnishings, garlands of gold chandeliers and a whole
wall of panelled mirror. Service is also fabulous and adds
to the charm of this elegant setting. The menu offers haute
cuisine overflowing with luxury ingredients. Try Cornish

Rhodes W1 Restaurant

LONDON W1   Plan 2 F2

British, French ▣

Rhodes' glamorous fine dining with superb Anglo-French cuisine

☎ 020 7616 5930
Great Cumberland Place W1H 7DL
e-mail: restaurant@rhodesw1.com
dir: Nearest station: Paddington/Marble Arch

Gary Rhodes' culinary flagship - which opened back in
May 2007 - is set in the Cumberland Hotel at Marble
Arch. Described by Rhodes as the restaurant he 'has
always dreamed of', the witty, glamorous interior of this
42-seat, fine-dining affair was created by celebrated
designer Kelly Hoppen. Twenty-four striking Swarovski
crystal chandeliers, antique French chairs and mirrors,
and lush taupe, black and deep-purple velvet fabrics set

a luxurious and sophisticated tone to the windowless
room. The seating in the bar area features another
individual twist, with Rhodes' recipes - in his own
handwriting - printed on the fabric. The food perfectly
matches the décor, with Rhodes and head chef Brian
Hughson's menus classically French based with modern
British influences. High-quality, seasonal ingredients are
treated with style and flair on a fixed-price repertoire of
lunch and carte, plus at dinner, there's a medley of
individually priced 'small tasting dishes' too. Expect
technical accuracy and clean, clear, full flavours in
well-executed dishes like a threesome: warm scallops
and langoustines with a caviar hollandaise; salt-roast
pigeon served with white asparagus, cabbage hearts and
lemon cumin, and perhaps a cherry trifle and Jersey ice
cream finish. (The Brasserie, the sister restaurant also
located at the Cumberland Hotel, takes a simpler, more
relaxed approach, see entry.)

Chef Gary Rhodes/Brian Hughson **Owner** Gary Rhodes
Times 12-2.30/7-10.30, Closed Xmas. New Year, BHs,
Closed Sun, Mon, Closed L Sat **Prices** Fixed L 2 course
£22-£28, Fixed D 3 course £55-£70, Tasting menu
£13-£21, Service added but optional 12.5% **Wines** 250
bottles over £20, 13 by glass **Notes** Dress restrictions,
Smart dress, no torn jeans or trainers, Air con **Seats** 46
Parking NCP at Marble Arch

poached lobster with butter beans, oxtail ravioli and almond velouté, or perhaps roast partridge with chestnut and foie gras pithivier, baby lettuce and Alsace bacon. An excellent wine list completes the package.

Chef John T Williams **Owner** The Ritz Hotel (London) Ltd **Times** 12.30-2.30/6-10.30 **Wines** 400+ bottles over £20, 9 by glass **Notes** Pre-theatre 3 course D £45, Sunday L, Vegetarian available, Dress restrictions, Jacket & tie requested, No jeans or trainers, Civ Wed 60, Air con **Seats** 90, Pr/dining room 14 **Children** Portions, Menu **Parking** NCP on Arlington Street

Roka

◉◉◉ – **see below**

Salt Yard

◉◉ Italian, Spanish   Plan 3 B4

Tapas restaurant offering vibrant little dishes for sharing

☎ 020 7637 0657
54 Goodge St W1T 4NA
e-mail: info@saltyard.co.uk
dir: Nearest station: Goodge St Near Tottenham Court Rd

At this very popular tapas restaurant (booking essential most nights) you can dine in the relative calm of the basement restaurant or join the hip and noisy crowd eating and drinking in the bar. Downstairs the tables are neatly laid between high-backed leather chairs, and you

can watch the kitchen buzz as you sample the fare. It's the same food wherever you sit, and the carefully sourced ingredients are sympathetically handled and cooked with flair. Meat, fish and vegetable selections include braised venison haunch with trinxat, crispy squid with aioli, and pumpkin gnocchi with brown butter and sage. Finish with house-made cantucci and bitter chocolate truffles served with a glass of Vin Santo.

Chef Benjamin Tish **Owner** Sanja Morris & Simon Mullins **Times** 12-3/6-11, Closed BHs, 25 Dec & 1 Jan, Closed Sun, Closed L Sat **Prices** Starter £1.95-£17, Main £3.50-£8.75, Dessert £4.50-£6.50, Service added but optional 12.5% **Wines** 43 bottles over £20, 6 bottles under £20, 15 by glass **Notes** Vegetarian available, Air con **Seats** 60 **Parking** NCP Cleveland St, meter parking Goodge Place

Sartoria

◉ Italian ▱   Plan 3 A2

Modern Italian at the heart of Savile Row

☎ 020 7534 7000 & 7534 7030
20 Savile Row W1S 3PR
e-mail: sartoriareservations@conran-restaurants.co.uk
dir: Nearest station: Oxford Circus/Green Park Tube to Oxford Circus, take exit 3, turn left down Regent St towards Piccadilly Circus, take 5th right into New Burlington St, end of street on left

Its Savile Row location has inspired a subtle tailoring theme to this sophisticated, contemporary Italian. Think

suited mannequins in the window, crockery with a button logo and a pinking scissor image fronting the menu. The large, open dining area - with plain white walls and big windows along one side - comes softened by table linen, standard lamps, taupe carpeting and modern sofas and chairs upholstered in grey. It's all as sleek and professional as the service and as clean cut as the seasonal Italian cooking driven by quality ingredients; think wild sea bass served with braised fennel. An extensive regional Italian wine list, separate bar area and fixed-price lunch/pre-theatre menu all catch the eye too.

Chef Alan Marchetti **Owner** Sir Terence Conran **Times** 12-3/6-11, Closed 25-26 Dec, Closed Sun, Closed L Sat **Prices** Food prices not confirmed for 2009. Please telephone for details. **Wines** 340 bottles over £20, 10 bottles under £20, 12 by glass **Notes** Vegetarian available, Dress restrictions, Smart casual preferred, Air con **Seats** 90, Pr/dining room 45 **Parking** On street

---

Roka

Roka

| LONDON W1 | Plan 3 B3 |

Japanese ▱

Stylish, friendly, funky Japanese grill

☎ 020 7580 6464
37 Charlotte St W1T 1RR
e-mail: info@rokarestaurant.com
dir: Nearest station: Goodge St/Tottenham Court Rd 5 min walk from Goodge St

Good design and impeccable style run through Roka as sure as the grain runs through a piece of wood. It makes a strong first impression, with floor-to-ceiling glass windows revealing the cool vibe of the interior. Various types of wood, stainless steel and glass combine to create an ultra-hip space dominated by the open kitchen and robata grill (traditional Japanese barbecue grill). There is counter seating in the Japanese style where you

can watch the chefs in action, or you can opt for wooden tables which fill the rest of the room. Downstairs, there's a more informal, cool, club-like vibe, with a central bar again, but this time, followed up by sofa-style seating and occasional tables. Service is friendly, upbeat and knowledgeable. The new-wave Japanese cooking - ideal for grazing and sharing - is delivered via an extensive menu (backed by a couple of tasting options) designed around dishes from the robatayaki grill alongside an impressive selection of fresh, vibrant sashimi and sushi, all based on top-quality produce. Note the food arrives in no particular order. Ebi no atama is sushi with crispy prawn, avocado, chilli, chrysanthemums and dark sweet soy, or there is rice hotpot with king crab and wasabi tobiko, and from the robata comes lamb cutlets with Korean spices. Roka is sibling to Rainer Becker's other restaurant Zuma, across town in Knightsbridge (see entry).

Times 12-3.30/5.30-11.30, Closed 25 Dec, 1 Jan

LONDON W1 *Continued*

RESTAURANT OF THE YEAR

Scott's Restaurant

◉◉ British 🖵   Plan 2 G2

Fashionable, glamorous seafood restaurant and oyster bar in the heart of Mayfair

☎ 020 7495 7309
20 Mount St W1K 2HE
dir: Nearest station: Bond Street Just off Grosvenor Sq, between Berkeley Sq and Park Ln

Dating back to 1851, this legendary fish restaurant - relaunched by Caprice Holdings (the people behind The Ivy, Le Caprice and J. Sheekey, see entries) - sees it return to its past glories in great style. The contemporary, fashionable remix of this classic oak-panelled restaurant comes inspired by its heyday, with rich burgundy-leather seating, an exquisite chandelier, specially commissioned modern art and a central crustacea bar in the style of a turn-of-the-century cruise liner. There's a doorman to greet, while table service is slick, attentive and polished. The kitchen uses top-notch ingredients in well-presented dishes, with the likes of oysters, caviar, crustacea, smoked fish, whole fish, meat and game finding a place. Think classics like Dover sole (grilled or meunière), lobster (américaine, grilled or thermidor), or maybe pan-fried skate with periwinkles, nut-brown butter and capers. The oyster bar offers more casual dining. **Scott's Restaurant is AA Restaurant of the Year for London.**

Times 12-3/5.30-11, Closed Xmas, Jan 1, Closed Aug BH

Sherlock's Bar & Grill

◉ Modern French 🖵   Plan 2 F4

Traditional methods for inspirational cuisine in detective-themed boutique hotel

☎ 020 7486 6161
Sherlock Holmes Hotel, 108 Baker St W1U 6LJ
e-mail: shh.fb@parkplazahotels.co.uk
web: www.parkplaza.com
dir: Nearest station: Baker Street Located on Baker St, close to the tube station. 10 mins from Wembley by underground

There's no escaping Sherlock Holmes at this elegant boutique hotel in Baker Street. Paintings on the wall and

a bronze cast remind diners of the famous fictional detective's roots. The restaurant's décor is chic and unfussy with warm colours and modern styling. A mesquite wood-burning stove and a charcoal grill are the main methods of cooking here. The modern Mediterranean-inspired menu makes use of good raw materials to produce dishes such as bouillabaisse soup, rouille and emmental crust, followed by grilled mallard duck breast, ceps and Jerusalem artichokes with port jus, and dessert of panaché of mixed berries, vanilla and lemongrass juices and pink champagne sorbet.

Sherlock's Bar & Grill

Chef Rachid Hammoum **Owner** Park Plaza Hotels **Times** 12-2.30/6-10.30 **Prices** Fixed L 2 course £12.50, Starter £7.25-£9.75, Main £14.25-£18.50, Dessert £5.50-£6.50, Service added 12.5% **Wines** 16 bottles over £20, 10 bottles under £20, 10 by glass **Notes** Sunday L, Vegetarian available, Civ Wed 60, Air con **Seats** 50, Pr/dining room 50 **Children** Portions, Menu **Parking** Chiltern St

Shogun, Millennium Hotel Mayfair

◉◉ Japanese   Plan 2 G1

Authentic Japanese food in the heart of Mayfair

☎ 020 7629 9400
Grosvenor Square W1A 3AN

This well-established Japanese restaurant is located in the lavishly decorated basement of the Millennium Hotel Mayfair, an impressive Georgian fronted building overlooking Grosvenor Square. Features of its interior décor are kyudo archery arrows, palms and a large statue of a Samurai warrior, and the simple wooden tables are set with bamboo place mats. Discreet service is provided by friendly staff in traditional Japanese attire, and the strength of the Japanese clientele is testimony to the authenticity of the cooking. Shogun produces some of the best Japanese food in the capital including a number of good-value set dinner menus, hand-rolled sushi, zenzai, dobin-mushi, sashimi, tempura, teriyaki and dessert options.

Times Closed Mon

Sketch (Lecture Room & Library)

◉◉◉◉◉ – *see opposite*

So Restaurant

◉ Japanese 🖵   Plan 3 B2

Modern Japanese with aspects of European cuisine

☎ 020 7292 0767 & 7292 0760
3-4 Warwick St W1B 5LS
e-mail: info@sorestaurant.com
dir: Nearest station: Piccadilly Circus Exit Piccadilly tube station via exit 1. Turn left along Glasshouse St, restaurant is situated next to The Warwick

Minimalist décor, clean lines, dark wood and artwork distinguishes this contemporary restaurant from the rest. There is an informal ground floor sushi bar with traditional irori tables seating eight, and a stylish basement dining area dominated by an open-to-view kitchen. Here you'll find lacquered tables and high-backed leather chairs. The cooking is contemporary Japanese uniquely infused with European flavours. Ingredients are top quality and the presentation simple and attractive. Expect scallop and daikon salad with yizu mayonnaise; grilled lobster with ponzu sauce; or Oxfordshire fillet steak with roasted seasonal vegetables and Goma sauce.

Chef Kaoru Yamamoto **Owner** Tetsuro Hama **Times** 12-3/5-10.30, Closed Xmas-New Year, Closed Sun **Wines** 33 bottles over £20, 5 bottles under £20, 4 by glass **Notes** Pre-theatre meal 3 courses £19.95. Tasting menu 3 courses, Vegetarian available, Air con **Seats** 70, Pr/dining room 6 **Children** Portions **Parking** On street

The Square

◉◉◉◉ – *see page 308*

Sumosan Restaurant

◉ Japanese   Plan 3 A1

Authentic Japanese cooking at an upmarket Mayfair address

☎ 020 7495 5999
26 Albermarle St, Mayfair W1S 4HY
e-mail: info@sumosan.com
dir: Nearest station: Green Park Please telephone for directions

This modern Japanese restaurant sits discreetly amongst the smart offices, boutiques and art showrooms of fashionable Mayfair. In keeping with its location and the majority of its clientele, the interior is stylish and business-like, with beige oak flooring, dark wooden tables

Continued on page 309

Sketch (Lecture Room & Library)

LONDON W1   Plan 3 A2

Modern European 🖥 V

Technical wizardry offers a unique experience

☎ 020 7659 4500

9 Conduit St W1S 2XG

web: www.sketch.uk.com

dir: Nearest station: Oxford Circus 4 mins walk from Oxford Circus tube station, take exit 3, down Regent St, Conduit St is 4th on right

Remarkably unassuming from outside, with its white-shuttered windows and iron railings, the un-savvy might easily walk on by, save for the evening doorman outside to catch the attention. Once inside though, this one-time HQ of Christian Dior comes brimful of surprises, outrageous flamboyancy and refinement. A collaboration between Algerian-born Mourad Mazouz and French super-chef Pierre Gagnaire that offers a multi-level food-based extravaganza, which includes the vibrant, ground-floor Gallery brasserie (opulent, exciting and bursting with signature art deco), plus the cool Parlour tea room by day, hyper-trendy bar by night. The fine-dining Lecture Room and Library upstairs - two parts of the same space (the Dining Room was the original Dior couture room) - is elegantly decorated in shades of orange, with ivory walls of studded leather and ornately plastered high ceilings, while thick-piled, brightly coloured carpets and long dangling lampshades cut a somewhat Middle Eastern edge. Well-spaced tables with crisp white linen and feather-cushioned armchairs - in purple and crimson - add comfort, while service is professional, attentive and necessarily knowledgeable of the elaborate dish compositions, and there's also a small lounge to enjoy the champagne trolley. Dishes bear the unmistakable creative genius of consultant Pierre Gagnaire's distinctive culinary style (delivered here by head chef and Gagnaire protégé, Pascal Sanchez); it's stunning, exciting, unmistakably innovative and technically superb. The very best quality fresh produce is transformed into an enormous range of textures and flavour sensations, ensuring a surprise at each turn. It's complex and deeply French, like the signature starter 'Langoustines Addressed in Five Ways', perhaps a main course of Sole (its series of elements including sole cooked meunière style/a sauce of champagne/onion and pink grapefruit marmalade, pear and hazelnut/black venere rice in a green crab bisque/and cucumber and chervil), while to finish, perhaps another signature offering 'Pierre Gagnaire Grand Desserts' which arrives as a combination of five miniatures. So dig deep into the pockets and be prepared to be wowed by the groundbreaking experience and sheer theatre of the place. (Note, the wallet-friendly 'Gourmet Rapid Lunch' offers fine value at this level.)

Chef P Gagnaire, P Sanchez **Owner** Pierre Gagnaire, Mourad Mazouz
Times 12-2.30/7-11, Closed 19 Aug-2 Sep, 23-30 Dec, 1 Jan and BHs, Closed Sun-Mon, Closed L Sat **Prices** , Fixed L 2 course £30, Tasting menu £65-£90, Starter £17-£45, Main £41-£52, Dessert £12-£35, Service added but optional 12.5% **Wines** 637 bottles over £20, 13 bottles under £20, 34 by glass **Notes** Tasting menu 8 courses, vegetarian tasting menu 7 courses, Vegetarian menu, Civ Wed 50, Air con **Seats** 50, Pr/dining room 24 **Children** Portions **Parking** Cavendish Sq, NCP Soho

The Square

LONDON W1 Plan 3 A1

Modern French 🖥 ⬥NOTABLE WINE LIST

A class culinary act in the heart of Mayfair

☎ 020 7495 7100
6-10 Bruton St W1J 6PU
e-mail: info@squarerestaurant.com
dir: Nearest station: Bond Street, Green Park Telephone for directions or refer to website

The Mayfair streets offer much opportunity for window shopping if you're in the market for a new Bentley or a designer suit or dress. Style and sophistication is essential if you are going to cut it in this part of town and The Square displays just the right degree without going overboard. The glass-frontage has discreetly frosted panels to keep out prying eyes and the welcome is professional without being intimidating. There is a small bar area before the large, high-ceilinged dining room, with its splendid parquet floor, mellow natural tones and splashes of colour from vivid canvases. Elegantly set tables are well spaced and the staff are impeccably turned out and completely on the ball. Philip Howard's cooking has developed and matured over the years - he was in his mid-twenties when he started the venture with Nigel Platts-Martin in 1991 - and the food, although underpinned by a classical French ethos, is dynamic and exciting without ever losing its way. Flavour and texture are paramount, the quality and integrity of the ingredients never lost in the mix. There is a tasting menu and carte and things start with the exceptional canapé and first-class bread. A starter of roast foie gras, given a sweet-and-sour citrus glaze, is a master-class in balance, and main-course roast calves' sweetbreads with cannelloni of rabbit is a virtuoso performance. Presentation is outstanding throughout, including in a dessert of Brillat-Savarin and blood orange cheesecake with a terrine of rhubarb and mascarpone. The superb wine list does justice to the food and the sommelier is on hand to help you through it.
Philip Howard is AA Chefs' Chef 2008-2009 (see pages 10-12).

Chef Philip Howard **Owner** Mr N Platts-Martin & Philip Howard
Times 12-2.45/6.30-10.45, Closed 24-26 Dec,1 Jan, Closed L Sat & Sun, BHs **Prices** Fixed D 3 course fr £65, Service additional but optional 12.5%
Wines 1400 bottles over £20, 3 bottles under £20, 14 by glass **Notes** Tasting menu £140 incs wine, Vegetarian available, Dress restrictions, Smart casual, jacket & tie preferred, Air con
Seats 75, Pr/dining room 18
Children Portions

LONDON W1 *Continued*

and comfortable banquette seating. Despite the understated exterior, it's a busy place, particularly buzzing at lunchtimes when the sushi and sashimi attract those with limited time, while those with plenty to discuss opt for teppan-yaki or the good value seven-course lunch selection. In fact, practically all variants of Japanese cuisine are represented, so you could begin with seared tuna tataki and mixed vegetable tempura, before moving on to black cod with miso, glass noodles with vegetables, and chicken yakitori.

Chef Bubker Belkhit **Owner** Janina Wolkow
Times 12-3/6-11.30, Closed Xmas, New Year, BHs, Closed L Sat-Sun **Wines** All bottles over £20, 14 by glass
Notes Tasting menu L, Fixed L 7 courses £22.50, Vegetarian available, Air con **Seats** 115, Pr/dining room 32 **Children** Portions **Parking** On street

Taman Gang

◎◎ South East Asian 🖥 Plan 2 F2

Vivacious, upmarket basement venue with late opening and elegant cuisine

☎ 020 7518 3160
141 Park Ln W1K 7AA
e-mail: info@tamangang.com
dir: Nearest station: Marble Arch

Leave the mayhem of Marble Arch behind and descend to this exotic, dimly-lit, split-level basement dining room and bar packed with Eastern promise. Hand-carved limestone walls, mahogany furniture, lanterns and low banquettes evoke the look and feel of ancient Indonesia. Flickering candles, white orchids, contemporary music and youthful, attentive staff add to the cool, trendy, upmarket vibe. The cuisine fits the surroundings, a fashionable, modern, sophisticated Pan-Asian mix - kind of Chinese by way of Japan and Thailand - utilising quality ingredients and skilful handling and presentation on a repertoire that promotes sharing. Expect dishes like honey-glazed lamb cutlets served with crispy lotus roots, or baked black cod with miso and mirin glaze.

Times 12-3.30/6-1, Closed L Mon-Sat

Tamarind

◎◎ Indian 🖥 Plan 4 H6

Contemporary, classy Indian in Mayfair

☎ 020 7629 3561
20 Queen St, Mayfair W1J 5PR
e-mail: manager@tamarindrestaurant.com
web: www.tamarindrestaurant.com
dir: Nearest station: Green Park Towards Hyde Park, take 4th right into Half Moon St to end (Curzon St). Turn left, Queen St is 1st right

The entrance may be a simple door leading on to a stone staircase, but it delivers you to this sophisticated and glamorous, designer-styled basement Indian in the heart of Mayfair, dressed in its contemporary best and graced by elegantly attired, knowledgeable and attentive staff. Muted

metallic colours, polished wood floor, modern seating, low lighting and cleverly placed mirrors subtly sporting the restaurant's logo - including the glass-fronted theatre kitchen - add to the sense of style, space and light. The skilful kitchen delivers an enticing medley of traditional and contemporary cuisine - focused around the tandoor oven - and cooked with panache in authentic North West Indian style. Expect neatly presented, intelligently subtly spiced, well-balanced dishes - using prime ingredients - to awaken the taste-buds; perhaps grilled chunks of monkfish in a marinade of ginger, yogurt, ground spices and saffron, while regular accompaniments - like breads, poppadoms, amuse-bouche, vegetables and wines - hold-up the stamp of quality throughout.

Tamarind

Chef Alfred Prasad **Owner** Indian Cuisine Ltd
Times 12-2.45/6-11.15, Closed 25-26 Dec, 1 Jan, Closed L Sat, BHs **Wines** 100 bottles over £20, 4 bottles under £20 **Notes** Pre-theatre D £24.50 6-7pm, Sunday L, Vegetarian available, Dress restrictions, No jeans or shorts, Air con **Seats** 90 **Parking** NCP

Texture Restaurant

LONDON W1 Plan 2 F2

Modern European 🖥 V 🍷

Exciting new opening from two talented young professionals of pedigree

☎ 020 7224 0028
Best Western Mostyn Hotel, 34 Portman St W1H 7BY
e-mail: info@texture-restaurant.co.uk
dir: Nearest station: Marble Arch/Bond St On the corner of Seymour St and Portman St

Located on a quiet corner just off Portman Square, this ambitious new restaurant hit the ground running when it opened back in 2007. It's the first venture for two young and enthusiastic professionals who originally met whilst working at Le Manoir aux Quat' Saisons; chef Agnar Sverrisson and manager and master sommelier Xavier Rousset - who runs the polished and knowledgeable front-of-house team. The ornate-ceilinged Georgian restaurant itself has a cool, elegant, modern tone with

leather chairs, polished-wood floors, large windows and a simple muted-cream décor, while a 30-seat champagne bar sympathetically divides the room. Sverrisson's European cuisine may have its roots in the classics, but the style is light and contemporary, driven by the best seasonal ingredients, and comes with creative twists and Icelandic influences from his Nordic homeland. Highly accomplished technical skill, immaculate attention to detail and presentation, fresh, clean flavours and, in tune with the restaurant's name, plenty of diverse textures, are all delivered on an appealing array of menus, including lunch (one-priced, starter-sized medley of dishes), carte and tasting options. So expect the likes of Scottish scallops with cauliflower textures to open, and perhaps Lancashire suckling pig (slow cooked for 12 hours) served with squid and bonito sauce for a main course. The wine list is a corker, with a cracking array of bubblies too.

Chef Agnar Sverrisson **Owner** Xavier Rousset & Agnar Sverrisson **Times** 12-2.30/6.30-11, Closed 2 wks Xmas, 2 wks Aug, Closed Sun-Mon **Prices** Fixed D 3 course £45, Tasting menu £55-£59, Service added but optional 12.5% **Wines** 110 bottles over £20, 12 by glass

Notes Tasting menu 7 courses, fish tasting option, Vegetarian menu, Dress restrictions, Smart casual, Air con **Seats** 55 **Parking** NCP Bryanston St

LONDON W1 *Continued*

Texture Restaurant

❀❀❀ – *see page 309*

Theo Randall @ InterContinental London

❀❀❀ – *see below*

La Trouvaille

❀❀ French 💻   Plan 3 A2

A modern approach to French bourgeois cooking in intimate surroundings

☎ 020 7287 8488
12a Newburgh St W1F 7RR
e-mail: contact@latrouvaille.co.uk
web: www.latrouvaille.co.uk
dir: Nearest station: Oxford Circus Off Carnaby St by Liberty's

As its name implies, La Trouvaille is quite the Soho find, set among the cobbled pedestrian lanes and boutiques off Carnaby Street. The chic ground floor wine bar serves mainly organic/biodynamic French wines alongside foie gras, charcuterie and cheese platters, while the light, bright and elegant dining room is upstairs. Check out the white linen, perspex

chairs, striking mirrors, stripped floorboards and tall windows - the perfect setting for some unconventional French cooking. Thoughtful but easygoing invention combines with well-sourced ingredients to produce the likes of seared tuna slices with vanilla dressing and smoked garlic purée, or fillet of Herdwick mutton and seared scallops with braised lettuce, cauliflower mash and cardamom sauce.

La Trouvaille

Chef Pierre Renaudeau **Owner** T Bouteloup
Times 12-3/6-11, Closed Xmas, BHs, Closed Sun
Prices Fixed L 2 course £16.50, Fixed D 3 course £35, Tasting menu £50, Service added but optional 12.5%
Wines 32 bottles over £20, 8 bottles under £20, 12 by glass **Notes** Tasting menu 5 courses, Vegetarian available **Seats** 45, Pr/dining room 30 **Children** Portions **Parking** NCP (off Broadwick St)

Umu

❀❀❀ – *see page 311*

Vasco & Piero's Pavilion Restaurant

❀❀ Italian   Plan 3 B2

Genuine taste of Umbria in intimate, family run restaurant

☎ 020 7437 8774
15 Poland St W1F 8QE
e-mail: vascosfood@hotmail.com
dir: Nearest station: Oxford Circus From Oxford Circus turn right towards Tottenham Court Rd, continue for 5min and turn right into Poland St. On corner of Great Marlborough St & Noel St

Unassuming from the outside, this snug and intimate Italian Soho restaurant stands out for all the right reasons; warm hospitality that brings this bijou, family-run eatery to life, and genuine regional cooking using quality ingredients imported from Italy. Closely-packed tables, subtle lighting, a warm terracotta colour scheme and attentive, helpful Italian service add to the authenticity. Simple, home-style cooking is based on traditional Umbrian ideas and lives up to its promise time and time again. Menus may change daily and pasta is hand-made, but clear, vivid flavours reign supreme in dishes like ravioli with pesto, calves' liver

Theo Randall @ InterContinental London

LONDON W1   **Plan 4 G5**

Italian 💻

Fresh, vibrant rustic-suave Italian cooking in a sophisticated modern setting

☎ 020 7318 8747
1 Hamilton Place, Hyde Park Corner W1J 7QY
e-mail: reservations@theorandall.com
dir: Nearest station: Hyde Park Corner Hyde Park Corner rdbt

Overlooking Hyde Park and the London skyline, this deluxe landmark hotel has undergone a multi-million pound refurbishment and features former River Café head chef Theo Randall's eponymous restaurant. Clean lined, modern, sophisticated and relaxed, the long beige and grey dining room uses lots of natural materials like wood and leather as a backdrop to the traditional regional

Italian cooking. There's also a long gleaming bar (at which diners can eat) and a visible kitchen too. Inspired by his passion for top quality and seasonal produce, the cooking takes on a rustic-suave theme. Ingredients are cooked with great care and skill, but without unnecessary fuss in well-conceived, well-presented, balanced and clear-flavoured dishes on daily-changing menus. Take the likes of smoked eel with beetroots, dandelion and fresh horseradish, perhaps a main course of chargrilled Aberdeen Angus beef sirloin (med rare) with borlotti beans from Lamon, spinach and salsa rossa, and to finish, maybe an Amalfi lemon tart, or a soft chocolate cake with crema di mascarpone. Unique Theo Randall wicker picnic hampers available, filled with freshly-prepared Italian goodies.

Chef Theo Randall **Owner** Intercontinental Hotels Ltd & Theo Randall **Times** 12-3/5.45-11.15, Closed Xmas, New Year, 1st wk Jan, BHs, Closed Sun **Prices** Fixed L 2 course £21, Fixed D 3 course fr £25, Starter £8-£12, Main £18-£30, Dessert £6-£7, Service added but optional 12.5% **Wines** 250 bottles over £20, 3 bottles under £20, 11 by glass **Notes** Pre-theatre menu available, Vegetarian available, Dress restrictions, Smart casual, Air con **Seats** 124, Pr/dining room 24 **Children** Portions **Parking** 100 **Parking** Car park

with sage and sautéed cabbage, and Umbrian sausages with cannellini beans.

Chef Vasco Matteucci **Owner** Tony Lopez, Paul Matteucci & Vasco Matteucci **Times** 12-3/6-11, Closed BHs, Closed Sun, Closed L Sat **Prices** Fixed D 3 course £27.50-£34.50, Starter £5-£10, Main £13.50-£20, Dessert £6.75-£8.50, Service added but optional 12.5% **Wines** 4 by glass **Notes** Tasting menu if requested, Vegetarian available, Dress restrictions, No shorts, Air con **Seats** 50, Pr/dining room 36 **Children** Min 5 yrs, Portions **Parking** NCP car park opposite

Veeraswamy Restaurant

◉ Indian 🖥 Plan 3 B1

Sophisticated, stylish Indian with refined, authentic cooking

☎ 020 7734 1401
Mezzanine Floor, Victory House, 99 Regent Street W1B 4RS
e-mail: veeraswamy@realindianfood.com
dir: Nearest station: Piccadilly Circus Entrance near junct of Swallow St and Regent St, in Victory House

Shimmering chandeliers and vibrant-coloured glass lanterns hang from ceilings, while plush Mogul-style carpets sit on gleaming black Indian granite speckled with gold or darkwood floors to deliver a chic, exotic vibe to London's oldest Indian restaurant, now dramatically restored to its glamorous former 1920s glory. Latticed silver screens, banquettes or upholstered chairs and large tables ooze comfort, alongside charming service and views over Regent Street. Classic Indian dishes ride alongside more contemporary offerings, all authentically and freshly prepared using high-quality ingredients and thoughtful presentation. Take prawn travancore (a spicy curry from southern Kerala), or gosht hara salan (a Hyderabadi dish of diced lamb, fresh green herbs and a hint of green chilli).

Veeraswamy Restaurant

Times 12-2.30/5.30-11.30, Closed D Xmas

Via Condotti

◎◎ Italian 🖥 Plan 3 A2

Stylish Italian with classical-based dishes and impeccable service

☎ 020 7493 7050
23 Conduit St W1S 2XS
e-mail: info@viacondotti.co.uk
dir: Nearest station: Oxford Circus, Piccadilly Circus

The lilac frontage, awning and planters pick this friendly and stylish Italian out from the crowd. Tucked away among the fashionable boutiques of Mayfair's Conduit Street (just off Bond Street), the peach décor, lightwood floors, tasteful posters, expensive leather chairs and dazzling white tablecloths add to its glamorous look. Service is charming and very Italian, unobtrusive and unpretentious, while the cooking comes based on classical roots with some southern influences. There is a pleasant, refreshing simplicity about the food, which showcases quality ingredients, some sourced direct from Italy. Think rabbit tortelli with black olive and wild onions or braised oxtail with celeriac purée.

Chef Andrea Francescato **Owner** Claudio Pulze, Pasquale Amico, Richard Martinez **Times** 12-3/6.30-11, Closed BHs, Closed Sun **Wines** 70 bottles over £20, 8 bottles under £20, 15 by glass **Notes** Lunch and pre-theatre 3 course menu £18.50, Vegetarian available, Air con **Seats** 90, Pr/dining room 18 **Children** Portions

Umu

LONDON W1 Plan 2 H2

Japanese 🖥

Sophisticated Japanese offering high-quality Kyoto cuisine

☎ 020 7499 8881
14-16 Bruton Place W1J 6LX
e-mail: reception@umurestaurant.com
dir: Nearest station: Green Park/Bond St Off Bruton St & Berkeley Sq

Tucked away just off Mayfair's Berkeley Square is London's first Kyoto restaurant - a classy affair, created from award-winning designer Tony Chi's vision of opulent Kyoto styling. An unobtrusive touch button slides open the wooden front door on to a sophisticated modern interior, with high-quality wood and mirrors, banquette seating and a chef's central sushi table. The staff are welcoming and attentive, necessarily knowledgeable and helpful in guiding diners through the intricacies of the menu. The cooking - from chef Ichiro Kubota - offers innovative classic and contemporary interpretations of Kyoto cuisine, delivered via a fixed-price lunch option, extensive carte, a separate sushi menu and six tasting options. The sheer quality of ingredients and the freshness, clarity, vibrancy and combinations of flavours strike through in every dish and combine with great attention to detail in superb presentation. So dig deep into your pockets and prepare to be wowed by sweet shrimp with sake jelly and caviar, or miso gratin with scallops, maitake and king oyster mushrooms. Main courses include delicious Wagyu beef in hoba leaf with seasonal vegetables, or grilled lobster with soy sauce velouté, with home-made white miso ice cream to close.

Chef Ichiro Kubota **Owner** Marlon Abela Restaurants Corporation **Times** 12-2.30/6-11, Closed between Xmas & New Year, Etr & BHs, Closed Sun, Closed L Sat **Prices** Fixed L 3 course £21-£45, Fixed D 4 course £60-£135, Starter £8-£22, Main £11-£57, Dessert £5-£9, Service added but optional 12.5% **Wines** 742 bottles over £20, 1 bottles under £20, 12 by glass **Notes** Chef Ichiro Kubota conducts series of cookery classes, Vegetarian available, Air con **Seats** 60, Pr/dining room 12

LONDON W1 *Continued*

Villandry

French, European 🖥   Plan 3 A4

Impressive restaurant, quality foodstore and bar

☎ 020 7631 3131
170 Great Portland St W1W 5QB
e-mail: contactus@villandry.com
web: www.villandry.com
dir: Nearest station: Great Portland Street/Oxford Circus
Entrance at 91 Bolsover St, between Great Portland St
tube station & Oxford Circus

This buzzy and lively bar, restaurant, shop and lunchtime
takeout prizes the quality of its ingredients, and entering
the restaurant through its upmarket foodstore really
whets the appetite. The glass-fronted, high-ceilinged
dining room is chic and modern, with tables dressed in
their best whites and friendly yet professional service.
The modern approach and accurate cooking makes the
most of quality, seasonal produce via classic, brasserie-
focused menus. Try hot-smoked salmon with Puy lentils
and artichoke purée, and to follow, perhaps seared black
bream with roasted vine tomatoes and olives. A child-
friendly attitude and separate bar menu add to the
upbeat package.

Times 12-3/6-10.30, Closed 25 Dec, Closed D Sun & BHs

Westbury Hotel

🏵🏵 Modern European 🖥   Plan 3 A2

Accomplished cooking in stylish modern hotel

☎ 020 7629 7755 & 8382 5450
Bond St W1S 2YF
e-mail: artisan@westburymayfair.com
dir: Nearest station: Oxford Circus, Piccadilly Circus,
Green Park Telephone for directions

Set in the heart of Mayfair just off Bond Street, this
stylish hotel is styled on the Westbury in New York and is
home to the renowned Polo Bar. The large, airy Artisan
restaurant overlooks Conduit Street, with its own street
entrance, and has a classy contemporary look resplendent
in creams and browns, with beautiful inlaid wooden
floors, wood panelled walls with frosted glass sheets,
stunning chandeliers, crisp white linen and cream leather
banquettes and chairs. The menus take an equally
appealing modern approach; take roasted black leg
chicken with pan-fried foie gras, potato gnocchi and
girolles, finishing, perhaps, with soft chocolate tart with
peanut ice cream.

Times 12-2.30/6.30-10.30, Closed L Sat, Closed D Sun

Wild Honey

🏵🏵 Modern European 🖥   Plan 3 A2

**Refined, intelligently straightforward and affordable
food and wine in Mayfair**

☎ 020 7758 9160
12 Saint George St W1S 2FB
e-mail: info@wildhoneyrestaurant.co.uk
dir: Nearest station: Oxford Circus, Bond St
Please telephone for directions

The second venture from Anthony Demetre and Will Smith
- the duo behind much-lauded sister restaurant Arbutus
(see entry) - certainly have the Midas touch, applying the
same winning formula here in Mayfair. Their London take
on the French bistrots de luxe theme sees the appealing
combination of modestly priced food (cooked with flair
and accuracy) and approachable wine list (served by
250ml carafe as well as bottle) delivered in informal,
friendly surroundings. Different in atmosphere and décor
to its Soho original, set just off Conduit and Bond Streets,
it oozes understated modernity. The high-ceilinged, well-
lit long room with rich oak panelling forms the backdrop
to banquettes, intimate booths and chairs, contemporary
artwork and an onyx-topped front bar (with stalls for bar
dining). The daily-changing menus display cooking of
refinement and flavour and the use of lesser-used cuts;
take line-caught Cornish pollack served with octopus and
shallots in red wine.

Chef Anthony Demetre **Owner** Anthony Demetre/Will Smith
Times 12-2.30/6-10.30, Closed 25-26 Dec, 1 Jan
Wines 40 bottles over £20, 10 bottles under £20, 50 by
glass **Notes** Pre-theatre D £17.50 (6-7pm), Vegetarian
available, Air con **Seats** 65 **Children** Portions **Parking** On
Street

The Wolseley

European   Plan 5 A6

**Bustling landmark brasserie offering stylish all-day
dining**

☎ 020 7499 6996
160 Piccadilly W1J 9EB
dir: Nearest station: Green Park 500mtrs from Green Park
Underground station

This European café-style phenomenon rightly continues to
be a massive crowd-pleaser. With revered owners in Chris
Corbin and Jeremy King and a high-impact redesign of
the one-time Wolseley car showroom and Barclays Bank
by David Collins, it has been reinvented as a buzzing,
fast-moving brasserie with multi-domed ceiling,
dramatic chandeliers and a black and cream colour
scheme. The show never stops from 7am to midnight; the
menus range from breakfasts to all-day snacks and
afternoon tea packages, right through to a full carte;
think fillet steak au poivre, grilled halibut with béarnaise,
and baked vanilla cheesecake. And it offers some great
people-watching too.

Chef Julian O'Neill **Owner** Chris Corbin & Jeremy King
Times 7am-mdnt/, Closed 25 Dec, 1 Jan, Aug BH, Closed
D 24 Dec, 31 Dec **Prices** Starter £5.75-£22.50, Main
£9.75-£23.50, Dessert £5.25-£7.50, Service added but
optional 12.5% **Wines** 55 bottles over £20, 4 bottles
under £20, 28 by glass **Notes** Vegetarian available, Air
con **Seats** 150 **Children** Portions

Yauatcha

🏵🏵 Chinese 🖥   Plan 3 B2

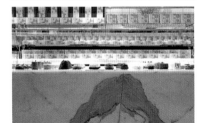

Top-rate dim sum in seductive room

☎ 020 7494 8888
15 Broadwick St W1F 0DL
e-mail: reservations@yauatcha.com
dir: Nearest station: Tottenham Ct Rd, Piccadilly, Oxford
Circus On the corner of Broadwick and Berwick St

In a building designed by Sir Richard Rogers and a
glamorous and hyper-trendy interior by Christian Liagre,
Yauatcha is a restaurant with style and attitude. On the
ground floor is a rather tranquil tea house serving over
150 different varieties of the leaf and a selection of
pastries, while the main action is in the basement where
diners sit at tightly packed tables on low banquettes and
chairs to feast on the first-class dim sum. There are
many traditional Cantonese dishes alongside more
modern Pan-Asian influences including Wagyu beef from

Japan. The classic stuff like har gau, shumai and chicken feet in chilli and black bean sauce are superb versions, while the lengthy menu also offers tender ostrich meat dumplings with black pepper and the signature baked venison puffs. Service zips along at speed and the level of consistency of the output from the kitchen is impressive.

Yauatcha

Times 12/11.30, Closed 24-25 Dec, Closed L 26 Dec, 1 Jan

YMing

◉ Chinese V　　　　　　　　　Plan 3 C2

Chinese regional specialities in theatreland

☎ 020 7734 2721
35-36 Greek St W1D 5DL
e-mail: cyming2000@blueyonder.co.uk
dir: Nearest station: Piccadilly Circus

Situated in the heart of Soho, this stylish Chinese is less frenetic than its Chinatown neighbours. Duck-egg blue walls with jade carvings surround well-spaced and crisply-clothed tables in the intimate setting of a series of small rooms. Helpful service makes a good impression, and the uninitiated are guided through the extensive carte and fixed-price menus of Cantonese and regional dishes. The kitchen adheres to traditional cooking methods but uses fresh, healthy ingredients and light oils. Lobster is a favourite, along with lean Tibetan garlic lamb, and prawns in spiced salt.

Chef Aaron Wong **Owner** Christine Yau
Times Noon-11.45/, Closed 25-26 Dec, 1 Jan, Closed Sun (ex Chinese New Year) **Wines** 15 bottles over £20, 19

bottles under £20, 7 by glass **Notes** Pre-theatre 3 course + coffee £10, Vegetarian menu, Dress restrictions, Clean and presentable, Air con **Seats** 60, Pr/dining room 25 **Parking** Chinatown car park

Yumi Restaurant

◉ Japanese　　　　　　　　　Plan 2 G3

Authentic Japanese cuisine, service and atmosphere

☎ 020 7935 8320
110 George St W1H 5RL
dir: Telephone for further details

This authentic Japanese, tucked away just off Gloucester Place, has more a neighbourhood vibe than West End experience. The décor's typically understated, but with plenty of pine and booth-style areas for privacy, while there's a sushi counter and the usual private dining rooms to bolster the small basement dining area. Service is formal Japanese, with attentive, polite kimono-clad staff presiding over a predominantly Japanese audience. The menu comes in Japanese and English, its lengthy array of authentic dishes driven by quality ingredients and bolstered by chef's recommendations, set-price offerings and a separate sushi menu. Think home-made seafood dumplings, belly pork cooked in sake and soy, or king prawn tempura.

Times 5.30-10.30

The Delhi Brasserie

☎ 020 7437 8261
44 Frith St W1D 4SB

Handy location off Soho Square. Traditional, elegant décor, and lots of old favourites on the menu.

Prices Food prices not confirmed for 2009. Please telephone for details.

Eat & Two Veg

☎ 020 7258 8595
50 Marylebone High St W1U 5HN

A super modern diner straight from a cosmopolitan vegetarian's dining dream. Open for breakfast, lunch and dinner seven days a week, serving delicious meat-free food in a lively, light-hearted atmosphere.

Prices Food prices not confirmed for 2009. Please telephone for details.

Angelus Restaurant

◉◉ Modern French 🍷 　　　　　Plan 2 D2

Smart, neighbourhood French brasserie of all-round class

☎ 020 7402 0083
4 Bathurst St W2 2SD
e-mail: info@angelusrestaurant.co.uk
dir: Nearest station: Lancaster Gate/Paddington Station Opposite Royal Lancaster Hotel

Set in a one-time pub, Thierry Tomasin (whose stellar CV includes general manager of renowned restaurant Aubergine and head sommelier at the legendary Le Gavroche) has brought a touch of chic Parisian brasserie to Bathurst Street - next door to the Hyde Park stables and just a short stroll from the Park itself. Smart, art deco interiors by French design company Gong feature darkwood, studded red-leather banquettes, elaborate art nouveau mirrors and high ceilings, while at the back, there's a boudoir bar. Tomasin is an enthusiastic, lively host and service is welcoming and relaxed, while Parisian chef Olivier Duret takes a contemporary approach to French brasserie classics, confidently using quality seasonal ingredients with skill to deliver clear flavours; take a Scottish rump steak pavé served with Jerusalem artichoke gratin, and perhaps a lemon tart with cacao sorbet finish. And, as you'd expect, the wine list catches the eye too.

Chef Olivier Duret **Owner** Thierry Tomasin
Times 12-2.30/5.30-11, Closed 23 Dec-4 Jan, Closed Mon
Prices Starter £7-£14, Main £15-£21, Dessert £7-£10, Service added but optional 12.5% **Wines** 800 bottles over £20, 11 bottles under £20, 4 by glass **Notes** Vegetarian available, Air con **Seats** 40, Pr/dining room 20

LONDON W2 *Continued*

Assaggi

◉◉ Italian ⬚ Plan 2 A2

Imaginative and authentic Italian dining in Notting Hill

☎ 020 7792 5501
39 Chepstow Place W2 4TS
e-mail: nipi@assaggi.demon.co.uk
dir: Nearest station: Notting Hill Gate Telephone for directions

Situated above the Chepstow pub in trendy Notting Hill, this small, colourful restaurant makes diners feel right at home with its simple pine furniture and wooden floors, Mediterranean colours, and white-clothed tables. Large floor-to-ceiling windows give the dining room a fresh, airy feel, and friendly staff offer a warm welcome and invaluable help with translating the menu. It's a great place for people-watching and the Italian food - leaning towards regional Sardinian cooking - is inventive, with the emphasis on flavour and the use of authentic ingredients, and good presentation too. Try starters like baby squid stuffed with risotto, with aubergine, basil and baby plum tomatoes, or perhaps pan-fried pecorino cheese with San Daniele ham and rocket leaves. Main courses include frito misto, or maybe gnocchi with wild boar ragout. Finish with a delicious signature dessert of flourless chocolate cake. Booking is essential.

Chef Nino Sassu **Owner** Nino Sassu, Pietro Fraccari **Times** 12.30-2.30/7.30-11, Closed 2 wks Xmas, BHs, Closed Sun **Prices** Starter £9.90-£13.90, Main £18-£23.90, Dessert £7.50, Service optional **Wines** All bottles over £20, 7 by glass **Notes** Vegetarian available, Air con **Seats** 35 **Children** Portions

Le Cafe Anglais

◉ French V ⬚NOTABLE WINE LIST Plan 2 B2

French brasserie-style cuisine in spacious, elegant surroundings

☎ 020 7221 1415
8 Porchester Gardens W2 4DB
e-mail: info@lecafeanglais.co.uk
dir: Nearest station: Bayswater or Queensway

An unassuming entrance at the side of Whiteley's Shopping Centre is the gateway to this stylish, art-deco style brasserie. The vast space - with room for 170 diners - has pale green leather banquettes, red satin curtains and linen tablecloths, while floor-to-ceiling lattice windows offer fabulous views over Bayswater. A giant rotisserie dominates a long open kitchen, where you can usually spot celebrated chef/owner Rowley Leigh, formerly of Kensington Place, manning the stoves. The mainly French menu is divided into apéritifs, hors d'oeuvres, first courses, fish, roasts, vegetables and desserts. Begin in adventurous mode with the parmesan custard and anchovy toasts, then move onto a starter of spaghetti with black and white pepper. Take your pick from rotisserie chicken or game, or scallops with Jerusalem artichoke purée, truffle and lemon for a main course.

Chef Rowley Leigh **Owner** Rowley Leigh & Charlie McVeigh **Times** 12-3/6.3-11.3, Closed 1 Jan **Prices** Fixed L 2 course £16.50, Starter £3-£14, Main £8-£25, Dessert £6-£7.50, Service added but optional 12.5% **Wines** 98 bottles over £20, 5 bottles under £20, 25 by glass **Notes** Vegetarian menu, Air con **Seats** 170, Pr/dining room 26 **Children** Portions

Hereford Road Restaurant

◉ British Plan 2 A2

Relaxed neighbourhood eatery offering the best of British from a chef of pedigree

☎ 020 7727 1144
3 Hereford Rd, Westbourne Grove W2 4AB
e-mail: www.herefordroad.org

Rather aptly occupying what in a previous incarnation was a Victorian butcher's shop in residential Notting Hill Gate, Tom Pemberton's Hereford Road offers straightforward, pared-down but innovative seasonal British cooking with a nod to his mentor Fergus Henderson (Tom worked at St John Bread & Wine, Spitalfields). The design offers a simple, small yet stylish, split-level room featuring mirrored walls, an open 'theatre' kitchen, wooden floors and small booth-style banquette tables, while down a few steps, the area at the back has a domed skylight. The twice-daily-changing menus of succinctly described, well-presented dishes (take braised hare leg with mash potato) pay faithful attention to seasonality, while to finish there's equally simple British desserts, like sticky date pudding. Informal but slick and attentive service fits the competitively priced bill too, while the big glass front window opens to pavement tables in summer.

Times 12-3/6-10.30 **Prices** Food prices not confirmed for 2009. Please telephone for details.

Island Restaurant & Bar

◉ Modern British ⬚ Plan 2 D2

Designer hotel restaurant with seasonal fare

☎ 020 7551 6070
Royal Lancaster Hotel, Lancaster Ter W2 2TY
e-mail: eat@islandrestaurant.co.uk
web: www.islandrestaurant.co.uk
dir: Nearest station: Lancaster Gate

This contemporary restaurant occupies a corner location within the Royal Lancaster Hotel with its own entrance from the street. There is a sleek bar (with great cocktails)

and open-plan kitchen in the split-level dining area where diners can view Hyde Park opposite through huge plate glass windows. In the evening, crisp white tablecloths and dramatic lighting bring an extra touch of glamour. The modern classical English cooking with European influences handles quality ingredients with skill to produce daily-changing dishes, presented in a pleasingly minimalist style. Sourcing from British suppliers, popular dishes sit alongside more sophisticated fare - carpaccio of tuna with wild rocket, truffle oil and shaved parmesan, followed by goat's cheese risotto and salsify, with custard tart and poached rhubarb to finish.

Times 12/10.30, Closed Xmas, BHs, between Xmas and New Year

Jamuna Restaurant

◉◉ Indian Plan 2 E3

Quality Indian in quiet part of town

☎ 020 7723 5056 & 020 7723 5055
38A Southwick St W2 1JQ
e-mail: info@jamuna.co.uk
web: www.jamuna.co.uk
dir: Nearest station: Paddington, Edgware Road Please telephone for directions

This neighbourhood Indian restaurant is located in what was once a private house, set rather off the beaten track in a small leafy parade of shops. A stylish, minimalist affair, it comes with wooden floors, suede chairs and painted walls decorated with traditional and modern art (all for sale). The lengthy carte (with chilli symbols illustrating medium and hot dishes) shows off the kitchen's skilfully prepared and well presented food, with its infusion of clean, subtle flavours and combination of traditional and less common North Indian and regional dishes. Expect the likes of black tiger prawns marinated with ginger, yogurt and ground spices, followed by mildly spiced Scottish lobster with saffron and garlic sauce, or familiar favourites like saffron chicken korma.

Chef Suresh Manandhar **Times** 12-2.30/6-11, Closed 25 Dec-1 Jan, 2 weeks in Aug, Closed L all week (unless prior notice given) **Prices** Fixed L 2 course £18.50-£49, Fixed D 3 course fr £24, Starter £5.50-£13, Main £13-£36, Dessert £5.50-£7.50, Service added 12.5% **Wines** 138 bottles over £20, 11 by glass **Notes** Reservation required for L, Vegetarian available, Dress restrictions, Smart dress, no jeans or T-shirts, Air con **Seats** 60 **Children** Min 12 yrs

Nipa Thai Restaurant

◉ Thai 🖵   Plan 2 D2

Genuine Thai cuisine with Hyde Park views

☎ 020 7551 6039
The Royal Lancaster Hotel, Lancaster Ter W2 2TY
e-mail: nipa@royallancaster.com
web: www.niparestaurant.co.uk
dir: Nearest station: Lancaster Gate Opposite Hyde Park
on Bayswater Rd. On 1st floor of hotel

Situated on the first floor of the Royal Lancaster Hotel,
this Thai restaurant, with its authentic décor of teak
panelling and original artefacts, offers an intimate
setting and views over Hyde Park. The à la carte menu
and three set menus provide a wide choice of intensely
flavoured quality dishes which include regional
specialities, with herbs and seasonings flown in direct
from Thailand. Mouthwatering Thai delicacies to tempt
the diner may include fried soft-shell crab served with
plum sauce, deep-fried marinated chicken wrapped in
pandanus leaves, or perhaps stir-fried scallops with
green asparagus.

Chef Nongyao Thoopchoi **Owner** Lancaster Landmark
Hotel Co Ltd **Times** 12-2.30/6.30-10.30, Closed week
between Xmas and New Year, BHs, Closed Sun, Closed L
Sat **Prices** Food prices not confirmed for 2009. Please
telephone for details. **Wines** 9 by glass **Notes** Fixed D 4
courses, Dress restrictions, Smart casual, Air con
Seats 55 **Children** Portions **Parking** 50

Royal China

◉ Chinese   Plan 2 B1

Ever popular traditional Bayswater Chinese

☎ 020 7221 2535
13 Queensway W2 4QJ
e-mail: royalchina@btconnect.com
dir: Nearest station: Bayswater, Queensway Stn Please
telephone for directions

The deceptively small shop front at the Royal China
restaurant opens into a spacious dining room that
stretches a long way back. The opulent interior features
black-and-gold lacquered walls, mirrors and etched

glass, and teak screens that create more intimate areas.
The large number of Chinese diners is a testimony to its
success. Classic Chinese food with quality ingredients
(especially seafood) comes together to produce clean-cut
dishes and flavours. The extensive menu is bolstered by
several set options, with dim sum a favourite and
available daily. Expect the likes of crispy aromatic duck
with pancakes and trimmings, stir-fried Szechuan tofu,
and Szechaun prawns.

Times 12/11, Closed 25-26 Dec

Urban Turban

◉ Modern Indian   Plan 2 A2

Vibrant, buzzy modern Indian with tapas for sharing

☎ 020 7243 4200
98 Westbourne Grove W2 5RU

This new contemporary Indian from the much-lauded
Vineet Bhatia (chef-patron of Rasoi Restaurant SW3, see
entry) has hit the ground running with its accessible
Indian tapas. It's a smart, trendy affair, with dark colours
softened by sub-continental soft furnishings; think
vibrant-coloured banquettes, low-slung chairs, pouffes
and banquettes, while mood lighting and a central bar
all catch the eye too. There's a big wrap-around glass
frontage on the buzzy ground floor, while the basement
dining area has a more intimate, sexier feel. The menu is
inspired by India's informal street eateries and quality
dishes come designed for sharing, with 'desi tapas' like
chicken lollipops served with spicy ketchup followed up
by larger 'classic helpings' such as lamb biryani. Cooking
is polished and spicing is as polite as the attentive
service.

Times Noon-mdnt **Prices** Food prices not confirmed for
2009. Please telephone for details.

LONDON W4

The Devonshire

◉ Traditional British   Plan 1 D3

**Gordon Ramsay pub serving unpretentious classic
British food**

☎ 020 7592 7962
126 Devonshire Rd, Chiswick W4 2JJ
e-mail: thedevonshire@gordonramsay.com
dir: Nearest station: Turnham Green 150yds from
Chiswick High Rd, opposite Turnham Green Terrace

Gordon Ramsay's second excursion into the pub scene
opened in October 2007 in residential Chiswick. The old
Victorian corner pub comes sympathetically refurbished
with a modern gastro-pub look. Think high ceilings, large
windows and original wood panelling, set against modern
chairs and varnished wood tables, dangling light shades
and wooden floors, while uncluttered white walls are
hung with vintage black-and-white photos. Casual
drinkers are not excluded, with modern sofas, armchairs
and high bar tables around the top-end of the L-shaped
room's big bar. The menu focuses on classic British
dishes driven by quality seasonal produce and intelligent

simplicity; take hake, chips and marrowfat peas or
bread-and-butter pudding with custard. A bar menu,
knowledgeable service and rear garden complete the
upbeat package.

Chef Chris Arkadieff, Mark Sargeant **Owner** Gordon
Ramsay Holdings **Times** 12-3/5-10.45 **Prices** Food prices
not confirmed for 2009. Please telephone for details.
Wines 37 bottles over £20, 16 bottles under £20, 11 by
glass **Notes** Sunday L, Vegetarian available **Seats** 45
Children Portions **Parking** On street

High Road Brasserie

◉ European   Plan 1 D3

Cool, bustling west London brasserie

☎ 020 8742 7474
162-164 Chiswick High Rd W4 1PR

French windows and canopied pavement seats pick out
this urban-chic High Road brasserie, the latest addition
to Nick Jones's blossoming empire. Pillars and mirrors,
pewter-topped tables, leather banquettes, patchwork-
coloured floor tiles and a marble bar make this a light,
modern, stylish venue with a very New York air. The food
fits the surroundings - informal, modern European
brasserie fare on an all-day menu. From breakfast or food
to run through the day, to more substantial dishes - like
halibut with clams, mussels and saffron, perhaps a
seafood platter, or Pyrenean Black Pig chop. (There's also
a private members' club and boutique hotel on site.)

Times 7/12

Sam's Brasserie & Bar

◉◉ Modern European 🖵   Plan 1 C3

**Modern, informal brasserie with friendly service and
quality food**

☎ 020 8987 0555
11 Barley Mow Passage W4 4PH
e-mail: info@samsbrasserie.co.uk
dir: Nearest station: Chiswick Park/Turnham Green
Behind Chiswick High Rd, next to the green, off Heathfield
Terrace

This converted, one-time paper factory is secreted away
down a narrow walkway just off the Chiswick High Road.
A New York loft-style edge and a timeless, relaxed urban
vibe are effortlessly created by the high ceilings, girders,
pillars, industrial piping, bare-brick walls, and the
contemporary furnishings that fill the vibrant space.

Continued

LONDON W4 *Continued*

There's a smaller mezzanine brasserie at the front and a semi-open kitchen to the back, while off to one side, the buzzy bar continues the theme. The cooking delivers clean-cut dishes and flavours driven by top-quality ingredients; take crisp sea bass with sautéed potatoes and horseradish cream and rump of lamb with creamed flageolet beans.

Chef Ian Leckie **Owner** Sam Harrison
Times 12-3/6.30-10.30, Closed 25-26 Dec **Prices** Fixed L 2 course £11.50, Fixed D 3 course £17, Starter £4.75-£10, Main £8.75-£17.50, Dessert £4-£7, Service added 12.5% **Wines** 43 bottles over £20, 21 bottles under £20, 20 by glass **Notes** Sunday L, Vegetarian available, Air con **Seats** 100 **Children** Portions, Menu **Parking** Metered parking

La Trompette

◉◉◉ – **see below**

Le Vacherin

◉ French 💻 Plan 1 C3

Smart bistro serving classic French cuisine

☎ 020 8742 2121 & 8742 0799
76-77 South Pde W4 5LF
e-mail: malcolm.john4@btinternet.com
dir: Nearest station: Chiswick Park Turn left and restaurant, 400mtrs on left

Blond-wood floors, a mirror-frieze above banquette-lined cream walls, foodie pictures and posters, attentive French staff clad in long white aprons and a backing track of Gallic music, evoke the atmosphere of a smart Parisian bistro. The cooking follows the script, with simple, classic French brasserie fare and an all-French wine list to match. The namesake soft mountain cow's milk cheese, Vacherin (in season November to February) makes a regular appearance on the menu. Organic produce is used wherever possible, with everything from bread to ice cream being made in-house. Tuck into the likes of milk-fed calves' liver with onions, Alsace bacon and creamed potatoes, or fillet of sea bass with gratin of truffled salsify, finishing off with a classic tarte Tatin.

Chef Malcolm John **Owner** Malcolm & Donna John
Times 12-3/6-11, Closed 25 Dec, BHs, Closed L Mon **Prices** Food prices not confirmed for 2009. Please telephone for details. **Wines** 20 bottles over £20, 17 bottles under £20, 8 by glass **Notes** Air con **Seats** 72, Pr/dining room 30 **Children** Portions

---

La Trompette

LONDON W4	Plan 1 C3

European

French-inspired cuisine at fashionable and chic restaurant

☎ 020 8747 1836
5-7 Devonshire Rd, Chiswick W4 2EU
e-mail: reception@latrompette.co.uk
dir: Nearest station: Turnham Green From station follow Turnham Green Tce to junct with Chiswick High Rd. Cross road & bear right. Devonshire Rd 2nd left

La Trompette is in eminent company as part of an eminent company with Chez Bruce in Wandsworth and The Glasshouse in Kew (see entries). The Chiswick operation cuts quite a dash on Devonshire Road with its immaculately trimmed hedge surrounding a few outside tables, large awning providing protection from the elements (rain or shine) and plenty of glass in the form of sliding doors which really open up the space when the weather allows. The room gives the impression of a brasserie with its oak floors, leather banquette seating, muted tones of brown and tables covered in white linen; it is all very understated and unpretentious yet smart and appealing. Service is confident and knowledgeable and the atmosphere positively buzzes with conviviality. The accomplished cooking has its roots in France, and the South West of the country specifically, although there are broader influences at work. Crisp-fried goujons of lemon sole with tartare sauce is a straightforward starter, or there might be boudin blanc with sautéed spinach, Madeira sauce and pistachio nuts. Main-course roast rump of veal comes with glazed potatoes, spring onions, lardons and veal jus, and desserts can be as globally inspired as iced yuzu parfait with mango sorbet and passionfruit.

Chef James Bennington **Owner** Nigel Platts-Martin, Bruce Poole **Times** 12-2.30/6.30-10.30, Closed 25-26 Dec, 1 Jan **Prices** Food prices not confirmed for 2009. Please telephone for details. **Wines** 500 bottles over £20, 30 bottles under £20, 15 by glass **Notes** Sunday L, Air con **Seats** 72 **Children** Portions **Parking** On street

LONDON W6

Agni

◉ Traditional Indian V   Plan 1 D3

Regional Indian cuisine in comfortable surroundings

☎ 020 8846 9191 & 8748 6611
160 King St W6 0QU
e-mail: info@agnirestaurant.com
dir: Nearest station: Hammersmith Broadway,
Ravenscourt Park Telephone for directions

Decked out in yellow and gold with a clear Indian theme,
Agni is set over two floors and has an unfussy bistro style
with wooden tables, cane-seated chairs and panelled
walls. It has pedigree too, with Gowtham Karingi (ex head
chef at Zaika and Veeraswamy) and Neeraj Mittra (ex
manager at Chutney Mary) at the helm, while service is
professional and very friendly. The traditional Indian
cuisine is well presented, reflecting the progression of
regional Indian food from its ancient roots, with
emphasis on quality ingredients, clever spicing and clear
flavours. Try one of the specialty Hyderabad biryani pots -
chicken, lamb, vegetable or tiger prawn - or maybe
chicken tikka tiranga, and to finish, rose petal and black
pepper kulfi. Plenty of vegetarian choices too.

Chef Gowtham Karingi **Owner** Neeraj Mittra & Gowtham
Karingi **Times** Closed 25 Dec, Closed L Mon-Sun
Prices Tasting menu £40, Starter £3.25-£6.50, Main
£7-£13.95, Dessert £3.50-£5, Service added but optional
10% **Wines** 6 bottles over £20, 14 bottles under £20, 8 by
glass **Notes** Vegetarian menu, Air con **Seats** 50, Pr/dining
room 45 **Children** Portions **Parking** On street, car park

Anglesea Arms

◉ British, French   Plan 1 D3

No-frills gastro-pub serving simple modern fare

☎ 020 8749 1291
35 Wingate Rd W6 0UR
e-mail: anglesea.events@gmail.com
dir: Nearest station: Goldhawk Road, Ravenscourt Park.
Off Goldhawk Road.

There's plenty of hustle and bustle at this small,
fashionably shabby-chic, neighbourhood gastro-pub,
popular with trendy locals and students alike. At the
front there are bare boards, panelling and a collection
of old wooden furniture to add atmosphere to the low-lit
bar, replete with the odd leather sofa or banquette.
Behind, the brighter dining area comes with skylight,
exposed brickwork and all the theatre of an open-to-
view kitchen to add to the unbuttoned, relaxed vibe.
Quality seasonal produce features on daily-changing
blackboard menus (served throughout, including the
terrace out front), delivering simple modern British food
with flair; take chargrilled onglet with chips, French
beans and béarnaise. (There's a no-bookings policy, so
arrive early.)

Chef Dion Scott **Owner** Michael Mann, Jill O' Sullivan
Times 12.30-2.45/7-10.30, Closed 24-31 Dec
Prices Starter £4.75-£9.95, Main £9.95-£15.50, Dessert

£5.25, Service optional, Groups min 8 service 12.5%
Wines 86 bottles over £20, 14 bottles under £20, 20 by
glass **Notes** Sunday L, Vegetarian available, Air con
Seats 70 **Children** Portions **Parking** On street, pay &
display (free at wknds)

The Brackenbury

◉ Modern European   Plan 1 D3

**Accomplished cooking in a friendly neighbourhood
environment**

☎ 020 8748 0107
129-131 Brackenbury Rd W6 0BQ
e-mail: info@thebrackenbury.com
dir: Nearest station: Goldhawk Road, Hammersmith
Please telephone for directions

The epitome of a neighbourhood restaurant, The
Brackenbury is set in a quiet residential street and has a
calm and friendly atmosphere. A front terrace is a fair-
weather bonus, while the split-level interior is decorated
in earthy tones with modern chairs or banquette seating,
flowers and candles. The style of cooking is modern
European with a nod to the Mediterranean and an
emphasis on fine basic ingredients, colourful
presentation and clear flavours. You can expect fish
dishes like John Dory with sautéed potatoes and
trompette mushrooms, and alternatives such as stuffed
pig's trotter, or rib-eye steak with hand-made chips.

Chef Matt Cranston **Owner** Lisa Inglis
Times 12.30-2.45/7-10.45, Closed 24-26 Dec, 1 Jan, Etr
Mon, Aug BH Mon, Closed D Sun **Prices** Food prices not
confirmed for 2009. Please telephone for details.
Wines 32 bottles over £20, 15 bottles under £20, 10 by
glass **Notes** Sunday L, Vegetarian available **Seats** 60
Children Portions **Parking** On street

Chez Kristof

◉ French 🖳   Plan 1 D4

Classic French cooking in a neighbourhood bistro

☎ 020 8741 1177
111 Hammersmith Grove W6 0NQ
e-mail: info@chezkristof.co.uk
dir: Nearest station: Hammersmith Please telephone for
directions

This popular neighbourhood restaurant occupies a corner
site in a quiet part of Shepherd's Bush. Squeeze on to one
of the closely packed tables and tuck into some well
executed rustic French dishes. Gallic classics include
snails with garlic butter, spatchcock coquelet with olives
and lemon, and pot au chocolat. A good choice of
crustacea also features, including duchess rock oysters,
razor clams, and ragout of cockles and mussels. If you
want to eat great French food at home, a visit to the
restaurant's delicatessen next door is a must.

Times 12-3/6-11.15, Closed 24-26 Dec, 1 Jan

The Gate

◉ Modern Vegetarian V   Plan 1 D3

Vegetarian restaurant offering inventive cuisine

☎ 020 8748 6932
51 Queen Caroline St W6 9QL
e-mail: hammersmith@thegate.tv
dir: Nearest station: Hammersmith Hammersmith Apollo
Theatre, continue down right side for approx 40 yds

The Gate is a gourmet vegetarian restaurant housed in
an unusual listed building, approached via a church
entrance hall. The former artist's studio is bright and airy
with high ceilings, large windows and dramatic artwork.
The cooking is an inspired alternative to the usual
vegetarian choices. It seeks out bold flavours, inventive
combinations and fresh ingredients to produce simple
but ingenious dishes, such as involtini (chargrilled
aubergine rolled in mozzarella, roasted red pepper and
basil pesto, served with lentil salsa), green Thai curry,
and pineapple and chilli crumble served with crème
anglaise.

Chef Adrian Daniel, Mariusz Wegrodski **Owner** Adrian &
Michael Daniel **Times** 12-3/6-11, Closed 23 Dec-3 Jan,
Good Fri & Etr Mon, Closed Sun, Closed L Sat **Prices** Fixed
L 2 course £18.75, Fixed D 3 course £23, Starter
£4.50-£6, Main £8.50-£14, Dessert £4.50-£6, Service
added but optional 12.5% **Wines** 2 bottles over £20, 8
bottles under £20, 10 by glass **Notes** Vegetarian menu,
Air con **Seats** 60 **Children** Portions **Parking** On street

The River Café

◉◉◉ – *see page 318*

Sagar

◉◉ Vegetarian, Indian V   Plan 1 D3

**Authentic south Indian vegetarian cooking in the heart
of Hammersmith**

☎ 020 8741 8563
157 King St, Hammersmith W6 9JT
dir: Nearest station: Hammersmith 10min from
Hammersmith Tube

This unpretentious restaurant with a modern glass frontage
is set among shops on a busy Hammersmith street. It's a
popular place with a lively atmosphere, close-set tables,
blond-wood floorboards and walls dotted with Indian
artefacts. The kitchen's lengthy vegetarian repertoire offers a
good range majoring on dishes from the Udipi region,
including starters such as kancheepuram idli (rice and lentil
dumplings with green chilli, pepper and cashew nuts),
special upma (wheat cooked with spices, tomato, peas and
nuts), and bhaji. Main meals include a choice of dosas,
uthappams (lentil pizzas) and curries such as brinjal bhajee
(aubergine cooked with tomato and South Indian spices). For
dessert, try srikand - a creamy yogurt with sugar, saffron
and cardamom. Dishes are skilfully crafted with clean-cut
presentation and distinct flavours, and prices are incredibly
low for the quality delivered.

Continued

LONDON W6 *Continued*

Chef Ramadas **Owner** S. Shurmielan **Times** 12-2.45/5.30-10.45, Closed 25-26 Dec **Prices** Food prices not confirmed for 2009. Please telephone for details. **Wines** 8 by glass **Notes** Vegetarian menu, Air con **Seats** 60 **Parking** On street

Snows-on-the-Green Restaurant

◉ Modern British 🍴 Plan 1 D3

Friendly, vibrant local restaurant with accomplished Mediterranean cuisine

☎ 020 7603 2142
166 Shepherd's Bush Rd, Brook Green, Hammersmith W6 7PB
e-mail: sebastian@snowsonthegreen.co.uk
dir: Nearest station: Hammersmith Broadway 300yds from station

A green awning and glass frontage distinguishes this long-established neighbourhood restaurant, which prides itself on its consistent delivery, honest pricing and gimmick-free business. The interior has a bright modern feel with black and white Bill Brandt photos, and the kitchen takes a modern approach with a sunny Mediterranean slant. Choose between the good-value, weekly set-price menu and a regularly changing carte, offering robust fare such as foie gras, fried egg and balsamic vinegar, daube of beef cheek in Chianti with snails, carrots, marrow toasts and truffled mash, and chocolate almond cake with crème fraîche.

Chef Sebastian Snow **Owner** Sebastian & Lana Snow **Times** 12-3/6-11, Closed BH Mon only, Closed Sun, Closed L Sat **Prices** Fixed L 2 course £13.50, Fixed D 3 course £16.50, Starter £5.95-£8.95, Main £14.95-£16.95, Dessert £5-£6, Service added but optional 12.5%, Groups min 6 service 12.5% **Wines** 20 bottles over £20, 17 bottles under £20, 12 by glass **Notes** Vegetarian available, Air con **Seats** 80, Pr/dining room 30 **Children** Portions, Menu **Parking** On street

LONDON W8

Babylon

◉◉ Modern British 🍴 Plan 4 B4

Minimalist chic, rooftop gardens and extraordinary views

☎ 020 7368 3993
The Roof Gardens, 99 Kensington High St W8 5SA
e-mail: babylon@roofgardens.virgin.co.uk
web: www.virginlimitededition.com
dir: Nearest station: High Street Kensington From High St Kensington tube station, turn right, then right into Derby St

The views over the London skyline from the seventh-floor decked terrace are framed by the lush greenery from the Roof Gardens below - a winning Kensington formula at Richard Branson's Babylon. Contemporary styling, a sleek, glass-sided dining room, booths, white linen and

The River Café

LONDON W6 Plan 1 D3

Italian 🍴 🌸 NOTABLE WINE LIST

The freshest food simply treated with reverence in Thames-side setting

☎ 020 7386 4200
Thames Wharf, Rainville Rd W6 9HA
e-mail: info@rivercafe.co.uk
dir: Nearest station: Hammersmith Restaurant in converted warehouse. Entrance on S side of Rainville Rd at junct with Bowfell Rd

Though celebrating some 20-plus years long-standing, the crowds still flock to Rose Gray and Ruth Rogers' enduringly famous Hammersmith Italian at the edge of the Thames. The place almost needs no description; a spacious, modern, minimalist white room (converted from an 18th-century warehouse) comes with plenty of steel and glass, and an urban vibe that successfully mixes a bustling, informal atmosphere with a fine-dining experience. Light floods in through floor-to-ceiling windows (opening up to the terrace in summer), and there's a long stainless-steel open kitchen with wood-burning oven, lively cocktail bar and close-set tables to add to the buzz. Menus change twice daily, so there's a sense of spontaneity to the flavour-driven cooking. The authentic, unfussy Italian cuisine - mainly Tuscan and Lombardian influenced - doesn't come cheap, but uses only the very best, freshest produce (with many ingredients specifically sourced for their rarity, locality and seasonality) simply treated and presented with skill and panache. Take wild sea bass roasted with lemon, capers and thyme and served with Castleluccio lentils and roasted trevise, and to finish, perhaps lemon tart or pannacotta with grappa and champagne rhubarb.

Chef R Gray, R Rogers, Sian Owen **Owner** Rose Gray, Ruth Rogers **Times** 12.30-3/7-11, Closed 24 Dec-1 Jan, Easter, BHs, Closed D Sun **Prices** Starter £11-£22, Main £27-£49, Dessert £7-£8, Service added but optional 12.5% **Wines** 155 bottles over £20, 13 bottles under £20, 18 by glass **Seats** 108 **Children** Portions **Parking** 29 **Parking** Valet parking in evening

even a sunken bar surrounded by fish-tanks, provide the stylish backcloth for slick, friendly service and those capital views. The menu's modern approach suits the surroundings and has a genuine focus on quality British produce and organic ingredients. A starter of wild mushroom and organic leek risotto is a well-made version demonstrating a sure hand in the kitchen, while main course griddled Kilravock free-range pork comes with bubble-and-squeak, caramelised baby onions, baby leeks and a well-judged Madeira jus.

Babylon

Chef Simon Davies **Owner** Sir Richard Branson **Times** 12-2.30/7-10.30, Closed Xmas, Closed D Sun **Prices** Fixed L 2 course £16, Starter £9-£14, Main £18-£24, Dessert £8-£15, Service added but optional 12.5% **Wines** 103 bottles over £20, 2 bottles under £20, 15 by glass **Notes** Sunday L, Vegetarian available, Dress restrictions, Smart casual, Civ Wed 28, Air con **Seats** 120, Pr/dining room 12 **Children** Portions, Menu **Parking** 10, NCP car park on Young St

Belvedere

◉◉ British 💻 Plan 1 D3

Jewel in Holland Park, with stunning interior and garden views

☎ 020 7602 1238
Abbotsbury Rd, Holland House, Holland Park W8 6LU
e-mail: sales@whitestarline.org.uk
dir: Nearest station: Holland Park Off Abbotsbury Rd entrance to Holland Park

The beautiful old orangery in pretty Holland Park - once the summer ballroom to its Jacobean mansion - is the setting for this achingly elegant and romantic restaurant. Dramatic interior design - from design-guru David Collins - evokes a glamorous 1920s feel; think high vaulted ceiling and arched windows, sparkling bevelled mirrors, ornate wallpaper, parquet flooring and huge oyster-shell lights. Add potted palms, brown leather seating, white linen and modern

artwork - plus a bar and marble staircase to a mezzanine and terrace - and the result is dramatic. An evening pianist and well orchestrated service complete the picture, and serve as the backdrop to the kitchen's understated modern brasserie approach. A backbone of classics and refined favourites drive the crowd-pleasing repertoire; from eggs Benedict to fillet of beef au poivre with French beans and fries, or tart Tatin to banana split.

Belvedere

Chef Billy Reid **Owner** Jimmy Lahoud **Times** 12-2.30/6-10.30, Closed 26 Dec, 1 Jan, Closed D Sun **Prices** Fixed L 2 course fr £14.95, Starter £7.95-£18.50, Main £11.50-£19.95, Dessert fr £6.50, Service added but optional 12.5%, Groups min 13 service 15% **Wines** 114 bottles over £20, 14 by glass **Notes** Sunday L, Vegetarian available, Dress restrictions, Smart casual, Air con **Seats** 90 **Parking** Council car park

Cheneston's Restaurant

◉◉ British 💻 Plan 4 B4

Intimate restaurant in elegant townhouse hotel

☎ 020 7917 1000
Milestone Hotel, 1 Kensington Court W8 5DL
e-mail: bookms@rchmail.com
dir: Nearest station: High St Kensington M4/ Hammersmith flyover, take 2nd left into Gloucester Rd, left into High St Kensington, 500mtrs on left

Enjoying a wonderful location opposite Kensington Palace and Gardens, this Victorian mansion has been transformed into a hotel of style and class, with many restored original features. Expect luxurious lounges and a sumptuous dining room with leaded Victorian windows, shining crystal and silverware and original cartoons on the walls. As befits the surroundings and the clientele, food is classically based and both cooking style and presentation are simple and unfussy, driven by quality seasonal ingredients. Take fillet of Aberdeen Angus beef

with woodland mushrooms, asparagus and truffle sauce, and perhaps a lemon tart with mascarpone cream finish. Service is formal and professional from an international team.

Chef David Smith **Owner** The Red Carnation Hotel **Times** 12-3/5.30-11 **Prices** Fixed L 2 course £21.50-£26.50, Fixed D 3 course £26.50-£29.50, Tasting menu £60-£95, Starter £8.50-£19.50, Main £15.50-£39.50, Dessert £9.50-£10.50, Service added but optional 12.5% **Wines** 250 bottles over £20, 12 by glass **Notes** Pre-theatre D £21.50, Tasting menu 7 courses, Sunday L, Vegetarian available, Dress restrictions, Smart casual, Civ Wed 30, Air con **Seats** 30, Pr/dining room 8 **Children** Portions, Menu **Parking** NCP Young Street off Kensington High Street

Clarke's

◉◉ Modern British, Mediterranean 💭 Plan 4 A5

The freshest food simply treated with reverence

☎ 020 7221 9225
124 Kensington Church St W8 4BH
e-mail: restaurant@sallyclarke.com
dir: Nearest station: Notting Hill Gate Telephone for directions

A popular haunt for Notting Hill residents and many a celebrity, Sally Clarke's influential restaurant is set amongst the well-known antique shops of Kensington Church Street, adjacent to her famous bread shop. Minimalist décor is chic and modern with crisply starched table linen, and staff are professional and diligent. The restaurant offers a choice at dinner (three at each turn) and it's no longer necessary to have all four courses (once a set four-course affair), plus there's also a brunch offering on Saturdays from 11am until 2pm. Menus change weekly and are posted on their website each Monday. Ingredients, skill and artistry take priority here, and it is this that makes the cooking so successful and enduring. Modern European-style dishes might include fillet of halibut baked in parchment with fennel, lemon and dill, finishing with apple strudel with raisins and cinnamon.

Chef Sally Clarke,Raffaele Colturi **Owner** Sally Clarke **Times** 12.30-2/7-10, Closed 8 days Xmas & New Year, Closed Sun **Prices** Food prices not confirmed for 2009. Please telephone for details. **Wines** 86 bottles over £20, 10 bottles under £20, 8 by glass **Notes** Fixed D 4 courses, Vegetarian available, Air con **Seats** 80, Pr/dining room 70 **Parking** On street

LONDON W8 *Continued*

Eleven Abingdon Road

◎◎ European 🖥 Plan 4 A4

Cool neighbourhood venue off High Street Kensington

☎ 020 7937 0120

11 Abingdon Rd, Kensington W8 6AH

e-mail: eleven@abingdonroad.co.uk

dir: Nearest station: Kensington High St Telephone for directions

This light, modern, glass-fronted restaurant is tucked away in a little road just off High Street Ken and proves quite a find; it shares ownership with Sonny's in Barnes. The stylish, restrained, clean-cut interior - with a small chic bar area up front decked out with leopard- and tiger-skin chairs - comes dominated by an eye-catching art collection set to a backdrop of sage-green walls, contemporary lighting, modern darkwood chairs and a friendly, upbeat vibe. Staff dressed in jeans and long black aprons deliver modern, Mediterranean-slant dishes using quality seasonal ingredients; think chargrilled halibut served with slow-cooked fennel, Swiss chard and salsa verde, or perhaps slow-cooked veal shin with risotto Milanese and gremolata.

Times 12.30-2.30/6.30-11, Closed 25 Dec, BHs

Geales

◎ Seafood 🖥 Plan 4 A6

Posh fish, chips and shellfish in a suave, modern setting

☎ 020 7727 7528

2 Farmer St W8 7SN

e-mail: www.geales.com

This long-time traditional chippie on the edge of Notting Hill (originally established back in 1939) has been given a smart makeover by new owners Mark Fuller and Garry Hollihead (of Mayfair restaurant and club fame, the Embassy London). The contemporary interior is fresh and sleek, with wooden floors and comfortable leather seating, while pavement terrace tables are popular in fair weather. The menu has been given an overhaul to match, offering an impressive selection of shellfish alongside traditional chippy cuisine; think cod, haddock or sole cooked in crispy batter with an array of side orders ranging from baby spinach to mushy peas, tartare sauce or sweet pickled onions. Desserts continue the homely theme with offerings like treacle tart, chocolate brownie or Eton Mess.

Times Closed L Mon

Kensington Place

◎◎ Modern British 🖥 Plan 4 A6

Busy brasserie-style restaurant with vibrant colour and atmosphere

☎ 020 7727 3184

201-9 Kensington Church St W8 7LX

e-mail: kpparty@egami.co.uk

dir: Nearest station: Notting Hill Gate Telephone for directions

Fish is a speciality at this popular Notting Hill restaurant, which even has its own elegant fish shop next door to cater for your every need. The restaurant's long plate-glass fascia lets you watch the world go by (and allows passers-by to get a good look in), and a revolving door leads onto a bustling, energetic bar. The main restaurant, which is decorated with a striking mural depicting nearby Kensington Gardens, has closely set tables and colourful wooden chairs. The cooking is modern British brasserie-style, served simply with an emphasis on fresh fish and game. Straightforward presentation allows the main ingredient to be the focus in dishes such as grilled smoked eel with fennel and horseradish sauce, or sea bass with crushed potatoes, chorizo and red wine sauce.

Times 12-3.30/6.30-11.15, Closed 24-26 Dec, 1 Jan

Launceston Place Restaurant

◎◎ Modern European 🖥 Plan 4 C4

Refurbished restaurant with exciting food

☎ 020 7937 6912

1a Launceston Place W8 5RL

e-mail: lpr@egami.co.uk

dir: Nearest station: Gloucester Road Just south of Kensington Palace

There have been changes at Launceston Place with the arrival of a new chef and refurbishment. The room, with its large windows letting the light flood in, is now painted a rich tone of brown and there are lots of stylish touches such as bold art on the walls and fibre-optic chandeliers. Staff are impeccably dressed in tones of brown and deliver highly professional service. New chef Tristan Welch has a track record at celebrated restaurants (notably Pétrus) and his menus are in the modern vein: seasonally inspired, grounded in classical France and with bags of creative ideas. Take a starter of hand-dived West Coast scallops with baby sorrel leaves and apple, strikingly served on a large, flat pebble. Main-course Tamworth suckling pig is served with Jersey Royals potato salad, creamed onion and a well flavoured jus.

Times 12.30-2.30/6-11, Closed Xmas, New Year, Etr, Closed L Sat

Park Terrace Restaurant

◎◎ Modern European ✍ Plan 4 B5

Imaginative modern cooking in a spacious room overlooking Kensington Gardens

☎ 020 7361 0602

Royal Garden Hotel, 2-24 Kensington High St W8 4PT

e-mail: dining@royalgardenhotel.co.uk

web: www.royalgardenhotel.co.uk

dir: Nearest station: Kensington High Street Next to Kensington Palace, Royal Albert Hall

The restaurant on the tenth floor of this hotel in fashionable Kensington, just a short walk from the Albert Hall, is undergoing total refurbishment as we go to press and will open as Min Jiang, focusing on provincial Chinese cooking. The Park Terrace Restaurant, located at lobby level, but still enjoying views over Kensington Gardens, is the place to sample well-sourced British produce, cooked with flair in a modern European style, and served by well trained and attentive staff. Floor-to-ceiling windows let the light flood in and fresh flowers add splashes of colour throughout the large and airy room. Warm salad of confit duck leg and foie gras Royale is a luxurious starter showing the ambition in the kitchen, while main-course pan-seared gilt head bream served with razor clam and hazelnut ragout, smoked garlic mash and buttered spinach is a successful combination of flavours.

Chef Steve Munkley **Owner** Goodwood Group
Times 12-3/6-10.30 **Prices** Fixed L 2 course fr £14.50, Fixed D 3 course fr £29.50, Starter fr £8.50, Main fr £15, Dessert fr £8.50, Service optional, Groups min 8 service 10% **Wines** 74 bottles over £20, 3 bottles under £20, 13 by glass **Notes** Sunday L, Vegetarian available, Dress restrictions, Smart casual, Air con **Seats** 92 **Children** Portions, Menu **Parking** 160

Timo

◉ Italian 🖥 Plan 1 D3

Stylish, authentic Italian dining

☎ 020 7603 3888
343 Kensington High St W8 6NW
e-mail: timorestaurant@tiscali.co.uk
dir: Nearest station: Kensington High St 5 mins walk
towards Hammersmith, after Odeon Cinema, on left of
street

Located on a quieter stretch of fashionable Kensington
High Street's western limits, this friendly, neighbourhood
Italian is worth seeking out for its authentic regional
cooking. The modern décor is smart and stylish but
relaxed too. The long, narrow, split-level space has
soothing pastel shades and blond-wood floors, while
high-backed suede chairs or banquettes and crisply
dressed tables provide the comforts. Two large paintings
of London park life add a splash of colour and interest.
The classical cooking and presentation comes driven by
prime ingredients. Linguine with clams, chilli, garlic and
parsley, or perhaps slow-cooked fillet of hake served with
capers, olives, chopped tomato and roasted radicchio are
fine examples of the fare.

Chef Franco Gatto **Owner** Piero Amodio
Times 12-2.30/7-11, Closed Xmas, New Year, BHs,
Closed L Sat, Closed D Sun **Prices** Fixed D 3 course
£17.50, Starter £6.90-£12.50, Main £14.50-£22.50,
Dessert £5-£7.50, Service added but optional 12.5%,
Groups min 10 service 15% **Wines** 3 bottles over £20, 3
bottles under £20, 8 by glass **Notes** Vegetarian available,
Air con **Seats** 55, Pr/dining room 18 **Children** Portions
Parking 3

Zaika

◉◉ Modern Indian 🖥 🍷NOTABLE WINE LIST Plan 4 B4

**Lively restaurant serving carefully prepared modern
Indian cuisine**

☎ 020 7795 6533
1 Kensington High St W8 5NP
e-mail: info@zaika-restaurant.co.uk
dir: Nearest station: Kensington High Street Opposite
Kensington Palace

Originally a bank, Zaika has maintained many original
features in its opulent, panelled interior and the design
recalls the style of British India. The restaurant is
decorated in a rich palette of colours, including the
contemporary chairs and banquettes. Blond-wood
floorboards, Indian artefacts, modern lighting and a bar
at the front add to the sophisticated styling, while
professional, informed service and an impressive wine
list complete the upbeat vibe. The kitchen's innovative
menu of modern Indian cuisine delivers well-executed,
vibrantly-flavoured and creatively presented dishes from
quality ingredients, as in seared marinated tuna with
Indian caviar, spicy chicken with watercress and spinach
and masala duck breast with rich black lentil sauce and
celeriac and parsnip mash.

Chef Sanjay Dwivedi **Owner** Claudio Pulze, Sanjay

Dwivedi Times 12-2.45/6-10.45, Closed BHs, Xmas, New
Year, Closed L Sat **Wines** 100+ bottles over £20, 8 bottles
under £20, 17 by glass **Notes** Fixed L 4 courses £19.50,
Pre-theatre 2/3 course £15/£18, Vegetarian available,
Dress restrictions, Smart casual preferred, Air con
Seats 84 **Children** Portions

The Ark

🖥

☎ 020 7229 4024
122 Palace Gardens Ter W8 4RT
web: http://www.theaa.com/travel/index.jsp

Small Italian restaurant where clever design has made
the dining area seem a lot bigger - there's also a decked
area for alfresco eating.

Prices Food prices not confirmed for 2009. Please
telephone for details.

The Warrington

◉ Modern British Plan 2 C5

Posh pub food in historically ornate surroundings

☎ 020 7592 7960
93 Warrington Crescent, Maida Vale W9 1EH
e-mail: warrington@gordonramsay.com
dir: Nearest station: Warwick Avenue, Maida Vale Please
telephone for directions

The third pub in the Gordon Ramsay empire, the main bar
of The Warrington is a glorious piece of old Victoriana:
dark-wood panelling, ornate cornices, leather sofas, and
all spruced up with a bit of Ramsay magic. The upstairs
dining room is equally as impressive, the cream-
coloured, high-ceilinged room a good contrast to the
bustling bar below. The menu is a broad selection of
British classics done with real style. Potted Goosnargh
duck and sourdough toast is a suitably luscious starter,
or there is the more cosmopolitan Sharpham spelt risotto
with butternut squash. Shredded duck shepherd's pie
provides a richly flavoured filling with a smooth cheesy
mash and desserts are as retro as knickerbocker glory
and as comforting as treacle tart with clotted cream. The
place buzzes with atmosphere on both floors and the
staff remain polite and friendly.

Chef Mark Sargeant **Owner** Gordon Ramsay
Times 12-2.3/6-10.30 **Prices** Starter £5.75-£11.75, Main
£7.25-£19.50, Dessert £4.50-£6.50, Service added but
optional 12.5% **Notes** Sunday L, Air con **Seats** 80, Pr/
dining room 14 **Children** Portions **Parking** On Street

E&O

◉ Pan Asian 🖥 Plan 1 D4

Fashionable oriental-style eatery and bar

☎ 020 7229 5454
14 Blenheim Crescent W11 1NN
e-mail: eando@rickerrestaurants.com
dir: Nearest station: Notting Hill Gate, Ladbroke Grove At
Notting Hill Gate tube station turn right, at mini rdbt turn
into Kensington Park Rd, restaurant 10min down hill

Oriental style combines with modern minimalist décor at
this trendy bar-restaurant. Think slatted darkwood, plain
white walls, giant oval lampshades, brown leather
banquettes or black lacquer chairs and polished
floorboards. Upfront there's a bustling red-walled bar
and, to the side, a few alfresco pavement tables, while
everywhere the atmosphere's vibrant and upbeat. The
modern pan-Asian fusion menu is divided into sections
for grazing and sharing from dim sum to tempura,
curries or sashimi, and specials like lobster Singapore
noodles and beef fillet bulgogi.

Chef Simon Treadway **Owner** Will Ricker **Times** 12-3/6-11,
Closed Xmas, New Year, Aug BH **Prices** Starter £5.50-£10,
Main £9.50-£21.50, Dessert £5.50-£6.50, Service added
but optional 12.5% **Wines** 80 bottles over £20, 8 bottles
under £20, 22 by glass **Notes** Sunday L, Vegetarian
available, Air con **Seats** 84, Pr/dining room 18
Children Portions, Menu **Parking** On street

Edera

◉◉ Modern Italian 🖥 Plan 1 D4

Good-value, modern and stylish neighbourhood Italian

☎ 020 7221 6090
148 Holland Park Av W11 4UE
e-mail: edera@btconnect.com
dir: Nearest station: Holland Park Please telephone for
directions

This clean-lined, minimally styled Holland Park Italian -
with glass frontage, awning and a few pavement tables
to catch the eye - proves a stylish yet friendly venue.
Decked out on tiered levels, the newly refurbished dining
areas and wine rooms provide the upmarket setting for
some accomplished Italian cooking, backed by attentive
Latin staff clad in long black aprons. The kitchen, like the
patriotic wine list, draws inspiration from the Italian
regions, with the occasional nod to Sardinia. Take
spaghetti bottarga and Sardinian couscous with
langoustine and cherry tomatoes. The style is
straightforward, clean-cut and creatively accomplished,
driven by high quality seasonal ingredients.

Chef Carlo Usai, Danilo Moi **Owner** A-Z Ltd/Mr Pisano
Times 12-2.30/6.30-11, Closed 25-26 & 31 Dec
Prices Starter £7-£15, Main £14-£20, Dessert £5-£8,
Service added but optional 12.5% **Wines** 140 bottles over
£20, 3 bottles under £20, 13 by glass **Notes** Air con
Seats 70, Pr/dining room 20 **Children** Portions
Parking On street parking

Notting Hill Brasserie

LONDON W11   Plan 4 D4

Modern Mediterranean 💻

Chic food, chic décor, chic location

☎ 020 7229 4481
92 Kensington Park Rd W11 2PN
e-mail: enquiries@nottinghillbrasserie.com
dir: Nearest station: Notting Hill Gate 3 mins walk from Notting Hill station

Who would have thought taking three townhouses and knocking them together into a single restaurant could result in something this stylish? The generously sized rooms of these former homes have been knocked together to create a series of inter-connected spaces, with high ceilings and moulded cornices and all painted a neutral off-white colour. The wooden floor, spot lighting, contemporary pieces of art and stunning flower arrangements result in a chic, classy restaurant. There is a separate cocktail bar and live jazz at Sunday lunchtimes. The accomplished kitchen impresses with execution and professionalism with both classic and original twists, while keeping things deceptively simple on crisply-scripted menus driven by quality seasonal ingredients. Seared tuna comes with soft-shelled crab and shellfish dressing among starters, followed by rack of Elwy Valley lamb with sweet potato purée, pithivier of shoulder and goat's cheese. Finish with milk ice cream with berry salad, lemon curd and crispy rice. Excellent breads and the likes of amuse-bouche match the upbeat performance.

Chef Karl Burdock **Owner** Carlo Spetale **Times** 12-4/7-11, Closed Xmas, New Year, Closed D Sun **Prices** Fixed L 2 course fr £17.50, Starter £9-£14.50, Main £19-£26.50, Dessert fr £7, Service added but optional 12.5% **Wines** 140 bottles over £20, 5 bottles under £20, 10 by glass **Notes** Sunday L, Air con **Seats** 110, Pr/dining room 44 **Children** Portions **Parking** On street

The Ledbury

Modern French 🖥 V 🍷

Highly accomplished French cooking in fashionable, residential Notting Hill

☎ 020 7792 9090
127 Ledbury Rd W11 2AQ
e-mail: info@theledbury.com
dir: Nearest station: Westbourne Park, Notting Hill Gate 5 min walk along Talbot Rd from Portobello Rd, on corner of Talbot and Ledbury Rd

The upbeat offering from Nigel Platts-Martin and Philip Howard (who together also own The Square in Mayfair, see entry) has a smart, refined vibe, and is set in the heart of residential Notting Hill. The interior is contemporary, sophisticated and luxurious, with cream leather chairs alongside long dark curtains and polished-wood floors. Tables are relatively closely set, but the room doesn't feel cramped, helped by a clever use of mirrors and floor-to-ceiling windows. In summer, a terrace provides a great space for alfresco dining with tables covered by parasols and a canopy. Service is professional and attentive without being stuffy or overbearing. The accomplished, sophisticated cooking from Philip Howard protégé, Oz-born Brett Graham, delivers high technical skill through modern dishes underpinned by a classical French theme and prime seasonal ingredients, with dazzling visual presentation, interesting combinations and textures to the fore. Peripherals like breads, amuse-bouche, pre-desserts and petits fours are all top form, while the fixed-price repertoire of lunch (great value), carte and eight-course tasting option are partnered by a high-class wine list. Expect the likes of roast sea bass served with potato gnocchi, pickled onions and a smoked butter emulsion, or perhaps loin of roe deer partnered by chervil and parsley root, Douglas fir and pepper.

Chef Brett Graham **Owner** Nigel Platts-Martin & Philip Howard **Times** 12-2/6.30-11, Closed 24-26 Dec, 1 Jan, Aug BH wk end **Prices** Fixed L 2 course fr £19.50, Fixed D 3 course fr £50, Tasting menu £60-£98, Service added but optional 12.5% **Wines** 661 bottles over £20, 5 bottles under £20, 12 by glass **Notes** Tasting menu 8 courses, Sunday L, Vegetarian menu, Air con **Seats** 62 **Parking** Talbot Rd, metered

---

LONDON W11 *Continued*

The Ledbury
◎◎◎ – *see above*

Lonsdale
◎ British, European 🖥 | Plan 1 D4

Trendy lounge-style eatery

☎ 020 7727 4080
48 Lonsdale Rd W11 2DE
e-mail: info@thelonsdale.co.uk
dir: Nearest station: Notting Hill/Ladbroke Grove One street parallel to Westbourne Grove. Between Portobello Rd and Ledbury Rd

This sophisticated, evening-only bar-restaurant stands out from the crowd in residential Notting Hill. The Lonsdale strips away conventional fine-dining formalities with bold retro styling, a fun and friendly atmosphere and youthful service. Close-set, darkwood tables are teamed with burgundy leather banquettes and large stools, and the mirror-lined walls, low-level lights and contemporary music hit all the right notes. The food is perfectly tuned to its surroundings with dishes like sweet and sour aubergine caponata with roasted cherry tomatoes and crisp celery; and rump of lamb with smashed root vegetables, chilli and thyme.

Chef Adam Penny **Owner** Adam & Charles Breeden **Times** Closed 25-26 Dec, 1 Jan, Closed L all wk **Prices** Starter £5.50-£8.50, Main £8.50-£18.50, Dessert £5.50, Service added but optional **Wines** 32 bottles over £20, 4 bottles under £20, 10 by glass **Notes** Vegetarian available, Air con **Seats** 80, Pr/dining room 24 **Children** Min 5 yrs **Parking** On street

Notting Hill Brasserie
◎◎◎ – *see opposite*

Notting Grill
🖥

☎ 020 7229 1500
123a Clarendon Rd, Holland Park W11 4JG
web: http://www.theaa.com/travel/index.jsp

Antony Worrall Thompson's eatery featuring quality meat dishes and produce from his own garden.

Prices Food prices not confirmed for 2009. Please telephone for details.

LONDON W14

Cibo
◎◎ Italian 🖥 | Plan 1 D3

Authentic Italian cooking to linger over

☎ 020 7371 2085 & 7371 6271
3 Russell Gardens W14 8EZ
e-mail: ciborestaurant@aol.com
dir: Nearest station: Olympia, Shepherds Bush Central Line Russell Gardens is a residential area off Holland Road, Kensington (Olympia) Shepherd's Bush

The décor certainly catches the eye at this long-established neighbourhood favourite close to Olympia - colourful, offbeat, abstract Renaissance-style nude paintings hang on the walls - and the room buzzes with energy from contented locals and lively staff. Tables are smartly laid with white linen and alongside modern

Continued

LONDON W14 *Continued*

blond-wood chairs and colourful crockery make for a confident impression. In summer, the full-length glass-front windows fold back so dining feels almost alfresco. Friendly waiting staff bring plenty of extras, from bread baskets to large olives and mini pizzas and petits fours. Menus are in Italian with English subtitles, with fish and shellfish a speciality and home-made filled pasta excellent. The cooking focuses on a straightforward but imaginative style driven by quality ingredients; think black pasta filled with crab in a light tomato and clam sauce, and grilled veal cutlet with rosemary and garlic.

Chef Alex Lombardi **Owner** Gino Taddei
Times 12.15-2.30/7-11, Closed Xmas, Etr BHs, Closed L Sat, Closed D Sun **Prices** Fixed L 2 course £17.50, Starter £7.50-£12.50, Main £12.50-£22.50, Dessert £3.95-£7, Service added but optional 12.5% **Wines** 41 bottles over £20, 5 bottles under £20, 4 by glass **Notes** Sunday L, Vegetarian available, Air con **Seats** 50, Pr/dining room 14 **Children** Portions **Parking** On street

LONDON WC1

Acorn House

⊛⊛ Modern 🖵 🕚 Plan 3 D5

Ground-breaking environmentally-friendly cooking in King's Cross

☎ 020 7812 1842
69 Swinton St WC1X 9NT

Acorn House is a restaurant aiming to leave its mark in the world by not leaving a mark on the planet - it is an environmentally friendly, sustainable establishment. There is an urban vegetable garden, composting bins, sustainable energy and a ban on mineral water. A future generation of chefs is trained here, too, so the ethos and skills are passed on. The setting is quietly cool and contemporary with an open-plan kitchen, shelves of produce and a take-away counter to service the local community. Candles come out in the evening. Not surprisingly, the food places a high emphasis on native produce, seasonality and sustainability. Salads are an appealing selection of the freshest ingredients - chargrilled and succulent red peppers infused with garlic and basil, and roast pumpkin with sage and shallots. Skill in the buying and the cooking is evident in duck cassoulet, the excellent meat falling off the bone, while the fish species served have to be endorsed by the Marine Stewardship Council. The philosophy is not force-fed to customers, but from little Acorns...

Times 12-3/6-10.30

Jurys Great Russell Street

⊛ Modern International 🖵 Plan 3 C3

Elegant 1930s setting for relaxed dining

☎ 020 7347 1000
16-22 Great Russell St WC1B 3NN
e-mail: restaurant_grs@jurysdoyle.com
dir: Nearest station: Tottenham Court Road Short walk from Tottenham Court Rd and tube station

Much is made of the association with renowned architect Sir Edwin Lutyens, who designed this impressive Neo-Georgian listed building in the 1930s. Many original features are retained and the building is home to a smart, spacious, basement restaurant (named after Lutyens). Its clean, traditional lines are in keeping with the surroundings, as is the adjacent small, classic cocktail bar for aperitifs. The crowd-pleasing menu delivers warm vichyssoise soup with smoked halibut and soft poached egg among starters, followed by rack of Welsh lamb with potato galette, lentils and rosemary sauce. Finish with banana tarte Tatin with maple syrup ice cream.

Chef Paul O'Brien **Owner** Jurys Doyle Hotel Group Ltd
Times Closed L all week **Prices** Starter £5.50-£12, Main £12-£22, Dessert £6.50-£8.50, Service optional **Wines** 19 bottles over £20, 31 bottles under £20, 11 by glass **Notes** Pre-theatre menu, seasonal menu, Vegetarian available, Civ Wed 180, Air con **Seats** 120, Pr/dining room 30 **Children** Portions **Parking** NCP opposite the Hotel

Matsuri High Holborn

⊛ Japanese 🖵 Plan 3 E3

Authentic Japanese food in a contemporary setting

☎ 020 7430 1970
Mid City Place, 71 High Holborn WC1V 6EA
e-mail: eat@matsuri-restaurant.com
web: www.matsuri-restaurant.com
dir: Nearest station: Holborn On the corner of Red Lion St. Opposite the Renaissance Chancery Court Hotel

This futuristic Japanese restaurant occupies a corner site on High Holborn. Three dining areas showcase the various styles of cuisine: the sushi counter, the teppan-yaki room and the main dining room with an open-plan kitchen. The Japanese ex-pats frequenting this restaurant are a clue to the quality and authenticity of the cooking. Menus are lengthy, yet good ingredients are simply prepared and well presented, with lots of memorable fresh fish, and the teppan-yaki set menus provide an overall flavour of

Japanese food. Not to be missed are the salmon and tuna sushi boat, the assorted tempura, and chicken teriyaki.

Chef H Sudoh, T Aso, S Mabalot **Owner** Matsuri Restaurant Group **Times** 12-2.30/6-10, Closed 25-26 Dec, 1 Jan, BHs, Closed Sun **Prices** Fixed L 2 course £8.50-£25, Fixed D 4 course £20-£75, Starter £4-£15, Main £16.50-£40, Dessert £3.50-£6.50, Service added but optional 12.5% **Wines** 93 bottles over £20, 2 bottles under £20, 5 by glass **Notes** Fixed D 5 courses, Vegetarian available, Air con **Seats** 120, Pr/dining room 10 **Parking** On street (pay & display)

The Montague on the Gardens

⊛ Modern British Plan 3 C4

Stylish hotel restaurant with modern cuisine

☎ 020 7637 1001
15 Montague St, Bloomsbury WC1B 5BJ
e-mail: bookmt@rchmail.com
dir: Nearest station: Russell Square 10 minutes from Covent Garden, adjacent to the British Museum

A swish boutique hotel in the heart of Bloomsbury and next to the British Museum, the Montague has two dining options - the Blue Room bistro or the fine-dining restaurant, the Chef's Table. The latter is a light, airy space with panoramic views over London and an outside terrace for alfresco dining. Attentive staff are on hand to make guests feel at ease and the cooking is modern British with some French influences. Expect dishes such as gazpacho with crayfish cocktail, followed by calves' liver, crisp bacon and spiced lentils, and a classic crème brûlée to finish.

Chef Neil Ramsey **Owner** Red Carnation Hotels
Times 12.30-2.30/5.30-10.30 **Prices** Fixed L 2 course £19.50, Fixed D 3 course £23.50, Starter £7.50-£13, Main £15-£33, Dessert £6-£11, Service added but optional 12.5% **Wines** 61 bottles over £20, 7 bottles under £20, 19 by glass **Notes** Pre-theatre menu available, Sunday L, Vegetarian available, Civ Wed 90, Air con **Seats** 45, Pr/dining room 100 **Children** Portions, Menu **Parking** On street, Bloomsbury Square

Pearl Restaurant & Bar

⊛⊛⊛ – *see opposite*

Pearl Restaurant & Bar

LONDON WC1   Plan 3 D3

Modern French

Metropolitan destination restaurant with modern French menu

☎ 020 7829 7000
Renaissance Chancery Court, 252 High Holborn WC1V 7EN
e-mail: info@pearl-restaurant.com
web: www.pearl-restaurant.com
dir: Nearest station: Holborn 200 mtrs from Holborn tube station

The old Pearl Assurance Building has been transformed into a glamorous, metropolitan destination restaurant. The achingly chic interior includes original marble pillars, while walnut, trails of hand-spun pearls (what else - over a million of them), cream leather chairs, well-spaced tables with expensive settings and a huge wooden wine cave to entertain the eye, too. Staff - including a sommelier - provide attentive, professional service, while the appealing medley of lunch, dinner, tasting option and vegetarian menus all come at fixed prices. The skilful kitchen takes a fresh, modern French approach, delivering exciting combinations with clear flavours driven by high quality produce - sprinkled with luxury - in dishes dressed to thrill. Take a chargrilled cutlet of black pig served with chorizo and lentil salsa, red pepper purée and roast langoustines, or perhaps John Dory with ginger

escabèche, crab croquettes and carrot purée, and to finish, maybe a Baileys parfait with profiteroles and an orange and yuzu foam. Peripherals like canapés, amuse-bouche, breads, pre-dessert and petits fours all hit form, too.

Chef Jun Tanaka **Owner** Hotel Property Investors **Times** 12-2.30/6-10, Closed Dec, BHs, 2 wks Aug, Closed Sun, Closed L Sat **Prices** Fixed L 2 course £26, Fixed D 3 course £50-£75, Service added but optional 12.5% **Wines** 200 bottles over £20, 10 bottles under £20, 200 by glass **Notes** Tasting menu available with wine or beer, Vegetarian available, Dress restrictions, Smart casual, Air con **Seats** 74, Pr/dining room 12 **Parking** NCP Drury Lane

LONDON WC2

The Admiralty Restaurant

⊛ French ⬚ Plan 3 D2

Contemporary restaurant in Somerset House

☎ 020 7845 4646
Somerset House, The Strand WC2R 1LA
e-mail: info@theadmiraltyrestaurant.com
dir: Nearest station: Temple, Covent Garden Telephone for directions, see website

Its Thames-side setting, off the courtyard at Somerset House, proves a grand prelude to lunch or dinner in the two high-ceilinged dining rooms that once played host to the Naval Headquarters. Today though, the smart, refurbished interior creates a contemporary dining experience. The cooking is French regional with modern twists; think roasted fillet of pork topped with a brie and pine-nut crust served with carrot and potato rösti, or perhaps grilled rump of English lamb teamed with wild mushrooms, spinach pommes Anna, roast cherry tomatoes and a red wine jus.

Chef Steve Gormersaff **Owner** Leiths-Compass Group **Times** 12-2.30/5.30-10.30, Closed 24-27 Dec, Closed D Sun **Prices** Fixed L 2 course £10-£25, Fixed D 4 course £49.50-£59.50, Starter £6.50-£10, Main £12.50-£18, Dessert £5.75-£6.50, Service added but optional 12.5% **Wines** 25 bottles over £20, 3 bottles under £20, 8 by glass **Notes** Pre-theatre D until 7pm, Vegetarian available **Seats** 90, Pr/dining room 60 **Children** Portions

Albannach

⊛⊛ Modern Scottish ⬚ Plan 5 C6

Highland chic meets city bustle with contemporary twists on Scottish favourites

☎ 020 7930 0066
66 Trafalgar Square WC2N 5DS
e-mail: bookings@albannach.co.uk
dir: Nearest station: Charing Cross SW corner of Trafalgar Sq, opposite Canada House

Overlooking Trafalgar Square, this fabulous mezzanine restaurant - on the former site of the Bank of Scotland - is adorned with purple sprouting heather in the windows and kilted staff, which provides major clues that you're in a Scottish-themed restaurant. The dark wood, open-plan dining areas are perhaps more like a bar or a nightclub than a fine-dining restaurant but it's a style that works, creating an atmospheric destination to imbibe generous amounts of whisky or enjoy a full-on foray into eclectic, modern Scottish cuisine with Caledonian produce championed with William Wallace-style fervour. Try roast saddle of wild roe deer with braised lentils, roast beetroot and game port sauce, followed by traditional Scottish raspberry cranachan.

Chef Iain Inman **Times** 12-3/5-10.30, Closed 25-26 Dec, 1 Jan, Closed Sun **Prices** Fixed D 3 course fr £18, Starter £5.50-£10.50, Main £16-£23, Dessert £6.50-£8.50, Service added but optional 12.5% **Wines** 44 bottles over £20, 3 bottles under £20, 10 by glass **Notes** Fixed D pre-theatre 12-7, Vegetarian available, Air con **Seats** 50, Pr/dining room 20 **Children** Min 8 yrs, Portions **Parking** NCP

L'Atelier de Joel Robuchon

⊛⊛⊛ – *see below*

Axis at One Aldwych

⊛⊛ Modern British ⬚ Plan 3 D2

Dramatic, contemporary dining in the heart of theatreland

☎ 020 7300 0300 & 7300 1000
1 Aldwych WC2B 4RH
e-mail: axis@onealdwych.com
dir: Nearest station: Covent Garden At point where Aldwych meets the Strand opposite Waterloo Bridge. On corner of Aldwych & Wellington St, opposite Lyceum Theatre

The Axis, one of two trendy dining options at One Aldwych hotel with its own street entrance, owes its dramatic appearance to its astonishingly high ceilings and an abstract cityscape mural, the 'Secret City' by Richard Walker. Muted colours combine with black leather upholstery and a

L'Atelier de Joël Robuchon

LONDON WC2 Plan 3 C2

French

Slick, sexy sophistication from French super-chef

☎ 020 7010 8600
13-15 West St WC2H 9HE
e-mail: info@joelrobuchon.co.uk
dir: Nearest station: Leicester Square/Covent Garden Left off Cambridge Circus and Shaftesbury Av

Joël Robuchon is a French super-chef who came out of early retirement to take the restaurant world by storm once again. His big idea, second time around, was L'Atelier concept, which translates as 'workshop'. Based around an open kitchen, restaurants from Paris to Tokyo offer small tasting plates of innovative and high quality food cooked before your eyes. The London operation is an impossibly glamorous place, spread over three floors with

the ground-floor L'Atelier dominated by the open kitchen and counter (sit up close on high stools or on nearby tables) and a wall of living ivy. With low-level lighting, dark red and black décor and everything stylised to the nth-degree, this futuristic look has a Japanese feel, which is not accidental. The first floor dining room, La Cuisine, has a black and white theme and is the place to eat if you want the more traditional three-course format. The top floor is a bar (Le Bar) with the glamour returning with a vengeance. The food can be simple - the quality of the produce is first class - and it can be innovative and complex. Inspiration is drawn mostly from France, Italy and Spain. Scottish lobster is served with spiced turnip in a dish that, like many, can be taken as a small tasting plate or a full-size course. Crispy langoustine fritters with basil pistou is made with the lightest imaginable tempura batter and the flavours perfectly judged. Service is as smart, hip and professional as everything else in this restaurant.

Chef Frederic Simonin, Olivier Limousin **Owner** Bahia UK Ltd **Times** 12-3/5.30-11 **Wines** 350 bottles over £20, 10 bottles under £20, 26 by glass **Notes** Tasting menu 9 courses, Pre-theatre 2/3 courses £19-£25, Vegetarian available, Air con **Seats** 43 **Children** Portions **Parking** Valet parking service

focal point of 92 slender birch trunks made of satin nickel to give the dining room great presence, along with a balcony bar and a sweeping staircase entrance. Quality ingredients are locally sourced and organic where possible and classic English seasonal dishes are prepared with imagination and simplicity. There are sections on the menu that include catch of the day, grills and roast for two. Try smoked eel with marinated beetroot and crispy pork to start, with pan-fried salmon, pot-roasted lobster, white beans and shellfish bisque, or perhaps sirloin of aged beef, bone marrow and shallot sauce to follow.

Chef Tony Fleming **Owner** Gordon Campbell Gray **Times** 12-2.30/5.45-10.45, Closed Xmas, New Year, Etr, Closed Sun, Closed L Sat **Wines** 16 by glass **Notes** Pre/Post-theatre D 2 courses £15.50, 3 courses £17.50, Vegetarian available, Civ Wed 60, Air con **Seats** 120, Pr/dining room 40 **Children** Portions, Menu **Parking** NCP - Wellington St

Christopher's

◉ Contemporary American 🖵   Plan 3 D2

Victorian grandeur meets contemporary American cooking

☎ 020 7240 4222
18 Wellington St, Covent Garden WC2E 7DD
e-mail: coventgarden@christophersgrill.com
dir: Nearest station: Embankment/Covent Garden Just by Strand, overlooking Waterloo Bridge

Situated smack bang in the middle of Covent Garden and theatreland, Christopher's is an American themed

establishment with a Martini bar downstairs, private dining and a large restaurant upstairs. The fascinating Victorian building, once London's first licensed casino, features a sweeping stone staircase, high, decorative ceilings and tall windows. Contemporary décor adds bold colours, polished wood floors and striking accessories. The huge menu offers lots of steak, fish and fresh seasonal fare, with starters like Caesar salad, followed by Midwestern veal meatloaf, and New York cheesecake to finish. Theatre and weekend brunch menus are popular options.

Times 12-3/5-11, Closed 24 Dec-2 Jan, Closed 25-26 Dec, 1 Jan, Closed D Sun

Clos Maggiore

◉◉◉ — *see below*

Imperial China

◉ Chinese V   Plan 3 B2

Sophisticated Cantonese cooking meets contemporary décor in Chinatown

☎ 020 7734 3388
White Bear Yard, 25a Lisle St WC2H 7BA
e-mail: mail@imperial-china.co.uk
dir: Nearest station: Leicester Sq From station into Little Newport St, straight ahead into Lisle St and right into White Bear Yard

Glass doors fronting Lisle Street lead through an inner courtyard complete with waterfall, bridge and pond to the

contemporary Chinese-designed dining room set on two floors. Think wooden panelling, lighting and artwork with slate, lightwood or blue-carpeted floors and upholstered chairs in gold. The sophisticated Cantonese cooking fits the place perfectly, drawing crowds of Chinese Londoners with its comprehensive dim sum menu and lengthy carte dotted with a few unfamiliar choices. Typical dishes are deep-fried soft shell crab with spicy salt and pepper, stir-fried fillet steak Cantonese-style with onion, and spicy aubergine and beancurd hot pot.

Chef Mr Wing Kei Wong **Times** 12/11.30, Closed 24-25 Dec **Prices** Fixed D 3 course £16.50-£31.50, Starter fr £2.90, Main fr £7.50, Dessert fr £2.90, Service added but optional 12.5% **Wines** 10 bottles over £20, 20 bottles under £20, 1 by glass **Notes** Vegetarian menu, Air con **Seats** 350, Pr/dining room 50 **Parking** China Town car park

Incognico

◉◉ French, Italian   Plan 3 C2

Franco-Italian food in the heart of theatreland

☎ 020 7836 8866
117 Shaftesbury Av, Cambridge Circus WC2H 8AD
e-mail: incognicorestaurant@gmail.com
dir: Nearest station: Leicester Sq Off Cambridge Circus at crossing with Charing Cross Rd, opposite the Palace Theatre

This French brasserie-style restaurant on Shaftesbury Avenue is a favourite among theatre-goers. The interior,

Continued

Clos Maggiore

LONDON WC2	Plan 3 C2

Modern French 🖵 V

Modern French fine dining in a romantic Covent Garden setting

☎ 020 7379 9696
33 King St, Covent Garden WC2E 8JD
e-mail: enquiries@closmaggiore.com
dir: Nearest station: Covent Garden 1 min walk from The Piazza and Royal Opera House

A Georgian townhouse with a discreet and unassuming mulberry-coloured awning and frontage picks out this sumptuous restaurant from the less glamorous razzmatazz of Covent Garden. Reminiscent of a stylish Provençal or Tuscan country property - with its warm colours and conservatory-style courtyard with fully opening glass roof that offers 'internal alfresco dining' in

the warmer months, or under the stars at night - it positively exudes romance, with real box hedging and flowers adding to the garden feel. In winter there's a roaring fire, while wooden floors, elegantly laid tables and smoked mirrors all contribute to the ambience. Service is impeccable - slick, friendly, professional and French - and there is an excellent wine list. Talented chef Marcellin Marc, previously at the two Michelin-starred Le Clos de la Violette in Aix-en-Provence, heads up the kitchen, his cooking modern-focused and underpinned by a classical theme. Classy, sophisticated and driven by high quality ingredients, this is French cooking at its best. Presentation is simple, portions generous and flavours bold, all accompanied by a superb wine list. Begin with a remoulade of Dorset crab and marjoram, with pickled cauliflower and brown shrimp, and follow with oven-roasted whole Maine lobster served with macaroni gratin and a light lobster and basil bisque.

Chef Marcellin Marc **Owner** Tyfoon Restaurants Ltd **Times** 12-2.30/5-11, Closed 24-26 Dec & 1 Jan, Closed L Sat-Sun **Prices** Food prices not confirmed for 2009. Please telephone for details. **Wines** 1900 bottles over £20, 50 bottles under £20, 15 by glass **Notes** Vegetarian menu, Dress restrictions, Smart casual, Civ Wed 150, Air con **Seats** 70, Pr/dining room 26 **Children** Portions **Parking** NCP, on street

LONDON WC2 *Continued*

designed by David Collins, is very handsome with red leather banquettes, oak panelling, globe lights, stripped wooden floors and light spilling in from large windows. There's also a spacious bar and an intimate private dining room in the basement. Cooking continues in the style of Nico Landenis, the restaurant's creator, with classic French dishes supplemented by some Italian options and lighter brasserie fare. It is all about quality raw materials cooked with great assurance and the minimum of fuss. Try escalope of foie gras with orange, sea bass with crushed potato, olives, tomato and pesto, or honey-roasted duck breast with pomme fondant.

Chef Daffyd Watkin **Owner** Sergio Rebecchi
Times 12-3/5.30-11, Closed 10 days Xmas, 4 days Etr, BHs, Closed Sun **Wines** 125 bottles over £20, 2 bottles under £20, 13 by glass **Notes** Pre-theatre 3 courses inc. champagne & coffee £32.50, Vegetarian available, Dress restrictions, Smart casual, Air con **Seats** 85, Pr/dining room 22 **Parking** NCP

Indigo

◉◉ Modern European 🖳   Plan 3 D2

Trendy mezzanine dining with a buzzy atmosphere

☎ 020 7300 0400 & 7300 1000
1 Aldwych WC2B 4RH
e-mail: indigo@onealdwych.com
dir: Nearest station: Covent Garden, Charing Cross Located where The Aldwych meets The Strand opposite Waterloo Bridge. On corner of Aldwych & Wellington St, opposite Lyceum Theatre

Overlooking the buzzy hotel Lobby Bar, sophisticated Indigo is set on a mezzanine balcony (perfect for people-watching), and is the epitome of modern chic and contemporary styling. Spotlights zoom down on to tables, seats are comfortable, service is focused and the atmosphere fashionable and relaxed. The kitchen follows the theme, with cosmopolitan, flavour-driven, clean-cut dishes delivered on creatively flexible menus that play to the gallery. There's the option to create your own salad dish, others can be taken as a starter or main course, while the more structured fine-dining options might deliver Bayonne ham, sauce gribiche, rocket salad and figs to start, followed by loin of monkfish with smoked garlic pomme purée and red wine jus.

Chef Tony Fleming **Owner** Gordon Campbell-Gray
Times 12-3/6-11.15 **Prices** Starter £6-£12.50, Main £15-£22.50, Dessert £5.50-£8, Service added but optional 12.5% **Wines** 79 bottles over £20, 2 bottles

under £20, 17 by glass **Notes** Sat & Sun brunch menu, Pre & Post-theatre D available, Vegetarian available, Civ Wed 60, Air con **Seats** 62 **Children** Portions, Menu **Parking** Valet parking

The Ivy

◉ British, International 🖳   Plan 3 C2

Theatreland legend with an accessible menu

☎ 020 7836 4751
1 West St, Covent Garden WC2H 9NQ
dir: Nearest station: Leicester Square Telephone for directions

Others may come and go, fall in and out of favour, but The Ivy manages to maintain its following among the rich and famous. Celebrities and various media types still pack out the place and getting a table against such competition is not always easy - booking in advance is essential. Given such a reputation, the room is remarkably low key with its club-like atmosphere of oak panelling, wooden floors and stained-glass windows. The staff are seemingly impervious to the fame and notoriety of the customers, and treat everyone the same. The lengthy menu is not ground-breaking or challenging, but it can be comforting (eggs Benedict or shepherd's pie) or rather more sophisticated (mixed sashimi or gnocchi with pumpkin, buffalo ricotta and pesto).

Times 12-3/5.30-12, Closed 25-26 Dec, 1 Jan, Aug BH, Closed L 27 Dec, Closed D 24 Dec

J. Sheekey

◉ Fish, Seafood   Plan 3 C2

Celebrity-favoured fish restaurant in theatreland

☎ 020 7240 2565
St Martin's Court WC2N 4AL
e-mail: reservations@j-sheekey.co.uk
dir: Nearest station: Leicester Square Telephone for directions

Remember to book early for a table at this enduringly popular fish and seafood restaurant in the heart of Londons West End. Celebrities come to relax and be seen, while their agents strike animated deals at the closely packed tables, or the dining bar. In this buzzing atmosphere the menu hits a traditional note, with its lists of caviar (Sévruga, Golden Oscietra, Beluga), oysters (Strangford Loch etc), crab and other shellfish, plus a dozen or so fish dishes including a handful of daily specials. There is also a meat menu upon request. The cooking is polished and perfectly timed to keep the fresh flavours and delicate textures intact, while the service is reassuringly old school.

Times 12-3/5.30-12, Closed 25-26 Dec, 1 Jan, Aug BH, Closed D 24 Dec

Mon Plaisir

◉ French 🖳   Plan 3 C2

A Francophile's delight in theatreland

☎ 020 7836 7243
21 Monmouth St WC2H 9DD
e-mail: monplaisirrestaurant@googlemail.com
dir: Nearest station: Covent Garden, Leicester Square Off Seven Dials

About as French as it comes this side of the Channel, with patriotic tricolour flag fluttering outside, this veteran of more than half a century still pulls in an adoring crowd. The entrance may be unassuming and the original front dining room little changed, but beyond there is a network of cosy rooms (including a mezzanine-style loft) decked out with a mix of French posters and artefacts, and modern abstracts and mirrors. The menu mixes the times too, offering classics such as coq au vin and côte de boeuf alongside more modern ideas like turbot with chicken jus and green asparagus or pork knuckle confit with chestnuts and lentils. Closely-packed tables and resolutely French service create a lively Gallic buzz.

Chef Frank Raymond **Owner** Alain Lhermitte
Times 12-2.15/5.45-11.15, Closed Xmas, New Year, BHs, Closed Sun, Closed L Sat **Prices** Fixed L 2 course £14.50, Fixed D 3 course £15.50, Starter £5.95-£13.90, Main £14.50-£23.50, Dessert £5.75-£7.50, Service added but optional 12.5% **Wines** 70 bottles over £20, 19 bottles under £20, 13 by glass **Notes** Pre-theatre menu inc. glass of house wine/coffee, Vegetarian available, Dress restrictions, Smart casual, Air con **Seats** 100, Pr/dining room 28 **Children** Portions

Orso Restaurant

◉ Modern Italian   Plan 3 D2

Italian food in a buzzing basement

☎ 020 7240 5269
27 Wellington St WC2E 7DB
e-mail: info@orsorestaurant.co.uk
dir: Nearest station: Covent Garden Please telephone for directions

Once through the discreet etched-glass doors, make your way downstairs past black-and-white photos of the stars of stage and screen. The cavernous basement dining room (once an orchid warehouse) at this long-established, all-day Covent Garden Italian reverberates with a buzz of conversation and the clinking of glasses. Herringbone floors, pastel tablecloths, fanciful frescoes and friendly staff - constantly flitting about - add to the lively, informal atmosphere. The crowd-pleasing bilingual menu showcases regional Italian cooking and offers bags of choice, from pizza and pasta to veal kidneys with mushrooms, parsley, garlic and white wine. A pre-theatre menu and weekend brunch offer excellent value.

Chef Martin Wilson **Owner** Orso Restaurants Ltd **Times** noon/midnight, Closed 24-25 Dec, Closed L Sat-Sun (Jul-Aug) **Wines** 46 bottles over £20, 3 bottles under £20, 16 by glass **Notes** Pre-theatre D available 2 or 3 courses £16/£18, Sunday L, Vegetarian available, Air con **Seats** 100 **Parking** On street

The Portrait Restaurant

◉ Modern British   Plan 3 C1

Stylish, contemporary dining with rooftop views

☎ 020 7312 2490
National Portrait Gallery, St Martins Place WC2H 0HE
e-mail: portrait.restaurant@searcys.co.uk
dir: Nearest station: Leicester Square, Charing Cross Just behind Trafalgar Square

The main drawcard at the gallery's sleek, light and contemporary top-floor restaurant are its stunning Nelson's-eye views up Whitehall to Westminster and over the capital's rooftops. A wall of windows means everyone gets an outlook, while its blond-wood floors, modern seating and grey and cream colour scheme hit just the right note, though hard surfaces and a bar crank up the decibels. The light, clean-cut modern bistro-style food suits the surroundings; think monkfish wrapped in smoked bacon with buttered samphire, asparagus, morels, spring greens and a roast garlic sauce, and to finish, perhaps blueberry and almond tart with lemon curd ice cream.

Times 11.45-2.45/5.30-8.30, Closed 24-26 Dec, 1 Jan, Closed D Sat-Wed

The Strand Terrace

◉ Modern, French   Plan 3 C1

Contemporary cooking in a classic dining environment

☎ 020 7747 8410
Charing Cross Hotel, The Strand WC2N 5HX
e-mail: concierge.charingcross@guoman.co.uk
web: www.guoman.com
dir: Nearest station: Charing Cross Station Located next to Charing Cross Station.

This centrally-located and historic landmark railway hotel provides a friendly welcome. Spacious in design, the original architecture recalls all the luxury of a bygone age, yet blends effortlessly with the modern décor. There's a choice of dining options: those in a hurry should try Co-Motion which offers a range of snacks and speedy service, while more leisurely dining can be enjoyed in the elegant Strand Terrace which affords superb views across the London skyline, especially at night. The contemporary European menu might feature a starter of artichoke barigoule with spinach, asparagus and truffled hollandaise, followed by lemon sole meunière with

parsley and potatoes, with mixed berry brûlée and raspberry sorbet to finish.

Times 12-3/5-10

Swissôtel The Howard, London

Rosettes not confirmed at time of going to press

Modern British   Plan 3 E2

New team in the kitchen at this smart Thames-side hotel

☎ 020 7836 3555 & 7300 1700
Temple Place WC2R 2PR
dir: Nearest station: Temple Telephone for directions (Opposite Temple Tube station

Formerly Jaan Restaurant, and now renamed 12 Temple Place, this riverside, city-based hotel offers excellent views of the river and the city. The restaurant has undergone a change from its former style although food continues to focus on quality and freshness. New Executive Chef Brian Spark has produced a menu that is based on modern British styles and which features regional, seasonal and fresh produce, with Hebridean crab, Galloway beef and even a London Gin and sloe berry parfait. There is also an eye for sustainability, with Shetland farmed cod on the menus, which offer a tasting option as well as the more flexible carte selections.

Chef Brian Spark **Owner** New Ray Ltd **Times** 12-2.30/5.45-10.30, Closed 1st wk Jan, BHs, Closed Sun, Closed L Sat **Prices** Fixed L 2 course fr £19.75, Fixed D 3 course fr £23.75, Tasting menu £46, Starter £8-£9, Main £8-£9, Dessert £8-£9, Service added 12.5% **Wines** 120 bottles over £20, 12 by glass **Notes** Tasting menu 5 courses, Vegetarian available, Dress restrictions, Smart, casual, Civ Wed 100, Air con **Seats** 56 **Parking** 30

32 Great Queen Street

◉ British   Plan 3 D3

Bustling, informal, fun venue serving simple, seasonal British fare

☎ 020 7242 0622
32 Great Queen St WC2B 5AA
e-mail: greatqueenstreet@googlemail.com
dir: Nearest station: Covent Garden, Holborn Telephone for directions

This new Covent Garden opening - set in a former pub - is now a bustling, informal, bohemian brasserie with blood-red walls, rustic unclothed tables and an open kitchen. Outside there's little to suggest its great food credentials, just a black awning and a handful of outside tables, while inside is a long, narrow space, with well-worn wooden floors and a long bar complete with high stools for more-informal eating. Friendly, attentive, knowledgeable and appropriately casually dressed staff don long butchers-style aprons. Ex-Eagle chef (touted as the first-ever gastro-pub) Tom Norrington-Davies' straightforward, less-is-more British cooking fits the bill perfectly, is deceptively simple and driven by prime

ingredients, seasonality and clear, gusty flavours. There's no flamboyancy, snobbery or flowery garnishes and menus are succinctly scripted and change daily; think rabbit saddle, black pudding and lentils, or mutton pie, and perhaps a rhubarb sponge finish.

Chef Tom Norrington-Davies **Owner** R Shaw, T Norrington-Davies, J Jones, M Belben **Times** 12-2.30/6-10.30, Closed last working day in Dec-1st working day in Jan, BHs, Closed Sun, Closed L Mon **Prices** Starter £4-£9, Main £9.80-£22, Dessert £3.20-£5.80, Service optional **Wines** 20 bottles over £20, 25 bottles under £20, 13 by glass **Notes** Vegetarian available **Seats** 70

Loch Fyne Restaurant, Covent Garden

🖥

☎ 020 7240 4999
2-4 Catherine St WC2B 5JS
web: http://www.theaa.com/travel/index.jsp

Quality seafood chain.

Prices Food prices not confirmed for 2009. Please telephone for details.

GREATER LONDON

BARNET
Map 6 TQ29

Dylan's

◎◎ Modern European

Modern surroundings for cutting-edge European cuisine

☎ 020 8275 1551 & 8275 1651
21 Station Pde, Cockfosters EN4 0DW
e-mail: dylan@dylansrestaurant.com
dir: M25 junct 24, follow A111 towards Cockfosters for 3m, Dylan's on left-hand side of Cockfosters Rd

A popular, contemporary high street eatery in the heart of Cockfosters. With two brightly-coloured dining areas, a fresh vibrant menu showcases seasonal and regional produce and unusual combinations making for an interesting dining experience. Expect classic dishes in an uncomplicated modern style, accompanied by service which is relaxed and informal, yet efficient and friendly. Cooking is deft and confident, producing the likes of pan-fried sea bass with braised lemon thyme potatoes and grilled vegetables, or guinea fowl with pumpkin risotto, chestnuts and glazed shallots. Desserts range from iced rhubarb parfait to sticky toffee pudding with rum and raisin ice cream. A cocktail menu is served in the comfortable lounge bar.

Chef Richard O'Connell **Owner** Dylan Murray, Richard O'Connell **Times** 12-2.30/6-10, Closed 26 Dec, 1 Jan, Closed Mon **Prices** Fixed L 2 course £12.95, Fixed D 3 course £15.95, Starter £3.95-£7.95, Main £11.50-£17.95, Dessert £4.95, Service added but optional 12.5% **Wines** 16 bottles over £20, 8 bottles under £20, 10 by glass **Notes** Sun L with live jazz band, Sunday L, Dress restrictions, Smart casual, Air con **Seats** 90, Pr/dining room 8 **Children** Portions, Menu **Parking** On street

Savoro

◎ Modern European 💻

Tucked-away modern restaurant well worth discovering

☎ 020 8449 9888
206 High St EN5 5SZ
e-mail: savoro@savoro.co.uk
web: www.savoro.co.uk
dir: M25 junct 23 to A1081, continue to St Albans Rd, at lights turn left to A1000

Cosily tucked away on a small alleyway off the High Street, the traditional frontage of this whitewashed hotel belies its modern interior, and the popular Savoro restaurant proves a little gem. A cool, contemporary décor sets the scene, with plenty of glass and mirrors and unobtrusive artwork, while leather banquettes line walls and come with comfy cushions that add to the relaxed tone. The kitchens modern approach produces intelligently simple, clean-cut, well-presented and executed dishes on an appealing carte with a large grill section driven by quality produce. Take roasted duck breast served with sweet potato purée, pak choi and a mustard seed and hoi sin dressing, while from the grill, perhaps whole wild sea bass cooked on a bed of fresh herbs, and to finish, treacle tart with bourbon ice cream (home-made ice creams being a speciality of the house).

Chef Robert Brown **Owner** Jack Antoni **Times** 12-3/6-11, Closed 1 Jan, 1 wk New Year **Wines** 30 bottles over £20, 12 bottles under £20, 12 by glass **Notes** Pre-theatre £15.95, early evening menu Mon-Thu, Sunday L, Vegetarian available, Air con **Seats** 68 **Children** Portions **Parking** 9

BECKENHAM

See LONDON SECTION plan 1- G1

Mello

◎◎ Modern European

Fashionable dining near suburban high street

☎ 020 8663 0994
2 Southend Rd BR3 1SD
e-mail: info@mello.uk.com
web: www.mello.uk.com
dir: 0.5m from Beckenham town centre, directly opposite Beckenham train station

Not quite where you might expect to find somewhere delivering such imaginative, clear-flavoured cuisine, but this ambitious modern restaurant - located in a Victorian listed building - is well worth uncovering. High-backed leather and suede chairs, contemporary art on deep red and warm sand coloured walls, white table linen and a red carpet cut a simple but effective style. The kitchen clearly has skill, potential and confidence, with presentation elegant and sophisticated, and ingredients of high quality. The appealing repertoire cuts a modern European line underpinned by classical roots; take roast cannon of Cornish lamb with confit shoulder, aubergine caviar, asparagus and roasting juices, and perhaps a hot chocolate fondant with pistachio ice cream to finish. One to watch.

Times 12-2.30/6-10, Closed D Sun

See advert opposite

BROMLEY

See LONDON SECTION plan 1- G1

Chapter One

◎◎◎◎ – *see page 332*

Tamasha

💻

☎ 020 8460 3240
131 Widmore Rd BR1 3AX
web: http://www.theaa.com/travel/index.jsp

Indian restaurant with Raj-inspired décor and a comprehensive collection of cricketing memorabilia. Live entertainment early in the week.

Prices Food prices not confirmed for 2009. Please telephone for details.

ENFIELD
Map 6 TQ39

Royal Chace Hotel

◎ Traditional British

Attractive hotel brasserie

☎ 020 8884 8181
The Ridgeway EN2 8AR
e-mail: reservations@royalchacehotel.co.uk
dir: 3m from M25 junct 24, 1.5m to Enfield

Not far from Enfield, the Royal Chace is set in 6 acres of grounds with woodland views just 3 miles from junction 24 of the M25. The refurbished public rooms are smartly appointed and the fine-dining option is the first-floor Chace Brasserie, a spacious restaurant with a warm colour scheme and great views of the surrounding countryside. Traditional English dishes, including scallops and steaks, are prepared from hand-picked ingredients and presented with imaginative flair. Less formal meals and snacks are served in the King's Bar and lounge.

Times Closed Xmas, BH Mon, Closed L Mon-Sat, Closed D Sun

Mello

Tel: 020 8663 0994
E-mail: info@mello.uk.com
Web: www.mello.uk.com

This modern European restaurant - just by Beckenham Junction - is easy to reach either by rail or tram link.

Having its own private car park makes it even more popular among its customers.

The decoration is classic, but still creative: modern oil paintings, leather and suede chairs and relaxing colours are making any meal even more enjoyable.

All the modern European dishes are cooked with quality ingredients and high skill.

The restaurant offers fantastic lunch and dinner set menus.

Chapter One

Modern European 🖳 🍷 NOTABLE WINE LIST

Sophisticated cooking meets contemporary décor at unbeatable prices

☎ 01689 854848
Farnborough Common, Locksbottom BR6 8NF
e-mail: info@chaptersrestaurants.com
dir: Situated on A21, 3m from Bromley. From M25 junct 4 onto A21 for 5m.

With its mock-Tudor appearance, Chapter One is handily located on the A21 and is home to Andrew McLeish's much-acclaimed cooking. The front door opens into a world of refinement, from the spacious dining room with its new metropolitan styling and serene pastel tones, to the suave, professional and welcoming service. Dark wooden floors, elegant tan-coloured seating, stylish food-related photographs, bevelled-mirror wall and crisp white linen continue the sophisticated theme, while a separate brasserie and stylish bar - also refurbished and with a louder buzz and more informal edge - attracts a wised-up crowd looking for culinary thrills at reasonable prices. McLeish's confident and accomplished cooking aptly suits the surroundings and takes a modern European approach based on classical techniques, with dishes displaying plenty of innovation alongside distinct flavours, balanced combinations and high skill. Tip-top seasonal ingredients are handled with consummate integrity here, and perfectly illustrate the maxim 'less is more'. Take pan-fried line-caught sea bass served with Puy lentils, pancetta, salsa verde and a red wine fish sauce, or perhaps roast rump of Kentish lamb with braised navarin, purple artichokes, tomato jus and bagna cauda, and to finish, maybe an organic lemon tart with crème fraîche sorbet and a millefeuille of passionfruit. The appealing repertoire is a fixed-price affair and reads like central London luxury with suburban prices - lunch offering fantastic value at this level. The wine list shows admirable pedigree, too, while its sister restaurant over in Blackheath, Chapters (see entry) is also well-worth checking out.

Chef Andrew McLeish **Owner** Selective Restaurants Group
Times 12-2.30/6.30-10.30, Closed 1-4 Jan **Prices** Fixed L 3 course fr £18, Starter fr £7, Main fr £16.50, Dessert fr £6, Service added but optional 12.5%
Wines 109 bottles over £20, 25 bottles under £20, 14 by glass **Notes** Sunday L, Vegetarian available, Dress restrictions, No shorts, jeans or trainers, Air con
Seats 120, Pr/dining room 55
Children Portions **Parking** 90

West Lodge Park Hotel, The Cedar Restaurant

◉◉ Modern British

Enjoyable dining in stylish country-house hotel with magnificent grounds

☎ 020 8216 3900
Cockfosters Rd EN4 0PY
e-mail: westlodgepark@bealeshotels.co.uk
dir: On the A111, 1m S of M25 junct 24

Just a few miles from the M25 and a short hop to central London, this splendid country house is set in stunning parkland and gardens. It was converted into a hotel in 1921 and is now decorated with a luxurious balance of modern and traditional themes. There are 35 acres of magnificent grounds, including an arboretum, to explore. The Cedar Restaurant is fairly traditional both in its formal style of service and in the cuisine, which looks to British classics for inspiration, with contemporary flourishes adding zest. You might start with Hertfordshire game terrine with red onion compote, then continue with line-caught wild sea bream with Parmesan gratin and chorizo saffron mash. Finish with cardamom and custard tartlet with crystallised ginger ice cream and pink peppercorns.

Chef Wayne Turner **Owner** Beales Ltd
Times 12.30-2.30/7-9.30 **Prices** Fixed L 2 course fr £15, Fixed D 3 course fr £25, Service optional **Wines** 51 bottles over £20, 24 bottles under £20, 7 by glass **Notes** Sunday L, Dress restrictions, Smart casual, jacket & tie recommended, Civ Wed 72, Air con **Seats** 70, Pr/dining room 54 **Children** Portions **Parking** 75

See LONDON SECTION Plan 1-B5

Incanto

◉ Modern Italian 💻 🕭

Stylish, relaxed modern Italian restaurant with deli and café

☎ 020 8426 6767
41 High St HA1 3HT
e-mail: info@incanto.co.uk
web: www.incanto.co.uk

Clean modern lines grace the long dining room of this Italian restaurant at the heart of Harrow on the Hill, opposite the village green. The former post office has wooden floors, ivory walls hung with modern art and a beautiful crystal chandelier. Other arresting features include full-length glass skylights and a spiral staircase. The simple, authentic Italian cooking utilises fresh, seasonal produce in dishes such as home-made oxtail raviolone in a light tarragon sauce and truffle butter, and oven-baked halibut wrapped in potato crust with garden pea purée, red wine and balsamic reduction.

Chef Franco Montone **Owner** David Taylor & Catherine Chiu **Times** 12-2.30/6.30-11, Closed 25-26 Dec, 1 Jan, Etr Sun, Closed Mon, Closed D Sun **Prices** Starter £4.95-£7.20, Main £13.95-£16.95, Dessert £5.75-£6.90, Service included **Wines** 24 bottles over £20, 13 bottles under £20, 10 by glass **Notes** Tasting menu available, Sunday L, Vegetarian available, Air con **Seats** 64, Pr/dining room 30 **Children** Portions, Menu **Parking** On street

The Glasshouse

Modern European 💻 🍷

Local favourite with sophisticated cooking

☎ 020 8940 6777
14 Station Rd TW9 3PZ
e-mail: info@glasshouserestaurant.co.uk
dir: Telephone for directions

Set in a parade of Kew Village shops close to Kew Bridge tube station, this sophisticated, smart and buzzy local restaurant is a class act and sister to the venerable Wandsworth eaterie Chez Bruce (see entry). Glass-fronted in keeping with its name (and probably inspired by its neighbour, the Royal Botanic Gardens), its sleek, contemporary décor has a light-and-airy appeal, drawing a loyal crowd of devotees with its vibrant atmosphere and bustling mix of diners. An eclectic mix of furniture, antiques, cushions and drapes blends with well-spaced tables and the appropriately relaxed and friendly yet professional service. The precision cooking is self assured and impressive too, taking an unfussy modern and seasonal approach, distinguished by a light touch, clean, clear flavours and some imaginative combinations. Take poached sea bass with gnocchi, crab, scallops and basil, or perhaps an assiette of pork served with apple tarte fine, choucroûte and Madeira, and to finish, maybe a hot chocolate fondant with coconut ice cream or a Pedro Ximenez sherry trifle might vie for attention. The appealing menu repertoire comes at fixed prices (and includes a seven-course tasting option), while the wine list is a notable affair, with many available by the glass.

Chef Anthony Boyd **Owner** Larkbrace Ltd
Times 12-2.30/6.30-10.30, Closed Xmas, New Year
Prices Fixed L 2 course £18.50, Fixed D 3 course £35, Tasting menu £50, Service added but optional 12.5% **Wines** 376 bottles over £20, 5 bottles under £20, 13 by glass **Notes** Sunday L, Vegetarian available, Air con **Seats** 60 **Children** Portions, Menu **Parking** On street; metered

HARROW WEALD

See LONDON SECTION plan 1- B6

Grim's Dyke Hotel

◉ Modern European

Peaceful country-house conveniently close to London

☎ 020 8385 3100
Old Redding HA3 6SH
e-mail: enquiries@grimsdyke.com
dir: 3m from M1 between Harrow and Watford

Once home to Sir William Gilbert, this Grade II listed mansion is filled with memorabilia from many well-known Gilbert and Sullivan productions. Now a country-house hotel, the property is set amid more than 40 acres of beautiful parkland and gardens. There are garden views from the sumptuously decorated dining room, which is accessed separately from the main hotel. Modern European cooking with occasional oriental influences might produce pan-roasted tiger prawns with sweet potato, turmeric and apple emulsion to start, followed by pan-fried Scotch fillet steak with truffled croquettes, oxtail ravioli and horseradish foam.

Chef Daren Mason **Owner** Skerrits of Nottingham Holdings **Times** 12.30-2/7-9.30, Closed L Sat **Prices** Fixed L 2 course fr £11.95, Fixed D 3 course fr £21, Service optional **Wines** 69 bottles over £20, 22 bottles under £20, 10 by glass **Notes** Sunday L, Vegetarian available, Dress restrictions, No jeans or trainers (Fri-Sat), Civ Wed 90 **Seats** 45, Pr/dining room 40 **Children** Portions, Menu **Parking** 100

KEW

See LONDON SECTION plan 1- C3

The Glasshouse

◉◉◉ – see page 333

KINGSTON UPON THAMES

See LONDON SECTION plan 1- C1

Ayudhya Thai Restaurant

◉ Thai

Authentic, neighbourhood Thai in the heart of suburbia

☎ 020 8546 5878 & 0208 5495984
14 Kingston Hill KT2 7NH
dir: 0.5m from Kingston town centre on A308, and 2.5m from Robin Hood rdbt at junction of A3

Set unassumingly in a small parade of shops, this charmingly authentic, long-established Thai transports you to another world with its pitched roof lines and traditional, darkwood-panelled interior. Wood carvings, original artefacts and Thai royal family pictures continue the illusion, complemented by oriental music and authentically costumed staff. The extremely extensive menu offers nearly 100 dishes including desserts, so be prepared to spend some time making your choice. Try gai phat bai kaprow (chicken with chilli and Thai speciality holy basil leaves). Order by dish number unless your Thai language skills are up to scratch.

Times 12-2.30/6.30-11, Closed Xmas, BHs, Closed L Mon

Frère Jacques

◉ French

Popular, friendly Thames-side brasserie offering French fare and atmosphere

☎ 020 8546 1332
10-12 Riverside Walk, Bishops Hall KT1 1QN
e-mail: john@frerejacques.co.uk
dir: 50 mtrs S of Kingston side of Kingston Bridge, by the river

A cracking position smack on the riverside promenade beside Kingston Bridge ensures this French-themed Thames-side brasserie is an all-weather magnet. Alfresco tables out front, a more rustic atmosphere under an awning, or inside in the contemporary-styled dining area, Jacques has the winning formula. It's a relaxed affair with red-clothed tables, friendly service and a backing track of Gallic music. The competent kitchen delivers a crowd-pleasing repertoire of French brasserie staples and more modern offerings, driven by quality ingredients and flavour on a value fixed-price menu and carte; expect classics like moules marinière to oven-roasted monkfish wrapped in bacon and served with dill-infused potatoes, wilted spinach and a shellfish bisque.

Times 12/11, Closed 25-26 Dec, 1 Jan, Closed D 24 Dec

Strada

🖵

☎ 020 8974 8555
1 The Griffin Centre, Market Place KT1 1JT
web: http://www.theaa.com/travel/index.jsp

One of the newest additions to this perennially popular chain of modern Italian restaurants, occupying two floors of a grand listed building near the Thames.

Prices Food prices not confirmed for 2009. Please telephone for details.

PINNER

See LONDON SECTION plan 1- B5

Friends Restaurant

◉ Modern British 🖵

Tudor property offering suburban brasserie dining

☎ 020 8866 0286
11 High St HA5 5PJ
e-mail: info@friendsrestaurant.co.uk
dir: In centre of Pinner, 2 mins walk from underground station

The black-and-white timber frontage entices impulse diners into the comfortably appointed, two-floor interior, complete with smartly dressed tables and leather-clad seating. The chef proprietor gained a wealth of experience during his early years at the Savoy and the Connaught, and has been at this high street restaurant for 16 years. The modern cuisine is inspired by timeless classics, dispensed by smartly dressed staff. Use of fresh ingredients and simple presentation is evident when you tuck into aubergine mousse with ratatouille dressing, followed by grilled sirloin of beef, wild mushrooms, red wine and sautéed potatoes. Finish with fig and almond tart with honey ice cream.

Chef Terry Farr **Owner** Mr Farr **Times** 12-3/6.30-10.30, Closed 25 Dec, BHs, Closed Mon in summer, Closed D Sun **Prices** Fixed L 2 course £16.50, Fixed D 3 course £29.50, Service added but optional 10% **Wines** 16 bottles over £20, 10 bottles under £20, 14 by glass **Notes** Sunday L, Vegetarian available, Air con **Seats** 40 **Children** Portions **Parking** Nearby car parks x3

RICHMOND UPON THAMES
See LONDON SECTION plan 1 C2

Bingham Hotel, Restaurant & Bar

◉◉ Modern British 🖳

Well-executed cuisine in stylish surroundings

☎ 020 8940 0902
61-63 Petersham Rd TW10 6UT
e-mail: reservations@thebingham.co.uk
web: www.thebingham.co.uk
dir: Please telephone for directions

Enjoying a wonderful Thames-side location, this Georgian townhouse now houses a boutique hotel and its romantic riverside restaurant. Having undergone a complete makeover, the two connecting dining rooms have an opulent air with gold fabrics and beige and brown décor. There are also balcony tables for summer evenings. The kitchen delivers the best in seasonal British cooking, with classic French influences, under the direction of new chef Shay Cooper (formerly head chef at Olga Polizzi's Hotel Endsleigh). With excellent technical ability, the cuisine is well refined with good clarity of flavour. Mains range from saddle back pork cheek and loin with black pudding, barbecue beans and smoked potato, to squab pigeon with Jerusalem artichoke purée, beetroot ravioli and coffee sauce. Service is knowledgeable and friendly.

Times 12.30-4/7-10, Closed 26 Dec-early Jan, Closed D Sun

La Buvette

◉ French, European

Stylish traditional French bistro

☎ 020 8940 6264
6 Church Walk TW9 1SN
e-mail: karen@brula.co.uk
dir: 3 mins from train station, opposite St Mary Magdalene church

A former church refectory built of York stone, La Buvette is the sister restaurant of Brula in Twickenham (see entry). The beautiful courtyard seats 40 in summer and is protected from the elements by brick walls, a canopied entrance and an enormous umbrella, while inside the intimate restaurant has traditional French bistro décor. The roots of the menus are in French cooking with dishes such as escargots de Bourgogne with garlic, Pernod and parsley butter, fillet of beef with potato rösti and red wine

and shallot jus. The formula is popular with discerning locals who return to savour the taste of France.

Chef Buck Carter **Owner** Bruce Duckett
Times 12-3/6-10.30, Closed 25-26 Dec, 1 Jan, Good Fri
Prices Fixed L 2 course £12, Fixed D 3 course £17, Starter £4.50-£9.50, Main £10-£22, Dessert £5-£7.50, Service added but optional 12.5% **Wines** 30 bottles over £20, 9 bottles under £20, 13 by glass **Notes** Sunday L, Vegetarian available **Seats** 50 **Children** Portions, Menu **Parking** NCP - Paradise Road

Petersham Nurseries

◉◉ Modern

Seasonal, fresh food with a rustic Italian slant, in a setting to match

☎ 020 8605 3627
Off Petersham Rd TW10 7AG

You need to book well in advance to eat at this quirky, upmarket café in the middle of a plant nursery in well-heeled Petersham. The restaurant may occupy a large, ramshackle greenhouse, with a dirt floor, wooden tables, rickety chairs and potted plants all around, but the seasonal, rustic Italian cooking of celebrated chef Skye Gyngell has made it a magnet for foodies. Open for lunch only, menus change daily and are based around the finest fresh produce (much of which is grown on site), given the lightest of treatments to bring out its distinctive flavours. Several dishes feature rare and unusual herbs and vegetables. Start with deep-fried baby globe artichokes with mint and anchovy crush, followed by halibut with black rice, spinacini, datterini tomatoes and raita, and perhaps squashed dark chocolate cake to finish. A cheaper alternative, with no need to book, is afternoon tea in the tea house.

Times 12.30-2.45, Closed Mon, Closed D all week
Prices Food prices not confirmed for 2009. Please telephone for details.

Restaurant at The Petersham

◉◉ British, European 🌸

Sophisticated dining and breathtaking Thames views

☎ 020 8940 7471 & 8939 1084
The Petersham, Nightingale Ln TW10 6UZ
e-mail: restaurant@petershamhotel.co.uk
web: www.petershamhotel.co.uk
dir: Telephone for directions

Perched on affluent Richmond Hill, this elegant hotel has fine architectural features, including a large Portland stone staircase, and offers magnificent views over a curving stretch of the Thames. The restaurant matches the classic-meets-contemporary style, with walnut panelling, mirrors and well-spaced tables, while the full-length windows make the best of those river views. A modern British approach, underpinned by French influences and plenty of luxury, graces the appealing, sensibly compact and clearly constructed carte. The sophisticated, accomplished cooking shows good technical skills combined with flair resulting in vibrant

dishes. Take terrine of foie gras with hare and smoked bacon with Muscat jelly, steamed halibut and crab ravioli with coconut and seaweed bouillon, and vanilla rice pudding with Armagnac prunes.

Chef Alex Bentley **Owner** The Petersham Hotel Ltd
Times 12.15-2.15/7-9.45, Closed 25-26 Dec, 1 Jan, Closed D 24 Dec **Prices** Fixed L 2 course £18.50, Starter £6.50-£12.50, Main £14.50-£26.50, Dessert £6.50 **Wines** 100 bottles over £20, 2 bottles under £20, 9 by glass **Notes** Sunday L, Vegetarian available, Dress restrictions, Smart casual, Civ Wed 40, Air con **Seats** 70, Pr/dining room 26 **Children** Portions, Menu **Parking** 60

Richmond Gate Hotel - Gates on the Park

◉◉ Traditional, International

Elegant restaurant in a prestigious hotel

☎ 020 8940 0061
Richmond Hill TW10 6RP
e-mail: richmondgate@foliohotels.com
web: www.foliohotels.com/richmondgate
dir: At top of Richmond Hill, opposite Star and Garter, just opposite Richmond Park

This elegant former Georgian country house stands on the crest of Richmond Hill, close to the 2,500-acre Royal Park and Richmond Terrace with its magnificent views over the River Thames. The intimate Gates on the Park Restaurant is light and airy and mixes an air of Georgian formality with contemporary style, complemented by friendly and attentive service. The seasonal menu is characterised by modern interpretations of classically-based ideas and the kitchen makes sound use of quality ingredients in unpretentious though not unadventurous dishes that deliver satisfying, clear flavours. Seared scallops with butternut squash and crispy pancetta makes a delightful starter, followed by a robust main course of aged Angus fillet of beef with wild mushroom, tomato, Pont-Neuf potatoes and béarnaise sauce. A smart leisure club and spa completes the upbeat package.

Chef Nenad Bibic **Owner** Folio Hotels
Times 12.30-2/7-9.30, Closed L Sat, BHs **Prices** Fixed L 2 course £19.50-£22, Fixed D 3 course £29-£34, Starter £6.50-£11.50, Main £16.50-£31.50, Dessert £6.50-£8.50, Service added but optional 10%, Groups min 6 service 10% **Wines** 37 bottles over £20, 17 bottles under £20, 8 by glass **Notes** Sunday L, Vegetarian available, Dress restrictions, Smart casual, Civ Wed 70, Air con **Seats** 30, Pr/dining room 70 **Children** Portions, Menu **Parking** 50

RICHMOND UPON THAMES *Continued*

Richmond Hill Hotel

◉ Modern European ▱

Sophisticated setting for accomplished cuisine

☎ 020 8939 0265
144-150 Richmond Hill TW10 6RW
e-mail: restaurant.richmondhill@foliohotels.com
dir: 1m town centre

Situated at the top of Richmond Hill, within walking distance of the town and park, this attractive and impressively refurbished Georgian manor enjoys elevated views of the Thames. Both the Pembrokes Restaurant and bar have been transformed with a stylish, contemporary décor. Floors and tables are in dark wood, set off by large-shaded lamps and smart table appointments. The menu changes seasonally and cooking is accomplished with tried-and-tested dishes like a classic Caesar salad or trio of soups, followed by rack of lamb with ratatouille and dauphinoise potatoes, or grilled Dover sole dusted with mild spices, lime herb butter and saffron potatoes, and dark chocolate tart to finish.

Chef Andrew Barrass **Owner** Folio Hotels
Times 10.30am/10.30pm **Prices** Starter £7.50-£14.50, Main £14.95-£28.95, Dessert £6.95-£7.95, Service added but optional 12% **Wines** 8 bottles over £20, 16 bottles under £20, 9 by glass **Notes** Sunday L, Vegetarian available, Dress restrictions, Smart casual, Civ Wed 80, Air con **Seats** 85, Pr/dining room 30 **Children** Portions, Menu **Parking** 150

RUISLIP

See LONDON SECTION plan 1- A5

Hawtrey's Restaurant at the Barn Hotel

◉◉ Modern French ▱

Imaginative, sophisticated cuisine in a smart hotel

☎ 01895 636057   & 679999
The Barn Hotel, West End Rd HA4 6JB
e-mail: info@thebarnhotel.co.uk
dir: From M40/A40 - exit at Polish War Memorial junct and follow A4180 towards Ruislip. After 2m turn right at mini rdbt into hotel entrance

A former farm, with parts dating back to the17th century, this impressive hotel sits in 3 acres of gardens. Its restaurant is an imposing affair styled in the fashion of a

Jacobean baronial hall, with tasteful mahogany panelling, chandeliers and gilt-framed oil paintings. With presentation a highlight, skilful cooking underpins the modern French menu with the five-course prestige tasting menu undoubtedly the best way to sample the talents of this Gordon Ramsay alumnus. Begin with haricot blanc velouté served with poached quail egg and truffle essence, followed perhaps by pan-fried fillet of Scottish beef with sautéed wild mushrooms, pomme Pont-Neuf, buttered spinach and red wine jus, or maybe lemon sole and prawns poached in coconut milk with cocotte potatoes, mixed grapes, aubergine caviar and shrimp sauce.

Chef Damien Leneff **Owner** Pantheon Hotels & Leisure
Times 12-2.30/7-10.30, Closed L Sat, Closed D Sun
Prices Fixed L 2 course fr £16.50, Fixed D 3 course £29-£42.50, Tasting menu £49.50, Service added but optional 10% **Wines** 68 bottles over £20, 52 bottles under £20, 9 by glass **Notes** Sunday L, Vegetarian available, Dress restrictions, Smart casual, Civ Wed 74, Air con **Seats** 44, Pr/dining room 20 **Children** Portions, Menu **Parking** 50

SURBITON

See LONDON SECTION plan 1- C1

The French Table

◉◉ French, Mediterranean ▱

Creative modern cuisine in warm, friendly local restaurant with ambition

☎ 020 8399 2365
85 Maple Rd KT6 4AW
e-mail: enquiries@thefrenchtable.co.uk
dir: 5 min walk from Surbiton station, 1m from Kingston

Set in a small parade of shops and eateries in leafy suburbia, this pretty little restaurant stands out from the crowd and is a deservedly popular affair. The interior is stylish and modern yet relaxed and unbuttoned. With banquette seating, simple blondwood chairs and white linen providing the comforts, a slate-tiled floor, modern art and friendly service hit just the right note too. The appealing, good value, creative French/Mediterranean cooking comes well presented and driven by fresh seasonal produce. Expect grilled sea bass served with sautéed Savoy cabbage, a tortellini of peas and wild mushrooms and morel foam, and perhaps a ginger bread-and-butter pudding with poached figs to finish.

Chef Eric Guignard **Owner** Eric & Sarah Guignard
Times 12-2.30/7-10.30, Closed 25-26 Dec, 1-3 Jan, Closed Mon, Closed D Sun **Prices** Fixed L 2 course fr £15.50, Starter £5.80-£9.80, Main £10.80-£17.50, Dessert fr £5.95, Service added but optional 12.5% **Wines** 50 bottles over £20, 11 bottles under £20, 9 by glass **Notes** Sunday L, Vegetarian available, Dress restrictions, Smart casual, Air con **Seats** 48 **Children** Portions **Parking** On street

TWICKENHAM

See LONDON SECTION plan 1- C2

La Brasserie McClements

◉◉ French

Enjoyable dining in suburban Twickenham

☎ 020 8744 9598
2 Whitton Rd TW1 1BJ
e-mail: info@labrasserietw1.co.uk
dir: Close to Twickenham Station

A discreetly located establishment in a modest parade of shops, this brasserie maintains its reputation for good French food. The interior is simply presented with dark polished tables set on plain wooden floorboards, though the fully stocked cheese table catches the eye. Choose between the carte or seven-course menu dégustation - with helpful staff on hand to assist. Simple dishes, carefully prepared and well executed, include seared scallops with cep cream and cauliflower purée to start, or a crab lasagne. Mains take in turbot with lobster sausage, or saddle of venison with parsnip purée, morels and port jus. At the time of going to press we understand there was a refurbishment and change of concept taking place.

Chef John McClements **Owner** John McClements/ Dominique Sejourne **Times** 12-2.30/7-11, Closed Sun **Wines** 30 bottles over £20, 20 bottles under £20, 12 by glass **Notes** Tasting menu £55, Air con **Seats** 40 **Children** Min 9 yrs **Parking** On street/train station

Brula

◉ French

Traditional, inviting French bistrot

☎ 020 8892 0602
43 Crown Rd TW1 3EJ
e-mail: info@brula.co.uk
dir: Join A305, go straight at lights over the A3004, turn left onto Baronsfield Rd. Restaurant is at the end of T-junct, immediately on the right

With its parquet floor, canopied entrance and stained glass, this former Victorian shop is faithful to the French tradition of eating out with its relaxed, inviting atmosphere. The restaurant's authentic look has seen it used as a film set for the Poirot series. Polite staff deliver keenly-priced French regional dishes to eager diners seated at plain wooden tables. Typically, start with a rustic fish soup with rouille, or foie gras and chicken liver parfait with Sauternes jelly, follow with roast lamb with rosemary jus, or grilled sea bass, served with Jerusalem artichoke, persillade and pancetta, then finish with a classic crème brûlée.

Chef Toby Williams & Jamie Russel **Owner** Lawrence Hartley **Times** 12-3/6-10.30, Closed Xmas, 1 Jan, Aug **Prices** Fixed L 2 course £15, Fixed D 3 course £17.95, Starter £6.50-£8, Main £13.50-£19, Dessert £5-£7.50, Service optional **Wines** 9 bottles under £20, 11 by glass **Notes** Sunday L, Vegetarian available **Seats** 40, Pr/dining room 24 **Children** Portions, Menu **Parking** On street & parking meters

Loch Fyne Restaurant & Oyster Bar

☎ 020 8255 6222
175 Hampton Rd TW2 5NG
web: http://www.theaa.com/travel/index.jsp

Quality seafood chain.

Prices Food prices not confirmed for 2009. Please telephone for details.

UXBRIDGE   Map 6 TQ08

Masala

☎ 01895 252925
61 Belmont Rd UB8 1QT
web: http://www.theaa.com/travel/index.jsp

Dining here is more than an experience, it's an education. Learn first-hand about the different cooking styles of India's various regions.

Prices Food prices not confirmed for 2009. Please telephone for details.

MERSEYSIDE

BIRKENHEAD   Map 15 SJ38

Fraiche

◉◉◉ – **see below**

HAYDOCK   Map 15 SJ59

Thistle Haydock

◉ Modern European

Popular hotel for crowd-pleasing modern dining

☎ 0870 333 9136
Penny Ln WA11 9SG
e-mail: haydock@Thistle.co.uk

This smart, purpose-built hotel - surrounded by landscaped gardens and close to Haydock Racecourse - offers a wide range of leisure and meeting facilities. Its two-tiered restaurant comes decked out in traditional hotel style and features a stained-glass domed ceiling. Service is friendly and efficient, while the kitchen's simple, well-presented, well-executed modern style is driven by local produce. Think slow-roast pork belly with Parma ham and tarragon rösti, or corn-fed breast of chicken stuffed with vine tomatoes and olives and served with Puy lentils, asparagus and sauce béarnaise, and to finish, perhaps a warm chocolate fondant with white ice cream.

Times 7-11

Fraiche

BIRKENHEAD   Map 15 SJ38

Modern French V

Intimate and elaborate fine dining in Merseyside

☎ 0151 652 2914
11 Rose Mount CH43 5SG
e-mail: contact@restaurantfraiche.com
dir: M53 junct 3 towards Prenton. Follow for 2m then take left towards Oxton, Fraiche on right

Chef-patron Marc Wilkinson's intimate, modern and relaxing little restaurant (of some dozen or so tables) is well worth tracking down. With an outside eating area in a seaside theme, soft muted beiges in linen and suede create warmth and subtlety inside. There's a seating area at the front for aperitifs and striking original artwork on the walls, which all create a simple backdrop for the well-trained, friendly service and elaborate, highly skilled

cooking. Expect the concise, crisply scripted, sensibly compact repertoire of fixed-priced menus to excite and surprise the palate and senses, with plenty of twists of flavours, colour, texture and temperature. The stimulating compositions feature tip-top produce, sourced locally or from the markets of France. A rib-eye of Dexter beef may come with salsify and fondant potato, or slow-cooked pork could be served with apple and olive cream. Innovative desserts take in lemongrass pannacotta. And for those dining alone, or the out-and-out foodie, there's a 'culinary box' brimful of the latest cookery books, articles, magazines and menus from great restaurants to peruse.

Chef Marc Wilkinson **Owner** Marc Wilkinson **Times** 12-1.30/7-9.30, Closed 25 Dec, 1 Jan, Closed Sun-Mon, Closed L Tue-Thu **Prices** Tasting menu £38-£58, Service optional **Wines** 232 bottles over £20, 24 bottles under £20, 6 by glass **Notes** Vegetarian menu **Seats** 20, Pr/dining room 20 **Children** Min 8 yrs, Portions **Parking** On street

LIVERPOOL
Map 15 SJ39

Malmaison Liverpool

◉ Modern British 🖳

Contemporary cuisine in relaxed surroundings on the waterfront

☎ 0151 229 5000
7 William Jessop Way, Princes Dock L3 1QZ
e-mail: liverpool@malmaison.com

A purpose-built hotel with cutting-edge, style, Malmaison Liverpool has a stunning location alongside the river and docks. It is particularly attractive at night with purple lights around the dockside illuminating the water. Inside, a yellow submarine suspended from the ceiling epitomise the sense of fun that is synonymous with this hotel group, while a champagne and cocktail bar completes the upbeat package. Dishes range from classic to contemporary; from terrine of ham hock and foie gras with sauce gribiche, or steak frites, to a choice of pizzas or braised shank of lamb shepherd's pie.

Times 12-2.30/6-11

Radisson SAS Hotel Liverpool - Filini

◉ Italian, Mediterranean 🖳

Stylish modern setting for authentic Italian cuisine

☎ 0151 966 1500 & 966 1600
107 Old Hall St L3 9BD
e-mail: info.liverpool@radissonsas.com
dir: Please telephone for directions

Diners can enjoy panoramic views over the bustling River Mersey at this smart hotel, formerly St Paul's Eye Hospital, which boasts the city's largest suite, The River Suite, as well as ocean- and urban-themed bedrooms. The smart Filini restaurant, created by restaurateur and commentator Roy Ackerman, offers imaginative, accomplished modern Italian cuisine in stylish

surroundings, making good use of the best local and Italian produce to create dishes like buffalo mozzarella with rocket and marinated tomatoes, or fillet of sole with cannellini beans, fennel, celery and capers. The trendy White Bar provides an alternative eating option.

Radisson SAS Hotel Liverpool - Filini

Chef Gavin Williams **Owner** Beetham Organisation Ltd **Times** 12-2.30/6-10.30, Closed Sun **Prices** Fixed L 2 course fr £14, Starter £8, Main £25, Dessert £8, Groups min 10 service 10% **Wines** 17 bottles over £20, 14 bottles under £20, 11 by glass **Notes** Vegetarian available, Civ Wed 100, Air con **Seats** 90, Pr/dining room 140 **Children** Portions, Menu **Parking** 25; 200 mtrs

See advert below

Simply Heathcotes

◉ Modern British 🖳 ◐

Modern eatery with extensive brasserie menu

☎ 0151 236 3536
Beetham Plaza, 25 The Strand L2 0XL
e-mail: liverpool@heathcotes.co.uk
dir: Opposite pier head, located on The Strand, near Princes Dock

The Liverpool branch of Paul Heathcote's laid-back dining destination is a contemporary concoction of granite, glass, cherrywood and Philippe Starck bucket chairs. There is a modern British menu to suit - think leg of

mutton with caper sauce, carrots and turnips, or grilled halibut with celeriac purée, baby spinach, vermouth and tarragon cream. Finish with classic sticky ginger pudding and clotted cream ice cream. Ingredients are fresh and seasonal, and come courtesy of the local area wherever possible, and the result is accomplished brasserie fare that should keep you popping in for more. Children's menu available.

Chef Steven Urquhart **Owner** Heathcotes Restaurants **Times** 12-2.30/6-10, Closed Xmas, BHs (except Good Fri) **Prices** Food prices not confirmed for 2009. Please telephone for details. **Notes** Sunday L, Vegetarian available, Air con **Seats** 75, Pr/dining room 30 **Children** Portions, Menu **Parking** On street

60 Hope Street Restaurant

◉ British 🖳 V 1⬛ NOTABLE WINE LIST

Minimalist setting for smart modern dining

☎ 0151 707 6060
60 Hope St L1 9BZ
e-mail: info@60hopestreet.com
web: www.60hopestreet.com
dir: From M62 follow city centre signs, then brown tourist signs for cathedral. Hope St near cathedral

A Grade II listed townhouse, 60 Hope Street stands on an avenue between Liverpool's two cathedrals, at the heart of the city's creative quarter. The building comprises a restaurant, basement bistro and private dining room for

special occasions, and the minimalist interior design provides the ideal gallery space for regular art shows. Cooking is simple and accurate using fresh local and seasonal ingredients in dishes such as Cumbrian ham croquettes with red pepper salsa, followed by roast breast of Goosnargh chicken with chicken liver pithivier, Savoy cabbage, pancetta and Madeira cream.

Chef Sarah Kershaw **Owner** Colin & Gary Manning **Times** 12-2.30/6-10.30, Closed BHs, Closed Sun, Closed L Sat **Prices** Fixed L 2 course fr £13.95, Starter £6.95-£14.95, Main £12.95-£42, Dessert £5.95-£8.95, Service optional, Groups min 8 service 10% **Wines** 70 bottles over £20, 18 bottles under £20, 6 by glass **Notes** Pre-theatre Mon-Sat 5-7pm, Vegetarian menu, Civ Wed 50, Air con **Seats** 90, Pr/dining room 40 **Children** Portions **Parking** On street

SOUTHPORT Map 15 SD31

Warehouse Brasserie

◎◎ International

Cool warehouse conversion with international flavours

☎ 01704 544662
30 West St PR8 1QN
e-mail: info@warehousebrasserie.co.uk
dir: Telephone for directions

This eye-catching, glass-and-chrome restaurant is moulded from a former warehouse, with a blend of art deco and contemporary design. Now in its 12th year of business, the restaurant delivers a consistent level of quality and draws a fashionable crowd who enjoy the vibrant atmosphere and the chefs on show in the theatre kitchen. The cooking takes up the modern theme, with an eclectic global repertoire of well-presented dishes produced from local ingredients wherever possible. A typical meal comprises curried Southport shrimps with raita and mango, home-smoked Bowland lamb with parsnip purée, and honey custard tart with pink Champagne-poached rhubarb to finish. A new private dining area seating 18 is available upstairs.

Chef Marc Verite, Darren Smith **Owner** Paul Adams **Times** 12-2.15/5.30-10.45, Closed 25-26 Dec, 1 Jan, Closed Sun **Prices** Fixed L 2 course £13.95, Fixed D 3 course £17.95, Starter £4.50-£9.95, Main £10.95-£21.95, Dessert £5.95-£7.95, Service optional, Groups min 8 service 10% **Wines** 57 bottles over £20, 15 bottles under £20, 5 by glass **Notes** Early D menu available Mon all night, Tue-Thu 5.30-7pm, Vegetarian available, Air con **Seats** 110, Pr/dining room 18 **Children** Portions **Parking** NCP - Promenade

THORNTON HOUGH Map 15 SJ38

The Italian Room Restaurant

◎◎ Modern British

Fine dining in a historic venue

☎ 0151 336 3938
Thornton Hall Hotel, Neston Rd CH63 1JF
e-mail: reservations@thorntonhallhotel.com
dir: M53 junct 4 onto B5151 & B5136 and follow brown tourist signs (approx 2.5m) to Thornton Hall Hotel

Dating back to the mid-1800s, this Victorian manor house turned country-house hotel has been sensitively extended and restored. The elegant Italian Room is so named because of its magnificent Italian leather ceiling, hand-tooled and inlaid with mother-of-pearl. Overlooking the stunning gardens, the restaurant is traditional country-house style in all other respects, with crisp linen and sparkling tableware. Slick, modern British cooking with excellent flavours and high technical skills is the order of the day, created from the freshest ingredients sourced from local suppliers. Try the ham hock terrine with sauce gribiche to start, perhaps followed by the poached halibut with tortellini of ox cheek and a bourguignon garnish, with chilled rice pudding and warm gooseberry compote to finish.

Chef Brian Heron **Owner** The Thompson Family **Times** 12-2/7-9.30, Closed 1 Jan, Closed L Sat **Prices** Fixed D 3 course £29, Starter £6.50-£8, Main £15.50-£24, Dessert £6.50-£8, Service included **Wines** 44 bottles over £20, 32 bottles under £20, 9 by glass **Notes** Sunday L, Vegetarian available, Dress restrictions, Smart casual, no T-shirts or jeans, Civ Wed 400 **Seats** 45, Pr/dining room 24 **Children** Portions, Menu **Parking** 250

NORFOLK

ALBURGH Map 13 TM28

The Dove Restaurant with Rooms

◎◎ French, European

Family-run restaurant with a classic menu

☎ 01986 788315
Holbrook IP20 0EP
dir: On South Norfolk border between Harleston and Bungay, by A143, at junct of B1062

This former inn turned smart restaurant with rooms is run by a husband-and-wife team who pride themselves on making the most of fresh, quality local and home-grown ingredients, with dishes straightforward and not overworked in French country style. You might try a main course of succulent pan-fried fillet of local beef served with sautéed mushrooms, roasted onion, rösti, French-style peas and a flavoursome jus, followed by apple and cinnamon crumble cake served with a light caramel sauce and home-made yogurt, passionfruit and peach ice cream. Service is relaxed but professional, and there's a cosy lounge for pre- or

post-dinner drinks and a terrace for alfresco dining in fine weather.

Times 12-2/7-9, Closed Mon-Tue, Closed L Wed-Sat, Closed D Sun

ATTLEBOROUGH Map 13 TM09

The Mulberry Tree

◎ Modern International

Trendy eatery with relaxed atmosphere and superb bedrooms

☎ 01953 452124
NR17 2AS
e-mail: relax@the-mulberry-tree.co.uk
dir: Turn off A11 to town centre. Continue around the one-way system, restaurant is on corner of Station Rd

Formerly 'The Royal' pub on the main road into Attleborough, this establishment has been transformed into a new style gastro-pub with rooms. Expect a contemporary, brasserie feel with darkwood floors, chunky wooden tables, smart, high-backed wicker chairs and quality table settings. Service is relaxed, friendly and professional from smartly dressed staff. Cooking is competent and modern, resulting in simple dishes with decent flavours, the short menu perhaps listing a pork belly with duck confit in hoi sin sauce starter, followed by chicken breast stuffed with mushrooms, served with cabbage and bacon and a mushroom sauce.

Chef Haydn Buxton **Owner** Philip & Victoria Milligan **Times** 12-2/6.30-9, Closed 25-26 Dec, Closed Sun **Prices** Starter £5.50-£8.50, Main £10.95-£19.95, Dessert fr £5.95, Service optional **Wines** 6 bottles over £20, 19 bottles under £20, 7 by glass **Notes** Vegetarian available **Seats** 50 **Children** Portions **Parking** 25

Sherbourne House Hotel

◎ British

Relaxed brasserie-style dining in friendly restaurant with rooms

☎ 01953 454363
8 Norwich Rd NR17 2JX
e-mail: stay@sherbourne-house.co.uk

Expect a warm welcome at this imposing, family-run Georgian hotel set in well-kept grounds, just a short stroll from the town centre. There's a cosy lounge, plus a bar and tastefully decorated conservatory restaurant with a relaxed brasserie style and mood, complete with lightwood tables and flooring, and friendly, informal service. Daily-changing menus offer a traditional British note with a modern twist, and come driven by well-sourced produce (beef and shellfish from the local Norfolk larder) delivered with intelligent simplicity. Expect seared fillet of halibut simply served with mash and spinach, or perhaps a seared sirloin steak with the time-honoured accompaniment of mushrooms and hand-cut chips.

Times 12-2/6.30-9.30, Closed 25 Dec, Closed Sun

BARNHAM BROOM — Map 13 TG00

Flints Restaurant

◎◎ Modern British, European

Country-club hotel with traditional-style restaurant and creative cooking

☎ 01603 759393 & 759522
Barnham Broom Hotel, Golf & Country Club, Honingham Road NR9 4DD
e-mail: enquiry@barnhambroomhotel.co.uk
dir: A47 towards Swaffham, turn left onto Honingham Rd, hotel 1m on left

As the name suggests, this hotel and country club is predictably set amid landscaped grounds and features a golf course and leisure facilities. Flints, the main restaurant, is where the fine-dining action takes place. Traditionally styled, it features white walls that form arches and individual seating areas, while a wall of glass windows looks out on to the golf-course action. Tables come laid with crisp white linen and staff are equally well turned out, while the kitchen deals in quality produce and some assured and creative cooking. Take roast rump of local Shropham lamb with champ mash, tomato fondue and a garlic-scented jus, while a Sweet Shop dessert assiette provides a clever take on those long-gone penny sweets.

Times 12-3/7-9.30

BLAKENEY — Map 13 TG04

The Blakeney Hotel

◎ Traditional British

Delightful dining with panoramic North Norfolk coastal views

☎ 01263 740797
The Quay NR25 7NE
e-mail: reception@blakeney-hotel.co.uk
dir: From the A148 between Fakenham and Holt , take the B1156 to Langham & Blakeney

Perched on Blakeney quay, this charming flint and brick fronted traditional Norfolk hotel enjoys impressive views across the National Trust estuary and salt marshes. Public rooms include a bar, a ground-floor lounge with an open fire for chilly winter days, and a first-floor sun lounge with wonderful views. There is also an elegant restaurant where service is friendly and the menu of British cuisine with a modern twist offers a wide choice. To start, perhaps try steamed local mussels in a white wine, tomato and garlic sauce, followed by roast fillet of Angus beef served with a potato cake, sautéed wild mushrooms and a Binham blue and tarragon butter.

Chef Martin Sewell **Owner** Michael Stannard
Times 12-2/6.30-8.45, Closed 24-27 Dec, Closed D 31 Dec
Wines 27 bottles over £20, 24 bottles under £20, 7 by glass
Notes TDH £25, Sunday L, Vegetarian available, Dress restrictions, Smart casual for D **Seats** 100, Pr/dining room 100 **Children** Min 8 yrs D, Portions **Parking** 60

The Moorings

◎ Modern British

Small, relaxed predominantly fish-based bistro

☎ 01263 740054 & 01328 878938
High St NR25 7NA
e-mail: reservations@blakeney-moorings.co.uk
dir: Off A149 where High St runs N to the quay

The Moorings is a relaxed, seaside bistro, situated on a busy side road adjacent to the quayside. Bright yellow walls, oiled wooden floorboards and closely-packed tables all add to the atmosphere and a sense of fun. The modern British menu places an emphasis on locally sourced seafood, as well as local meat and game and home-grown fruit and vegetables. Cooking is straightforward and accurate, with simple dishes and strong flavours. Recommendations include spicy Norfolk crabcakes with lime, coriander and chilli relish, baked fillet of sea bass with a pine nut, parsley and sea salt crust, and white chocolate raspberry tart.

Chef Richard & Angela Long **Owner** Richard & Angela Long **Times** 10.30-5/7-9.30, Closed 2 wks Jan, Closed Mon-Thu (Nov-Mar), Closed D Sun **Prices** Starter £4.75-£7.95, Main £11-£18, Dessert £4.75-£5.75, Service optional **Wines** 8 bottles over £20, 18 bottles under £20, 8 by glass **Notes** Sunday L, Vegetarian available, Air con **Seats** 50 **Children** Portions, Menu **Parking** On street, car park 50mtrs

---

Morston Hall

BLAKENEY — Map 13 TG04

Modern British, French V

Inspired cooking in small country house

☎ 01263 741041
Morston, Holt NR25 7AA
e-mail: reception@morstonhall.com
dir: On A149 coast road

This intimate flint-and-brick country-house hotel dates from the 17th century and is tucked away on the north Norfolk coast - just across the road from the sea. Set in delightful walled gardens, it enjoys a tranquil, relaxed setting and is well known for its award-winning chef-patron, Galton Blackiston, and as something of a food lover's paradise, with a whole range of cookery demonstrations, courses and wine tastings on offer. Inviting lounges - with roaring log fire on winter days

- lead through to the airy, elegant restaurant, resplendent with its bright conservatory. Galton's inspired cooking continues to go from strength to strength, delivered via a daily-changing six-course tasting dinner menu (with a choice at dessert) that includes some classics alongside new ideas. The style aims for skilful and intelligent simplicity, with the focus on fresh, high quality local seasonal produce and clean, clear flavours, as in pan-fried curried plaice fillet with gremolata, lemongrass and ginger froth, or perhaps roast tournedos of beef served on horseradish mash with fine bean parcels and sprouting broccoli. Superb desserts like Rothschild soufflé with white chocolate and almond ice cream, excellent breads and petits fours complete the inspired package.

Chef Galton Blackiston **Owner** T & G Blackiston
Times 12.30/7.30, Closed 2 wks Jan, Closed L Mon-Sat (ex party booking) **Prices** Fixed L course £32, Fixed D 4 course £50, Service optional **Wines** 160 bottles over £20, 8 bottles under £20, 15 by glass **Notes** Sunday L, Vegetarian menu, Dress restrictions, Smart casual

Seats 50, Pr/dining room 20 **Children** Portions, Menu **Parking** 40

Morston Hall

◉◉◉ – *see opposite*

◉◉◉ – *see opposite*

BRANCASTER STAITHE   Map 13 TF74

The White Horse

◉◉ Modern, Traditional British ☺

Seafood beside the tidal marsh

☎ 01485 210262
PE31 8BY
e-mail: reception@whitehorsebrancaster.co.uk
dir: On A149 coast road, midway between Hunstanton & Wells-next-the-Sea

In a stunning location on the edge of the tidal marshes, with the sea in the far distance, the views from the stylish conservatory restaurant, bar or sunny terrace are outstanding. Tourists and locals alike flock here throughout the year to relax in informal comfort so you need to book early for a window seat. Locally-sourced fish and shellfish are the lure here, and their simple handling allows the impeccably fresh flavours full expression; Cyril's Brancaster Staithe mussels cooked in a white wine, cream and parsley sauce is a good example. The menus change frequently to take maximum advantage of a variety of seasonal produce, including meat as well as seafood. Try a main of slow roast belly of Norfolk pork with caramelised apples and dressed leaves, with a selection of Norfolk cheeses to follow.

Chef Nicholas Parker **Owner** Clifford Nye
Times 12-2/6.30-9 **Prices** Starter £4.45-£7.60, Main £10.45-£17.85, Dessert £5.75, Service optional **Wines** 28 bottles over £20, 29 bottles under £20, 17 by glass **Notes** Sunday L, Vegetarian available **Seats** 100 **Children** Portions, Menu **Parking** 85

BRUNDALL   Map 13 TG30

The Lavender House

◉◉ Modern British V ☺

Quintessentially English thatched cottage offering a gourmet experience

☎ 01603 712215
39 The Street NR13 5AA
dir: 4m from Norwich city centre

The pretty thatched cottage dates from around 1540 and has been a restaurant for over fifty years. Now in the hands of Richard Hughes, it is run with dedication and commitment as both restaurant and cookery school. Heavy oak beams give a clue to the antiquity of the building, while sympathetic restoration and extension have created a light modern interior. There are comfortable sofas in the bar and high-backed wicker dining chairs and crisp white table settings in the restaurant areas. The modern British cooking takes advantage of products from artisan local suppliers. There is a tasting menu alongside the sensibly concise fixed-price menu. Things start with canapés before an amuse-bouche and then the starter, something like terrine of pheasant with figs and pickled vegetables. Main-course poached turbot comes with fricassée of mussels and brown shrimps.

Chef Richard Hughes, Richard Knights **Owner** Richard Hughes **Times** Closed 24-30 Dec, Closed Sun & Mon, Closed L all week **Prices** Fixed D 6 courses £39.95, Tasting menu £55, Service optional **Wines** 50 bottles over £20, 16 bottles under £20, 8 by glass **Notes** Tasting menu 10 courses, Vegetarian menu **Seats** 50, Pr/dining room 36 **Children** Portions **Parking** 16

BURNHAM MARKET   Map 13 TF84

Fishes Restaurant & Rooms

◉ Modern International ☺

A fish-lover's paradise

☎ 01328 738588
Market Place PE31 8HE
e-mail: info@fishesrestaurant.co.uk
dir: From Fakenham take B1065. 8m to Burnham Market, restaurant on the green

The relaxed, contemporary, brasserie-style surroundings of a Georgian double-fronted building on the village green is the setting for sampling superb quality locally-sourced fish and shellfish, all intelligently and simply cooked to allow flavours to shine through. The restaurant has a light, modern area with contemporary art, while there is also a more traditional décor with Lloyd Loom chairs and dark red walls. The kitchen's classical underpinning is matched with an occasional nod to India and Asia; think deep-fried octopus in beetroot tempura, mango, coconut and mint chutney, or perhaps a more classic offering like fish soup with rouille and roast Brancaster skate wing in oatmeal crust, brown shrimps, capers, parsley and beurre noisette. This is the place to come for the catch of the day.

Chef M Owsley-Brown **Owner** Matthew & Caroline Owsley-Brown **Times** 12-2.15/6.45-10, Closed Xmas for 4 days, Closed Mon (except BHs), Closed D Sun **Prices** Fixed L 2 course £19-£22, Fixed D 3 course £38-£43, Service optional, Groups min 8 service 10% **Wines** 150 bottles over £20, 8 bottles under £20, 23 by glass **Notes** Sunday L, Vegetarian available, Air con **Seats** 42, Pr/dining room 12 **Children** Portions **Parking** On street

Hoste Arms Hotel

◉◉ Modern British, Pacific Rim ✦ ☺

Stylish inn with impressive menu

☎ 01328 738777
The Green PE31 8HD
e-mail: reception@hostearms.co.uk
dir: 2m from A149 between Burnham & Wells

Local man Lord Nelson was once a regular visitor here, but he'd hardly recognise this stylish place now. Choose between the gallery and the garden room at this very relaxed inn close to the north Norfolk coast, and you'll get the same easygoing but professional service. There is also further private dining and an orangery. The walled garden is designed with Indian and Moroccan touches, with all-year-round alfresco dining a bonus. The modern British menu with Pacific Rim influences includes quality snacks and fine dining. Start with a half dozen of Richard Loose's Brancaster oysters, followed by 21-day New York rib steak and hand-cut chips. Finish with the assiette of desserts.

Chef Rory Whelan **Owner** Paul Whittome **Times** 12-2/7-9, Closed D 25 Dec **Prices** Starter £4.75-£8.75, Main £10.95-£24.25, Dessert £6.75-£10, Service optional **Wines** 153 bottles over £20, 14 bottles under £20, 21 by glass **Notes** Sunday L, Dress restrictions, Smart casual, Air con **Seats** 140, Pr/dining room 24 **Children** Menu **Parking** 45

CROMER
Map 13 TG24

See also **Sheringham**

Elderton Lodge Hotel & Langtry Restaurant

Modern British

Romantic retreat serving the best Norfolk produce

☎ 01263 833547
Gunton Park NR11 8TZ
e-mail: enquiries@eldertonlodge.co.uk
web: www.eldertonlodge.co.uk
dir: On A149 (Cromer/North Walsham road), 1m S of village

A former shooting lodge set in six acres of gardens, the hotel was once frequented by Lillie Langtry, who lends her name to the elegant, traditional-styled restaurant. Here, painted panel walls, clothed tables and crisp napkins set the scene for dishes majoring on fresh local produce, notably venison from the Gunton Hall Deer Park next door and locally farmed Wickmere beef. Dishes to delight include smooth chicken liver and venison parfait with red onion marmalade and Letheringsett granary toast, and pan-fried free-range chicken breast served with crisp Parmentier potatoes, baby leeks and wild mushroom fricassée.

Chef Daniel Savage **Owner** Rachel & Patrick Roofe
Times 12-2.30/6.30-9 **Prices** Fixed L 2 course £12.50, Starter £5-£8, Main £12-£20, Dessert £5-£8, Service optional **Wines** 11 bottles over £20, 25 bottles under £20, 6 by glass **Notes** Sunday L, Vegetarian available, Dress restrictions, Smart casual, Civ Wed 55 **Seats** 50, Pr/dining room 25 **Children** Portions **Parking** 100

Sea Marge Hotel

Modern British

Fantastic sea views with modern restaurant and cuisine

☎ 01263 579579
16 High St NR27 0AB
e-mail: info@mackenziehotels.com

Built in 1908 as a gentleman's seaside residence, this charming Grade II listed house has had a fascinating history. Perched on the cliff tops and offering stunning views of the sea, the hotel has been lovingly restored and retains many period features and original fireplaces. Relaxed, with a modern vibe, the conservatory-feel restaurant comes with leather high-backed chairs and crisply-clothed tables, its professional staff smartly

turned out in long aprons. A lengthy menu takes an equally modern approach offering dishes such as seared lambs' liver with mash and roast red onions, or whole grilled lemon sole with purple broccoli and new potatoes.

Chef Jack Woolner **Owner** Mr & Mrs MacKenzie
Times 12-2/6.30-9.30 **Prices** Food prices not confirmed for 2009. Please telephone for details. **Wines** 6 bottles over £20, 25 bottles under £20, 5 by glass **Notes** Sunday L, Vegetarian available, Dress restrictions, Smart casual **Seats** 80, Pr/dining room 40 **Children** Portions, Menu **Parking** 50

FRITTON
Map 13 TG40

Fritton House

Modern British

Lakeside dining in smart surroundings

☎ 01493 484008
Church Ln NR31 9HA
e-mail: frittonhouse@somerleyton.co.uk

This charming 15th-century property is set amidst parkland on the banks of Fritton Lake. The dining room is contemporary in style with plain dark tables, wooden floors and smart leather chairs. The same menu is also available in the large open-plan lounge bar and outside on the terrace, and casually-dressed staff offer relaxed but very efficient service. Using the best of local produce, you might start with smoked eel, bacon and Anya potato salad with sumac and parsley dressing, moving on to rump of lamb, white bean and ham hock ragout with braised Savoy cabbage and mint salsa.

Seats 70

GREAT BIRCHAM
Map 13 TF73

The Kings Head Hotel

Modern British

Great food in stylish village hotel

☎ 01485 578265
PE31 6RJ
e-mail: welcome@the-kings-head-bircham.co.uk
dir: Telephone for directions

Situated in a peaceful little village close to Sandringham and the north Norfolk coastline, The Kings Head may look like a very well kept inn, but this stylish hotel and restaurant is one of the new gems of Norfolk. The contemporary restaurant overlooks a sheltered courtyard which is perfect for alfresco dining in summer. Lots of local, seasonal produce appears on the simple menu of British and Mediterranean dishes. Try slow-cooked free-range belly pork with Puy lentil purée, apple and cinnamon purée, followed by roast fillet of sea bass with marinated vegetable salad, Parmentier potatoes and rocket pesto.

Times 12-2/7-9

GREAT YARMOUTH
Map 13 TG50

Café Cru Restaurant

Modern British

Family-run seaside hotel serving quality cuisine

☎ 01493 842000
Imperial Hotel, North Dr NR30 1EQ
e-mail: reception@imperialhotel.co.uk
dir: North end of Great Yarmouth seafront

An imposing Victorian hotel on the seafront is the location for the refurbished Café Cru, a welcoming restaurant with a contemporary feel, decked out in neutral shades, with modern chandeliers and a choice of open-plan and booth seating. Guests can enjoy a drink in the upstairs Savoie Bar before taking their place for dinner, where they can expect a good choice of honest, unfussy British dishes. Prime ingredients are cooked well and simply, and the seasonally-changing menu with daily specials includes a range of mature, locally-reared steaks from the chargill, and grilled Lowestoft plaice with lemon and parsley butter. An alternative choice of classic dishes includes baked belly of pork with bubble-and-squeak, Braeburn apple sauce and thyme gravy.

Chef Stephen Duffield **Owner** Mr N L & Mrs A Mobbs
Times 12-4.30/6.30-10, Closed 24-28 & 31 Dec, Closed L Mon-Sat, Closed D Sun **Prices** Starter £4.50-£9, Main £8.50-£18, Dessert £5.50-£8, Service optional **Wines** 25 bottles over £20, 68 bottles under £20, 10 by glass **Notes** Sunday L, Vegetarian available, Dress restrictions, Smart casual, No shorts or trainers, Civ Wed 140, Air con **Seats** 60, Pr/dining room 140 **Children** Portions **Parking** 45

The Seafood Restaurant

Seafood V

Traditional-style seafood restaurant with simply prepared fresh fish

☎ 01493 856009
85 North Quay NR30 1JF
dir: Please telephone for directions

Situated on a corner in Great Yarmouth, The Seafood Restaurant is slightly rounded in shape giving the dining room a characterful, curved appearance. This popular traditional-style seafood restaurant, run by the same Greek husband-and-wife owners for 29 years, impressively claims to be the first seafood restaurant in Norfolk. Top-quality fish from Lowestoft market is simply cooked, or with a sauce, allowing freshness and flavour to speak for themselves. Dishes are served in generous proportions and service is friendly. Choose your fish from a chilled cabinet, or pick a lobster straight from the tank, then enjoy dishes such as wild sea bass with chilli, garlic and soy sauce.

Chef Christopher Kikis **Owner** Christopher & Miriam Kikis **Times** 12-1.45/6.30-10.30, Closed 2 wks Xmas, 2 wks May, BHs, Closed Sun, Closed L Sat **Prices** Food prices not confirmed for 2009. Please telephone for details. **Wines** 39 bottles over £20, 19 bottles under £20, 6 by glass **Notes** Vegetarian menu, Dress restrictions, Smart casual, Air con **Seats** 42 **Children** Min 6 yrs **Parking** On street

---

Congham Hall

◎◎ Modern British **V**

Imaginative, seasonal cooking in Georgian setting

☎ 01485 600250
Lynn Rd PE32 1AH
e-mail: info@conghamhallhotel.co.uk
dir: 6m NE of King's Lynn on A148, turn right towards Grimston. Hotel 2.5m on left (do not go to Congham)

This elegant Georgian manor is set amid 30 acres of parkland, with beautiful landscaped gardens and renowned herb garden, a working kitchen garden with over 700 varieties of herbs. Traditional features have been maintained, as has a style of décor throughout the inviting and tastefully furnished public rooms, with log fires, fresh flowers and fine ceramics creating a warm, homely atmosphere. Imaginative cooking is served in the Orangery restaurant, an intimate, summery room with French windows leading on to the terrace and gardens. Local and seasonal produce feature prominently on classically inspired modern menus, which include a tasting gourmand option. Game comes from the nearby Sandringham Estate, while fish is delivered fresh from the day boats at King's Lynn. Starters may feature goat's cheese wonton salad with home-cured tomatoes, Portobello mushrooms, onion confit and balsamic vinegar. For mains, try darne of halibut with a fève and bacon risotto, glazed baby onions and parsley jus. Cookery classes are offered.

Chef Jamie Murch **Owner** von Essen Hotels **Times** 12-1.45/7-9.15 **Wines** 60 bottles over £20, 10 bottles under £20, 10 by glass **Notes** Gourmand menu L £31.95, D £59, Sunday L, Vegetarian menu, Dress restrictions, Smart casual, Civ Wed 100 **Seats** 50, Pr/dining room 18 **Children** Min 7 yrs D, Portions, Menu **Parking** 50

Rushmore's

◎ Modern British

Assured cooking of traditional British food

☎ 01485 579393
14 High St PE31 7ER
dir: A149 towards Hunstanton. At Heacham, turn left at Lavender Fields. Follow into village, take 1st left into High St

Good honest service with a smile is offered at this traditional restaurant, with its proper tablecloths and linen napkins. The eponymous chef hails from Norfolk and his monthly menu is drawn from seasonal local ingredients, including shellfish from the coast and game from Sandringham. Utterly British in style, this is simple, effective cooking with a classic feel. Recommended dishes are oven-baked pancake filled with prawns and glazed with cheese sauce, rack of lamb with minted mash and rosemary gravy, or sea bass with pak choi and lime dressing.

Chef Colin Rushmore **Owner** P Barrett, D Askew **Times** 12-2/6.30-9.30, Closed Mon-Tue, Closed L Sat, Closed D Sun **Prices** Fixed L 2 course £10.95, Fixed D 3 course £22.95, Service optional **Wines** 6 bottles over £20, 15 bottles under £20, 3 by glass **Notes** Sunday L, Vegetarian available **Seats** 42, Pr/dining room 6 **Children** Min 5 yrs, Portions **Parking** 25

Park Farm Hotel

◎ British

Attractive restaurant serving a relaxed style of food

☎ 01603 810264
NR9 3DL
e-mail: enq@parkfarm-hotel.co.uk
dir: 6m S of Norwich on B1172

This Georgian former farmhouse is now an elegant hotel set in landscaped grounds surrounded by open countryside. The smart orangery-style restaurant overlooks the garden. Plain white walls are hung with bright, unframed canvases, and tables are neatly clothed and laid with contemporary crockery and cutlery. There's a set-price menu for lunch and dinner, and dishes make good use of seasonal local produce. Typical examples include wild mushroom and parmesan risotto topped with crispy leek, and pan-fried pork fillet filled with apple and

sage mousseline and arranged on a potato rösti with Madeira jus.

Chef David Bell **Owner** David Gowing **Times** 12-2/7-9.30 **Prices** Fixed L 2 course £12.95-£13.50, Fixed D 3 course £23.95-£24.95, Service optional **Wines** 26 bottles over £20, 38 bottles under £20, 12 by glass **Notes** Sunday L, Vegetarian available, Dress restrictions, Smart casual, Civ Wed 100, Air con **Seats** 60, Pr/dining room **Children** Portions, Menu **Parking** 150

The Victoria at Holkham

◎◎ British, French

Norfolk hideaway with an interesting colonial feel

☎ 01328 711008
Park Rd NR23 1RG
e-mail: victoria@holkham.co.uk
dir: 3m W of Wells-next-the-Sea on A149. 12m N of Fakenham

Part of the Holkham Estate, home to the Earls of Leicester, the Victoria was built to house the entourage of visiting aristocracy and sports a smart colonial theme inspired by Sikh Maharajah, who visited the estate in the 1800s. Expect an informal bar decked out in carved wooden furniture, huge sofas and a wealth of Indian artefacts, and a contemporary brasserie-style restaurant that extends into a conservatory. Simple, classic British food abounds on the menu with dishes that stress the inclusion of local ingredients - roasted saddle of estate rabbit with chorizo and root vegetable cassoulet, or medallions of Holkham beef fillet with tempura of Thornham oysters, champ potato and Guinness cream.

Chef Ricardo Juanico **Owner** Viscount & Viscountess Coke **Times** 12-2.30/7-9.30 **Prices** Food prices not confirmed for 2009. Please telephone for details. **Wines** 54 bottles over £20, 19 bottles under £20, 10 by glass **Notes** Dress restrictions, Smart casual, Civ Wed 80 **Seats** 80 **Children** Portions, Menu **Parking** 50

Butlers Restaurant

◎ Modern European ⚭

Contemporary café bar and restaurant offering bistro-style dining

☎ 01263 710790
9 Appleyard NR25 6BN
e-mail: eat@butlersofholt.com
dir: Just off High Street, signed Appleyard

The atmosphere is relaxed and friendly at this bright modern restaurant, with its part glass roof and glazed doors letting the light flood in. Customers can enjoy a drink at the large oak bar or relax in the courtyard and garden beneath the shade of a 200-year-old tree. Dishes are full of fresh flavours and vibrant colours, using seasonal and local produce. With everything prepared in

Continued

HOLT *Continued*

the open kitchen, expect the likes of duck confit terrine wrapped in Parma ham and accompanied by piccalilli and rustic bread, followed by pan-fried pigeon breast on warm salad of peas, pancetta and baby gems.

Chef Sean Creasey **Owner** Sean & Ruth Creasey **Times** 12-3/6-9, Closed 25, 26 Dec **Prices** Starter £4.50-£6.95, Main £6.95-£17.95, Dessert £3.95-£4.95, Service optional **Wines** 13 bottles over £20, 20 bottles under £20, 12 by glass **Notes** Monthly events with special menu, Sunday L, Vegetarian available, Air con **Seats** 50 **Children** Portions **Parking** On street (free after 6pm)

The Lawns

◉ Modern European

☎ 01263 713390
26 Station Rd NR25 6BS
e-mail: mail@lawnsatholt.co.uk

A splendid Georgian house at the centre of this bustling north Norfolk market town, The Lawns is a stylish wine bar and restaurant with rooms. Total refurbishment presents a modern, open-plan face, with bar decked out in plush leather sofas, smart dining room with matching high-backed leather chairs and a conservatory area. Outside there's the fair-weather bonus of an alfresco terrace and garden. The atmosphere's relaxed and unstuffy throughout, though service is suitably professional. The kitchen deals in quality local and

seasonal produce on a simple, traditional, crowd-pleasing menu that's served in all areas. Expect Morston mussels marinière to start, followed by mixed game pie or pan-fried sea bass on wilted spinach with a butter sauce.

Chef Nick Hare, Jack Watts **Owner** Mr & Mrs Daniel Rees **Times** 12-2.30/6-9 **Prices** Starter £4.50-£6.95, Main £7.95-£17.50, Dessert £5-£5, Service optional **Wines** 6 bottles over £20, 29 bottles under £20, 9 by glass **Notes** Wine tasting D available, Sunday L, Vegetarian available **Seats** 24 **Children** Portions **Parking** 18

The Pigs

◎◎ British

Local pub with refreshing attitude and high standards

☎ 01263 587634
Edgefield NR24 2RL

The Pigs puts great importance on its status as a pub. That means real ales, pub quizzes, bar billiards and a welcome lack of stuffiness. The white-painted building has been extended over the years and there are a number of informal rooms to choose from, including one for children which is full of toys and games. Staff are kitted out with black aprons and keep things running with a cheerful efficiency. The philosophy of good, fresh food, local wherever possible, extends to the choice of bar snacks ('Iffits'), which include a mixed pickle pot, and small plates ('Peckish') such as devilled whitebait with gentleman's relish. All food is ordered at the bar. Start

with potted shrimps with toasted granary bread before slow-cooked belly of pork, smoky bacon beans, apple chutney and black pudding, finishing with chocolate custard with rum-soaked raisins and brown sugar meringue.

Times 11-2.30/6-9, Closed Mon except BHs, Closed D Sun **Prices** Food prices not confirmed for 2009. Please telephone for details.

HORNING   Map 13 TG31

Taps

◉ Modern, Traditional

Consistency and good value from an intimate local restaurant

☎ 01692 630219
25 Lower St NR12 8AA
web: www.tapsrestaurant.com
dir: From Norwich follow signs to The Broads on A1151. Through Wroxham and turn right to Horning & Ludham. After 3m turn right into Horning, Lower St 500yds on left

With its welcoming cosy neighbourhood restaurant atmosphere, Taps attracts diners from far and near. The décor - amber and ivory walls and wicker furniture - gives it a pleasant, airy feel, while crisp table linen and candlelight add a touch of formality. The modern British menu is peppered with stylistic borrowings from a range of culinary styles, all using good quality local produce.

The Neptune Inn & Restaurant

HUNSTANTON   Map 12 TF64

Modern British

New owner with a culinary pedigree for relaxed country inn

☎ 01485 532122
85 Old Hunstanton Rd PE36 6HZ
e-mail: reservations@theneptune.co.uk
dir: Please telephone for directions

Kevin Mangeolles has been a big fish on the Isle of Wight for the last decade and now, with his wife Jacki, he has moved across the country from the critically acclaimed George to the Norfolk coast. The 18th-century, red-brick Neptune, a former coaching inn, has a New England feel on the inside, blended with touches of old Norfolk: think white-painted clap-board walls, model boats, framed black-and-white photos of the surrounding coast and the

laid-back charm of Lloyd Loom sofas and chairs in the bar. The dining room is a civilised space, with crisp linen tablecloths and high-backed chairs, and suitably professional-yet-friendly service. The sensibly short menu - five at each course - is appealing and inventive, and makes use of the significant regional larder. Local mussels in a risotto with apple and a light curry flavour sits alongside grilled Crottin goat's cheese tart with pickled beetroot among starters. Main courses are equally well considered, such as a roasted free-range chicken (superb flavour) with a ballotine of the thigh meat enriched with black pudding, sweet potato purée and a luscious chicken jus. The all-round high quality starts with the home-made bread and continues through to desserts such as a trio of chocolate that includes a tart, soup and white chocolate and thyme ice cream.

Chef Kevin Mangeolles **Owner** Kevin & Jacki Mangeolles **Times** 12-2/7-11, Closed 2 wks Nov & Jan, Closed Mon (except BHs), Closed L Tue-Wed **Prices** Fixed L 2 course £15.50, Starter £6-£9.50, Main £15.50-£20, Dessert £6.50-£9, Service optional **Wines** 20 bottles over £20, 20 bottles under £20, 12 by glass **Notes** Sunday L, Vegetarian available **Seats** 32 **Children** Min 10 yrs **Parking** 8

Starters might include smooth chicken liver parfait served with a compote of fruit, dressed mixed leaves and Melba toast, and mains such as pan-fried breast of Norfolk chicken on a potato rösti with creamed leeks and a panaché of vegetables.

Taps

Times 12-2/7-9.30, Closed Mon, Closed D Sun

HUNSTANTON   Map 12 TF64

Luigi's (@ Sutton House Hotel)

◎ Italian, Mediterranean ✪

Authentic Italian cuisine by the sea

☎ 01485 532552
24 Northgate PE36 6AP
e-mail: benelli@freeuk.com
dir: A149 Hunstanton, left into Greevegate, right into Northgate

The authentic and family-owned Luigi's Trattoria is situated in a small hotel adjacent to the seafront in Hunstanton. The homely dining room has plain wood floors, sage green walls and simple tables. Service is both attentive and very friendly, and there's an emphasis on fresh fish and seafood. You could expect to tuck into Tuscan bean soup to start, followed by a hearty main course of tagliatelle with wild boar sausages and pancetta in a red wine sauce, a traditional lasagne, or whole sea bass with garlic olive oil, tomatoes, basil and clams, with a decent tiramisù to finish.

Owner Tony & Karen Lombari **Times** 12-3/6-11, Closed Mon **Wines** 3 bottles over £20, 15 bottles under £20, 2 by glass **Notes** Pre-theatre menu 2 courses £14.50, Sunday L, Vegetarian available, Dress restrictions, Smart casual, no shorts **Seats** 30, Pr/dining room 10 **Parking** Ample parking on street within 100 mtrs

---

The Neptune Inn & Restaurant

◎◎◎ – **see opposite**

KING'S LYNN   Map 12 TF62

Spread Eagle Inn

◎ British, French

Delightful country inn serving wholesome fare

☎ 01366 347995
Church Rd, Barton Bendish PE33 9GF
e-mail: info@spreadeaglenorfolk.co.uk
dir: From A1122 take Barton Bendish turning. 1st left into Church Rd, continue past church on left and straight ahead into cul-de-sac, Spread Eagle is on left

Nestling in a rural hamlet in picturesque West Norfolk, this simple village inn has gained a reputation for good quality food made with the best of local seasonal produce. Small country-style rooms feature open fires, low-beamed ceilings, exposed brickwork and murals of the local area. The bar has plain tables and wooden floors, while the restaurant tables are neatly clothed and accompanied by high-backed leather chairs. Service is typically relaxed and friendly but attentive. The kitchen's wholesome modern approach might deliver smoked haddock and prawn gratin with mixed leaves, local fillet of beef, mushroom and red wine sauce, creamed potatoes and wilted greens, as well as favourites like home-made steak burgers topped with bacon and cheese.

Chef Austin Chapman **Owner** Martin & Lori Halpin **Times** 12.30-2.30/6.30-11, Closed Mon, Closed L Tue-Wed, Closed D Sun **Prices** Food prices not confirmed for 2009. Please telephone for details. **Wines** 7 bottles over £20, 25 bottles under £20, 8 by glass **Notes** Sunday L, Vegetarian available, Dress restrictions, **Seats** 46 **Children** Portions **Parking** 30

NORTH WALSHAM   Map 13 TG23

Beechwood Hotel

◎◎ British, Mediterranean ✪

A passion for local produce in elegant surroundings

☎ 01692 403231
Cromer Rd NR28 0HD
e-mail: enquiries@beechwood-hotel.co.uk
dir: From Norwich on B1150, 13m to N Walsham. Turn left at lights and next right. Hotel 150 mtrs on left

Agatha Christie was a frequent visitor to this gracious ivy-clad 18th-century property, and fans can see letters to the family displayed in the hallway. The Beechwood has a strong focus on food, and the kitchen makes the best use of the abundant Norfolk larder; notably

---

shellfish from Cromer, Sheringham, Thornham and Morston as well as local meat and the freshest of vegetables. Modern British dishes with a Mediterranean influence are served in the smartly appointed restaurant; take Walsingham cheese tartlet with bacon and mustard ice cream, followed by fillet of beef on bubble-and-squeak with wild mushroom jus and onion marmalade. Drinks can be taken in the garden or the clubby lounge bar.

Beechwood Hotel

Chef Steven Norgate **Owner** Don Birch & Lindsay Spalding **Times** 12-1.45/7-9, Closed L Mon-Sat **Prices** Fixed L course £22, Fixed D 3 course £36, Service optional **Wines** 220 bottles over £20, 10 bottles under £20, 5 by glass **Notes** Sunday L, Vegetarian available, Dress restrictions, Smart casual **Seats** 60, Pr/dining room 20 **Children** Min 10 yrs, Portions **Parking** 25

NORWICH   Map 13 TG20

Adlard's Restaurant

◎◎ Modern

New owners at city-centre favourite producing good modern European food

☎ 01603 633522
79 Upper St Giles St NR2 1AB
e-mail: info@adlards.co.uk
dir: City centre, 200yds behind the City Hall

The renowned and respected David Adlard sold his restaurant to MJB Hotels and so begins a new era for this city centre venue. There are seemingly no significant changes to the room - the smart, bright décor remains the same - and locals and visitors to the city still flock here for the modern European food based around good local produce. Pumpkin soufflé is an imaginative starter, served with creamed leeks and roasted pumpkin seeds, while main-course slow-cooked pork is served with baby turnips and cabbage mixed with bacon and caraway seeds. Chocolate mousse with caramelised blood orange and candied peel is a successful finish. Service is by a professional, smartly turned-out team.

Times 12.30-1.45/7.30-10.30, Closed 1st wk Jan, Closed Sun, Mon

NORWICH *Continued*

Ah-So Japanese Restaurant

◉ Japanese

Authentic taste of the land of the rising sun in Norwich

☎ 01603 618901
16 Prince of Wales Rd NR1 1LB
e-mail: booking@ah-so.co.uk
dir: From station, cross bridge, restaurant in 600yds on right, near Anglia TV

This smart, modern restaurant is popular with business types, and a friendly and relaxed atmosphere pervades. Specialising in teppan-yaki, the chefs cook meals in front of you on a large stainless steel griddle, providing some flamboyant culinary theatrics. The menu is authentically Japanese, assembling fresh, simple ingredients - miso soup with tofu, or vegetable tempura for example, followed by fillet steak cooked in butter and served with Japanese onion soup, seasonal grilled vegetables and fried rice. The set meals are an economical option, as well as offering the chance to sample a number of dishes at one sitting.

Times 12-9/6-12, Closed Mon, Closed L Tue-Sat

Arlington Grill & Brasserie

◉ Modern British **V**

Enjoyable dining at historic city-centre venue

☎ 01603 617841
The George Hotel, 10 Arlington Ln, Newmarket Road NR2 2DA
e-mail: reservations@georgehotel.co.uk
web: www.arlingtonhotelgroup.co.uk
dir: 1m from Norwich city centre, 1m from Norwich city station, 1m from A140

Just a short walk from the city centre, behind the frosted glass frontage of this family-run Victorian hotel lies a contemporary dining room with leather banquette seating, darkwood panelling and mirrors which give a bright but intimate atmosphere while the open-plan grill adds a touch of theatre. Expect formal service from friendly, uniformed staff. Simply cooked dishes make good use of fresh seasonal produce such as steamed Brancaster mussels with white wine and parsley, and main courses of roast breast and confit leg of guinea fowl with a ragout of shallots, bacon lardons and mushrooms. Desserts include pineapple tarte Tatin with ginger ice cream.

Chef Paul Branford **Owner** David Easter/Kingsley Place Hotels Ltd **Times** 12-2/6-10 **Prices** Fixed L 2 course fr £7.95, Fixed D 3 course fr £19.95, Starter £4.50-£6.50, Main £9.95-£17.95, Dessert £4.75-£5.50, Service optional **Wines** 7 bottles over £20, 19 bottles under £20, 5 by glass **Notes** Sunday L, Vegetarian menu, Air con **Seats** 44, Pr/dining room 60 **Children** Portions, Menu **Parking** 40

Best Western Annesley House Hotel

◉◉ Modern International 🍽

Conservatory dining in charming surroundings

☎ 01603 624553
6 Newmarket Rd NR2 2LA
e-mail: annesleyhouse@bestwestern.co.uk
dir: On A11, close to city centre

This delightful Grade II listed Georgian property is set in 3 acres of landscaped gardens and grounds within a tree-lined conservation area, just a short walk from the historic city centre. There's a comfortable lounge bar for pre-dinner drinks, while the smart conservatory restaurant is furnished with Mediterranean-style décor and ornate white and black cast-iron chairs (cushioned for comfort), with views over the charming water garden and waterfall. The modern food with European influences benefits from straightforward handling that allows quality ingredients to shine. On the short fixed-price menu you might find pan-seared hand-dived scallops with Burgundy-poached pear and Binham blue cheese with confit tomato and rocket salad, or perhaps pan-fried fillet of sea bass with wholegrain mustard mash, creamed leeks, softly poached egg and mustard sauce.

Chef Philip Woodcock, Steven Watkin **Owner** Mr & Mrs D Reynolds **Times** 12-2/6-9.30, Closed Xmas & New Year, Closed D Sun **Prices** Fixed D 4 course £27.50, Starter £5.50, Main £18.50, Dessert £5.50, Service optional **Wines** 6 bottles over £20, 19 bottles under £20, 9 by glass **Notes** Pre-theatre menu available from 6pm by arrangement, Vegetarian available **Seats** 30, Pr/dining room 18 **Children** Portions **Parking** 25

Brummells Seafood Restaurant

◉◉ International, Seafood

Quaint restaurant for fresh seafood

☎ 01603 625555
7 Magdalen St NR3 1LE
e-mail: brummell@brummells.co.uk
web: www.brummells.co.uk
dir: In city centre, 2 mins walk from Norwich Cathedral, 40yds from Colegate

Located in the oldest part of the city, Brummells is in a 17th-century building just a short walk from the cathedral. Exposed beams and stonework give it charm and character, while the atmosphere is relaxed and rather romantic in the evening when the tables glow under candlelight. Seafood is the basis of the menu and it is sourced with conviction and cooked with care. Start with six native oysters served naturally over ice, or creamed fish soup with coconut milk. Main courses include skate wing with black butter, or chargrilled tuna with compôte of fruity curry marmalade. Non-fish alternatives include beef or venison steaks. Finish with rich Amaretto and dark chocolate pot.

Chef A Brummell, J O'Sullivan **Owner** Mr A Brummell **Times** Flexible, Closed L (bookings only) **Prices** Starter £6-£16, Main £16-£35, Dessert £6.50, Service optional, Groups min 7 service 10% **Wines** 56 bottles over £20, 27 bottles under £20, 3 by glass **Notes** Vegetarian available, Dress restrictions, Smart casual or jacket & tie, Air con **Seats** 30 **Children** Portions

By Appointment

◉ British, Mediterranean V

Dinner in an Aladdin's cave

☎ 01603 630730
27-29 St George's St NR3 1AB
web: www.byappointmentnorwich.co.uk
dir: City centre. Entrance rear of Merchants House

This restaurant occupies three 15th-century merchants' houses and has a multitude of nooks and crannies. There are four intimate dining rooms, all very theatrical, with the added luxury of two comfortable drawing rooms. The whole house is filled with antique furniture, and tables are embellished with Victorian silver-plated cutlery and fine china. Dishes are classically English with continental influences, and everything is freshly made on the premises from local produce wherever possible. Favourites are pistachio nut and apricot stuffed loin of Sheringham lamb, and fillet of English beef wrapped in Parma ham and served with Burgundy sauce.

Chef Timothy Brown **Owner** Timothy Brown, R Culyer **Times** Closed 25 Dec, Closed Sun-Mon, Closed L all week **Prices** Starter £6.95-£7.95, Main £19.95-£21.95, Dessert £6.95, Service optional **Wines** 40 bottles over £20, 19 bottles under £20, 3 by glass **Notes** Vegetarian menu, Dress restrictions, Smart casual **Seats** 50, Pr/dining room 36 **Children** Min 12 yrs **Parking** 4; Colegate car park

---

De Vere Dunston Hall

◉ Modern British

Accomplished cuisine in grand hotel

☎ 01508 470444
Ipswich Rd NR14 8PQ
e-mail: dhreception@devere-hotels.com
dir: On A140 between Norwich & Ipswich

Located in 170 acres of landscaped grounds, this imposing Grade II listed building is just a short drive from the centre of Norwich. Diners choosing the intimate atmosphere of La Fontaine restaurant can expect a contemporary take on classic British and French cuisine prepared from produce that mainly comes from within a 30-mile radius, including regular farmers markets on site. Try grilled pigeon breast, caramelised endive, oranges and raspberry vinegar, or roasted loin of wild boar, served with its own sausage and pancetta. Typical desserts include mango soufflé with pineapple and peppercorn syrup. The Brasserie bar and grill offers a more informal option.

Times Closed Sun, Closed L Mon-Sat

Marriott Sprowston Manor Hotel

◉◉ International

Fine dining in elegant hotel

☎ 01603 410871
Sprowston Park, Wroxham Rd NR7 8RP
e-mail: debbie.phillips@marriotthotels.com
dir: From A47 take Postwick exit onto Norwich outer ring road, then take A1151. Hotel approx 3m and signed

This imposing, refurbished hotel is built around a stately manor house that dates back to the 16th century. Set in well-tended landscaped gardens and surrounded by open parkland, it combines historic charm with modern comforts, including golf and leisure facilities. The elegant Manor Restaurant, with its crystal chandeliers and mahogany reeded columns, offers traditional international cuisine using good quality, locally-sourced produce. To start, try pressed tomato flavoured with basil, drizzled with olive oil and served with slivers of red onion, followed by fillet of beef with wild mushrooms and a potato stack. Desserts include a trio of brûlées - traditional, chocolate and strawberry. For more informal fare, there is the contemporary Zest Café.

Times 12.30-2/6-10, Closed L Sat, Closed D Sun

Old Rectory

◉◉ Modern British V ☺

A Georgian haven in the heart of Norwich

☎ 01603 700772
103 Yarmouth Rd, Thorpe St Andrew NR7 0HF
e-mail: enquiries@oldrectorynorwich.com
dir: From A47 take A1042 to Thorpe, then A1242. Hotel right after 1st lights

This ivy-clad Georgian house sits in pretty grounds overlooking the River Yare. Take an aperitif on the pool terrace in summer or by the cosy drawing room fire in winter, and then move through to the elegant, panelled restaurant, a period room lit by candles. The concise menu changes daily but consistently impresses; expect modern British dishes conjured from good-quality local ingredients, seared fillet of marinated sea bass perhaps, on a bed of roasted fennel, cherry vine tomatoes, saffron potatoes and green olive tapenade, or heartier options such as marinated, roasted local wild pheasant breast and stuffed leg with braised Savoy cabbage, thyme mash and reduced juices, or marinated, roasted medallions of Attleborough beef with roasted root vegetables, red wine jus and wilted spinach.

Chef James Perry **Owner** Chris & Sally Entwistle **Times** Closed Xmas & New Year, Closed Sun, Mon, Closed L all week **Prices** Fixed D 3 course £25-£28, Service optional **Wines** 14 bottles over £20, 7 bottles under £20, 5 by glass **Notes** Vegetarian menu **Seats** 18, Pr/dining room 16 **Children** Portions **Parking** 16

1 Up @ The Mad Moose

◉◉ Modern British 🖥

Contemporary restaurant and modern food above a popular pub

☎ 01603 627687
The Mad Moose Arms & 1Up, 2 Warwick St NR2 3LD
e-mail: madmoose@animalinns.co.uk
web: www.themadmoose.co.uk
dir: A11 onto A140. Turn right at lights onto Unthank Rd, then left onto Dover/Warwick St

The first-floor restaurant of a popular gastro-pub, 1 Up is the fine dining part of the operation. Open at dinner only (plus Sunday lunch), the elegant, chic space offers a twist on the classical - where modern wallpaper rubs shoulders with chandeliers and luxurious velvet curtains. The atmosphere is intimate, sophisticated and unpretentious and comes backed by appropriately professional yet relaxed service. The food fits the bill too, the accomplished cooking is big on clear flavours and balance, and committed to the use of high quality seasonal ingredients from the abundant local larder. Start with confit of Norfolk rabbit with quince and lemon aïoli with watercress, raisins and grain mustard dressing, followed by pan-fried organic salmon with truffled ratte potatoes, roasted fennel, crayfish tails and roasted red pepper dressing.

Chef Eden Derrick **Owner** Mr Henry Watt **Times** 12-3/7-9.30, Closed 25-26 Dec, 1 Jan, Closed L Mon-Sat, Closed D Sun **Prices** Fixed D 3 course £20, Starter £5.95-£8.50, Main £10.50-£15.95, Dessert £5.50-£6.50, Service optional **Wines** 32 bottles over £20, 24 bottles under £20, 11 by glass **Notes** Sunday L, Vegetarian available **Seats** 48 **Children** Portions **Parking** On street

NORWICH *Continued*

St Benedicts Restaurant

☺ Modern British 💻

Centrally located, welcoming setting with quality cuisine

☎ 01603 765377
9 St Benedicts St NR2 4PE
e-mail: stbens@ukonline.co.uk
dir: Just off inner ring road. Turn right by Toys-R-Us, 2nd right into St Benedicts St. Restaurant is on left by pedestrian crossing

Situated on a bustling street in the city centre, the contemporary blue interior of this local restaurant offers an intimate and relaxed atmosphere, while service is helpful, professional and unobtrusive. The kitchen conjures up an eclectic and imaginative choice of dishes, with an emphasis on good, clean flavours, using fresh, local, seasonal ingredients. Perhaps try the simple, but succulent starter of local brown shrimps on toast with herb mayonnaise and a sweet and sour orange dressing, followed by roast Norfolk pheasant with Savoy cabbage, parsnips and Puy lentils, and be tempted by desserts such as sticky toffee pudding with caramelised pear and pecan nuts.

Chef Stuart Duffield **Owner** Nigel & Joyne Raffles **Times** 12-2/7-10, Closed 25-31 Dec, Closed Sun-Mon **Prices** Fixed L 2 course fr £7.95, Fixed D 3 course fr £16.95, Starter £4.95-£6.95, Main £10.95-£15.95, Dessert £4.95, Groups min 10 service 10% **Wines** 15 bottles over £20, 34 bottles under £20, 8 by glass **Notes** Vegetarian available, Air con **Seats** 42, Pr/dining room 24 **Children** Portions **Parking** On street, Car parks nearby

St Giles Restaurant

☺ British

Relaxed dining in stylish city-centre hotel

☎ 01603 275180 & 275182
St Giles House Hotel, 41-45 St Giles St NR2 1JR
e-mail: reception@stgileshousehotel.com
web: www.stgileshousehotel.com
dir: A11 into Norwich, turn left at rdbt signed Chapelfield shopping. At nxt rdbt take 3rd exit & keep left as road forks. St. Giles House on left.

This impressive Grade II listed building with its sandstone façade is conveniently located in the centre of town. Original wood panelling, ornamental plasterwork and elegant marble floors have been complemented in unique style with a mixture of modern design and stunning chandeliers to give the place a sense of sumptuous individuality. Sip a cocktail in the bar or on the Parisian-style terrace before going through to dinner, which is an intimate affair, set against an art deco style backdrop. The kitchen makes the most of locally-sourced ingredients to create an inviting selection of classic dishes, simply prepared to let the flavours speak for themselves. For starters, try crab fishcakes with red pepper aïoli accompanied by good home-made bread,

and follow with deliciously tender slow-roasted belly pork with roasted root vegetables and celeriac purée, Parmentier potatoes and jus.

St Giles Restaurant

Chef Daniel Savage & Leigh Taylor **Owner** Norfolk Hotels Ltd **Times** 11-10 **Prices** Fixed L 2 course £12.50-£14.50, Starter £4.95-£7.95, Main £13.95-£18.95, Dessert £4.50-£7.50, Service optional **Wines** 38 bottles over £20, 25 bottles under £20, 9 by glass **Notes** Sunday L, Vegetarian available, Air con **Seats** 50, Pr/dining room 48 **Children** Portions **Parking** 30

Shiki

☺ Modern Japanese

Sushi with style whether you want to eat in or takeaway

☎ 01603 619262
6 Tombland NR3 1HE
e-mail: bookings@shikirestaurant.co.uk
dir: Norwich city centre. From Castle Meadow onto Upper Kings St continue straight onto Tombland, restaurant on left

A Victorian building conceals this minimalist Japanese restaurant, with its stripped pine floors, bench seating and generally uncluttered interior. Freshly prepared sushi and the tapas-style menus are the main attractions, including blackboard specials. The choice of fish includes the popular types and extends to eel, turbot and yellow tail tuna. Japanese specialities include miso soup and other classic appetisers, with main courses such as Japanese curries, chicken teriyaki and seafood tempura. Fresh ingredients and clean flavours more than live up to expectations. The all-in-one bento boxes are great value for money.

Times 12-2.30/5.30-10.30, Closed Xmas, Closed Sun

Stower Grange

☺ Traditional British, European

Welcoming surroundings for an enjoyable meal

☎ 01603 860210
School Rd, Drayton NR8 6EF
e-mail: enquiries@stowergrange.co.uk
dir: From Norwich take A1065 to Drayton Village. Turn right at lights. Continue to small rdbt, bear left into School Rd for 100 yds.

Set in pretty grounds just a mile or so from Norwich airport, this imposing ivy-clad building dates back to the 17th century and is a good choice for special occasions. The restaurant overlooks the gardens and is an elegant setting for some well-executed favourites. Cooking is straightforward and reassuring, with just about everything made on the premises. You might start with seared fillet of beef served with a tomato and chilli salsa and a parmesan and rocket salad, and then tuck into baked chicken breast stuffed with wild mushroom, or rump of lamb served with a thyme and shallot polenta cake and thyme jus. Save room for dessert, which could include honey pannacotta with brandied apricots and a brandy snap cone.

Chef David Kilmister, Gary Taylor **Owner** Richard & Jane Fannon **Times** 12-2.30/7-9.30, Closed 26-30 Dec, Closed D Sun **Prices** Fixed L 2 course £14.50-£16, Fixed D 3 course £25-£33, Starter £5.50-£7.50, Main £12.50-£21, Dessert £5.50-£6.25, Service optional **Wines** 15 bottles over £20, 28 bottles under £20, 4 by glass **Notes** Sunday L, Vegetarian available, Civ Wed 100 **Seats** 40, Pr/dining room 20 **Children** Portions **Parking** 40

The Sugar Hut

☺ Thai V

Relaxed Thai dining in this smart city-centre restaurant

☎ 01603 766755
4 Opie St NR1 3DN
e-mail: lhongmo@hotmail.co.uk
dir: City centre next to Castle Meadow and Castle Mall car park.

Smart yet informal Thai restaurant in the heart of Norwich, offering authentic cooking using good quality ingredients, some imported and some sourced locally. Expect a tasteful yellow and blue décor, with high ceilings, balcony, wicker chairs, blue tablecloths and gold linen napkins, and polite, friendly and efficient service from uniformed staff. Vibrant, well-flavoured dishes include steamed pork and king prawn dumplings with sweet chilli and soy dipping sauce, duck with seaweed and tamarind sauce, and deep-fried sea bass with sweet and sour chilli sauce. Good value set menus available for two to four people.

Chef Chartchai Fodsungnoen **Owner** Leelanooch Hongmo **Times** 12-2.30/6-10.30, Closed Sun **Prices** Fixed L 2 course £6.95-£8.95, Fixed D 3 course £25, Starter £4.15-£6.50, Main £7.95-£15.95, Dessert £3.75-£4.50, Service optional, Groups min 7 service 10% **Wines** 6 bottles over £20, 24 bottles under £20, 7 by glass **Notes** Vegetarian available, Vegetarian menu, Air con **Seats** 40 **Children** Portions **Parking** Castle Mall

Tatlers

◉◉ Modern British

Relaxed and stylish brasserie dining

☎ 01603 766670
21 Tombland NR3 1RF
e-mail: info@tatlers.com
web: www.tatlers.com
dir: In city centre in Tombland. Next to Erpingham Gate by Norwich Cathedral

Not far from Norwich's beautiful cathedral, this bustling restaurant is a laid-back, friendly place to dine. A converted Edwardian townhouse, it is split into several eating areas, each decorated in colourful shades and furnished with chunky oak tables. Upstairs, there's a bar with an old leather Chesterfield and an array of newspapers where you can enjoy a light meal from the express menu, while downstairs serves a range of traditional British classics with a modern twist: pan-fried squid with sweetcorn relish and crisp pancetta, for example, or mains like rump of lamb in Parma ham with spring greens, five bean cream sauce and salsa verde. The odd international touch adds excitement and sees confit Barbary duck leg with Szechuan-fried aubergine, wok-seared potatoes and pak choi.

Chef Brendan Ansbro **Owner** Annelli Clarke
Times 12-2/6.30-10, Closed 25-26 Dec, BHs, Closed Sun
Prices Fixed L 2 course £14.95, Starter £6.95-£7.95, Main £14-£18, Dessert £7-£7.50, Service optional, Groups min 10 service 10% **Wines** 33 bottles over £20, 15 bottles under £20, 15 by glass **Notes** Vegetarian available **Seats** 75, Pr/dining room 33 **Children** Portions **Parking** Law courts, Elm Hill, Colegate, St Andrews

Thailand Restaurant

◉ Thai

Deservedly popular authentic Thai

☎ 01603 700444
9 Ring Rd, Thorpe St Andrew NR7 0XJ

This Thai eatery's mouthwatering cooking has made it something of a favourite with the Norwich natives, so book ahead to avoid disappointment. It's located just off the ring road in a huge detached, white-painted house. Inside, the tables are neatly clothed with dark bamboo-style chairs, and walls are decorated with pictures of Thailand. The staff are smartly dressed in silks, shirts and bow ties, and attentive no matter how busy it gets. The kitchen delivers superb traditional cuisine using excellent quality produce. A typical main sees beef Musaman (beef slow braised in coconut cream with fresh chillies, cinnamon and shallots), while green curry is vibrant and flavoursome.

Times Please telephone for details

RINGSTEAD Map 12 TF74

The Gin Trap Inn

◉ Modern British

Charming 17th-century inn turned gastro-pub

☎ 01485 525264
6 High St PE36 5JU
e-mail: thegintrap@hotmail.co.uk
dir: A149 from King's Lynn towards Hunstanton. After 15m turn right at Heacham for Ringstead

This delightful 17th-century coaching inn is now very much a charming, modern-day gastro-pub. Set in a tranquil village on the outskirts of Hunstanton, the rustic bar boasts a huge fireplace with wood-burning stove, exposed brickwork and beams and is simply furnished with plain wooden tables. The tables in the intimate candlelit restaurant are more formally attired in crisp linen. There is also a new conservatory dining area available. The British menu draws on good quality produce, locally sourced where possible. Clean-flavoured dishes are pleasingly presented, as in organic saddleback pork belly with creamed leeks and wholegrain mustard velouté, or hand-made saffron pasta with sautéed wild mushrooms, Madeira herb sauce and fresh parmesan.

Chef Ethan Rodgers **Owner** Steve Knowles & Cindy Cook
Times 12-2/6-9 **Prices** Starter £5-£8.50, Main £8.50-£13, Dessert £5.50-£7, Service optional **Wines** 8 bottles over £20, 25 bottles under £20, 8 by glass **Notes** Sunday L, Vegetarian available **Seats** 60, Pr/dining room 18 **Children** Menu **Parking** 20

SHERINGHAM Map 13 TG14

Marmalade's Bistro

◉ British, International **V**

Relaxed, rustic bistro serving quality, simply-cooked produce

☎ 01263 822830
5 Church St NR26 8QR
e-mail: marmaladesbistro@aol.com
dir: A149 into town centre then left at clock tower

An old, one-time fishing cottage with Tudor beams provides the inspiration for this simple, rustic, husband-and-wife run bistro. Plain pine tables, cream paintwork, wood flooring and chalkboards set a friendly, informal, relaxed tone. The kitchen comes driven by quality, seasonal, locally-sourced produce, including fish on a daily basis, all intelligently simply cooked with clean flavours. Take a fricassée of local seafood with garden herbs, or perhaps roasted local sea bass served on roasted aubergine and plum tomatoes with a basil sauce, or locally shot pheasant with roasted shallots, bacon and a thyme jus. A pecan nut cheesecake with toffee sauce might round things off.

Chef Ben Mutton **Owner** Mr & Mrs B Mutton
Times 12-2/6-9, Closed seasonal closures, Closed Wed, Closed L Mon, Closed D Sun **Prices** Starter £4.50-£5.95, Main £7.75-£15, Dessert £4.95, Service optional **Wines** 1 bottles over £20, 19 bottles under £20, 6 by glass **Notes** Pre-theatre D available, Sunday L, Vegetarian

---

menu, Dress restrictions, Smart casual, Air con **Seats** 30 **Children** Min D 7.30pm, Portions **Parking** On street & town car parks

No. 10 Restaurant

◉ Modern British

Seasonal dishes served in elegant surroundings

☎ 01263 824400
10 Augusta St NR26 8LA
e-mail: eat@no10sheringham.com
dir: Please telephone for directions

Two neatly curved windows form the frontage of this appealing restaurant, with its high ceiling, paintings, gold-framed mirrors and candles twinkling in and around the large fireplace. Smartly-dressed staff, in black and white with long aprons, present unfussy food prepared from wonderfully fresh local ingredients. Excellent home-made breads are followed by dishes such as duck breast with smashed potatoes, spinach and port sauce; and sea bass fillet with chorizo, butterbeans and coriander. Vegetarian alternatives include roasted aubergine and yellow pepper filled with risotto and parmesan and served with tomato compôte.

Chef Mustapha Fassih **Owner** Mustapha & Sonya Fassih
Times 12-2/6.30-9, Closed Sun, Mon-Tue (Winter)
Prices Food prices not confirmed for 2009. Please telephone for details. **Notes** Vegetarian available **Seats** 32 **Children** Portions

Upchers Restaurant

◉ British, European

Country-house dining in delightful parkland surroundings

☎ 01263 824555
Dales Country House Hotel, Lodge Hill NR26 8TJ
e-mail: dales@mackenziehotels.com
dir: On B1157, 1m S of Sheringham. From A148 Cromer to Holt road, take turn at entrance to Sheringham Park. Restaurant 0.5m on left

Near to the North Norfolk coast, this impressive Grade II listed country house is set in its own 4 acres of gardens on the edge of the National Trust grounds of Sheringham Park. Attractive public rooms include the intimate Upchers restaurant with its inglenook fireplace, oak panelling and formal yet relaxed atmosphere. The menu, which includes fresh fish board choices, offers uncomplicated dishes with superb flavours, making good use of quality local produce including game from local estates. Expect grilled scallops in the shell served with salmon, toasted hazelnuts and coriander dressing, followed by perhaps fillet steak served with fricassée of wild mushrooms, shallots, dauphinoise potatoes and juniper berry sauce.

Chef Grant Thorley **Owner** Mr & Mrs Mackenzie
Times 12-2/7-9.30 **Prices** Food prices not confirmed for 2009. Please telephone for details. **Wines** 16 bottles over £20, 28 bottles under £20, 8 by glass **Notes** Vegetarian available, Dress restrictions, No shorts or sportswear **Seats** 70, Pr/dining room 40 **Children** Portions **Parking** 50

SNETTISHAM · Map 12 TF63

Rose & Crown

◉ Modern British 🌱

Bustling local with culinary verve

☎ 01485 541382
Old Church Rd PE31 7LX
e-mail: info@roseandcrownsnettisham.co.uk
dir: From King's Lynn take A149 N towards Hunstanton.
After 10m into Snettisham to village centre, then into Old
Church Rd towards church. Hotel is 100yds on left

This lovely 14th-century village inn is full of character
with its cosy warren of nooks and crannies, old beams,
uneven floors and log fires. Now a smart gastro-pub, the
décor is colourful and contemporary throughout the many
dining areas, which include a garden room opening on to
a walled garden with a children's play area. The menu
offers pub favourites, often with global influences,
prepared to a high standard with good quality, locally
sourced ingredients. Classic dishes include Cumberland
sausages, celeriac mash, confit shallot and red wine jus,
or grilled black back gammon steak, hand-cut chips and
Heacham duck egg. Bar snacks are also available in the
two bars.

Chef Keith McDowell **Owner** Anthony & Jeanette Goodrich
Times 12-2/6.30-9 **Prices** Starter £4.50-£6.50, Main
£7.50-£14.50, Dessert £4.50-£5.50, Service optional,
Groups min 10 service 10% **Wines** 10 bottles over £20,
27 bottles under £20, 10 by glass **Notes** Sunday L,
Vegetarian available **Seats** 60, Pr/dining room 30
Children Portions, Menu **Parking** 70

STOKE HOLY CROSS · Map 13 TG20

The Wildebeest Arms

◉◉ Modern British 📖

Modern take on a traditional pub with enticing menus

☎ 01508 492497
82-86 Norwich Rd, Stoke Holy Cross NR14 8QJ
e-mail: wildebeest@animalinns.co.uk
web: www.thewildebeest.co.uk
dir: From A47, take A140 turn off towards Ipswich. Turn
first left signposted byway to Dunston. Continue to end of
the road and turn left at the T-junct, restaurant on right

The building may look like a traditional pub, but the name
and the choice of fencing (think African Savannah) give
the impression of something a little different. The theme
is not over-played - it still feels like a pub with bare
floorboards, beams, panelling and open fires, but the
open-plan room is filled with African motifs and artefacts
to add a touch of exoticism. The accomplished kitchen
takes a modern approach - underpinned by a classical
French theme - on appealing carte and menu du jour
offerings. Staff are friendly and well informed about the
quality, locally-sourced produce on offer. Start with pan-
fried pigeon breast with braised lentils, crisp Alsace
bacon, celeriac and red wine jus before main-course
herb-crusted local smoked haddock with potato purée,
confit beetroot, buttered courgettes and herb nage.

Chef Daniel Smith **Owner** Henry Watt
Times 12-3.30/6-11.30, Closed 25-26 Dec **Prices** Fixed
L 2 course fr £12.95, Fixed D 3 course fr £18.50, Starter
£4.95-£8.95, Main £12.50-£19.50, Dessert £5.25-£6.75,
Service optional **Wines** 30 bottles over £20, 40 bottles
under £20, 14 by glass **Notes** Sunday L, Vegetarian
available, Air con **Seats** 65 **Children** Portions
Parking 40

SWAFFHAM · Map 13 TF80

Best Western George Hotel

◉ European

Relaxed dining overlooking the busy high street

☎ 01760 721238
Station Rd PE37 7LJ
e-mail: georgehotel@bestwestern.co.uk
web: www.arlingtonhotelgroup.co.uk

This Georgian hotel, standing directly opposite the
Saturday market in this bustling market town, is a
300-year-old institution. The Green Room restaurant is
the setting for local and international food prepared from
quality produce. Here you can expect dark green seating
and carver chairs, crisp napery, clothed tables and
traditional-style crockery. Lovely local asparagus makes
an enjoyable starter served with home-made hollandaise
sauce, followed perhaps by slow-roasted belly pork with
crackling and a full flavoured jus. Conclude with pear
and almond tart with a frangipane filling, accompanied
by home-made custard.

THETFORD · Map 13 TL88

The Elveden

◉ Modern

Relaxed café-style dining on the Elveden Estate

☎ 01842 898068
London Rd, Elveden IP24 3TQ

This smart café on the Elveden Estate near Center Parcs
is set in a large courtyard of converted red-brick farm
buildings that also house a range of shops. There's an
open-plan alfresco barbecue zone and large outdoor
dining area too, all tastefully set out with patio heaters.
Inside it's equally light and airy with vaulted ceiling and
beams, natural-wood floors, cream walls and black
marble-topped tables partnered by modern-style wooden
chairs. Staff offer an informal but professional service in
a relaxed, upbeat atmosphere. Regularly-changing menus
range from restaurant-style meals and daily specials to

lovely home-made sandwiches and cakes, all using local
produce. Expect an Elveden Estate burger (made from
21-day hung beef) with a rum truffle cake finish. (Open
until early evening.)

Seats 60

THORNHAM · Map 12 TF74

Lifeboat Inn

◉ Traditional British

Fish features strongly at this historic alehouse

☎ 01485 512236
Ship Ln PE36 6LT
e-mail: reception@lifeboatinn.co.uk
dir: Take A149 from King's Lynn to Hunstanton follow
coast road to Thornham, take 1st left

This lovely 16th-century building, with superb views
across open fields to Thornham Harbour, has long been
providing a warm welcome to travellers. A smugglers'
alehouse turned gastro-pub, its open fires, exposed
brickwork and ancient oak beams add extra character.
The smart restaurant, with white-clothed, candlelit
tables, offers an interesting daily-changing menu, while
a bar snack menu is available for lighter fare. Fish is a
highlight here, with starters such as pan-fried tiger
prawns with chargrilled Mediterranean vegetables and
yellow pepper sauce. Meat-eaters are also well catered
for, with dishes like breaded lamb cutlets with a clove
and redcurrant jus accompanied by parsley mash.

Chef Michael Sherman **Owner** Maypole Group plc
Times 12-2.30/7-9.30, Closed L all week **Prices** Fixed D 3
course £29.95, Starter £4-£7, Main £9.50-£18.50,
Dessert £4.20-£4.50, Service optional **Wines** 16 bottles
over £20, 19 bottles under £20, 8 by glass **Seats** 70, Pr/
dining room 18 **Children** Portions, Menu **Parking** 100

The Orange Tree

◉◉ British, Pacific Rim

Stylish gastro-pub in a Norfolk coastal village

☎ 01485 512213
High St PE36 6LY
e-mail: email@theorangetreethornham.co.uk
web: www.theorangetreethornham.co.uk
dir: On A149 between Holme-next-the-Sea and
Brancaster Staithe

This smart, popular gastro-pub, situated on the main
coast road in the lovely village of Thornham, offers warm

and friendly hospitality. Enjoy a meal in the bar, with its exposed beams and quarry-tiled floor, or choose between two dining areas with stylish leather chairs, natural wood tables and contemporary décor. Service is relaxed but professional and the kitchen delivers modern cuisine with good, clear flavours, featuring top-notch local produce. Starters may include seared scallops with slow honey-roasted pork belly and pineapple carpaccio, followed by main courses such as crispy fried local sea bass with potted marsh samphire and Norfolk brown shrimps and pepperdew coulis

Chef Philip Milner **Owner** Paul Bishop
Times 12-2.30/6-9.30, Closed D Sun **Prices** Fixed L 2 course £10, Starter £4.50-£8, Main £8.50-£25, Dessert £3.50-£6, Service optional **Wines** 11 bottles over £20, 21 bottles under £20, 13 by glass **Notes** Sunday L, Vegetarian available **Seats** 50, Pr/dining room 20 **Children** Portions, Menu **Parking** 20

THURSFORD
Map 13 TF93

The Old Forge Seafood Restaurant

🏵 Seafood **V**

Charming, relaxed seafood restaurant with rooms

☎ 01328 878345
Seafood Restaurant, Fakenham Rd NR21 0BD
e-mail: sarah.goldspink@btconnect.com
dir: Located on A418

It's all in the name - this is a popular, relaxed seafood restaurant (with rooms) in what was once an old forge with an adjoining coaching station. The front door opens into a small bar area with comfy sofas, while the intimate dining room is a cosy, rustic affair, decked out with pine tables and chairs and featuring original ironwork from the 14th-century forge. As expected of a family-run outfit, service is friendly and relaxed but attentive. Menus change almost daily driven by the availability of fresh fish, although some items make a regular appearance. The approach is intelligently simple, allowing the sea-fresh produce centre stage; take grilled halibut with lemon and parsley butter, or perhaps a medley of lobster, salmon and sea bass in a creamy lobster sauce.

Chef Colin Bowett **Owner** Colin Bowett
Times 12-2/6.30-9.30, Closed Mon **Prices** Fixed L 2 course fr £17.50, Fixed D 3 course fr £21.75, Starter £4.50-£8.50, Main £12-£32, Dessert £3.95-£4.95, Service optional **Wines** 5 bottles over £20, 10 bottles under £20, 5 by glass **Notes** Vegetarian menu **Seats** 28 **Children** Min 5yrs, Portions **Parking** 12

TITCHWELL
Map 13 TF74

Titchwell Manor Hotel

🏵🏵 Modern European 🍷

Innovative cooking in splendid coastal hotel

☎ 01485 210221
PE31 8BB
e-mail: margaret@titchwellmanor.com
dir: On the A149 coast road between Brancaster and Thornham

A former Victorian gentlemen's club on North Norfolk's unspoilt coast, this charming hotel has stunning views across wild salt marshes to the sea and provides a comfortable base for exploring the coastline. The light, modern décor of white walls, wooden floors and leather furniture goes well with the seaside atmosphere. Meals can be taken in the bar or in the attractively presented conservatory dining room with its neatly clothed tables and relaxing atmosphere. Local and seasonal ingredients, notably seafood, are skilfully prepared to produce dishes with interesting combinations and clear flavours. Expect crispy salt cod with salt cod chowder, young carrots and saffron to start, followed by rack of Norfolk lamb with dauphinoise potatoes, Alsace bacon, rosemary jelly, cavolo nero and sautéed lamb's kidney, with pineapple tarte Tatin and basil ice cream to finish.

Chef Eric Snaith **Owner** Margaret and Ian Snaith
Times 12-2.30/6-9.30 **Prices** Food prices not confirmed for 2009. Please telephone for details. **Wines** 27 bottles over £20, 25 bottles under £20, 9 by glass **Notes** Vegetarian available, Dress restrictions, Smart casual, Air con **Seats** 50 **Children** Min 7 yrs D, Portions, Menu **Parking** 25

WELLS-NEXT-THE-SEA
Map 13 TF94

The Crown Hotel

🏵 Modern British, Pacific Rim

Great location for modern cooking

☎ 01328 710209
The Buttlands NR23 1EX
e-mail: reception@thecrownhotelwells.co.uk
dir: 9m from Fakenham. At the top Buttlands Green

Standing at the foot of a tree-lined green, the Buttlands, the Crown is a former coaching inn and oozes 16th-century charm, with ancient beams in the bar and a lovely open fireplace. Close to the beach and bustling quay, it's the place to come for modern classic dishes using an abundance of local produce, served in the sophisticated, contemporary-styled restaurant. Try seared scallops with green bean salad and chive butter sauce, or caramelised red onion tart to start, perhaps followed by brill with tapenade crust on herb cous cous, or beef fillet with horseradish cream. A sheltered sun deck is available for alfresco dining.

The Crown Hotel

Chef Chris Coubrough **Owner** Chris Coubrough
Times Closed L all week **Prices** Food prices not confirmed for 2009. Please telephone for details. **Wines** 25 bottles over £20, 19 bottles under £20, 12 by glass **Seats** 30, Pr/dining room 22 **Children** Portions, Menu

---

WIVETON
Map 13 TG04

Wiveton Bell

🏵 Modern 🍷

Food-driven pub serving simply prepared, local produce in relaxed atmosphere

☎ 01263 740101
Blakeney Rd NR25 7TL
e-mail: bernimorritt@btconnect.com
dir: Please telephone for directions

Situated on the village green, this traditional 18th-century inn turned gastro-pub stays true to its roots with a large bar area for locals. Heavily beamed it may be, with an open inglenook fire, but refurbishment has brought cream walls, contemporary art and a mix of natural-wood tables and seating very much in the modern food-pub idiom. Friendly staff don black aprons, while alfresco dining is a summer bonus. The crowd-pleasing, seasonal menus are driven by quality local produce (think Morston mussels, Blakeney crabs or Holkham game) and a simply prepared, clear-flavoured approach. Take traditional classics like fisherman's pie and bangers and mash or slow-roasted local Briston pork belly with sage pomme purée and creamy apple and cider sauce.

Chef Nick Anderson **Owner** Berni Morritt & Sandy Butcher
Times 12-2.45/6-9, Closed D Sun (Oct-May)
Prices Starter £4.95-£6.95, Main £8.95-£16.95, Dessert £4.95-£6.95, Service optional **Wines** 2 bottles over £20, 28 bottles under £20, 21 by glass **Notes** Sunday L, Vegetarian available **Seats** 60 **Children** Portions, Menu **Parking** 5, village green 50yds away

| **WYMONDHAM** | **Map 13 TG10** |

Number Twenty Four Restaurant

◉◉ Modern British

Sound cooking in listed townhouse

☎ 01953 607750
24 Middleton St NR18 0AD
dir: Town centre opposite war memorial

This family-run restaurant is just the place for a relaxed evening with a bottle of wine. There's nothing pretentious or stuffy about the operation, instead it's a low-key affair with a friendly ambience, housed in a pretty row of listed cottages. The décor teams period features with pale cream walls, and tables are neatly clothed and well-spaced for conversation. Changing daily to reflect quality market choice, expect a compact menu of British dishes with the occasional international touch: seared fillet of beef with bubble-and-squeak, Portobello wild mushroom and whisky gravy for example, or grilled breast of duck with parsnip mash, leeks and pancetta wine gravy. Round things off with an old favourite like sticky toffee pudding or something more involved: dark chocolate parfait perhaps, served with white chocolate sauce and pistachio ice cream.

Chef Jonathan Griffin **Owner** Jonathan Griffin **Times** 12-2/7-9, Closed 26 Dec, 1 Jan, Closed Mon, Closed L Tue, Closed D Sun **Prices** Fixed L 2 course £14.50, Fixed D 3 course £24.95 **Wines** 10 bottles over £20, 26 bottles under £20, 6 by glass **Notes** Sunday L, Vegetarian available, Dress restrictions, Smart casual, No shorts **Seats** 60, Pr/dining room 55 **Children** Portions **Parking** On street opposite. In town centre car park

NORTHAMPTONSHIRE

| **COLLYWESTON** | **Map 11 SK90** |

The Collyweston Slater

◉ Modern British 🖥

Smart, modern brasserie within a handsome village inn

☎ 01780 444288
87 Main Rd PE9 3PQ
e-mail: info@thecollywestonslater.co.uk
dir: 4m S of Stamford, A43, 2m off A1

With splendid views over the Wetland Valley and Fineshade Woods, this traditional village inn has undergone a stylish but sensitive makeover. Named after the slate industry in the village, the original oak beams and slate flooring combine beautifully with the modern décor and furnishings. The brasserie-style restaurant has wooden tables, leather seating and contemporary lighting. Serving modern British fare with a focus on seasonal, local produce, the emphasis is on quality and flavour. Typical well-presented dishes on the monthly-changing menu might include chicken, tarragon and white grape terrine with a creamy celeriac remoulade to start, Gressingham duck breast with spiced red cabbage and parsnip purée to follow and vanilla pannacotta with exotic fruit salad for dessert.

Chef Simon Turner **Owner** Richard & Nikki Graham **Times** 12-2/6-9, Closed 25 Dec, 2 Jan, Closed D Sun **Prices** Fixed L 2 course fr £12, Starter £4.50-£6.95, Main £9-£17, Dessert £5.50, Service optional **Wines** 10 bottles over £20, 10 bottles under £20, 7 by glass **Notes** Sunday L, Dress restrictions, No shorts or baseball caps **Seats** 34, Pr/dining room 10 **Children** Portions, Menu **Parking** 32

| **DAVENTRY** | **Map 11 SP56** |

Equilibrium

◉◉◉ – *see below*

Equilibrium

| **DAVENTRY** | **Map 11 SP56** |

Modern British

High gastronomic ambition in stunning grand Tudor manor

☎ 01327 892000
Fawsley Hall, Fawsley NN11 3BA
e-mail: reservations@fawsleyhall.com
dir: From M40 junct 11 take A361 (Daventry), follow for 12m. Turn right towards Fawsley Hall

Fawsley Hall looks more like a stately home than a mere country-house hotel, boasting a garden designed by Capability Brown and receiving Queen Elizabeth I as a visitor way back in 1575. The 2000 acres of rolling countryside are a picturesque setting and the house has a splendid interior with a grand hall and smart furnishings. The Knightley Restaurant is one dining option, but changes are planned, while the new Equilibrium Restaurant is a bold venture delivering a highly modern and creative menu. A Taste of Equilibrium is available for the whole table and includes wines, while the carte offers four choices at each course over three courses. Technical wizardry and bold innovation are evident in a pigeon starter consisting of three dishes - the main plate containing a breast of the bird rolled in bacon and stuffed with foie gras alongside a small bowl of consommé, with a perfect square of confit leg wrapped in gold leaf and placed in the bowl at table by the waiter and, on the third plate, a mini-parfait and mini-brioche. This is a dramatic, involved and successful start to a meal. Innovation continues at main course stage with poached and roasted lamb turning up with sweetbreads, kidney and parsley jus. Desserts play with our perceptions with an artichoke crème alongside delightfully silky truffle ice cream and olive oil gel. The canapés, breads and pre-desserts are equally as creative, and the drama starts when the pre-starter of langoustine with frozen lime is smoked before your eyes at the table. Service is refined and formal.

Chef Nigel Godwin **Times** 7-9.30, Closed Sun-Mon **Prices** Fixed D £59, Taste of Equilibrium £79

The Falcon Inn

◉ British, European

Vibrant cooking in rural Northamptonshire

☎ 01832 226254
PE8 5HZ
e-mail: info@thefalcon-inn.co.uk
dir: From A605 at Warmington follow signs to
Fotheringhay. Situated centre of village

Situated in the mellow stone-built village where Mary,
Queen of Scots ended her days, the pub has immense
character and a lovely garden with the views of the
church especially enchanting from the conservatory
restaurant at night. The Falcon successfully combines
the roles of village local and smart, comfortable
restaurant. British classics are served in the bar, and the
restaurant menu is Anglo-Italian, starting perhaps with
beef carpaccio with roast beetroot and horseradish crème
fraîche before main-course roast fillet of salmon with
cannellini beans and spinach. Finish with vanilla
pannacotta with preserved cherries or excellent local
cheeses.

Chef Danny Marshall & Chris Kipping **Owner** Harry Facer
& Jim Jeffries **Times** 12-2.15/6.15-9.15, Closed 2 Jan
Prices Starter £5.50-£6.95, Main £10-£17.50, Dessert
£5-£7, Service optional, Groups min 10 service 10%
Wines 21 bottles over £20, 28 bottles under £20, 14 by
glass **Notes** Sunday L, Vegetarian available **Seats** 45, Pr/
dining room 30 **Children** Portions, Menu **Parking** 50

The New French Partridge

◉◉ Modern British, French

Confident cooking in stylish country-house restaurant

☎ 01604 870033
Newport Pagnell Rd NN7 2AP
e-mail: info@newfrenchpartridge.co.uk
dir: On B526 between Milton Keynes and Northampton, in
village of Horton

Situated in private grounds in the lovely rural village of
Horton, this former coaching inn was extended into a
traditional country manor in 1622. The current owners have
stylishly restored it to its original splendour, including ten
individually designed bedrooms and a bar in the vaulted
cellar. A well-balanced menu of modern French and British
dishes perfectly suits the surroundings and makes good
use of high quality ingredients. You could start with belly
pork braised in orange and vanilla, served on a bed of
segmented oranges with apple purée and ale foam,
followed by roast fillet of Scottish beef served with beef
hash, squash purée and a foie gras ballotine. To finish,
maybe a vanilla pannacotta.

Times 11.30-2.30/6.30-10.30, Closed L Sat, Closed D Sun

Kettering Park Hotel

◉ Modern British

Impressive cuisine in a smart hotel restaurant

☎ 01536 416666
Kettering Parkway NN15 6XT
e-mail: kpark.reservations@shirehotels.com
dir: Off A14 junct 9

This modern hotel combines old world charm with up-to-
date comfort. In the split-level Langberry's restaurant
you'll find traditional décor with subtle lighting, a

---

welcoming fire in winter and formal table service from
well-trained staff; there's an outdoor terrace for alfresco
eating in warmer months. The kitchen works hard to source
seasonal produce from local suppliers for a cooking style
that is light, direct and with vibrant flavours handled with
restraint and harmony. Favourite combinations are given a
modern twist; these might include River Exe mussel pot
with shallots, cream and garlic, best-end Stamford lamb
with a shallot and rosemary tart and a splendid selection
of classic desserts.

Chef Stephen Robinson **Owner** Shire Hotels
Times 12-2/7-9.30, Closed Xmas & New Year (ex
residents), Closed L Sat **Prices** Starter £5.95-£8.95, Main
£13.50-£21.50, Dessert £6.50-£11.50, Service optional
Wines 14 bottles over £20, 14 bottles under £20, 15 by
glass **Notes** Sunday L, Civ Wed 100 **Seats** 90, Pr/dining
room 40 **Children** Portions, Menu **Parking** 200

Rushton Hall Hotel

◉◉ Modern British

**Highly accomplished cooking in magnificent
surroundings**

☎ 01536 713001
NN14 1RR
e-mail: enquiries@rushtonhall.com
web: www.rushtonhall.com
dir: A14 junct 7. A43 to Corby, A6003 to Rushton, turn off
after bridge

The epitome of an elegant country-house hotel, the
imposing Rushton - dating back to 1438 - is set in acres
of parkland. The interior is kitted out in the grand style,
from its large, heavy-timbered entrance doors to huge
stone and timber fireplaces, ornate plasterwork and
stained glass. The impressive oak, linenfold panelled
dining room continues the theme, its modern British
approach - underpinned by classical influences -
delivering highly accomplished cuisine with fine depth of
flavour, utilising high-quality well-sourced produce. Take
duck and pistachio sausage with Puy lentils and parsnip
purée, followed by poached halibut with potato and herb
gnocchi and butternut squash, and dark chocolate
mousse with lime jelly.

Chef Adrian Coulthard **Owner** Tom & Valerie Hazelton
Times 12-2/7-9 **Prices** Fixed L 2 course £15.95, Starter
£8.50-£14, Main £19-£27, Dessert £8.95-£10.95, Service
optional **Wines** 76 bottles over £20, 17 bottles under £20,
11 by glass **Notes** Sunday L, Vegetarian available, Dress
restrictions, No jeans or trainers, Civ Wed 160 **Seats** 46,
Pr/dining room 60 **Children** Min 10yrs, Portions, Menu
Parking 140

ROADE
Map 11 SP75

Roade House Restaurant

◉ Modern French

Popular village restaurant serving simple lunches and more serious evening fare

☎ 01604 863372
16 High St NN7 2NW
e-mail: info@roadehousehotel.co.uk
dir: M1 junct 15 (A508 Milton Keynes) to Roade, left at mini rdbt, 500yds on left

Set in a rural Northamptonshire village, this 18th-century, stone-built pub has expanded to encompass a large, comfortable lounge bar and restaurant. Seasonally based menus offer produce sourced from all over the country, including Cornish lamb, Scottish beef and local game. With clear flavours throughout, a starter of carpaccio of tuna with guacamole, melon and citrus fruits could be followed by baked fillet of pork with Irish black pudding, caramelised apple and wild mushroom sauce, with shortcake and summer berries to finish. There are good value set menus at lunch and dinner, and special dining evenings are held throughout the year.

Chef Chris Kewley **Owner** Mr & Mrs C M Kewley **Times** 12-2/7-9.30, Closed 1 wk Xmas, Closed L Sat, Closed D Sun **Prices** Fixed L 2 course fr £20, Fixed D 3 course fr £31, Service optional **Wines** 40 bottles over £20, 30 bottles under £20, 4 by glass **Notes** Sunday L, Vegetarian available, Dress restrictions, No shorts, Air con **Seats** 50 **Children** Portions **Parking** 20

TOWCESTER
Map 11 SP64

Vine House Hotel & Restaurant

◉◉ Modern British

Fresh local ingredients in a home-from-home atmosphere

☎ 01327 811267
100 High St, Paulerspury NN12 7NA
e-mail: info@vinehousehotel.com
dir: 2m S of Towcester, just off A5

Set in a tranquil Northamptonshire village, this charming 300-year-old property - now a homely restaurant with rooms - was lovingly created by converting two limestone cottages. Run by husband-and-wife team Marcus and Julie Springett, the emphasis is on relaxed, informal dining in a friendly atmosphere. Original features have been preserved throughout, enhanced by tasteful décor, modern art and polished wood floors. Outside there's a carefully tended cottage garden and a delightfully romantic table in the folly for an intimate lunch or dinner for two. The food is rustic and full bodied, offered from a daily-changing menu using as much local and organic produce as possible. Prime examples are traditional potted Dexter salt beef with toasted sour dough, or locally-cured smoked bacon sausage and black pudding terrine topped with a warm poached egg and home-made ketchup.

Chef Marcus Springett **Owner** Mr M & Mrs J Springett **Times** 12-2/6-10, Closed Sun, Closed L Mon **Prices** Fixed D 2 course £26.95-£29.95, Service added 12.5% **Wines** 47 bottles over £20, 26 bottles under £20, 2 by glass **Seats** 26, Pr/dining room 10 **Parking** 20

WHITTLEBURY
Map 11 SP64

Murray's

◉◉ British, European

Fine-dining restaurant dedicated to Formula 1 commentator Murray Walker

☎ 01327 857857 & 0845 400 0001
Whittlebury Hall Hotel and Spa NN12 8QH
e-mail: sales@whittleburyhall.co.uk
dir: A43/A413 to Whittlebury, through village, hotel at far end on right

Just around the corner from Silverstone, Murray's Restaurant is named after Murray Walker and is home to a series of Formula 1 anecdotes from his commentary years, as well as photos from Formula 1 drivers and teams. It provides an intimate, sophisticated dining venue with formal service, offering modern British cooking with classical and international influences. Try a starter like smoked ham hock and white bean soup, then follow with roast rump of lamb with creamed Savoy cabbage, honey-roasted vegetables and lamb jus, or sea bass with scallops, shellfish and citrus risotto. Desserts are 'The Finale' on the menu and may include warm pear tarte Tatin with a red sorbet and cinnamon foam.

Chef Craig Rose **Owner** Macepark (Whittlebury) Ltd **Times** Closed 24-26, 31 Dec, 1-7 Jan, Closed Sun, Mon, Closed L all wk **Notes** Fixed D 5 courses £65, Vegetarian available, Dress restrictions, Smart casual, No jeans, trainers or shorts **Seats** 32, Pr/dining room 400 **Children** Min 12 yrs, Portions, Menu **Parking** 300

NORTHUMBERLAND

CORNHILL-ON-TWEED
Map 21 NT83

Tillmouth Park Country House Hotel

◉◉ British ⟨⟩

Modern cuisine in Victorian elegance

☎ 01890 882255
TD12 4UU
e-mail: reception@tillmouthpark.force9.co.uk
dir: A698, 3m E from Cornhill-on-Tweed

Set on the banks of the River Till in secluded woodland, this imposing Victorian manor recalls a leisurely country-house age. Think stone and marble fireplaces, stained glass, oil paintings, chandeliers, antiques and objets d'art, all backed by relaxed but attentive service. The intimate, wood-panelled Library Dining Room with its crisp white linen overlooks the garden, while aperitifs are served in the stunning galleried lounge or elegant drawing room. And the food? Less traditional than you'd expect, given the surroundings, and distinguished by plenty of flair and a commitment to local suppliers. Celery

and stilton soup is a typical starter, served with a chicken and blue cheese dumpling, while mains might include corn-fed chicken breast with Savoy cabbage, bacon Parmentier potatoes and a mushroom cream sauce.

Chef Tony McKay **Owner** Tillmouth Park Partnership **Times** 12-2/7-8.45, Closed 26-28 Dec, Jan-Mar, Closed L Mon-Sat **Prices** Fixed L 2 £15.50, Fixed D 4 course £35, Service optional **Wines** 50 bottles over £20, 8 bottles under £20, 8 by glass **Notes** Sunday L, Dress restrictions, Smart casual, No jeans, Civ Wed 60 **Seats** 40, Pr/dining room 20 **Children** Portions **Parking** 50

HEXHAM
Map 21 NY96

De Vere Slaley Hall

◉ British

Fine dining and informal eating choices within a stunning parkland setting

☎ 01434 673350
Slaley NE47 0BX
e-mail: slaley.hall@devere-hotels.com
dir: A1 from S to A68. Follow signs for Slaley Hall. From N A69 to Corbridge then take A68 S and follow signs to Slaley Hall

Set in 1000 acres of parkland with two renowned golf courses, spa facilities and stunning views over the Tyne Valley, this much extended old hall is popular with both leisure and corporate guests. Expect several comfortable lounges, informal eating in a former golf club, The Claret Jug and the fine-dining Duke's Grill restaurant, which is furnished with striking colour schemes, deep purple chairs, mirrors and chandeliers. The daily set menu, Grill menu and brasserie-style carte all feature local seasonal produce and offer well-executed dishes. Take ham hock terrine with plum chutney, Northumbrian lamb cutlets with Madeira jus, or tournedos of rabbit with caramelised onions and roasted salsify, and pear and rosemary tarte Tatin.

Times 1-2.30/7-9.30, Closed L Mon-Sat

Langley Castle Hotel

◉ Modern, European

Medieval castle dining laced with atmosphere

☎ 01434 688 888
Langley on Tyne NE47 5LU
e-mail: manager@langleycastle.com
web: www.langleycastle.com
dir: From A69 take A686 S, restaurant 2m on right

A genuine 14th-century castle plays host to this modern-day hotel and restaurant. Stained-glass windows and an open fire dominate the magnificent drawing room with an adjacent oak-panelled cocktail bar, while the original garderobe staircase leads to the Josephine Restaurant. Here, window alcoves are set into seven-feet thick walls, while rich drapes, tapestries, high-backed leather chairs and formally laid tables provide the comforts. Service is formal too, but with a friendly edge, while the skilful kitchen's modern approach comes with a strong regional accent, driven by quality local seasonal produce, with fish and game a feature. Roasted saddle of rabbit with a wild mushroom and chestnut farce, butternut squash chips and roasting juices is a fine example of the fare.

Times 12-2.30/7-9

LONGHORSLEY Map 21 NZ19

Dobson Restaurant

◎◎ Modern International

Grade II listed country property set amid extensive parkland

☎ 01670 500000
Macdonald Linden Hall, Golf & Country Club NE65 8XF
e-mail: general.lindenhall@macdonald-hotels.co.uk
dir: 7m NW of Morpeth on A697 off A1

This Georgian mansion is set in 450 acres of park and woodland surrounded by beautiful countryside. Facilities include a golf course, a recently refurbished country pub and conference suites. The hotel's Dobson Restaurant, which offers superb views, observes the civilised formalities in terms of dress code. The menu is priced for two or three courses, and the same format applies for lunch and dinner but with a more extensive choice in the evening. Recommended dishes include carefully-cooked scallops set on an aubergine purée with a crisp ratatouille dice, or a lovely local beef fillet, accurately cooked and served with fondant potato, caramelised onions and carrots. For dessert, take a hot chocolate fondant with chocolate sauce and orange curd ice cream, or 'singin hinnies' with a rhubarb compôte and cardamom ice cream.

Times 12-2.30/6.30-9.30, Closed L Mon-Sat

MATFEN Map 21 NZ07

Matfen Hall

◎◎ Modern International

Satisfying dining in elegant country-house surroundings

☎ 01661 886500 & 855708
NE20 0RH
e-mail: info@matfenhall.com
dir: A69 signed Hexham, leave at Heddon on the Wall. Then B6318, through Rudchester & Harlow Hill. Follow signs on right for Matfen

An imposing Regency mansion set in 250 acres of classic parkland, Matfen Hall is still owned by the Blackett family who built it in the 1830s. These days it has its own championship golf course as well as a high-tech spa and leisure facilities. The spacious, elegant book-lined Library and adjoining Print Room Restaurant ooze atmosphere, especially by candlelight, with floor-length tablecloths, fine glassware and lovely views. Imaginative modern dishes with an international flavour are prepared from fresh local produce. Organically reared lamb from the Matfen Home Farm and local game and fish feature strongly. Not to be missed dishes are twice-baked wild

mushroom and thyme soufflé, roast rump of Matfen lamb with rosemary dauphinoise, and mini cinnamon doughnuts.

Matfen Hall

Chef Phil Hall **Owner** Sir Hugh & Lady Blackett **Times** 12.15-2.30/7-10, Closed L Mon-Sat **Prices** Starter £6.25-£7.25, Main £14.95-£23.95, Dessert £5.95-£6.95, Service optional **Wines** 56 bottles over £20, 37 bottles under £20, 6 by glass **Notes** Vegetarian available, Dress restrictions, Smart casual, Civ Wed 160 **Seats** 90, Pr/dining room 120 **Children** Portions **Parking** 120

PONTELAND Map 21 NZ17

Café Lowrey

◎ British, French

Relaxed, bistro-style dining

☎ 01661 820357
35 The Broadway, Darras Hall NE20 9PW
web: www.cafelowrey.co.uk
dir: From A696, follow signs for Darras Hall. Left at mini rdbt, restaurant in 200yds

This bistro-style restaurant is situated in a small shopping precinct in a residential area of Ponteland, not far from Newcastle airport. The simple interior includes quarry-tiled floors, clothed tables and Victorian-style wooden chairs, and the atmosphere is warm, relaxed and inviting. It offers an extensive menu of modern British and French-style dishes prepared from the finest, fresh local produce. Favourite dishes of the house include cheddar cheese and spinach soufflé to start; followed by simply grilled halibut with mushy peas, chips and tartare sauce. Finish with a traditional plum crumble.

Chef Ian Lowrey **Owner** Ian Lowrey **Times** 12-2/5.30-10, Closed BHs, Closed Mon, Closed L Tue-Fri, Closed D Sun **Prices** Fixed L 2 course £13.50, Fixed D 3 course fr £15.50, Starter £4.50-£10.50, Main £10.50-£20.50, Dessert £4.50-£7, Service optional, Groups min 10 service 10% **Wines** 12 bottles over £20, 18 bottles under £20, 6 by glass **Notes** Sunday L, Vegetarian available, Dress restrictions, Smart casual, Air con **Seats** 68 **Children** Portions **Parking** 15

NOTTINGHAMSHIRE

GUNTHORPE Map 11 SK64

Tom Browns Brasserie

◎ Modern International 🍸

Popular brasserie with splendid river views

☎ 0115 966 3642
The Old School House, Trentside NG14 7FB
e-mail: info@tombrowns.co.uk
dir: A6097, Gunthorpe Bridge

Housed in a converted Victorian schoolhouse on the banks of the River Trent, this restaurant has several dining areas and popular outside decking for warmer weather. Dark chocolate high-backed leather chairs and simply dressed linen-clad tables with flickering candles and lively music set a vibrant atmosphere. The contemporary feel of the décor extends to the modern brasserie-style menu, which takes in starters like local game and wild mushroom terrine with apricot and peppercorn chutney and main courses such as chicken breast stuffed with pistachio and pork, wrapped in pancetta with potato rösti, fine beans and a red wine and thyme jus.

Chef Chris Hooton **Owner** Adam & Robin Perkins **Times** 12-2.30/6-9.30, Closed D 25-26 Dec **Prices** Fixed L 2 course £13.95, Fixed D 3 course £15.95, Starter £4.95-£8.95, Main £9.95-£19.95, Dessert £5.75-£7.50, Service optional **Wines** 30 bottles over £20, 30 bottles under £20, 18 by glass **Notes** Sunday L, Dress restrictions, Smart casual, Air con **Seats** 100, Pr/dining room 20 **Children** Portions **Parking** 9

Langar Hall

◎◎◎ Modern, Traditional British 💻 ⌑

Country-house hotel with delightful views

☎ 01949 860559
NG13 9HG
e-mail: imogen@langarhall.co.uk
web: www.langarhall.com
dir: Signed off A46 & A52 in Langar village centre (behind church)

This delightful country-house hotel enjoys a secluded rural location at the end of a long avenue of lime trees next to a 12th-century church - with views of gardens, parkland and ancient fishponds. The elegant lounges, library and dining room are furnished with antiques and works of art, retaining the feel of a country residence, complemented by warm and welcoming service. The garden conservatory offers a lighter menu, while the gracious, pillared dining room is the perfect setting for fine dining - complete with smartly appointed tables, fresh flowers and candlelight. Here you can expect to enjoy seasonal British dishes using the best of local produce. Take a starter of seared scallops with squid-ink risotto and saffron and chive sauce, and follow with chargrilled fillet of beef with potato cake and truffle and thyme butter.

Chef Gary Booth **Owner** Imogen Skirving **Times** 12-2/7-10 **Prices** Fixed L 2 course fr £14.50, Fixed D 3 course £25, Starter £5-£12, Main £12.50-£20, Dessert £5-£7.50, Service added but optional 10% **Wines** 20 bottles over £20, 30 bottles under £20, 4 by glass **Notes** Sunday L, Vegetarian available, Civ Wed 50 **Seats** 30, Pr/dining room 20 **Children** Portions **Parking** 40

Cutlers at The Grange

◎ Modern, British

Good, honest food in an elegant Victorian setting

☎ 01636 703399
The Grange Hotel, 73 London Rd NG24 1RZ
e-mail: info@grangenewark.co.uk
dir: From A1 follow signs for Balderton, the hotel is opposite the Polish War Graves

As the name suggests, Cutlers Restaurant at The Grange Hotel follows a theme, with prints and display cabinets of antique cutlery adorning the walls. The

high-ceilinged Victorian dining room with its gold, blue and red furnishings provides an elegant setting, and service is friendly. The emphasis is on good, honest, unpretentious food, focusing on seasonal and natural flavours, sympathetically handled and carefully cooked. Simple dishes with great flavours abound, such as slow-roasted belly pork and dauphinoise potatoes, which is complemented by a deliciously tart Bramley apple sauce. Desserts, made using locally-grown fruit, arrive with home-made ice cream or sorbet, such as Bramley apple crumble tartlet with blackberry ice cream.

Chef Sharon Haney **Owner** Tom & Sandra Carr **Times** 12-2/6.30-9.30, Closed 25 Dec-5 Jan, Closed L Mon-Sat **Prices** Fixed L 2 course fr £13.50, Starter £4.75-£8.50, Main £10.95-£18.50, Dessert £4.75-£6.50, Service optional **Wines** 26 bottles over £20, 19 bottles under £20, 6 by glass **Notes** Sunday L, Vegetarian available **Seats** 40 **Children** Portions **Parking** 17

Hart's Restaurant

◎◎ Modern British V

Skilfully prepared dishes in a modern, urban, brasserie setting

☎ 0115 988 1900
Standard Hill, Park Row NG1 6FN
e-mail: ask@hartsnottingham.co.uk
web: www.hartsnottingham.co.uk
dir: M1 junct 24, follow A453 to city centre. Follow signs to the castle. Once on Maid Marion Way turn left at the Gala Casino, continue to top of the hill and turn left through black gates

Hart's hotel is located in a beautiful modern building close to Nottingham Castle, in what used to be part of the emergency section of the General Hospital. The lively, modern brasserie restaurant is situated just 30 metres away and features booths and banquettes, warm colours and a lighting scheme that highlights the contemporary art. Expect a comfortable, intimate and sophisticated atmosphere. Skilfully prepared modern British dishes make extensive use of local produce whenever possible. Subtle presentation only augments the pleasure; take pan-fried lambs' sweetbreads with pea purée and crispy shallots, or perhaps pan-fried wild sea bass with poached clams and mussels, spinach and saffron potatoes. Finish with a banana parfait with lime froth.

Hart's Restaurant

Chef Mark Osborne **Owner** Tim Hart **Times** 12-1.45/6-10.30, Closed 26 Dec & 1 Jan, Closed L 31 Dec, Closed D 25 Dec **Wines** 57 bottles over £20, 23 bottles under £20, 6 by glass **Notes** Pre-theatre 3 courses £18, Sunday L, Vegetarian menu, Civ Wed 100 **Seats** 80, Pr/dining room 100 **Children** Portions **Parking** 15

The Lobster Pot

◎ Seafood

A gem of a seafood restaurant

☎ 0115 947 0707
199 Mansfield Rd NG1 3FS
dir: From Nottingham city centre N on A60 for 0.5m, restaurant on left at the lights where Huntingdon St joins Mansfield Rd

Although unassuming from the outside, you walk by this friendly, relaxed seafood restaurant at your peril! The simple décor features fish-themed objets d'art and Middle Eastern carvings, alongside chunky wooden tables. A range of different smoked salmons is available, and there's also a daily specials board. Saucing is subtle and takes care not to dominate the main ingredient. Starters include the likes of calamari rings deep-fried in batter with a spicy dip, while for mains you could expect smoked fish and mushroom pasta with white wine and cream sauce. Early booking is advised.

Chef Mr & Mrs Pongsawang **Owner** Mr & Mrs Pongsawang **Times** 12-2/6-10.30, Closed BHs, Closed Mon, Closed L Sun **Prices** Food prices not confirmed for 2009. Please telephone for details. **Wines** 2 bottles over £20, 30 bottles under £20, 3 by glass **Notes** Air con **Seats** 40 **Children** Portions

Restaurant Sat Bains with Rooms

Modern International 🖥️ 🍷NOTABLE WINE LIST 👐

Thrilling food by top chef in stylish restaurant with rooms

☎ 0115 986 6566
Lenton Ln, Trentside NG7 2SA
e-mail: info@restaurantsatbains.net
web: www.restaurantsatbains.com
dir: From M1 junct 24 take A453 for approx 8 m. Through Clifton, road divides into 3 - take middle lane signed 'Lenton Lane Industrial Estate', then 1st left and left again - brown signpost Restaurant Sat Bains

The setting down a quiet lane means it can be a little difficult to find, but even if you have to cross a stormy ocean or climb a windswept mountain, press on, for it is well worth the effort in the end. A car will suffice, of course, but check the directions first or turn on your sat-nav. The building, a converted farmhouse, sits on the banks of the Trent and has had a smart, contemporary make-over, with Sat and Amanda Bains leaving no stone unturned to create a stylish and unpretentious restaurant with rooms. There is a bar area with comfortable leather chairs and solid oak tables and two inter-connecting dining rooms, one a conservatory with exposed brickwork and a view of the garden, the other a smaller and more intimate space. Frosted glass panels reveal shadows

from the chef's table. Sat Bains is a chef with a creative mind, a sure touch, refined technical ability, and attention to detail as his default setting. The sourcing of produce is second to none and the menus are designed to take the diner on a journey of taste, texture and temperature. This big claim is firmly realised, whether opting for the Tasting Menu or choosing dishes from the carte - this is a chef who delivers the wow factor and then some. An amuse-bouche of leek and potato soup with clams is bursting with flavour, before a first course, first class wood pigeon in a dish with pearl barley, caramelised cauliflower, rhubarb purée and lemon confit that delivers phenomenal textural contrasts and flavours, followed by main-course Cornish brill with morels, bacon, salsify, crispy onion, wild garlic and fennel. A pre-dessert passionfruit with yogurt and liquorice is a tantalisingly delicious combination, while presentation dazzles in a dessert of chocolate, banana, coffee and grapefruit. The smartly attired waiting staff are knowledgeable about the menu and polite and professional all round.

Chef Sat Bains **Owner** Sat Bains, Amanda Bains **Times** Closed 2 wks Jan & 2 wks Aug, Closed Sun, Mon, Closed L all week **Wines** 120 bottles over £20, 6 bottles under £20, 30 by glass **Notes** Suprise menu 12 courses £89, Chef's table £95, Air con **Seats** 34, Pr/dining room 14 **Parking** 22

NOTTINGHAM *Continued*

Merchants Restaurant & Bar

⊛⊛ Modern French 💻

Classic French brasserie with chic interior

☎ 0115 958 9898 & 952 3211
Lace Market Hotel, 31 High Pavement NG1 1HE
e-mail: dine@merchantsnottingham.co.uk
dir: Follow city centre signs for Galleries of Justice, entrance is opposite

Situated in the vibrant Lace Market area of Nottingham, this former Georgian lace factory has found a new lease of life as a classic brasserie restaurant. The stylish yet unstuffy décor was designed by the world-renowned David Collins, interior architect to many of Marco Pierre White's restaurants, and includes a Canadian pressed tin ceiling and an eye-catching frieze of Nottingham lace panels. The award-winning waiting staff are relaxed but attentive, serving up seasonal, wholesome French cooking with a modern edge. Try a starter of seared St Mawes diver scallops with fennel purée, followed perhaps by a main course of cannon of lamb with red onion and pinto bean tart, accompanied by one of the wines from the superb list.

Times 12-2.30/7-10.30, Closed 26 Dec, 1 Jan, Closed Sun-Mon, Closed L Sat & Mon

Restaurant Sat Bains with Rooms

⊛⊛⊛⊛ – *see page 357*

World Service

⊛⊛ Modern British

International décor and fine food in a Georgian property

☎ 0115 847 5587
Newdigate House, Castle Gate NG1 6AF
e-mail: enquiries@worldservicerestaurant.com
dir: 200mtrs from city centre, 50mtrs from Nottingham Castle

Set in the historic and elegant Newdigate House, this fine dining restaurant and lounge bar is a Nottingham favourite. A chic, buzzy eatery, World Service is designed to look like the home of an eccentric traveller, and teams country-house comfort with exotic artefacts to create a relaxed, contemporary, designer interior. Entry is via an oriental garden to a lounge where gilt armchairs, a roaring fire and coconut shell tables await, plus a decadent list of cocktails. Dining tables are darkwood, seating comes in brown leather and walls are lined with low-level mirrors. The food fits the bill with a fusion theme and takes an equally modern approach punctuated by precision and finesse; take honey and mustard roast ham hock and chicken liver parfait terrine with hazelnut, green bean and quail egg salad, followed by local fillet of beef with blackcurrant onion, rosti potato, portabello mushroom and red wine sauce. Great wine list available.

Chef Preston Walker **Owner** Daniel Lindsay, Phillip Morgan, Ashley Walter, Chris Elson **Times** 12-2.15/7-10, Closed 1-7 Jan **Prices** Fixed L 2 course £12, Starter £5-£12.50, Main £12.50-£21, Dessert £5.50-£8, Service added but optional 10% **Wines** 90 bottles over £20, 15 bottles under £20, 10 by glass **Notes** Sunday L, Vegetarian available **Seats** 80, Pr/dining room 34 **Children** Min 12 yrs D, Portions, Menu **Parking** NCP

OXFORDSHIRE

ARDINGTON Map 5 SU48

The Boar's Head

⊛⊛ British, European 🍴

Enjoyable, leisurely dining in peaceful village surroundings

☎ 01235 833254
Church St OX12 8QA
e-mail: info@boarsheadardington.co.uk
dir: 2 m E of Wantage on A417, next to village church

Standing alongside the church in the delightful Downland village of Ardington, The Boar's Head has been serving customers for over 150 years. This attractive, half-timbered pub and restaurant provides friendly service and also offers comfortable accommodation with three well-appointed bedrooms. The cosy, rustic-style restaurant supplies good British cooking with French and Spanish overtones, using quality, seasonal and local produce. Dishes are cooked with care and simplicity and may include starters such as terrine of pigeon and sun blushed tomato with grapes in Muscat, or mackerel and black pudding salad with walnut vinaigrette, and main courses like fillets of halibut with oxtail, squid chips and Shiraz sauce, or roast rack of English lamb with dauphinoise and garlic confit. To finish, perhaps try Grand Marnier soufflé with iced chocolate cream.

Chef Bruce Buchan **Owner** Boar's Head (Ardington) Ltd **Times** 12-2/7-10, Closed 25 Dec **Wines** 70 bottles over £20, 30 bottles under £20, 12 by glass **Notes** Gastronomic menu 6 courses £39.50, Sunday L, Vegetarian available **Seats** 40, Pr/dining room 24 **Children** Portions **Parking** 20

BICESTER
Map 11 SP52

Bignell Park Hotel

◉ Modern British V

Creative cooking in a relaxed country setting

☎ 01869 326550 ☎ 0870 0421024
Chesterton OX26 1UE
e-mail: enq@bignellparkhotel.co.uk
dir: M40 junct 9, follow A41 towards Bicester, turn off at Chesterton and hotel is signed at turning

Originally a farmhouse, dating from 1740, Bignell Park combines period charm with modern facilities to provide a small hotel in peaceful countryside near Bicester Shopping Village. The Oaks Restaurant, with its superb oak beams, open fire and minstrels' gallery, is housed in a converted barn; the perfect setting for great local food cooked with flair and passion by a skilled team, including a vegetarian menu. Impressive dishes include full-flavoured Mediterranean vegetable terrine with olive tapenade, or roast rack of lamb served with pan-fried rump of lamb and braised shoulder of lamb samosa.

Chef Chris Coates **Owner** Caparo Hotels
Times 12-2/7-9.30, Closed D Sun **Prices** Fixed L 2 course £10-£18.95, Fixed D 3 course £24-£25.50, Service optional **Wines** 16 bottles over £20, 30 bottles under £20, 4 by glass **Notes** Sunday L, Vegetarian menu, Civ Wed 60 **Seats** 60, Pr/dining room 20 **Children** Portions **Parking** 50

BRITWELL SALOME
Map 5 SU69

The Goose

◉◉ Modern French

18th-century gastro-pub offering accomplished cuisine

☎ 01491 612304
OX49 5LG
e-mail: info_thegoose@btconnect.com
dir: M40 junct 6 take B4009 to Watlington, then towards Benson. Restaurant on left 1.5m

A warm, characterful brick and flint building set below the Chiltern Hills sporting a simple, modern décor with olive green walls, wooden floors, original beams and fireplaces, and comfortable seating. Service is attentive from an enthusiastic young team who contribute to a great overall experience. Serious, high-quality cooking is offered here with refined presentation and tip-top seasonal produce. Cooking skills are accomplished with the exciting carte offering dishes like lasagne of braised oxtail with truffled celeriac purée and horseradish cream to start, followed by fillet of wild Scottish halibut with caramelised salsify, buttered spinach, crispy potato and wild mushrooms. For dessert, try the warm rice pudding tart, served with fig purée, candied pecans and maple syrup. Good accompaniments include lovely home-made bread.

Chef Matthew Tomkinson **Owner** Lisa Inglis & Andrew Bonnell **Times** 12-3/7-11, Closed Mon, Closed D Sun **Prices** Fixed L 2 course £10.95, Fixed D 3 course £19, Starter £6.50-£12, Main £16-£24, Dessert £6.95-£8.50, Service optional **Wines** 57 bottles over £20, 28 bottles under £20, 11 by glass **Notes** Tasting menu on request, Sunday L, Vegetarian available **Seats** 40, Pr/dining room 25 **Children** Portions **Parking** 35

BURFORD
Map 5 SP21

The Angel at Burford

◉◉ Modern European V

Simple, effective brasserie fare in a pretty village restaurant with rooms

☎ 01993 822714
14 Witney St OX18 4SN
e-mail: paul@theangelatburford.co.uk
dir: From A40, turn off at Burford rdbt, down hill 1st right into Swan Lane, 1st left to Pytts Lane, left at end into Witney St

Formerly a 16th-century coaching inn, this bijou Cotswold restaurant with rooms is a delicious haven of rustic elegance, situated down a quiet street in the picturesque village. There's a sunny courtyard and walled garden to explore outside, while inside the white-painted walls create a bright-and-breezy feel, with open stonework, oak beams and log fires, an old church pew in the bar, and a host of interesting artefacts to let the eye wander over while sampling the excellent brasserie-style food. Service is relaxed, friendly and efficient, while the modern cuisine uses local and seasonal produce, offering good, well-balanced flavours, with varied and appropriate presentation. Take a starter of Scottish herb pancake with smoked trout and lemon sabayon, perhaps followed by a main course of breast of pheasant with forest mushrooms, pickled walnuts and swede and parsnip mash, with white chocolate crème brûlée to finish.

Chef David Latter **Owner** Paul Swain **Times** 12-2/7-9, Closed Early Jan -15 Jan, Closed Mon, Closed D Sun **Prices** Fixed D 3 course fr £22.50, Starter £4.95-£7.50, Main £10.50-£17.50, Dessert £4.95-£6.95, Service optional **Wines** 18 bottles over £20, 17 bottles under £20, 11 by glass **Notes** Sunday L, Vegetarian menu, Dress restrictions, Smart casual **Seats** 34, Pr/dining room 18 **Children** Min 9 yrs, Portions **Parking** On street

The Bay Tree Hotel

◉ Traditional British ✪

Stylish woodland retreat with skilful kitchen

☎ 01993 822791
Sheep St OX18 4LW
e-mail: info@baytreehotel.info
web: www.cotswold-inns-hotels.co.uk/baytree
dir: From Oxford, A40, take right at Burford rdbt. Continue half way down the hill and turn left into Sheep St. Hotel is 200yds on right

Visitors have been welcomed through the solid oak doors of this stone-built inn since 1565, and you can relax before dinner with a drink in the Woolsack bar, with its open fire and comfy leather armchairs. In the restaurant, tapestry hangings, a flagstone floor and original leaded windows overlooking the patio and garden, combine to create an elegant country feel. Produce is locally sourced and features in dishes of carrot and coriander soup with smoked goat's cheese fritter, grilled duck breast with pine nut and sun-blushed tomato jus, and desserts like bread-and-butter pudding with whisky custard.

Chef Brian Andrews **Owner** Cotswold Inns & Hotels **Times** 12-2/7-9.30 **Prices** Fixed L 2 course £12.95, Fixed D 3 course £27.95, Service optional **Wines** 40 bottles over £20, 23 bottles under £20, 5 by glass **Notes** Sunday L, Vegetarian available, Dress restrictions, No jeans or trainers, Civ Wed 80 **Seats** 70, Pr/dining room 24 **Children** Portions **Parking** 55

BURFORD *Continued*

The Lamb Inn

◎◎ Traditional British 🕯

Traditional coaching inn with imaginative menu

☎ 01993 823155
Sheep St OX18 4LR
e-mail: info@lambinn-burford.co.uk
web: www.cotswold-inns-hotels.co.uk/lamb
dir: 1st left as you descend on the High St

This enchanting old inn is just a short walk from the centre of the delightful Cotswold village and dates from 1420, when the inn was originally built as weavers' cottages. The spacious restaurant overlooks a lovely courtyard with Cotswold stone walls and a sitting area that positively buzzes in the summer. Inside, cream walls, mullioned windows and frosted skylights make for a bright, cheerful room decorated with food-related pictures, wooden tables and chairs and large floral displays. The food is imaginative and the flavours concise and well balanced using the best of local produce, such as Gloucestershire Old Spot pork, Hereford beef, Bibury trout and Cerney goat's cheese. House specialities include a trio of pork with cider jus, followed by a quirky chocolate tart with parsnip ice cream.

Chef Sean Ducie **Owner** Cotswold Inns & Hotels
Times 12-2.30/7-9.30 **Prices** Fixed D 3 course £32.50, Service added but optional 10% **Wines** 37 bottles over £20, 17 bottles under £20, 9 by glass **Notes** Sunday L, Vegetarian available, Dress restrictions, Smart casual, no jeans or T-shirts **Seats** 55 **Children** Portions **Parking** Care of The Bay Tree Hotel

The Navy Oak

◎ British, European

Traditional surroundings, inventive modern dishes

☎ 01993 878496
Lower End, Leafield OX29 9QQ
e-mail: thenavyoak@aol.com
dir: Telephone for directions

The open-plan kitchen in the restaurant of this 400-year-old village pub allows diners to view the chefs at work while enjoying the fruits of their labours. Elsewhere, open fires and cosy lighting contribute to a traditional country inn feel. The cooking style draws on a range of influences to create interesting modern dishes, with the lunch menu taking in baguettes and snacks, while the dinner menu focuses on more complex fare. Starters might include

queen scallops with rocket and hazelnut butter, while mains range from spiced Moroccan fish tagine with coriander rice, to pan-fried saddle of Wychwood venison with crushed potatoes, prunes and bacon.

Times 12.30-2.30/7-9.30, Closed 1-10 Jan, Closed Mon, Closed D Sun

CHARLBURY   Map 11 SP31

The Bell at Charlbury, Hotel & Restaurant

◎ Modern British 🖳 🕯

Fine cuisine in a former inn

☎ 01608 810278
Church St OX7 3PP
e-mail: reservations@bellhotel-charlbury.com
dir: Situated 3m off A44 between Oxford and Chipping Norton 5m NW of Woodstock. From London via M40 follow signs for Blenheim Palace, then A44 N. Take 1st left after Woodstock. Hotel is near church

This mellow Cotswold stone inn dates from the 18th century, when it was home to Customs and Excise, and is set in over an acre of grounds. The traditional oak-beamed bar and lounge offer a warm welcome and the dining room has a friendly, informal ambience. Modern British cooking with European influences makes use of fine local produce in an appealing carte. Typical dishes include horseradish rarebit with buttered leeks, smoked salmon and tapenade dressing, and Mr Hook's 28-day Aberdeen Angus sirloin steak served with fat chips, grilled tomatoes, mushrooms, onion rings and salad or with Oxford blue cheese sauce.

Chef Pete Southey **Owner** Fergus & Sarah McVey
Times 12-2.30/6.30-9.30 **Prices** Fixed L 2 course £10-£25, Fixed D 3 course £15-£50, Starter £5-£8, Main £10-£22, Dessert £5-£8, Service optional, Groups min 8 service 10% **Wines** 10 bottles over £20, 17 bottles under £20, 8 by glass **Notes** Tasting menu available, Sunday L, Vegetarian available **Seats** 30, Pr/dining room 20 **Children** Portions, Menu **Parking** 40

CHECKENDON   Map 5 SU68

The Highwayman

◎ British, International 🕯

Country pub with good food and creative ideas

☎ 01491 682020
Exlade St RG8 0UA
dir: Exlade St signed off Reading/Wallingford Rd, A4074 0.4m

Hanging baskets on a whitewashed façade give this country pub a traditional demeanour on the outside, but once through the door, although not modern or overworked, the inside has a rather stylish look. It is still countrified - low-beamed ceilings, open fireplaces, exposed brick walls - but tastefully appointed. There are various dining areas and service throughout is relaxed and unstuffy. The menus consist of a set price and long carte with around 10 choices per course. The food is a

mix of British and international ideas with an inevitable twist. Start with sardines on chargrilled crostini served with a Bloody Mary ketchup, followed by very slow cooked (their words) belly of pork, bacon and egg risotto and Worcestershire sauce jus.

Chef Matt Clarke/Michael Keating **Owner** Mr Ken O'Shea/Matt Clarke **Times** 12-2.30/6-10, Closed 26 Dec, 1 Jan, Closed Mon, Closed D Sun **Prices** Fixed L 2 course £12.95, Starter £4.95-£8.95, Main £10.95-£18, Dessert fr £5.50, Service optional, Groups min 8 service 10% **Wines** 15 bottles over £20, 25 bottles under £20, 11 by glass **Notes** Sunday L, Vegetarian available, Dress restrictions, No work clothes or vests **Seats** 55, Pr/dining room 60 **Children** Portions, Menu **Parking** 30

CHINNOR   Map 5 SP70

Sir Charles Napier

◎◎ British, French 🌶

Accomplished cooking at a country inn of great character

☎ 01494 483011
Sprigg's Alley OX39 4BX
e-mail: info@sircharlesnapier.co.uk
dir: M40 junct 6 to Chinnor. Turn right at rdbt, up hill for 2m to Sprigg's Alley

Perhaps the nicest way to arrive at this popular country pub in the Chiltern Hills is on foot from Chinnor village, a two-mile climb through the surrounding beechwoods, which provide its chef with wild garlic in the spring and mushrooms in autumn. When it's cold, you'll be greeted by huge fires and comfy sofas, while sunny days bring an exodus to a wisteria-shaded terrace outside. Unusual sculptures dotted around the bar and dining room provide a talking point for visitors. Here, you'll be treated to some seriously accomplished cooking. The kitchen delivers a menu underpinned by classical French cuisine, and shows a dedication both to quality local produce and clean, accurate flavours. Try a fricassée of white asparagus, crayfish and morels to start, followed by open lasagne of John Dory with lobster and lemongrass sauce.

Chef Sam Hughes **Owner** Julie Griffiths
Times 12-3.30/6.30-10, Closed 25-27 Dec, Closed Mon, Closed D Sun **Prices** Fixed L 2 course fr £15.50, Fixed D 3 course fr £23.25, Tasting menu £45, Starter £7.50-£13.50, Main £16.50-£24.50, Dessert £6.25-£8.50, Service added but optional 12.5% **Wines** 200 bottles over £20, 23 bottles under £20, 9 by glass **Notes** Sunday L, Vegetarian available, Air con **Seats** 75, Pr/dining room 45 **Children** Min 6 yrs D, Portions, Menu **Parking** 60

CHOLSEY — Map 5 SU58

The Sweet Olive

◉ French

French restaurant in charming pub

☎ 01235 851272
Baker St OX11 9DD

Quintessential English pub meets Gallic charm at this country restaurant, which pulls in crowds of diners thanks to its honest French cooking from a mainly French team. Wine cases and bottles decorate the walls of the rustic interior and, thankfully, there is still a bar, so you can have a drink and eat there if you'd prefer to. Sautéed sweetbreads with wild mushrooms makes an impressive starter; followed by venison with port sauce, creamed cabbage and chips. For dessert, three large quenelles of chocolate mousse are served with classic sauce anglaise and espresso ice cream.

Times 12-2/7-9, Closed Feb, 1 wk Jul, Closed Sun, Wed

DEDDINGTON — Map 11 SP43

Deddington Arms

◉ Traditional British

Traditional but stylish coaching inn offering fine food

☎ 01869 338364
Horsefair OX15 0SH
e-mail: deddarms@oxfordshire-hotels.co.uk
web: www.deddington-arms-hotel.co.uk
dir: Telephone for directions

Located just off the market square, this old Cotswold stone coaching inn has been converted and extended into a popular modern venue that attracts diners from across the counties. While retaining the original oak-beamed bar with flagstone floor and cosy fireplace, the contemporary, air-conditioned restaurant features high-backed leather chairs and carved wood panelling and archways. You'll find classic-style cooking with local beer-battered fish and chips and braised blade of beef with parsnip Tatin, along with more intricate dishes of tian of crab, avocado and pink grapefruit, as well as chicken and basil roulade, woodland mushrooms, potato fondant, wilted spinach and fèves. For dessert, try Madagascan vanilla bean and mascarpone cheesecake with cane sugar caramel ice cream.

Chef Nick Porter **Owner** Oxfordshire Hotels Ltd
Times 12-2/6.30-9.45 **Prices** Starter £4.50-£7.70, Main £9.95-£16.75, Dessert £5.25-£6.95, Service optional,

Groups min 6 service 10% **Wines** 20 bottles over £20, 22 bottles under £20, 9 by glass **Notes** Sunday L, Vegetarian available, Air con **Seats** 60, Pr/dining room 30 **Children** Portions, Menu **Parking** 36

DIDCOT — Map 5 SU59

Splitz Restaurant

◉ Modern European 🖵 V

Enjoyable dining in smart surroundings

☎ 01235 817711
32/34 Wantage Rd OX11 0BT
e-mail: info@splitzdidcot.co.uk
dir: A34/A4130 after 3m straight on at 1st rdbt, right at 2nd, continue to next rdbt & take 3rd exit into Wantage Rd. Restaurant 500 yds on right

A substantial double-fronted building in a small parade on the edge of town. Once a classic motorcycle shop, now a smart, modern restaurant and bar, Splitz has roared onto the neighbourhood dining scheme. A long contemporary bar replete with leather seating leads to the spacious dining room, both with a buzzy, upbeat atmosphere. Service is suitably relaxed but attentive, while the sophisticated menu (including a chef's table) offers classic and modern dishes using prime produce from a talented young chef; think an assiette of suckling pig, slow-cooked loin, belly and shoulder served with warm apple jelly, crushed black pudding potatoes and new season asparagus. Look out for the wine tasting evenings.

Chef Chris Finnigan **Owner** Sue Crowther, Dave King, Keith Metris **Times** 12-3/6.30-10, Closed Mon, Closed D Sun **Prices** Fixed L 2 course £12.50, Fixed D 3 course £14.95, Starter £4.95-£7.95, Main £11.75-£18.95, Dessert £5.95, Service optional, Groups min 6 service 10% **Wines** 30 bottles over £20, 6 bottles under £20, 10 by glass **Notes** Tasting menu 7 courses, Sunday L, Vegetarian menu, Air con **Seats** 50 **Children** Portions, Menu **Parking** 6

DORCHESTER (ON THAMES) — Map 5 SU59

White Hart Hotel

◉ British, French

Historic coaching inn serving simply presented fare

☎ 01865 340074
High St OX10 7HN
e-mail: whitehart@oxfordshire-hotels.co.uk
web: www.oxfordshire-hotels.co.uk
dir: Village centre. Just off A415/ A4074. 3m from Wallingford, 6m from Abingdon

Set in the heart of a picturesque village, this 17th-century coaching inn retains its original façade, period charm and character, complete with beams and brickwork. Inside, the décor is warm and inviting, complementing the flagstone floors, stone fireplaces and vaulted timber ceiling in the atmospheric restaurant. The carte demonstrates a serious approach through dishes prepared from quality ingredients, such as salad of Oxford Blue cheese with pear compôte and toasted walnuts, braised belly of pork with crispy crackling, smooth mash, Savoy cabbage, caramelised onion and Madeira jus, and Belgian chocolate terrine with orange salad.

Times 12-2.30/6.30-9.30

FARINGDON — Map 5 SU29

The Folly Restaurant

◉ British, International

Popular hotel restaurant with menu to match

☎ 01367 241272
Sudbury House Hotel & Conference Centre, London Street SN7 8AA
e-mail: stay@sudburyhouse.co.uk
dir: Off A420 signposted Folly Hill & Market Place

Set in nine acres of pleasant grounds on the edge of the Cotswolds, this once fine Regency residence now blends modern facilities with traditional good looks. The elegant, comfortable, light-and-airy Folly Restaurant offers a tranquil outlook over patio and gardens, while its crowd-pleasing menu comes driven by seasonal produce, simplicity and well-balanced flavours. Expect seared calves' liver on braised Savoy cabbage with lardons of smoked bacon in a red wine sauce, or rosemary-scented rump of lamb served with vegetable couscous and caramelised tomatoes. Menus helpfully indicate

Continued

FARINGDON *Continued*

vegetarian, vegan and low-fat options, plus dishes suitable for coeliac and diabetic sufferers. (A lounge and bar menu is also available.)

Chef Clifford Burt, J Massey, K Arlott, M Murray, J Gilmore **Owner** Cranfield University **Times** 12.30-2/7-9.15, Closed 26-30 Dec **Prices** Fixed L 2 course £15.50-£18.25, Fixed D 3 course £23.50, Starter fr £5.25, Main fr £13, Dessert fr £5.25, Service optional **Wines** 9 bottles over £20, 23 bottles under £20, 11 by glass **Notes** Sunday L, Vegetarian available, Dress restrictions, Smart-casual, Civ Wed 160, Air con **Seats** 100, Pr/dining room 40 **Children** Portions, Menu **Parking** 100

GORING Map 5 SU68

The Leatherne Bottel

◉◉ British, French 🖥

Unique Thames-side location for enjoyable eating

☎ 01491 872667
RG8 0HS
e-mail: leathernebottel@aol.com
dir: M4 junct 12 or M40 junct 6, signed from B4009 towards Wallingford

With its glorious views over the River Thames and the Berkshire Downs, The Leatherne Bottel enjoys a truly tranquil setting. The addition of a paved terrace and conservatory extension has created a feeling of spaciousness, at the same time extending the wonderful views from the decked alfresco area. Inside, the dining room is no less impressive, combining exposed brickwork and lemon-coloured walls with vibrant artwork and fresh flower displays. Youthful service is enthusiastic and attentive, and there's a small cosy bar. The chef adds Pacific Rim ideas, inspired by her time in New Zealand, to generous-sized modern British and French dishes, handling quality produce with care. Start with steak tartare and horseradish ice cream, and follow with poached monkfish, roast cherry tomatoes and baby leeks, saffron potatoes, lemongrass, ginger and shellfish sauce.

Chef Julia Storey & John Abbey **Owner** John Madejski **Times** 12-2/7-9, Closed 1st 3 wks Jan, Closed Mon (Jan-Apr & Sep-Nov), Closed D Sun **Prices** Fixed L 2 course £19.50, Tasting menu £58, Starter £7.50-£13.50, Main £17.50-£24, Dessert £7.50, Service added 10% **Wines** 181 bottles over £20, 7 bottles under £20, 14 by glass **Notes** Sunday L, Vegetarian available **Seats** 45 **Children** Min 10 yrs **Parking** 40, extra parking available

GREAT MILTON Map 5 SP60

Le Manoir aux Quat' Saisons

◉◉◉◉◉ – *see opposite*

HENLEY-ON-THAMES Map 5 SU78

The Cherry Tree Inn

◉ Modern British, European 🌿

Popular inn with a modern menu

☎ 01491 680430
Stoke Row RG9 5QA
e-mail: info@thecherrytreeinn.com
dir: On the A4155 from Henley-on-Thames exit B481 to Sonning Common. Follow signs for Stoke Row, turn right for pub

Taking its name from the pretty cherry tree that grows outside, this 400-year-old inn is set in the hamlet of Stoke Row, not far from Henley. Beams and flagstone floors provide an old world backdrop for contemporary furnishings, while a nearby barn has been converted into four chic bedrooms. The inn is popular locally for everything from a quick pint to a special meal, and dinner brings imaginative and hearty fare such as grilled sea bass with vegetable couscous, lamb tagine with tzatziki, and steamed mussels in a coconut and chilli broth.

Chef Richard Coates **Owner** Richard Coates **Times** 12-3/7-10, Closed 25-26 Dec **Prices** Starter £4.50-£6.75, Main £10.50-£16.95, Dessert £5.50-£6.50, Service optional **Wines** 12 bottles over £20, 27 bottles under £20, 11 by glass **Notes** Sunday L, Vegetarian available **Seats** 76 **Children** Portions, Menu **Parking** 25

Hotel du Vin and Bistro

◉◉ British, French 🖥 V

Stylishly converted old brewery with classic bistro fare

☎ 01491 848400
New St RG9 2BP
e-mail: info@henley.hotelduvin.com
dir: M4 junct 8/9, situated in town centre close to river

The Henley branch of this boutique hotel chain is as sleek and upmarket as ever. Housed in a stylish conversion of the former Brakspear Brewery, just a splash away from the waterfront, it boasts a comfy bar with walk-in humidor, and a small courtyard for alfresco dining with a new pavilion for smokers. Inside, the bistro-style restaurant is decorated with wine ephemera. It is a relaxed and lively setting for some top-notch cooking from a kitchen team who consistently impress. Expect classic combinations with a twist: chicken liver and foie gras parfait to start perhaps, served with toasted brioche and tomato chutney, followed by confit duck leg with spinach, gnocchi, beetroot purée and aromatic honey, and vanilla poached pear with praline and honey ice cream.

Chef Neil Falzon **Owner** MWB Group **Times** 12-2.30/6-10 **Prices** Food prices not confirmed for 2009. Please telephone for details. **Wines** 700 bottles over £20, 30 bottles under £20, 16 by glass **Notes** Sunday L, Vegetarian

menu, Civ Wed 60, Air con **Seats** 90, Pr/dining room 60 **Children** Portions, Menu

Number 28 at the White Hart

◉◉ Modern British

Historic inn with contemporary style and flavour

☎ 01491 641245
28 High St, Nettlebed RG9 5DD
e-mail: info@whitehartnettlebed.com
dir: From Henley take A4130 towards Wallingford. Approx 5m

On the outside an historic inn dating from the 15th century, but once inside the spacious bistro reveals itself as a thoroughly modern space: inlaid spot lighting, clean lines and natural colours. Both menu du jour and bistro menus offer good value and simple, honest food, carefully sourced and organic where possible. With vibrancy and colour on the plate, starters feature smoked Oxford partridge served with new potatoes in a light walnut dressing, following on with main-course roast Stonor pheasant, braised leg, artichokes and thyme jus, or braised local lamb shoulder with lentils and red wine orange sauce. Iced banana parfait with chocolate ravioli and rum syrup is an ambitious dessert.

Times 12-2.30/6.30-9.30, Closed Mon-Wed, Closed L all week, Closed D Sun

KINGHAM Map 10 SP22

The Kingham Plough

◉ Modern, Traditional British 🌿

Simple cooking, big flavours and top-notch local ingredients in revamped village pub

☎ 01608 658327
The Green OX7 6YD
e-mail: book@thekinghamplough.co.uk
dir: On village green in Kingham, 3m from Stow-on-the-Wold

Transformed from a run-down village local to a contemporary dining pub in 2007 by Emily Watkins, former sous-chef at The Fat Duck in Bray, the new-look Kingham Plough is making waves in the pub-food world. Although still very much a pub, with Hooky on tap and decent bar bites, the emphasis is on the short, innovative daily menu. Cooking is simple, concentrating on the depth of flavours from the best local ingredients available, much of it sourced from local farms and the adjacent Daylesford Estate. A memorable meal could start with a perfectly timed crisp duck egg on bacon with a rich watercress sauce, followed by Cotswold lamb pudding with purple sprouting broccoli, or monkfish, hake and tomato stew. Finish with Bramley apple and cinnamon doughnut with condensed milk and toffee ice cream, or a plate of local Cotswold cheeses.

Chef Emily Watkins **Owner** Emily Watkins & Miles Lampson **Times** 12-3/6-11.30, Closed 25 Dec **Prices** Starter £6, Main £10-£20, Dessert £5, Service optional **Wines** 16 bottles over £20, 9 bottles under £20, 7 by glass **Notes** Sunday L, Vegetarian available **Seats** 70, Pr/dining room 20 **Children** Portions, Menu

Le Manoir aux Quat' Saisons

Modern French

An absolute dream of a place

☎ 01844 278881
OX44 7PD
e-mail: lemanoir@blanc.co.uk
dir: M40 junct 7 follow A329 towards Wallingford. After 1m turn right, signed Great Milton and Le Manoir aux Quat' Saisons

Whatever the season, a visit to this mellow stone, 15th-century manor-house hotel, set in beautiful grounds, is one of life's not-to-be-missed experiences - it's the epitome of luxury and good taste, where modern style and classic virtues combine with truly memorable cooking and exemplary service. And, though Le Manoir may have been accumulating top accolades for more than twenty years, its iconic chef-patron, Raymond Blanc, still fizzes with enthusiasm. On warm summer days you can enjoy aperitifs on the lawn, while during winter months lounges pamper with sophistication and modernity. The dining room is in three parts, with the principal room being a conservatory, plus the Grand Salle, that both continue the contemporary theme. But no visit here would be complete without a stroll round the stunning gardens dotted with life-size bronze statues and, among the delights beyond the garden wall, there's a Japanese garden and teahouse and the all-important organic potager. Producing some 90 types of vegetables and over 70 varieties of herbs for the kitchen, it's fundamental to the Blanc cooking philosophy - freshness, quality and seasonality are vital to the ethos here. This extends to the use and sourcing of local produce - organic where possible - reconnecting gastronomy with local producers. So expect classic French dishes in a modern, light, fresh style with clear, precise flavours, balance and subtlety, delivered with breathtaking skill and immaculate presentation. Take the likes of an assiette of milk-fed lamb from the Pyrenees served with pea purée and roasting jus, and to finish, perhaps tiramisù flavours with cocoa sauce and cream and coffee bean ice cream. And do save room for the dazzling selection of oven-fresh breads, canapés and petits fours that line up alongside a superb wine list. The number of fine chefs who have learned their trade here is a testament to Raymond's supreme commitment to training and ultimately a tribute to the man and the high esteem in which his kitchen and renowned hotel are held. This is a must-do experience.

Chef Raymond Blanc & Gary Jones **Owner** Mr R Blanc **Times** 12-2.30/7-10 **Prices** Fixed L 3 course fr £49, Starter £34, Main £32-£38, Dessert £17-£19, Service optional **Wines** 1000 bottles over £20, 5 bottles under £20, 16 by glass **Notes** Menu Découverte available daily, Menu Classiques 5 courses, Sunday L, Vegetarian menu, Dress restrictions, No jeans, trainers or shorts, Civ Wed 50, Air con **Seats** 100, Pr/dining room 50 **Children** Portions, Menu **Parking** 70

KINGHAM *Continued*

Mill House Hotel

◉◉   Modern British

Charming hotel with an accomplished menu

☎ 01608 658188
OX7 6UH
e-mail: stay@millhousehotel.co.uk
dir: Just off B4450, between Chipping Norton and Stow-on-the-Wold. On S outskirts of village

Set in 10 acres of well-kept gardens with a trout stream, this Cotswold-stone former mill house makes a relaxing setting for country-house dining. The building dates back to the time of the Domesday Book and was rebuilt in 1770. British dishes make good use of fresh ingredients and the cooking shows skill and imagination. Take a starter of pan-seared smoked salmon with potato and herb pancake, and move on to belly pork with cider fondant, parsnip chip and apple jus or perhaps butternut squash and white bean lasagne with spinach sauce. Round things off with hot chocolate fondant with Amaretto cream, or choose from the extensive English cheese menu that features some regional favourites.

Chef Michael Burns **Owner** John Parslow
Times 12-2/6.30-10 **Prices** Fixed L 2 course £10-£15, Fixed D 3 course fr £32, Starter £5-£6.95, Main £7.50-£13.95, Dessert fr £5, Service optional **Wines** 26 bottles over £20, 36 bottles under £20, 9 by glass **Notes** Sunday L, Vegetarian available, Dress restrictions, Smart casual, Civ Wed 80 **Seats** 70, Pr/dining room 50 **Children** Portions, Menu **Parking** 60

MURCOTT   **Map 11 SP51**

The Nut Tree Inn

◉◉   Modern European

Assured cooking in a characterful country inn

☎ 01865 331253
Main St OX5 2RE
dir: M40 junct 9. A34 towards Oxford, take 2nd exit for Islip. At Red Lion pub turn left and then take right towards Murcott

Dating back to the 14th century, this pretty thatched stone inn overlooks the village pond and sits beside a paddock area complete with the restaurant's own pigs. Popular with local foodies, there are two cosy dining rooms with stripped oak beams and wood-burning stoves, as well as an airy conservatory hung with modern art. Dishes are well executed and uncomplicated, showing plenty of skill and an awareness of seasonality with good use made of high-quality ingredients from regional suppliers and artisan producers. Take a main course of olive-oil poached fillet of wild Scottish halibut with green herb risotto and confit garlic, or maybe grilled cutlet of Nut Tree-reared pork with salt and pepper potatoes, parsnip purée and apple gravy. Then move on to hot passionfruit soufflé with passionfruit sorbet for dessert.

Chef Michael North **Owner** Michael North, Imogen Young
Times 12-2.30/6.30-11, Closed D Sun (Winter)
Prices Fixed L 2 course £15, Fixed D 3 course £18, Starter £4.50-£10, Main £14-£22, Dessert £5.50-£7.50, Service optional, Groups min 6 service 10% **Wines** 72 bottles over £20, 27 bottles under £20, 15 by glass **Notes** Tasting menu available Mon-Sat eve, Sunday L, Vegetarian available **Seats** 60, Pr/dining room 24 **Children** Portions **Parking** 30

OXFORD   **Map 5 SP50**

Arezzo Restaurant

◉   Modern Italian

Popular Italian-influenced food served in conservatory-style restaurant

☎ 01865 749988
Hawkwell House Hotel, Church Way, Iffley Village OX4 4DZ
e-mail: info@hawkwellhouse.co.uk
dir: A34 follow signs to Cowley, at Littlemore rdbt take A4158 onto Iffley Rd. After lights turn left into Iffley village

Set in a peaceful residential location, Hawkwell House Hotel provides the setting for Arezzo, an Italian bistro-influenced restaurant. The décor has an understated Mediterranean feel, light and airy with white-tiled floor. With friendly, smartly-attired staff, Italian-style carefully prepared comfort food is the order of the day. Starters like mozzarella bocconcini, with tomato salad and basil oil, or carpaccio of beef, with walnut, red onion and roasted garlic dressing, precede a pasta and pizza selection, with main courses such as lamb al forno: roasted lamb steak,

marinated in mint with shallots and garlic, served with creamed potatoes and redcurrant sauce.

Chef Christopher Kennedy **Owner** Bespoke Hotels
Times 12-2.30/7-9.30 **Prices** Fixed D 3 course £23.50, Starter £4.95-£5.50, Main £10.95-£17.95, Dessert £3.95-£5.25, Service optional **Wines** 6 bottles over £20, 21 bottles under £20, 6 by glass **Notes** Sunday L, Civ Wed 120, Air con **Seats** 55, Pr/dining room 20 **Children** Portions, Menu **Parking** 85

Brasserie Blanc

◉   French

Accomplished cuisine at popular French-style brasserie

☎ 01865 510999
71-72 Walton St OX2 6AG
e-mail: oxford@brasserieblanc.com
dir: From city centre. N along St Giles, left into Little Clarendon St and right at end of Walton St

This popular French-style brasserie, which is part of a small chain, is situated in the bustling city suburb of Jericho. The attractive and welcoming two-roomed restaurant provides a smart, spacious setting with contemporary furnishing, colourful prints, wooden floors and full-length windows. Service is skilled and friendly, and children are positively welcomed. A menu of accomplished bistro-style dishes offers thoroughly French fare found in starters such as Burgundian snails in garlic herb butter, followed by main courses like Toulouse sausages with smooth mash and onion gravy, while a choice of Gallic desserts might include tarte Tatin.

Times 12-2.45/6-10.30, Closed 25 Dec

Cotswold Lodge Hotel

◉   Modern 🖥

Elegant dining near city centre

☎ 01865 512121
66a Banbury Rd OX2 6JP
e-mail: aa@cotswoldlodgehotel.co.uk
dir: Take A4165 (Banbury Road) off A40 ring road, hotel 1.5m on left

There is a relaxed country-house feel to this family-run Victorian hotel close to the centre of Oxford. In the dining room, the contemporary décor - wooden flooring and cerise-coloured walls hung with pictures - combines with period features to provide an informal ambience, while high-backed chairs and crisp white linen provide the comforts. Straightforward modern classic British dishes, with a hint of European influence, are the focus of the brasserie-style menu; try fresh scallops with deep-fried anchovies, sun-blushed tomatoes and olive salsa, followed by breaded chicken fillet with beetroot and onion timbale and a port wine sauce, while fig and almond tart with crème anglaise might prove the finale for dessert. Alfresco dining is available in the Mediterranean-style garden.

Times 12-2.30/6.30-10

The Lemon Tree

◉ British, Mediterranean

Attractive restaurant with a Mediterranean feel

☎ 01865 311936
268 Woodstock Rd OX2 7NW
e-mail: info@thelemontreeoxford.co.uk
dir: 1.5m from city centre heading N

Expect a warm, relaxing ambience at this spacious, bright-and-airy restaurant, the flagstone flooring, wicker chairs, larger-than-life ferns, big mirrors and conservatory-style ceiling giving an impression of sunnier climes. The Mediterranean influence can be seen in some of the dishes on the modern, brasserie-style menu but most tend towards home-grown fare. Take seared pigeon breast with spring onion mash, black pudding and mustard sauce, braised lamb shank with colcannon and root vegetables, or monkfish with crayfish and rocket risotto and lemon oil, and perhaps treacle and almond tart for dessert.

Chef Johnny Pugsley **Owner** Clinton Pugh **Times** 12/11, Closed Xmas, New Year, Closed Mon-Tue, Closed L Wed, Closed D Sun **Prices** Fixed L 2 course fr £10, Service added but optional 12.5% **Wines** 29 bottles over £20, 12 bottles under £20, 14 by glass **Notes** Sunday L, Vegetarian available, Civ Wed 90 **Seats** 90 **Children** Portions **Parking** 19

Macdonald Randolph

◉◉ Traditional British 🖥

Classic Oxford dining experience

☎ 0844 879 9132 & 01865 256400
Beaumont St OX1 2LN
e-mail: general.randolph@macdonald-hotels.co.uk
dir: M40 junct 8 onto A40 towards Oxford, follow signs towards city centre, leads to St Giles, hotel is on right

Built in 1864, this neo-Gothic mansion turned elegant hotel is superbly situated in the heart of Oxford. The high-ceilinged restaurant stylishly combines traditional and modern décor, while its large picture windows offer diners wonderful views of the Ashmolean Museum and St Giles Memorial. The service is friendly and knowledgeable, while the menu focuses on British cuisine - underpinned by a classical base - making the most of quality seasonal ingredients, simply prepared and beautifully presented. Take seared hand-dived scallops with pork belly and pear purée to start, with thyme roast free-range chicken breast, confit leg and truffle dressing, or fillet of wild sea bass,

fennel purée and langoustine sauce to follow, and perhaps the classic Randolph trifle to finish.

Chef Tom Birks **Owner** Macdonald Hotels **Times** 12-2.30/5.30-10 **Prices** Fixed L 2 course £28.80, Starter £8.50-£11.50, Main £21.60-£31.80, Dessert £9.50-£11.50, Service optional **Wines** 100 bottles over £20, 3 bottles under £20, 12 by glass **Notes** Sunday L, Vegetarian available, Dress restrictions, Smart casual, Civ Wed 300 **Seats** 90, Pr/dining room 30 **Children** Portions, Menu **Parking** 50

Malmaison Brasserie Oxford

◉ Modern 🖥 🔊

Contemporary brasserie dining in former prison

☎ 01865 268400
3 Oxford Castle, New Rd OX1 1AY
e-mail: oxford@malmaison.com
dir: M40 junct 9 (signed Oxford A34). Follow A34 S to Botley Interchange and then take A420 to the city centre

Once the city's prison, this popular hotel is now a city destination, with many of the rooms actually old cells complete with original door and bars. Its popular, relaxed, subterranean brasserie comes decked out in shades of dark brown and aubergine, while waiting staff are clad in black. The bright, clean-cut food follows the blueprint of other Malmaisons, with the emphasis on accomplished, modern brasserie-style fare with a French twist, plus a Home Grown & Local menu. Take a starter of steak tartare with pomme allumette, followed by fillet of sea bass with vitelotte potato and watercress sauce, with white chocolate and Amaretto fondue to finish.

Chef Russell Heeley **Owner** MWB **Times** 12-2.30/6-10.30 **Prices** Food prices not confirmed for 2009. Please telephone for details. **Wines** 150 bottles over £20, 50 bottles under £20, 21 by glass **Notes** Civ Wed 50, Air con **Seats** 100, Pr/dining room 10 **Children** Portions, Menu

Old Parsonage Restaurant

◉ Modern British

Memorable Oxford setting for modern and ambitious cooking

☎ 01865 292305 & 310210
The Old Parsonage Hotel, 1 Banbury Rd OX2 6NN
e-mail: restaurant@oldparsonage-hotel.co.uk
dir: M40 junct 8, A40. Turn right onto ring road, first left into Banbury Road. Hotel & restaurant on right just before St Giles Church.

The wisteria-clad Old Parsonage dates back to 1659 and is full of character, style and charm inside and out. The lively all-day bar and restaurant is a traditional space with polished oak tables and Russian red walls hung with paintings, but in the summer months the focus switches to the splendid terrace, where white linen-clothed tables maintain the air of refinement. The menu offers a sensibly concise choice of five dishes at each course and the approach is distinctly modern, the presentation unfussy. Home-smoked wood pigeon salad or sea trout ballotine with pickled girolles and mixed baby cress are typical starters, while main courses might include stuffed saddle of rabbit served with crushed potatoes and mustard sauce.

Chef Nick Seckington **Owner** Jeremy Mogford **Times** 12/10.30 **Prices** Fixed L 2 course £12.95, Starter £6-£10, Main £10-£25, Dessert £6-£8.50, Service optional, Groups min 5 service 12.5% **Wines** 40 bottles over £20, 5 bottles under £20, 10 by glass **Notes** Sunday L, Dress restrictions, Smart casual, Civ Wed 20, Air con **Seats** 75, Pr/dining room 15 **Children** Portions **Parking** 14

Quod Brasserie & Bar

◉ Modern Mediterranean 🔊

Busy city-centre brasserie

☎ 01865 202505
Old Bank Hotel, 92-94 High St OX1 4BN
e-mail: quod@oldbank-hotel.co.uk
web: www.quod.co.uk
dir: Approach city centre via Headington. Over Magdalen Bridge into High St. Hotel 75yds on left

A stylish former banking hall with an amazing collection of contemporary British art, stone floors, ink blue leather banquettes and a huge zinc-topped bar, this open-all-day brasserie is part of the Old Bank Hotel. Expect the sort of robust food you might find on the Mediterranean coast: wonderful pizza, bread, pasta, bar snacks, steak frites, grilled lobster and great wine by the glass. Not to be missed are the Quod home-made hamburgers, Caesar salad and pizza Vincenzo. The large outdoor terrace seating a hundred on various levels is an added bonus.

Chef Michael Wright **Owner** Mr J Mogford **Times** 7am/11 pm **Prices** Fixed L 2 course £10.25, Starter £5.95-£8.95, Main £6.95-£18.95, Dessert £5.50-£8.50, Service optional, Groups min 5 service 10% **Wines** 6 bottles over £20, 6 bottles under £20, 17 by glass **Notes** Sunday L, Vegetarian available, Air con **Seats** 164, Pr/dining room 24 **Children** Portions, Menu **Parking** 50

OXFORD *Continued*

Cherwell Boathouse Restaurant

☎ 01865 552746
60 Bardwell Rd OX2 6ST

Enjoy international dishes at this small and intimate restaurant, right on the banks of the Isis in a truly scenic spot.

Prices Food prices not confirmed for 2009. Please telephone for details.

The Crazy Bear

◉◉ Modern British

Contemporary dishes in imaginative surroundings

☎ 01865 890714
Bear Ln OX44 7UR
e-mail: enquiries@crazybear-oxford.co.uk
web: www.crazybeargroup.co.uk
dir: From M40 junct 7 turn left onto A329, continue for 4m, left after petrol station & left again into Bear Lane

This traditional 16th-century inn has something of an art deco theme with leather-bound tables, lots of mirrors, atmospheric lighting, and a ceiling of binned wine bottles combining with the original features. The bedrooms are decorated in dramatic style, making an overnight stay after dinner an attractive option. It's a relaxing and popular place, with well-informed and friendly staff. Modern British dishes with lots of international influences are prepared using the best ingredients, and dishes are simply but effectively presented. Start with mackerel pâté on toasted sour dough, before a main course of braised ox cheek with creamed potato, mushrooms, orange and red wine braising juices, or smoked haddock with colcannon mash and poached egg. Finish with rhubarb crumble and custard.

Chef Martin Picken **Owner** Jason Hunt **Times** 12/10 **Prices** Fixed L 2 course fr £15, Fixed D 3 course fr £19.50, Starter £6.50-£45, Main £12-£42, Dessert £6.70-£9.50, Service added but optional 12.5% **Wines** 130 bottles over £20, 12 bottles under £20, 16 by glass **Notes** Sunday L, Vegetarian available, Civ Wed 100, Air con **Seats** 40, Pr/dining room 140 **Children** Portions **Parking** 100

Thai Thai at the Crazy Bear

◉◉ Modern Thai

Authentic Thai cuisine in the heart of rural Oxfordshire

☎ 01865 890714
The Crazy Bear, Bear Ln OX44 7UR
e-mail: enquiries@crazybear-oxford.co.uk
web: www.crazybeargroup.co.uk
dir: M40 junct 7 turn left onto A329, continue for 4m, left after petrol station and 2nd left again into Bear Lane

This 16th-century former coaching inn never fails to excite with its unique and flamboyant décor, including a restaurant decorated like a Moroccan Bedouin tent, with mirror-panelled ceiling and luxurious velvet walls. Thai Thai's chefs create modern cuisine using traditional methods and the freshest, organic ingredients, including some flown in from Thailand to produce the genuine taste of the Far East. The long and varied menu includes a dedicated dim sum section and an adventurous tasting menu. Start with the chargrilled marinated Aberdeen Angus beef wrapped in cha poo leaf perhaps, followed by slow pot-roasted ox cheek, braised lettuce, shiitake mushrooms, spring onions and roasted garlic. Desserts are more Western orientated, such as salted butter caramel, pistachios, peanuts and chocolate sorbet.

Chef Chalao Mansell **Owner** Jason Hunt **Times** 12-3/6-12, Closed L Sun **Prices** Starter £6-£9, Main £7.50-£18.50, Dessert £6.70-£9.50, Service added but optional 12.5% **Wines** 130 bottles over £20, 12 bottles under £20, 16 by glass **Notes** Vegetarian available, Civ Wed 100, Air con **Seats** 30, Pr/dining room 140 **Children** Portions **Parking** 100

The Mason's Arms

◉ Modern British 🍷

Country restaurant with skilfully produced dishes

☎ 01608 683212
Banbury Rd OX7 4AP
e-mail: themasonschef@hotmail.com
dir: Situated between Banbury and Chipping Norton on A361

A classic stone-built inn with a dining room extension, The Mason's Arms has maintained its traditional identity enhanced by a complete refurbishment a few years ago. Produce is locally sourced where possible and breads, terrines, pastries and desserts are all home made. The meat is rare breed and traceable, poultry is free range, and fish is delivered daily. Fresh, lively and well-presented dishes include smoked duck breast and smooth duck terrine with chutney and oatcakes, and a main course of 20-hour roasted shoulder of Gloucestershire Old Spot pork with honey-roasted parsnips. Finish with a delightful raspberry and Drambuie crème brûlée.

Chef Bill Leadbeater **Owner** B & C Leadbeater, Tom Aldous **Times** 12-3/7-11, Closed 25-26 Dec, Closed D 24 Dec, Sun **Prices** Fixed L 2 course £12.95, Fixed D 3 course £19.95, Starter £4.50-£8.50, Main £9.95-£18.95, Dessert £5.50, Service optional, Groups min 10 service 10% **Wines** 13 bottles over £20, 26 bottles under £20, 6 by glass **Notes** Sunday L, Vegetarian available **Seats** 75, Pr/dining room 40 **Children** Portions, Menu **Parking** 60

The Swan at Tetsworth

◉ Modern British

Antique inn with a timeless atmosphere and accomplished cuisine

☎ 01844 281182
High St, Tetsworth OX9 7AB
e-mail: restaurant@theswan.co.uk
dir: 3m from M40 junct 6.5m from M40 junct 8

The Swan, an Elizabethan coaching inn dating back to 1482, retains all its rustic charm and old-world atmosphere. Successfully combining a renowned antiques centre with the restaurant, you can be assured that the menu is thoroughly modern. Whether eating alfresco in the pretty garden or in the intimate, candlelit dining room, expect an ambitious menu, utilising top quality, seasonal ingredients. Try the home-smoked venison, with a salad of beetroot and pickled mushrooms to start, perhaps followed by the line-caught sea bass, tagliatelle, sea asparagus and lobster beurre blanc. Leave room for apple bavarois with apple jam doughnut and Granny Smith sorbet.

Chef Derek Muircroft **Owner** Solution Culinaire **Times** 12-3/7-9.30, Closed D Sun **Prices** Fixed L 2 course fr £13.50, Starter £7.50-£10, Main £15-£22, Dessert £7-£7.50, Service added but optional 10% **Wines** 84 bottles over £20, 35 bottles under £20, 11 by glass **Notes** Bistro menu/light L available Sun-Fri, Sunday L, Vegetarian available **Seats** 55, Pr/dining room 12 **Children** Portions **Parking** 120

WALLINGFORD Map 5 SU68

Lakeside Restaurant

◉ Modern European

A popular restaurant in an attractive setting

☎ 01491 836687
The Springs Hotel & Golf Club, Wallingford Rd, North Stoke OX10 6BE
e-mail: info@thespringshotel.com
web: www.thespringshotel.com
dir: Edge of village of North Stoke

Set in beautiful grounds overlooking the spring-fed lake, the mock-Tudor style Springs Hotel was often visited by Edward VIII. Built in 1874, there is plenty of period detail, including crackling fires in open hearths, comfortable lounges and exposed oak beams. Situated in the glass-enclosed Winter Garden, the Lakeside Restaurant offers the attentiveness of formal service with a friendly, unobtrusive feel. With good attention to detail especially in presentation, the modern European menu offers a good variety and choice using quality, seasonal produce in dishes like breast of wood pigeon with caramelised apple and Clonakilty black pudding, port and redcurrant dressing, followed by Butlers Farm slow-roasted pork belly, tortellini of pig's cheek and pea purée.

Chef Paul Franklin **Owner** Lakeside Restaurant **Times** 12-2.30/7-9.45 **Prices** Fixed L 2 course £11.50, Fixed D 3 course £27.50, Starter £5.95-£8.50, Main £15.95-£23.50, Dessert £6.50, Service optional, Groups min 10 service 10% **Wines** 71 bottles over £20, 15 bottles under £20, 12 by glass **Notes** Sunday L, Vegetarian available, Dress restrictions, No denim, trainers or T-shirts, Civ Wed 90 **Seats** 80, Pr/dining room 30 **Children** Portions **Parking** 150

WESTON-ON-THE-GREEN Map 11 SP51

The Manor Restaurant

◉◉ Modern British

Enjoyable dining in impressive medieval manor-house hotel

☎ 01869 350621
Weston Manor Hotel OX25 3QL
e-mail: reception@westonmanor.co.uk
dir: 2 mins from M40 junct 9, via A34 (Oxford) to Weston-on-Green; hotel in village centre

This historic medieval manor, which was used during World War II as an officer's mess for American airmen, exudes an air of character and charm. Set in well-tended gardens, Weston Manor Hotel retains a wealth of original features. The restaurant, with its impressive linenfold oak-panelling, high-vaulted ceiling and minstrels' gallery, is the oldest part of the building and was once the baronial hall, making it a popular venue for weddings and functions. The kitchen demonstrates accomplished cooking skills, delivering impressive dishes with creative flair. To start, why not try pan-fried fillet of mackerel with warm potato salad and grain mustard sauce? Expect mains such as rack of locally-reared lamb with roasted garlic, and artichoke-shallot tart, and desserts may include apple and cider soup with blackcurrant sorbet.

Chef Michael Keenlyside **Owner** Mr & Mrs Osborn **Times** 12-2/7-9.30, Closed L Sat **Prices** Fixed L 2 course £23-£27, Fixed D 3 course £35-£39.50, Starter £6.45-£8.50, Main £14.70-£21.20, Dessert £7.10-£9.40, Service optional, Groups min 8 service 12.5% **Wines** 32 bottles over £20, 18 bottles under £20, 6 by glass **Notes** Coffee incl, Sunday L, Vegetarian available, Dress restrictions, Smart Casual; no jeans, Civ Wed 90 **Seats** 60, Pr/dining room 32 **Children** Portions **Parking** 50

WOODCOTE Map 5 SU68

Woody Nook at Woodcote

◉ British, International V

Hearty cooking with Australian flair and wines in relaxed, informal atmosphere

☎ 01491 680775
Goring Rd RG8 0SD
e-mail: info@woodynookatwoodcote.co.uk
web: www.woodynookatwoodcote.co.uk
dir: Opposite the village green

This cosy restaurant takes its unusual name from its owners' award-winning winery in Western Australia and,

as you might expect, offers an excellent list of wines. Wooden beams, low ceilings and leaded windows create a rustic ambience, while a village-green setting means you might be treated to a game of cricket while you wait for your food. The hearty range of international, country-style dishes is distinguished by an occasional nod to the Pacific Rim. Kick off with a foie gras, chicken and truffle terrine perhaps, before sampling the likes of breast of Barbary duck served with sweet potato, smoked bacon and an orange and honey sauce, or roast best end of lamb with root vegetables and tarragon jus.

Chef Stuart Shepherd **Owner** Jane & Peter Bailey **Times** 12-2.30/7-9.30, Closed 1st 2 wks Jan, 1st 2 wks Aug, Closed Mon & Tue, Closed D Sun **Prices** Fixed L 2 course fr £19.75, Fixed D 3 course fr £25, Starter £5.95-£9.95, Main £13.95-£18.95, Dessert £4.95-£6.95, Service optional, Groups min 6 service 10% **Wines** 18 bottles over £20, 15 bottles under £20, 6 by glass **Notes** Sunday L, Vegetarian menu **Seats** 50 **Children** Portions **Parking** 25

WOODSTOCK Map 11 SP41

The Feathers

◉◉ Modern British ⌨

Accomplished modern British cuisine at a sophisticated townhouse hotel

☎ 01993 812291
Market St OX20 1SX
e-mail: enquiries@feathers.co.uk
web: www.feathers.co.uk
dir: 8m from Oxford on A44, follow signs for Evesham & Blenheim Palace. In Woodstock take 2nd left into the town, hotel 20mtrs on left

The Feathers is an intimate and individual hotel formed from five 17th-century townhouses in a historic market town not far from Blenheim Palace. For grazing or a light meal you can eat in the bar or bistro, but the atmospheric restaurant is the main attraction, comprising three richly decorated interconnected rooms with wood-panelled walls, traditional fittings and elegantly appointed tables. The kitchen draws on the local larder for seasonal produce, preparing dishes with classical origins and a modern twist. Pickled courgette adds an extra dimension to a terrine of minestrone with home-made ciabatta, followed by a well-timed Kelmscott pork belly and tenderloin served with sweet potato. Finish with millefeuille of banana, vanilla mousse and banana ice cream.

Times 12.30-2.30/7-9.30, Closed D Sun

WOODSTOCK *Continued*

Macdonald Bear Hotel

◉◉ Modern British

Modern cooking in historic inn

☎ 0844 8799143
Park St OX20 1SZ
e-mail: bear@macdonald-hotels.co.uk
web: www.bearhotelwoodstock.co.uk
dir: Town centre, facing the market square

The Bear has been around for 800 years which makes it one of England's oldest coaching inns. With its ivy-clad exterior, it oozes old world charm and character. The smart restaurant is entirely in keeping with the antiquity of the building and has all the oak beams, stone walls and open fireplaces you would expect. Service is warm, relaxed and good humoured. The kitchen takes a modern direction on its seasonal, well-balanced menus, combining skill with quality ingredients. Ballotine of rabbit comes with pear chutney and apple purée among starters, and hand-dived scallops with garlic and coriander purée. Main courses extend to poached fillet of wild rainbow trout with chargrilled fennel and lemon butter, and slow-roasted belly of pork with roasted onion purée and green peppercorn sauce.

Chef Adrian Court **Owner** Macdonald Hotels
Times 12.30-2/7-9.30 **Prices** Fixed L 2 course £17-£25, Fixed D 3 course £20-£32, Starter £7-£12, Main £15-£32, Dessert £7-£10, Service optional **Wines** 70 bottles over £20, 18 bottles under £20, 12 by glass **Notes** Sunday L **Seats** 80, Pr/dining room 30 **Children** Portions, Menu **Parking** 45

RUTLAND

CLIPSHAM   Map 11 SK91

The Olive Branch

◉◉ British, European ☺

Stone-flagged gastro-pub showcasing the best local produce

☎ 01780 410355
Main St LE15 7SH
e-mail: rooms@theolivebranchpub.com
dir: 2m from A1 at Stretton junct, 5m N of Stamford

A village inn extending into a barn conversion, The Olive Branch is furnished with an eclectic mixture of antiques, French monastery pews, pine tables and open fires. The atmosphere throughout is relaxed and informal, with service provided by friendly and informative staff. There is a great emphasis on local produce here, some of which is available for sale: eggs, butter, breads and other baked goods, meats, sauces and dressings. Picnic hampers and gift boxes can also be provided. The menu offers an innovative modern take on traditional pub fare, with some European influences, as in shallot Tatin with smoked duck salad, or venison (from Clipsham Woods) casserole with juniper fondant potato and roast root vegetables.

Chef Sean Hope, Tim Luff **Owner** Sean Hope, Ben Jones
Times 12-2/7-9.30, Closed 26 Dec, 1 Jan, Closed L 31 Dec, Closed D 25 Dec **Prices** Fixed L 2 course fr £15.50, Starter £4.50-£9.50, Main £12.75-£22.50, Dessert £4.50-£6.95, Service optional, Groups min 12 service 10% **Wines** 20 bottles over £20, 25 bottles under £20, 8 by glass **Notes** Sunday L **Seats** 45, Pr/dining room 20 **Children** Portions, Menu **Parking** 15

OAKHAM   Map 11 SK80

Barnsdale Lodge Hotel

◉ Modern British

Attractively converted farmhouse hotel on the shores of Rutland Water

☎ 01572 724678
The Avenue, Rutland Water, North Shore LE15 8AH
e-mail: enquiries@barnsdalelodge.co.uk
dir: Turn off A1 at Stamford onto A606 to Oakham. Hotel 5m on right. (2m E of Oakham)

Originally a farmhouse, this attractive hotel still retains the 17th-century bread ovens and stone floors, which

blend well with the country-house style furnishings. Being built around a courtyard gives the hotel a series of dining rooms, plus the courtyard itself for alfresco meals in summer. The style of cooking is modern British with European influences and good use is made of seasonal, local ingredients. Expect starters such as trio of scallops, black pudding, broad beans and Colbert butter, followed by breast and confit leg of guinea fowl with roasted winter vegetables, and desserts like mulled wine poached pears and yogurt and honey pannacotta to finish.

Chef Richard Carruthers **Owner** The Hon Thomas Noel
Times 12-2.15/7-9.30 **Prices** Fixed L 2 course £12.95, Fixed D 3 course £27.50-£40, Starter £4.50-£7.95, Main £11.95-£21.95, Dessert £4.95-£5.95, Service added but optional 10% **Wines** 45 bottles over £20, 33 bottles under £20, 10 by glass **Notes** Sunday L, Vegetarian available, Civ Wed 100 **Seats** 120, Pr/dining room 50 **Children** Portions, Menu **Parking** 250

Hambleton Hall

◉◉◉◉ – *see opposite*

Nick's Restaurant at Lord Nelson's House

◉◉ Modern European V

Innovative cooking in an elegant setting full of character

☎ 01572 723199
11 Market Place LE15 6HR
e-mail: simon@nicksrestaurant
dir: Off A606 in town centre

Located in the corner of the town's market square, this medieval timber-framed restaurant with rooms is tastefully appointed with an abundance of period features. There are bold red walls in the comfortable lounge and large prints adorn the light mustard and red walls of the sumptuous dining room, where a huge original fireplace is the main focal point. The modern cooking demonstrates skill and technical ability with an eclectic style: a starter of crab and tarragon risotto with brown crab ice cream and parmesan velouté could be followed by roast turbot with buttered leek, butternut squash purée and a ravioli of scallop, or pan-fried venison with beetroot dauphinoise, smoked garlic, beetroot purée and chocolate jus. Dégustation and vegetarian dégustation menus also available.

Chef Dameon Clarke **Owner** Simon McEnery
Times 12-2.30/6-9, Closed 25-26 Dec, Closed Mon, Closed D Sun **Prices** Fixed L 2 course £16-£23, Fixed D 3 course £27.95-£35, Service optional **Wines** 22 bottles over £20, 13 bottles under £20, 9 by glass **Notes** Tasting menu available, Sunday L, Vegetarian menu **Seats** 45 **Children** Portions **Parking** 4

Hambleton Hall

OAKHAM Map 11 SK80

Modern British 📺 V 🍷 NOTABLE WINE LIST

Romantic retreat serving the best of English country-house cuisine

☎ 01572 756991
Hambleton LE15 8TH
e-mail: hotel@hambletonhall.com
web: www.hambletonhall.com
dir: 8m W of the A1 Stamford junct (A606), 3m E of Oakham

Set in sweeping landscaped grounds overlooking Rutland Water, Hambleton Hall remains the epitome of the English country-house hotel. Established in 1980 by Tim and Stefa Hart, Hambleton weaves its spell and bestows an immediate impression of relaxation and confidence that everything will run with absolute aplomb. All the sophisticated, traditional comforts are here, from deep-cushioned sofas and log fires to magazines to peruse in the spacious, elegant drawing room over aperitifs. The dining room is intimate and comfortable and comes dressed in warm traditional colours with crisp white linen, fresh flowers, heavy brocade drapes and oil paintings, enhanced by the lovely backdrop of the garden and lake. Service is professional and friendly and the wine list appropriately extensive, while chef Aaron Patterson's inspired cooking delivers a superb, subtly modern take on classic country-house cooking. His style echoes that of his

mentor, Raymond Blanc, in its focus on the finest quality produce, seasonality and clarity of flavour, together with the use of the freshest vegetables, herbs and salads from the hotel's own kitchen garden. Local game is a speciality, while luxury items pepper the sophisticated repertoire of fixed-price menus where technical excellence reigns supreme. The menu might start with ballotine of foie gras with spiced pineapple and pistachio nuts. Main courses may offer poached fillet of sea bass with tempura fried langoustines, hazelnuts and chervil root purée, or roast breast of Goosnargh duck with caramelised endive and white raisins. Finish with black Périgord truffle and white chocolate ice cream or chocolate and olive oil truffle with salted caramel, pistachios and baked banana.

Chef Aaron Patterson **Owner** Mr T Hart **Times** 12-1.30/7-9.30 **Prices** Fixed L 2 course fr £21.50, Fixed D 3 course £40-£50, Starter £16-£25, Main £34-£39, Dessert £13-£16, Service added but optional 12.5% **Wines** 375 bottles over £20, 10 bottles under £20, 10 by glass **Notes** Tasting menu available, Sunday L, Vegetarian menu, Dress restrictions, Smart dress, no jeans, T-shirts or trainers, Civ Wed 64 **Seats** 60, Pr/dining room 20 **Children** Portions, Menu **Parking** 36

The Lake Isle

◉◉ British, French

Quality food in a sleepy market town

☎ 01572 822951
16 High Street East LE15 9PZ
e-mail: info@lakeislehotel.co.uk
web: www.lakeislehotel.co.uk
dir: Located on main High St

Situated in the pretty market town of Uppingham, this hotel and restaurant was once a shop and still retains many of the original features, including panelled walls and mahogany shop fittings. These are complemented by the heavy wooden tables in the otherwise chic, up-to-date interior. Clean, simple and fresh flavours abound, with an emphasis on quality ingredients, and the menu changes regularly to make full use of local produce and seasonal fruit and vegetables. Typical dishes might be fine tartlet of sliced tomatoes and goat's cheese drizzled with pesto rosso sauce, followed by supreme of halibut baked on a bed of summer vegetables with a lemon and basil sauce. Finish with white chocolate pannacotta with poached peach and a peach and vanilla sorbet. Look out for the regular wine dinners.

Chef Stuart Mead **Owner** Richard & Janine Burton **Times** 12-2.30/7-9, Closed L Mon, Closed D Sun **Prices** Starter £4.25-£6.50, Main £12.95-£20, Dessert £5.25-£6.25, Service optional **Notes** Sunday L, Air con **Seats** 40, Pr/dining room 16 **Children** Portions **Parking** 7

Kings Arms Inn & Restaurant

◉ Modern British ◉

Traditional country inn with modern cooking

☎ 01572 737634
13 Top St LE15 8SE
e-mail: info@thekingsarms-wing.co.uk
dir: 1m off A6003, between Oakham and Uppingham

It may be a modern-style operation these days, but this popular, extended 17th-century village pub has all the charm and character of a traditional country inn with its open fires, low beams and flagstone floors. The recently refurbished dining room boasts improved lighting above tables and fresh new white, yellow and blue décor. The kitchen shows a commitment to fresh, quality produce with everything made in-house, while the lengthy repertoire takes a modern approach and plays to the gallery with something for everyone. Take a starter of confit Gressingham duck leg with spicy chorizo and five bean cassoulet, with a main course of cod loin baked in Chardonnay with mussels also catching the eye.

Chef James Goss **Owner** David, Gisa & James Goss **Times** 12-2.30/6.30-9, Closed Mon **Prices** Fixed L 2 course fr £10, Starter £4-£7.50, Main £8.50-£22, Dessert £5.75-£6.25, Service optional, Groups min 7 service 10% **Wines** 20 bottles over £20, 28 bottles under £20, 20 by glass **Notes** Sunday L, Vegetarian available **Seats** 30, Pr/dining room 24 **Children** Portions **Parking** 30

Old Vicarage Hotel and Restaurant

Modern European

Accomplished cooking in a one-time vicarage

☎ 01746 716497
WV15 5JZ
e-mail: admin@the-old-vicarage.demon.co.uk
dir: Off A454, approx 3.5m NE of Bridgnorth 5m S of Telford on A442 follow brown signs

This elegant Edwardian property is set in 2 acres of wooded farmland in a peaceful village location. The interior features fresh flowers and polished wood floors and tables, and the relaxing lounge is perfect for pre-dinner drinks. Lovely views of Shropshire countryside are afforded from the Orangery Restaurant, and service is as friendly and unobtrusive as the atmosphere. The highly accomplished, modern-focused kitchen is firmly driven by flavour and intelligent simplicity, which is entirely appropriate to the surroundings. This refreshing approach allows high quality produce to shine. The light lunch menu is a useful introduction to the Old Vicarage experience but, for the full effect, try house specialities from the dinner menu, such as a starter of pan-fried king scallops with a salad of French beans, tomato and truffles, and a main course of pan-fried gilthead bream with coconut and green curry jelly, vegetable spring rolls and coriander foam. Finish your meal with a dessert of warm cherry and almond clafoutis with basil ice cream, or raspberry cheesecake with orange and Drambuie jelly and vanilla ice cream. If you have room, the artisan cheeses from the trolley are not to be missed.

Chef Simon Diprose **Owner** Mr & Mrs D Blakstad **Times** 12-2.30/7-9.30, Closed L Mon Tue Sat (by reservation only), Closed D 24-26 Dec **Prices** Fixed L 3 course fr £29.50, Fixed D 3 course £45-£50, Tasting menu £55, Service included **Wines** 50 bottles over £20, 20 bottles under £20, 10 by glass **Notes** Sunday L,

Vegetarian available **Seats** 64, Pr/dining room 20 **Children** Portions, Menu **Parking** 30

SHROPSHIRE

BRIDGNORTH   Map 10 SO79

Old Vicarage Hotel and Restaurant

@@@ – *see opposite*

CHURCH STRETTON   Map 15 SO49

The Pound at Leebotwood

@ Modern British 🍴

Local produce cooked with flair in a modern, country-inn setting

☎ 01694 751477
SY6 6ND
e-mail: info@thepound.org.uk
web: www.thepound.org.uk
dir: On A49 9m S of Shrewsbury.

This former thatched roadside inn, and one of half-timbered Leebotwood's oldest buildings, has been sympathetically remodelled to offer a fresh, contemporary face within the traditional framework of its listed building. The stylish minimalist interior décor comes enlivened by modern artwork, subtle lighting and wood-block floors, while the bar is decked out with occasional seating and the open-plan dining area with polished-wood tables and its mix of modern and period seating. The kitchen's modern approach, with the occasional Mediterranean nod, is driven by quality local and seasonal produce and intelligent restraint; expect grilled breast of organic chicken with an olive oil, caper and lemon sauce served with sautéed new potatoes and seasonal vegetables.

Chef Wessel Van Yaarsveld **Owner** Paul & Barbara Brooks **Times** 12-2.30/6.30-9.30, Closed 25 & 26 Dec **Prices** Starter £4.95-£6.95, Main £7.95-£14.95, Dessert £4.95-£5.95, Service optional **Wines** 10 bottles over £20, 30 bottles under £20, 9 by glass **Notes** Food served all day Sat & Sun, Vegetarian available **Seats** 60 **Children** Portions **Parking** 60

The Studio

@ British, French 🍴

Food with imaginative flair in a former art studio

☎ 01694 722672
59 High St SY6 6BY
e-mail: info@thestudiorestaurant.net
web: www.thestudiorestaurant.net
dir: Off A49 to town, left at T-junct onto High Street, 300 yds on left

Decorative reminders of this restaurant's previous life as an artist's studio can be seen in an interesting array of art and ceramics, and the original paint-palette sign which still swings outside the building. A small, welcoming bar awaits within and a lovely patio garden, overlooking the Shropshire hills, offers alfresco dining on warm evenings. Modern, bistro-style food is the order of the day, and all dishes are created from carefully selected, local, seasonal produce, prepared with the classical and traditional skills of the husband-and-wife team. Picture roast rack of Shropshire lamb with an onion marmalade and goat's cheese tart and a thyme and red wine jus.

Chef Tony Martland **Owner** Tony & Sheila Martland **Times** Closed 2 wks Jan, 1 wk Apr, 1 wk Nov, Closed Sun-Tue, Closed L all week **Prices** Fixed D 3 course £26-£28, Service optional **Wines** 13 bottles over £20, 27 bottles under £20, 6 by glass **Notes** Fixed min price Wed-Fri, Max price Sat only, Vegetarian available, Dress restrictions, Smart casual **Seats** 34 **Children** Portions **Parking** On street parking available

HADNALL   Map 15 SJ52

Saracens at Hadnall

@ Modern British

Skilful cooking at an elegant restaurant with rooms

☎ 01939 210877
Shrewsbury Rd SY4 4AG
e-mail: reception@saracensathadnall.co.uk
dir: On A49 5m N of Shrewsbury

A Grade II listed building, the Saracens was originally a Georgian farmhouse, later a pub and today a smart restaurant with rooms. There are two dining rooms, the Georgian-style front room, with its polished-wood floor, panelled walls and stone fireplace, or the conservatory, which features a capped well. The kitchen deals in skilfully prepared fare, with the emphasis on quality, locally-sourced ingredients. Think pan-fried fillet of Welsh Black beef, with root vegetable mash, sautéed oyster mushrooms and a bacon and horseradish reduction, or pan-fried loin of Attingham Park venison, while an oven-baked apple with pecan and orange crumble and sweet sabayon might tempt at dessert. Children under 12 years not allowed at dinner Fridays and Saturdays.

Times 11.30-2.30/6.30-9.30, Closed Mon, Closed L Tue, Closed D Sun

IRONBRIDGE   Map 10 SJ60

Restaurant Severn

@@ British, French 🍴

Fine food to match the views in famous Ironbridge

☎ 01952 432233 & 510086
33 High St TF8 7AG
e-mail: ericbruce@talktalk.net
web: www.restaurantsevern.co.uk
dir: Please telephone for directions or check website

Following a career in top hotels (and a first venture, the Navigation Inn and Warehouse Restaurant near Oswestry), chef-patron Eric Bruce and wife Beb (who makes all the desserts and breads) have brought their innovative cooking to historic Ironbridge. Restaurant Severn is set in a Grade II listed converted cottage, its minimalist interior décor highlighting many retained features, including a wealth of oak beams, while subtle lighting and warm colours create an intimate atmosphere. Lacquered tables and stylish high-backed leather chairs provide the comforts, while service is suitably attentive and friendly. The cooking's modern approach, underpinned by classical French roots, is driven by well-sourced, fresh local seasonal ingredients, supplemented by produce from their own kitchen garden. Dishes are not over embellished and allow flavours to shine: Welsh lamb shank served with a sweet potato and rosemary sauce, or duo of Shropshire venison and Lord Forester Estate pheasant with sloe damson and Cognac sauce.

Chef Eric & Beb Bruce **Owner** Eric & Beb Bruce **Times** 12-2/6.30-9, Closed BHs, Closed Mon-Tue, Closed L Wed-Sat, Closed D Sun **Prices** Fixed D 3 course £23.95-£26.95, Service optional, Groups min 8 service 5% **Wines** 10 bottles over £20, 30 bottles under £20, 5 by glass **Notes** Midweek promotion Wed & Thu, Sunday L, Vegetarian available, Dress restrictions, Smart casual **Seats** 30 **Children** Portions **Parking** On street & car park opposite

La Bécasse

French 🖥 V 🐦

New and exciting addition to Ludlow's dining scene

☎ 01584 872325
17 Corve St SY8 1DA
e-mail: info@labecasse.co.uk
dir: Town centre, opposite side of rd to Feathers Hotel, bottom of hill.

Chef-restaurateur Alan Murchison, of L'ortolan restaurant (Shinfield, Berkshire) fame, bought Claude and Claire Bosi's much-acclaimed Hibiscus restaurant site back in 2007 (after they relocated Hibiscus to London's Mayfair) and renamed it La Bécasse (the Woodcock). From outside little seems to have changed at this one-time 17th-century coaching inn on the town's Corve Street, except a new sign perhaps, but those who knew the old Hibiscus will spot a few changes inside to this unassuming but stylish and sophisticated restaurant. Refurbishment has brought changes to the kitchen, and, out front, there's an additional small dining area to the rear with a bar upstairs. Stylish chairs and table appointments find their place alongside the retained oak panelling and exposed brick. Heading up the kitchen is Will Holland (previously head chef at L'ortolan) and there's continuity here as many of the brigade also worked there. His cooking takes a modern French line

with stylish dishes driven by prime seasonal produce, clean-cut flavours and balanced combinations; take Mortimer Forest venison loin wrapped in pancetta with whimberry preserve and sauce grand veneur, and to finish, perhaps a plum crumble soufflé served with vanilla ice cream. The fixed-price menu repertoire includes a value lunch option.

Chef Will Holland **Owner** Alan Murchison Restaurants Ltd
Times 12-2.30/6.45-9.30, Closed Xmas, New Year, Closed Mon, Closed L Tue, Closed D Sun **Prices** Fixed L 2 course £20, Tasting menu £55, Service optional **Wines** 123 bottles over £20, 4 bottles under £20, 12 by glass **Notes** Tasting menu 7 courses, Sunday L, Vegetarian menu **Seats** 36 **Children** Portions **Parking** 6

LLANFAIR WATERDINE Map 9 SO27

The Waterdine

◎◎ Modern British

Charming countryside dining

☎ 01547 528214
LD7 1TU

The Waterdine is a former drover's inn, dating back over 400 years. Set in wonderful Shropshire countryside, and with the River Teme running at the bottom of the garden, it's full of charm and character. The main restaurant has two different areas, The Garden Room and The Taproom - the oldest part of the building. Friendly, efficient hospitality from the owners puts you at your ease immediately. Here you'll find an experienced chef making great use of quality local produce, including fruit and vegetables from the inn's own garden. The menu is seasonal and changes regularly. Expect starters like fillet of sea bass on marinated cucumber with basil sauce, and mains such as fillet of beef on a crisp rösti with Cognac-marinated mushrooms and wilted spinach. Finish with blackcurrant and almond tart.

Times 12-1.45/7-9, Closed 1 wk spring, 1 wk autumn, Closed D Sun, Mon

LUDLOW Map 10 SO57

La Bécasse

◎◎◎ – *see opposite*

The Clive Bar and Restaurant with Rooms

◎◎ Modern British 🍴

Bright, modern restaurant in former farmhouse

☎ 01584 856565 & 856665
Bromfield SY8 2JR
e-mail: info@theclive.co.uk
web: www.theclive.co.uk
dir: 2m N of Ludlow on A49, near Ludlow Golf Club, racecourse and adjacent to Ludlow food centre

This 18th-century farmhouse was once home to Clive of India, who now gives his name to the smart restaurant with rooms that occupies the property today. It's an airy modern eatery, think light wood, large windows and sparkling glassware, with a wide-ranging contemporary menu that suits the setting. Modern British dishes predominate, although there's the occasional nod to the

Mediterranean and farther flung climes: you might start with Shropshire ham hock and parsley terrine with apple and cider chutney for example; then move on to lightly spiced roast monkfish tails with vegetable pilaf and coconut curry sauce, or a 28-day aged rib of Bridgnorth steak with oyster mushrooms, dauphinoise potatoes and a pink peppercorn sauce. Desserts are pleasingly decadent and might include warm pistachio and cherry crumble with organic butterscotch ice cream.

Chef Soames Whittingham **Owner** Paul & Barbara Brooks
Times 12-3/6.30-9.30, Closed 25-26 Dec **Prices** Starter £4.95-£8.95, Main £7.95-£17.95, Dessert £4.95-£5.95, Service optional **Wines** 30 bottles over £20, 38 bottles under £20, 9 by glass **Notes** Sunday L, Vegetarian available **Seats** 90 **Children** Portions **Parking** 80

The Feathers Hotel

◎ Modern British, French

Historic building with up-to-the-minute food

☎ 01584 875261
The Bull Ring SY8 1AA
e-mail: enquiries@feathersatludlow.co.uk
web: www.feathersatludlow.co.uk
dir: The hotel is in the centre of town

The hotel, described by Nikolaus Pevsner in The Buildings of England as 'that prodigy of timber-frame houses' and more recently in The New York Times as 'the most handsome inn in the world', is internationally recognised for its beautiful Jacobean architecture and medieval heritage. The kitchen balances traditional and innovative contemporary cooking, using fresh local produce, in dishes such as pan-seared scallops with cauliflower and vanilla purée, honey-roast duck with leek and pearl onion tarte Tatin and fondant potato; and chilled melon and pear soup with almond tuile and elderflower sorbet.

Chef Martin Jones **Owner** Ceney Developments
Times 12.30-2/6.30-9.30, Closed L Mon-Sat
Prices Starter £4.95-£7.50, Main £12.95-£19.95, Dessert £4.95-£6.95, Service optional, Groups min 12 service 10% **Wines** 25 bottles over £20, 26 bottles under £20, 10 by glass **Notes** Vegetarian available, Dress restrictions, Smart casual, Civ Wed 80 **Seats** 60, Pr/dining room 30 **Children** Portions, Menu **Parking** 36

Fishmore Hall

◎◎ Modern European V 🍴

Imaginative cooking in smartly renovated Georgian-house hotel

☎ 01584 875148
Fishmore Rd SY8 3DP
e-mail: reception@fishmorehall.co.uk
dir: A49 from Shrewsbury, follow signs for Ludlow & Bridgnorth. 1st left towards Bridgnorth, at next rdbt turn left onto Fishmore Rd. Hotel 0.5m on right after golf course

Set in a rural area within easy reach of the town centre, this Palladian-styled Georgian house-turned-smart-hotel, opened back in October 2007, has been sympathetically renovated and extended. The contemporarily styled minimalist interiors enhance its many retained period features, including polished-wood floors, ceiling roses and moulded cornices. The restaurant is bright and airy with unrivalled views of Clee Hill and the Shropshire countryside, while service is professional, well informed and friendly. The kitchen exudes skill and imagination, driven by quality local seasonal produce (the majority sourced within a 30-mile radius) with suppliers admirably listed with the menu, while seafood and fish is from the Isle of Skye or Brixham. Accuracy, flair and skilled presentation come without over-embellishment, intelligently allowing flavours to shine. Expect dishes like a loin of venison served with marjoram gnocchi, blackberries and liquorice, or perhaps line-caught sea bass with thyme-crushed potatoes, sweet-and-sour onions and a hazelnut foam.

Chef Marc Hardiman **Owner** Laura Penman
Times 12-2.30/7-9.30 **Wines** 100 bottles over £20, 8 bottles under £20, 11 by glass **Notes** Gourmand menu £65, Sunday L, Vegetarian menu, Civ Wed 60, Air con **Seats** 60, Pr/dining room 20 **Children** Portions **Parking** 36

Mr Underhills

◎◎ Modern International 🍴

Unpretentious dining on the riverbank

☎ 01584 874431
Dinham Weir SY8 1EH
dir: From Castle Square: with castle in front, turn immediately left, proceed round castle, turn right before bridge, restaurant on left

This is a very English setting: right on the banks of the River Teme, lush with greenery and over-hanging trees, the sound of water flowing over the weir and the towers of Ludlow Castle looming up behind. The pretty courtyard garden of this attractive restaurant with rooms offers an ideal vantage point, as do the bright-and-airy dining room's large picture windows, allowing views over both garden and the river. Dinner is a fixed-price menu of six courses as well as amuse-bouche, coffee and petits fours, and the only choice to be made is at dessert stage. Chef-patron Chris Bradley enquires about dietary

Continued

LUDLOW *Continued*

requirements or dislikes when booking. His style of cooking is intelligently simple, concentrating on bringing the best out of prime, seasonal ingredients, the emphasis on freshness and natural flavours rather than cutting-edge cuisine. A cone of marinated salmon kicks things off, followed by pavé of halibut on a bed of julienne vegetables, then fillet of local venison with a fine combination of butternut squash and black pudding. Service is relaxed and friendly.

Chef Christopher Bradley **Owner** Christopher & Judy Bradley **Times** Closed 1 wk Jan, 1 wk Jul, Closed Mon-Tue, Closed L all week **Prices** Tasting menu £45-£52, Service optional **Wines** 90 bottles over £20, 35 bottles under £20, 12 by glass **Notes** Fixed D 7 courses, Tasting menus only, Dress restrictions, Smart casual **Seats** 30 **Children** Min 8 yrs, Portions **Parking** 7

Overton Grange Country House & Restaurant

◉◉ Modern British, European

Impressive cuisine on the outskirts of Ludlow

☎ 01584 873500 & 0845 4761000
Old Hereford Rd SY8 4AD
e-mail: info@overtongrangehotel.com
web: www.overtongrangehotel.com
dir: M5 junct 5. On B4361 approx 1.5m from Ludlow towards Leominster

Standing in mature grounds on the outskirts of Ludlow, Overton Grange is popular with locals and gastro-tourists alike and offers lovely views over the Shropshire countryside from the handsome Edwardian house. The contemporary dining room is in two parts at the rear, with light flooding through large windows dressed with Roman blinds. Aubergine and cream is the modern colour theme, tables are elegantly laid, chairs are high-backed suede and service highly polished and professional. Classically-based, French-style cuisine uses locally-sourced produce where possible. A feuillette of langoustine with buttered baby spinach and crustacé coulis is a good choice for starters, followed by paupiette of wild sea bass with red mullet farce. An extensive, well-chosen wine list offers the perfect accompaniment, as does a pre-meal stroll on the lawns in summer.

Chef Christophe Dechaux-Blanc **Owner** Indigo Hotels Ltd **Times** 12-2.30/7-10, Closed 27 Dec-7 Jan **Prices** Fixed L 2 course £17.50-£22.50, Fixed D 4 course £32.50-£38.50, Tasting menu £59.50, Starter £7.50-£12.50, Main £12.50-£22.50, Dessert £7.50-£12.50, Service optional, Groups min 10 service 10% **Wines** 150 bottles over £20, 20 bottles under £20, 12 by glass **Notes** Sunday L, Vegetarian available, Dress restrictions, Smart casual, Civ Wed 50 **Seats** 40, Pr/dining room 24 **Children** Min 6 yrs **Parking** 50

The Roebuck Inn

◉◉ Modern

Elegant, minimalist setting for imaginative, French-biased cooking

☎ 01584 711230
Brimfield SY8 4NE
e-mail: info@theroebuckludlow.co.uk
dir: Just off A49 between Ludlow & Leominster

This 15th-century former rural village inn has been sympathetically remodelled and offers comfortable accommodation and a choice of formal and casual dining. The lounge bar retains many original features including exposed beams, and is decked out in rustic style with polished-oak tables and tapestry-upholstered chairs. By contrast, the separate dining room and bar crank up the ante with contemporary spin, the elegant minimalist styling enhanced by modern art and furnishings, crisp linen and subtle lighting. Chef-patron Olivier Bossut (ex Ludlow's Overton Grange) shows his pedigree here, the imaginative repertoire's modern approach intertwined with his classical French roots and fresh, quality seasonal produce. Dishes are intelligently not over embellished, with skilful cooking and clear flavours to the fore. Expect classic favourites like coq au vin or cassoulet Toulousain to rub shoulders with a rack of lamb served with oriental couscous and smoked garlic sauce, and perhaps a warm chocolate fondant and pistachio sauce finish.

Times 12-2.30/7-9, Closed Xmas, Closed D Sun

MARKET DRAYTON **Map 15 SJ63**

The Cottage Restaurant at Ternhill Farm House

◉ Modern International ✋

Local fresh produce served in cottage-style restaurant

☎ 01630 638984
Ternhill TF9 3PX
e-mail: info@ternhillfarm.co.uk
dir: On x-rds of A41 & A53, 3m W of Market Drayton

Set in an acre of gardens, Ternhill is a Grade II listed Georgian farmhouse full of character with oak beams and floors. The cottage-style restaurant has well-spaced rustic tables, high-backed leather chairs and a huge inglenook fireplace. Cooking is modern British in style with international influences and lots of fresh seasonal produce. A good variety of dishes includes peppered beef salad (pan-fried strips of English beef fillet seasoned with cracked black pepper, finished with a balsamic dressing and served on a croûton with mixed salad leaves), and herb-crusted fillet of sea bass with a chilli and toasted sesame dressing.

Chef Michael Abraham **Owner** Michael & Joanne Abraham **Times** Closed Sun & Mon, Closed L all week **Prices** Fixed D 3 course £14.95, Starter £4.50-£6.25, Main £9.95-£16.95, Dessert £4.50-£5.95, Service optional

Wines 4 bottles over £20, 20 bottles under £20, 6 by glass **Notes** Fixed D Tue-Thu, Vegetarian available, Dress restrictions, Smart casual **Seats** 20, Pr/dining room 12 **Children** Before 8pm **Parking** 16

Goldstone Hall

◉◉ Modern British

Modern cooking amidst period charm

☎ 01630 661202
Goldstone TF9 2NA
e-mail: enquiries@goldstonehall.com
web: www.goldstonehall.com
dir: From A529, 4m S of Market Drayton, follow signs for Goldstone Hall Hotel

This comfortable, family-run country-house hotel in an elegant Georgian property is set in extensive and well-maintained gardens and woodland, and comes complete with original beams, exposed timbers and open fires. Follow in the footsteps of PG Wodehouse and enjoy a glass of Pimms in the garden, before going through to dinner in the oak-panelled dining room, where service is relaxed but attentive. The carefully evolving menus are based on seasonal and local produce, notably home-grown herbs and vegetables from the well-stocked walled garden. Fixed-price dinner menus and the light 'Upper Crust' supper choice list simple, contemporary British dishes. Try grilled fillet of 32-day matured South Yorkshire beef with port wine sauce and wild mushrooms, or grilled sea bass with chargrilled fennel, palm heart salad and lemon vinaigrette.

Chef Andrew Keeling **Owner** Mr J Cushing & Mrs H Ward **Times** 12-2.30/7.30-11 **Prices** Fixed L 2 course £18.50-£26.50, Starter fr £6.50, Main £12-£20, Dessert fr £6.50, Service included **Wines** 36 bottles under £20, 9 by glass **Notes** Sunday L, Vegetarian available, Dress restrictions, Smart casual, Civ Wed 100 **Seats** 40, Pr/dining room 20 **Children** Portions **Parking** 40

Rosehill Manor

◉ Modern, Traditional

Traditional country-house style restaurant

☎ 01630 638532 & 637000
Rosehill, Ternhill TF9 2JF
dir: On A41 4m from Market Drayton

Privately owned and personally run, this charming manor house hotel is set in 1.5 acres of mature gardens. Parts of it date back to the 16th century and the bar has lovely exposed beams reflecting the character of the original house. The restaurant enjoys garden views, an open fire in winter and a relaxing atmosphere. The emphasis is on a mix of traditional and modern cooking using freshly prepared ingredients, complemented by professional service. Dishes from the seasonal menu include smoked salmon and trout mousse served with melba toast and cucumber in crème fraîche, followed by pan-fried fillet of beef on a spring onion and red pepper potato cake with a port jus and mangetout.

Chef Jane Eardley **Owner** Mr & Mrs P Eardley
Times 12-2/7-9.30, Closed L Mon-Sat, Closed D Sun
Prices Food prices not confirmed for 2009. Please
telephone for details. **Wines** 7 bottles over £20, 12
bottles under £20, 4 by glass **Notes** Dress restrictions,
Smart casual, Civ Wed 100 **Seats** 70, Pr/dining room 30
Children Portions **Parking** 60

MUCH WENLOCK — Map 10 SO69

Raven Hotel

◉ British, Mediterranean

Fresh cooking in historic location

☎ 01952 727251
30 Barrow St TF13 6EN
e-mail: enquiry@ravenhotel.com
dir: 10m SW from Telford on A4169, 12m SE from
Shrewsbury. In town centre

This town-centre hotel brings together several 15th-
century almshouses and a medieval great hall, with a
17th-century coaching inn at its heart. The cosy warren
of rooms are dotted with oak beams and open fires, and
the friendly and intimate restaurant looks out over an
inner courtyard where you can dine alfresco on warm
summer evenings. Local, seasonal produce and fresh
ingredients are key to the cooking here, which is honest
and not over ambitious. Classic dishes are given modern
European interpretations along the lines of pan-fried
Morville beef with red onion and olive chutney and port
wine jus, and whole grilled Brixham plaice with a chive
and caper butter.

Times 12-2.30/6.45-9.30, Closed 25 Dec

MUNSLOW — Map 10 SO58

Crown Country Inn

◉◉ British 🌱

Historic, charming inn with modern, sophisticated food

☎ 01584 841205
SY7 9ET
e-mail: info@crowncountryinn.co.uk
dir: On B4368 between Craven Arms & Much Wenlock

This impressive three storey pastel-coloured, half-
timbered Tudor inn is full of character and charm, with
stone floors, exposed beams and logs blazing in inglenook
fireplaces in the winter. But that's only half of it, as this
was once a 'Hundred House' where the infamous Judge
Jeffries presided, passing sentence on local villains.
Today though, the only crime would be not to sample
chef-patron Richard Arnold's accomplished cuisine in the
Corvedale restaurant. A Master Chef of Great Britain,
Richard's cooking oozes pedigree and deals in quality
local produce and clear flavours. Take crispy slow-cooked
belly of Muckleton Gloucestershire Old Spot pork with
rosti potatoes and onion marmalade and do save room
for the likes of vanilla pannacotta with poached oranges,
mango coulis and bitter orange ice cream.

Chef Richard Arnold **Owner** Richard & Jane Arnold
Times 12-2/6.45-9, Closed Xmas, Closed Mon, Closed D
Sun **Prices** Fixed L 2 course £14.95, Starter £4.75-£7.50,
Main £11.95-£16.50, Dessert £4.95, Service included
Wines 13 bottles over £20, 29 bottles under £20, 5 by
glass **Notes** Sunday L, Vegetarian available **Seats** 65, Pr/
dining room 42 **Children** Portions **Parking** 20

NORTON — Map 10 SJ70

Hundred House Hotel

◉◉ British, European

**Historic backdrop and quirky charm meets modern
cuisine**

☎ 01952 730353
Bridgnorth Rd TF11 9EE
e-mail: reservation@hundredhouse.co.uk
web: www.hundredhouse.co.uk
dir: Midway between Telford & Bridgnorth on A442. In
centre of Norton village

The oldest part of this primarily Georgian former
coaching inn dates back as far as the 14th century and
was used as a courthouse. Stained glass panels on the
front door declaring 'Temperance Hall' suggest this

building has had a long and interesting life, and these
days it is a friendly, family-run hotel set in pretty grounds
complete with herb and flower gardens. Inside it is rich
with original features, including exposed beams, open
fires, quality rustic furnishings and memorabilia, and a
warren of formal or informal rooms for dining. Service is
friendly and well informed and the food essentially
modern British with some European touches. Expect
fresh, well sourced produce and clear flavours in dishes
such as rich and spicy venison terrine to start, followed
by breast and confit of Hereford duck with orange sauce
and black pudding.

Times 12-2.30/6-10, Closed D 26 Dec

OSWESTRY — Map 15 SJ22

Best Western Wynnstay Hotel

◉◉ Modern European

Modern cooking in elegant period-style surroundings

☎ 01691 655261
Church St SY11 2SZ
e-mail: info@wynnstayhotel.com
dir: In centre of town, opposite the church

Dating from 1727, this listed Georgian property was once
a coaching inn and posting house, and surrounds a
unique 200-year-old crown bowling green. The hotel's
elegant Four Seasons Restaurant comes decorated in
pastel shades along with hues of yellow and gold, backed
by equally smartly turned-out staff who provide suitably
attentive, professional and friendly service. A mixture of
traditional dishes with modern interpretations
incorporating European influences is the kitchen's style,
supported by good use of the best available produce, as
much as possible locally sourced. Try seared scallops
with crispy pancetta and toasted pine kernels to start,
followed by a main course of pan-fried loin of cod,
cannellini beans and fire-roasted tomatoes, and to finish,
maybe iced berry parfait with berry compôte and tuile
biscuit.

Chef Ecky Griffiths **Owner** Mr N Woodward
Times 12-2/7-9.30, Closed 25 Dec, Closed D Sun
Prices Fixed L 2 course fr £14.50, Starter £4.50-£6.50,
Main £9.95-£18.50, Dessert £4.95-£6.95, Service
optional **Wines** 20 bottles over £20, 36 bottles under £20,
7 by glass **Notes** Sunday L, Vegetarian available, Dress
restrictions, Smart casual, Civ Wed 90, Air con **Seats** 46,
Pr/dining room 200 **Children** Portions, Menu **Parking** 80

OSWESTRY *Continued*

Pen-y-Dyffryn Country Hotel

⊛⊛ Modern British

Quality cooking in a hillside haven

☎ 01691 653700
Rhydycroesau SY10 7JD
e-mail: stay@peny.co.uk
dir: 3m W of Oswestry on B4580

Built as a rectory in 1845, this alluring stone property stands amid lush grounds in a stunning valley, with glorious views of rolling countryside. There's a homely feel about the place, with its real fires and comfortable lounges. In the intimate dining room, with huge south-facing sash windows, the fixed-price dinner menu offers a handful of options at each course. In line with the kitchen's commitment to sourcing quality ingredients, dishes are prepared from fresh local produce, much of it organic. Particularly impressive dishes include best end of Welsh lamb with apricot and orange couscous, minted natural yogurt with honey, or pan-fried king scallops, cauliflower and spinach risotto and parmesan tuile.

Chef David Morris **Owner** MJM & AA Hunter **Times** Closed 20 Dec–21 Jan, Closed L all week **Prices** Fixed D 3 course £35, Service optional **Wines** 30 bottles over £20, 40 bottles under £20, 3 by glass **Notes** Vegetarian available **Seats** 25 **Children** Min 3 yrs, Portions, Menu **Parking** 18

Sebastian's Hotel & Restaurant

⊛⊛ French

Relaxed, personally-run outfit with accomplished French fare

☎ 01691 655444
45 Willow St SY11 1AQ
e-mail: sebastian.rest@virgin.net
dir: Telephone for directions

A former merchant's house dating back to the 16th century is the setting for this privately-owned and personally-run small hotel. As you'd expect, the place exudes period charm and character, with original features like exposed beams and oak panelling in its comfortable lounge, bar and popular bistro-style restaurant. Here, smart high-backed leather chairs come with linen-clothed tables, while walls are adorned with plenty of pictures. Traditional French cooking is the kitchen's stock in trade, delivering skilfully prepared, balanced-flavoured dishes that utilise quality ingredients on a repertoire of sensibly compact, fixed-price, weekly-changing market menus and monthly-changing carte. Start with fillet of red mullet on a bed of spicy couscous with red pepper coulis, and follow with iced banana parfait with pistachio praline, caramelised bananas and watermelon sorbet.

Chef Mark Sebastian Fisher, Richard Jones **Owner** Mark & Michelle Fisher **Times** Closed 25-26 Dec, 1 Jan, Closed Sun-Mon, Closed L all week **Wines** 16 bottles over £20, 38 bottles under £20, 6 by glass **Notes** Fixed D 5 courses £37.50, Vegetarian available **Seats** 35 **Children** Portions **Parking** 25 **Parking** Street parking

---

SHREWSBURY Map 15 SJ41

Albright Hussey Manor Hotel & Restaurant

⊛ Modern British 🖐

Enchanting, historic manor with punchy food

☎ 01939 290571 & 290523
Ellesmere Rd SY4 3AF
e-mail: info@albrighthussey.co.uk
dir: On A528, 2m from centre of Shrewsbury

This moated, timbered manor dates from 1524 and stands in landscaped gardens with country views. Although sympathetically renovated, modernised and extended over the years, the restaurant remains full of original character with a wealth of oak beams, panelling and leaded windows, with some quirky nooks and crannies providing plenty of privacy. The cooking style is an imaginative blend of traditional and modern with a strong emphasis on quality local ingredients. Simply presented dishes may include rump of Shropshire yearling lamb with honey and rosemary-glazed root vegetables and a robust marjoram jus, and to finish, perhaps a sloe gin and ginger nut brûlée.

Chef Michel Nijsten **Owner** Franco, Vera & Paul Subbiani **Times** 12/10 **Prices** Fixed L 2 course £12-£20, Fixed D 3 course fr £24.95, Starter £5.95-£14, Main £12.50-£22.50, Dessert £5.95-£8.50, Service optional, Groups min 6 service 10% **Wines** 53 bottles over £20, 43 bottles under £20, 5 by glass **Notes** Sunday L, Dress restrictions, No jeans, trainers or T-shirts, Civ Wed 200 **Seats** 80, Pr/dining room 40 **Children** Portions **Parking** 100

Mercure Albrighton Hall

⊛⊛ International

Notable food in formal setting

☎ 0870 1942129
Albrighton SY4 3AG

This former ancestral home dates back to 1630 and is set in 15 acres of attractive gardens. An established hotel currently undergoing extensive refurbishment, it boasts a well equipped health and fitness centre and its elegant public rooms feature rich oak panelling and a long gallery-style dining room. Well dressed and well spaced tables make for a formal setting, although service is friendly. The accomplished cooking is classically based, although contemporary flourishes appear in starters like crab and chive risotto with poached hen's egg, or a main

---

course of pan-fried sea bream with tiger prawn beignets and saffron cream. Desserts are a particular strength and could include rich dark chocolate mousse with griottine cherries and toffee sauce, or walnut and dark chocolate brownie with chocolate orange sauce.

Times 7am-9.45pm

Mytton & Mermaid Hotel

⊛⊛ Modern British V 🖐

Historic riverside inn serving contemporary cuisine

☎ 01743 761220
Atcham SY5 6QG
e-mail: admin@myttonandmermaid.co.uk
dir: Just outside Shrewsbury on the B4380 (old A5). Opposite Attingham Park

This Grade II listed hotel enjoys an enviable local reputation for the quality of its food. Located within easy reach of Shrewsbury, the ivy-clad building dates back to the early 18th century and offers pretty views across the River Severn. Its brasserie restaurant is a convivial place to dine, furnished with antique oak tables set with candles and fresh flowers. A list of nearby suppliers on the menu shows the commitment to local produce. Pan-seared scallops are among typical starters, served with cauliflower purée, apple salad and cumin velouté, while mains might include pan-fried fillet of rare breed beef with parmesan and thyme mash, buttered spinach, watercress purée and wild mushroom jus, or roast saddle of juniper-spiced venison with celeriac purée, fondant potato, Savoy cabbage and pancetta casserole and gin and sloe berry jus.

Chef Adrian Badland **Owner** Mr & Mrs Ditella **Times** 11.30-2.30/6.30-10, Closed 25 Dec, Closed D 26 Dec, 1 Jan **Prices** Food prices not confirmed for 2009. Please telephone for details. **Wines** 26 bottles over £20, 30 bottles under £20, 12 by glass **Notes** Sunday L, Vegetarian menu, Civ Wed 90 **Seats** 100, Pr/dining room 12 **Children** Portions, Menu **Parking** 80

Rowton Castle Hotel

◉ Modern British

Fine dining in a superbly renovated 17th-century castle

☎ 01743 884044
Halfway House SY5 9EP
e-mail: post@rowtoncastle.com
dir: From Birmingham take M6 west. Follow M54 & A5 to Shrewsbury. Continue on A5 and exit at 6th rdbt. Take A458 to Welshpool. Rowton Castle 4m on right

Retaining many of its original features, including a handsome carved oak fireplace, this sympathetically restored 17th-century castle stands in 17 acres on the site of a Roman fort. Oak panelling and velvet chairs add to the warm and intimate ambience in the Cedar Restaurant, where a seasonal menu that utilises fresh local produce is offered. Accurate modern British cooking reveals a terrine of salmon and cod mousse with avocado and walnut salad, a tender, well-timed duck breast served with a rich chorizo and butterbean casserole, and a delicious lemon syllabub with a blueberry compôte for dessert.

Times 12-2/7-9.30

TELFORD   Map 10 SJ60

Best Western Valley Hotel & Chez Maws Restaurant

◉◉ Modern British V

Imaginative menus in historic surroundings

☎ 01952 432247
TF8 7DW
e-mail: info@thevalleyhotel.co.uk
dir: From M6 on to M54, take junct 6 and follow A5223 to Ironbridge for 4m. At mini island turn right, hotel 80 yds on left

Situated in the World Heritage site of Ironbridge, this Grade II listed Georgian building sits on the banks of the River Severn, surrounded by stunning parkland. Once the home of the Maws family who manufactured ceramic tiles, the hotel features fine examples of their craft and the restaurant is named after them. An adjacent bar leads on to the patio, while the bright, contemporary-designed restaurant is a stylish venue, with high-backed chairs and well-spaced tables complemented by friendly and efficient service. Quality local and seasonal ingredients speak for themselves in imaginative daily-changing menus. A variety of dishes with British and continental influences include pan-seared red mullet with black pudding, creamed potatoes and fresh pea velouté, or braised blade of Welsh Black beef with sautéed Lyonnaise potatoes, spinach and bourguignon sauce.

Chef Barry Workman **Owner** Philip & Leslie Casson
Times 12-2/7-9.30, Closed 26 Dec-2 Jan, Closed L Sat & Sun **Prices** Fixed L 2 course fr £14.50, Fixed D 3 course fr £22, Starter £4.95-£7, Main £11.95-£19.50, Dessert £4.75-£6.50, Service optional **Wines** 2 bottles over £20,

27 bottles under £20, 7 by glass **Notes** Vegetarian menu, Dress restrictions, Smart casual, Civ Wed 120, Air con **Seats** 50, Pr/dining room 30 **Children** Portions, Menu **Parking** 100

Hadley Park House

◉ Modern British ✋

Conservatory restaurant offering modern cuisine

☎ 01952 677269
TF1 6QJ
e-mail: info@hadleypark.co.uk
web: www.hadleypark.co.uk
dir: M54 junct 5 take A5 Rampart Way, at rdbt take A442 towards Hortonwood, over double rdbt, next rdbt take 2nd exit, hotel at end of lane

Built by Thomas Telford's chief engineer, this Georgian mansion has an airy conservatory dining room complemented by a traditional oak-panelled bar. Modern cooking with an Australian twist is reflected in a good choice of dishes prepared from locally sourced ingredients. Options from the seasonal menu include good quality, fresh seared scallops, tomato and cucumber salsa to start, followed by seared Moroccan spiced yellow fin tuna with couscous and fennel salad, or perhaps Szechuan spiced duck breast with spring greens, honey and soy dressing. Steamed chocolate pudding with chocolate sauce and ice cream is an indulgent way to end the meal.

Chef Tim Wesley **Owner** Mark & Geraldine Lewis
Times 12-2/7-9.30, Closed L Sat (subject to availability), Closed D Sun (subject to demand) **Prices** Starter £4.65-£7.95, Main £12.95-£19.95, Dessert £5.50 **Wines** 18 bottles over £20, 28 bottles under £20, 8 by glass **Notes** Sunday L, Vegetarian available, Dress restrictions, Smart casual, Civ Wed 80, Air con **Seats** 80, Pr/dining room 12 **Children** Portions, Menu **Parking** 40

SOMERSET

BATH   Map 4 ST76

Bailbrook House Hotel

◉ Modern British

Relaxed dining in contemporary surroundings

☎ 01225 855100
Eveleigh Av, London Road West BA1 7JD
e-mail: bbridgeman@hilwoodresorts.com
dir: M4 junct 18, A46 towards Bath continue for 8m. Take slip rd signed Bath Centre, left onto the A4, Bailbrook Lodge is 200m on left

The contemporary restaurant at Bailbrook House has a light and airy feel with warm modern décor, and both the atmosphere and service are friendly and relaxed. Fresh local produce is delivered daily and all the dishes are hand made. The style of cooking is modern British, with good use of herbs and spices to produce vibrant, memorable flavours. House favourites are grilled fillet mignon with mushroom fricassée, fondant potato and baby vegetables, and Cotswold Bampton chicken with truffle mash, fine beans and rosemary oil dressing. Vegetarians might plump for red onion tarte Tatin with petit salad.

Times 12.30-2.30/7-9.30, Closed 24-26 Dec

Barcelo Combe Grove Manor Hotel

◉ International

Georgian country-house hotel dining

☎ 01225 834644
Brassknocker Hill, Monkton Combe BA2 7HS
e-mail: julianebbutt@combegrovemanor.com
dir: Telephone for directions

Set in over 80 acres of gardens, this delightful hotel has magnificent views and a wealth of leisure and therapy treatments to tempt guests. The Cellars Bistro and Bar (open for lunch and dinner daily) is located in the basement with adjoining terrace and gardens where guests can dine alfresco in summer. The main restaurant, the elegant Georgian Rooms with its high ceiling and large windows and notable countryside views, offers finer dining in a more traditional style. The menu includes the likes of Scottish smoked salmon, warm blinis, lemon and caviar crème fraîche, followed by guinea fowl supreme with mashed potato cake, braised endive and lemongrass jus, with raspberry and white chocolate cheesecake and poached kumquats to finish.

Times 12-2/7-9.30, Closed Mon-Wed, Closed L Thu-Sat, Closed D Sun

The Bath Priory Hotel, Restaurant & Spa

◉◉◉ – see page 378

The Bath Priory Hotel, Restaurant & Spa

BATH Map 4 ST76

Modern French 🖥 🕙

Intimate country-house restaurant with highly innovative cooking

☎ 01225 331922
Weston Rd BA1 2XT
e-mail: mail@thebathpriory.co.uk
web: www.thebathpriory.co.uk
dir: Please telephone for directions or see website

Set on a tree-lined residential road behind high walls, you'll find all the trappings of a country-house retreat at this Gothic-style Bath-stone mansion set in 4 acres of impeccably maintained gardens. Although only a few minutes from the city, this tranquil place is enhanced further by the luxurious and sophisticated style. A collection of oil paintings adorns the walls, there are deep sofas and roaring winter fires, and yet the mood is thoroughly relaxed with a friendly but professional approach from staff. The intimate, formal restaurant continues the theme, with white-clothed tables, deep burgundy and gold soft furnishings, high ceilings and views over the gardens. The kitchen, under chef Chris Horridge (ex Le Manoir aux Quat' Saisons, and appearing on BBC Two's 'Great British Menu' programme in 2008), shows pedigree, delivering highly innovative dishes created and presented with imagination and flair. Tip-top

ingredients, interesting combinations (with the focus on nutrition), clean flavours and high skill deliver on the contemporary French repertoire. Perhaps warm John Dory slow-poached in rape oil with pea purée and mace, and to finish, a lemon verbena crème brûlée with kifir sorbet. A beautifully presented extensive wine list offers good tasting notes.

Chef Chris Horridge **Owner** Mr A Brownsword **Times** 12-1.45/7-9.45 **Prices** Food prices not confirmed for 2009. Please telephone for details. **Wines** 180 bottles over £20, 60 bottles under £20, 12 by glass **Notes** Tasting menu 8 courses, Sunday L, Vegetarian available, Dress restrictions, No jeans, T-shirts or trainers, Civ Wed 64 **Seats** 64, Pr/dining room 64 **Children** Portions, Menu **Parking** 40

BATH *Continued*

Cavendish Restaurant

⊛⊛ Modern British 🍴

Georgian splendour meets highly creative cooking

☎ 01225 787960 & 787963
Dukes Hotel, Great Pulteney St BA2 4DN
e-mail: info@dukesbath.co.uk
dir: M4 junct 18 take A46 to Bath. At lights turn left
towards A36, at next lights turn right and right again into
Gt Pulteney St

There is no shortage of fine Georgian houses in Bath and
Dukes Hotel is certainly one of them: Grade I listed,
effortlessly elegant in true Palladian style, and located just
a few minutes walk from the city's Pulteney Bridge. The
Cavendish Restaurant is on the lower-ground level but
light, airy and understated, and has access to the secluded
walled garden for alfresco eating on the patio. The white
table linen, cream walls and botanical prints provide a
suitably genteel and refined setting. A change of chef in
the kitchen has not resulted in a change of direction and
the cooking is still highly creative, reflects the seasons,
and is defined by classical cooking underpinned by modern
ideas and presentation. High quality produce, much of it
organic and from the West Country, is used to good effect.
The confidence of the kitchen is evident in a starter of
hand-dived scallops in a dish with cauliflower tempura, a
purée of the same vegetable and a truffle-flavoured honey;
a successful combination. The farm providing the beef
fillet is name-checked on the menu and the meat is cooked
perfectly and served with a wonderfully intense ceps purée,
fondant potato, roasted root vegetables, baby onions and
spring greens.

Chef Fran Snell **Owner** Alan Brookes, Michael Bokenham
Times 12-2.30/6.30-10, Closed L Mon **Prices** Fixed L 2
course £12.95, Starter £8.95-£10.95, Main
£17.95-£24.95, Dessert £7.95-£8.95, Service optional
Wines 34 bottles over £20, 10 bottles under £20, 9 by
glass **Notes** Sunday L, Vegetarian available **Seats** 28, Pr/
dining room 16 **Children** Portions **Parking** On street

The Dower House Restaurant

⊛⊛ Modern British 🖥 V

Contemporary fine dining in Georgian splendour

☎ 01225 823333
The Royal Crescent Hotel, 16 Royal Crescent BA1 2LS
e-mail: info@royalcrescent.co.uk
dir: Please telephone for directions

John Wood the Younger's masterpiece of Georgian
architecture provides the sublime setting for this elegant

and luxurious hotel in the centre of the world-famous
Royal Crescent. Extensive refurbishment has resulted in a
chic art deco style bar and inviting lounge, while the
contemporary restaurant overlooks the secluded gardens
and is bathed in natural light from large windows
swathed in mink-coloured silk. Comfortable armchair
seating and a central banquette make a strong visual
statement, enhanced by distinctive fabrics, splendid
works of art and attractive light olive décor. The cooking
style here is creative and ambitious, underpinned by
strong technical skills, with Mediterranean and oriental
influences evident on the modern British menu. Crab
tortellini, cauliflower purée, shellfish dressing and crisp
celeriac makes an excellent starter, with perhaps a
signature dish of roast grouse tart served with Puy
lentils, creamed leeks and choux rouge for main course.

Chef Gordon Jones & Mark Brega **Owner** von Essen Hotels
Times 12.30-2/7-9.45 **Prices** Food prices not confirmed
for 2009. Please telephone for details. **Wines** 270 bottles
over £20, 8 by glass **Notes** Sunday L, Vegetarian menu,
Dress restrictions, Smart casual, No denim, Civ Wed 60,
Air con **Seats** 70, Pr/dining room 40 **Children** Portions,
Menu **Parking** 17

Four Seasons Restaurant

⊛ Traditional, International

Imaginative cuisine in traditional country-house setting

☎ 01225 723226
**Best Western The Cliffe Hotel, Cliffe Dr, Crowe Hill,
Limpley Stoke BA2 7FY**
e-mail: cliffe@bestwestern.co.uk
dir: A36 S from Bath for 4m at lights turn left onto B3108
towards Bradford-on-Avon. Before railway bridge turn
right into Limpley Stoke, hotel is 0.5m on right

This stylish restaurant was once the billiard room of a
private gentleman's residence just south of Bath. The
building is now a country-house hotel set in peaceful
grounds with stunning views across the valley. The
traditional-styled restaurant overlooks the gardens and
offers a choice of imaginative dishes with international
influences on a seasonally-changing menu, using
produce sourced locally. Service is relaxed and friendly. A
meal might begin with country house soup, home-made
daily, followed by crispy fried sea bass with roasted
fennel bulb and watercress sauce. Desserts include
marmalade and Cointreau-flavoured bread-and-butter
pudding or, for chocoholics, rich chocolate mousse with
Grand Marnier served in a dark chocolate cup.

Chef Martin Seccombe, Andrea Colla **Owner** Martin &
Sheena Seccombe **Times** 12-2.30/7-9.30 **Prices** Fixed L 2

course £10.80-£15, Starter £4.50-£7.50, Main
£14-£21.50, Dessert £5-£6, Service optional **Wines** 6 by
glass **Notes** Sunday L, Vegetarian available, Dress
restrictions, Smart casual **Seats** 50, Pr/dining room 15
Children Portions, Menu **Parking** 30

Macdonald Bath Spa Hotel, Vellore Restaurant

⊛⊛ Traditional International V

A grand setting for ambitious cooking

☎ 0870 400 8222
Sydney Rd BA2 6JF
e-mail: sales.bathspa@macdonald-hotels.co.uk
dir: A4 and follow city-centre signs for 1m. At lights turn
left towards A36. Turn right after pedestrian crossing
then left into Sydney Place. Hotel 200yds on right

Just a short walk from the city centre, this grand hotel is
set amid seven acres of landscaped grounds and boasts
an array of facilities including a spa, indoor pool and
croquet lawn. It's a luxurious affair, rich with neo-
classical styling, from the grandiose entrance to the
murals that adorn the two restaurants: the conservatory-
style Alfresco and the opulent fine-dining venue The
Vellore, once a ballroom. With efficient and entertaining
service, dinner at the latter showcases the kitchen's
culinary skills. Your choice of starters might include pan-
fried foie gras with gingerbread croûton and roast figs, or
roast mallard salad with Puy lentils, celeriac and apple,
while main courses range from loin of venison with
chestnut purée, cabbage and bacon and juniper juices, to
darne of brill with buttered kale, root vegetables,
shellfish and horseradish cream.

Chef Andrew Hamer **Owner** Macdonald Hotels plc
Times 12-2/7-9.45, Closed L Mon-Sat **Prices** Starter
£9.50-£14.95, Main £24.50-£28, Dessert £9-£9.95,
Service optional **Wines** 140 bottles over £20, 12 by glass
Notes Sunday L, Vegetarian menu, Dress restrictions, No
jeans preferred, Civ Wed 120 **Seats** 80, Pr/dining room
120 **Children** Portions, Menu **Parking** 160

BATH *Continued*

The Olive Tree at the Queensberry Hotel

◉◉ Modern British 🖥 ⚜ ☕

Confident modern cooking in stylish hotel restaurant

☎ 01225 447928
Russel St BA1 2QF
e-mail: reservations@thequeensberry.co.uk
web: www.thequeensberry.co.uk
dir: City centre. 100yds N of Assembly Rooms in Lower Lansdown

Set within a stylish 18th-century townhouse hotel hidden in the centre of Georgian Bath, The Olive Tree restaurant combines Georgian opulence with contemporary simplicity. Floors are wooden and soft grey walls are hung with modern artworks, with brown leather banquettes and unclothed tables adding to the relaxed feel. Attentive service from polo-shirted staff is a real strength. Innovative modern British menus are based on quality ingredients and competent cooking with creative flair. Particular attention is paid to seasonality and named local producers. Expect a starter of smoked loin of venison with apple piccalilli and celeriac chips, with mains such as Madgetts Farm breast of duck with sweet potato, thyme Tatin and onion marmalade, and a dessert of toffee rice pudding with apple and pear compote.

Chef Marc Salmon **Owner** Mr & Mrs Beere
Times 12-2/7-10, Closed L Mon **Prices** Fixed L 2 course £16-£18, Starter £7.50-£12, Main £16-£23, Dessert £7.50-£9.50, Service optional, Groups min 10 service 10% **Wines** 270 bottles over £20, 30 bottles under £20, 34 by glass **Notes** Sunday L, Vegetarian available, Air con **Seats** 60, Pr/dining room 30 **Children** Portions
Parking Residents' valet parking; Street pay/display

Woods Restaurant

◉ Modern British, French

Modern cooking amidst period charm

☎ 01225 314812 & 422493
9-13 Alfred St BA1 2QX
e-mail: claude@woodsrestaurant.fsnet.co.uk
dir: Please telephone for directions

John Wood was the architect and builder of much of Georgian Bath and the restaurant bearing his name occupies the ground floor of five of his townhouses. Just a short walk from the historic town centre, a small reception area leads into the large brasserie-style dining room, which has a wooden floor and walls decorated with horse-racing prints. The cooking style is simple and uncluttered, making good use of well-sourced produce in starters like guinea fowl and prune rillette with honey-pickled vegetables and red pepper syrup. Follow on with a properly cooked calves' liver, pink and full of flavour, with a balsamic reduction adding a touch of sharpness, and finish with a well-made dessert such as maple and coffee parfait served with a sticky espresso and whisky syrup.

Chef Stuart Ash **Owner** David & Claude Price
Times 12-2.30/6-10, Closed 25-26 Dec, 1 Jan, Closed Sun (open for special request) **Wines** 32 bottles over £20, 12 bottles under £20, 9 by glass **Notes** Pre-theatre D 5.30-6.45pm 2 courses £12.95, Vegetarian available **Seats** 100, Pr/dining room 40 **Children** Portions, Menu **Parking** On street, car park nearby

No. 5 Bistro

🖥

☎ 01225 444499
5 Argyle St BA2 4BA
web: http://www.theaa.com/travel/index.jsp

Modern British cooking in a relaxed, informal atmosphere. Specials change daily, main menu changes seasonally. There's a great 'bring your own wine' offer - no corkage - on Monday and Tuesday evenings.

Prices Food prices not confirmed for 2009. Please telephone for details.

BRIDGWATER **Map 4 ST23**

The Lemon Tree Restaurant

◉ Modern British

☎ 01278 662255
Walnut Tree Hotel, Fore St, North Petherton TA6 6QA
e-mail: sales@walnuttreehotel.com
dir: M5 junct 24, A38, hotel 1m on right opposite St Mary's Church

This establishment was awarded its Rosette/s just as we went to press. Therefore we are unable to provide a description for it - visit www.theAA.com for the most up-to-date information.

Chef Mark Roy, Luke Nicholson, Debbie & Vagelis
Owner Kristine & Stephen Williams
Times 12-2.30/6.30-9.30 **Prices** Fixed L 2 course £22-£31, Fixed D 3 course £27-£36, Service optional **Wines** 14 bottles over £20, 21 bottles under £20 **Notes** Sunday L, Vegetarian available, Civ Wed 100, Air con **Seats** 40, Pr/dining room 100 **Children** Portions **Parking** 70

BRUTON **Map 4 ST63**

Bruton House Restaurant

◉◉ British ⒱ ☕

Fine dining and contemporary style in historic village

☎ 01749 813395
2-4 High St BA10 0AA
e-mail: info@brutonhouse.co.uk
dir: A303, exit signed Bruton, follow signs to Bruton, restaurant at end of High St, opposite pharmacy

The intimate lounge bar welcomes with comfortable sofas and armchairs in which to peruse the menu at this High Street village restaurant. The small, elegant dining room retains character features too, including a huge stone fireplace and oak beams, alongside more contemporary touches such as bright artwork, wood flooring and leather chairs. Service is formal and discreet but also friendly. The accomplished and passionate chef-proprietor duo have rightly built a strong reputation, with their focus on uncomplicated, modern seasonal cuisine driven by prime local produce, flavour and fine attention to detail. Expect precisely timed and well presented dishes like rabbit loin, rack and ravioli served with wild rabbit consommé, and to finish, perhaps a rhubarb crumble soufflé with rhubarb sorbet.

Chef Scott Eggleton **Owner** Christie-Miller Andrews Ltd
Times 12-2/7-9.30, Closed Sun-Mon **Prices** Fixed L 2 course fr £18.50, Fixed D 3 course fr £39, Service optional, Groups min 8 service 10% **Wines** 77 bottles over £20, 12 bottles under £20, 15 by glass **Notes** Vegetarian menu **Seats** 26 **Children** Portions **Parking** on street

Truffles

◉ British ⒱ ☕

Popular, picturesque rural restaurant with delightful dining

☎ 01749 812255
95 High St BA10 0AR
e-mail: mark@trufflesbruton.co.uk
dir: Near A303, in town centre, at start of one-way system, on left

This charming, creeper-clad family-run village restaurant is spread over two floors and retains many original features. Offering efficient, extremely friendly service in an intimate setting, menus are created around the seasonal availability of excellent local produce, much of which is sourced within a 5 mile radius. The kitchen delivers accomplished, hearty modern British cuisine with clear flavours. To start try diver-caught Lyme Bay scallops simply served with garlic and parsley butter, followed by pan-roasted fillet of bream served with parsnip purée and purple sprouting broccoli, and be sure to make room for tempting desserts such as rhubarb crème brûlée. Monthly gourmet nights tend to sell out early.

Chef Mark Chambers **Owner** Mr & Mrs Chambers
Times 12-2/7-9.30, Closed Mon, Closed L Tue-Wed, Closed D Sun **Prices** Fixed L 3 course fr £21.95, Fixed D 3

course fr £29.95, Service optional **Wines** 13 bottles over £20, 23 bottles under £20, 3 by glass **Notes** Sunday L, Vegetarian menu, Dress restrictions, Smart casual preferred, Air con **Seats** 30, Pr/dining room 10 **Children** Portions **Parking** On street opposite

CHARD
Map 4 ST30

Bellplot House Hotel & Thomas's Restaurant

◉ Modern European

Classic Georgian townhouse offering West Country fare

☎ 01460 62600
High St TA20 1QB
e-mail: info@bellplothouse.co.uk
dir: M5 junct 25/A358 signposted Yeovil. At rdbt take 4th exit A358 from Taunton, follow signs to Chard town centre. 500 mtrs from Guildhall

This Grade II listed property originally stood on a bell-shaped piece of land - hence the name. There's an emphasis on good friendly service in the Georgian-style dining room, where guests enjoy drinking from Royal Brierley cut-glass crystal. The emphasis is on fresh, local and seasonal ingredients, with the suppliers proudly listed on the back of the menu. Modern European dishes with an individual twist might include crème brûlée of asparagus, or seared medallion of veal on rösti potatoes served with veal jus and spinach. Finish with lemon meringue pie.

Times Closed Sun, Closed L all week

CREWKERNE
Map 4 ST40

Kempsters Restaurant

◉ Modern British

Restored Somerset longhouse providing excellent cooking using local produce

☎ 01935 881768
Lower St, West Chinnock TA18 7PT
e-mail: debbie@kempsters.fslife.co.uk
dir: From A303 take Crewkerne junct, follow A356 to Chiselborough/West Chinnock, turn left, over hill into West Chinnock

A lovingly restored Somerset longhouse with heavy new oak doors, old beams, pine and slate floors and Somerset country life black and white photographs on the walls. Comfortable furnishings and warm décor reflect the high standards and friendly welcome offered here. Cooking is accomplished, making excellent use of predominantly locally and regionally sourced ingredients, right down to local tea and coffee merchants. At dinner, enjoy canapés on arrival, then tuck into a starter of hand-dived seared scallops and main course of rack of Dorset lamb with mustard grain mash. Vegetarians are well catered for and there is a good selection of cider brandy.

Times 12-3/7-11.30, Closed 2 wks after 14 Feb, Closed Mon, Closed D Sun

DULVERTON
Map 3 SS92

Tarr Farm Inn

◉ Modern British

Historic inn in stunning setting with focus on excellent cuisine

☎ 01643 851507
Tarr Steps, Exmoor National Park TA22 9PY
e-mail: enquiries@tarrfarm.co.uk
dir: Leave M5 junct 27, signed Tiverton. Follow signs to Dulverton, from Dulverton take B3223 signed Tarr Steps for approx 6.5m

Almost hidden away from the outside world, this charming riverside inn really is the place to escape from it all. Dating back to the 16th century, it sits in a wooded valley at Exmoor's heart by the famed Tarr Steps, and offers relaxed and informal dining in addition to stylish accommodation. Meals can be taken in the bar areas or in the stylish restaurant with its high-backed chairs and candlelit tables. The accomplished, confident cooking displays good technical skills, showcasing impressive, locally-sourced ingredients. Expect risotto of squid, mussels and red mullet with tomato concasse and a light curry sauce, or perhaps guinea fowl wrapped in Parma ham with a mustard velouté for main course.

Chef Edward Heard **Owner** Richard Benn & Judy Carless **Times** 12-3/6.30-12, Closed 1-10 Feb **Prices** Food prices not confirmed for 2009. Please telephone for details. **Wines** 41 bottles over £20, 39 bottles under £20, 8 by glass **Notes** Sunday L **Seats** 50, Pr/dining room 20 **Children** Min 14yrs D, Portions **Parking** 40

Woods Bar & Dining Room

◉◉ British

Unpretentious setting for accomplished cooking

☎ 01398 324007
4 Banks Square TA22 9BU
dir: Telephone for directions

Food-lovers are beating a path to this charming pub/restaurant (once an old bakery), where the passion for good food and wine is obvious. Inside, a lovely log fire warms the cosy interior, which is split-level with a popular bar at the top of the restaurant and a refined barn-style feel, with beams, exposed timbers and hand-made wood furniture. Clean, accurate, straightforward modern British cooking with French influences - using quality West Country produce - is the draw here with a great choice of eating options from simple light lunches to the full carte, which might include roast tenderloin of Somerset pork and slow-cooked belly stuffed with boudin noir. Ask for help in choosing a wine and you won't be disappointed either.

Times 11-3/6-11.30, Closed 25 Dec

DUNSTER
Map 3 SS94

The Luttrell Arms Hotel

◉ Traditional British

Historic setting for interesting dishes using fresh local produce

☎ 01643 821555
High St TA24 6SG
e-mail: info@luttrellarms.fsnet.co.uk
dir: A39 to Minehead, Turn S towards Tiverton on the A396. Hotel is in centre of Dunster village

The historic setting lends plenty of character to the restaurant within this 15th-century hotel. The split-level restaurant has a contemporary, quality feel with attractive styling and comfortable seating, while the bar area has some lovely old features and interesting nooks and crannies. It also serves meals in the garden in the summer months. Friendly local staff offer professional service. The menu changes every few weeks and is supplemented by a special of the day and vegetarian option. Dishes are intelligently straightforward allowing the quality local produce to shine. Take pan-fried fillet of John Dory with pappardelle, chargrilled fennel and tomato sauce, followed by glazed apple tart with elderflower sorbet.

Chef Paul Hepburn **Owner** Paul Toogood **Times** 12-3/7-10 **Prices** Food prices not confirmed for 2009. Please telephone for details. **Wines** 28 bottles over £20, 18 bottles under £20, 6 by glass **Notes** Vegetarian available **Seats** 70, Pr/dining room 24 **Children** Portions **Parking** Market Place or Pay & Display

EXFORD
Map 3 SS83

Crown Hotel

◉◉ Modern British ⌖

Confident cooking in famous Exmoor hotel

☎ 01643 831554
Park St TA24 7PP
e-mail: info@crownhotelexmoor.co.uk
web: www.crownhotelexmoor.co.uk
dir: From Taunton take A38 to A358. Turn left at B3224 & follow signs to Exford

This famous old hotel is situated in lovely gardens in the middle of Exmoor and is a favoured haunt of the country sports set although others find it irresistible too, and the welcome is warm and genuine. Reputedly the moor's

Continued

EXFORD *Continued*

oldest coaching inn, it has a cocktail bar and romantic candlelit dining room with formal table settings. With an Exmoor theme to the dishes, the arrival of a new chef has seen a real focus on quality local ingredients. Local venison is sure to be found, perhaps pan-fried and served on celeriac dauphinoise and served with a fig tart and a game and cassis jus, along with pan-fried wild sea bass with fennel and red chard with roasted salsify and vanilla sauce.

Crown Hotel

Chef Darren Edwards **Owner** Mr C Kirkbride & S & D Whittaker **Times** Closed L all week **Prices** Starter £6.50-£10, Main £13.95-£22.95, Dessert £6.50-£8.75, Service optional, Groups min 8 service 10% **Wines** 25 bottles over £20, 16 bottles under £20, 19 by glass **Notes** Sunday L, Vegetarian available, Dress restrictions, Smart casual, No jeans, T-shirts, swimwear **Seats** 30, Pr/dining room 14 **Children** Portions **Parking** 30

Homewood Park

◉◉ Modern British, European 💻

Elegant atmosphere for fine cuisine

☎ 01225 723731
Abbey Ln BA2 7TB
e-mail: info@homewoodpark.co.uk
dir: 6m SE of Bath off A36, turn left at second sign for Freshford

Traditional country-house comforts abound at this lovely period hotel which sits in 10 acres of award-winning gardens just a few miles from Bath. Its smart restaurant makes the most of the pretty views and has been newly refurbished in a classic, contemporary style, complete with high-backed chairs, sparkling glassware and fine china. Food is the main focus of the operation and shows no shortage of ambition, the kitchen delivering plenty of flair and finesse. Sautéed scallops are a typical starter, served with braised pork belly, black pudding and an apple compôte, while mains might include roast loin of Mendip venison with St Moores goat's cheese potato, chestnut purée and venison jus. Food and wine matching guide available.

Chef Daniel Moon **Owner** von Essen Hotels **Times** 12-1.45/6.30-9.30 **Wines** 130 bottles over £20, 15 bottles under £20, 6 by glass **Notes** Early bird menu 3 courses £22, Sunday L, Vegetarian available, Dress restrictions, Smart casual, No jeans or trainers, Civ Wed 50 **Seats** 60, Pr/dining room 40 **Children** Portions, Menu **Parking** 50

Combe House Hotel

◉ Modern European

Big flavours and fresh local ingredients in a relaxed and comfortable dining room

☎ 01278 741382
TA5 1RZ
e-mail: info@combehouse.co.uk
web: www.combehouse.co.uk
dir: Telephone for directions

The tranquil setting of this country-house hotel combines with the integrity of the cooking to produce an all round feel good factor. Set in four acres of gardens tucked away in a quiet valley in the Quantock Hills, it is an idyllic location. The beamed restaurant has a huge stone ornamental fireplace and modern Cornish maple and walnut tables. The organic kitchen garden provides the chefs with vegetables and soft fruit while other ingredients are sourced locally - meat and game from local farms and shoots, fish from Brixham and, of course, Somerset cheeses. The food is sometimes classic, sometimes innovative, and extends to Parma ham stuffed with pigeon, rabbit and butter beans and Neapolitan sauce, and a main-course grilled brill with Somerset shrimps, lobster tail and chive velouté.

Times 12-2.30/7-9

Hunstrete House Hotel

◉◉ Modern European

A peaceful setting for enjoyable hotel cuisine

☎ 01761 490490
BS39 4NS
e-mail: info@hunstretehouse.co.uk
dir: On A368 - 8m from Bath

This fine Georgian mansion has its own deer park and is situated on the edge of the beautiful Mendips. It provides a genuine country-house experience inside and out, the interior bedecked with period paintings and furniture. The Terrace dining room is decorated in white and shades of green with sparkling chandeliers. Cooking is contemporary in style and uses the best of local, seasonal ingredients in well conceived dishes accurately executed. Much of the freshly picked produce comes from the hotel's own Victorian walled garden, and free-range meat from Wiltshire farms. Start with salad of Wiltshire duck with pickled beetroot and apple dressing before fillet of Stokes Marsh Farm beef, served with the braised cheeks and root vegetables, finishing with a trio of sticky toffee desserts or a selection of West Country cheeses.

Chef Matthew Lord **Owner** von Essen hotels **Times** 12-2/7-9.30 **Prices** Fixed L 2 course £17.50, Fixed D 3 course £50, Service optional **Wines** 92 bottles over £20, 17 bottles under £20, 7 by glass **Notes** Sunday L, Vegetarian available, Dress restrictions, No jeans, smart casual, Civ Wed 60 **Seats** 35, Pr/dining room 50 **Children** Portions, Menu **Parking** 50

The Vobster Inn

◉ Modern Mediterranean, European ☺

Spanish-influenced food in a rural English setting

☎ 01373 812920
BA3 5RJ
e-mail: info@vobsterinn.co.uk
dir: 4m W of Frome, between Wells & Leigh on Mendip

Dating back to the 17th century, this traditional village inn is set in 4 acres of Somerset countryside and has a welcoming, relaxed feel. Inside the décor is thoroughly modern, and diners can choose between the bar, lounge or more formal restaurant, where the service is genuinely friendly and efficient. There's a distinctly Spanish flavour to the cooking, reflecting the influence of the chef-proprietor, with Spanish ingredients sourced from specialist suppliers. Fish is delivered daily from Cornwall and there's a strong emphasis on local West Country produce. Firm British favourites also feature on the seasonal menu, which offers high-quality, simply prepared dishes with robust flavours. Take a main course of Catalan fish and chorizo stew, or perhaps featherblade of beef with cheddar parsnip purée and buttered Savoy.

Chef Mr Rafael F Davila **Owner** Mr Rafael F Davila
Times 12-3/6.30-11, Closed 25 Dec, Closed D Sun
Prices Starter £5-£9, Main £9.50-£16, Dessert £4.95,
Service optional **Wines** 9 bottles over £20, 18 bottles under £20, 12 by glass **Notes** Sunday L, Vegetarian available **Seats** 40, Pr/dining room 40 **Children** Portions, Menu **Parking** 60

Ash House Country Hotel

◉ British, French

A friendly, family-run hotel and restaurant

☎ 01935 822036 & 823126
41 Main St, Ash TA12 6PB
e-mail: reception@ashhousecountryhotel.co.uk
dir: Leave A303 at Tintinhull Forts junct. After slip road turn left. Continue for approx. 0.75m, hotel on right

Diners have a choice of venues at this family-run Georgian country-house hotel: a traditionally-styled restaurant or a more informal conservatory overlooking pretty grounds. The food's great either way - a range of classic French dishes with some modern British twists. All the ingredients are sourced from named local suppliers, who provide the chef with ample material for dishes such as pork tenderloin stuffed with apricot and apple, or pan-seared venison with dauphinoise potato, courgette gratin and glaze de viande. Black cherry chocolate mousse with chocolate cup or lemon mousse round things off nicely.

Chef Michael Scarborough **Owner** Nick & Gill McGill
Times 12-2/6.30-9, Closed 25-26 Dec, 31 Dec, 1 Jan,
Closed Sun-Mon **Prices** Fixed L 2 course £10-£12, Starter £4.50-£6.50, Main £13.95-£19.95, Dessert £4.50-£5.95,

Service optional **Wines** 7 bottles over £20, 16 bottles under £20, 4 by glass **Notes** Vegetarian available, Civ Wed 60 **Seats** 40, Pr/dining room 20 **Children** Portions **Parking** 35

The Moody Goose At The Old Priory

◉◉ Modern British 🖳 V

Historic setting for innovative modern cooking

☎ 01761 416784 & 410846
Church Square BA3 2HX
e-mail: info@theoldpriory.co.uk
dir: Along High St, right at lights, right at rdbt in front of church

This former 12th century priory is one of the oldest buildings in Somerset. Bursting with character, inglenook fireplaces, flagstone floors and oak beams all add to the ambience. The bright and airy décor of the Moody Goose restaurant complements the building's period features and contemporary cuisine, with deep burgundy chairs, whitewashed walls and modern French watercolours displayed alongside a 100-year-old cooking range. Expect considered dishes based around fresh seasonal produce, locally sourced where possible, with herbs, fruit and vegetables coming from their own kitchen garden. Dishes are cooked to order with the emphasis on simplicity - perhaps start with the cannelloni of chicken and walnuts with pan-fried chicken livers and balsamic glaze, followed by the pan-fried fillet of beef with a Roquefort mousseline, roasted salsify and Madeira sauce. Round off with the warm chocolate and griottine clafoutis with whisky ice cream.

Chef Stephen Shore **Owner** Stephen Shore
Times 12-1.30/7-9.30, Closed Xmas, New Year, BHs,
Closed Sun-Mon **Prices** Fixed L 2 course fr £16, Fixed D 3 course fr £25, Starter £9-£11.50, Main £15-£22, Dessert £6-£6.50, Service optional **Wines** 81 bottles over £20, 13 bottles under £20, 9 by glass **Notes** Vegetarian menu, Dress restrictions, Smart casual **Seats** 34, Pr/dining room 22 **Children** Portions **Parking** 12

The Oaks Hotel

◉ British, French

Elegant Edwardian house dining with sea views

☎ 01643 862265
TA24 8ES
e-mail: info@oakshotel.co.uk
dir: At bottom of Dunstersteepe Road, on left on entering Porlock from Minehead

A small hotel overlooking Porlock towards the sea, The Oaks is personally run by a husband-and-wife team, Tim and Ann Riley. The restaurant is light with large windows enabling virtually every table to enjoy the splendid view. The daily-changing menu places the emphasis firmly on local produce in simply prepared dishes. A cream of pear and watercress soup starter might be followed by tenderloin of organic Somerset pork with grain mustard and Marsala. Perhaps banana and stem ginger ice cream for dessert.

Times Closed Nov-Mar

Charlton House

◉◉ Modern British ☺

Innovative cuisine in wonderfully elegant surroundings

☎ 01749 342008
Charlton Rd BA4 4PR
e-mail: enquiries@charltonhouse.com
dir: On A361. Hotel is located 1m before Shepton Mallet

This chic hotel is the epitome of stylish contemporary country-house living. Owned by the founders of upmarket design label, Mulberry, their exquisite fabrics and sumptuous furnishings abound, creating a luxurious yet relaxed atmosphere. The smart and spacious conservatory-style Sharpham Park restaurant overlooks the delightful grounds, while the kitchen makes the most of high quality local produce, much from their own organic and rare breed farm. Dishes impress with their skill, flavour and artistic presentation; take the lightly grilled Cornish red mullet with pesto to start, with poached fillet of Sharpham beef, braised brisket and mushroom consommé to follow. A seven-course tasting menu supports carte and lunch offerings, while the extensive wine list has been personally chosen by the proprietor.

Continued

SHEPTON MALLET *Continued*

Charlton House

Chef Elisha Carter **Owner** Roger Saul
Times 12.30-2.30/7.30-9.30 **Prices** Food prices not
confirmed for 2009. Please telephone for details.
Wines 130 bottles over £20, 10 bottles under £20, 8 by
glass **Notes** Sunday L, Vegetarian available, Civ Wed 120,
Air con **Seats** 84, Pr/dining room 70 **Children** Portions,
Menu **Parking** 70

Thatched Cottage

◎ Modern British, European ✲

Modern dining in a traditional-style inn

☎ 01749 342058
63-67 Charlton Rd BA4 5QF
e-mail: david@thatchedcottage.info
dir: 0.6m E of Shepton Mallet, at lights on A361

The main building is 370 years old, thatched and listed
Grade II, but the interior is not what you might expect.
You'll find oak beams, tiled floors, panelled walls, open
stonework and log fires alongside a stylish modern décor,
squashy sofas and pale-wood tables. Dishes are
attractively presented making good use of quality local,
seasonal produce. With European and some international
influences, and plenty of steaks on offer, crab pâté, pan-
fried sea bass with sauce vierge, confit of duck with
poached pear and fondant potato, and chocolate
mascarpone cheesecake are fine examples of the fare.

Chef Fabrice Belier, Madan Pandley **Owner** David Pledger
Times 12-2.30/6.30-9.30 **Prices** Fixed L 2 course £7.95,
Starter £3.95-£5.95, Main £9.95-£16.95, Dessert
£3.20-£5.95, Service optional, Groups min 8 service 9%
Wines 7 bottles over £20, 27 bottles under £20, 23 by
glass **Notes** Sunday L, Vegetarian available **Seats** 56, Pr/
dining room 35 **Children** Portions **Parking** 35

The Three Horseshoes Inn

◎ European ✲

**Honest cooking and real ale in a 17th-century coaching
inn**

☎ 01749 850359
Batcombe BA4 6HE
dir: Signed from A359 Bruton/Frome

Full of rustic charm, this honey-coloured 17th-century
coaching inn has an inglenook fireplace, wood-burning
stove, solid wood tables and chairs, exposed beams and
stone walls to welcome the diner. The cooking style is
modern British and service is relaxed and friendly. Expect
mains like local free-range supreme of chicken stuffed
with reblochon cheese and wrapped in Parma ham
accompanied by sautéed potatoes and zuchini fritti. Or
for an interesting vegetarian alternative try fricassée of
wild mushrooms, celeriac, white of leek, Madeira and
cream in a Brittany crêpe basket served with parsnip,
sweet potato and beetroot crisps. There is a patio for
alfresco dining.

Chef Mike Jones, Bob Wood **Owner** Bob Wood & Shirley
Greaves **Times** 12-2/7-9, Closed 25 Dec, Closed Mon,
Closed D Sun **Prices** Starter £4.75-£7.25, Main
£10.50-£18.75, Dessert £4.50-£5.50, Service optional,
Groups min 10 service 10% **Wines** 8 bottles over £20, 28
bottles under £20, 8 by glass **Notes** Sunday L, Vegetarian
available, Dress restrictions, Smart casual **Seats** 40, Pr/
dining room 40 **Children** Min 12yrs+ D, Portions
Parking 30

The Devonshire Arms

◎ Modern British

**Hunting lodge turned stylish gastro-pub with modern
brasserie-style cooking**

☎ 01458 241271
Long Sutton TA10 9LP
e-mail: mail@thedevonshirearms.com
dir: A303 Podimore rdbt. Take A372, continue for 4m and
turn left towards Long Sutton

Step inside and you will be surprised by the
unexpectedly contemporary, light and airy interior of
this Grade II listed former hunting lodge, in its idyllic
location on the village green. Chunky modern tables and
leather chairs or upholstered benches provide the
comforts, plus there are a few sofas for relaxing over
drinks or coffee. The menu offers modern brasserie-style
fare with Mediterranean influences: hand-picked crab
crème brûlée with fennel and rocket salad,
Gloucestershire Old Spot belly pork with crackling, black
truffle mash and parsnip chips, and ricotta mousse with
prune compote and brandy snap.

Chef Sasha Matkevich **Owner** Philip & Sheila Mepham
Times 12-2.30/7-9.30, Closed 25 Dec, 1 Jan **Prices** Fixed
L 2 course fr £10.95, Starter £4.50-£7.50, Main
£12.95-£22.95, Dessert £4.95-£6.50, Service added but
optional 10% **Wines** 10 bottles over £20, 16 bottles under

£20, 10 by glass **Notes** Sunday L, Vegetarian available
Seats 40 **Children** Portions, Menu **Parking** 6 **Parking** On
street

The Priory House Restaurant

◎◎ Modern British

Enjoyable dining at a smart high-street restaurant

☎ 01935 822826
1 High St TA14 6PP
e-mail: reservations@theprioryhouserestaurant.co.uk
dir: 0.5m from A303 in the centre of Stoke Sub Hamdon

Originally an 18th-century guest house to the local priory,
this intimate high-street restaurant is decked out in
smart contemporary shades of blue and beige. Take a
drink in the bar or on the pretty garden terrace in
summer, and then move through to the restaurant for
some accomplished modern British cuisine, distinguished
by technical mastery, attentive sourcing of ingredients,
and plenty of flavour. Dishes are gutsy, yet refined, and
deliver on both taste and texture. Seared Lyme Bay
scallops and smoked haddock soufflé with crispy leeks
and thermidor sauce show the style, perhaps followed by
a main course of loin of West Country venison with sweet
potato purée, confit garlic and caramelised baby onions,
and hot apricot and almond tart with Amaretto ice cream
to finish. Wines are supplemented by an interesting
selection of Somerset cider brandies.

Chef Peter Brooks **Owner** Peter & Sonia Brooks
Times 12-2/7-9.30, Closed 25 Dec, BHs, 2 wks May, 2wks
Nov, Closed Sun & Mon, Closed L Tue-Fri **Prices** Fixed L 2
course £16, Starter £7-£10.50, Main £19.50-£20.50,
Dessert £7-£10, Service optional **Wines** 37 bottles over
£20, 10 bottles under £20, 7 by glass **Notes** Vegetarian
available **Seats** 25 **Children** Min 7 yrs **Parking** Free car
park 200yds & street parking

Ston Easton Park

◎◎ Modern British 🛏

Fine dining in a Palladian mansion

☎ 01761 241631
BA3 4DF
e-mail: info@stoneaston.co.uk
dir: Follow A39 from Bath for approx. 8m. Turn onto A37
(Shepton Mallet), Ston Easton is next village

Set within 36 acres of glorious parkland, this grand
Palladian mansion belongs to one of the West Country's
most romantic estates. The wonderful grounds designed
by the great 18th-century landscape gardener, Humphry
Repton, reward exploration; take a stroll before dinner
and you might stumble upon a ruined grotto, sham
castle, or an 18th-century ice house. Inside is as opulent
as you'd expect, with dinner served in a number of
magnificent dining rooms. The Cedar Tree Restaurant
serves an imaginative menu of modern dishes, drawing
its ingredients from the estate's large Victorian kitchen

garden and the best of local producers. Start with plaice and tiger prawn spring roll perhaps, and then move on to steamed fillet of wild sea bass with braised baby leeks, champagne and lemongrass sauce. End on a high note with Bramley apple crumble soufflé served with thyme jelly and apple brandy.

Times 12-2/7-9.30

TAUNTON   Map 4 ST22

Corner House Hotel

◉ Modern

Enjoyable bistro dining in tastefully updated Victorian surroundings

☎ 01823 284683
Park St TA1 4DQ
e-mail: res@corner-house.co.uk
dir: Please telephone for details

The impressive turrets and stained glass of this Victorian building conceal a contemporary interior of innovation, quality and style. The 4DQ bistro (trendily named after part of its postcode) combines modern comfort with original features to produce a dining venue that has a pleasing, relaxed ambience. The simple, well-executed dishes ride with the surroundings, and come based on fresh Somerset ingredients. Take Thai fishcakes with sweet chilli dressing, chargrilled rib-eye steak with herb butter and chips, or herb-crusted cod with ratatouille and new potatoes, and to finish, perhaps rich chocolate pot with vanilla cream.

Owner Hatton Hotels **Times** 12-2/6.30-9.30
Prices Starter £3.95-£6.95, Main £7.20-£13.95, Dessert £2.50-£6.95, Service optional **Wines** 8 bottles over £20, 13 bottles under £20, 7 by glass **Notes** Sunday L, Vegetarian available **Seats** 100, Pr/dining room 55 **Children** Portions **Parking** 30

Farthings Country House Hotel and Restaurant

◉ Modern British 🍃

Country-house hotel providing local and regional ingredients

☎ 01823 480664 & 0785 668 8128
Village Rd, Hatch Beauchamp TA3 6SG
e-mail: info@farthingshotel.co.uk
web: www.farthingshotel.co.uk
dir: M5 junct 25 towards Ilminster, Yeovil, Chard on A358.

Built in 1762, Farthings is a fine example of a country-house hotel. In an English village setting, the grounds are suitably picturesque, the atmosphere relaxing and the staff genuinely attentive and considerate. Peruse the menu in the traditionally decorated bar or dining room and note the predominance of local produce: duck eggs from the garden, lamb from nearby Neroche Farm and fish from the south coast. Start with a terrine of duck and chicken livers with spiced fruit chutney, followed by roasted loin of cod, cheese and herb mash and vegetable

panaché. Comforting desserts include classic crème brûlée and bread-and-butter pudding.

Chef Simon Clenlow **Owner** John Seeger, Kevin Groves **Times** 12-3/6.30-9.15 **Prices** Fixed L 2 course £20-£26, Fixed D 3 course £30-£34, Starter £6-£10, Main £17-£30, Dessert £6-£9, Service optional **Wines** 38 bottles over £20, 6 bottles under £20, 4 by glass **Notes** Sunday L, Civ Wed 50 **Seats** 60, Pr/dining room 30 **Children** Portions **Parking** 25

The Mount Somerset Hotel

◉◉ British, French

Elegant Regency property with interesting contemporary food

☎ 01823 442500
Henlade TA3 5NB
e-mail: info@mountsomersethotel.co.uk
dir: From M5 junct 25 take A358 (Chard); turn right in Henlade (Stoke St Mary), then turn left at T-junct. Hotel 400yds on right

From its elevated and rural position, this impressive Regency house has wonderful views over Taunton Vale. Italian-designed, the house retains its original grandeur and the restaurant is splendid, with a magnificent central chandelier and two superb mirrors. Chairs are large and very comfortable and tables are smartly appointed with crisp linen, sparkling silver and contemporary crockery. The likes of a terrine of crab, lobster, sole and John Dory, a trio of Gloucestershire Old Spot pork (served with mustard mash, creamed Savoy cabbage and apple Tatin), and several peripheral courses (canapés, West Country cheeses and petits fours) all add to the sense of occasion. Finish, perhaps, with warm chocolate tart with mint ice cream and raspberry compote.

Times 12-2/7-9.30

The Willow Tree Restaurant

◉◉ Modern British 🍃

Imaginative regional cooking in a period restaurant

☎ 01823 352835
3 Tower Ln, Off Tower St TA1 4AR
dir: 200 yds from Taunton bus station

Housed in a 17th-century former moat house, handy for the town centre, this delightful little restaurant has plenty of atmosphere, with exposed beams, inglenook fireplaces and colourful contemporary artwork. There is

also a charming waterside terrace for alfresco drinks and dining. The fixed-price, three-course menu is drawn from carefully sourced local produce, and the classically French-based modern British food offers clarity of flavours in dishes such as velouté of Jerusalem artichoke with smoked haddock and macaroni to start, followed by fillet of beef with oxtail jus served with parsnip purée and braised root vegetables. Finish with dessert - perhaps pistachio crème brûlée with a cocoa sablé - or a selection of pasteurised and unpasteurised cheeses.

Chef Darren Sherlock **Owner** Darren Sherlock & Rita Rambellas **Times** Closed Jan, Aug, Closed Sun-Mon, Closed L all week **Prices** Fixed D 3 course £27.50-£32.50, Service optional, Groups min 7 service 10% **Wines** 20 bottles over £20, 25 bottles under £20, 4 by glass **Notes** Vegetarian available, Dress restrictions, Smart casual **Seats** 25, Pr/dining room 15 **Children** Min 10 yrs **Parking** 20 yds, 300 spaces

---

WELLS   Map 4 ST54

Best Western Swan Hotel

◉◉ Traditional British

Generous and imaginative dishes in a traditional setting

☎ 01749 836300
Sadler St BA5 2RX
e-mail: info@swanhotelwells.co.uk
dir: A39, A371, on entering Wells follow signs for Hotels & Deliveries. Hotel on right opposite Cathedral

Nestling in the shadow of Wells Cathedral, this former coaching inn is situated in a spectacular location. Full of character and steeped in over 500 years of history, the hotel has been sympathetically restored and extended in recent years, combining period features with modern comfort. The long, narrow dining room, with magnificent linen-fold oak panelling and interesting antiques, provides a very traditional setting with a formal but friendly style of service, while the walled garden and garden room are perfect for alfresco dining in summer. Imaginative dishes, traditional but with a modern twist, are served in good country portions, the careful cooking making use of fresh local produce. Daily-changing menus include the likes of warm tartlet of Exmoor Blue cheese with toasted pine nuts, with braised blade of Somerset beef and horseradish mash with sweet red wine jus to follow.

Chef Paul Mingo-West **Owner** Kevin Newton
Times 12-2/7-9.30 **Prices** Fixed L 2 course £13.50-£15.50, Fixed D 3 course £25.50-£27.50, Starter £4.95-£6.95, Main £12.95-£19.50, Dessert £5.50-£5.95, Service optional **Wines** 20 bottles over £20, 23 bottles under £20, 7 by glass **Notes** Sunday L, Vegetarian available, Civ Wed 70 **Seats** 60, Pr/dining room 100 **Children** Portions, Menu **Parking** 25

WELLS *Continued*

Goodfellows

◎◎ European

Family-run top quality pâtisserie and fish restaurant

☎ 01749 673866
5 Sadler St BA5 2RR
e-mail: goodfellows@btconnect.com
dir: Town centre near Market Place

The mulberry-coloured shop front of this establishment houses an informal pâtisserie and coffee shop. Downstairs provides a modern, bright main restaurant with an open-plan kitchen and there's further restaurant space upstairs with a glass atrium, and an adjoining courtyard. The technically accomplished and skilled modern European cooking offers top-notch fish and seafood with Mediterranean influences - a light style with intense flavours from oils and vinaigrettes using the likes of black olives, capers and anchovy or truffle oil. A six-course tasting menu is also available, and typical dishes might include local purple potato and Chew Valley smoked eel terrine with caper vinaigrette to start, followed by roast cod and sea bass with squid ink linguine and bouillabaisse sauce, with excellent pâtisserie, perhaps a summer fruit tart, to finish.

Chef Adam Fellows **Owner** Adam & Martine Fellows **Times** 12-2/6.30-9.30, Closed 25-27 Dec, 1 Jan, Closed Sun & Mon, Closed D Tue **Prices** Fixed L 2 course £17, Fixed D 3 course fr £35, Tasting menu £55, Starter £6-£12, Main £13-£25, Dessert £7-£9, Service optional, Groups min 8 service 8% **Wines** 45 bottles over £20, 12 bottles under £20, 13 by glass **Notes** Tasting menu 6 courses, Vegetarian available, Air con **Seats** 30, Pr/dining room 20 **Children** Portions

The Old Spot

◎ European

Contemporary restaurant with friendly, relaxed bistro vibe

☎ 01749 689099
12 Sadler St BA5 2SE
dir: On entering village, follow signs for Hotels & Deliveries. Sadler St leads into High St, Old Spot on left opposite Swan Hotel

The large window frontage of this period-style stone building picks out this light-and-airy, contemporary city-centre restaurant. Pale green walls, framed menus and wooden floorboards add fashionable touches to the high

ceilings, while a few steps down, an extension overlooks the cathedral. Informal yet professional table service and unclothed tables add to the relaxed, friendly atmosphere. The kitchen takes an intelligently simple approach driven by local seasonal produce, with well presented, clean-cut, bistro-style dishes. Try saffron risotto with peas, mozzarella and basil, or breast of chicken with Parma ham, polenta and wild mushrooms, with orange cake, citrus fruit and mascarpone to close.

Chef Ian Bates **Owner** Ian & Clare Bates **Times** 12.30-2.30/6.30-10.30, Closed 1 wk Xmas, Closed Mon, Closed L Tue, Closed D Sun **Prices** Fixed L 2 course £15, Fixed D 3 course £26.50, Service optional, Groups min 6 service 10% **Wines** 56 bottles over £20, 14 bottles under £20, 9 by glass **Notes** Sunday L, Vegetarian available **Seats** 50 **Children** Portions **Parking** On street, Market Square

The Walnut Tree Hotel

◎ British, French

Fine food in friendly village hotel

☎ 01935 851292
Fore St BA22 7QW
e-mail: info@thewalnuttreehotel.com
dir: Just off A303 between Sparkford & The RNAS Yeovilton Air Base

This small hotel has all the character and atmosphere of a village inn. There is a family-orientated restaurant, with a different kitchen and team to the fine-dining Rosewood Restaurant. Here lightwood panelling and white table settings give a clean, airy feel. Accomplished cooking and sound techniques show in a starter of white crabmeat and smoked oysters with avocado and lemon vinaigrette. Main courses like roast English lamb rump with broad bean, pea and mint cassoulet could be followed by brandy snap basket with fresh figs, pecan and honey ice cream.

Times 12-2/6-8.45, Closed 25-26 Dec, 1 Jan, Closed L Mon

Holbrook House

◎◎ British, French

Elegant hotel with stylish restaurant

☎ 01963 824466 & 828844
Holbrook BA9 8BS
e-mail: enquiries@holbrookhouse.co.uk
dir: From A303 at Wincanton, turn left on A371 towards Castle Cary & Shepton Mallet

The handsome country-house hotel stands in 23 acres of parkland and formal gardens, not far from Wincanton. Plush leather sofas, antique furniture and open fires invite diners to linger over drinks in the lounge before moving into the elegant Cedar Restaurant, where the warm colour scheme creates a calming atmosphere.

Menus, based on local and organic produce, offer an innovative selection of dishes prepared with enthusiasm and served by caring staff. Expect the likes of seared scallops with chive mash and black pudding, followed by tournedos of West Country beef fillet with braised oxtail and shallot purée. For dessert, make room for traditional treacle sponge and clotted cream ice cream.

Holbrook House Hotel & Spa

Times 12.30-2/7-9, Closed L Sat, Closed D Sun

Karslake House

◎ Modern British

Fresh local produce in charming country-house style

☎ 01643 851242
Halse Ln TA24 7JE
e-mail: enquiries@karslakehouse.co.uk
dir: A396 to Winsford, then left up the hill

A 15th-century former malthouse in a peaceful Exmoor village has been sympathetically restored to create this comfortable guest house and restaurant. The attractive restaurant is open to non-residents on Friday and Saturday evenings or by prior arrangement and has crisply-set tables with cut glass and fresh flowers. The style of cooking is British with a focus on fresh, locally sourced produce, including fish, meat and game. Typical dishes include Brixham halibut on a carrot pattie with spinach cream, cannon of Bridgwater salt marsh lamb with ratatouille-filled courgette and rosemary jus, and Somerset plum crème brûlée with shortbread stars.

Chef Juliette Mountford **Owner** Mr & Mrs F N G Mountford **Times** Closed Nov-Apr, Closed D Sun-Thu (ex residents) **Prices** Fixed D 3 course £30, Service optional **Wines** 15 bottles over £20, 18 bottles under £20, 2 by glass **Notes** Vegetarian available, Dress restrictions, Smart casual **Seats** 18 **Children** Min 12 yrs **Parking** 12

WOOKEY HOLE — Map 4 ST54

Wookey Hole Inn

Modern International

Good, wholesome food in a quirky Somerset inn

☎ 01749 676677
BA5 1BP

A relaxed, café atmosphere pervades behind the traditional pub exterior of Wookey Hole Inn. There is a quirky assortment of styles, with banquette seating, whitewashed tables, log fires, and Moroccan type fabrics and cushions in the lounge area, while service is welcoming and friendly. The kitchen provides uncomplicated, wholesome modern-style dishes, using locally sourced produce wherever possible, with generous helpings proving great value. Bolstered by blackboard specials, expect dishes like roasted organic salmon over potato rösti, wilted baby leaves and a tomato and langoustine bisque with mussels and clams, followed by rhubarb and plum frangipane served with crème anglaise and stem ginger ice cream. A wide choice of Belgian beers is also available.

Times 12-2.30/7-9.30, Closed L Sun

YEOVIL — Map 4 ST51

Helyar Arms

British

Accomplished cooking in a Somerset haven

☎ 01935 862332
Moor Ln, East Coker BA22 9JR
e-mail: info@helyar-arms.co.uk
dir: 3m from Yeovil. Take A37 or A30. Follow signs for East Coker. Helyar Arms is 50 mtrs from church

Made famous by TS Eliot in the poem of the same name, East Coker is one of Somerset's prettiest villages. Its inn dates back to the 15th century and boasts all the character and warm atmosphere one might expect, as well as attractive gardens for alfresco dining. Simple, homely, crowd-pleasing modern cooking is the order of the day, so expect straightforward comfort dishes like pan-seared calves' liver with grilled bacon, caramelised shallots and mash potato, or perhaps chargilled lamb chops with curly kale, rosemary potatoes and a Madeira jus. Ingredients are from local producers whenever possible, while daily blackboard specials bolster the repertoire.

Times 12-2.30/6.30-9.30, Closed 25 Dec

Lanes

Modern British

Imaginative, modern cooking in contemporary surroundings

☎ 01935 862555
West Coker BA22 9AJ
e-mail: stay@laneshotel.net
web: www.laneshotel.net
dir: 2m W of Yeovil, on A30 towards Crewkerne

A splendid Victorian property, this former rectory has a magnificent carved oak fireplace, high ceilings, spacious lounges and a piano bar. Through the stylish chrome bar, you'll find the brasserie-style restaurant in a modern extension, with floor-to-ceiling windows, wooden floors, mirrors, high-backed cream leather chairs and striking works of art on plain white walls. The crowd-pleasing menu evolves with the seasons and offers an imaginative range of dishes, including a few options in smaller or

Continued

Little Barwick House

YEOVIL — Map 4 ST51

Modern European

Delightful house, wonderful gardens, unfussy service and great food

☎ 01935 423902
Barwick Village BA22 9TD
e-mail: reservations@barwick7.fsnet.co.uk
dir: Turn off A371 Yeovil to Dorchester opposite Red House rdbt, 0.25m on left

This listed Georgian dower house has everything you might desire in a restaurant with rooms: just over 3 acres of beautiful grounds to unwind in, elegant and eminently civilised decoration and furnishings, and first-class food. Timothy and Emma Ford run the place with enthusiasm and dedication, and their restoration of the property has shown sensitivity to the period charm of the building

while giving it a stylish and contemporary edge. Sumptuous fabrics, Farrow and Ball colours, huge windows overlooking the garden and terrace, and sympathetic modern touches provide an unobtrusive backdrop for fine eating and drinking. Tim's food shows a welcome absence of fuss and gimmickry, but this does not mean it lacks punch or panache: dishes are well crafted, considered and demonstrate a steady hand in the kitchen. Top-quality seasonal produce is used throughout and presentation is a strong suit. Start with warm terrine of lamb's sweetbreads, chicken and tarragon with Madeira sauce, or grilled fillet of Cornish mackerel with fennel escabèche and lemon chilli syrup. Rump of local lamb is served with Savoy cabbage, parsnip purée and rosemary sauce in a typically well-considered main course, while rum baba served with poached pineapple and cream and black pepper ice cream is a fine, inventive finish. There is an excellent wine list available.

Chef Timothy Ford **Owner** Emma & Timothy Ford
Times 12-2/7-9.30, Closed New Year, 2wks Jan, Closed Mon, Closed L Tues, Closed D Sun **Prices** Fixed L 2 course fr £19.95, Fixed D 3 course fr £36.95, Service optional **Wines** 179 bottles over £20, 21 bottles under £20, 6 by glass **Notes** Sunday L, Vegetarian available, Air con **Seats** 40 **Children** Min 5 yrs, Portions **Parking** 25

YEOVIL *Continued*

larger portions. Using good technical skills, the kitchen delivers dishes such as potage of clams and mussels, seared calves' liver with grilled bacon and bubble-and-squeak and apple, cider and vanilla soufflé.

Chef Jason Eland **Owner** John & Alison Roehrig **Times** 12-2.30/7-9.30, Closed L Sat **Prices** Starter £4.25-£6, Main £8.50-£18.50, Dessert £3.50-£5, Service optional **Wines** 27 bottles over £20, 21 bottles under £20, 10 by glass **Notes** Sunday L, Vegetarian available **Seats** 85, Pr/dining room 40 **Children** Portions **Parking** 65

Little Barwick House

◉◉◉ – *see page 387*

Yeovil Court Hotel & Restaurant

◉◉ Modern European

Enjoyable dining in a modern, family-run hotel

☎ 01935 863746
West Coker Rd BA20 2HE
e-mail: unwind@yeovilhotel.com
dir: On A30, 2.5m W of town centre

With its modern décor and convivial bar area, this friendly, family-run hotel has a welcoming ambience. The dining room is also decorated in a modern style with white tablecloths and good quality settings. The kitchen takes a modern approach with an enjoyable menu, which includes the classics, built on the use of quality local produce. Expect the likes of smoked haddock and salmon fishcake with herb cream for a starter, followed by pan-seared calves' liver with pancetta and a port and shallot reduction, or maybe fillet of sea bass with saffron creamed potatoes, braised fennel and lemon butter, while a caramelised rice pudding with glazed banana and caramel sauce might head-up the tempting list of desserts.

Chef Simon Walford **Owner** Brian & Carol Devonport **Times** 12-1.45/7-9.30, Closed 24 Dec, 26-28 Dec, 1-2 Jan, Closed L Sat **Prices** Starter £3.50-£8, Main £8-£19, Dessert £4.25-£5.75, Service optional **Wines** 12 bottles over £20, 27 bottles under £20, 5 by glass **Notes** Sunday L, Air con **Seats** 50, Pr/dining room 80 **Children** Portions **Parking** 65

STAFFORDSHIRE

BURTON UPON TRENT Map 10 SK22

The Grill Room

◉ Traditional British ℃

Victorian-themed hotel restaurant serving simple, flavourful food

☎ 01283 523800 & 0845 230 1332
Three Queens Hotel, One Bridge St DE14 1SY
e-mail: restaurant@threequeenshotel.co.uk
dir: On A511, at junct of High St and Bridge St

Reputedly named after the English queens, Elizabeth, Mary and Anne, the oldest part of this comfortable hotel dates back to 1531. The Grill Room restaurant is a characterful, intimate affair, reminiscent of a Victorian gentlemen's dining club with its hardwood panelling and screens. Terracotta and cream walls blend with small tapestries and bold-coloured carpets, while high-backed dining chairs provide the comforts. The kitchen's suitably traditional style - delivered with modern, clean-cut presentation - focuses on fresh local produce, simplicity and flavour. Expect dishes like fillet steak from the grill, served with a horseradish crust and wild mushrooms, or perhaps seared fillet of red mullet partnered by baby vegetables, fondant potato and a beurre blanc sauce.

Chef Stuart Robotham **Owner** Three Queens Hotel Ltd. **Times** 12-2.15/6.15-10, Closed L Sat-Sun **Prices** Fixed L 2 course £8.95-£14.50, Fixed D 3 course £16.50, Starter £4.50-£6.50, Main £9.95-£17.50, Dessert £4.50-£6.50, Service optional **Wines** 7 bottles over £20, 29 bottles under £20, 8 by glass **Notes** Air con **Seats** 36, Pr/dining room 60 **Parking** 40

Meynell and Deer Park Restaurant

◉ Modern, International

Traditional inn with a very rural location

☎ 01283 575202
Hoar Cross DE13 8RB
e-mail: info@themeynell.co.uk
dir: 7m W of Burton on Trent, 2 minute drive off the A515 main road between Lichfield on the A50

This handsome brick-built country inn stands at a quiet village crossroads and boasts a traditional pub interior with exposed beams, oak floors and open fires. The Deer Park Restaurant offers a comprehensive à la carte menu featuring locally-sourced produce. Included on the menu are some timeless classics with international influences,

such as tempura of king prawns with lemon and fennel salad to begin, followed by Gressingham duck breast served with confit barrel potatoes and an orange and green peppercorn sauce. Finish off with Bailey's brioche bread-and-butter pudding with vanilla ice cream.

Times 12-2/6.30-9.30, Closed 25 Dec

LEEK Map 16 SJ95

Three Horseshoes Inn & Country Hotel

◉ Modern British, Thai

Traditional inn offering an oriental twist to a modern British menu

☎ 01538 300296
Buxton Rd, Blackshaw Moor ST13 8TW
e-mail: enquiries@threeshoesinn.co.uk
dir: M6 junct 15 or 16 onto A500. Exit A53 towards Leek. Turn left onto A50 (Burslem)

This family-run, ivy-clad inn stands in immaculate grounds complete with a children's play area. Exposed beams, polished brass and rustic furniture set the scene and you can dine in either the bustling brasserie or more formal restaurant. The menu offers hearty British and fragrant Thai specialities, and everything is cooked before your eyes in the open, glassed kitchen. Seasonal ingredients from local suppliers are favoured in dishes such as soy-roasted chicken wings with watercress, red cabbage, fried leeks, shallots, soy and hazelnuts starter, followed by braised oxtail Wellington with Madeira sauce.

Chef Mark & Stephen Kirk **Owner** Bill, Jill, Mark & Stephen Kirk **Times** 12.30-2/6.30-9, Closed 26-30 Dec, Closed L Mon-Sat **Prices** Starter £4.10-£8.20, Main £10.50-£15, Dessert £3.95-£5.75 **Wines** 30 bottles over £20, 50 bottles under £20, 10 by glass **Notes** Tasting menu available, Dress restrictions, Smart casual, Civ Wed 150 **Seats** 50, Pr/dining room 150 **Children** Portions, Menu **Parking** 100

LICHFIELD Map 10 SK10

The Four Seasons Restaurant

◉◉ Modern British ℃

Stunning mansion and impressive cuisine

☎ 01543 481494
Swinfen Hall Hotel, Swinfen WS14 9RE
e-mail: info@swinfenhallhotel.co.uk
web: www.swinfenhallhotel.co.uk
dir: 2m S of Lichfield on A38 between Weeford rdbt and Swinfen rdbt. Follow A38 to Lichfield, hotel is 0.5m on right

Dating back to 1757, this lavishly decorated mansion has been painstakingly restored to create an exquisite country-house hotel. Set in 100 acres of parkland which includes a deer park, diners may well be amazed by the stunning entrance hall but the sumptuous public rooms with carved ceilings and original oil paintings will impress even further. Despite its opulence, Swinfen Hall is warm and welcoming. The oak-panelled Four Seasons restaurant offers a three-course fixed-price menu, showcasing the kitchen's contemporary approach, underpinned by classical French themes. Locally sourced, top quality ingredients are to the fore in dishes such as pan-fried John Dory with spinach and leek fondue and mussel cappuccino to start, followed by organic loin of grass-fed venison from their own deer park, served with honey-roast parsnips, chicory, orange and espresso sauce.

The Four Seasons Restaurant

Chef Matthew Warburton **Owner** Helen & Vic Wiser **Times** 12.30-2.30/7-9.30, Closed L Sat, Closed D Sun **Prices** Fixed L 2 course fr £19.95, Fixed D 3 course fr £42.50, Service optional **Wines** 108 bottles over £20, 9 bottles under £20, 6 by glass **Notes** Sunday L, Vegetarian available, Dress restrictions, No trainers or jeans, Civ Wed 120 **Seats** 50, Pr/dining room 20 **Children** Portions **Parking** 80

LONGNOR   Map 16 SK06

The Black Grouse

◉ Modern International

Skilfully prepared food in stylishly renovated Georgian inn with great views

☎ 01298 83205 & 83194
SK17 0NS
e-mail: food@theblackgrouse.co.uk
dir: In village centre on B5053

Previously called The Crewe and Harpur Arms and set in the heart of the Peak District National Park six miles south of Buxton, this charming Georgian inn has been sympathetically renovated to a high standard. The rustic, oak-panelled bar is the friendly, relaxed setting for a wide range of wines and real ales to complement locally-sourced food, handled with skill. Traditional bar favourites such as steak and kidney pie make way for more ambitious dishes in the stylish, more formal restaurant. Start with scallops and pak choi with ginger sauce, followed by roasted cod with potted shrimp risotto and tarragon and pea velouté, or calves' liver and champ with smoked bacon jus.

Chef Todd Carroll **Owner** Todd Carroll & Sophie Mitchell **Times** 12-2/6-9.30 **Prices** Starter £4-£9.95, Main £6.95-£16.50, Dessert £3.50-£6, Service optional **Wines** 39 bottles over £20, 21 bottles under £20 **Notes** Sunday L, Vegetarian available, Civ Wed 50 **Seats** 36 **Children** Portions **Parking** 100

RUGELEY   Map 10 SK01

The Plum Pudding

◉ Modern British 🖵

Innovative cooking, canal-side location

☎ 01543 490330
Rugeley Rd, Armitage WS15 4AZ
e-mail: enquiries@theplumpudding.co.uk
dir: M6 junct 11 follow signs for Cannock to Rugeley. Situated on A513 through Rugeley to Lichfield

With a large terrace alongside the Trent and Mersey canal, the atmosphere in this modern-rustic, heavily-beamed gastro-pub is relaxed and intimate, with friendly and attentive service. Plum Pudding was a popular name given to canal-side pubs. Fresh, locally sourced produce, from organic meats through to local cheeses, is found throughout a modern British menu that changes with the seasons and might take in smoked haddock fishcakes with cucumber and dill salsa for starters. Follow with chargrilled rib-eye steak with parsley mash and tarragon, or rump of Staffordshire lamb with Italian bean gremolata and celeriac chips, and Bakewell cheesecake with strawberry jam ice cream to finish.

Chef Carl Jones **Owner** Mr & Mrs J Takhar **Times** 12-3/6-11.30, Closed 1 Jan **Prices** Starter £3.95-£7.95, Main £8.95-£18.95, Dessert £4.50-£5.95, Service optional **Wines** 15 bottles over £20, 29 bottles under £20, 9 by glass **Notes** Sunday L, Vegetarian available **Seats** 70 **Children** Portions **Parking** 50

STAFFORD   Map 10 SJ92

Moat House

◉◉ Modern British

Cutting-edge menu meets conservatory dining in canal-side hotel

☎ 01785 712217
Lower Penkridge Rd, Acton Trussell ST17 0RJ
e-mail: info@moathouse.co.uk
web: www.moathouse.co.uk
dir: M6 junct 13 towards Stafford, 1st right to Acton Trussell, hotel by church

As the name suggests, this well restored hotel occupies a 17th-century former moated manor house. Situated in a picturesque village in an idyllic canal-side location, the main building is full of oak panelling and exposed beams. The informal Lounge Bar offers a range of snacks, while the more spacious and stylish fine-dining

Conservatory Restaurant is a modern, luxurious affair with high-backed seating and generous-sized tables, set to a backdrop of barges plying the canal. The enticing menu comes dotted with luxury items, promoting an agony of choice on a classically-based, modern-focused repertoire. Fresh, high-quality seasonal ingredients combine with a sense of flair to deliver skilfully-crafted, flavour-driven dishes that show the kitchen's pedigree. For starters, try smoked salmon and king prawn ravioli with pak choi, guacamole, lemon grass foam, pea shoots and chervil, while main courses might feature a rosette of Staffordshire beef fillet with beef daube, oxtail bon bon, swede and thyme purée, ceps, shallots and red wine.

Moat House

Chef Matthew Davies **Owner** The Lewis Partnership **Times** 12-2/7-9.30, Closed 25 Dec **Prices** Fixed L 2 course £14.50, Fixed D 3 course £18.50, Tasting menu £42, Starter £7.95-£10.50, Main £16-£21.95, Dessert £6.50-£7.50 **Notes** Vegetarian available, Civ Wed 120, Air con **Seats** 120, Pr/dining room 150 **Children** Portions, Menu **Parking** 200

STOKE-ON-TRENT   Map 10 SJ84

The Elms, Passion of India

◉ Indian

Welcoming Indian restaurant serving healthy dishes

☎ 01782 266360 & 07774 119983
Snowhill, Shelton ST1 4LY
dir: Telephone for directions

Once home to the famous potter John Ridgway, the building is an impressive sight with original cornices, windows and staircase. Today, this warm and friendly Indian restaurant produces regional Indian cooking with a healthy approach (most of it is less than five percent fat), introducing soft, light flavours with spices and herbs to enhance quality core ingredients. Take Pathar kebab, comprising marinated chicken cooked and served on stones; or The Elms special lamb cooked in a saffron sauce. One of the many vegetarian options is Hyderabadi baingan, an aubergine dish with tomatoes and a sweet, tangy taste.

Chef Harish Kumar, Mahboob Hussain **Owner** Pritpal Singh Nagi **Times** Closed 25 Dec, Closed Sun, Closed L Mon-Sat **Prices** Fixed D 3 course £20-£25, Starter £3.95-£10.95, Main £7.95-£12.95, Dessert £3.75-£4.50, Service optional **Wines** 8 bottles over £20, 2 by glass **Notes** Dress restrictions, Smart casual **Seats** 120, Pr/dining room 30 **Children** Portions **Parking** 80

STOKE ON TRENT *Continued*

Haydon House Hotel

◉ Modern British, European

Family-run hotel with a sound reputation

☎ 01782 711311
Haydon St, Basford ST4 6JD
e-mail: enquiries@haydon-house-hotel.co.uk
dir: From M6 take either junct 15 or 16, follow A500 to A53, take A53 signed Newcastle, take 2nd left before lights onto Haydon St

Standing like a sentry, this hotel watches over the district of Etruria, home to the workforce of Josiah Wedgwood's celebrated pottery for 200 years. The late Victorian townhouse retains many of the elegant original features and is a popular haunt for locals lured by the gracious décor and reputation for quality cuisine in the Townhouse restaurant. The carte and flambé menus change seasonally, with a weekly-changing fixed-price menu. Expect mains such as roast rack of Welsh lamb set on a mint and honey-enhanced wine sauce, or julienne of beef wrapped in a Staffordshire oatcake with a rich bordelaise wine sauce.

Times 12-2/7-9.30, Closed 26 Dec, 1 Jan, Closed L Sat

UTTOXETER	Map 10 SK03

Restaurant Gilmore at Strine's Farm

◉◉ Modern British ◔

Friendly, family-run farmhouse restaurant

☎ 01889 507100
Beamhurst ST14 5DZ
e-mail: paul@restaurantgilmore.com
web: www.restaurantgilmore.com
dir: 1.5m N of Uttoxeter on A522 to Cheadle. Set 400yds back from road along fenced farm track

This serious husband and wife-run establishment, the second incarnation of Restaurant Gilmore, occupies three separate rooms of a traditional Staffordshire farmhouse. (The original was in Birmingham a few years back.) The property is set in acres of open grounds, including cottage gardens, herb and vegetable plots, making it a popular venue for weddings. The kitchen uses local produce, along with home-grown fruits and vegetables from the garden, in modern British dishes with bold flavours and lighter touches. Recommendations include classic risotto Milanese with stewed porcini mushrooms flavoured with saffron and garlic juices, roast 'Packington Poultry' chicken with parsnip soufflé and Swiss chard, and praline rose nougat glacé with tayberry sauce.

Chef Paul Gilmore **Owner** Paul & Dee Gilmore
Times 12.30-2/7.30-9, Closed 1 wk Jan, 1 wk Etr, 1 wk Jul, 1 wk Oct, Closed Mon & Tue, Closed L Sat & Wed, Closed D Sun **Prices** Fixed L 2 course £19.50, Fixed D 3 course £38.50, Service optional, Groups min 8 service 10% **Wines** 30 bottles over £20, 20 bottles under £20, 10 by glass **Notes** Sunday L, Vegetarian available, Dress restrictions, Smart casual **Seats** 24 **Children** Portions **Parking** 12

YOXALL	Map 10 SK11

Foresters At Yoxall

◉ Modern British

Informal dining with simple flair in rural surroundings

☎ 01283 575939
62 Wood Ln DE13 8PH
e-mail: theforesters@hotmail.com
dir: On A515 Litchfield to Ashbourne road, 1m outside village of Yoxall

The Foresters is a modern-styled pub-restaurant, set in rural surroundings - as the name indicates - on the main road north of the village. Spread over three rooms - with one decked out with some comfy sofas - with a mix of wooden and carpeted floors. Tables are plain wood as are chairs, all helping to cultivate a relaxed, informal atmosphere, as does the polite and helpful service. The kitchen shows confident form, with simply prepared, clean-flavoured dishes from quality produce; take a starter of Archie's vintage cheese soufflé with two tomato dressing, followed by Staffordshire fillet of beef with Stilton fondant potato, crisp pancetta and red wine sauce.

Times 11.30-3/6.30-11.30, Closed 25-28 Dec, Closed Mon, Closed D Sun

SUFFOLK	
ALDEBURGH	**Map 13 TM45**

Best Western White Lion Hotel

◉ Modern British 🖥 ◔

Elegant dining by the sea

☎ 01728 452720
Market Cross Place IP15 5BJ
e-mail: info@whitelion.co.uk
dir: Please telephone for directions

Sympathetically furnished and retaining some of its 16th-century features, this popular hotel is situated at the quiet end of town, overlooking the shingle beach and the sea. There are two lounges, and the elegant, oak-panelled Restaurant 1563 (the year in which the hotel was built) featuring an intricately carved inglenook fireplace. Traditional British cooking with modern twists uses fresh, seasonal and locally sourced produce in dishes such as pot au feu of salt marsh beef with Suffolk onion pudding, or deep-fried Lowestoft haddock in Adnams Broadside batter served with mushy peas and chips cooked in dripping. Finish with rhubarb and apple charlotte.

Chef David Edward **Owner** Thorpeness and Aldeburgh Hotels Ltd **Times** 12-2.30/6.30-9.30 **Prices** Food prices not confirmed for 2009. Please telephone for details. **Wines** 27 bottles over £20, 26 bottles under £20, 22 by glass **Notes** Sunday L, Vegetarian available, Civ Wed 90 **Seats** 60, Pr/dining room 80 **Children** Portions, Menu **Parking** 15

The Brudenell

◉◉ Modern European 🖥

Chic modern brasserie just a few steps from the sea

☎ 01728 452071
The Parade IP15 5BU
e-mail: info@brudenellhotel.co.uk
dir: Please telephone for directions

The glass-fronted brasserie certainly makes the most of its fabulous location on an unspoiled stretch of Suffolk coast, a pebble's skim from the beach in the beautiful seaside town of Aldeburgh. The split-level restaurant has an informal, contemporary feel thanks to wooden tables, pastel shades and Mediterranean shutters, and you can dine on the terrace in summer. Culinary influences from around the world sit side by side on an extensive menu that sidesteps the usual fare to offer clever variations on the bistro theme. Start with chicken liver parfait with home-made Suffolk rusks, before sampling the fish of the day, perhaps fillet of plaice with home-made gnocchi and smoky bacon emulsion.

Chef Justin Kett **Owner** Thorpeness & Aldeburgh Hotels Ltd **Times** 12-2.30/6.30-9.30 **Prices** Fixed L 2 course £12.95, Starter £3.95-£9, Main £8.95-£17.95, Dessert £4.95, Service optional **Wines** 41 bottles over £20, 20 bottles under £20, 32 by glass **Notes** Sunday L, Vegetarian available **Seats** 100 **Children** Portions, Menu **Parking** 15

See advert opposite

152 Aldeburgh

◉ Modern British, European ◔

Well-tuned cooking in popular resort

☎ 01728 454594
152 High St IP15 5AX
e-mail: info@152aldeburgh.co.uk
web: www.152aldeburgh.co.uk
dir: Please telephone for details

Located through an archway from the High Street to the beach, this bustling brasserie exactly fits the Aldeburgh bill. Light and clean cut, the stripped wooden floors, cream panelling, pine tables and chairs, fresh flowers and informal, helpful and cheerful service, create a relaxed atmosphere that ticks all the right boxes. The compact seasonal European menus make good use of quality ingredients, with locally landed fish appearing with game in season and quality meats. Take baked leek and blue cheese tart, baby leaf with green pesto and balsamic, followed by sea bass, crushed potato and sprouting broccoli, and finish with sticky toffee pudding and caramel sauce.

Chef Mark Clements **Owner** Andrew Lister **Times** 12-3/6-10 **Prices** Fixed L 2 course £12.50-£16, Fixed D 3 course £18-£25, Starter £4.50-£7.50, Main £9.50-£18.50, Dessert £4.50, Service optional **Wines** 13 bottles over £20, 24 bottles under £20, 7 by glass **Notes** Sunday L, Vegetarian available **Seats** 56 **Children** Portions, Menu **Parking** On street parking on High St & Kings St

Regatta Restaurant

◉ Modern British

Busy, refurbished bistro-style restaurant featuring locally-caught fish

☎ 01728 452011
171 High St IP15 5AN
e-mail: regatta.restaurant@aldeburgh.sagegost.co.uk
dir: Middle of High St, town centre

Recently refurbished with comfortable banquette seating, clean lines and stylish décor, this contemporary bistro-style restaurant features locally-caught fish and seafood as its mainstay. A blackboard gives a daily update on the freshly caught offerings, while the menu lists the alternatives. Staff are stylishly dressed and service is very relaxed. Food comes simply cooked and presented with clear flavours from the wonderfully fresh ingredients. Expect starters like bruschetta of crayfish with wild mushrooms, then perhaps a trio of smoked organic

salmon with smoked prawns and bradan rost from the smoke house specialities, or excellent tempura of local sole with saffron fricassée. Look out for special gourmet evenings.

Chef Robert Mabey **Owner** Mr & Mrs R Mabey **Times** 12-2/6-10, Closed 24-26 Dec, Closed D Sun (Nov-Feb) **Prices** Starter £3.50-£7.50, Main £9.50-£21.50, Dessert £4-£5.50 **Wines** 6 bottles over £20, 40 bottles under £20, 6 by glass **Notes** Vegetarian available, Air con **Seats** 90, Pr/dining room 30 **Children** Portions, Menu **Parking** On street

Wentworth Hotel

◉◉ Modern British

Traditional values with modern twists in seafront hotel

☎ 01728 452312
Wentworth Rd IP15 5BD
e-mail: stay@wentworth-aldeburgh.co.uk
dir: From A12 take A1094 to Aldeburgh. In Aldeburgh straight on at mini rdbt, turn left at x-roads into Wentworth Rd. Hotel on right

Managed by the same family for more than 80 years, this reassuringly traditional hotel exudes a real sense of quality and retains the charm of a private residence. It overlooks the beach at the quiet end of town, and has three stylish lounges and a cocktail bar in addition to the dining room with superb sea views. Elegantly decorated in Etruscan red, complemented by well-dressed tables

and high-quality settings, the smart dining room is a beacon of excellence locally, with its mixture of firm favourites and an upbeat modern approach. Seasonal changes and local suppliers keep the food fresh and interesting on daily-changing menus. Steamed Brancaster mussels with white wine, onion and cream starter might feature alongside an assiette of salmon, sea bream and sea bass with black olive and tomato sauce for main course.

Chef Graham Reid **Owner** Wentworth Hotel Ltd/Michael Pritt **Times** 12-2/7-9 **Prices** Fixed L 2 course £12-£18, Fixed D 3 course £17-£32, Service optional **Wines** 13 bottles over £20, 41 bottles under £20, 10 by glass **Notes** Sunday L, Vegetarian available **Seats** 90, Pr/dining room 20 **Children** Portions, Menu **Parking** 33

BARNBY · Map 13 TM48

The Swan Inn

◉ Seafood

Unpretentious pub serving a stunning array of fresh fish

☎ 01502 476646
Swan Ln NR34 7QF
dir: Telephone for directions

A traditional inn with its distinctive pink walls and village bar, The Swan is also very well known for its fish restaurant called the Fisherman's Cove. In this low-beamed room, the nautical memorabilia includes the bow of a small dinghy mounted on the wall, where blackboards list the day's choice. Owned by a family of Lowestoft fish merchants, it offers a variety of the freshest fish, simply pan fried, grilled or cooked in batter, and served with chips or new potatoes, salads or peas. Expect scallops sautéed in garlic butter, or deep-fried codling in crisp beer batter served with chips, peas and a mixed salad.

Times 12-2/7-9

BILDESTON — Map 13 TL94

The Bildeston Crown

@@@ – *see below*

BUNGAY — Map 13 TM38

Earsham Street Café

@@ Modern British, Mediterranean 🍷

Modern cooking in busy neighbourhood café

☎ 01986 893103
11-13 Earsham St NR35 1AE
e-mail: www.earshamstcafe@aol.com
dir: In the centre of Bungay

This bustling café has an informal and relaxed atmosphere and the chic décor provides the perfect setting for modern cooking with Mediterranean influences, delivering simple flavours using the freshest ingredients. Dishes are well executed and the daily-changing menus have an emphasis on fresh fish and seafood. Start with pan-fried oysters, chorizo, fennel and butter bean salad, followed by a main course of roast sea bass with pea and goat's cheese risotto and chargrilled fennel, or sticky pork belly with mango, spring onion and cherry tomatoes. Hot chocolate black forest fondant with sloe gin and damson ice cream might prove a fitting finale, accompanied by a recommended dessert wine. A big favourite with the locals, there's often a queue out the door, so be sure to book a table.

Chef Christopher Rice, James Stewart **Owner** Rebecca Mackenzie, Stephen David **Times** 9.30-4.30/7-9, Closed Xmas, New Year, BHs, Closed D ex last Fri & Sat of month **Prices** Starter £4.50-£9.95, Main £9.95-£18.95, Dessert fr £6, Service optional **Wines** 27 bottles over £20, 22 bottles under £20, 16 by glass **Notes** Sunday L, Vegetarian available **Seats** 55, Pr/dining room 16 **Children** Portions, Menu **Parking** Parking opposite

BURY ST EDMUNDS — Map 13 TL86

Angel Hotel - The Eaterie

@@ Modern British 🍷

Accomplished cooking in historic building

☎ 01284 714000
Angel Hill IP33 1LT
e-mail: sales@theangel.co.uk
dir: Town centre, right from Northgate St traffic lights

A short walk from the centre of Bury St Edmunds, this impressive coaching inn has a long history of hospitality and boasts Charles Dickens among former guests. It stands in a pretty square looking across to the cathedral, and has a cosy contemporary feel despite its heritage charms. The place has undergone a complete facelift in recent months. Both the refurbished Angel eaterie, with its stunning artwork and stylish design, and the 12th-century stone Vaults restaurant below the ground floor are relaxed in style, and serve accomplished food along modern British lines. Starters might include a warm salad of pigeon with chorizo and pine nuts, with pork tenderloin stuffed with black pudding a typical main, served with bubble-and-squeak and cider jus.

Chef Simon Barker **Owner** Robert Gough **Times** 7am/10pm **Prices** Fixed L 2 course fr £12.95, Starter £4.95-£8.95, Main £12.95-£21.50, Dessert £5.95-£8.50, Service optional **Wines** 48 bottles over £20, 18 bottles under £20, 24 by glass **Notes** Vegetarian available, Dress restrictions, Smart casual/dress, Civ Wed 85 **Seats** 85, Pr/dining room 80 **Children** Portions **Parking** 30

The Bildeston Crown

BILDESTON — Map 13 TL94

Modern British 🍷

Highly accomplished cooking in a stylish country inn

☎ 01449 740510
104 High St IP7 7EB
e-mail: hayley@thebildestoncrown.co.uk
dir: A12 junct 31. B1070 to Hadleigh, B1115 to Bildeston

This 15th-century coaching inn has survived successive generations to become a 21st-century gem. The owners have got the balance just right, maintaining a sense of the original from the sensitive refurbishment of the exterior to the retention inside of the heavy beams and large fireplaces, and by choosing colours from the traditional local palette. The introduction of contemporary furniture and solid oak tables, and a good use of space, results in a successful balance of old and new. And it is still very much a pub - a drink at the bar is an option. The food is taken seriously here whether it's a sandwich in the bar or a full meal in the restaurant (the main menu is available in the bar as well), and local and seasonal produce are to the fore. There is a British flavour to the menu, but the dishes are modern, imaginative and prepared with a high degree of skill. A starter of seared scallops - nicely caramelised - comes with lobster tail, cauliflower, as both purée and beignet, and spiced date chutney in an impressive starter, while Gloucestershire Old Spot pork belly is partnered with lobster ravioli and pollack in a compelling combination. Finish with a zesty lemon posset and lemon olive oil cake served with an orange and basil salad. Service is efficient and well informed about the menu.

Chef Chris Lee **Owner** Mrs G Buckle, Mr J K Buckle **Times** 12-7/3-10, Closed D 25 Dec, 1 Jan **Prices** Fixed L 2 course fr £16, Fixed D 3 course fr £20, Starter £7-£11, Main £10-£20, Dessert £7-£10, Service optional, Groups min 10 service 12.5% **Wines** 118 bottles over £20, 18 bottles under £20, 17 by glass **Notes** Tasting menu available, Sunday L, Vegetarian available, Civ Wed 24 **Seats** 100, Pr/dining room 16 **Children** Portions **Parking** 36

Best Western Priory Hotel

◎◎ Modern, Traditional British

Accomplished manor-house hotel dining

☎ 01284 766181
Mildenhall Rd IP32 6EH
e-mail: reservations@prioryhotel.co.uk
web: www.prioryhotel.co.uk
dir: From Bury St Edmunds follow signs for Mildenhall
A1011. 1m out of town centre

This 18th-century Grade II listed property in a pretty
location on the edge of town was built on the remains of
a 13th-century priory - hence the name. The equally
aptly-named Garden Restaurant lies beyond the
landscaped gardens, where modern artwork and
contemporary décor create a comfortable environment.
After pre-dinner drinks in the lounge, the well-executed
blend of British and Europe-influenced cuisine
incorporating the finest, locally-sourced ingredients
ensures an accomplished meal. Try a starter of ravioli of
crab and sweetcorn, with chilli and shellfish oil and
chervil, or chargrilled peach with basil sorbet, frisée,
crushed pistachios and parmesan tuile, followed by pan-
seared sea trout with fennel carpaccio, roast cherry vine
tomatoes, Anya potatoes and caper and orange dressing.

Chef Graham Smith **Owner** Priory Hotel Ltd.
Times 12.30-2/7-10, Closed L Sat **Prices** Fixed L 2 course
fr £15, Fixed D 3 course fr £17, Starter fr £5, Main fr £12,
Dessert fr £5, Service added but optional 10% **Wines** 20
bottles over £20, 12 bottles under £20, 6 by glass
Notes Coffee inc, Sunday L, Vegetarian available, Civ
Wed 55 **Seats** 74, Pr/dining room 26 **Children** Portions
Parking 60

Clarice House

◎ Modern European

Upmarket health and beauty spa with modern menu

☎ 01284 705550
Horringer Court, Horringer Rd IP29 5PH
e-mail: bury@claricehouse.co.uk
web: www.claricehouse .co.uk
dir: From Bury St Edmunds on A143 towards Horringer
and Haverhill, hotel 1m from town centre on right

This attractive neo-Jacobean mansion, now doubles as
relaxed country-house hotel and spa. As you'd expect,
healthy eating is the order of the day in the intimate oak-
panelled restaurant, complemented with modern
artworks. With nicely adorned and well-spaced tables,
you can expect lighter options, such as a warm salad of
herbed omelette ribbons, grilled asparagus spears, fried
potatoes, orange segments and hazelnut vinaigrette, as
well as more hearty fare: pan-roasted breast of corn-fed
chicken served with a root vegetable and chestnut torte,
garlic and herb mashed potatoes and red wine sauce, for
example. After lunch, take a stroll in the beautiful
landscaped gardens.

Chef Steve Winser **Owner** King Family **Times** 12-2/7-9,
Closed 25-26 Dec, 1 Jan **Prices** Fixed L 2 course £16.95,
Fixed D 3 course £24.95, Service optional **Wines** 13 bottles

over £20, 28 bottles under £20, 7 by glass **Notes** Sunday L,
Vegetarian available, Dress restrictions, Smart casual D,
Air con **Seats** 40, Pr/dining room 20 **Parking** 82

The Leaping Hare Restaurant & Country Store

◎◎ Modern British 🌱

Seasonal local produce served in a vineyard restaurant

☎ 01359 250287
Stanton IP31 2DW
e-mail: info@wykenvineyards.co.uk
dir: 8m NE of Bury St Edmunds, 1m off A143. Follow
brown signs at Ixworth to Wyken Vineyards

A vineyard restaurant, part of the Wyken Hall estate, The
Leaping Hare is set in a 400-year-old Suffolk barn. The
barn, which also houses the Country Store, has high
ceilings, old beams, wooden flooring and large windows
looking south over fields and woods. The place is warmed
by wood-burning stoves and adorned with paintings and
tapestries of leaping hares. Simple modern cooking with
the emphasis on flavour is based on quality produce,
usually from within a five-mile radius, and some home-
grown (including lamb, venison and pheasant from the
estate, and wine too). There is also a commitment to
seasonality, with Suffolk asparagus in April and May, for
example. Simpler meals are served in the on-site café.

Chef Jon Ellis **Owner** Kenneth & Carla Carlisle
Times 12-2.30/7-9, Closed 2 wks Xmas, Closed D Sun-
Thu **Prices** Fixed L 2 course £16.95, Starter £5.95-£6.95,
Main £12.95-£17.95, Dessert £5.50, Service optional,
Groups min 6 service 10% **Wines** 16 bottles over £20, 24
bottles under £20, 27 by glass **Notes** Vegetarian
available **Seats** 55 **Children** Portions **Parking** 50

Maison Bleue

◎◎ French

Upbeat French seafood brasserie

☎ 01284 760623
30-31 Churchgate St IP33 1RG
e-mail: info@maisonbleue.co.uk
dir: Town centre, Churchgate St is opposite cathedral

With a local reputation as a convivial and stylish place to
dine, a refurbishment in early 2008 has given this chic
seafood restaurant a smart makeover. Served by
charming French staff, seafood is the speciality, but
carnivores aren't forgotten as options such as roast rack
of lamb with garlic sauce, or pan-fried Gressingham

duck with lime sauce testify. Expect accomplished, well-
presented cooking: pot-roast monkfish tail with smoked
pork belly and Savoy cabbage for example, or perhaps
poached wild turbot and rainbow trout mousse wrapped
in carrots with sorrel sauce. The bargain 'plat du jour
with coffee' lunch is not to be missed, and it's well worth
booking ahead for the plateau de fruits de mer.

Chef Pascal Canevet **Owner** Regis Crepy
Times 12-2.30/7-9.30, Closed Jan, 2 wks in summer,
Closed Sun-Mon **Wines** 80 bottles over £20, 62 bottles
under £20, 7 by glass **Notes** Pre-theatre 2 courses
£16.95 from 6.15pm, Vegetarian available, Dress
restrictions, Smart casual preferred **Seats** 65, Pr/dining
room 35 **Children** Portions **Parking** On street

Nazar

◎ Turkish

**Authentic Turkish cuisine in relaxed, lively
surroundings**

☎ 01284 704870
19-21 Angel Hill IP33 1UZ
e-mail: info@nazar-bse.co.uk

Situated on Angel Hill, this traditional-style building with
wooden beams and furniture is brought to life with Turkish
music and tapestry-style tablecloths, creating a relaxing
atmosphere in which to enjoy some authentic cuisine. For a
simple fresh starter, try squid rings in crunchy batter with
lightly dressed leaves, while mains include the likes of
shish kebab - tender pieces of marinated lamb on skewers,
cooked on the charcoal grill and served with rice, tomatoes
and pepper. Try the Turkish rice pudding made with milk
and rose water for dessert.

Times 12-2.30/6-11, Closed Mon

Ravenwood Hall Hotel

◎◎ Traditional Mediterranean

Tudor hall with traditional food

☎ 01359 270345
Rougham IP30 9JA
e-mail: enquiries@ravenwoodhall.co.uk
dir: 3m from Bury St Edmunds, just off A14 junct 45
signed Rougham

With its origins in the reign of Henry VIII, this historic
property is set in 7 acres of tranquil countryside. The hall
itself has been restored over the years but retains an
ornate carved oak structure, inglenook fireplaces and rare
15th-century wall paintings. Accommodating staff and
accomplished cuisine make dining here a truly relaxed
and unpretentious affair, with prime local produce to the
fore. The cooking style tends toward more familiar
classics with seasonal twists, while home-smoked fish
and meats and herbs from the garden add a homely
touch. Expect starters such as confit of duck leg and foie
gras terrine, with mains like pan-fried breast of guinea
fowl served on a bed of garlic tagliatelle. Round off the
meal with a lemon and crystallised ginger syllabub.

Times 12-2.30/7.30-9.30

IXWORTH
Map 13 TL97

Theobalds Restaurant

◉ Modern British

Village restaurant full of character

☎ 01359 231707
68 High Street IP31 2HJ
web: www.theobaldsrestaurant.co.uk
dir: 7m from Bury St Edmunds on A143 Bury/Diss road

Simon and Geraldine Theobald's long established restaurant is housed in a 16th-century timber-framed property, beamed throughout, with a large inglenook fireplace in the bar lounge area. There is also a pretty patio garden for drinks in warmer weather. The menu changes with the seasons to use quality ingredients at their best. Classical cooking methods are used to produce dishes such as potted dressed crab and smoked salmon, with avocado and cucumber, served with lime juice and walnut oil dressing, and noisette of venison, wrapped in pancetta, with celeriac mash and game sauce.

Chef Simon Theobald **Owner** Simon & Geraldine Theobald **Times** 12.15-1.30/7-9, Closed 10 days in Summer, Closed Mon, Closed L Tue, Thu, Sat, Closed D Sun **Prices** Fixed L 2 course fr £21, Fixed D 3 course £28, Starter £6.95-£8.95, Main £15.95-£19.95, Dessert £6.95, Service optional **Wines** 44 bottles over £20, 19 bottles under £20, 6 by glass **Notes** Sunday L, Vegetarian available **Seats** 42, Pr/dining room 16 **Children** Min 8 yrs D, Portions **Parking** On street

---

LAVENHAM
Map 13 TL94

The Angel

◉ Modern British

Medieval inn with lip-smacking food

☎ 01787 247388
Market Place CO10 9QZ
e-mail: angel@maypolehotels.com
web: www.maypolehotels.com
dir: Between Bury St Edmunds and Sudbury on A1141. In town centre, Market Place just off High St

The Angel stands at the centre of one of England's finest medieval villages overlooking the market place, and was first licensed in 1420. The décor is in keeping with the period of the building, which has lots of oak beams, a large inglenook fireplace with log fires in winter and sturdy wooden tables and chairs. The cooking has a

traditional English base (soups, pies, casseroles and roasts) but has evolved to suit more sophisticated palates with some continental and oriental influences. Steak and ale pie, roast loin of lamb, and steamed syrup sponge pudding are still favourites.

Chef Michael Pursell **Owner** Mr Alastair McEwen **Times** 12-2.15/6.45-9.15 **Prices** Starter £4.50-£6.95, Main £7.95-£15.95, Dessert £4.50-£5.75, Service optional, Groups min 10 service 10% **Wines** 15 bottles over £20, 26 bottles under £20, 10 by glass **Notes** Sunday L, Vegetarian available, Dress restrictions, Smart casual **Seats** 100, Pr/dining room 16 **Children** Portions **Parking** 5

Lavenham Great House Restaurant with Rooms

◉◉ French

Gallic charm in Tudor setting

☎ 01787 247431
Market Place CO10 9QZ
e-mail: info@greathouse.co.uk
web: www.greathouse.co.uk
dir: In Market Place turn onto Market Lane from High Street

Built in the 14th and 15th centuries for an important weaving family, this impressive house with a Georgian façade occupies an imposing position in this important medieval wool town, opposite the historic Guildhall, overlooking the market square. In this most English of settings, The Great House is a resolutely French restaurant with rooms, offering high-quality rural cuisine served by friendly French staff. Recent extensive refurbishment has resulted in a classic contemporary look that enhances the period charm of the beamed Tudor dining room, with its huge inglenook, oak floors, exposed brickwork and uneven walls. In the kitchen an accomplished team favours well-sourced luxury ingredients and an elaborate style, delivering carefully prepared dishes like Scottish monkfish tail poached in red wine, with garlic and potato mousseline and red wine butter.

Chef Regis Crepy **Owner** Mr & Mrs Crepy **Times** 12-2.30/7-9.30, Closed Jan, Closed Mon, Closed L Tue, Closed D Sun **Prices** Fixed L 2 course fr £14.95, Fixed D 3 course £26.95, Starter £6.95-£12.95, Main £15.95-£23.95, Dessert £5.50, Service optional, Groups min 10 service 10% **Wines** 65 bottles over £20, 75 bottles under £20, 10 by glass **Notes** Sunday L, Vegetarian available **Seats** 40, Pr/dining room 15 **Children** Portions **Parking** Market Place

---

The Swan Hotel

◉◉ Modern, Traditional 💻

Dine surrounded by medieval splendour

☎ 01787 247477
High St CO10 9QA
e-mail: info@theswanatlavenham.co.uk
dir: From Bury St Edmunds take A134 for 6m. Lavenham is 6m along B1071

Nestling in the picturesque Suffolk countryside, this quintessential English timber-framed property, dating from the 15th century, stands out even amongst its medieval and Tudor village setting. Once key to the town's famous wool trade, it is formed from a collection of delightful listed buildings and the interior is a riot of ancient oak beams, panelled walls, leaded lights and inglenook fireplaces. The elegant medieval great hall, complete with a minstrels' gallery, is populated by well-spaced tables, comfortably upholstered chairs, expensive table linen and formal settings. Attentive staff serve accomplished, well-presented modern British and European dishes using prime local produce. Ballotine of salmon with sweet potato rémoulade and mustard dressing, followed by main courses like pan-fried sirloin of beef topped with a Paris mushroom, with rösti potato, cherry vine tomatoes and Madeira jus are fine examples of the fare. There's also an informal brasserie and rustic bar.

Chef David Ryan **Owner** Thorpeness & Aldeburgh Hotels Ltd **Times** 12-2.30/7-9.30 **Prices** Fixed L 2 course £11.95, Fixed D 3 course £29.95-£37.95, Starter £6.50-£9.50, Main £16.95-£21.99, Dessert £6-£9.50, Service optional **Wines** 85 bottles over £20, 40 bottles under £20, 12 by glass **Notes** Sunday L, Dress restrictions, No jeans or trainers, Civ Wed 100, Air con **Seats** 90, Pr/dining room 32 **Children** Portions, Menu **Parking** 50

See advert opposite

LONG MELFORD Map 13 TL84

The Black Lion Hotel

🏵 Traditional, Mediterranean 🍃

Stylish hotel dining overlooking the village green

☎ 01787 312356
Church Walk, The Green CO10 9DN
e-mail: enquiries@blacklionhotel.net
dir: From Bury St Edmunds take A134 to Sudbury. Turn right onto B1064 to Long Melford. Right onto A1092 to Cavendish. Black Lion on the green

Overlooking the village green, this charming Georgian building combines contemporary furnishings, warm colours and crisp white linen with exquisite antiques and oil paintings, giving the restaurant a formal, elegant feel. Local, flavoursome produce is used to the full in British dishes that have a Mediterranean twist. Try rabbit and spiced gammon steamed suet pudding, or whole sea bass baked with rosemary, lemon and sea salt. Desserts are a treat too and might include steamed plum sponge pudding with custard. The same innovative seasonal menu is also available in the cosy lounge-bar.

Chef Annette Beasant **Owner** Craig Jarvis
Times 12-2/7-9.30 **Prices** Starter £5.95-£7.50, Main £11.95-£22.95, Dessert fr £5.50, Service optional
Wines 53 bottles over £20, 31 bottles under £20, 10 by glass **Notes** Sunday L, Vegetarian available, Civ Wed 50 **Seats** 50, Pr/dining room 20 **Children** Portions, Menu **Parking** 10

Scutchers Restaurant

🏵🏵 Modern British 🍃

Confident cooking in bright and bustling bistro

☎ 01787 310200
Westgate St CO10 9DP
e-mail: info@scutchers.com
dir: About 1m from Long Melford towards Clare

A bright and lively bistro where coloured fabrics, pine furnishings, artwork and modern lighting combine seamlessly with the old beams of this ancient building, which dates back to the 16th century. It may look smart but the atmosphere is relaxed, unpretentious and friendly. Modern British cooking gets positive treatment, the style being simple, with the quality and freshness of the raw ingredients enhancing competently cooked dishes. Typical choices on the extensive carte include grilled fillet of halibut on crushed potatoes with crab butter sauce, roast breast of Gressingham duck with caramelised apple compote and marsala gravy and white, dark and milk chocolate truffle terrine with coffee bean sauce. A good-value fixed price weekday menu is also available.

Chef Nicholas Barrett **Owner** Nicholas & Diane Barrett
Times 12-2/7-9.30, Closed 25 Dec, 2wks Mar, last wk Aug, Closed Sun-Mon **Prices** Fixed L 2 course £15, Fixed D 3 course £20, Starter £5-£12, Main £12-£23, Dessert £6, Service optional **Wines** 90 bottles over £20, 7 bottles under £20, 17 by glass **Notes** Air con **Seats** 70 **Children** Portions **Parking** 12

LOWESTOFT Map 13 TM59

Carlton Manor Hotel

🏵 Modern V

Smart restaurant in attractive manor house

☎ 01502 566511
Chapel Rd, Carlton Colville NR33 8BL
e-mail: reservations@thecarltonmanor.com
dir: off A146 Beccles/Lowestoft follow signs to Carlton Manor & Transport Museum

Set in beautiful countryside, this delightful Victorian manor house has recently undergone an impressive refurbishment. The smart lounge bar is perfect for aperitifs, and the light-and-airy restaurant, complete with a variety of different tables and chairs, opens onto a sunny terrace. With professional yet relaxed service, the à la carte and set menus make the most of fresh, seasonal ingredients. Typical starters might include creamy crab bisque with a home-baked wholemeal roll, followed by ribeye steak with French onion rings, roasted vine tomatoes and hand-cut chips, and Bakewell tart with home-made crème anglaise and Cointreau to finish.

Chef Jonathan Nicholson **Owner** Jonathan & Charlotte Nicholson **Times** 12-2.3/6-9.3 **Prices** Fixed L 2 course £6.95-£8.95, Starter £3.95-£5.95, Main £7.95-£17.95, Dessert £4.50 **Wines** 6 by glass **Notes** Vegetarian menu, Civ Wed 70 **Seats** 60, Pr/dining room 70 **Children** Portions, Menu **Parking** 50

LOWESTOFT *Continued*

The Crooked Barn

◉◉ Modern European ✤

Characterful dining in a restful Broads setting

☎ 01502 501353
Ivy House Country Hotel, Ivy Ln, Oulton Broad NR33 8HY
e-mail: aa@ivyhousecountryhotel.co.uk
web: www.ivyhousecountryhotel.co.uk
dir: A146 into Ivy Lane

Complete with creaking floorboards and crooked beams, this converted 18th-century thatched barn at the Ivy House Country Hotel makes a delightful dinner venue. Local artists' work is displayed on the walls and tables are clad in pale green with crisp linen napkins. There are views over the beautiful gardens and ornamental lily ponds, and a courtyard for summer dining. Modern British and European dishes - made with fresh, predominantly local ingredients - revel in their simplicity and freshness. Try an paupiette of local smoked chicken and king prawns, followed by pan-fried fillet of Suffolk beef with horseradish mash, black pudding and red wine jus. Finish with the speciality Ivy House baked Alaska.

Chef Martin Whitelock **Owner** Caroline Coe
Times 12-1.45/7-9.30, Closed 24 Dec-8 Jan **Prices** Fixed L 2 course £16.95-£18.95, Starter £4.95-£12.95, Main £14.95-£26.95, Dessert £5.50-£11.95, Service included **Wines** 12 bottles over £20, 23 bottles under £20, 4 by glass **Notes** Sunday L, Vegetarian available, Dress restrictions, Smart casual, No shorts, Civ Wed 80 **Seats** 45, Pr/dining room 24 **Children** Portions **Parking** 50

MONKS ELEIGH Map 13 TL94

The Swan Inn

◉◉ Modern, Traditional British, European ✤

Attractive pub with culinary clout

☎ 01449 741391
The Street IP7 7AU
e-mail: carol@monkseleigh.com
dir: On B1115 between Sudbury & Hadleigh

Situated in the heart of a 'chocolate-box' Suffolk village, this pretty 16th-century thatched pub is driven by culinary aspirations while remaining true to its local roots. The refurbished light modern bar area comes decked out with oak floors, beamed ceilings and an open

fire, while blackboard menus confirm the kitchen's serious intent. Driven by quality local seasonal produce, the cooking's modern bistro-style approach is intelligently unfussy, allowing the main ingredient to shine. Start with a simple dish of dressed Cromer crab with lemon and mayonnaise, or perhaps pan-fried scallops with crispy sage leaves, capers and pink grapefruit. Follow with whole roast sea bass with ginger and coriander butter, and for dessert you may not be able to resist an excellent chocolate pot with a quenelle of cream.

Chef Nigel Ramsbottom **Owner** Nigel Ramsbottom
Times 12-2/7-9.30, Closed 25-26 Dec, 1-2 Jan, Closed Mon-Tue (except BHs) **Prices** Fixed L 2 course £12.50-£15.50, Fixed D 3 course £16.50-£20.50, Starter £5-£9, Main £10-£20, Dessert £5-£8, Service optional **Wines** 10 bottles over £20, 30 bottles under £20, 10 by glass **Notes** Sunday L, Vegetarian available **Seats** 30, Pr/dining room 24 **Children** Portions **Parking** 12

NAYLAND Map 13 TL93

The White Hart Inn

◉◉ French, Italian, Mediterranean

First-rate gastro-pub cuisine with a French twist

☎ 01206 263382
High St CO6 4JF
e-mail: reservations@whitehart-nayland.co.uk
dir: 6m N of Colchester on A134 towards Sudbury

Situated in the heart of Constable country, this 15th-century coaching inn has all the charm you would expect of a delightful English village in this area. Heavy wooden beams, tiled floors and feature fireplaces add character, while the restaurant is a more elegant affair, formally laid at dinner, and there's a terrace for alfresco summer dining, too. The kitchen's French flair is complemented by polished, friendly and mostly Gallic service, and the extensive repertoire of assured dishes uses good quality local seasonal produce. Expect chicken liver parfait with a salad of dressed mixed leaves and a quenelle of home-made chutney to start, with mains such as chargrilled Denham Estate beef and hand-cut chips, and a chocolate fondant with home-made white chocolate ice cream to finish. Lunchtimes see a lighter selection.

Times 12-2/7-9

NEWMARKET Map 12 TL66

Bedford Lodge Hotel

◉◉ Modern International

A perfect place to dine during Newmarket races

☎ 01638 663175
Bury Rd CB8 7BX
e-mail: info@bedfordlodgehotel.co.uk
dir: From town centre follow A1303 towards Bury St Edmunds for 0.5m

Based around an 18th-century Georgian hunting lodge, imposing Bedford Lodge is popular with the racing

fraternity, who enjoy its combination of period elegance and leisurely informality as well as the proximity to the gallops at Newmarket. The Orangery restaurant, decorated in sympathy with the original property, offers an inventive and distinguished menu. Well-executed dishes may take in scallops with pea and parmesan risotto and chorizo foam to start, with trio of lamb (herb-crusted rack, roast shoulder, mini shepherd's pie) with sweet potato purée and shallot and red wine sauce, or spiced monkfish with clam and vanilla chowder for main course. To finish, try the coconut pannacotta with spicy pineapple sorbet.

Chef Paul Owens **Owner** Barnham Broom Golf Club
Times 12-2.30/7-9.30, Closed L Sat **Prices** Fixed L 2 course £16.50, Fixed D 3 course £29, Starter £7.50-£9.95, Main £15.50-£25, Dessert £6.50-£8.50, Service optional **Wines** 141 bottles over £20, 22 bottles under £20, 9 by glass **Notes** Sunday L, Dress restrictions, No shorts, sandals, vests, Civ Wed 120, Air con **Seats** 47, Pr/dining room 150 **Children** Portions, Menu **Parking** 100

The Rutland Arms Hotel

◉ British, Mediterranean

Relaxed wine bar and restaurant in the heart of this popular racing town

☎ 01638 664251
High St CB8 8NB
e-mail: reservations.rutlandarms@ohiml.com

Part of the Rutland Arms Hotel and with its own separate entrance just off the high street, the aptly-named Carriages restaurant and wine bar recalls the days when this was the entrance for horses and coaches. Today, the surroundings could not be more different. There's a smart bar area with comfy contemporary-style armchairs and stools, and light solid wood floors leading through to the dining area, where darkwood tables and coffee-coloured chairs contrast with cream walls. Simple, fresh ingredients feature on the good-value modern European menu. Crowd-pleasing starters include the likes of freshly baked Camembert with celery and onion soldiers and roasted cherry tomato and onion jam, or chargrilled chicken breast with green beans, gratin potatoes, and forestière sauce, and glazed lemon tarte with crème fraîche to close.

Prices Food prices not confirmed for 2009. Please telephone for details.

Tuddenham Mill

◉ Modern European

Relaxed, stylish brasserie in a former mill

☎ 01638 713552
Tuddenham St Mary IP28 6SQ

Set in idyllic countryside, this smart new restaurant is a mix of rustic charm and modern-day sophistication. It is set over two floors of a converted mill with a large illuminated wooden wheel dramatically covering one wall; the ground floor incorporates the reception and bar, with the main dining room upstairs. Huge exposed beams blend with contemporary prints, modern dark-lacquered tables and brown suede chairs, while staff are relaxed and don long black aprons. The cooking follows the modern European theme using the best of local produce; take duck parfait, breast and confit spring rolls to open, followed by lamb - shank, lamb with roasted vegetables and shepherd's pie.

Times 12-2.30/6.30-10.30

ORFORD
Map 13 TM45

The Crown & Castle

◎◎ Modern V

Quality cooking on the Suffolk coast

☎ 01394 450205
IP12 2LJ
e-mail: info@crownandcastle.co.uk
web: www.crownandcastle.co.uk
dir: 9m E of Woodbridge, off A12

This red-brick Victorian inn stands on Orford's old market square, next to the castle keep, overlooking the estuary. Proprietor, food writer Ruth Watson, has put this bistro on the culinary map. There is a relaxed style to the Trinity restaurant with its plush bench seating and dark wooden floors and tables. Staff wear long black aprons, and service is professional but laid back. The emphasis is on local produce and many of the dishes are featured in Ruth's cookbooks. The menu divides into raw, cold and hot dishes, including Orford-caught sea bass with Moorish-style cauliflower, saffron and barberries, or rump of Suffolk lamb and roast Niçoise salad and aioli. Warm fig and frangipane tart with proper custard or crushed meringue, fresh pomegranate and vanilla ice cream sundae might catch the eye at dessert.

Chef Ruth Watson, Max Dougal **Owner** David & Ruth Watson **Times** 12.15-2.15/7-9.30, Closed 7-11 Jan **Prices** Fixed L 2 course £14.95, Starter £4.95-£9.50, Main £12.95-£19.50, Dessert £6.50, Service optional, Groups min 8 service 10% **Wines** 98 bottles over £20, 24 bottles under £20, 14 by glass **Notes** Fixed D Sat & BHs only, Sunday L, Vegetarian menu **Seats** 60, Pr/dining room 10 **Children** Min 8 yrs D, Menu **Parking** 20

SOUTHWOLD
Map 13 TM57

The Crown

◎ Modern British ♨ ✋

A modern twist on traditional fare at a seaside inn

☎ 01502 722275
90 High St IP18 6DP
e-mail: crown.reception@adnams.co.uk
dir: Take A1095 from A12; hotel in the middle of the High Street

This early 19th-century coaching inn provides the services of a pub, wine bar, restaurant and small hotel, with Adnams ales, a celebrated wine list and good food prepared from fresh, locally-sourced ingredients, organic where possible. There's a panelled snug with a nautical

---

theme at the back, a main bar at the front with a lively cosmopolitan atmosphere, and a restaurant full of character. An appealing menu offered throughout includes daily specials such as hot smoked rock eel with horseradish mayo and salad, and seared venison with curly kale and mash finished with ruby port jus.

The Crown

Chef Robert Mace **Owner** Adnams plc
Times 12-2/6.30-9.30 **Prices** Starter £5-£6.50, Main £12-£17, Dessert £5.50-£6.50, Service optional **Wines** 144 bottles over £20, 73 bottles under £20, 14 by glass **Notes** Sunday L, Vegetarian available **Seats** 65, Pr/dining room 30 **Children** Portions, Menu **Parking** 15 **Parking** Free car parks within 5 mins walking distance

The Randolph

◎ Modern, Traditional British

Chic gastro-pub meets upmarket restaurant

☎ 01502 723603
41 Wangford Rd, Reydon IP18 6PZ
e-mail: reception@randolph.co.uk
dir: 1m from Southwold

A former pub, this welcoming restaurant with rooms is located in the village of Reydon on the outskirts of Southwold, perfect for exploring the Suffolk coast. The traditional bar has been retained, but high-backed leather chairs, wood-stripped flooring and comfortable sofas have been added to create a gastro-pub ambience. Modern British menus offer simple dishes full of flavour, such as Cantonese braised shin of beef salad with spring onions and cucumber; saltimbocca of grey mullet served with herb polenta and a pepper salpicon; and rhubarb and stem ginger mousse with ginger biscuits.

Chef Paul Buck **Owner** David Smith **Times** 12-2/6.30-9, Closed D 25 Dec **Prices** Food prices not confirmed for 2009. Please telephone for details. **Wines** 2 bottles over £20, 12 bottles under £20, 6 by glass **Notes** Vegetarian available **Seats** 65 **Children** Portions, Menu **Parking** 40

Sutherland House

◎◎ Modern British ♨

Trendy eatery in the heart of town

☎ 01502 724544
56 High St IP18 6DN
e-mail: enquiries@sutherlandhouse.co.uk
dir: A1095 into Southwold, on High St on left after Victoria St

This smart, 16th-century townhouse in the heart of the bustling town centre plays host to this contemporary-styled restaurant. Its two beamed dining areas are decked out with modern darkwood tables, mauve padded chairs and trendy carpeting. Staff are relaxed, casually dressed and friendly, while the kitchen takes an appropriately modern approach driven by local seasonal produce, with daily game and fish specials bolstering menus that highlight 'food miles' against dishes - everything is sourced locally. Expect the likes of roast chicken terrine with garlic and tarragon, braised lamb shoulder with liver and sweetbreads, red cabbage and lamb jus, and perhaps an apple crumble tart with vanilla cream finale.

Chef Alan Paton **Owner** Peter & Anna Banks **Times** 12-3/7-9.30, Closed 25 Dec, 1st 2 wks Jan, Closed Mon-Tues **Prices** Starter £3-£10, Main £4-£23.50, Dessert £6-£6.50, Service optional **Wines** 35 bottles over £20, 15 bottles under £20, 6 by glass **Notes** Sunday L, Vegetarian available **Seats** 50, Pr/dining room 60 **Children** Portions, Menu **Parking** On street

---

Swan Hotel

◎◎ Modern British ♨

Accomplished cooking in a seaside inn

☎ 01502 722186
Market Place IP18 6EG
e-mail: swan.hotel@adnams.co.uk
dir: Turn right off A12 signed Southwold/Reydon, continue for 4m into Southwold. Follow main street into Market Place, hotel on left

This charming 17th-century coaching inn has been at the heart of Southwold social life for centuries. Revelling in its contemporary styling but retaining many original features, the elegant, bay-fronted restaurant looks out over the town square, while the drawing room is the place to relax over afternoon tea. The accomplished kitchen's modern approach makes the most of fresh local produce in dishes such as Suffolk game terrine served with onion compote and mustard bread, roasted fillet of Suffolk beef with truffle-scented mash potatoes, buttery curly kale, roasted cherry tomatoes and roast garlic jus, with rhubarb and ginger polenta crumble to finish. There's an excellent wine list and range of Adnams ales, too, and if staying over, the Admiral's Room comes complete with telescope to survey the sea.

Chef Robert Mace **Owner** Adnams plc
Times 12-2.30/7-9.30 **Prices** Fixed L 2 course £14.95, Fixed D 3 course £35, Service optional **Wines** 60 bottles over £20, 75 bottles under £20, 8 by glass **Notes** Pre-theatre picnic hampers, Sunday L, Vegetarian available, Dress restrictions, Smart casual - no jeans, Civ Wed 40 **Seats** 65, Pr/dining room 36 **Children** Min 12 yrs D, Portions, Menu **Parking** 36

STOKE-BY-NAYLAND — Map 13 TL93

The Angel Inn

◉ Modern British

Traditional coaching inn with innovative cooking

☎ 01206 263245
Polstead St CO6 4SA
e-mail: theangel@tiscali.co.uk
dir: From A12, take Colchester right turn, then A135, 5m
to Nayland from A125, take B1068

A 16th-century well is an unusual feature of the smart
restaurant at this charming oak-beamed former coaching
inn. Popular with the locals, it has a wealth of character,
its relaxed style mixing period features side by side with
modern art and leather sofas. With daily-changing
specials, the same menu for restaurant and bar draws on
locally-sourced ingredients to produce both traditional
and contemporary pub-style dishes, including starters
like chicken liver pâté with red onion marmalade and
granary bread, followed by succulent tiger prawns in a
sesame batter with chilli-flavoured mayonnaise, dressed
mixed salad and crisp fries. Vegetarian options are also
on offer.

Times 12-2/6.30-9.30

The Crown

◉◉ Modern British ⬡

**Smart, friendly village gastro-pub with great
atmosphere and food**

☎ 01206 262001 & 01206 262346
CO6 4SE
e-mail: thecrown@eoinns.co.uk
dir: Off A12 onto B1068 signed Higham, 5m to village,
The Crown on right.

Though dating back to the 1500s, this friendly gastro-pub
has undergone a stylish refurbishment and is now very
much contemporary in style, decked out in smart soft
furnishings and relaxing pastel colours. The pub is split
into areas with each room offering a mix of different
styles - from more formal to casual - while a glass wine
cellar catches the eye in the dining area. Service is
suitably relaxed and friendly but professional, with orders
taken at the bar to keep that unbuttoned, pubby feel. The
menu's modern approach comes driven by quality,
locally-sourced produce; think Blythburgh free-range pork
chop served with roasted pumpkin, chilli and sage, pan
juices and salad, while the daily catch-of-the-day fish
selection comes chalked up on the blackboard.

Chef Mark Blake **Owner** Edward Oliver Inns Ltd
Times 12-2.30/6-10, Closed 25 & 26 Dec **Prices** Food
prices not confirmed for 2009. Please telephone for
details. **Wines** 134 bottles over £20, 67 bottles under
£20, 27 by glass **Notes** Sunday L, Vegetarian available
Seats 130 **Children** Portions **Parking** 49

STOWMARKET — Map 13 TM05

The Firecracker Grill

◉ Mexican

Authentic Mexican cuisine on a Suffolk chilli farm

☎ 01449 766677
Chilli Farm, Norwich Rd, Mendlesham IP14 5NQ
e-mail: info@chillicompany.com
dir: From A14 take A140 towards Norwich, 7 miles on left.
From Norwich A140 towards Ipswich for 26 miles.

Named after a variety of chilli, this interesting Mexican
restaurant is located in a cream-painted converted barn
complete with traditional thatched roof on a chilli farm
near the popular village of Mendlesham. Inside the
décor's traditional too, with darkwood cottage-style
furniture and tiled floor, an upstairs seating area and an
open-plan kitchen on view to diners. The food is authentic
Mexican, with much of the produce - including the chillis
- grown on the farm or sourced direct. Traditional Mexican
dishes include the likes of courgette and cactus stew, or
pan-fried salmon with lime and coriander sauce, followed
by chocolate and pecan pie with a quenelle of cream.
There's a large selection of vegetarian dishes and light
bites, as well as a children's menu, and an array of
Mexican food products is available from the shop.

Chef Duncan Pearcy **Owner** Adrian & Denise Nuttall
Times 12-2/7-9.30, Closed 25-26 Dec **Prices** Starter
£3.95-£7.95, Main £7.95-£16.95, Dessert £2.95-£4.50,
Service optional **Wines** 4 bottles over £20, 10 bottles
under £20, 10 by glass **Notes** Vegetarian available
Seats 50 **Children** Portions, Menu **Parking** 50

The Shepherd and Dog

◉ Modern British

Relaxed gastro-pub atmosphere with cooking to match

☎ 01449 711361 & 710464
Forward Green IP14 5HN
e-mail: marybruce@btinternet.com
web: www.theshepherddanddog.com
dir: On A1120 between A14 and A140

A recent refurbishment and extension has given this
Suffolk gastro-pub a smart new interior that teams
lightwood furniture with comfy leather chairs in cream
and brown, and themes of racehorses and sheep and
sheep dogs. It is split into the bar and two restaurants,
where quality local produce is handled simply and
delivered to the table in tempting combinations. Kick off

with salmon and crab spring rolls served with crispy
seaweed and a sweet chilli crème fraîche, and then tuck
into pan-fried breast of chicken with a Parmesan cream
sauce, and a potato and truffle terrine, followed by warm
chocolate brownie with hot chocolate sauce and vanilla
ice cream.

Chef Christopher Bruce & Daniela Bruce
Owner Christopher & Mary Bruce **Times** 12-2/7-11,
Closed mid Jan, Closed Mon, Closed D Sun **Prices** Fixed L
2 course £10.50-£17, Fixed D 3 course £21, Starter
£5-£7, Main £13-£19, Dessert £5.50-£6.50, Service
optional **Wines** 28 bottles over £20, 25 bottles under £20,
19 by glass **Notes** Sunday L, Vegetarian available
Seats 50, Pr/dining room 24 **Children** Portions
Parking 35

WALBERSWICK — Map 13 TM47

The Anchor

◉◉ Modern British ⬡

**Gastro-pub serving unpretentious modern- and
traditional-influenced food**

☎ 01502 722112
Main St IP18 6UA
e-mail: info@anchoratwalberswick.com
dir: On entering village The Anchor is on the right,
immediately after MG garage

In the 1920s Arts and Crafts style, The Anchor boasts
good sea views, a relaxed atmosphere and a gastro-pub
feel. Like the service, the cooking is unpretentious,
striking an interesting modern note. Simpler comfort food
is also available. The menu displays the owners' vast
knowledge of beer and wines, as each dish is matched
with one or the other. The kitchen insists upon the
freshest seasonal local produce, with many ingredients
coming directly from the owners' allotments. Expect the
accomplished dishes to include caramelised scallops
served on a bed of purée of artichoke, followed by deep-
fried local cod with a crisp golden beer batter, served
with home-made fat chips and jalapeno tartare sauce,
while desserts might include lemon curd mousse with
brandy snaps.

Chef Sophie Dorber **Owner** Sophie & Mark Dorber
Times 11-4/6-11, Closed 25 Dec, Closed Mon (from Nov
2008) **Prices** Fixed L 2 course £16.50-£22.50, Starter
£4.75-£7.75, Main £10.25-£16.75, Dessert £3.50-£5.25,
Service optional **Wines** 18 by glass **Notes** Sunday L,
Vegetarian available **Seats** 55, Pr/dining room 26
Children Portions, Menu **Parking** 60

WESTLETON — Map 13 TM46

The Westleton Crown

Modern British

Great British food in a great British setting

☎ 01728 648777
The Street IP17 3AD
e-mail: reception@westletoncrown.co.uk
dir: From Ipswich head N on A12, turn right past Yoxford, follow tourist signs for 2m

With its origins extending back to the 12th century, this traditional coaching inn succeeds in retaining its rustic, historic charm with the comfort you'd expect of contemporary dining. Diners can choose between the cosy parlour, elegant dining room or large airy conservatory. With an emphasis on the best of local produce, an extensive menu includes daily specials and offers classic dishes with a twist. Typically, start with confit duck and apricot terrine and follow with whole grilled East Coast plaice with a prawn, caper and herb butter, or roast chump of lamb with jus Niçoise. For dessert, why not try caramelised banana tarte Tatin with hazelnut ice cream. The pretty terrace also provides the perfect setting for alfresco dining.

Chef Richard Bargewell **Owner** Agellus Hotels Ltd **Times** 12-2.30/7-9.30, Closed 25 Dec **Prices** Starter £4.95-£9.50, Main £9.50-£21.95, Dessert £3.50-£7.50, Service optional **Wines** 29 bottles over £20, 22 bottles under £20, 9 by glass **Notes** Sunday L, Vegetarian available **Seats** 85 **Children** Portions, Menu **Parking** 50

WOODBRIDGE — Map 13 TM24

The Captain's Table

Modern

Busy, friendly and relaxed cottage restaurant

☎ 01394 383145 & 388508
3 Quay St IP12 1BX
e-mail: eat@captainstable.co.uk
dir: From A12. Quay St opposite rail station and theatre. Restaurant 200m on left

A heavily beamed 16th-century property that was originally three cottages, this charming restaurant has a 100-year-old Grande Flora magnolia and an 80-year-old rose over the front door. Relaxed and friendly, its interconnecting rooms are light and airy by day and romantic at night by candlelight. Honest and simple, the food is prepared from fresh, quality local ingredients (organic where possible) and there's always a mixture of old favourites and more unusual dishes. Try twice-baked goat's cheese soufflé, roast Suffolk pork tenderloin with baked apple, dauphinoise potatoes and Madeira sauce, and apple and blackberry crumble with custard.

Chef Pascal Pommier **Owner** Mr P & Mrs J M Pommier **Times** 12-2.30/6.30-10, Closed 25-26 Dec, Closed Sun-Mon (except BHs) **Prices** Starter £3-£7.95, Main £10.50-£13.95, Dessert fr £5.50, Service included **Wines** 11 bottles over £20, 22 bottles under £20, 5 by glass **Notes** Sun L served BH wknds only, Vegetarian available **Seats** 50, Pr/dining room 34 **Children** Portions, Menu **Parking** 6

Seckford Hall Hotel

Modern British

Sound cooking amid Elizabethan splendour

☎ 01394 385678
IP13 6NU
e-mail: reception@seckford.co.uk
dir: Hotel signposted on A12 (Woodbridge bypass). Do not follow signs for town centre

Dating back to the mid 1500s, this imposing ancestral home has been in the same family for over 500 years, and today its commanding red-brick Tudor façade with tall chimneys and huge carved oak entrance door is no less impressive than when Queen Elizabeth I held court here. The stately feel extends to the elegant oak-panelled restaurant - an intimate setting for sumptuous dining, decorated with rich tapestries, wood carvings and fresh flower displays. An extensive menu of modern British cuisine is served, and the accomplished kitchen makes good use of local produce, with lobster dishes and farmed local Suffolk duckling among the specialities. Start with a timbale of Uig Lodge smoked salmon with Cromer crab and confit citrus segments, followed by roast loin of Suffolk pork with black pudding boudin and trompette des mort sauce.

Chef Mark Archer **Owner** Mr & Mrs Bunn **Times** 12.30-1.45/7.30-9.30, Closed 25 Dec, Closed L Mon **Prices** Food prices not confirmed for 2009. Please telephone for details. **Wines** 40 bottles over £20, 45 bottles under £20, 11 by glass **Notes** Sunday L, Vegetarian available, Dress restrictions, Smart casual, No jeans or trainers, Civ Wed 120, Air con **Seats** 70, Pr/dining room 100 **Children** Portions, Menu **Parking** 100

YAXLEY
Map 13 TM17

The Auberge

◉◉ Traditional International 🖥

Great cooking at a family-run restaurant with rooms

☎ 01379 783604
Ipswich Rd IP23 8BZ
e-mail: deestenhouse@fsmail.net
dir: 5m S of Diss on A140

This 16th-century inn has been lovingly converted by the present owners into a smart restaurant with rooms, the extended dining room and tasteful improvements retaining the cosiness of the building. Exposed brickwork and oak beams testify to its age, but there's nothing old-fashioned about the food: expect simple, almost rustic dishes, packed with flavour and created from the best of local ingredients. A starter of twice-baked cheddar soufflé topped with cream and served on truffle-scented croûte might be followed by chargrilled entrecote of prime Norfolk beef with a medley of mushroom and shallot confit, and garlic-baked baby potatoes, complemented by Amaretto pannacotta with apricot frangipane and zabaglione for dessert. It's all served in an intimate dining room, where candles create a cosy ambience and the tables are smartly laid with crisp napkins.

Chef John Stenhouse **Owner** John & Dee Stenhouse **Times** 12-2/7-9.30, Closed Xmas, Closed Sun & Mon, Closed L Sat **Prices** Food prices not confirmed for 2009. Please telephone for details. **Wines** 35 bottles over £20, 25 bottles under £20, 8 by glass **Notes** Air con **Seats** 60, Pr/dining room 20 **Children** Portions **Parking** 25

YOXFORD
Map 5 TM36

Satis House

◉◉ Modern British 🍽

Relaxed modern cuisine in a country house setting

☎ 01728 668418
Satis House Hotel IP17 3EX
e-mail: enquiries@satishouse.co.uk
dir: Between Ipswich and Lowestoft on A12, N of village

Tucked away in rural Suffolk, this impressive Grade II listed Georgian country house, now a privately-owned hotel, is set in 3 acres of parkland. Charles Dickens, a family friend of the owners at that time, was a regular visitor and the property's name features in his book Great Expectations. Offering 18th-century character and 21st-century comforts, the service is relaxed but formal and

elegant. The cuisine is modern British with European and Pacific Rim influences, with locally-produced seasonal ingredients used to create imaginative dishes that will please all tastes. Starters include pan-fried scallops with sweet chilli jam and crème fraîche, and mains such as steamed rabbit and rosemary pudding with braised red cabbage, green beans and game gravy, or Thai beef curry with pineapple, fragrant jasmine rice and crispy noodles. Finish with pear and almond tart with vanilla ice cream.

Chef David Little, Brian Rant **Owner** David Little, Kevin Wainwright **Times** 12-3/6.30-11, Closed L Mon, Tue, Closed D Sun **Prices** Fixed L 2 course £14.95-£20, Starter £5.50-£11.50, Main £9.50-£25, Dessert £5.95-£6.95, Service optional **Wines** 20 bottles over £20, 10 bottles under £20, 6 by glass **Notes** Sunday L, Vegetarian available, Civ Wed 30 **Seats** 30, Pr/dining room 25 **Children** Min 8 yrs, Portions **Parking** 30

See advert on page 401

SURREY

ABINGER HAMMER
Map 6 TQ04

Drakes on the Pond

◉◉ Modern British 🖥

Skilful cooking in a classy village restaurant

☎ 01306 731174
Dorking Rd RH5 6SA
dir: On the A25 between Dorking and Guildford

This charming cottage situated on the A25 is run with attention to detail and dedication by the friendly proprietors. There are views across the Surrey hills and the eponymous pond is nearby. The recently refurbished dining room has pale terracotta walls and chocolate brown furnishings, creating a comfortable and unpretentious space. The seasonally-changing menu is modern in approach with a clear respect for classical preparation. Thus roasted cauliflower soup is presented in a straightforward manner but is big on flavour and main-course pan-fried halibut combines well with a creamy potato purée and a cheesy fennel fondue. 'Old fashioned' lemon posset is given a modern twist with a lemon meringue ice cream and a lemon and nut biscotti. Service is formal but not stuffy.

Chef John Morris **Owner** John Morris & Tracey Honeysett **Times** 12-2/7-10, Closed 2 wks Aug-Sep, Xmas, New Year, BHs, Closed Sun (except Mothering Sun), Mon, Closed L Sat **Prices** Fixed L 2 course fr £19.50, Fixed D 3 course fr £41, Service optional, Groups min 8 service 10% **Wines** 65 bottles over £20, 9 bottles under £20, 9 by glass **Notes** Dress restrictions, Smart casual, Air con **Seats** 32 **Children** Min 10 yrs **Parking** 20

BAGSHOT
Map 6 SU96

The Brasserie

◉◉ Modern British

Skilful modern cooking in five-star hotel setting

☎ 01276 471774
Pennhill Park Hotel & Spa, London Rd GU19 5EU
e-mail: enquiries@pennyhillpark.co.uk
dir: M3 junct 3, continue through Bagshot village & turn left onto A30. Hotel is 0.5m past Notcutts on right

The Brasserie is the more informal option to the smaller fine-dining Latymer restaurant at this renowned five-star hotel (see entry). Overlooking manicured lawns and boasting a grand spa, the hotel has a spacious lounge for pre- or post-meal drinks, while the restaurant's décor has something of a Mediterranean tone, the large open room decked out with marble floor, big leather armchairs and well spaced darkwood tables, all set around a central white statue. The dinner carte offers an eye-catching modern approach driven by tip-top produce. Take cannelloni of Devon crab claw meat with sweet red pepper purée and shiso dressing, followed by seared fillet of halibut with smoked clams, crushed new potatoes, dandelions and shellfish vinaigrette, with poached white peach, rose champagne sabayon and toasted almonds for dessert.

Times 12-2.30/7-10.30

The Latymer

◉◉◉ – *see opposite*

The Latymer

Modern British NOTABLE WINE LIST

Innovative cuisine in peaceful, relaxed surroundings

☎ 01276 471774
Pennyhill Park Hotel & Spa, London Rd GU19 5EU
e-mail: enquiries@pennyhillpark.co.uk
dir: M3 junct 3, through Bagshot village, take left onto A30. 0.5m on right

This delightful ivy-clad former Victorian manor house - now comfortable country-house hotel - is set in 123 acres of rolling Surrey parkland, complete with state-of-the-art spa. There's an undeniable grandeur about the place, with its formal terraced gardens inspired by a French château in Tours. This year has seen the arrival of Michael Wignall (ex Devonshire Arms in Yorkshire). To coincide, the intimate fine-dining Latymer restaurant has undergone a complete and impressive refurbishment. Set in the original part of the house, many of the original features such as the oak panelling, leaded windows and wooden beams have been retained and are now combined with many contemporary touches and an overall modern feel. Expect innovative and skilful modern cooking underpinned by a classical theme on a fixed-price repertoire centred around tip-top, seasonal, fresh produce with clean, clear flavours. Take cumin-scented

seared tuna with poached Scottish langoustines, wild leeks, smoked eel beignets and tapioca vinaigrette, or perhaps fillet of red mullet and sardine with boudin of salt cod, confit tomato and golden beetroot with bouillabaisse emulsion. Exquisite desserts like mango parfait, lychee with rosewater, passionfruit and banana ice cream are not to be missed. Early visits have impressed and it is clear that Michael has quickly established a very high level of consistency and will be one to watch. As anticipated, service is formal yet friendly from a highly professional front of house team. The wine list is extensive and offers numerous wines by the glass, with examples to suit each dish on the menu.

Chef Michael Wignall **Owner** Exclusive Hotels **Times** 12-2/7-9.30, Closed Xmas-13 Jan, Closed Mon, Closed L Sat & Sun **Prices** Fixed L course £28, Fixed D 3 course fr £55, Tasting menu £78, Main £55, Service optional **Wines** 220 bottles over £20, 220 by glass **Notes** ALC 3 courses, Tasting menu 9 courses, Vegetarian available, Dress restrictions, Smart casual, Civ Wed 160, Air con **Seats** 48, Pr/dining room 10 **Children** Min 12 yrs **Parking** 500

BANSTEAD
Map 6 TQ25

Post
◎◎ Modern

First-class Post arrives in leafy Banstead

☎ 01737 373839
28 High St SM7 2LQ
e-mail: enquiries@postrestaurant.co.uk
web: www.postrestaurant.co.uk

Celebrity chef-patron Tony Tobin (who also owns sister restaurant, The Dining Room, in Reigate - see entry) has created this cosmopolitan-style brasserie, restaurant and delicatessen operation in the former Post Office on the High Street. Contemporary design and buzzy atmosphere is the style, with the deli up front, airy all-day brasserie (with separate menu) to the rear, and the intimate, fine-dining restaurant on the first floor. Here, cream leather banquettes, funky swivel leather tub chairs and a small bar complete the upbeat, modern setting. A fixed-price repertoire includes a carte and tasting option to excite the palate and eye, using top quality ingredients and bags of skill; take pan-seared halibut served with boulangère potato, cauliflower silk and a light thyme sauce.

Times 11/10

CAMBERLEY
Map 6 SU86

Macdonald Frimley Hall Hotel & Spa
◎◎ Modern European

Smart country-house dining

☎ 0844 879 9110
Lime Av GU15 2BG
e-mail: gm.frimleyhall@macdonald-hotels.co.uk
dir: From M3 junct 3 follow signs for Bagshot. Turn left onto A30 signed Camberley/Basingstoke. At rdbt branch left onto A325, then right into Conifer Dr & Lime Ave to hotel

The epitome of English elegance, this dignified, ivy-clad Victorian manor is set in beautiful grounds. The interior combines a modern décor with traditional features and the stylishly decorated Linden Restaurant has established an excellent reputation as a fine-dining venue. It offers pretty views over a woodland garden from well-spaced tables and looks elegant by candlelight in the evening. Quality seasonal ingredients are a feature of the modern European menu, where classical dishes are presented with a modern twist. Starters might include chicken liver and foie gras parfait served with pineapple chutney and brioche, followed by sea bass with saffron fondant potato, salsify and red wine butter sauce, with Valrhona chocolate tart with orange ice cream to finish.

Chef Max Pettini **Owner** Macdonalds Hotels
Times 12.30-2/7-9.45, Closed L Sat **Prices** Starter £6-£10.50, Main £16.50-£23.50, Dessert £6.50-£8.50, Service added but optional 12.5% **Notes** Sunday L, Vegetarian available, Civ Wed 120, Air con **Seats** 70 **Children** Portions, Menu **Parking** 100

CHARLWOOD

For restaurant details see under Gatwick Airport (London), (Sussex, West)

DORKING
Map 6 TQ14

Mercure Burford Bridge Hotel
◎◎ Modern European

Historic hotel offering contemporary design and accomplished dining

☎ 01306 884561
Burford Bridge, Box Hill RH5 6BX
dir: M25 junct 9. Towards Dorking, the hotel is on the A24 at the Burford Bridge rdbt

Sitting at the foot of beautiful Box Hill, the hotel dates back to the 16th century and is reputedly where Lord Nelson and Lady Hamilton met for the last time before the Battle of Trafalgar. Today, it's a smart, contemporary hotel, with comfortable armchairs and sofas in the bar and an elegant modern restaurant with low ceilings and candlelit tables overlooking the gardens. The modern cooking, underpinned by a classical theme, encompasses quality produce alongside excellent presentation and succinct flavours on crisply-scripted menus. Take roast salmon with spicy chorizo and confit tomatoes, or braised lamb shank served with mashed potato, and perhaps a tonka bean brûlée with white coffee ice cream and coffee sauce to finish.

Times 12-2.30/7-9.30

Two To Four
◎◎ Modern **V**

Skilled cooking in a chic town-centre restaurant

☎ 01306 889923
2-4 West St RH4 1BL
e-mail: eliterestaurants@hotmail.com
dir: M25, exit at Leatherhead junct, follow signs to Dorking town centre

Dining on three floors is offered at this charming Grade II listed building, originally three cottages, in a special street full of lovely old properties and antique shops. The interior has a clean contemporary feel, with bare wooden tables, ceramic-tiled floors and natural decorations, and there's a friendly, bustling atmosphere with professional service. Dishes from the short carte and daily blackboard are modern in style with Mediterranean influences. From the carte, try seared scallops with beetroot purée, cumin velouté, shredded apple and pea shoots to start; and a main course of whole Dover sole with lemon mash, buttered peas and spring onion; alternatively, côte de boeuf from the blackboard specials.

Chef Rob Gathercole **Owner** Elite Restaurants
Times 12-2.30/6.30-10, Closed Xmas, Etr, BHs, 2 wks Aug, Closed Sun **Prices** Fixed L 2 course £12, Fixed D 3 course £30-£33.50, Starter £8.50, Main £18.50, Dessert £6.50-£12, Service added but optional 10% **Wines** 23 bottles over £20, 9 bottles under £20, 4 by glass **Notes** Vegetarian menu, Air con **Seats** 70, Pr/dining room 18 **Children** Portions **Parking** West St car park

EGHAM
Map 6 TQ07

The Oak Room at Great Fosters
◎◎ Modern British ▲NOTABLE WINE LIST

Regal Elizabethan setting for accomplished cuisine

☎ 01784 433822
Stroude Rd TW20 9UR
e-mail: enquiries@greatfosters.co.uk
web: www.greatfosters.co.uk
dir: M25 junct 13

Set within a Grade I listed Elizabethan manor house, this former royal retreat is steeped in history. Sitting in acres of celebrated landscaped grounds, the interior of the hotel is rich with dark woods, deep sofas and magnificent tapestries and the elegant Oak Room restaurant cleverly blends modern design with more traditional features. Think vaulted oak-beamed ceiling, ornate wood-carved fireplace and mullioned windows versus high-backed chairs, large contemporary tapestry and friendly, polished service. The kitchen's modern approach flirts with the classical, delivering accomplished dishes showcasing quality produce. Expect the likes of smoked eel and foie gras terrine with apple textures, followed by slow-cooked feather blade of beef with hot pot vegetables and herb dumplings, with banana tarte Tatin and liquorice cream to finish. Excellent wine list available.

The Oak Room at Great Fosters

Chef Simon Bolsover **Owner** Great Fosters (1931) Ltd
Times 12.30-2/7-9.30, Closed L Sat **Prices** Fixed L 2
course £21.50, Fixed D 3 course £36.50, Starter £9-£13,
Main £22-£28, Dessert £9, Service added but optional
10% **Wines** 285 bottles over £20, 2 bottles under £20, 22
by glass **Notes** Sunday L, Vegetarian available, Civ Wed
170 **Seats** 60, Pr/dining room 20 **Children** Portions
Parking 200

EPSOM — Map 6 TQ26

Chalk Lane Hotel

◎◎ British, French ☙

**Accomplished cooking a short walk from Epsom
racecourse**

☎ 01372 721179
Chalk Ln, Woodcote End KT18 7BB
e-mail: smcgregor@chalklanehotel.com
web: www.chalklanehotel.com
dir: M25 junct 9 then A24 towards Ashtead & Epsom. Just
in Epsom turn right at BP garage, then left into Avenue
Rd & follow hotel signs

This endearing, privately-owned hotel enjoys a peaceful,
tucked-away location a short walk from Epsom
Racecourse. It's a Grade II listed building, dating from
1805 and the restaurant is cosy and comfortable with
mood lighting. Food is imaginative and accomplished
using great ingredients cooked with obvious technical
ability. There's a dine-with-wine lunch Monday to Friday
with a free glass of wine thrown in, and a tasting menu
of many courses. Interesting options from the regular
menu include seared king scallops with cream of
haddock, baby spinach, carrot and leek julienne, or a trio
of beef with three different sauces and garnishes. Finish
with a caramel soufflé with Armagnac and prune ice
cream.

Chef Vincent Hiss **Owner** Steven McGregor
Times 12.30-2.30/7-10, Closed L Sat **Prices** Fixed L 2
course £12.50, Service added but optional 12.5%
Wines 75 bottles over £20, 25 bottles under £20, 10 by
glass **Notes** Sunday L, Vegetarian available, Dress
restrictions, Smart casual **Seats** 40, Pr/dining room 20
Children Portions **Parking** 60

GODALMING — Map 6 SU94

La Luna

◎◎ Modern Italian

Stylish two-tone Italian of all-round quality

☎ 01483 414155
10 Wharf St GU7 1NN
e-mail: info@lalunarestaurant.co.uk
dir: In centre of Godalming, junct of Wharf St & Flambard
Way

This sophisticated, light and airy, contemporary Italian -
smack in the centre of town - comes with a striking
black-and-white interior design that speaks quality.
Expect black leather high-backed chairs, white-clothed
tables with black undercloths and white or black walls,
all set on polished wooden floorboards. Service is
effortless, charming, warm and very Italian - as is the
patriotic and impressive wine list. There's an equally
serious approach to the seasonal menus too, combining
the classic flavours of Italy. Quality, daily-delivered
produce is handled with flair and imagination, and
dishes come stylishly presented; take pan-fried calves'
liver on a bed of sautéed cavolo nero and pancetta with
parsnip purée and aged balsamic vinegar, or organic
Shackleford pork fillet in puff pastry crust with Sicilian
aubergine caponata and mashed potato.

Chef Valentino Gentile **Owner** Daniele Drago & Orazio
Primavera **Times** 12-2/7-10, Closed early Jan, 2 wks in
Aug, Closed Sun-Mon **Prices** Fixed L 2 course £13.95,
Tasting menu £65, Starter £7-£10, Main £15-£21,
Dessert £6-£8 **Wines** 136 bottles over £20, 9 bottles
under £20, 6 by glass **Notes** Tasting menu 5 courses,
Sunday L, Air con **Seats** 58, Pr/dining room 24
Children Portions **Parking** Public car park behind
restaurant

HASLEMERE — Map 6 SU93

Lythe Hill Hotel & Spa

◎◎ French

Sumptuous hotel dining in the countryside

☎ 01428 651251
Petworth Rd GU27 3BQ
e-mail: lythe@lythehill.co.uk
web: www.lythehill.co.uk
dir: 1 mile E of Haslemere on B2131

Created from a collection of distinctive farm buildings,
which include a splendid Elizabethan house, plus stylish,
newer additions, Lythe Hill is set in 30 acres of glorious
parkland. The Auberge de France restaurant is located in
the timbered farmhouse and oozes historic charm, with
mellow oak panelling and ancient beams creating an
evocative dining ambience. The French-based menu
acknowledges modern-day trends and classic dishes are
given a fusion twist. Expect the likes of pressed seafood
bisque and crispy duck leg with Oriental salad and plum
dressing to start, followed by braised leg of English lamb
with roasted confit of garlic, baby leeks and fondant
potato. Finish with a peach and raspberry tiramisu or an
assiette of chocolate. The contemporary Italian Garden
restaurant offers lighter dishes.

Chef Neil Wackrill **Owner** Lythe Hill Hotel Ltd
Times 12.30-2.15/7.15-9.45, Closed L Sat **Prices** Fixed L
2 course fr £15.50, Service optional **Wines** 200 bottles
over £20, 7 bottles under £20, 6 by glass **Notes** Sunday L,
Vegetarian available, Dress restrictions, Smart casual,
Civ Wed 128 **Seats** 60, Pr/dining room 35
Children Portions, Menu **Parking** 150

HORLEY

For restaurant details see Gatwick Airport (London),
(Sussex, West)

LIMPSFIELD — Map 6 TQ45

Alexander's at Limpsfield

⌾⌾ Modern

Sophisticated food with relaxed and friendly service

☎ 01883 714365
The Old Lodge, High St RH8 0DR
e-mail: info@alexanders-limpsfield.co.uk
dir: N of A25 on B269

This 16th-century building has undergone a major refurbishment to offer a modern, contemporary style. Next to the small bar and brasserie area serving its simple bistro fare, the fine-dining restaurant boasts a high vaulted ceiling, dark oak-panelled walls and candlelit tables. Plenty of local and seasonal produce makes an appearance and the cooking is confident and simply presented on both the tasting menu and carte. Take a starter of roasted langoustine, macaroni of pork and langoustine bisque, followed by roast rump of Cornish lamb with root vegetables, Puy lentils and raspberry vinegar, or maybe Scottish halibut with tomato and olive crushed potatoes, bouillabaisse sauce and anchovy beignet. Finish with a well-made Valrhona chocolate fondant with salted caramel and caramel ice cream.

Times 10/mdnt, Closed Mon

OCKLEY — Map 6 TQ14

Bryce's Seafood Restaurant & Country Pub

⌾ Modern British, Seafood

Rural fish destination with pub and restaurant options

☎ 01306 627430
The Old School House RH5 5TH
e-mail: bryces.fish@virgin.net
dir: From M25 junct 9 take A24, then A29. 8m S of Dorking on A29

Housed in the former gymnasium of a boys' boarding school dating from 1750, this beamed restaurant and pub has been recently refurbished, retaining its character but is now furnished with comfortable high-backed leather chairs. The menu offers the very best fresh fish and seafood, much of it from Shoreham, an hour away on the South Coast. Typical dishes from the fixed-price menu, priced for two or three courses, include natural smoked haddock on potato purée with pancetta and mushroom cream sauce, and fillet of sea bream on prawn and basil risotto. Daily specials feature some non-fish alternatives.

Chef B Bryce and Ashley Sullivan **Owner** Mr B Bryce **Times** 12-2.30/7-9.30, Closed 25-26 Dec, 1 Jan, Closed D Sun (Nov & Jan-Feb) **Prices** Fixed L 2 course £25, Fixed D 3 course £31, Service optional, Groups min 8 service 10% **Wines** 15 bottles over £20, 29 bottles under £20, 15 by glass **Notes** Sunday L **Seats** 50 **Children** Portions **Parking** 35

REDHILL — Map 6 TQ25

Nutfield Priory - Cloisters Restaurant

⌾⌾ Modern European

Unique and grand setting to enjoy fine modern food

☎ 0845 0727486
Nutfield Rd RH1 4EL
e-mail: nutfieldpriory@handpicked.co.uk
dir: On A25, 1m E of Redhill, off M25 junct 8 or M25 junct 6, follow A25 through Godstone

This imposing building was built in 1872 to resemble a priory and it would have been grand enough to satisfy any religious order. A host of original features remains including elaborate stone carvings, wood panelling and stunning stained glass. With panoramic views across three counties and an imposing cathedral-style arched ceiling, the Cloisters Restaurant makes a lasting impression. The capable kitchen offers seasonal menus using locally-sourced produce where possible, the provenance of much of it name-checked on the menu, and delivers appealing European-influenced dishes. Start with Kyle of Lochalsh hand-dived scallops with potato fondant, black truffle and fine cress, before moving on to belly of Shakleford pork with langoustines, roasted sweet potato purée finished with a tomato and broad bean vinaigrette. Desserts include the Priory's Black Forest trifle.

Chef Roger Gadsden **Owner** Hand Picked Hotels **Times** 12-2/7-9.30, Closed L Sat **Prices** Fixed L 2 course fr £15, Fixed D 3 course fr £36, Starter £9.50-£13, Main £18.50-£29, Dessert £8-£12, Service optional **Wines** 90 bottles over £20, 2 bottles under £20, 18 by glass **Notes** Sunday L, Vegetarian available, Dress restrictions, No jeans or trainers, Civ Wed 80 **Seats** 60, Pr/dining room 100 **Children** Portions **Parking** 130

REIGATE — Map 6 TQ25

The Dining Room

⌾⌾ Modern British

Inspirational cooking in contemporary setting

☎ 01737 226650
59a High St RH2 9AE
dir: First floor restaurant on Reigate High St

Newly refurbished, this contemporary and stylish restaurant brings a touch of the London scene to Reigate. The bar, with leather sofas and soft lights, is creating a stir as a fabulous location for pre- and post-dinner drinks. In the restaurant, Tony Tobin continues to offer imaginative British dishes using fresh, seasonal ingredients. His fusion cooking draws inspiration from the Mediterranean and further afield from Thailand and Australia. So, dishes along the lines of seared spicy beef salad with wasabi mayonnaise, followed by Parma ham wrapped roast chicken breast with sun-blushed tomato and caper dressing might be on offer. The weekly-changing four-course 'Sunday Roast at the Dining Room' proves popular, and vegetarians have their own interesting selection of dishes.

Times 12-2/7-10, Closed Xmas & BHs, Closed L Sat, Closed D Sun

The Westerly

⌾⌾ Modern European

Modern neighbourhood bistro delivering affordable, refined rustic-themed cooking

☎ 01737 222733
2-4 London Rd RH2 9AN

A wallet-friendly, unpretentious bistro de luxe, The Westerly has pedigree. Chef-patron Jonathan Coomb (with wife Cynthia at front of house) previously ran the Stephen Langton Inn at nearby Abinger Common, but cranks up the ante here, with his Mediterranean-inspired cooking taking a more refined slant. Dishes adopt an intelligently straightforward, well-presented approach on frequently-changing, great-value menus driven by quality fresh seasonal produce from local suppliers, with clean flavours and some innovative and unusual combinations Take a starter croquette of pig's head served with sauce gribiche, while a cracking main course of bourride of monkfish, red mullet, bream, prawns, mussels and clams proves an eye-catching signature dish. The bistro interior befittingly follows an understated modern theme, with light walls, blond-wood floorboards, red banquettes or brown leather chairs and modern artwork.

Times 12-2.30/7-10, Closed Sun, Mon **Prices** Food prices not confirmed for 2009. Please telephone for details.

RIPLEY — Map 6 TQ05

Drake's Restaurant

⌾⌾⌾ — *see opposite*

SHERE — Map 6 TQ04

Kinghams

⌾⌾ Modern British

Local produce showcased in attractive cottage restaurant surroundings

☎ 01483 202168
Gomshall Ln GU5 9HE
e-mail: paul@kinghams-restaurant.co.uk
dir: On A25 between Guildford and Dorking. 12 mins from M25 junct 10

Set in a picturesque Surrey village, this pretty red-brick cottage dates back to the early 17th century and once played home to a family of sheep thieves. It's gone upmarket since then and now houses a relaxed and friendly, intimate restaurant with low ceilings and beams, crisp white linen and sparkling glassware. Cosy in the winter with a roaring log fire, the summer brings a heated gazebo into use, where guests can dine alfresco in the carefully tended garden. Cooking is imaginative with excellent presentation and uses seasonal produce from local suppliers. You might begin with pan-fried lamb's kidneys on black pudding with a Madeira sauce and crispy fried onions, and then tuck into fillet of pork wrapped in bacon and chorizo, served with a coriander pancake and pineapple and chilli salsa. Fish specials change daily depending on the catch of the day.

Kinghams

Chef Paul Baker **Owner** Paul Baker
Times 12.15-2.30/7-9.30, Closed 25 Dec-4 Jan, Closed Mon, Closed D Sun **Prices** Fixed L 2 course £16.50, Fixed D 3 course £22.45, Starter £7.95-£9.95, Main £13.95-£19.95, Dessert £5.95, Service optional, Groups min 8 service 10% **Wines** 12 bottles over £20, 26 bottles under £20, 6 by glass **Notes** Sunday L, Vegetarian available **Seats** 48, Pr/dining room 24 **Children** Portions **Parking** 16

STOKE D'ABERNON   Map 6 TQ15

Woodlands Park Hotel

◉ Modern British, French

Victorian grandeur with contemporary cuisine

☎ 01372 843933
Woodlands Ln KT11 3QB
e-mail: woodlandspark@handpicked.co.uk
dir: From M25 junct 10, A3 towards London. Through Cobham centre and Stoke D'Abernon, left at garden centre into Woodlands Lane. Hotel 0.5m on left

This elegant Victorian mansion is set in over 10 acres of attractive parkland in the Surrey countryside and was originally built for the Bryant family who founded the match company Bryant & May. The original house retains many period features including a grand hall with dramatic marble fireplace, minstrels' gallery and impressive carved staircase, perfectly complemented by antiques, chandeliers and quality furnishings. Whether you're dining in the relaxed Quotes Bar and Brasserie or in the more formal Oak Room, you can enjoy a pre-dinner drink in the cocktail bar while you peruse the menu. A nice balance of imagination and classically-rooted technique is evident in dishes like duo of scallop and prawn on squid ink pasta and saffron vinaigrette, or an equally imaginative main course of fillet of red mullet with braised potato and minestrone garnish. Finish with orange soufflé with dark rum sorbet.

Chef Peter Wallner **Owner** Hand Picked Hotels
Times 12-2.30/7-10, Closed Mon, Closed L Tue-Sat, Closed D Sun **Prices** Starter £6.50-£11, Main £17-£36, Dessert £7.50-£9, Service optional **Wines** 125 bottles over £20, 4 bottles under £20, 10 by glass **Notes** Jazz evenings in brasserie, Sunday L, Vegetarian available, Dress restrictions, No jeans or trainers, Civ Wed 200 **Seats** 35, Pr/dining room 130 **Children** Portions, Menu **Parking** 150

Drake's Restaurant

RIPLEY   Map 6 TQ05

Modern British 🖥️

Skilled, artisan cooking in village restaurant

☎ 01483 224777
The Clock House, High St GU23 6AQ
web: www.drakesrestaurant.co.uk
dir: M25 junct 10/A3 towards Guildford. Follow Ripley signs off A3, restaurant in centre of village

An imposing, red-brick Georgian house, with its old restored clock set above the doorway, picks out this Surrey culinary high-flyer. Home to chef-patron Steve Drake (one time of Drakes on the Pond at Abinger Hammer), the eponymous, two-roomed restaurant has fine pedigree and goes from strength to strength, driven by a committed young team who show clear dedication and passion to their craft. Warm earthy tones are complemented by ornately framed pictures, while the open-plan space has an unstuffy vibes, smart but in an unpretentious and relaxed way. Tables are formally laid while service is knowledgeable and attentive, and there's a small seating area for aperitifs plus the added bonus of a pretty walled garden for summer drinks. Steve's cooking takes a light modern approach (he likes to describes it as 'artisan cooking') and oozes skill, flair and finesse, creating dishes presented with elegant simplicity and clean, clear flavours from the freshest, high quality seasonal produce. Take roasted John Dory served with a mushroom casserole and herb gnocchi, or perhaps lamb cooked in a herb crumble with onion purée, fondant potato and braised fillet. And do save room for the cracking petits fours.

Chef Steve Drake **Owner** Steve & Serina Drake
Times 12-1.30/7-9.30, Closed 2 wks Jan, 2 wks Aug, Closed Sun-Mon, Closed L Sat **Prices** Fixed L 2 course fr £21, Fixed D 3 course fr £46, Tasting menu £60, Service optional **Wines** 200 bottles over £20, 16 bottles under £20, 9 by glass **Notes** Vegetarian available **Seats** 34, Pr/dining room 10 **Children** Min 12 yrs **Parking** 2

SUSSEX, EAST

ALFRISTON
Map 6 TQ50

Harcourts Restaurant

◉ Modern British 🖥

Elegant dining with the best of local produce

☎ 01323 870248
Deans Place Hotel, Seaford Rd BN26 5TW
e-mail: mail@deansplacehotel.co.uk
web: www.deansplacehotel.co.uk
dir: On A27 follow signs for Alfriston & Drusillas zoo and
continue through village, hotel is on left upon exiting

Located on the edge of one of England's prettiest villages
in the heart of the Sussex countryside, 14th-century
Deans Place is set in attractive gardens. The elegant,
classically-styled Harcourts Restaurant is traditional with
a warm, relaxing ambience, serving English cuisine with
a French influence. The kitchen goes to great lengths to
source as much local produce as possible, particularly
fish from the Sussex coast. Imaginative dishes might
include roasted herb-crusted pork fillet stuffed with
Sussex blue cheese, soused apple purée, spinach and
celeriac mash, or Romney Marsh rump of lamb, creamy
pea and mint risotto and griddled leeks. The Friston Bar
offers a more informal choice of dishes.

Chef Stuart Dunley **Owner** Peter Bramich
Times 12-2.30/6.30-9.30 **Prices** Fixed L 2 course £15.95,
Fixed D 3 course fr £29.50, Service optional **Wines** 59
bottles over £20, 47 bottles under £20, 11 by glass
Notes Sunday L, Dress restrictions, Smart casual, Civ
Wed 200 **Seats** 60, Pr/dining room 30 **Children** Portions,
Menu **Parking** 100

BATTLE
Map 7 TQ71

Powder Mills Hotel

◉ Modern British

**Modern menu in a well-appointed conservatory dining
room**

☎ 01424 775511
Powdermill Ln TN33 0SP
e-mail: powdc@aol.com
dir: A21/A2100 past Battle Abbey. Turn into Powdermill
Lane, first right

Nestling in 150 acres of landscaped grounds with lakes
and woodland, just outside the historic town of Battle,
this stunning 18th-century country-house hotel was
originally the site of a gunpowder works. Today, guests
and diners can enjoy the walks and wildlife on the many
woodland trails. The large conservatory restaurant is
sumptuously Georgian and has a colonial style, with
marble floors, Greek statues and huge windows looking
out on to the terrace and swimming pool. The food,
however, is resolutely modern. Take seared scallops with
broccoli and hazelnut purée and Enoki mushrooms,
followed by confit red mullet fillets on Grand Marnier à la
Grecque vegetables.

Times 12-2/7-9

BRIGHTON & HOVE
Map 6 TQ30

Due South

◉ Modern British 🌱

**Seaside dining, committed to organic and local
produce**

☎ 01273 821218
139 Kings Road Arches BN1 2FN
e-mail: eat@duesouth.co.uk
web: www.duesouth.co.uk
dir: On seafront, beneath cinema

Set into the Victorian arches underneath Brighton
promenade, this former fishermen's net-mending shed is
now a modern restaurant with superb views of the beach.
Inside, the style is contemporary, with banquette seating
and polished pine tables, with an outside terrace for
alfresco dining. The restaurant's strong commitment to
the environment is reflected in the weekly-changing
menu. The majority of dishes are made up of organic and
free-range, seasonal produce from local sources, such as
the seared scallops with a clear beetroot broth and
medley of Sussex guinea fowl with braised Puy lentils.
They also serve English and European wines to cut down
on import distances.

Chef Michael Bremner **Owner** Robert Shenton
Times 12-4/6-9.30, Closed 25 Dec **Prices** Starter
£4.50-£11.50, Main £10.50-£28.50, Dessert £5.50-£7.50,
Service added but optional 10% **Wines** 36 bottles over
£20, 22 bottles under £20, 9 by glass **Notes** Tasting
menu 7 courses incl wine D Mon-Thu, Sunday L,
Vegetarian available, Civ Wed 50, Air con **Seats** 55,
Pr/dining room 12 **Children** Portions **Parking** NCP
Churchill Sq

The Gingerman Restaurant (Norfolk Square)

◉◉ Modern British 🌱

Impressive cuisine at a busy bistro-style eatery

☎ 01273 326688
21A Norfolk Square BN1 2PD
e-mail: info@gingermanrestaurants.com
dir: A23 to Palace Pier rdbt. Turn right onto Kings Rd. At
Art Deco style Embassy building turn right into Norfolk Sq

This small, popular, relaxed Brighton bistro-style eatery
has an easy-on-the-eye modern décor of stripped pine
floorboards, white walls and smartly dressed tables.
Lunch is good value, but dinner brings a varied British
menu of well-executed dishes, with textures,
accompaniments and garnishes absolutely spot on.
Expect an appealing modern repertoire created from
quality local ingredients - with fresh fish from the boats a
daily speciality - delivered with minimum fuss and eye-
catching presentation. Think Rye Bay scallops with crispy
pig's cheek, or perhaps rack of South Downs lamb with
fondant potato and rosemary, while desserts such as a
rich chocolate fondant with a tangy mango and
passionfruit sorbet make the perfect finale.

Chef Ben McKellar/David Keates **Owner** Ben & Pamela
McKellar **Times** 12.30-2/7-10, Closed 1 wk Xmas, Closed
Mon **Prices** Fixed L 2 course £15-£27, Fixed D 3 course
£30, Service optional, Groups min 6 service 10%
Wines 12 bottles over £20, 7 bottles under £20, 8 by
glass **Notes** Sunday L, Air con **Seats** 32 **Children** Portions

Graze Restaurant

◉ British, European 🖥 V

Stylish dining at taster only restaurant

☎ 01273 823707
42 Western Rd BN3 1JD
e-mail: bookings@graze-restaurant.co.uk
dir: A23/A259 Brighton Pier. E 2km, onto Lansdowne
Place. Situated on Western Rd, Restaurant on right

This stylish and popular restaurant attracts a well-heeled
local following and is unusual in that it serves entirely
taster dishes. Situated just off the main road, it
resembles a French café from the outside with its slide-
back doors, but the comfortable interior on two floors is
decked out in glamorous yet elegant Rococo style. An
enticing menu of modern British dishes with strong
Mediterranean and Australian influences lives up to the
stylish surroundings. Two- and three-course fixed-price
menus feature alongside the carte and grazing and taster
menus, the starter-sized portions enabling diners to enjoy
a wide combination of finely balanced, exciting dishes.
Kick off with Jerusalem artichoke soup with chanterelles
and confit duck, follow with crab risotto, and then with
beetroot carpaccio and walnut and lentil salad. Nougat
parfait with passionfruit dessert rounds things off in
style.

Chef Adrian Geddes **Owner** Kate Alleston, Adrian Geddes,
Neil Mannifield **Times** 12-3/6-10, Closed 25-26 Dec, 1

Jan, Closed Mon, Closed D Sun **Prices** Fixed L 2 course £10-£16.50, Tasting menu £25.95-£49.50, Starter £5.95-£7.95, Main £6.95-£8.50, Dessert £5.95, Service added but optional 12% **Wines** 26 bottles over £20, 19 bottles under £20, 4 by glass **Notes** Tasting menu 5, 7 & 9 courses available., Sunday L, Vegetarian menu **Seats** 50, Pr/dining room 24

Hotel du Vin Brighton

French, European

Stylish brasserie dining in Metropolitan hotel setting

☎ 01273 718588
Ship St BN1 1AD
e-mail: info@brighton.hotelduvin.com
dir: A23 to seafront, at rdbt take right, then right onto Middle St, bear right until Ship St, hotel is at sea end, on the right

High on anyone's list of Brighton's many attractions must be its beach and its shopping, and this boutique hotel - set just a few minutes' walk from both the seafront and The Lanes - is perfectly positioned to let you make the most of both. Its décor has a strong wine theme, from the individually designed bedrooms through to the buzzy, split-level bar and relaxed brasserie, where cooking is in the classic bistro style. Seasonal ingredients are used throughout, with an emphasis on meat, game and fish from local farms and fisheries. Kick off with ham hock and foie gras terrine, perhaps, and then tuck into boeuf bourguignon with a parsley mash, or grilled Rye Bay cod with Salamanca lentils and chorizo with salsa verde. Excellent wine list.

Chef Rob Carr **Owner** M.W.B **Times** 12-2/7-10, Closed D 31 Dec **Prices** Starter £4.95-£10.75, Main £15.50-£19.50, Dessert £6.75-£8.50, Service added but optional 10% **Wines** 300 bottles over £20, 50 bottles under £20, 12 by glass **Notes** Sunday L, Vegetarian available **Seats** 85, Pr/dining room 36 **Children** Portions, Menu **Parking** The Lanes NCP

The Meadow Restaurant

British

Modern cooking with local produce to the fore

☎ 01273 721182
64 Western Rd BN3 2JQ

A former bank on Hove's main thoroughfare is now a light and bright restaurant with the focus firmly set on Sussex produce. Chef-proprietor Will Murgatroyd lists his suppliers with pride and they include his own parents who contribute produce from their Sussex garden. Blond-wood tables and chairs, white walls and high ceilings combine to create a vibrant and airy space, while the easy-going and friendly service is entirely in keeping. The menu treads a path through Britain and mainland Europe, so, among starters, English pea and watercress soup (enriched with crème fraîche and enhanced with mint oil and sorrel) appears alongside a salad of beetroot, barrel-aged feta and toasted pine nuts. Main-course pan-fried bream, caught off the south coast,

comes with pink fir potatoes, chunks of braised beetroot and wilted spinach.

Times 12-2.30/6-9.30/Closed Mon, Closed D Sun **Prices** Food prices not confirmed for 2009. Please telephone for details.

Pintxo People

Catalan

Modern spin on traditional Basque tapas-style dining

☎ 01273 732323
95-99 Western Rd BN1 2LB
e-mail: info@pintxopeople.co.uk
dir: Close to junct with Montpelier Rd, Opposite Waitrose

Here is a thoroughly modern concept: a bar and deli with casual scrubbed tables on the ground floor and an intimate restaurant on the first floor, both with a Catalan (and Brighton) flavour. A wrought iron spiral staircase leads up to the dining room, where red leather banquettes and black leather chairs provide the seating at white clothed tables. An impressive array of tapas and dishes to share includes Hanger steak with sweet and sour piquillos and pintxo crisps, and octopus with broken potatoes and chorizo. The award-winning bar offers an intriguing cocktail menu.

Chef Miguel Jessen **Owner** Miguel Jessen, Jason Fendick **Times** 12-4/6-10.30, Closed 25-26 Dec, 1 Jan, Closed Mon, Closed L Tue-Fri, Closed D Sun **Prices** Fixed L 3 course £28-£35, Fixed D 3 course £28-£35, Starter £5-£8, Main £9-£15, Dessert £5-£7, Service added but optional 12% **Wines** 53 bottles over £20, 17 bottles under £20, 27 by glass **Notes** Sunday L, Vegetarian available, Civ Wed 75, Air con **Seats** 75

Promenade Restaurant at Thistle Brighton

Modern British

Exciting dining with amazing sea views

☎ 0870 3339129 & 01273 206700
King's Rd BN1 2GS
e-mail: brighton@thistle.co.uk
web: www.thistlehotels.com/brighton
dir: M23 leading onto A23, continue to seafront. At rdbt turn right, hotel is 200 yds on right

The hotel stands right on the promenade and the second floor restaurant offers stunning sea views from floor-to-ceiling windows. The interior design is contemporary, and diners are seated in high-backed chairs at smart wooden tables. Classic English and French techniques are employed to produce an arresting menu showcasing regional produce, including locally caught fish. You might start with a salad of roasted quail with baked squash, seasonal leaves and sauce vièrge, moving on to line-caught wild sea bass with crushed new potatoes, chicory, baby spinach and crème légère. Finish with impressively-decorated desserts like apple frangipane served with caramelised almond and cinnamon ice cream. Imaginative vegetarian dishes are offered.

Chef Seref Ozalp **Owner** Thistle Company **Times** 12.30-2.30/7-9.30 **Prices** Starter £6.50-£7.50, Main £14.50-£22.50, Dessert £6.50-£7.50, Service optional **Wines** 15 bottles over £20, 23 bottles under £20, 13 by glass **Notes** Sunday L, Vegetarian available, Dress restrictions, Smart casual, Civ Wed 120, Air con **Seats** 77, Pr/dining room 30 **Children** Portions, Menu **Parking** 68

Sevendials

Modern European

Modern cuisine in a stylish former bank building

☎ 01273 885555
1-3 Buckingham Place BN1 3TD
e-mail: info@sevendialsrestaurant.co.uk
dir: From Brighton station turn right 0.5m up hill, restaurant situated at Seven Dials rdbt

This former Lloyds bank on the busy Seven Dials junction is now a stylish contemporary restaurant. High ceilings feature deep cornicing and the beige walls are punctuated by dark-stained window surrounds. Darkwood tables, modern art from local artists and a buzzy atmosphere contribute to a clubby feel. Its simple, modern brasserie-style European cookery suits the surroundings and deals in top-notch ingredients and flavour-packed, imaginative dishes. Take duck ham with celeriac remoulade, orange and watercress, followed by breast of free-range chicken with crushed broad beans, courgettes and dill and mustard sauce, or perhaps an apple tart fine with cinnamon ice cream to finish. A fair-weather decked terrace completes the upbeat act.

Chef Sam Metcalfe, Martin Moore **Owner** Sam Metcalfe **Times** 12-3/6-10.30, Closed 25 Dec, 1 Jan, Closed D Sun **Wines** 30 bottles over £20, 14 bottles under £20, 8 by glass **Notes** Early eve ALC menu 6-7pm £10-£15, Sunday L, Vegetarian available, Civ Wed 80 **Seats** 55, Pr/dining room 20 **Children** Portions, Menu **Parking** 2 & 2 mins from restaurant

BRIGHTON & HOVE *Continued*

Terre à Terre

◉◉ Modern Vegetarian ▢ V ◐

Creative vegetarian cooking in a contemporary setting

☎ 01273 729051
71 East St BN1 1HQ
e-mail: mail@terreaterre.co.uk
web: www.terreaterre.co.uk
dir: Town centre near casino, close to Palace Pier & The Lanes

A funky shop-fronted restaurant, Terre à Terre is a haven of imaginative vegetarian cooking and constantly full. Recently refurbished, the deep-coloured walls are finished with damask and candy striped details lending a contemporary feel. The service here is slick and the food almost defies description. Nothing is straightforward - including the quirky descriptions - and the kitchen's daring and imagination can be breathtaking. A vast array of ingredients is skilfully combined to create dishes with intense flavours and sublime textures. An example is the YumUmplum Sushi Rice Tempura, where sushi rice is crammed full of pickled ginger and sweet pepper, dipped in nori and black studded tempura, served with kohlrabi blankets wrapped around siso, daikon and bean shoots, splashed with Uzu lime dressing and Umboshi chilli and red capsicum dunk!

Chef Glen Lester **Owner** Ms A Powley & Mr P Taylor **Times** 12/10.30, Closed 25-26 Dec, 1 Jan, Closed Mon (open some BH's) **Wines** 30 bottles over £20, 12 bottles under £20, 17 by glass **Notes** Pre-theatre menu 12-7pm 2 courses £16, Vegetarian menu, Air con **Seats** 110 **Children** Portions, Menu **Parking** NCP, on street

Leonardo Restaurant

☎ 01273 328888
55 Church Rd, Hove BN3 2BD

A welcoming, exuberant place with a great atmosphere. The menu is Italian all the way, with a combination of old favourites and new inventions.

Prices Food prices not confirmed for 2009. Please telephone for details.

EASTBOURNE   Map 6 TV69

Grand Hotel (Mirabelle)

◉◉ Modern, Classic ▢ ♦NOTABLE WINE LIST

Seaside grandee serving sophisticated cuisine

☎ 01323 412345 & 435066
King Edward's Pde BN21 4EQ
e-mail: reservations@grandeastbourne.com
web: www.grandeastbourne.com
dir: Western end of the seafront, 1m from Eastbourne station

This celebrated Victorian hotel veteran of the Eastbourne seafront successfully integrates late 19th-century charm and grandeur with modern comforts. Tastefully restored to its former glory, it's a suitably palatial venue that comes complete with spacious lounges, luxurious health club and a Grand Hall, where afternoon tea is served amid marble-columned splendour. The Mirabelle is the light-and-airy fine-dining restaurant and its décor and atmosphere follows the traditional theming, though the kitchen takes a more modern approach via its repertoire of fixed-price menus, which include a tasting option and supplemented seasonal classics. Take roast marinated rump of lamb served with broccoli purée and a thyme sauce, and perhaps a stilton pannacotta with mini muffins to finish.

Grand Hotel (Mirabelle)

Chef Keith Mitchell, Gerald Roser **Owner** Elite Hotels **Times** 12.30-2/7-10, Closed 1-14 Jan, Closed Sun-Mon **Prices** Fixed L 2 course fr £18.50, Fixed D 3 course £36.50-£55, Tasting menu £65, Starter £8.50-£17, Main £24-£38, Dessert fr £8, Service added but optional 10% **Wines** 360 bottles over £20, 42 bottles under £20, 17 by glass **Notes** Tasting menu 6 courses, Vegetarian available, Dress restrictions, Jacket or tie for D, Civ Wed 200, Air con **Seats** 50 **Children** Min 12 yrs **Parking** 50

FOREST ROW   Map 6 TQ43

Anderida Restaurant

◉◉ Modern, Traditional British, European V

Grand hotel dining in a country-house setting

☎ 01342 824988
Ashdown Park Hotel, Wych Cross RH18 5JR
e-mail: reservations@ashdownpark.com
dir: A22 towards Eastbourne, pass through Forest Row, continue on A22 for 2m. At Wych Cross turn left, hotel 0.75m on right

Situated in 186 acres of landscaped gardens and parkland, this impressive Victorian country house enjoys a peaceful countryside setting in the heart of the Ashdown Forest. An extensive range of facilities includes a cocktail bar and 18-hole golf course. Reached via a long corridor, the restaurant is a grand and formal affair, enjoying stunning views over the lake and grounds. Professional, friendly staff put their silver service skills to good use, with cloches used for main courses, and soups served from tureens. Traditional dishes like chateaubriand and Dover sole are carved and filleted respectively at the table. The menu is firmly rooted in classical dishes, with the occasional foray into something more adventurous, such as Cromer crab tian with cured tomato petals, mango carpaccio and shellfish sauce, or roast cod on chorizo risotto with smoked paprika foam.

Anderida Restaurant

Chef Jerry Davies **Owner** Elite Hotels **Times** 12-2/7-10 **Prices** Food prices not confirmed for 2009. Please telephone for details. **Wines** 334 bottles over £20, 14 bottles under £20, 16 by glass **Notes** Sunday L, Vegetarian menu, Dress restrictions, Jacket and tie for gentlemen after 7pm, Civ Wed 150 **Seats** 120, Pr/dining room 160 **Children** Portions, Menu **Parking** 120

HERSTMONCEUX   Map 6 TQ61

Sundial Restaurant

◎ French

Pretty cottage setting for classic French cuisine

☎ 01323 832217
BN27 4LA
e-mail: sundialrestaurant@hotmail.com
dir: In village centre, on A271, between Bexhill & Hailsham

This charming red-brick country cottage combines ancient oak beams and Tudor-style windows with modern décor. Tables are well appointed, with fine napery, china, silver and glassware. Classical French cooking features seasonal delicacies like pheasant, partridge, guinea fowl and venison, as well as fresh fish from nearby Rye and Hastings. Diners can choose between the carte, monthly and seasonal fixed-price menus. With skilled presentation, from the carte comes an entrée of beef carpaccio with summer truffle and parmesan shavings, and a main course of roast pigeon and pan-fried duck liver foie gras with Perigourdine sauce.

Chef Vincent Rongier **Owner** Mr & Mrs V & M Rongier **Times** 12-2/7-10, Closed Mon, Closed D Sun **Prices** Fixed L 2 course fr £18, Fixed D 3 course £22-£37, Tasting menu £47.50, Starter £8.50-£19.75, Main £17.75-£21, Dessert £5.55-£10.75, Service added but optional 10% **Wines** 150 bottles over £20, 12 bottles under £20, 4 by glass **Notes** Menu dégustation 5 courses, Vegetarian available, Dress restrictions, Smart casual preferred, Civ Wed 150 **Seats** 50, Pr/dining room 22 **Children** Portions **Parking** 16

JEVINGTON   Map 6 TQ50

Hungry Monk Restaurant

◎ British, French 🖥

Charming, long-established 14th-century cottage restaurant

☎ 01323 482178
BN26 5QF
web: www.hungrymonk.co.uk
dir: A22, turn towards Wannock at Polegate x-rds. Continue for 2.5m, restaurant on left

This 14th-century flint building was once a monastic retreat, and original oak beams and log fires continue to set a traditional tone in antique-furnished lounges and the intimate, candlelit dining room. Accomplished, classic French country cooking draws on wider European influences to offer quality ingredients - presented without unnecessary fuss - on daily fixed-price menus. Expect squid and mussel stew, roast pork belly with Puy lentils, pan-fried beef sirloin with olive oil mash, and to finish, Sue's chocolate cake or their famous banoffee pie. French bottles dominate the varied wine list.

Chef Gary Fisher, Matt Comben **Owner** Mr & Mrs N Mackenzie **Times** 12-2/6.45-9.45, Closed 24-26 Dec, BHs, Closed Mon, Sat **Prices** Fixed L 2 course £16.95, Fixed D 3 course £33.95, Groups min 7 service 12.5% **Wines** 101 bottles over £20, 43 bottles under £20, 9 by glass **Notes** Sunday L, Vegetarian available, Air con **Seats** 38, Pr/dining room 16 **Children** Min 4 yrs, Portions **Parking** 14

LEWES   Map 6 TQ41

The Real Eating Company

◎◎ Modern British

Assured modern cooking in informal deli-restaurant

☎ 01273 402650
18 Cliffe High St BN7 2AJ
e-mail: lewes@real-eating.co.uk
dir: Please telephone for directions

Set in the heart of town, The Real Eating Company is a deli-restaurant outfit, an outpost of the original model in Hove. The classic shop frontage leads into a spacious food/deli shop, leading to the restaurant - a long, oblong room that looks out onto a small-decked alfresco area. The décor is modern, clean and simple, with stripped wood floors, plain walls enlivened by colourful prints and ceiling skylights to add natural light. Tables and chairs are modern wood and service is relaxed, while the cooking's highly assured with chef Darren Velvick's impressive pedigree (ex-head chef at renowned London restaurant Pétrus) to drive things. As you'd expect with his background, the cooking is underpinned by a classical repertoire driven by quality local seasonal produce. His modern, simple approach and clean presentation is underscored by fine attention to detail, with lunch a simpler affair. Take herb-crust halibut served with crushed Peruvian potatoes, warm fennel salsa and crayfish tails.

Chef Darren Velvick **Owner** Helena Hudson **Times** 12-3/6.30-11.30, Closed 25-26 Dec, 1 Jan, Closed D Sun-Mon **Prices** Fixed D 3 course fr £12, Starter £5-£8, Main £12-£16, Dessert £6-£7, Service added but optional 10%, Groups min 10 service 10% **Wines** 12 bottles over £20, 6 bottles under £20, 10 by glass **Notes** Sunday L, Vegetarian available, Air con **Seats** 72 **Children** Portions, Menu **Parking** Harveys Way (behind restaurant)

The Shelleys

◎◎ Modern British

Elegant market town hotel dining

☎ 01273 472361
High St BN7 1XS
e-mail: reservations@the-shelleys.co.uk
dir: From Brighton take A27 towards Eastbourne. Follow signs for Lewes town centre

Centrally located on the historic high street, the classically proportioned exterior of this elegant 16th-

Continued

LEWES *Continued*

century hotel is echoed within, with public rooms graced by beautiful chandeliers and fine oil paintings. It takes its name from the poet Shelley whose family once lived here. The airy, spacious dining room is romantically lit by candles and overlooks a peaceful private garden. A confident kitchen sources quality Sussex ingredients and produces simply presented, yet appealing dishes that are listed on a modern British menu with European influences. Twice-baked goat's cheese soufflé and fresh white crabmeat with asparagus and citrus salad are typical starters. Roast partridge features in a main course with glazed walnuts, celeriac purée and a rich jus made from the roasting juices.

The Shelleys

Chef Simon Thomas **Owner** Shelton & Ragu Fernando **Times** 12-2.15/7-9.15 **Prices** Starter £6.50-£9.95, Main £17.50-£23, Dessert £7-£8.50, Service added 10% **Wines** 60 bottles over £20, 8 bottles under £20, 6 by glass **Notes** Sunday L, Vegetarian available, Civ Wed 60 **Seats** 40, Pr/dining room 40 **Children** Portions **Parking** 30

NEWICK	**Map 6 TQ42**

Newick Park Hotel & Country Estate

◉◉◉ – *see opposite*

Two Seven Two

◉◉ Modern European

Sophisticated cooking in stylish surroundings

☎ 01825 721272
20/22 High St BN8 4LQ
e-mail: twoseventwo@hotmail.co.uk
web: www.272restaurant.co.uk
dir: On A272, 7m E of Haywards Heath and 7m N of Lewes

This former whitewashed village hardware store on the A272 (hence the name) has been transformed into a stylish modern restaurant, with a simple cream and beige colour scheme. Polished light oak flooring, painted brickwork, pine tables and hand-made, high-backed Italian chairs make a smart impression. Appealing, fixed-price menus offer good value and complement the more serious modern European carte. Top-notch ingredients and stylish presentation showcase the highly accomplished, sophisticated cooking; take grilled fillet of beef topped with a blue cheese and herb crust on a bed of stir-fried greens and beets, served with wine and shallot sauce. Finish with passionfruit parfait rolled in

coconut flakes, served with a coconut sauce and sesame seeds. Service is relaxed, informal and friendly and suits this upbeat act.

Chef Neil Bennett **Owner** Simon Maltby **Times** 12-2.30/7-9.30, Closed 25-26 Dec, 1-2 Jan, Closed Mon, Closed L Tue, Closed D Sun **Prices** Fixed L 2 course fr £12.95, Fixed D 3 course fr £16.95, Starter £5.25-£8.75, Main £13.50-£22.50, Dessert £5.25-£7.50, Groups min 8 service 10% **Wines** 52 bottles over £20, 35 bottles under £20, 6 by glass **Notes** Sunday L, Vegetarian available, Air con **Seats** 60 **Children** Portions **Parking** 10

RYE	**Map 7 TQ92**

Mermaid Inn

◉ British, French **V**

Local legend with a traditional menu

☎ 01797 223065 & 223788
Mermaid St TN31 7EY
e-mail: info@mermaidinn.com
dir: Rye is situated on A259 between Ashford and Hastings

Situated on a magnificent cobbled side street, the Mermaid is one of England's oldest inns and the building oozes charm and history. Its former guests include Queen Elizabeth I and Johnny Depp, although not at the same time. Uneven floors, creaky staircases and heavily timbered ceilings are testament to its advanced age, while the open fires and comfy sofas are welcoming and inviting. The linenfold panelled restaurant is an airy room with graciously appointed tables and a romantic feel. Take your seat for a menu of traditional fare with a French bias in dishes such as timbale of crab with light curry oil, followed by roast cannon of venison with creamed Savoy cabbage and bacon, dauphinoise potatoes, pear spring roll and sauce grand veneur.

Chef Robert Malyon, Roger Kellie **Owner** Mrs J Blincow & Mr R I Pinwill **Times** 12-2.30/7-9.30 **Prices** Fixed L 2 course £19, Fixed D 4 course £39.50, Starter £6.50-£10.50, Main £17.50-£31, Dessert £7, Service added but optional 10% **Wines** 35 bottles over £20, 21 bottles under £20, 14 by glass **Notes** Sunday L, Vegetarian menu, Dress restrictions, Smart casual, no jeans or T-shirts **Seats** 64, Pr/dining room 14 **Children** Portions, Menu **Parking** 26

Webbes at The Fish Café

◉ Modern British

Fish and seafood restaurant in an upbeat and lively setting

☎ 01797 222226 & 222210
17 Tower St TN31 7AT
e-mail: info@thefishcafe.com
web: www.thefishcafe.com
dir: 100mtrs before Landgate Arch

This converted warehouse once housed a toy factory but it has been tastefully restored with many of the old warehouse-style features of the original building remaining - the exposed brickwork and high ceilings are particularly impressive. The restaurant is laid out over three floors: a lively café-style ground floor, a more formal first floor for dinner, and a private function room on the second floor. The kitchen takes an appealing modern approach using fresh local seafood; ceviche of scallop and salmon with fennel, caviar and lime dressing, or perhaps loin of monkfish wrapped in prosciutto with crushed new potatoes, pan-fried leeks and sage sauce show the style.

Chef Paul Webbe, Mathew Drinkwater **Owner** Paul & Rebecca Webbe **Times** Closed 25-26 Dec, 2-11 Jan, Closed Mon, Closed L all week, Closed D Sun **Prices** Starter £5.50-£7.50, Main £12.50-£23, Dessert £4.75-£6, Service optional **Wines** 52 bottles over £20, 16 bottles under £20, 6 by glass **Notes** Vegetarian available, Air con **Seats** 52, Pr/dining room 70 **Children** Portions, Menu **Parking** Cinque Port Street

TICEHURST	**Map 6 TQ63**

Dale Hill Hotel & Golf Club

◉ Modern European

Formal dining in modern golfing hotel

☎ 01580 200112
TN5 7DQ
e-mail: info@dalehill.co.uk
web: www.dalehill.co.uk
dir: At junction of A21 & B2087 follow signs for Ticehurst & Flimwell; Dale Hill is 1m on left

This smart, modern golfing hotel is situated just a short drive from the village and the views from the formal Wealden restaurant take in the 18th green and the broad expanse of the Kentish Weald. The hotel boasts two golf courses and a swimming pool and gym, as well as a

Continued on page 414

Newick Park Hotel & Country Estate

Modern European

Highly accomplished cooking in elegant country house

☎ 01825 723633
BN8 4SB
e-mail: bookings@newickpark.co.uk
web: www.newickpark.co.uk
dir: From village green on A272, turn right into Church Ln. Continue along lane for 1m, past pubs and garage to T-junct. Turn left and continue to entrance on right

This delightful Grade II listed Georgian mansion - set in over 200 acres of landscaped gardens and parkland - offers a quintessential country-house experience. Interiors are grand, with tasteful fabrics and genteel colours, while open fires cosset in winter and a terrace beckons in summer. Floor-to-ceiling windows, high ceilings, bright summery colours, striking flower displays and artwork grace the elegant restaurant. Staff are suitably professional and knowledgeable, but have a friendly, unstuffy style, while the highly accomplished kitchen comes driven by quality, local fresh seasonal ingredients, including produce from its own organic walled kitchen garden - including fruit and vegetables - and game from the estate (duck, pheasant, partridge and venison). The cooking impresses with an intelligent simplicity

and highly skilled execution, with its modern approach delivered with fine presentation, balance and flavour. Take South Coast brill served with braised oxtail, creamed cabbage and pommery mustard croquette, or perhaps a rump of South Downs lamb accompanied by a spiced aubergine and tomato salad with lemon-crushed potato, and to finish, maybe a pistachio parfait, with bitter-chocolate sorbet and almond tuile.

Chef Chris Moore **Owner** Michael & Virginia Childs **Times** 12-2.30/7-9, Closed New Year **Prices** Fixed L 2 course £18.50, Fixed D 3 course £38.50, Service optional **Wines** 85 bottles over £20, 25 bottles under £20, 9 by glass
Notes Sunday L, Vegetarian available, Civ Wed 120 **Seats** 40, Pr/dining room 74 **Children** Portions, Menu **Parking** 100

TICEHURST *Continued*

lounge bar, conservatory brasserie, and the Spike Bar which has a lively atmosphere. The kitchen offers an interesting range of modern dishes on an extensive carte or a three-course fixed-price menu. Kick off with lobster and girolle tortellini with Noilly Prat and vanilla sauce, and follow with a main course of beef fillet Rossini with fondant potato and wilted spinach topped with chicken liver parfait and red wine sauce.

Times 12-2.30/6.30-9, Closed L Mon-Sat

UCKFIELD
Map 6 TQ42

The Dining Room

◎◎ Modern, Traditional 💻 V

Masterful cooking in classical surroundings

☎ 01825 733333
Buxted Park Hotel, Buxted Park, Buxted TN22 4AY
e-mail: buxtedpark@handpicked.co.uk
dir: Turn off A22 Uckfield bypass (London-Eastbourne road), then take A272 to Buxted. Cross lights, entrance to hotel 1m on right

The Palladian Georgian façade of Buxted Park stands impressively in 300 acres of beautiful parkland and formal gardens. The restaurant, located in the original Victorian orangery, retains many original features but still feels modern and bright. It's a stylish and relaxing place in which to dine, with views over the gardens. Accomplished modern British and European cuisine blends classic and modern ideas and is based around top-quality ingredients. Simply-presented dishes may include ballotine of foie gras with herb jus and a sweet and sour reduction, followed by grilled fillet of sea bream with warm artichoke and sorrel salad, broad beans and fresh herbs, and a deliciously smooth chocolate fondant with caramelised orange ice cream for dessert.

Chef Mark Murphy **Owner** Hand Picked Hotels
Times 12-2/7-9.30 **Prices** Fixed L 2 course fr £12.95, Fixed D 3 course £28-£38, Service optional **Wines** 130 bottles over £20, 8 bottles under £20, 20 by glass **Notes** Vegetarian menu, Dress restrictions, Smart casual, Civ Wed 130, Air con **Seats** 40, Pr/dining room 60 **Children** Portions, Menu **Parking** 100

Horsted Place

◎◎ Modern British

Opulent country-house restaurant, formal but friendly

☎ 01825 750581
Little Horsted TN22 5TS
e-mail: hotel@horstedplace.co.uk
dir: 2m S on A26 towards Lewes

Built in 1850, the house is one of the country's finest examples of the Gothic-style of architecture. The magnificent pile is gloriously set in its own 1,000-acre estate, which includes the East Sussex National Golf Club. Within, there's a splendid Pugin staircase and smart public rooms, including an elegant, traditional

country house-style dining room. The kitchen's modern approach produces plenty of interest in generously proportioned dishes created from good regional and seasonal produce; take duck breast with confit leg and shallot sauce, or perhaps roast wild sea bass on braised yellow beans in tomato, garlic and olive oil. Mascarpone dumplings might provide the finish, served with lime and crème fraîche ice cream.

Chef Allan Garth **Owner** Perinon Ltd **Times** 12-2/7-9.30, Closed L Sat **Prices** Fixed L 2 course £15.95, Starter £9.50, Main £20, Dessert £8.50, Service optional **Wines** 120 bottles over £20, 8 bottles under £20, 8 by glass **Notes** Sunday L, Vegetarian available, Dress restrictions, No jeans, Civ Wed 100 **Seats** 40, Pr/dining room 80 **Children** Min 7 yrs, Portions **Parking** 50

WESTFIELD
Map 7 TQ81

The Wild Mushroom Restaurant

◎ Modern British 🐝

Impressive cuisine in a converted Victorian farmhouse

☎ 01424 751137
Woodgate House, Westfield Ln TN35 4SB
e-mail: info@wildmushroom.co.uk
dir: From A21 towards Hastings, turn left onto A28 to Westfield. Restaurant 1.5m on left

Situated on the ground floor of a converted 19th-century farmhouse, this cosy L-shaped restaurant, with its linen-clothed tables, wooden floors, soft brown tones and mushroom ornaments, has a relaxed and welcoming atmosphere with friendly service to match. You can also enjoy a pre-dinner drink in the delightful garden or in the bar. The kitchen serves simple, unfussy food cooked with self-assured skill, and good use is made of quality seasonal ingredients to create impressive, well-presented dishes. Expect roast breast and confit of Gressingham duckling with caramelised black plums and Chinese five spice sauce, followed by vanilla mousse with rhubarb and shortbread. (Sister establishment is Webbes at The Fish Café, Rye. See entry.)

Chef Paul Webbe **Owner** Mr & Mrs P Webbe
Times 12-2.30/7-10, Closed 25 Dec, 2 wks at New Year, Closed Mon, Closed L Sat, Closed D Sun **Prices** Fixed L 2 course £15.95, Tasting menu £32, Starter £5.50-£8.50, Main £11-£20, Dessert £6-£6.95, Service optional **Wines** 46 bottles over £20, 33 bottles under £20, 6 by glass **Notes** Tasting menu 6 courses, Sunday L, Vegetarian available, Dress restrictions, Smart casual **Seats** 40 **Children** Portions **Parking** 20

WILMINGTON
Map 6 TQ50

Crossways

◎◎ Modern British

Relaxed and welcoming country-house dining

☎ 01323 482455
BN26 5SG
e-mail: stay@crosswayshotel.co.uk
dir: On A27, 2m W of Polegate

A charming country house, Crossways is set in the heart of the Cuckmere Valley and its own attractive gardens, and was once home to Elizabeth David's parents. A friendly and relaxed atmosphere is assured by the proprietors and the restaurant is very much the focus of the hotel. Food is prepared with love and affection from fresh ingredients, local where possible. Dishes are offered from a set monthly menu, including a daily home-made soup and fresh fish from the day's catch. Typically impressive dishes are hot game sausage with onion relish to start, followed by roast Gressingham duck with mango, ginger and sun-dried cranberry sauce, or parmesan-crusted pork schnitzel served with sweet-and-sour prunes.

Chef David Stott **Owner** David Stott, Clive James **Times** Closed 24 Dec-24 Jan, Closed Sun-Mon, Closed L all week **Prices** Fixed D 4 course £35.95-£36.95, Service optional **Wines** 18 bottles over £20, 25 bottles under £20, 10 by glass **Notes** Vegetarian available **Seats** 24 **Children** Min 12 yrs **Parking** 20

SUSSEX, WEST

AMBERLEY
Map 6 TQ01

Queens Room at Amberley Castle Hotel

◎◎◎ – *see opposite*

ARUNDEL
Map 6 TQ00

The Bay Tree

◎ British, Mediterranean

Relaxed bistro-style dining

☎ 01903 883679
21 Tarrant St BN18 9DG
dir: A27 between Chichester and Worthing. Restaurant is in Tarrant St just off High St

This friendly family-run restaurant in the town centre is housed within a charming 16th-century timber-framed building. A stylish calming cream and pale green décor means diners can relax in the contemporary interior, or on a pretty sun-dappled terrace, while the chefs create modern British dishes with a Mediterranean or Pacific Rim twist. Successful combinations include a starter of garlic battered tiger prawns set on red pepper angel hair noodles and a wasabi dressing. Seasonal and local produce form the basis of more traditional dishes like roasted garlic and herb-scented lamb noisettes with leek and onion purée and redcurrant and sherry sauce.

Chef David Partridge, Kate Holle, Karen Bowley **Owner** Valerie & Mike Moore **Times** 11-3/7-9.30, Closed Mon, Closed D Sun **Prices** Starter £4.95-£8.25, Main £12.95-£22.95, Dessert £5.25-£5.75, Service optional **Wines** 10 bottles over £20, 16 bottles under £20, 6 by glass **Notes** Sunday L, Vegetarian available, Dress restrictions, Smart casual **Seats** 40 **Children** Min 5yrs, Portions **Parking** On street & car park nearby - free after 6pm

---

The Townhouse

◉ Modern Mediterranean

Precise cooking in a stunning setting

☎ 01903 883847
65 High St BN18 9AJ
e-mail: enquiries@thetownhouse.co.uk
dir: A27 to Arundel. Follow road to High Street

This splendid Grade II Regency building in the heart of Arundel is situated opposite the castle that dominates the town. The crowning glory of the building, the carved and gilded walnut ceiling in the restaurant, dates from the Italian Renaissance and reputedly comes from a Medici palace. Informal but sophisticated, the restaurant also has a large picture window which, together with gilded mirrors and stripped wood floors, creates a sense of space. The modern Mediterranean menu is up to date and rooted in classical combinations, as in langoustine

and tiger prawn risotto, followed by roasted Angmering partridge with lightly spiced cabbage, wild mushroom ravioli and game chips. Finish with a warm chocolate fondant and vanilla sauce, or maybe hazelnut parfait with chocolate sorbet. There's a good range of dessert wines to choose from.

Chef Lee Williams **Owner** Lee & Kate Williams **Times** 12-2.30/7-9.30, Closed 2 wks Oct, Xmas, 2 wks Jan, Closed Sun-Mon **Prices** Fixed L 2 course £12.50, Fixed D 3 course £27.50, Service optional **Wines** 29 bottles over £20, 15 bottles under £20, 6 by glass **Notes** Vegetarian available **Seats** 24 **Children** Portions **Parking** On street or nearby car park

---

Millstream Hotel

◉◉ ◉ Modern British 🖳

Indulgent dining in a gorgeous village setting

☎ 01243 573234
Bosham Ln PO18 8HL
e-mail: info@millstream-hotel.co.uk
dir: Take A259 exit from Chichester rdbt and in village follow signs for quay

Its picturesque setting in the harbourside village of Bosham, near Chichester, makes this hotel and restaurant a popular destination for the sailing crowd. At dinner, the ambitious kitchen pulls out all the stops to

deliver a luxurious meal. The chef here clearly has high aspirations - the food is both innovative and technically accomplished and quality ingredients are used with care and sensitivity throughout the large menu. Try the great balance of flavours of seared Shetland scallops with a pea and mint purée, pancetta and foie gras cream to start, followed by best end of lamb, garlic potatoes, baby vegetables, basil jus, spinach, tapenade and tomato fondue. Finish with white chocolate fondant, kumquat coulis and dark chocolate syrup.

Millstream Hotel

Times 12.30-2/6.45-9.15

Queens Room at Amberley Castle Hotel

❀ ❀ ❀

AMBERLEY Map 6 TQ01

Modern European V 🎗

Serious and complex fine dining in fairytale castle surroundings

☎ 01798 831992
BN18 9LT
e-mail: info@amberleycastle.co.uk
dir: Off B2139 between Storrington and Houghton

Anyone with fantasies of medieval knights on white chargers or maidens in distress in need of rescue will find all their desires satisfied at the 900 year-old Amberley Castle. It is a true castle - castellated walls and towers, barrel-vaulted ceilings and a working portcullis - and since 1988 it has been owned by the Cummings who turned it into luxury hotel, while keeping the sense of antiquity. Antiques and suits of armour are dotted around

the place, huge fireplaces roar away and then there are the grounds: 12 acres of stunning parkland with gardens, pond and even a thatched tree house with a rope bridge. The Queens Room is the main fine-dining room of the hotel, dating from the 12th century, and is suitably refined and romantic. Chef James Dugan is not overawed by the fabulous setting, in fact his food lives up to it. The cooking is broadly speaking modern European in approach and in presentation; there are pre-starters and pre-desserts, all adding to the sense of occasion. Salt-cod brandade is a light and garlic-free version paired with a twice-cooked hen's egg and a crisp piece of Iberian cured ham, and the creativity continues with a main-course dish of brill poached in carrot juice with a 'salad' of carrot and wild garlic and oxtail dumplings, which are a Polish pierogi rather than the traditional British version. Service is knowledgeable and friendly and the team includes a sommelier to help with the extensive wine list.

Chef James Dugan **Owner** Amberley Castle Hotel Ltd **Times** 12-2/7-9.30 **Prices** Fixed L 2 course £20, Fixed D 3 course £50, Tasting menu £65, Service optional, Groups min 10 service 10% **Wines** 155 bottles over £20, 4 bottles under £20, 14 by glass **Notes** Tasting menu 8 courses, Sunday L, Vegetarian menu, Dress restrictions, Smart casual, jacket or tie, Civ Wed 55 **Seats** 70, Pr/dining room 40 **Children** Min 12 yrs, Portions **Parking** 30

BRACKLESHAM Map 5 SZ89

Cliffords Cottage Restaurant

◉ British, French

Cosy cottage restaurant offering reliably good seafood and game

☎ 01243 670250

Bracklesham Ln PO20 8JA

dir: From A27 follow signs for The Witterings. A286 to Birdham, B2198 to Bracklesham

This little gem of a restaurant is set unobtrusively beside the road, and easily mistaken for a homely cottage. Inside is as unspoilt as outside, with plenty of exposed beams and original features adding to its charm. Outside, a large garden provides many of the vegetables used in the kitchen, while the sea and nearby estates yield the fish and game that dominate the French menu. A separate blackboard lists the seafood specials, usually around six choices including perhaps Dover sole, fillet of sea bass with a herb crust, and pan-fried skate with capers. Flavoursome traditional and modern desserts are not to be missed.

Chef Peter Gray **Owner** Peter & Carolyn Gray
Times 12.30-5/7-9.30, Closed Jan **Prices** Fixed L 2 course £14.95-£22, Fixed D 3 course £24-£38, Service optional, Groups min 10 service 10% **Wines** 4 bottles over £20, 25 bottles under £20, 5 by glass **Notes** Sunday L, Vegetarian available **Seats** 28 **Children** Portions **Parking** 16

BURGESS HILL Map 6 TQ31

Taylor's Restaurant

◉ Modern

Popular town-centre restaurant serving simply great food

☎ 01444 233311

2 Church Hill, Burgess Hill RH15 9AE

e-mail: michelle@taylorsrestaurant.uk.com

dir: M3 junct 11, A23 towards Brighton. Left onto A2300 towards Burgess Hill. Take Jane Murray Way (A273) towards town centre, B2113

Set in a parade of shops near the station, this popular restaurant has simple cream décor, modern artwork and plain pine tables. Good raw ingredients are skilfully and simply prepared with European and some Asian influences. The deli board is a nice idea, you can choose a selection of nibbles, starters or tasters to share, or have a selection chosen for you. Starters and light bites feature soups, salads and dishes like creamy seafood tagliatelle with tarragon. Main courses might include slow-roasted belly of pork with red cabbage and star anise, red wine and juniper berry sauce. Taylor's also provides an outside catering service.

Times 12-3/6.30-10, Closed 1st week Jan, Closed Sun, Closed L Sat, Closed D Mon

BURPHAM Map 6 TQ00

George & Dragon

◉ British, French

Idyllically-located old inn on the South Downs

☎ 01903 883131

BN18 9RR

dir: 2.5m along no-through road signed Burpham off A27, 1m E of Arundel

Perfectly placed at the end of a lane on the South Downs, this inn is ideal for a walk before or after dinner. Old beams, stone floors and bags of atmosphere draw a crowd, particularly at weekends, so come early for a good table. Expect honest pub grub from a kitchen that does the basics well: a smoked chicken and duck terrine with orange chutney and Melba toast to start perhaps, followed by walnut-crusted cod loin with parsnip purée and minted new potatoes. A short carte is supplemented by a lengthy specials board, with an additional bar selection served at lunchtime.

Times 12-2/7-9, Closed 25 Dec, Closed D Sun

CHICHESTER Map 5 SU80

Comme Ça

◉ French

Classic French cooking in a friendly restaurant

☎ 01243 788724 & 536307

67 Broyle Rd PO19 6BD

e-mail: comme.ca@commeca.co.uk

dir: On A286 near Festival Theatre

A long-established French restaurant with a strong local following, Comme Ça is housed in a Georgian inn across the park from the Chichester Festival Theatre. The cosy beamed interior is decorated in bold colours, with an interesting collection of prints and objets d'art. There is also a bar-lounge and garden room with French doors leading onto a patio and sunken garden. With a variety of cooking methods creating an interesting menu, classic French dishes - Gascogne duck foie gras terrine with walnuts, baked cod with seared scallop topped with shrimp butter and dark Belgian chocolate mousse - are simply presented.

Chef Michael Navet, Mark Howard **Owner** Mr & Mrs Navet **Times** 12-2/6-10.30, Closed Xmas wk & New Year wk, BHs, Closed Mon, Closed L Tue, Closed D Sun **Prices** Fixed L 2 course £19.95, Fixed D 3 course £22.95, Starter £6.75-£12.95, Main £15.95-£18.95, Dessert £6.65, Service

optional, Groups min 8 service 10% **Wines** 60 bottles over £20, 60 bottles under £20, 7 by glass **Notes** Sunday L, Dress restrictions, Smart casual **Seats** 100, Pr/dining room 14 **Children** Portions, Menu **Parking** 46

Croucher's Country Hotel & Restaurant

◉ Modern

Modern cooking in bright, characterful surroundings

☎ 01243 784995

Birdham Rd PO20 7EH

e-mail: crouchers@btconnect.com

dir: From A27, S of Chichester, take A286 to The Witterings. Hotel 2m on left

The hotel is a former farmhouse incorporating more recently built barn-style public rooms housing the restaurant and bar. Relax on leather sofas in the bar-lounge before dining in the restaurant with its high beamed ceilings. Large windows overlook the courtyard and fields, and pre-dinner drinks can be enjoyed on the terrace in summer. Modern cooking offers imaginative combinations and fresh flavours in an aesthetically pleasing starter of scallops served with asparagus, parsnip purée and shellfish cream, followed by tender rump of lamb with champ potato and rosemary jus. For dessert, take spiced poached pear served with vanilla crème brûlée and red wine sorbet, or perhaps a selection of cheeses.

Times 12.30-2.30/7-11, Closed 26 Dec, 1 Jan

Hallidays

◉◉ Modern European ☺

A charming traditional village restaurant serving modern cuisine

☎ 01243 575331

Funtington PO18 9LF

e-mail: hallidaysdinners@aol.com

dir: Please telephone for directions

Three 13th-century flint and thatched cottages at the foot of the South Downs have been transformed to create this intimate two-room restaurant with a wealth of original features and a pale green and yellow décor. Family-run, it offers friendly service and is well patronised by a local clientele. Weekly-changing menus based on quality, local seasonal ingredients, including farm meats and fish from day boats, offer a range of modern European dishes with a classical theme. Take home-smoked local sea trout with watercress for starters, followed by Racton Park lamb shoulder with morels and broad beans, or baked turbot with cider, mustard and thyme, while a lemon verbena crème brûlée might catch the eye at dessert.

Chef Andrew Stephenson **Owner** Mr A & Mrs J Stephenson **Times** 12-1.45/7-9.45, Closed 2 wks Mar, 1 wk Aug, Closed Mon-Tue, Closed L Sat, Closed D Sun **Prices** Fixed L 2 course fr £17.50, Fixed D 3 course fr £33.50, Starter £7.50-£9, Main £17-£20, Dessert £7.50-£9, Service optional **Wines** 65 bottles over £20, 25 bottles under £20, 5 by glass **Notes** Sunday L, Vegetarian available, Dress restrictions, No shorts **Seats** 26 **Children** Portions **Parking** 12

Royal Oak Inn

◉ Modern European

Traditional food and buzzy atmosphere with a sophisticated twist

☎ 01243 527434
Pook Ln PO18 0AX
e-mail: info@royaloakeastlavant.co.uk
dir: From Chichester take A286 towards Midhurst, 2m to mini rdbt, take right, signposted East Lavant. Royal Oak is on the left

A tastefully converted inn, Sussex barn and flint cottage provide the setting for this relaxing restaurant and bar, situated in a quiet village 2 miles north of the city. Original beams, bare brick walls, open fires and an intimate bar area combine with comfortable leather sofas and armchairs to create a smart, sophisticated ambience. The restaurant continues the theme, with pine tables and tall, modern leather chairs, while the crowd-pleasing menu marries tradition with Mediterranean touches, bolstered by daily blackboard specials. Try warm English apple and goat's cheese tartlet with watercress and sun-blushed tomato salad, follow with incredibly fresh black-olive-crusted fillet of sea bass with warm tomato, chorizo, potato salad and salsa verde.

Chef Sam Baker **Owner** Charles Ullmann
Times 10-2/6-9.30 **Prices** Starter £5.25-£9.50, Main £12.50-£19.50, Dessert £3.95-£5.95, Service optional **Wines** 45 bottles over £20, 12 bottles under £20, 20 by glass **Notes** Sunday L, Vegetarian available, Air con **Seats** 55 **Children** Portions, Menu **Parking** 25

West Stoke House

◉◉◉ – *see below*

CHILGROVE   Map 5 SU81

The Fish House (formerly White Horse)

◉◉ Modern British, International **V** ☻

Accomplished seafood cooking at a pretty, rural restaurant with rooms

☎ 01243 519444
PO18 9HX
e-mail: info@thefishhouse.co.uk
web: www.thefishhouse.co.uk
dir: 7m N of Chichester on B2141. W of A286 on to B2141, at Lavant restaurant 4m on right

Located on the edge of the South Downs, this former 18th-century inn makes a pretty destination, its whitewashed walls decked with blooms of lilac wisteria. David Barnard, who owned The Crab at Chieveley in Berkshire, where he gained two Rosettes, bought the former White Horse in spring 2008 and plans to create a fish and oyster bar with a crustacean cabinet and revamp the dining area into a classy, contemporary restaurant. So expect big changes and a predominantly seafood menu.

The Fish House (formerly White Horse)

Chef Alan Gleeson **Owner** David Barnard
Times 12-3/6-11 **Prices** Fixed L 2 course £14.50, Fixed D 3 course fr £24, Tasting menu £60, Starter £7-£12, Main £14-£27, Dessert £5-£7, Service optional **Wines** 270 bottles over £20, 30 bottles under £20, 15 by glass **Notes** Sunday L, Vegetarian menu, Civ Wed 100, Air con **Seats** 100, Pr/dining room 24 **Children** Portions, Menu **Parking** 70

West Stoke House

CHICHESTER   Map 5 SU80

Modern British, French

Sophisticated but relaxed dining for creative modern cuisine

☎ 01243 575226
Downs Rd, West Stoke PO18 9BN
e-mail: info@weststokehouse.co.uk
dir: N of Chichester leave A286 at Lavant church and continue to West Stoke

Set on the edge of the Sussex Downs, this Georgian mansion surrounded by beautiful countryside - now a country-house restaurant-with-rooms - offers sophisticated dining but in a relaxed atmosphere bereft of traditional pomp and fuss. The décor follows the theme, is stylish with a classic appeal, featuring French antiques and contemporary artwork, while dining tables come dressed in their best whites. Menus are sensibly compact, fixed-price, well-conceived affairs - a tasting option is also available at dinner when things crank up a notch or two - and come explained in detail by the professional front-of-house team; but like the atmosphere here, they're not at all starchy. The kitchen's modern approach - underpinned by a classical theme - understandably utilises fresh, prime local and seasonal produce. Visually strong, technically adept dishes come intelligently simply prepared, but offer ambition, excitement and wow elements. Expect a threesome like lobster tortellini with cauliflower purée, pea shoots and shellfish bisque, roasted rump of Welsh lamb served with creamed potato, spinach, chervil root and a red wine sauce, and to finish, perhaps an apple crumble soufflé accompanied by cinnamon ice cream and sauce anglaise.

Chef Darren Brown **Owner** Rowland & Mary Leach
Times 12-2/7-9.30, Closed Xmas, 1 Jan, Closed Mon-Tue, Closed D Sun **Prices** Fixed L 2 course fr £17.50, Fixed D 3 course £42.50-£49.50, Service optional, Groups min 8 service 12.5% **Wines** 85 bottles over £20, 14 bottles under £20, 8 by glass **Notes** Sunday L, Vegetarian available, Civ Wed 60 **Seats** 40, Pr/dining room 26 **Children** Min 12 yrs, Portions **Parking** 20

CLIMPING — Map 6 SU90

Bailiffscourt Hotel & Spa

Modern British

A fascinating architectural folly offering creative modern cooking

☎ 01903 723511
BN17 5RW
e-mail: bailiffscourt@hshotels.co.uk
web: www.hshotels.co.uk
dir: From A27 (Arundel), take A284 towards Littlehampton. Continue to the A259, Bailiffscourt is signed towards Climping Beach

Set in 30 acres of parkland with moats and small streams, this architectural gem was built in 1927 by Lord Moyne in the style of an authentic medieval manor house, using reclaimed stone and woodwork gathered from across England. Gothic-style mullioned windows overlook the rose-clad courtyard, while narrow passageways lead you through a series of intimate lounges and sitting rooms. The restaurant, with its heavy wooden ceiling, stone window frames with leaded lights, and walls adorned with rich tapestries, continues the medieval illusion. The cooking style, however, is definitely in the present with classical underpinning, sharp and precise, concentrating on simple effective flavours from quality ingredients. Expect main courses like grilled sea bass served with herb purée, purple sprouting broccoli, baby leeks and tomato consommé.

Chef Russell Williams **Owner** Pontus & Miranda Carminger **Times** 12-1.30/7-9.30 **Prices** Fixed L 2 course £15, Fixed D 3 course £44.50, Service optional **Wines** 120 bottles over £20, 6 bottles under £20, 12 by glass **Notes** ALC 3 courses, Sunday L, Vegetarian available, Dress restrictions, Smart casual, no jeans or T-shirts, Civ Wed 60 **Seats** 70, Pr/dining room 70 **Children** Portions, Menu **Parking** 80

COPTHORNE

For restaurant details see Gatwick Airport (London), (Sussex, West)

CRAWLEY

For restaurant details see Gatwick Airport (London), (Sussex, West)

CUCKFIELD — Map 6 TQ32

Ockenden Manor

– *see below*

EAST GRINSTEAD — Map 6 TQ33

Anise

Modern British

Contemporary restaurant with cuisine to match

☎ 01342 337768 & 337766
The Felbridge Hotel & Spa, London Rd RH19 2BH
e-mail: info@felbridgehotel.co.uk
web: www.felbridgehotel.co.uk
dir: A22 (southbound), 200m passed East Grinstead Boundary sign

This elegant restaurant has recently benefited from a tasteful makeover. The contemporary colour scheme, in

---

Ockenden Manor

CUCKFIELD — Map 6 TQ32

Modern French V

Creative cuisine in an elegant manor house

☎ 01444 416111
Ockenden Ln RH17 5LD
e-mail: reservations@ockenden-manor.com
web: www.hshotels.co.uk
dir: Village centre

The setting in a beautiful village in the heart of the Sussex countryside is enough to induce feelings of peace and tranquillity, but sight of the Elizabethan manor house itself might result in a slight intake of breath. The perfectly manicured grounds and the elegant building are the stuff of an American tourist's dreams. Guests are warmly welcomed and the service is knowledgeable and professional throughout. The wood-panelled dining room has stained-glass windows and an ornate painted ceiling, which is a suitably formal setting for the French-focused food. Expect all the bells and whistles from canapé, amuse bouche (thinly sliced braised beef, perhaps, with horseradish creamed potato, half a cherry tomato and pea shoot) to an array of petits fours. Plump, succulent and sweet scallops are glazed with parsley oil and served with smoked bacon and garlic crisps in a simple and vibrant starter, while a main course saddle of Balcombe venison is artfully partnered with apple beignets, creamed celeriac, golden roasted butternut squash and some buttered spinach. The quality of the produce is evident throughout and the creativity in the kitchen runs all the way to dessert: warm chocolate tart is beautifully made and served with a shot glass of lychee foam with excellent depth of flavour. The extensive international wine list is worth exploring.

Chef Steve Crane **Owner** The Goodman & Carminger Family **Times** 12-2/7-9 **Prices** Fixed L 2 course £14.95-£15.95, Fixed D 3 course £47.50, Tasting menu £65, Service optional, Groups min 10 service 10% **Wines** 204 bottles over £20, 14 bottles under £20, 11 by glass **Notes** ALC fixed price, Sunday L, Vegetarian menu, Dress restrictions, No jeans, T-shirts, Civ Wed 74 **Seats** 40, Pr/dining room 75 **Parking** 45

subtle tones of grey, cream and black, perfectly compliments the high-backed leather chairs, starched white table linen and fine silverware. Offering modern European cuisine with interesting French and British influences, the menu emphasises local, seasonal ingredients creating simply prepared, imaginative dishes that are beautifully presented. Start with tian of Dorset crab with lime and avocado, plum tomato, roasted pepper and chervil jelly, followed by loin of Romney Marsh lamb, served with rosemary dauphinoise, baby spinach, sweetbread fritters and sloe gin jus, or roast fillet of local Limousin beef, ravioli of the blade and rib and kidney suet pudding.

Chef Matthew Budden **Owner** New Century, East Grinstead Ltd. **Times** 12-2.30/6-10 **Wines** 75 bottles over £20, 11 bottles under £20, 11 by glass **Notes** Business L £22.95, Sunday L, Vegetarian available, Civ Wed 50, Air con **Seats** 34, Pr/dining room 20 **Children** Portions, Menu **Parking** 200

Gravetye Manor Hotel

◎◎◎ – *see below*

GATWICK AIRPORT (LONDON)   Map 6 TQ24

Langshott Manor

◎◎   Modern British ▭ **V** ✤

Fine dining in elegant Elizabethan manor house

☎ 01293 786680
Langshott Ln, Horley RH6 9LN
e-mail: admin@langshottmanor.com
dir: From A23, Horley, take Ladbroke Rd turning off Chequers Hotel rdbt, entrance 0.75m on right

Sitting in 3 acres of beautifully landscaped grounds, this delightful timber-framed manor house dates back to 1580 and, despite its rural location, is only 5 minutes from Gatwick Airport. The elegant Mulberry restaurant has a baronial feel, with original features that include leaded windows overlooking the gardens and picturesque

pond enhanced by contemporary artwork, discreet modern décor and smart linen-clad tables. This elegant setting is the venue for some serious and impressive cooking, with its roots firmly in the modern British camp and a keen eye on quality and seasonality. Some ingredients are provided by the kitchen garden. Bold flavour combinations feature on the carte and tasting menu, as in a nage of turbot and mussels with thyme and garlic potatoes with chive emulsion, or slow-cooked blade of beef with mushroom ravioli.

Chef Phil Dixon **Owner** Peter & Deborah Hinchcliffe **Times** 12-2.30/7-9.30 **Prices** Fixed L 2 course fr £15, Fixed D 3 course fr £40, Tasting menu £55, Service added 12.5%, Groups service 12.5% **Wines** 80 bottles over £20, 4 bottles under £20, 11 by glass **Notes** Sunday L, Vegetarian menu, Dress restrictions, No jeans or shorts, jacket, Civ Wed 60 **Seats** 55, Pr/dining room 22 **Children** Min 12 yrs, Portions **Parking** 25

Gravetye Manor Hotel

EAST GRINSTEAD   Map 6 TQ33

Modern British ♦ NOTABLE WINE LIST ✤

Fabulous country-house hotel with historic gardens and memorable cuisine

☎ 01342 810567
RH19 4LJ
e-mail: info@gravetyemanor.co.uk
dir: From M23 junct 10 take A264 towards East Grinstead. After 2m take B2028. After Turners Hill, follow signs

This stunning Elizabethan stone mansion was built in 1598 and has a timeless quality, enjoying a truly tranquil setting. One of Gravetye's most notable owners was the celebrated Victorian horticulturalist William Robinson, who created the 30 acres of gardens as the National English Garden as well as restoring the house, which

later became a hotel in 1958. The current owners continue the custodianship of house and gardens and the tradition of country-house hospitality with care and affection. Inside, the traditional oak-panelled restaurant has a carved white ceiling and winter log fires. Chef Mark Raffan has his culinary roots in classical French cuisine from his time with the Roux brothers, plus a stint as personal chef to the late King Hussein of Jordan. This background and his considerable experience at Gravetye ensure an interesting and eclectic menu of broadly modern English cuisine delivered with high skill and top-class local ingredients, with fruit and vegetables coming from the hotel's own kitchen garden and peach house. Fresh fish is also a particular strength, with typical dishes including the likes of steamed charlotte of lemon sole and organic salmon with creamed leek and langoustine cappuccino, or roast fillet of West Coast turbot with autumn ceps, roasted salsify and creamy cep sauce.

Chef Mark Raffan **Owner** A Russell & M Raffan **Times** 12.30-1.45/7-9.30, Closed 25 Dec pm **Prices** Fixed L 2 course £19, Fixed D 3 course £35, Starter £12, Main £28, Dessert £9, Service added but optional 12.5% **Wines** 500 bottles over £20, 15 bottles under £20, 25 by glass **Notes** Sunday L, Vegetarian available, Dress restrictions, Jacket & tie preferred, Civ Wed 45 **Seats** 50, Pr/dining room 20 **Children** Min 7 yrs, Portions **Parking** 45

GATWICK AIRPORT (LONDON) *Continued*

The Old House Restaurant

◉ Traditional

Fine dining in surroundings of great character

☎ 01342 712222
Effingham Rd, Copthorne RH10 3JB
e-mail: info@oldhouserestaurant.co.uk
dir: From M23 junct 10 follow A264 to East Grinstead, take 1st left at 2nd rdbt, left at x-rds, restaurant 0.75m on left

This delightful beamed 16th-century house oozes rustic charm and features a collection of cosy lounges with intimate lighting and comfortable seating. The sunny, elegant dining room is suitably grand, in gold, cream and navy, without being intimidating. The emphasis is on good quality ingredients, locally sourced wherever possible. From the fairly traditional menu, begin with duck liver parfait with fig chutney or shellfish bisque and move on to fillet of gilt head bream served with vegetable spaghetti and a light butter sauce, or chump of lamb with boulangère potatoes and Madeira sauce, and round off with orange pannacotta with caramelised oranges.

Chef Alan Pierce **Owner** Mr & Mrs C Dormon
Times 12.15-2/6.30-9.30, Closed Xmas, New Year, 1 wk spring, BHs, Closed Mon, Closed L Sat, Closed D Sun
Prices Fixed L 2 course £15, Fixed D 3 course £35.50-£42.50, Starter £7.75-£9.75, Main £21.50-£29, Dessert £7.50-£8.50, Service added but optional 10%
Wines 112 bottles over £20, 18 bottles under £20
Notes Sunday L, Vegetarian available, Dress restrictions, Smart casual, no jeans or trainers, Air con **Seats** 80, Pr/dining room 35 **Children** Min 10 yrs **Parking** 45

Restaurant 1881

◉◉ Modern French, Mediterranean **V**

Fine dining in elegant surroundings

☎ 01293 862166
Stanhill Court Hotel, Stanhill Rd, Charlwood RH6 0EP
e-mail: enquiries@stanhillcourthotel.co.uk
dir: Please telephone for directions

This attractive country house, within easy reach of Gatwick Airport, is surrounded by 35 acres of ancient woodland, including an amphitheatre and Victorian walled garden. The romantic, wood-panelled Restaurant 1881 is elegantly appointed and has wonderful views over the grounds. The food is largely classical French in inspiration, with European influences and some innovative ideas. Well-presented dishes prepared from quality ingredients include honey roast wood pigeon with pancetta crisp and a light jus, followed by perfectly cooked turbot fillet with a rich sauce of fish, ceps and garlic. Glazed lemon tart is a perfect finale with its delicate pastry and exuberantly fruity lemon cream, topped with lime crème fraîche and fresh raspberries.

Chef Lloyd Williams **Owner** Antony Colas
Times 12-3/7-11, Closed L Sat **Prices** Food prices not confirmed for 2009. Please telephone for details.
Wines 80 bottles over £20, 20 bottles under £20, 15 by glass **Notes** Sunday L, Vegetarian menu, Civ Wed 250, Air con **Seats** 120, Pr/dining room 260 **Children** Portions **Parking** 150

GOODWOOD Map 6 SU80

The Richmond Arms/The Goodwood Park Hotel

◉◉ British

Local food at a sport and leisure hotel close to Goodwood

☎ 01243 775537
PO18 0QB
e-mail: reservations@thegoodwoodparkhotel.co.uk
dir: Just off A285, 3m NE of Chichester. Follow signs for Goodwood, once in Estate follow signs for hotel

It is no surprise that this smart modern hotel and country club has a leaning toward sport and leisure, given its setting in the 12,000-acre Goodwood Estate. In fact the facilities are excellent with a golf course, swimming pool and spa and a cocktail bar bedecked with motor sport memorabilia. The country-style Richmond Room restaurant, housed in the entrance archway of the original 17th-century coaching inn, is the fine-dining option here. The forward-thinking modern British menu offering imaginative dishes using the finest local ingredients. Start with pressed skate and potato with lemon and parsley, followed by Sussex pork cutlet with baked potato, roast apple and black pudding. Conclude, perhaps, with lemon tart and raspberry sorbet.

Chef Nick Funnell, Alex Wood **Owner** The Goodwood Estate Company Ltd **Times** 12-2.30/6-10.30 **Prices** Fixed L 2 course fr £15, Fixed D 3 course fr £17.50, Starter £4.95-£8.50, Main £12.50-£17.50, Dessert £6-£7, Service optional **Notes** Sunday L, Vegetarian available, Civ Wed 120 **Seats** 80, Pr/dining room 120 **Children** Portions **Parking** 350

HAYWARDS HEATH Map 6 TQ32

Jeremy's at Borde Hill

◉ Modern European

Attractive restaurant with a creative kitchen

☎ 01444 441102
Balcombe Rd RH16 1XP
e-mail: reservations@jeremysrestaurant.com
dir: 1.5m N of Haywards Heath. From M23 junct 10a take A23 through Balcombe

Jeremy's is housed in a converted stable block in the grounds of the Borde Hill Estate, approached by a cobbled courtyard. The restaurant overlooks a Victorian walled garden and has a fabulous south-facing terrace for outdoor dining in summer. The vibrant interior combines wooden floors and high-backed leather chairs with a striking collection of contemporary art. A menu of modern European cooking is built around fresh seasonal produce, with dishes such as salad of portobello mushrooms with roasted beetroot, globe artichoke and watercress, pan-fried fillet of Rye Bay brill with bouillabaisse jus, and rhubarb tart with rhubarb jelly.

Chef J & V Ashpool, Andre Ebert **Owner** Jeremy & Vera Ashpool **Times** 12-2.30/7-9.30, Closed 1st wk Jan, Closed Mon, Closed D Sun **Prices** Fixed L 2 course £17.50, Fixed D 3 course fr £22.50, Tasting menu £32.50, Starter £8-£10.50, Main £13.50-£22, Dessert £5-£6.50, Service optional, Groups min 8 service 10% **Wines** 70 bottles over £20, 18 bottles under £20, 10 by glass **Notes** Sunday L, Vegetarian available, Civ Wed 55 **Seats** 55 **Children** Portions **Parking** 20

The Camellia Restaurant at South Lodge Hotel

LOWER BEEDING Map 6 TQ22

French, Mediterranean

Country-house cuisine overlooking the South Downs

☎ 01403 891711
Brighton Rd RH13 6PS
e-mail: enquiries@southlodgehotel.co.uk
dir: A281 Brighton road out of Horsham, through Monksgate. Hotel is on right past Leonardslee Gardens on left

A haven of gracious living, this impeccably presented Victorian country-house hotel stands in 90 acres of mature gardens and grounds, and offers stunning views over the South Downs. With its wood panelling, oil paintings, heavy fabrics and sense of space, it was built to impress and it certainly does. The extended, sumptuous candlelit restaurant - named after the 100-year-old camellia which still grows against the terrace wall - continues the theme, with ornate ceilings, wood panelling and floors and crisp white tablecloths, while large windows offer views over the Downs. Service is formal but appropriately friendly. The kitchen's approach is intelligently simple, with the emphasis on allowing tip-top seasonal produce to shine. The style is modern-focused and underpinned by a classical theme, with the fixed-price menu repertoire refreshingly unpretentious. Dishes are delivered with

flair and a lightness of touch and enjoy well-defined flavours and combinations. For mains, take slow-cooked fillet of Sussex beef served with braised oxtail, creamed potato and mushroom purée, or monkfish tail with spiced lentils, smoked salmon ravioli and parsley sauce, and for dessert, perhaps treacle tart with gingerbread ice cream.

Chef Lewis Hamblet **Times** 12-2/7-9.45

HORSHAM   Map 6 TQ13

Stan's Way House Restaurant

◉ Modern European ♥

Smart setting for modern European dining with a twist

☎ 01403 255688
3 Stan's Way, East St RH12 1HU
e-mail: sl@stanswayhouse.co.uk
web: www.stanswayhouse.co.uk
dir: Telephone for directions

The impressive 600-year-old Grade II listed building has oak floors throughout, with a solid oak staircase leading to the first-floor restaurant. Here, oak beams, wooden furnishings, candlelight and crisp white napery add to the atmosphere, making it a lovely venue for a special meal. Cooking is generally modern European in style using the best of local produce, with an eclectic combination of New World ingredients combined with classical techniques and smart presentation. Try ham hock and parsley terrine with cauliflower parfait and apple purée, and pan-fried fillet of red mullet with cep mushrooms, pearl barley risotto and cucumber relish.

Chef Mr Steven Dray Owner Steven & Stephanie Dray
Times 12-3/7-10, Closed BHs, 2 wks summer, 1 wk New Yr, Closed Sun, Mon, Closed L Tue-Thu Prices Fixed D 3 course fr £28.50, Service added but optional 10%
Wines 15 bottles over £20, 12 bottles under £20, 5 by glass Notes Vegetarian available Seats 40 Parking Piries Place free after 6pm

LICKFOLD   Map 6 SU92

The Lickfold Inn

◉ Modern International

Ancient inn with thoroughly modern food

☎ 01798 861285 & 861342
Lickfold GU28 9EY
e-mail: thelickfoldinn@aol.com
dir: Signposted from A272, 6m E of Midhurst. From A285 6m S of Haslemere, follow signs for Lurgashall Winery and continue on to Lickfold village

Dating back to the 15th century, this charming inn oozes style and sophistication. Built in a herringbone brick pattern, it boasts an abundance of original features - not least a large inglenook fireplace, flagstone floors and sturdy oak beams - and the large terrace is the perfect place for summer dining. Crowd-pleasing menus focus on fish and seafood, and include quality pub food alongside more sophisticated dishes. Wok-fried samphire with crayfish tails in a lemon and garlic butter and 8-hour braised shank of South Downs lamb with French beans , roast garlic mash and mint and redcurrant jus are fine examples of the fare.

Times 12-2.30/7-9.30, Closed 25-26 Dec, Closed Mon, Closed D Sun

LOWER BEEDING   Map 6 TQ22

The Camellia Restaurant at South Lodge Hotel

◉◉◉ – see page 421

MANNINGS HEATH   Map 6 TQ22

Goldings Restaurant

◉ Modern British

Fine dining with a magnificent golf course backdrop

☎ 01403 210228
Mannings Heath Golf Club, Hammerpond Rd RH13 6PG
e-mail: enquiries@manningsheath.com
dir: From Horsham A281, for 2m. Approaching Mannings Heath, left at the Dun Horse. Follow road to T-junct, left, then follow road past village green. At T-junct, right, then right again

Located at this members-only golf club housed in a lovely 17th-century mansion, lodge-style Goldings Restaurant is open to all. With its beamed ceiling, wooden panels and open log fire, the elegant dining room offers fine views across the South Downs and, when weather allows, you can dine on the terrace. On a menu of predominantly British, well-prepared dishes, using mostly regional produce, the emphasis is on clarity of flavours. Tee off with roasted parsnip and cider soup with crispy deep-fried shallot, followed by pan-fried fillets of black bream on wilted spinach with garlic fondant potato and tapenade sauce. To finish, try rich Belgian chocolate tart served with white chocolate ice cream.

Chef Robbie Pierce Owner Exclusive Hotels
Times 12-3/7-9, Closed D Sun-Wed Prices Food prices not confirmed for 2009. Please telephone for details.
Wines 32 bottles over £20, 3 bottles under £20, 4 by glass Notes Vegetarian available, Dress restrictions, Smart casual, collared shirt required, Civ Wed 100 Seats 43, Pr/dining room 12 Children Portions, Menu Parking 120

MIDHURST   Map 6 SU82

Spread Eagle Hotel and Spa

◉◉ Modern British

Accomplished classical cooking in a character setting

☎ 01730 816911
South St GU29 9NH
e-mail: reservations@spreadeagle-midhurst.com
dir: Town centre

Dating from 1430, this beautiful old property occupies a prime position at the foot of the town, yet enjoys the seclusion of its own delightful grounds. The building retains many original features, including ancient beams, sloping floors and oak panelling. Two interconnecting rooms make up the restaurant, separated by a large stone fireplace complete with a copper canopy adorned with old copper pots. The hospitality here is renowned and the food is similarly spot-on, with appealing dishes delivered with good technical skill and clear flavours. Typical of these are Thai spiced crab cake with crab and vanilla soup, and steak and oyster pudding with slow-roasted root vegetables, glazed onions and Guinness gravy.

Times 12.30-2/7-9.30

ROWHOOK   Map 6 TQ13

Neals Restaurant at The Chequers Inn

◉ Traditional British

Enjoyable rural pub dining

☎ 01403 790480
RH12 3PY
e-mail: thechequers1!@aol.com
dir: From Horsham take A281 towards Guildford. At rdbt take A29 signposted for London. After 200 mtrs turn left, follow signs for Rowhook

Set in the heart of rural West Sussex in the hamlet of Rowhook, The Chequers Inn is traditionally decorated in rustic style with open fires, oak beams, flagstone floors and wooden tables. There is also a large garden with picturesque views. Relaxed, efficient service and a warm, friendly atmosphere complete the picture. Expect good home traditional British cooking with a twist. Using the best of local produce, tempting dishes might include chicken liver parfait with crab apple jelly, followed by roast loin of South Downs venison with bubble-and-squeak and a chestnut jus, or pan-seared salmon with buttered salsify and Portobello mushrooms.

Chef Tim Neal Owner Mr & Mrs Neal Times 12-2/7-9, Closed 25 Dec, Closed D Sun Prices Starter £5.50-£9.50, Main £8.50-£16.75, Dessert £5.50, Service optional, Groups min 8 service 10% Wines 22 bottles over £20, 29 bottles under £20, 8 by glass Notes Sunday L, Vegetarian available Seats 40 Children Portions Parking 40

Ghyll Manor

◎◎ Modern European 🖥

Creative and accomplished cooking at peaceful country-house hotel

☎ 0845 345 3426
High St RH12 4PX
e-mail: reception@ghyllmanor.com
dir: M23 junct 11, join A264 signed Horsham. Continue to 3rd rdbt, take 3rd exit towards Faygate and Rusper

This 16th-century mansion house turned country-house hotel is set in 45 acres of idyllic grounds, in the pretty and peaceful village of Rusper. Enjoy a drink in the light-and-airy conservatory - or in summer on the terrace overlooking the lake - before going through to dinner in the fine-dining Purus Restaurant. Located in the original part of the house, the restaurant retains many period features and with its oak beams and spacious seating exudes a warm, cosy ambience. Service is efficient and friendly, and the kitchen's modern European style is delivered via fixed-price dinner, carte and six-course tasting menus. Try poached monkfish with young leeks in a light lime leaf and lemongrass broth, followed perhaps by pan-fried fillet of beef with Jerusalem artichoke purée, crispy potato galette and baby carrots with port and Madeira jus.

Chef Alec Mackins **Owner** Civil Service Motoring Association **Times** 12-2/6.30-9.30 **Prices** Fixed L 2 course fr £14.95, Fixed D 3 course fr £35, Service optional **Wines** 76 bottles over £20, 16 bottles under £20, 8 by glass **Notes** Sunday L, Vegetarian available, Dress restrictions, Smart casual, Civ Wed 80 **Seats** 40, Pr/dining room 30 **Children** Min 10 yrs, Portions **Parking** 100

The Crab & Lobster

◎ British, Mediterranean

Stylish waterside hideaway

☎ 01243 641233
Mill Ln PO20 7NB
e-mail: enquiries@crab-lobster.co.uk
dir: A27 S onto B2145 towards Selsey. At Sidlesham turn left onto Rockery Ln, continue for 0.75m.

Hidden away on the picturesque banks of the Pagham Harbour Nature Reserve is this stylish restaurant with rooms in a 350-year-old former pub. Recently refurbished, the smart restaurant is a comfortable blend of old and new, combining flagstone floors, beams and open fires with contemporary plum and beige upholstered chairs and a small bar area. Open for lunch and dinner, the restaurant offers a varied menu with a strong emphasis on locally-caught fish and regionally-sourced seasonal produce, with some traditional as well as Mediterranean dishes to tempt the taste buds. Start with excellent pan-seared diver-caught Scottish scallops with puréed celeriac and red wine jus with pancetta, and for a main course try devilled local crab with a gratinated herb crust on crushed new potatoes and pea leaf salad.

Chef Antony Phillips **Owner** Sam & Janet Bailese **Times** 12-2.30/6-10 **Prices** Starter £5.50-£10.50, Main £11.95-£27, Dessert £5-£7, Service optional, Groups min 7 service 10% **Wines** 41 bottles over £20, 16 bottles under £20, 14 by glass **Notes** Sunday L, Vegetarian available **Seats** 54 **Children** Portions **Parking** 12

see advert below

Old Forge

◎ Modern International

Fine food and wine in a historic setting

☎ 01903 743402
6 Church St RH20 4LA
e-mail: contact@oldforge.co.uk
dir: On side street in village centre

The restaurant comprises three small dining rooms in what was originally a forge and adjacent cottages, dating from the 16th century. The old-world beams and low ceilings make for a cosy atmosphere, and husband-and-wife team Cathy and Clive Roberts offer a warm welcome. The modern cooking draws on traditional British and international cuisine, with dishes ranging from halibut fillet poached in olive oil and served with herb risotto, to spiced and roasted duck breast with quince jelly glaze, wilted spring greens and rosemary mash. Look out for special food and wine evenings.

Chef Cathy Roberts **Owner** Mr & Mrs N C Roberts **Times** 12.15-1.30/7.15-9, Closed Xmas-New Year, 2 wks spring, 2 wks autumn, Closed Mon-Wed, Closed L Sat, Closed D Sun **Prices** Fixed L 2 course £14.50-£26, Fixed D 3 course £34, Service included **Wines** 42 bottles over £20, 39 bottles under £20, 10 by glass **Notes** Sunday L, Dress restrictions, Smart casual **Seats** 34, Pr/dining room 12 **Children** Portions **Parking** On street

TURNERS HILL   Map 6 TQ33

Alexander House Hotel & Utopia Spa

◉◉   Modern European ▱

French cuisine in a grand country house

☎ 01342 714914
East St RH10 4QD
e-mail: info@alexanderhouse.co.uk
web: www.alexanderhouse.co.uk
dir: On B2110 between Turners Hill & East Grinstead; 6m from M23 junct 10

This grand 17th-century country mansion-turned-hotel is set in over 100 acres of parkland and landscaped gardens. Sensitively restored, it has a modern opulence with understated luxury, with a recently added sumptuous spa. The restaurant is in the oldest part of the hotel and its plush furnishings and splendid works of art are country-house grandeur at its finest. Service is formal, but the atmosphere is relaxed and friendly. The cooking style is classical French with some European influences. Try the terrine of oriental spiced duck with plum and five spice coulis and micro leaf salad to start, then opt for the duo of lamb, ballotine of the shoulder and noisettes, with wilted spinach, warm potato and mint mousse and pot au feu of baby vegetables. Millefeuille of rhubarb and strawberries and strawberry coulis makes a fitting finale.

Chef Kirk Johnson **Owner** Alexander Hotels Ltd
Times 12-3/7-10, Closed Mon, Closed D Sun **Prices** Fixed L 2 course £16, Fixed D 3 course £35, Starter £8-£12, Main £20-£30, Dessert £8.50-£10, Service added but optional 12.5% **Wines** 130 bottles over £20, 4 bottles under £20, 18 by glass **Notes** Sunday L, Vegetarian available, Dress restrictions, No jeans or trainers, Civ Wed 90 **Seats** 40, Pr/dining room 90 **Children** Min 7 yrs, Portions **Parking** 150

TYNE & WEAR

GATESHEAD   Map 21 NZ26

Eslington Villa Hotel

◉   Modern British **V**

Relaxed and inviting dining in a charming setting

☎ 0191 487 6017   & 420 0666
8 Station Rd, Low Fell NE9 6DR
e-mail: home@eslingtonvilla.co.uk
dir: From A1 (M) turn off to Team Valley Trading Estate, up Eastern Avenue. Turn left at PDS car showroom. Hotel is 100 yds on left

This smart hotel combines a bright contemporary atmosphere with the period style of a fine Victorian villa, with high ceilings, fireplaces and cornices. It stands in its own two acres of beautiful garden in a quiet leafy district. Eat in the classical dining room, or the conservatory overlooking the Team Valley, decorated in a more modern style. Modern British and European-influenced dishes are offered from a choice of fixed-price and carte menus, such as crab ravioli with avocado pesto and sauce vièrge to start, followed by peppered pork fillet with bubble-and-squeak and honey-roasted roots.

Chef Andy Moore **Owner** Mr & Mrs N Tulip
Times 12-2/7-9.45, Closed 25-26 Dec, 1 Jan, BHs, Closed L Sat, Closed D Sun **Prices** Fixed L 2 course £16-£18, Fixed D 3 course £20-£22, Starter £6.75-£8.75, Main £16.50-£21, Dessert £5.75-£8.50, Service optional **Wines** 17 bottles over £20, 24 bottles under £20, 8 by glass **Notes** Sunday L, Vegetarian menu **Seats** 80, Pr/dining room 30 **Children** Portions **Parking** 30

NEWCASTLE UPON TYNE   Map 21 NZ26

Black Door

◉◉   Modern British, French ▱ **V**

Smart, contemporary venue with innovative cuisine

☎ 0191 260 5411
32 Clayton Street West NE1 5DZ
e-mail: justine.ladd@blackdoorgroup.co.uk
dir: Opposite St Mary's Cathedral, close to Newcastle Central stn

Though hidden away somewhat unobtrusively behind a namesake black door in a Georgian-style city-centre townhouse, it hasn't stopped this restaurant making waves in the North East. Inside has a very modern edge, with brown leather sofas, suede stools, wooden floors and leather-topped tables. Cream-painted walls are hung with black and white artwork of famous Newcastle landmarks and tables are clothed, while the well-stocked bar proves a prominent feature. Service is friendly and knowledgeable, while the kitchen delivers a repertoire of innovative modern French cuisine that uses the best local ingredients. Technical skill, timings and balance are spot on, and dishes have a certain air of excitement. At the time of going to press we understand there were changes taking place at this restaurant, please telephone for details.

Chef David Kennedy **Owner** David Ladd & David Kennedy
Times 12-2/7-10, Closed Sun & Mon **Prices** Fixed L 2 course £15.50, Fixed D 3 course £42.50, Service optional, Groups min 6 service 10% **Wines** 50 bottles over £20, 18 bottles under £20, 11 by glass **Notes** Vegetarian menu **Seats** 34 **Children** Portions

---

Blackfriars Restaurant

◉   Traditional British ▱ ☕

Modern dining in ancient surroundings

☎ 0191 261 5945
Friars St NE1 4XN
e-mail: info@blackfriarsrestaurant.co.uk
web: www.blackfriarsrestaurant.co.uk
dir: Take the only small cobbled road off Stowel St (China Town). Blackfriars 100yds on left

Once the refectory of an early 13th-century monastery, Blackfriars is full of medieval charm, accentuated by masses of candles, massive stone walls, ancient beams, inglenooks and the staff who occasionally wear period costume. The place was once used extensively by King Henry III, and might well be considered as the oldest restaurant in the UK. The traditional and modern British dishes are based on fresh local ingredients, with interesting flavours and simple, contemporary presentation. Try Northumbrian black pudding beignet with apple compote and mustard sauce, followed by Tritlington Hall lamb with heritage dauphinoise potatoes and shallot purée. There is also a peaceful courtyard for summer dining.

Chef David Mitchell **Owner** Andy & Sam Hook
Times 12-2.30/6-12, Closed BHs except Good Fri, Closed D Sun **Prices** Fixed L 2 course fr £11.50, Fixed D 3 course fr £16, Starter £4.50-£10.50, Main £11.50-£20, Dessert £5.50-£7.50, Service added but optional 10% **Wines** 29 bottles over £20, 17 bottles under £20, 7 by glass **Notes** Sunday L, Vegetarian available, Air con **Seats** 80, Pr/dining room 50 **Children** Portions, Menu **Parking** Car park next to restaurant

Café 21 Newcastle

◉ French, International V 🍴

Busy bistro in Newcastle's trendy Quayside area

☎ 0191 222 0755
Trinity Gardens NE1 2HH
e-mail: bh@cafetwentyone.co.uk
dir: Please telephone for directions

This city-centre bistro has contemporary colour and style, where the walls are hung with large mirrors, little pictures and old French recipes. White clothed wooden tables are set on wooden floors, each with a bowl of olives, tea lights, and branded crockery with the Café 21 logo. Well presented and accurately cooked French bistro dishes with British and Asian influences, with regularly changing specials, are based on local produce where possible. Try grilled taleggio cheese with new potatoes and Parma ham, or dill-cured salmon and sweet pickled herrings in lemon and chive crème fraîche, followed by fillets of red mullet with sweet carrot broth and parsley mash. Service is informal and friendly.

Chef Christopher Dobson **Owner** Mr and Mrs T Laybourne **Times** 12-2.30/5.30-10.30, Closed Xmas **Prices** Fixed L 2 course fr £14, Fixed D 3 course fr £16.50, Starter £7-£11.50, Main £14.40-£23, Dessert £5-£8.50, Service added but optional 10% **Wines** 82 bottles over £20, 21 bottles under £20, 24 by glass **Notes** Sunday L, Vegetarian menu, Air con **Seats** 129, Pr/dining room 40 **Children** Portions **Parking** NCP

The Fisherman's Lodge

◉◉ British, French 🖥

Tranquil setting for imaginative cooking

☎ 0191 281 3281
Jesmond Dene, Jesmond NE7 7BQ
e-mail: enquiries@fishermanslodge.co.uk
dir: 2.5m from city centre, off A1058 (Tynemouth road). Turn into Jesmond Rd then 2nd right on Jesmond Dene Rd. Follow signs

Lord Armstrong's former private dwelling enjoys a wonderfully secluded parkland location, but is only a five-minute drive from the city centre. The décor is,

appropriately enough, in the style of a smart, shooting lodge, but very modern with it. Fine linen and glassware add extra sparkle to the dining room and the effect is all very tasteful and elegant. The accomplished kitchen takes a modern focus - underpinned by a classical French theme - to deliver carefully presented, imaginative menus (dotted with luxury ingredients and showcasing a penchant for fish). Among starters seared scallops come with celeriac and truffle purée, apple jelly and cumin foam, and carrot, honey and ginger soup is enlivened further with a coriander cream. Main course fillet of turbot with Niçoise garnish and basil vierge confirms that fish is still a favourite here.

Chef Ashley Paynton **Owner** Tom and Jocelyn Maxfield **Times** 12-2/7-10.30, Closed 25 Dec, BHs, Closed Sun-Mon, Closed L 31 Dec **Wines** 205 bottles over £20, 8 bottles under £20, 12 by glass **Notes** ALC 2-3 courses £40-£50, Dress restrictions, Smart casual, Civ Wed 60 **Seats** 60, Pr/dining room 40 **Children** Portions **Parking** 40

Jesmond Dene House

◉◉ Modern British V 🍴

Impeccable fine dining in Grade II listed hotel with a contemporary theme

☎ 0191 212 3000
Jesmond Dene Rd NE2 2EY
e-mail: info@jesmonddenehouse.co.uk
dir: From city centre follow A167 to junct with A184. Turn right towards Matthew Bank. Turn right into Jesmond Dene Rd

Built in the early 1820s, this fine Grade II listed Arts and Crafts house overlooks the wooded valley of Jesmond Dene in a charming rural location, while being only 5 minutes from the centre of town. A sympathetic conversion programme has transformed it into a trendy contemporary hotel, with many original features retained and pristine décor throughout. Comfortable wood-panelled lounges with fine antiques create a sense of elegance and understated luxury, while the restaurant is split into two handsome dining areas - the former music room with its delicate plasterwork and dramatic colour scheme, and the light-and-airy Garden Room with impressive oak floors. The cooking is generous and skilful, with a seasonally-inspired menu concentrating on well-matched flavours with dashes of thoughtful innovation. Home-made pappardelle, rare-breed pork belly cooked soubise style and Perigord truffle, or braised turbot with lasagne of langoustines and champagne sauce are fine examples of the cuisine's style. Tantalising desserts create an agony of choice for those with a sweet tooth. Dither over warm chocolate tart with blood orange ice cream, or millefeuille of pink pralines, banana butter and yogurt with bitter chocolate sorbet. Exceptional breads, amuse-bouche and petits fours complete the package. To do the cooking justice, try the tasting menu with wine matching.
Jesmond Dene House is AA Hotel of the Year for England.

Chef Pierre Rigothier **Owner** Terry Laybourne, Peter Candler **Times** 12-2.30/7-10.30 **Prices** Fixed L 2 course £18.50-£22, Starter £10.50-£14.50, Main £19.50-£25.50, Dessert £4-£9.50, Service added but optional 10%

Wines 222 bottles over £20, 22 bottles under £20, 17 by glass **Notes** Sunday L, Vegetarian menu, Dress restrictions, Smart casual, Civ Wed 100 **Seats** 60, Pr/ dining room 18 **Children** Portions, Menu **Parking** 64

Malmaison Hotel

◉ French 🖥

Good brasserie dining in trendy location

☎ 0191 245 5000
Quayside NE1 3DX
e-mail: newcastle@malmaison.com
dir: Telephone for directions

Enjoy stunning views of the Millennium Bridge from this stylish hotel on the fashionable Newcastle quayside. Formerly a warehouse, it now has a first-floor bar with stripped wood floors, oversized sofas, bustling atmosphere and views of the River Tyne. The equally contemporary brasserie-style restaurant has bold colours, mood lighting and giant picture windows setting the relaxing scene for sampling some traditional classics. Take smoked mackerel, quail's egg and chicory salad as a starter, or a main of braised belly pork with soy dressing and pak choi, with Malmaison crème brûlée to finish. Vegetarians have their own section on the menu and there's a Sunday brunch menu, too.

Times 12-2.30/6-11

The Plate

◉ Traditional British

Formal hotel dining room overlooking Gosforth Park

☎ 0191 236 4111
Newcastle Marriott Hotel, High Gosforth Park, Gosforth NE3 5HN
e-mail: frontdesk.gosforthpark@marriotthotels.co.uk
dir: From A1 take A1056 (Killingworth/Wideopen) 3rd exit to hotel ahead

What a splendid location for a smart modern hotel: on the outskirts of the city amid 12 acres of woodland, handy for the bypass, airport and racecourse. The recently refurbished Plate restaurant, named after the Northumberland Plate trophy, has rich walnut panelling, deep reds and golds and leather upholstery, and - reflecting the hotel's long association with horseracing - there's racing paraphernalia, including a silver replica of the Centenary Plate. At dinner there's a daily fixed-price menu of fairly straightforward dishes and a more ambitious carte studded with luxury items. Representative dishes include pan-fried foie gras, pot-roasted guinea fowl or saddle of venison from the carving trolley.

Chef Simon Devine **Owner** Marriott International **Times** 12.30-2/5.30-10.30, Closed 31 Dec, Closed L Sat (Mon-Fri for conferences only) **Prices** Fixed L 2 course £16.95, Fixed D 3 course £29, Starter £5.70-£9, Main £14-£20, Dessert £5.50-£6.75, Service optional **Wines** 38 bottles over £20, 31 bottles under £20, 19 by glass **Notes** D & dance every Sat evening, Sunday L, Vegetarian available, Civ Wed 200, Air con **Seats** 140, Pr/dining room 6 **Children** Portions, Menu **Parking** 300

NEWCASTLE UPON TYNE *Continued*

Vermont Hotel

British, European 💻

Elegant location for quayside dining

☎ 0191 233 1010
Castle Garth NE1 1RQ
e-mail: info@vermont-hotel.co.uk
dir: City centre, by high level bridge and castle keep

Plumb in the city centre next to the castle and close to the bustling quay, the Vermont is a highly distinctive building. Built of Portland stone in 1910 and originally the County Hall, it is Grade II listed and enjoys spectacular views of the Tyne and Millennium bridges. The aptly-named Bridge Restaurant, with its smart leather chairs and banquette seating, is the fine-dining option, where you can expect some interesting combinations using seasonal local produce on the modern British and European inspired menu. Cooked with flair by a chef who shows great promise, dishes include ham hock terrine with red pepper chutney and pan-seared chicken with mushroom duxelle and tarragon jus, with banana parfait with raspberry coulis for dessert.

Owner Lincoln Group **Times** 12-2.30/6-11 **Prices** Fixed L 2 course fr £14 **Wines** 123 bottles over £20, 54 bottles under £20, 17 by glass **Notes** Sunday L, Dress restrictions, Very smart; no casual dress, no jeans, Civ Wed 150, Air con **Seats** 80, Pr/dining room 80 **Children** Portions **Parking** 70

TYNEMOUTH Map 21 NZ36

Sidney's Restaurant

Modern British

Buzzing bistro in Tynemouth town centre

☎ 0191 257 8500 & 213 0284
3-5 Percy Park Rd NE30 4LZ
e-mail: bookings@sidneys.co.uk
dir: A1058 & follow signs for Tynemouth Village. Restaurant on corner of Front St & Percy Park Rd

With its wooden floors, leather benches, displays of local art and unclothed tables with simple settings, you would never guess that this cosy modern bistro was a grocery shop during the war. Current customers tell lovely stories of working in the shop years ago. The lively atmosphere is helped along by friendly and efficient staff while the modern menu relies on fresh local ingredients, including locally-landed fish, and everything is home made. Accurate bistro-style dishes with clear flavours include Sidney's black pudding with scallops and brioche croutons, local halibut with brown shrimp and crab bouillabaisse, and warm banana and chocolate fondant.

Chef A O'Kane, Jessica Mossman **Owner** A O'Kane **Times** 12-2.30/6-12, Closed 24-26 Dec, BHs ex Good Friday, Closed Sun **Prices** Fixed L 2 course £12, Fixed D 3 course £15, Starter £5-£7, Main £12-£19.50, Dessert

£5-£7, Service optional, Groups min 6 service 10% **Wines** 5 bottles over £20, 16 bottles under £20, 6 by glass **Notes** Vegetarian available, Air con **Seats** 50, Pr/dining room 20 **Children** Portions **Parking** On Front Street

---

WARWICKSHIRE

ABBOT'S SALFORD Map 10 SP05

Best Western Salford Hall Hotel

Modern, Traditional

Modern food in a historic setting

☎ 01386 871300
WR11 5UT
e-mail: reception@salfordhall.co.uk
dir: Off A46 between Stratford-upon-Avon & Evesham. Take road signed Salford Priors 1.5m on left

Steeped in history with spectacular views of the Severn Valley, this building is full of character. It was a former retreat for the Abbot of Evesham, a Tudor family home and then a nunnery before becoming a hotel. The traditional-styled restaurant has oak panelling, a large fireplace, mullioned windows, chandeliers and matching wall lights. The modern British menu offers simply-presented dishes using the best of fresh ingredients, locally sourced. Try spiced winter vegetable and orange soup to start, followed by loin of venison with smoked bacon mash and beetroot jus, and dark chocolate tart with a raspberry and rhubarb syrup to finish.

Times 12.30-2/7-10, Closed Xmas, Closed L Sat

ALDERMINSTER Map 10 SP24

Ettington Park Hotel

British, French

Dine in Gothic splendour

☎ 01789 450123
CV37 8BU
dir: M40 junct 15/A46 towards Stratford-upon-Avon, then A439 into town centre onto A3400 5m to Shipston. Hotel 1/2m on left

Set in 40-acre grounds in the Stour Valley, this imposing Victorian-Gothic manor offers the best of both worlds - the peace of the countryside and easy access to the motorway network. Tables clothed in formal white linen, polished glassware and cutlery, and views across the garden to the 12th-century family chapel set a traditional note in the stately Oak Room restaurant. By contrast, there's a sense of adventure about the cooking, though the food remains classically French based, with the skilled kitchen delivering some complex cooking: maybe brandade of salt cod with teriyaki langoustine and garlic crisps, followed by pot-roast breast of partridge with a pumpkin and watercress risotto and Madeira jus, with iced whisky parfait served with red berry compote and white coffee sauce to finish.

Times 12-2/7-9.30, Closed L Mon-Fri

ATHERSTONE Map 10 SP39

Chapel House Restaurant with Rooms

French, European

Elegant surroundings for imaginative cooking

☎ 01827 718949
Friar's Gate CV9 1EY
e-mail: info@chapelhousehotel.co.uk
web: www.chapelhousehotel.co.uk
dir: Off Market Sq in Atherstone, behind High St

Tucked away in the corner of the historic market square, this smart townhouse with lovely walled gardens was built in 1728 as the dower house to Atherstone Hall. Florence Nightingale was a frequent visitor here. Extended and upgraded over the years, many period features have been preserved, retaining the elegance of a bygone age. The restaurant is a light, elegant Georgian dining room with views over the garden and patio, and smartly appointed tables. The cooking style is mainly classical French but with a modern, light touch, using locally-sourced produce wherever possible. Starters on the daily-changing menu might feature smoked salmon paupiettes, while for main course try the likes of local fillet steak with a creamy stilton sauce, garnished with walnuts and roasted vegetables.

Chef Richard Henry Napper **Owner** Richard & Siobhan Napper **Times** Closed 24 Dec-3 Jan, Etr wk, late Aug-early Sep, Closed Sun, Closed L all week **Prices** Starter £4.95-£8.50, Main £17.95-£21.25, Dessert £5.95-£7.95, Service optional **Wines** 61 bottles over £20, 44 bottles under £20, 9 by glass **Notes** Vegetarian available, Dress restrictions, Smart casual **Seats** 24, Pr/dining room 12 **Children** Portions **Parking** On street

---

FARNBOROUGH Map 11 SP44

The Inn at Farnborough

British, French 🌢

Skilful cooking in the heart of a small village

☎ 01295 690615
Main St OX17 1DZ
e-mail: enquiries@innatfarnborough.co.uk
dir: M40 junct 11 - (Banbury). 3rd rdbt turn right onto A423 to Southam. After 4m turn left down road signed Farnborough. After 1m turn right into the village - The Inn at Farnborough is on right

The traditional and the contemporary sit happily together in this former butcher's shop, which dates from around 1700. Now a stylish restaurant and pub, the owners have created a relaxed atmosphere in which to eat and drink, and service comes with a smile. Essentially French, the bistro-style menu is based on local produce and features some interesting choices. Sautéed Scottish king scallops with grilled Parma ham, coriander and mint dressing, followed by braised shin of beef with shallots, red wine and ginger, or roast fillet of sea bass with chargrilled artichokes and roasted peppers show the style of the kitchen.

Chef Anthony Robinson **Owner** Oyster Inns Ltd
Times 12-3/6-10, Closed 25 Dec **Prices** Fixed L 2 course
fr £10.95, Starter £3.95-£12, Main £7.95-£19.95, Dessert
fr £5, Service added but optional 10% **Wines** 15 bottles
over £20, 15 bottles under £20, 16 by glass **Notes** Sunday
L **Seats** 80, Pr/dining room 16 **Children** Portions
Parking 40

KENILWORTH Map 10 SP27

Simply Simpsons

◎ Modern British

Stylish bistro serving classically-based modern dishes

☎ 01926 864567
101-103 Warwick Rd CV8 1HL
e-mail: info@simplysimpsons.com
dir: A452. In main street in Kenilworth centre

Situated in the main street of the historic market town,
this fashionable bistro has quarry-tiled floors, polished
wooden tables, artwork and painted bricks. Its name says
it all - it is sister restaurant to the fine-dining Simpsons
in Birmingham (see entry), but here you'll find simpler
cooking with a good balance of flavours and friendly
informal service. Fresh local produce and stylish
presentation combine in accomplished dishes like
chicken liver parfait, Cumberland sauce and toasted
brioche, or organic cod with black olive tapenade,
chorizo, new potatoes and pesto. For dessert, perhaps
praline crème brûlée or warm cherry and frangipane tart
with chocolate ice cream.

Times 12.30-2/6.30-10, Closed Last 2 wks of Aug, BHs,
Closed Sun, Mon

Coconut Lagoon

💻

☎ 01926 864500
149 Warwick Rd CV8 1HY
web: http://www.theaa.com/travel/index.jsp

Southern Indian cuisine from Goa, Kerala, Karnataka, and
Andhra Pradesh.

Prices Food prices not confirmed for 2009. Please
telephone for details.

Raffles

💻

☎ 01926 864300
57 Warwick Rd CV8 1HN
web: http://www.theaa.com/travel/index.jsp

Malaysian cuisine, including Indian and Chinese.
Colonial atmosphere and Singapore Slings a must.

Prices Food prices not confirmed for 2009. Please
telephone for details.

LEAMINGTON SPA (ROYAL) Map 10 SP36

The Brasserie at Mallory Court

◎ Modern European V

Elegant dining in country manor house

☎ 01926 453939
Harbury Ln, Bishop's Tachbrook CV33 9QB
e-mail: thebrasserie@mallory.co.uk
dir: 2m S off B4087 towards Harbury

Set within an elegant Lutyens-style country manor house,
this welcoming restaurant is surrounded by 10 acres of
landscaped grounds. The Brasserie exudes a unique sense
of style, with its art deco inspired interior, private gardens
for alfresco dining, a stunning cocktail bar, and upstairs
areas for private dining. Take a starter of twice-baked
goat's cheese soufflé with apple and hazelnut salad, and
for mains perhaps slow-cooked blade of beef with mashed
potato and braising juices, or wild mushroom risotto, with
truffle oil and rocket and parmesan salad. Enticing
desserts include favourites like sticky toffee pudding with
toffee sauce and vanilla ice cream.

Chef Nick Chappell **Owner** Sir Peter Rigby
Times 12-2.30/6.30-10.45, Closed D Sun **Prices** Fixed L 2
course £15, Fixed D 3 course £25, Service optional
Wines 37 bottles over £20, 5 bottles under £20, 6 by
glass **Notes** Sunday L, Vegetarian menu, Air con
Seats 80, Pr/dining room 12 **Children** Portions, Menu

Mallory Court Hotel

◎◎◎ — *see page 428*

Restaurant 23

◎◎ Modern European 💻

**Interesting and confident cooking in a modern
restaurant**

☎ 01926 422422
23 Dormer Place CV32 5AA
e-mail: info@restaurant23.co.uk
web: www.restaurant23.co.uk
dir: M40 junct 13 onto A452 towards Leamington Spa.
Follow signs for town centre

Located in the busy town of Leamington Spa - across the
road from Jefferson Park - this tiny gem of a restaurant is
dominated by an open-plan kitchen. There is a spacious
feel to the restaurant, with its subtle citrus décor, artwork
and large windows. An eclectic modern European style of
cooking is offered; ingredients are well sourced, dishes are
well balanced and presentation is interesting. Free-range
belly pork appears as a starter in ravioli with chorizo,
served with squid and baby spinach. For mains, a sirloin of
beef is cooked in a salt crust with boulangère potatoes,
braised shallots and a black pepper sauce. Finish with
poached rhubarb cheesecake with rhubarb sorbet.

Chef Peter Knibb **Owner** Peter & Antje Knibb
Times 12.15-2.30/6.15-9.45, Closed 25 Dec, 2 wks Jan, 2
wks Aug, Closed Sun-Mon **Prices** Fixed L 2 course £13,
Fixed D 3 course £23-£33, Service optional, Groups min 6

service 10% **Wines** 50 bottles over £20, 14 bottles under
£20, 9 by glass **Notes** Vegetarian available, Air con
Seats 24 **Children** Min 12 yrs **Parking** On street opposite

---

STRATFORD-UPON-AVON Map 10 SP25

Barcelo Billesley Manor Hotel

◎◎ Modern, Traditional British

Modern cooking in historic manor house

☎ 01789 279955 & 767103
Billesley, Alcester B49 6NF
e-mail: billesleymanor@barcelo-hotels.co.uk
dir: M40 junct 15, then take A46 S towards Stratford/
Worcester. Follow the A46 E over three rdbts. Continue for
2m then take a right for Billesley

Shakespeare is believed to have written part of As You Like
It in this lovely Elizabethan manor house set in 11 acres of
delightful grounds and parkland close to Stratford-upon-
Avon. The Stuart Restaurant is a splendid oak-panelled
room with a huge stone fireplace, chandeliers and silver
pheasants, enjoying pleasant views across the gardens,
including the stunning yew topiary. A modern approach is
taken to the food and ingredients are carefully sourced.
You might start with a salad of venison with spiced plums
and red wine reduction, before moving on to a main course
of fillet of sea bass with baby vegetables and tomato juice.
Hot chocolate fondue with dipping fruits and
marshmallows might prove a fitting finale.

Chef Wayne Asson **Owner** Barcelo Hotels
Times 12.30-2/7-9.30 **Prices** Fixed L course £24.95,
Fixed D 3 course £39.95, Starter £8.75-£12, Main
£17.95-£32, Dessert £9-£12, Service added but optional
5% **Wines** 46 bottles over £20, 4 by glass **Notes** Sunday
L, Vegetarian available, Dress restrictions, No denim,
trainers or T-shirts, Civ Wed 100 **Seats** 42, Pr/dining
room 40 **Children** Portions, Menu **Parking** 100

Macdonald Alveston Manor

◎ Modern British

Modern dining in an Elizabethan manor

☎ 01789 205478
Clopton Bridge CV37 7HP
e-mail: events.alvestonmanor@macdonald-hotels.co.uk
dir: 6m from M40 junct 15, just on edge of town, across
Clopton Bridge towards Banbury

This charming well-established hotel has a striking red-
brick and half-timbered façade, and the main house
retains much of its Elizabethan charm, with leaded
windows and splendid original panelling. Well-tended
grounds include a giant cedar, under which it's said that
A Midsummer Night's Dream was first performed. The
traditional country-house style restaurant offers reliable
modern British dishes with French influences from a daily
menu and a seasonal carte. Try hand-dived sea scallops
with creamed leeks to start, followed by fillet of Aberdeen
Angus beef with caramelised onions and nutmeg and
potato soufflé, with glazed lemon tart with crème fraîche
ice cream to finish.

Continued on page 429

Mallory Court Hotel

Modern British V

Exquisitely prepared dishes in country-house splendour

☎ 01926 330214
Harbury Ln, Bishop's Tachbrook CV33 9QB
e-mail: reception@mallory.co.uk
dir: M40 junct 13 N-bound. Turn left, and left again towards Bishop's Tachbrook. Continue for 0.5m and turn right up Harbury Ln. M40 junct 14 S-bound. Follow A452 for Leamington. At 2nd rdbt take left into Harbury Ln

This magnificent Lutyens-style country-house hotel was built during World War I for a wealthy cotton merchant, and is an idyllic rural retreat, situated as it is amid picturesque countryside, in 10 acres of landscaped grounds and manicured lawns. Its harmonious blend of country-house splendour and contemporary design creates a wonderfully relaxed, homely atmosphere. You can relax over drinks or coffee in the sumptuous lounges, or take advantage of the pool and tennis court. There are two dining options: the formal oak-panelled Dining Room, or the contemporary art deco-style Brasserie converted from the former groundskeeper's cottage, offering lighter meals. In summer, guests can also dine in the charming walled garden. The accomplished modern

British cooking is underpinned by classical French themes, bringing together top-class ingredients in sophisticated and tempting combinations that are beautifully conceived on the plate. Flavours are clear, and presentation designed to impress, with fine quality produce treated with admirable technical skill. The fixed-price menu is intelligently compact and enticing; try a starter of Torbay crab, mildly curried and served with lime-marinated scallops, followed by braised blade of beef with mash potato, bacon and mushrooms. An array of tempting desserts includes chocolate and cherry pastilla with banana purée and pistachio ice cream. Canapés, breads and petits fours are all superb and showcase the kitchen's skills.

Chef Simon Haigh **Owner** Sir Peter Rigby **Times** 12-1.45/6.30-8.45 **Prices** Fixed L course £27.50, Fixed D 3 course £39.50, Starter £7.50-£12.50, Main £22-£28, Dessert £10.50-£14, Service optional **Wines** 2 bottles under £20, 7 by glass **Notes** Sunday L, Vegetarian menu, Dress restrictions, No jeans or sportswear, Civ Wed 160 **Seats** 56, Pr/dining room 30 **Children** Portions, Menu **Parking** 100

STRATFORD-UPON-AVON *Continued*

Owner Macdonald Hotels plc **Times** 12-2.30/6-9.30, Closed L Mon-Sat **Prices** Fixed D 4 course £28, Starter fr £7.50, Main fr £17, Dessert fr £7.50, Service included **Wines** 69 bottles over £20, 14 bottles under £20, 15 by glass **Notes** Pre-theatre menu available, Sunday L, Vegetarian available, Civ Wed 120 **Seats** 110, Pr/dining room 40 **Children** Portions, Menu **Parking** 120

Menzies Welcombe Hotel and Golf Course

◉◉ Modern International **V**

Delightful cooking in traditional manor house setting

☎ 01789 295252
Warwick Rd CV37 0NR
e-mail: welcombe@menzieshotels.co.uk
dir: M40 junct 15, A46 to Stratford-upon-Avon. 1st rdbt take left onto A439, hotel is 3m on right

Set within 157 acres of landscaped parkland, the Trevelyan restaurant is located within this Jacobean-style manor house hotel. The restaurant is traditional in style with French glass chandeliers, and the seasonally-changing menu of English and European dishes is complemented by superb views over the Italian gardens, golf course and water features. For starters you could expect the likes of pan-fried smoked salmon, lemon and herb risotto with caviar dressing, while mains might feature loin of Charlecote Park venison, braised red cabbage, parsnip purée and bitter chocolate sauce. Save room for a dessert like pear and almond tart with butternut squash purée, milk chocolate and cinnamon ice cream or the platter of British and continental cheeses.

Chef Dean Griffin **Owner** Menzies Hotels
Times 12.30-2/7-9.30, Closed L Sat **Prices** Fixed L 2 course fr £18, Starter £6.75-£10.50, Main £18.50-£28, Dessert £7.50-£8.50, Service optional **Wines** 125 bottles over £20, 5 bottles under £20, 16 by glass **Notes** Pre-theatre D menu available, Sunday L, Vegetarian menu, Dress restrictions, Smart casual, shirt with collar, no jeans, Civ Wed 120 **Seats** 70, Pr/dining room 40 **Children** Portions, Menu **Parking** 150

Mercure Shakespeare

◉ Modern British

Contemporary cuisine in Tudor surroundings

☎ 01789 294997 & 01789 294997
Chapel St CV37 6ER
e-mail: h6630@accor.com
dir: Follow signs to town centre. Round one-way system, into Bridge St. At rdbt turn left. Hotel 200yds on left

Dating back to the 17th-century, this is one of the oldest hotels in Shakespeare's historic home town. With a traditional Tudor-timbered façade, the smart interior is just as authentic, with original beams, log fires and rich fabrics adding to the traditional feel. The menu, however, is up to the minute, and makes the most of top-quality ingredients. Try the terrine of pressed game and juniper

with blackberry and apple compote to start, perhaps followed by the poached red mullet, braised celeriac fondant and clam and sweet potato chowder. Make room for a dessert such as the rich dark chocolate fondant or vanilla pannacotta with redcurrant ice cream.

Chef Paul Smith **Owner** Mercure Hotels **Times** 12-2/6-9.30, Closed L Mon-Sat (ex by arrangement) **Prices** Fixed D 3 course £25, Starter £4.25-£7.95, Main £11.50-£24.25, Service included **Wines** 84 bottles over £20, 25 bottles under £20, 12 by glass **Notes** Fixed L 3 courses, Sunday L, Vegetarian available, Dress restrictions, Smart casual, Civ Wed 100 **Seats** 80, Pr/dining room 25 **Children** Portions **Parking** 35

Stratford Manor

◉ Modern British

Assured cooking in a relaxed modern brasserie

☎ 01789 731173
Warwick Rd CV37 0PY
e-mail: stratfordmanor@qhotels.co.uk
dir: M40 junct 15, A46 signposted Stratford-Upon-Avon, A439 travel 1m located on left

Just outside Stratford, this modern, purpose-built hotel is set against a rural backdrop with lovely gardens and ample parking. Facilities include conference rooms, a leisure centre with a gym, pool, spa, sauna and tennis courts. The atmosphere in the stylish dining room is relaxed and the service polished. Honest, straightforward dishes are prepared from quality, fresh ingredients. Try blade of beef with truffle mash, shallots and tarragon jus, roast pheasant breast with Anna potatoes, or fillet of cod with pea, asparagus and leek ragout. Light meals are served in the Terrace Bar.

Chef Richard Marshall **Owner** Qhotels
Times 12-2.30/6-9.30, Closed L Sat **Prices** Fixed L 3 course fr £14.95, Starter fr £5, Main fr £15.95, Dessert fr £5.95, Service optional **Wines** 35 bottles over £20, 15 bottles under £20, 20 by glass **Notes** Sunday L, Vegetarian available, Dress restrictions, Smart casual, Civ Wed 200 **Seats** 140, Pr/dining room 250 **Children** Portions, Menu **Parking** 200

Stratford Victoria

◉ British, Mediterranean

Victorian-style modern hotel serving classic cuisine

☎ 01789 271000
Arden St CV37 6QQ
e-mail: stratfordvictoria@qhotels.com
dir: From town centre, follow A3400 towards Birmingham. Turn left at lights towards Arden St, hotel is 150 yds on right

Situated next to the hospital, this eye-catching red-brick modern hotel has a Victorian appearance and is within walking distance of the town centre. The spacious Traditions Restaurant comes with exposed beams and ornately carved furniture, and the cooking is an honest, straightforward mix of old and new, where dish presentation and the quality of ingredients are taken seriously. The crowd-pleasing range of dishes might include as a starter fishcake with tomato and chilli jam,

with main courses taking in slow-roast duck with herb and garlic mash, and pan-fried sea bass with red pepper and basil coulis.

Times 12.30-2/6-9.45

The Lodge Restaurant at Ardencote Manor

◉◉ British, International ◔

Lakeside restaurant with lively menu

☎ 01926 843111 & 843939
The Cumsey, Lye Green Rd CV35 8LT
e-mail: hotel@ardencote.com
dir: Off A4189. In Claverdon follow signs for Shrewley & brown tourist signs for Ardencote Manor, approx 1.5m

Originally built as a 19th-century gentleman's residence, this smart hotel is set in 45 acres of landscaped grounds. Strikingly done out in sleek, contemporary style with an open-plan layout, The Lodge Restaurant has a modern bistro look and is situated on the shoreline of a small lake - its plentiful windows and patio doors open on to the waterside terrace with impressive views. On less clement days, there's a cocktail bar at the entrance to the restaurant and a huge stone fireplace at the far end of the dining room. The extensive carte delivers the likes of roasted whole lemon sole with crayfish and organic Shetland salmon mousse, confit of baby fennel and sauce Choron, alongside less elaborate grilled fish and meat dishes on 'La Plancha' menu, served with a choice of sauces - steak with pan-fried wild mushrooms and grilled balsamic tomatoes, perhaps.

Chef Luciano Catalinotto **Owner** TSB Developments Ltd **Times** 12-3/6-11 **Prices** Starter £5.50-£6.80, Main £15.95-£23.95, Dessert £5.50-£6.25, Service included **Wines** 50 bottles over £20, 40 bottles under £20, 8 by glass **Notes** Sunday L, Vegetarian available, Civ Wed 180 **Seats** 75, Pr/dining room 40 **Children** Portions, Menu **Parking** 200

WEST MIDLANDS

BALSALL COMMON   Map 10 SP27

Nailcote Hall

◉ Modern

Delightful cooking in an attractive country house with great facilities

☎ 024 7646 6174
Nailcote Ln, Berkswell CV7 7DE
e-mail: info@nailcotehall.co.uk
web: www.nailcotehall.co.uk
dir: On B4101 towards Tile Hill/Coventry, 10 mins from NEC/Birmingham Airport

Dating back as far as 1640, Nailcote Hall stands in 15 acres of grounds with its own 9-hole championship golf course within easy reach of the Midlands motorway network. The Oak Room restaurant with its dark beams is spacious and comfortable and the food is both ambitious and accomplished. Try the goats' cheese and walnut parfait with redcurrant and onion relish for example, or duo of pork for main course - Asian spiced pork belly and medallions wrapped in pimento and spinach, served with apple-scented fondant potato and Savoy cabbage. Round off with vanilla bean brûlée with glazed pineapple and chilli jam.

Chef Lee Childs **Owner** Mr R W Cressman
Times 12-2/7-9.30, Closed L Sat, Closed D Sun
Prices Fixed L 2 course fr £19.50, Starter £5-£10.95, Main £15.95-£28, Dessert £5.95-£18, Service optional **Wines** 80 bottles over £20, 23 bottles under £20, 5 by glass **Notes** Vegetarian available, Dress restrictions, Smart casual, no jeans or trainers, Civ Wed 120 **Seats** 45, Pr/dining room 140 **Children** Portions, Menu **Parking** 100

BARSTON   Map 10 SP27

The Malt Shovel at Barston

◉ Traditional British

Popular local foodie pub in a rural setting

☎ 01675 443223
Barston Ln B92 0JP
web: www.themaltshovelatbarston.com
dir: M42 junct 5, take turn towards Knowle. 1st left on Jacobean Lane, right turn at T-junct (Hampton Lane). Sharp left into Barston Lane. Restaurant 0.5m

This delightful country pub comes complete with log fires, heavy fabrics, lime-green paintwork, stripped wooden floors and a lovely garden for alfresco lunches in summer. The bar menu is supplemented by blackboard specials from the fine-dining restaurant, which is situated in a stylishly converted barn. Portions are hearty, with good quality fish of all kinds featuring strongly, as well as a variety of dishes for meat-lovers. Take a starter of wild crayfish and pea risotto with rocket, followed by roast turbot on the bone with tarragon crush, béarnaise sauce, asparagus and Parma ham, and to finish, morello cherry brioche bread-and-butter pudding with Kirsch custard. Vegetarian options include Mediterranean vegetable and aubergine cannelloni with haloumi and tomato passata.

Chef Max Murphy **Owner** Caroline Furby & Chris Benbrook
Times 12-2.30/6.30-9.30, Closed 25 Dec, Closed D Sun
Prices Fixed D 3 course fr £25.50, Starter £3.95-£7.50, Main £9.95-£18.95, Dessert £5.50-£5.95, Service optional, Groups min 6 service 10% **Wines** 12 bottles over £20, 14 bottles under £20, 6 by glass **Notes** Sunday L, Vegetarian available, Air con **Seats** 40 **Children** Min 10 yrs, Portions **Parking** 30

BIRMINGHAM   Map 10 SP08

Birmingham Marriott

◉ Modern British, French

Elegant brasserie in traditional hotel

☎ 0121 452 1144
12 Hagley Rd, Five Ways B16 8SJ
e-mail: pascal.demarchi@marriotthotels.com
dir: City end of A456, at the Five Ways rdbt

A prominent landmark on the edge of the city centre, this large, comfortable Edwardian hotel has a feel of fin-de-siècle elegance throughout. The well-presented public areas include an informal restaurant, West 12, popular with the city's businessmen and leisure guests alike. Service is typically up-front and helpful for the UK's second city. The brasserie-style menu comprises traditional dishes with some modern influences. Start with the goat's cheese and tapenade filo with red onion jam before trying either the penne with chargrilled chicken, artichokes, courgettes and tarragon cream or the butternut squash risotto with chilli and oregano. Finish with classic Bakewell tart with clotted cream ice cream.

Chef James Carrol **Owner** Marriott International Ltd
Times 12-2.30/6-10, Closed L Sat **Prices** Fixed L 2 course £18-£26, Service optional **Wines** 20 bottles over £20, 10 bottles under £20, 10 by glass **Notes** Sunday L, Vegetarian available, Civ Wed 80, Air con **Seats** 60, Pr/dining room 60 **Children** Portions, Menu **Parking** 60

Hotel Du Vin

◉ Mediterranean, French 🖥

Chic hotel with a winning bistro menu

☎ 0121 200 0600
25 Church St B3 2NR
e-mail: info@birmingham.hotelduvin.com
dir: Telephone for directions

Located in the Jewellery Quarter, Birmingham's outpost of the Hotel du Vin chain is as chic and trendy as its sister establishments. A former eye hospital, the building dates from the early Victorian era and retains many original features including a sweeping staircase and granite pillars. The hotel's well-stocked bar is popular with residents and locals alike, while its bistro upholds the classic Hotel du Vin philosophy of quality food cooked simply from the freshest ingredients and good attention to detail. Mains might include a perfectly chargrilled rib-eye steak with pommes frites and sauce béarnaise, or pan-fried sea bass with baby fennel and green asparagus in a chive velouté.

Times 12-2/6-10

Opus Restaurant

◎◎ Modern British 🖥

Chic modern eatery with crustacea counter

☎ 0121 200 2323
54 Cornwall St B3 2DE
e-mail: restaurant@opusrestaurant.co.uk
dir: Please telephone for directions

This smart, modern restaurant is close to the City Chambers in Birmingham city centre. Floor-to-ceiling windows, wine racks and a crustacea counter set the scene for an upbeat and contemporary dining experience, while warm colours, linen table cloths and friendly but professional service mark it out as one of Birmingham's growing number of serious restaurants. Much emphasis is placed on sourcing quality seasonal produce on the daily-changing menu, from freshly caught wild fish (shellfish is a speciality here) and a commitment to free-range meats. The accomplished kitchen's modern approach is seen in a warm salad starter containing roast quail, Clonakilty black pudding and a grain mustard cream sauce, and in a main course of roasted Cornish monkfish, lemon thyme and wild garlic risotto. The menu also delivers more traditional dishes such as prawn cocktail and braised faggots with mash and mushy peas.

Chef David Colcombe **Owner** Ann Tonks, Irene Allan, David Colcombe **Times** 12-2.30/6-10, Closed between Xmas and New Year, Closed Sun, Closed L Sat **Prices** Fixed L 2 course £15.50, Fixed D 3 course £17.50, Starter £6.50-£12.50, Main £13-£22, Dessert £6.50, Service added but optional 12.5% **Wines** 65 bottles over £20, 12 bottles under £20, 28 by glass **Notes** Vegetarian available, Air con **Seats** 85, Pr/dining room 64 **Children** Portions, Menu **Parking** On street

---

Pascal's

◎◎ Modern French

Unmissable dining experience in a leafy Birmingham suburb

☎ 0121 455 0999
1 Montague Rd, Edgbaston B16 9HN
e-mail: info@pascalsrestaurant.co.uk
dir: Please telephone for directions

Set in the beautiful grounds of Asquith House on the outskirts of Birmingham's bustling centre, Pascal's offers city dining with a country feel. Enjoying views over the garden, the conservatory-style restaurant provides an intimate setting with friendly, professional service. The kitchen delivers modern French cuisine with skill and flair, making good use of quality, local produce. Expect starters such as langoustines with chicken wings, white coco bean purée, chicken jus and shellfish foam, or parfait of smoked eel with Granny Smith purée and roast almonds, followed by mains like braised shoulder of pork with Iberian morcilla, crispy trotter and mustard, or skate tapenade with confit potato, broccoli, curry and vanilla and, for a thoroughly superb finish, try apricot tartlet served with plum ripple ice cream.

Owner P Cuny **Times** 12-2/7-10, Closed 1 wk Xmas, 1 wk Etr, last 2 wks Jul, Closed Sun-Mon, Closed L Sat **Wines** 50 bottles over £20, 7 bottles under £20, 8 by glass **Notes** Fixed ALC 3 courses £27.95, Vegetarian available, Dress restrictions, Smart casual, Air con **Seats** 40 **Children** Portions **Parking** On street

---

Purnell's

◎◎ Modern European

Imaginative fine dining in city centre

☎ 0121 2129799
55 Cornwall St B3 2DH

This new fine-dining venture from Brummie Glynn Purnell is set in a former furniture warehouse, and builds on his previous successes. A stylish, modern affair of well-spaced tables and comfortable contemporary seating, with different floor levels and alcoves creating added interest alongside eye-catching local photographs and large windows that let in plenty of light. Service is professional and knowledgeable with a touch of formality that suits the venue. Glynn's highly imaginative cooking displays bags of thought and technical skill on a fixed-price repertoire that also includes a couple of tasting options. Expect the likes of unusual-sounding combinations like slow-cooked shoulder of lamb with a

Continued

Simpsons

BIRMINGHAM   **Map 10 SP08**

Modern 🖥

A serious restaurant with sophisticated cuisine

☎ 0121 454 3434
20 Highfield Rd, Edgbaston B15 3DU
e-mail: info@simpsonsrestaurant.co.uk
dir: 2m from city centre, opposite St Georges Church, Edgbaston

Andreas Antona's restaurant in a Grade II listed Georgian villa in Edgbaston is widely regarded as one of the best restaurants in the Birmingham area. There are four individually-themed dining rooms - French, Venetian, Oriental and Colonial - adding a touch of the theatrical to the surroundings. The chic rooms are decorated in subtle hues of cream and beige, contemporary artworks hang on the walls, and artful floral arrangements are in the bar and salon. The sense of occasion is heightened by discreetly attentive service from professional staff who are well informed on the menu and wine list. The modern menu focuses on quality seasonal ingredients from the best UK sources (Salcombe crab, Lyme Bay lemon sole, Aberdeenshire beef, Loch Fyne smoked salmon, etc) presented in dishes cooked with a high degree of culinary expertise by a talented team. Start with poached duck egg, pea purée, white and green asparagus and pea shoots, before a main course such as slow-cooked halibut served with sweet-and-sour onions, caramelised parsnip purée and smoked bacon, and finishing with fresh raspberry millefeuille with milk ice cream. There are vegetarian and children's menus.

Chef/patron Andreas Antona, Luke Tipping **Times** 12.30-2/7-10, Closed 24-26, 31 Dec, 1-2 Jan, BHs, Closed D Sun

BIRMINGHAM *Continued*

trompette de la mort purée, leek braised barley, natural yogurt and roasted sweetbreads, and to finish, perhaps a dark chocolate mousse with mango leather, black olive and passionfruit rice pudding and mango sorbet.

Chef Glynn Purnell **Times** 12-4.30/7-1am, Closed Mon

Simpsons

◉◉◉ – *see page 431*

Thai Edge Restaurant

◉ Thai

Authentic Thai cooking in a contemporary setting

☎ 0121 643 3993
Brindley Place B1 2HS
e-mail: birmingham@thaiedge.co.uk
dir: Brindley Place is just off Broad St (approx 0.5m from B'ham New Street station)

Designed to emphasise the four elements (earth, air, fire and water), this contemporary oriental restaurant is decorated with Thai artefacts and water features, and divided up with glass and wooden screens. Well-spaced linen-dressed tables and smart, well-informed staff complete the picture. Authentic Thai dishes from the four main regions of Thailand are presented on the typically lengthy menu, each with its own individual style and clear translations, and dishes are served together so are ideal for sharing. Expect vibrant dishes with clear flavours of the ingredients evident, say, in stir-fried lamb with red chilli, red and green peppers and sweet basil, or perhaps deep-fried snapper with sweet chilli sauce.

Chef Mit Jeensanthia **Owner** Harish Nathwani
Times 12-2.30/5.30-11, Closed 25-26 Dec, 1 Jan
Prices Fixed L 2 course £7.95, Fixed D 3 course £29.80-£38.50, Service added but optional 10% **Wines** 14 bottles over £20, 26 bottles under £20, 6 by glass **Notes** Air con **Seats** 100 **Parking** Brindley Place

Bank Restaurant & Bar

⌨

☎ 0121 633 4466
4 Brindley Place B1 2JB
web: http://www.theaa.com/travel/index.jsp

Prices Food prices not confirmed for 2009. Please telephone for details.

The Bucklemaker

⌨

☎ 0121 200 2515
30 Mary Ann St, St Paul's Square B3 1RL
web: http://www.theaa.com/travel/index.jsp

Tucked into a former Georgian silversmiths' workshop, this delightful restaurant is traditional, contemporary and welcoming all at once. The atmosphere is businessy at lunch, romantic in the evenings, with modern European menus and a friendly, buzzy bar area.

Prices Food prices not confirmed for 2009. Please telephone for details.

Metro Bar and Grill

⌨

☎ 0121 200 1911
73 Cornwall St B3 2DF
web: http://www.theaa.com/travel/index.jsp

A sumptuous, modern meeting and eating place that attracts a loyal crowd of regulars. The bright, slightly rustic modern European menu seems to please just about everyone, and there are daily blackboard specials.

Prices Food prices not confirmed for 2009. Please telephone for details.

Forest Hotel

◉◉ Modern European

Impressive cooking in modern, boutique surroundings

☎ 01564 772120
25 Station Approach B93 8JA
e-mail: info@forest-hotel.com
web: www.forest-hotel.com
dir: From M42 junct 5, go through Knowle village, right to Dorridge village, turn left before bridge

Directly opposite the station, at the end of a classic suburban parade of shops, the red-brick and ornate scrolling of the late Victorian façade gives way to a sophisticated, easy-on-the-eye modern look within, with its boutique-style rooms and designer décor in the airy bar and restaurant. The crowd-pleasing, broadly European style of cooking suits the contemporary surroundings. Well-conceived dishes are prepared from quality seasonal ingredients, and cooking is precise, simple and intelligent. Start with lamb sweetbreads with tartare sauce, move on to grilled halibut with artichokes, salsify, clams and basil linguine, and finish with dark chocolate fondant with pistachios and Turkish delight. Competitive pricing and informal, professional service hit just the right note, too.

Chef Dean Grubb **Owner** Gary & Tracy Perkins
Times 12-2.30/6.30-10, Closed 25 Dec, Closed D Sun
Prices Fixed L 2 course £12, Fixed D 3 course £15, Starter £4.25-£5.95, Main £8.50-£17.95, Dessert £4.75-£5.90, Service added but optional 10% **Wines** 12 bottles over £20, 30 bottles under £20, 9 by glass **Notes** Fixed L & D Mon to Fri only, Sunday L, Vegetarian available, Civ Wed 100, Air con **Seats** 70, Pr/dining room 150
Children Portions, Menu **Parking** 40

Nuthurst Grange Country House Hotel

◉◉ British, French

Fine dining with all the trimmings in country-house style

☎ 01564 783972
Nuthurst Grange Ln B94 5NL
e-mail: info@nuthurst-grange.com
dir: Off A3400, 0.5 mile S of Hockley Heath, turn at sign into Nuthurst Grange Ln

The tree-lined drive makes for a fabulous first impression when arriving at Nuthurst Grange, a creeper-covered country house set in extensive landscaped gardens and woodland. In the light and bright dining room, guests are comfortably seated at candlelit tables set with crystal glassware and roses from the garden. A range of highly imaginative classic and modern French and British cuisine is offered from a choice of fairly-priced menus, with canapés and pre-desserts adding to the sense of value. Ballotine of quail and foie gras with poached egg yolk and a grape salad shows precision and skill, while main-course fillet of brill comes with crushed potatoes, baby vegetables and a light vermouth velouté served separately. Finish with green apple soufflé - a dessert showing good balance of flavours and technical ability.

Times 12-2/7-9.30, Closed 25-26 Dec, Closed L Sat

MERIDEN | Map 10 SP28

Manor Hotel

◉ Modern British, French

Modern cooking in elegant Georgian building

☎ 01676 522735
Main Rd CV7 7NH
e-mail: reservations@manorhotelmeriden.co.uk
dir: M42 junct 6 take A45 towards Coventry then A452, signed Leamington. At rdbt join B4102, signed Meriden, hotel 0.5m on left

Within easy reach of the National Exhibition Centre, this sympathetically extended Georgian manor house is located in the heart of the sleepy village of Meriden. There are two dining options - the informal Triumph Buttery for light lunches and snacks and the more formal Regency Restaurant for fine dining. The latter specialises in classically-inspired dishes with a light, modern touch and good presentation. Try wild mushroom ravioli with wilted baby spinach and morel jus to start, followed perhaps by roast duck breast, confit of leg, caramelised pear and sweet potato fondant.

Chef Peter Griffiths **Owner** Mr R Richards
Times 12-2/7-9.45, Closed 27-30 Dec, Closed L Sat
Prices Fixed L 2 course £24, Fixed D 3 course £28, Starter £6.50-£11.50, Main £12.95-£19.95, Dessert £4.95-£5.50, Service included **Wines** 14 bottles over £20, 18 bottles under £20, 6 by glass **Notes** Sunday L, Vegetarian available, Civ Wed 120, Air con **Seats** 150, Pr/dining room 220 **Children** Portions, Menu **Parking** 180

SUTTON COLDFIELD | Map 10 SP19

New Hall

◉◉ Modern British

Moated manor house serving accomplished cuisine

☎ 0121 378 2442
Walmley Rd B76 1QX
e-mail: sales@newhall.co.uk
dir: On B4148, E of Sutton Coldfield, close to M6 & M42

Although new owners have taken over at New Hall, little changes at this 800-year-old Grade I listed building, reputed to be the oldest inhabited moated house in England. Outside there are 26 acres of mature grounds and inside flagstone floors, open fires, exposed beams and mullioned windows. Good quality décor and furnishings highlight the building's intrinsic charm, and the intimate restaurant overlooks the moat that surrounds the hotel. In the kitchen, ingredients are carefully sourced and sympathetically cooked using classical techniques. Try potted ham hock with warm potato terrine and pea shoots, followed by Aberdeenshire beef served three ways. Finish with a citrus dessert of orange millefeuille, lime cheesecake and lemon sherbert.

Chef Wayne Thompson **Owner** Hand Picked Hotels
Times 12-2/7-9.30, Closed L Sat, Closed D Sun
Prices Starter £7.50-£13.50, Main £16-£26, Dessert £7.50-£9.50, Service optional **Wines** 65 bottles over £20, 14 bottles under £20, 10 by glass **Notes** Sunday L, Vegetarian available, Civ Wed 150 **Seats** 30, Pr/dining room 50 **Children** Portions, Menu **Parking** 60

WALSALL | Map 10 SP09

Fairlawns Hotel and Spa

◉◉ Modern British

Elegant hotel with robust modern cooking

☎ 01922 455122
178 Little Aston Rd, Aldridge WS9 0NU
e-mail: reception@fairlawns.co.uk
web: www.fairlawns.co.uk
dir: Outskirts of Aldridge, 400yds from junction of A452 (Chester Rd) & A454

This popular family-run hotel is set in 9 acres of landscaped gardens, located in an extended Victorian building complete with fitness centre and spa. The restaurant's contemporary elegance, with cream décor,

---

comfortable seating and white-clothed tables, sets the scene for some accomplished cooking. International influences are evident on the essentially British menu, which makes the most of fresh, seasonal ingredients from local producers where possible. Simply prepared yet imaginative and well-presented dishes feature on the two- and three-course dinner menus, and on the wide-ranging brasserie-style lunch menu available Monday to Friday. For mains, take a delightful tranche of halibut cooked and served on the bone, perhaps preceded by a starter of accurately cooked scallops on dauphinoise potatoes with pomegranate seeds and sweet vinegar dressing.

Chef Neil Atkins **Owner** John Pette **Times** 12-2/7-10, Closed 25-26 Dec, 1 Jan, Good Fri, Etr Mon, May Day, BH Mon, Closed L Sat **Prices** Fixed L 2 course £15-£29.50, Fixed D 3 course £26.50-£37.50, Service optional **Wines** 32 bottles over £20, 34 bottles under £20, 12 by glass **Notes** Sunday L, Vegetarian available, Dress restrictions, No jeans, trainers, sports clothing, Civ Wed 100, Air con **Seats** 80, Pr/dining room 100 **Children** Portions, Menu **Parking** 120

◉ WIGHT, ISLE OF

FRESHWATER | Map 5 SZ38

Farringford

◉ Modern V

Country-house dining overlooking Tennyson Downs

☎ 01983 752500
Bedbury Ln PO40 9PE
e-mail: enquiries@farringford.co.uk
web: www.farringford.co.uk
dir: Follow signs for Yarmouth, over bridge for 1m, take left at Pixie Hill. Continue for 2m. At rdbt take left into Afton Rd. Turn left at the bay. Turn into Bedbury Ln. Farringford is 0.5m from bay

The former home of Alfred, Lord Tennyson, Farringford is set in 33 acres of mature parkland and remains a relaxed country-house retreat, with cosy log fires in winter and marvellous year-round views. The restaurant, with its large picture windows, brings a contemporary touch to the period property. Generous portions of straightforward modern British cooking are served using quality fresh ingredients. Island produce is to the fore in dishes like timbale of lemon-dressed crab served with cucumber gazpacho to start, followed by poached fillet of beef with oxtail ravioli, rösti potato and ruby port wine jus.

Chef Ross Hastings **Owner** Martin Beisly & R Fitzgerald **Times** 12-2/6.30-9, Closed Nov-Mar **Prices** Fixed D 3 course £29.50, Service optional **Wines** 30 bottles over £20, 39 bottles under £20, 5 by glass **Notes** Sunday L, Vegetarian menu, Dress restrictions, No sports clothes or denim, Civ Wed 150 **Seats** 100, Pr/dining room 20 **Children** Portions, Menu **Parking** 50

RYDE Map 5 SZ59

The St Helens

◉ Modern British ☙

The best of fresh local produce in seaside village setting

☎ 01983 872303 & 0771 7175 444
Lower Green Rd, St Helens PO33 1TS
e-mail: mark@bonnebouchee.co.uk
dir: Follow B3330 to St Helens

Overlooking one of England's largest village greens, the St Helens has a modern seaside/New England design and feel. Think wooden floors, tables and chairs, blue-and-white paintwork, aqua-coloured window shutters and simple nautical-themed artwork. During winter months there's an open fire, while a few outside tables beckon in summer. Service is suitably unobtrusive, relaxed and knowledgeable, while the kitchen comes admirably driven by the best local island produce from land and sea, with menus changing daily to match availability. The modern approach delivers rustic-style dishes and unfussy presentation that allow flavours to shine; take pan-fried, line-caught Isle of Wight sea bass fillet served with a pancetta and parmesan risotto, leaf salad and lemon oil.

Chef Mark Young, Iain Wilson **Owner** Mark Young, Lian Beadell **Times** 12-2.30/6.30-9.30, Closed 25-26 Dec, Closed Mon (Nov-Mar), Closed L Mon-Sat **Prices** Fixed D 3 course £22.50, Starter £4.50-£7.95, Main £11.50-£21.50, Dessert £4.75-£6.95, Service optional, Groups min 8 service 10% **Wines** 9 bottles over £20, 13 bottles under £20, 4 by glass **Notes** Sunday L, Vegetarian available, Dress restrictions, Shirt & shoes must be worn **Seats** 40 **Children** Portions, Menu **Parking** on street, car park 100yds

See advert below

SEAVIEW Map 5 SZ69

Priory Bay Hotel

◉ Modern

Tranquil country-house dining with wonderful views

☎ 01983 613146
Priory Dr PO34 5BU
e-mail: enquiries@priorybay.co.uk
web: www.priorybay.co.uk
dir: On B3330 to Nettlestone, 0.5 miles from St Helens

This 14th century priory turned holiday haven once played home to a community of monks, who no doubt made the most of its peaceful location. Offering remarkable views of the Solent and Spithead, the house is still a good place to get away from it all, although these days tranquillity comes with an array of temptations that include a private beach, 6-hole golf course and outdoor swimming pool. The Regency-styled, candlelit Island Room is a romantic dinner setting for some flavourful food: white island tomato soup with asparagus ravioli and extra virgin olive oil, for example, followed by cassoulet of locally-farmed chicken with spring cabbage and fondant potatoes.

Chef Ashleigh Harris **Owner** Mr R Palmer & Mr J Palmer **Times** 12.30-2.15/7-9.30 **Prices** Fixed L 2 course £18.50, Fixed D 3 course £32.50, Service optional, Groups min 8 service 12% **Wines** 29 bottles over £20, 14 bottles under £20, 8 by glass **Notes** Sunday L, Vegetarian available, Dress restrictions, Smart/smart casual recommended, Civ Wed 100 **Seats** 70, Pr/dining room 50 **Children** Portions, Menu **Parking** 50

Seaview Hotel & Restaurant

◉◉ Modern British ☙

Bright and lively hotel with a choice of restaurants

☎ 01983 612711
High St PO34 5EX
e-mail: reception@seaviewhotel.co.uk
dir: Take B3330 from Ryde to Seaview, left into Puckpool Hill, follow signs for hotel

An extensive programme of refurbishment and expansion has seen this charming and relaxed hotel, in a quiet location just a short stroll from the seafront, undergo a complete transformation. As its name suggests, fantastic views of the Solent can be enjoyed from selected vantage points, and there's a choice of dining options - the quaint Victorian dining room, or the smart, contemporary brasserie-style Sunshine Restaurant which is decked out in blue and white and comes with its own conservatory. The seasonally-inspired menus, including a five-course gastronomic menu, list modern choices using the freshest local ingredients. You might start with roasted island lobster with potato and carrot fettuccine and saffron sauce, and follow with a main course of superbly fresh

line-caught sea bass served on a bed of new potatoes with broad bean purée and herb oil.

Chef Graham Walker **Owner** Techaid Facilities Ltd **Times** 12-2/6.30-9.30, Closed L weekdays during winter **Prices** Fixed L course £26.95, Fixed D 3 course £26.95, Service optional, Groups min 8 service 12.5% **Wines** 22 bottles over £20, 14 bottles under £20, 4 by glass **Notes** Sunday L, Vegetarian available, Air con **Seats** 100, Pr/dining room 100 **Children** Min 5 yrs, Portions, Menu **Parking** On street, car park nearby

VENTNOR
Map 5 SZ57

Hambrough Hotel

Modern European

Skilful cooking in stylishly renovated seaside hotel

☎ 01983 856333
Hambrough Rd PO38 1SQ
e-mail: info@thehambrough.com
dir: Please telephone for directions

Extensive refurbishment has created a sophisticated, contemporary interior at this Victorian villa, set on a hillside overlooking Ventnor with memorable sea views. The regularly-changing, short fixed-price modern European menu makes good use of seasonal ingredients, sourced from the island wherever possible. Dishes are highly appealing, imaginatively conceived and skilfully cooked, with eye-catching presentation. Try pressed confit duck and foie gras served with pear purée and poached cherries to start. Superbly fresh sea bass impresses as a main course with braised fennel, fricassée of new season morels and asparagus, freshwater crayfish and sauce Nantua. A separate chef's table, just feet from the kitchen, is provided for guests choosing the impressive tasting menu.

Chef Craig Atchinson **Owner** H Madeira **Times** 12-2.30/7-9.30, Closed Tue, Closed D Sun **Prices** Food prices not confirmed for 2009. Please telephone for details. **Wines** 80 bottles over £20, 20 bottles under £20, 6 by glass **Notes** Sunday L, Air con **Seats** 26, Pr/dining room 14 **Children** Min 10 yrs **Parking** On street

The Pond Café

Modern European

Accomplished restaurant in a scenic village setting

☎ 01983 855666
Bonchurch Village Rd, Bonchurch PO38 1RG
e-mail: info@thepondcafe.com
dir: Please telephone for directions

The celebrated pond is just across the road from this Victorian property, and on fine days it can be admired from the patio tables. Inside, the pleasantly understated décor is simple and sophisticated. Quality ingredients for the fortnightly-changing menu are carefully sourced and the bread is freshly baked each day. Modern European food is imaginatively prepared and presented, bringing a touch of excitement to dishes such as pavé of salmon with mussels, clams and creamed winter vegetables, or Gressingham duck breast with honey-roasted figs and braised red cabbage. Iced passionfruit parfait with a chocolate case and caramelised bananas makes a fitting finale.

Chef Luke Borley **Owner** H Madeira **Times** 12-2.30/6.30-9.30, Closed Mon **Prices** Starter £4.95-£5.95, Main £10.50-£18.95, Service optional **Wines** 27 bottles over £20, 8 bottles under £20, 6 by glass **Notes** Sunday L **Seats** 26 **Children** Portions **Parking** On street

The Royal Hotel

Modern British

Sophisticated cuisine in smart surroundings

☎ 01983 852186
Belgrave Rd PO38 1JJ
e-mail: enquiries@royalhoteliow.co.uk
dir: On A3055 coastal road, into Ventnor. Follow the one way system, turn left at lights into Church St. At top of hill bear left into Belgrave Rd, hotel on right

Purpose built in 1832, the hotel stands in tranquil gardens affording glimpses of the sea. An air of sophistication pervades the elegant restaurant with its blue and peach décor, high ceilings, heavy drapes, oil paintings and crystal chandeliers, and formalities are observed by the smartly attired staff. A menu of modern British dishes includes good, honest cooking focusing on local and seasonal produce, with good technical skills. A smooth foie gras and chicken liver parfait comes with a light brioche and apple and ginger chutney, and there's a wonderful sea-fresh flavour to poached fillet of sole served with a nage of fresh seafood - mussels, clams and prawns - seasoned with garlic and chervil.

Chef Alan Staley **Owner** William Bailey **Times** 12-1.45/6.45-9, Closed 2 wks Jan, Closed Mon-Sat in Apr-Oct, Sun also Jul-Sep **Prices** Fixed L 3 course £28-£35, Fixed D 3 course £37.50-£52, Service optional **Wines** 46 bottles over £20, 18 bottles under £20, 6 by glass **Notes** Sunday L, Vegetarian available, Dress restrictions, Smart casual, no shorts, Civ Wed 150 **Seats** 100, Pr/dining room 40 **Children** Min 5 yrs, Portions **Parking** 50

YARMOUTH
Map 5 SZ38

Brasserie at The George Hotel

British, Mediterranean

Waterside views and fresh fish and seafood with an Italian influence

☎ 01983 760331
The George Hotel, Quay St PO41 0PE
e-mail: jeremy@thegeorge.co.uk
web: www.thegeorge.co.uk
dir: Situated between the castle and pier

The historic, colour-washed George Hotel stands on Yarmouth Square close to the ferry terminal in attractive shoreline grounds abutting the old castle walls. Located at the rear of the 17th-century property, with great views across the Solent, the bright, sunny and informal brasserie has recently been refurbished in contemporary style, with dark wood and leather seats, to reflect the new style of food on offer. Freshness, simplicity and flavour are the focus of the seasonal Italian-inspired menu, which uses top-notch ingredients. Expect to be wowed, perhaps by crab and scallop lasagne with shellfish cappuccino and basil to start, and a main course of whole Dover sole with rissole potatoes and organic mixed vegetables. Try the honey pannacotta with caramelised fruits for dessert.

Chef Jose Graziosi **Owner** John Illsley, Jeremy Willcock **Times** 12.30-3/7-10 **Prices** Fixed L 2 course £27.95-£29.95, Fixed D 3 course £35.95-£44.95, Starter £6.75-£12.50, Main £16.50-£27.50, Dessert £6.50-£9.50, Service optional **Wines** 40 bottles over £20, 20 bottles under £20, 10 by glass **Notes** Sunday L, Vegetarian available, Dress restrictions, Smart casual, Air con **Seats** 60, Pr/dining room 20 **Children** Portions, Menu **Parking** The Square

WILTSHIRE

BRADFORD-ON-AVON — Map 4 ST86

The Tollgate Inn

◉◉ Modern British ⌾

Traditional character inn offering notable cooking

☎ 01225 782326
Ham Green BA14 6PX
e-mail: alison@tollgateholt.co.uk
web: www.tollgateholt.co.uk
dir: M4 junct 18, take A46 and follow signs for Bradford-on-Avon, take A363 then turn left onto B3105, in Holt turn left onto B3107 towards Melksham. The Tollgate Inn is 100 yds on right

Just a short drive from Bath, this quintessential English country pub offers a choice of several dining areas. Downstairs, there's a cosy room furnished with pews and cushions and a wood-burning stove, while upstairs, the larger first-floor restaurant occupies what was originally a chapel for the weavers who worked below. The menu is a lengthy affair that's sure to provoke some pleasurable dithering. The fine modern British cuisine is underpinned by produce carefully sourced from the local area including fish delivered daily from Brixham. Eggs Benedict and sausage and mash make an appearance at lunchtime, but there's also more complex fare: pan-fried pheasant breast with a cider and apple cream sauce, for example, or sea bass with a smoked haddock fish cake and a crayfish sauce.

Chef Alexander Venables **Owner** Alexander Venables, Alison Ward-Baptiste **Times** 11-2.30/5.30-11, Closed 25-26 Dec, Closed Mon, Closed D Sun **Prices** Fixed L 2 course £11.95-£14.95, Starter £4.50-£8, Main £13.50-£18.80, Dessert £4.50-£6.75, Service optional, Groups min 6 service 10% **Wines** 12 bottles over £20, 23 bottles under £20, 9 by glass **Notes** Sunday L, Air con **Seats** 60, Pr/dining room 38 **Children** Min 12 yrs **Parking** 40

Widbrook Grange

◉ Modern British, European ⌾

Imaginative cooking in comfortable country house

☎ 01225 864750
Trowbridge Rd, Widbrook BA15 1UH
e-mail: stay@widbrookgrange.com
dir: 1m S of Bradford-on-Avon on A363

This former farmhouse, nestling by the Kennet and Avon Canal in 11 acres of gardens and fields, was built as a model farm in the 18th century. The Bee Bole Conservatory (named after the set of five bee boles at the front of the house) is the venue for more casual dining, while the Medlar Tree Restaurant is named after the ancient tree in the gardens and is decorated in relaxing shades of cinnamon, sage and cream to create an intimate fine-dining experience. High-quality ingredients are sourced by a kitchen that concentrates on modern British and European dishes, delivered by friendly, attentive staff. Oven-baked kedgeree fishcake with a lightly curried crème fraîche, and chargrilled halibut with lobster ravioli, roasted vine tomatoes, watercress and chablis cream are fine examples of the fare.

Chef Peter Stollett, Lee Williams **Owner** Peter & Jane Wragg **Times** 11.30-2.30/7-11, Closed 21-30 Dec, Closed L Sun **Prices** Starter £5-£6.25, Main £14.50-£18.50, Dessert £5.50-£6.50, Service included **Wines** 15 bottles over £20, 13 bottles under £20, 6 by glass **Notes** Vegetarian available, Dress restrictions, Smart casual, Civ Wed 50 **Seats** 45, Pr/dining room 12 **Children** Portions, Menu **Parking** 50

Woolley Grange

◉◉ Modern British, French V

Child-friendly atmosphere and excellent dining in Jacobean manor

☎ 01225 864705
Woolley Green BA15 1TX
e-mail: info@woolleygrangehotel.co.uk
dir: Please telephone for directions

Children are made especially welcome at this splendid Jacobean Cotswold manor house and there is much for them to do, from exploring the attractive gardens to other child-focused activities; there is always a trained nanny on duty, too. The restaurant is split into two rooms - the Orangery leading on to the garden, and the main dining room, with its fun pictures of life at Woolley. The kitchen is able to make use of vegetables and herbs from the hotel's own walled garden, which is certified as organic by the Soil Association, and the seasons are clearly respected. Dinner features the works from appetisers through to petits fours and a sure hand in the kitchen is evident throughout. Presentation is a strong point, as in a pressing of salmon, potato and leek with a fennel salad and herb and lemon dressing, and highly successful combinations include pan-fried sea bass with duck confit, sweet carrot purée and red wine sauce.

Owner Luxury Family Hotels & von Essen Hotels **Times** 12-2/7-9.30 **Prices** Fixed D 3 course £35.50, Service optional **Wines** 72 bottles over £20, 10 bottles under £20, 8 by glass **Notes** Sunday L, Vegetarian menu, Dress restrictions, Smart casual, Civ Wed 50 **Seats** 40, Pr/dining room 22 **Children** Portions, Menu **Parking** 25

CASTLE COMBE — Map 4 ST87

The Bybrook at the Manor

◉◉◉ — see opposite

COLERNE — Map 4 ST87

Lucknam Park

◉◉◉ — see page 438

HIGHWORTH — Map 5 SU29

Jesmonds of Highworth

◉◉ Modern European

Stylish, contemporary restaurant with skilfully prepared cuisine to match

☎ 01793 762364
Jesmond House SN6 7HJ
e-mail: info@jesmondsofhighworth.com
dir: Please telephone for directions

The stylish and contemporary refurbishment of this Grade II listed restaurant with rooms, on the edge of the Cotswolds, is a successful blend of old and new. From the modern bar to lounge and restaurant, the upbeat theme is set, backed by professional but friendly service. The enthusiastic kitchen team has pedigree, their modern European approach driven by high quality produce and delivering intelligently simple, skilfully prepared dishes with a fine combination of textures and flavours. There are various menu options, including lunch, lite bite and square meal offerings, while the dinner carte might deliver beetroot bavarois, goat's cheese foam and basil pesto to start, then halibut with crispy Parma ham, crushed olive potatoes and orange butter sauce, and to finish, perhaps dark chocolate delice, griottine cherries and mascarpone ice cream.

Chef William Guthrie **Owner** Andrew Crankshaw **Times** 12-2.30/7-9.15, Closed Mon, Closed D Sun **Prices** Fixed D 3 course £26.50-£34.50, Service optional **Wines** 20 bottles over £20, 40 bottles under £20, 12 by glass **Notes** Sunday L

The Bybrook at the Manor

Map 4 ST87

Modern British 💻

Innovative cooking in imposing surroundings

☎ 01249 782206
Manor House Hotel SN14 7HR
e-mail: enquiries@manorhouse.co.uk
dir: M4 junct 17, follow signs for Castle Combe via Chippenham

Built on the site of a Norman castle, this delightful country-house hotel sits in peaceful grounds in the picturesque village of Castle Combe. Exuding tranquillity and calm, it's the perfect place to curl up with a book by the fire, and then perhaps work up an appetite before dinner with a round of golf or croquet. Named after the river crossing the estate, the elegant Bybrook restaurant affords stunning views across the Italian gardens, lawns and woodland, and, as befits its location, comes complete with many original features, including stained-glass windows and carved stonework enhanced by rich tapestries and classical décor. If you can take your eyes off the lovely views, you'll find a menu as accomplished as the setting demands. Expect artful modern dishes from a kitchen that knows its stuff and consistently impresses with its imaginative approach and clever combinations. Local produce is used where possible, with vegetables and

herbs often arriving courtesy of the manor's gardens. A tian of Cornish crab with smoked sweetcorn, pink grapefruit and pistachio dressing makes an excellent starter, followed by pan-fried red mullet with pearl barley risotto and scallop beignet.

Chef Richard Davies **Owner** Exclusive Hotels **Times** 12.30-2/7-10, Closed L Sat **Prices** Fixed L 2 course £19-£36, Fixed D 3 course fr £52, Tasting menu £65-£95, Service optional **Wines** 252 bottles over £20, 76 by glass **Notes** Tasting menu 6 courses, Sunday L, Dress restrictions, Smart casual, Civ Wed 90 **Seats** 80, Pr/dining room 90 **Children** Portions, Menu **Parking** 175

HORNINGSHAM — Map 4 ST84

The Bath Arms at Longleat

◉ British

Boutique-style inn with unpretentious cooking of local produce

☎ 01985 844308 & 07770 268359
Longleat Estate BA12 7LY

Set in a quintessential English village deep in the heart of the Longleat Estate, this traditional stone-built inn is now a stylish and quirky boutique hotel. It serves unpretentious British cuisine from home-grown or Estate-reared produce and locally sourced ingredients in an ornate dining room, casual bar or terrace overlooking the garden. The main dining room is certainly opulent, with dramatic chandeliers, French-style wallpaper, wooden tables and floor and huge candlesticks. The kitchen's fixed-price menus change daily with lunch a lighter affair, while dinner cranks up the ante; think Longleat Estate venison served with parsnip purée and red cabbage, and perhaps a nougat parfait with sticky fruit-and-nut compote.

Prices Food prices not confirmed for 2009. Please telephone for details.

LITTLE BEDWYN — Map 5 SU26

The Harrow at Little Bedwyn

◉◉◉ – see opposite

LOWER CHICKSGROVE — Map 4 ST92

Compasses Inn

◉ Modern

Carefully prepared, quality produce in charming country inn

☎ 01722 714318
SP3 6NB
e-mail: thecompasses@aol.com
dir: On A30 W of Salisbury, take 3rd right after Fovant, after 1/2m turn left into Lagpond Lane, Inn 1m on left

This 14th-century thatched inn comes brimful of character and atmosphere. Its original beams derive from decommissioned galleons, while stone walls, uneven flagstones and high settle booths add further charm, and, with only two windows, candlelight adds to the timeless quality, punctuated with helpings of relaxed and friendly service. The cooking's certainly not stuck in a time warp though, the modern approach making intelligent use of carefully sourced produce, including fish from Brixham. Menus come chalked up on blackboards, changing regularly to focus on seasonal and local availability; perhaps Cornish lobster thermidor, Chateaubriand with béarnaise sauce with home-made chips or lamb shoulder with red wine and mint sauce and celeriac mash.

Compasses Inn

Chef Ian Evans, Ian Chalmers, Damian Trevett
Owner Alan & Susie Stoneham **Times** 12-3/6-11, Closed 25-26 Dec **Prices** Starter £5-£7.50, Main £9-£18, Dessert £5-£6, Service optional **Wines** 17 bottles over £20, 19 bottles under £20, 20 by glass **Notes** Sunday L, Vegetarian available **Seats** 50, Pr/dining room 14 **Children** Portions, Menu **Parking** 35

Lucknam Park

COLERNE — Map 4 ST87

Modern British 🖵 V 🕙

Faultless country-house cuisine

☎ 01225 742777
SN14 8AZ
e-mail: reservations@lucknampark.co.uk
web: www.lucknampark.co.uk
dir: From M4 junct 17/A350 to Chippenham, then A420 towards Bristol for 3m. At Ford turn towards Colerne. After 4m turn right into Doncombe Ln, then 100yds on right

Set in 500 acres of parkland and beautiful gardens, this magnificent Palladian mansion - now a notable country-house hotel - exudes luxury, its mile-long drive lined with mature beech and elm trees creating the perfect first impression. A choice of lounge areas, from the luxurious splendour of the 17th-century drawing room with its chandeliers, ornate cornicing, oil paintings and deep sofas to the atmospheric library, deliver the anticipated comforts and style. The formal dining room, in the mansion's former ballroom, is an elegant bow-fronted affair with lovely views across the estate, gardens and that avenue of trees. Well-spaced tables, crisp napery and fine glassware fit the bill, as does the attentive, professional and knowledgeable service, while chef Hywel Jones's highly accomplished, clean-cut cooking more than matches expectations. The approach is modern-focused, underpinned by a classical French theme, with great emphasis placed on sourcing high quality seasonal ingredients and clarity and harmony of flavour. The fixed-price menus come dotted with luxury (and there's a vegetarian version of the tasting Gourmet Menu too); take a fillet of line-caught sea bass with barigoule artichoke, tortellini of Cornish crab and black olive paste perhaps, and to finish, an iced honeycomb parfait with banana tart and bitter chocolate sorbet. (Note: the spa restaurant - currently under construction - is due to become the hotel's main dining option, with the current restaurant turned into an evening-only fine-dining affair.)

Chef Hywel Jones **Owner** Lucknam Park Hotels Ltd **Times** 12-2.30/6.30-10, Closed Mon, Closed D Sun **Prices** Fixed L course £30, Fixed D 3 course £65, Service included **Wines** 300 bottles over £20, 15 by glass **Notes** Sunday L, Vegetarian menu, Dress restrictions, Smart casual, no denim or trainers, Civ Wed 64 **Seats** 80, Pr/dining room 30 **Children** Min 5 yrs, Portions, Menu **Parking** 80

The Harrow at Little Bedwyn

LITTLE BEDWYN   Map 5 SU26

Modern British V   🍷 NOTABLE WINE LIST

Stylish dining in former village pub with emphasis on stunning seafood, game and wine

☎ 01672 870871
SN8 3JP
e-mail: bookings@harrowinn.co.uk
web: www.harrowinn.co.uk
dir: Between Marlborough & Hungerford, well signed

Secreted away down winding country lanes in the hamlet of Little Bedwyn, what was once the village pub is now a classy country restaurant of some note. The dining room - split into two sections - is bright and contemporary, featuring dark leather high-backed chairs and neatly dressed tables laid with Riedel glasses and colourful Villeroy & Boch crockery. Service, led by Sue Jones, is friendly and relaxed, and husband Roger mans the stove. There's also a small garden at the rear for summer alfresco dining and aperitifs. Roger's approach in the kitchen is equally modern, with great emphasis on the freshness and sourcing of quality ingredients. Fish is caught on day boats landed at Brixham, while meat and game is from specialist farmers and butchers (perhaps 28-day hung Aberdeen Angus from Moray or new season Norfolk woodcock), and salads and herbs are specifically grown in North Devon. Roger's cooking style is

thus intelligently straightforward, allowing ingredients to shine with clean-cut flavours. Subtle new Asian flavours are also in evidence on the repertoire, as in a fabulous tranche of sea bass on aubergine and peppers with Asian spices and cauliflower purée. The stunning wine list displays plenty of passion and high quality, and the introduction of two wine options alongside the gourmet tasting menu gives diners even greater chance to explore one of the finest wine lists in the UK.

Chef Roger Jones **Owner** Roger & Sue Jones **Times** 12-3/7-11, Closed 3 wks Jan & Aug, Closed Mon-Tue, Closed D Sun **Prices** Fixed L course £30, Fixed D 3 course £30, Tasting menu £60-£120, Starter £12-£15, Main £24-£28, Dessert £7-£12, Service optional **Wines** 900 bottles over £20, 25 bottles under £20, 20 by glass **Notes** Vegetarian menu, Dress restrictions, Smart casual **Seats** 34 **Children** Portions, Menu **Parking** On street

Whatley Manor

Modern French ▲NOTABLE WINE LIST

French cuisine in new-style, luxury country-house hotel

☎ 01666 822888
Easton Grey SN16 0RB
e-mail: reservations@whatleymanor.com
dir: Please telephone for directions

This impressive Cotswold-stone country house has been lovingly renovated by its Swiss owners to provide the highest levels of luxury. Set amid 12 acres of gardens, meadows and woodland, it's designed to soothe and restore, with luxurious furnishings and fabrics, beautiful gardens and a magnificent spa, complemented by professional yet understated service. Diners can choose between Le Mazot (named after and reflecting the old-fashioned Swiss mountain chalet) - the more informal brasserie open for lunch and dinner (though suitably sophisticated in its own right with an appealing menu), and the Dining Room - the dinner-only fine-dining option which has recently been refurbished to create a more contemporary feel. Soft yellow walls contrast with brightly-coloured chairs and strand-woven bamboo flooring, while the use of mirrors and subtle spot lighting adds to the ambience and blown-glass chandeliers create a focal point. The cuisine is classic French with

a contemporary theme, focusing on top-class produce, and, like everything else here, luxury. Light, complex, beautifully presented dishes are delivered via a fixed-price carte and tasting option. You might start with a lovely dish of hand-dived scallops, perfectly cooked, and served with brown shrimps glazed in their own stock and a light parsley foam, and follow with contre fillet of veal caramelised in herbs and butter, with slow-braised cheek, hazelnut purée and roasted ceps. Winter truffle ice cream dressed with lightly creamed roquefort, deep-fried goat's cheese with candied walnut makes an intriguing dessert. Ancillaries like canapés, amuse-bouche, pre-desserts, breads and petits fours all hold top form too, complemented by a notable wine list.

Chef Martin Burge **Owner** Christian & Alix Landolt **Times** Closed Mon-Tues, Closed L all week **Prices** Fixed D 3 course £65, Tasting menu £80-£140, Service added but optional 10% **Wines** 15 by glass **Notes** Civ Wed 120 **Seats** 40, Pr/dining room 30 **Children** Min 12 yrs, Portions **Parking** 120

MALMESBURY
Map 4 ST98

Best Western Mayfield House Hotel

◉ Modern British

Fresh, modern dishes in a country-house setting

☎ 01666 577409
Crudwell SN16 9EW
e-mail: reception@mayfieldhousehotel.co.uk
dir: 3m N of Malmesbury on A429, in the village of Crudwell. Hotel is on left

Situated in a small Cotswold village, this stone-built country-house hotel has a spacious walled garden and is an ideal location for exploring many of the nearby attractions. The chef takes a modern approach to cooking and presentation, turning out imaginative, simply prepared dishes using local produce. Starters might include a warm North Cerney goat's cheese tart with pesto oil, while main courses typically feature dishes like slow-roasted Gloucestershire Old Spot pork belly on herb mash with Bramley apple compôte, or poached salmon and sole with sautéed sea kale and a chive cream sauce. For dessert, try the gooey treacle tart, served with lashings of clotted cream.

Times 12-2/6.15-9, Closed L Mon-Sat

Old Bell Hotel

◉◉ British, French

Traditional fare in Cotswold setting

☎ 01666 822344
Abbey Row SN16 0BW
e-mail: info@oldbellhotel.com
dir: In town centre, next to Abbey. 5 m from M4 junct 17

The central part of this Cotswold hotel was built in 1220 in order to accommodate scholars studying the manuscripts at the nearby Abbey. Reputedly the oldest purpose-built hotel in England, The Old Bell has provided rooms and food ever since although visitors will note that facilities have improved greatly since then! Older rooms are furnished with antiques - new ones have a more contemporary feel. Service is friendly and efficient. The dining room is an elegant Edwardian addition offering imaginative dishes using local ingredients. To start, try sautéed Cornish scallops, crushed parsnips and truffle dressing, followed by poached breast of Cotswold chicken with mushroom ravioli and foie gras velouté. Comforting desserts include apple and raisin crumble or Valrhona chocolate fondant with mint chocolate chip ice cream.

Chef Tom Rains **Owner** The Old Bell Hotel Ltd
Times 12.15-2/7-9.30 **Prices** Starter £7.50-£8.95, Main £15.50-£21.50, Dessert £6.75-£8.75, Service optional **Wines** 109 bottles over £20, 8 bottles under £20, 8 by glass **Notes** Tasting menu 7 courses available, Vegetarian available, Dress restrictions, Smart dress preferred, Civ Wed 80 **Seats** 60, Pr/dining room 48 **Children** Portions, Menu **Parking** 31

Whatley Manor

◉◉◉◉ – see opposite

OAKSEY
Map 4 ST99

The Wheatsheaf Inn

◉◉ Modern British ✿

Friendly gastro-pub in tranquil village setting

☎ 01666 577348
Wheatsheaf Ln SN16 9TB
e-mail: info@thecompletechef.co.uk
dir: Off A429 towards Cirencester, near Kemble

Dating back to the 14th century, this Cotswold stone pub has a traditional feel, with a big inglenook fireplace, flagstone floors and dark beams. The restaurant has a light, modern feel with sisal carpet, wooden tables and painted walls decorated with wine racks and jars of preserved vegetables. Modern British pub food is the order of the day, from a kitchen team with a strong commitment to local produce. With daily specials from the blackboard available, begin with a delicately flavoured chestnut soup, followed by succulent belly pork with braised red cabbage, rich, creamy mash and a shallot jus, with a baked rice pudding with cinnamon and cranberry jam to finish. Expect quality ales on tap and a varied wine selection.

Chef Guy Opie **Owner** Tony & Holly Robson-Burrell
Times 12-2/6.30-9.30, Closed Mon, Closed D Sun **Prices** Starter £4-£6.95, Main £8-£15.95, Dessert £4.25-£5.95, Service optional **Wines** 12 bottles over £20, 16 bottles under £20, 7 by glass **Notes** Sunday L, Vegetarian available **Seats** 44, Pr/dining room 8 **Children** Portions, Menu **Parking** 15

PURTON
Map 5 SU08

The Pear Tree at Purton

◉◉ Modern British 💻

Charming Cotswold stone hotel with superior food

☎ 01793 772100
Church End SN5 4ED
e-mail: stay@peartreepurton.co.uk
dir: From M4 junct 16, follow signs to Purton. Turn right at Spa shop, hotel 0.25m on right

This handsome 15th-century former vicarage looks out over 7.5 acres of well-tended gardens, and beyond that lies the rolling Wiltshire countryside. The house was originally associated with the unique twin towers church of St Mary's in the village of Purton. The airy conservatory restaurant perfectly complements the serene setting, with fine linen and elegant tableware adding to the air of genteel refinement. The kitchen uses quality ingredients - many locally sourced - to good effect and ambition is shown when it comes to marrying flavours. A starter of oak-smoked chicken mousse comes with chilli caramelised apple, while a main course of superbly fresh steamed halibut is complemented, not over-powered, by

ginger and teriyaki sauce. Pistachio parfait served with dark chocolate sauce and pistachio tuile is an equally ambitious dessert.

Chef Alan Postill **Owner** Francis and Anne Young **Times** 12-2/7-9.15, Closed 26-30 Dec, Closed L Sat **Prices** Fixed L course £19.50, Fixed D 4 course £34.50, Service optional **Wines** 76 bottles over £20, 24 bottles under £20, 11 by glass **Notes** Sunday L, Vegetarian available, Dress restrictions, No shorts, Smart casual, Civ Wed 50 **Seats** 50, Pr/dining room 50 **Children** Portions **Parking** 70

ROWDE
Map 4 ST96

The George & Dragon

◉◉ Modern British, Italian V

Charming old pub with a relaxed gastro-pub atmosphere

☎ 01380 723053
High St SN10 2PN
e-mail: thegandd@tiscali.co.uk
dir: On A342, 1m from Devizes towards Chippenham

This charming old inn, which dates back to the 14th century when it was a meeting house, mixes original features with a relaxed gastro-pub atmosphere. With dark wooden beams throughout, a log fire strikes a homely note in the bar, while the restaurant is decked out with wooden furniture and simple table appointments. The carte is supplemented by blackboard specials, plus a separate fish menu featuring daily fresh fish deliveries from Cornwall. Expect starters such as spicy crab risotto topped with crème fraîche for contrasting coolness, while mains might include sea bass on pesto mash with pancetta. Choose from a selection of home-made ice creams, including vanilla, coffee and chocolate chip kiwi fruit for dessert.

Chef Christopher Day **Owner** Christopher Day, Philip & Michelle Hale **Times** 12-3/7-10, Closed 25 Dec & BHs, Closed D Sun **Prices** Fixed L 2 course fr £13, Starter £5-£9, Main £10.50-£32.50, Dessert fr £5.75, Service optional **Wines** 35 bottles over £20, 13 bottles under £20, 9 by glass **Notes** Sunday L, Vegetarian menu **Seats** 35 **Children** Portions, Menu **Parking** 14

SALISBURY — Map 5 SU12

Anokaa Restaurant

Modern Indian **V**

Contemporary Indian cuisine in colourful, stylish surroundings

☎ 01722 414142
60 Fisherton St SP2 7RB
e-mail: info@anokaa.com/bookings@anokaa.com
dir: Adjoined to The Salisbury Playhouse & City Hall

Anokaa means something out of the ordinary, and this restaurant challenges the idea that Indian recipes are set in stone, believing that Indian food should adapt and evolve. With waiters wearing traditional Moghul costumes and service slick and confident, this modern split-level restaurant is simply decorated. Dishes are based on the freshest of ingredients, using a fusion of Asian and European ideas, providing a twist to traditional Indian cooking. Options from an extensive menu include hand-picked crab cake with roasted coconut, chilli and dill, avocado stuffed roast chicken masala with basil and tomato sauce and a hint of chilli. Rose and lime cheesecake on a semi freddo makes a fitting finale.

Chef Puban Kumar Bhaniya & Asad ur Rahman
Owner Mohammed Odud, Solman Farsi
Times 12-2/5.30-11, Closed 25-26 Dec **Wines** 19 bottles over £20, 18 bottles under £20, 9 by glass **Notes** Pre/post theatre D, 2 courses with wine £15, Sunday L, Vegetarian menu, Dress restrictions, Smart casual, Air con **Seats** 80 **Children** Min 5 yrs **Parking** Main car park to rear of restaurant

Best Western Red Lion Hotel

Modern European

Imaginative cooking in eclectic surroundings

☎ 01722 323334
Milford St SP1 2AN
e-mail: reception@the-redlion.co.uk
web: www.the-redlion.co.uk
dir: Please telephone for directions

The old and the new blend effortlessly at the welcoming Red Lion, built to accommodate draughtsmen working on Salisbury Cathedral 750 years ago and thought to be the oldest purpose-built hotel in Britain. It has been owned by the same family for 100 years. The elegant and relaxed Vine Restaurant has an ancient wattle-and-daub wall and offers an interesting mixture of modern and traditional dishes, with English and European influences, using fresh local produce whenever possible. Typically, follow spiced foie gras terrine with roast monkfish tail and a saffron butter sauce, and finish with chocolate tart with Cointreau cream custard.

Chef Noel Malnoe **Owner** Maidment Family
Times 12.30-2/7-9.30, Closed L Mon-Sat **Prices** Food prices not confirmed for 2009. Please telephone for details. **Wines** 9 bottles over £20, 22 bottles under £20, 9 by glass **Notes** Sunday L, Vegetarian available, Civ Wed 80 **Seats** 85, Pr/dining room 80 **Children** Portions **Parking** Brown St. Pay & display car park

206 Brasserie

Modern

Modern setting for straightforward, honest cooking

☎ 01722 417411 & 424111
Milford Hall Hotel, 206 Castle St SP1 3TE
e-mail: simonhughes@milfordhallhotel.com
dir: From A36 at rdbt on Salisbury ring road, right onto Churchill Way East. At St Marks rdbt left onto Churchill Way North to next rdbt, left in Castle St

This smart brasserie-style restaurant adjoins the hotel and has the feel of a substantial conservatory. The interior is light and airy with pastel rag-rolled walls and ceiling, and the tables are simply set. External decking provides space for outside seating in summer. Simple, honest and skilfully-cooked dishes might include a starter of crispy duck and watercress salad, followed by pork medallions with celeriac and apple mash and a Calvados reduction, or baked red snapper marinated in lemongrass and ginger, with the likes of baked lemon, raisin and ricotta cheese pie for dessert.

Chef James Noyce **Owner** Simon Hughes
Times 12-2/6.30-10, Closed 26 Dec **Prices** Starter £4.95-£8.95, Main £9.95-£18.95, Dessert £4.95-£5.95, Service optional **Wines** 6 bottles over £20, 27 bottles under £20, 6 by glass **Notes** Sunday L, Civ Wed 50 **Seats** 40, Pr/dining room 20 **Children** Portions, Menu **Parking** 50

STANTON ST QUINTIN — Map 4 ST97

Stanton Manor Country House Hotel

Modern European

Contemporary cooking in country-house hotel

☎ 01666 837552 & 0870 890 02880
SN14 6DQ

Set in 5 acres of lovely gardens with a short golf course, this charming manor house, mentioned in the Domesday Book, has easy access to the M4. The recently refurbished restaurant offers a short carte of imaginative dishes, complemented by an interesting wine list. A good use of local produce can be found in the simple, unfussy food. Crab ravioli could be followed by roast breast of Gressingham duck with a confit of its leg and served with sautéed potatoes and wild garlic. Round things off with a well made banana and chocolate mousse.

Prices Food prices not confirmed for 2009. Please telephone for details.

SWINDON — Map 5 SU18

Chiseldon House Hotel

Modern International

Comfortable country-house dining delivering carefully prepared seasonal produce

☎ 01793 741010 & 07770 853883
New Rd, Chiseldon SN4 0NE
e-mail: info@hiseldonhousehotel.co.uk
web: www.chiseldonhousehotel.co.uk
dir: M4, junct 15, A346 signed Marlborough. After 0.5m turn right onto B4500 for 0.25m, hotel on right

Conveniently located for the M4, this charming Grade II listed Regency house is set in peaceful manicured grounds with a courtyard for alfresco dining. Overlooking the garden, the traditional country-house style dining room provides the comfortable setting in which to sample carefully prepared modern European dishes. Using high quality seasonal produce, including local meats and game from nearby shoots, the monthly-changing set dinner menu may offer ragout of pigeon with wild mushroom and thyme jus to start, then a main course of herb-crusted cod with sweet-and-sour red pepper sauce and butter beans with coconut sauce, with hot chocolate and chestnut fondant for dessert.

Chef Rob Avery **Owner** John & Sarah Sweeney
Times 12-5.30/7-9.30 **Prices** Fixed L 2 course £10, Fixed D 3 course £24.95, Starter £5-£6.50, Main £14.95-£17.95, Dessert £5-£6.50, Service optional **Wines** 7 bottles over £20, 24 bottles under £20, 11 by glass **Notes** Sunday L, Vegetarian available, Civ Wed 120 **Seats** 65, Pr/dining room 25 **Children** Portions **Parking** 85

Menzies Swindon

◉ British

☎ 01793 528282
Fleming Way SN1 1TN
e-mail: swindon@menzieshotels.co.uk

This establishment was awarded its Rosette/s just as we went to press. Therefore we are unable to provide a description for it - visit www.theAA.com for the most up-to-date information.

Prices Food prices not confirmed for 2009. Please telephone for details.

WARMINSTER · Map 4 ST84

Bishopstrow House Hotel

◉◉ Modern British V 🕯

Skilled cooking in country-house surroundings

☎ 01985 212312
BA12 9HH
e-mail: info@bishopstrow.co.uk
dir: From Warminster take B3414 (Salisbury). Hotel is signed

A fine example of a Georgian country home, Bishopstrow House is set in 27 acres of landscaped grounds. The hotel retains a host of period features, enhanced by a sensitive modern approach to décor. It also houses one of the biggest collections of antique firearms in the country. The modern British menu presents a mixture of straightforward and more interesting dishes, delivered with consummate skill and creativity. On the more complicated side is a flavoursome starter of seared scallops with pig's cheek tortellini, garnished with a selection of sauces and garden peas. Equally impressive is olive-crusted monkfish accompanied by a risotto of tomato and chorizo, and basil-infused rocket.

Chef Ross Hadley **Owner** von Essen Hotels
Times 12-2.30/7-9.30 **Prices** Fixed L 2 course fr £12, Fixed D 3 course £40, Tasting menu £50, Starter £4.95-£10.50, Main £7.95-£26.50, Dessert £5.95-£8.95, Service added but optional 15% **Wines** 220 bottles over £20, 12 by glass **Notes** Tasting menu 7 courses, Sunday L, Vegetarian menu, Dress restrictions, Smart casual, Civ Wed 70 **Seats** 65, Pr/dining room 28 **Children** Portions, Menu **Parking** 100

WHITLEY · Map 4 ST86

The Pear Tree Inn

◉◉ Modern British

Attractive inn serving local produce

☎ 01225 709131
Top Ln SN12 8QX
e-mail: enquiries@thepeartreeinn.com
dir: Please telephone for directions

Set within lovely grounds, the inn was once a farm and the décor reflects its history, using old agricultural implements and simple stripped-wooden tables. The mellow stone building has been transformed with a rustic yet contemporary feel, with the interior divided into a bar, dining area and garden room. Modern British cuisine with European influences and fresh, locally-sourced seasonal produce are the draw here. Dishes are straightforward and the menu offers an appealing choice. Try fresh Brixham crab gratin for starters, followed by fillet of beef served with creamy dauphinoise potatoes, spinach and a mushroom stuffed with shallots in red wine. Recommended desserts include excellent home-made ice creams, with some unusual flavours such as marmalade.

Chef Kevin Chandler **Owner** Maypole Group plc
Times 12-2.30/6.30-9.30, Closed 25-26 Dec, 1 Jan
Prices Food prices not confirmed for 2009. Please telephone for details. **Wines** 28 bottles over £20, 26 bottles under £20, 12 by glass **Notes** Sunday L, Vegetarian available **Seats** 60, Pr/dining room 40 **Children** Portions, Menu **Parking** 60

WORCESTERSHIRE

ABBERLEY · Map 10 SO76

The Elms Hotel & Restaurant

◉◉ Modern, Traditional British V 🕯

English country elegance and fining dining

☎ 01299 896666
Stockton Rd WR6 6AT
e-mail: info@theelmshotel.co.uk
web: www.theelmshotel.co.uk
dir: Located on A443 near Abberley, 11m NW of Worcester

This imposing Queen Anne house was built in 1710 by a pupil of Sir Christopher Wren and has recently been brought up-to-date with the addition of a luxurious health spa. Overlooking beautifully kept grounds, the lavish interiors complement the grandiose exteriors, with ornate ceilings, carved fireplaces, antique furnishings and stained-glass windows creating an atmosphere of elegant sophistication. With an elegant restaurant overlooking the gardens, the technically adept kitchen creates accomplished modern British dishes, aspiring to even greater heights with clear flavours and the imaginative use of first-class ingredients. Think roast squab pigeon and spiced lentils to start, perhaps followed by roast monkfish, pancetta and sardine and mussel dressing, and tiramisu, vanilla-poached pear and coffee croquant to finish.

Chef Daren Bale **Owner** von Essen Hotels
Times 12-2.30/7-9.30 **Prices** Food prices not confirmed for 2009. Please telephone for details. **Wines** 111 bottles over £20, 21 bottles under £20, 10 by glass **Notes** ALC 3 courses, Sunday L, Vegetarian menu, Dress restrictions, Smart casual, no jeans, no T-shirts, Civ Wed 70 **Seats** 50, Pr/dining room 50 **Children** Portions, Menu **Parking** 100

The Mug House Inn & Angry Chef Restaurant

◉ Modern British ✿

Imaginative cooking in historic riverside setting

☎ 01299 402543
12 Severnside North DY12 2EE
e-mail: drew@mughousebewdley.co.uk
web: www.mughousebewdley.co.uk
dir: B4190 to Bewdley. On riverside, just over bridge on right hand side

This delightful inn on the banks of the River Severn has welcomed locals and travellers alike since the 17th century. Part of a terrace of period properties, it has been sympathetically renovated to create a relaxed, comfortable ambience, complete with original beams, pastel colours and fresh flowers. The amusingly named Angry Chef Restaurant is an elegant, classically-styled venue, complemented by friendly service from smart, yet informally dressed staff. The kitchen delivers a good range of imaginative modern British dishes with a Mediterranean twist. There's a dedicated fish menu, as well as meat, game and vegetarian options, all using locally-sourced produce wherever possible. A house specialty is fresh lobster (diners can select their own) grilled simply in garlic butter and served with new potatoes, or meat-eaters might opt for a satisfying chargrilled fillet of beef with confit of wild mushrooms, marquis potatoes and Burgundy sauce.

Chef Stewart Hiorns, Drew Clifford **Owner** Drew Clifford **Times** 12-2.30/6.30-9, Closed D Sun **Prices** Starter £4.15-£7.95, Main £10.95-£30, Dessert £4.95-£6.25, Service optional **Wines** 24 bottles over £20, 23 bottles under £20, 9 by glass **Notes** Sunday L, Vegetarian available, Dress restrictions, Smart casual **Seats** 26, Pr/dining room 16 **Children** Min 10 yrs **Parking** Car park 100mtrs along river

Barcelo The Lygon Arms

◉◉ Modern European ⚫WINE LIST ✿

Accomplished cuisine in Elizabethan surroundings

☎ 01386 852255 & 854400
High St WR12 7DU
e-mail: info@thelygonarms.co.uk
dir: A44 to Broadway

A hotel with a wealth of historic charm and character, The Lygon Arms has been welcoming guests since the

16th century. Boasting a choice of restaurants, a cosy bar and an array of lounges, as well as a smart spa and fitness centre, the hotel is undergoing an ongoing programme of sympathetic refurbishment. The refurbished Elizabethan Great Hall - complete with oak floor, barrel-vaulted ceiling, minstrels' gallery, huge stone fireplace and suits of armour - is the hotel's baronial-themed main dining room. Sophisticated fabrics and tailor-made furnishings lend a sense of drama and occasion to the dining experience, complemented by the recent addition of mirrors and chandeliers to create a somewhat more contemporary feel. The cooking takes a modern approach, driven by the best possible quality ingredients in skilful, well-executed dishes; take twice-baked goats' cheese soufflé with basil pesto and tomato coulis, followed by herb-crusted rump of lamb on a provençale aubergine galette, with garlic fondant potato, and perhaps dark chocolate torte with butterscotch ice cream and chocolate syrup to finish.

Barcelo The Lygon Arms

Chef Chris Lelliot **Owner** Barceló Hotels & Resorts **Times** 12-2/7-9.30 **Prices** Fixed L 2 course £15-£17, Fixed D 3 course £42.50-£48, Starter £8-£15, Main £19-£30, Dessert £9-£11, Service optional **Wines** 100+ bottles over £20, 4 bottles under £20, 14 by glass **Notes** Gourmet 7 courses with wine £75 on request, Sunday L, Vegetarian available, Dress restrictions, Smart casual, no jeans, T-shirts or trainers, Civ Wed 80, Air con **Seats** 80, Pr/dining room 110 **Children** Portions, Menu **Parking** 150

Dormy House Hotel

◉◉ British, French

Enjoyable dining at this luxurious Cotswold retreat

☎ 01386 852711
Willersey Hill WR12 7LF
e-mail: reservations@dormyhouse.co.uk
dir: From A44 take turn signed Saintbury, after 0.5m turn left

Located in extensive grounds in the heart of the Cotswolds, this tastefully converted 17th-century farmhouse overlooks the picturesque town of Broadway. The best country-house traditions are observed, with luxurious rooms, real fires, comfy sofas and afternoon teas and a traditional approach to dining making a winning combination. Smart dress is required, but there's no stuffiness here: staff throughout provide excellent, friendly service. High quality, locally sourced produce is used to create simple yet elegant traditional dishes with the occasional contemporary twist. Stuffed morels with

chicken and sorrel mousse, garden pea risotto and pea cappuccino makes a fine starter, perhaps followed by seared king scallops with San Daniele ham, basil mashed potato, angel hair vegetables and saffron and lemon beurre blanc.

Times 12-2/7-9.30, Closed 24-27 Dec, Closed L Mon-Sat

Russell's

◉◉ Modern British

Fine dining in a chic restaurant with rooms

☎ 01386 853555
20 High St WR12 7DT
e-mail: info@russellsofbroadway.com
dir: A44 follow signs to Broadway, restaurant on High St opposite village green

On the picturesque high street, this stylish restaurant with rooms takes its name from Gordon Russell, the renowned furniture designer, who once had his headquarters here. Carefully restored, Russell's combines the period features of this historic building with subtle contemporary décor. In the front room, a stone fireplace is used to display fine wines and during summer a courtyard and front patio supply alfresco dining space. The kitchen delivers a good choice of modern British dishes with Mediterranean influences, including a fixed-price menu. Expect starters such as whole roasted quail with parsnip rösti, pickled mushrooms and a honey sauce, followed by mains like grilled John Dory with smoked trout and spring onion mash, creamed salsify and a grain mustard sauce.

Chef Matthew Laughton **Owner** Andrew Riley, Barry Hancox **Times** 12-2.30/6-9.30, Closed D Sun **Prices** Fixed L 2 course £14-£16, Fixed D 3 course £18-£25, Starter £7-£12, Main £10-£26, Dessert £6-£9, Service optional **Wines** 38 bottles over £20, 12 bottles under £20, 12 by glass **Notes** Sunday L, Air con **Seats** 55, Pr/dining room 14 **Children** Portions **Parking** 16

Grafton Manor Restaurant

◉ Modern British, Indian V

Modern cuisine dotted with Indian dishes in elegant period setting

☎ 01527 579007
Grafton Ln B61 7HA
e-mail: stephen@graftonmanorhotel.co.uk
dir: Off B4091, 1.5m SW of Bromsgrove

Built in 1567 by the Earl of Shrewsbury, this impressive manor house is set in manicured grounds with its own lake and retains many original features. Moulded ceilings, open fires and a sumptuous period drawing room set the scene, together with the country-house style dining room finished with crisp white linen. The monthly-changing modern menu has an Indian influence, as in Bombay prawns with three-herb raita, followed by chicken caffreal with Indian vegetables, or roast breast and confit leg of partridge, Brussels sprouts and chestnuts cooked in port with beetroot purée and orange glaze for a more conventional main course. A separate vegetarian menu offers fricassée of wild mushrooms with roasted Jerusalem artichokes, while Hyderabadi apricots with mango and coriander sorbet makes an interesting dessert.

Chef Adam Harrison, Tim Waldon **Owner** The Morris Family **Times** 12.30-1.30/7-9.30, Closed New Year, BHs, Closed L Sat, Closed D Sun **Prices** Fixed L 3 course £18.50-£20.50, Fixed D 3 course £28.95, Service optional **Wines** 46 bottles over £20, 24 bottles under £20, 3 by glass **Notes** Sunday L, Vegetarian menu, Dress restrictions, Smart casual, Civ Wed 120 **Seats** 60, Pr/dining room 60 **Children** Portions **Parking** 60

CHADDESLEY CORBETT   Map 10 SO87

Brockencote Hall

◎◎ Modern French **V**

Divine French cooking at an elegant manor house

☎ 01562 777876
DY10 4PY
e-mail: info@brockencotehall.com
web: www.brockencotehall.com
dir: On A448 just outside village, between Kidderminster & Bromsgrove

Glorious countryside surrounds this magnificent Victorian mansion set in 70 acres of landscaped parkland just a thirty minute drive from Birmingham. Inside has the feel of a provincial French château - all pastel shades, chandeliers and elegant drapes - while a stroll around the grounds reveals all-weather tennis courts, a croquet lawn and a pretty lake. But it's the food that really delights - passionate and artistic, yet without any pretension, this is cooking to savour from a chef who really knows his stuff. Have a flutter on the six-course tasting menu, or choose from the modern French carte: a starter of dodine of Perigord duck foie gras perhaps, served with an Armagnac and salt flower and truffle salad, followed by noisette of Scottish wild venison with forestière potato, creamed Jerusalem artichoke, bitter chocolate and an old balsamico jus. One to watch.

Chef Didier Philipot **Owner** Mr & Mrs Petitjean **Times** 12-1.30/7-9.30, Closed L Sat **Wines** 160 bottles over £20, 26 bottles under £20, 13 by glass **Notes** Dégustation menu 6 courses £55, Sunday L, Vegetarian menu, Dress restrictions, Smart casual, no jeans, Civ Wed 70 **Seats** 60, Pr/dining room 30 **Children** Portions, Menu **Parking** 45

EVESHAM   Map 10 SP04

The Evesham Hotel

◎ International

Relaxed Georgian style, with plenty of choice

☎ 01386 765566
Coopers Ln, Off Waterside WR11 1DA
e-mail: reception@eveshamhotel.com
dir: Coopers Lane is off road along River Avon

Dating from 1540 and set in extensive grounds, this former Tudor farmhouse was modernised in 1810 in Georgian style. Today it's a well-maintained family-run hotel with a wealth of memorabilia including newspaper cuttings, toys and teddy bears striking a humorously eccentric note. The aptly-named Cedar Restaurant - an elegant Georgian room that looks out on to a 200-year-old cedar of Lebanon - has well-appointed tables, comfortable chairs and striking gold and green décor. The menu is pleasingly lengthy and wide-ranging, and the cooking style straightforward. Expect the likes of filo pastry filled with white crabmeat, tomato and roasted peppers in mayonnaise with sweet red pepper sauce, and griddled Cotswold beef fillet with stilton-topped fondant potato, creamy mushrooms and a port reduction.

Chef Adam Talbot **Owner** John Jenkinson **Times** 12.30-2/7-9.30, Closed 25-26 Dec **Wines** 391 bottles over £20, 303 bottles under £20, 5 by glass **Notes** Buffet L available £9.50, Sunday L **Seats** 55, Pr/dining room 12 **Children** Portions, Menu **Parking** 45

Northwick Hotel

◎ British

Traditional dining in welcoming hotel

☎ 01386 40322
Waterside WR11 1BT
e-mail: enquiries@northwickhotel.co.uk
dir: M5 junct 9, A46 Evesham, follow signs for town centre. At River Bridge lights turn left, hotel 50yds on left.

Overlooking the River Avon and its adjacent park, this modernised but classically-designed hotel is situated just a short stroll from the town centre. Its aptly-named contemporary-style fine-dining Courtyard Restaurant has an airy garden feel, overlooking the courtyard and raised beds and pond. The straightforward carte delivers simple, well-presented traditional dishes of flavour,

based on home-made and local ingredients. Take cod goujons with lemon and caper mayonnaise to start, followed by seared beef fillet with horseradish pomme purée and green peppercorn jus, or perhaps lamb medallions with roasted vegetables and mint jus.

Times 12-2/7-9.30, Closed Xmas

KIDDERMINSTER   Map 10 SO87

The Granary Hotel & Restaurant

◎◎ Modern European ♨

Modern cuisine in a setting to match

☎ 01562 777535
Heath Ln, Shenstone DY10 4BS
e-mail: info@granary-hotel.co.uk
web: www.granary-hotel.co.uk
dir: Situated on A450 between Worcester and Stourbridge. 2m outside Kidderminster

This smart hotel has an airy contemporary restaurant decorated in dark woods and muted colours, and furnished with Lloyd Loom chairs and well-spaced tables. Modern dishes, using the very best of local produce, are the mainstay of the menu: kick off with seared king scallops, for example, served with a sweet potato purée and oven-dried grapes, before tucking into slow-cooked pork belly with champ potatoes, carrots, parsnips and apple sauce, or Herefordshire beef fillet wrapped in pancetta with carrot and coriander purée and sautéed button mushrooms. There's simpler fare too, in the form of steaks served with chips and an array of sauces, or a carvery at weekends.

Chef Tom Court **Owner** Richard Fletcher **Times** 12-2.30/7-11, Closed 25 Dec, Closed L Mon & Sat, Closed D Sun **Prices** Fixed L 2 course £9.25-£9.75, Fixed D 3 course £18.50-£20.50, Starter £4.25-£8.50, Main £10.50-£22.50, Dessert £4.50-£5.50, Service optional **Wines** 11 bottles over £20, 31 bottles under £20, 9 by glass **Notes** Sunday L, Vegetarian available, Civ Wed 200, Air con **Seats** 60, Pr/dining room 40 **Children** Portions **Parking** 95

MALVERN   Map 10 SO74

Cotford Hotel & L'Amuse Bouche Restaurant

◉ British, French ✆

French-style cooking in a quaint English setting

☎ 01684 572427
51 Graham Rd WR14 2HU
e-mail: reservations@cotfordhotel.co.uk
dir: M5 junct 7. 250mtrs from Malvern town centre

Nestling at the foot of the beautiful Malvern Hills with landscaped grounds and stunning views, this gothic-style property was originally built in 1851 for the Bishop of Worcester. The high-ceilinged Amuse Bouche Restaurant boasts a wealth of wonderful architecture to complement its modern décor, and as its name suggests brings a taste of French cuisine to the Worcestershire countryside, accompanied by fittingly formal and efficient service. Daily-changing menus feature locally-sourced and organic produce with suppliers duly noted, and there's a strong emphasis on quality with everything from sorbets to petits fours made on the premises. A trio of Colchester oysters, smoked salmon and crayfish shows the style, followed by pan-fried French Barbary duck breast with piquant orange and rocha pear sauce.

Chef Christopher Morgan **Owner** Christopher & Barbara Morgan **Times** 12.30-2/7-9 **Prices** Fixed L 2 course £21.50, Fixed D 3 course £25, Starter £4.95-£12, Main £14.50-£24, Dessert £4.95-£6.50, Service optional **Wines** 1 bottles over £20, 8 bottles under £20, 4 by glass **Notes** Sunday L **Seats** 36, Pr/dining room 12 **Children** Portions, Menu **Parking** 15

The Cottage in the Wood Hotel and Outlook Restaurant

◉◉ British, European 🏅 NOTABLE WINE LIST

Country retreat with imaginative food and stunning views

☎ 01684 588860
The Cottage in the Wood Hotel, Holywell Rd, Malvern Wells WR14 4LG
e-mail: john@cottageinthewood.co.uk
web: www.cottageinthewood.co.uk
dir: 3m S of Great Malvern off A449. From Great Malvern, take 3rd turning on right after Railway pub

The Cottage is a cluster of three white-painted buildings, gloriously situated high on the steep wooded slopes of the Malvern Hills, with the recently refurbished restaurant located in the heart of the elegant Georgian dower house. Views across the Severn Plain from the floor-to-ceiling windows are stunning but the ambitious cooking does its best to distract, with a British menu that focuses on quality local seasonal produce and imaginative flavours. Take sea bass with saffron-crushed potatoes, fennel and parsley juices, or perhaps lamb rump with pea purée and redcurrant jus. The thoughtfully compiled wine list is packed with interest, enthusiasm and a refreshing lack of pretension.

The Cottage in the Wood Hotel and Outlook Restaurant

Chef Dominic Pattin **Owner** The Pattin Family **Times** 12.30-2/7-9.30 **Prices** Starter £5.70-£11.90, Main £10.45-£22.85, Dessert £5.55-£6.95, Service optional **Wines** 374 bottles over £20, 59 bottles under £20, 10 by glass **Notes** Pre-theatre D available from 6pm, Sunday L, Vegetarian available, Air con **Seats** 70, Pr/dining room 20 **Children** Portions **Parking** 40

Holdfast Cottage Hotel

◉ Modern

Beautifully simple, quality dishes in a charming cottage setting

☎ 01684 310288
Marlbank Rd, Welland WR13 6NA
e-mail: enquiries@holdfast-cottage.co.uk
dir: On A4104 midway between Welland & Little Malvern

Well-executed dishes with clear, concise flavours can be experienced in the pretty dining room at this lovely 17th-century wisteria-clad cottage, set at the foot of the Malvern Hills. Enlarged in Victorian times, it boasts 2 acres of gardens and woodland. Oak tables, fresh flowers and simple cutlery and glassware set the mood in the elegant, cottage-style restaurant, and service is relaxed and welcoming. Seasonality and quality are evident on the set four-course menu, which may list smoked salmon terrine to start, followed by herb-crusted lamb chump with mustard mash and mint sauce, and vanilla pannacotta with black cherry compôte for dessert.

Times 12-2.30/7-9

Seasons Restaurant at Colwall Park Hotel

◉◉ Modern British ✆

Stylish restaurant serving excellent local produce

☎ 01684 540000
Walwyn Rd, Colwall WR13 6QG
e-mail: hotel@colwall.com
dir: On B4218, off A449 from Malvern to Ledbury

This attractive country-house hotel is located in a quiet village at the foot of the Malvern Hills and enjoys splendid views from the gardens. Light meals and snacks are served in the Lantern Bar. In contrast to the generally traditional décor in the public rooms, the fine-dining restaurant is quite contemporary in shades of cream with light-oak panelling and bespoke artwork. The kitchen delivers accomplished, technically well-executed dishes, with good use made of seasonal produce and local producers duly acknowledged. Typical starters might include pan-fried hand-dived scallops with cauliflower purée and sherry caramel, and for main course, guinea fowl breast with wild mushroom and asparagus risotto, and white wine and truffle froth. Round things off with lime and ginger crème brûlée with ginger biscuit ice cream, and if you have room, sample the impressive cheeseboard.

Chef James Garth **Owner** Mr & Mrs I Nesbitt **Times** 12-2/7-9, Closed L all week ex by arrangement **Prices** Fixed L 2 course £16.95, Starter £6.95-£7.95, Main £17.95-£21.50, Dessert £6.50-£7.75, Service included **Wines** 32 bottles over £20, 40 bottles under £20, 9 by glass **Notes** Sunday L, Vegetarian available, Air con **Seats** 40, Pr/dining room 100 **Children** Portions, Menu **Parking** 40

OMBERSLEY   Map 10 SO86

The Venture In Restaurant

◉◉ British, French

Modern British dining in medieval draper's house

☎ 01905 620552
Main Rd WR9 0EW
dir: From Worcester N towards Kidderminster - A449 (approx 5m). Turn left at Ombersley turning - 0.75m on right

Attractive historical features abound at this lovely old building, which dates from 1430, and there is a resident ghost, too. Fresh flowers and gentle colours enhance the comfortable dining venue, and service is thoughtful and attentive. Breads, ice creams and petits fours are all made in-house and dishes are skilfully prepared from the best quality ingredients and simply presented. The fixed-price dinner menu offers the likes of seared home-cured gravad lax fillet with warm potato salad and dill crème fraîche, and slow-braised medallion of lamb served with sautéed lambs' kidneys and rosemary sauce. Classic desserts include glazed lemon tart with vanilla ice cream, or rich chocolate mousse with griottine cherries.

Chef Toby Fletcher Owner Toby Fletcher
Times 12-2/7-9.30, Closed 25 Dec-1 Jan, 2 wks summer
& 2 wks winter, Closed Mon, Closed D Sun Prices Fixed L
2 course £22, Fixed D 3 course £37, Service optional
Wines 40 bottles over £20, 20 bottles under £20, 6 by
glass Notes Sunday L, Vegetarian available, Dress
restrictions, Smart casual, Air con Seats 32, Pr/dining
room 32 Children Min 12 yrs D Parking 15 Parking on
street

Cadmore Lodge

◉ Modern British ✊

Enjoyable dining in rural retreat

☎ 01584 810044
Berrington Green, St Michaels WR15 8TQ
e-mail: reception.cadmore@cadmorelodge.com
dir: Off A4112 from Tenbury Wells to Leominster. 2m from
Tenbury Wells, turn right opposite St Michael's Church

This former fishing lodge turned friendly, family-run hotel
is set in an idyllic rural location, surrounded as it is by a
70-acre private estate, featuring a 9-hole golf course and
overlooking a lake. The country-style restaurant has a
peaceful and relaxing atmosphere, with lovely views of
the countryside, a warm colour scheme and a log fire. The
daily-changing dinner menu has a contemporary
approach; take smoked salmon on rocket salad with a
poached egg and horseradish cream to start, with mains
such as baked supreme of corn-fed chicken with crisp
chorizo and port jus, rounded off with apple fritters and
vanilla ice cream.

Chef Mark Griffiths, Russell Collins Owner Mr & Mrs J
Weston Times 12-2/7-9.15, Closed 25 Dec, Closed L Mon
Prices Fixed L 2 course £11.50, Fixed D 3 course £22.95
Wines 3 bottles over £20, 13 bottles under £20, 6 by
glass Notes Sunday L, Civ Wed 100, Air con Seats 50, Pr/
dining room 50 Children Portions, Menu Parking 100

Whites @ the Clockhouse

◉◉ Modern British ✊

Contemporary high-street bistro serious about food

☎ 01584 811336
14 Market St WR15 8BQ
e-mail: whites@theclockhouse.net
web: www.whites@theclockhouse.net
dir: A456/A4112 into Tenbury Wells. Continue over the
bridge and along the main street. Restaurant on right
adjacent to The Royal Oak

Whites is a stylish wine bar and restaurant on the town's
pretty main street. Enjoy a drink in the downstairs wine
bar while you look at the menu, then make your way up
the spiral staircase to the light-and-airy loft-style
restaurant. Here, polished-wood tables are set on wooden
floors against a backdrop of beams, lathes and plaster.
Fresh local seasonal produce is used wherever possible
and the kitchen team delivers modern cuisine with
artistic flare, making everything from the canapés to the
petits fours, including bread, ice cream and biscuits.

Accomplished cooking and stylish presentation combine
in well-executed dishes, such as Whites gravadlax and
steak and chips (local fillet steak served on a bed of
roasted cherry tomatoes and ragout of mushroom and
shallot pie).

Whites @ the Clockhouse

Chef Jonathan Waters Owner Sarah MacDonald, Chris
Whitehead Times 10.30am/11pm, Closed 2 wks mid Jan,
Closed Mon, Closed L Tue-Wed, Closed D Sun
Prices Starter £5-£8, Main £13-£20, Dessert £6-£6.50,
Service optional Wines 20 bottles over £20, 19 bottles
under £20, 7 by glass Notes Sunday L, Vegetarian
available Seats 45 Children Portions, Menu Parking On
street, car park on Teme St

White Lion Hotel

◉ Modern British

**Historic hotel of character, with modern décor and
cooking**

☎ 01684 592551
21 High St WR8 0HJ
e-mail: info@whitelionhotel.biz
dir: From A422 take A38 towards Tewkesbury. After 8m
take B4104 for 1m, after bridge turn left to hotel

Famed for being the inn depicted in Henry Fielding's
novel Tom Jones, this historic 16th-century hotel in the
heart of town blends old beams and timbers with
contemporary design. The restaurant follows the theme,
its solid oak-finished tables dressed with fresh flowers,
and some have views over the High Street. Service is
friendly, relaxed and knowledgeable, while the kitchen's
modern approach - via carte, two-course lunch and
dinner menus - is driven by fresh local ingredients and
accuracy. Take pan-fried fillet of halibut served with a
pea and mint risotto and crispy pancetta, and perhaps a
warm prune and Armagnac tart finish with vanilla cream.

Chef Jon Lear, Richard Thompson Owner Mr & Mrs Lear
Times 12-2/7-9.15, Closed 31 Dec-1 Jan, Closed L few
days between Xmas & New Year Wines 5 bottles over
£20, 26 bottles under £20, 4 by glass Notes Sun L 2
courses £13.25, 3 courses £16 Seats 45
Children Portions Parking 16

Brown's Restaurant

◉◉ Modern British V ✊

Skilful modern cooking in former corn mill

☎ 01905 26263
The Old Cornmill, South Quay WR1 2JJ
e-mail: enquiries@brownsrestaurant.co.uk
dir: From M5 junct 7 to city centre, at lights turn into
Copenhagen St

This former Victorian corn mill is situated in a stunning
location overlooking the River Severn, enjoying tranquil
views over the water and swan sanctuary. Newly
refurbished with chic, modern décor, feature lighting and
interesting architectural features, it comes complete with
a mezzanine balcony where guests can relax over pre-
dinner drinks before going through to dinner in the
downstairs restaurant. Here, well-spaced linen-clad
tables, artwork and mirrors set the scene, while the
accomplished cooking takes an equally modern approach
with some Mediterranean and classical influences,
making sound use of high-quality, locally-sourced
ingredients. Clean-cut starters like shellfish ragout with
fennel cream, crab beignet and chervil velouté feature
alongside robust main courses like dry-aged beef fillet
and braised short rib with smoked mushrooms, shallot
confit, port-roasted turnips and beef jus.

Chef Martin Lovell, Ian Courage Owner Mr & Mrs R
Everton Times 12-2.30/6.30-10, Closed Mon, Closed D
Sun Prices Fixed L 2 course £19.95, Fixed D 3 course
£31.95, Starter £4.95-£10.95, Main £15.95-£24.95,
Dessert £6.95-£7.95, Service optional Wines 93 bottles
over £20, 30 bottles under £20, 7 by glass Notes Sunday
L, Vegetarian menu, Dress restrictions, Smart casual
preferred, Civ Wed 80 Seats 110, Pr/dining room 20
Children Portions Parking Large car park adjacent to the
Restaurant

The Glasshouse

◉◉ Modern British ✊

Bustling town-centre brasserie with cathedral views

☎ 01905 611120
55 Sidbury WR1 2HU
e-mail: eat@theglasshouse.co.uk
dir: M5 junct 7 towards Worcester. Continue straight over
2 rdbts, through 2 sets of lights. At 3rd set of lights turn
left into car park, restaurant is opposite

Owned by Shaun Hill (see entry for The Walnut Tree,
Abergavenny), this restaurant occupies a converted
antique shop in the centre of town. Immediately beyond
the large plate-glass windows is a small bar leading into
the downstairs dining area with striped banquette
seating and leather chairs. The upstairs dining room,
with views of the cathedral, is open to the ground floor
and retains the great atmosphere. A Shaun Hill-designed
menu is always going to be about good ingredients and
simplicity of cooking and presentation. An extensive
choice of brasserie classics and signature dishes is

Continued

WORCESTER *Continued*

offered, prepared from local produce. Recommendations include pheasant pudding with crispy sage and bacon, sautéed monkfish with pickled cucumber and mustard, and warm chocolate cake with blood orange sorbet.

Chef Dwight Clayton **Owner** Brandon Weston, Shaun Hill **Times** 12-2.30/5.30-10, Closed D Sun **Prices** Fixed L 2 course fr £15, Starter £5-£9, Main £14-£19, Dessert £6, Groups min 8 service 10% **Wines** 18 bottles over £20, 5 bottles under £20 **Notes** Sunday L, Vegetarian available, Air con **Seats** 100, Pr/dining room 16 **Children** Portions **Parking** Pay & display 100yds

YORKSHIRE, EAST RIDING OF

BEVERLEY   Map 17 TA03

The Pipe and Glass Inn

⊛ Modern British **V** 🍷

Charming countryside inn serving hearty food

☎ 01430 810246
West End, South Dalton HU17 7PN
e-mail: email@pipeandglass.co.uk
dir: Just off B1248

The 17th-century inn effortlessly blends modern and traditional styles, with an open fire in the beamed snug bar, leather chesterfields in the lounge area, and bespoke wooden dining tables in the interconnecting dining areas and large conservatory dining room. A good range of dishes, from classic to modern British, is offered from the seasonally changing menu. Real effort is made to use as much locally sourced produce as possible in dishes such as potted Hornsea crab with spiced butter, crab sticks, sorrel and blood orange to start, followed by Barnsley chop with devilled kidneys, or grilled Filey Bay sea bass with wilted samphire, and crab and lovage beignet.

Chef James MacKenzie **Owner** James MacKenzie, Kate Boroughs **Times** 12-2/6.30-9.30, Closed 25 Dec, 2 wks Jan, Closed Mon, Closed D Sun **Prices** Starter £4.95-£9.95, Main £8.95-£19.95, Dessert £5.95-£8.95, Service optional **Wines** 71 bottles over £20, 26 bottles under £20, 10 by glass **Notes** Sunday L, Vegetarian menu, Air con **Seats** 70, Pr/dining room 26 **Children** Portions, Menu **Parking** 60

Tickton Grange Hotel

⊛⊛ Modern British 🍷

Elegant Georgian country-house retreat with exciting dining

☎ 01964 543666
Tickton HU17 9SH
e-mail: info@ticktongrange.co.uk
dir: From Beverley take A1035 towards Bridlington. After 3m hotel on left, just past Tickton

Dating back to the 1820s, this charming Georgian country-house hotel is set in 4 acres of grounds and beautiful landscaped gardens. The large bay windows of the elegant dining room offer superb views over the hillside. Suppliers

of local produce get a prominent listing on the seasonal menus, where the carefully selected ingredients are skilfully transformed into light modern British dishes. Notable for clever combinations, clean flavours and attractive presentation, expect dishes such as Yorkshire Wolds wild venison and chicken terrine with carrot and coriander chutney to start, perhaps followed by Skipsea sea bass fillet with spinach, champagne, dill weed and saffron, with assiette of Wakefield rhubarb to finish. Don't forget the wonderful Tickton truffles served with coffee and, for special occasions, there's the champagne dinner.

Chef David Nowell, John MacDonald **Owner** Mr & Mrs Whymant **Times** 12-2/7-9.30, Closed 26 Dec **Wines** 33 bottles over £20, 32 bottles under £20, 8 by glass **Notes** Champagne D £39.50, Sunday L, Vegetarian available, Civ Wed 150 **Seats** 45, Pr/dining room 20 **Children** Portions, Menu **Parking** 75

KINGSTON UPON HULL   Map 17 TA02

Boars Nest

⊛ Modern British 🍷

Accomplished cooking in a one-time butcher's shop

☎ 01482 445577
22 Princes Av HU5 3QA
e-mail: boarsnest@boarsnest.karoo.co.uk
dir: 1m from Hull city centre. From Ferensway onto Spring Bank, turn right onto Princes Ave

An Edwardian former butcher's shop, complete with ceramic wall-and-floor tiles, the Boars Nest sits in a rejuvenated area of fashionable boutiques, artisan and ethnic food shops and popular eateries. The old front shop is filled with smaller tables, while the former drawing room at the back acts as an intimate dining area and upstairs there is a sumptuous champagne/wine bar. The kitchen offers honest local British cooking with dishes such as wild boar brawn and home-made piccalilli, Goosnargh corn-fed duck with bubble-and-squeak, and hot chocolate pudding with chocolate ice cream.

Chef Simon Rogers, M Bulamore, H Pepper **Owner** Simon Rogers, Dina Hanchett **Times** 12-2/6.30-10, Closed 26 Dec, 1 Jan **Prices** Fixed L 2 course £8, Fixed D 3 course £20, Starter £4.75-£6.95, Main £13.50-£21.95, Dessert £4.95-£5.95, Service added but optional 10% **Wines** 22 bottles over £20, 19 bottles under £20, 13 by glass

Notes Sunday L, Vegetarian available, Dress restrictions, Smart casual **Seats** 50, Pr/dining room 16 **Children** Portions

Cerutti's

⊛ Traditional, Seafood

Long-established fish restaurant with estuary views

☎ 01482 328501
10 Nelson St HU1 1XE
e-mail: ceruttis@ceruttisltd.karoo.co.uk
dir: Please telephone for directions

Set beside the old Humber Ferry ticket office with views over the river, Cerutti's appropriately specialises in fresh local fish from the docks, and has been at the forefront of the town's dining scene for over 20 years. On the ground floor there's a small bar, while the restaurant - decked out in coral paintwork and '70s-style furniture creating an easy and comfortable feel - is on the first floor to make the best of those estuary views. Italian ownership lends Mediterranean flavour and enthusiasm to the careful cooking built around the freshness of ingredients. Take pan-fried sea bass served with capers in a lemon butter sauce, or perhaps a medley of seafood - steamed with sun-blushed tomatoes - and served with a pesto dressing. (Meat eaters are not forgotten.)

Chef Tim Bell **Owner** Anthony Cerutti **Times** 12-2/7-9.30, Closed 1 wk Xmas & New Year, Closed Sun, Closed L Sat **Prices** Starter £4.75-£11.85, Main £12.25-£19.75, Dessert £5.65-£7.50, Service optional **Wines** 18 bottles over £20, 28 bottles under £20, 8 by glass **Notes** Vegetarian available, Dress restrictions, Smart casual **Seats** 40 **Children** Portions **Parking** 6

WILLERBY   Map 17 TA03

Best Western Willerby Manor Hotel

⊛⊛ Modern European

Quality cooking in a slick modern setting

☎ 01482 652616
Well Ln HU10 6ER
e-mail: willerbymanor@bestwestern.co.uk
dir: M62/A63, follow signs for Humber Bridge, then signs for Beverley until Willerby Shopping Park. Hotel signed from rdbt next to McDonald's

Set in a quiet residential area, amid well-tended gardens, this popular hotel was originally the home of a wealthy shipping merchant. Renovated in sympathetic modern style, the hotel has two dining options: the Everglades brasserie in a sunny conservatory, or the more formal Icon restaurant in a thoroughly contemporary dining room. The latter leans toward the Mediterranean in style. To start, try oriental salad with pan-fried monkfish cheeks and soy dressing, and follow with a main course of local beef fillet with wild mushrooms, globe artichoke and baked Yorkshire blue ravioli. Rather than the traditional separation into starters and mains, the menu gives the option of small or large portions for several of the dishes - a nice idea.

Times 12.30-2.30/7-9.30, Closed 1st wk Jan, last 2 wks Aug, BHs, Closed Sun, Closed L Mon-Sat

YORKSHIRE, NORTH

ALDWARK — Map 19 SE46

Aldwark Manor

◉◉ Modern British

19th-century manor house with a contemporary dining room

☎ 01347 838146 & 838251
YO61 1UF
e-mail: aldwarkmanor@qhotels.co.uk
dir: From A1, A59 towards Green Hammerton, then B6265 towards Little Ouseburn, follow signs Aldwark Bridge/Manor. A19 through Linton on Ouse to Aldwark

Mature parklands form the impressive backdrop for this rambling 19th-century mansion house within easy reach of York and Harrogate. The hotel is set amid 100 acres of grounds on the River Ure, which flows through an 18-hole golf course. Located in the bright and airy modern extension, the restaurant's minimalist décor makes full use of the picture windows overlooking the gardens, and large modern artwork depicting wine bottles dominates the room. The cooking style is modern with good saucing, and there's a focus on local and British produce. Start with fresh dressed crab, asparagus and lemon salad and follow it with roasted rump of lamb served with champ mash potatoes, swede purée and rosemary gravy.

Chef Bruce McDowell **Owner** Q Hotels **Prices** Food prices not confirmed for 2009. Please telephone for details. **Wines** 69 bottles over £20, 30 bottles under £20, 12 by glass **Notes** Vegetarian available, Dress restrictions, No trainers, Civ Wed 140, Air con **Seats** 90, Pr/dining room 150 **Children** Portions, Menu **Parking** 200

ARNCLIFFE — Map 18 SD97

Amerdale House Hotel

◉◉ British, European

Imaginative modern cuisine in a gorgeous Dales village

☎ 01756 770250
BD23 5QE
e-mail: amerdalehouse@littondale.com
dir: On the outskirts of village

This delightful former Victorian manor house enjoys a truly idyllic location in an Area of Outstanding Natural Beauty. Surrounded by immaculately maintained gardens, the hotel affords wonderful views of the dales and fells from every room. Many original features have

been retained, complemented by beautiful décor and period furniture, while the elegant dining room has a more contemporary feel. The imaginative modern menu is very much influenced by seasonality and freshness with home-grown and local ingredients making appearances throughout. The chef's modern British approach leans toward the traditional with consistently well-cooked and thoughtful dishes. A starter of superb oak-roasted salmon with samphire tossed in lemon vinaigrette might feature alongside pan-roasted Whitby cod with mashed potato, pea butter sauce and crispy courgettes.

Times Closed mid Nov-mid Mar, Closed L all week

ASENBY — Map 19 SE37

Crab and Lobster Restaurant

◉◉ British, European

Character restaurant serving mainly seafood

☎ 01845 577286
Dishforth Rd YO7 3QL
e-mail: enquiries@crabandlobster.co.uk
web: www.crabandlobster.co.uk
dir: From A19/A168 take A167, drive through Topcliffe follow signs for A1. On left, 8m from Northallerton

From its low-ceilinged bar to the main dining room and bright pavilion conservatory, the whole of this highly individual thatched establishment is festooned in a riot of memorabilia. Seafood is the speciality of the lengthy, crowd-pleasing menu, which offers both traditional and more unusual fare, from lobster, scallop and prawn thermidor, or posh fish and chips, to korma fish curry with squid, tiger prawns and mussels, or roast Thai-spiced lobster with scallops and king prawns, green salad and basil mayonnaise. Alternatives include prime Yorkshire fillet steak, or confit of Yorkshire lamb, hotpot potatoes and pickled red cabbage. Dishes are accomplished and well conceived, portions generous and the atmosphere relaxed.

Chef Steve Dean **Owner** Vimac Leisure **Times** 12-2.30/7-9.30 **Prices** Fixed L 2 course fr £14.50, Fixed D 3 course fr £35, Starter £6.50-£11, Main £10.50-£24.50, Dessert £6.30-£11.50, Service optional **Wines** 8 bottles over £20, 8 bottles under £20, 8 by glass **Notes** Sunday L, Civ Wed 24 **Seats** 55, Pr/dining room 24 **Children** Portions **Parking** 80

AUSTWICK — Map 18 SD76

The Austwick Traddock

◉ Modern British V ☺

Georgian country-house hotel with organic cuisine

☎ 015242 51224
Nr Settle LA2 8BY
e-mail: info@austwicktraddock.co.uk
dir: From Skipton take A65 towards Kendal, 3m after Settle take right signed Austwick, cross hump back bridge, hotel 100yds on left

Set in the heart of the Yorkshire Dales National Park, this charming country-house hotel dates back to the 1700s, when it was built as a private residence. Inside, there are two comfortable lounges with fine furnishings and real fires, as well as a cosy bar. The former library is now an elegant, candlelit restaurant serving modern British dishes using only organic and wild ingredients. Try starters such as roasted pigeon breasts, Puy lentils and bacon crisp, and mains like sustainably farmed organic roast salt cod with clam chowder and wilted sorrel. Desserts might include almond and apple crumble with bay leaf custard.

Chef Tom Eunson **Owner** Bruce & Jane Reynolds **Times** 12-3/6.45-9.45 **Prices** Fixed L 2 course £12.95, Starter £4.95-£9.50, Main £14.95-£19.95, Dessert £5.25-£8.50, Service optional **Wines** 18 bottles over £20, 21 bottles under £20, 8 by glass **Notes** Sunday L, Vegetarian menu **Seats** 36, Pr/dining room 16 **Children** Portions, Menu **Parking** 20

BOLTON ABBEY — Map 19 SE05

The Burlington Restaurant

See page 450

BOROUGHBRIDGE — Map 19 SE36

The Dining Room

◉◉ Modern British

Quality cooking in relaxed surroundings

☎ 01423 326426
20 St James Square YO51 9AR
e-mail: chris@thediningrooms.co.uk
dir: A1(M), Boroughbridge junct, sign to town. Opposite fountain in the town square

Behind the restaurant's shop-style, bow-fronted exterior lies a traditional lounge-style bar, perfect for pre- and

Continued

BOROUGHBRIDGE *Continued*

post-dinner drinks. In contrast, the dining room is a more light, spacious and contemporary affair, decked out with wooden beams, high-backed chairs, crisp linens and good quality crockery and silverware. In fine weather, the new terrace is perfect for relaxed alfresco dining. The owner-chef is passionate about cooking with the freshest produce and his intelligent, compact menus (supplemented by specials) deliver fresh, clean-flavoured dishes that allow the top quality ingredients to speak for themselves. Typical starters might include lobster bisque, with fillet of Yorkshire beef to follow and rounded off with home-made liquorice ice cream and rhubarb.

Chef Christopher Astley **Owner** Mr & Mrs C Astley **Times** 12-2/7-9.30, Closed 26-28 Dec, 1 Jan, BHs, Closed Mon, Closed L Tue-Sat, Closed D Sun **Prices** Fixed D 3 course £26.50, Starter £5.75-£6.95, Main £12-£17.50, Dessert £5-£6.95, Service optional **Wines** 48 bottles over £20, 37 bottles under £20, 9 by glass **Notes** Sunday L, Vegetarian available **Seats** 32 **Children** Min 3 yrs, Portions **Parking** On street/Private on request

---

BURNSALL   Map 19 SE06

Red Lion Hotel & Manor House

@ Modern British 🍷

Picturesque old inn serving hearty favourites

☎ 01756 720204
By the Bridge BD23 6BU
e-mail: info@redlion.co.uk
dir: 10m from Skipton on B6160

Set beside a five-arch bridge over the River Wharfe, this delightful, 16th-century Dales village inn has avoided the trend to modernise, and retains real charm and character. Expect flagstone floors, hand-pump ales, roaring winter fires, low ceilings and exposed beams. Dine in the elegant restaurant, or more casually in the oak-panelled bar. The cooking is straightforward and bold from a committed kitchen. Using fresh, local ingredients, Queenie scallops with gruyère cheese and breadcrumbs, Wharfedale fillet of beef with asparagus and hollandaise, and tangy lemon tart with lemon sorbet are fine examples of the fare.

Chef James Rowley, Olivier Verot, Charles Brown **Owner** Andrew & Elizabeth Grayshon **Times** 12-2.30/6-9.30 **Prices** Starter £4.25-£8.50, Main £13.50-£19.25, Dessert £5.50-£8, Service included **Wines** 26 bottles over £20, 56 bottles under £20, 12 by glass **Notes** Sunday L, Vegetarian available, Civ Wed 125 **Seats** 50, Pr/dining room 90 **Children** Portions, Menu **Parking** 70

CRATHORNE   Map 19 NZ40

Crathorne Hall Hotel

@@ British 🍷

Edwardian country house with impressive cuisine

☎ 01642 700398
TS15 0AR
e-mail: crathornehall@handpicked.co.uk
dir: Off A19, 2m E of Yarm. Access to A19 via A66 or A1, Thirsk

Savour the stunning period elegance of Crathorne Hall, a magnificent Edwardian property set in 15 acres of landscaped grounds with views of the Leven Valley and the Cleveland Hills. Wood panelling, an impressive carved stone fireplace, ornate ceilings and imposing oil paintings are just some of the original features in the formal Leven Restaurant, forming the period backdrop for white-linen dressed tables, darkwood leather chairs and stunning views. The formal service is appropriately skilled and professional but friendly. Impressive British cooking - underpinned by classical roots - is characterised by interesting combinations with the emphasis on high quality local and seasonal ingredients and accomplished simplicity. Grand reserve blade of beef served with roasted foie gras and pumpkin mash, and Yorkshire curd tart accompanied by elderflower ice cream and sloe gin jelly show the style.

Chef James Cooper **Owner** Hand Picked Hotels **Times** 12.30-2.30/7-9.30 **Prices** Fixed D 3 course fr £35,

---

The Burlington Restaurant

Rosettes not confirmed at time of going to press

BOLTON ABBEY   Map 19 SE05

Modern French 🖥 V 🍷

Quietly located hotel with a strong local reputation

☎ 01756 718111 & 710441
The Devonshire Arms, Country House Hotel & Spa BD23 6AJ
e-mail: res@devonshirehotels.co.uk
web: www.devonshirehotels.co.uk
dir: On B6160 to Bolton Abbey, 250 yds N of junct with A59 rdbt junct

Set on the Duke and Duchess of Devonshire's 30,000-acre Bolton Abbey Estate, this classic country-house hotel has stunning views of the delightful Wharfedale countryside. Originally a 17th-century coaching inn, it oozes the atmosphere of a private country mansion - think wellies and fishing rods by the door, open winter fires, sumptuous lounges, antique furniture and large Devonshire family oil paintings. The fine-dining Burlington Restaurant continues the theme, with its refined, traditional edge, where large, highly-polished antique tables come appropriately set with the finest table appointments and service is professional but friendly. The dining room spreads over into the extended conservatory, with its wicker chairs and stone floor and views over the Italian courtyard garden. The highly accomplished kitchen uses top-notch, luxury ingredients and the best available seasonal local produce on an evolving and exciting modern menu. Under the new kitchen team, expect the likes of slow-cooked loin of rabbit with morels, asparagus purée, glazed carrot and quinoa, followed by loin of Lakeland venison with parsnip purée, Alsace bacon and warm black pudding, with warm chocolate fondant with praline anglaise, nougat cone and pistachio ice cream. A truly outstanding wine list is full of top-class producers. At the time of going to press there was a recent change of chef. A new award will be in place once our inspectors have completed their meal assessments at the restaurant.

Chef Stephen Smith **Owner** Duke & Duchess of Devonshire **Times** 12.30-2.30/7-10, Closed Mon, Closed L Tue-Sat **Prices** Fixed L course £35, Fixed D 4 course £58, Tasting menu £68, Service added but optional 12.5% **Wines** 2300 bottles over £20, 30 bottles under £20, 12 by glass **Notes** Sunday L, Vegetarian menu, Civ Wed 90 **Seats** 70, Pr/dining room 90 **Children** Menu **Parking** 100

Starter £8.50–£10.50, Main £18.50–£23.50, Dessert £7–£9.50, Service optional **Wines** 98 bottles over £20, 1 bottles under £20, 18 by glass **Notes** Sunday L, Vegetarian available, Civ Wed 90 **Seats** 45, Pr/dining room 26 **Children** Portions, Menu **Parking** 80

ESCRICK   Map 16 SE64

The Parsonage Country House Hotel

◎ Modern British **V**

Quality service and cooking in a delightful country house

☎ 01904 728111
York Rd YO19 6LF
e-mail: sales@parsonagehotel.co.uk
dir: S from York on A19, Parsonage on right, 4m out of town in Escrick village

A 19th-century former parsonage, the hotel is set in over six acres of beautiful grounds just minutes from the city of York. The elegant fine-dining restaurant has recently been refurbished with bright red high-backed leather chairs and clothed tables set against dark cream walls. The Yorkshire Farmers' menu sets great store by locally grown and produced ingredients. Dishes to satisfy include terrine of foie gras with toasted brioche and plum and apple chutney, pan-roasted saddle of venison with creamed potatoes and juniper jus, and sticky toffee pudding with caramelised ice cream.

Chef Neal Birtwell **Owner** P Smith **Times** 12-2/6.30-9, Closed L Sat **Prices** Fixed L 3 course £15.50–£19.95, Fixed D 3 course £25–£35, Starter £5.95–£8.50, Main £15.50–£22.50, Dessert £5–£8.50, Service included **Wines** 20 bottles over £20, 26 bottles under £20, 10 by glass **Notes** Sunday L, Vegetarian menu, Dress restrictions, No jeans, Civ Wed 120 **Seats** 70, Pr/dining room 40 **Children** Portions **Parking** 80

GRASSINGTON   Map 19 SE06

Gamekeeper's Inn

◎ Modern British

Robust, simple cuisine in leisure park inn

☎ 01756 752434
Long Ashes Park, Threshfield BD23 5PN
e-mail: info@gamekeeperinn.co.uk

This restaurant is situated in a traditional inn in Long Ashes Park, a caravan/leisure park, in the heart of Wharfedale. Originally built as a gamekeeper's cottage

for nearby Netherlands Hall, the inn blends traditional oak beams and wooden floors with a modern-style bar. Its Poacher's restaurant offers an interesting selection of dishes prepared with a robust but gentle and simple approach using local produce. Try twice-baked Swaledale cheddar soufflé with pepper and tomato chutney, followed by roast rack of lamb with braised shoulder, white bean purée, glazed carrots and port jus. Finish with classic egg custard tart with honeyed fig.

Times 5-9.30 (Bar 12-9)

GREAT AYTON   Map 19 NZ51

The Cook's Room

◎◎ Modern British ◎

Confident cuisine at popular, stylish and relaxed village restaurant

☎ 01642 724204
113a High St TS9 6BW
e-mail: thecooksroom@yahoo.co.uk
dir: Take A172 from Middlesbrough signed to Stokesley, take B1292 to Great Ayton

Overlooking the village green and appropriately looking down on the statue of Captain Cook, this popular village restaurant is accessed off the High Street and up a flight of stairs. The décor is modern with splashes of colour coming from artwork, while pale wood, white fittings and paintwork create a relaxed, stylish setting. Expect accomplished, classically-inspired, modern British cooking with international influences. Quality local seasonal produce is prepared with skill and enthusiasm; think seared king scallops with broad bean and pancetta risotto and vanilla sauce, roasted local beef fillet with oxtail ravioli and a Puy lentil and thyme jus, and hot chocolate fondant and tart with milky bar ice cream.

Chef Neal Bullock **Owner** Neal & Fiona Bullock **Times** 12-3/6.30-10, Closed 1st wk Jan, Closed Mon, Closed L Tue-Sat **Prices** Fixed L 2 course £12.95–£19.95, Fixed D 3 course £15.95–£24.95, Service optional **Wines** 4 bottles over £20, 6 bottles under £20, 4 by glass **Notes** Sunday L, Vegetarian available **Seats** 46 **Children** Portions **Parking** On street

---

GUISBOROUGH   Map 19 NZ61

Macdonald Gisborough Hall

◎ Modern British

Well prepared local produce at an elegant Victorian house

☎ 0870 400 8191
Whitby Ln TS1 6PT
e-mail: general.gisboroughhall@macdonald-hotels.co.uk

This Victorian country-house hotel is situated on the edge of the North Yorkshire Moors, close to the historic market town of Guisborough. The building has retained its period charm, and Tockett's dining room has a traditional feel with large windows overlooking the stunning formal

gardens. Service is friendly, and the menus feature classically-based cuisine with a modern slant. Take cream of celeriac soup, followed by beef and foie gras Wellington served with a good red wine jus. Make room for desserts such as sticky toffee pudding served with a thick butterscotch sauce.

Pinchinthorpe Hall

◎ Modern British ◎

Cooking with a punch in a vibrant bistro setting

☎ 01287 630200
Pinchinthorpe TS14 8HG
e-mail: nybrewery@pinchinthorpe.wanadoo.co.uk
web: www.pinchinthorpehall.co.uk
dir: 10m S of Middlesbrough

Located in a spectacular woodland setting, this delightful country-house hotel dates from the 17th century and stands in 3 acres of landscaped gardens, complete with a Victorian vegetable garden and a working farm. The Brewhouse Bistro has its own organic micro brewery and offers unpretentious fare in a rustic setting, complete with flagstone floors, bare brick walls and unclothed timber tables. The Manor restaurant is a more formal affair, offering a daily-changing menu of modern British dishes using organic herbs and vegetables from the kitchen garden. Typical dishes include the likes of Yoadwarth Mill smoked salmon with grilled asparagus spears, or sautéed suprême of pheasant with glazed apple, bacon crisp and elderberry jus, while a dessert of warm chocolate mousse with a liquid chocolate centre and clotted cream might prove a perfect finale.

Chef Jenny Tombs **Owner** George Tinsley, John Warnock & Alison Foster **Times** Noon/9.30 **Prices** Fixed L 2 course £8.95, Fixed D 3 course £17.95, Starter £3.95–£11.95, Main £10.95–£22, Dessert £5.95–£8.95, Service optional **Wines** 20 bottles over £20, 50 bottles under £20, 8 by glass **Notes** Sunday L, Vegetarian available, Dress restrictions, Smart casual, Civ Wed 80 **Seats** 45, Pr/dining room 40 **Children** Portions **Parking** 150

HAROME   Map 19 SE68

The Star Inn

◎◎ Traditional British

Creative cuisine at a popular village inn

☎ 01439 770397
YO62 5JE
e-mail: starinn@bt.openworld.com
dir: From Helmsley take A170 towards Kirkbymoorside, after 0.5m turn right towards Harome. After 1.5m Inn is 1st building on right

The Star, built around the 14th century and a fine example of a cruck-framed longhouse, is a thriving family-run business with high standards of hospitality and excellent cooking. The opening of a shop to sell their dishes as well as local produce perhaps demonstrates their desire not to stand still and how much the pub is part of the community. Full of original features, nooks

Continued

HAROME *Continued*

and crannies, it is possible to eat in the bar or the garden if the dining room is full. The title of chef-owner Andrew Pern's new book, 'Black Pudding and Foie Gras', sums up the cooking style: a mix of humble and fine ingredients, and much importance is placed on using local produce. Expect starters like black pudding and foie gras in a stack with apple and vanilla chutney and a scrumpy reduction, followed by calves' liver with bubble-and-squeak, local Felixkirk beetroot and York ham lardons.

Times 11.30-3/6.30-11, Closed 25 Dec, 2 wks early spring, BHs, Closed Mon, Closed D Sun

---

HARROGATE   **Map 19 SE35**

The Boar's Head Hotel

◉◉   Modern British

Charming British setting and food

☎ 01423 771888
Ripley Castle Estate HG3 3AY
e-mail: reservations@boarsheadripley.co.uk
dir: On A61 (Harrogate/Ripley road). In village centre

A taste of fine British cuisine is on offer at this former coaching inn set in the privately-owned village of Ripley alongside the castle, owned by the current castle occupiers, Sir Thomas and Lady Ingilby. The restaurant is adorned with paintings of past Ingilby ancestors and still life paintings of food. With the ambience of a hunting, shooting and fishing lodge, expect vibrant red walls, comfortable seating and well-drilled staff. The skilful British cuisine with modern French influences concentrates on local produce executed with flair. Expect ballotine of guinea fowl with onion tart and truffle cream, or monkfish poached in red wine with glazed leeks and salsify and vanilla-scented kohlrabi. (The Bistro here is less formal with a simpler menu.)

Times 12-2/7-9

Clocktower

◉◉   Modern British ✿

Elegant, modern hotel with excellent dining to match

☎ 01423 871350
Rudding Park, Follifoot HG3 1JH
e-mail: reservations@ruddingpark.com
web: www.ruddingpark.com
dir: A61 at rdbt with A658 follow signs 'Rudding Park'

Rudding Park House, with its mixture of elegant Regency style and contemporary décor, is the stylish location for the refurbished Clocktower restaurant, situated in the converted stable block in 200-year-old landscaped parkland. A striking French hand-made pink glass chandelier forms the centre piece of the contemporary dining room, which also boasts bare-wood tables with quality settings, modern artwork, hand-painted Brazilian wallpaper, and an adjacent lively bar area. The seasonal menu uses oodles of fresh Yorkshire produce and offers modern British dishes with plenty of creativity. Tuck into a starter of Yorkshire blue cheese spring roll with beetroot and baby spinach salad, and follow with grilled lemon sole fillets served with winter squash, red pepper piperade and sauce gribiche. The conservatory - with its 400-year-old olive tree - offers an informal setting to enjoy excellent Yorkshire tapas. There's a vast alfresco terrace, too.

Chef Stephanie Moon **Owner** Simon Mackaness
Times 12-2.30/7-9.30 **Prices** Fixed L course £25, Fixed D 3 course £25, Starter £5-£9.50, Main £14-£20, Dessert £6.50-£9.50, Service optional **Wines** 69 bottles over £20, 15 bottles under £20, 14 by glass **Notes** Sunday L, Vegetarian available, Civ Wed 180, Air con **Seats** 170, Pr/dining room 240 **Children** Portions, Menu **Parking** 250

Hotel du Vin & Bistro

◉◉   British, Mediterranean **V** ✿

Luxurious surroundings for fine food and wine

☎ 01423 856800
Prospect Place HG1 1LB
e-mail: info.harrogate@hotelduvin.com
dir: From A1 follow signs for Harrogate & town centre. Take 3rd exit on Prince of Wales rdbt (marked town centre). Hotel is 400yds on right

The hotel was created from a row of eight Georgian town houses overlooking the 200-acre common, The Stray. It has operated as a hotel since the 1930s and Hotel du Vin Harrogate offers a luxurious experience. Both food and

wine are very important here, and the bistro menu changes daily and is available throughout the day. Classic dishes are featured, supporting the HdV philosophy of quality food cooked simply, using the freshest of local ingredients. Kick off with seared scallops with celeriac purée, Cox's apple and parsnip crisps, followed by a main course of roast rabbit loin with tagliatelle, broad beans, girolle mushrooms and Pommery mustard and tarragon velouté. In summer you can dine outside in the courtyard.

Chef Tom Van Zeller **Owner** Hotel du Vin Ltd
Times 12-2/6.30-10 **Prices** Fixed L 2 course £15.50, Fixed D 3 course £17.50-£35, Starter £4.95-£11.25, Main £10.50-£24, Dessert £6.75, Service optional, Groups service 10% **Notes** Sunday L, Vegetarian menu, Civ Wed 75 **Seats** 86, Pr/dining room 60 **Children** Portions, Menu **Parking** 33

Orchid Restaurant

◉   Pacific Rim

Authentic Pacific Rim cuisine in stylish setting

☎ 01423 560425
Studley Hotel, 28 Swan Rd HG1 2SE
e-mail: info@orchidrestaurant.co.uk
dir: Telephone for directions

Set within the Studley Hotel, the Orchid Restaurant provides a dynamic and authentic approach to Pacific Rim and Asian cuisine. The décor is contemporary and smart with Asian influences - elegant lacquered tables, rattan bamboo steamers and Asian clay pots. Expect a culinary trip through Asia, the kitchen delivering well-balanced, accurately cooked dishes using high-quality ingredients - some coming direct from Thailand. Start with chicken satay or sweet and sour tiger prawns, followed by fried sea bass fillet covered with a subtle but richly spiced curry, or black-peppered sizzling beef with lemongrass. Sushi and sashimi are served on Tuesdays, and there's a good-value buffet lunch on Sundays.

Chef Kenneth Poon **Owner** Bokmun Chan
Times 12-2/6.30-10 **Prices** Fixed L 2 course £10.95, Fixed D 3 course £19.95-£27.95, Starter £4.50-£8, Main £6.50-£18, Dessert £4.50-£6, Service added but optional 10% **Wines** 13 bottles over £20, 15 bottles under £20, 8 by glass **Notes** Tue D sushi & sashimi, Vegetarian available, Air con **Seats** 72, Pr/dining room 18 **Parking** 18

HELMSLEY   **Map 19 SE68**

Black Swan Hotel

◉◉◉   *– see opposite*

Feversham Arms Hotel & Spa

◉◉ British, French V

Refined dining in a smart and friendly hotel

☎ 01439 770766
1 High St YO62 5AG
e-mail: info@fevershamarmshotel.com
dir: From A1(M) take A168 to Thirsk then A170 for 14 miles to Helmsley

This old coaching inn, formerly owned by the Feversham family, is now a well-established hotel with a new spa and a recently refurbished and extended restaurant, which has its own snug bar. At dinner there is a set-price menu, a carte and a tasting menu offering plenty of choice. Dishes are based on produce from the local landscape; game, shellfish, lamb, beef and farmhouse cheeses are plentiful in the area. You might start with Whitby crab salad with orange segments and hazelnuts, followed by trio of Helmsley lamb with potato dauphinoise and rosemary jus. Innovative desserts include pistachio mousse with prune and cherry flapjack, or poached pear with warm parkin and aniseed ice cream.

Chef Simon Kelly **Owner** Simon Rhatigan
Times 12-2/7-9.30 **Prices** Fixed D 3 course £33, Starter £7.50-£11.50, Main £18-£24, Dessert £7.50-£9, Service optional **Wines** 200 bottles over £20, 22 bottles under £20, 12 by glass **Notes** Tasting menu & afternoon tea available, Sunday L, Vegetarian menu, Dress restrictions, Smart casual, No jeans, no T-shirts, Civ Wed 120 **Seats** 70, Pr/dining room 25 **Children** Portions, Menu **Parking** 50

Stone Trough Inn

◉ Modern British

Satisfying gastro-pub dining amid splendid scenery

☎ 01653 618713
Kirkham Abbey, Whitwell on the Hill YO60 7JS
e-mail: info@stonetroughinn.co.uk
dir: 1.5m off the A64, between York & Malton

This red-roofed, yellow stone country inn occupies a wonderful elevated position close to Kirkham's romantic castle ruins. Log fires, flagstone floors, walls full of bric-à-brac or country-pursuit cartoons and comfortable seating fill the labyrinth of cosy rooms and restaurant at this a popular dining destination. Service is thoughtful and friendly. The hard-working kitchen takes a modern approach producing dishes like pan-fried calves' liver on black pudding mash with crisp pancetta and sage and redcurrant jus, or roast rack of Flaxton lamb with crab apple sauce and mint, with a warm apricot and frangipane tart to finish. Home-made breads, brioches and petits fours bolster the accomplished act.

Times 12-2.15/6.45-9.30, Closed 25 Dec, 2-5 Jan, Closed Mon, Closed L Tue-Sat, Closed D Sun

---

General Tarleton Inn

◉◉ Modern British 🍃

Foodie destination in North Yorkshire countryside

☎ 01423 340284
Boroughbridge Rd, Ferrensby HG5 0PZ
e-mail: gti@generaltarleton.co.uk
dir: A1(M) junct 48 at Boroughbridge, take A6055 to Knaresborough. Continue into Ferrensby inn on right

This tastefully redesigned coaching inn boasts a stylish, contemporary setting with a buzzy atmosphere. This is a destination for food-lovers trying exciting pub dining in the bar brasserie, or enjoying the more formal atmosphere of the dining room restaurant. Original beamed ceilings and rustic walls are accompanied by modern black-and-white still life pictures to create an inviting and intimate atmosphere. Brasserie-style menus *Continued*

Black Swan Hotel

Modern British

Charming country-house hotel with first-class food

☎ 01439 770466
Market Place YO62 5BJ
e-mail: enquiries@blackswan-helmsley.co.uk
web: www.blackswan-helmsley.co.uk
dir: A170 towards Scarborough, on entering Helmsley hotel at end of Market Place, just off mini-rdbt

People have been visiting this charming, creeper-clad historic hotel - whose building dates back to the 14th century - for some 200 years, and it has become a local landmark that dominates the Market Place. And, while its refurbished Rutland Restaurant is sympathetic to the building's traditional charms, it delivers a more up-to-date edge with its contemporary colours and fabrics.

There's a series of lounges offering comfortable seating pre- and post-meal plus views over the pretty rear walled garden, and there's a new champagne bar planned too. The kitchen under Andrew Burton shows real pedigree and a modern touch, with the emphasis on using fresh, high quality locally-sourced seasonal ingredients. Tempting combinations (classic dishes with modern twists), precision and clarity of flavour all shine in intelligently restrained, beautifully presented dishes. Take a daube of beef with bubble-and-squeak, Savoy cabbage and bourguignon garnish, or wild sea bass with shellfish and crab bubbles, while to finish, perhaps a chocolate orange fondant served with Grand Marnier parfait and cardamom brûlée. Service is slick and attentive, but also with a friendly, relaxed face. There's also an all-day tearoom and pâtisserie serving teas from around the world. (The Black Swan is sister to the town's Feversham Arms Hotel & Spa - see entry.)

Chef Andrew Burton **Owner** Simon Rhatigan
Times 12.30-2.30/7-9.15, Closed L Mon-Sat **Prices** Fixed L course £25, Fixed D 3 course fr £30, Tasting menu £55, Starter £9-£10.95, Main £19.50-£22.50, Dessert £8.50 **Wines** 169 bottles over £20, 9 bottles under £20, 19 by glass **Notes** Tasting menu 7 courses, Sunday L, Vegetarian available, Dress restrictions, Smart casual, Civ Wed 100 **Seats** 85, Pr/dining room 30 **Children** Portions, Menu **Parking** 40

KNARESBOROUGH *Continued*

and daily specials offer the best of local and seasonal produce, delivering honest modern British dishes. Nidderdale oak-roast hot smoked salmon with fennel and pear salad, tapenade and Bloody Mary dressing might be followed by pan-roast breast of Goosnargh cornfed duckling with fondant potato, braised red cabbage, port and thyme jus. If you have room, try trio of rhubarb - brûlée, crumble and compôte - for dessert.

Chef John Topham **Owner** John & Claire Topham **Times** 12-1.45/6-9.15, Closed L Mon-Sat, Closed D Sun **Prices** Fixed L course £22.95, Starter £4.95-£9.95, Main £9.50-£17.95, Dessert £5.25-£6.75, Service optional, Groups min 6 service 10% **Wines** 70 bottles over £20, 29 bottles under £20, 15 by glass **Notes** Sunday L, Vegetarian available, Dress restrictions, Smart casual **Seats** 64, Pr/dining room 36 **Children** Portions, Menu **Parking** 40

MARTON   Map 19 SE78

The Appletree

◉ Modern British 🍃

Quality food in cosy, country gastro-pub

☎ 01751 431457
YO62 6RD
e-mail: info@appletreeinn@virgin.net
dir: 2m from Kirkbymoorside on A170 towards Pickering, turn right to Marton

The Appletree was once a working farm and became a pub when the farmer's wife first started serving beer to workers in earthernware jugs in the front room. Now an inviting and friendly restaurant, its freshly-painted warm red walls, ubiquitous candles and roaring fire create a cosy ambience for diners whose well-spaced tables, tucked away in private nooks and window alcoves throughout the ground floor, create a peaceful haven. The daily-changing menu takes in some specials, offering simple and unfussy modern British dishes with some unusual flavour combinations and good use of local seasonal produce, particularly meat and game in season. Start with Whitby crab cheesecake with tomato salsa and parmesan crisp perhaps, before moving on to Wintringham pheasant breast, with chestnuts and bacon in a rich red wine sauce.

Chef TJ Drew **Owner** TJ & Melanie Drew **Times** 12-2/6-9.30, Closed Xmas, 2 weeks Jan, Closed

---

Mon-Tue **Prices** Starter £4-£8, Main £8-£17, Dessert £3-£7.50, Service optional **Wines** 68 bottles over £20, 56 bottles under £20, 17 by glass **Notes** Booking essential, Vegetarian available **Seats** 24, Pr/dining room 8 **Children** Portions **Parking** 18

MASHAM   Map 19 SE28

Samuel's at Swinton Park

◉◉◉ – *see below*

Vennell's

◉◉ Modern British

Accomplished modern cooking in local village restaurant

☎ 01765 689000
7 Silver St HG4 4DX
e-mail: info@vennellsrestaurant.co.uk
dir: 8m from A1 Masham exit

The décor in this Grade II listed, shop-front style restaurant, which overlooks the main street through the village, is traditional and comes in muted shades of beige, while plenty of artwork adorns the walls. There's a snug-style lounge downstairs to peruse the sensibly concise, appealing, classically-inspired menus and, while wife Laura runs front of house with relaxed informality, chef-patron Jon (who worked for many years at Haley's

---

Samuel's at Swinton Park

MASHAM   Map 19 SE28

Modern British 🍃

Elegant and atmospheric luxury castle hotel

☎ 01765 680900
HG4 4JH
e-mail: enquiries@swintonpark.com
dir: A1 take B6267, from Masham follow brown signs for Swinton Park

Swinton Park has been a family home since the late 1800s, although the earliest part of the castle dates from the late 1600s. Though extended during the Victorian and Edwardian eras, the original part of this castle hotel comes complete with turrets, gatehouse, sweeping drive and a 200-acre estate. Everything about Swinton Park oozes elegance; beautiful day rooms, huge windows, high ceilings, heavy drapes, antiques and portraits, and swish

sofas. There's a real sense of grandeur, and Samuel's restaurant doesn't disappoint, with its ornate gold-leaf ceiling, chandeliers, comfortable seating, crisp white linen, impeccable service and sweeping views over lake and parkland. The cooking - underpinned by a classical French theme - draws heavily on fresh produce from the walled kitchen garden and estate, particularly game, herbs and vegetables. Clean, distinct flavours, fine combinations and balance, accuracy, seasonality and luxury all parade on the fixed-price menu repertoire. So expect roast chump of local lamb, kidney with sage and pancetta, corn purée, winter greens and devilled lamb sauce, or vanilla-oil poached organic salmon, crisp potato with apple and roasted beetroot, and to finish, perhaps a hot chocolate fondant served with pistachio biscotti and milk ice cream.

Chef Simon Crannage **Owner** Mr and Mrs Cunliffe-Lister **Times** 12.30-2/7-9.30 **Prices** Fixed L 2 course £19, Fixed D 4 course £42-£52, Service optional **Wines** 120 bottles over £20, 18 bottles under £20, 10 by glass **Notes** Sunday L, Vegetarian available, Civ Wed 100 **Seats** 60, Pr/dining room 20 **Children** Min 8 yrs D, Portions, Menu **Parking** 80

Hotel in Leeds) is at the stove. Quality local ingredients and assured skill are evident throughout the menu; think home-smoked salmon, followed by hare saddle and ravioli with beetroot purée and wild mushrooms. Finish with a trio of passionfruit desserts: a soufflé, sorbet and posset.

Chef Jon Vennell **Owner** Jon & Laura Vennell **Times** 12-2/7.15-9.15, Closed 26-29 Dec, 1-14 Jan, 1 wk Sep, BHs, Closed Mon, Closed L Tue-Thu, Closed D Sun **Prices** Fixed L 2 course fr £16.95, Fixed D 3 course £26.50-£26.95, Service optional **Wines** 54 bottles over £20, 18 bottles under £20, 4 by glass **Notes** Sunday L, Vegetarian available **Seats** 30 **Children** Min 4 yrs, Portions **Parking** On street and in Market Sq

MIDDLESBROUGH   Map 19 NZ41

Thistle Middlesbrough

◉ International

Honest modern European cooking in stylish surroundings

☎ 01642 232000
Fry St TS1 1JH
e-mail: middlesbrough@thistle.co.uk
web: www.thistlehotels.com/middlesbrough

Housed within the centrally-located Thistle Middlesbrough, this stylish restaurant is called Gengis (after Ghenghis Khan) and takes inspiration from this era. Accessed via a café bar, the restaurant combines chunky mock architectural features and clean-lined wooden floors to create an unusual dining venue, while the kitchen delivers straightforward dishes focused on clear flavours and quality ingredients. A starter of mussels with chilli, garlic and lemongrass shows the style, finished with coconut milk and double cream, with perhaps pan-seared sea bass, lemon-crushed potatoes, braised leeks and caviar velouté, with a warm chocolate fudge brownie and marmalade ice cream finale.

Prices Food prices not confirmed for 2009. Please telephone for details.

OLDSTEAD   Map 19 SE57

The Black Swan at Olstead

◉ Modern British ◔

Charming country inn with elegant yet understated restaurant

☎ 01347 868387
YO61 4BL
e-mail: enquiries@blackswanoldstead.co.uk
dir: A1 junct 49, A168, A19 S (or from York A19 N), then Coxwold, Byland Abbey, Oldstead

This 16th-century recently refurbished country inn on the edge of Oldstead is surrounded by rolling countryside with views of the North York Moors. The stone-flagged bar has an open fire, oak 'Mousey' Thompson furnishings and Copper Dragon on tap, while the upstairs restaurant sports a rug-strewn oak floor and antique tables and chairs, and has a fresh, airy feel. Expect British cooking with some modern twists, with the monthly menu and daily specials making good use of local seasonal produce, notably meats from surrounding farms. Carefully presented dishes may take in ham hock terrine with pease pudding, a beautifully cooked confit lamb shoulder with sweet potato purée, and vanilla pannacotta with Yorkshire rhubarb.

Chef Adam Jackson **Owner** The Banks Family **Times** 12-2/6-9, Closed 1 wk Jan, Closed Mon **Prices** Starter £4.25-£7.95, Main £9.95-£19.95, Dessert £4.50-£6.50, Service optional **Wines** 20 bottles over £20, 24 bottles under £20, 12 by glass **Notes** Sunday L, Vegetarian available **Seats** 30, Pr/dining room 20 **Children** Portions, Menu **Parking** 25

PICKERING   Map 19 SE78

Fox & Hounds Country Inn

◉ Modern British ◔

Village pub with interesting menu

☎ 01751 431577
Main St, Sinnington YO62 6SQ
e-mail: foxhoundsinn@easynet.co.uk
web: www.thefoxandhoundsinn.co.uk
dir: In centre of Sinnington, 300 yds off A170 between Pickering & Helmsley

This civilised 18th-century coaching inn nestles in a sleepy village below the North York Moors. Beyond the mellow-stone frontage lies a comfortably modernised interior, including a popular beamed bar and a light and spacious dining room with well-spaced tables, upholstered chairs and oak panelling. Freshly cooked, modern British dishes draw on quality local produce and might include goats' cheese soufflé with honey and walnut chutney and shoulder of lamb, root vegetable and rosemary casserole, or chargrilled rib-eye steak with pepper sauce, and apricot clafoutis, stem ginger and honey ice cream for dessert.

Chef Mark Caffrey **Owner** Mr & Mrs A Stephens **Times** 12-2/6.30-9, Closed 25-26 Dec **Prices** Starter £4.50-£7.75, Main £9.25-£19.95, Dessert £4.50-£5.25, Service optional **Wines** 6 bottles over £20, 26 bottles under £20, 7 by glass **Notes** Sunday L, Vegetarian available, Dress restrictions, Smart casual, No shorts **Seats** 40, Pr/dining room 12 **Children** Menu **Parking** 35

PICKERING *Continued*

The White Swan Inn

British

Welcoming inn with pleasing food

☎ 01751 472288
Market Place YO18 7AA
e-mail: welcome@white-swan.co.uk
web: www.white-swan.co.uk
dir: Just beyond junct of A169/A170 in Pickering, turn right off A170 into Market Pl

Owned and personally run by the Buchanan family for 22 years, the unassuming exterior of this charming 16th-century coaching inn belies its sophisticated and modern interior. A place of great character with flagstone floors, log fires and a cosy, intimate dining room, it was once a refuge for salt smugglers. The classic gastro-pub style cooking features locally-sourced ingredients, including meat produce from The Ginger Pig in Levisham. Dishes include local game terrine with onion chutney, poached monkfish, salmon, mussel, leek and saffron stew, pan-fried haunch of venison with bubble-and-squeak and redcurrant jelly, and poached pear and ginger ice cream.

Chef Darren Clemmit **Owner** The Buchanan Family
Times 12-2/6.45-9 **Prices** Fixed L 2 course £12, Fixed D 3 course fr £25, Starter £4.25-£10.95, Main £11.95-£17.95, Dessert £2.70-£6.95, Service optional **Wines** 80 bottles over £20, 28 bottles under £20, 17 by glass **Notes** Sunday L, Vegetarian available, Civ Wed 50 **Seats** 50, Pr/dining room 18 **Children** Portions, Menu **Parking** 35

Nags Head Country Inn

Modern British

Charming countryside inn with great food, fine wines and real ales

☎ 01845 567 391 & 567570
YO7 4JG
e-mail: reservations@nagsheadpickhill.co.uk

Convenient for the A1, this charming 200-year-old country inn is situated in the centre of the village and offers superb hospitality and an extensive range of food in the country-style bars or the more formal Library Restaurant. Attractive wooden tables and elegant chairs set the scene for some imaginative cooking with some international influences and an emphasis on seafood and

local game. Baked queenie scallops, herb butter and glazed with gruyère cheese and calves' liver with crispy bacon and red wine gravy show the style. Smartly uniformed staff are attentive and friendly.

Prices Food prices not confirmed for 2009. Please telephone for details.

Frenchgate Restaurant & Hotel

Modern British

Restored gentleman's residence with a modern menu

☎ 01748 822087
59-61 Frenchgate DL10 7AE
e-mail: info@thefrenchgate.co.uk
web: www.thefrenchgate.co.uk
dir: Please telephone for details

A stylishly restored, three-storey Georgian townhouse, the Frenchgate Hotel is set in a quiet cobbled street. In the restaurant, contemporary style combines with period features - antique pieces, oak tables, restored floorboards, modern artwork, sophisticated lighting and fine table appointments. The constantly-changing menu draws on as much local produce as possible to offer modern British dishes with a continental twist. Cream of parsnip soup with light curry oil might be followed by roast loin of Yorkshire venison with red onion and chive rösti, celeriac purée, caramelised figs and Pedro Ximénez jus. Finish with iced nougatine parfait, sherry anglaise and fresh raspberries.

Chef John Paul **Owner** David & Luiza Todd
Times 12-2.30/7-10 **Prices** Fixed L 2 course £9-£12, Fixed D 3 course £29-£34, Service optional **Wines** 58 bottles over £20, 36 bottles under £20, 9 by glass **Notes** Sunday L, Vegetarian available, Civ Wed 50 **Seats** 24, Pr/dining room 16 **Children** Min 6 yrs D, Portions **Parking** 12

Beiderbecke's Hotel

Modern British, International

Buzzing atmosphere with jazz music while you eat

☎ 01723 365766
1-3 The Crescent YO11 2PW
e-mail: info@beiderbeckes.com
dir: 200mtrs from rail station

Situated in a beautiful Georgian crescent in the heart of the town, and named after the famous American jazz cornet player, Bix Beiderbecke, this hotel includes the restaurant Marmalade's, offering international cuisine with a modern twist. Red walls set off jazz pictures and there's a stage for the musicians as it hosts live music acts at weekends, including the resident jazz band. Diners can enjoy the lively atmosphere while they choose from an extensive menu and range of daily specials. Typical dishes include fried Atlantic squid with tartare sauce to start, followed by home-made Yorkshire beef and ale pie with duck fat roast potatoes and pease pudding. Desserts might include orange bread-and-butter pudding with Cointreau custard.

Chef Paul Spruce **Owner** Vladimir Kishenin
Times 12-3/6-9.30 **Prices** Fixed D 3 course £19.50, Starter £3.95-£7.95, Main £8.95-£19.50, Dessert £4.25-£4.75, Service included **Wines** 20 bottles over £20, 15 bottles under £20, 15 by glass **Notes** Sunday L, Vegetarian available, Dress restrictions, Smart casual, Air con **Seats** 100, Pr/dining room 20 **Children** Portions, Menu **Parking** 15

Best Western Ox Pasture Hall Country Hotel

British, European

Relaxed, country-house hotel dining with imaginative cuisine

☎ 01723 365295
Lady Edith's Dr, Raincliffe Woods YO12 5TD
e-mail: oxpasturehall@btconnect.com

This charming country-house hotel is stunningly located in the North Riding Forest Park, in 17 acres of landscaped gardens and grounds just a few miles from the coast. Diners can choose between the brasserie or more formal Courtyard Restaurant, which has a welcoming, relaxed atmosphere, complemented by a split-level bar and comfortable lounge. On fine summer days you can also dine or take a drink on the terrace overlooking the gardens and delightful courtyard. Imaginative dishes make the most of seasonal and local produce, as in a starter of fillet of gilt head bream with cauliflower purée, confit tomato and sauce vièrge, followed by a main course of rack of lamb served with dauphinoise potatoes, pea purée and Paloise sauce, with date crème brûlée to finish.

Times 12-2.30/6-9.45

Pepper's Restaurant

◉ Modern British 🎨

Carefully sourced produce served in a welcoming atmosphere

☎ 01723 500642
11 York Place YO11 2NP
e-mail: peppers.restaurant@virgin.net
web: www.peppersrestaurant.co.uk
dir: Please telephone for directions

This impressive late Georgian townhouse with split-level dining and cellar bar area is decked out with spacious wooden tables, brown leather chairs, intimate lighting and contemporary artwork. Service is relaxed and unobtrusive, yet attentive. With a nose-to-tail ethos, British dishes are reinterpreted using classical techniques, taking advantage of the best seasonal produce from the local area and proprietor's own farm. Excellent, freshly baked breads are made on the premises. Starters might include a warm salad of local wood pigeon, hand-made black pudding and crispy Old Spot bacon, while roast loin of Stewardship lamb and pressing of lamb breast with mint and brown barley juices may be on offer as a main course.

Chef Jonothon Smith **Owner** Jonothon & Katherine Smith **Times** 12-2/6-10, Closed 5 days over Xmas, Closed Sun-Mon, Closed L Tue-Wed **Prices** Fixed D 3 course £16, Starter £6-£9.50, Main £14-£22, Dessert £6.50-£7.50,

Service optional **Wines** 10 bottles over £20, 13 bottles under £20, 6 by glass **Notes** Pre-theatre tasting menus available, Vegetarian available **Seats** 45 **Children** Portions, Menu **Parking** On street

---

SUTTON-ON-THE-FOREST   Map 19 SE56

The Blackwell Ox Inn

◉ Modern European 🖥 🎨

Gastro-pub cooking in refurbished village inn

☎ 01347 810328 & 690758
Huby Rd YO61 1DT
e-mail: enquiries@blackwelloxinns.com
dir: A1237 take B1363 to Sutton-on-the-Forest, turn left at T-junct, Inn 50m on right

This 1820s inn, named after a famous Shorthorn Teeswater ox, has been modernised and refurbished to provide a bar, lounge bar and smart restaurant. Based on seasonal local produce, the daily-changing menu offers honest hearty cooking with big rustic flavours, rich stews, steak, chops and bangers with suppliers listed, and a great range of charcuterie, cheeses and old fashioned puddings. Think Wensleydale blue cheese and poached pear tart, followed by roast rack of venison with buttered greens, creamed celeriac and spiced pear, or roast fillet of cod with olive oil mash and gremolata.

Chef Steven Holding **Owner** Blackwell Ox Inns (York) Ltd **Times** 12-2/6-9.30, Closed 25 Dec, 1 Jan, Closed D Sun **Prices** Fixed L 2 course £8.95, Fixed D 3 course £13.95, Tasting menu £38, Starter £3.95-£6.95, Main £8.95-£14.95, Dessert £3.95-£5.95, Service optional **Wines** 36 bottles over £20, 32 bottles under £20, 17 by glass **Notes** Sunday L, Vegetarian available **Seats** 36, Pr/dining room 16 **Children** Portions **Parking** 19

Rose & Crown

◉ Modern British 🖥

Relaxed, country-dining pub

☎ 01347 811333
Main St YO61 1DP
e-mail: ben@rosecrown.co.uk
dir: 8m N of York towards Helmsley on B1363

This dining pub in a village setting midway between York and Helmsley has old world charm with a simple beamed interior, wooden floors and tables and open fires. The warm and cosy décor of the dining room has contemporary features and has been extended into a conservatory. There are African-inspired thatched parasols on the terrace where you can enjoy alfresco dining. Dishes are attractively presented and there is an emphasis on fresh fish and seafood. Perhaps try the crab salad with beetroot pickle and mixed leaf salad, followed by pan-fried fillet of pollack with champ potato, shallot and caper butter.

Chef Adam Jackson, Danny Jackson **Owner** Ben & Lucy Williams **Times** 12-2/6-9.30, Closed 1st wk Jan, Closed Mon, Closed D Sun **Prices** Starter £4.25-£8.95, Main £10.95-£19.95, Dessert £4.95-£7.95, Service optional **Wines** 50 bottles over £20, 20 bottles under £20, 12 by glass **Notes** Vegetarian available **Seats** 80 **Children** Portions **Parking** 12

WEST WITTON — Map 19 SE08

The Wensleydale Heifer

◉ Traditional, International

Great seafood restaurant in the Dales

☎ 01969 622322
DL8 4LS
e-mail: info@wensleydaleheifer.co.uk
dir: On A684 (3m W of Leyburn)

This 17th-century former coaching inn hides a smart, modern seafood restaurant offering two different dining experiences. The fish bar is less formal, with its seagrass flooring, wooden tables and rattan chairs, while the restaurant has a contemporary tone with chocolate leather chairs and linen cloths. The kitchen shows its pedigree via a repertoire awash with the fruits of the sea. Well-sourced, high quality fresh fish and seafood are handled with simplicity and come full of flavour. Take warm salad of chilli salt squid with lime-marinated fennel and French bean salad, roast Whitby cod cordon bleu with tomato fondue, basil pesto and spring onion mash, or fish pie, including salmon, cod, tiger prawns and scallops. (Meat dishes are also available.)

Times 12-2.30/6-9.30
See advert on page 457

WHITBY — Map 19 NZ81

Dunsley Hall

◉ Modern, Traditional

Modern culinary delights in a fine country house

☎ 01947 893437
Dunsley YO21 3TL
e-mail: reception@dunsleyhall.com
dir: 3.5m from Whitby off A171 Teeside road

This delightful mellow-stone Victorian country-house hotel is set amid 4 acres of landscaped gardens on the Whitby coastline. The traditional-style dining room comes complete with original wooden panelling and fireplaces; there's also a separate bar, and the atmosphere is relaxed and friendly. An amuse-bouche and an intermediate course inject an unhurried feel, and the modern menus with French influences are well worth lingering over. An enthusiastic team makes the most of the fine produce harvested locally from the land and sea. A sample menu offers starters like crab and prawn platter with capers, lemon and petit salad, or seared diver picked scallops with pea and lemongrass cream, truffled asparagus and pea shoots, while mains include grilled Whitby crab with fresh tomato fondue, wilted spinach and crayfish tails.

Times 12-2/7.30-9.30

Estbek House

◉ Modern British

Restaurant with rooms by the sea

☎ 01947 893424
East Row, Sandsend YO21 3SU
e-mail: info@estbekhouse.co.uk
web: www.estbekhouse.co.uk
dir: From Whitby follow A174 towards Sandsend, Estbek just before bridge

Once the office for the local mine, this listed Georgian building on the village seafront is now a popular restaurant with rooms. The pretty cobbled courtyard is perfect for alfresco dining in summer; alternatively, dine upstairs in the contemporary restaurant - a chic and romantic room decked out with mirrors, sparkling glassware and high-backed leather chairs. Local fish is the mainstay of the menu, with dishes like Estbek's seafood pie, but there's plenty of other fare to tempt, including Shiraz-glazed steak - local fillet steak with red onions and mushrooms cooked in red wine glaze. The wine list focuses on speciality Australian wines.

Chef Tim Lawrence, James Nelson **Owner** D Cross, T Lawrence **Prices** Starter £6.95-£8.95, Main £15.95-£28.95, Dessert £5.95, Service optional **Wines** 91 bottles over £20, 15 bottles under £20, 10 by glass **Notes** Tasting menu available, Vegetarian available **Seats** 36, Pr/dining room 16 **Children** Min 14 yrs **Parking** 6
See advert below

The White Horse & Griffin

⊛ Modern, Traditional European

Bistro fare in historic coaching inn

☎ 01947 825026 & 604857
Church St YO22 4BH
e-mail: info@whitehorseandgriffin.co.uk

Dating from the 17th century, this former coaching inn retains many original features. There are three dining areas, each with a different mood, and the kitchen delivers crowd-pleasing bistro cooking using locally-sourced meat and fish direct from the boats. Good quality breads are freshly made daily, alongside dishes such as seafood medley on a stick with rocket and wasabi mayo, or pot-roast pheasant with cider, creamed cabbage and good old-fashioned mashed potato. A fun dessert for two or more diners is Swiss chocolate fondue with exotic fruits.

Times 12-3/5-9, Closed D 25 Dec

YARM   Map 19 NZ41

Judges Country House Hotel

⊛⊛⊛ – *see below*

YORK   Map 16 SE65

Best Western York Pavilion Hotel

⊛ Modern European

Relaxed, brasserie-style dining in Georgian surroundings

☎ 01904 622099
45 Main St, Fulford YO10 4PJ
e-mail: reservations@yorkpavilionhotel.com
dir: S from city centre on A19 (Selby), hotel 2m on left. On A1 from N or S take A64 to York, then take Selby/York city centre A19 junct

The elegant Pavilion is a Grade II listed Georgian property set in its own grounds just over a mile from the city walls. The hotel's Langton Brasserie is true to its name with floorboards, polished wood tables and lots of pictures, and candlelit in the evenings. It's light and airy, too, thanks to high ceilings and large garden windows. A seasonal carte and a weekly fixed-price menu offer dishes such as caramelised duck breast on sweet potato and pumpkin seed rösti with redcurrant jus, medallions of beef with wild mushrooms, and fresh lemon tart with ice cream and candied citrus fruits.

Chef Paul Sellers **Owner** Irene & Andrew Cossins
Times 12-1.45/6.30-9.30 **Prices** Food prices not confirmed for 2009. Please telephone for details.
Wines 25 bottles over £20, 20 bottles under £20, 11 by glass **Notes** Civ Wed 90 **Seats** 60, Pr/dining room 150
Children Portions, Menu **Parking** 50

Blue Bicycle

⊛ Modern European 💻

Popular bistro-style city-centre restaurant

☎ 01904 673990
34 Fossgate YO1 9TA
e-mail: info@thebluebicycle.com
web: www.thebluebicycle.com
dir: Located in centre of York, just off Parliament St

A buzzy city-centre eatery with a big personality, the Blue Bicycle is one of York's most talked about restaurants. You'll easily spot the namesake blue bicycle propped up outside the bright shop-front style window. Deep colours, subtle lighting and secluded corners set the scene in the two-floored restaurant. The kitchen brings creative touches to popular dishes, delivering a wide-ranging modern European menu with an emphasis on local ingredients, including fish and game in season. You

Continued

Judges Country House Hotel

YARM   Map 19 NZ41

Modern British

Delightful conservatory restaurant offering bold, accomplished cooking

☎ 01642 789000
Kirklevington TS15 9LW
e-mail: enquiries@judgeshotel.co.uk
dir: 1.5m from junct W A19, take A67 towards Kirklevington, hotel 1.5m on left

Built in 1881 as a rural retreat for a prominent family in the north east, the house was later used as a residence for circuit judges, hence its current name. The 42 acres of landscaped grounds provide a truly peaceful environment, and it's easy to imagine those judges were sorry to see it become a sumptuous country-house hotel. Their loss is our gain. Traditionally and elegantly furnished, the house is the setting for some bold and imaginative cooking in the conservatory restaurant. The fixed-price carte (with supplements) is based around classical French cooking but demonstrates an eye for innovation and presentation. Mosaic of guinea fowl and foie gras comes with pickled mouli and figs in a starter, while main-course fillet of locally reared beef is partnered with ox cheek, wild mushroom cannelloni and bordelaise sauce. Finish with lemongrass and cardamom soup with plum compôte and chilli sorbet. The genuinely friendly and professional service helps make for a memorable experience all round.

Chef John Schwarz **Owner** Mr M Downs
Times 12-2/7-9.30 **Prices** Fixed L 2 course £14.95, Fixed D 3 course £44-£58, Service optional **Wines** 117 bottles over £20, 45 bottles under £20, 12 by glass **Notes** Sunday L, Vegetarian available, Dress restrictions, Jacket & tie preferred, No jeans, Smart dress, Civ Wed 200 **Seats** 60, Pr/dining room 50 **Children** Portions, Menu **Parking** 110

YORK *Continued*

might start with smoked haddock and mushy pea cakes with tartare sauce, and then move on to fillet of Yorkshire beef with fondant potato, beetroot purée, red wine jus and a horseradish crisp.

Blue Bicycle

Chef Simon Hirst **Owner** Lawrence Anthony Stephenson **Times** 12-2.30/6-9.30, Closed 24-26 Dec, 1-11 Jan, Closed L 31 Dec, 12 Jan **Prices** Starter £6.75-£9.75, Main £14.75-£19.75, Dessert £5.50-£9.75, Service added but optional 10% **Wines** 50 bottles over £20, 31 bottles under £20, 20 by glass **Notes** Vegetarian available **Seats** 83, Pr/dining room **Parking** On street & NCP

D.C.H

◎◎ Modern British 🖥 🍃

Fine dining with great views of York Minster

☎ 01904 625082
Best Western Dean Court Hotel, Duncombe Place YO1 7EF
e-mail: sales@deancourt-york.co.uk
web: www.deancourt-york.co.uk
dir: City centre, directly opposite York Minster

Overlooking York Minster, this smart hotel was originally built to house the clergy. It has been sensitively refurbished in an elegant, contemporary style and offers two dining options - the popular D.C.H. restaurant for fine dining and the café-bistro, The Court. The former offers a fairly extensive menu with a wonderful array of modern British favourites cooked expertly - king scallop ceviche with pink grapefruit and watercress salad or seared pigeon breast with horseradish quinoa and caramelised apple to start, for example, followed by rib of beef with potato purée and morel and port jus or grilled brill with braised leeks and hollandaise sauce. Finish with a classic bread-and-butter pudding with crème anglaise.

D.C.H.

Owner Mr B A Cleminson **Times** 12.30-2/7-9.30, Closed L 31 Dec, Closed D 25 Dec **Prices** Fixed L 2 course £13-£15, Starter £5.75-£7.65, Main £13-£19.50, Dessert £5.75-£6.25 **Wines** 79 bottles over £20, 22 bottles under £20, 19 by glass **Notes** Sunday L, Vegetarian available, Civ Wed 50, Air con **Seats** 60, Pr/dining room 40 **Children** Portions, Menu **Parking** Car park nearby belonging to hotel

Hotel du Vin Hotel

◎ European, French

Luxury bistro with exciting food and wine to match

☎ 01904 557350
89 The Mount YO24 1AX
e-mail: info.yorke@hotelduvin.com

Sheer luxury permeates this latest addition to the Hotel du Vin stable. The opulence of the bedrooms is matched by the exciting bistro, which is based on the old French style but with a few contemporary twists. Staff are knowledgeable, especially with recommendations from the impressive wine list, and the slick service is complemented by the food which has a strong classical influence. A starter of seared scallops with black pudding and cauliflower purée could make way for French duck breast with chicory Tatin, a haricot vert and bacon parcel and red wine jus. Finish with a classic crème brulée.

Times 12-2.30/6.30-10.30 **Prices** Food prices not confirmed for 2009. Please telephone for details.

Ivy Brasserie

◎◎ Brasserie classics 🖥

Chic Regency townhouse hotel with bar and brasserie

☎ 01904 644744
The Grange Hotel, 1 Clifton YO30 6AA
e-mail: info@grangehotel.co.uk
dir: A19 York/Thirsk road, approx 400 yds from city centre

Guests and visitors to this smart townhouse hotel in the heart of the city have a choice of two dining venues: the Cellar Bar, a cosy space that is sophisticated yet relaxed, or the Ivy Brasserie, a more formal affair with slate grey walls, black leather chairs and modern art. Both serve a tempting brasserie menu of modern classics, with mains ranging from the straightforward - Yorkshire rib-eye steak with horseradish croquette potato, roast mushroom and tomato - to classier creations, such as roast English partridge with bread sauce and game chips, for example,

or halibut with clam ragout and a Jerusalem artichoke dauphinoise. Rice pudding served with steeped prunes is a typical dessert, or delicious fig fritters with vanilla ice cream.

Ivy Brasserie

Chef James Brown **Owner** Jeremy & Vivien Cassel **Times** 12-2/6-10.30, Closed L Mon-Sat, Closed D Sun **Prices** Fixed L 2 course £12.50, Starter £5.60-£7.50, Main £12.75-£19.50, Dessert £5.25-£7.50, Service optional **Wines** 19 bottles over £20, 24 bottles under £20, 14 by glass **Notes** Sunday L, Vegetarian available, Civ Wed 60 **Seats** 60, Pr/dining room 60 **Children** Portions **Parking** 26

Marmadukes Hotel

◎ Traditional British V 🍃

Stunning views from an elegant restaurant

☎ 0845 460 2020
St Peters Grove, Bootham YO30 6AQ
e-mail: mail@marmadukesworld.com
dir: Please telephone for directions

Located on a quiet road a short walk from York Minster, this elegant Victorian townhouse is a small but stylish hotel with plenty of antiques and a walled Roman garden. The Victorian chop house restaurant, Monty's Grill, serves satisfying Yorkshire cuisine with a choice of British rare breeds such as Longhorn beef, Gloucestershire Old Spot pork and Wensleydale lamb, as well as fresh fish and lobsters landed daily at Whitby. With an emphasis on freshness and simplicity, expect starters such as potted prawns with lemon butter, followed by English Longhorn steak and ale pudding with pan-fried lamb's kidneys and ale gravy, or Gloucestershire Old Spot pork T-bone with apple chutney and cider gravy.

Chef John Griffiths **Owner** De Bretton Hospitality Ltd **Times** 12-2/6-10 **Prices** Starter £4.95-£7.95, Main £11.95-£24.95, Dessert £5.95, Service optional **Notes** Pre-theatre meals available, Sunday L, Vegetarian menu **Seats** 20 **Children** Portions **Parking** 14

Melton's

◉◉ British

Top-notch home cooking in a relaxed setting

☎ 01904 634341
7 Scarcroft Rd YO23 1ND
e-mail: greatfood@meltonsrestaurant.co.uk
web: www.meltonsrestaurant.co.uk
dir: South from centre across Skeldergate Bridge, restaurant opposite Bishopthorpe Road car park

The Victorian terraced frontage conceals a bright and modern dining room with a bustling ambience. A long and narrow room, Melton's walls are covered with mirrors and large murals depicting the chef and his customers going about their business to a backdrop of city scenes. Unclothed tables, polished-wood floors, banquette seating or chairs and friendly service complete the picture. Flavourful modern cooking is the order of the day - expect creative and simply prepared dishes such as local trout and bacon with a red wine sauce and purple broccoli, or confit pork belly with pease pudding and glazed apples. A wide-ranging menu covers all the bases, but Tuesdays see extra vegetarian dishes on offer, while Thursdays bring additional treats for fish lovers.

Chef Michael Hjort, Annie Prescott **Owner** Michael & Lucy Hjort **Times** 12-2/5.30-10, Closed 23 Dec-9 Jan, Closed Sun, Closed L Mon **Prices** Fixed L 2 course £18, Starter £5.90-£9, Main £13.50-£21, Dessert £5.50-£6.90, Service optional **Wines** 62 bottles over £20, 21 bottles under £20, 6 by glass **Notes** Pre-theatre D available, early evening, Vegetarian available, Air con **Seats** 30, Pr/dining room 16 **Children** Portions **Parking** Car park opposite

Middlethorpe Hall & Spa

◉◉ Modern British V 🅰 NOTABLE WINE LIST

Elegant, country-house surroundings with imaginative cuisine

☎ 01904 641241
Bishopthorpe Rd, Middlethorpe YO23 2GB
e-mail: info@middlethorpe.com
dir: A64 exit York West. Follow signs Middlethorpe & racecourse

Dating from the reign of William and Mary, this magnificent red-brick country house sits in 20 acres of beautifully landscaped grounds. Conveniently located adjacent to York racecourse and just a mile and a half outside the city centre, Middlethorpe Hall also offers a luxury health and fitness spa. The elegant, candle-lit, oak-panelled dining room, with its long windows overlooking the gardens, offers an accomplished menu of classical and regional cuisine, using top-quality ingredients. Choose from starters such as poached wood pigeon breast with wild mushroom mousse, lentils, baby onions and a red wine and shallot sauce, perhaps followed by roast Yorkshire fallow deer loin with rösti, pumpkin purée, red cabbage, shallots and a bitter chocolate sauce.

Chef Nicholas Evans **Owner** Historic House Hotels Ltd **Times** 12.30-2/7-9.45 **Wines** 221 bottles over £20, 17 bottles under £20, 9 by glass **Notes** Gourmet 6 course menu £55, Sunday L, Vegetarian menu, Dress restrictions, Smart, no trainers, tracksuits or shorts, Civ Wed 56 **Seats** 60, Pr/dining room 56 **Children** Min 6 yrs **Parking** 70

One 19 The Mount

◉ British

Quality cooking in a popular hotel

☎ 01904 619444
Mount Royale, The Mount YO24 1GU
dir: W on B1036, towards racecourse

Its position in a hotel close to the town centre makes this an ideal dining venue for tourists, locals and business people alike. Delightful gardens overlooked by a bright, modern restaurant and separate bar have their own appeal, while beauty treatments, swimming pool, sauna and hot tub are attractions for residents. The menu offers a good balance with daily specials and vegetarian choices, and the modern cooking is based on sound ingredients and good technical skills. Expect the likes of

sautéed king scallops or Thai fishcakes to start, with mains such as sea bass provençale or succulent rack of lamb.

Times 12-2.30/6-9.30, Closed 1-6 Jan, Closed Sun

The Lime House

🖳

☎ 01904 632734
55 Goodramgate YO1 7LS
web: http://www.theaa.com/travel/index.jsp

Excellent food and wine, a relaxed and friendly atmosphere and a regularly changing menu with an international flavour. Good vegetarian choices too.

Prices Food prices not confirmed for 2009. Please telephone for details.

YORKSHIRE, SOUTH

CHAPELTOWN   Map 16 SK39

Greenhead House

◉ European

Exciting food of consistent quality in country-style restaurant

☎ 0114 246 9004
84 Burncross Rd S35 1SF
dir: 1m from M1 junct 35

A 300-year-old stone built house with a pretty walled garden set in a Sheffield suburb. Period charm has been preserved inside and you'll find country-style furnishings, a comfortable lounge, oak beams and an open fire. The cooking is equally accurate, stylish and refined, with Mediterranean flair and skill evident throughout the set monthly-changing menu. Fancy presentation is eschewed; this is good, tasty food prepared from quality local produce. Expect a starter of open ravioli with braised pheasant with salmi sauce, wild duck casserole with polenta mixed with gorgonzola cheese for main course, with lemon pannacotta to finish.

Chef Neil Allen **Owner** Mr & Mrs N Allen **Times** 12-1/7-9, Closed Xmas-New Year, 2wks Etr, 2wks Aug, Closed Sun-Tue, Closed L Wed, Thu & Sat **Prices** Fixed L 3 course £10-£22, Fixed D 4 course £39.50-£43.25, Service included **Wines** 30 bottles over £20, 15 bottles under £20, 7 by glass **Notes** Vegetarian available **Seats** 32 **Children** Min 7 yrs, Portions **Parking** 10

ROSSINGTON
Map 16 SK69

Best Western Premier Mount Pleasant Hotel

🎕 Modern British

Country-house hotel with a tempting menu

☎ 01302 868696 & 868219
Great North Rd, Rossington DN11 0HW
e-mail: reception@mountpleasant.co.uk
dir: Located S of Doncaster, adjacent to Robin Hood Airport, on A638 between Bawtry and Doncaster

This charming 18th-century country-house hotel is set in 100 acres of wooded parkland and well-tended gardens. Decorated with tapestries, the elegant restaurant delivers a traditional menu of well-cooked, flavoursome dishes. Begin with ravioli of pigeon with cep butter, move on to a classic beef Wellington, or roast monkfish with herb mousse wrapped in Parma ham, saffron and mussel sauce, and round things off with chocolate and caramel soufflé with blood orange sherbet, or a plate of Yorkshire cheeses served with fruit cake. Steaks, chicken and salmon are available from the grill with a variety of sauces.

Chef Dave Booker **Owner** Richard McIlroy
Times 12-2/6.45-9.30, Closed 25 Dec **Prices** Starter £5.75-£8.25, Main £14.25-£25.95, Dessert fr £6.25, Service optional **Wines** 38 bottles over £20, 15 bottles under £20, 7 by glass **Notes** Sunday L, Vegetarian available, Dress restrictions, Smart casual preferred, Civ Wed 150, Air con **Seats** 72, Pr/dining room 200 **Children** Portions, Menu **Parking** 140

SHEFFIELD
Map 16 SK38

Artisan

🎕🎕 British, European 🕙

Classic, chic Parisian-bistro style

☎ 0114 266 6096
32-34 Sandygate Rd, Crosspool S10 5RY
e-mail: info@artisan.com
dir: Just off A57 Glossop, in Crosspool shopping centre

Richard Smith's one-time Thyme restaurant is now split into two venues. Upstairs, there is the seafood restaurant Catch (see entry), and on the ground floor, there is Artisan, which comes bathed in Parisian bistro-chic. Think darkwood floors, dark brown leather chairs and foodie memorabilia adorning walls, while there's a bar at the front and a semi open-plan kitchen at the rear. The service suits the surroundings, is fittingly friendly, attentive but relaxed like the atmosphere. The kitchen delivers rustic, accomplished dishes where the freshness of local produce is showcased at its best. Expect the likes of pigeon pie with beetroot and game jus or a starter of 'plate of pig' - pork belly, black pudding and ham hock, apple purée, crackling and cider reduction. For mains, try the braised lamb shoulder, served with a chargrilled lamb cutlet, Scotch broth and brown butter mash.

Chef Simon Wild **Owner** Richard & Victoria Smith, Simon

Wild **Times** 12-2.30/6-10, Closed 25-26 Dec, 1 Jan **Prices** Fixed L 2 course fr £12, Fixed D 3 course £18, Starter £5-£9, Main £12-£19, Dessert £6-£9, Service optional **Wines** 60 bottles over £20, 60 bottles under £20, 12 by glass **Notes** Sunday L, Vegetarian available, Air con **Seats** 60 **Children** Portions **Parking** On street

Catch Seafood Café

🎕🎕 Modern, Traditional, Seafood 🕙

Modern, vibrant seafood café

☎ 0114 266 6096
34 Sandygate Rd, Crosspool S10 5RY
e-mail: info@catchofsheffield.com
dir: Just off A57 Glossop, in Crosspool shopping centre

This modern seafood café runs in tandem with the Artisan bistro (see entry) downstairs in this parade of shops on Sandygate. This aptly named eatery has a buzzy, laidback feel. A fish market provides the inspiration for the interior design, with metal-topped tables, white-tiled walls and daily-changing blackboard menus suspended from metal racks by meat hooks. Its kitchen is dedicated to delivering fresh, high quality seafood and has its own in-house fishmonger who buys in daily. Whether you come for a quick snack or a leisurely meal, you'll find bold and accomplished cooking distinguished by influences from around the globe. The daily changing chalkboard menu could feature Old Bay crab cakes with spicy ketchup and lemon oil, or pan-fried plaice with butternut squash tortellini, spinach and sage butter.

Chef Simon Wild **Owner** Richard & Victoria Smith, Simon Wild **Times** 12-2.30/6-10, Closed 25-26 Dec, 1 Jan, Closed Sun **Prices** Fixed L 2 course fr £12, Fixed D 3 course £15, Starter £5-£8, Main £10-£35, Dessert £5-£8, Service optional **Wines** 20 bottles over £20, 20 bottles under £20, 10 by glass **Notes** Vegetarian available, Air con **Seats** 30, Pr/dining room 30 **Children** Portions **Parking** On street

Nonna's Ristorante Bar and Cucina

🎕 Modern Italian 🖥 V 🔖

Friendly, relaxed trattoria with a passion for Italian cooking

☎ 0114 268 6166
535-41 Ecclesall Rd S11 8PR
e-mail: info@nonnas.co.uk
dir: Large red building situated on Ecclesall Rd

Hugely popular trattoria-style restaurant with a lively and informal front bar for a quick espresso or leisurely latte, and a bustling restaurant that draws local foodies in for authentic and enthusiastic Italian cooking. Many of the ingredients come direct from Italy, arriving at the table in classic dishes such as melanzana parmigiana, pasta puttanesca and tiramisu. And there's less familiar fare too, including regional specialities from a different area every week, perhaps red wine baked halibut with braised leeks. Visit the deli and take some of the high-quality ingredients home with you. Look out for the regular wine events.

Nonna's Ristorante Bar and Cucina

Chef Jamie Taylor **Owner** Gian Bohian, Maurizio Mori **Times** 12-3.30/6-9.45, Closed 25 Dec **Prices** Fixed L 2 course £21.95, Fixed D 3 course £24.95, Starter £5.50-£9.95, Main £8.95-£21.50, Dessert £5.75, Service optional, Groups min 6 service 10% **Wines** 90 bottles over £20, 23 bottles under £20, 18 by glass **Notes** Sunday L, Vegetarian menu, Air con **Seats** 75, Pr/dining room 32 **Children** Portions, Menu **Parking** On street

Rafters Restaurant

🎕🎕 Modern European

Popular neighbourhood restaurant in a leafy area

☎ 0114 230 4819
220 Oakbrook Rd, Nethergreen S11 7ED
dir: 5 mins from Eccleshall road, Hunters Bar rdbt

Situated in a well-known and quieter suburb of the city, this popular restaurant is located above a parade of shops. Original rafters echo the restaurant's name, while oak beams and exposed brickwork feature too, along with contemporary soft furnishings and overhanging lighting to create a bright and cosy vibe. The fixed-price menus make good reading and take a fashionably modern approach dotted with influences from around the world. For starters, take a tian of dressed white crabmeat with freshwater crayfish tails, avocado, oriental cress and shellfish oil dressing, or a filo roll of salmon and Japanese seaweed with red pepper mayonnaise and pickled ginger with watercress salad. Baked fillet of Whitby cod with steamed prawn dumplings and shrimp and spring onion butter sauce is a fine main course.

Times Closed 25-26 Dec, 1wk Jan, 2 wks Aug, Closed Sun, Tue, Closed L all week

Staindrop Lodge Hotel

◉ British, European

Art deco-style brasserie in a smart hotel

☎ 0114 284 3111
Lane End, Chapeltown S35 3UH
e-mail: info@staindroplodge.co.uk
dir: Take A629 towards Huddersfield, go straight at first rdbt, at mini rdbt take right fork. Restaurant is 0.5m on the right

This bar, brasserie and hotel occupies an extended and refurbished 200-year-old building on the north side of the city, handy for the M1. The split-level restaurant is in art deco style with lots of glass and a solid floor. The menu reflects influences from around Europe, with dishes such as oxtail terrine with home-made piccalilli, roast monkfish with curried prawns and mussels, and roast loin of English venison haunch with garlic spinach and sautéed potatoes. Desserts include baked egg custard with cider apples. A similar menu is also available in the bar.

Times 12/9.30

Whitley Hall Hotel

◉ Modern British ⊛

Country-house dining using the best of local produce

☎ 0114 245 4444
Elliott Ln, Grenoside S35 8NR
e-mail: reservations@whitleyhall.com
dir: Please telephone for directions

This 16th-century ivy-clad country-house hotel stands in 20 acres of landscaped grounds with lakes and immaculate gardens. Expect high levels of comfort and a modern approach to traditional and contemporary dishes from an enthusiastic young kitchen team who are passionate about local produce. Imaginative and flavoursome dishes are served in the oak-panelled restaurant and might include Isle of Shuna mussels with sauce vièrge, followed by braised shoulder of lamb with sticky mint jus, or whiting in tempura batter with pea purée. Desserts may take in Yorkshire curd tart with orange and whisky marmalade.

Prices Fixed L 2 course £13.95, Fixed D 3 course £23.25, Service optional **Wines** 50 bottles over £20, 30 bottles under £20, 14 by glass **Notes** Sunday L, Vegetarian available, Civ Wed 80 **Seats** 80, Pr/dining room 16 **Children** Portions **Parking** 80

Montagu's at the Wortley Arms

◉◉ Modern British ⊛

Intimate restaurant serving imaginative modern fare

☎ 0114 288 8749
Halifax Rd S35 7DB
e-mail: thewortleyarms@aol.com
dir: M1 junct 36. Follow Sheffield North signs, right at Tankersley garage, 1m on right

While this renovated traditional village inn on the Wharncliffe Estate serves carefully prepared, informal meals daily (nothing so unusual there), its fine-dining Montagu's restaurant upstairs really ups the ante. Bookings are essential at Montagu's though, as there are just forty covers in this formally set, upmarket affair. The skilful kitchen's modern approach shows flair and innovation, and takes its cue from prime local produce on a fixed-price, three-course menu that includes canapés, amuse bouche, coffee and petits fours. So expect stylishly presented dishes to excite the taste buds, such as pan-fried foie gras served with glazed baby pears and toasted brioche to start, perhaps a Yorkshire Parkin with dandelion and burdock ice cream to finish, and in between, local Round Green Farm venison liver with braised Savoy cabbage, pomme purée and orange and onion marmalade.

Chef Mark Turner **Owner** Andy Gabbitas **Times** Closed Mon, Closed L Tue-Sat, Closed D Sun **Prices** Food prices not confirmed for 2009. Please telephone for details. **Wines** 34 bottles over £20, 19 bottles under £20, 7 by glass **Notes** Sunday L, Dress restrictions, Smart casual, Air con **Seats** 40, Pr/dining room 10 **Children** Portions **Parking** 30

Black Horse Inn Restaurant with Rooms

◉ British, Mediterranean ⊛

Welcoming Yorkshire coastal inn with enjoyable dining

☎ 01484 713862
HD6 4HJ
e-mail: mail@blackhorseclifton.co.uk
dir: M62 junct 25, Brighouse and follow signs

A traditional village inn with a cheerful pub atmosphere and good coastal views. The white linen tablecloths and

---

brown leather chairs, mixing easily with the oak beams and open fires, don't seem out of place in this former Luddite meeting house. Once the refuge of top entertainers on the variety club circuit, Shirley Bassey, Roy Orbison, Lulu and other celebrity guests of the 1960s and 1970s have been replaced by today's guests who come here for traditional dishes with the occasional Mediterranean flourish, such as leek and pea tartlet, or slow-roasted rare breed pork belly, whole grain mustard mash, apple purée, swede fondant and red wine jus. To finish, try the summer pudding with berry coulis.

Chef Darren Marshall **Owner** Andrew & Jane Russell **Times** 12-3/5.30-9.30, Closed 25-26 Dec **Prices** Starter £4.95-£8.50, Main £13.95-£19.95, Dessert £5.50-£6.50, Service optional **Wines** 53 bottles over £20, 50 bottles under £20, 18 by glass **Notes** Sunday L, Dress restrictions, Smart casual, Civ Wed 60 **Seats** 80, Pr/dining room 60 **Children** Portions, Menu **Parking** 60

See advert on page 464

Healds Hall Hotel

◉ Modern British ⊛

Charming 18th-century family-run hotel with bistro and restaurant

☎ 01924 409112
Leeds Rd, Liversedge WF15 6JA
e-mail: enquire@healdshall.co.uk
dir: M1 junct 40, A638, From Dewsbury take the A652 (signed Bradford). Turn left at A62 and then 50 yds on right

Formerly a mill owner's residence, this attractive stone-built country house dates from 1765 and has strong associations with the Brontë family. There's a lively bistro and cosy bar, but the fine-dining Harringtons Restaurant is at the heart of the establishment. A strong focus on quality local produce is evident in dishes such as slow-roast belly of locally farmed pork with caramelised apple, or roast best end of Bolton Abbey estate lamb with a little shepherd's pie of lamb neck. Alternatively, try pan-fried skate wing with capers, lemon, brown butter and shrimps. Daily specials, a good range of Yorkshire cheeses and polite, friendly service complete the package.

Chef Phillip McVeagh, David Winter **Owner** Mr N B & Mrs T Harrington **Times** 12-2/6-10, Closed 1 Jan, BHs, Closed L Sat, Closed D Sun (ex residents) **Prices** Fixed L 2 course £8.50, Fixed D 3 course £16.95, Starter £3.95-£7.95, Main £8.95-£21, Dessert £5.25-£5.50, Service optional **Wines** 21 bottles over £20, 31 bottles under £20, 8 by glass **Notes** Sunday L, Vegetarian available, Civ Wed 100, Air con **Seats** 46, Pr/dining room 30 **Children** Portions **Parking** 90

"The Black Horse Inn, once a coaching inn, now a self-styled restaurant with rooms, offers a rare level of old-style hospitality. It all adds up to professionalism with a human face."

Robert Cockroft, Yorkshire Post.

The Black Horse Inn, Coalpit Lane, Clifton – Brighouse, West Yorkshire, HD6 4HJ

Telephone: 01484 713862   Fax: 01484 400582

Website: www.blackhorseclifton.co.uk

Email: mail@blackhorseclifton.co.uk

Restaurant

Our award winning restaurant recently achieved 'Yorkshire Post Dining Pub of the Year' and was accredited as highly commended by Yorkshire Life in their category – 'Yorkshire Dining Pub of the Year'.

Fresh food sourced locally and a team of classically trained chefs combine to create a menu of style and flair whilst not ignoring some traditional Yorkshire dishes.

To compliment our menus we have a personally selected wine list with more than 100 bins to choose from. Some of these wines are imported directly from the vineyard to our door.

Rooms

Our 21 individually designed rooms are located in sympathetically restored 16th century cottages. Whilst they do have all the warmth and modern facilities expected of today's busy traveller, they retain their original charm and character.

Special Occasions

At The Black Horse Inn we have a number of options for private dining depending on the size of your party. For that special celebration – birthday – anniversary you may wish to hire our Wellington Suite – a self contained function suite which opens on to a beautiful courtyard setting. We have many years experience providing weddings, and are licensed for civil ceremonies and partnerships.

Conference Facilities

In response to the age of remote working, The Black Horse Inn caters for all types of conferences, meetings, seminars and interview rooms.

Our location – ½ mile off junction 25, M62 provides access to the major motorway networks. We have all the modern facilities expected of today's corporate world including wireless internet access.

HALIFAX
Map 19 SE02

Holdsworth House Hotel

◉◉ Modern British ◉

Delightful 17th-century manor-house dining

☎ 01422 240024
Holdsworth HX2 9TG
e-mail: info@holdsworthhouse.co.uk
dir: From Halifax take A629 (Keighley), 2m turn right at garage to Holmfield, hotel 1.5m on right

Set in beautifully-tended gardens, this magnificent Jacobean manor house comes complete with exposed beams, oil paintings and real fires. The stone cross of St John, above the central gable of the house, is also of particular interest. The restaurant consists of three appropriately-named adjoining rooms - the oak-panelled Panel Room, the Mullion Room with leaded windows, and the informal Stone Room. The kitchen caters for both business guests and those celebrating special occasions, with dishes such as walnut-crusted hake fillet with parsnip purée, herb mash and roasted cherry vine tomatoes, or pan-fried breast of corn-fed chicken with goat's cheese and confit garlic, sweet potato purée and cumin-scented Savoy cabbage, and irresistible desserts like lemon and raspberry mousse layered with tuile and white chocolate.

Chef Gary Saunders **Owner** Gail Moss, Kim Wynn **Times** 12-2/7-9.30, Closed Xmas (open 25-26 Dec L only), Closed Sun, Closed L Sat **Prices** Fixed L 2 course £13.95, Fixed D 3 course £16.95, Starter £5-£8.50, Main £14.95-£22, Dessert £6-£11.25, Service optional, Groups min 10 service 10% **Wines** 40 bottles over £20, 32 bottles under £20, 13 by glass **Notes** Vegetarian available, Dress restrictions, Smart casual, No shorts, Civ Wed 120 **Seats** 45, Pr/dining room 120 **Children** Portions **Parking** 60

The Old Bore at Rishworth

◉ British ◉

Traditional coaching inn with a growing reputation for fine food

☎ 01422 822291
Oldham Rd, Rishworth HX6 4QU
e-mail: chefhessel@aol.com
dir: M62 junct 22 take A672 towards Halifax, 3m on left after reservoir

This converted 200-year-old coaching inn stands in the pretty Pennine countryside. The traditional décor comes replete with flagstone floors, stuffed animals and antler chandeliers, while in the restaurant area there's a more formal tone, with oak floors, exposed wooden beams, antique or high-backed leather chairs, candlelight and white linen - in the style of a shooting lodge. The well-conceived menu delivers a modern cooking style with a nod to seafood, fish and game, while quality ingredients are sourced from a strong network of local suppliers. Typically, tuck into steamed rabbit, ham and cider brandy pudding with wild mushrooms and celeriac purée, or wild halibut with roast prawn and lemongrass cream.

Chef Scott Hessel **Owner** Scott Hessel **Times** 12-2.15/6-9.30, Closed 2 wks in Jan, Closed Mon-Tue **Prices** Fixed L 2 course £10, Starter £6.50-£9.95, Main £12.95-£19.95, Dessert £4.95-£6, Service optional **Notes** Sunday L **Seats** 80, Pr/dining room 20 **Children** Portions **Parking** 20

Shibden Mill Inn

◉ Modern British

Secluded inn with a menu to draw the crowds

☎ 01422 365840
Shibden Mill Fold, Shibden HX3 7UL
e-mail: enquiries@shibdenmillinn.com
web: www.shibdenmillinn.com
dir: A58 turn onto Kell Lane after 0.5m turn left onto Blake Hill, located bottom of Blake Hill on left

Nestling in a fold of Shibden Dale away from the hustle and bustle of Halifax, this sympathetically renovated 17th-century inn has a cosy, friendly bar where you can sample hearty, traditional fare warmed by log fires, and an intimate, fine-dining restaurant in the loft conversion with original oak beams, raftered ceiling and candlelight to complete the mood. In summer, you can also dine alfresco on the riverside terrace. Expect an appealing, crowd-pleasing menu with imaginative modern twists to classic combinations using quality produce. Take chicken liver parfait with port wine jelly and toasted brioche to start, and follow with seared suprême of salmon with sautéed wild mushrooms and spinach, roast new potatoes and red wine jus.

Chef Ian Booth **Owner** Mr S D Heaton **Times** 12-2/6-9.30, Closed 25-26 Dec & 1 Jan **Prices** Fixed L 2 course £10.95, Starter £4.25-£7.25, Main £11.50-£19.95,

HAWORTH
Map 19 SE03

Weavers Restaurant with Rooms

◉ Modern, Traditional British ◉

Friendly family-run eatery with Northern flavours and produce

☎ 01535 643822
15 West Ln BD22 8DU
e-mail: weaversinhaworth@aol.com
web: www.weaversmallhotel.co.uk
dir: From A629 take B6142 towards Haworth, follow signs for Brontë Parsonage Museum, use museum car park

Set on the cobbled main street, this family-run restaurant is converted from 18th-century weavers' cottages. Inside, an eclectic collection of mismatched furniture contributes to the relaxed and informal atmosphere. The menu mixes creative new ideas with popular traditional and regional dishes. Using produce sourced from excellent local suppliers, typical options include pan-seared scallops with yellow split pea purée, Yorkshire pancetta with balsamic reduction, followed by pan-fried breast of local chicken with sweetcorn potato cake, banana fritter, crisp-fried pancetta and fruit chutney sauce, and apple and Wensleydale filo basket with fruitcake ice cream for dessert. Service is provided by young, friendly staff.

Chef Colin & Jane Rushworth **Owner** Colin & Jane Rushworth and family **Times** 11.30-2.30/6.30-9.30, Closed 10 days Xmas/New Year, Closed Mon, Closed L Tue & Sat, Closed D Sun **Prices** Fixed L 2 course £12.95-£15.95, Fixed D 3 course £16.95, Starter £5-£7.50, Main £12.50-£18.50, Dessert £4.50-£5.50, Service optional, Groups min 6 service 10% **Wines** 8 bottles over £20, 56 bottles under £20, 8 by glass **Notes** Sunday L, Vegetarian available, Dress restrictions, Clean & tidy, Air con **Seats** 65, Pr/dining room 14 **Children** Portions **Parking** Brontë Museum car park (free 6pm-8am)

HUDDERSFIELD   Map 16 SE11

The Weavers Shed Restaurant with Rooms

◎◎ Modern British ▮ NOTABLE WINE LIST

Enjoyable regional dining with home-grown ingredients

☎ 01484 654284
86-88 Knowl Rd, Golcar HD7 4AN
e-mail: info@weaversshed.co.uk
dir: 3m W of Huddersfield off A62. (Please telephone for further directions)

This converted 18th-century wool mill now has a contemporary style, yet retains plenty of the original features, including stone and bare wood. The comfortable lounge leads on to an atmospheric, barn-style dining room with banquettes and chairs and clothed tables. There's a wonderful kitchen garden to drive the menus, which provides herbs, fruit, vegetables and over 70 varieties of wild edibles. Dishes are cooked in the modern British style and based almost without exception on home-grown and local produce. Expect wild and cultivated mushroom risotto, truffle-cep caramel and pickled mushrooms as a starter, followed by chargrilled pigeon breast, grilled polenta, Medjool dates and game reduction, with perhaps freshly baked Eccles cakes with Kirkham Lancashire cheese to finish. There is an excellent wine list, too.

Chef S Jackson, I McGunnigle, C Sill **Owner** Stephen & Tracy Jackson **Times** 12-2/7-9, Closed 25 Dec-7 Jan,

Closed Sun-Mon, Closed L Sat **Prices** Fixed L 2 course fr £14.95, Starter £7.95-£13.95, Main £16.95-£26.95, Dessert £8.25-£12.50, Service optional **Wines** 56 bottles over £20, 22 bottles under £20, 6 by glass **Notes** Vegetarian available **Seats** 26, Pr/dining room 16 **Parking** 30

ILKLEY   Map 19 SE14

Best Western Rombalds Hotel & Restaurant

◎ Modern International

Modern cuisine in a relaxing atmosphere

☎ 01943 603201
11 West View, Wells Rd LS29 9JG
e-mail: reception@rombalds.demon.co.uk
dir: From Leeds take A65 to Ilkley. At 3rd main lights turn left & follow signs for Ilkley Moor. At junct take right onto Wells Rd, by bank. Hotel 600yds on left

The elegantly furnished hotel is a converted Georgian townhouse in a peaceful terrace on the edge of Ilkley Moor. Delightful day rooms include an attractive restaurant with a relaxed atmosphere. The kitchen is committed to local produce and offers an imaginative choice of modern European dishes. A starter of king prawns, wok-fried with sherry and garlic, is served with a herbed salad, and might be followed with roasted breast of guinea fowl with caramelised orange sauce, warm

spinach and orange salad and wild rice. Finish with white chocolate basket and dark chocolate and rum mousse.

Best Western Rombalds Hotel & Restaurant

Times 12-2/6.30-9, Closed 28 Dec-2 Jan

Box Tree

◎◎◎ – **see below**

Box Tree

ILKLEY   Map 19 SE14

Modern British, French ▱ ▮ NOTABLE WINE LIST

Culinary legend that still delivers

☎ 01943 608484
35-37 Church St LS29 9DR
e-mail: info@theboxtree.co.uk
dir: On A65 from Leeds through Ilkley, main lights approx. 200 yds on left

The old stone farmhouse dates back 300 years and first made its mark as a serious restaurant in 1962. It has had a few owners since then and many chefs have passed through the door, but it maintained a reputation for good food for most of that time. The current incumbents, Simon and Rena Gueller, are clearly respectful of the past while taking the restaurant forward. Box trees - topiary in tubs - mark the entrance

before the recently refurbished upmarket rooms where log fires and gilt-edged mirrors create a tasteful but not over-worked setting. Service is highly professional and, while a touch old school, the atmosphere is friendly and unstuffy. There is a good value prixe fixe at lunch and dinner or choose from the carte. Simon's menus are based around French classical cooking, with the use of first-rate produce evident throughout, and creative flair and precision on show. Risotto of Canadian lobster is combined with braised fennel and fresh tarragon in a well judged first course, and roasted squab pigeon stars in a main course with buttered Savoy cabbage with lardons, étuvée of baby leeks and carrots, fondant potato and sauce chocolat Amer. Vanilla pannacotta is a fine version and comes with a scoop of pink grapefruit sorbet, poached fruits and rhubarb. The wine list has something for everyone and the sommelier is on hand if needed.

Chef Mr S Gueller **Owner** Mrs R Gueller
Times 12-2/7-9.30, Closed 27-31 Dec & 1-5 Jan, Closed Mon, Closed L Tue-Thu, Closed D Sun **Prices** Fixed L 2 course fr £20, Fixed D 3 course fr £30, Starter £9-£16, Main £24-£29, Dessert £9.50-£10, Groups min 8 service 10% **Wines** 256 bottles over £20, 8 bottles under £20, 7 by glass **Notes** Sunday L, Vegetarian available, Dress restrictions, Smart casual, Air con **Seats** 50, Pr/dining room 16 **Children** Min 10 yrs **Parking** NCP

KEIGHLEY Map 19 SE04

The Harlequin Restaurant

◉ Modern British

Cosmopolitan cooking served in style

☎ 01535 633277
139 Keighley Rd, Cowling BD22 0AH
e-mail: enquiry@theharlequin.org.uk
dir: On A6068 in Cowling village, between Crosshills and Colne. 6m from M65

On the edge of the Dales, this stylish restaurant is located in a converted Victorian property built with traditional Yorkshire stone. The smart restaurant has comfortable banquette seating and spacious, well-dressed tables. The menu, which attracts diners from near and far, concentrates on straightforward and enjoyable flavours. Start with goujons of haddock with lemon mayonnaise and baby leaves, followed by mains such as pine nut and spinach risotto with grilled goat's cheese and balsamic vinegar. Desserts are a particular highlight, so leave some room to enjoy the likes of delice of blackcurrant with a shortbread base.

Times 12-3/5.30-11, Closed 4 days at Xmas, BHs, Closed Mon-Tue

LEEDS Map 19 SE23

Anthony's Restaurant

◉◉◉ – **see below**

Brasserie Forty 4

◉◉ British, European 🖥

Buzzing brasserie overlooking the canal

☎ 0113 234 3232
44 The Calls LS2 7EW
e-mail: info@brasserie44.com
web: www.brasserie44.com
dir: From Crown Point Bridge, left past Church, left into High Court Lane. On river

A former grain store situated on the waterfront, this lively brasserie has a balcony overlooking the canal. The stylish décor comes based around a modern colour scheme of cream and terracotta, creating a warm, welcoming, airy feel that - coupled with a fashionable, cosmopolitan menu and informal, friendly service - plays to the gallery and offers appeal for all. Accomplished brasserie standards sit alongside more modish combinations to deliver an appealing nod to the Mediterranean; take classics like pan-fried scallops with cauliflower purée and crispy pancetta and confit leg of duck with dauphinoise potatoes and red wine sauce, to the likes of fillet of sea bass with buttered spinach and Avruga caviar lemon sauce. An interesting wine list complements the upbeat package.

Chef Antoine Quentin **Owner** Steve Ridealgh
Times 12-2/6-10, Closed BHs, Closed Sun **Prices** Fixed D 3 course £19.95, Starter £3.75-£7.50, Main £7.90-£19.50, Dessert £3.75-£5, Service added but optional 10% **Wines** 125 bottles over £20, 35 bottles under £20, 17 by glass **Notes** Fixed D early bird option & incl 1/2 bottle of wine, Vegetarian available, Air con **Seats** 130, Pr/dining room 42 **Children** Portions **Parking** On street, NCP

Brontë Restaurant

◉◉ Modern European

Grand dining room offering classic cuisine

☎ 0113 282 1000
De Vere Oulton Hall, Rothwell Ln, Oulton LS26 8HN
e-mail: oulton.hall@devere-hotels.com
dir: M62 junct 30 signed Rothwell, or M1 junct 44 signed Pontefract

Surrounded by the Yorkshire Dales yet within 15 minutes of the city, this elegant Grade II listed mansion dates back more than 150 years. It has been lovingly restored to combine traditional features with modern comforts and facilities, including an adjacent 27-hole golf course, while the formal gardens have been faithfully returned to their original design. The Brontë restaurant is very impressive with its velvet-clad walls and décor in shades of cream, dark red and claret. A striking central feature

Continued

Anthony's Restaurant

LEEDS Map 19 SE23

Modern European

One of the city's most exciting restaurants

☎ 0113 245 5922
19 Boar Ln LS1 6EA
e-mail: reservations@anthonysrestaurant.co.uk
dir: 500 yds from Leeds Central Station towards The Corn Exchange

Chef Anthony Flinn's bold, modern cuisine sits well with the chic surroundings and both are designed to wow and excite diners at this ambitious and highly praised city restaurant. Stairs lead down from the swish ground-floor bar, with its floor-to-ceiling windows and large, deep leather sofas, to the curved basement dining room. Decorated in clean, modern minimalist lines, its simple colours of cream and chocolate contrast well with modern art and high-quality cutlery and glassware that grace well-spaced tables. Anthony has an impressive pedigree, having trained with John Campbell (of The Vineyard at Stockcross, see entry) and worked at the internationally acclaimed El Bulli restaurant in Spain. The approach is via a compact, crisply-scripted carte, with the kitchen's superbly-presented, light style bursting with flavours and surprise. Think braised pig cheek with garlic squid and sour cream ice cream, or red mullet with pineapple and tarragon jelly and crab sandwich, while a chocolate mousse with peanut ice cream and fennel caramel might head-up dessert offerings. Much effort goes into the amazing tasters and inter-courses that pepper the repertoire, with pre-starters, amuse-bouche, pre-desserts, petits fours and breads all hitting top form. There's also a good-value fixed-price lunch option and a tasting menu (for the whole table) to complete the exciting package.

Chef Anthony Flinn **Owner** Anthony Flinn
Times 12-2/7-9.30, Closed Xmas-New Year, Closed Sun, Mon **Prices** Fixed L 2 course £19.95, Fixed D 3 course £42, Tasting menu £60, Service optional **Wines** 100 bottles over £20, 8 bottles under £20, 6 by glass **Notes** Tasting menu, Air con **Seats** 40 **Children** Portions **Parking** NCP 20 yds

LEEDS *Continued*

light also creates a starlight effect, and mahogany pillars and panels add to the ambience. The skilful English and European cooking is flavour-driven, using fine local ingredients, which might include steaks from the late Queen Mother's estate in the Castle of Mey. Signature dishes and matching wines are recommended at each course. Take a starter of smoked haddock risotto topped with parmesan cheese, or a main course of pot-roasted belly pork with wild mushrooms.

Times 12.30-2/7-10

Malmaison Hotel

◉ Traditional French 🖵 🍷 🌰

French brasserie fare in stylish hotel

☎ 0113 398 1000 & 398 1001
1 Swinegate LS1 4AG
e-mail: leeds@malmaison.com
dir: City centre. 5 mins walk from Leeds railway station. On junct 16 of loop road, Sovereign St & Swinegate

The Leeds offshoot of the chic modern hotel chain is located in an old converted tram company station on Sovereign Quay. It's stylish, intimate and design-led, a fashionable venue with a smart, contemporary interior that features a true brasserie-style dining room with panelling, stone floors, vaulted ceilings, comfortable booths and a relaxed atmosphere. Choose between the carte or the noteworthy 'home grown and local' menu. Uncomplicated but innovative traditional French cooking produces fresh and full flavoured dishes, perhaps pan-fried scallops with chorizo and champ mash, followed by venison Wellington with pickled cabbage, and baked ginger Parkin with braised rhubarb or an excellent plate of cheese to finish.

Chef Peter Conlin **Owner** Malmaison **Times** 12-2.30/6-11, Closed L 26 Dec, Closed D 25 Dec **Prices** Fixed L 2 course £13.50-£16.50, Fixed D 3 course 15.50-£18.50, Starter £4.75-£7.50, Main £9.50-£25, Dessert £5.95-£7.50, Service added but optional 10% **Wines** 90% bottles over £20, 10% bottles under £20, 25 by glass **Notes** Sunday L, Vegetarian available, Air con **Seats** 95, Pr/dining room 12 **Children** Portions **Parking** Criterion Place car park

Simply Heathcotes Leeds

◉ Modern French 🖵

Converted warehouse with a friendly bistro feel

☎ 0113 244 6611
Canal Wharf, Water Ln LS11 5PS
e-mail: leeds@heathcotes.co.uk
dir: 0.5m from M621 junct 3; follow signs to city centre, left into Water Lane, right onto Canal Wharf. On Canal Basin

This trendy brasserie is located in a former warehouse overlooking the Leeds-Liverpool canal. Nowadays the old stone walls and exposed beams are complemented by low-key modern décor with an upstairs bar lounge for reclining and imbibing. The food is contemporary in style with a

bistro feel and plenty of straightforward comfort dishes. Using the best of local produce, the emphasis is still firmly on big, satisfying flavours. Expect hearty servings of crispy duck confit with baby onions, smoked bacon, red wine and balsamic, citrus-seared sea bass with braised fennel, spinach and garlic butter, and desserts like bread-and-butter pudding with compôte of apricots.

Times 12-2.30/6-10, Closed 25-26 Dec, 1-2 Jan, BH Mons

Thorpe Park Hotel & Spa

◉ Modern British

Chic modern dining showcasing local produce

☎ 0113 264 1000
Century Way, Thorpe Park LS15 8ZB
e-mail: thorpepark@shirehotels.com
dir: Telephone for directions

A range of dining options can be found at this modern hotel with its state-of-the-art spa which provides superb treatments. The terrace and courtyard offer all-day casual dining and refreshments while the spacious open-plan restaurant - furnished with lightwood and leather - features a Mediterranean-themed menu, using seasonal ingredients from local suppliers. Try a starter of confit of duck, black pudding and chorizo salad, followed by escalope of veal Milanese with fennel and tomato salad and asparagus. Finish with white chocolate pannacotta with fresh raspberries.

Times 12-2/6.45-9.30, Closed L Sat & Sun

The Olive Branch Restaurant with Rooms

◉ Modern French

Popular roadside inn with accomplished cuisine

☎ 01484 844487
Manchester Rd HD7 6LU
e-mail: mail@olivebranch.uk.com
web: www.olivebranch.uk.com
dir: Located on A62 between Slaithwaite and Marsden

This old roadside coaching inn, situated on the edge of Marsden Moor and surrounded by historic attractions, is a comfortable restaurant with rooms offering a cosy atmosphere and warming log fires in winter. The menu of modern French dishes features the best of seasonal and local ingredients adeptly prepared with imagination and style. The generous choice of options might include starters such as seared diver-caught king scallops with parmesan shavings, white truffle oil and mixed leaf salad, followed by main courses like confit leg of duck with red onion and sultana marmalade and red wine jus. For dessert, perhaps try treacle and lime tart with crème anglaise.

Chef Paul Kewley **Owner** Paul Kewley & John Lister **Times** 12-2/6.30-9.30, Closed 26 Dec, 1st 2 wks Jan, Closed L Mon, Tue, Sat **Prices** Fixed L 2 course £11.95, Fixed D 3 course £18.95-£19.95, Starter £5.50-£9.95,

Main £14-£25, Dessert £6.50-£7.50, Service optional **Wines** 100 bottles over £20, 30 bottles under £20, 16 by glass **Notes** Sunday L, Vegetarian available **Seats** 65, Pr/dining room 40 **Children** Portions **Parking** 20

Chevin Country Park Hotel

◉ Modern European

Scandinavia comes to Yorkshire

☎ 01943 467818
Yorkgate LS21 3NU
e-mail: chevin@crerarhotels.com
dir: Take A658 towards Harrogate. Left at 1st turning towards Carlton, turn 2nd left towards Yorkgate

Conveniently located for both major road links and the airport, this log-built, Finnish-style hotel is peacefully situated in attractive woodland by a lake. Its pine-clad modern restaurant with views of the lake makes an impact with black high-backed chairs and white-clothed tables, and offers an extensive range of dishes with a set price for two or three courses. Kick things off with pea risotto with poached egg and mixed salad, before tucking into breast of Gressingham duck, boulangère potatoes, Savoy cabbage and carrot purée. Finish with vanilla crème brûlée with shortbread fingers.

Chef Debbie Rhodes **Owner** Crerar Hotels **Times** 12-2/6.30-9.15, Closed L Mon, Sat **Prices** Fixed L 2 course fr £16.95, Fixed D 3 course fr £25, Starter £4.95-£9.95, Main £12.95-£24.95, Dessert £4.95-£7.95, Service included **Wines** 19 bottles over £20, 36 bottles under £20, 10 by glass **Notes** Sunday L, Vegetarian available, Dress restrictions, Smart casual minimum, Civ Wed 120 **Seats** 70, Pr/dining room 30 **Children** Portions, Menu **Parking** 100

Wentbridge House Hotel

◉ Modern British ⓥ 🍷 🌰

Classically-influenced cuisine in a country-house setting

☎ 01977 620444
Wentbridge WF8 3JJ
e-mail: info@wentbridgehouse.co.uk
dir: 0.5m off A1, 4m S of M62/A1 junct

Steeped in history, this well established country-house hotel is set in landscaped grounds located just a short drive from the A1 in the picturesque Went Valley. Enjoy a drink by the fire in the bar, and then move through to the restaurant, a traditional, candlelit venue where some dishes are cooked in the dining room adding the element of 'table theatre'. Produce is well sourced on the varied menu of modern British and French dishes and arrives at the table in tempting combinations: try rack of lamb with asparagus, wild mushrooms and white truffle foam perhaps, or lobster thermidor, followed by carpaccio of pear with vanilla-bean ice cream and hot chocolate sauce to finish.

Chef Steve Turner **Owner** Mr G Page **Times** Closed 25 Dec eve, Closed L Mon-Sat, Closed D Sun **Prices** Starter £6.50-£15, Main £18-£30, Dessert £7-£10, Service optional **Wines** 100 bottles over £20, 30 bottles under £20, 10 by glass **Notes** Sunday L, Vegetarian menu, Civ Wed 130 **Seats** 60, Pr/dining room 24 **Children** Portions **Parking** 100

SHIPLEY
Map 19 SE13

Marriott Hollins Hall Hotel & Country Club

🌸 Traditional British

Traditional dining venue with stunning views

☎ 01274 530053
Hollins Hill BD17 7QW
e-mail: mhrs.lbags.frontdesk@marriotthotels.com
dir: From A650 follow signs to Salt Mill. At lights in Shipley take A6038. Hotel 3m on left

Built in 1858, Hollins Hall was constructed in the Elizabethan style and is set in 200 acres of grounds with stunning views over the Pennines. Set in the original drawing room, Heathcliff's Restaurant looks out across the garden; the atmosphere is warm and relaxed, helped along by friendly and attentive staff. The menus deliver a balance of traditional and contemporary culinary styles with international influences. Expect the likes of butternut squash and saffron soup, spiced halibut steak with Chinese wonton broth, or rack of lamb with sweet potato rosti and black cherry jus.

Times 12-2/6.30-9.30, Closed L Sat, Closed D BHs

WAKEFIELD
Map 16 SE32

Brasserie Ninety Nine

🌸 Modern British, European

Bright, fresh brasserie in a business park

☎ 01924 377699
Trinity Business Park WF2 8EF
e-mail: brasserie99@lawsonleisure.com
dir: Please telephone for directions

This sleek modern restaurant is unexpectedly located beyond the security gates of a high-tech business park. Stainless steel and glass are the featured materials for the interior, and there is a fully equipped function suite and conference facilities on site. The carte offers a comprehensive choice of modern European dishes, such as lobster, salmon and tarragon ravioli in its own bisque, available as a starter or main course, and Manor House free-range belly pork with crushed new potatoes and pea purée. Early bird and rapid lunch menus are also available.

Times 12-2.30/5.30-10, Closed 25 Dec, 1 Jan, BHs, Closed Sun, Closed L Sat, Closed D Mon, Tue

WETHERBY
Map 16 SE44

Wood Hall Hotel

🌸🌸 Modern International V 🍷

Classic country house with modern food and décor

☎ 01937 587271
Trip Ln, Linton LS22 4JA
dir: From Wetherby take A661(Harrogate road) N for 0.5m. Left to Sicklinghall/Linton. Cross bridge, left to Linton/Woodhall, right opp Windmill Inn, 1.25m to hotel, (follow brown signs)

As soon as you turn off the main road onto the long sweeping drive that leads to this delightful Georgian manor, you know you're in for a treat. Set on a hillside amid 100 acres of lush parkland, it's at first sight a classic country house, but inside there's a contemporary feel to the décor. The modern theme extends to the food, which is conjured by a kitchen team with no shortage of passion or ambition. Expect high-quality ingredients and dishes designed to impress: red-legged partridge with apple and thyme purée, kalamata olive and radicchio risotto and a red wine and black olive sauce, for example, or fillet of beef with ox cheek ravioli, creamed Savoy, root vegetables and morels.

Chef Darren Curson **Owner** Hand Picked Hotels **Times** 12-2.30/6.30-9.30, Closed L Mon-Sat **Prices** Fixed D 3 course £35, Tasting menu £55, Starter £10-£14.50, Main £17.50-£29.50, Dessert £7.50, Service optional **Wines** 78 bottles over £20, 4 bottles under £20, 21 by glass **Notes** Sunday L, Vegetarian menu, Dress restrictions, Smart casual, no jeans or trainers, Civ Wed 100 **Seats** 32, Pr/dining room 100 **Children** Portions, Menu **Parking** 100

CHANNEL ISLANDS
GUERNSEY

CASTEL
Map 24

La Grande Mare Hotel Golf & Country Club

◎ Modern

Resort hotel restaurant serving accomplished cuisine

☎ 01481 256576
The Coast Rd, Vazon Bay GY5 7LL
e-mail: simon@lagrandemare.com
dir: From airport turn right. 5 mins to reach Coast Rd. Turn right again. Hotel another 5 min drive

Set in 110 acres of private grounds, La Grande Mare is a family-owned and run resort hotel set next to a sandy bay and incorporating a golf course and health suite. With its granite fireplaces, the restaurant has several arches and oak floors, with friendly but professional service. New head chef Chris Sloan has pedigree, his modern approach driven by fresh seasonal produce and a passion for locally-caught fish. Intelligently simple dishes deliver clean flavours and eye-catching presentation; take pan-seared sea bass served with saffron risotto and red wine fumet, perhaps seared local scallops with Lyonnaise potatoes and a tomato and pesto dressing, or roast rack of lamb served with wilted spinach, pomme purée and tarragon jus.

Times 12-2/7-9.30

COBO
Map 24

Cobo Bay Restaurant

◎ European, International

Great views of the bay from this popular restaurant

☎ 01481 257102
GY5 7HB
e-mail: reservations@cobobayhotel.com
dir: From St Peter Port follow signs for Castel/Cobo/West Coast. At coast road turn right, hotel 100m on right

As the name suggests, this popular seaside holiday destination is situated on the seafront, overlooking a picture-postcard bay. Comfortable and modern, it somehow recalls the golden age of British holiday-making. Guests can enjoy a drink in the Chesterfield bar with its comfy leather sofas and armchairs, while the welcoming restaurant makes the most of the stunning

sea views. The food is undoubtedly a highlight for diners who enjoy contemporary cuisine prepared from fresh local ingredients. Unsurprisingly there's an emphasis on seafood, with dishes of roasted suprême of wild Irish salmon on creamed leeks with salsa verde dressing and a freshly steamed langoustine, or grilled fillet of brill on a purée of petit pois with carrot and coriander broth and a panaché of baby vegetables, but meat-lovers are catered for too.

Chef John Chapman **Owner** Mr D Nussbaumer
Times 12-2/7-9.30, Closed Jan & Feb, Closed L Mon-Sat
Prices Fixed L 3 course fr £17.50, Fixed D 3 course fr £19.95 **Wines** 21 bottles over £20, 24 bottles under £20, 6 by glass **Notes** Sunday L, Vegetarian available, Dress restrictions, Smart casual, Air con **Seats** 110
Children Portions, Menu **Parking** 50

ST MARTIN
Map 24

The Auberge

◎◎ Modern European

Exciting modern cooking with stunning ocean views

☎ 01481 238485
Jerbourg Rd GY4 6BH
e-mail: dine@theauberge.gg
web: www.theauberge.gg
dir: End of Jerbourg Rd at Jerbourg Point

The elevated setting of the Auberge allows for stunning views over the bay to the neighbouring islands, which are every bit as memorable as the cuisine. An unassuming exterior belies the sleek, contemporary styling inside. A long bar dominates the entrance, which leads into the conservatory-style dining area with its floor-to-ceiling windows and decked terrace for alfresco eating. Tables are unclothed and service is relaxed and efficient, while the cooking is contemporary and innovative. Take a starter of smoked haddock risotto with pea sorbet and horseradish sour cream, and a main such as local lobster and prawn ravioli with roast cherry tomatoes, basil, fennel and endive salad. To finish try soft centre chocolate and banana bread pudding with milk chocolate ice cream.

Chef Daniel Green **Owner** Lapwing Trading Ltd
Times 12-2/7-9.30, Closed 25 Dec, 1 Feb, Closed Mon (Winter), Closed D Sun (Winter) **Prices** Fixed L 3 course £15-£24.95, Starter £6.50-£7.95, Main £13.95-£18, Dessert £6.95, Service optional **Wines** 19 bottles over £20, 16 bottles under £20, 12 by glass **Notes** Sunday L
Seats 70 **Children** Portions, Menu **Parking** 25

La Barbarie Hotel

◎ British, French

Quietly located hotel with a strong local reputation

☎ 01481 235217
Saints Rd, Saints Bay GY4 6ES
e-mail: reservations@labarbariehotel.com
web: www.labarbariehotel.com
dir: At traffic lights in St Martin take road to Saints Bay - hotel on right at end of Saints Rd

An old stone-built former priory, this delightful hotel is named after 17th-century pirates from the Barbary Coast who kidnapped a previous owner. With charm and style, the hotel offers a comfortable stay and great food served in the attractively decorated restaurant. Fresh local ingredients form the basis of the interesting menus - the steak board and Marine Cuisine selection of fresh fish have a strong local following, with a short carte adding to the variety. Typical dishes are Guernsey brill with soft parsley crust, young leaf spinach, mashed potato and chive beurre blanc, or roast rack of lamb with spring greens, gratin dauphinoise and thyme jus.

Chef Colin Pearson **Owner** La Barbarie Ltd
Times 12-1.45/6-9.30, Closed 2 Nov-13 Mar **Prices** Fixed D 4 course £19.95, Starter £5.95-£7.50, Main £9.95-£18.50, Dessert £4.95-£5.95, Service optional **Wines** 6 bottles over £20, 16 bottles under £20, 6 by glass **Notes** Sunday L, Vegetarian available **Seats** 70
Children Menu **Parking** 60

ST PETER PORT
Map 24

The Absolute End

◎ Mediterranean, International

Cottage restaurant serving fresh fish straight from the boat

☎ 01481 723822
Longstore GY1 2BG
e-mail: theabsoluteend@cwgsy.net
dir: Less than 1m from town centre, going N on seafront road to St Sampson

Housed in a converted fisherman's cottage, opposite the sea on the road out of town, the restaurant's main dining room has half-panelled walls on rough plaster dotted with small paintings, and upstairs there's a private dining room with a covered terrace. Candles and tablecloths formalise the atmosphere in the evening. The chef concentrates on fresh fish along with specials from his native Italy, and the results go down well with a loyal clientele. For starters, why not try the home-smoked seafood platter, including brill, scallops, salmon, mackerel and trout, while an impressive main course is the grilled local sea bass, perfectly timed, with a well-judged hollandaise sauce.

Times 12-2/7-10, Closed Jan, Closed Sun

Christophe

◉◉ Modern French ⬛

Quality food, relaxed, friendly service and spectacular sea views

☎ 01481 230725
Fort Road GB GY1 1ZP

The view through the trees and out to sea beyond Fermain Bay is best taken in from the terrace, which has the prime summer tables, but it can still be enjoyed from inside the dining room. Set just off the main road between the airport and St Peter Port, this smart hotel restaurant has a stylish, contemporary feel, and the chic dining room has modern wooden panels around the walls, darkwood pillars, cappuccino-coloured leather chairs, white-linen clothed tables and quality table appointments. The kitchen delivers modern French cooking, displaying some accomplished technical skills and eye-catching presentation. Flavours are clean, with quality ingredients allowed to speak up and be counted. Start with foie gras ballotine with banana tarte Tatin and peanut dentelle, followed by turbot with artichoke and vibrant herb foam. There are gourmand and dégustation menus available.

Times 12-2/7-10, Closed 2 wks Nov, 2 wks Feb, BHs, Closed Mon, Closed D Sun

Da Nello

◉ Italian, Mediterranean

Popular Italian just off the High Street

☎ 01481 721552
46 Le Pollet GY1 1WF
e-mail: danello@cwgsy.net
dir: In town centre, 100 yds from North beach car park

Located in the heart of the historic town, this characterful restaurant is housed in a 500-year-old residence which

has been much extended and smartly renovated over the years. The narrow frontage of the old granite house opens out into a series of dining areas, leading to the delightful covered Mediterranean-style piazza at the rear, decked out in marble and terracotta - reflecting its historic past as an ancient Roman encampment. The lengthy menu covers all the Italian favourites and has a separate fish section. Why not try the signature dish of lobster linguine as a starter or main course, or perhaps fettuccine with hand-picked Guernsey crab, tossed in olive oil, chilli, garlic and parsley.

Da Nello

Chef Tim Vidamour **Owner** Nello Ciotti
Times 12-2/6.30-10, Closed 25 Dec-23 Jan **Prices** Fixed L 3 course £13.25-£13.95, Fixed D 3 course £23.95, Starter £4.25-£8.95, Main £9.95-£19.50, Dessert £4.95-£5.50, Service optional **Wines** 19 bottles over £20, 31 bottles under £20, 8 by glass **Notes** Sunday L, Vegetarian available, Air con **Seats** 90, Pr/dining room 20 **Children** Portions **Parking** Public car park

Governor's

◉◉ Traditional French

Formal hotel dining with fine views over St Peter Port harbour

☎ 01481 738623
Old Government House Hotel, St Ann's Place GY1 2NU
e-mail: governors@theoghhotel.com
dir: Located off St Julian's Av, N of town centre

Once the residence of the Governor of Guernsey, the property dates back to 1748 and has been a hotel since 1857. The location is superb, overlooking the harbour and town. The Governor's fine-dining restaurant is a warm, intimate, beautifully decorated, traditionally themed room full of memorabilia and photographs of former island governors. Shaped seating, rich fabrics and patterned wallpaper recollect the glorious décor of the early 19th century. The classic cooking fits the bill, influenced by the French chef, who offers a seven-course

dégustation surprise menu in addition to carte and lunch. Local produce features strongly, take pan-seared fillets of brill with asparagus crown, herb risotto and morel cream, and honey roast apple and cinnamon pie served with crumble ice cream.

Times 12-2/7.30-10, Closed L Sat, Sun, Closed D Mon

Mora Restaurant & Grill

◉ British, French

Contemporary eatery in 18th-century wine cellars overlooking the harbour

☎ 01481 715053
The Quay GY1 2LE
e-mail: eat@mora.gg
dir: Facing Victoria Marina

Two storeys of an 18th-century vaulted wine cellar on the historic seafront have been converted to create this restaurant, sister venture to Da Nello (see entry). Furnishings are contemporary and the walls are hung with black-and-white portraits of local fishermen. Little Mora, downstairs, is perfect for a lighter meal, but go upstairs for the full dining experience and views of the open-plan kitchen. Classic cooking with contemporary influences is inspired by fresh local ingredients and clean flavours. Try lobster risotto, Mora fish and chips (bass, brill, scallops and king prawns) and oven-baked breast of Breton duck.

Chef Chris Marshall **Owner** Nello Ciotti
Times 12-2/6.30-10, Closed Sun **Prices** Fixed L 2 course £12.90, Fixed D 3 course £21.50, Starter £4.50-£9.50, Main £14.50-£19.90, Dessert £5.75, Service optional **Wines** 31 bottles over £20, 29 bottles under £20, 12 by glass **Notes** Vegetarian available, Air con **Seats** 90 **Children** Portions **Parking** On pier

Le Nautique Restaurant

◉ French, International **V**

Nautical-themed restaurant with sea views

☎ 01481 721714
Quay Steps GY1 2LE
dir: Seafront opposite harbour and Victoria Marina

Converted from a warehouse, this harbourside establishment overlooks the marina, Castle Cornet and the islands beyond. There are around 15 steps to the restaurant door, at first floor level. Inside there's a snug-style bar and main restaurant decorated with nautical

Continued

ST PETER PORT *Continued*

memorabilia, with a private dining room on the second floor with magnificent sea views from a huge window. The menu offers French cooking with international influences, featuring fresh local produce. Hitting the spot are lobster ravioli on steamed leeks and shellfish sauce, and roast fillet of sea bass with ginger, chilli, pineapple and coriander.

Chef G Botzenhardt & J Flemming **Owner** Gunter Botzenhardt **Times** 12-2/6.30-10, Closed Sun, Closed L Sat **Prices** Fixed L 2 course fr £14, Starter £5.50-£9.50, Main £9.50-£23.50, Dessert £5.50-£8.50, Service optional **Wines** 51 bottles over £20, 25 bottles under £20, 16 by glass **Notes** Vegetarian menu, Dress restrictions, Smart casual, Air con **Seats** 56, Pr/dining room 30 **Children** Portions **Parking** On street

Saltwater

◎ Traditional, Seafood

Contemporary restaurant with great harbour views

☎ 01481 720823
Albert Pier GY1 1AD
e-mail: info@saltwater.gg

This popular local restaurant overlooks the outer harbour. Stylish décor with wooden floors, whitewashed panelled walls, a bright conservatory and an understated nautical theme achieve an unpretentious chic. The extensive carte, fixed-price menu and daily specials offer plenty of choice. As you might expect, the menu favours seafood dishes, many of the simple, classic variety like moules marinière or crab thermidor, or perhaps Thai-style fishcakes served with a citrus mayonnaise and chilli jam. For mains, tuck into an impressively fresh, moist sea bass with hollandaise sauce, while for dessert vanilla crème brûlée hits all the right spots for texture and creaminess.

Times 12-2/6-10, Closed 23 Dec-5 Jan, Closed L Sat (Nov-Mar), Closed D Sun (Nov-Mar)

HERM

HERM	Map 24

White House Hotel

◎ Modern, Mediterranean

Island hotel with sea views and accomplished cooking

☎ 01481 722159
GY1 3HR
e-mail: hotel@herm-island.com
dir: By regular 20 min boat trip from St Peter Port, Guernsey

From its island setting and well-tended gardens, this attractive hotel has wonderful views out to sea. Relax in one of the lounges, enjoy a drink in one of the two bars and choose between two dining options. The fine dining room is light and airy with sea views from most tables, and the conservatory area overlooks the garden. The daily fixed-price four-course dinner is served by relaxed but attentive staff and offers the likes of warm figs baked

with Parma ham and parmesan, and poached fillet of plaice with asparagus and crab mousse and rich sea scallop cream.

Chef Neil Southgate **Owner** Wood of Herm Island **Times** 12.30-1.30/7-9, Closed Oct-Apr **Prices** Food prices not confirmed for 2009. Please telephone for details. **Wines** 74 bottles over £20, 101 bottles under £20, 7 by glass **Notes** Vegetarian available, Dress restrictions, Jacket & tie at D **Seats** 100 **Children** Portions

JERSEY

GOREY	Map 24

Suma's

◎◎ Modern Mediterranean

Stylish Jersey dining with superb scenery

☎ 01534 853291
Gorey Hill JE3 6ET
e-mail: info@sumasrestaurant.com
dir: Take A3 E, continue for 5m from St Helier to Gorey. Before castle take sharp left. Restaurant 100yds up hill on left. (Look for blue & white blind)

Overlooking Mont Orgueil Castle and Gorey fishing harbour, this stylish modern restaurant - sister establishment to Longueville Manor (see entry) - provides stunning views from its terrace and from inside. The blue-themed contemporary décor, with a selection of artwork adorning the walls, provides a suitably bright, refreshing setting to enjoy the modern cuisine with a touch of Mediterranean flair. Top-notch local produce, with an emphasis on seafood, is used to create wonderfully uncomplicated, beautifully-presented fare. Choose from dishes such as roasted lobster tail on a crab and prawn risotto with shellfish foam and asparagus, or loin of venison on a celeriac gratin with root vegetables, braised baby leeks and glazed chestnuts. Desserts might include poached mandarin set in a pecan crumble and mandarin foam.

Chef Daniel Ward **Owner** Mrs Butts & Mr M Lewis **Times** 12-3/6.15-10, Closed mid Dec-mid Jan (approx) **Prices** Fixed L 2 course fr £15, Fixed D 3 course fr £30, Starter £4.75-£12.50, Main £15-£25, Dessert £5.75-£12.50, Service included **Wines** 47 bottles over £20, 22 bottles under £20, 16 by glass **Notes** Early supper Mon-Sat 6.15-8pm, Sunday L, Vegetarian available, Dress restrictions, Smart casual, Air con **Seats** 40 **Children** Portions, Menu **Parking** On street

The Village Bistro

◎ Modern British, Mediterranean V

Welcoming restaurant in a converted church with carefully prepared cuisine

☎ 01534 853429
Gorey Village JE3 9EP
e-mail: thevillagebistro@yahoo.co.uk
dir: Take A3 E from St Helier to Gorey. Restaurant in village centre

Situated in the quiet seaside village of Gorey in a converted church, this popular husband-and-wife run bistro has a relaxed and welcoming atmosphere. Outdoor seating in the front garden offers alfresco dining while inside, wooden tables, beams and old farm implements set the scene. The menu of carefully prepared rustic bistro-style cuisine makes good use of quality Jersey produce and a daily blackboard offers popular fish specials. Dishes may include pan-roasted fillet of sea bass with sautéed local scallop on a parsley potato cake with Jerusalem artichokes and a tomato and chive dressing. A three-course set lunch with coffee also provides good value for money.

Chef Sarah Copp **Owner** Sean & Sarah Copp **Times** 12-2.30/7-10.30, Closed Mon, Closed D Sun **Prices** Fixed L course £14.50, Fixed D 3 course £17.50, Starter £6.95-£8.50, Main £13.50-£19.50, Dessert £3.75-£5.50, Service optional, Groups min 8 service 10% **Wines** 14 bottles over £20, 20 bottles under £20, 4 by glass **Notes** Sunday L, Vegetarian menu, Dress restrictions, Smart casual **Seats** 40 **Children** Portions **Parking** On street and public car park

ROZEL	Map 24

Château La Chaire

◎◎ Traditional British, French

Victorian country retreat offering creative cuisine

☎ 01534 863354
Rozel Bay JE3 6AJ
e-mail: res@chateau-la-chaire.co.uk
dir: From St Helier NE towards Five Oaks, Maufant, then St Martin's Church & Rozel; 1st left in village, hotel 100mtrs

Built in 1843, this gracious château nestles within a secluded wooded valley a short walk from Rozel's picturesque harbour. The architecture and opulent features have been sensitively restored and the two dining areas - one oak- panelled, the other a light and airy conservatory - offer diners a choice of relaxed and intimate settings. The imaginative menu combines French culinary techniques with traditional English dishes, making the best use of local produce. Try the home-made linguine with hand picked chancre crab, lime chilli and garlic to start, and perhaps the roast fillet of beef with stilton soufflé, roast vegetables and pesto gravy to follow, and make sure to leave room for the Valrhona chocolate marquise with espresso sauce and chocolate sorbet.

Chef Simon Walker **Owner** The Hiscox Family **Times** 12-3/7-10 **Prices** Fixed L 3 course £12.50-£35, Fixed D 3 course £16.50-£35, Starter £7.95-£9.95, Main £17.95-£24.95, Dessert £6.95, Service added but optional 10% **Wines** 51 bottles over £20, 18 bottles under £20, 12 by glass **Notes** Sunday L, Vegetarian available, Dress restrictions, No jeans or trainers, Civ Wed 60 **Seats** 60, Pr/dining room 28 **Children** Portions **Parking** 30

ST AUBIN Map 24

The Boat House

◉ Modern European 🍴

Striking seafront venue specialising in seafood

☎ 01534 744226 & 747141
Sails Brasserie & Quay Bar, 1 North Quay JE3 8BS
e-mail: enquiries@jerseyboathouse.com
dir: Please telephone for directions

There are stunning views from this sleek, recently built venue at the harbour edge, occupying the site of a former boat repair yard. Casual dining is available in the ground floor bar and terrace, while the serious dining is upstairs. Wood and glass is the theme, with wooden floors and tables, large windows and a glass-enclosed kitchen. Modern European cooking, specialising in island seafood, takes a straightforward modern approach: fresh oysters on crushed ice with shallot vinegar or shellfish soup, with mains like pan-fried fillet of sea bass with wild mushrooms and tarragon cream.

Chef Adrian Goldsborough **Owner** Mill Holdings (St Brelade) Ltd **Times** 12-2/6-9.30, Closed 25 Dec & 31 Dec to 1st wk in Feb, Closed Mon-Tue (Winter), Closed L Wed-Sat (Winter), Closed D Sun (Winter) **Notes** Early bird menu available 6-7pm 2 courses £16.95, Sunday L, Vegetarian available **Seats** 96 **Children** Portions, Menu **Parking** On street, public car park

The Salty Dog Bar & Bistro

◉ Modern International V 🍴

Lively bistro with an enjoyable, eclectic menu

☎ 01534 742760
Le Boulevard, St Aubins Village JE3 8AB
e-mail: info@.saltydogbistro.com
web: www.saltydogbistro.com
dir: Walking from centre of St Aubin Village along harbour, approx halfway along, slightly set back

This vibrant bistro, situated in a courtyard set back from St Aubin's scenic harbour, offers a stylish and relaxed

setting with an inviting maritime décor featuring driftwood, shells and Caribbean prints. An eclectic menu, specialising in New World fusion cuisine, features enjoyable international flavours and excellent Jersey produce. Seafood dishes take centre stage with starters such as pan-seared local hand-dived scallops in a light ginger and spring onion sauce with a rocket and toasted sesame dressing, and mains like steamed local turbot fillet served simply on sautéed greens with a salsa verde, tuna Creole, or whole sea bass in banana leaf.

Chef Damon James Duffy **Owner** Damon & Natalie Duffy **Times** 12.30-6/6-1.30am, Closed 2 wks Xmas, Closed Mon (Jan-Feb), Closed L Tue-Fri (Jan-Mar) **Prices** Fixed L course £18.95, Fixed D 3 course £27.95, Starter £6.90-£9.40, Main £11.50-£26.95, Dessert £3.95-£5.25, Service added but optional 10% **Wines** 28 bottles over £20, 24 bottles under £20, 7 by glass **Notes** Sunday L, Vegetarian menu **Seats** 60 **Children** Portions, Menu **Parking** Car parks & on street parking nearby

Somerville Hotel

◉◉ International V

Stunning views over the bay, and serious modern cooking

☎ 01534 741226
Mont du Boulevard JE3 8AD
e-mail: somerville@dolanhotels.com
dir: From village follow harbour, then take Mont du Boulevard

Settings just don't come much better than this: on the hillside overlooking St Aubin's harbour, with glorious views over the gardens all the way to St Helier enjoyed from both the lounge and the smart, classic country-house atmosphere of the Tides restaurant. Service is formal and reserved, and the smart table settings are in keeping with this serious approach to dining. The extensive choice on the modern menu makes fine use of the abundant local larder, including the fruits of the sea, in complex, accomplished dishes. Take warm tart of Jersey crab thermidor, roast rack and braised shoulder of lamb with parsnip hash brown and rosemary jus, and dark chocolate tart with vanilla mascarpone and candied orange.

Chef Wayne Pegler **Owner** Mr W Dolan **Times** 12.30-2/7-9 **Prices** Fixed L 2 course £12.50, Fixed D 4 course £29.50, Starter £7-£9, Main £15-£21, Dessert £6-£8, Service optional **Wines** 35 bottles over £20, 29 bottles under £20, 6 by glass **Notes** Sunday L, Vegetarian menu, Dress restrictions, Smart casual at D, Civ Wed 40, Air con **Seats** 120, Pr/dining room 40 **Children** Portions **Parking** 30

ST BRELADE Map 24

L'Horizon Hotel and Spa

◉◉ British, French

Lovely views and classical cooking

☎ 01534 743101
Route de la Baie JE3 8EF
e-mail: lhorizon@handpicked.co.uk
dir: 2m from Jersey Airport, 5m from St Helier

An abundance of glass and mirrors enhances the impression of light and space at this stylish hotel restaurant, while clever use of partitions and alcoves imparts an air of intimacy. A sliding glass door opens to reveal wonderful views of St Brelade's Bay, while crisp white linen and small flower arrangements create a formal setting. A classical base underpins the cooking, though the interpretation of most dishes is modern and light, especially when it comes to seafood. Quality local produce stars in well-presented dishes such as tian of Jersey crab with coriander guacamole and bisque dressing, and wild line-caught sea bass with Jersey Royal and goat's cheese terrine and a clementine reduction.

Chef Nicholas Valmagna **Owner** Hand Picked Hotels **Times** Closed Xmas, Closed Sun-Mon, Closed L all wk **Prices** Food prices not confirmed for 2009. Please telephone for details. **Wines** 75 bottles over £20, 14 bottles under £20, 8 by glass **Notes** Civ Wed 200, Air con **Seats** 46, Pr/dining room 250 **Children** Min 12 yrs, Portions, Menu **Parking** 150

Hotel La Place

◉ Modern British

Classic cooking in a beamed dining room

☎ 01534 744261
Route Du Coin, La Haule JE3 8BT
e-mail: hotlaplace@aol.com
dir: Telephone for directions

The hotel is a conversion of a 17th-century farmhouse located in lovely countryside a short walk from St Aubin's Harbour and St Brelade's beach. Enjoy a drink in the cocktail bar overlooking the pool in fine weather, or by the log fire in the lounge, and then head through to the beamed Retreat Restaurant. The menu suits the setting and makes good use of local produce in dishes like honey lemon chicken and crab terrine with asparagus spaghetti and truffle vinaigrette, and fried beef fillet with shallot and cep purée and red wine jus.

Times 12-2/7-9

Ocean Restaurant at the Atlantic Hotel

◉◉◉ – *see page 474*

Ocean Restaurant at the Atlantic Hotel

ST BRELADE   Map 24

Modern British ⚘ NOTABLE WINE LIST

Sophisticated dining with Atlantic views

☎ 01534 744101
Le Mont de la Pulente JE3 8HE
e-mail: info@theatlantichotel.com
web: www.theatlantichotel.com
dir: From St Brelade take the road to Petit Port, turn into Rue de Sergente and right again, signed to hotel

Built in 1970 as a bespoke hotel, the Atlantic is in a spectacular, peaceful position overlooking St Ouen's Bay, surrounded by sub-tropical gardens and next to the immaculate fairways of the La Moye championship golf course. Owned and run by the same family since it opened, an air of luxury and sophistication pervades throughout, including in the Ocean Restaurant. The dining room is spacious, light and stylish, and the smartly dressed staff hit the right balance between formality and friendliness. The kitchen's modern approach delivers beautifully presented dishes based on first class produce from the abundant local Jersey larder, including the fruits of the sea. The cooking is accurate, consistent, innovative, full of flavour and draws inspiration from all over the world. Start with terrine of rabbit with pickled vegetables and truffled celeriac purée followed by pot-roasted poussin with

foie gras, morels and peas. Finish with milk pudding with vanilla syrup and cinnamon doughnuts or the selection of English, French and Jersey cheeses.

Chef Mark Jordan
Times 12.30-2.30/7-10,
Closed 5 Jan-8 Feb

ST CLEMENT — Map 24

Green Island Restaurant

 Mediterranean

Contemporary beachside café with alfresco tables

☎ 01534 857787
Green Island JE2 6LS
e-mail: greenislandrestaurant@jerseymail.co.uk
dir: Telephone for directions

A jazzed-up beach café/restaurant that's very popular locally, especially in the summer, while a takeaway window serving quality food does a roaring trade. The views out over Green Island are well worth savouring, as is the stylish modern Mediterranean cooking with much emphasis on fresh fish dishes. Expect sardines, crab, and lobster to be on the menu. Fresh squid with soy sauce and sesame seeds with an oriental salad might be followed by an accurately cooked breast of chicken stuffed with emmental cheese and wrapped in Parma ham. Staff in white tee shirts and jeans are relaxed and helpful.

Times 12-3/7-10, Closed 21 Dec-Mar, Closed Mon, Closed D Sun

ST HELIER — Map 24

Bohemia Restaurant

⊕⊕⊕⊕ – see page 476

Grand Jersey

⊕⊕⊕ – see below

La Petite Pomme

⊕⊕ Modern European

Convivial dining with good views

☎ 01534 880110
Pomme d'Or Hotel, Liberation Square JE1 3UF
e-mail: enquiries@pommedorhotel.com
dir: 5m from Airport, 0.5m from ferry terminal

The Pomme d'Or Hotel was the German naval headquarters during the World War II occupation, and is a focal point of the annual liberation celebrations (9th May). La Petite Pomme, the hotel's fine dining area, occupies the first floor overlooking Liberation Square and St Helier harbour. The restaurant is richly decorated with well-spaced tables and classy settings. Dishes are modern, imaginative and skilfully prepared from the freshest Jersey produce (the kitchen is committed to reducing food miles and supporting the local community). Recommendations include ballotine of sea bass with scallops, glazed baby vegetables and chive butter sauce, or aged fillet of beef served with dauphinoise potatoes, sautéed spinach and thyme jus.

Chef James Waters, Chris Morris **Owner** Seymour Hotels **Times** Closed 26-30 Dec, Closed Sun, Closed L all week **Prices** Fixed D 3 course £15-£19.95, Starter £4.95-£7.95, Main £9.95-£16.95, Dessert £5.95-£6.95, Service optional **Wines** 17 bottles over £20, 41 bottles under £20, 10 by glass **Notes** Vegetarian available, Dress restrictions, Smart casual, Air con **Seats** 50, Pr/dining room 50 **Children** Portions, Menu **Parking** 100 yds from hotel

Radisson SAS Waterfront Hotel - Jersey

⊕ French, European

Contemporary waterfront restaurant

☎ 01534 471100
The Waterfront, La Rue de L'Etau JE2 4HE

This modern purpose-built hotel is set on the waterfront in St Helier with fabulous views of the coastline. Enjoy a drink in the cocktail bar before dining in the contemporary restaurant, where you will find a neutral décor with minimalist clean lines and friendly relaxed service. The crowd-pleasing menu changes seasonally with daily specials available. This is simple brasserie fare with classics included. For starters, try fresh and vibrant tuna Niçoise, followed by calves' liver with bacon and mashed potatoes, with apple tarte Tatin to finish.

Grand Jersey

ST HELIER — Map 24

Modern European

Refurbished landmark hotel offering modern ambience and food to match

☎ 01534 722301
The Esplanade JE4 8WD
e-mail: kmcalpine@hilwoodresorts.com
dir: On outskirts of town overlooking Victoria Park

A local landmark, the newly refurbished Grand Jersey is set on The Esplanade with the bustling streets of St Helier to the rear and views across the bay at the front. Tassili restaurant is a stylish, chic and contemporary affair, with linen tablecloths and sophisticated, knowledgeable service, plus great views of the bay and Elizabeth Castle. (There's also an adjoining modern brasserie and Champagne Bar.) At the time of going to press new chef Richard Allen had arrived at the helm (previously 3 Rosettes at the Cavendish in Bath, see entry) and early visits suggest a high standard of cooking, using the finest available ingredients, offering a sophisticated yet intelligently simple approach that allows subtle flavours to shine. Think Jersey beef fillet served with ox cheek, horseradish and celeriac, langoustine tails with pork belly, choucroûte and butternut squash.

Chef Richard Allen **Owner** Hilwood Resorts & Hotels **Times** 7-9.45, Closed Sun-Mon **Prices** Fixed D 3 course fr £47, Service optional **Wines** 118 bottles over £20, 6 bottles under £20, 9 by glass **Notes** Vegetarian available, Dress restrictions, Smart casual, Civ Wed 200, Air con **Seats** 32 **Parking** 30

Bohemia Restaurant

Modern British, French

Confident classical cooking in contemporary Jersey restaurant

☎ 01534 880588 & 876500
**The Club House & Spa, Green St
JE2 4UH**
e-mail: bohemia@huggler.com
dir: Located on Green St in centre of St Helier

Bohemia would make a splash in any major town or city and in St Helier it is a veritable tidal wave. Located in The Club Hotel & Spa, a stylish and impossibly fashionable boutique hotel near the centre of town, Bohemia is a destination restaurant. There is a bold and brilliant bar - to see and be seen - while the dining room is a refined and elegant space, the colours chosen from a natural palette. Leather chairs, banquette seating, wooden finishes, Lalique glass and tables smartly set and clothed in linen make for a contemporary and eminently moneyed look. Chef Shaun Rankin's menus are based around classic and modern British and French preparations, some contemporary innovations and first class produce. There is a tasting menu with the option of suggested wines, a kitchen table if you want to get up close and personal, and a fantastically good value set lunch. All the bells and whistles are present - amuse-bouche,

pre-desserts and petits-fours - and strong technical skill is evident throughout. Luxury ingredients are used to great effect in a starter of lightly poached Royal Bay oysters, Sévruga caviar, saffron noodles and lemon butter, and contemporary ideas figure in another starter of goat's cheese ice cream with carrot and tomato jelly and a celery salad. Main-course squab pigeon is served with a Roquefort risotto and an Asian pear, and Jersey lobster with home-made macaroni and crab and fennel céviche. A selection of mini desserts for two people will prevent a difficult decision: rhubarb crumble soufflé with white chocolate cannelloni or Valrhona's Caraïbe chocolate tart with whisky cream, semi-fredo and espresso granité? Service is professional but not at all stuffy.

Chef Shaun Rankin **Owner** Lawrence Huggler **Times** 12-2.30/6.30-10, Closed Sun, Closed L BH Mon **Prices** Fixed L 2 course fr £18.50, Fixed D 3 course £49-£55.50, Tasting menu £60, Starter fr £17, Main £27-£33, Dessert fr £8.50, Service added but optional 10% **Wines** 3 bottles over £20, 3 bottles under £20, 16 by glass **Notes** Tasting menu 7 courses, Vegetarian available, Dress restrictions, Smart casual, Air con **Seats** 60, Pr/dining room 20 **Children** Portions **Parking** 20

ST HELIER *Continued*

Restaurant Sirocco @ The Royal Yacht

◉◉ Modern

Serious modern cooking overlooking the harbour

☎ 01534 720511
The Weighbridge JE2 3NF
e-mail: reception@theroyalyacht.com
dir: Adjacent to Weighbridge Park overlooking Jersey Harbour

Overlooking St Helier's bustling marina and steam clock, Jersey's oldest established hotel, The Royal Yacht, has been extensively refurbished and now includes a range of dining options. Newly created on the first floor, the contemporary-styled Restaurant Sirocco enjoys views over the harbour and offers summer alfresco dining on a heated patio. The kitchen takes a serious, modern approach to cooking high-quality local produce. Seasonal menus list innovative dishes, all simply prepared to maintain the flavour of the main ingredient, as seen in a tasting of Jersey beef - silverside, liver and fillet - or pan-roasted black bream and langoustine with basil gnocchi and sauce vierge. Precede with seared king scallops with cider-braised pork belly and leek purée and finish with a light mint mousse with melting chocolate topping, served with a peppermint sorbet.

Chef Fred Tobin/Peter Brewer **Owner** Lodestar Group
Times 12-2/7-8.30, Closed D Sun **Prices** Fixed L 2 course fr £16.50, Fixed D 3 course fr £25.50, Service optional **Wines** 175 bottles over £20, 23 bottles under £20, 16 by glass **Notes** Sunday L, Vegetarian available, Dress restrictions, Smart casual, Civ Wed 300, Air con **Seats** 65 **Parking** Car park

Seasons

◉ British, International 🍃

Long-established hotel with a kitchen focused on local produce

☎ 01534 726521
Best Western Royal Hotel, Davids Place JE2 4TD
e-mail: manager@royalhoteljersey.com
dir: Please telephone for directions

The Royal is centrally located in the town and has been undergoing improvements over recent years, the latest of which is the opening of the Seasons restaurant. The dining room is now a contemporary space with wooden floorboards and well-spaced white-clothed tables and a relaxed, friendly atmosphere. The menu is focused on local produce, including local butternut squash in the form of a velouté with chicken and leek tortellini, wild mushrooms and parmesan crisp, and Jersey oysters served traditionally. Dishes are modern British with European overtones. The main-course trio of Welsh lamb is perfectly cooked, while for dessert pears are poached in local cider and come with home-made Jersey black butter ice cream.

Chef Alun Williams **Owner** Morvan Hotels
Times 12-2/6.30-9, Closed L Mon-Sat (unless by prior arrangement) **Prices** Fixed L 2 course £10-£14, Fixed D 3 course £17.50-£21.50, Starter £5-£8, Main £11-£18, Dessert £4-£6, Service optional **Wines** 6 bottles over £20, 39 bottles under £20, 5 by glass **Notes** Sunday L, Vegetarian available, Dress restrictions, Smart casual, Civ Wed 35 **Seats** 100, Pr/dining room 50 **Children** Portions, Menu **Parking** 14

ST LAWRENCE   Map 24

Indigos

◉ Modern

Eclectic cooking coupled with breathtaking views

☎ 01534 758024
Hotel Cristina, Mont Felard JE3 1JA
e-mail: cristina@dolanhotels.com
dir: Please telephone for directions

There's a contemporary, chic vibe in this delightful hotel and restaurant, perched on a hillside with lovely gardens and far reaching views over St Aubin's Bay. Its peaceful location is ideal - the beach is minutes away, and some of Jersey's unique heritage sites are on the doorstep. The restaurant has a modern bistro-style atmosphere and offers simply prepared, thoughtfully sourced fresh ingredients put to good use in dishes with Mediterranean influences. Take grilled fillet of cod, minted pea purée, boulangère potatoes, balsamic reduction and crisp pancetta, or Chinese spiced duck breast, stir-fried greens, spring onions and ginger, noodles and miso broth. On a warm evening, eat on the stunning terrace.

Chef Mark Rowan **Owner** W G Dolan **Times** Closed Nov-Mar, Closed L all week **Prices** Fixed D 3 course £20.50-£23.50, Starter £6.30-£9, Main £16-£19.50, Dessert £4.50-£6.50, Service optional **Wines** 25% bottles over £20, 75% bottles under £20 **Notes** Vegetarian available, Dress restrictions, Smart casual, Civ Wed 60 **Seats** 120 **Children** Portions **Parking** 60

ST PETER   Map 24

Greenhills Country Hotel

◉ European

Fine dining in peaceful period surroundings

☎ 01534 481042
Mont de L'Ecole JE3 7EL
e-mail: greenhills@messages.co.uk
dir: A1 signed St Peters Valley (A11). Continue for 4m and thurn right onto E112

This delightful 17th-century country-house hotel is set amidst award-winning gardens in the tranquil heart of St Peter's Valley. Retaining the unique atmosphere and intimacy of a period house, the light, traditional restaurant serves European-influenced cuisine, with the accent on fresh local produce and seafood. Try the duo of scallops and king prawns seared with fresh thyme and bacon on cauliflower purée, red bell pepper coulis and basil pesto to start, followed by Jersey line-caught sea bass on a truffled lobster and fine garden pea risotto with saffron crème fraîche, with perhaps the iced passionfruit and white chocolate terrine, glazed with champagne on a cinnamon and Amaretto syrup to finish.

Chef Ronny Friedrich **Owner** Peter Bromley
Times 12.30-2/7-9.30, Closed 20 Dec - 6 Feb
Prices Fixed L 2 course £12.50, Fixed D 4 course £30.25, Starter £5.95-£12.95, Main £17.95-£25.50, Dessert £7.95-£8.50, Service optional **Wines** 37 bottles over £20, 37 bottles under £20, 4 by glass **Notes** Sunday L, Vegetarian available, Dress restrictions, Smart casual, Civ Wed 50, Air con **Seats** 90, Pr/dining room 40 **Children** Portions, Menu **Parking** 45

ST SAVIOUR   Map 24

Longueville Manor

◉◉◉ – *see page 478*

Longueville Manor

Modern British NOTABLE WINE LIST

Historic manor with sophisticated cuisine

☎ 01534 725501
JE2 7WF
e-mail: info@longuevillemanor.com
web: www.longuevillemanor.com
dir: From St Helier take A3 to Gorey, hotel 0.75m on left

This grand Norman manor house - dating from the 13th century - is an imposing dinner venue and a hotel of international renown. Clad in wisteria, it stands in 15 acres of woodland that invite exploration - take a stroll before dinner and you may stumble across a game of croquet on the lawn, a spectacular rose garden, or a lake with a flock of majestic black swans. Inside, everything is decorated in understated country-house style, and guests are treated to very high standards of comfort and care. The two dining rooms cater for different moods, from the Jacobean dark-panelled Oak Room to the more relaxed and modern Garden Room, rich in fabrics and antiques. Whichever you choose, you're in for a treat; the cuisine at Longueville is confident and accomplished, and makes intelligent use of top-notch ingredients from the walled kitchen garden and local area (Taste of Jersey menu available). Combinations are deft and

flavours balanced; the result is an assured menu of classical dishes. Take poached tronçon of turbot served with confit cabbage, calamari, lardons, morels and braised baby onions, and to finish, perhaps a hot chocolate fondant 'Guanaja' with passionfruit pastille and coconut ice cream.

Chef Andrew Baird **Owner** Malcolm Lewis **Times** 12.30-2/7-10 **Prices** Fixed L 2 course fr £15, Fixed D 3 course £55-£67, Service included **Wines** 300+ bottles over £20, 20 bottles under £20, 23 by glass **Notes** Sunday L, Vegetarian available, Dress restrictions, Smart casual, jacket minimum, Civ Wed 40 **Seats** 65, Pr/dining room 22 **Children** Portions, Menu **Parking** 45

TRINITY Map 24

Water's Edge Hotel

◉◉ Modern British

Stunning coastal setting for enjoyable cuisine

☎ 01534 862777
Bouley Bay JE3 5AS
e-mail: mail@watersedgehotel.co.je
web: www.watersedgehotel.co.je
dir: 10-15 mins from St Helier, A9 N to the A8 to the B31, follow signs to Bouley Bay

Nestling in the tranquil surroundings of Bouley Bay on the island's north coast, this art deco style hotel enjoys panoramic views over the bay across to the distant French coastline. The split-level Waterside Restaurant makes the most of those views, complemented by the hotel's own Black Dog pub and alfresco dining area. Modern British cuisine with a nod to the classics is offered on the restaurant's carte or fixed-price market menu, with fresh local fish and seafood not surprisingly the order of the day. Local lobster comes with a choice of thermidor sauce or grilled garlic butter, served, of course, with Jersey Royals, while pan-roast halibut with boulangère potatoes, baby vegetables and fennel butter sauce also makes a memorable main course, with an assiette of apple to finish. Flambés are a speciality. Formal service and crisp table linen complete the experience.

Chef Gael Maratier **Owner** Water's Edge Hotel Ltd
Times Closed Nov-Mar, Closed L all week **Prices** Fixed D
4 course £26-£28, Starter £7.50-£12, Main £17-£21,
Dessert £7.50-£9.50, Service included **Wines** 40 bottles
over £20, 50 bottles under £20, 14 by glass
Notes Vegetarian available, Dress restrictions, Smart
casual, No trainers, jeans or T-shirts, Civ Wed 100
Seats 100, Pr/dining room 40 **Children** Min 7 yrs,
Portions, Menu **Parking** 20

SARK

SARK Map 24

Hotel Petit Champ

◉ Modern British

Relaxed, country-house dining with amazing sea views

☎ 01481 832046
GY9 0SF
e-mail: info@hotelpetitchamp.co.uk
dir: 20 min walk from village, signed from Methodist
Chapel

Guests can expect a warm welcome at this delightful secluded hotel on Sark's west coast. Set in well-tended grounds, the hotel has a fascinating history, having served as a private home, boatyard and German observation post during the Occupation. These days, the only thing guests come to watch are the magnificent views across the sea and neighbouring islands, which are particularly stunning at sunset. The restaurant delivers a menu of modern British dishes with an international twist: roasted breast of chicken with morels, Puy lentils and capers in port sauce, for example, or pan-fried fillet of sea bass with freshwater prawns and champagne and chervil velouté. Fresh crab, scallops and lobster from the harbour are a speciality, the latter offered with an array of sauces, and there's a good selection of meatier options too.

Owner Chris & Caroline Robins **Times** 12.15-1.45/8,
Closed Oct-Etr **Wines** 8 bottles over £20, 69 bottles under
£20, 4 by glass **Notes** Fixed D 5 courses £21.75, Sunday
L, Vegetarian available, Dress restrictions, Smart casual
Seats 50 **Children** Min 7 yrs D, Portions, Menu
Parking No cars on Sark

La Sablonnerie

◉◉ Modern, Traditional International

Creative cuisine in an idyllic setting

☎ 01481 832061
GY9 0SD
e-mail: lasablonnerie@cwgsy.net
dir: On southern part of island. Horse & carriage is
transport to hotel

The idyllic island of Sark is car-free, so access to this cosy gem of a restaurant comes courtesy of the hotel's very own horse and carriage which will deliver you to the door of a white-washed cottage half-hidden in summer by a mass of flowers. The oak-beamed restaurant retains the original style and charm of the 400-year-old farmhouse, and delivers a menu of modern international dishes with a strong French influence: fresh Sark lobster with lime and ginger butter, caramelised duck breast with green peppercorn and sage sauce, pan-fried fillet of home-grown beef with a soubise glaze, rosti potatoes and Madeira sauce. Fresh local fish and shellfish are a speciality.

La Sablonnerie

Chef Martin Cross **Owner** Elizabeth Perrée
Times 12-2.30/7-9.30, Closed mid Oct-Etr **Prices** Fixed L
2 course £16.80-£22.30, Fixed D 3 course £23.60-£30.10,
Starter £5.80-£7.80, Main £11-£14.50, Dessert
£5.80-£6.80, Service added 10% **Wines** 9 bottles over
£20, 41 bottles under £20, 6 by glass **Notes** Sunday L,
Vegetarian available **Seats** 39 **Children** Portions, Menu

ISLE OF MAN

DOUGLAS Map 24 SC37

Sefton Hotel

◉ Modern European

Fine dining beside the sea

☎ 01624 645500
Harris Promenade IM1 2RW
e-mail: info@seftonhotel.co.im
dir: 1m along Promenade from the sea terminal

A Victorian seafront hotel with a contemporary, comfortable fine-dining restaurant, decorated with bright artwork and enjoying fine views out to sea. Modern cooking is the order of the day with fine ingredients in a mix of European-style and classic French dishes. Typically, start with caramelised pear and dolcelatte tart with roasted vine tomatoes and balsamic syrup, or pan-seared scallops coated with polenta, before moving on to pan-roasted fillet of Manx beef with celeriac and potato mash, onion marmalade tart, red wine and vegetable broth, or perhaps simply grilled Dover sole. Finish with hot chocolate pudding served with warm anglaise and vanilla pod ice cream.

Times 12-2/6-10, Closed L Sun

Scotland

Loch Long

SCOTLAND

CITY OF ABERDEEN

ABERDEEN   Map 23 NJ90

Atlantis at the Mariner Hotel

Modern British, Seafood V

Established hotel with excellent local seafood and meats

☎ 01224 588901
349 Great Western Rd AB10 6NW
e-mail: info@themarinerhotel.co.uk
web: www.themarinerhotel.co.uk
dir: From S, 400yds right off A90 at Great Western Rd lights

This family-run hotel is situated to the west of the city centre. Dine in the Atlantis Restaurant, a split-level affair with a conservatory area, subtle nautical theme, rich coloured furnishings and a wide-ranging menu. The emphasis is on fresh local seafood, including a cold seafood platter and selection of lobster dishes, and, inevitably for Aberdeen, there are steaks too. Portions are hearty and a light touch lets the quality of regional produce speak for itself. Try perhaps Cullen skink with oatcakes, followed by battered calamari with lemon mayonnaise and, for carnivores, pan-fried fillet of venison with whisky, honey and mustard sauce. To close, tiramisu and cappuccino ice cream might catch the eye.

Chef George Bennett **Times** 12-2.30/6-10, Closed 26 Dec, 1-2 Jan, Closed L Sat **Prices** Fixed L 2 course £16, Fixed D 3 course £19.50, Starter £3.25-£8, Main £13-£33, Dessert £5-£5.50, Service optional **Wines** 29 bottles over £20, 15 bottles under £20, 8 by glass **Notes** Sunday L, Vegetarian menu **Seats** 50 **Children** Portions, Menu **Parking** 50

The Caledonian by Thistle

Modern British

Enjoyable dining in the heart of the city

☎ 0870 333 9151
10-14 Union Ter AB10 1WE
e-mail: aberdeencaledonian@thistle.co.uk

Centrally located overlooking Union Terrace Gardens and within walking distance of many shops and local attractions, this elegant Victorian building has comfortable, well-appointed public areas in keeping with the building's age and style. There's a cocktail bar and upbeat café bar for light bites and hearty lunches, while upstairs in the Terrace Restaurant a more formal dining experience is on offer, with smart leather chairs and stylish darkwood tables setting the tone. Simple but effective, well-constructed dishes are prepared from quality local produce, skilfully executed with good, clear flavours. Start with haggis and Stornoway black pudding croquettes with shallot sauce, and perhaps follow with pan-fried venison saddle braised with red cabbage, served with sweet potato mash. Desserts include a delightful crème brûlée.

Norwood Hall

British, European

Fine dining on a grand scale

☎ 01224 868951
Garthdee Rd, Cults AB15 9FX
e-mail: info@norwood-hall.co.uk
dir: From S, off A90 at 1st rdbt cross bridge and turn left at rdbt into Garthdee Road, continue 1.5m

An imposing Victorian mansion in 7 acres of grounds, with roaring winter fires, sweeping staircases and an oak-panelled dining room, aptly named the Tapestry restaurant after the ornate tapestry work on the walls. Well-spaced candlelit tables grace this richly furnished room, displaying fine crockery and glassware befitting the magnificent scale of the house. A selection of traditional and more adventurous dishes is the kitchen's style, driven by quality local seasonal produce, with an emphasis on game and seafood. The slick cooking majors on flavour and simplicity; perhaps medallions of beef served with a wild mushroom sauce and haggis, followed by chocolate brownie and vanilla ice cream to finish.

Owner Monument Leisure **Times** 12-2.30/7-9.45 **Prices** Food prices not confirmed for 2009. Please telephone for details. **Wines** 43 bottles over £20, 23 bottles under £20, 9 by glass **Notes** Vegetarian available, Dress restrictions, Smart casual, Civ Wed 180 **Seats** 28, Pr/dining room 180 **Children** Portions, Menu **Parking** 100

The Silver Darling

French, Seafood

Romantic seafood restaurant with stunning harbour views

☎ 01224 576229
Pocra Quay, North Pier AB11 5DQ
dir: Situated at Aberdeen Harbour entrance

Located at the entrance to Aberdeen harbour, the building which was once the customs house is now a restaurant with its focus firmly on the fruits of the sea. The name is a reference to the rather romantic colloquial term for herring. From the large windows of the first-floor conservatory restaurant you can see passing ships and even dolphins sometimes. Fresh locally-landed seafood appears on a menu with a decidedly French influence, and there are meat options for those that insist. A starter of salmon rillette is served with horseradish and chive cream, pickled beetroot and apples, chicory and grilled toast, while main courses include beautifully cooked seared king scallops with cauliflower and ratte potato purée with a raisin and caper dressing.

Times 12-1.45/6.30-9.30, Closed Xmas-New Year, Closed Sun, Closed L Sat

Thistle Aberdeen Airport

Scottish, European

Traditional Scottish cooking in an airport setting

☎ 0870 333 9149
Aberdeen Airport, Argyll Rd AB21 0AF
e-mail: aberdeenairport@thistle.co.uk

Ideally located at the entrance to the airport, the Thistle Hotel Aberdeen Airport offers fine Scottish cuisine in a convenient setting for both business and leisure travellers. The Osprey restaurant utilises first-class ingredients, pairing simple flavour combinations with high standards of presentation. Typical starters on the varied menu include fillet of sole, crab mousse and spinach salad, served with delicious home-made parmesan bread. Try the lamb rack with roast garlic jus, crispy leeks, carrots and dauphinoise potatoes to follow, rounding off with rhubarb and ginger crumble tart with double cream.

Times 12-2/7-10

Howies Restaurant - Chapel Street

☎ 01224 639500
50 Chapel St AB10 1SN
web: http://www.theaa.com/travel/index.jsp

The Aberdeen member of the successful Edinburgh-based group of modern Scottish restaurants. Monthly-changing menus of fantastic seasonal and local food made on the premises every day.

Prices Food prices not confirmed for 2009. Please telephone for details.

ABERDEENSHIRE

BALLATER Map 23 NO39

Darroch Learg Hotel

@@@ — *see below*

The Green Inn

@@ Modern British 🖥 V

Intimate, family-run conservatory-style restaurant

☎ 013397 55701
9 Victoria Rd AB35 5QQ
e-mail: info@green-inn.com
dir: in centre of village

A historic landmark and former temperance hotel, The Green Inn is a family affair. Trevor O'Halloran entertains at front of house, while son Chris is in charge of the kitchen, ably assisted by mum, Evelyn. With only seven well-spaced tables, the atmosphere is relaxed at this dinner-only affair, where the table is yours for the night. The cooking is contemporary in approach underpinned by classical techniques, reflecting the chef's training at Le Manoir aux Quat' Saisons. Artistically presented dishes utilise fresh, local produce, home-grown when available. Try the pressed organic salmon, leek and potato terrine with crushed peas, oyster and rocket emulsion to start, followed by the roasted rack of Scottish lamb with black

mustard seeds, roasted garlic purée and asparagus. Round off with the hot chocolate fondant with cookies, cinnamon stick ice cream and chocolate sauce.

Chef Chris & Evelyn O'Halloran **Owner** Trevor & Evelyn O'Halloran **Times** Closed 2 wks Nov, 2 wks Jan, Closed Sun, Mon **Prices** Food prices not confirmed for 2009. Please telephone for details. **Wines** 52 bottles over £20, 9 bottles under £20, 7 by glass **Notes** Vegetarian menu, Dress restrictions, Smart casual **Seats** 30, Pr/dining room 24 **Parking** On Street & car park nearby

Loch Kinord Hotel

@ Modern British 🖥

Stylish, elegant dining in woodland setting

☎ 013398 85229
Ballater Rd, Dinnet AB34 5JY
e-mail: stay@lochkinord.com
dir: From Aberdeen take A93 W towards Braemar, hotel on A93 between Aboyne & Ballater

Situated on the edge of the Highlands in an attractive woodland setting, this family-run roadside hotel has lots of character and a friendly, informal atmosphere. Set in pretty gardens, it has a choice of comfortable lounges and bars and a formally laid, elegant dining room with attentive service. The kitchen's style is intelligently uncomplicated, delivering well presented dishes and honest flavours that make good use of the abundant local larder. Expect starters such as smoked Scottish venison,

thinly sliced on a Cumberland sauce, or darne of Scottish salmon, grilled and served with asparagus and smoky bacon on a cream sauce, followed by mains like fillet of halibut topped with Scottish cheese and wrapped in bacon and baked in puff pastry.

Loch Kinord Hotel

Chef Dominic Brennan **Owner** Andrew & Jenny Cox **Times** Closed L all week **Prices** Food prices not confirmed for 2009. Please telephone for details. **Wines** 15 bottles over £20, 15 bottles under £20, 4 by glass **Notes** Civ Wed 40 **Seats** 30 **Children** Portions, Menu **Parking** 20

Darroch Learg Hotel

BALLATER Map 23 NO39

Modern Scottish

Flawless cooking in stunning Highland retreat

☎ 013397 55443
Braemar Rd AB35 5UX
e-mail: enquiries@darrochlearg.co.uk
dir: On A93 at the W end of village

Situated on a wooded hillside, this Victorian country-house hotel has fine views over the Dee valley and the Cairngorm National Park. The house is comfortably and traditionally furnished and the two lounges, one with a welcoming log fire, enjoy views through large bay windows. The conservatory dining room is a light, bright and contemporary space with muted colours, modern art on the walls, and windows that open out to the trees. Tables are smartly dressed in white linen, and the service

is friendly and knowledgeable. The chef takes a modern approach to Scottish cooking and delivers an exciting menu using the best of the national produce to good effect. Pan-fried scallops are paired with Stornoway black pudding in a starter, the dish finished with sweetcorn purée, while roast partridge comes with caramelised red cabbage, smoked bacon, wild mushrooms and pear purée in a seductive main course. Finish with classic lemon tart with a berry sauce or a selection of fine cheeses with oatcakes (of course) and digestive biscuits. The wine list is excellent and has a truly global reach.

Chef David Mutter **Owner** The Franks Family **Times** 12.30-2/7-9, Closed Xmas, last 3wks Jan, Closed L Mon-Sat **Prices** Fixed L course £24, Fixed D 3 course £44-£50, Tasting menu £47, Service included **Wines** 186 bottles over £20, 4 by glass **Notes** Sunday L, Vegetarian available, Dress restrictions, Smart casual **Seats** 48 **Children** Portions, Menu **Parking** 15

BANCHORY — Map 23 NO69

Raemoir House Hotel

🏵🏵 Scottish, French 💻

Romantic setting for accomplished cuisine

☎ 01330 824884
Raemoir AB31 4ED
e-mail: relax@raemoir.com
dir: A93 to Banchory then A980, hotel at x-rds after 2.5 m

Raemoir House enjoys a romantic setting in 3,500 acres of parkland and forest. It was built in 1817 but extensively developed in the Victorian era, when Balmoral first became a favourite royal retreat, and has been a hotel since 1943. Dramatic changes have recently taken place, including the swapping of the dining room with the drawing room. The new dining room is the majestic wood panelled room at the end of the main corridor. Cuisine is Scottish with French influences and uses prime local produce. You might start with hot smoked salmon tian with red onion and caper relish, and follow with Gressingham duck breast served with dauphinoise potato, braised Savoy cabbage and rosemary jus.

Times 12-2/6.30-9, Closed 26-30 Dec

OLDMELDRUM — Map 23 NJ82

Meldrum House Hotel Golf & Country Estate

🏵 Modern British

Elegant dining in a splendid country mansion

☎ 01651 872294
AB51 0AE
e-mail: enquiries@meldrumhouse.co.uk
dir: 11m N of Aberdeen (from Aberdeen to Dyce), A947 towards Banff, through Newmachen along outskirts of Oldmeldrum, main entrance large white archway

Tastefully restored to highlight its original character, this substantial baronial country mansion stands in 350 acres of wooded parkland with a golf course. The traditional Scottish cooking - with international twists - has a flare for presentation in well-constructed dishes using quality Scottish produce. Expect panache of fish (salmon, sea bass, smoked haddock and halibut) with a light curry sauce to start, breast of guinea fowl with truffle mash and cep cream, or breast of Gressingham duck with tarragon sauce for main course, and desserts like apple tart with caramel sauce and green apple sorbet.

Chef Grant Walker **Owner** Sylvia Simpson
Times 12-2.30/6.30-9 **Prices** Fixed L 3 course fr £19, Fixed D 4 course fr £37, Service optional **Wines** 46 bottles over £20, 25 bottles under £20, 4 by glass **Notes** Sunday L, Vegetarian available, Dress restrictions, Smart casual, Civ Wed 80 **Seats** 40, Pr/dining room 16 **Children** Portions, Menu **Parking** 60

STONEHAVEN — Map 23 NO88

Carron Art Deco Restaurant

🏵 Modern British

Impressive food served in a stylish art deco setting

☎ 01569 760460
20 Cameron St AB39 2HS
e-mail: jacki@cleaverhotels.eclipse.co.uk
dir: From Aberdeen, right at town centre traffic lights, 2nd left onto Ann St, right at road end, 3rd building on right.

This glass-fronted restaurant, dating from 1937, has been beautifully restored to its former glory as an impressive example of art deco design, with objets d'art, mirrored tiles and wooden panels providing an authentic period feel. Service is friendly and alfresco dining is available, weather permitting. The kitchen impresses with modern British cuisine using local produce, and seafood features well on the menu. Great combinations of flavours hit home in dishes like chef's special crab soup and local haddock fillet topped with cheese, bacon, cumin and pesto served on a bubble-and-squeak cake. Prepare to be wowed by desserts such as sticky pear and carrot pudding with butterscotch sauce and vanilla ice cream.

Chef Robert Cleaver **Owner** Robert Cleaver
Times 12-2/6-9.30, Closed 24 Dec-10 Jan, Closed Sun-Mon **Prices** Starter £3.45-£5.85, Main £10.50-£19.95, Dessert £4.95-£5.10, Service optional **Wines** 12 bottles over £20, 15 bottles under £20 **Seats** 80, Pr/dining room 30 **Children** Portions, Menu **Parking** Town Square

Tolbooth Restaurant

🏵 Modern British, Seafood

Quay-side restaurant serving fish straight from the sea

☎ 01569 762287
Old Pier, Stonehaven Harbour AB39 2JU
e-mail: enquiries@tolbooth-restaurant.co.uk
dir: 15m S of Aberdeen on A90, located in Stonehaven harbour

The oldest building in Stonehaven, dating from 1600, was originally a store used during the building of nearby Dunnottar Castle. It is right on the harbour and has also been a jail and courthouse. These days there's a museum on the ground floor and a restaurant upstairs, accessed by a steep outside staircase, with whitewashed walls, wooden floors and modern table settings. Wonderfully fresh seafood is the house speciality, simply prepared in dishes such as Tolbooth crab soup enriched with sherry, grilled local lobster or langoustines, and a collection of local grilled fish with dauphinoise potatoes, buttered fève beans and chive oil.

Chef Craig Somers **Owner** J Edward Abbott
Times 12-2.30/6-10, Closed 2 wks Xmas & Jan, Closed Sun & Mon **Prices** Fixed L 2 course £12.50, Starter £3.95-£7.95, Main £13.95-£19.95, Dessert £5.95-£6.95, Service optional, Groups min 10 service 10% **Wines** 24 bottles over £20, 8 bottles under £20, 3 by glass **Notes** Vegetarian available **Seats** 46 **Children** Portions **Parking** Public car park, 100 spaces

ANGUS

CARNOUSTIE — Map 21 NO53

Dalhousie Restaurant

🏵 Traditional British

Fining dining in a wonderful location

☎ 01241 411999
Carnoustie Hotel, The Links DD7 7JE
e-mail: reservations.carnoustie@ohiml.com
dir: A92 exit at Upper Victoria junct, follow signs for town centre and then signs for golf course

This modern hotel is adjacent to the 1st and 18th greens of the magnificent Carnoustie golf course, which was home of the 2007 British Open. Overlooking the course, the traditional-styled, bright-and-airy Dalhousie restaurant is attractively presented and has a modern elegance with well appointed tables set off with quality silver and sparkling glassware. Service is attentive and friendly, and the cooking style is traditional Scottish. Simply presented dishes are well balanced and seasonality playing a strong part. Haggis wontons with clapshot and whisky jus, and pork tenderloin with duo of cabbage, château potatoes and apple slices show the style.

Times Closed L all week

GLAMIS — Map 21 NO34

Castleton House Hotel

🏵🏵 Modern & Traditional British 💻 V 🖐

Victorian country house with culinary flair

☎ 01307 840340
Castleton of Eassie DD8 1SJ
e-mail: hotel@castletonglamis.co.uk
dir: On A94 midway between Forfar & Coupar Angus, 3m W of Glamis

A moated Victorian property surrounded by tall trees, this impressive hotel provides a great sense of seclusion and tranquillity. Beautiful grounds include a croquet lawn and a menagerie of ducks, chickens and pigs. Vases of seasonal flowers adorn the conservatory dining room, overlooking the garden which also supplies the kitchen with vegetables and herbs. Highest quality ingredients are used and there is a strong emphasis on local produce. Contrasting flavours work well in a starter of wood pigeon with Puy lentils, quails' eggs, lardons and truffle vinaigrette, while roast fillet of monkfish served on a crab and saffron risotto is perfectly complemented by fragrant baby fennel and young courgettes in a well-presented main course.

Chef Kevin MacGillivray Owner David & Verity Webster Times 12-2/6.30-9, Closed 25 Dec, New Year Prices Fixed L 2 course £10.90–£21.50, Fixed D 3 course £35, Service included Wines 30 bottles over £20, 17 bottles under £20, 8 by glass Notes Sunday L, Vegetarian menu, Civ Wed 50 Seats 50, Pr/dining room 35 Children Portions, Menu Parking 50

Gordon's

◉◉ Modern British 🖥 🖐

Scottish cooking from a friendly family team

☎ 01241 830364

Main St DD11 5RN

e-mail: gordonsrest@aol.com

dir: On A92, turn off at signs for village of Inverkeilor, between Arbroath and Montrose

This charming Georgian property is a cosy affair with bags of character - beamed ceiling, huge open fire and rugs on wooden floors. But the name of this family-run establishment only tells half the story, as the eponymous Gordon is joined in the kitchen by son Garry whose cooking is now cutting edge with that all-important wow-factor. The imaginative modern cooking is underpinned by a classical theme and makes good use of seasonal produce from the abundant Scottish larder on its appealing, sensibly compact menus. Jerusalem artichoke and pancetta velouté with roasted scallops and chestnut purée might feature alongside the likes of pan-fried line-caught sea bass with saffron potato mousseline, and mussel, clam and oyster broth, while for dessert you might try hot Valrhona chocolate fondant with basil ice cream and passionfruit and guava coulis.

Chef Gordon Watson & Garry Watson Owner Gordon & Maria Watson Times 12-1.45/7-9, Closed 1st 2 wks Jan, Closed Mon, Closed L Sat, Closed D Sun Prices Fixed L 3 course fr £27, Fixed D 4 course fr £43, Service optional Wines 19 bottles over £20, 25 bottles under £20, 3 by glass Notes Sunday L, Vegetarian available, Dress restrictions, Smart casual Seats 24, Pr/dining room 8 Children Min 12 yrs Parking 6

Loch Melfort Hotel

◉◉ Modern British 🖥

Wonderful views and a menu specialising in fresh seafood

☎ 01852 200233

PA34 4XG

e-mail: reception@lochmelfort.co.uk

dir: From Oban, 20 m S on A816; from Lochgilphead, 19 m N on A816

This family-run hotel enjoys a spectacular location on the West Coast with views across Asknish Bay towards the islands of Jura, Scarba and Shuna. The setting is the

perfect complement to the wonderful seafood on offer in the attractive dining room. Skilful cooking makes excellent use of local produce in starters such as shellfish bisque, or tian of melon and crab topped with tapenade, herb oil and toasted pine nuts. Mains include slices of monkfish tail gently steamed with a warm red wine and herb vinaigrette, or roast saddle of Morayshire lamb with rosemary and garlic. An alternative dining choice, popular with visiting yachtsmen, is the Skerry Bistro.

Loch Melfort Hotel

Times Closed 2 Jan-15 Feb, Closed L all week

Dunvalanree

◉ Modern British V 🖐

Local seafood in stunning location

☎ 01583 431 226

Port Righ Bay PA28 6SE

e-mail: stay@dunvalanree.com

dir: On B879, in Carradale turn right at X-rds, restaurant is situated at end of rd

Standing in delightful gardens and an ideal place to explore the Mull of Kintyre, Dunvalanree enjoys stunning views across the Kilbrannan Sound to the hills of Arran. This is a genuine family-run operation with mum in the kitchen and father and daughter welcoming guests in the traditional restaurant. With skill and imagination, simple Scottish cuisine is conjured from the very best that the local larder has to offer and traditional dishes stand shoulder to shoulder with more innovative fare. The daily-changing menu might include locally-landed langoustines with dill mayonnaise followed by honey-roasted duck with bramble fruit poached in red wine, and chocolate mousse cake with butterscotch sauce.

Chef Alyson Milstead Owner Alan & Alyson Milstead Times Closed Jan-Feb, Closed L all week Prices Fixed D 3 course £25, Service optional Wines 12 bottles under £20, 4 by glass Notes Vegetarian menu Seats 20 Children Portions Parking 8

Balinakill Country House Hotel

◉ Scottish, French

Victorian setting for contemporary cuisine

☎ 01880 740206

PA29 6XL

e-mail: info@balinakill.com

dir: 10m S of Tarbert Loch Fyne. The entrance is located on the left off A83 travelling S towards Campbeltown

This magnificent house on the Kintyre peninsula was built by William Mackinnon, founder of the British India Line. It has had a chequered history, but there is no evidence of this in the beautiful Victorian plasterwork and panelling, antiques and period pieces. The cooking is classical Scottish and French in style, using free-range, organic and local produce wherever possible. Typical dishes from the concise, fixed-price menu include grilled mackerel salad with sweet chilli dressing, rack of lamb with creamy mash, ratatouille and roast garlic jus, and dark chocolate brownie with vanilla ice cream.

Chef Angus MacDiarmid Owner Angus & Susan MacDiarmid Times Closed L all week Prices Fixed D 3 course £28.95, Service optional Wines 12 bottles over £20, 23 bottles under £20, 3 by glass Seats 24 Children Min 12 yrs, Portions Parking 20

CLACHAN-SEIL — Map 20 NM71

Willowburn Hotel

British, French 🖥️ NOTABLE WINE LIST 🍷

Welcoming country-cottage hotel offering local produce and fine dining

☎ 01852 300276
PA34 4TJ
e-mail: willowburn.hotel@virgin.net
dir: 11m S of Oban via A816 and B844 (Easdale) over Atlantic Bridge, restaurant 0.5m after bridge on left

This welcoming small hotel enjoys a peaceful setting, with grounds stretching down to the shores of Clachan Sound. There is a friendly, homely feel to this relaxed place and you can watch the wildlife from the dining room window. Service is unobtrusive, and there's a dinner party atmosphere with all guests congregating at 7pm for aperitifs and canapés. The cooking style brings together French, Scottish and British cuisine, producing good clean flavours using the very best of local produce. Try a starter like salmon and turbot in seaweed with chervil broth, followed by a main course of loin of local Barrichbeyan pork roasted with garlic, rosemary and cream. Finish with lemon, raspberry and chocolate roulade. An excellent wine list completes the upbeat package.

Chef Chris Wolfe **Owner** Jan & Chris Wolfe **Times** Closed Dec-Feb **Prices** Fixed D 4 course £39, Service optional **Wines** 74 bottles over £20, 64 bottles under £20, 4 by glass **Notes** Gourmet & wine wknds available, Vegetarian available **Seats** 20 **Children** Min 8 yrs **Parking** 20

COVE — Map 20 NS28

Knockderry House Hotel

Modern Scottish, International 🖥️

Scottish country-house dining in an idyllic setting

☎ 01436 842283
Shore Rd G84 0NX
e-mail: info@knockderryhouse.co.uk
dir: From A814 follow signs to Coulport, then take sharp left at rdbt and continue for 2m along Shore Rd

Looking out over the majestic shores of Loch Long, this fine Victorian country-house hotel has a wealth of period features, and even provides five moorings for guests wishing to arrive by sea. Wood-panelled walls and stained glass windows set the scene in the restaurant, which supplies relaxed, friendly service and impressive views of the Clyde sea lochs and beyond. The kitchen conjures up accomplished cuisine, with great attention to detail, using excellent seasonal local produce. Try breast of corn-fed chicken served with Peaton Hill venison stovies and buttered Savoy cabbage, or perhaps Wick-landed lythe fillet served with mushroom and artichoke risotto, spinach and brown shrimp sauce.

Chef Beth MacLeod, Johnny Aitken **Owner** Beth & Murdo MacLeod **Times** 12.30-2.30/6-9, Closed 25 Dec **Prices** Fixed L 2 course £13.95, Starter £4.95-£9.95, Main £9.95-£24, Dessert £4.95-£7.95, Service optional, Groups min 6 service 12% **Wines** 6 by glass **Notes** Sunday L, Vegetarian available, Dress restrictions, Smart casual, Civ Wed 80 **Seats** 36 **Children** Portions, Menu **Parking** 20

ERISKA — Map 20 NM94

Isle of Eriska

⊕⊕⊕ – see below

KILCHRENAN — Map 20 NN02

The Ardanaiseig Hotel

French, British

An idyllic lochside location, with a rugged romantic feel and excellent food

☎ 01866 833333
by Loch Awe PA35 1HE
e-mail: info@ardanaiseig.com
dir: Take A85 to Oban. At Taynuilt turn left onto B845 towards Kilchrenan. In Kilchrenan turn left by pub. Hotel in 3m

The reward for a beautiful, long and winding drive down a single-track road is this early Victorian mansion, gloriously located on the shores of Loch Awe, amid truly

Isle of Eriska

ERISKA — Map 20 NM94

Traditional British 🖥️ NOTABLE WINE LIST 🍷

Flawless blend of service, style and cuisine in luxurious island retreat

☎ 01631 720371
PA37 1SD
e-mail: office@eriska-hotel.co.uk
dir: A82 from Glasgow to Tyndrum. A85 towards Oban; at Connel bridge take A828 to Benderloch village for 4m

It's hard to beat the Isle of Eriska. First, it's a private island with stunning sea views and amazing sunsets - a real romantic getaway. Linked to the mainland by a causeway, it has a remote and secluded feel that belies its proximity to Glasgow and Edinburgh. Secondly, there's the house - a Scottish baronial pile decorated in an opulent yet tasteful style with rich colours, heavy curtains

and plenty of dark, polished wood. Not to mention the thoroughly modern addition of a luxurious spa. The restaurant continues the fine balance of old-school formality and current dining sensibilities with highly professional staff offering knowledgeable and friendly service. The kitchen's daily-changing dinner menu is modern, classically underpinned, and comes driven by some of the finest Scottish and locally sourced produce available. Take Argyll roe deer with quince purée, crottin ravioli and wild juniper jus, followed by Oban-landed turbot with its own lightly smoked consommé, soft herb gnocchi and braised leaves, and perhaps a baked black olive madeleine covered with orange chiboust with a passionfruit sorbet. A cheese trolley follows dessert and coffee and petits fours wrap things up in the Hall, while an impressive wine list pays due reverence to the memorable cuisine. And don't miss the badgers that come to feed at the terrace door in the evening.

Chef Robert MacPherson **Owner** Mr Buchanan-Smith **Times** 12.30-1.30/8-9, Closed Jan **Prices** Fixed D 4 course £35-£39.50, Service optional **Wines** 136 bottles over £20, 43 bottles under £20, 10 by glass **Notes** Dress restrictions, Smart casual, Civ Wed 110, Air con **Seats** 40, Pr/dining room 20 **Children** Portions, Menu **Parking** 50

breathtaking scenery. Interiors are very much in keeping with the period, with gorgeous antiques and fine art, all very understated and uncluttered. The kitchen produces innovative food, skilfully and faultlessly cooked with good use made of local produce. Dinner is a complete five-course experience, with dishes such as Inverawe smoked trout with potato salad, trout caviar and herb oil, fillet of Aberdeen Angus Wellington with shallot purée, wild mushrooms and Madeira jus, and vanilla pannacotta with pear jam and rice pudding croquettes.

Times 12-2/7-9, Closed 2 Jan- 10 Feb

Taychreggan Hotel

@@ Traditional British 🖳 V
- -
Imaginative dining in Highland country house

☎ 01866 833211 & 833366
PA35 1HQ
e-mail: info@taychreggan.co.uk
dir: W from Glasgow on A82 to Crainlarich. W on A85 to Taynuilt. Hotel on B845 towards Kilchrenan & Taychreggan

Surrounded by stunning Highland scenery, this former cattle drovers' inn enjoys an idyllic location in 40 acres of grounds on the shores of Loch Awe. Now a comfortable country-house hotel, diners can enjoy courteous and winningly old-fashioned service as they admire spectacular views from the arched windows of the elegant dining room. The imaginative cuisine is skilfully prepared and makes extensive use of high quality Scottish and locally sourced ingredients. Start with marinated Mull Bay scallops with lemon and lime, served with chilli and coriander noodles and an oriental dressing, then tuck into roast loin of Highland beef fillet with fondant potato, ratatouille of vegetables, braised shallot and a Madeira and thyme jus. Finish with apple, cinnamon and raisin crumble with toasted walnuts served with sauce anglaise and vanilla pod ice cream.

Chef Alan Hunter **Owner** North American Country Inns **Times** Closed 24-26 Dec **Wines** 23 bottles over £20, 16 bottles under £20, 2 by glass **Notes** Fixed D, 5 courses £40.00, Vegetarian menu, Dress restrictions, Smart casual, Civ Wed 60 **Seats** 45, Pr/dining room 18 **Children** Min 5 yrs **Parking** 40

Cairnbaan

@ British, European 🖳
- -
Canal-side dining strong on seafood

☎ 01546 603668
Crinan Canal, Cairnbaan PA31 8SJ
e-mail: info@cairnbaan.com
dir: Cairnbaan is 2m N of Lochgilphead on A83, hotel first on left

In a delightful location on the Crinan Canal, this small hotel has wide picture windows making the most of the views. While alfresco dining is popular in the warmer months, winter is made cosy by the tartan décor in the

restaurant, and a wealth of creature comforts. Fresh seafood is a powerful draw throughout the seasons, with dishes such as home-made fishcakes with fresh herb sauce and salad garnish, and fillet of halibut in a herb crust with braised fennel, black olives and rocket oil. Meat-eaters are not forgotten.

Cairnbaan

Times 12-2.30/6-9.30

Colquhoun's

@@ Modern British
- -

Idyllic Loch Lomond location with inspired cuisine

☎ 01436 860201
The Lodge on Loch Lomond, Hotel & Restaurant G83 8PA
e-mail: res@loch-lomond.co.uk
dir: N of Glasgow on A82

In an idyllic setting with stunning views across the loch, Colquhoun's is the fine-dining restaurant at The Lodge on Loch Lomond. Traditional Scottish décor blends with Scandinavian-style touches of pinewood walls and pillars in this refurbished venue. There is also a split-level lounge bar and a balconied terrace where guests can dine alfresco in the summer. The restaurant has glass-topped tables, good table appointments and an open-plan kitchen. The brasserie-style modern menu has strong Scottish flair and features good quality, locally-sourced produce, while service is friendly and efficient. To start, try spiced pumpkin ravioli with red onion marmalade, parsnip crisps and beetroot dressing, followed by roast North Sea halibut with sauté potatoes, fennel confit, smoked aubergine purée and roasted red pepper coulis.

Colquhoun's

Chef Donn Eadie **Owner** Niall Colquhoun
Times 12-5/6-9.45 **Prices** Main £29.95, Service optional
Wines 29 bottles over £20, 20 bottles under £20, 7 by glass **Notes** ALC 3 courses, Sunday L, Vegetarian available, Civ Wed 100 **Seats** 100, Pr/dining room 40
Children Portions, Menu **Parking** 70

Bachler's Conservatory

@ French, International
- -
Sophisticated dining overlooking Oban Bay

☎ 01631 571115
13 Dalriach Rd PA34 5EQ
e-mail: info@kimberley-hotel.com
dir: Telephone for directions

The stunning Bachler's Conservatory restaurant overlooks the garden, the harbour and the waters of Oban Bay, with a sophisticated décor of green tablecloths, red striped seating and plenty of fresh flowers. The building was a maternity hospital until 1995, and the hotel name is linked to the South African Kimberley Diamond Mine. The cooking has a distinctly modern French flair but the ingredients are decidedly top-of-the-range Scottish. Seafood straight from the sea is a strength (monkfish roasted in herb butter with leaf spinach), but local game (roasted venison) and meat (Aberdeen Angus beef and Scottish lamb) are well represented too.

Times Closed Nov-Etr, Closed L all week

Coast

@ Modern
- -
Contemporary restaurant serving prime local seafood and meats

☎ 01631 569900
104 George St PA34 5NT
e-mail: coastoban@yahoo.co.uk
dir: Situated on Oban's main street

True to its name, this contemporary restaurant's interior - originally a bank, on the town's main street - has been transformed into a smart, welcoming space with the use of textiles and colours that reflect its surrounding coastline. The warm, calming colour palette combines with a mix of metal, wood and modern artwork that's pleasing to the eye. The kitchen's modern, simple yet

Continued

OBAN *Continued*

imaginative approach suits the surroundings, driven by high-quality Oban-landed fish and seafood from the day's catch, while the likes of lamb and game find a place alongside seasonal produce from the abundant Scottish larder. Seared West Coast scallops served with a compôte of Jerusalem artichokes, borlotti beans, spinach and confit tomatoes or pot roast shoulder of lamb are fine examples of the cuisine.

Chef Richard Fowler **Owner** Richard & Nicola Fowler **Times** 12-2/5.30-9.30, Closed 25 Dec, Closed L Sun **Prices** Fixed L 2 course £12, Starter £4.25-£7.95, Main £14.95-£21.50, Dessert £4.95, Service optional **Wines** 19 bottles over £20, 22 bottles under £20, 6 by glass **Notes** Vegetarian available **Seats** 46 **Parking** On street

Eeusk

◉ Seafood 🖥

Impeccably fresh seafood and great sea views

☎ 01631 565666
North Pier PA34 5QD
e-mail: eeusk.fishcafe@virgin.net
dir: Close to ferry terminal, on opposite pier (North)

Eeusk is a modern building in a fantastic location, right on one of Oban's piers. Unrestricted views of the bay and islands are afforded from the large glass windows and, as the pier is busy with fishermen and visitors, there is

plenty to see as you eat. Simple cooking makes the best of fine fresh local seafood. A good selection would be Thai fishcakes with chilli and ginger dressing and salad, baked wild halibut served with creamed leeks and sautéed potatoes, and sticky toffee pudding with butterscotch and fresh cream.

Eeusk

Chef Wayne Keenan **Owner** The Macleod Family **Times** 12-3/6-9.30, Closed 25-26 Dec, 1 Jan, 2 wks mid Jan **Prices** Food prices not confirmed for 2009. Please telephone for details. **Notes** Vegetarian available, Air con **Seats** 100, Pr/dining room 24 **Children** Min 10 yrs D, Portions **Parking** Public car park at rear

Manor House Hotel

◉ Traditional European

Elegant Georgian dower house with quality local produce

☎ 01631 562087
Gallanach Rd PA34 4LS
e-mail: info@manorhouseoban.com
web: www.manorhouseoban.com
dir: 300 mtrs W of Oban ferry terminal

Looking out over the harbour, The Manor House dates back to around 1780, when it was built by the Duke of Argyll for his family. Now a hotel, it retains the charm and atmosphere of its Georgian origins. The elegant, cosy dining room has deep green walls and heavy curtains, and provides a five-course dinner menu of Scottish cuisine with a European influence, which makes good use of seasonal local produce, including fresh herbs from the garden. Starters might include smoked haddock and leek

Airds Hotel and Restaurant

PORT APPIN   Map 20 NM94

Modern British 🖥 V 🍷

A lochside gastronomic treat

☎ 01631 730236
PA38 4DF
e-mail: airds@airds-hotel.com
web: www.airds-hotel.com
dir: On A828 (Oban to Fort William road) follow signs for Port Appin. 2.5m, hotel on left

This small luxury hotel sits at the edge of the waters of the Sound of Lismore, enjoying breathtaking views of Loch Linnhe. Originally an 18th-century ferry inn, today it combines country-house comfort with modern chic to create a relaxed, intimate atmosphere. Richly furnished lounges come replete with cosy sofas, log fires and interesting artwork, while the small cottage-style

restaurant continues the theme with designer fabrics, candlelit tables and huge windows framing the views over the loch and mountains. Service is highly professional, but retains a personal and welcoming touch, while the cooking takes a modern approach imbued with a Scottish twist. Tip-top ingredients are treated with due respect, featuring an abundance of fish and seafood with the focus squarely on local luxury produce. The kitchen's intelligently simple, clean-cut style and uncomplicated combinations allow the flavours of key ingredients to shine on the seasonal, daily-changing fixed-price menus. Try a starter of halibut with scallop, crispy artichokes and pan juices, followed perhaps by roast fillet of cod with langoustines, tapenade crust, herb mash and chive velouté, or seared wild salmon and scallop with soft herb and parmesan risotto and shellfish cappuccino.

Chef J Paul Burns **Owner** Mr & Mrs S McKivragan **Times** 12-1.45/7.30-9 **Wines** 151 bottles over £20, 13 bottles under £20, 6 by glass **Notes** Gourmet menu 7 courses £75, Sunday L, Vegetarian menu, Dress restrictions, Smart casual at D, no jeans/trainers/T-shirts, Civ Wed 40 **Seats** 32, Pr/dining room 8 **Children** Min 8 yrs, Portions, Menu **Parking** 20

risotto with sea scallops and sweet basil oil, followed by mains such as roast loin of venison with thyme Anna potatoes and creamed Savoy cabbage with bacon and mustard.

Chef Patrick Freytag, Shaun Squire **Owner** Mr P L Crane **Times** 12-2.30/6.45-8.45, Closed 25-26 Dec **Prices** Fixed L course £22, Fixed D 4 course £36, Starter £3-£8, Main £15-£21, Dessert £7, Service optional **Wines** 21 bottles over £20, 21 bottles under £20, 7 by glass **Notes** Sunday L, Vegetarian available, Dress restrictions, Smart casual, no trainers, Civ Wed 30 **Seats** 34 **Children** Min 12 yrs, Portions **Parking** 12

PORT APPIN   Map 20 NM94

Airds Hotel and Restaurant

◉◉◉ – see opposite

STRACHUR   Map 20 NN00

Creggans Inn

◉ Modern British 🖳

Local produce showcased in spectacular lochside setting

☎ 01369 860279
PA27 8BX
e-mail: info@creggans-inn.co.uk
dir: From Glasgow A82, along Loch Lomond, then W on A83, onto A815 to Strachur. Or by ferry from Gourock to Dunoon onto A815

Overlooking Loch Fyne, in a picture-perfect location next to some of the most remote and unspoilt countryside in Scotland, sits this charming, historic country hotel. Stunning views, open fires and a restaurant that showcases local produce make it a destination venue for tourists and business travellers alike. The dining room boasts stripped floors, terracotta walls and fabulous views, complemented by roaring log fires in the winter months. Scottish dishes predominate on a menu that offers the likes of grilled fillet of salmon with braised Savoy cabbage, butternut squash and bacon, or pot-roasted chicken with mashed potatoes, carrots, garlic confit and gremolata. For dessert, try pear and almond cake with home-made stem ginger ice cream.

Times Closed 25-26 Dec, Closed L all week

TARBERT LOCH FYNE   Map 20 NR86

Stonefield Castle Hotel

◉ Modern British

Enjoyable waterside dining in baronial keep

☎ 01880 820836
PA29 6YJ
e-mail: reservations.stonefieldcastle@ohiml.com
dir: 2m N of Tarbert Village

Set in beautiful woodland gardens - justly famous for their rhododendrons - on the loch shore, this impressive baronial castle dates back to 1837. The elegant dining room boasts picture windows offering unrivalled views over Loch Fyne. Serving modern Scottish dishes with the occasional oriental influence, good use is made of local ingredients like Buccleuch beef, Argyll lamb, salmon and home-grown vegetables. Try the lobster shavings with a lightly dressed fennel salad to start, followed by roasted darne of salmon served with pork belly, and lime and chilli dressing. Round off with chocolate assiette and one of the fifty listed malts.

Chef Aaron Hartman **Owner** Oxford Hotels & Inns **Times** 12-2/6-9 **Prices** Starter £4.50-£9, Main £9.50-£23, Dessert £3-£6, Service optional **Wines** 23 bottles over £20, 38 bottles under £20, 6 by glass **Notes** Dress restrictions, Smart casual, Civ Wed 120 **Seats** 120, Pr/dining room 10 **Children** Portions, Menu **Parking** 33

TIGHNABRUAICH   Map 20 NR97

An Lochan

◉◉ Modern Scottish 🍃

Fine Scottish fare beside the loch

☎ 01700 811239
Shore Rd PA21 2BE
e-mail: info@anlochan.co.uk
dir: From Strachur, on A886, right onto A8003 to Tighnabruaich. Hotel on right at bottom of hill. From Dunoon ferry terminal left onto B8000

In an idyllic location on the loch shore, this delightfully cosy 18th-century coaching inn offers magnificent views over the water to the Kyles of Bute. Open log fires and bare-stone walls add to the relaxed and informal atmosphere, and the small team are warm and welcoming. With a choice of dining areas, the elegant main restaurant marries tradition with a modern Scottish gastro-style approach, putting the emphasis on quality ingredients and named suppliers. Game and beef, fresh from local estates, and freshly-caught fish are treated with integrity in starters such as pan-fried scallops 'caught by Mary' and served with sweet potato purée and pancetta cream froth, perhaps followed by fillet of Buccleuch beef Rossini with pommes Anna, baby vegetables and onion three ways. Not forgetting desserts, like Seville orange soufflé with hot chocolate and malt ice cream.

Chef Paul Scott **Owner** The McKie Family **Times** 12-2.30/6-9, Closed Xmas **Prices** Starter £4-£8, Main £18-£24, Dessert £4-£8, Service optional **Wines** 50 bottles over £20, 14 bottles under £20, 6 by glass **Notes** Sunday L, Vegetarian available **Seats** 35, Pr/dining room 20 **Children** Portions **Parking** 20

AYRSHIRE, EAST

SORN   Map 20 NS52

The Sorn Inn

◉◉ Modern British

Refurbished coaching inn offering modern cuisine

☎ 01290 551305
35 Main St KA5 6HU
e-mail: craig@sorninn.com
dir: From A77, take the A76 to Mauchline join B743, 4m to Sorn

Don't let appearances deceive you. On the outside this may look like an 18th-century coaching inn, but on the inside it's very much in the present day with modern styling and a warm, rustic colour scheme throughout that's very inviting. There are two dining options, the more informal Chop House for bistro-style food in a cosy pub area, and the fine-dining restaurant with its comfy leather seats and interesting artwork. Here you will find modern British cooking with an emphasis on fresh produce from the abundant local larder, including game, meat and fish. Seasonally-changing menus, including daily specials and grazing options, include the likes of warm oak-smoked salmon with pea purée, potato fritter and horseradish cream, and pan-fried cod served with red wine, tomato and chorizo risotto, with bramble apple compôte, brandy savarin and advocaat ice cream to finish.

Chef Craig Grant **Owner** The Grant Partnership **Times** 12-2.30/6.30-9.30, Closed 2 wks Jan, Closed Mon, Closed D Sun **Prices** Starter £4-£5.80, Main £8.25-£23, Dessert £4-£5, Service optional, Groups min 8 service 10% **Wines** 35 bottles over £20, 17 bottles under £20, 13 by glass **Notes** Sunday L, Vegetarian available **Seats** 42 **Children** Portions, Menu **Parking** 9

AYRSHIRE, NORTH

DALRY — Map 20 NS24

Braidwoods

◎◎ Modern Scottish 🖳

Creative flair in a beautiful setting

☎ 01294 833544
Drumastle Mill Cottage KA24 4LN
e-mail: keithbraidwood@btconnect.com
dir: 1 mile from Dalry on the Saltcoats road

This charming group of old millers' cottages, transformed into a modern-looking restaurant with two dining rooms, offers rustic dining in a relaxed yet formal environment. A popular venue for 'ladies who lunch', but equally a romantic setting for dinner. Skilled cooking by the chef/patron brings modern Scottish dishes of high quality and good value to the menu. Try a starter of smoked chicken, prawn and avocado salad with garlic and anchovy dressing. Main courses might include the likes of whole roasted boneless quail stuffed with black pudding or baked fillet of West Coast turbot on smoked salmon risotto. To finish, try the vanilla pannacotta with passionfruit, pineapple and mango soup.

Times 12-1.45/7-9, Closed 25-26 Dec, 1st 3 wks Jan, 1st 2 wks Sep, Closed Mon, Closed L Tue (Sun Etr-Sep), Closed D Sun

AYRSHIRE, SOUTH

AYR — Map 20 NS32

Enterkine Country House

◎◎ Traditional 🖳 V

The best of Scottish produce in a country-house setting

☎ 01292 520580
Annbank KA6 5AL
e-mail: mail@enterkine.com
dir: 5m E of Ayr on B743

An elegant art deco property dating from the 1930s, Enterkine is set within its own 350-acre estate with views over woodland, meadows and the Ayr valley. Drinks are served in the library or garden room, and food in the large, open-plan restaurant with low ceilings, a blazing fire in winter and Shaker-style panelling. The Scottish country house-style cooking with French influences takes full advantage of excellent local produce, including pork from the estate, local berries and Buccleuch organic beef. Recommendations include terrine of Scottish hare with 'crabbies' wine jelly, beetroot and ginger muffin, and fillet of turbot with pigs' cheeks, artichokes and Alsace bacon.

Chef Paul Moffat **Owner** Mr Browne **Times** 12-2/7-9 **Prices** Fixed L 2 course fr £16.50, Fixed D 4 course £30-£45, Service optional **Wines** 36 bottles over £20, 14 bottles under £20, 4 by glass **Notes** Tasting menu available, Sunday L, Vegetarian menu, Dress restrictions, Jackets required, Civ Wed 70 **Seats** 40, Pr/dining room 14 **Children** Portions, Menu **Parking** 20

Fairfield House Hotel

◎◎ Traditional British

Modern, relaxed dining and great views

☎ 01292 267461
12 Fairfield Rd KA7 2AS
e-mail: reservations@fairfieldhotel.co.uk
dir: From A77 to Ayr South. Follow signs for town centre. Left into Miller Rd. At lights turn left, then right into Fairfield Rd

Once home to a Glasgow tea merchant, this luxury seafront hotel has spectacular views across the Firth of Clyde to the Isle of Arran. Martin's Bar and Grill has leather seating, Grecian-style pillars, feature plants and original artwork across the bar and restaurant areas, plus an outside terrace making the most of the views. The cuisine style is simple, using local produce to create Scottish dishes with a twist. Try duo of oak-smoked Shetland salmon and gravad lax, followed by Fairfield steak pie with potatoes and seasonal vegetables. Finish, perhaps, with hot chocolate

Glenapp Castle

BALLANTRAE — Map 20 NX08

Modern British V

Elegant castle hideaway offering accomplished, innovative cuisine

☎ 01465 831212
KA26 0NZ
e-mail: info@glenappcastle.com
dir: Drive S through Ballantrae, cross bridge over River Stinchar, turn 1st right, gates & lodge house 1m.

This is a gem of a castle, built in 1870 as a private home and restored to splendour by Fay and Graham Cowan, and now a luxury hotel. The grounds are breathtaking, with 36 acres of gardens and woodland to explore, including terraced formal gardens, azalea pond and walled garden with magnificent 150ft Victorian glasshouses. The castle is opulently furnished in a traditional manner including the dining room with its elegantly set tables and views

out over the garden. The kitchen team, with new head chef at the helm, deliver six-course menus based on first-class produce and demonstrating considerable craftsmanship. There are two choices at main course and dessert, otherwise you are in the capable hands of the chef. An amuse-bouche of langoustine in tomato essence precedes seared foie gras, perfectly timed, with red pepper purée and balsamic reduction in a confident beginning. The fish course is next, perhaps seared scallops partnered with lightly spiced aubergine purée and sauce vierge. The balance of the meal is well judged, the ideas sharp and innovative. Main-course fillet of beef is served with white onion and dauphinoise and a light yet intensely flavoured red wine jus. Scottish cheeses are perfectly kept and precede dessert: rhubarb crumble soufflé with vanilla ice cream. Service is excellent throughout and lunch offers imaginative dishes in a three-course format.

Chef Adam Stokes **Owner** Graham & Fay Cowan **Times** 12.30-2/7-10, Closed 2 Jan-14 Mar, Xmas **Wines** 200 bottles over £20, 8 by glass **Notes** Fixed D 6 courses £55, Sunday L, Vegetarian menu, Civ Wed 40 **Seats** 34, Pr/dining room 20 **Children** Min 5 yrs, Portions, Menu **Parking** 20

fondant with vanilla ice cream. There is a wide selection of fine wines, plus a good collection of single malts.

Times 11-9.30
See advert below

Fouters

French, Scottish

Intimate basement restaurant and ambitious cooking

☎ 01292 261391
2A Academy St KA7 1HS
e-mail: chef@fouters.co.uk
dir: Town centre, opposite Town Hall, down Cobblestone Lane

Given this basement restaurant's location down a narrow, cobbled lane in the heart of this seaside town, it's easy to miss the flight of steps leading down to a series of intimate cellar rooms that operated as a bank vault in the 18th century. The vaulted ceiling, flagstone floors, linen-clothed tables and colourful local seascapes give the place an appealing atmosphere, while service is relaxed and friendly. Fish landed at the local quay and meat and game from the surrounding hills are skilfully handled, the honest and unpretentious cooking allowing the fresh flavours to shine through. Deliciously tender roast pigeon with Stornoway black pudding and pancetta makes a great starter, with a main course of roast halibut served with basil butter sauce, grilled asparagus and roast vine tomatoes, and iced Grand Marnier and orange parfait with caramelised orange to finish.

Chef George Ramage **Owner** Barry Rooney, George Ramage **Times** 12-2/6-9, Closed 2 wks Feb, 2 wks Nov, 1 Jan, Closed Sun-Mon **Prices** Fixed L 2 course £10.95, Fixed D 3 course £21.50, Starter £4.25-£7.50, Main £14.95-£21.50, Dessert £5.25-£7.25, Service optional **Wines** 22 bottles over £20, 10 bottles under £20, 3 by glass **Notes** Fixed D midweek only, Vegetarian available, Air con **Seats** 36, Pr/dining room 22 **Children** Min 5-10 yrs, **Portions Parking** On street

The Western House Hotel

Traditional British

Race-goers' haven with a winning formula and accomplished cuisine

☎ 0870 055 5510
2 Craigie Rd KA8 0HA
e-mail: msimpson@ayr-racecourse.co.uk
dir: A77 at Whitletts rdbt take Ayr North, to lights. At racecourse left then 2nd left

An impressive hotel alongside Ayr Racecourse provides the setting for the Jockey Club Restaurant, which overlooks the splendid gardens to the racecourse beyond. Here, a light-and-airy modern look has been introduced to the traditional wood-panelled room decked out with plenty of equestrian pictures. The emphasis is on fresh local produce, with dishes such as trio of seafood (smoked Burns House salmon with lemon cream and caviar, seared scallops on leek cream, and roast smoked salmon cake with cucumber dressing) or prime fillet of Scottish beef with Madeira and thyme jus, roasted parsnips, creamed Savoy cabbage, carrots and celeriac dauphinoise.

Chef Charles Price **Owner** Alan MacDonald, Richard Johnstone **Times** 12-2/7-9.30 **Prices** Food prices not confirmed for 2009. Please telephone for details. **Wines** 22 bottles over £20, 26 bottles under £20, 9 by glass **Notes** Sunday L, Vegetarian available, Dress restrictions, Smart casual, Air con **Seats** 40, Pr/dining room 60 **Children** Portions **Parking** 200

BALLANTRAE Map 20 NX08

Glenapp Castle

– *see opposite*

TROON Map 20 NS33

Lochgreen House

– *see page 492*

MacCallums of Troon

British

Seafood restaurant in a working harbour

☎ 01292 319339
The Harbour KA10 6DH
dir: Please telephone for directions

A former pump station has been transformed to create this spacious modern restaurant in a stunning harbourside location, where diners can watch the fishing fleet come and go. Décor in the high-raftered, wooden-floored interior is themed around America's Cup memorabilia. Expect great fish from a kitchen confident enough to take a simple approach and let the freshness of its produce shine through. Expect dishes like cullen skink, grilled langoustines with garlic butter, and baked halibut with mushy peas and lemon vinaigrette. A takeaway and deli sells everything from wet fish to fish and chips.

Chef Ewan McAllister, Scott Muir **Owner** John & James MacCallums **Times** 12-2.30/6.30-9.30, Closed Xmas, New Year, Closed Mon, Closed D Sun **Prices** Fixed L 2 course fr £10.50, Starter £3.95-£10.95, Main £9.50-£26.50, Dessert £4.85-£5.85, Service optional, Groups min 12 service 10% **Wines** 9 bottles over £20, 17 bottles under £20, 4 by glass **Notes** Sunday L **Seats** 43 **Children** Portions **Parking** 12

TURNBERRY | Map 20 NS20

Malin Court

◉ Scottish 💻

Modern cooking with views of the Firth of Clyde

☎ 01655 331457
KA26 9PB
e-mail: info@malincourt.co.uk
dir: On A719 one mile from A77 on N side of village

This friendly and comfortable hotel enjoys delightful views over the Firth of Clyde and the famous Turnberry golf courses. The restaurant, Cotters, which has wonderful views along the coast, offers a good value lunch and supper menu and a set six-course dinner including canapés and coffee. Modern British dishes are presented alongside traditional Scottish fare, all using quality local ingredients. Typical of these are carrot soup flavoured with lemon, honey and coriander to start, followed by seared red snapper with a chive mash and onion sauce, or braised shank of Ayrshire lamb on parsnip purée.

Times 12.30-2/7-9

The Westin Turnberry Resort Hotel

◉◉ Traditional

Fine dining with coastal views across famous golf courses

☎ 01655 331000
KA26 9LT
e-mail: turnberry@westin.com
web: www.westin.com/turnberry
dir: Just off A77 S towards Stranraer, through Maybole. 2m after Kirkoswald turn right & follow signs for Turnberry. Hotel 0.5m on right

Situated on a spectacular stretch of the Atlantic coastline, this imposing hotel is a popular resort destination and comes with all mod cons, including a golf academy, spa and choice of eateries. Dramatic sunset views of the Isle of Arran and misty Mull of Kintyre are on offer at the elegant Turnberry restaurant (book ahead for a window table). Here, there's a choice of traditional classic dishes, or a six-course Cuisine Creative menu that features more innovative contemporary fare. The cooking is faultless, with a good balance of flavours based around the finest local ingredients. Starters include lobster bisque with brioche croûtons, or mains such as Dornoch lamb with tomato and herb crust served with bean Chartreuse and mini fondant potatoes. Finish with a trio of mango, raspberry and blueberry brûlées.

Times Closed Xmas, Closed L Mon-Sun

DUMFRIES & GALLOWAY

AUCHENCAIRN | Map 21 NX75

Balcary Bay Hotel

◉◉ Modern French 🍷 NATIONAL WINE LIST

Top-notch food in an idyllic setting

☎ 01556 640217 & 640311
DG7 1QZ
e-mail: reservations@balcary-bay-hotel.co.uk
web: www.balcary-bay-hotel.co.uk
dir: on A711 between Dalbeattie & Kirkcudbright. In Auchencairn follow signs to Balcary along shore road for 2m

Located beside beautiful Balcary Bay, this country-house hotel commands stunning views across the Solway coast. With its genteel atmosphere, few would suspect its shady origins as the 17th-century headquarters of a band of

---

Lochgreen House

TROON | Map 20 NS33

Modern British 💻

Winning country house and highly rated restaurant

☎ 01292 313343
Monktonhill Rd, Southwood KA10 7EN
e-mail: lochgreen@costleyhotels.co.uk
dir: From A77 follow signs for Prestwick Airport, take B749 to Troon, Lochgreen is situated on left 1m from junct

Views across golf links to the sea and Ailsa Craig give Lochgreen House a truly Ayrshire vista. The house itself has been sympathetically restored and extended, and it looks decidedly grand standing in 16 acres of beautifully tended grounds. Andrew Costley has built up a solid reputation for good Scottish food and he has the ideal setting in which to showcase local dishes. The light-and-airy formal Tapestry Restaurant comes with a high vaulted ceiling, stunning chandeliers, namesake wall-hung tapestries and furniture to match, and overlooks the fountain garden. The cooking is in the classic vein but with a modern approach. The kitchen deals with the freshest seasonal produce from the abundant Scottish larder and produces consistent results. Crown of quail is stuffed with Stornoway black pudding and served atop a potato and thyme blini, plus macerated grapes and apples and finished with a Calvados jus in a sophisticated and appealing starter. There is an intermediate course - spiced winter vegetable soup, perhaps - before main-course seared escalope of salmon with langoustine tempura, oriental-style vegetables and rice laced with cashew nuts. Attentive and personal service is as much a feature of the place as the fine food.

Chef Andrew Costley **Times** 12-2.30/7-9.30

smugglers. In the elegant dining room, a menu of modern French cuisine consistently impresses. The kitchen comes up trumps with clever combinations and clean, clear flavours, such as the starter of tortellini of wild mushroom fricassée with foie gras, Agen prune purée and chive butter sauce, while the main course of venison is perfectly partnered with swede fondant, spinach, chestnuts and pea sauce vierge. Vegetarian dishes are also well represented. A tempting cheese menu and seductive desserts make for a difficult choice, but how about white chocolate mousse with passionfruit jelly and pistachio bitter chocolate sauce?

Balcary Bay Hotel

Chef Stuart Matheson **Owner** Graeme A Lamb & Family **Times** 12-2/7-8.30, Closed early Dec-early Feb, Closed L prior booking only Mon-Sat **Prices** Fixed D 4 course £33.25, Starter £6.75-£8.25, Main £15.50-£19.50, Dessert £6.75-£7.50, Service optional **Wines** 60 bottles over £20, 25 bottles under £20, 8 by glass **Notes** Fixed D 4 courses, Sunday L, Vegetarian available, Dress restrictions, Smart casual **Seats** 55 **Children** Portions, Menu **Parking** 45

DUMFRIES — Map 21 NX97

The Linen Room

◎◎◎ Modern French

Refreshingly unpretentious restaurant with imaginative food

☎ 01387 255689
53 St. Michael St DG1 2QB
e-mail: enquiries@linenroom.com
web: www.linenroom.com
dir: Please telephone for directions

Just a short stroll from the centre of town, The Linen Room's décor is striking in its simplicity - black walls and carpet setting off fresh white table linen, white cushioned captain's-style chairs and black-and-white framed prints dotting the walls. Fine dining certainly, but refreshingly unpretentious with friendly, relaxed and informed service. The innovative cuisine makes good use of local seasonal produce in well-presented modern French dishes that reveal strong flavours and a light touch. Take a starter of hand-dived scallops with white onion, rocket hot shot, crunchy mushrooms and cep vinaigrette, followed by seared sea bass with salt cod brandade, mussels and tarragon, and to finish off, 'obsession in chocolate MkII'. Two tasting menus and a comprehensive wine list complete an assured package.

Chef Daniel Hollern **Owner** P & D Byrne, R Robertson **Times** 12.30-2.30/7-10, Closed 25 & 26 Dec, 1 & 2 Jan, 2 wks in Jan & Oct, Closed Mon **Wines** 150 bottles over £20, 60 bottles under £20, 12 by glass **Notes** Indulgence menu £45, Tasting menu £39.50 **Seats** 32 **Parking** 10

GATEHOUSE OF FLEET — Map 20 NX55

Cally Palace Hotel

◎ Traditional **V**

Quality British cuisine in a grand setting

☎ 01557 814341
DG7 2DL
e-mail: info@callypalace.co.uk
dir: From A74(M) take A75, at Gatehouse take B727. Hotel on left

An imposing country manor house, Cally Palace dates from 1763 and is set in extensive forest and parkland including its own 18-hole golf course. The opulent décor befits its stately past; a pianist plays most evenings and a jacket and tie are obligatory for men. The menu is concise, but changes daily and puts a winning emphasis on quality local ingredients. Typical dishes are roast pepper, chicken and mozzarella terrine with pesto, and pan-fried Castle of Mey beef fillet on a horseradish mash with cocotte grandmère and a red wine shallot sauce.

Chef Jamie Muirhead **Owner** McMillan Hotels **Times** 12-1/6.45-9, Closed 3 Jan-early Feb **Prices** Food prices not confirmed for 2009. Please telephone for details. **Wines** 34 bottles over £20, 48 bottles under £20, 7 by glass **Notes** Vegetarian menu, Dress restrictions, Jacket, collar and tie, Air con **Seats** 110 **Children** Portions, Menu **Parking** 70

GRETNA — Map 21 NY36

Smiths at Gretna Green

◎◎◎ Modern Scottish, International

Renowned rural setting for contemporary hotel with modern, globally-inspired food

☎ 01461 337007
Gretna Green DG16 5EA
e-mail: info@smithsgretnagreen.com
web: www.smithsgretnagreen.com

These days anyone thinking of running away to get married is just as likely to think of Las Vegas as Gretna Green, but Smiths has added a dose of contemporary glamour to the Scottish town in the form of a stylish,

modern hotel. Situated within an agricultural estate, it overlooks the old blacksmith's shop which has been famous for runaway weddings since 1745. The successful blend of contemporary minimalism with modern art and quality fabrics has resulted in a quietly luxurious setting. The brasserie-style dining room has slick and professional service and delivers a menu of well crafted dishes using Scottish produce where appropriate and drawing inspiration from around the world. Thus chicken liver parfait with kumquat compôte is among starters alongside seared scallops with langoustine gnocchi and beetroot fondue. Main-course duck breast with stir-fried noodles is given an Eastern flavour with five spice lychee syrup. The hotel is also a wedding and conference venue.

Times noon/9.30 **Prices** Food prices not confirmed for 2009. Please telephone for details.

KIRKBEAN — Map 21 NX95

Cavens

◎ British, French ✿

Consistent cooking at a beautiful country-house hideaway

☎ 01387 880234
DG2 8AA
e-mail: enquiries@cavens.com
dir: From Kirkbean, follow signs for Cavens

Set in landscaped grounds, this charming country-house hotel was built in 1752 as a private residence for a Glasgow tobacco baron with strong links to Robert Burns. The intimate dining room has a limited number of well-spaced tables, and a daily set menu of dinner party fare offers a choice of two dishes at each course, plus alternatives on request. Impressive dishes include a classic rendition of a salmon and dill risotto; and rack of Galloway lamb with a thyme and oatmeal crust delivering all its promised flavour. Finish with an exemplary lemon crème brûlée.

Chef A Fordyce **Owner** A Fordyce **Times** Closed Dec-1 Mar, Closed L all week **Prices** Fixed D 3 course £30, Service included **Wines** 20 bottles over £20, 7 bottles under £20, 2 by glass **Notes** Vegetarian available, Dress restrictions, Smart casual, Civ Wed 100 **Seats** 14, Pr/dining room 20 **Children** Min 12 yrs **Parking** 20

MOFFAT
Map 21 NT00

Hartfell House & The Limetree Restaurant

⊛ Modern British 🖐

Relax in the friendly traditional dining room and enjoy the food

☎ 01683 220153
Hartfell Crescent DG10 9AL
e-mail: enquiries@hartfellhouse.co.uk
dir: Off High Street at War Memorial onto Well Street and Old Well Road, Hartfell Crescent on right

Built in 1850, this impressive Victorian house is situated in a peaceful terrace high above the town, having lovely views of the surrounding countryside. The Limetree Restaurant was previously in the high street but has moved into Hartfell House. The traditionally-styled dining room has an ornate ceiling with crystal chandeliers and local art on the walls. There is a simple, intuitive approach to the traditional and modern cooking here, big on taste and flavour with great combinations. Risotto of smoked haddock, braised neck and pan-fried loin of Cumbrian blackface lamb with garlic-infused mashed potatoes and rosemary cream show the style.

Chef Matt Seddon **Owner** Robert & Mhairi Ash
Times 12.30-2.3/6.30-9, Closed Xmas, Closed Mon, Closed L Tue-Sat, Closed D Sun **Prices** Fixed L 2 course £16.50, Fixed D 3 course £25, Service optional, Groups min 8 service 10% **Wines** 8 bottles over £20, 16 bottles under £20, 4 by glass **Notes** Sunday L **Seats** 26 **Children** Portions **Parking** 6

Well View

⊛⊛ Modern European **V**

Intimate dining, lovely views and personal service

☎ 01683 220184
Ballplay Rd DG10 9JU
e-mail: johnwellview@aol.com
dir: M74 junct 15, enter Moffat. Continue out of Moffat on A708 for 0.5m, turn left into Ballplay Rd, restaurant is 300 yds on right

Set in delightful gardens in a wonderful location on the Scottish Borders, this well-appointed house enjoys fabulous views both over the town to the hills beyond, and to the wild open fells. Tastefully and traditionally decorated and furnished, it comes with well-presented bedrooms and many personal pieces. Service and attention to detail are key features, with the accomplished, traditionally-based fare personally cooked by the proprietors. The kitchen makes fine use of the abundant Scottish larder, with quality local produce a feature of the intimate restaurant's repertoire. Dining is dinner-party style with everyone seated around one large

table. Take a starter of stilton and apricot tart, and for main course perhaps roast breast of guinea fowl on sautéed mushrooms, with sun-blushed tomatoes and courgettes with pink peppercorn sauce.

Chef Janet & Lina Schuckardt **Owner** Janet & John Schuckardt **Times** 12.30/7.30, Closed L Mon-Sat **Prices** Fixed L course £22, Fixed D 4 course £35, Service included **Notes** Sunday L, Vegetarian menu, Dress restrictions, Smart dress **Seats** 10, Pr/dining room 10 **Children** Min 6 yrs **Parking** 4

NEWTON STEWART
Map 20 NX46

Kirroughtree House

⊛⊛ Modern European

Formal dining in Scottish mansion

☎ 01671 402141
Minnigaff DG8 6AN
e-mail: info@kirroughtreehouse.co.uk
dir: From A75 turn onto A712 (New Galloway), hotel entrance 300 yds on left

Standing in 8 acres of landscaped grounds on the edge of Galloway Forest Park, this historic country mansion house is rich with antiques and architectural features, including a 'modesty staircase' designed to hide a lady's ankles as she climbs the steps. Opulent, formal decoration extends to the dining rooms where good quality china, linen and glassware combine with professional and friendly service. The chef seeks out local specialist suppliers to bring the

---

Knockinaam Lodge

PORTPATRICK
Map 20 NW95

Modern Scottish 🖥 **V** 🏆

Idyllic location with cooking of real grace and refinement

☎ 01776 810471
DG9 9AD
e-mail: reservations@knockinaamlodge.com
dir: From A75, follow signs to Portpatrick, follow tourist signs to Knockinaam Lodge

It is easy to overuse adjectives when describing the position of Knockinaam Lodge: idyllic and stunning are two that do the job perfectly well. Surrounded by cliffs and woodland with views out over the sea, and even its own private sandy cove, the hotel has an enviable location. Inside, there is oak panelling, rich fabrics and antique furniture, all impeccably tasteful and in keeping

with the house. The bight and airy dining room has views over the lawn to the sea, linen-clothed tables and displays of antique china. With a four-course, no-choice menu, the cooking is modern Scottish with local flavours dominating, plus plenty of exciting ideas and an artful style of presentation. Meals are complemented with home-made crisps before lively and imaginative canapés, excellent bread, plus pre-starter, pre-desserts and petits-fours. Balance and integrity is maintained throughout in starters such as grilled fillet of salted cod with chive butter sauce - simple and perfect. Roast breast of Gressingham duck features in a complex main course with haggis beignet, creamed celeriac, potato fondant and a coriander jus.

Chef Antony Pierce **Owner** David & Sian Ibbotson
Times 12.30-2/7-9 **Wines** 335 bottles over £20, 18 bottles under £20, 10 by glass **Notes** Fixed D 5 courses £50.00, Sunday L, Vegetarian menu, Dress restrictions, No jeans, Civ Wed 40 **Seats** 32, Pr/dining room 18 **Children** Min 12 yrs, Menu **Parking** 20

best of Galloway's larder to his kitchen, such as Kirroughtree venison, Wigtown Bay wildfowl and Cairnsmore cheese. Otherwise, expect a fillet of Castle Mey beef with pont-neuf potatoes and baked shallot sauce, and to finish, perhaps a nougatine glace with fruit coulis.

Kirroughtree House

Chef Rolf Mueller **Owner** Mr D McMillan
Times 12-1.30/7-9, Closed 2 Jan-mid Feb **Prices** Fixed D 3 course £35, Service optional **Wines** 73 bottles over £20, 21 bottles under £20, 5 by glass **Notes** Sunday L, Vegetarian available, Dress restrictions, Jacket must be worn after 6.30pm **Seats** 45 **Children** Min 10 yrs **Parking** 50

PORTPATRICK — Map 20 NW95

Fernhill Hotel

⊛ Modern V

Conservatory restaurant with stunning views

☎ 01776 810220
Heugh Rd DG9 8TD
e-mail: info@fernhillhotel.co.uk
dir: A77 from Stranraer, right before war memorial. Hotel 1st left

On a clear day, the coast of Ireland, 21 miles away, can be seen from this hotel, which is set high above the village of Portpatrick. This family-run hotel overlooks the harbour and an airy conservatory houses the restaurant where the concise menu changes daily and offers the likes of Ayrshire bacon and chicken terrine with fruit chutney, followed by beef fillet with balsamic reduction and garden leaves. The selection of Scottish cheeses is particularly fine - or turn

your attention to the sweet treats promised by the dessert menu, such as millefeuille of meringue and strawberry.

Chef Andrew Rankin **Owner** McMillan Hotels
Times 12-1.45/6.30-9, Closed mid Jan-mid Feb
Prices Fixed L 2 course £13.50-£16, Fixed D 3 course £32.50-£34.50, Service optional **Wines** 17 bottles over £20, 38 bottles under £20, 3 by glass **Notes** Vegetarian menu, Dress restrictions, No jeans or shorts, Civ Wed 40, Air con **Seats** 70, Pr/dining room 24 **Children** Portions, Menu **Parking** 45

Knockinaam Lodge

⊛ ⊛ ⊛ – *see opposite*

STRANRAER — Map 20 NX06

North West Castle Hotel

⊛ British

Enjoyable dining in long-established hotel overlooking a loch

☎ 01776 704413
DG9 8EH
e-mail: info@northwestcastle.co.uk
web: www.mcmillanhotels.com
dir: From Glasgow N take A77 to Stranraer. From S follow M6 to Gretna then A75 to Stranraer. Hotel in town centre opp ferry terminal

Built in 1820 for Sir John Ross, the renowned arctic explorer, North West Castle enjoys a position overlooking
Continued

De Vere Deluxe Cameron House

BALLOCH — Map 20 NS38

Modern French ▮NOTABLE WINE LIST

Chic environment for fine dining on the shores of Loch Lomond

☎ 01389 755565
G83 8QZ
e-mail: reservations@cameronhouse.co.uk
dir: M8 junct 30, over toll bridge and follow signs for Loch Lomond (A82). Hotel is on right

Idyllically set on the shores of Loch Lomond in extensive grounds, this elegant, leisure-orientated mansion-house hotel - boasting wonderful views and an array of facilities - has undergone a chic, multi-million pound facelift, where style and quality are the watchwords. Originally built in the Scottish baronial style, it dates back to the 17th century and has played host to countless dignitaries, with Winston Churchill and Queen Victoria

listed among former guests. As the name suggests, the elegant, fine-dining Lomond's Restaurant and Bar looks directly across the loch and offers a chance to sample the highlife; the style is very contemporary but understated, cleverly blending the old house architecture with modern fabrics and furnishings. A mix of leather, velvet and contemporary tartan furnishings and dark-framed black-and-white photos of the loch add a backdrop to those views. Service is friendly and skilled - with helpful sommelier advice to guide you through the wine list - and keen to deliver a memorable experience. The accomplished kitchen's modern approach works well with the surroundings and comes driven by high-quality produce from the abundant Scottish larder on a seasonally-changing repertoire, which also includes a seven-course tasting option. Skill, precision and deft execution deliver accomplished, well-constructed dishes; perhaps scallops with pumpkin purée and apple caviar followed by poached halibut served with clams and razor clams, apricot purée and potato layers.

Times 12-2.30/7-9.30, Closed Mon, Tue, Closed L Wed-Sat

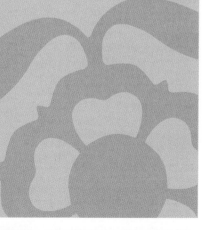

STRANRAER *Continued*

Loch Ryan and was the first hotel to have its own indoor curling rink. The traditionally decorated, spacious Regency dining room, with gleaming chandeliers and a resident pianist, adjoins a comfortable lounge with large leather armchairs and a warming fire in winter. The menu of honest fare, featuring fresh, seasonal ingredients, may include mains such as grilled fillet of Shetland salmon with creamed potatoes, asparagus tips, broccoli spears, cherry tomatoes and sun-dried tomato dressing, and desserts like Malibu and coconut parfait.

North West Castle Hotel

Chef Bruce McLean **Owner** H C McMillan **Times** 12-2/7-9 **Prices** Fixed D 4 course fr £23.50, Starter £2.95-£5.25, Main £11.30-£15.85, Dessert £3, Service optional **Wines** 29 bottles over £20, 55 bottles under £20, 3 by glass **Notes** Sunday L, Vegetarian available, Dress restrictions, Smart casual, No jeans, Civ Wed 130 **Seats** 130, Pr/dining room 180 **Children** Portions, Menu **Parking** 100

DUNBARTONSHIRE, WEST

BALLOCH
Map 20 NS38

De Vere Deluxe Cameron House
☺☺☺ – *see page 495*

CLYDEBANK
Map 20 NS47

Arcoona at the Beardmore
☺ Modern

Fine dining in a modern setting

☎ 0141 951 6000
Beardmore Hotel, Beardmore St G81 4SA
e-mail: info@beardmore.scot.nhs.uk
web: www.thebeardmore.com
dir: M8 junct 19, follow signs for Clydeside Expressway to Glasgow road, then Dumbarton road (A814), then signs for Clydebank Business Park. Hotel on left

Set on the banks of the Clyde, a convenient fifteen minutes from Glasgow International Airport, this stylish, modern hotel offers fine dining in the newly refurbished restaurant. The Arcoona was the name of a passenger ship, a throwback to when shipbuilders, William Beardmore & Co, occupied the site. The stylish décor is coupled with friendly and efficient service and the menus focus on modern British and French-style cooking with classical elements. Perhaps try the pan-fried loin of

lamb, black pudding mash, glazed vegetables and thyme jus. There are lots of extras too, such as home-made vegetable crisps and warm nuts as well as a selection of great home-baked breads.

Arcoona at the Beardmore

Chef Iain Ramsay **Owner** Scottish Executive **Times** Closed Festive period, Closed L all week **Prices** Starter £4.25-£6.95, Main £8.95-£19.75, Dessert £4.95-£5.85, Service optional **Wines** 39 bottles over £20, 30 bottles under £20, 12 by glass **Notes** Vegetarian available, Civ Wed 174, Air con **Seats** 60, Pr/dining room 16 **Children** Min 12 yrs, Portions, Menu **Parking** 400

CITY OF DUNDEE

DUNDEE
Map 21 NO43

Alchemy Restaurant
☺☺ French, Scottish

Creative cooking on the quayside

☎ 0845 365 0002 & 01382 202902
Apex City Quay Hotel & Spa, 1 West Victoria Dock Rd DD1 3JP
e-mail: alchemy@apexhotels.co.uk
dir: From A90 Perth, A85 to Dundee. Cross 2 rdbts, follow signs to City Quay

At the heart of Dundee's regenerated quayside, Apex City Quay is a smart modern hotel. First-rate facilities include a decadent spa and range of restaurants, while the open-plan public areas offer panoramic views. Alchemy is the hotel's fine-dining option with a modern menu based around quality Scottish produce. The inventive cooking tends towards complexity. A starter of langoustine comes with celeriac remoulade and confit potato, while carpaccio of Inverurie beef fillet is topped with a coffee crust and parmesan. Main course belly of pork is served with kale and hazelnut foam and for dessert pop corn crème brûlée is partnered with toffee ice cream and maple oil. Scottish cheeses are served with walnut bread and a good selection of petits fours rounds things off.

Chef Michael Robinson **Owner** Mr Norman Springford **Times** Closed Sun-Wed, Closed L all week **Prices** Fixed D 3 course £32.50-£35, Groups service 10% **Wines** 13 bottles over £20, 9 bottles under £20, 3 by glass **Notes** Vegetarian available, Civ Wed **Seats** 30, Pr/dining room 10 **Parking** 50

CITY OF EDINBURGH

EDINBURGH
Map 21 NT27

Agua
☺ Modern

Stylish, modern hotel bistro with food to match

☎ 0845 365 0002 & 0131 243 3456
Apex City Hotel, 61 Grassmarket EH1 2JF
e-mail: agua@apexhotels.co.uk
dir: Continue towards W end of Princes St, at main junct turn into Lothian Rd, then turn left onto Kings Stables Rd which leads into Grassmarket

This stylish bistro draws a trendy crowd with its combination of popular bar and dining room. Large expanses of dark wood and marble with modern art unite to create a calm, comfortable and contemporary feel. The modern theme continues on the eye-catching menu. Allowing for some mixing and matching, it creates something for everyone. Quality ingredients - locally-sourced and organic where possible - and light, clear flavours deliver in dishes such as cullen skink (smoked haddock and potato soup with parsley crème fraiche) and rosemary-roasted rump of Dornoch lamb, bashed parsnip and basil with roasted shallot jus. Friendly and eager-to-please staff complete the picture.

Chef John Paul Persighetti **Owner** Norman Springford **Times** 12-4.30/5-10, Closed 20-28 Dec **Prices** Fixed L 3 course £17-£20, Fixed D 3 course £17-£20, Starter £3.95-£6.95, Main £9.95-£16.50, Dessert £5.95, Service optional, Groups min 8 service 10% **Wines** 16 bottles under £20, 7 by glass **Notes** Vegetarian available, Civ Wed **Seats** 60 **Children** Menu **Parking** NCP

Apex Grassmarket Hotel
☺☺ Modern Scottish

Fabulous castle views meets refined cooking

☎ 0845 365 0002 & 0131 300 3456
31/35 Grassmarket EH1 2HS
e-mail: heights@apexhotels.co.uk
dir: From Princes St turn into Lothian Rd and then King Stables Rd. Follow this road winding round the foot of the castle, then into Grassmarket

Boasting panoramic views of Edinburgh Castle and the city skyline, the aptly named Heights Restaurant is set on the fifth floor of this modern boutique hotel. The contemporary décor combines floor-to-ceiling windows with glass and chrome, wood and marble and subdued lighting in a stylish minimalist way, while the service is slick but friendly. The kitchen's concise carte has a modern approach that matches the surroundings. The focus is on the freshest of seasonal Scottish ingredients, with plentiful seafood and game. Expect accomplished, considered and clean-flavoured dishes like carpaccio of diver-caught scallops, tian of Crail crab and rock chive salad, and fillet of Aberdeen Angus beef wrapped in Ayrshire sweet-cured bacon with cep mushroom and potato pavé and red onion marmalade.

Chef John Paul Persighetti **Owner** Norman Springford **Times** Closed Sun, Closed L all week **Prices** Fixed D 3 course £22.50-£25, Starter £6.50-£11.95, Main £16-£23.50, Dessert £5.95-£10.95, Service optional **Wines** 12 bottles over £20, 16 bottles under £20, 6 by glass **Notes** Vegetarian available, Civ Wed **Seats** 85 **Parking** 65

The Atholl at The Howard Hotel

Modern, Traditional Scottish 🖥 🖐

Stylish Georgian townhouse with intimate dining room

☎ 0131 557 3500
34 Great King St EH3 6QH
e-mail: reception@thehoward.com
dir: Please telephone for directions

Just a short walk from Princes Street, this intimate, elegant restaurant is located in the splendidly luxurious Howard Hotel, which comprises three linked Georgian houses. Why not enjoy pre-dinner cocktails in the drawing room, with its ornate chandeliers, lavish drapes and views of the wide cobbled streets, then dine in the exclusive Georgian setting of The Atholl, with its hand-painted murals dating back to the 1820s. An innovative menu offers modern interpretations of classic dishes, with a taste of traditional Scottish fare. Think caramelised pork belly with cashew nam jim and grilled tiger prawns, followed by roast monkfish tail with sweet carrot purée and confit duck tortellini.

Chef Steven Falconer **Owner** Peter Taylor **Times** 12-2/7-9 **Prices** Starter £7-£12.50, Main £13.50-£26, Dessert £6-£8.50, Service optional **Wines** 40 bottles over £20, 6 bottles under £20, 10 by glass **Notes** Sunday L, Vegetarian available, Civ Wed 45 **Seats** 18, Pr/dining room 40 **Children** Portions, Menu **Parking** 10

Atrium

Modern Scottish 🖥 🖐

Modish contemporary dining in the city centre

☎ 0131 228 8882
10 Cambridge St EH1 2ED
e-mail: eat@atriumrestaurant.co.uk
web: www.atriumrestaurant.co.uk
dir: From Princes St, turn into Lothian Rd, 2nd left & 1st right, by the Traverse Theatre, Blu Bar Café and Usher Hall

Situated in the heart of the city, Atrium represents the modern face of Scottish dining. The dining room is chic, unselfconsciously trendy, with colours and surfaces

chosen from the modern template of natural and earthy colours. In the evening, candlelight flickers against the darkwood tables. Ingredients are locally sourced where possible, the suppliers name-checked on the menu, and the produce deftly handled by a kitchen confident in its skills. Combinations on the daily-changing menu can be ambitious, flavours bold, such as a starter of seared Campbeltown scallops paired with confit chicken wings, lemon chutney and a cumin jus. The produce shines in a main course of wild halibut, accurately cooked, and Hugh Grierson's organic lamb served three ways, while a chocolate and pine nut tart is a simple and successful dessert. There is a tasting menu and an extensive wine list.

Chef Neil Forbes **Owner** Andrew & Lisa Radford **Times** 12-2/6-10, Closed 25-26 Dec, 1-2 Jan, Closed Sun (apart from Aug), Closed L Sat (apart from Aug & international rugby matches) **Prices** Fixed L 2 course £15.50, Fixed D 3 course £27, Tasting menu £55-£90, Starter £8-£12.50, Main £18.50-£25, Dessert £7-£8, Service optional, Groups min 5 service 10% **Wines** 250+ bottles over £20, 10 bottles under £20, 250 by glass **Notes** Tasting menu 6 courses, Civ Wed 100, Air con **Seats** 80, Pr/dining room 20 **Children** Portions **Parking** Castle Terrace Car Park and on Cambridge St

Le Café St Honore

Scottish, French **V**

Rustic French food in a genuine bistro

☎ 0131 226 2211
34 North West Thistle Street Ln EH2 1EA
dir: City centre, between Hanover & Frederick St

Le Café St Honore is the genuine article when it comes to authentic Parisian-style bistros. It is set in a quiet cobbled side street five minutes from Princes Street. Black and white tiled floors, smoked-glass mirrors and wine racks on the walls add to the Bohemian charm of the place. Ingredients are well sourced to produce good, honest, flavoursome and well proportioned food. Well worthy of consideration are the baked oysters with smoked haddock and hollandaise sauce, saddle of venison with beetroot and Stornoway black pudding, and the classic crème brûlée.

Chef Chris Colverson, Ben Radford **Owner** Jim Baird **Times** 12-2.15/7-10, Closed 24-26 Dec, 3 days at New Year **Prices** Fixed D 3 course £21, Starter £3.95-£10.50, Main £9.95-£23, Dessert £5.50, Service optional, Groups min 8 service 10% **Wines** 45 bottles over £20, 19 bottles under £20, 9 by glass **Notes** Pre-theatre menu available 5.30-6.45pm, Sunday L, Vegetarian menu **Seats** 56, Pr/dining room 18 **Children** Portions **Parking** On street - Thistle St

Channings Bar and Restaurant

Modern British 🖥

Honest, well prepared food in a bright basement restaurant

☎ 0131 315 2225
15 South Learmonth Gardens EH4 1EZ
e-mail: restaurant@channings.co.uk
dir: From Princes St follow signs to Forth Bridge (A90), cross Dean Bridge and take 4th right into South Learmonth Ave. Follow road to bottom of hill

A traditional townhouse property, Channings is the former home of the polar explorer Sir Ernest Shackleton and offers a peaceful retreat just minutes from the city centre. The modern basement restaurant, located next to the bar, faces the terraced gardens. The chefs have developed a repertoire of exciting modern dishes focusing on seasonality and using high-quality organic produce. Good examples of these are Jerusalem artichoke velouté with slow-roasted garlic and white truffle oil, fillet of Buccleuch beef with fondant potato, braised chicory and squash purée, and espresso crème brûlée. Interesting vegetarian alternatives include pumpkin, coriander and pine nut samosa with spiced aubergine and crème fraîche.

Chef Karen MacKay **Owner** Mr P Taylor **Times** 12-2.30/6-10 **Prices** Fixed L 2 course £13-£15, Starter £5-£9, Main £12-£23, Dessert £5-£7, Service optional, Groups min 10 service 10% **Wines** 26 bottles over £20, 16 bottles under £20, 6 by glass **Notes** Sunday L, Vegetarian available **Seats** 40, Pr/dining room 30 **Children** Portions **Parking** on street

Dalhousie Castle and Aqueous Spa

Modern European

Creative cuisine in a truly unique setting

☎ 01875 820153
Bonnyrigg EH19 3JB
e-mail: info@dalhousiecastle.co.uk
dir: From A720 (Edinburgh bypass) take A7 south, turn right onto B704. Castle 0.5m on right

The fantastic setting under the castle in a vaulted dungeon makes this a unique restaurant choice. The imposing medieval castle, which sits amid lawns and parkland, is also a popular wedding venue. In the part of the castle that dates back to the 13th century, exposed stonework, high-arched stone-vaulted ceilings, suits of armour, antique swords and tapestries, and bountiful

Continued

EDINBURGH *Continued*

candlelight add to the atmosphere of the Dungeon restaurant. Before descending the ancient steps to the restaurant, you can enjoy a complimentary glass of champagne in the wood-panelled library, which hides a secret bar. The menu gives a modern twist to traditional dishes and showcases creative combinations with French influences; take mille-feuille of crab with home-made ketchup and coriander oil, followed by medallions of monkfish with saffron risotto and langoustine cream sauce, with baked chocolate mousse with blood orange sorbet to finish.

Dalhousie Castle and Aqueous Spa

Times Closed L all week

Duck's at Le Marché Noir

◉◉ Modern Scottish, French 🖳 🍷NOTABLE WINE LIST 🕐

Modern cooking in an inviting restaurant

☎ 0131 558 1608
14 Eyre Place EH3 5EP
e-mail: enquiries@ducks.co.uk
dir: Princes St, Hanover St, Dundas St, right at lights

Both intimate and vibrant in turn, this charming restaurant is distinguished by its crisp white linen, fine tableware and candlelight (no stainless steel here). Ducks appear everywhere, in the décor as well as on the menu, by association with their namesake, owner Malcolm Duck. The good-value repertoire combines a hint of French-brasserie style with a modern Scottish flavour. Take ballontine of foie gras and chicken with green beans, lentils, golden raisins and truffled toast, followed by loin of Perthshire venison with pan-fried Brussels sprouts, chestnuts, pancetta, beetroot, potato fondant and pear.

Chef Rob Mitchell **Owner** Mr M K Duck
Times 12-2.30/7-10.30, Closed 25-26 Dec, Closed Sun-Mon, Closed L Sat-Mon **Prices** Fixed L 2 course £12, Fixed D 3 course £28, Service optional, Groups min 8 service 10% **Wines** 150 bottles over £20, 28 bottles under £20, 7 by glass **Notes** Vegetarian available **Seats** 60, Pr/dining room 51 **Parking** On street

La Garrigue

◉◉ Traditional French 🖳

Authentic French regional cuisine with fine views

☎ 0131 557 3032
31 Jeffrey St EH1 1DH
e-mail: lagarrigue@btconnect.com
web: www.lagarrigue.co.uk
dir: Halfway down Royal Mile towards Holyrood Palace, turn left at lights into Jeffrey St

A little piece of Languedoc can be found at this traditional French neighbourhood restaurant. Other features are the outstanding hill views, Tim Stead furniture and paintings of the South of France by Andrew Walker. The restaurant is deservedly popular, and the wooden floor, chunky wooden tables and chairs and cool blue walls have a sophisticated Mediterranean feel. The regional cooking style delivers simple, rustic dishes using fresh local produce as well as specialist ingredients sourced by the chef. Signature dishes are fish soup, cassoulet and lavender crème brûlée,

The Kitchin

AA RESTAURANT OF THE YEAR

| EDINBURGH | Map 21 NT27 |

Scottish, French 🖳 🍷NOTABLE WINE LIST 🕐

Slick, modern décor and ambitious cooking on the waterfront

☎ 0131 555 1755
78 Commercial Quay, Leith EH6 6LX
e-mail: info@thekitchin.com
dir: Short drive from city centre, opposite Scottish Executive building

The Kitchin - not some glib play on words - but home to Edinburgh-born chef-patron, Tom Kitchin, whose impressive CV includes stints in the lofty kitchens of the likes of Pierre Koffmann in London and Alain Ducasse and Guy Savoy in France (Tom also appeared on BBC Two's 'Great British Menu' TV series in 2008). Set on Leith's rejuvenated waterfront, The Kitchin was once a whisky

distillery and has a fine outlook on to the smart maritime piazza and stylish waterfront houses. It's a delightful modern, dining venue, with stylish grey décor, original stone pillars and high-quality furniture, together with a feature window offering views of the kitchen at work. Simple table appointments, soft lighting, highly comfortable leather seating and refreshingly informal but attentive and knowledgeable service complete the understated but upbeat package. Meanwhile, the slick, modern cooking from a dedicated team showcases a successful marriage of fresh, seasonal quality Scottish produce and classical French technique. From 'nature to plate' is Tom's strapline and cooking philosophy here. It's ambitious with impressive presentation to create a focal point on every plate; take hare from the Borders cooked à la royale and served with soft polenta, celeriac purée and tomato chutney, and to finish, perhaps chunky apple compote with a caramel parfait, chestnuts and salted almond ice cream.

The Kitchin is AA Restaurant of the Year for Scotland.

Chef Tom Kitchin **Owner** Tom & Michaela Kitchin
Times 12.30-1.45/6.45-10, Closed Xmas, New Year, 1st wk Jul **Prices** Fixed L 3 course £19.50-£22.50, Tasting menu £60-£100, Starter £9-£16, Main £21-£30, Dessert £6.50-£10.50, Service optional, Groups min 8 service 10% **Wines** 116 bottles over £20, 15 bottles under £20, 28 by glass **Notes** Tasting menu 7 courses, Vegetarian available **Seats** 45 **Children** L only, Portions **Parking** On site parking eve. Parking nearby daytime

but other options might be fresh crab and potato cake with garlic dip and red pepper coulis

Chef Jean Michel Gauffre, Hubert Lamort **Owner** J M Gauffre **Times** 12-3/6.30-10.30, Closed 25-26 Dec, 1-2 Jan, Closed Sun **Prices** Fixed L 2 course £12.50-£15.50, Fixed D 3 course £29.50, Service added but optional 10% **Wines** 24 bottles over £20, 10 bottles under £20, 11 by glass **Notes** Vegetarian available, Air con **Seats** 48, Pr/ dining room 11 **Children** Portions **Parking** On street, NCP

Haldanes

◉◉ Modern

Intimate basement restaurant in an Edinburgh townhouse

☎ 0131 556 8407
13B Dundas St EH3 6QG
e-mail: dinehaldanes@aol.com
dir: Telephone for directions

Located on the edge of the new town, this quirky basement restaurant with an upstairs bar-lounge has a regular and loyal following. Vettriano prints and objets d'art, smart white-clothed tables, subdued lighting and exposed natural stone combine to create an elegant and intimate setting with a contemporary vibe. Three small interconnected eating areas make for cosy dining, while upstairs guests can enjoy pre-dinner drinks or during the day coffees, pastries and good-value lunches. The finest seasonal Scottish produce features on a monthly-changing menu of modern dishes, simply prepared, with fish always well represented. For starters, take smoked haddock and leek fishcake with pan-fried baby spinach and fresh tomato coulis, and follow with baked fillet of salmon with a Shetland crab and spring onion sabayon, panaché of green beans and confit tomatoes.

Times 12-2.15/5.30-10.15, Closed Mon, Closed L Sat-Sun

Iggs

◉ Spanish ▱

Convivial and welcoming taste of Spain near the Royal Mile

☎ 0131 557 8184
15 Jeffrey St EH1 1DR
e-mail: info@iggs.co.uk
dir: At the heart of Edinburgh's Old Town 0.5m from castle, just off the Royal Mile

This modern glass-fronted restaurant is the more formal dining option to the next-door tapas bar (Barioja) under

the same ownership. Situated just a stone's throw from the Royal Mile, the restaurant brings a touch of the Mediterranean to the city, with its warm shades of terracotta complemented by large cast-iron candlesticks and antique dressers, and oils and mirrors adorning the walls. The cooking also speaks with a Spanish accent, creating simple, well-constructed modern dishes that deliver quality ingredients and good flavours. Try a traditional dish from Northern Spain like white bean soup with chorizo and jamon, and for main course perhaps pan-fried fillet of sea bass with carrot and heather honey sauce. The wine list is equally patriotic.

Iggs

Chef Mark Ishaq **Owner** Mr I Campos
Times 12-2.30/6-10.30, Closed Sun **Prices** Fixed L 2 course fr £14.50, Service added but optional 10% **Wines** 10 by glass **Notes** Vegetarian available **Seats** 80, Pr/dining room 40 **Children** Portions **Parking** On street, NCP

The Indian Cavalry Club

◉ Indian

Settle in for the night and enjoy a traditional Indian feast

☎ 0131 220 0138 & 343 1712
22 Coates Crescent EH3 7AF
e-mail: shahid@indiancavalryclub.co.uk
dir: 3 mins walk from Haymarket Railway Stn on west end of Princess St

Now in new premises just across the road from the restaurant of 21 years, there are four distinctly different dining spaces offering a modern taste of Indian cuisine. The dishes are lighter and less fiery, relying on the finest ingredients that are steamed or cooked fat-free in tandoori fashion. The dining areas are all very impressive and then there's the extensive menu; you might get through a drink and a few poppadums just deciding what to order. Luckily the wide-ranging selection is helpfully annotated with suggested side orders and drinks for each dish. There are various banquet options and also a carte offering authentic tandoori, biryani, vegetarian, chicken, lamb and seafood dishes.

Chef Muktar Miah, Firoz Hossain **Owner** Shahid Choudhury **Times** 12-4/5.30-11.30 **Prices** Food prices not confirmed for 2009. Please telephone for details. **Wines** 15 bottles over £20, 16 bottles under £20, 2 by glass **Notes** Vegetarian available **Seats** 120, Pr/dining room 50 **Parking** On street

The Kitchin

◉◉◉ – *see opposite*

Macdonald Holyrood Hotel

◉ Modern British

Relaxed dining in the shadow of Holyrood Palace

☎ 0131 550 4500
Holyrood Rd EH8 6AU
e-mail: holyrood@macdonald-hotels.co.uk
dir: Holyrood area parallel to the Royal Mile

Right at the heart of Edinburgh's Old Town, this large hotel just a stroll from the Scottish Parliament Building is right in the heart of the action. The split-level Opus 504 Restaurant features Scottish produce on its daily market menu and enthusiastic staff help create a relaxed atmosphere. The food takes a modern approach with some traditional and international influences. Thus roll mop herrings come with prawns, sun-dried tomatoes and apple salsa, and creamed pearl barley risotto is flavoured with tarragon. Main-course pan-fried lamb is served with bean and artichoke compôte, fondant potato and mint jus, and desserts include chocolate tart with raspberry cream and fruit coulis.

Chef David Robertson **Owner** Macdonald Hotels
Times 12-2/6.30-10, Closed D 25 Dec **Prices** Fixed L 2 course £15.95-£24.95, Fixed D 3 course £24.95-£29.95, Service optional **Wines** 43 bottles over £20, 3 bottles under £20, 9 by glass **Notes** Sunday L, Vegetarian available, Dress restrictions, Smart casual, Civ Wed 120, Air con **Seats** 95, Pr/dining room 20 **Children** Portions, Menu **Parking** 20

Malmaison Hotel & Brasserie

◉◉ Scottish, French ▱ ◐

Slick style, simple food and friendly service on the waterfront

☎ 0131 468 5000
One Tower Place, Leith EH6 7DB
e-mail: edinburgh@malmaison.com
dir: From the city centre follow Leith Docklands, through 3 sets of lights and left into Tower St

The Malmaison began life as a seamen's mission on the Leith waterfront. Built in 1883, its castle-like appearance gives way to a slick interior, with wooden floors, leather chairs and banquettes giving it a bold, contemporary feel. The relaxed, ground-floor brasserie looks out across the cobbles to the quayside. It specialises in classic, simple dishes created using fresh local ingredients from named suppliers, many of whom are listed on the 'Home-grown and Local' menu. Start with the Iberico ham with fig or mackerel and beetroot tartlet, perhaps followed by rack of lamb with clapshot red wine jus, or confit of duck with red cabbage and Comice pear. It's also the perfect place for Sunday brunch.

Chef Matthew Powell **Owner** Malmaison Hotels Ltd
Times 12-2/6-10.30, Closed D 25 Dec **Prices** Fixed L 2

Continued

EDINBURGH *Continued*

course £13.50, Fixed D 3 course £15.50, Starter £4.75–£7, Main £11.95–£25, Dessert £5.95, Service added but optional 10% **Wines** 146 bottles over £20, 14 bottles under £20, 12 by glass **Notes** Sun brunch menu available, Sunday L, Vegetarian available, Air con **Seats** 62, Pr/dining room 60 **Children** Portions **Parking** 48

Marriott Dalmahoy Hotel & Country Club

◎◎ Modern, Traditional

Fine dining in a Scottish mansion

☎ 0131 333 1845
Kirknewton EH27 8EB
e-mail: fandb.dalmahoy@marriotthotels.co.uk
dir: On A71 city bypass. Take Calder exit & follow signs for A71. 7m and hotel clearly signed on left.

This hotel and country club is beautifully situated amongst the rolling Pentland Hills and bounded by two championship golf courses and extensive grounds. The Adams-designed mansion retains many of its original features and has been brought up-to-date with the addition of an impressive health and beauty spa. There's a choice of formal and informal dining options: the smart, classically decorated Pentland Restaurant, overlooking the 18th hole, is where the serious eating takes place. Successfully combining a strong Scottish theme and the

use of quality seafood and game in modern and classic dishes such as Arbroath smoked fish, wilted spinach, poached hen's egg and Arran mustard hollandaise, and ballotine of chicken, truffled stuffing, spring cabbage and Madeira sauce.

Chef Alan Matthew **Owner** Marriott Hotels
Times 12.30–2/7–10 **Prices** Fixed L 2 course £14, Fixed D 3 course £35–£50, Starter £5.50–£8.50, Main £16.50–£32, Dessert £5.50–£8.50, Service optional **Wines** 20 bottles over £20, 14 bottles under £20, 18 by glass **Notes** Sunday L, Vegetarian available, Dress restrictions, Smart casual, Civ Wed 200, Air con **Seats** 120, Pr/dining room 16 **Children** Portions, Menu **Parking** 350

Norton House Hotel

◎◎◎ – *see below*

Number One, The Balmoral Hotel

◎◎◎ – *see opposite*

Plumed Horse

◎◎◎ – *see opposite*

The Restaurant at the Bonham

◎◎ Modern Scottish 💻

Enjoyable dining in stylish urban setting

☎ 0131 274 7444
35 Drumsheugh Gardens EH3 7RN
e-mail: restaurant@thebonham.com
dir: Located to the W end of Princes St

Originally built as a private residence, this grand stone house in the heart of fashionable New Town is these days a smart boutique hotel with an excellent restaurant. The spacious and chic dining room has handsome wooden floors and panelling, high ceilings with ornate cornicing and some neat contemporary touches including modern artworks on the walls. Darkwood tables are set with fine glassware, cutlery, linen napkins and candles, and staff provide attentive service. The French chef uses his classical training to transform local and seasonal ingredients into dishes with flair and individualism. The menu is sensibly concise with five or so choices per course. Smoked mackerel rillette with toasted sourdough bread and pan-fried Scottish rump steak with spring onion and pancetta mash, green olive and anchovy butter suggest the Auld Alliance is alive and well.

Times 12–2.30/6.30–10

Restaurant Martin Wishart

◎◎◎◎ – *see page 502*

Norton House Hotel

Modern British

Sophisticated fine-dining restaurant in elegant hotel

☎ 0131 333 1275
Ingliston EH28 8LX
e-mail: nortonhouse@handpicked.co.uk
dir: M8 junct 2, off A8, 0.5m past Edinburgh Airport

Situated outside the city and tucked away up a long tree-lined drive, this elegant, extended Victorian mansion - now a stunning country-house hotel - is set in 55 acres of beautiful parkland, woods and manicured lawns. Original features blend delightfully with a relaxed, contemporary edge here. Ushers is the elegant fine-dining restaurant, an intimate, candlelit, 22-seat affair smartly decked out in soft creamy-latte coloured walls, subdued lighting, white linen and armchairs, while service is

impeccable but with a relaxed charm. The kitchen's modern approach comes underpinned by a classical French theme, delivered via an appealing, sensibly compact carte. Skilled, precise cooking allows fine quality Scottish ingredients to shine with deceptive simplicity and clean, clear, balanced flavours. Take a starter of seared Loch Duart salmon served with tomato and wakame water, poached oysters, micro basil, baby leeks and parsley oil, and to follow, perhaps fillet of Aberdeen Angus teamed with onion ice cream, turnip fondant and a ravioli of shin. A prune and Armagnac soufflé with walnut cream and gorgonzola ice cream might catch the eye at dessert. A good cheese selection, first-class breads and interesting canapés hold up standards, and make a walk around the grounds almost mandatory. (The hotel's more relaxed Brasserie offers a contemporary menu and décor.) **Norton House Hotel is AA Hotel of the Year for Scotland**

Chef Graeme Shaw & Glen Bilins **Owner** Hand Picked Hotels **Times** Closed 26 Dec, 1 Jan, Closed Sun–Mon, Closed L all week **Prices** Food prices not confirmed for 2009. Please telephone for details. **Wines** 168 bottles over £20, 12 by glass **Notes** Vegetarian available, Civ Wed 140, Air con **Seats** 22, Pr/dining room 40 **Children** Portions **Parking** 100

Number One, The Balmoral Hotel

Modern Scottish, French 🖥 ✑

Fine dining in luxury hotel

☎ 0131 557 6727
1 Princes St EH2 2EQ
e-mail: numberone@thebalmoralhotel.com
dir: Hotel at E end of Princes St, next to Waverley station

The magnificent Edwardian Balmoral Hotel, with its landmark clock tower, is right in the heart of the city. The vast entrance hall reveals it as a building on a grand scale and the quality of the refurbishment sets it apart in the city - this is a hotel of considerable class. There is a Roman-style health spa, champagne bar, a light and bright brasserie called Hadrians, and the star culinary attraction: Number One restaurant. The basement room where Jeff Bland and his team produce refined and

assured modern Scottish cuisine is a chic space styled by Olga Polizzi, with red and gold dominating, a rich pile carpet, modern art and well spaced, immaculately set tables giving a sense of comfort and timeless sophistication. Service is formal, slick and engaging. Scottish produce is prominent on the menus, the ideas and preparations classically inspired and interpreted in a modern way. Haddock fish cake and blue cheese fritter are two canapés showing some wit before a starter of Isle of Skye scallops with artichokes and spiced lentils, and main-course fillet of halibut - perfectly cooked - with lemon pommes mousseline, fresh asparagus tips and brown shrimps. Apple tarte Tatin is a modern version with spiced apple jelly, walnuts and vanilla ice cream, each element beautifully made and well considered. Jackets must be worn, although you can leave your tie at home.

Chef Jeff Bland **Owner** Rocco Forte Hotels **Times** Closed 1st 2 wks Jan, Closed L all week **Prices** Tasting menu £60-£110, Starter £13-£16.95, Main £25-£28.50, Dessert £9.75-£10.50, Service optional, Groups min 6 service

12.5% **Wines** 350 bottles over £20, 8 by glass **Notes** Tasting menu 6 courses, Vegetarian available, Dress restrictions, Smart casual preferred, Civ Wed 60, Air con **Seats** 50, Pr/dining room 50 **Children** Portions **Parking** NCP: Greenside/St James Centre

Plumed Horse

Modern European 🖥 ✑

Creative cooking using first-class produce

☎ 0131 554 5556 & 05601 123266
50-54 Henderson St, Leith EH6 6DE
e-mail: plumedhorse@aol.com
dir: From city centre N on Leith Walk, left into Great Junction St & 1st right into Henderson St. Restaurant 200mtrs on right

After relocating from rural Dumfries & Galloway, Tony Borthwick's classy and highly individual enterprise is now well and truly settled in Leith. The large, discreetly screened windows grab the attention of passers-by while the menus draw in a crowd from across the city and further afield. The dining room is smartly decorated, the tables set with quality glassware and cutlery;

contemporary paintings add splashes of colour. The menu uses top quality produce, much of it local or regional, to good effect in dishes of a modern European vein. Cauliflower soup is a seemingly simple starter but displays real depth of flavour and is partnered with a quenelle of lightly herbed sour cream. If lots of flavours appear on the same plate they are soundly judged, such as in a main-course loin of free-range pork topped with a mousseline of foie gras, a piece of pork belly rolled and stuffed with apricots and prunes, mashed potato and a Pedro Ximenez sauce with raisins. Poached pear stuffed with prunes, encased in a wafer-thin brioche, is served with a prune and Armagnac ice cream in a skilfully made dessert.

Chef Tony Borthwick **Owner** Company of The Plumed Horse Ltd **Times** 12-1.30/7-9, Closed Xmas, New Year, 2 wks Summer, 1 wk Nov, Closed Sun-Mon **Prices** Fixed L 2 course £17.50, Fixed D 3 course £39, Service optional **Wines** 165 bottles over £20, 24 bottles under £20, 10 by glass **Notes** Vegetarian available, Air con **Seats** 36, Pr/dining room 10 **Parking** On street

Restaurant Martin Wishart

Modern French 🖥 V ⚡NOTABLE WINE LIST

Imaginative, memorable French cooking in intimate, fashionable waterfront venue

☎ 0131 553 3557
54 The Shore, Leith EH6 6RA
e-mail: info@martin-wishart.co.uk
dir: Please telephone for directions/map on website

Leith has been fashionable for a few years now and the rejuvenation and reinvention of the area has been well and truly successful. There are lots of bars and restaurants, a real buzz about the place and, behind an unassuming frontage by the water's edge, a world class restaurant. Restaurant Martin Wishart opened in 1999 and has built a reputation that spreads beyond the city, across the borders into England and throughout the country. This is not provincial cuisine, although fine Scottish produce is prominent on the menu, but refined, complex and exciting cooking, based on a modern French foundation. The dining room has the look of a serious venue: mature but not stuffy, chic but subtle. Colours are chosen from the in vogue natural palette of browns and beige, with elegant panelling, eye-catching contemporary artworks and well-designed light fittings giving it an air of sophistication. Tables are elegantly

dressed in crisp white linen and immaculately set, while the service is appropriately professional, focused and unstuffy. A combination of acute technical ability and an appreciation of texture and balance of flavours results in menus of innovative and appealing dishes. There are tasting, lunch and à la carte menus, even a vegetarian version, all at fixed prices and each preceded by fabulous canapés (haggis bonbon among them) and amuse-bouche (poached quail's egg with beetroot, black pudding and bacon tuile). Calves' kidney, potato and Epoisses cream comes with winter cabbage and Armagnac jus in a starter displaying fine flavours and demonstrating the creative skills of the kitchen. Main-course John Dory, mussel and almond gratin is no less inventive, served as it is with leeks, salsify and Sauternes and curry jus, and a dessert of fromage frais and lemon curd served with sablé biscuit and camomile sauce makes a beautifully crafted finish. The seriously impressive wine list does justice to the food.

Chef Martin Wishart **Owner** Martin Wishart **Times** 12-2/6.30-10, Closed 25-26 Dec, 1 Jan, 1 wk Jan, Closed Sun-Mon **Prices** Fixed L course £22.50, Fixed D 3 course £50, Tasting menu £60, Service optional, Groups min 6 service 10% **Wines** 200+ bottles over £20, 2 bottles under £20, 11 by glass **Notes** Tasting menu 6 courses, Vegetarian menu, Dress restrictions, Smart casual **Seats** 50, Pr/dining room 10 **Children** Portions **Parking** On street

EDINBURGH *Continued*

Rhubarb - the Restaurant at Prestonfield

@@ Traditional British 🖥 ⚑NOTABLE WINE LIST

Opulent setting for impressive food

☎ 0131 225 1333
Prestonfield, Priestfield Rd EH16 5UT
e-mail: reservations@prestonfield.com
web: www.rhubarb-restaurant.com
dir: Leave city centre on Nicholson St, join Dalkeith Rd. At lights turn left into Priestfield Rd. Prestonfield is on the left

Richly decadent, stylish and very glamorous, Prestonfield's interior is the epitome of opulence. Situated within a remarkable Regency house set in 20 acres of parkland, Rhubarb (rhubarb was first grown in this area) is the hotel's luxurious and opulent restaurant, comprising a matching pair of oval dining rooms, both with fine views, crisp linen, comfortable seating and massive oil paintings. The very best seasonal Scottish produce is handled with flair and panache in dishes like beef fillet and braised cheeks served with baked potato mousseline, carrots with star anise and port jus, or pan-fried halibut with leek risotto, smoked bacon and clams, while a rhubarb jam doughnut with rhubarb and custard parfait, ginger and white chocolate might delight at the finish.

Chef John MacMahon **Owner** James Thomson OBE **Times** 12-2/6-11 **Wines** 400 bottles over £20, 20 bottles under £20, 12 by glass **Notes** Theatre D 2 courses £16.95, Sunday L, Vegetarian available, Civ Wed 500 **Seats** 90, Pr/dining room 500 **Children** Min 12 yrs, Portions **Parking** 200

Santini

@@ Italian 🖥

Chic venue for modern Italian food

☎ 0131 221 7788
Sheraton Grand Hotel & Spa, 8 Conference Square EH3 8AN
e-mail: info@santiniedinburgh.co.uk
dir: City centre. From Lothian Rd onto West Approach Rd. Entrance to car park 1st left. Santini within One Spa building

Santini is a fresh, modern and elegant Italian-themed restaurant and bistro that provides an informal dining venue for the Sheraton Grand's impressive One Spa. With a large cocktail bar to enjoy pre- or post-dinner drinks, the bistro has diners sitting high on padded stools, while more traditional seating fills the restaurant - a bright, contemporary space decked out in glass, chrome and low-key neutral shades and presided over by attentive staff. Dishes are well executed using Scottish ingredients and full of Italian flavours. Menus follow a traditional format (antipasti, primi, pesce and carne), typically including potato and garlic soup with sage and mussels to start, while mains might include linguine with seafood, white wine and chilli, alongside beef fillet with fried polenta and green peppercorn sauce.

Chef Marco Terranova **Owner** Sheraton Grand Hotel & Spa **Times** 12-2.30/6-10, Closed Sun, Closed L Sat **Prices** Fixed L 2 course fr £9.50, Fixed D 3 course fr £18.50, Starter £3.50-£11, Main £7.50-£26, Dessert £4.50-£6.50, Service added but optional 10% **Wines** 58 bottles over £20, 7 bottles under £20, 7 by glass **Notes** Vegetarian available **Seats** 80 **Children** Portions **Parking** 120

Stac Polly

◉ Modern Scottish

Modern Scottish cuisine in relaxed atmosphere

☎ 0131 229 5405 & 558 3083
8-10 Grindlay St EH3 9AS
e-mail: bookings@stacpolly.com
dir: In city centre beneath castle, near Lyceum Theatre

Within strolling distance of the Princes Street shops, the unassuming façade of this restaurant hides a sociable warren of richly-furnished and softly-lit rooms. This Edinburgh chain has proved so successful with tourists and locals alike, it now has three branches (the others are in Dublin Street (see entry) and St Mary's Street). Quality Scottish cuisine dominates the menu, with many traditional dishes given a modern twist using local seasonal produce where possible. Try organic fillet of salmon stuffed with lobster mousse, fondant potato with fine beans and red pepper coulis.

Chef Steven Harvey, Stanislas Andre **Owner** Roger Coulthard **Times** 12-2/6-10, Closed Xmas, New Year, Closed Sun, Closed L Sat **Prices** Fixed L 2 course £14.95, Starter £6.95-£8.35, Main £17.95-£21.95, Dessert £6.65, Service added but optional 10% **Wines** 50 bottles over £20, 6 bottles under £20, 6 by glass **Seats** 98, Pr/dining room 50 **Children** Portions **Parking** NCP - Castle Terrace

Stac Polly

◉ Modern Scottish

Modern Scottish cuisine in atmospheric surroundings

☎ 0131 556 2231
29-33 Dublin St EH3 6NL
e-mail: enquiry@stacpolly.com
dir: On corner of Albany St & Dublin St

Taking its name from a Scottish mountain, there are three restaurants of this name in the city centre (see above). Set in a 200-year-old building at basement level, this restaurant features a labyrinth of rough stone-walled cellars, combining traditional and modern décor. The same menu is served at both restaurants, and features modern Scottish dishes with a traditional twist and some French influences. Take baked filo parcels of finest haggis served on a sweet plum and red wine sauce, followed by a mouthwatering main course of roast breast of mallard with confit leg, honey-roast vegetables and game sauce.

Times 12-2/6-10, Closed 25-26 Dec, 1 Jan, Closed Sun, Closed L Sat

EDINBURGH *Continued*

The Stockbridge Restaurant

Modern European 🖥 🕙

Stylish, dramatic basement restaurant driven by fine local produce

☎ 0131 2266766
54 St Stephen St EH3 5AL
e-mail: jjase74@aol.com
dir: From A90 towards city centre, left Craigleith Rd B900, 2nd exit at rdbt B900, straight on to Kerr St, turn left onto St Stephen St

Set in the heart of bohemian Stockbridge (in a street of unusual shops), this intimate, romantic and relaxed basement restaurant comes with oodles of character and charm. Dramatic black walls, large over-sized artwork, mirrors, feature fireplace and low ceilings are set to a backdrop of flickering candles and formally set tables. The kitchen passionately sources prime, seasonal, fresh local produce and delivers them with flair and imagination while intelligently not overcomplicating things. Take grilled fillet of wild halibut with a crab crust served with courgette ribbons, sautéed potatoes, cherry tomatoes and a citrus butter sauce, and to finish, perhaps a trio of chocolate - fondant, brûlée and white chocolate sorbet.

Chef Jason Gallagher **Owner** Jason Gallagher & Jane Walker **Times** 12.30-2.30/7-9.30, Closed 1st 2 wks Jan, Closed Mon, Closed L Tue, Sat **Prices** Fixed L 2 course fr £12.95, Fixed D 3 course fr £21.95, Starter £4.95-£11.95, Main £12.95-£24.95, Service optional, Groups min 6 service 10% **Wines** 23 bottles over £20, 19 bottles under £20, 5 by glass **Notes** Sunday L, Vegetarian available **Seats** 40 **Children** Portions **Parking** On street

Tower Restaurant & Terrace

Modern British 🍴 NOTABLE WINE LIST

Cultural and culinary delights combined in a striking modern venue

☎ 0131 225 3003
Museum of Scotland, Chambers St EH1 1JF
e-mail: reservations@tower-restaurant.com
dir: Above Museum of Scotland building at corner of George IV Bridge & Chambers St, on level 5

A chic, contemporary restaurant, the Tower is situated on the top floor of the Museum of Scotland with impressive views over the cathedral and castle. The colourful décor is elegant and luxurious, with striking aluminium furniture and banquettes creating a clubby feel. Cooking is accomplished and continues to impress, the modern menu offering the likes of ham and pig's cheek terrine with poached foie gras and pickled fennel, bouillabaisse with saffron rouille, and vanilla crème brûlée with home-made shortbread. Good value light lunch and early supper menus, and a super terrace for summer alfresco dining.

Times Closed 25-26 Dec

The Vintners Rooms

French, Mediterranean

Candlelit restaurant with vintage charm

☎ 0131 554 6767
The Vaults, 87 Giles St, Leith EH6 6BZ
e-mail: enquiries@thevintersrooms.com
dir: At the end of Leith Walk; left into Great Junction St, right into Henderson St. Restaurant in old warehouse on right

An atmospheric restaurant, lit only by flickering candles, is housed in the old wine merchants' auction room of this 16th-century former warehouse. The dining room is exquisitely adorned with hand-worked stucco and is set over historic vaults, which have stored imported barrels of fine wines from France since the 12th century. This is rustic cuisine presented with great artistry, with modern French dishes conjured from quality Scottish produce - foie gras and lobster terrine; saddle of lamb stuffed with haggis and spinach; and lemon tarte meringue with passion fruit sorbet - complemented by an extensive wine list. A bar area with a bistro feel provides an alternative to the formal restaurant.

The Vintners Rooms

Chef P Ginistière **Owner** Patrice Ginistière **Times** 12-2/7-10, Closed 1-16 Jan, Closed Sun-Mon **Prices** Fixed L 2 course £16.50, Fixed D 3 course £35-£40, Starter £6.50-£11.50, Main £16.50-£25, Dessert £6, Service added but optional 10%, Groups min 5 service 10% **Wines** 160 bottles over £20, 12 bottles under £20, 4 by glass **Notes** Sunday L, Vegetarian available **Seats** 64, Pr/dining room 34 **Children** Portions **Parking** 4

Waterfront Gastro Bar & Grill

Seafood, Scottish

Waterfront dining with an emphasis on grills and seafood

☎ 0131 554 7427
1c Dock Place, Leith EH6 6LU

A former waiting room for steamship passengers on the Leith to Aberdeen route has been converted to provide a lively wine bar and grill in the vibrant Leith Docks area. It shares a berth with the Scottish Office building and offers dockside conservatory restaurant dining with great views and an intimate wine bar with interesting maritime objets d'art and cosy booths. Good use is made of local produce, especially seafood such as Loch Etive oysters, and Aberdeen Angus steaks from the grill. Other favourites include baked Finnan haddie topped with melted brie, Serrano ham and white truffle oil.

Times 12/11, Closed 25-26 Dec

The Witchery by the Castle

Traditional Scottish

Destination dining in historic location

☎ 0131 225 5613
Castlehill, Royal Mile EH1 2NF
e-mail: mail@thewitchery.com
web: www.thewitchery.com
dir: At the gates of Edinburgh Castle, at the top of the Royal Mile

Dating back to 1595, The Witchery takes its name from the hundreds of people burnt at the stake as witches on Castlehill in the 16th and 17th centuries. Now a renowned romantic hotel, the unique combination of décor reflects the building's fascinating past. Choose between the rich baroque surroundings of the oak-panelled Witchery, or the elegant charms of the Secret Garden, reached via a stone staircase from the courtyard above. The very best of Scottish produce, including Angus beef, lamb, game and seafood, features on a classic menu with a relaxed and unfussy style. Scottish lobster and rock oysters sit alongside seared Western Isles scallops with boudin noir, orange glaze and pea shoots, while main courses might include the likes of chateaubriand of Borders beef for two, or braised oxtail with horseradish mousseline and seared foie gras. The sense of quality, luxury and theatre cannot help but impress.

Times 12-4/5-11.30, Closed 25-26 Dec

Bellini - Edinburgh

☎ 0131 476 2602
8b Abercromby Place EH3 6LB
web: http://www.theaa.com/travel/index.jsp

Regional Italian cuisine in a Georgian dining room in the heart of New Town, with a relaxed and friendly atmosphere.

Prices Food prices not confirmed for 2009. Please telephone for details.

Daniel's Restaurant

☎ 0131 553 5933
88 Commercial St EH6 6LX
web: http://www.theaa.com/travel/index.jsp

A bright, light warehouse conversion on the lovely Leith waterfront, offering consistently high-quality French and Scottish food and a friendly atmosphere.

Prices Food prices not confirmed for 2009. Please telephone for details.

First Coast

☎ 0131 313 4404
97-101 Dalry Rd EH11 2AB
web: http://www.theaa.com/travel/index.jsp

An intimate, relaxed shop-front restaurant with a frequently-changing modern Scottish menu, offering meat and fowl as well as fish. Short, thoughtful wine list, good vegetarian choices and warm service.

Prices Food prices not confirmed for 2009. Please telephone for details.

Fishers Bistro

☎ 0131 554 5666
1 The Shore, Leith EH6 6QW
web: http://www.theaa.com/travel/index.jsp

A long-time favourite in Leith, with views over the water. From superb raw Loch Fyne oysters, to seared tuna steak with chilli and lime couscous salad, the fish, as you would expect, is excellent.

Fishers Bistro

Prices Food prices not confirmed for 2009. Please telephone for details.

Fishers in the City

☎ 0131 225 5109
58 Thistle St EH2 1EN
web: http://www.theaa.com/travel/index.jsp

A smart, stylish, modern bistro in New Town with all the virtues of the original Fishers Bistro in Leith: superb ingredients, memorable cooking, swift, caring service, and a great atmosphere.

Prices Food prices not confirmed for 2009. Please telephone for details.

The Gallery Restaurant & Bar

☎ 0131 624 6579
National Gallery, The Mount EH2 2EL
web: http://www.theaa.com/travel/index.jsp

A fantastic location and great views in the stunning new Weston link joining the National Gallery and the Royal Scottish Academy. Décor is smart and up to the minute, and so is the modern Scottish menu.

Prices Food prices not confirmed for 2009. Please telephone for details.

Howies Restaurant - Alva Street

☎ 0131 225 5553
1a Alva St EH2 4PH
web: http://www.theaa.com/travel/index.jsp

Monthly-changing menus offer modern Scottish dishes, superb local ingredients and seasonal fare. As much as possible - desserts and warm crusty bread included - is made on the premises.

Prices Food prices not confirmed for 2009. Please telephone for details.

EDINBURGH *Continued*

Howies Restaurant - Victoria Street

☎ 0131 225 1721
10-14 Victoria St EH1 2HG
web: http://www.theaa.com/travel/index.jsp

Part of a thriving chain of acclaimed modern Scottish restaurants, this branch is characteristically modern and atmospheric; popular for quick lunches by day, and leisurely candlelit dinners by night.

Prices Food prices not confirmed for 2009. Please telephone for details.

Howies Restaurant - Waterloo Place

☎ 0131 556 5766
29 Waterloo Place EH1 3BQ
web: http://www.theaa.com/travel/index.jsp

This particular Howies occupies a 200-year-old Georgian building and reliably serves up the classic Howies' mix of a laidback atmosphere and quality, good-value modern Scottish cooking served by friendly staff in bright, light surroundings.

Prices Food prices not confirmed for 2009. Please telephone for details.

No.3 Restaurant

☎ 0131 477 4747
3 Royal Ter EH7 5AB
web: http://www.theaa.com/travel/index.jsp

A narrow, airy dining room serving great Scottish produce.

Prices Food prices not confirmed for 2009. Please telephone for details.

The Olive Branch Bistro

☎ 0131 557 8589
91 Broughton St EH1 3RX
web: http://www.theaa.com/travel/index.jsp

Lunch, dinner, weekend brunches all from a Mediterranean menu. Informal, relaxed, friendly and romantic.

Prices Food prices not confirmed for 2009. Please telephone for details.

Petit Paris

☎ 0131 226 1890
17 Queensferry St EH2 4QP
web: http://www.theaa.com/travel/index.jsp

A cosy, traditional French bistro with a whitewashed dining room and checked tablecloths.

Prices Food prices not confirmed for 2009. Please telephone for details.

FALKIRK

BANKNOCK — Map 21 NS77

Glenskirlie House and Castle

⊛⊛ Modern British

Elegant hotel with an imaginative kitchen

☎ 01324 840201
Kilsyth Rd FK4 1UF
e-mail: macaloneys@glenskirliehouse.com
web: www.glenskirliehouse.com
dir: From Glasgow take A80 towards Stirling. Continue past Cumbernauld, at junct 4 take A803 signed Kilsyth/Bonnybridge. At T-junct turn right. Hotel 1m on right

An Edwardian country house set in acres of parkland, Glenskirlie offers a selection of dining options - the formal Glenskirlie House Restaurant and the more relaxed Castle Grill. Luxurious fabrics and striking wall coverings give the restaurant an intimate feel, with well-spaced tables and unobtrusive staff making it an ideal destination for both romantic and business assignations. And the cuisine matches the sumptuous setting: a blend of classic and contemporary, conjured from the finest Scottish ingredients. Imaginative dishes might include pan-fried scallops, aubergine purée, slow-roasted pork belly with apple compôte and pea sorbet to start, with steamed halibut stuffed with scallop mousse with a grilled herb and sesame nut crust, spiced red wine sauce, bok choi and fennel purée to follow.

Chef Daryl Jordan **Owner** John Macaloney, Colin Macaloney **Times** 12-2/6-9.30, Closed 26-27 Dec, 1-3 Jan, Closed D Mon **Prices** Fixed L 2 course £17.50, Starter £7.50-£11.50, Main £19.95-£22, Dessert £8.25, Service

optional **Wines** 40 bottles over £20, 20 bottles under £20, 8 by glass **Notes** Sunday L, Vegetarian available, Civ Wed 94, Air con **Seats** 54, Pr/dining room 150 **Children** Portions, Menu **Parking** 100

GRANGEMOUTH — Map 21 NS98

The Grange Manor

⊛ Modern

Family-run manor-house hotel with imaginative cooking

☎ 01324 474836
Glensburgh FK3 8XJ
e-mail: info@grangemanor.co.uk
dir: M9 (eastward) junct 6 200 mtrs on right, M9 (westward) junct 5, then A905 for 2m

This stylish country-house hotel is set in lovely gardens on the outskirts of Grangemouth. Located in the former stables, Wallace's bar and restaurant retains its original stone walls and old beams and offers an informal setting for enjoying popular international dishes. (Le Chardon is an elegant restaurant for more formal dining.) Using the finest local ingredients, well-presented dishes take in traditional favourites like quality pork and herb sausages with mustard mash and confit onion, alongside roasted king prawns in garlic and chilli butter, and grilled Cajun salmon with mango and coriander salsa.

Times 12-2/7-9.30, Closed 26 Dec, 1-2 Jan, Closed Sun, Closed L Sat

FIFE

ANSTRUTHER — Map 21 NO50

The Cellar

◉◉◉ — *see page 508*

CUPAR — Map 21 NO31

Ostlers Close Restaurant

◉◉ Modern British **V**

Modern, elegant restaurant making good use of excellent local ingredients

☎ 01334 655574
Bonnygate KY15 4BU
dir: In small lane off main street, A91

Amongst its previous incarnations, this long established, family-run restaurant was a 17th-century dwelling and part of a temperance hotel. These days it attracts a loyal following for its confident cooking, relaxed atmosphere and charming service. The owners are passionate about fresh, local ingredients, many of which they grow in their own garden. They have a particular fondness for wild mushrooms, which they pick themselves from local woodland, and locally landed sea-fresh fish. The menu sees classic dishes given a modern makeover: take the roast fillet of Pittenweem halibut with buttered garden kale and parsley potato velouté to start, roast saddle of Perthshire roe venison with red cabbage and fondant potatoes on beetroot port sauce to follow, with a pear tarte Tatin to finish.

Chef James Graham **Owner** James & Amanda Graham **Times** 12.15-1.30/7-9.30, Closed 25-26 Dec, 1-2 Jan, 2 wks Oct, 2 wks Apr, Closed Sun-Mon, Closed L Tue-Fri **Wines** 60 bottles over £20, 31 bottles under £20, 6 by glass **Notes** Supper menu Nov-Apr Tue-Fri 3 courses £26, Vegetarian available, Vegetarian menu **Seats** 26 **Children** Min 6 yrs D, Portions **Parking** On street, public car park

DUNFERMLINE — Map 21 NT08

Cardoon

◉ Modern, Traditional

Contemporary cooking in relaxed conservatory restaurant

☎ 01383 736258
Best Western Keavil House, Crossford KY12 8QW
e-mail: sales@keavilhouse.co.uk
web: www.keavilhouse.co.uk/ConservatoryRestaurant.asp
dir: M90 junct 3, 7m from Forth Road Bridge, take A985, turning right after bridge. From Dunfermline, 2m W on A994

Set in gardens and parkland, this 16th-century former manor house has a stylish, conservatory restaurant, Cardoon, which overlooks the gardens and has a terrace for fair-weather aperitifs. Rich colours and a bright, airy, relaxed atmosphere create the mood, while the kitchen's

crowd-pleasing, modern, brasserie-style repertoire suits the surroundings, the conventional three-course format enhanced by a range of light dish options and grills. Expect tandoori chicken terrine or vanilla and vodka cured salmon with horseradish coleslaw, followed by juniper-crusted loin of venison with turnip dauphinoise, garlic confit and pomme purée, with bourbon and vanilla parfait with spiced syrup to finish.

Cardoon

Chef Phil Yates **Owner** Queensferry Hotels Ltd **Times** 12-2/6.30-9.30 **Prices** Fixed L 2 course £11.45-£12.50, Fixed D 3 course £25, Starter £3.95-£4.95, Main £9.95-£14.95, Dessert £3.95-£4.95, Service optional **Wines** 11 bottles over £20, 23 bottles under £20, 6 by glass **Notes** Sunday L, Vegetarian available, Dress restrictions, No football colours, Civ Wed 200 **Seats** 80, Pr/dining room 22 **Children** Portions, Menu **Parking** 175

ELIE — Map 21 NO40

Sangsters

◉◉ Modern British

Enjoy great Scottish dishes in relaxed surroundings

☎ 01333 331001
51 High St KY9 1BZ
e-mail: bruce@sangsters.co.uk
dir: From St Andrews on the A917, take the B9131 to Anstruther, turn right at rdbt and follow A917 to Elie. 11m from St Andrews

A seaside village restaurant, Sangsters has a relaxed and peaceful atmosphere with a comfortable lounge for pre-dinner drinks and after-dinner coffees. The dining room has bright, clean and simple lines, the walls hung with local prints and watercolours. Cooking is precise, showing attention to detail and considerable skill in a menu of modern British cooking prepared from quality raw ingredients. Impressive dishes include Ross-shire diver scallops with ginger, lime and peppercorn butter, served with Thai coconut sauce, followed by oven-baked fillet of North Sea halibut, the sea-fresh fish complemented by an Arbroath smokie and chive crust with a vegetable risotto and vermouth sauce. Cinnamon pannacotta with apple vanilla and lemon compôte and an apple and cider sorbet might catch the eye at dessert,

or chocolate-lovers might succumb to the chocolate cheesecake with cherry compôte home-made ice cream.

Times 12.30-1.30/7-9.30, Closed 25-26 Dec, early Jan, mid Feb/Oct, mid Nov, Closed Mon, Closed L Tue & Sat, Closed D Sun

MARKINCH — Map 21 NO20

Balbirnie House

◉◉ Classic ▲ NOTABLE WINE LIST

Impressive Scottish cuisine in a grand mansion

☎ 01592 610066
Balbirnie Park KY7 6NE
e-mail: info@balbirnie.co.uk
dir: M90 junct 13, follow signs for Glenrothes and Tay Bridge, right onto B9130 to Markinch and Balbirnie Park

An imposing Georgian mansion, set in beautiful landscaped parkland, Balbirnie House is one of Scotland's most important listed buildings, dating back to 1777. Now a luxurious country-house hotel, it boasts sumptuous décor, a modern health spa and a choice of restaurants to suit your mood. Both the refurbished Orangery restaurant and the more informal bistro serve top-notch food. The contemporary dining room focuses on accomplished classical cuisine under the supervision of new chef James Stocks, using the very best of Scottish and locally-sourced produce. Beautifully presented dishes might include sea bream, poached langoustine, ratatouille and langoustine cappuccino, or shoulder of Blackface lamb, sweetbreads and dauphinoise potatoes. Leave room for a tempting dessert such as passionfruit and mango soufflé, sorbet and crumble.

Chef James Stocks **Owner** The Russell family **Times** 12-1.30/7-9, Closed Mon-Tue **Prices** Fixed L course £16, Fixed D 4 course £36.50, Tasting menu £50-£80, Service added 10% **Wines** 100 bottles over £20, 43 bottles under £20, 10 by glass **Notes** Vegetarian available, Civ Wed 200, Air con **Seats** 65, Pr/dining room 216 **Children** Portions **Parking** 100

The Cellar

Seafood

Superb seafood served in atmospheric restaurant

☎ 01333 310378
24 East Green KY10 3AA
dir: Located behind Scottish Fisheries Museum

This renowned seafood restaurant, close to the picturesque fishing village of Anstruther, is accessed by a delightful cobbled courtyard. A 400-year-old former cooperage, where barrels were made for the herring industry, it retains an old, rustic feel with roaring log fires, beams, stone floors and walls, and an eclectic décor featuring local art and pottery. The real draw is of course Peter Jukes' superb food and the restaurant has an established reputation, so it's worth booking in advance. The philosophy is simple and extremely successful, the very best fresh fish and other produce, cooked with care to allow the flavours to shine through. A daily-changing array of dishes uses consistently excellent produce, as in the chef's recommended creamy tart of lobster and smoked salmon served with warm dressed leaves, or steamed mussels with shallot, thyme and garlic broth. Exquisite main courses include pesto-crusted fillet of cod, pak choi with basil mash and balsamic dressing, or you might try one of the meat options -

griddled fillet of Scottish beef perhaps, with caramelised onions, wild mushrooms and 'stovies' with grain mustard sauce. Terrific desserts feature the likes of layered terrine of chocolate mousses with orange liqueur custard. Front of house, Susan Jukes offers a warm welcome and can help you match suitable wines with the various dishes from a well chosen list.

Chef Peter Jukes **Owner** Peter Jukes **Times** 12.30-1.30/7-9.30, Closed Xmas (5 days), Closed Sun (Sun & Mon Winter), Closed L Mon-Tue **Prices** Fixed L course £23.50, Fixed D 3 course fr £38.50, Service optional **Wines** 5 by glass **Seats** 38 **Children** Portions **Parking** On street

PEAT INN Map 21 NO40

The Peat Inn

◉◉ Modern British 🖥

Restaurant with rooms with fine, locally-sourced cuisine

☎ 01334 840206
KY15 5LH
e-mail: stay@thepeatinn.co.uk
dir: At junction of B940/B941, 6m SW of St Andrews

Geoffrey and Katherine Smeddle are now well and truly settled at this 300-year-old former coaching inn, which was put on the Scottish culinary map by David Wilson, who ran it for over 30 years. The white-washed building is now a smart restaurant with rooms, full of character on the inside. Service is relaxed, approachable and charming. The muted tones of the rooms are chosen from nature's palette and the tables are laid with crisp white linen and fresh flowers. Geoffrey's cooking is based around the wonderful local produce, and he is dedicated to supporting small producers and suppliers. The food is modern in focus and presentation, beginning with well-made canapés and amuse-bouche and finishing with an array of petits fours. A starter of foie gras and ham hock might be followed by main-course red mullet with chorizo, crushed ratte potatoes, and carrot and orange purée.

Times 12.30-2/7-9.30, Closed 25-26 Dec, 1-4 Jan, Closed Sun-Mon

ST ANDREWS Map 21 NO51

Fairmont St Andrews

◉◉ Mediterranean V ☌

Mediterranean cooking in luxuriously appointed hotel restaurant

☎ 01334 837000
KY16 8PN
e-mail: standrews.scotland@fairmont.com
dir: 1.5m outside St Andrews on A917 towards Crail

Enjoying breathtaking coastal views, this modern resort hotel is flanked by its two golf courses, with a central atrium as its focal point. Esperante is the well presented restaurant overlooking the atrium with an opulent Mediterranean atmosphere, deep ruby red décor and luxurious upholstery. Staff are professional and friendly. The generous menu is heavily influenced by French and Italian classics with contemporary British touches.

Dishes are prepared with skill and care and good use is made of top quality ingredients. Take seared yellowfin tuna with pickled cucumber and sweet mustard dressing, followed by lobster and prawn risotto, or perhaps black sambuca-marinated salmon with crushed green peas and caper berry beignets, and to finish, raspberry soufflé with Tahitian vanilla ice cream.

Chef Kelly Jackson **Owner** Apollo European Real Estate
Times Closed Mon-Tues, Closed L all week **Prices** Starter £9-£15, Main £20-£29, Dessert £9-£12, Service optional **Wines** 67 bottles over £20, 3 bottles under £20, 6 by glass **Notes** Dégustation menu available with selected wines, Vegetarian menu, Dress restrictions, No denim, Civ Wed 600, Air con **Seats** 60, Pr/dining room 80 **Children** Min 14 yrs **Parking** 250

Inn at Lathones

◉◉ Modern European 🖥

Exquisite local produce, imaginative menus and an ancient inn

☎ 01334 840494
Largoward KY9 1JE
e-mail: lathones@theinn.co.uk
web: www.theinn.co.uk
dir: 5m SW of St Andrews on A915. In 0.5m before Largoward on left, just after hidden dip

Situated near the famous golfing town of St Andrews, the town's oldest coaching inn comes complete with its own resident ghost. But don't let that put you off - during its 400-year-old history the premises have been extended, today providing a mix of modern style with traditional country-house flair, with a relaxed and friendly atmosphere pervading throughout. The colourful, cosy restaurant is the main focus, offering modern interpretations of Scottish and European dishes with refined technique, and making the most of the abundant local larder. Take roast salmon fillet with cherry confit tomatoes and citrus dressing, or roast turbot with Mediterranean ratatouille and olive oil. The market menu, carte and intriguing Trilogy menu provide the best ways of sampling the kitchen's skill and creativity.

Inn at Lathones

Chef Marc Guibert **Owner** Mr N White
Times 12-2.30/6-9.30, Closed 26 Dec, 1st 2 wks Jan
Prices Food prices not confirmed for 2009. Please telephone for details. **Wines** 89 bottles over £20, 13 bottles under £20, 5 by glass **Notes** Sunday L, Vegetarian available, Dress restrictions, Smart casual, Civ Wed 40 **Seats** 40, Pr/dining room 40 **Children** Menu **Parking** 35

Macdonald Rusacks Hotel

◉◉ Traditional British

Accomplished cooking in legendary golfing setting

☎ 0870 400 8128
Pilmour Links KY16 9JQ
e-mail: general.rusacks@macdonald-hotels.co.uk
dir: From M90 junct 8 take A91 to St Andrews. Hotel on left on entering the town

This long-established St Andrews' hotel enjoys an unrivalled location close to the 18th hole with superb views across the famous golf course. Take your eyes off the green and you'll find the food's not bad either, served in the smart restaurant with huge windows to take in those views. The traditional Scottish and international cuisine offers a tempting range of sophisticated, contemporary, weekly-changing dishes, including the likes of scallops with sweet potato tortellini, langoustine and langoustine foam as a starter, or mains such as venison and Agen prune, corn-fed chicken and foie gras boudin with port glaze, turnip croustillant, sautéed potato, amaretto jelly and Valrhona chocolate jus. For those with a sweet tooth, the chocolate cake with caramelised banana and pistachio ice cream will definitely appeal.

Times 12-2.30/6.30-9

The Road Hole Grill

ST ANDREWS — Map 21 NO51

British NOTABLE WINE LIST

Amazing setting over the 17th hole and first-class food

☎ 01334 474371
Old Course Hotel, Golf Resort & Spa KY16 9SP
e-mail: reservations@oldcoursehotel.co.uk
dir: M90 junct 8, close to A91. 5 mins from St Andrews

The huge Old Course Hotel stands proudly overlooking the town of St Andrews, the sea and, most importantly of all, the legendary golf course. The grand hotel has a number of dining options including a pub, a contemporary restaurant called Sands (see entry), and the Road Hole Grill, the newly refurbished restaurant on the fourth floor with its coveted views over the famous 17th hole. It now has new floor-to-ceiling windows to maximise the impact of the view, and is an opulent space with oak-panelled walls, chandeliers, leather and carved wooden chairs and tables smartly laid with crisp white linen and quality silverware. A new chef has arrived amid the changes and hit the ground running. Expect all the bells and whistles from canapés to petits fours; what comes between is based on the best Scottish produce cooked with considerable flair. There is an 8-course Tasting Menu and a carte with six dishes per course plus a choice of steaks cooked on the chargrill. Foie gras ballotine with smoked duck, blood orange, pickled rhubarb and watercress is a dish displaying impeccably modern credentials, as is suckling pig - cured leg and braised belly - with carrot purée, spring cabbage, fennel, apple and liquorice jus. These are well crafted and impressive dishes showing good technical skill and balance of flavours. Valrhona Araguani chocolate fondant pudding with vanilla parfait and sour cherry foam makes a stunning finish. Service is formal, professional and friendly. Adjacent is a great bar also refurbished with those fabulous new windows.

Chef Paul Hart **Owner** Kohler Company
Times 12.30-2/7-10, Closed L Mon-Sat **Prices** Food prices not confirmed for 2009. Please telephone for details. **Wines** 220 bottles over £20, 8 by glass
Notes Sunday L, Vegetarian available, Dress restrictions, Smart dress, no jeans, shirt with collar, Civ Wed 200
Seats 80, Pr/dining room 20 **Children** Portions, Menu
Parking 100

The Seafood Restaurant

ST ANDREWS — Map 21 NO51

Modern Seafood

Accomplished cooking in a stunning glass building by the bay

☎ 01334 479475
The Scores KY16 9AS
e-mail: reservations@theseafoodrestaurant.com
dir: Please telephone for directions

Take a look out of the windows of this restaurant and you will see the source of what is to follow: the sea. In fact, this building, an impressive modernist structure of glass, wood and metal, is virtually suspended over the bay and seemingly floats on the water. The open-plan kitchen and stylish fixtures and fittings make for a lively and appealing backdrop for some fresh, local seafood. The clean, crisp cooking style is flavour-driven, allowing the wonderfully fresh produce to shine. The menu is as up-to-the-minute as the building, so among starters pan-seared scallops appear in a fashionable partnership with cauliflower purée, and honey- and soy-braised pork belly comes with lobster, shizo cress and truffle vinaigrette. Main-course grilled fillet of halibut is served with crushed ratte potatoes, soy-scented vegetables and smoked bacon dressing, and there is loin of venison for those who don't want to get on board with the seafood theme. Finish with rhubarb parfait with ginger pastille and hazelnut biscuit. There is a sister restaurant down the coast at St Monans (see entry).

Chef Craig Millar, Scott Miller **Owner** Craig Millar, Tim Butler **Times** 12-2.30/6.30-10, Closed 25-26 Dec, Jan 1
Wines 180 bottles over £20, 5 bottles under £20, 8 by glass **Notes** Oct-Mar fixed L menu 3 courses £12.95 Mon-Fri, Sunday L, Vegetarian available, Air con **Seats** 60
Children Min 12 yrs, Portions **Parking** 50mtrs away

ST ANDREWS *Continued*

The Road Hole Grill

@@@ – *see opposite*

Rufflets Country House & Terrace Restaurant

@@ Modern British

Stylish country-house dining in a friendly atmosphere

☎ 01334 472594
Strathkinness Low Rd KY16 9TX
e-mail: reservations@rufflets.co.uk
web: www.rufflets.co.uk
dir: 1.5m W of St Andrews on B939

This stylish Edwardian country house with delightful formal gardens and woodland makes a wonderful retreat. The restaurant features a simple and stylish traditional décor with lots of colourful artwork. Service is particularly friendly and attentive making the diner feel really at ease. Cooking style is Scottish with influences from the Mediterranean, using the freshest local produce available. Typical dishes include a starter of venison and pigeon terrine with quince purée and toasted brioche. Likewise, a main course might be halibut with spring onion risotto, baby leeks and a tomato and dill velouté. To finish, try the chocolate, brandy and ginger cheesecake with coconut ice cream, or a plate of Scottish cheeses.

Chef Mark Nixon **Owner** Ann Murray-Smith
Times 12.30-2.30/7-9, Closed L Mon-Sat **Prices** Fixed L 2 course £10-£15, Fixed D 3 course £39.75-£49.75, Service optional, Groups min 20 service 10% **Wines** 88 bottles over £20, 18 bottles under £20, 9 by glass **Notes** Sunday L, Vegetarian available, Dress restrictions, No shorts, Civ Wed 130 **Seats** 80, Pr/dining room 130 **Children** Portions, Menu **Parking** 50

Russell Hotel

@ Scottish, International

Imaginative cooking in an intimate setting

☎ 01334 473447
26 The Scores KY16 9AS
e-mail: russellhotel@talk21.com
dir: A91 to St Andrews. At 2nd rdbt take 1st exit onto Golf Place. After 200 yds turn right into The Scores, hotel is 200 yds on right

With lovely views over the east bay, this comfortable and intimate hotel restaurant prides itself on the sort of

Russell Hotel

convivial atmosphere usually only found in Paris bistros. The international cooking draws on French and British influences and high-quality local ingredients appear in Loch Fyne salmon and Crail crab fritters served on sweet-and-sour cherry tomatoes, followed by peppered saddle of Auchtermuchty venison with Roquefort cheese butter, or pan-seared king scallops with coriander and spring onion blinis and a garlic- and herb-infused olive oil. Desserts could include white chocolate and strawberry crème brûlée.

Times 12-2/6.30-9.30, Closed Xmas

St Andrews Golf Hotel

@@ Scottish

Modern Scottish fine-dining restaurant

☎ 01334 472611
40 The Scores KY16 9AS
e-mail: reception@standrews-golf.co.uk
dir: Enter town on A91, cross both mini rdbts, turn left at Golf Place and 1st right into The Scores. Hotel 200 yds on right

There is no hiding the target market for this hotel - the clue is in the name - and anyone looking to bring their clubs will not be disappointed. The family-run hotel has splendid views of the famous golf course and the coastline, but the restaurant is worth a visit too. The Number Forty restaurant is a light and bright space with muted tones of cream and brown and well-spaced, formally dressed tables. It cuts a contemporary dash. The menu deals in fashionable ideas (cappuccino of white bean) and more traditional fare such as steaks from the grill, and presentation is a strength. Butternut squash soup demonstrates a steady hand in the kitchen when it comes to the balance of flavours, as does main-course halibut served with crab risotto and a pea purée.

Times 12.30-2/7-9.30, Closed 26-28 Dec

Sands Restaurant

@ International, Mediterranean

Elegant, stylish restaurant within golf-resort hotel complex

☎ 01334 474371 & 468228
The Old Course Hotel, Golf Resort & Spa KY16 9SP
e-mail: reservations@oldcoursehotel.co.uk
dir: M90 junct 8. Situated close to A91 and 5 mins walk from St Andrews

The hotel borders the 17th fairway of the legendary Old Course, and the Sands Restaurant is its second dining option. It has a stylish, sophisticated décor with lots of dark wood and black leather - shades of a luxury ocean-going liner of yesteryear - and an upbeat atmosphere. The cooking is accurate yet unpretentious with a good smattering of Mediterranean-influenced brasserie-style dishes. Twice-baked mini goat's cheese soufflé with red onion confit, daube of beef on roasted garlic mash with red wine jus, or whole sea bass from the grill are fine examples of the fare. Attentive, professional table service.

Chef Mark Lindsey **Owner** Kohler Company
Times 12-6/6-10 **Prices** Food prices not confirmed for 2009. Please telephone for details. **Wines** 25 bottles over £20, 8 by glass **Notes** Vegetarian available, Dress restrictions, Smart casual, Civ Wed 200 **Seats** 80, Pr/dining room 40 **Children** Portions, Menu **Parking** 100

The Seafood Restaurant

@@@ – *see opposite*

ST MONANS   Map 21 NO50

The Seafood Restaurant

@@ Modern Scottish, Seafood

The freshest seafood by the harbour

☎ 01333 730327
16 West End KY10 2BX
e-mail: info@theseafoodrestaurant.com
dir: Take A959 from St Andrews to Anstruther, then head W on A917 through Pittenweem. In St Monans to harbour then right

Under the same ownership as the restaurant of the same name at St Andrews (see entry), this place occupies an old fisherman's cottage and features an 800-year-old freshwater well with mythical healing powers. There's an open fire in the Victorian bar, a terrace for sitting outside, and picture windows in the modern restaurant extension overlooking the harbour and the Firth of Forth across the Isle of May. The cooking deals in the freshest fish simply cooked, a light touch allowing the main ingredient to shine. Start with smoked haddock and leek tart with sweetcorn purée and herb salad, or half-dozen Kilbrandon oysters, before pan-fried collops of monkfish with leek and pancetta risotto. Finish with pear tarte Tatin with vanilla ice

Continued

ST MONANS *Continued*

cream, and note there is usually one meat dish on the fixed-price repertoire.

Chef Craig Millar, Roy Brown **Owner** Craig Millar, Tim Butler **Times** 12-2.30/6-9.30, Closed 25-26 Dec,1-2 Jan, Closed Mon-Tue **Wines** 40 bottles over £20, 18 bottles under £20, 6 by glass **Notes** Oct-1 Apr fixed L menu 3 courses £14.95 Wed-Fri, Sunday L, Vegetarian available **Seats** 44 **Children** Portions **Parking** 10

CITY OF GLASGOW

GLASGOW   Map 20 NS56

An Lochan

◉ Scottish Seafood

Simple café style in a trendy residential area, serving Scottish produce

☎ 0141 338 6606
340 Crow Rd G11 7HT
e-mail: glasgow@anlochan.co.uk
dir: Please telephone for directions

This busy shop-front-style establishment was once a bank. With blue walls, white leather chairs and white tablecloths, the décor has a seafood theme. The restaurant serves modern Scottish food, simply cooked to make the most of fresh local produce. Light snacks, a blackboard tapas menu and pre-theatre dinners feature alongside the evening carte. Majoring on seafood, a sample evening menu might include hand-dived scallops wrapped in pancetta for starters, followed by a main course of whole sea bass served with dauphinoise potatoes, roasted red peppers and saffron butter, or maybe a platter of langoustine, scallops, oysters and hot-smoked salmon. Service is relaxed and friendly.

Chef Claire McKie, Andrew Moss **Owner** The McKie Family **Times** 12-3/6-11.30, Closed 24-26 Dec, 1-3 Jan, Closed Mon, Closed D Sun **Prices** Fixed L 2 course fr £8.95, Fixed D 3 course fr £15.95, Tasting menu £29.95, Service added but optional, Groups min 6 service 10% **Wines** 17 bottles over £20, 8 bottles under £20, 5 by glass **Notes** Tasting menu Fri-Sat, Fixed evening menu 3 courses Tue-Thu, Sunday L, Vegetarian available, Air con **Seats** 40 **Children** Portions **Parking** On street

La Bonne Auberge

◉ French, Mediterranean 🖥

Classic French cuisine in a modern hotel

☎ 0141 352 8310
Holiday Inn Theatreland, 161 West Nile St G1 2RL
e-mail: info@higlasgow.com
dir: Please telephone for directions

Handy for the shops and close to the Theatre Royal Concert Hall, this popular French brasserie-style restaurant is found in the contemporary Holiday Inn. The repertoire plays to the crowds with a wide range of accomplished, honest, modern dishes. Menus take in fixed-price options, a pre-

theatre menu and speciality dishes, perhaps including a spicy fish soup packed with seafood, a tender, five-spiced pork fillet, served with wilted spinach, creamed chanterelles and curried risotto, and a well-presented chocolate and praline torte. There are also wonderful North Highlands steaks, traditionally aged, served from the grill. Staff are friendly and attentive.

Chef Gerry Sharkey **Owner** Chardon Leisure Ltd **Times** 12-2.15/5-10 **Prices** Food prices not confirmed for 2009. Please telephone for details. **Wines** 26 bottles over £20, 23 bottles under £20, 8 by glass **Notes** Air con **Seats** 90, Pr/dining room 100 **Children** Portions, Menu **Parking** NCP opposite

Brian Maule at Chardon d'Or

◉ French, Mediterranean 🖥 V 🔖

Confident cooking in a slick city-centre venue

☎ 0141 248 3801
176 West Regent St G2 4RL
e-mail: info@brianmaule.com
dir: 10 minute walk from Glasgow central station

Situated in a converted Victorian city-centre townhouse, this classy restaurant is elegant and modern, with a warm and relaxed atmosphere. Suede and leather banquette seating, high-backed chairs and vibrant pictures on cream walls contrast with high ceilings and other original features. There is an upstairs bar area and an extended area downstairs with three private dining rooms, which can be opened up into one large room. From a regularly-changing menu, accomplished dishes, made with the best Scottish produce using classical French techniques, include pan-fried scallops with pancetta and aged balsamic, and local fillet of beef with rich red wine sauce.

Chef Brian Maule **Owner** Brian Maule at Chardon d'Or **Times** 12-2/6-10, Closed 25-26 Dec, 1-2 Jan, 2 wks Jan, 2 wks Aug, BHs, Closed Sun, Closed L Sat **Prices** Fixed L 2 course £16.50, Tasting menu £48.50, Service optional, Groups service 10% **Wines** 280 bottles over £20, 6 by glass **Notes** Tasting menu 6 courses, Vegetarian menu, Dress restrictions, Smart casual, Air con **Seats** 90, Pr/dining room 60 **Children** Portions **Parking** Metered parking on street

Gamba

◉◉ Scottish, Seafood

One of Glasgow's most established fish restaurants

☎ 0141 572 0899
225a West George St G2 2ND
e-mail: info@gamba.co.uk
dir: Please telephone for directions

Named after the Spanish word for 'prawn', this perennial favourite enjoys a well deserved reputation locally as a fine seafood restaurant, providing attentive service and consistent food in an intimate and stylish basement setting. Located in the heart of the city's West End, there's a striking Mediterranean theme to the décor - warm colours, terracotta floor tiles, stylish fish-themed artwork and polished-wood

Gamba

tables, plus a cosy cocktail area. This theme also extends to the food - though with some subtle Asian influence too - on the well-balanced menu. Portions are generous and the no-nonsense approach is a winning formula, but it's the classics like Gamba fish soup - for which they are deservedly renowned - that win the day. Other interesting options include grilled fillets of bream with crayfish tails, honey and Pommery mustard, or fillet of Angus beef with crushed peppercorns, shiitake mushrooms and mash.

Chef Derek Marshall **Owner** Mr A C Tomkins & Mr D Marshall **Times** 12-2.30/5-10.30, Closed 25-26 Dec, 1-2 Jan, BHs, Closed L Sun **Wines** 60 bottles over £20, 8 bottles under £20, 8 by glass **Notes** Pre-theatre £15 inc wine 5-6pm, Vegetarian available, Air con **Seats** 66 **Children** Min 14 yrs **Parking** On street

Hotel du Vin Bistro at One Devonshire Gardens

◉◉◉ – **see opposite**

Ho Wong Restaurant

◉ Chinese V

Stylish design, warm hospitality and an emphasis on seafood

☎ 0141 221 3550 & 221 4669
82 York St G2 8LE
e-mail: ho.wong@amserve.com
dir: Off Argyle St. 2 mins from Glasgow Central station

A popular upmarket restaurant close to the city centre, the Ho Wong has quite a buzz about it. Impressive surroundings, modern décor and friendly, skilled service all contribute to the atmosphere. Fish dishes are a real highlight on the sophisticated, traditional Cantonese-style menu. In addition to a range of set menus, a seafood gourmet table selection is available for a minimum of four diners. From the carte, you can push the boat out with fresh lobster baked in spicy chilli oil, or whole sea bass, steamed or grilled with ginger, spring onion and soy.

Ho Wong Restaurant

Chef S Wong **Owner** David Wong **Times** 12-2/6-11, Closed L Sun **Prices** Food prices not confirmed for 2009. Please telephone for details. **Wines** 42 bottles over £20, 30 bottles under £20, 4 by glass **Notes** Vegetarian menu, Air con **Seats** 90, Pr/dining room 35 **Children** Portions **Parking** 8

Killermont Polo Club

◉ Traditional Indian

Creative Indian cooking in a setting fit for a maharaja

☎ 0141 946 5412
2002 Maryhill Rd, Maryhill Park G20 0AB
dir: Please telephone for directions or visit website

Not your everyday Indian eatery this, either in terms of décor - inspired by the East's centuries-long fascination with the sport of polo - or food. Dum pukht is the speciality - an unusual cuisine thought to have originated with the arrival of the Moghul emperors in India. It's said they blended the best of Indian spices with those brought from the legendary city of Samarkand in Uzbekistan to create a new style of cooking. Now a byword for great-value, top-notch Indian cuisine, the restaurant delivers a lengthy list of dishes, from the ubiquitous chicken tikka masala to murgh wajid ali - braised chicken breast stuffed with pomegranates, mint, cheese and onions served in an orange and saffron gravy.

Chef Belbir Farwaha **Owner** P Thapar
Times 12-2.30/5-11.30 **Prices** Fixed L 3 course £6.95-£7.95, Fixed D 3 course £11.95, Starter £2.95-£5.95, Main £5.50-£14.95, Dessert £2.95-£3.50 **Wines** 6 bottles over £20, 22 bottles under £20, 4 by glass **Notes** Sunday L, Dress restrictions, Smart casual **Seats** 80, Pr/dining room 30 **Children** Portions, Menu **Parking** 40

The Left Bank

◉ Modern International ✍

Great value, international food in contemporary setting

☎ 0141 339 5969
33-35 Gibson St, Hillhead G12 8NU
e-mail: contact@theleftbank.co.uk
dir: M8 junct 17, A82. After Kelvinbridge turn left onto Otago St, left onto Gibson St. Restaurant on right

A welcome addition to the burgeoning Glasgow foodie-scene and set on a bustling residential road in the West End, there's an informal and vibrant vibe in this coolly modern restaurant, but there are quiet corners too. It's split level, with some exposed brick walls, lots of wood and glass, muted and natural colours with occasional highlights like designer wallpaper, murals by local artists and a unique concrete bar by sculptor Chris Bannerman. The food is funky too; the diverse menu takes you round the world and back again. Asian influences are noted with very good execution - no frills presentation lets the food do the talking - think sticky pork belly with ginger, tamarind and port, cashews and prunes, or garlic masala fried fish on a Goan seafood curry.

Chef Liz McGougan **Owner** Catherine Hardy, Jacqueline Fennessy, George Swanson **Times** 9/mdnt, Closed 25 Dec, 1 Jan **Prices** Fixed L 2 course fr £9.50, Fixed D 3 course £19.50, Starter £2.95-£5.50, Main £6.50-£19.95, Dessert £2.95-£4.50, Service optional, Groups min 6 service 10% **Wines** 1 bottles over £20, 17 bottles under £20, 17 by glass **Notes** Brunch menu available Sat-Sun, Vegetarian available **Seats** 75 **Children** Min 14yrs D, Portions

The Living Room

◉ Modern, Traditional International ▣

Laid-back piano bar and restaurant that aims to please

☎ 0870 220 3028
150 St Vincent St G2 5NE
e-mail: glasgow@thelivingroom.co.uk
web: www.thelivingroom.co.uk
dir: City centre location between Hope St & Wellington St

This laid-back piano bar and restaurant has a chic décor that brings a touch of Manhattan to Glasgow with an

Continued

Hotel du Vin Bistro at One Devonshire Gardens

British, French ▣

Elegant bistro with fine-dining style in sophisticated townhouse hotel

☎ 0141 339 2001
1 Devonshire Gardens G12 0UX
e-mail: bistro.odg@hotelduvin.com
dir: M8 junct 17, follow signs for A82 after 1.5m turn left into Hyndland Rd

Set in a series of Victorian townhouses on a tree-lined terrace in Glasgow's fashionable West End, the Hotel du Vin group has remodelled this contemporary boutique hotel in its usual fine style. The refurbished interior is sympathetic to the original architecture while adding all the modern comforts. The bar-lounge has deep sofas and comfortable chairs, while the popular, atmospheric, oak-panelled bistro follows the theme, though it isn't as typically relaxed as the usual HDV style, offering a more formal fine-dining note here, with tables dressed in their best whites. Staff are well drilled, but relaxed, helpful and knowledgeable, and, as the hotel name suggests, wine is a hallmark theme, with a list to delight backed by a strong sommelier service. The kitchen's repertoire of modern and classic dishes supports the group's philosophy - quality food cooked simply with the freshest local ingredients and attractive presentation. But again, they've cranked up the ante here, with excellent flavours and consistency and all the extra trappings of a fine-dining restaurant, with peripherals like amuse-bouche, breads and petits fours all hitting the spot. Expect dishes like crab and chorizo ravioli to start, followed by butter-roasted loin of border lamb with anchovy beignet, with an almond macaroon served with pistachio ice cream to finish. There's a cosy and inviting whisky snug to be enjoyed too.

Chef Paul Tamburrini **Owner** MWB/Hotel Du Vin **Times** 12-2.30/6-10.30, Closed L Sat **Prices** Fixed L 2 course fr £14.50, Tasting menu £65, Starter £6.50-£12, Main £15-£32, Dessert £9-£16, Service added but optional 10% **Wines** 600 bottles over £20, 12 bottles under £20, 12 by glass **Notes** Tasting menu 6 courses, Sunday L, Vegetarian available, Civ Wed 70 **Seats** 78, Pr/dining room 70 **Children** Portions, Menu

GLASGOW *Continued*

array of secluded booths and alcoves, and a menu to suit most pockets and occasions. Its lengthy selection ranges from home comforts (corned beef hash with fried eggs, or fish and chips) to classier fare - seared pepper tuna with lemon aioli and baby herb salad, for example, or slow-roast shoulder of lamb with creamed potatoes and rosemary. There's a good mix of local and European dishes, and an extensive range of cocktails and wines by the glass to wash it all down.

Chef Alan Watts **Owner** Ultimate Leisure **Times** 11-4.30/5-10, Closed 25-26 Dec, 1-2 Jan **Prices** Food prices not confirmed for 2009. Please telephone for details. **Wines** 24 bottles over £20, 14 bottles under £20, 12 by glass **Notes** Vegetarian available, Dress restrictions, Smart casual, no sportswear, Air con **Seats** 140, Pr/dining room 12 **Children** Portions, Menu **Parking** On street

Lux

◎◎ Modern Scottish **V**

Stylish, formal fine dining in a converted railway station

☎ 0141 576 7576
1051 Great Western Rd G12 0XP
e-mail: luxstazione@bt.connect.com
dir: At traffic lights signed Gartnavel Hospital, on Great Western Rd. 0.25m E of Anniesland Cross

Kelvinside railway station, a listed JJ Burnet Victorian building, has been converted into two stylish restaurants. Lux, on the upper floor, has a minimalist look, with wooden floors, comfortable leather chairs, subtle lighting and a muted colour scheme. The food is resolutely modern and consistently good. Quality ingredients are imaginatively prepared: perfectly cooked baked cod sits on a bed of linguine with oysters and king prawns mixed with chilli and a light toasted sesame seed dressing; and the chocolate bread and butter pudding is simply divine, the richness kept in check by a vanilla cream sauce and a thick raspberry purée. Stazione, with a Mediterranean feel, is the informal dining alternative.

Chef Stephen Johnson, Julie Johnson **Owner** Stephen Johnson **Times** Closed 25-26 Dec, 1-2 Jan, Closed Sun ex by arrangement, Closed L all week ex by arrangement **Prices** Main £29.50-£34.50, Service optional, Groups min 6 service 10% **Wines** 60 bottles over £20, 6 bottles under £20, 4 by glass **Notes** ALC 2-3 courses, Vegetarian menu, Air con **Seats** 64, Pr/dining room 14 **Children** Min 12 yrs **Parking** 16

Malmaison

◎ French, British 🖳 ✋

French brasserie fare in an atmospheric boutique hotel

☎ 0141 572 1001
278 West George St G2 4LL
e-mail: glasgow@malmaison.com
dir: From George Square take St.Vincent St to Pitt St. Hotel on corner with West George St

Built around a 19th-century Greek Orthodox church in the historic Charing Cross area, the Glasgow offshoot of the boutique Malmaison chain isn't short on atmosphere or style. Its chic restaurant is housed in the crypt and decked out with smart leather banquettes and chairs and a subtle lighting scheme that keeps things intimate. Expect a lengthy selection of French brasserie fare to suit most tastes - pan-fried calves' liver with crisp pancetta, creamed potatoes and red wine jus, for example, or confit of duck with red cabbage and spiced pear - underpinned by a serious commitment to fresh local produce that sees many suppliers listed on the menu.

Chef Donald McInnes **Owner** Malmaison Hotels Ltd **Times** 12-2.30/5.30-10.30 **Prices** Fixed L 2 course £13.50, Fixed D 3 course £15.50, Starter £4.95-£8, Main £11.95-£25, Dessert £5.95-£7.50, Service added but optional 10%, Groups min 10 service 10% **Wines** 160 bottles over £20, 20 bottles under £20, 20 by glass **Notes** Sun Brunch menu available, Sunday L, Vegetarian available **Seats** 85, Pr/dining room 22 **Children** Portions, Menu **Parking** Q Park Waterloo St

Manna Restaurant

◎ Modern British

New style at city-centre bistro

☎ 0141 332 6678
104 Bath St G2 2EN
e-mail: info@mannarestaurant.co.uk
dir: City centre. At junct of Bath St & Hope St

Formerly known as Papingo, this restaurant presents a new image and a welcome to a new head chef. The décor has clean lines with cream walls, leather banquette seating and clothed tables. Much attention is focused on sourcing Scottish produce as the Buccleuch Estate steaks bear witness - Chateaubriand for two, fillet, sirloin and rib-eye are all offered on the menu. Other dishes include chargrilled tiger prawns with chilli, lime, roasted red peppers and mixed leaves, followed by fillet of sea bass in paper with pak choi, spring onions and ginger, while tempting desserts could include toasted coconut and banana iced parfait with caramel sauce.

Chef Brian Smith **Owner** Alan Tomkins **Times** 12-2.30/5-10.30, Closed 25-26 Dec, 1-2 Jan, Closed L Sun **Notes** Pre-theatre D £11.95, Vegetarian available, Air con **Seats** 80 **Children** Min 14 yrs, Portions

Menzies Glasgow Hotel

◎ Traditional Scottish

Brasserie fare in the heart of Glasgow

☎ 0871 472 4017
27 Washington St G3 8AZ
e-mail: glasgow@menzies-hotels.co.uk
dir: Continue on Broomliean, turn right before Kingston Bridge

Enjoying a prime position on the site of a historic rice mill, this strikingly contemporary hotel is just a short walk from the city centre, and comes complete with impressive indoor leisure facilities. Service in the new contemporary-style brasserie restaurant is friendly and attentive with a relaxed atmosphere. Continental and British classics appear alongside more complex combinations on the appealing modern menu. A starter of grilled chorizo, pancetta and poached egg salad might be followed by a hearty main course of grilled Toulouse sausage with parsley mash and grain mustard sauce, or pan-seared trout fillet with asparagus wrapped in Parma ham with cherry confit tomatoes and cream sauce. Desserts like boozy raspberry crème brûlée with lemon shortcake are sure to please.

Times 12-2.30/6-10

Michael Caines Restaurant

◎◎ Modern European 🖳 ♦NOTABLE WINE LIST

Stylish city hotel with accomplished cuisine

☎ 0141 572 6011 & 221 6789
Abode Hotel Glasgow, 129 Bath St G2 2SZ
e-mail: restaurantmanagerglasgow@michaelcaines.com
dir: Please telephone for directions

Set in the heart of the city, this stylish hotel, with original Edwardian features, boasts a café-bar with low-level lighting, leather seating, table service and a cocktail menu for pre-dinner drinks. The accomplished cooking in the Michael Caines Restaurant has built up a formidable reputation. Here you'll find darkwood flooring, comfortable chairs and banquettes, stylish table appointments, and an eye-catching glass-screened wine cave. A starter of pan-fried scallops with parsnip and vanilla purée and vanilla and ginger jus, followed by loin of venison with braised baby gem, belly pork, fig galette and chestnut purée sets the style. The passionfruit mousse with exotic salad and rice pudding ice cream makes a fabulous finale.

Owner Abode Hotels **Times** 12-2.30/7-10, Closed 1st 2 wks Jan, 14-28 Jul, Closed Sun-Mon **Prices** Fixed L 2 course fr

£14, Fixed D 3 course fr £25, Tasting menu £55, Starter £9-£12.95, Main £16-£24, Dessert £7, Service added but optional 11% **Wines** 100 bottles over £20, 8 bottles under £20, 8 by glass **Notes** Vegetarian available, Air con **Seats** 40, Pr/dining room 40 **Children** Min 5 yrs, Portions

Rococo

◉◉ ◉ Modern European 🖳 ✋

Confident cooking in intimate and stylish place to be seen

☎ 0141 221 5004
48 West Regent St G2 2RA
e-mail: res@rococoglasgow.co.uk
dir: City centre

One of the most stylish eateries in Glasgow's city centre, Rococo has recently relocated. The cooking style is modern British with French and Italian influences, and there is a firm emphasis on fine quality seasonal, local produce. Pan-fried fillet of red mullet with clam and sweet pepper chowder and creamed cabbage might feature as a starter on the dinner menu, with perhaps oven-roasted chump of lamb with salardaise potatoes, wilted spinach and confit garlic as a main course. Round things off with a dessert of passionfruit mousse. The more simple lunch and pre-theatre menu is excellent value for money.

Chef Mark Tamburrini **Owner** Alan & Audrey Brown **Times** 12-3/5-10.30, Closed 26 Dec, 1 Jan **Prices** Fixed L 2 course £15, Fixed D 3 course £42, Tasting menu £65,

Starter £4.95-£8.50, Main £13.95-£18.75, Dessert £4.50-£7.50, Service added but optional 10% **Wines** 100 bottles over £20, 12 by glass **Notes** Tasting menu 6 courses, Pre theatre menu available, Sunday L, Vegetarian available, Air con **Seats** 60, Pr/dining room 30 **Children** Menu **Parking** On street parking or NCP

See advert below

Shish Mahal

◉ Modern European, Indian

Consistently hitting the mark with fine Indian cuisine

☎ 0141 339 8256 & 334 7899
60-68 Park Rd G4 9JF
e-mail: reservations@shishmahal.co.uk
dir: From M8/A8 take exit towards Dumbarton, drive along Great Western Rd and turn 1st left into Park Rd

After almost 40 years in business, the charming Shish Mahal continues to go from strength to strength. In three sections, with Moorish-themed décor, this consistently good Indian restaurant is popular with local residents, business people and students alike. And the menu is as eclectic as the clientele, covering the varied cooking styles of the sub-continent from the Himalayas to Madras and beyond. Typical starters include spicy chicken tikka and mince samosas, followed by lamb amrat mirchi Punjabi khoya (lamb simmered in cream with spices). Leave room for extras, such as chawal e khas (rice fried in saffron) and the excellent naan bread.

Chef Mr I Humayun **Owner** Ali A Aslam, Nasim Ahmed **Times** 12-2/5-11, Closed 25 Dec, Closed L Sun

Prices Fixed D 4 course £16.95-£19.95, Starter £1.95-£6.95, Main £6.95-£16.95, Dessert £1.95-£3.95, Service optional, Groups min 5 service 10% **Wines** 3 bottles over £20, 13 bottles under £20, 1 by glass **Notes** Fixed L 4 courses, Vegetarian available, Air con **Seats** 95, Pr/dining room 14 **Children** Portions **Parking** Side street, Underground station car park

Stravaigin

◉◉ ◉ Modern International 🖳

Lively, relaxed basement restaurant with exciting, eclectic cooking

☎ 0141 334 2665
30 Gibson St G12 8NX
e-mail: stravaigin@btinternet.com
web: www.stravaigin.com
dir: Next to Glasgow University. 200 yds from Kelvinbridge underground

Spanning three floors of a Glasgow tenement, this popular restaurant has a distinctly contemporary style, with a lacquered tiled floor, stone and leather-covered walls - decorated with modern art and quirky antiques - and lightwood tables throughout. Whether eating in the informal bar or the main basement dining area, expect a daring and exciting menu cooked with flair and imagination. The chef makes the best use of fresh Scottish ingredients, adding an international twist in keeping with the restaurant's 'think global, eat local'

Continued

GLASGOW *Continued*

motto. Try the Aberdeenshire haddie, mussel and sweetcorn velouté and Gruyère fugu to start, followed by the Acharacle venison osso bucco, pan-fried ricotta and sage and parmesan gnocchi. There are also interesting vegetarian dishes available.

Stravaigin

Chef Daniel Blencowe **Owner** Colin Clydesdale **Times** 12/11, Closed 25-26 Dec, 1 Jan, Closed L Tue-Thu **Prices** Fixed D 3 course fr £15.95, Starter £6.25-£11.95, Main £13.65-£22.45, Dessert £4.95-£6.25, Service optional **Wines** 28 bottles over £20, 20 bottles under £20, 9 by glass **Notes** Pre-theatre and Sun brunch menus available, Sunday L, Vegetarian available, Air con **Seats** 76 **Children** Portions, Menu **Parking** On street, car park 100yds

Two Fat Ladies

◎ Modern Seafood

Intimate seafood restaurant in the city centre

☎ 0141 847 0088
118a Blytheswood St G2 4EG
e-mail: mr_james2fl@msn.com
dir: Please telephone for directions

The name of this small street-level restaurant comes from its founding premises at 88 Dumbarton Road (two fat ladies - 88). It has a polished parquet floor and the yellow walls are hung with colourful paintings of coastal scenes. The variety and freshness of the food dictates the style of cooking. Seafood is the speciality, presented in uncomplicated dishes with a degree of innovation. Expect dishes like pan-seared, hand-dived scallops with

Stornoway black pudding and Strathdon blue cheese cream, or whole red snapper stuffed with roasted peppers, basil and lime. Pre and post theatre menu available.

Chef David Monaghan **Owner** Ryan James **Times** 12-3/5.30-10.30, Closed 25 Dec, 1 Jan **Prices** Fixed L 2 course £12.50, Fixed D 3 course £14.50, Starter £3.50-£8.50, Main £12.95-£18.50, Dessert £4.95-£5.95, Service optional **Wines** 15 bottles over £20, 17 bottles under £20, 6 by glass **Notes** Pre-theatre menu available, Sunday L, Vegetarian available **Seats** 30 **Children** Portions **Parking** On street - metered

Ubiquitous Chip

◎◎ Traditional Scottish ♦ NOTABLE WINE LIST

Reliable Scottish cuisine in a unique setting

☎ 0141 334 5007
12 Ashton Ln G12 8SJ
e-mail: mail@ubiquitouschip.co.uk
dir: In the West End of Glasgow, off Byres Rd. Beside Hillhead subway station

Set in a cobbled mews in the city's West End, this has been a Glasgow institution for over 30 years. With its spectacular glass-covered courtyard and fabulous array of lush green plants, it's a unique venue. A mezzanine level overlooks the tables and foliage below, and there's also a more formal dining room. There are three bars, too, each with its own atmosphere. The cooking is a mixture of traditional and original Scottish recipes using local ingredients. Menus are constantly evolving with the seasons, but favourite dishes include venison (or vegetarian) haggis with mashed potato, carrot crisps and turnip cream, followed by organic Orkney salmon with lime and vanilla mash, finishing with whisky mac parfait with rhubarb compôte.

Chef Ronnie Clydesdale **Owner** Ronnie Clydesdale **Times** 12-2.30/5.30-11, Closed 25 Dec, 1 Jan **Prices** Fixed L 2 course fr £23.85, Fixed D 3 course fr £39.85, Service optional **Wines** 330 bottles over £20, 49 bottles under £20, 31 by glass **Notes** Sunday L, Vegetarian available, Civ Wed 60, Air con **Seats** 200, Pr/dining room 45 **Children** Portions, Menu **Parking** Lilybank gardens (50m)

Urban Bar and Brasserie

◎◎ Modern French

Contemporary bar-brasserie with food to match

☎ 0141 248 5636
23/25 St Vincent Place G1 2DT
e-mail: info@urbanbrasserie.co.uk
dir: Located in city centre between George Sq and Buchanan St

One-time home to the Bank of England's Scottish headquarters, this imposing building has been transformed into a chic modern restaurant and champagne bar. A grand façade sets the scene and leads into the large bar, off which is an intimate lounge and spacious dining area. Here white walls are hung with

colourful modern artwork, and there's brown banquette seating, smart wood flooring, a glass skylight and tables dressed in their best whites. It's a tall order, but the food lives up to the surroundings: expect accomplished cooking distinguished by quality produce and clean flavours - monkfish steamed in paper for example, served with ginger and spring onions, or roast saddle of venison with beetroot, redcurrant, port and pink peppercorns. Rum and raisin crème brûlée rounds things off nicely, and there's a well chosen wine list too.

Chef Derek Marshall **Owner** Alan Tomkins, Derek Marshall **Times** 12-10/12-10, Closed 25-26 Dec, 1-2 Jan **Wines** 60 bottles over £20, 20 bottles under £20, 10 by glass **Notes** Pre-theatre menu 5-6pm £15, Sunday L, Vegetarian available, Air con **Seats** 110, Pr/dining room 18 **Children** Min 14 yrs, Portions **Parking** NCP West Nile St

The Big Blue

🖥

☎ 0141 357 1038
445 Great Western Rd G12 8HH
web: http://www.theaa.com/travel/index.jsp

The entrance is on one of the West End's busier streets, but this bar is three flights down, in an old archway which opens out onto the Kelvin walkway and overlooks the river. The menu is predominantly Italian with a few seafood dishes thrown in.

Prices Food prices not confirmed for 2009. Please telephone for details.

Red Onion

🖥

☎ 0141 221 6000
257 West Campbell St G2 4TT
web: http://www.theaa.com/travel/index.jsp

A charming restaurant in the heart of the City, with an eclectic menu and open from breakfast throughout the day.

Prices Food prices not confirmed for 2009. Please telephone for details.

ACHILTIBUIE Map 22 NC00

The Summer Isles Hotel

◎◎ Modern British 🖥

Food from land and sea in stunning location

☎ 01854 622282
IV26 2YG
e-mail: info@summerisleshotel.co.uk
dir: 10 m N of Ullapool. Turn left off A835 onto single track road. 15m to Achiltibuie. Hotel 100 yds after post office on left

This one-time fishing inn has retained a friendly and informal feel despite its transformation into a chic and comfortable hotel. Run by the same family since the late 1960s, it's a perfect base for exploring the stunning scenery of Achiltibuie, particularly during the summer when the long northern days stretch until 10.30pm. A single five-course menu is served every night, but with cooking this good you're in safe hands; flavours are clean, combinations refreshingly straightforward, and almost all the ingredients are home produced or locally caught. Warm scallop mousse with herb and tomato loaf, followed by grilled fillet of Lochinver halibut with local mussels steamed in saffron and white wine are fine examples of the fare.

Times 12.30-2/8, Closed mid Oct-Etr

BOAT OF GARTEN   Map 23 NH91

Boat Hotel - The Capercaille

◎◎ Modern British

Scottish cuisine with a modern twist amidst beautiful scenery

☎ 01479 831258
Deshar Rd PH24 3BH
e-mail: holidays@boathotel.co.uk
dir: Turn off A9 N of Aviemore onto A95. Follow signs to Boat of Garten

Located in the heart of the Cairngorms, the restaurant overlooks the Spey Valley, next to the Speyside Steam Railway. This Victorian station hotel has been tastefully modernised while retaining many period features. The intimate, stylish restaurant is lit by a fire and wall sconces, emphasising the dark blue walls and striking avant-garde artwork, and there's a refurbished bar and comfortable lounge in which to enjoy canapés or after-dinner drinks. Scottish cuisine is prepared with a contemporary twist, making the most of local produce. Interesting combinations might include a terrine of Aberdeenshire smoked ham hock with Dublin Bay langoustines, saffron and dill coulis, or cannon of Spey Valley lamb with boulangère potatoes and braised Puy lentils with rosemary, sage and pancetta.

Chef John Dale **Owner** Mr J Erasmus & Mr R Drummond **Times** Closed Dec-Feb, Closed L all week **Prices** Fixed D 3 course £35-£40, Tasting menu £42-£68, Starter £8-£10, Main £18-£20, Dessert £6-£8, Service optional **Wines** 40 bottles over £20, 6 bottles under £20, 4 by glass **Notes** Tasting menu 7 courses, Sunday L, Vegetarian available, Dress restrictions, No jeans **Seats** 30, Pr/dining room 40 **Children** Min 8 yrs **Parking** 36

BRORA   Map 23 NC90

Royal Marine Hotel

◎ Modern British

Traditional Highland hotel with reliable cooking

☎ 01408 621252
Golf Rd KW9 6QS
e-mail: info@highlandescape.com
dir: Turn off A9 in village toward beach and golf course

This Edwardian country house has been sensitively restored and is a popular choice with the many tourists

lured by the area's reputation for good shooting, fishing, golf and whisky. Three dining options are on offer: a bustling bistro, a café-bar overlooking the pool, and the formal Lorimer Dining Room, which delivers a modern British menu of solid, dependable fare with a sprinkling of traditional Scottish favourites. You might start with Cullen skink or hot-smoked roast and whisky-cured salmon, and then tuck into collops of best Scottish beef, pan-fried and served on a crispy haggis cake with a creamy malt whisky sauce.

Times 12-2/6.30-8.45, Closed L (pre booking only)

CONTIN   Map 23 NH45

Achilty Hotel

◎ Traditional, Mediterranean

Traditional Scottish fare in a family-run hotel

☎ 01997 421355
IV14 9EG
e-mail: info@achiltyhotel.co.uk
dir: A9 N of Inverness onto A835 to Contin, hotel is 0.5m W of village

Originally a drovers' inn dating back to the 1700s, this hotel's friendly owners contribute much to the relaxed and hospitable atmosphere. The spacious open-plan restaurant is located in a former still, lending a traditional appearance with high ceilings and stone walls. Tables are well appointed and service is attentive and friendly. The menu is identifiably Scottish, with a starter like a trio of Scottish smoked salmon - Inverawe smoked salmon, gravad lax and Salar smoked salmon served with dill mustard, and a main course of chicken breast on a bed of haggis finished with a whisky, green peppercorn and cream sauce.

Times 12-2/5-8.30, Closed L Mon-Tue

Coul House Hotel

◎ Modern British V ◎

Georgian country-house hotel with superb views and fine dining

☎ 01997 421487
IV14 9ES
e-mail: stay@coulhousehotel.com
dir: A835 signed Ullapool, 12m Contin. Hotel drive 100yds right after petrol station

Built in 1821, this impressive country-house hotel is set in extensive grounds with stunning views of the distant mountains. A wealth of period features and welcoming log fires await within, and the distinctive Octagonal Restaurant offers contemporary Scottish cuisine with classic French overtones, accompanied by an extensive wine list. Starters may include hickory smoked rabbit saddle served warm with pan-fried gnocchi, French beans, café de Paris butter and lamb jus, followed by mains such as pan-fried calves' liver with mashed potato and sour apple crisp, chef's vegetable caponata and raspberry vinegar jus, topped with flaky pastry.

Chef G Kenley **Owner** Stuart MacPherson **Times** 12-2.30/6.30-9, Closed 24-26 Dec **Prices** Starter £4-£10.50, Main £12-£22, Dessert £4.50-£5.95, Service optional **Wines** 53 bottles over £20, 25 bottles under £20, 9 by glass **Notes** Sunday L, Vegetarian menu, Civ Wed 120 **Seats** 70, Pr/dining room 40 **Children** Portions, Menu **Parking** 60

DORNOCH   Map 23 NH78

Dornoch Castle Hotel

◎ Scottish, Fusion ◎

Refreshing brasserie food in the castle conservatory

☎ 01862 810216
Castle St IV25 3SD
e-mail: enquiries@dornochcastlehotel.com
dir: 2m from A9 in the centre of Dornoch

Situated opposite the cathedral, the purpose-built Garden Restaurant is attached to the fine 15th-century castle and overlooks the immaculate walled castle gardens. The rich décor is Scottish-influenced, successfully marrying traditional and modern styles, while the modern Scottish menu offers a straightforward brasserie-style choice using quality ingredients, locally sourced wherever possible. Kick off with a traditional dish of Cullen skink, or maybe haggis cake with whisky cream sauce, before moving on to pan-fried sea bass and queen scallops with chargrilled fennel, black caviar cream and fondant potatoes, or perhaps roasted breast of chicken wrapped in Parma ham and stuffed with saffron cream cheese in red wine jus. Service is informal, but attentive.

Chef Michael Middleton **Owner** Colin Thompson **Times** 12-3/6-9.30, Closed 25-26 Dec **Prices** Fixed L 2 course fr £11.95, Fixed D 3 course fr £20.95, Starter £5.50-£7.95, Main £13.25-£21, Dessert £4.95-£7.25, Service optional **Wines** 25 bottles over £20, 22 bottles under £20, 6 by glass **Notes** Early D special menu, Sunday L, Vegetarian available **Seats** 75, Pr/dining room 25 **Children** Portions, Menu **Parking** 12

2 Quail Restaurant & Rooms

◎◎ International

Classic cooking in tiny Highland restaurant

☎ 01862 811811
Inistore House, Castle St IV25 3SN
e-mail: theaa@2quail.com
dir: 200 yds past war memorial on left side of main street, just before Cathedral

You'll need to make a reservation at this small, book-lined restaurant with rooms located in a Victorian Highland townhouse. It has a homely feel and as it is run by a husband-and-wife team, you can be sure of personal attention. Everything is made in-house using locally-sourced produce where possible. The four-course dinner menu offers a choice between dessert and cheese, with the other dishes being fixed. You might start with dived West Coast scallops in a Thai broth, followed by roast best end of Ross-shire lamb with provençale vegetables

Continued

DORNOCH *Continued*

and thyme gravy. Finish with vanilla bavarois served with a raspberry coulis. Good quality wines are served by the glass or bottle.

Chef Michael Carr **Owner** Michael and Kerensa Carr **Times** Closed Xmas, 2 wks Feb-Mar, Closed Sun-Mon **Prices** Fixed D 4 course £38, Service optional **Wines** 47 bottles over £20, 10 bottles under £20, 8 by glass **Notes** Dress restrictions, Smart casual **Seats** 14 **Children** Min 10 yrs **Parking** On street

---

FORT AUGUSTUS	Map 23 NH30

Lovat Arms, Hotel Bar Restaurant

◉ Modern British

Intimate bistro-style dining with the best of local produce and views

☎ 0845 450 1100 & 01456 459250
Hotel Bar Restaurant, Loch Ness PH32 4DU
e-mail: info@lovatarms-hotel.com
dir: A82 between Fort William and Inverness

A family-run Victorian hotel, the Lovat Arms is surrounded by beautiful scenery: Loch Ness, the mountains and the five-lock canal staircase of the Caledonian Canal. The bistro-style restaurant, while cosy and intimate, has a contemporary feel with subdued lighting and an informal atmosphere. Local produce is used wherever possible, including fish and seafood sourced direct from Mallaig.

Good examples of dishes are seared scallops with garlic and cherry tomato fettuccine and basil dressing; and best end of Highland lamb with clapshot potato, Lochaber haggis, and rosemary and malt whisky jus.

Chef Jim Murphy **Owner** David, Geraldine & Caroline Gregory **Times** Closed Hogmany (Jan) - guests only **Prices** Fixed D 3 course £30, Starter £4.50-£9.50, Main £10.50-£22.50, Dessert £5.50-£7.50, Service optional, Groups min 8 service 10% **Wines** 20 bottles over £20, 20 bottles under £20, 7 by glass **Notes** Vegetarian available **Seats** 50, Pr/dining room 40 **Children** Portions, Menu **Parking** 30

FORT WILLIAM	Map 22 NN17

Inverlochy Castle Hotel

◉◉◉ – *see below*

Lime Tree Hotel & Restaurant

◉ Modern European

Stylish small hotel with art gallery and modern menu

☎ 01397 701806
Lime Tree Studio, Achintore Rd PH33 6RQ
e-mail: info@limetreefortwilliam.co.uk
web: www.limetreefortwilliam.co.uk
dir: Please telephone for directions

This old stone manse, enjoying fine views over both loch and mountains, is now a small boutique hotel, restaurant and art gallery. Original artwork is displayed throughout. The artistic eye of the owner is evident in the stylish contemporary décor, but with real fires in the lounges and clever use of natural materials there is a successful balance of traditional and modern. Similarly, the menu is a blend of traditional ingredients and modern European touches: Loch Linnhe shellfish risotto is infused with lobster bisque and topped with rocket and truffle oil, while a starter of perfectly pink wood pigeon is served with lightly dressed salad leaves. Service from a young team is friendly and efficient.

Lime Tree Hotel & Restaurant

Chef Robert Ramsay **Owner** David & Charlotte Wilson **Times** 12-2.30/6.30-9, Closed Nov **Prices** Starter £2.95-£6, Main £5.95-£20, Dessert £3.50-£6, Service optional **Wines** 14 bottles over £20, 17 bottles under £20, 5 by glass **Notes** Sunday L, Vegetarian available, Civ Wed 50 **Seats** 30 **Children** Portions **Parking** 10

Inverlochy Castle Hotel

FORT WILLIAM	Map 22 NN17

Modern British 🖳 V 📖

Luxurious Highland castle setting for fine dining

☎ 01397 702177
Torlundy PH33 6SN
e-mail: info@inverlochy.co.uk
web: www.inverlochycastlehotel.com
dir: 3m N of Fort William on A82, just past Golf Club, N towards Inverness

Nestling in the foothills of Ben Nevis in over 500 acres of grounds, this majestic castle sits amidst some of Scotland's finest scenery. Built in 1863, it remained a private residence for over 100 years before being converted into a luxury hotel. Lavishly appointed in classic country-house style, it makes a truly impressive setting for fine dining - aperitifs are taken in the sumptuous lounge or on

the terrace on warm sunny days, while dinner is an experience to savour in any of the three dining rooms, each with elaborate period furniture and stunning mountain views. Genuine comfort and luxury abound, while service is highly professional but with a relaxed and friendly note. The kitchen's accomplished modern approach - underpinned by a classical theme - suits the surroundings and makes fine use of the abundant Highland larder, as well as produce from the estate's walled garden, on its repertoire of daily-changing five-course dinner and tasting menus. Expect high-level technical skill and clear flavours in dishes like grilled tranche of turbot with cauliflower salad, horseradish mousseline and yogurt beignets, or Scottish blue lobster with lemon and honey dressing, navet and truffle, followed by seared fingers of John Dory with soured cabbage and chorizo gnocchi, or crispy fillet of sea bass with Jerusalem artichoke ravioli and fish velouté. There's a notable wine list with an extensive range of half-bottles to enjoy, but remember your jacket and tie gentlemen, it's the required dress code here.

Chef Matthew Gray **Owner** Inverlochy Ltd **Times** 12.30-1.15/6.30-10 **Prices** Fixed L 2 course fr £32.50, Fixed D 4 course fr £67.50, Service optional **Wines** 283 bottles over £20, 8 by glass **Notes** Fixed D 4 courses, Vegetarian menu, Dress restrictions, Jacket & tie for D, Civ Wed 80 **Seats** 40, Pr/dining room 20 **Children** Portions, Menu **Parking** 20

Moorings Hotel

🏵 Modern, Traditional

Popular Highland hotel with contemporary cooking

☎ 01397 772797
Banavie PH33 7LY
e-mail: reservations@moorings-fortwilliam.co.uk
dir: From A82 take A830 W for 1m. 1st right over
Caledonian Canal on B8004, signed Banavie

With wonderful views of Ben Nevis, this popular hotel sits alongside the Caledonian Canal, overlooking the series of locks known as Neptune's Staircase. The spacious restaurant, complete with beams and artwork aplenty, provides friendly service and a menu of carefully prepared British and European cuisine using quality local ingredients. Perhaps start with Mallaig seafood soup, or red mullet served with couscous, red pepper sauce, herb pesto and rouille, followed by warm salad of seared scallops with mallard duck served with orange, honey and grain mustard dressing, or asparagus risotto with roasted vegetables and grilled halloumi. Desserts might include iced raspberry parfait with sugar toasted hazelnuts and fresh fruit sauce.

Chef Paul Smith **Owner** Mr S Leitch **Times** Closed 24-26 Dec, Closed L all week **Prices** Fixed L 2 course £8.95-£15.95, Fixed D 3 course £13.95-£28, Starter £4.95-£7.95, Main £11.50-£18.95, Dessert £4.95-£7.95, Service optional **Wines** 17 bottles over £20, 28 bottles under £20, 4 by glass **Notes** Sunday L, Vegetarian available, Dress restrictions, Smart casual, Civ Wed 120 **Seats** 60, Pr/dining room 120 **Children** Portions **Parking** 50

GLENFINNAN Map 22 NM88

The Prince's House

🏵🏵 Modern British 🍷

Welcoming 17th-century coaching inn with skilful Scottish cooking

☎ 01397 722246
PH37 4LT
e-mail: princeshouse@glenfinnan.co.uk
dir: From Fort William N on A82 for 2m. Turn left on to A830 Mallaig Rd for 15m to hotel

In a beautiful Highland setting, surrounded by mountains and woodland, this delightful old coaching inn dates back to 1658, and sits in the heart of 'Bonnie Prince Charlie' country. The hospitality at this family-run hotel is legendary and the restaurant, with its half-panelled walls and warming winter log fire, offers inspiring mountain views. The simplicity of the cooking here really shines through, with the best-quality seasonal local produce, including excellent game and seafood, used to create dishes with clear flavours. Take Mallaig seafood soup, followed by loin of Kinlochmoidart venison with celeriac and potato rösti, roast root vegetables and port wine jus and, for dessert, perhaps Ardbeg malt whisky and heather honey ice cream with Aberfeldy oatmeal tuile and Scottish raspberries.

Chef Kieron Kelly **Owner** Kieron & Ina Kelly **Times** Closed Xmas, Jan-Feb, Low season - booking only, Closed L all week **Prices** Fixed D 3 course £30-£35, Service included **Wines** 50 bottles over £20, 15 bottles under £20, 8 by glass **Notes** Vegetarian available **Seats** 30 **Children** Portions **Parking** 18

GRANTOWN-ON-SPEY Map 23 NJ02

Craggan Mill

🏵 Modern Scottish, International 🍷

A 17th-century mill restaurant serving carefully-prepared modern fare

☎ 01479 872288
PH26 3NT
e-mail: info@cragganmill.co.uk
web: www.cragganmill.co.uk
dir: 1m S of Grantown-on-Spey

No shortage of charm here as Craggan Mill is a restored 17th-century mill with a working wheel and art gallery, located just south of town and offering stunning views of the Cairngorms. Artisan tools adorn the walls, while great cross cuts from mature trees form lounge tables; further on, the natural-wood dining tables are dotted with place mats made from the ends of French wine boxes. Modern Scottish dishes predominate with an emphasis on the abundant local produce: roast belly of Craggie Farm pork arrives with Kailkenny mash, sauerkraut and cider gravy. Interest comes courtesy of the occasional nod to farther flung climes - durum wheat and sweet potato patties with a coconut sauce for example, or lamb rogan josh.

Chef Graham Harvey & Sheila McConachie **Owner** Graham Harvey & Sheila McConachie **Times** 12-2.30/6-11, Closed Tues **Prices** Starter £4-£8, Main £10-£25, Dessert £5.25-£8, Service optional **Wines** 16 bottles over £20, 25 bottles under £20, 8 by glass **Notes** Tasting menu 5 courses inc whisky, booked in advance, Sunday L **Seats** 50, Pr/dining room 20 **Children** Portions, Menu **Parking** 18

Culdearn House

🏵 Traditional Scottish 🍷

Quality local ingredients cooked with flair in homely small hotel

☎ 01479 872106
Woodlands Ter PH26 3JU
e-mail: enquiries@culdearn.com
dir: Enter Grantown from SW on A95, left at 30mph sign

This large Victorian villa set in a quiet residential street has beautifully proportioned rooms with ornate ceilings, open fires and many period features. The small dining room at the front of the house is colourful and comfortable, offering lovely views of the garden from white-clothed tables. Good-quality local ingredients are simply cooked with care and skill, especially beautifully fresh fish and fully traceable beef. Perhaps try breast of guinea fowl with green pepper and brandy sauce, or fillet of haddock with tomato and black olive relish. Service is efficient but unobtrusive making this a relaxing place to dine. An excellent wine list is available, too.

Chef Sonia Marshall **Owner** Mr & Mrs Marshall **Times** Closed L all week **Prices** Fixed D 4 course £34, Service optional **Wines** 28 bottles over £20, 9 bottles under £20, 4 by glass **Notes** Vegetarian available, Dress restrictions, Smart casual, no jeans, sportswear/T-shirts **Seats** 14 **Children** Min 10 yrs **Parking** 11

The Glass House Restaurant

🏵🏵 Modern British V 🍷

Ambitious cooking in a conservatory setting

☎ 01479 872980
Grant Rd PH26 3LD
e-mail: enquiries@theglasshouse-grantown.co.uk
dir: Turn off High St between the bank and Co-op into Caravan Park Rd. First left onto Grant Rd.

Set in an unusual double conservatory attached to a stone-built bungalow, this light-and-airy restaurant provides a contemporary setting for an accomplished menu of modern British dishes. There are just four choices at each course but you're in safe hands; the food here is full of flavour and makes good use of seasonal local produce. Better still, it's great value for money even in the evening when the cooking gets more adventurous, with dishes such as hot peat-smoked salmon on an avocado, pea and cucumber salad with lime oil dressing and crème fraîche; followed by seared Morayshire beef with asparagus spears on a wild mushroom and sorrel cream with parmesan potato cake.

Chef Stephen Robertson **Owner** Stephen and Karen Robertson **Times** 12-1.45/7-9, Closed 2 wks Nov, 1 wk Jan, 25-26 Dec, 1-2 Jan, Closed Mon, Closed L Tue, Closed D Sun **Wines** 10 bottles over £20, 12 bottles under £20, 2 by glass **Notes** Oct-Mar 2 courses £9.95, 3 courses £13.50, Sunday L, Vegetarian menu **Seats** 30 **Children** Portions **Parking** 10

INVERGARRY   Map 22 NH30

Glengarry Castle

🌸 British, International

Scottish country-house style in a dramatic setting

☎ 01809 501254
PH35 4HW
e-mail: castle@glengarry.net
dir: 1m S of Invergarry on A82

Set above the shores of Loch Oich, the Victorian Glengarry Castle stands surrounded by tall trees in 50 acres of grounds, with great views all around. A panelled reception hall, marble fireplaces and a traditionally furnished dining room are features of this comfortable and welcoming hotel. The fixed-price dinner menu showcases the best of Scottish produce in dishes such as a starter of traditional haggis with neeps and tatties and a whisky and redcurrant jus. Then comes soup or sorbet before main courses such as chargrilled fillet of prime Scottish beef served with shallots and wild mushrooms in a creamy paprika and brandy sauce. Finish with rhubarb fool or a plate of Scottish cheeses.

Chef John McDonald **Owner** Mr & Mrs MacCallum **Times** 12-1.45/7-8.30, Closed mid Nov to mid Mar, Closed L Mon-Sun **Prices** Starter £5, Main £16, Dessert £5, Service included **Wines** 32 bottles over £20, 20 bottles under £20, 9 by glass **Notes** Vegetarian available **Seats** 40 **Children** Portions, Menu **Parking** 30

INVERGORDON   Map 23 NH76

Kincraig House Hotel

🌸 Modern French

Fine dining in a lovingly restored period house

☎ 01349 852587
IV18 0LF
e-mail: info@kincraig-house-hotel.co.uk
web: www.kincraig-house-hotel.co.uk
dir: Situated off A9, past Alness towards Tain. Hotel is 0.25m on left past church

A charming country house set in landscaped grounds with sea views, the hotel has been totally refurbished in recent years. The restaurant, looking over the grounds to the Cromarty Firth, boasts a large original fireplace, while crisp white linen, sparkling glassware and fresh flowers all add to the ambience. Skilfully prepared dishes make use of the finest Scottish produce. Original presentation

---

particularly appeals in a main course of grilled halibut with braised fennel, crispy polenta parcels and sauce vièrge, followed by an equally impressive tarte Tatin with excellent vanilla ice cream. The sympathetically restored lounge has open fires and comfortable seating, as does the bar, where informal meals are served.

Times 12.30-2/6.45-9

INVERNESS   Map 23 NH64

Abstract Restaurant

🌸🌸🌸 – **see below**

Bunchrew House Hotel

🌸🌸 Modern, Traditional V 🕲

Confident cooking in imposing Highland manor

☎ 01463 234917
Bunchrew IV3 8TA
e-mail: welcome@bunchrew-inverness.co.uk
dir: 3m W of Inverness on A862 towards Beauly

A carefully restored and upgraded 17th-century Scottish baronial mansion set alongside the Beauly Firth in 20 acres of woodland and pretty gardens. The stately, well-proportioned restaurant makes the most of the view towards Ben Wyvis and the Black Isle across the water - book ahead for a window table as the summer sunsets are stunning. There's nothing whimsical about the food or the dedication to combining quality Scottish

---

Abstract Restaurant

INVERNESS   Map 23 NH64

Modern French 🖳

Refined French dining in elegant townhouse hotel

☎ 01463 223777
Glenmoriston Town House Hotel, 20 Ness Bank IV2 4SF
e-mail: reception@glenmoristontownhouse.com
web: www.glenmoristontownhouse.com
dir: 2 mins from city centre, on river opposite theatre

Bold contemporary designs blend seamlessly with the classical architecture of this stylish townhouse hotel on the banks of the River Ness. Elegantly dressed tables, quality glassware, lots of wood and leather, mood lighting and fresh flowers contribute to the chic modern elegance of the sophisticated restaurant Abstract, which includes Scotland's first chef's table in its kitchen. Service is friendly and attentive, while the fine-dining experience

offers a refined modern French flavour. High quality Scottish ingredients - with a strong emphasis on seasonality - are prepared and presented with flair, skill and attention to detail, with interesting combinations and beautifully blended flavours that don't overpower the principal ingredient. There's an eight-course tasting menu too, bolstering an appealing carte, while excellent ancillaries - including amuse-bouche, pre-dessert and petits fours - all hold form. Expect roasted John Dory perhaps served with white asparagus and ox kidney and wholegrain-mustard jus, or roasted fillet of Scottish hare and pâté of leg accompanied by apple and passionfruit compote and brandy sauce, and to finish, maybe a hot banana soufflé teamed with chocolate ice cream. The hotel's bistro-style restaurant 'Contrast' offers a stylish but less formal alternative.

Chef Geoffrey Malmedy **Owner** Larsen & Ross South **Times** Closed 26-28 Dec, Closed Sun-Mon, Closed L all week **Prices** Tasting menu £50, Starter £7-£11, Main £14-£19.50, Dessert £8, Service optional, Groups min 6

service 12.5% **Wines** 90% bottles over £20, 10% bottles under £20, 11 by glass **Notes** Vegetarian available **Seats** 50, Pr/dining room 15 **Children** Portions, Menu **Parking** 50

ingredients with accomplished technique. Contemporary dishes on daily dinner menus may include ragout of seafood spiked with pink caviar and fresh herbs, followed by loin of pork wrapped in Parma ham with local black pudding and pancetta sauce, and to finish, perhaps a banana and mascarpone cheesecake with hot toffee sauce.

Chef Walter Walker **Owner** Terry & Irina Mackay **Times** 12-1.45/7-9, Closed 23-26 Dec **Prices** Fixed L course £25.50, Fixed D 4 course £39.50, Service optional **Wines** 4 by glass **Notes** Sunday L, Vegetarian menu, Civ Wed 92 **Seats** 32, Pr/dining room 14 **Children** Portions, Menu **Parking** 40

Culloden House Hotel

ⓐⓐ Traditional British

Serious Scottish cuisine in historic setting

☎ 01463 790461
Culloden IV2 7BZ
e-mail: info@cullodenhouse.co.uk
dir: From A96, take left turn at junction of Balloch, Culloden, Smithton. Continue for 2m, hotel is on right

'Bonnie' Prince Charlie lodged at this grand Palladian mansion before the battle of Culloden Moor in 1746. High ceilings and intricate cornices are particular features of the public rooms, including the elegant Adam dining room. Scottish produce is served in a five-course extravaganza, commencing with canapés and finishing with hand-made petits fours. Perfectly cooked risotto of smoked haddock is served with a lemon dressing, to cut through the strong fish flavour, and another well balanced dish is grilled fillet of halibut set on courgette provençale with tomato jus. For dessert, an interesting combination of flavours comes together in an attractively presented lemon crème brûlée with cardamom and pistachio ice cream.

Times 12.30-2/7-9, Closed 2 wks Jan/Feb

The Drumossie Hotel

ⓐⓐ Modern British

Country-house hotel producing high-quality food

☎ 01463 236451
Old Perth Rd IV2 5BE
e-mail: stay@drumossiehotel.co.uk
dir: Telephone for directions

An art deco building on a hillside south of Inverness houses this comfortable hotel. It has been refurbished to country-house standard, and features an elegant restaurant with well-dressed tables where the crisp white linen and polished silverware lend a touch of formality. The food is several notches above the ordinary, and has been very well received locally. Notable among the daily-changing set dishes are an Isle of Skye fish pie featuring salmon, halibut and sole, and a seared tournedos of Castle Mey tenderloin of beef and braised ribs with caramelised red onion and Burgundy infusion. Dessert may come in the form of pear tarte Tatin with liquorice ice cream and star anise anglaise.

Times 12.30-2/7-9.30

Riverhouse

ⓐ British ⓒ

Relaxed riverside dining

☎ 01463 222033
1 Greig St IV3 5PT
e-mail: riverhouse.restaurant@unicombox.co.uk
dir: On corner of Huntly Street and Greig Street

Situated on the banks of the River Ness, this small bistro-style restaurant is close to the city centre and the main shopping district. The wood-panelled interior has an intimate atmosphere, and from here you can watch the chefs at work in the open kitchen. Classic dishes are simply prepared using quality produce. Particularly impressive is a terrine of rabbit, boudin noir and pheasant served with home-made sweet chutney, followed by a main course of steamed halibut with smoked salmon on a bed of crushed potatoes, given bite from a pineapple and sweet pepper salsa.

Chef Allan Little, Mark Chisholm **Owner** Allan Little **Times** 12-2.15/5.30-10, Closed Mon, Closed L Sun **Prices** Fixed L 2 course £11.50, Starter £6.95-£10.50, Main £14.50-£19.50, Dessert £5.25-£6.95 **Wines** 3 bottles over £20, 5 bottles under £20, 10 by glass **Notes** Dress restrictions, Smart Casual **Seats** 30 **Children** Min 8 yrs, Portions **Parking** Parking available 200 yds

---

Rocpool

ⓐⓐ Modern European

Lively cosmopolitan atmosphere meets classic dishes with contemporary twist

☎ 01463 717274
1 Ness Walk IV3 5NE
e-mail: info@rocpoolrestaurant.com
dir: Please telephone for details

A busy city-centre brasserie with sleek contemporary interior, riverside views and an energetic atmosphere, Rocpool brings a touch of modern style and glamour to town. Lots of wood and glass - with windows the entire length of the long, slim room - comes decked out with wood tables, crisp white linen and leather banquettes, backed by attentive but unobtrusive service. The food is in the equally fashionable modern European vein, delivering quality ingredients cooked with simplicity and flair. Dishes come attractively presented but

sensibly not over embellished as in chump of lamb roasted with garlic and thyme and served with Lyonnaise potatoes, oven-roasted tomato, zucchini and spinach. While the carte cranks things up a gear, the fixed-price lunch and early-evening options offer excellent value.

Chef Steven Devlin **Owner** Mr Devlin **Times** 12-2.30/5.45-10, Closed 25-26 Dec, 1-2 Jan, Closed Sun Oct-Mar, Closed L Sun Apr-Sep **Prices** Fixed L 2 course fr £9.95, Starter £3.95-£7.95, Main £8.95-£19.95, Dessert £4.95-£5.95, Service optional **Wines** 25 bottles over £20, 17 bottles under £20, 11 by glass **Notes** Vegetarian available, Air con **Seats** 55 **Children** Portions **Parking** On street

---

KINGUSSIE Map 23 NH70

The Cross at Kingussie

ⓐⓐⓐ – **see page 522**

KYLE OF LOCHALSH Map 22 NG72

The Seafood Restaurant

ⓐ Modern, Traditional Seafood ⓒ

Wonderful setting for fine food and great views

☎ 01599 534813 & 577230
Railway Station Buildings, Station Rd IV40 8AE
e-mail: seafoodrestaurant@btinternet.com
dir: Off A87

This restaurant is found in one of the railway buildings on the pier, looking over one platform towards the Skye bridge, and across the other towards Loch Duich. Parking is on the pier at the end of the buffers. The simply furnished restaurant seats 35 at pinewood tables and there is a dispense bar with counter. Naturally the menu relies heavily on fresh seafood and the portions are generous. Try the seafood chowder to start, served piping hot. Main courses might include Isle of Skye smoked haddock with clapshot and a white wine and parsley sauce.

Chef Jann MacRae **Owner** Jann MacRae **Times** 11-3/5-9.30, Closed end Oct-beginning Mar, Closed Sun (please phone to confirm opening hrs) **Prices** Fixed L 2 course £17-£36, Starter £3.95-£7.95, Main £11.95-£19.95, Dessert £4.95-£6.95, Service optional **Wines** 2 bottles over £20, 15 bottles under £20, 2 by glass **Notes** Vegetarian available **Seats** 35 **Children** Portions **Parking** 5

The Cross at Kingussie

Modern Scottish

Top-notch restaurant with rooms in a pretty setting

☎ 01540 661166
**Tweed Mill Brae, Ardbroilach Rd
PH21 1LB**
e-mail: relax@thecross.co.uk
dir: From lights in centre of Kingussie, uphill along Ardbroilach Rd for 300 mtrs

The River Gynack flows past this former mill, the tranquil setting now a place of relaxation and enjoyment, the industrial endeavours of the tweed industry long forgotten. Enjoy a glass of champagne by the water and contemplate the past whilst looking forward to dinner. The four acres of grounds are peaceful and worth exploring, revealing woodland and wild flowers. David and Katie Young have created a comfortable and eminently civilised restaurant with rooms which fits in with the surrounding landscape - the stone building has been sensitively restored and elegantly refurbished with an absence of pretension. The restaurant with its exposed stone walls and heavy beams is brought up to date with some modern art on the walls and natural wood tables. The fabulous food is just as in keeping with its locale: the best Scottish produce stars on a menu based around the seasons and showing a contemporary edge. Cured fillet of

Fraserburgh mackerel is served simply with a spiced aïoli and a green leaf salad in a starter which neatly demonstrates the uncluttered simplicity of the approach. Timing is spot on in the searing of a cutlet of Borders rose veal, the meat served with garlic leaves, comfrey, morels and a purée of Yukon Gold potatoes. Baked Alaska makes a fitting finale and everything from canapés to petits-fours show the passion and skill underlying the whole establishment. The hospitality and service is second to none.

Chef Becca Henderson, David Young
Owner David and Katie Young
Times Closed Xmas & Jan (excl New Year), Closed Sun-Mon, Closed L all week **Prices** Fixed D 4 course £45-£50, Service included, Groups min 6 service 10% **Wines** 200 bottles over £20, 20 bottles under £20, 4 by glass
Notes Vegetarian available **Seats** 20
Children Min 10 yrs **Parking** 12

LOCHINVER
Map 22 NC02

Inver Lodge

@@ Modern British

Relaxed fine dining in wonderful location

☎ 01571 844496
IV27 4LU
e-mail: stay@inverlodge.com
dir: A835 to Lochinver, left at village hall, private road for 0.5m

Nestled in a far corner of the Scottish Highlands, the Western Isles can be seen through the large picture windows of this delightful modern hotel. Diners at this high quality modern hotel are treated to spectacular views over the small harbour and the ocean beyond. The kitchen makes sound use of the abundant local larder - fish is landed at the quayside below, while Aberdeen Angus beef might also feature on the fixed-price, daily-changing dinner menu. Descriptions are not short on adjectives and the cooking's equally ambitious; take Inver Lodge gravadlax with capers, lemon oil and hand-made soda bread, followed by brandy-roasted pork fillet with creamy mash potato, Stornoway black pudding, apple, mushroom and Calvados jus.

Chef Peter Cullen **Owner** Robin Vestey **Times** Closed Nov-Mar, Closed L Mon-Sun **Prices** Fixed D 3 course fr £38, Service included **Wines** 23 bottles over £20, 41 bottles under £20, 5 by glass **Notes** Dress restrictions, No jeans, shorts, tracksuit trousers, Civ Wed 60 **Seats** 50 **Children** Min 10 yrs, Portions **Parking** 30

MUIR OF ORD
Map 23 NH55

Ord House Hotel

@ Traditional British, French

Home comforts and fresh local produce in listed country house

☎ 01463 870492
IV6 7UH
e-mail: admin@ord-house.co.uk
dir: A832 to Muir of Ord. Over x-rd and rail bridge, 1st left signed Ullapool & Ord Distillery. Hotel 0.5m on left

Husband-and-wife team John and Eliza Allen offer a warm welcome to Ord House, which was built in 1637 as the laird's residence. Now a comfortable country-house hotel, the property is set in 60 acres of grounds, which provide some of the fruit, vegetables and herbs used in the kitchen. Among the inviting day rooms are a cosy snug bar and elegant dining room serving traditional fare with an emphasis on fresh, local, seasonal produce. Try pan-seared scallops with ginger, basil and lime, or chargrilled venison fillet with redcurrant and port sauce.

Chef Eliza Allen **Owner** Eliza & John Allen **Times** Closed Nov-end Feb **Prices** Fixed D 3 course £25, Starter £6.50-£12, Main £12-£21, Dessert £4.95-£7.25, Service included **Wines** 14 bottles over £20, 18 bottles under £20, 4 by glass **Notes** Vegetarian available **Seats** 26 **Children** Portions **Parking** 24

NAIRN
Map 23 NH85

The Boath House

@@@@ – **see page 524**

Newton Hotel

@ Traditional European

Traditional and modern cuisine in ancient surroundings

☎ 01667 453144
Inverness Rd IV12 4RX
e-mail: salesnewton@ohiml.com
dir: West of the town centre, 10 minutes walk

This ancient building has been on the site since 1640 and was once a holiday haunt of Charlie Chaplin. Today's visitor can choose from the traditional restaurant or the more contemporary bistro. The cooking style is traditional, as reflected in starters like Orkney herring marinated in dill and sherry, or prawn cocktail, while main courses feature a selection of steaks (chargrilled with wild mushrooms), plus something like breast of duckling with colcannon and black cherry jus. Vegetarians are well catered for.

Times 12-2.30/6-9

NETHY BRIDGE
Map 23 NJ02

The Restaurant at The Mountview Hotel

@@ Modern British ☙

Confident Highland cooking amidst amazing scenery

☎ 01479 821248
Grantown Rd PH25 3EB
e-mail: mviewhotel@aol.com
dir: From Aviemore follow signs for Nethy Bridge, through Boat-of-Garten. In Nethy Bridge over humpback bridge & follow hotel signs

This Edwardian country-house hotel perched on top of a hill offers panoramic views of the Cairngorms from its elevated position on the edge of the village. The building has been sensitively extended with a modern dining room with large picture windows allowing guests to drink in the breathtaking scenery. The cooking is characterised by flashes of contemporary flair underpinned by traditional influences and wonderful seasonal ingredients from a region renowned for its produce, including the hotel's own organic kitchen garden. Expect assured, imaginative cooking on a menu that might include starters such as chicken livers cooked in Marsala on home-made brioche, followed by pan-fried medallions of Glebe Farm beef with shallot purée, and Bramley apple pudding with caramel sauce to finish.

Chef Lee Beale **Owner** Kevin & Caryl Shaw **Times** 12-2/6-11, Closed 25-26 Dec, Closed Mon-Tue, Closed L Mon-Sat **Prices** Starter £4.50-£6.50, Main £13.75-£19, Dessert £5.25-£7, Service optional **Wines** 4 bottles over £20, 14 bottles under £20, 4 by glass **Notes** Sunday L, Vegetarian available **Seats** 24 **Children** Portions, Menu **Parking** 20

ONICH
Map 22 NN06

Onich Hotel

@ Traditional

Formal dining with wonderful loch views

☎ 01855 821214
PH33 6RY
e-mail: enquiries@onich-fortwilliam.co.uk
dir: Beside A82. Located in village of Onich, 9m S of Fort William

This friendly hotel is set in pretty gardens on the shores of Loch Linnhe. A choice of inviting public rooms includes a cocktail bar and a sun lounge with panoramic views of the loch, which can also be enjoyed from the attractive restaurant. Using local produce such as West Coast seafood and Highland game, there's plenty on the menu to tempt. You might try pressed game terrine or pan-fried scallops to start, followed by braised lamb shank or grilled salmon. In summer you can dine alfresco in the hotel's landscaped grounds.

Times Closed Xmas, Closed L all week

POOLEWE
Map 22 NG88

North by North West

@@ Modern European

Stunning location for fine Scottish cuisine

☎ 01445 781272
Pool House IV22 2LD
e-mail: enquiries@poolhousehotel.com
dir: 6m N of Gairloch on A832. Hotel by bridge on River Ewe

This white-painted country-house hotel sits right on the shore of Loch Ewe, with spectacular hills rising up all around. The location is second to none in terms of the archetypal Scottish vista, and the interior of the building is traditionally decorated to a high standard. The panoramic views are visible from the North by North West dining room, which is the backdrop for the imaginative cuisine. A concise menu provides well-balanced food, influenced by elements of the light, natural style of food found in California and modern European cooking. Tartare of sashimi-grade tuna with a salad of Enoki mushrooms and 'Japanese flavours' is an Eastern-inspired starter, followed by Loch Ewe langoustines and John Dory in a risotto with parmesan and main-course Buccleuch beef - fillet and cheek - comes with heirloom

Continued on page 525

The Boath House

NAIRN **NAIRN** Map 23 NH85

Modern French

Stunning food and effortless service in small country-house hotel

☎ 01667 454896
Auldearn IV12 5TE
e-mail: wendy@boath-house.com
dir: 2m E of Nairn on A96 (Inverness to Aberdeen road)

One of Scotland's finest small hotels, this lovingly restored, classic Georgian mansion sits in 20 acres of peaceful lawns, mature woodlands and streams. Its walled garden provides produce for chef Charles Lockley's inspired cooking, while ebullient, hands-on owners the Mathesons greet guests and diners like old friends. The ornamental lake here is stocked with brown and rainbow trout (in the early evening, when the flies are about, they can be seen jumping), while in the grounds, badgers and roe deer can be spotted. Inside, open fires flicker, while lounges and dining room abound with colourful ceramics and vibrant paintings - Boath acts as a permanent exhibition for contemporary Highland art. The elegant, candlelit dining room comes with well-spaced tables, high quality appointments and comfortable high-backed chairs, with views over garden and lake through large French windows. Service suits the winning formula here, being attentive, skilled and efficient but suitably relaxed and friendly. Charles Lockley's modern approach is classically based with a strong Scottish influence, using quality produce from the abundant Highland larder. Think red deer with wheat grain, shallots and bacon, or monkfish served with a haricot bean stew and pork belly, while a white chocolate and cardamom mousse with madeleines might feature at dessert. The approach at dinner is a fixed-price, five-course set affair, but with a choice offered at mains and dessert. The emphasis here is on allowing the superb quality produce to shine. High technical skills, imagination, balance, a light touch and clean, clear flavours parade in style. Make a night of it and stay in one of six beautiful bedrooms, enjoy a spa treatment, or just stroll in the lovely grounds.

Chef Charles Lockley **Owner** Mr & Mrs D Matheson **Times** 12.30-1.45/7-8.30, Closed Xmas, Closed L Mon-Wed **Wines** 153 bottles over £20, 15 bottles under £20, 7 by glass **Notes** Fixed D 5 courses £55, Vegetarian available, Dress restrictions, Smart casual, no shorts/T-shirts/jeans, Civ Wed 30 **Seats** 28, Pr/dining room 8 **Children** Portions **Parking** 20

POOLEWE *Continued*

carrots, horseradish and Merlot sauce. Finish with popcorn pannacotta, caramel jelly and olive oil gelato.

Chef Daniel Gordon Hall **Owner** Peter & Margaret Harrison **Times** Closed Jan, 1st 2 wks Feb, Closed L all week **Prices** Tasting menu £52, Service optional **Wines** 130 bottles over £20, 2 bottles under £20, 6 by glass **Notes** Tasting menu 6 courses, Dress restrictions, No jeans or T-shirts **Seats** 14, Pr/dining room 10 **Children** Min 16 yrs **Parking** 12

SHIELDAIG   Map 22 NG85

Tigh an Eilean Hotel Restaurant

◉◉ Modern British V ✿

Accomplished cooking in a welcoming hotel

☎ 01520 755251
IV54 8XN
e-mail: tighaneilean@keme.co.uk
dir: From A896 follow signs for Shieldaig. Hotel in village centre on water's edge

However long your journey to reach Sheildaig, an 18th-century fishing village perched on the shore of Loch Torridon, you'll know it was worth it when you arrive at this delightful small white-painted hotel. The restaurant is airy and light, with an atmosphere of relaxed chic, and fabulous views across the loch to the open sea beyond. The hotel centres around the original substantial house, built around 1800 when the village was constructed using a government grant. Modern Scottish cuisine with French and Spanish influences offers straightforward, accurately prepared dishes where nothing is more important than flavour. Daily-changing dinner menus rely on local produce, demonstrating a passion for fine ingredients and a commitment to quality. Expect mains like fillet of Kinlochbervie sea bass served with a vanilla vinaigrette, perhaps followed by a trio of rhubarb puddings.

Chef Christopher Field & Margaret Kirk **Owner** Christopher & Cathryn Field **Times** Closed end Oct-mid Mar (except private booking), Closed L all week **Prices** Fixed D 3 course £44, Service optional **Wines** 50 bottles over £20, 20 bottles under £20, 14 by glass **Notes** Vegetarian menu, Civ Wed 40 **Seats** 28, Pr/dining room 28 **Children** Portions, Menu

---

SPEAN BRIDGE   Map 22 NN28

Russell's at Smiddy House

◉◉ Modern Scottish

Top-notch cooking in a convivial setting

☎ 01397 712335
Roy Bridge Rd PH34 4EU
e-mail: enquiry@smiddyhouse.co.uk
dir: Located in Spean Bridge, 9m N of Fort William, on A82 towards Inverness

Set within the 'Great Glen' which stretches from Fort William to Inverness, this was once the village smithy and is now a friendly guesthouse. Russell's restaurant occupies the two front rooms and seats its diners at tables decked with candles, sparkling glasses, quality china and fresh flowers. It's an intimate venue with modern-classic design, and the knack for turning the best of local seasonal produce into high-quality, well-presented and well-balanced cuisine. Start with crispy duck salad with a honey and sesame dressing, and then tuck into herb-crusted rack of lamb with carrot and parsnip mash and hollandaise sauce, or pancetta-wrapped chicken with sun-blushed tomatoes, couscous and pesto dressing. Don't miss warm date pudding with toffee sauce for dessert, or a plate of Scottish cheese and fruit with home-made chutney.

Chef Glen Russell **Owner** Glen Russell, Robert Bryson **Times** Closed 2 wks Jan, 2 wks Nov, Closed 2 days a week (Nov-Apr), Closed L all week **Prices** Fixed D 3 course £28.95-£36.45, Service optional **Wines** 21 bottles over £20, 11 bottles under £20, 5 by glass **Notes** Vegetarian available, Dress restrictions, Smart casual **Seats** 38 **Children** Portions, Menu **Parking** 15

STRONTIAN   Map 22 NM86

Kilcamb Lodge Hotel & Restaurant

◉◉ Modern European 🖥 ✿

Fine country-house cooking in a lochside setting

☎ 01967 402257
PH36 4HY
e-mail: enquiries@kilcamblodge.co.uk
dir: Take the Corran ferry off A82. Follow A861 to Strontian. First left over bridge after village

Historic Kilcamb Lodge was a military barracks around the time of the Jacobite uprising. Today, the chic country-house hotel is a peaceful, woodland retreat on the shores of Loch Sunart. The restaurant is an intimate, romantic, candlelit affair where accomplished cooking benefits from the careful sourcing of fresh seasonal ingredients from local suppliers. Typical starters on the modern European menu include confit duck leg with orange jelly and beetroot carpaccio, and well-flavoured main courses such as pan-seared line-caught halibut, pickled ginger, pea purée, roasted leek and saffron velouté. The tempting dessert menu might include hot chocolate pudding, tonka bean ice cream, white chocolate mousse, orange caviar and chocolate dust. Round things off with fresh cafetière coffee and petits fours in the drawing room.

Chef Mark Greenaway **Owner** Sally & David Fox **Times** 12-1.30/7.30-9.30, Closed 1 Jan-1 Feb **Prices** Fixed L 2 course £14.75, Fixed D 4 course £48, Service optional, Groups min 10 service 10% **Wines** 45 bottles over £20, 20 bottles under £20, 10 by glass **Notes** Sunday L, Vegetarian available, Dress restrictions, Smart casual, no jeans, T-shirts or trainers, Civ Wed 60 **Seats** 26 **Children** Min 12 yrs **Parking** 28

Glenmorangie Highland Home at Cadboll

⊛⊛ French, International V ✆

Home-from-home dining from Scotland's larder

☎ 01862 871671
Cadboll, Fearn IV20 1XP
e-mail: relax@glenmorangie.co.uk
dir: N on A9, at Nigg Rdbt turn right onto B9175 (before Tain) & follow signs for hotel

This exclusive hideaway, owned by the Glenmorangie whisky company, is formed from a 17th-century farmhouse and an 18th-century castle, with its own beach, walled orchards and gardens providing produce for the house. Diners eat together, house-party style, at one long table, after introductions in the drawing room over drinks. Impressive cuisine capitalises on wonderful local produce, including fresh seafood and venison from neighbouring estates. Dinner is a six-course meal (with just one choice at an interim course), produced by classically trained chefs. Expect the likes of lightly spiced West Coast scallops with mango and avocado salsa, haggis, neeps and tatties with a wee dram, and chocolate soufflé with Ardbeg ice cream.

Chef David Graham **Owner** Glenmorangie Ltd
Times Closed 23-26 Dec, 4-27 Jan, Closed L by prior arrangement **Wines** 38 bottles over £20, 5 bottles under £20, 15 by glass **Notes** Fixed D 5 courses £45, Vegetarian menu, Dress restrictions, Smart casual, no jeans or T-shirts, Civ Wed 60 **Seats** 30, Pr/dining room 12 **Children** Min 16 yrs, Portions **Parking** 60

Forss House Hotel & Restaurant

⊛ Modern Scottish ✆

Elegant dining in spectacular Highland surroundings

☎ 01847 861201
Forss KW14 7XY
e-mail: anne@forsshousehotel.co.uk
dir: On A836, 5m outside Thurso

Set in a 200 year-old shooting lodge, the tastefully refurbished Forss House Hotel is ensconced in a tree-lined glen below a waterfall. The intimate dining room has an elegant period feel, complete with an Adams fireplace and a superb view of the meandering River Forss. Uncomplicated modern Scottish dishes use the finest locally-sourced seasonal ingredients. Try the home oak-smoked salmon with warm potato cakes, horseradish crème fraîche and wild leaves, followed by line-caught Dunnet Bay sea bass with creamed cauliflower, cauliflower croquettes and red wine sauce, rounded off with roast fig iced soufflé and caramelised figs.

Chef Kevin Dalgleish, Gary Leishman **Owner** Ian & Sabine Richards **Times** Closed 23 Dec-4 Jan, Closed L All week **Prices** Food prices not confirmed for 2009. Please telephone for details. **Wines** 26 bottles over £20, 9 bottles under £20, 4 by glass **Notes** Vegetarian available, Civ Wed **Seats** 26, Pr/dining room 14 **Children** Portions **Parking** 14

See advert below

Ben Loyal Hotel

⊛ Modern, Traditional

Food with flair in a magnificent setting

☎ 01847 611216
Main St IV27 4XE
e-mail: benloyalhotel@btinternet.com
web: www.benloyal.co.uk
dir: Hotel in centre of village at junction of A836 & A838

Following the stunning highland and coastal drive it takes to get to the hotel, you can relax in the restaurant and enjoy magnificent views of the Kyle of Tongue. Alongside informal, friendly service, quality, simply prepared and presented food is offered with an emphasis on local Scottish produce, particularly seafood. Home-made squash soup with good consistency and depth of flavour is served with freshly baked bread, followed by perfectly cooked wild salmon served with seasonal vegetables and a subtly flavoured tarragon sauce. Finish with rich, smooth chocolate mousse flavoured with a touch of mint.

Owner Mr & Mrs P Lewis **Times** 12-2.30/6-8.30, Closed 30 Nov -1 Mar, Closed L all week **Prices** Starter £4.25-£5.50, Main £11.50-£16.50, Dessert £5.50, Service optional **Wines** All bottles under £20, 4 by glass **Notes** Sunday L, Vegetarian available **Seats** 50 **Children** Portions, Menu **Parking** 20

Borgie Lodge Hotel

◉ Modern British

Cosy hotel offering accomplished cooking

☎ 01641 521332
Skerray KW14 7TH
e-mail: info@borgielodgehotel.co.uk
web: www.borgielodgehotel.co.uk
dir: 0.5m off A836 6m from Tongue

This Victorian sporting lodge lies in a glen close to the river of the same name, and continues to provide a welcome retreat for today's sportsmen, particularly anglers. There's a relaxed and friendly atmosphere in the cosy lounge and bar, where you can settle down by the fire and listen to tales about 'the one that got away'! A skilful kitchen makes good use of local produce in modern British and Scottish dishes. The concise menu changes daily depending on what's in season, but might include crab claws with pink grapefruit and herb dressing, followed by fillet of local beef with onion marmalade and port sauce, and bitter chocolate fondant pudding.

Times 12-2/7-8.30, Closed 25 Dec

TORRIDON — Map 22 NG95

The Torridon Restaurant

◉◉ Modern British V ⬗ ☙

Victorian shooting lodge with fine dining and superb scenery

☎ 01445 791242
IV22 2EY
e-mail: info@thetorridon.com
dir: From Inverness take A9 N, follow signs to Ullapool (A835). At Garve take A832 to Kinlochewe; take A896 to Torridon. Do not turn off to Torridon Village. Hotel on right after Annat village

The impressive lochside location and spectacular mountain scenery make this Victorian country-house hotel the perfect destination for a romantic retreat or relaxing break. A former shooting lodge, The Torridon has been beautifully restored and recently refurbished, making the most of its many original features. The restaurant, complete with pine panelling and ornate ceilings, has a formal yet relaxed atmosphere with friendly service, and a conservatory area overlooks the view. There is also a bar with over 320 whiskies, and a noteworthy wine list. The menu has a modern British theme with a French twist, providing skilfully prepared,

intricate dishes using top-quality, local ingredients, including produce from the hotel's garden. Expect grilled West Coast halibut with local wild woodland mushrooms, poached chicken wings and verjus jus, or roast rib of 30-day aged Torridon beef with smoked garlic, pickled walnut jus and marrowbone soufflé.

Chef Kevin Broome **Owner** Daniel & Rohaise Rose-Bristow **Times** 12-2/7-9, Closed 2 Jan for 3 wks, Closed L Bar only **Prices** Fixed D 4 course £40-£60, Service optional **Wines** 156 bottles over £20, 27 bottles under £20, 8 by glass **Notes** Tasting menu available, Vegetarian menu, Dress restrictions, No jeans or trainers, Civ Wed 42 **Seats** 38, Pr/dining room 16 **Children** Min 10 yrs, Portions, Menu **Parking** 20

INVERCLYDE

KILMACOLM — Map 20 NS37

Windyhill Restaurant

◉ Modern British V ☙

Contemporary British cuisine in a relaxed setting

☎ 01505 872613
4 St James Ter, Lochwinnoch Rd PA13 4HB
e-mail: matthewscobey@hotmail.co.uk
dir: From Glasgow Airport, A737 taking Bridge of Weir exit. Join A761 to Kilmacolm turning left into main High Street.

Based on Charles Rennie Macintosh's house, Windyhill, the imposing black shop front with frosted glass leads into a contemporary restaurant with subdued lighting, dark wooden furniture and white walls scattered with modern artwork. Using top quality, locally-sourced ingredients, the simple but effective cuisine allows interesting flavour combinations to shine through. The monthly-changing menu offers starters such as steamed Shetland mussels with tarragon cider cream and garlic sourdough bread, with baked halibut with herb butter crust, lemon and asparagus risotto and caper dressing to follow. Leave room for a home-made dessert such as raspberry shortbread baked cheesecake.

Chef Matthew Scobey **Owner** Matthew Scobey & Careen McLean **Times** 12-3/6-10, Closed Xmas-New Year, last wk Jul, 1st wk Aug, Closed Sun-Mon, Closed L Sat **Prices** Starter £4.95-£6.95, Main £11.95-£19.95, Dessert £5.50-£6.95 **Wines** 5 bottles over £20, 18 bottles under £20, 6 by glass **Notes** Vegetarian menu **Seats** 45 **Children** Portions, Menu **Parking** On street, car park opposite

LANARKSHIRE, NORTH

MOTHERWELL — Map 21 NS75

Alona Hotel

◉ Modern

Fabulous loch-side setting for Mediterranean-influenced food

☎ 0870 112 3888
Strathclyde Country Park ML1 3RT

'Alona' is a Celtic word meaning 'exquisitely beautiful', and the building and setting at this hotel certainly live up to its name. The modern open-plan bar and restaurant is located just off the entrance to the hotel, with a stunning glass atrium overlooking Strathclyde Loch which is especially impressive over the bar area. Tables are well spaced, set with crisp linen and flower displays. The food here is modern with an emphasis on seasonality and fresh local produce, with Mediterranean style and flair evident in a number of dishes. A main course of salmon with chorizo tortilla, salsa verde and poached cherry tomato might feature alongside monkfish wrapped in Ayrshire cured ham with cauliflower froth and haricot blanc cassoulette, while tempting desserts include chocolate and cherry fondant with white chocolate parfait.

Prices Food prices not confirmed for 2009. Please telephone for details.

LANARKSHIRE, SOUTH

BIGGAR — Map 21 NT03

Chancellors at Shieldhill Castle

◉◉ Modern, International ⬗ ☙

Fine food and wine in an impressive castle

☎ 01899 220035
Quothquan ML12 6NA
e-mail: enquiries@shieldhill.co.uk
dir: From Biggar take B7016 to Carnwath. After approx 2.5m turn left on to Shieldhill Road. Castle 1m on right

This imposing fortified mansion, set among acres of woodland and landscaped parkland, dates back almost 800 years. Providing a seamless fusion of historic architecture and modern cooking, the atmospheric public areas include the oak-panelled lounge and Chancellor's Restaurant, a classic high-ceilinged room resplendent in

Continued

BIGGAR *Continued*

baronial furnishings. A technically-skilled kitchen delivers imaginative dishes with a focus on clean, simple flavours. Utilising fresh local seasonal produce - including the estate game - all dishes are available as starters or mains, and combine with an award-winning wine list designed by the proprietors. Expect dishes such as pan-seared black cod marinated in honey, ginger and Pernod on celeriac mash with a Périgourdine sauce, or Shieldhill Castle sporting venison on a confit of carrot with an oxtail pudding and broad beans in a wood sorrel dressing.

Chef Christina Lamb **Owner** Mr & Mrs R Lamb
Times 12-1.45/7-8.45 **Prices** Fixed L 2 course £15.95, Fixed D 3 course £19.95, Starter £5.95-£13.95, Main £13.95-£19.95, Dessert £8.95, Service optional, Groups min 10 service 5% **Wines** 20 bottles under £20, 30 by glass **Notes** Sunday L, Civ Wed 150 **Seats** 52, Pr/dining room 30 **Children** Portions **Parking** 60

EAST KILBRIDE   Map 20 NS65

Macdonald Crutherland House

◉◉ Scottish, International ☺

Honest, clear flavours in country-house hotel

☎ 01355 577000
Strathaven Rd G75 0QZ
e-mail: general.crutherland@macdonald-hotels.co.uk
dir: From East Kilbride take A726 towards Strathaven. Continue for 1.5m beyond Torrance rdbt, hotel on left

This 18th-century property, set in 37 acres of landscaped grounds just 20 minutes from the town centre, has been converted into a relaxing country-house hotel. Its richly furnished dining room is a haven of elegant good taste and offers an extensive range of dishes. Those on the carte showcase the kitchen's flair, while a fixed-price selection offers simpler choices at keener prices. Expect honest, flavourful cooking with a Scottish twist - baked fillet of trout with Ugie smoked salmon, Black Forest ham and fresh crab perhaps, followed by pan-fried delice of halibut with pickled fennel, gruyère cheese, grain mustard croquette and parsley sauce. For dessert, try chocolate mocha torte with cappuccino parfait and vanilla bean sauce.

Chef Joe Queen **Owner** Macdonald Hotels
Times 12-2.30/7-9.30 **Prices** Fixed L 2 course £14.95, Fixed D 3 course £27.50-£28.50, Starter £4.95-£8.95, Main £14.50-£22.95, Dessert £3.95-£8.95, Service optional **Wines** 62 bottles over £20, 14 bottles under £20, 14 by glass **Notes** Sunday L, Vegetarian available, Civ Wed 250, Air con **Seats** 80, Pr/dining room 200 **Children** Portions, Menu **Parking** 60

STRATHAVEN   Map 20 NS74

Rissons at Springvale

◉ Modern Scottish ☺

Relaxed restaurant with modern Scottish cuisine

☎ 01357 520234 & 521131
18 Lethame Rd ML10 6AD
e-mail: rissons@msn.com
dir: From M74 junct 8 follow A71, through Stonehouse and onto Strathaven

Situated in a Victorian-style house just outside the town, this light-and-airy modern restaurant comes with an intimate conservatory overlooking the local park. The atmosphere is relaxed and friendly, and the service informed, while the kitchen's modern-bistro output matches the mood, delivering simple, unfussy, well-presented dishes that concentrate on clean flavours and the use of quality produce. Typically, warm pigeon salad with beetroot crème fraîche, or perhaps shin of beef served with root vegetables in Strathaven ale, with marmalade pudding and whisky custard for dessert.

Chef Scott Baxter, Leonard Allen, Stephen Conway **Owner** Scott Baxter, Anne Baxter **Times** 12-2.30/6-9.30, Closed New Year, 1 wk Jan, 1st wk July, Closed Mon-Tue **Prices** Fixed L 2 course £13.95, Starter £4-£8, Main £9-£19, Dessert £4.50-£5.50, Service optional **Wines** 13 bottles over £20, 23 bottles under £20, 6 by glass **Notes** Sunday L, Vegetarian available **Seats** 40 **Children** Portions, Menu **Parking** 10

LOTHIAN, EAST

DIRLETON   Map 21 NT58

The Open Arms Hotel

◉ Modern Scottish

Charming country hotel with relaxing atmosphere and enjoyable dining

☎ 01620 850241
EH39 5EG
e-mail: openarmshotel@clara.co.uk
dir: From A1 (S) take A198 to North Berwick, then follow signs for Dirleton - 2 miles W. From Edinburgh take A6137 leading to A198

A long established hotel, the Open Arms lies across the green from the 13th-century Dirleton Castle. Inviting public areas include a choice of lounges and a cosy bar, and you can eat in either Deveau's Brasserie or the fine-dining Library Restaurant. The latter has soft lighting, clothed tables and formal settings. Staff are helpful and friendly, and the menu offers a variety of carefully prepared dishes. Local flavours are apparent in rollmop herring with potato salad and herb oil, and pan-fried fillet of beef with haggis and wild mushroom jus.

Times 12-2/7-9, Closed D Sun

GULLANE   Map 21 NT48

La Potinière

◉◉ Modern British ☺

Ambitious cooking in cottage-style restaurant

☎ 01620 843214
Main St EH31 2AA
dir: 20m SE of Edinburgh. 3m from North Berwick on A198

Set in a charming cottage, La Potinière is a two-partner operation, with both owners sharing the kitchen, while Keith also acts as host and wine waiter. Accordingly, the meal is a leisurely four-course affair at dinner, plus an amuse-bouche and pre-dessert, and three courses at lunch. Smart, crisp linen and quality tableware reinforce the kitchen's serious intent, while the cooking lends a contemporary touch with artistic presentation and makes fine use of local seasonal produce. There are just two choices at each course, perhaps featuring Thai coconut soup with poached scallops, followed by braised fillet of brill or roast fillet of Scotch beef with parsnip mash, winter vegetables and shallot sauce. Round things off in style with praline parfait or warm chocolate fondant.

Chef Mary Runciman & Keith Marley **Owner** Mary Runciman **Times** 12.30-1.30/7-8.30, Closed Xmas, Jan, Closed Mon-Tue, Closed D Sun (Oct-May) **Prices** Fixed L 2 course fr £17.50, Fixed D 4 course fr £38, Service optional **Wines** 28 bottles over £20, 8 bottles under £20, 4 by glass **Notes** Sunday L, Dress restrictions, Smart casual **Seats** 30 **Children** Portions **Parking** 10

NORTH BERWICK   Map 21 NT58

Macdonald Marine Hotel

◉◉ French

Impressive fine-dining restaurant with stunning sea views

☎ 0870 400 8129
Cromwell Rd EH39 4LZ
e-mail: sales.marine@macdonald-hotels.co.uk
dir: From A198 turn into Hamilton Rd at lights, 2nd right into Cromwell Rd

This refurbished Grade II listed Victorian property is located on East Lothian's famous championship golf course overlooking the Firth of Forth. The restaurant - with oak panelling, deep plum-coloured walls and portraits - enjoys an equally impressive setting, its formal décor creating a regal feel. Diners enjoy canapés and pre-starters in addition to choices from the classically-based menu, featuring the freshest local and seasonal ingredients. A pressing of smoked salmon with lobster, crabmeat and lime and saffron dressing shows the style, followed by a pavé of wild halibut with new potatoes and mussel vermouth, or perhaps fillet of Scottish beef with potato gratin, asparagus and Balvenie whisky jus. Finish in style with an assiette of chocolate (warm dark chocolate tarte, white chocolate brownie cheesecake and chocolate tiramisù torte).

Chef John Paul McLachlan **Owner** Donald Macdonald **Times** 12.30-2.30/6.30-9.30 **Prices** Fixed L course £17.95, Fixed D 3 course £35, Service optional **Notes** Sunday L, Dress restrictions, Smart casual, Civ Wed 250 **Seats** 80, Pr/dining room 20 **Children** Portions, Menu **Parking** 50

LOTHIAN, WEST

LINLITHGOW   Map 21 NS97

Champany Inn

◎◎ Traditional British

Impressive steak restaurant in a country lodge

☎ 01506 834532 & 834388
EH49 7LU
e-mail: reception@champany.com
dir: 2m NE of Linlithgow. From M9 (N) junct 3, at top of slip road turn right. Champany is 500yds on right

Just 20 minutes from Edinburgh, the Davidson family have taken a collection of buildings - some dating back to Mary, Queen of Scots - and turned them into a unique hotel. The restaurant itself is an octagonal affair with exposed stone walls and timbered ceiling, while tapestries, gleaming copper and elegant portraits abound alongside an open kitchen. An extensive wine choice is stored on a mezzanine floor. A temple to prime beef and the Rolls Royce of steakhouses, Champany specialises in cuts from cattle sourced and prepared by the restaurant's own butchery and hung for three weeks. Shetland salmon also finds its place on the charcoal grill, but it's the full-flavoured, tender beef that takes pride of place, such as Aberdeen Angus sirloin, fillet or rib-eye. The old farmer's cottage has now been converted into a shop selling Champany produce.

Chef C Davidson, D Gibson, Liam Ginname **Owner** Mr & Mrs C Davidson **Times** 12.30-2/7-10, Closed 25-26 Dec, 1-2 Jan, Closed Sun, Closed L Sat **Prices** Food prices not confirmed for 2009. Please telephone for details. **Wines** 650 bottles over £20, 8 bottles under £20, 8 by glass **Notes** Vegetarian available, Dress restrictions, No jeans or T-shirts **Seats** 50, Pr/dining room 30 **Children** Min 8 yrs **Parking** 50

Livingston's Restaurant

◎◎ Modern Scottish V

Superb Scottish cooking in a delightful rural restaurant

☎ 01506 846565
52 High St EH49 7AE
e-mail: contact@livingstons-restaurant.co.uk
dir: Opposite post office

Once the stables for Linlithgow Palace during the reign of Mary, Queen of Scots, family-run Livingston's provides an authentic Scottish experience. Set partly in a conservatory looking on to the garden with a glimpse of the loch through the trees, ruby red fabrics, tartan carpets and soft candlelight unite to create a relaxed, Caledonian atmosphere. The modern Scottish menu showcases local ingredients such as Inverurie lamb, Highland venison and

Stornoway black pudding. Among the highlights are dishes such as the spiced parsnip and pear soup, followed by fillet of sea bass with a winter green pea risotto and fresh parmesan, making room for a tasting of Celtic cheeses with home-made sweet oatcakes and apple chutney.

Livingston's Restaurant

Chef Julian Wright **Owner** Ronald & Christine Livingston **Times** 12-2.30/6-9.30, Closed 1 wk Jun, 1 wk Oct, 2wks Jan, Closed Sun(except Mothering Sun)-Mon **Prices** Food prices not confirmed for 2009. Please telephone for details. **Wines** 37 bottles over £20, 24 bottles under £20, 6 by glass **Notes** Vegetarian menu, Dress restrictions, Smart casual **Seats** 40 **Children** Min 8 yrs, Portions **Parking** NCP Linlithgow Cross, on street

UPHALL   Map 21 NT07

The Tower

◎ Traditional British ◔

Fine dining in beautiful surroundings

☎ 0844 879 9043
Macdonald Houstoun House EH52 6JS
e-mail: houstoun@macdonald-hotels.co.uk
dir: M8 junct 3 follow signs for Broxburn. Continue straight over rdbt the turn right at mini rdbt towards Uphall, Hotel 1m on right

Set in beautifully landscaped grounds, this historic 16th-century tower house is bang up-to-date with its modern leisure club and spa. It also offers a choice of dining options, including a vaulted cocktail bar with an impressive selection of whiskies, and an elegant, formal dining room with period features and lovely views of the garden. The fixed-price menu provides good value traditional fare, or opt for the carte if you're feeling more adventurous. Innovative dishes are underpinned by uncomplicated, clean flavours and use only the finest Scottish ingredients. Expect mains like roasted wild cod with a chervil and chive butter sauce, or poached guinea fowl supreme with Puy lentils and silverskin jus.

Chef Cameron Robertson **Owner** Macdonald Hotels **Times** 12-2/7-9.30, Closed L Sat-Sun **Prices** Fixed L 2 course £20, Fixed D 3 course £29.50-£32.50, Service optional **Wines** 74 bottles over £20, 16 bottles under £20, 13 by glass **Notes** Vegetarian available, Dress restrictions, Smart casual, no jeans or trainers, Civ Wed 200 **Seats** 65, Pr/dining room 30 **Children** Portions, Menu **Parking** 200

MORAY

ARCHIESTOWN   Map 23 NJ24

Archiestown Hotel

◎ Modern British, International

Well-prepared local produce at a small, friendly hotel

☎ 01340 810218
AB38 7QL
e-mail: jah@archiestownhotel.co.uk
dir: Turn off A95 onto B9102 at Craigellachie

Taking pride of place in the village square, this small Victorian country house is in the heart of the whisky and salmon fishing country of Speyside, and comes with a delightful walled garden. Popular with locals and visitors alike, the cosy bistro-style restaurant offers a seasonally-changing international menu full of interesting dishes. Twice-baked garlic and cheese soufflé makes an impressive starter, followed by an equally enjoyable main course of pan charred sirloin steak with local haggis on peppercorn and whisky jus. Puddings are satisfyingly traditional - you might try Cranachan cheesecake with raspberry compôte or chocolate pudding with home-made ice cream.

Chef Robert Aspden, Ian Fleming **Owner** Alan & Jane Hunter **Times** 12-2/7-9, Closed Xmas, 3 Jan-10 Feb **Prices** Starter £5-£8, Main £16.50-£21, Dessert £5.50-£6.50, Service optional, Groups min 10 service 10% **Wines** 24 bottles over £20, 11 bottles under £20, 6 by glass **Notes** Sunday L, Dress restrictions, Smart casual, Civ Wed 20 **Seats** 35, Pr/dining room 16 **Children** Portions **Parking** 30

CRAIGELLACHIE   Map 23 NJ24

Craigellachie Hotel

◎ Traditional Scottish

Formal dining with Scottish flavour and atmosphere

☎ 01340 881204
AB38 9SR
e-mail: info@craigellachie.com
dir: 12m S of Elgin, in the village centre

This impressive Victorian hotel enjoys a village setting in the heart of Speyside's whisky distilling area - no surprises then that the bar features almost 700 malts. The Ben Aigan Restaurant encompasses several rooms, each with its own decorative style. Here, regional ingredients are to the fore - Aberdeen Angus beef, Cabrach lamb, Moray Firth seafood - in dishes such as

Continued

CRAIGELLACHIE *Continued*

citrus-cured salmon and hot smoked salmon rillette with horseradish cream and cucumber, and lamb rump on parsley crushed new potatoes with braised red cabbage, root vegetable jus and shallot purée.

Craigellachie Hotel

Chef Addy Daggert **Owner** Oxford Hotels & Inns **Times** 12-2/6-10 **Prices** Food prices not confirmed for 2009. Please telephone for details. **Wines** 64 bottles over £20, 30 bottles under £20, 7 by glass **Notes** Sunday L, Vegetarian available, Dress restrictions, Smart casual, Civ Wed 60, Air con **Seats** 30, Pr/dining room 60 **Children** Portions, Menu **Parking** 25

| **CULLEN** | **Map 23 NJ56** |

Cullen Bay Hotel

◎ Traditional Scottish 🕯

Restaurant with views and traditional Scottish fare

☎ 01542 840432
AB56 4XA
e-mail: stay@cullenbayhotel.com
dir: On A98, 0.25 m W of Cullen

Sitting on a hillside west of the town, this small family-run hotel overlooks Cullen Bay, taking in the beach, golf course and Moray Firth. The relaxed, spacious, traditionally-styled restaurant takes full advantage of the views. Menus offer simply prepared and presented dishes focusing on quality Scottish produce, especially seafood from the local port. You might start with smoked haddock, bacon and mussel chowder served with chopped chives and home-made bread or Cullen skink, followed by 'Bonnie Prince Charlie's trampled trio' - slices of mealie pudding, black pudding and haggis layered with steak medallions, topped with cheese and drizzled with mushroom and Drambuie jus.

Chef Gail Meikle **Owner** Mr & Mrs Tucker & Sons **Times** 12-2/6.30-9, Closed From 2 Jan for 10 days **Prices** Food prices not confirmed for 2009. Please telephone for details. **Wines** 5 bottles over £20, 48 bottles under £20, 8 by glass **Notes** Vegetarian available, Civ Wed 150 **Seats** 60, Pr/dining room 40 **Children** Portions, Menu **Parking** 100

| **AUCHTERARDER** | **Map 21 NN91** |

Andrew Fairlie @ Gleneagles

◎◎◎◎ – *see opposite*

AA WINE AWARD WINNER

The Strathearn

◎◎ Classic 🏅 NOTABLE WINE LIST

Grand ballroom-style setting with classic dining and impressive service

☎ 01764 694270
The Gleneagles Hotel PH3 1NF
e-mail: resort.sales@gleneagles.com
web: www.gleneagles.com
dir: Just off A9, well signed. Between Stirling and Perth

Residing in the world-renowned resort and conference hotel of Gleneagles, The Strathearn restaurant is a stronghold of sheer elegance and classic dining. The massive, grand ballroom-style room, with high ceilings, pillars and a pianist, provides an impressively sophisticated setting. Classical dishes are given a contemporary slant on the seasonal menu, while service, by a whole brigade of staff, is formal but by no means stuffy and helps make the occasion memorable, especially with the showpiece carving and flambé trolleys, and award-winning wine list. Expect ham hock and foie gras terrine with Madeira jelly and apricot and apple chutney, followed by pan-seared monkfish with confit belly pork and saffron velouté.

The Strathearn is AA Wine Award Winner for Scotland

Times 12.30-2.30/7-10, Closed L Mon-Sat

| **COMRIE** | **Map 21 NN72** |

Royal Hotel

◎ Traditional British 🕯

Traditional food in an elegant environment

☎ 01764 679200
Melville Square PH6 2DN
e-mail: reception@royalhotel.co.uk
web: www.royalhotel.co.uk
dir: In main square, 7m from Crieff, on A85

You'll find this 18th-century former coaching inn on Comrie's central square, at a point where the verdant lowlands meet the Perthshire Highlands. Polished-wood

floors, stylish soft furnishings, log fires and antique pieces characterise the stylish, elegant interior, and there's a choice of dining venues, including the lounge bar, conservatory brasserie, open-hearthed library and beautifully appointed formal dining room. In fine weather you can eat outside in the walled garden. Menus of Scottish fare offer Cullen skink, fillet of beef topped with Strathdon Blue gratin, and baked salmon steak with basil crust.

Royal Hotel

Chef David Milsom **Owner** The Milsom Family **Times** 12-2/6.30-9, Closed Xmas **Prices** Fixed D 3 course fr £26.50, Starter £4.75-£6.95, Main £7.25-£17.50, Dessert £5.50, Service optional **Wines** 46 bottles over £20, 47 bottles under £20, 7 by glass **Notes** Sunday L, Vegetarian available **Seats** 60 **Children** Portions **Parking** 25

| **CRIEFF** | **Map 21 NN82** |

The Bank Restaurant

◎◎ British, French

Original features and classic cuisine

☎ 01764 656575
32 High St PH7 3BS
e-mail: mail@thebankrestaurant.co.uk
dir: Please telephone for directions

Even without the clue in the name it might be possible to guess this restaurant had a moneyed former life - it was indeed a bank, and the work of Washington Brown no less, who also designed the Caledonian Hotel in Edinburgh. The ornate, red sandstone listed building has a prominent position on the main street. Today, the original wood panelling and cornices can still be seen in the charming, genteel atmosphere of the dining room, with its wooden floors, lofty ceiling and print-adorned walls. Run by a husband-and-wife team, the kitchen takes a fittingly serious approach to cooking. Its accomplished classical French-influenced cuisine delivers the likes of mussel, bacon and leek croustade, followed perhaps by slow-

Continued on page 532

Andrew Fairlie @ Gleneagles

Modern French 🖥 🍷NOTABLE WINE LIST

Dramatic setting, inspired food

☎ 01764 694267
PH3 1NF
e-mail: andrew.fairlie@gleneagles.com
web: www.andrewfairlie.com
dir: Take Gleneagles exit from A9, continue for 1m

Gleneagles is a huge and imposing hotel of considerable class, one that is big enough and bold enough to host a G8 summit and the Ryder Cup. Within its walls are many dining options, including the Strathearn Restaurant (see entry), but the star attraction is an independent business located on the ground floor, open only for dinner, and catering for the well-heeled, five-star international clientele - Andrew Fairlie. The elegant dark-panelled walls, bespoke artworks by Archie Frost, floor to ceiling silk drapes and banquette seating sumptuously covered in rich fabrics with a stylish leaf motif make for an eminently civilised space despite the lack of natural light. Tables are well-spaced, laid with crisp white linen, high quality glassware and crockery, and beautifully lit with chic lamps. Service runs with precision and gentle jazz music plays in the background. Andrew Fairlie is a class act and this room in this hotel is a fitting place for him to deliver his style of refined and

intricate French-focused cooking. A dégustation menu and menu du marché are alternatives to the carte and on each first-class produce is used to create dishes underpinned by classical French cooking but elevated skywards by superb technique and intelligent, creative ideas. The simple menu descriptions belie the complexity and immaculate presentation of what is to follow - dishes dazzle and impress. Scallops from the Isle of Skye are pan-fried with precision and partnered with braised pork cheeks and sweet potato purée among starters, or there is home-smoked lobster with lime and herb butter. Main-course pork comes as fillet, cheek, belly and black pudding, and apple as soufflé, sorbet, crumble and parfait among desserts.

Chef Andrew Fairlie **Owner** Andrew Fairlie **Times** Closed 24-25 Dec, 3 wks Jan, Closed Sun, Closed L all week **Prices** Tasting menu £85, Starter £21-£31, Main £32, Dessert £12, Service optional **Wines** 250 bottles over £20, 12 by glass **Notes** Dress restrictions, Smart casual, Air con **Seats** 54 **Children** Min 12 yrs **Parking** 300

CRIEFF *Continued*

roasted neck of lamb with olive mash, and finishing with lemon tart with Greek yogurt and honey or Scottish cheeses.

Chef Bill McGuigan **Owner** Mr B & Mrs L McGuigan **Times** 12-1.30/7-9.30, Closed 25-26 Dec, 2 wks mid Jan, 1 wk Jul, Closed Mon-Sun, Closed L Tue-Fri **Prices** Starter £4.50-£6.50, Main £15.50-£20, Dessert £5.25-£5.75, Service optional **Wines** 34 bottles over £20, 21 bottles under £20, 4 by glass **Notes** Air con **Seats** 22 **Children** Portions **Parking** Parking available 150 yds

---

DUNKELD
Map 21 NO04

Kinnaird

◉◉◉ – *see below*

FORTINGALL
Map 20 NN74

Fortingall Hotel

◉ Modern Scottish

☎ 01887 830367 & 830368
PH15 2NQ
e-mail: hotel@fortingallhotel.com

This establishment was awarded its Rosette/s just as we went to press. Therefore we are unable to provide a description for it - visit www.theAA.com for the most up-to-date information.

Prices Food prices not confirmed for 2009. Please telephone for details.

GLENDEVON
Map 21 NN90

An Lochan Tormaukin

◉ Modern Scottish V ◑

High quality local produce served in relaxed, rustic surroundings

☎ 01259 781252
FK14 7JY
e-mail: tormaukin@anlochan.co.uk
dir: From the A9 take A823 towards Dollar

Set in splendid seclusion amongst the rolling Ochil hills close to Gleneagles, this delightful country inn dates back to the 17th century, and the team behind the An Lochan brand have given it a sensitive modern makeover. Dine in the snug or the airy conservatory; their open-fires, bare-stone walls and wooden tables contrasting with vibrant artwork. Both table settings and service are suitably relaxed and informal, while the modern Scottish fare is underpinned by top quality, locally sourced, produce and clean flavours. Both carte and fixed-price menus offer generous portions; choose from Highland beef, Perthshire lamb, venison, game and seafood.

Chef Gary Noble **Owner** Roger & Bea McKie **Times** 12-3/5.30-9.30, Closed Please telephone for details **Prices** Fixed L 2 course £10.95, Fixed D 3 course £24.95, Starter £4.25-£8.95, Main £10.95-£31.95, Dessert £5.25, Service optional **Wines** 25 bottles over £20, 6 bottles under £20 **Notes** Early evening menu available 5.30-6.30, Sunday L, Vegetarian menu, Air con **Seats** Pr/dining room **Children** Portions

---

KENMORE
Map 21 NN74

Taymouth Restaurant

◉ Traditional British

Tay views and quality Scottish fare

☎ 01887 830205
The Kenmore Hotel, The Square PH15 2NU
e-mail: reception@kenmorehotel.co.uk
dir: A9 N, A827 Ballinluig, A827 into Kenmore, hotel is at centre of village

The historic Kenmore Hotel, built in 1572, is Scotland's oldest inn. Set on the banks of the Tay, this historic building has a cosy Poets' bar with log fire, while the modern, spacious conservatory-style restaurant boasts panoramic views of the tranquil river and surrounding forests. The menus offer traditional Scottish fare with a seasonal focus, and simply and cleanly presented dishes make full use of fresh, local ingredients. Good examples include Cullen skink to start, followed by beef fillet with haggis and whisky jus. Make room for desserts like raspberry and Glayva crème brûlée.

Chef Duncan Shearer **Owner** Kenmore Estates Ltd **Times** 12-6/6-9.30 **Wines** 14 bottles over £20, 35 bottles under £20, 11 by glass **Notes** Taste of Scotland menu £29.50, Sunday L, Vegetarian available, Civ Wed 80, Air con **Seats** 100, Pr/dining room 80 **Children** Portions, Menu **Parking** 40

Kinnaird

DUNKELD
Map 21 NO04

Modern European

Exquisite country house in glorious setting serving innovative food

☎ 01796 482440
Kinnaird Estate PH8 0LB
e-mail: enquiry@kinnairdestate.com
dir: From A9 N take B898 for 4.5m. Hotel on right

It is easy to lose oneself in the grounds of this 7,000-acre estate of prime Perthshire countryside. Don't, though, miss dinner. The imposing baronial mansion is built on a grand scale and its position overlooking the wooded valley of the River Tay is breathtaking. The public rooms of the house are traditionally furnished with fine antiques, an impressive collection of art and inviting lounges with roaring log fires. The dining room is

wonderfully plush, with ornate Italian frescoed walls, marble fireplace, a central chandelier and views out on to the garden through the huge bay windows. Jacket and tie are required at dinner, but with the formal service and grand scale of the place, that doesn't seem entirely out of keeping. Despite the arrival of a new head chef in the kitchen, the style of food remains focused on local produce and puts a modern spin on classically-based ideas. There is a Tasting Menu and carte, backed up with an excellent wine list. Roasted breast of quail comes with crispy leg and cardamom potato in an attractively presented and well balanced first course, while main-course sea bass is poached in vanilla oil and served with baby carrots, Swiss chard and black olive and potato purée. Hot orange and Grand Marnier soufflé with vanilla nougat ice cream and honeycomb makes for a distinguished finish.

Chef Jean-Baptiste Bady **Owner** Mrs C Ward **Times** 12.30-1.45/7-9.30 **Prices** Fixed L 2 course £20-£25, Fixed D 3 course £59, Tasting menu £65, Service optional **Wines** 158 bottles over £20, 2 bottles under £20, 7 by glass **Notes** Tasting menu 6 courses, Sunday L, Dress restrictions, Smart dress, jackets at D, Civ Wed 45 **Seats** 35, Pr/dining room 20 **Children** Min 10 yrs, Portions **Parking** 15

Killiecrankie House Hotel

◉◉ Modern British ▱ ⓘ

Modern cooking in a delightful country-house hotel

☎ 01796 473220
PH16 5LG
e-mail: enquiries@killiecrankiehotel.co.uk
dir: From A9 take B8079 N of Killiecrankie, hotel is 3m on right, just past village signpost

Overlooking the River Garry and the Pass of Killiecrankie, this relaxing, small country hotel was built as a dower house in 1840. Take a stroll in the mature landscaped gardens before dinner. Run with genuine passion and enthusiasm, the hotel maintains consistently high standards and has a sound reputation for accomplished modern Scottish cooking. The compact fixed-price dinner menu changes daily and is driven by fresh local produce, including game and fish as well as herbs and vegetables from the kitchen garden. Start with terrine of venison, pigeon and rabbit, studded with pistachio and served with red onion chutney before main-course crispy-skinned fillet of salmon with potato and beetroot rösti. Each dish has a wine recommendation from the excellent list. Finish with marmalade sponge pudding with brandy Anglaise or opt to carry on to the cheese course. (Lunches are served in the bar.)

Chef Mark Easton **Owner** Henrietta Fergusson
Times Closed Jan- Feb, Closed L all week **Prices** Fixed D 3 course £31, Service optional **Wines** 125 bottles over £20, 44 bottles under £20, 8 by glass **Notes** Pre-theatre meals available, Dress restrictions, No shorts **Seats** 30, Pr/dining room 12 **Children** Portions, Menu **Parking** 20

Ballathie House Hotel

◉◉ Modern Scottish

Splendid Scottish country-house dining with River Tay views

☎ 01250 883268
PH1 4QN
e-mail: email@ballathiehousehotel.com
dir: From A9 take Luncarty/Stanley exit, follow the B9099 through Stanley, follow signs for Ballathie after 0.5m

Situated on its own delightful Perthshire estate, this splendid Scottish former shooting lodge now country-house hotel combines contemporary comfort with

classical grandeur. The elegant dining room, with its traditional décor, enjoys impressive views across lawns to the River Tay. Service is friendly and seasonal Scottish produce, including ingredients grown on the estate and beef from the Ballathie Estate pedigree herd, feature on creative menus. Starters might include pressed terrine of fresh, cured and smoked salmon on a salad of crushed new potatoes with chives and crème fraîche, followed by mains like pan-fried medallions of Scotch beef with a Welsh rarebit glaze, pomme fondant and cracked black peppercorn cream. To finish, perhaps try white chocolate and raspberry mousse with orange curd ice cream and warm cherry muffin.

Chef Andrew Wilkie **Owner** Ballathie House Hotel Ltd
Times 12.30-2/7-9 **Prices** Fixed L 2 course £18.50, Fixed D 3 course £41.50, Service optional **Wines** 220 bottles over £20, 10 bottles under £20, 6 by glass **Notes** Sunday L, Dress restrictions, Jacket & tie preferred, No jeans/T-shirts, Civ Wed 75 **Seats** 70, Pr/dining room 32 **Children** Min 12 yrs, Portions **Parking** 100

Dunalastair Hotel

◉ Modern British ⓖ

Traditional Highland hotel with expertly prepared food

☎ 01882 632323 & 632218
PH16 5PW
e-mail: info@dunalastair.co.uk
dir: From Pitlochry N, take B8019 to Tummel Bridge then B846 to Kinloch Rannoch

Dating back to 1770, this traditional Highland hotel was formerly a staging post and barracks for Jacobite troops. The impressive Schiehallion restaurant, with its wood-panelling and log fire lit in a feature fireplace, has a definite baronial atmosphere to it. Service is friendly and the menu provides traditional dishes with a contemporary touch, using quality Scottish produce. Cooking and presentation are wonderfully uncomplicated with beautifully balanced flavours. Enjoy smoked trout with crisp salad leaves and a lime mayonnaise followed by seared sea bass fillet served with saffron cocotte, roast cherry tomatoes and a soya and sesame seed dressing.

Chef Kevin Easingwood **Owner** R Gilmour
Times 12-2.30/6.30-9 **Prices** Fixed L 2 course £12-£21, Fixed D 3 course £30-£37, Starter £5-£8.50, Main £15-£21, Dessert £5-£7.95, Service optional **Wines** 55 bottles over £20, 25 bottles under £20, 6 by glass **Notes** Sunday L, Vegetarian available, Civ Wed 70 **Seats** 70, Pr/dining room 20 **Children** Portions **Parking** 50

The Green Hotel

◉ Modern International

Contemporary restaurant with classic-based modern cuisine

☎ 01577 863467
2 The Muirs KY13 8AS
e-mail: reservations@green-hotel.com
dir: M90 junct 6 after 1m, turn left onto The Muirs. Hotel located 0.5 m on left.

Originally a staging post, this aptly named hotel comes with its own golf course and sits at the heart of the small town in extensive grounds and gardens. Basil's is its light and spacious contemporary restaurant, with colourful artwork and floral displays adding interest. There's a small cocktail bar for aperitifs with views over a landscaped courtyard, too. Service is friendly, while the accomplished kitchen's modern interpretations are delivered on a seasonal menu backed by daily specials. Take smoked haddock and leek risotto with Parmesan crisps, followed by loin of venison, dauphinoise potatoes and cranberry tea jus, with blueberry crème brûlée with biscotti to finish.

Prices Fixed D 3 course fr £29.50, Service optional **Wines** 24 bottles over £20, 26 bottles under £20, 6 by glass **Notes** Vegetarian available, Dress restrictions, Smart casual, Civ Wed 120, Air con **Seats** 90, Pr/dining room 22 **Children** Portions, Menu **Parking** 80

Acanthus Restaurant

◉◉ Modern Scottish

Imaginative, accomplished cuisine in a Victorian setting

☎ 01738 622451
Parklands Hotel, St Leonards Bank PH2 8EB
e-mail: info@acanthusrestaurant.com
dir: Adjacent to Perth station, overlooking South Inch Park

With clear views over the South Inch, this former home of the Lord Provost is also conveniently located close to the town centre. Public areas at the Parklands Hotel include a choice of restaurants, with the stylish Victorian Acanthus Restaurant providing the fine dining option. Service here is formal and a menu of creative, well-prepared dishes features top-notch local and seasonal ingredients. Enjoy starters such as escabèche of red mullet and langoustine with an organic leaf and local herb salad, perhaps followed by mains like roast Gressingham duck oriental with rhubarb compôte and pak choi. For a stylish finale, why not try passionfruit soufflé with coconut ice cream and chocolate sauce?

Chef Graeme Pallister **Owner** Scott and Penny Edwards
Times Closed 26 Dec-7 Jan, Closed Sun-Tue, Closed L Wed-Sat **Prices** Fixed D 3 course £28.95-£33.95, Service

Continued

PERTH *Continued*

optional, Groups min 8 service 10% **Wines** 33 bottles over £20, 55 bottles under £20, 6 by glass
Notes Vegetarian available, Dress restrictions, Smart casual, no shorts or jeans, Civ Wed 30 **Seats** 36, Pr/dining room 22 **Children** Portions, Menu **Parking** 25

Best Western Huntingtower Hotel

Traditional British

Edwardian country-house hotel with enjoyable fine dining

☎ 01738 583771
Crieff Rd PH1 3JT
e-mail: reservations@huntingtowerhotel.co.uk
dir: 10 minutes from Perth on A85 towards Crieff

Set in 6 acres of secluded landscaped grounds on the outskirts of Perth, this country-house hotel dates back to 1892. Period features abound in this former mill owner's house and the traditional décor adds to the ambience. Lunch is served in the conservatory, while the elegant oak-panelled dining room provides a formal and intimate setting for dinner. A traditional menu of Scottish cuisine with European influences might include starters such as smoked salmon with red onions and capers, or celeriac soup with crispy pancetta, followed by loin of venison with dauphinoise potatoes, baby asparagus, caramelised beetroot and bramble jus, or fillet of cod with fine beans, spinach, sautéed potatoes and a prawn beurre noisette. Chocolate and raspberry mousse completes the fine dining experience.

Chef Bill McNicoll **Times** 12-2/6-9.30 **Prices** Fixed L 2 course £12.95-£17.95, Fixed D 3 course £29.50-£50, Starter £4.50-£10.50, Main £12.50-£50, Dessert £4.50-£12, Service optional **Wines** 23 bottles over £20, 26 bottles under £20, 4 by glass **Notes** Sunday L, Civ Wed 135 **Seats** 34, Pr/dining room 24 **Children** Portions, Menu **Parking** 200

Deans @ Let's Eat

Modern Scottish

Modern, friendly bistro serving imaginative Scottish food

☎ 01738 643377
77/79 Kinnoull St PH1 5EZ
e-mail: deans@letseatperth.co.uk
dir: On corner of Kinnoull St & Atholl St, close to North Inch

This lively, welcoming bistro run by a husband-and-wife team is housed in a converted 19th-century theatre, the warm, rich décor adds to the cosy and informal atmosphere, with squishy sofas perfect for pre- or post-dinner drinks. Contemporary Scottish cooking with a continental twist makes the most of the freshest seasonal ingredients, locally sourced where possible, and everything from the delicious bread to the post-dinner chocolates is home made. Try the rillettes of duckling with ginger and beetroot to start, followed perhaps by monkfish on slow-cooked pork belly with white bean

fricassee, vermouth, tomato and basil. It's a great local favourite, so be sure to book ahead.

Deans @ Let's Eat

Chef Willie Deans, Simon Lannon **Owner** Mr & Mrs W Deans **Times** 12-2/6.30-9.30, Closed Sun-Mon **Prices** Fixed L 2 course £13.95, Starter £3.95-£9.25, Main £11.50-£21.50, Dessert £5.25-£6.50, Service optional **Wines** 40 bottles over £20, 23 bottles under £20, 8 by glass **Notes** Vegetarian available, Dress restrictions, Smart casual **Seats** 70 **Children** Portions **Parking** Multi-storey car park (100 yds)

Murrayshall Country House Hotel

Modern British V

Fine Scottish cuisine with stunning views

☎ 01738 551171
New Scone PH2 7PH
e-mail: info@murrayshall.co.uk
dir: From Perth A94 (Coupar Angus) turn right signed Murrayshall before New Scone

This imposing country-house hotel boasts lovely views of the Grampian Hills. Set on a hillside in 350 acres of grounds, you can work up an appetite on one of the hotel's two golf courses and then visit the Old Masters restaurant. The elegant dining room also enjoys those countryside views and the friendly attentive staff combine to create a relaxed ambience. Expect traditional combinations with a contemporary twist from a kitchen that makes full use of Scotland's bountiful larder. Try risotto of roast sweetcorn and crab served with soft poached duck egg and parmesan to start, perhaps followed by seared Isle of Skye scallops with apple and Calvados, black pudding, parsnip purée and sauce Jacqueline.

Chef Jonathan Greer **Owner** Old Scone Ltd
Times 12-2.30/7-9.45, Closed 26 Dec, Closed L Sat
Prices Fixed L 2 course £11.75, Fixed D 3 course £26, Starter £5-£9, Main £14-£21, Dessert £5-£8.75, Service optional **Wines** 30 bottles over £20, 20 bottles under £20, 8 by glass **Notes** Sunday L, Vegetarian menu, Civ Wed 100, Air con **Seats** 55, Pr/dining room 40 **Children** Portions, Menu **Parking** 90

63 Tay Street

Modern Scottish

Chic city dining in Tayside

☎ 01738 441451
63 Tay St PH2 8NN
e-mail: info@63taystreet.com
dir: In town centre, on river

The setting in a fine stone building overlooking the Tay is second to none in the city, and the change of ownership in 2007 has seen it go from strength to strength. The stylish modern dining room is accessed via a flight of steps next door to Perth's council offices and it remains a popular choice for both dinner and the good-value lunch, with friendly and attentive waiting staff. Local produce figures large on the ambitious menu, from Stornoway black pudding to Carnoustie pork, and with European influences very much in evidence, the result is confident modern Scottish cooking. Carpaccio of Scrabster haddock comes with lightly scrambled eggs on chick pea toast in a successful starter, and main-course duck is pink and moist and complemented by a fragrant barbecue dipping sauce, cherries and orzo.

Chef Graeme Pallister **Owner** Scott & Penny Edwards, Graeme Pallister **Times** 12-2/6.30-9, Closed Xmas, New Year, 1st wk Jul, Closed Sun, Mon **Prices** Food prices not confirmed for 2009. Please telephone for details. **Wines** 59 bottles over £20, 25 bottles under £20, 8 by glass **Seats** 35 **Children** Portions

PITLOCHRY — Map 23 NN95

Green Park Hotel

Modern, Traditional British

Fine cuisine in a lochside country-house hotel

☎ 01796 473248
Clunie Bridge Rd PH16 5JY
e-mail: bookings@thegreenpark.co.uk
dir: Off A9 at Pitlochry, follow signs along Atholl road to Inverness

This family-run country-house hotel enjoys an enviable location on the shore of Loch Faskally. The traditional dining room - in soothing colours of beige and purple - looks out over gardens towards the loch, providing a relaxing setting for some fine traditionally-inspired cuisine. The menu makes the most of local and specialist produce - so seafood and game feature strongly - alongside seasonal herbs and salads from the kitchen garden. Think a salad of hot roast guinea fowl suprême served with coleslaw, plum tomatoes and olive oil dressing, or perhaps a roast rib of beef with horseradish mash and onion and sherry gravy.

Times 12-2/6.30-8.30, Closed L all week (ex residents)

Pine Trees Hotel

◎ Traditional British 🍷

Honest food served in an elegant hotel

☎ 01796 472121
Strathview Ter PH16 5QR
e-mail: info@pinetreeshotel.co.uk
dir: N through Pitlochry to far end of town, turn right into Larchwood Road. Hotel on left just below golf course

A Victorian mansion house set within spacious grounds on the edge of Pitlochry, this elegant hotel retains many period features including a marble staircase and stained glass windows. The country-house style dining room overlooks attractive gardens, woodland and hills, and the atmosphere is relaxed with soft music and candlelight. Dishes are prepared from the finest ingredients, such as fillet of Campbell's Gold certified Scotch beef served on roast vegetables with a rich red wine sauce flavoured with fresh thyme, or saddle of Highland venison with braised red cabbage and juniper berry jus.

Chef Cristian Cojocaru, Eric Toralba **Owner** Mr & Mrs Kerr **Times** 12-2/6.30-9, Closed L Mon-Sat **Prices** Fixed D 3 course £25.50, Service included **Wines** 17 bottles over £20, 11 bottles under £20, 4 by glass **Notes** Pre-theatre D from 5.45pm, Vegetarian available, Dress restrictions, Smart casual **Seats** 50 **Children** Min 8 yrs, Menu **Parking** 40

ST FILLANS Map 20 NN62

Achray House Hotel

◎ Traditional British

Family-run hotel, loch views and traditional cooking

☎ 01764 685231
PH6 2NF
e-mail: info@achray-house.co.uk
dir: Please telephone for directions

Set in pretty gardens, Achray House is a family-run establishment in an idyllic location at the eastern end of Loch Earn, where Perthshire gives way to the Highlands within the Loch Lomond and Trossachs National Park. The restaurant is interconnected with a conservatory-style bar that offers the best of the views. Service is friendly and relaxed and the menu, popular with discerning tourists, showcases fresh Scottish produce. With confident cooking, simple dishes generate bold flavours. Features of the daily-changing menu might be tart of Mull brie with red onions and mushrooms, baked fillet of halibut with an oatmeal herb crust and raspberry cinnamon baked rice.

Chef Andrew J Scott **Owner** Andrew J Scott **Times** 12-2.30/6-8.30, Closed 3-31 Jan **Prices** Starter £3.95-£6.95, Main £9.95-£17.95, Dessert £3.95-£4.95, Service optional **Wines** 11 bottles over £20, 24 bottles

under £20, 9 by glass **Notes** Sunday L, Vegetarian available, Civ Wed **Seats** 70, Pr/dining room 30 **Children** Portions, Menu **Parking** 20

The Four Seasons Hotel

◎◎ Modern European

Breathtaking scenery and bold cuisine

☎ 01764 685333
Loch Earn PH6 2NF
e-mail: info@thefourseasonshotel.co.uk
web: www.thefourseasonshotel.co.uk
dir: From Perth take A85 W, through Crieff & Comrie. Hotel at west end of village

Tucked away beneath steeply forested hills on the edge of Loch Earn, this hotel has a range of comfortable lounges, log fires and stunning views where you really can appreciate the seasons throughout the year. Originally built in the early 1800s for the manager of the limekilns, it was also a schoolmaster's house before becoming a hotel. The lochside Meall Reamhar fine-dining restaurant serves up modern Scottish and European dishes based on great Scottish produce. Bold flavours and imaginative combinations might produce a starter of Highland game terrine with bitter leaves and dowerhouse chutney. Soup or sorbet precede main courses such as baked paupiette of East Coast haddock with roasted vine tomatoes, Welsh rarebit and pesto dressing. Finish with chocolate chestnut truffle cake with brandy-soaked raisins, served with cream.

Times 12-2.30/6-9.30, Closed Jan-Feb

SPITAL OF GLENSHEE Map 23 NO17

Dalmunzie Castle Hotel

◎◎ Traditional, British

Cooking worthy of the laird in a highland mansion

☎ 01250 885224
PH10 7QG
e-mail: reservations@dalmunzie.com
dir: N of Blairgowrie on A93 at the Spittal of Glenshee

Situated in a secluded glen on a 6,500-acre estate, this turreted country-house hotel was once a Highland laird's mansion. It's within easy reach of the ski slopes at Glenshee, making it the perfect destination after a hard day on the piste. The house is furnished with antiques, and logs burn in the original fireplaces, while the spacious dining room has well-appointed tables and a classic blue and cream colour scheme where you can soak up the fine-dining experience. Top-quality seasonal ingredients are sourced for dishes with a British approach, underpinned by classic French influences. Take pan-fried wood pigeon with winter vegetable ragout and thyme jus, followed by pork fillet and mustard roulade with fennel mash and braised cabbage and apple balsamic glaze. More informal meals are available in the bar.

Times 12-2.30/7-9, Closed 1-28 Dec

RENFREWSHIRE

HOWWOOD Map 20 NS36

Country Club Restaurant

◎ Modern British

Stylish modern cooking in old-world surroundings

☎ 01505 705225
Bowfield Hotel & Country Club PA9 1DZ
e-mail: enquiries@bowfieldhotel.co.uk
dir: From M8 take A737 (Irvine Rd), exit at Howwood, take 2nd right up country lane, turn right at top of hill

Occupying a converted 17th-century bleaching mill, this hotel oozes character, with beamed ceilings, brick and white-painted walls and open fires. Simple, clear presentation belies the complexity of the cooking, but all the skill and effort is evident in the flavours. Seasonal Scottish produce is respectfully prepared so expect an emphasis on local fish, game and shellfish. Take a confit duck starter served with pearl barley risotto and jus, or roast Orkney salmon with celeriac purée and a caper and tomato dressing for main course, followed by a plate of Scottish cheeses.

Chef Ronnie McAdam **Owner** Bowfield Hotel & Country Club Ltd **Times** 12-2.30/6.30-9 **Prices** Fixed L 2 course £12, Fixed D 3 course £22.50, Starter £3.95-£7.50, Main £12.50-£22.50, Dessert £3.95-£5.95, Service optional **Wines** 39 bottles over £20, 24 bottles under £20, 11 by glass **Notes** Sunday L, Vegetarian available, Dress restrictions, Smart casual, Civ Wed 120 **Seats** 40, Pr/dining room 20 **Children** Portions, Menu **Parking** 100

RENFREWSHIRE, EAST

UPLAWMOOR Map 10 NS45

Uplawmoor Hotel

◎◎ Modern Scottish 🍷

Friendly inn serving traditional and modern Scottish cuisine

☎ 01505 850565
Neilston Rd G78 4AF
e-mail: info@uplawmoor.co.uk
web: www.uplawmoor.co.uk
dir: From Glasgow follow M8 & M77 to junct 2, follow signs for Barrhead & Irvine A736. 5m past Barrhead take village road left signposted to Uplawmoor

Established in 1759, this former coaching inn was once frequented by smugglers travelling between Glasgow and

Continued

UPLAWMOOR *Continued*

the Ayrshire coast. The old beamed barn is now the restaurant, where rich furnishings and subtle lighting create an intimate atmosphere, and a Charles Rennie Mackintosh-inspired look was incorporated in the late 1950s by architect James Gray. The cocktail bar, with its large copper canopied fireplace and displays of modern art, has an impressive cocktail list designed by the resident mixologist. A regular carte and monthly fixed-price menus offer a good range of Scottish fare - roast loin of venison with thyme-scented sweet potato, crispy leeks and redcurrant jus, or Gaelic steak Uplawmoor with haggis croûton, flamed in whisky - and feature home-grown herbs and meats supplied by five local farms.

Chef Paul Brady **Owner** Stuart & Emma Peacock **Times** 12-3/6-9.30, Closed 26 Dec, 1 Jan, Closed L Mon-Sat **Prices** Fixed L 2 course £14-£16, Fixed D 3 course £17-£23, Starter £4-£8.50, Main £12.50-£21, Dessert £5.25-£6.25, Service optional **Wines** 7 bottles over £20, 19 bottles under £20, 9 by glass **Notes** Early evening menu available 5.30-7 Sun-Fri, Sunday L, Vegetarian available, Dress restrictions, Smart casual **Seats** 30 **Children** Min 12 yrs, Portions, Menu **Parking** 40

SCOTTISH BORDERS

EDDLESTON — Map 21 NT24

The Horseshoe Inn

⊛⊛⊛ – *see opposite*

KELSO — Map 21 NT73

The Roxburghe Hotel & Golf Course

⊛ Modern, Traditional ⓖ

Scottish country-house sporting destination with fine dining

☎ 01573 450331
TD5 8JZ
e-mail: hotel@roxburghe.net
dir: From A68, 1m N of Jedburgh, take A698 for 5m to Heiton

Owned by the Duke of Roxburghe, this impressive Jacobean country-house hotel nestles in woodlands with grounds incorporating a championship golf course. Inside, luxurious décor and log fires set the scene and the dining room, with its crisp white linen and sparkling glassware, provides formal yet friendly service. The kitchen makes good use of local produce and ingredients from the estate. Expect starters like smoked salmon, cream cheese and black olive ravioli with fine bean and shallot salad dressed with lemon and olive oil, followed by grilled breast of guinea fowl wrapped in pancetta with fondant potato, creamed leeks and apple coulis. A fine choice of wines, from the Duke's cellar, provides a fitting accompaniment.

Chef Keith Short **Owner** Duke of Roxburghe **Times** 12-2/7.30-9.45 **Prices** Fixed L 2 course £18-£20, Fixed D 3 course £39-£42, Service optional **Wines** 120 bottles over £20, 12 bottles under £20, 6 by glass

Notes Sunday L, Vegetarian available, Dress restrictions, No jeans, trainers or T-shirts, Civ Wed 50 **Seats** 40, Pr/dining room 18 **Children** Portions, Menu **Parking** 150

MELROSE — Map 21 NT53

Burt's Hotel

⊛⊛ Modern British

Tempting cooking at a family-run hotel

☎ 01896 822285
The Square TD6 9PL
e-mail: enquiries@burtshotel.co.uk
web: www.burtshotel.co.uk
dir: Town centre in Market Sq

This smart hotel is something of a local legend, having been run by the same family for more than 35 years. Built in 1722, it sits in the picturesque heart of a small market town and is easy to spot thanks to its distinctive white-washed exterior and flower-filled window boxes. Inside, there's a clubby feel to the restaurant, with its dark green striped wallpaper, sporting prints and high-backed chairs. The menu is a modern British affair, distinguished by fresh local produce. Kick off with ballotine of foie gras to start perhaps, served with Sauternes poached pear, toasted pistachios and balsamic vinegar, and then tuck into line-caught sea bass served with pomme ecresse, plum tomato sorbet, black olive caramel and a langoustine foam. Leave room for caramelised pineapple pain perdu, rum and raisin sorbet and warm coconut foam for dessert.

Chef Alisdair Stewart **Owner** The Henderson Family **Times** 12-2/7-9, Closed 26 Dec, 2-3 Jan **Prices** Fixed L 2 course £21.50, Fixed D 3 course £33.95, Service optional **Wines** 40 bottles over £20, 20 bottles under £20, 6 by glass **Notes** Sunday L, Vegetarian available, Dress restrictions, Jacket & tie preferred **Seats** 50, Pr/dining room 25 **Children** Min 10 yrs, Portions **Parking** 40

PEEBLES — Map 21 NT24

Castle Venlaw Hotel

⊛ Traditional British

Classical dining in a romantic setting

☎ 01721 720384
Edinburgh Rd EH45 8QG
e-mail: stay@venlaw.co.uk
dir: From Peebles at east end of High Street, turn left at rdbt signed A703 to Edinburgh. After 0.75m hotel is signed on right

This family-owned castle-style hotel is located in the scenic Borders, overlooking the historic town of Peebles. Built on the site of Old Smithfield Castle, it dates from the 18th century and its elegant restaurant boasts tall Georgian windows affording lovely views over the town, as well as an ornamental fireplace and corniced ceiling. The kitchen's technical skills are evident in well-balanced, full-flavoured dishes offered on traditional British and Scottish fixed-price menus, with the occasional nod to the Mediterranean. House specialties include starters like lemon- and lime-scented crab claw cake set on tomato and spring onion compôte with coriander syrup, with chargrilled fillet of Scottish beef, thyme fondant potatoes, wild mushrooms and port-glazed onions to follow. Service is friendly and obliging.

Chef David Harrison **Owner** PAG Hotels Ltd **Times** 12-2.30/7-9 **Prices** Fixed L 2 course £13, Fixed D 3 course £30, Service optional **Wines** 73 bottles over £20, 9 bottles under £20, 6 by glass **Notes** Vegetarian available, Dress restrictions, Smart casual, Civ Wed 35 **Seats** 35, Pr/dining room 30 **Children** Min 5 yrs, Portions, Menu **Parking** 25

Cringletie House

⊛⊛ Modern British **V**

Fine dining in baronial splendour

☎ 01721 725750
Edinburgh Rd EH45 8PL
e-mail: enquiries@cringletie.com
dir: 2.5m N of Peebles on A703

Set in 28 acres of gardens and woodlands, this romantic Scottish baronial mansion enjoys stunning views of the countryside. The grand dining room is timelessly elegant, combining oak floors and a trompe l'oeil ceiling with contemporary fabrics and furniture. The focus on the carte and tasting menu is on local Scottish produce, with

Continued on page 538

The Horseshoe Inn

EDDLESTON   Map 21 NT24

Modern French

Glamorous venue and food make this a destination restaurant

☎ 01721 730225
EH45 8QP
e-mail: reservations
@horseshoeinn.co.uk
web: www.horseshoeinn.co.uk
dir: On A703, 5m N of Peebles

The unassuming converted village blacksmiths house takes on a very different personality on the inside. Gone are any thoughts of its past life, for inside it is lavishly furnished with gilded mirrors and smart fabrics. There is a stylish bar-bistro and a fine dining restaurant, Bardoulet's, named after the chef-director of this rejuvenated inn. The setting is luxurious and bold, mixing old and new to create a comfortable environment in which to sample the cooking of Patrick Bardoulet. The French origins of the chef are reflected in the menu and high quality Scottish produce figures large. A thin tart of crab and scallops is served as a starter with a spiced mango tartar, sweet beetroot and orange oil, while marinated foie gras is set in a rhubarb jelly and served with gingerbread. This is inventive and creative food. Main-course Scottish beef, fillet and shoulder, comes with creamed wild mushrooms and morel jus, and the originality continues at dessert:

crème caramel with pecan cake, praline and ginger sorbet. Service is knowledgeable, helpful and attentive.

Chef Patrick Bardoulet **Owner** Border Steelwork Structures Ltd
Times 12-2.30/7-9, Closed 25 Dec, early Jan, mid Oct, Closed Mon, Closed D Sun
Prices Fixed L course £17.50, Starter £9-£14, Main £14.50-£24.50, Dessert £7-£9, Service optional **Wines** 55 bottles over £20, 32 bottles under £20
Notes Sunday L, Vegetarian available, Dress restrictions, Smart casual, Jackets for men preferred **Seats** 40
Parking 20

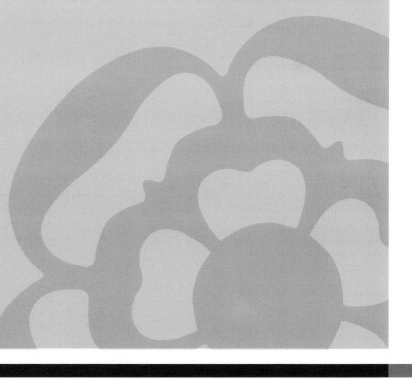

PEEBLES Continued

much of the fruit and vegetables coming from the kitchen garden. Imaginative dishes might include a starter such as lime ceviche scallop tart, apple jelly, pumpkin and apple, followed by duo of pork (belly and fillet) with caramelised apple purée, pomme maxim, anise jus and creamed Savoy cabbage. The chestnut pannacotta, butternut ice cream and chestnut Madeleine makes a fitting finale.

Chef Craig Gibb **Owner** Jacob & Johanna van Houdt **Times** Closed L Mon-Sat **Prices** Fixed D 3 course £41.50, Tasting menu £55, Service optional **Wines** 76 bottles over £20, 7 bottles under £20, 7 by glass **Notes** Sunday L, Vegetarian menu, Dress restrictions, Smart casual, No jeans or trainers, Civ Wed 55 **Seats** 55, Pr/dining room 12 **Children** Portions, Menu **Parking** 30

Renwicks

⊚ British

Accomplished cooking with stunning views

☎ 0844 879 9024 & 01896 833600
Macdonald Cardrona Hotel, Golf & Country Club, Cardrona Mains EH45 6LZ
e-mail: general.cardrona@macdonald-hotels.co.uk
dir: From Edinburgh on A701 signposted Penicuik/Peebles. Continue on A703, 1st rdbt next to garage turn left onto A72, hotel 3m on right

Situated in the beautiful Tweed Valley, with exceptional views of the dramatic Borders countryside, this smart, modern hotel enjoys a unique setting. Aside from the golf course, guests can work up an appetite in the state-of-the-art gym or pool. Glorious views are afforded from the light-and-airy second-floor Renwicks restaurant, where diners can keep an eye on the fairways and greens, or cast their eyes further to the rolling Scottish hills. The set-price seasonal menu offers excellent Scottish produce like fresh seafood and well-hung game. The cooking style is crisp and precise, so simple concepts are delivered with a high degree of accuracy, accompanied by delightful service from a strong, professional team. Try a starter like artichoke tortellini in white wine with sun-blushed tomato and tarragon sauce, and perhaps grilled organic salmon fillet for mains, with saffron and shellfish risotto.

Chef Ivor Clark **Owner** Macdonald Hotels **Times** 12-2.30/6.30-9.45, Please telephone for details **Prices** Fixed L 2 course £12.50-£15.75, Fixed D 3 course £34.95, Service included **Wines** 50 bottles over £20, 14 bottles under £20, 14 by glass **Notes** Sunday L, Vegetarian available, Dress restrictions, Smart casual, Civ Wed 150 **Seats** 70, Pr/dining room 24 **Children** Portions, Menu **Parking** 100

SWINTON Map 21 NT84

The Wheatsheaf at Swinton

⊚⊚ Modern British 🖥 V 🐾

Attractive restaurant with rooms on a peaceful village green

☎ 01890 860257
Main St TD11 3JJ
e-mail: reception@wheatsheaf-swinton.co.uk
web: www.wheatsheaf-swinton.co.uk
dir: From Edinburgh turn off A697 onto B6461. From East Lothian turn off A1 onto B6461

All around are reminders of the rural locality of this traditional country inn which stands on the edge of the village green. Although very much a destination venue for its food, The Wheatsheaf remains at the heart of village life. A pine-clad conservatory, traditional dining room and bar lounge are among the cosy eating areas, warmed by log fires in winter. The menu offers a broad choice with dishes reflecting the seasons and the emphasis firmly placed on the sourcing of ingredients from within the region - seafood is from Eyemouth harbour, while Borders beef, lamb and organic pork come from local traditional butchers. Wild salmon, venison and game birds add further local flavour when in season. The provenance is evident in dishes like seared Scottish scallops with roast cherry vine tomatoes and lemon butter sauce, and main courses such as roast rack of Border lamb served with spring onion mash.

Chef John Kier **Owner** Mr & Mrs Chris Winson **Times** 12-2/6-9, Closed 25-27 Dec **Prices** Starter £5.20-£11.25, Main £10.90-£21, Dessert £5.10-£6.15, Service optional, Groups min 12 service 10% **Wines** 84 bottles over £20, 34 bottles under £20, 12 by glass **Notes** Sunday L, Vegetarian menu, Civ Wed 50 **Seats** 45, Pr/dining room 29 **Children** Portions, Menu **Parking** 6

STIRLING

CALLANDER Map 20 NN60

Callander Meadows

⊚ Modern British

☎ 01877 330181
24 Main St FK17 8BB
e-mail: mail@callandermeadows.co.uk
web: www.callandermeadows.co.uk
dir: M9 junct 10, A8 for 15 miles, restaurant 1m into village on left past traffic lights

This establishment was awarded its Rosette/s just as we went to press. Therefore we are unable to provide a description for it - visit www.theAA.com for the most up-to-date information.

Chef Nick & Susannah Parkes **Owner** Nick & Susannah Parkes **Times** 12-2.30/6-9, Closed 25-26 Dec, Closed Tue-Wed **Prices** Fixed L 2 course £7.95-£12.95, Fixed D 3 course £20-£35, Starter £3.95-£5.95, Main £11.95-£21.95, Dessert £4.50-£4.95 **Wines** 10 bottles over £20, 17 bottles under £20, 4 by glass **Notes** Vegetarian available **Seats** 40, Pr/dining room 16 **Children** Portions **Parking** 6

Roman Camp Country House Hotel

⊚⊚⊚ – **see opposite**

STRATHYRE Map 20 NN51

Creagan House

⊚⊚ French, Scottish 🍷 NOTABLE WINE LIST

17th-century former farmhouse with welcoming hospitality and admirable food

☎ 01877 384638
FK18 8ND
e-mail: eatandstay@creaganhouse.co.uk
web: www.creaganhouse.co.uk
dir: 0.25m N of village, off A84

This carefully restored 17th-century farmhouse, set in the Loch Lomond and the Trossachs National Park, offers very warm hospitality and a sizeable baronial dining room with an impressive fireplace and polished refectory tables. The kitchen creates accurately cooked classical French dishes with strong Scottish influences using fresh, seasonal ingredients - many of which are produced on local small-holdings specifically for Creagan House. Choose from dishes such as collop of venison with poached pear and skirlie potato cake and Malbec red wine sauce, or fillet of organic cod with tournedos of hand-dived scallops and light curry sauce. There is also an exceptional wine list and a noteworthy selection of whiskies to ponder over.

Chef Gordon Gunn **Owner** Gordon & Cherry Gunn **Times** Closed 1-19 Nov, Xmas, 21 Jan-5 Mar, Closed Wed-Thu, Closed L (ex parties) **Prices** Fixed D 3 course £29.50-£32.50, Service optional **Wines** 42 bottles over £20, 26 bottles under £20, 8 by glass **Notes** Dress restrictions, Smart casual **Seats** 15, Pr/dining room 6 **Children** Min 10 yrs, Portions **Parking** 25

Roman Camp Country House Hotel

CALLANDER   Map 20 NN60

Modern French V

Innovative cooking in splendid riverside setting

☎ 01877 330003
FK17 8BG
e-mail: mail@romancamphotel.co.uk
dir: N on A84 through Callander Main St turn left at East End into drive

Built as a hunting lodge for the Dukes of Perth in 1625, this charming country-house hotel is set in 20 acres of tranquil woodland gardens and grounds leading down to the River Teith in the heart of the Trossachs National Park. It became the Roman Camp Country House Hotel in 1939, taking its name from the nearby earthworks - believed to be Roman. In keeping with its historic past, decorative tapestries grace the walls of the oval dining room and real fires warm the atmospheric public rooms in true country-house fashion. Softly decorated in a modern, classical style and overlooking the garden, the restaurant's well-spaced tables are lit by tall candles and decorated with fresh flowers. The service is suitably professional yet friendly. The talented kitchen's modern approach is underpinned by a classical theme, the repertoire dominated by high quality Scottish produce from the abundant local larder. Expect creative, exciting and innovative dishes with clear

flavours, such as smoked eel lasagne with sauté langoustines and carrot escabèche to start, and to follow perhaps loin of hare, date purée and dark chocolate sauce. Finish with Turkish delight, poached rhubarb and rosewater foam. There's an extensive wine list and pre-dinner canapés, pre-desserts and petits fours to enjoy.

Chef Ian McNaught **Owner** Eric Brown **Times** 12-1.45/7-8.30 **Prices** Fixed L 3 course £25-£30, Fixed D 4 course £45-£49, Starter £9.50-£19.50, Main £25-£35, Dessert £9.50-£12.50, Service optional **Wines** 185 bottles over £20, 15 bottles under £20, 16 by glass **Notes** Sunday L, Vegetarian menu, Dress restrictions, Smart casual, Civ Wed 100 **Seats** 120, Pr/dining room 36 **Children** Portions **Parking** 80

SCOTTISH ISLANDS

ARRAN, ISLE OF

BRODICK
Map 20 NS03

Auchrannie Country House Hotel

◎◎ Modern, Traditional ☜

Fine dining on Arran Isle

☎ 01770 302234
KA27 8BZ
e-mail: info@auchrannie.co.uk
dir: From Brodick Pier turn right on to main road. Continue for 0.5m, turn left at signs for Auchrannie

The Isle of Arran is the romantic setting for this imposing country-house hotel, part of a luxury resort complex. The renamed eighteen69 restaurant is tastefully housed in the conservatory, where beautiful table settings and subtle lighting create an appealing atmosphere for the fine Scottish dining. Traditional recipes - using the best of local produce - are given a modern makeover on the imaginative seasonal menu. Take a starter of duck rillettes with prune brioche and beetroot and ginger chutney, followed by rack of Arran lamb with creamed layered potato, tomato and vegetable stew, or perhaps monkfish wrapped in bacon with celeriac purée, white beans, tomato and basil, with malt whisky baba with Arran Gold ice cream for dessert.

Chef Gregg Russell **Owner** Mr I Johnston **Times** Closed L all week **Prices** Tasting menu £45, Starter £4.25-£12.50, Main £14.50-£22.50, Dessert £6-£9.50, Service optional **Wines** 34 bottles over £20, 24 bottles under £20, 13 by glass **Notes** Tasting menu 7 courses, Civ Wed 100, Air con **Seats** 64, Pr/dining room 22 **Children** Portions **Parking** 25

Kilmichael County House Hotel

◎◎ Modern British ☜

Exciting local dining in country-house surroundings

☎ 01770 302219
Glen Cloy KA27 8BY
e-mail: enquiries@kilmichael.com
dir: Turn right on leaving ferry terminal, through Brodick & left at golf club. Follow brown sign. Continue past church & onto private drive

The handsome, white-painted house is the oldest on the island and has plenty of period features to prove it. The hotel is furnished with a mix of antiques, interesting artworks and fabulous china collected during the owners' extensive travels and there are 4 acres of gardens to explore amid the stunning rolling, wooded countryside. The restaurant is elegant and semi-formal but with an emphasis on guests' comfort and relaxation. Everything is made in-house using fresh produce from the hotel's own gardens or from the island. Dinner starts with canapés before a starter of rocket, watercress and goat's cheese mousse served with a quail Scotch egg, sun-blushed tomatoes and rocket salad. Then comes the sorbet - Pimm's, perhaps - before the main course

Gressingham duck, stuffed with wild rice, walnuts and raspberries and served with a port wine sauce and superb vegetables.

Chef Antony Butterworth **Owner** G Botterill & A Butterworth **Times** Closed Nov-Mar, Closed Tue **Prices** Fixed D 3 course £38.50, Service optional **Wines** 32 bottles over £20, 23 bottles under £20, 3 by glass **Notes** Vegetarian available, Dress restrictions, Smart casual, no T-shirts or bare feet **Seats** 18 **Children** Min 12 yrs **Parking** 12

HARRIS, ISLE OF

SCARISTA
Map 22 NG09

Scarista House

◎◎ Modern Scottish

Remote country house with great views and island produce

☎ 01859 550238
HS3 3HX
e-mail: timandpatricia@scaristahouse.com
dir: On A859 15m S of Tarbert

A Georgian former manse with stunning views of the Atlantic, heather-covered mountains and the nearby shell and sand beach, Scarista House is the perfect base for gastronomes wanting to explore the magnificent island of Harris. The dining room is elegantly presented with silver cutlery and candlesticks, oak dining tables and original art on the walls. Drinks are served in two sitting rooms, both with open fires. Immediately available island seafood, lamb, beef and game are cooked with skill to produce dishes like local langoustines with garlic mayonnaise, crushed olive potatoes and garden salad, or navarin of Harris lamb with dauphinoise potatoes, aubergine purée and fine beans. Finish with iced Drambuie praline parfait with fresh raspberries.

Chef Tim Martin **Owner** Tim & Patricia Martin **Times** Closed 25 Dec, Jan-Feb **Prices** Fixed D 3 course £39.50, Service optional **Wines** 25 bottles over £20, 25 bottles under £20, 2 by glass **Notes** Vegetarian available, Civ Wed 40 **Seats** 20, Pr/dining room 14 **Children** Min 7 yrs, Portions, Menu **Parking** 10

ISLAY, ISLE OF

BOWMORE
Map 20 NR35

The Harbour Inn

◎◎ Scottish, International 🖳 ☜

Must-visit dining experience on this magnificent island with wonderful views

☎ 01496 810330
The Square PA43 7JR
e-mail: info@harbour-inn.com
dir: Bowmore is situated approx 8m from both ports of Port Ellen & Port Askaig

This modest whitewashed inn is set in an idyllic fishing village, with views over the harbour to the loch beyond.

Inside lies a sizeable modern restaurant decorated with style and sophistication. The menu relies heavily on premium local produce with many of the dishes focusing around one or two key ingredients, including world-class seafood and fish and fantastic cheeses. The varied menu offers much to deliberate over. Perhaps try Loch Gruinart oysters, simply served with wedges of lemon and Tabasco to start, with medallions of local venison on spiced red cabbage, garnished with a poached pear and a Burgundy and juniper sauce to follow, rounded off with a hot chocolate and ginger soufflé, decorated with fresh strawberries and home-made basil ice cream.

The Harbour Inn

Chef Paul Lumby **Owner** Carol Scott, Neil Scott **Times** 12-2.30/6-9.30 **Prices** Food prices not confirmed for 2009. Please telephone for details. **Wines** 33 bottles over £20, 8 by glass **Notes** Dress restrictions, Smart casual **Seats** 44 **Children** Min 10 yrs, Portions

MULL, ISLE OF

TOBERMORY
Map 22 NM55

Highland Cottage

◎◎ Modern Scottish, International 🖳 ☜

A traditional Mull hotel with enticing local menu

☎ 01688 302030
Breadalbane St PA75 6PD
e-mail: davidandjo@highlandcottage.co.uk
web: www.highlandcottage.co.uk
dir: Opposite fire station. Main St up Back Brae, turn at top by White House. Follow road to right, left at next junct

This traditional, countrified restaurant, located in a small family-run hotel close to Tobermory's working pier, is regarded by locals as the fine dining and special occasion venue. It certainly lives up to its reputation, the cosy and homely dining room has a welcoming atmosphere, and the food is simple, honest and home cooked using quality local produce, notably seafood landed on the pier. Expect a Scottish menu with international influences, sound culinary skills and well-balanced dishes; perhaps a warm leek and red onion tart with Mull cheddar and apple and mint jam or tea-smoked Inverlussa mussels with mango mayonnaise, followed by seared diver-caught scallops served with sautéed leeks and ginger cream, and coffee and walnut brownie with pistachio ice cream.

Chef Josephine Currie **Owner** David & Josephine Currie **Times** Closed Nov-Feb, Closed L all week **Prices** Fixed D 4 course £45, Service included **Wines** 33 bottles over £20, 21 bottles under £20, 11 by glass **Notes** Vegetarian available, Dress restrictions, Smart casual **Seats** 24 **Children** Min 10 yrs, Portions **Parking** On street

Tobermory Hotel

◉ Modern Scottish 🖥 ✋

Delightful seafront retreat on the Isle of Mull

☎ 01688 302091
53 Main St PA75 6NT
e-mail: tobhotel@tinyworld.co.uk
dir: Please telephone for directions

With its pretty pink frontage, this friendly, small hotel sits on the seafront overlooking Tobermory Bay, and was once a row of fishermen's cottages. The attractive and aptly-named Water's Edge restaurant is laid out with solid-wood furniture, while local artists' sea sculptures brighten up the walls. The kitchen follows an intelligent and refreshingly simple modern Scottish line, allowing the quality local produce to shine, notably the wonderful seafood landed on the quay. Crab ravioli with local ling and a lemon and herb sauce, Iona lamb with black pudding and rosemary stuffing, or home-smoked wild venison with a bramble, candied walnut, blue cheese and baby spinach salad are typical examples of the fare.

Chef Helen Swinbanks **Owner** Mr & Mrs I Stevens **Times** Closed Xmas, Jan, Closed L all week **Prices** Fixed D 3 course fr £22.50, Service optional **Wines** 18 bottles over £20, 24 bottles under £20, 5 by glass **Notes** Vegetarian available **Seats** 30 **Children** Portions, Menu **Parking** On street

ORKNEY ISLANDS

ST MARGARET'S HOPE   Map 24 ND49

Creel Restaurant

◉◉ Modern, Seafood

Family-run seafront restaurant

☎ 01856 831311
Front Rd KW17 2SL
e-mail: alan@thecreel.freeserve.co.uk
dir: 13m S of Kirkwall on A961, on seafront in village

Overlooking the lovely seafront in the picturesque village of St Margaret's Hope, the Creel is a charming island restaurant with rooms, specialising in local produce. The dining room is informal in style and looks out across the sea. A large collection of local artwork is displayed on the walls, and the atmosphere is warm and friendly. Fresh and simple is the philosophy behind the cooking and the menu is constantly changing according to the supply of seafood, Orkney meat and vegetables. Seafood figures strongly, and favourites are grilled new season mackerel with warm beetroot relish and toasted oatmeal, followed by pan-fried North Atlantic hake with squid and haddock stew. For a fitting finish, try the glazed baked lemon tart with marmalade ice cream.

Chef Alan Craigie **Owner** Alan & Joyce Craigie **Times** Closed Jan-Mar, Nov, Closed Mon & Tues (Apr, May, Sep, Oct), Closed L all week, Closed D Mon **Prices** Starter £7-£7.50, Main £18.50-£26.50, Dessert £6.50-£7.50, Service optional **Wines** 10 bottles over £20, 18 bottles under £20, 4 by glass **Seats** 34, Pr/dining room 14 **Children** Portions **Parking** 12

SKYE, ISLE OF

COLBOST   Map 22 NG24

The Three Chimneys

◉◉◉ – **see page 542**

The Three Chimneys

COLBOST Map 22 NG24

Modern Scottish NOTABLE WINE LIST

Foodie hideaway on Skye serving the freshest seafood

☎ 01470 511258
IV55 8ZT
e-mail: eatandstay@threechimneys.co.uk
web: www.threechimneys.co.uk
dir: 5m W of Dunvegan take B884 signed Glendale. On left beside loch

A visit to this delightful property will make a trip to Skye even more memorable. Housed within the stone walls of an original crofter's cottage, close to the shores of Loch Dunvegan, this magical little restaurant is set in glorious wilderness, nestled between the hills and the sea. The whitewashed building's interconnecting rooms pick up on the natural theme to create a feeling of chic simplicity. Take the candlelit restaurant's bare stone walls, low ceilings and polished-wood tables, with their slate tablemats and high-backed chairs. It's intimate and cosy, while service is suitably relaxed and friendly, but professional and well informed. As you'd expect, the menus change daily to make the best of the abundant local larder, with seafood a highlight. Superb quality produce is simply cooked to let the freshness and quality shine through. The finely-tuned style marries traditional Scottish ideas with a more modern approach, delivering skilful combinations and clean, crisp flavours - as in Loch Dunvegan langoustines with organic leaves and lemon and olive oil vinaigrette, or pan-fried monkfish and Sconser scallops with root dauphinoise, purple sprouting broccoli and claret jus. For dessert, succumb to the temptations of hot marmalade pudding with Drambuie custard. Add an impressive wine list and fantastic views that money can't buy, and a walk along the loch to see the seals is a must.

Chef Michael Smith **Owner** Eddie & Shirley Spear **Times** 12.30-2/6.30-9.30, Closed 4-30 Jan, Closed L Sun & end Oct-Easter **Prices** Fixed L 2 course £23-£35, Fixed D 3 course £55-£60, Service optional, Groups min 8 service 10% **Wines** 150 bottles over £20, 4 bottles under £20, 11 by glass **Notes** Tasting menu 7 courses, Vegetarian available, Dress restrictions, Smart casual preferred **Seats** 40, Pr/dining room 10 **Children** Min 8 yrs D, Portions

ISLEORNSAY — Map 22 NG71

Hotel Eilean Iarmain

◉◉ Traditional Scottish

Impressive cuisine on Skye

☎ 01471 833332
IV43 8QR
e-mail: hotel@eileaniarmain.co.uk
dir: Mallaig & cross by ferry to Armadale, 8m to hotel or via Kyle of Lochalsh.

A hotel of charm and character, this 19th-century former inn is set above the beach by the pier, overlooking the bay and sea lochs beyond. Enjoy pre-dinner drinks in front of a roaring fire in the cosy lounge before moving into the elegant panelled restaurant with its view of Ornsay Lighthouse. Scottish fare prepared from high quality local ingredients is offered from a daily menu, including venison from their own estate. Specialities include Loch Eishort mussels steamed open in a sauce of fresh chopped tomatoes, organic basil, white wine and coriander, and tournedos of Aberdeen Angus beef fillet with rosemary jus and sautéed courgettes. Finish with mango pineapple sorbet in a vanilla-marinated pineapple ring.

Chef Graham Smith **Owner** Sir Ian Andrew Noble **Times** 12-2.30/6.30-8.45 **Prices** Fixed L 2 course £12.95-£18, Fixed D 3 course £31-£35, Starter £4.50-£12, Main £14.95-£28, Dessert £4.25-£6.50, Service optional **Wines** 60 bottles over £20, 10 bottles under £20, 6 by glass **Notes** Sunday L, Vegetarian available, Dress restrictions, Smart casual, Civ Wed 80 **Seats** 40, Pr/dining room 22 **Children** Portions, Menu

Iona Restaurant

◉ Modern Scottish **V**

Stylish haven of peace serving Skye's wonderful produce

☎ 0845 055 1117 & 01471 833231
Toravaig House Hotel, Knock Bay, Sleat IV44 8RE
e-mail: info@skyehotel.co.uk
web: www.skyehotel.co.uk
dir: Travel to Isle of Skye by bridge, continue towards Broadford for 4m, turn left for Armadale & Sleat. Torvaig is on main A851, 11m beyond this junct

Expect the freshest ingredients from the abundant Highland larder at this elegant restaurant set within the stylishly refurbished Toravaig House Hotel, a haven of peace with panoramic views to the Knoydart Hills. White-

clothed tables and high-backed modern leather chairs set the inviting scene in which to sample Skye's wonderful fish, game or lamb from the daily menu, perhaps hand-dived West Coast scallops with an orange and basil beurre blanc and loin of lamb with a thyme and whisky jus, or the intriguing gateau of MacBeth's beef fillet. The style is straightforward, with clear flavours that intelligently allow the quality produce to take centre stage. Look out for sailings on the hotel's own yacht.

Chef Peter Woods, Richard Glass **Owner** Anne Gracie & Ken Gunn **Times** 12.30-2/6.30-11.30 **Prices** Fixed D 4 course £32.50-£37.50, Tasting menu £42.50, Service optional **Wines** 20 bottles over £20, 20 bottles under £20, 6 by glass **Notes** Sunday L, Vegetarian menu, Dress restrictions, Smart casual, Civ Wed 18 **Seats** 30 **Children** Min 14yrs **Parking** 20

See advert on page 541

PORTREE — Map 22 NG44

Bosville Hotel

◉◉ Modern British ◕

Masterful cooking of truly local produce with harbour views

☎ 01478 612846
Bosville Ter IV51 9DG
e-mail: bosville@macleodhotels.co.uk
dir: 200mtrs from bus station, overlooking Portree Harbour

A popular hotel with fine views over Portree Harbour, the Bosville offers stylish public areas including a smart bar, bistro and the Chandlery Restaurant. The Chandlery has a modern, luxurious feel and draws on an abundance of fresh local and seasonal island produce, especially seafood and game. Great produce, skilful modern Scottish cooking - with French influence - and inspirational combinations feature in chef John Kelly's dishes. Take butter-poached Mallaig halibut accompanied by wilted pak choi, baby gem lettuce, peas and bacon lardons and finished with a saffron, mussel and scallop broth topped with garlic chips, and to finish, perhaps fried porridge served with raspberries and lemon cream.

Chef John Kelly **Owner** Donald W Macleod **Times** Closed L all week **Prices** Fixed D 3 course £40, Service optional **Wines** 20 bottles over £20, 20 bottles under £20, 12 by glass **Notes** Vegetarian available **Seats** 30 **Children** Portions **Parking** 10

Cuillin Hills Hotel

◉◉ French, European

Highland hotel with stunning views and fine local produce

☎ 01478 612003
IV51 9QU
e-mail: info@cuillinhills-hotel-skye.co.uk
dir: 0.25m N of Portree on A855

Built in the 1870s as a hunting lodge for Lord Macdonald of the Isles, the hotel stands in mature grounds and enjoys spectacular views over Portree Bay to the Cuillin Hills from its split-level restaurant. In summer you can enjoy drinks on the lawn, and service is friendly and professional. The imaginative cuisine combines modern European and classical French dishes on a daily-changing menu, and takes full advantage of fresh, local produce, including local seafood, Highland game and home-made breads. Traditional Scottish dishes are set alongside the likes of pan-fried cod with a pea crust and white wine cream, finished off with a dessert of lemon tart with fruit coulis, or a plate of Scottish cheeses. There's an extensive wine list.

Chef Robert Macaskill **Owner** Wickman Hotels Ltd **Times** 12-2/6.30-9, Closed 6-26 Jan, Closed L Mon-Sat **Prices** Fixed D 3 course £32.50, Service optional **Wines** 40 bottles over £20, 15 bottles under £20, 6 by glass **Notes** Sunday L, Vegetarian available, Civ Wed 70 **Seats** 48, Pr/dining room 20 **Children** Portions, Menu **Parking** 56

PORTREE *Continued*

Rosedale Hotel

◎ Traditional Scottish

Welcoming waterfront hotel with seafood a speciality

☎ 01478 613131
Beaumont Crescent IV51 9DB
e-mail: rosedalehotelsky@aol.com
dir: On harbour front

Once a group of fishermen's cottages, this delightful, family-run waterfront hotel offers a wonderfully warm, intimate atmosphere. Inside, a labyrinth of corridors and stairs connects the lounges, bar and restaurant which are set on different levels. A window seat is a must in the charming first-floor restaurant with fine views overlooking the bay and Portree's busy harbour. An inspired Scottish menu supplies local produce, including a good smattering of seafood, prepared with panache. To start try a terrine of duck, orange and brandy on dressed local leaves served with oat biscuits, followed by oven-baked fillet of sea bass on a bed of buttered leeks and spinach in a prawn bisque sauce.

Chef Kirk Moir **Owner** Mr & Mrs P Rouse **Times** Closed 1 Nov-1 Mar, Closed L all week **Prices** Fixed D 3 course £26-£31, Service optional **Wines** 10 bottles over £20, 20 bottles under £20, 7 by glass **Notes** Vegetarian available **Seats** 30 **Children** Portions, Menu **Parking** On street

---

Loch Bay Seafood Restaurant

◎ British Seafood 🍷

Excellent local seafood in a bistro-style setting

☎ 01470 592235
IV55 8GA
e-mail: david@lochbay-seafood-restaurant.co.uk
dir: 4m off A850 by the B886

A terrace of 18th-century fishermen's cottages is the setting for this intimate seafood restaurant, located close to the loch shore near Waternish Point. The atmosphere is wonderfully welcoming and the need to book for both lunch and dinner really says it all. The blackboard advertises the freshest of seafood from the catch landed at nearby Dunvegan, and supplements an extensive carte. Everything is simply cooked with almost nothing added to mask the natural flavours. Try scallop and lobster risotto, Stein shellfish extravaganza, and Drambuie and vanilla pannacotta with passionfruit syrup.

Chef David Wilkinson **Owner** David & Alison Wilkinson **Times** 12-2/6-9, Closed Nov-Etr (excl. 1wk over Hogmanay), Closed Sun-Mon **Prices** Starter £3.60-£10.10, Main £11.25-£18.50, Dessert £4.80-£5.25, Service optional **Wines** 13 bottles over £20, 20 bottles under £20, 5 by glass **Notes** Extensive blackboard choices **Seats** 26 **Children** Portions **Parking** 6

Ullinish Country Lodge

◎◎◎ – *see opposite*

Ullinish Country Lodge

Map 22 NG33

Modern French V

Culinary paradise for foodies in an idyllic, hidden-away Skye setting

☎ 01470 572214
IV56 8FD
e-mail: ullinish@theisleofskye.co.uk
web: www.theisleofskye.co.uk
dir: 9m S of Dunvegan on A863

Set at the end of a track amid some of Scotland's most dramatic scenery (lochs on three sides and breathtaking views of the Black Cuillins and MacLeod's Tables), Ullinish Lodge is a haven of peace and tranquillity and boasts the celebrated Samuel Johnson and James Boswell among former guests. Unsurprisingly, the interior has a country-house feel, with a peaceful lounge and efficient, pleasant service. Tables in the wood-panelled dining room feature pristine white linen against a backdrop of tartan carpet and curtains, the intimate atmosphere heightened by candlelight. The chef's modern approach - underpinned by classical roots - is driven by the freshest quality produce from the abundant local larder, with fish and seafood from the surrounding waters, and meat and game from the hills. High technique, passion, a light touch, clean-cut flavours, clever and interesting combinations and striking presentation set the taste-buds soaring on a sensibly

compact, fixed-price repertoire. A light lunch is served, but it's dinner that really cranks up the ante on the culinary front and shows the kitchen's true credentials. Take Mallaig turbot for instance, perhaps poached in red wine and served with spinach, pomme purée, duck en crepinette and a vinaigrette of smoked bacon and ketchup, and to finish, maybe a soufflé of local blueberries served with vanilla and blueberry ripple ice cream and a lemonade shot.

Chef Bruce Morrison **Owner** Brian & Pam Howard **Times** 12-2.30/7.30-8.30, Closed Jan, 1 wk Nov **Prices** Fixed L 2 course £13.95, Fixed D 4 course £45, Service optional **Wines** 24 bottles over £20, 14 bottles under £20 **Notes** Sunday L, Vegetarian menu, Dress restrictions, Smart casual, No T-shirts **Seats** 22 **Children** Min 16 yrs **Parking** 10

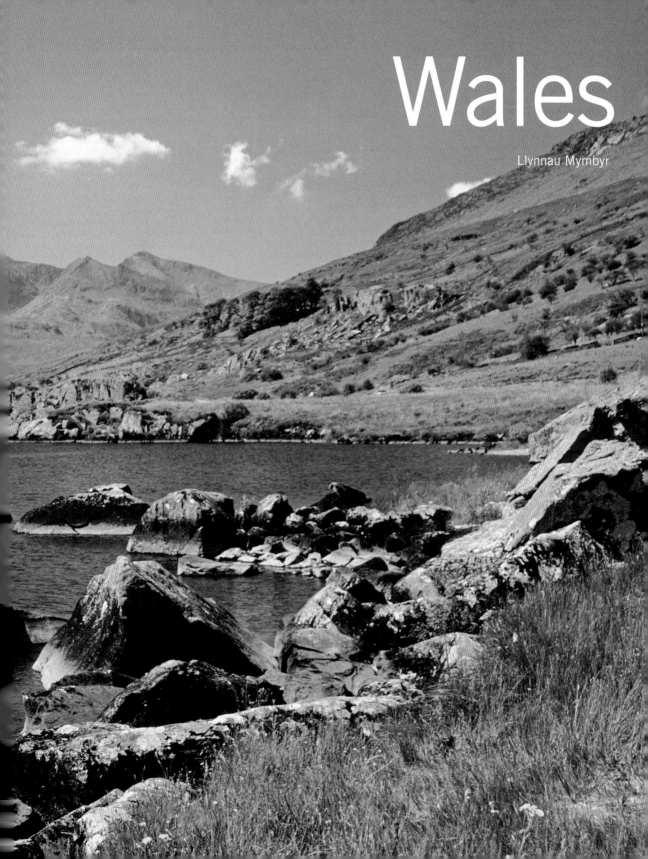

Wales

Llynnau Mymbyr

ANGLESEY, ISLE OF

BEAUMARIS — Map 14 SH67

Bishopsgate House Hotel

Traditional Welsh 🖥 🖐

Fine Welsh cooking in a historic setting

☎ 01248 810302
54 Castle St LL58 8BB
e-mail: hazel@bishopsgatehotel.co.uk
dir: From Britannia Bridge follow A545 into town centre.
Hotel is 2nd on left in the main street

An immaculately maintained Georgian townhouse, this
privately owned hotel features original wood panelling and
a Chinese Chippendale staircase, one of the finest in the
country. Fresh local produce is served in the elegant
restaurant, including fish, salt marsh lamb and beef from
the Lleyn Peninsula. A choice of carte and fixed-price
traditional Welsh menus is offered. Typical dishes are oak-
smoked salmon and white crabmeat parcels served with
cherry tomatoes and wholemeal bread, rack of lamb set on
bubble-and-squeak, finished with mint and onion sauce.
Puddings range from lemon cheesecake to jam roly poly.

Chef H Johnson Ollier & I Sankey **Owner** Hazel Johnson
Ollier **Times** 12.30-2.30/7-9.30, Closed L Mon-Sat
Prices Fixed L 2 course £12.50-£14.45, Fixed D 3 course
£17.95-£19.90, Starter £4.50-£5.95, Main £9.50-£19.95,
Dessert £4.95-£5.75, Service optional **Wines** 14 bottles
over £20, 20 bottles under £20, 3 by glass **Notes** Sunday
L, Dress restrictions, Smart dress **Seats** 40
Children Portions **Parking** 10

Ye Olde Bulls Head Inn

Modern British 🖐

Historic inn serving punchy food

☎ 01248 810329
Castle St LL58 8AP
e-mail: info@bullsheadinn.co.uk
dir: Town centre, main street

A historic 14th-century coaching inn, visited by Charles
Dickens and Samuel Johnson. Exposed beams and
antique weaponry bear testament to its heritage,
although the rest of the décor is smart and contemporary,
particularly the Loft restaurant, the more formal of the
two dining options. The food is confident, progressive and
demonstrates creativity - lightly cooked pigeon breast
with home-made plum chutney, toasted hazelnut salad
and sherry vinegar dressing perhaps, followed by Brian's

Ye Olde Bulls Head Inn

fillet of Anglesey Welsh Black beef with fondant potato,
red wine shallot, cep, green beans, pancetta and Madeira
jus. To finish, try traditional bara brith and Welsh butter
pudding with semi-dried grapes and Madeira and clotted
cream.

Chef Keith Rothwell, Craig Yardley **Owner** D Robertson,
K Rothwell **Times** Closed 25-26 Dec, 1 Jan, Closed Sun,
Closed L Mon-Sat **Prices** Fixed D 3 course £38.50-£40,
Service optional **Wines** 93 bottles over £20, 28 bottles
under £20, 6 by glass **Notes** Vegetarian available
Seats 45 **Children** Min 7 yrs **Parking** 10

CARDIFF

CARDIFF — Map 9 ST17

Elements

Modern

**Deft cooking at a popular restaurant and champagne
bar on Cardiff Bay**

☎ 029 2047 0780
Harbour Dr, (off Pierhead Street), Cardiff Bay CF10 4DQ

It's a wise chef who knows not to overwork the ingredients
and it's that restraint which distinguishes the cooking at
this glass-fronted restaurant and champagne bar on the
edge of Cardiff Bay. With contemporary art on the walls
and long, hanging lighting, tables are well spaced and
glass topped with the restaurant's insignia. Fresh local
produce arrives at the table in well-judged and flavourful
combinations. Brunch is served from 8am till 2pm
(American pancakes, boiled eggs and Marmite soldiers,
Welsh rarebit and proscuitto), with a combined grazing
menu and à la carte, and nine-course tasting
extravaganza available in the evening. Roast sea bass
with beetroot, pine nut and dill crème fraîche, or rib-eye
steak accompanied by braised oxtail and horseradish
beignet, are fine examples of the fare.

Times 8/mdnt, Closed Sun, Closed L Sat, Closed D Mon-Tue

First Floor Restaurant

Modern European

**European cooking to match a stylish modern hotel
restaurant**

☎ 0870 122 0020
Mercure Holland House, 24-26 Newport Rd CF24 0DD
e-mail: H6622-am@accor.com
dir: Newport Road 300mtrs from Queen St. Adjacent to
Institute for the Blind and Cardiff University buildings

There's an exciting buzz at this modern tower-block city-
centre hotel, not least in the First Floor restaurant where
there are views over city life through floor-to-ceiling
windows. Expect contemporary styling with bags of natural
light by day and coloured lighting by night casting a glow
on high-quality furnishings (bistro-style seating and
unclothed tables) and an open 'theatre' kitchen. The menu
provides plenty of Welsh produce, given contemporary
appeal with European inspiration; take a loin of Welsh
lamb with anchovy crust and braised shoulder, served with
a white bean purée, confit of baby leeks, butternut squash,
baby fondant potatoes and a rosemary-garlic jus, and to
finish, perhaps a pear and thyme tart partnered by
chocolate and cardamom ice cream.

Owner Accor Hotels **Times** 12-2/6-10, Closed L 1 Jan,
Closed D 25 Dec **Prices** Fixed L 2 course £18, Fixed D 3
course £22, Starter £5.95-£7.50, Main £13.95-£20.95,
Dessert £5.50-£6.95 **Wines** 21 bottles over £20, 16
bottles under £20, 11 by glass **Notes** Sunday L,
Vegetarian available, Civ Wed 700, Air con **Seats** 120, Pr/
dining room 500 **Children** Portions, Menu **Parking** 90

Le Gallois-Y-Cymro

French, European 🖥

Popular culinary venue in Cardiff's Canton district

☎ 029 2034 1264
6-10 Romilly Crescent CF11 9NR
e-mail: info@legallois-ycymro.com
dir: From town centre, follow Cowbridge Rd East. Turn
right to Wyndham Crescent, then to Romilly Crescent.
Restaurant on right

Within walking distance of the castle and the Millennium
Stadium, this popular Franco-Welsh family-run
restaurant is bustling on international rugby days. The
décor is minimalist, with the huge picture windows,
wooden flooring and large mirrors bringing lots of light
into the split-level dining area. The French and Welsh
staff are welcoming and knowledgeable, making it a
friendly and relaxed experience. The menu offers modern
European dishes based on innovative combinations, with
quality ingredients being the guiding factor. Try a starter
of pan-fried duck's liver and mesclun salad with a
flavoursome aged balsamic dressing. Follow with pan-
fried hake served with pomme purée, beurre noisette and
lemon parsley, and for dessert, chocolate marquise and
hazelnut ice cream.

Times 12-2.30/6.30-10.30, Closed Xmas, 1 wk Aug, New
Year, Closed Sun

Gilby's Restaurant

◉◉ Modern European 🖳 V ✪

Converted tithe barn with delightful dining and excellent service

☎ 029 2067 0800
Old Port Rd, Culverhouse Cross CF5 6DN
e-mail: gilbysrestaurant@btconnect.com
web: www.gilbysrestaurant.co.uk
dir: From M4 junct 33 follow signs for Airport/Cardiff West. Take A4050 Barry/Airport road and right at 1st rdbt

On the outskirts of Cardiff and set in an acre of grounds, this converted tithe barn is secluded from the main road and yet is within easy access of the city centre and the Welsh coastline. The dining area, with its stylish décor, exposed beams and pillars, provides a relaxed atmosphere and an open-plan kitchen gives glimpses of the culinary activities within. Service is friendly and the menu of modern European-style cuisine, using quality locally sourced produce, offers accurately cooked dishes with clear and vibrant flavours such as seafood and saffron risotto with parmesan cream, followed by braised shank of Welsh lamb with macédoine of vegetables, Puy lentils and a sticky honey glaze. A vegetarian à la carte menu and good value lunch and early evening menus are also available.

Chef Darren John, Robert Sharp, Kurt Fleming **Owner** Michael Standerline & Xavier Le Bellego **Times** 12-2.30/5.45-10, Closed 26-27 Dec, 1 Jan, Closed D Sun **Prices** Fixed L 2 course £14.95, Fixed D 3 course £19.95-£34.95, Starter £4.95-£12.95, Main £12.95-£42, Dessert £5.95-£6.50, Service optional, Groups min 6 service 10% **Wines** 80 bottles over £20, 18 bottles under £20, 14 by glass **Notes** Sunday L, Vegetarian menu, Civ Wed 50 **Seats** 100 **Children** Min 8 yrs, Portions **Parking** 50

The Laguna Kitchen & Bar

◉ Traditional European ✪

Enjoyable dining in contemporary surroundings

☎ 029 2011 1103
Park Plaza Cardiff, Greyfriars Rd CF10 3AL
e-mail: ppcres@parkplazahotels.co.uk
dir: City centre, next to New Theatre

Laguna is far from your typical hotel restaurant, being a large contemporary space done out in shades of browns and cream with wooden floors, low lighting, unclothed tables, an open-plan kitchen and huge windows affording river views. An impressive wine wall divides the brasserie-style restaurant area from the bar. The extensive menu lists simple snacks alongside skilfully-prepared dishes, but quality, local ingredients bring out vibrant flavours throughout. Choose from old favourites - steaks with a choice of sauces, or fish and chips - or plump for classier fare; your choice might include pan-fried confit of pork belly with Savoy cabbage and hot mustard mash, or Gressingham duck breast with butternut squash, slow-cooked lentils and balsamic.

Chef Mark Freeman **Owner** Martin Morris **Times** 12-2.30/5.30-10.30 **Prices** Fixed L course £15.50, Starter £4.50-£6.95, Main £8-£19.50, Dessert £4.50-£6, Service added but optional 10% **Wines** 44 bottles over £20, 36 bottles under £20, 9 by glass **Notes** Sunday L, Vegetarian available, Civ Wed 140, Air con **Seats** 110, Pr/dining room 150 **Children** Portions, Menu **Parking** NCP

Manor Parc Country Hotel & Restaurant

◉ Modern European

Welcoming hotel serving fresh local fare

☎ 029 2069 3723
Thornhill Rd, Thornhill CF14 9UA
e-mail: enquiry@manorparc.com
dir: A469 Thornhill Road, 200 yds past the crematorium, left hand side

The Manor Parc is a delightful hotel, where traditional values of hospitality and service are upheld. It is set in open countryside just on the outskirts of Cardiff. The orangery-style restaurant, overlooking the grounds, is rather grand and sumptuously decorated. Dishes from the fixed-price menu might include tian of fresh crab and smoked salmon with lemon and dill mayonnaise; and shank of Welsh lamb, slowly braised with rosemary, and

served with a leek and parsnip mash and port jus. To finish, take your choice from the dessert trolley.

Chef Mr D Holland, Alun Thomas **Owner** Mr S Salimeni & Mrs E A Salimeni **Times** 12-2/6-9, Closed 26 Dec-2 Jan, Closed D Sun **Prices** Fixed L 2 course £19.50, Fixed D 3 course £19.50-£24, Service optional, Groups min 6 service 10% **Notes** Sunday L, Vegetarian available, Civ Wed 100 **Seats** 70, Pr/dining room 100 **Children** Portions **Parking** 85

The Old Post Office Restaurant

◉ British, European

Modern European dining in a contemporary Welsh conservatory setting

☎ 029 2056 5400
Greenwood Ln, St Fagans CF5 6EL
e-mail: info@theoldpostofficerestaurant.co.uk
dir: A48 E through Cardiff to St Fagans sign. Right at lights, 1.4m, in village turn right into Croft-y-Genau Rd, right into Greenwood Lane

Its days as the village post office may be long gone, but people are still queuing up for the food at this contemporary Welsh restaurant with rooms based on New England style. The conservatory dining room boasts clean lines with high-backed chairs and dark unclothed tables. Staff are friendly but service retains an element of formality. Dishes are modern European in style with distinct French influences. Strong, clear flavours allow best quality ingredients, brought in from near and far, to speak for themselves. Start with local wild rabbit with spinach salad and thyme sauce before a main course of braised pig's cheeks with purple sprouting broccoli and Jerusalem artichokes. Puddings include orange tart with marmalade ice cream and there's a selection of Welsh cheeses.

Chef Simon Kealy **Owner** Simon Kealy, Cressida Slater **Times** 12-3/7-9.30, Closed Xmas, 1st 2 wks Jan, Closed Mon, Closed D Sun **Prices** Fixed L 2 course £11.95, Starter £5.50-£7.95, Main £9.95-£18.50, Dessert £5.50-£7.50, Service optional **Wines** 16 bottles over £20, 18 bottles under £20, 4 by glass **Notes** Sunday L, Vegetarian available, Air con **Seats** 38 **Children** Portions, Menu **Parking** 30

Raglans Restaurant

◉◉ Modern European 🖳

Fine-dining restaurant in a comfortable modern hotel

☎ 029 2059 9100
Copthorne Hotel Cardiff, Copthorne Way, Culverhouse Cross CF5 6DH
e-mail: sales.cardiff@millenniumhotels.co.uk
dir: M4 junct 33 take A4232 (Culverhouse Cross), 4th exit at rdbt (A48), 1st left

This popular modern hotel, situated four miles outside the city centre, within easy access of the airport and motorway, offers views over the nearby lake, which can be enjoyed from its Raglans Restaurant. Décor of stained

Continued

CARDIFF *Continued*

glass, wood panelling and comfortable seating creates a traditional feel, and service is attentive and friendly. The menu of modern European cuisine includes some sophisticated touches with dishes such as roasted monkfish tail with shiitake mushrooms, spiced crab tortellini and aromatic lemongrass nage, followed by smoked dark chocolate and pecan nut brownie with lavender ice cream and candied kumquats.

Chef Daniel James **Owner** Millennium & Copthorne Hotels **Times** 12.30-2/6.30-9.45, Closed 25 Dec **Prices** Starter £6.25-£10.25, Main £12.95-£17.95, Dessert £5.50-£6.95, Service optional **Wines** 33 bottles over £20, 27 bottles under £20, 14 by glass **Notes** Sunday L, Vegetarian available, Dress restrictions, Smart casual, Civ Wed 200, Air con **Seats** 100, Pr/dining room 220 **Children** Portions, Menu **Parking** 225

The Thai House Restaurant

◉ Thai V

First-rate Thai cooking in Cardiff

☎ 029 2038 7404
3-5 Guildford Crescent, Churchill Way CF10 2HJ
e-mail: info@thaihouse.biz
dir: At junct of Newport Rd & Queen St turn left past Queen St station, before lights turn left into Guildford Crescent

Wales's first Thai restaurant has gone from strength to strength for 22 years. Now one of the country's leading Thai eateries, it delivers a lengthy menu of fragrant dishes conjured from a mix of locally sourced Welsh produce and herbs, spices and vegetables flown in from Bangkok. Located in one of the oldest crescents in Cardiff but with a contemporary décor, high standards of hospitality from waiting staff in traditional dress create an expectation of authenticity: expect top-notch cooking from a native-born chef who started out as an apprentice to her mother on a small market stall back home. Expect

dishes like roasted crispy duck with tamarind sauce or hor moak - fillet of cod with broccoli marinated in red curry paste and steamed in banana leaves.

Chef Sujan Klingson **Owner** Noi & Arlene Ramasut **Times** 12-2.30/6-11, Closed Xmas, 1 Jan, Closed Sun **Prices** Fixed D 3 course £23-£38, Starter £4.95-£9.95, Main £8.50-£35, Dessert £4.25-£5.95, Service optional, Groups min 8 service 10% **Wines** 32 bottles over £20, 29 bottles under £20, 16 by glass **Notes** Vegetarian menu, Dress restrictions, Smart casual **Seats** 130, Pr/dining room 20 **Children** Portions **Parking** On street & NCP opposite

Woods Brasserie

◉ Modern European

Honest hearty food in regenerated Cardiff Bay

☎ 029 2049 2400
Pilotage Building, Stuart St, Cardiff Bay CF10 5BW
e-mail: serge@woods-brasserie.com
dir: In heart of Cardiff Bay. M4 junct 33, then towards Cardiff Bay, big stone building on the right

One of the oldest buildings in Cardiff Bay, this former customs and excise office houses this contemporary brasserie. Enormous glass windows enhance the restaurant's sense of light and space, and seating on the patio is great for outdoor dining. There's a strong French influence to the modern European cooking, which appeals to shoppers, business people and tourists alike. Typical dishes include ravioli of salmon and crab with lobster bisque, chargrilled Aberdeen Angus rib-eye steak with turnip and thyme gratin and sauce bordelaise, and prune and Armagnac crème brûlée with shortbread.

Chef Sean Murphy **Owner** Choice Produce **Times** 12-2/5.30-10, Closed 25-26 Dec & 1 Jan, Closed D Sun (Sep-May) **Prices** Fixed L 2 course fr £13.50, Fixed D 3 course fr £35, Starter £4.95-£9.95, Main £9.95-£19.95, Dessert £5.50-£6.95, Service optional, Groups min 6 service 10% **Wines** 35 bottles over £20, 25 bottles under

£20, 20 by glass **Notes** Pre-theatre meals available, Sunday L, Air con **Seats** 90, Pr/dining room 40 **Children** Portions, Menu **Parking** Multi-storey car park opposite

CARMARTHENSHIRE

LAUGHARNE
Map 8 SN31

The Cors Restaurant

◉◉ Modern

Great food in a quirky former vicarage

☎ 01994 427219
Newbridge Rd SA33 4SH
e-mail: nickpriestland@hotmail.com
web: www.the-cors.co.uk
dir: From Carmarthen follow A40, turn left at St Clears & 4m to Laugharne

Hidden from the main street behind exotically landscaped grounds, this intimate restaurant is located within a former Victorian vicarage in the village made famous by Dylan Thomas. Once simply a bog ('cors' in Welsh), the glorious garden now provides a delightful setting with ponds and modern sculptures. The unremarkable exterior doesn't prepare first-time visitors for what's inside, however. With no credit cards, no printed menus and walls painted with bold colours, the place exudes an air of Bohemian splendour, with Modernist paintings placed alongside antiques to create a quirky, eclectic feel. The

kitchen makes fine use of produce from the region: smoked haddock crème brûlée perhaps, accompanied by excellent home-made bread, or tournedos of organic Pembrokeshire beef fillet with a gratin of wild mushrooms and red wine jus.

Times Closed Sun-Wed, 25 Dec

see advert opposite

LLANDEILO · Map 8 SN62

The Angel Salem

◉◉ Modern

Enjoyable dining in the Carmarthenshire countryside

☎ 01558 823394
Salem SA19 7LY
dir: Please telephone for directions or see website.

This welcoming Welsh inn, set in lovely rural surroundings, has much to make a visit worthwhile. Large comfortable sofas and a mix of modern and antique furniture all help to create a homely atmosphere, and service is relaxed and friendly. A regularly-changing menu and lunchtime blackboard specials offer contemporary dishes with classical influences, prepared carefully with good technical skills. Fresh, local produce is used wherever possible and everything, including the breads and ice cream, is home made. Starters might include Swansea Bay mussels with basil pesto cream, followed by main courses such as duo of Welsh beef with celeriac, pancetta and béarnaise sauce, or roast cannon of lamb with sweet minted aubergine.

Chef Rod Peterson **Owner** Rod Peterson & Liz Smith **Times** 12-3/7-9, Closed 2 wks in Jan, Closed Mon (ex BHs), Closed L Tues, Closed D Sun **Prices** Starter £4.25-£7.50, Main £10.95-£19.95, Dessert £5.25-£7.95, Service optional **Wines** 18 bottles over £20, 21 bottles under £20, 5 by glass **Notes** Sunday L, Vegetarian available **Seats** 70 **Children** Portions **Parking** 25

The Plough Inn

◉ Modern Welsh

☎ 01558 823431
Rhosmaen SA19 6NP

This establishment was awarded its Rosette/s just as we went to press. Therefore we are unable to provide a description for it - visit www.theAA.com for the most up-to-date information.

Prices Food prices not confirmed for 2009. Please telephone for details.

LLANELLI · Map 8 SN50

Fairyhill Bar & Brasserie

◉ Modern ✿

Modern brasserie and views over the estuary

☎ 01554 744994
Machynys Golf Club, Nicklaus Av SA15 2DG
e-mail: machynys@fairyhill.net
dir: M4 junct 48 onto A4138 towards Llanelli. Follow signs to Machynys Golf Club

The restaurant is housed in the impressive clubhouse of a Jack Nicklaus-designed golf course on the Machynys Peninsula, from where there are fabulous views over the bay and the course. The atmosphere is relaxed and staff provide efficient, informal service. Everything on the menu is fairly easy on the pocket, with local produce and specialities to the fore. A wide range of good, hearty dishes takes in salads, vegetarian dishes and snacks, while typical mains might include Machynys fishcakes with tartare sauce and steamed greens, or braised Welsh lamb shank with parsley mash and red wine sauce.

Chef Nick Jones **Owner** Paul Davies, Andrew Hetherington **Times** 12-3/6-10, Closed 25 Dec **Prices** Starter £3.55-£6.55, Main £9.95-£16.95, Dessert £3.65-£5.65, Service included **Wines** 12 bottles over £20, 18 bottles under £20, 4 by glass **Notes** Sunday L, Vegetarian available **Seats** 70, Pr/dining room 125 **Children** Min 5 yrs, Portions **Parking** 100

NANTGAREDIG · Map 8 SN42

Y Polyn

◉◉ Modern British ✿

A simple, unpretentious regional restaurant of distinction

☎ 01267 290000
SA32 7LH
e-mail: ypolyn@hotmail.com
dir: Follow brown tourist signs to National Botanic Gardens, Y Polyn is signed from rdbt in front of gardens

Located in tranquil countryside a few miles outside Carmarthen, Y Polyn is a cosy bar and restaurant with a serious approach to food, and a setting which oozes rustic, unpretentious charm. Think shabby chic, with solid farmhouse-style tables and a miscellany of comfy chairs set on quarry-tiled floors and sisal-style carpet runners, and dark terracotta painted walls hung with paintings by local artists and menus from renowned restaurants. Service is very personable, suitably relaxed but efficient. The kitchen delivers modern, British-themed bistro-style fare using the best local produce. Dishes and flavours are clean cut and unfussy, with the main ingredient allowed to shine; think fish soup with rouille, croûtons and gruyère cheese, followed by roast rump of salt marsh lamb with onion, garlic and thyme purée.

Chef Susan Manson, Maryann Wright **Owner** Mark & Susan Manson, Simon & Maryann Wright **Times** 12-2/7-9, Closed Mon, Closed D Sun **Prices** Fixed D 3 course

---

£27.50, Starter £4-£7.50, Main £8.50-£15, Dessert £5.50, Service optional **Wines** 20 bottles over £20, 31 bottles under £20, 7 by glass **Notes** Sunday L, Vegetarian available **Seats** 40 **Children** Portions **Parking** 25

CEREDIGION

ABERAERON · Map 8 SN46

Harbourmaster Aberaeron

◉ Modern Welsh ✿

Enjoyable Welsh cuisine in an historic harbourside hotel

☎ 01545 570755
Pen Cei SA46 0BA
e-mail: info@harbour-master.com
dir: A487 coastal road, once in town follow signs for tourist information centre. Restaurant next door on the harbourside.

Located right on the harbour, this Grade II listed building was previously the harbourmaster's house. It has been sympathetically updated and benefits from a dramatic quayside location. Eat at the bar tables or in the bright, airy brasserie with its ships' chandlery décor and magnificent spiral staircase. Relaxed, bilingual service delivers modern Welsh dishes based on local produce to eager diners. Start with the smoked haddock and cockle chowder before a main course of venison hash with warm kale and beetroot salad, or pan-fried fillet of Gower sea bass with skinny fries and hollandaise. Try some excellent Welsh cheeses to finish.

Chef Stephen Evans **Owner** Glyn & Menna Hevlyn **Times** 12-2.30/6-9, Closed 25 Dec, Closed L Mon **Prices** Starter £4.50-£8.50, Main £12.50-£19.50, Dessert £5.50, Service optional, Groups min 8 service 10% **Wines** 30 bottles over £20, 30 bottles under £20, 12 by glass **Notes** Sunday L, Vegetarian available **Seats** 40 **Children** Portions **Parking** 8

Ty Mawr Mansion

◉◉ Modern British, Welsh ✿

Peaceful, relaxed country-house dining showcasing quality local produce

☎ 01570 470033
Cilcennin SA48 8DB
e-mail: info@tymawrmansion.co.uk
dir: 4m from Aberaeron on A482 to Lampeter road

Offering its guests a very personal and friendly welcome, this Grade II listed mansion in 12 acres of countryside

Continued

ABERAERON *Continued*

grounds, just a few miles from Wales's heritage coastline, has been carefully renovated with rich fabrics and sumptuous furnishings. There's a choice of three lounges for aperitifs while the restaurant comes smartly decked out in period colours that coordinate with furniture, pictures and prints. Expect top-notch cooking from the imaginative kitchen team who work hard to deliver a menu of classic dishes enlivened by a contemporary Welsh twist. Cardigan Bay seafood chowder with a crab beignet is a typical starter, while mains might include pan-fried cannon of lamb with a rosemary butter crust, boulangère potatoes and a red wine jus.

Chef Jeremy Hywel Jones **Owner** Martin & Catherine McAlpine **Times** Closed 26 Dec-7 Jan, Closed Sun, Closed L all week **Prices** Fixed D 3 course £29.95-£32.95, Starter £6.95-£10.95, Main £17.95-£24.95, Dessert £6.95-£9.95, Service optional **Wines** 23 bottles over £20, 13 bottles under £20, 6 by glass **Notes** Vegetarian available, Dress restrictions, Smart casual **Seats** 35, Pr/dining room 12 **Children** Min 12 yrs **Parking** 20

ABERPORTH	Map 8 SN25

The Penrallt

◎ Modern British

Fine cuisine in a country-house setting

☎ 01239 810227 & 810927
SA43 2BS
e-mail: info@hotelpenrallt.co.uk
dir: From Carmarthen take A484 to Cardigan, take A487 towards Aberystwyth. Continue for 6m then take left to Aberporth on B4333. Hotel 200yds on right

Peacefully set in 42 acres of grounds, this one-time Edwardian mansion turned country-house hotel (with self-catering cottages) has been recently refurbished and overlooks Aberporth Bay. Its elegant Bay Restaurant presents a traditional face, with a magnificent ornately beamed ceiling and matching wood panelling, while a fireplace and plum-coloured walls catch the eye too. The kitchen's modern British approach deals in fresh local ingredients, with dishes not over-worked to deliver clean flavours; take flambé medallions of Welsh beef fillet served with garlic mash, sweet 'n' sour shallots, turned courgettes and pan jus. Full-length doors from the Bay dining room open onto a conservatory area, and there's also a terrace bar with separate, more informal menu.

Times Closed D Sun

ABERYSTWYTH	Map 8 SN58

Conrah Hotel

◎◎ Modern French

Innovative food at a refurbished country hotel

☎ 01970 617941
Ffosrhydygaled, Chancery SY23 4DF
e-mail: enquiries@conrah.co.uk
dir: On A487, 3m S of Aberystwyth, between Llanfarian & Blaenpluf

Standing in 22 acres of mature grounds, this privately owned country-house hotel has undergone extensive refurbishment while losing none of its Georgian charm and character. The elegant public areas include a choice of comfortable lounges with inviting open fires, and the combination of country-house comforts, quality décor and furnishings and wonderful views of the Ystwyth Valley is a winning one. Harry's Restaurant is the stylish setting for uncomplicated, modern British fare that relies extensively on Welsh produce including much grown in the hotel's own garden. Try a starter of Welsh cheese frittata with tomato and basil salad, followed by Welsh beef medallion with cocotte potatoes, celeriac purée and Madeira jus. Service is very professional and attentive.

Times 12-2/7-9, Closed 26-28 Dec, Closed D 25 Dec

Ynyshir Hall

EGLWYSFACH	Map 14 SN69

Modern British 🏆 🍴

Adventurous and stunning country-house cuisine

☎ 01654 781209
SY20 8TA
e-mail: ynyshir@relaischateaux.com
dir: On A487, 6m S of Machynlleth

This charming, white-painted Tudor manor house hideaway, set in 14 acres of glorious gardens amid the splendour of the Dovey estuary and once owned by Queen Victoria as a shooting lodge, offers one of Wales' great gastronomic and country-house experiences. The original 1,000-acre estate that surrounds the hotel is now an RSPB reserve, while Ynyshir's gardens are ablaze with azaleas and rhododendrons in spring, and the drive is flanked by sequoia and Wellingtonia trees. An intimate

retreat of high quality, though there's a modern twist on the country-house theme here, with a bold and vibrant colour scheme and walls adorned with bright canvasses. The restaurant is the epitome of a country-house dining room, small and decked out with crisp linen and comfortable high-backed chairs, while offering views over the garden. Head chef Shane Hughes' cooking oozes pedigree, his modern approach underpinned by classical French technique and driven by high quality seasonal Welsh produce, including herbs and vegetables from Ynyshir's walled garden. His innovative, creative, sharp cooking allows flavours to shine in dishes like braised pork ballotine served with Cardigan Bay lobster and a wild garlic and spiced aromatic consommé, or monkfish and mushroom tortellini with butternut squash, lemon and chervil, and to finish, perhaps a wild berry soufflé accompanied by bay leaf ice cream.

Chef Shane Hughes **Owner** von Essen Hotels, Rob & Joan Reen **Times** 12.30-1.30/7-8.45, Closed Jan **Prices** Fixed L 2 course fr £25, Fixed D 4 course fr £65, Tasting menu £65-£75, Service optional **Wines** 250 bottles over £20, 5 bottles under £20, 14 by glass **Notes** Sunday L, Vegetarian available, Dress restrictions, No jeans, beachwear or shorts, Civ Wed 40 **Seats** 30, Pr/dining room 16 **Children** Min 9 yrs **Parking** 15

DEVIL'S BRIDGE

The Hafod Hotel

◉ Modern Welsh

Local produce cooked with flair in former hunting lodge

☎ 01970 890232
SY23 3JL
e-mail: hafodhotel@btconnect.com

This former hunting lodge overlooking the renowned Devil's Bridge beauty spot dates back to the 17th century and is set in 6 acres of grounds. Now a family-owned and run hotel, it offers fine dining at well-spaced tables and ladder-back chairs backed by attentive, friendly service. The accomplished kitchen's modern approach is driven by fresh seasonal produce from the abundant local Welsh larder on daily-changing menus delivered with flair. Take a rosette of local Welsh lamb served with fondant potato, swede purée, braised red cabbage and a tarragon jus, and to finish, perhaps a blueberry and almond tart with vanilla ice cream.

EGLWYSFACH   Map 14 SN69

Ynyshir Hall

◉◉◉ – *see opposite*

LAMPETER   Map 8 SN54

Valley Restaurant at the Falcondale Mansion

◉◉ Modern British V ☕

Mansion house offering fine dining with great views

☎ 01570 422910
Best Western Falcondale Mansion, Falcondale Drive SA48 7RX
e-mail: info@falcondalehotel.com
dir: 1m from Lampeter take A482 to Cardigan, turn right at petrol station, follow for 0.75m

Surrounded by rare varieties of exotic and native trees and shrubs in 14 acres of gardens and parkland, this charming Victorian mansion was originally the country residence of the Harford family, founders of the NatWest bank. Built in the Italianate style, it is now transformed into a country hotel. Peterwells Brasserie offers informal dining, while the candlelit Valley Restaurant is the main act with its fine views and daily-changing menu of classical dishes with a modern edge, using the best of local produce. Expect home-cured gravadlax with king prawns and sweet mustard dressing, followed by Celtic Pride fillet steak with dauphinoise potatoes, beef samosa and wild mushroom and basil sauce. To finish, an indulgent sticky ginger pudding with lime sauce and vanilla ice cream might catch the eye.

Chef Michael Green **Owner** Chris & Lisa Hutton
Times 12-2/6.30-10 **Prices** Fixed L 2 course fr £9.95, Fixed D 4 course fr £34, Starter £5-£10, Main £12-£20, Dessert £5.50-£8, Service optional, Groups min 10

service 10% **Wines** 18 bottles over £20, 24 bottles under £20, 12 by glass **Notes** Sunday L, Vegetarian menu, Dress restrictions, Smart casual, no shorts, Civ Wed 60 **Seats** 36, Pr/dining room 20 **Children** Portions **Parking** 60

CONWY

ABERGELE   Map 14 SH97

The Kinmel Arms

◉ Modern Welsh

Popular gastro-pub serving regional produce

☎ 01745 832207
The Village, St George LL22 9BP
e-mail: info@thekinmelarms.co.uk

Set in the beautiful Elwy valley, light open-plan spaces have been created by the conversion of this 17th-century inn. Featuring oak floors, a conservatory with marble tables and a central slate-topped bar with a stained glass header, mountain photography and paintings by the owner adorn the walls, reflecting an interest in climbing and travel. The food is well balanced and presented, based on local ingredients, and offered alongside a good wine selection and real ales. With daily fish specials, recommendations include Conwy crab and salmon cake with crunchy Asiatic salad and mango salsa, or rump of spring organic Welsh lamb with a timbale of chargrilled Mediterranean vegetables.

Times 12-2/6.30-9.30, Closed 25 Dec, 1-2 Jan, Closed Mon, Closed D Sun

BETWS-Y-COED   Map 14 SH75

Craig-y-Dderwen Riverside Hotel & Restaurant

◉ Traditional, International ☕

Relaxing country-house dining in picturesque Snowdonian surroundings

☎ 01690 710293
LL24 0AS
e-mail: info@snowdoniahotel.com
dir: On A5 near Waterloo Bridge

Surrounded by dramatic wooded slopes and set in 16 acres of well-tended grounds, this Victorian country-house hotel offers a tranquil and relaxing atmosphere. Overlooking the river Conwy, the formal restaurant provides expertly prepared dishes with an emphasis on seasonal local ingredients, including produce from their own kitchen garden. To start, try seared tartar of Ynys Mon pigeon set on corn bread with a port and redcurrant sauce, followed by fillet of Tremeirchion trout with Welsh goats' cheese wrapped in Carmarthen ham, and for a fitting finale perhaps try Welsh cake and honeycomb millefeuille. There is also a substantial wine list with helpful tasting notes.

Chef Paul Goosey **Owner** Martin Carpenter
Times 12-2.30/6.30-9.30, Closed 25 Dec, 2 Jan-1 Feb,

Closed L Mon-Fri **Prices** Starter £4.95-£7.50, Main £12.95-£18.75, Dessert £4.25-£6.95, Service optional **Wines** 18 bottles over £20, 40 bottles under £20, 2 by glass **Notes** Sunday L, Vegetarian available, Dress restrictions, Smart casual, Civ Wed 50 **Seats** 82, Pr/dining room 40 **Children** Portions, Menu **Parking** 50

Llugwy Restaurant

◉ Modern British, Welsh ☕

Former coaching inn with quality Welsh cuisine

☎ 01690 710219
Royal Oak Hotel, Holyhead Rd LL24 0AY
e-mail: royaloakmail@btopenworld.com
web: www.royaloakhotel.net
dir: Situated on A5 trunk road

Located in the picturesque village of Betws-y-Coed, in the midst of Snowdonia National Park, this former coaching inn once housed a 19th-century artists' colony led by renowned painter David Cox. Inside this popular hotel, mountain trekkers mingle with hotel guests in the modern bistro and through the comfortable bar, the more formal Llugwy restaurant awaits with white linen-clad tables and an ornate plaster ceiling. Service is helpful and the menu of modern Welsh cuisine with global influences includes starters like confit of local wild rabbit on vanilla pod risotto with port wine reduction, followed by lightly pan-fried fillet of Anglesey halibut with a vegetable broth of Menai mussels and herbs.

Chef Dylan Edwards **Owner** Royal Oak Hotel Ltd
Times 12-3/6.30-9, Closed 25-26 Dec, Closed Mon-Tue, Closed L Wed-Sat, Closed D Sun **Prices** Fixed L 2 course fr £11.95, Fixed D 4 course £25-£29.50, Starter £4.95-£7.85, Main £12.95-£18.95, Dessert £4.95-£8.50, Service optional **Wines** 16 bottles over £20, 40 bottles under £20, 11 by glass **Notes** Welsh tasting menu available 4-5 courses, Sunday L, Vegetarian available, Dress restrictions, Smart casual, no jeans, shorts or T-shirts, Civ Wed 85 **Seats** 60, Pr/dining room 20 **Children** Portions, Menu **Parking** 100

BETWS-Y-COED *Continued*

Tan-y-Foel Country House

⊛⊛⊛ – *see below*

CONWY	Map 14 SH77

Dawsons @ The Castle Hotel Conwy

⊛⊛ Modern British ☺

Welsh produce and solid cooking in landmark building

☎ 01492 582800
High St LL32 8DB
e-mail: mail@castlewales.co.uk
dir: From A55 junct 18 towards town centre. Follow signs for town centre and continue on one-way system. Hotel halfway up High St

Nestling within the walls of the Unesco World Heritage town of Conwy, with its imposing 13th-century castle, this family-run coaching inn is one of the town's most distinguished buildings. A popular modern bar offers light meals, but the recently refurbished and renamed Dawsons is the main event, a fine-dining restaurant that takes its name from the distinguished Victorian artist John Dawson-Watson who designed the impressive frontage of the hotel. Local Welsh produce is the driving force behind the lengthy carte of modern British dishes. Expect the likes of Conwy Valley lamb hot pot with bacon and tarragon dumplings or whole North Wales coast sea bass on grilled fennel with baby roast potatoes and a tomato, olive and caper sauce.

Dawsons @ The Castle Hotel Conwy

Chef Graham Tinsley **Owner** Lavin Family & Graham Tinsley **Times** 12/10, Closed 26 Dec **Prices** Fixed L 2 course fr £15, Fixed D 3 course fr £22.50, Starter £4.75-£6.95, Main £10.25-£15.95, Dessert £5.95, Service added but optional 10% **Wines** 12 bottles over £20, 24 bottles under £20, 12 by glass **Notes** Sunday L, Vegetarian available **Seats** 70 **Children** Portions, Menu **Parking** 36

The Groes Inn

⊛ Traditional British ☺

Honest, wholesome food in a characterful inn

☎ 01492 650545
Tyn-y-Groes LL32 8TN
e-mail: reception@groesinn.com
web: www.groesinn.com
dir: On B5106, 3m from Conwy

This ancient inn, said to be the first establishment to be granted a licence in Wales (in 1573), oozes charm and character. Its cosy warren of nooks and crannies preserves an authentic sense of history. A warm welcome is part of the attraction, enhanced by a beautiful restaurant with a conservatory extending into the garden with stunning mountain views. Fresh seasonal ingredients, creatively handled, make for an irresistible choice. Look out for Bryn Dowsi lamb, pheasant and game from nearby estates, as well as Conwy crab

Tan-y-Foel Country House

BETWS-Y-COED	Map 14 SH75

Modern British

Gourmet sanctuary in Snowdonia

☎ 01690 710507
Capel Garmon LL26 0RE
e-mail: enquiries@tyfhotel.co.uk
dir: A5 onto A470; 2m N towards Llanrwst, then turning for Capel Garmon. Country House on left 1m before village

Perched in the hills above the pretty village of Betws-y-Coed, this family-run hotel offers stunning views of the Conwy valley. Its unassuming 17th-century façade conceals a chic and sophisticated interior which blends country-house comfort with minimalist modern design in a series of intimate and individual rooms, including a cosy restaurant which seats only a dozen diners at a time. Daughter Kelly and husband Peter serve, while mum Janet (Pitman) conjures up some of the finest cuisine in Wales, intelligently allowing quality local organic produce to speak for itself in accomplished, well presented and executed dishes. The short, fixed-price dinner menu changes daily and features a choice of two dishes at each course, with wine recommendations accompanying mains. Take a loin of Cambrian Hills lamb served with parsnip pomme purée, sautéed red onions, balsamic reduction and roasted hazelnut oil, while at dessert, a panettone bread-and-butter pudding might offer an agony of choice alongside poached fresh fig with Welsh goat's cheese lemon cream and Merlot syrup.
Tan-y-Foel Country House is AA Guest Accommodation of the Year for Wales

Chef Janet Pitman **Owner** Mr & Mrs P Pitman **Times** Closed Dec-Jan, Closed Mon, Closed L all week **Prices** Fixed D 3 course £42, Service optional **Wines** 81 bottles over £20, 7 by glass **Notes** Dress restrictions, No jeans, trainers, tracksuits, walking boots **Seats** 12 **Children** Min 12 yrs **Parking** 14

and plaice, wild salmon, oysters and mussels from nearby waters. For mains, expect the likes of lamb steak slowly baked with capers and garlic, followed by orange and Cointreau bread-and-butter pudding.

Chef Ray Jones **Owner** Dawn & Justin Humphreys **Times** 12-2.15/6.30-9, Closed 25 Dec **Prices** Fixed D 4 course £28, Starter £4.50-£7.50, Main £8.50-£17.50, Dessert £5.10-£6.95, Service optional, Groups min 8 service 10% **Wines** 10 by glass **Notes** Sunday L, Vegetarian available, Dress restrictions, Smart casual **Seats** 54, Pr/dining room 20 **Children** Min 12 yrs **Parking** 100

Sychnant Pass House

◉ Modern British

Country house in peaceful setting with good British cooking

☎ 01492 596868

Sychnant Pass Rd LL32 8BJ
e-mail: bre@sychnant-pass-house.co.uk
dir: Travel past Visitors Centre in Conwy, take 2nd left into Uppergate St. Continue up hill for 2m, restaurant on right

Surrounded by large trees and situated in the foothills of the Snowdonia National Park, this recently refurbished family-run country house hotel built in 1890 has good facilities including a smart swimming pool and a restaurant which prides itself on delivering freshly cooked modern British food. The hotel is traditionally and stylishly furnished while the attractive dining room has a relaxed and informal feel with wooden tables, slate place mats and a large marble fireplace. The fixed-price menu offers good choice at each course. Goat's cheese and endive salad starter and sorbet precede main-course cannon of Welsh lamb with creamy mashed potato and a light peppercorn sauce.

Times 12.30-2.30/7-9, Closed Xmas & Jan, Closed L Mon-Sat

DEGANWY — Map 14 SH77

The Vue

◉◉ Modern British ▣ V

Panoramic views, contemporary surrounds and innovative food

☎ 01492 564100

Quay Hotel & Spa, Deganwy Quay LL31 9DJ
e-mail: info@quayhotel.com
dir: From S, M6 junct 20 signed North Wales/Chester, From N, M56 onto A5117 then A494. Continue on A55 to junct 18 (Conwy). Continue straight over 2 rdbts, at lights turn left over railway crossing, right at mini rdbt, hotel is on right.

With chic, large airy spaces and clever use of light, this sophisticated hotel enjoys stunning views over rolling hills and the beautiful Conwy estuary and castle. With the Quay's first-floor restaurant and cocktail bar - aptly called The Vue - continuing the contemporary approach,

its two dining areas separated by cleverly lit glass partitions that bring the nautical theme indoors. It's an informal, brasserie-style experience, backed by relaxed and friendly service. The cooking is suitably modern too, focusing on quality local produce; take a trio of Welsh lamb, fondant potato with creamed cabbage and parsnip purée, or roast halibut with herb crust and buttered prawns.

Chef Jimmy Williams **Owner** Alan Waldron **Times** 12-2/6.30-9.30 **Wines** 76 bottles over £20, 18 bottles under £20, 19 by glass **Notes** Gourem menu £45-£55, Sunday L, Vegetarian menu, Civ Wed 120, Air con **Seats** 120, Pr/dining room 100 **Children** Portions, Menu **Parking** 120

LLANDUDNO — Map 14 SH78

Bodysgallen Hall and Spa

◉◉◉ — **see page 556**

Empire Hotel

◉ Modern British ▣

Family-run hotel restaurant offering seasonal cuisine

☎ 01492 860555

Church Walks LL30 2HE
e-mail: reservations@empirehotel.co.uk
web: www.empirehotel.co.uk
dir: From Chester take A55 junct 19, then follow signs towards Llandudno. Follow signs to town centre, head through town centre to Millennium rdbt, take 2nd exit, hotel at end facing main street

The hotel, which occupies an imposing position, dates from 1854 when it was built as the town's first block of shops. It has been run by the Maddocks family for 61 years, assisted by long-serving staff. The elegant restaurant was formerly a wine and spirits merchant's and now showcases traditional cooking of local produce using modern techniques. Recommendations include grilled local sea bass fillet with roasted vegetables, toasted flaked almonds and wild rocket pesto, or tender braised shoulder of Welsh lamb with seasonal root vegetables, mustard mash and rosemary-scented port jus.

Empire Hotel

Chef Michael Waddy, Larry Mutisyo **Owner** Len & Elizabeth Maddocks **Times** 12.30-2/6.45-9.30, Closed 20-30 Dec, Closed L Mon-Sat **Prices** Fixed D 4 course £19.95-£22.50, Service optional **Wines** 39 bottles over £20, 47 bottles under £20, 7 by glass **Notes** Sunday L, Vegetarian available, Dress restrictions, Smart casual, Air con **Seats** 110, Pr/dining room 18 **Children** Portions **Parking** 44

Imperial Hotel

◉ Modern British

Trustworthy cooking with a Welsh bias on the seafront

☎ 01492 877466

The Promenade LL30 1AP
e-mail: reception@theimperial.co.uk
web: www.theimperial.co.uk
dir: On the Promenade

Set back from the promenade, this imposing traditional seaside hotel has a grandiose façade and dominates the Victorian seafront. Interiors are decorated in a more unassuming contemporary style. The modern British menu at the elegant Chantrey's restaurant changes monthly and takes full advantage of seasonal local produce; expect reliable cooking and a range to suit most tastes. Typically, start with Welsh vegetable cawl with herb dumplings, follow with venison casserole in red wine, slow-cooked belly pork with braised trotter, herb gnocchi, charcutiére sauce and parsnip purée, or a steak from the grill, and finish with a passionfruit tart and chocolate sorbet.

Chef Wayne Roberts, Joanne Williams **Owner** Greenclose Ltd **Times** 12.30-3/6.30-9.30 **Prices** Fixed L 3 course £17.50-£25, Fixed D 3 course £25-£35, Service optional **Notes** Sunday L, Vegetarian available, Dress restrictions, Smart casual, Civ Wed 120 **Seats** 150, Pr/dining room 30 **Children** Portions, Menu **Parking** 20

Bodysgallen Hall and Spa

Modern **NOTABLE WINE LIST**

Sumptuous dining in classic country-house setting

☎ 01492 584466
LL30 1RS
e-mail: info@bodysgallen.com
dir: From A55 junct 19 follow A470 towards Llandudno. Hotel 2m on right

Standing in over 200 acres of its own parkland and formal gardens to the south of Llandudno with spectacular views of Snowdonia, Bodysgallen started life as a look-out tower for nearby Conwy Castle. This traditional country-house hotel grew to its current proportions in the 17th century and today still enjoys a wonderful elevated position. There is a comfortable and welcoming foyer-lounge doubling as a bar with two formal yet intimate dining rooms. The well-established service makes this a wonderful dining venue with staff operating like a well-oiled machine. The best of local Welsh produce is competently showcased on the fixed-price menus of modern British dishes. Take a velouté starter of spiced pumpkin with lobster dumplings, sweetbread fritter and curry spice, followed by grilled fillet of sea bass served with caramelised cauliflower roast scallops, sliced truffle and a red wine reduction, and to close, a tonka bean parfait with warm chocolate

madeleines. Ancillaries like canapés, home-made breads, petits fours and an exceptional wine list round off an accomplished package.

Chef Gareth Jones **Owner** Historic House Hotels Ltd **Times** 12.30-1.45/7-9.30 **Prices** Fixed L 2 course fr £19, Fixed D 4 course £43-£47, Service included **Wines** 100 bottles over £20, 30 bottles under £20, 8 by glass **Notes** Pre-theatre D, Sunday L, Vegetarian available, Dress restrictions, Smart casual, no trainers/T-shirts/tracksuits, Civ Wed 55, Air con **Seats** 60, Pr/dining room 40 **Children** Min 6 yrs, Portions **Parking** 40

LLANDUDNO *Continued*

Osborne House

◉ Modern British 🖥

Small luxury hotel with bistro-style food

☎ 01492 860330
17 North Pde LL30 2LP
e-mail: sales@osbornehouse.com
web: www.osbornehouse.co.uk
dir: A55 at junct 19, follow signs for Llandudno then
Promenade, at War Memorial turn right, Osborne House
on left opposite entrance to pier

Opulently restored, this Victorian townhouse overlooks the
seafront at Llandudno and is sumptuously decorated with
rich fabrics, crystal chandeliers and Roman-style pillars
that add a Palladian glamour to the elegant, high-
ceilinged dining room. Helpful, formal service comes from
uniformed staff which, despite the grand surroundings,
manages to feel both personal and pleasantly relaxed.
The bistro-style menu consists largely of modern cuisine,
using local ingredients wherever possible. Typically, order
Menai mussels in white wine and garlic sauce to start,
follow with pan-roasted calves' liver and bacon with
mushroom and onion gravy, and finish with baked
Bramley apple tart with custard.

Chef Michael Waddy & Rob Parry **Owner** Len & Elizabeth
Maddocks **Times** 12-4/5-10, Closed 20-31 Dec **Wines** 17
bottles over £20, 24 bottles under £20, 6 by glass
Notes Pre-theatre menu 5pm £17.95, Sunday L,
Vegetarian available, Dress restrictions, Smart casual,
Air con **Seats** 70, Pr/dining room 18 **Children** Portions
Parking 6

St George's Hotel

◉ Modern, Traditional 🕙

Refined seaside dining in luxurious surroundings

☎ 01492 877544 & 862184
The Promenade LL30 2LG
e-mail: info@stgeorgeswales.co.uk
dir: A55 exit at Glan Conwy for Llandudno. A470 follow
signs for seafront, look out for distinctive tower to locate
hotel

An elegant Victorian property overlooking Llandudno Bay,
this impressive hotel offers two eating options, the
contemporary-style Terrace restaurant with sea views,
and the magnificent Wedgwood Room, with ornate
Jasper-style décor. Both serve the same menu and every
dish highlights the qualities of fresh local produce. For a
great combination of flavours try gratinated leek and
stilton tart with mizuna, sunblushed tomato and pine
nuts to start, followed by pink and succulent calves' liver
on creamy mash with pan-fried shallots and robust red
wine jus, and for a perfect finale pannacotta with home-
made pistachio ice cream.

Chef Danny Mountain **Owner** Anderbury Ltd **Prices** Fixed
L 2 course £10-£15, Fixed D 3 course £20-£30, Starter
£4-£7, Main £9-£18, Dessert £4-£7, Service optional
Wines 18 bottles over £20, 32 bottles under £20, 10 by
glass **Notes** Pre-theatre menu, market choice ALC,
Sunday L, Vegetarian available, Dress restrictions, Smart
casual, Civ Wed 150, Air con **Seats** 110, Pr/dining room
12 **Children** Portions, Menu **Parking** 36

St Tudno Hotel and Restaurant

◉◉ Modern British

**Accomplished cuisine in elegant surroundings by
the sea**

☎ 01492 874411
The Promenade LL30 2LP
e-mail: sttudnohotel@btinternet.com
dir: Town centre, on Promenade opposite the pier
entrance (near the Great Orme)

This elegant, family-owned hotel enjoys fine sea views
and caters to a genteel clientele. Perched on the seafront
opposite the Victorian pier, it offers classical cuisine and
a magnificent afternoon tea. Ornate columns and arches
provide glimpses of Lake Como - in mural form - prettily
complemented by imposing Italian chandeliers and a
working fountain. Quality ingredients are brought
together in intriguing combinations to form an appealing

St Tudno Hotel and Restaurant

modern seasonal carte, plus a list of daily specials.
Expect starters like Stinking Bishop cheese soufflé with
celery sorbet, walnuts and crème fraîche, followed by
slow-poached baby halibut with haricot blanc, fennel
chardonnay and Pacific oysters, while white chocolate
and plum parfait with iced vanilla and chocolate makes
a superb dessert.

Times 12.30-1.45/7-9.30

DENBIGHSHIRE

LLANDRILLO Map 15 SJ03

Tyddyn Llan

◉◉ Modern British V 🏅 NOTABLE WINE LIST

Relaxed and stylish North Wales dining destination

☎ 01490 440264
LL21 0ST
e-mail: tyddynllan@compuserve.com
dir: Take B4401 from Corwen to Llandrillo. Restaurant on
right leaving village

A small, elegant Georgian house that was once a
shooting lodge for the Duke of Westminster is the setting
for this stylish restaurant with rooms, in a peaceful
corner of North Wales. Comfortable, thoughtfully
furnished bedrooms with restful views of the gardens and
Berwyn Mountains beyond provide the perfect excuse to
stay over, and the relaxing lounges come complete with
roaring log fires. The dining room enjoys particularly
attractive views over the gardens, and there's a terrace
for alfresco dining. The emphasis is on quality local
produce with the chef-proprietor offering a daily-
changing repertoire to reflect availability, with a tasting
option bolstering the choice. Expect the likes of roast
turbot with leek risotto and red wine sauce, or maybe
excellent roast breast of Gressingham duck with potato
pancake, apple and cider. Service is informal and

Continued

LLANDRILLO *Continued*

efficient, and an impressive wine list rounds things off in fine style.

Chef Bryan Webb **Owner** Bryan & Susan Webb **Times** 12.30-2.30/7-9.30, Closed 3 wks Jan/Feb, Closed L Mon-Thu **Prices** Fixed L 2 course fr £21.50, Fixed D 3 course fr £45, Tasting menu £60 **Wines** 184 bottles over £20, 24 bottles under £20, 16 by glass **Notes** Sunday L, Vegetarian menu, Civ Wed 40 **Seats** 40, Pr/dining room 40 **Children** Portions, Menu **Parking** 20

Barratt's at Ty'n Rhyl

@@ British, French

Historic house serving imaginative food

☎ 01745 344138 & 0773 095 4994
Ty'n Rhyl, 167 Vale Rd LL18 2PH
e-mail: EBarratt@aol.com
dir: From A55 take Rhyl exit onto A525. Continue past Rhuddlan Castle, supermarket, petrol station, 0.25 on right

A family-run establishment, this stone-built 16th-century property is set well back from the road surrounded by mature gardens. Bard Angharad Llwyd once lived here and the house - the oldest in Rhyl - is full of charm with oak panelling, comfortable sofas and a separate bar. The soft lemon-coloured restaurant is country house in style with original wooden floors, well-spaced tables and crisp linen. The daily-changing menu utilises local ingredients and reflects the seasons with well-balanced dishes and classic sauces. Good examples are crab and dill cakes with spinach for starters, followed by the likes of pigeon breast with a blackcurrant and fennel sauce, or fillet of Welsh Black beef with caramelised onion and truffle-flavoured jus. For dessert, why not try creamed rhubarb tart with red wine ice cream, or perhaps passionfruit crème brûlée.

Times 12-2.30/7.30-9, Closed 26 Dec, Closed 1 wk for holiday

Bertie's @ Ruthin Castle

@ Modern European

Upmarket modern cooking in historic surroundings

☎ 01824 702664
Castle St LL15 2NU
e-mail: reservations@ruthincastle.co.uk
web: www.ruthincastle.co.uk
dir: From Ruthin town square take road to Corwen for 100 yds

This impressive castle dates from the 13th century, but most of what you see today was built in the early 19th century. It makes the perfect setting for a luxury hotel, complete with ghostly grey lady strolling the battlements. Elegant public rooms include a bar, medieval banqueting hall and a wood-panelled restaurant with five chandeliers. Making the most of local ingredients are dishes such as duo of scallops with sweetcorn purée and truffle emulsion, trio of Conwy lamb with fondant potato and red wine jus, and classic lemon tart with raspberry soufflé.

Chef Phillip Ashe **Owner** Mr & Mrs Saint Claire **Times** 12.30-2/7-9.30, Closed L Sat **Prices** Food prices not confirmed for 2009. Please telephone for details. **Wines** 60 bottles over £20, 30 bottles under £20, 12 by glass **Notes** Sunday L, Vegetarian available, Dress restrictions, Smart casual, Civ Wed 120 **Seats** 60, Pr/dining room 26 **Children** Portions, Menu **Parking** 120

The Wynnstay Arms

@@ Traditional, International

Popular town-centre brasserie in former coaching inn

☎ 01824 703147
Well St LL15 1AN
e-mail: reservations@wynnstayarms.wanadoo.co.uk
web: www.wynnstayarms.com
dir: Please telephone for directions

Once a secret Jacobite meeting place, this former coaching inn was established in 1549. Extensive renovation has transformed it into a smart restaurant with rooms with quality accommodation, an attractive café-bar and contemporary Fusions Brasserie. Here service is friendly and informal, but always professional. Local ingredients, including Welsh lamb and Black beef, are used to produce well-flavoured dishes, often quite lightly sauced so as not to mask the main item. Typical of the style are pan-fried pigeon breast with aubergine

pickle, sea bass fillets with seared scallop and saffron cream, or spinach and goats' cheese tagliatelle with tomato salsa.

Chef Jason Jones **Owner** Jason & Eirian Jones, Kelvin & Gaye Clayton **Times** 12-2/6-9.30, Closed Mon **Prices** Fixed D 3 course £17.95-£23.50, Starter £4.25-£7, Main £15.50-£23.50, Dessert £4.50-£5.50, Service optional **Wines** 6 bottles over £20, 31 bottles under £20, 6 by glass **Notes** Sunday L, Vegetarian available **Seats** 40 **Children** Portions **Parking** 12

The Oriel Country Hotel & Spa

@ Modern British

Formal dining in fabulous surroundings

☎ 01745 582716
Upper Denbigh Rd LL17 0LW
e-mail: reservations@orielhousehotel.com
dir: Please telephone for directions

Originally built as a gentleman's residence in the 1760s, the Oriel became a boys' school which closed its doors in the 1970s when it was converted into a hotel. Since changing hands in 1998, the hotel has been refurbished and given a new lease of life. The stylish Terrace Restaurant adjoins a sunny terrace where guests can dine alfresco. Imaginative food is served here, relying on fresh local produce in dishes like Conwy mussels poached in white wine with tomatoes and garlic, or roasted poussin with russet apple and Calvados. For dessert, try dark chocolate and orange kumquat truffle, or if you have room choose from the selection of Welsh cheeses.

Chef Ray Williams **Owner** Gary Seddon **Times** 12-6/6-9.30 **Prices** Fixed L 2 course £9.95-£14.95, Fixed D 3 course £27.95, Service included **Wines** 37 bottles over £20, 17 bottles under £20, 6 by glass **Notes** Sunday L, Vegetarian available, Dress restrictions, Smart casual, Civ Wed 220 **Seats** 30, Pr/dining room 240 **Children** Portions **Parking** 100

Neigwl Hotel

@ British, European

Enjoyable dining in well-established hotel with sea views

☎ 01758 712363
Lon Sarn Bach LL53 7DY
e-mail: relax@neigwl.com
dir: A499 from Pwllheli to Abersoch. On entering village turn right at bank. Hotel is 400yds on left

Just a short stroll from the town, harbour and beach, this delightful, privately owned and run hotel offers magnificent views over Abersoch Bay from both its attractive restaurant and comfortable lounge. Good use is made of local produce in the imaginative modern British dishes with European influences. Try fresh tasting crab cakes on coriander and tomato salsa to start, followed by peppered fillet of beef accompanied by Lyonnaise potatoes, aubergine bake and cauliflower cheese. Highly recommended is the chocolate cheesecake as a fitting finale. Book ahead for a window table.

Times Closed Jan, Closed L all week

Porth Tocyn Hotel

◎◎◎ Modern, Traditional

Ambitious cooking in country hotel with stunning views

☎ 01758 713303
Bwlch Tocyn LL53 7BU
e-mail: bookings@porthtocyn.fsnet.co.uk
dir: 2m S of Abersoch, through Sarn Bach & Bwlch Tocyn. Follow brown road signs

Originally converted from a row of lead miners' cottages, this welcoming hotel has been run by the same family for 60 years. Marine watercolours adorn the walls of the dining room, with large picture windows providing impressive views over Cardigan Bay and across to Snowdonia. A daily-changing menu is short, contemporary and dictated by local, seasonal produce. Bold flavours can be enjoyed in simple, well balanced dishes like crab and king prawn cannelloni with wilted spinach in a robust crab bisque, followed by seared venison with beetroot potato cake, sautéed wild mushrooms and raspberry and Madeira jus, with a zesty lemon tart with Chantilly cream to finish. Service is relaxed and friendly from hands-on owners.

Chef L Fletcher-Brewer, J Bell **Owner** The Fletcher-Brewer Family **Times** 12.15-2/7.30-9, Closed mid Nov, 2 wks before Etr, Closed L Mon-Sat **Prices** Fixed D 3 course £39, Service included **Wines** 63 bottles over £20, 37 bottles under £20, 4 by glass **Notes** Sunday L, Vegetarian available, Dress restrictions, Smart casual preferred **Seats** 50 **Children** Min 7 yrs D, Portions

---

BARMOUTH Map 14 SH61

Bae Abermaw

◎ Modern British

Modern cuisine and wonderful sea views

☎ 01341 280550
Panorama Rd LL42 1DQ
e-mail: enquiries@baeabermaw.com
dir: From Barmouth centre towards Dolgellau on A496, 0.5m past garage turn left into Panorama Rd, restaurant 100yds

Set in landscaped grounds overlooking Cardigan Bay, the Bay View restaurant certainly lives up to its name, complete with French doors that open on to the garden. There is no hint of its wonderfully bright, contemporary interior from the imposing dark-stone Victorian façade of the hotel but, once inside, wooden floors, fresh white walls, exposed brickwork, marble and slate fireplaces and modern art prints set the upbeat scene. The modern British cuisine comes with French influences and makes fine use of local produce in dishes like pan-fried fillet of local mackerel on warm crushed new potatoes with crème fraîche and chives, or roast rack of new season local mountain lamb with rosemary and honey jus, cabbage and garlic-scented potatoes.

Times Closed 2 wks Jan, Closed Mon, Closed L all week (ex parties of 10+ pre booked)

CAERNARFON Map 14 SH46

Seiont Manor Hotel

◎◎ Modern British V ☜

Culinary hideaway near Snowdonia

☎ 01286 673366
Llanrug LL55 2AQ
e-mail: seiontmanor@handpicked.co.uk
dir: From Bangor follow signs for Caernarfon. Leave Caernarfon on A4086. Hotel 3m on left

This friendly hotel is an imaginative development of original farm buildings and a Georgian manor house. Contemporary fabrics and pastel colours are teamed with original features such as stone slabs and exposed brickwork in the public areas, while the beamed dining room is appointed with crisp linen cloths, fresh flowers and sparkling glassware. Local ingredients and classical cooking techniques are used to create modern dishes, offered from a seasonal carte and a daily fixed-price menu. Recommendations include pressed terrine of confit

---

rabbit, wrapped in Parma ham and served with plum and brandy compote to start; followed by roasted rack of peninsula lamb with a herb crumb, sweet potato, ginger leeks, roasted shallots and rosemary sauce.

Chef Martyn Williams **Owner** Hand Picked Hotels **Times** 12-2/7-9.30 **Prices** Fixed L 2 course £13.95-£15.95, Fixed D 3 course £29.50, Starter £6.95-£8.95, Main £19.95-£24.95, Dessert £6.50, Service optional **Wines** 98 bottles over £20, 3 bottles under £20, 19 by glass **Notes** Tasting menu available, Sunday L, Vegetarian menu, Dress restrictions, Smart casual, Civ Wed 100 **Seats** 55, Pr/dining room 20 **Children** Portions, Menu **Parking** 40

CRICCIETH Map 14 SH53

Bron Eifion Country House Hotel

◎ Modern British ☜

Stylish dining in conservatory restaurant

☎ 01766 522385
LL52 0SA
e-mail: enquiries@broneifion.co.uk
dir: A497 Between Porthmadog and Pwllheli

Set in peaceful grounds with breathtaking views of the sea and formal gardens, the interior of this imposing Grade II listed country house has been completely and sympathetically refurbished. Enjoy a pre-dinner drink in the new cocktail bar or in the Great Hall, a stately room with minstrels' gallery and lofty timbered roof, then dine in the elegant, candlelit conservatory restaurant in comfortable air-conditioned surroundings. British and international cuisine features dishes such as crab ravioli with saffron risotto and main course Bron Eifion duck with a redcurrant and red pepper sauce. Chocolate fondant, banana beignets and peanut ice cream might catch the eye for dessert.

Chef Steven Burnham **Owner** John & Mary Heenan **Times** 12-2/6.30-9 **Prices** Fixed D 3 course fr £30, Service included **Notes** Sunday L, Vegetarian available, Dress restrictions, No jeans, T-shirts, Civ Wed 50, Air con **Seats** 50, Pr/dining room 16 **Children** Portions, Menu **Parking** 50

DOLGELLAU Map 14 SH71

Dolserau Hall Hotel

◎ Traditional

Enjoyable British cooking in a country-house setting

☎ 01341 422522
LL40 2AG
e-mail: welcome@dolserau.co.uk
dir: 1.5m from Dolgellau on unclass road between A470/ A494 to Bala

Built in 1863, this charming hotel is set in five acres of peaceful woodland extending to the river. The elegant dining room of the Winter Garden Restaurant, newly refurbished in tones of gold and red, has wonderful views

Continued

DOLGELLAU *Continued*

over Snowdonia. Fresh local and seasonal produce is a major focus for the owners and the daily-changing dinner menu features local lamb and venison, fish from a private fleet in Anglesey and locally produced fruit and vegetables. Typical dishes range from a starter of sweet pepper crostini with cheddar cheese to a main course of grilled fillet of haddock with herbs, served on a bed of garlic rustic potatoes, rounded off with a selection of Welsh cheeses.

Chef John Charnley **Owner** Tim & Susan Langdon **Times** Closed Nov-Feb, Closed L all week **Prices** Fixed D 4 course fr £28.95, Service optional **Wines** 3 by glass **Notes** Vegetarian available, Dress restrictions, Smart casual, no jeans, sweatshirts, trainers **Seats** 40 **Children** Min 12 yrs **Parking** 20

Penmaenuchaf Hall Hotel

◉◉ Modern British ⬥

Imaginative cooking in an elegant conservatory-style dining room

☎ 01341 422129
Penmaenpool LL40 1YB
e-mail: eat@penhall.co.uk
dir: From A470 take A493 (Tywyn/Fairbourne), entrance 1.5m on left by sign for Penmaenpool

Built in 1860 as a summer home for a Bolton cotton magnate, this impressive manor house stands in 20 acres of terraced gardens and woodlands. The high-ceilinged garden room restaurant has a light, contemporary feel, with Gothic windows offering pretty rural views. It provides an elegant backdrop for a modern British menu with Mediterranean and French influences featuring dishes such as seared scallop and monkfish wrapped in Parma ham with ratatouille and rosemary, or fillet of Welsh Black beef with foie gras, honey-roasted parsnips, wild mushrooms and a Barolo jus. Expect confidence, flair and plenty of fresh local produce. A sensibly priced wine list sourced with considerable care by the proprietors and an alfresco area for summer dining completes the package.

Chef J Pilkington, T Reeve **Owner** Mark Watson, Lorraine Fielding **Times** 12-2/7-9.30 **Prices** Fixed L 2 course fr £15.95, Fixed D 4 course fr £35, Starter £7.50-£8.50, Main £19.95-£24.50, Dessert £7.50-£8.50, Service optional **Wines** 65 bottles over £20, 37 bottles under £20, 5 by glass **Notes** Sunday L, Vegetarian available, Dress restrictions, Smart casual, no jeans or T-shirts, Civ Wed 50 **Seats** 36, Pr/dining room 16 **Children** Min 6 yrs, Portions **Parking** 36

HARLECH   Map 14 SH53

Maes y Neuadd Country House Hotel

◉◉ Modern, Traditional ⬥ ☺

Family-run hotel with fine food

☎ 01766 780200
LL47 6YA
e-mail: maes@neuadd.com
web: www.neuadd.com
dir: 3m NE of Harlech, signed off B4573

This attractive 14th-century manor house enjoys fine views over the mountains, across the bay to the Lleyn Peninsula. It has been extended over the centuries and yet all parts of the building sit together in harmony. Comfortable and tranquil, the house is furnished with antiques throughout, while service is formal but friendly. The elegant Georgian panelled dining room is decorated in deep blue and gold, while the modern British menu showcases top-quality Welsh produce, with many of the vegetables and herbs coming from the hotel's extensive gardens. The four-course dinner menu might feature crab cakes with oriental leaves, horseradish butter sauce and king prawn fritter and perhaps local organic sea bass with wilted greens and red basil sauce to follow. Don't miss 'The Grand Finale' - a selection of three desserts preceded by quality Welsh cheeses. Look out for the notable wine list.

Chef Peter Jackson, John Owen Jones **Owner** Mr & Mrs Jackson & Mr Payne **Times** 12-1.45/7-8.45 **Prices** Fixed D 3 course £35, Service optional, Groups min 15 service 10% **Wines** 100 bottles over £20, 46 bottles under £20, 10 by glass **Notes** Sunday L, Vegetarian available, Dress restrictions, Smart casual, no jeans for D or Sun L, Civ Wed 65 **Seats** 50, Pr/dining room 12 **Children** Portions, Menu **Parking** 60

PORTMEIRION   Map 14 SH53

Castell Deudraeth

◉ Modern Welsh

Stylish hotel dining in the North Wales fantasy village

☎ 01766 772400
LL48 6EN
e-mail: castell@portmeirion-village.com
dir: Off A487 at Minffordd. Between Porthmadog & Penrhyndeudraeth

This castellated mansion is set in the heart of Clough Williams-Ellis' Italianate village of Portmeirion. The renovated, elegant former private residence combines traditional materials, such as oak and slate, with up-to-the-minute design and technology. The light and airy brasserie-themed dining room affords views of the garden and distant sea, and the wooden tables and simple settings add to the air of informality. The seasonal menu draws on the best of local produce, especially seafood, as in a starter of seared scallops with bubble-and-squeak and smoked bacon. Mains might include duck breast, cooked pink and tender, set on braised red cabbage and apple with plum and ginger sauce.

Chef Peter Hedd Williams **Owner** Portmeirion Ltd **Times** 12-2/6.30-9.30 **Prices** Fixed L 2 course £15-£19, Service optional **Notes** Sunday L, Vegetarian available, Civ Wed 40, Air con **Seats** 80, Pr/dining room 40 **Children** Portions, Menu **Parking** 40

Hotel Portmeirion

◉ Modern British

Famed Italianate village setting with accomplished Welsh cuisine

☎ 01766 770000 & 772440
LL48 6ET
e-mail: hotel@portmeirion-village.com
dir: Off A487 at Minffordd

Opened in 1926, the hotel was built on a river estuary in Clough Williams-Ellis' Italianate village, which achieved fame when it was featured in the 1960s classic cult series The Prisoner. Recently refurbished by Sir Terence Conran, the art deco style dining room has the air of an ocean liner about it, with columns, large windows and views over the estuary. A bilingual menu offers modern Welsh cuisine with an emphasis on good quality, local produce. Expect noisette of Welsh lamb with root vegetable mash, caramelised sweetbreads and red onion tartlet and jus, followed by Welsh Merlyn liqueur and peanut butter iced parfait with chocolate macaroon.

Chef David Doughty **Owner** Portmeirion Ltd **Times** 12-2.30/6.30-9, Closed 11-22 Jan **Prices** Fixed L 3 course £17.50-£20.50, Fixed D 3 course fr £35.50, Starter £5.50-£12.50, Main £14.50-£22.95, Dessert £5.50-£8.50, Service optional **Wines** 60 bottles over £20, 40 bottles under £20, 8 by glass **Notes** Sunday L, Dress restrictions, Smart dress, no trainers, T-shirts, Civ Wed 130 **Seats** 100, Pr/dining room 36 **Children** Portions, Menu **Parking** 130

PWLLHELI   Map 14 SH33

Plas Bodegroes

◉◉ Modern British ⬛

Destination restaurant with rooms on the Llyn Peninsula

☎ 01758 612363
Nefyn Rd LL53 5TH
e-mail: gunna@bodegroes.co.uk
dir: On A497, 1m W of Pwllheli

A small, sympathetically converted Georgian house, hidden away in woodland on the beautiful Llyn Peninsula, is the setting for this stylish restaurant with rooms. There's a covered terrace, a walled garden and a ha-ha, and an elegant, contemporary dining room that doubles as a showcase for paintings by famous local artists. Modern British dishes are cooked with care and flavours are deftly balanced using the best of North Wales produce. Start perhaps with a warm salad of monkfish with Carmarthen ham and mushrooms before the roast loin of mountain lamb with herbs, served with a robust rosemary jus. Finish with poached pear with chocolate sauce and hazelnut ice cream. Service is personable and efficient.

Times 12-2.30/7-9, Closed Dec-Feb, Closed Mon, Closed L Tue-Sat, Closed D Sun

MONMOUTHSHIRE

ABERGAVENNY
Map 9 SO21

Angel Hotel

◉ European

Elegant, popular venue with a wide-ranging menu

☎ 01873 857121
15 Cross St NP7 5EN
e-mail: mail@angelhotelabergavenny.com
dir: From A4042/A465/A40 rdbt S of Abergavenny, follow signs for town centre. Continue past railway and bus station on left

Once a coaching inn on the London to Fishguard route, the Angel Hotel has long been popular with both locals and visitors, and offers Georgian elegance with a touch of contemporary chic. A relaxed bar, attractive courtyard and a smart restaurant provide a choice of dining options, and on Friday and Saturday nights a pianist serenades diners. The European menu offers a generous choice of quality dishes such as organic salmon spiced with caraway and cardamom with green cabbage, caramelised salsify and an orange beurre blanc, or roast rump of Welsh lamb, braised green beans and potato gratin. Afternoon tea, with freshly-baked cakes, is also a speciality of the house.

Chef Mark Turton **Owner** Caradog Hotels Ltd
Times 12-2.30/7-10, Closed 25 Dec, Closed D 24 & 26 Dec **Prices** Food prices not confirmed for 2009. Please telephone for details. **Wines** 50 bottles over £20, 48 bottles under £20, 6 by glass **Notes** Vegetarian available, Civ Wed 200 **Seats** 80, Pr/dining room 120 **Children** Portions **Parking** 40

The Foxhunter

◉◉ Modern British 🔖 🍷

A delightful combination of service, surroundings and excellent food

☎ 01873 881101
Nantyderry NP7 9DN
e-mail: info@thefoxhunter.com
dir: Just off A4042 between Usk & Abergavenny

An old stationmaster's house, sensitively restored and decorated in contemporary style, creates the setting for this charming restaurant. The Foxhunter has an excellent reputation both locally and nationally for its imaginative food, engaging service and excellent wine list. Modern cooking using fresh, local ingredients provides clean flavours and eye-catching presentation. The menus, which change twice a day, leave you spoilt for choice, but you won't go wrong with the well-textured house terrine of pork, chicken and foie gras, followed by whole grilled plaice served with coriander butter, new potatoes and

distinctively flavoured rock samphire. Two cottages are now available for overnight stays.

Chef Matt Tebbutt **Owner** Lisa & Matt Tebbutt
Times 12-2.30/7-9.30, Closed Xmas, 1 Jan, Closed Mon (exceptions apply), Closed D Sun **Prices** Fixed L 2 course £18.95-£19.95, Starter £6.95-£9.95, Main £12.95-£20.95, Dessert £5.95-£7.95, Service optional, Groups min 8 service 10% **Wines** 50 bottles over £20, 26 bottles under £20, 5 by glass **Notes** Sunday L, Vegetarian available **Seats** 50, Pr/dining room 50 **Children** Portions **Parking** 25

The Hardwick

◉◉ Modern British

Modern, gastro-pub dining from a renowned chef

☎ 01873 854220
Old Raglan Rd NP7 9AA

The Hardwick is located just outside town and manages to retain the character of a pub (you can still pop in for a pint) while offering the modern ambience and quality of food you'd expect from a restaurant. Renowned chef Stephen Terry owns the place, so it's not surprising that it has been attracting attention. Stephen's accomplished cooking delivers simply prepared, bold and appealing dishes using quality local ingredients, and there is plenty of choice. Start with smoked chicken and pancetta salad with grilled courgettes and sun-dried tomato dressing; moving on to slow-cooked shoulder of lamb and sautéed Anya potatoes with rosemary and garlic, served with Swiss chard, poached carrots, braised lentils, capers and parsley.

Times 12-3/6.30-10, Closed Mon (exc BHs), Closed D Sun

Llansantffraed Court Hotel

◉◉ Modern British 🔖 🍷

Stylish country-house hotel with winning menus

☎ 01873 840678
Llanvihangel Gobion, Clytha NP7 9BA
e-mail: reception@llch.co.uk
dir: From junction of A40 & A465 at Abergavenny, take B4598 signed to Usk. Hotel 4.5m on left (with white gates). 0.5m along drive

In a commanding position with enviable views of the Brecon Beacons, this impressive Grade II listed former manor house, now elegant country-house hotel, is set in 20 acres of landscaped gardens. Located in the oldest part of the building is the Court Restaurant, traditionally

decorated with exposed beams, warm colours, country-style furniture and pretty floral prints. The south-facing terrace is perfect for alfresco dining in summer. Attentive but friendly service, crisp linen and candles make dining a romantic affair. The menu comprises stylish, classical dishes with unfussy modern presentation based on quality local and home-grown produce. Belly of Richard Vaughan's middlewhite pork, roast scallops, pumpkin and maple syrup, and caramelised John Dory with butternut squash purée and trompette mushrooms show the style.

Chef Steve Bennett **Owner** Mike Morgan
Times 12-2/7-8.45 **Prices** Fixed L 2 course fr £14.50, Fixed D 3 course fr £27.50, Tasting menu fr £42.50, Starter £4-£9.50, Main £14-£22, Dessert £4-£9, Service optional **Wines** 57 bottles over £20, 25 bottles under £20, 22 by glass **Notes** Tasting menu 8 courses, Sunday L, Vegetarian available, Civ Wed 150 **Seats** 50, Pr/dining room 30 **Children** Portions, Menu **Parking** 250

Llanwenarth Hotel & Riverside Restaurant

◉ Modern British

Stylish riverside dining

☎ 01873 810550
Brecon Rd NP8 1EP
e-mail: info@llanwenarthhotel.com
dir: A40 from Abergavenny towards Brecon, hotel 3m past hospital on left

Midway between the market towns of Abergavenny and Crickhowell in the Brecon Beacons National Park, this 16th-century former coaching inn has spectacular views of the Usk Valley. This spacious, popular restaurant with well-spaced tables has floor-to-ceiling windows and a terrace overlooking the River Usk. Local, seasonal produce is carefully prepared and there are some well thought out combinations of ingredients and flavours on the lengthy modern British menu with European influences. Take fillet of beef with wild mushroom pâté served with rosti potato, roast shallots and red wine sauce with truffle oil and perhaps a dark chocolate tart with pistachio ice cream to finish.

Chef Rob Scrimgeour **Owner** Richard Wallace & Jon West
Times 12-2/5.30-9.30, Closed 26 Dec, 1 Jan, Closed L 31 Dec, Closed D 24-25 Dec **Prices** Fixed L 2 course £11.95, Fixed D 3 course £16.25, Starter £4.25-£5.45, Main £9.45-£16.95, Dessert £4.75, Service optional **Wines** 11 bottles over £20, 24 bottles under £20, 4 by glass **Notes** Sunday L, Vegetarian available, Air con **Seats** 60 **Parking** 30

ABERGAVENNY *Continued*

1861

@@ Modern British 🌙

Well balanced menu and flavours at a country inn

☎ 0845 388 1861
Cross Ash, Abergavenny NP7 8PB
dir: On B4521 9m from Abergavenny, 15m from Ross-on-Wye, on the outskirts of Cross Ash.

Peacefully set just a few miles outside Abergavenny, this friendly gastro-pub opened in 2007 and has already built a reputation for top-notch cuisine. It takes its name from its year of construction, but no longer looks its age following a serious sprucing-up by new owners. Inside has a rustic feel with well-spaced tables, black-painted beams and white-washed walls, and is presided over by a small but knowledgeable staff. The kitchen teams technical skill with a knack for eye-catching presentation, delivering a modern British menu that doesn't disappoint. Fresh local ingredients are used wherever possible, including vegetables from the family's market garden, and are treated with a confident simplicity that lets quality speak for itself. Start with chicken liver and foie gras parfait with ruby port jelly, then tuck into rainbow trout with caviar cream, or honey-glazed pork belly with sage cream. A tasting menu is also available.

Chef Simon King **Owner** Simon & Kate King
Times 12-2/7-9, Closed Mon, Closed D Sun **Prices** Fixed L 2 course fr £14.50, Fixed D 3 course fr £26.50, Tasting menu £40, Service optional **Wines** 25 bottles over £20, 14 bottles under £20, 8 by glass **Notes** Tasting menu 7 courses, Sunday L **Seats** 32 **Children** Portions **Parking** 20

Walnut Tree Inn

@@@ – **see below**

ROCKFIELD Map 9 SO41

The Stonemill & Steppes Farm Cottages

@@ British, French

A unique dining experience with modern, flavour-driven cooking

☎ 01600 716273
NP25 5SW
e-mail: enquiries@thestonemill.co.uk
dir: B4233, 2.5m from Monmouth town

A 16th-century barn in a hamlet west of Monmouth has been converted to create the Stonemill Restaurant. Oak beams, vaulted ceilings and an old cider press provide the backdrop for contemporary furnishings. The kitchen takes a modern approach and uses the very best of fresh local produce for wholesome and accomplished dishes offered from a choice of fixed-price and carte menus. You might start with fresh steamed mussels in coconut milk, lemon grass and root ginger; and follow with fillet of Longhorn beef, wild seasonal mushrooms, crushed herb potato and Café de Paris butter. Interesting vegetarian options are also available. The complex includes six well-appointed cottages let as self-catering or bed and breakfast accommodation.

The Stonemill & Steppes Farm Cottages

Chef Mr Michael Fowler **Owner** Mrs M L Decloedt
Times 12-2/6-9, Closed 25-26 Dec, 2 wks Jan, Closed Mon, Closed D Sun **Prices** Food prices not confirmed for 2009. Please telephone for details. **Wines** 15 bottles over £20, 28 bottles under £20, 8 by glass **Notes** Civ Wed 60 **Seats** 56, Pr/dining room 12 **Children** Portions **Parking** 40

Walnut Tree Inn

ABERGAVENNY Map 9 SO21

RESTAURANT OF THE YEAR

Italian, Mediterranean

Top chef at the stove in legendary venue

☎ 01873 852797
Llandewi Skirrid NP7 8AW
e-mail: mail@thewalnuttreeinn.com
dir: 3m NE of Abergavenny on B4521

The Walnut Tree forever has a place in the culinary lexicon. For nearly 40 years Franco Taruschio's cooking represented the best of ingredient-led seasonally-inspired simple food. He's been gone for eight years and the restaurant has had its ups-and-downs since then. Until now. Shaun Hill is a man with a big reputation, not based on ego or acts of culinary showmanship, but on being an excellent chef, and now he's back at the stove, hands-on, getting down and dirty. The location among the Black Mountains doesn't change and is as beautiful as ever but the building itself has been smartened up and given a lick of cream paint. The bar provides a central focus and the dining room is simply and unpretentiously decorated in muted colours. The staff are well informed about the menu and their friendly and positive attitude creates confidence all round. Shaun's menu is based around superb produce and a sure hand is evident in the delivery. Scallop tartare with scallop wonton fritters sits alongside mussel and cockle pie among starters, while main-course saddle of rabbit includes the liver and kidneys. Grilled halibut with herb dumplings stars a superb piece of fish perfectly cooked; and chocolate and brandy torte is a luxurious finish. **Walnut Tree Inn is AA Restaurant of the Year for Wales.**

Chef Shaun Hill **Times** 12-2.30/7-10, Closed Sun, Mon

SKENFRITH Map 9 SO42

The Bell at Skenfrith

◎◎ Modern British 🍷 ✸

Restaurant with rooms and all-round appeal

☎ 01600 750235
NP7 8UH
e-mail: enquiries@skenfrith.co.uk
dir: N of Monmouth on A466 for 4m. Left on B4521
towards Abergavenny, 3m on left

This delightful former coaching inn with bags of
character is set beside the River Monnow in a pretty
village setting. Stylishly refurbished, its décor teams the
best of the old - oak beams, flagstone floors, open fires -
with the comforts of the new, in the form of sumptuous
sofas and an accomplished menu of British cuisine.
Expect keen attention to seasonality and the quality of
ingredients, with much of the produce arriving fresh from
The Bell's new organic kitchen garden. Seared red mullet
is a typical starter, served with roast red pepper
gazpacho, oyster tempura and watercress purée, while
mains might include an assiette of lamb comprising pan-
roast cutlet, pan-seared liver, braised leg fillet and
sweetbread. For dessert, try rhubarb and apple charlotte,
accompanied by a rhubarb and champagne sorbet and
Calvados anglaise. A large walk-in wine cellar and
award-winning wine list completes the picture.

Chef David Hill **Owner** Mr & Mrs W Hutchings
Times 12-2.30/7-9.30, Closed last wk Jan, 1st wk Feb,
Closed Mon (Nov-Mar) **Prices** Starter £4.50-£8.75, Main
£13-£19.50, Dessert £5.95, Service optional **Wines** 214
bottles over £20, 71 bottles under £20, 13 by glass
Notes Sunday L, Vegetarian available, Dress restrictions,
Smart casual **Seats** 55, Pr/dining room 40 **Children** Min 8
yrs **Parking** 35

USK Map 9 SO30

Raglan Arms

◎ Modern

Unpretentious restaurant serving honest food

☎ 01291 690800
Llandenny NP15 1DL
e-mail: raglanarms@aol.com
dir: M4 junct 26. Llandenny is situated halfway between
the market towns of Usk and Raglan

This cosy, stone-floored flint-built pub is tucked away in
a beautiful village setting in scenic Monmouthshire. Dine
at rustic tables around the bar or in the conservatory
extension, with the short and imaginative lunch and
dinner menus listing modern British dishes with a
distinct Gallic influence. Menus change with the seasons
and make good use of fresh local ingredients. Expect
unfussy presentation and good, clean flavours, as seen in
a starter of beef carpaccio with shaved beetroot and
parmesan, a main course of fishcakes with wilted
spinach and parsley sauce, and a deliciously creamy
crème brûlée with red berry compôte.

Times 12-2.30/7-9.30, Closed 25-26 Dec, Closed Mon
except BHs, Closed D Sun

WHITEBROOK Map 4 SO50

WINE AWARD OF THE YEAR

Crown at Whitebrook

◎◎ Modern British 🖥 🍷

**Stylishly restored old drover's inn with skilfully
prepared food**

☎ 01600 860254
NP25 4TX
e-mail: info@crownatwhitebrook.co.uk
web: www.crownatwhitebrook.co.uk
dir: From Monmouth take B4293 towards Trellech,
continue for 2.7m. Take left towards Whitebrook, continue
for 2m

Situated in the heart of the Wye Valley Area of
Outstanding Natural Beauty, the Crown at Whitebrook
may be off the beaten track, but is well worth seeking
out. This carefully renovated 17th-century drover's inn
retains many original features, like old beams (although
now whitewashed with lime ash), but the minimalist
décor, elegantly dressed tables and original artwork
create a fresh, contemporary feel. Service is attentive and
friendly. The memorable menu, with bold interpretations
of modern British ideas, is underpinned by a classical
French theme, and the intelligent use of fresh, local
ingredients produces some exhilarating results. Perhaps
start with terrine of pork cheek and foie gras with chorizo
and fig, followed by Welsh lamb three ways with truffle,
shallot and Pommery mustard.
**Crown at Whitebrook is AA Wine Award Winner for
Wales.**

Chef James Sommerin **Owner** The Crown Hotels &
Restaurants Ltd **Times** 12-2/7-9.30, Closed 2 wks Xmas,
New Year, Closed Mon-Tue, Closed D Sun **Prices** Fixed L 2
course £25, Fixed D 3 course £45, Tasting menu £65,
Service optional, Groups min 6 service 12.5% **Wines** 216
bottles over £20, 14 bottles under £20, 11 by glass
Notes Tasting menu 8 courses, Sunday L, Vegetarian
available, Dress restrictions, Smart casual, No T-shirts,
shorts or sandals **Seats** 36, Pr/dining room 12
Children Min 12 yrs **Parking** 20

NEWPORT

NEWPORT Map 9 ST38

The Chandlery

◎◎ Modern, Traditional

Skilful cooking in historic maritime surroundings

☎ 01633 256622
77-78 Lower Dock St NP20 1EH
e-mail: food@thechandleryrestaurant.com
dir: Situated on A48, 0.5m from the Royal Gwent Hospital
at the foot of George St Bridge

A former ships' chandlery, this Grade II listed building
has been transformed into a restaurant at the heart of
Newport's commercial centre. The interior combines
smart décor with original Georgian features and offers a
comfortable bar area and airy dining rooms with well-
spaced tables. Top quality local and Welsh produce is used
for the carefully prepared modern dishes, which are well-
presented, allowing the main ingredient to shine through.
A starter of succulent fresh scallops and miniature Thai
fishcakes is perfectly complemented by chilli jam and
crème fraîche. Clean and fleshy pan-fried hake works well
as a main course with diced new potatoes and tomatoes in
a fish sauce of mussels, clams and cockles.

Chef Simon Newcombe, Carl Hammet **Owner** Simon
Newcombe, Jane Newcombe **Times** 12-2/7-10, Closed 1
wk Xmas, Closed Mon, Closed L Sat-Mon, Closed D Sun-
Mon **Prices** Fixed L 2 course fr £11.95, Starter
£3.95-£7.95, Main £10.95-£16.95, Dessert £4.95-£6.50,
Service optional, Groups min 6 service 10% **Wines** 19
bottles over £20, 21 bottles under £20, 8 by glass
Notes Sunday L, Vegetarian available, Air con **Seats** 80,
Pr/dining room 60 **Children** Portions **Parking** 20

Junction 28

◎ Traditional European

**Busy, popular, informal dining just a diversion from
the M4**

☎ 01633 891891
Station Approach, Bassaleg NP10 8LD
e-mail: enquiries@junction28.com
dir: M4 junct 28, follow signs Risca-Brymawr, then left in
0.5m signed Caerphilly. Right at mini-rdbt, then 1st left
beyond St Basil's church

Taking its name from the nearby M4 motorway junction,
this informal restaurant (formerly a railway station)

Continued

NEWPORT *Continued*

draws the crowds with its extensive modern European repertoire while service and hospitality is both professional and friendly. With bamboo screens separating the dining areas, cane seating and mirrors on the walls create an inviting ambience. The brasserie-style dishes offer something for everyone, delivered via value fixed-price lunch and evening 'Flying all Night' menus that come bolstered by an equally generous carte. Expect the likes of Cajun salmon fishcakes with hollandaise sauce, cannon of Brecon lamb with rosemary sauce, and a more traditional range of grills and homely desserts like bread-and-butter pudding.

Chef Jon West **Owner** Jon West/Richard Wallace **Times** 12-2/5.30-9.45, Closed last wk July, 1st wk Aug, Closed D Sun **Prices** Fixed L 2 course £11.95, Fixed D 3 course £16.25-£19.95, Starter £3.50-£7.95, Main £11.95-£18.95, Dessert £3.50-£5.95, Service optional **Wines** 23 bottles over £20, 38 bottles under £20, 6 by glass **Notes** Early evening menu 5.30-7, Sunday L, Vegetarian available, Dress restrictions, Smart casual, Air con **Seats** 165, Pr/dining room 12 **Children** Portions **Parking** 50

ST BRIDES WENTLOOGE Map 9 ST28

The Inn at the Elm Tree

◉ Modern British ☙

Contemporary inn serving fresh local produce in a peaceful location

☎ 01633 680225
St Brides Wentlooge NP10 8SQ
e-mail: inn@the-elm-tree.co.uk
dir: From M4 junct 28 take A48 towards Castleton. At 1st rdbt turn left, continue 1.5m, right onto Morgan Way. Turn right at T-junct onto B4239. Inn 2.5m

This stylish barn conversion in a tranquil setting on the Wentlooge Flats is quite an unexpected find. The barn dates from the 19th century and the original conversion to a restaurant has since developed into an inn. The restaurant has a contemporary feel with a cool minimalist note, and the tropical courtyard is the perfect place to be on a warm summer evening. Good use is made of fresh local produce, including fish and game (pheasant, partridge, woodcock and venison) from local estates in season, and specialities of the house are rack of Welsh lamb and Welsh Black beef.

Chef David Goddard **Owner** Shaun Ellis **Times** 12-2.30/6-9.30 **Prices** Fixed D 3 course £11,

---

Starter £4.60-£8.95, Main £12.50-£18.95, Dessert £4.95-£6.50, Service optional **Wines** 16 bottles over £20, 27 bottles under £20, 11 by glass **Notes** Sunday L, Vegetarian available, Civ Wed 60 **Seats** 45, Pr/dining room 20 **Children** Min 12 yrs **Parking** 30

PEMBROKESHIRE

HAVERFORDWEST Map 8 SM91

Wolfscastle Country Hotel

◉ Traditional, International

Freshly cooked local food in comfortable surroundings

☎ 01437 741225 & 741688
Wolf's Castle SA62 5LZ
e-mail: info@wolfscastle.com
dir: From Haverfordwest take A40 towards Fishguard. Hotel in centre of Wolf's Castle

This 19th-century stone-built former vicarage commands a prominent position in the village and has a good reputation locally for its food. The same menu is offered in the bar and restaurant and is divided into a choice of traditional dishes, like salmon fishcakes with sweet chilli sauce, and lamb's liver with bacon and sage sauce, and a more international selection of dishes. With an emphasis on the freshest local produce, start with a Spanish tapas platter to share, follow with rack of Welsh lamb with sweet potato gratin and rosemary-scented jus, and round off with chocolate and pecan tart with champagne sorbet.

Times 12-2/7-9, Closed 24-26 Dec

PORTHGAIN Map 8 SM83

The Shed

◉ Traditional British, Mediterranean ☙

Local seafood dining in sea-going surroundings

☎ 01348 831518
SA62 5BN
e-mail: caroline@theshedporthgain.co.uk
web: www.theshedporthgain.co.uk
dir: 7m from St David's. Off A40

This one-time carpenter's workshop and fisherman's lock-up has an enviable position by the quay, where local fish are landed and appear on the menu in the blink of an eye. The décor has a simple, rustic feel with slate floors and pictures of the local landscape, and the restaurant has expanded to both floors of the building, doubling

---

capacity. Local seafood and other regional produce is the focus of the menu, so Porthgain crab mornay is topped with Llangloffan cheese among starters, and wonderfully fresh sea bass is a main course with roast tomato fondue and fresh herb beurre blanc. Finish with 'Shed' apple tart served with fresh vanilla custard. Service is relaxed and informal.

Chef Caroline Jones **Owner** Rob & Caroline Jones **Times** 11-4.30/6-11.30, Closed Nov-Apr open only weekends (except half term & Xmas hols), Closed D Mon **Prices** Starter £5.95-£7.95, Main £17.50-£24.95, Dessert £4.95-£6.50 **Wines** 26 bottles under £20, 6 by glass **Seats** 36 **Children** Portions, Menu **Parking** On village street

---

ST DAVID'S Map 8 SM72

Morgan's

◉ Modern British ☙

Family-run restaurant serving fresh local fare

☎ 01437 720508
20 Nun St SA62 6NT
e-mail: eat@morgans-restaurant.co.uk
web: www.morgans-restaurant.co.uk
dir: Haverfordwest 16m. On A487 to Fishguard, just off main square, 100m from cathedral

It may be Britain's smallest city, but St David's has a growing reputation for its food. Husband-and-wife team Tara and David run the show at this chic little eatery, offering a modern British menu that makes the most of fresh local ingredients, with a number of fish specials depending on the day's catch. Ratatouille and Pembrokeshire goats' cheese tian gets things started, followed by fillet of Welsh beef Montpellier with butter sauce, onion compote, beetroot crisps and dauphinoise potatoes. Save room for the likes of pineapple, passionfruit and cardamom crème brûlée.

Chef Tara Pitman **Owner** David & Tara Pitman **Times** Closed Jan, Closed Tue, Closed L all week, Closed D Wed (Oct-Mar) **Prices** Starter £4.75-£8.50, Main £12.95-£20, Dessert £4.50-£6.50, Service optional **Wines** 8 bottles over £20, 31 bottles under £20, 4 by glass **Notes** Vegetarian available **Seats** 36, Pr/dining room 12 **Children** Portions **Parking** Car park opposite

---

Warpool Court Hotel

◎◎ Modern British

Enjoyable dining with impressive coastal scenery

☎ 01437 720300
SA62 6BN
e-mail: info@warpoolcourthotel.com
dir: From Cross Sq in centre of St David's, left by HSBC bank into Goat St, at fork follow hotel signs

Set in extensive grounds in a stunning location, overlooking a beautiful expanse of the Pembrokeshire coast, the Warpool Court Hotel dates back to 1860, when it was built as the St David's Cathedral choir school. Of notable interest are the 3,000 hand-painted tiles decorating the downstairs and the original bedrooms. Crisp white linen and carefully coordinated design set the scene in the spacious dining room and service is friendly and relaxed. Locally sourced produce is used wherever possible, and ingredients are accurately cooked to create a menu of tempting choices such as Pant Ysgawn goats' cheese soufflé with walnut dressing, followed by Welsh Black beef fillet with horseradish crust, fondant potato and red wine jus, and perhaps crème brûlée with shortbread and hibiscus to finish.

Chef Barry Phillips **Owner** Peter Trier
Times 12-1.45/7-9.15, Closed Jan **Prices** Fixed L 2 course £16.95-£25, Fixed D 3 course £42-£47, Service included **Wines** 101 bottles over £20, 21 bottles under £20, 4 by glass **Notes** Sunday L, Vegetarian available, Civ Wed 130 **Seats** 50, Pr/dining room 22 **Children** Portions, Menu **Parking** 100

| TENBY | Map 8 SN10 |

Penally Abbey Hotel

◎ Traditional, Modern

Enjoy local produce in charming country-house setting

☎ 01834 843033
Penally SA70 7PY
e-mail: penally.abbey@btinternet.com
dir: From Tenby take A4139 to Penally

This ivy-fronted, country-house hotel is set in five acres of grounds and has impressive views across Carmarthen Bay. Renovation and upgrading has done nothing to diminish the charm of the place. The restaurant is spacious, well decorated with good garden and sea views. Service is pleasant and unhurried. The menu comprises modern British dishes with good use of local produce. To start, try the smoked salmon and trout gateau with asparagus followed by the Welsh Black beef with stilton and red wine jus. Finish with the crème caramel with red berries.

Times 12.30-2/7.30-9.30, Closed L (ex by arrangement only)

| POWYS |
| BRECON | Map 9 SO02 |

The Felin Fach Griffin

◎◎ British 🖥 V ⭐ 🌿

High-quality dining in a wonderful upland setting

☎ 01874 620111
Felin Fach LD3 0UB
e-mail: enquires@eatdrinksleep.ltd.uk
dir: 3.5m N of Brecon on A470. Large terracotta building on left, on edge of village

At the junction of the Brecon Beacons and the Black Mountains sits this delightful restaurant with rooms, with its distinctive red exterior and extensive garden. Inside,

an open fire and large sofas welcome guests in the bar, while the dining areas display a wealth of rustic charm, each with its own theme or colour and an array of artwork and photos by local artists. The modern British cooking comes underpinned by classical French influences, and local organic ingredients are used wherever possible - the inn's kitchen garden is the first in Wales to achieve organic certification. Dishes are simply prepared, letting flavours speak for themselves. Smoked salmon tartare from the Black Mountains Smokery served with Crickhowell crème fraîche and black pepper tuile makes an excellent starter, followed by an equally impressive breast of local pheasant with Yukon Gold potato mash and sauerkraut.

Chef Ricardo Van Ede **Owner** Charles Inkin, Edmund Inkin **Times** 12.30-2.30/6.30-9.30, Closed 24-25 Dec, few days Jan, Closed L Mon (in winter excl BHs) **Prices** Starter £4.90-£11.90, Main £13.50-£17.90, Dessert £6-£9.50, Service optional **Wines** 65 bottles over £20, 25 bottles under £20, 10 by glass **Notes** Vegetarian menu **Seats** 45, Pr/dining room 20 **Children** Portions **Parking** 60

Peterstone Court

◎◎ Modern British, European 🖥

Accomplished modern British cooking overlooking the River Usk

☎ 01874 665387
Llanhamlach LD3 7YB
e-mail: info@peterstone-court.com
dir: 1m from Brecon on A40 to Abergavenny

Set on the edge of the Brecon Beacons with stunning views over the River Usk, this comfortable Georgian manor is eclectic, with a blend of traditional country house and contemporary style. Quality produce, good technical skills and eye-catching presentation make for a memorable meal in the high-ceilinged restaurant, which prides itself on sourcing meat and poultry direct from the nearby family farm. Ingredients are treated sympathetically by a talented kitchen and delivered to the table in flavoursome combinations - roast breast of quail with braised onions and potato galette for example, or honey-roast parsnip and parmesan risotto. Mains are similarly tempting and might include caramelised duck with red onion tarte Tatin and wilted baby gem.

Chef Sean Gerrard & Robert Taylor **Owner** Jessica & Glyn Bridgeman, Sean Gerrard **Times** 12-2.30/7-9.30 **Prices** Starter £4.95-£9.95, Main £14.95-£17.95, Dessert £5.75-£7.95, Service optional **Wines** 30 bottles over £20, 31 bottles under £20, 12 by glass **Notes** Sunday L, Vegetarian available, Civ Wed 120 **Seats** 45, Pr/dining room 120 **Children** Portions, Menu **Parking** 40

BRECON *Continued*

The Usk Inn

◉ British, French 🖥

Imaginative menu at a traditional inn

☎ 01874 676251
Station Rd, Talybont-on-Usk LD3 7JE
e-mail: dine@uskinn.co.uk
dir: 250 yds off A40, 6m E of Brecon

From the open log fires, polished wooden tables and flagstone floors at this traditional looking inn, situated in the quiet village of Talybont-on-Usk, you'd never guess that it was once a bank. The bright, airy restaurant has a Mediterranean feel, while the bar area is more traditional. Local Welsh produce and seasonal ingredients are used to create an imaginative menu supplemented by blackboard specials. Look out for starters like fillet of salmon with saffron and herb sauce, or baked field mushroom stuffed with onion, peppers and melted stilton, with a main course of roasted fillet of monkfish served with a trio of rice and Pernod sauce.

Times 12-3/6.30-9.30, Closed 25-27 Dec

The White Swan

◉ Modern British, Mediterranean

Charming old pub with bags of character

☎ 01874 665276
LD3 7BZ
dir: 3m E of Brecon, off A40. Take B4558 following signs for Llanfrynach

The Brecon Beacons provide the stunning backdrop to this row of converted rough-stone cottages opposite the church. The former coaching inn is now a relaxing gastro-style pub with accomplished cooking appealing to locals and tourists alike. Inside, you'll find a cosy bar and a spacious restaurant, decked out with painted beams, flagstone floors, modern artwork and well-appointed tables. The modern British menu makes good use of fresh local ingredients, the simply presented dishes taking in chicken, smoked ham and leek terrine with minted pea sorbet, chargrilled Welsh Black beef with Rhymney beer jus, sticky toffee pudding or a slate of Welsh cheeses to finish.

Chef L Havard **Owner** Richard Griffiths
Times 12-2/7-11.30, Closed 25-26 Dec, 1 Jan, Closed Mon **Prices** Starter £4.95-£8.50, Main £12.50-£18.95, Dessert £4.95-£5, Service included **Wines** 6 by glass **Notes** Sunday L, Vegetarian available **Seats** 60, Pr/dining room 50 **Children** Portions, Menu **Parking** 40

The Drawing Room

◉◉ Modern British 🖥 🍴 ✋

Stylish restaurant with rooms starring local produce

☎ 01982 552493
Cwmbach, Newbridge-on-Wye LD2 3RT
e-mail: post@the-drawing-room.co.uk
dir: From Builth Wells, take A470 towards Rhayader, 3m on left

Close to the market town of Builth Wells, this attractive restaurant with rooms is set in a graceful, beautifully refurbished Georgian country residence. The intimate dining room has a refined feel with subtle wall colours adorned with eye-catching French prints and an uncluttered atmosphere. The kitchen's modern British approach - underpinned by a classical French theme - delivers clean, unfussy flavours using quality local ingredients. Take Cardigan Bay crab salad with king prawns, Avruga caviar and mustard mayonnaise to start, followed by pan-roasted breast of Goetre Farm duck and confit leg with boudin blanc, braised red cabbage and pan jus with blueberries and Herefordshire cassis, with perhaps a hot apple, Calvados and praline soufflé with caramel ice cream to finish.

Chef Colin & Melanie Dawson **Owner** Colin & Melanie Dawson **Times** Closed Sun-Mon, Closed L all week **Prices** Fixed D 3 course £40, Service added but optional 10% **Wines** 45 bottles over £20, 2 bottles under £20, 4 by glass **Notes** Dress restrictions, Smart casual **Seats** 12, Pr/dining room 8 **Children** Min 12 yrs **Parking** 14

The Talkhouse

◉◉ British, European

Seasonal cooking at a former coaching inn

☎ 01686 688919 & 07876 086183
Ty Siarad, Pontdolgoch SY17 5JE
e-mail: info@talkhouse.co.uk
dir: 1.5m W of Caersws on A470 Machynlleth road

This stone-built inn dates from around 1909 and was formerly known as the Mytton Arms. It retains much of its original character enhanced by warm Laura Ashley fabrics. The inviting restaurant has French windows opening on to a secluded garden for summer dining, and large, individual tables provide plenty of space and comfort. The welcoming sitting room comes with deep

---

sofas and armchairs and a beamed bar with a log fire. There is a frequently changing menu of rustic British cooking, served in generous portions, including poached home-grown pear with melting Perl-wen brie; local Welsh Pride fillet beef on a horseradish rösti; and chilled bread-and-butter pudding with a vanilla pod sauce.

Chef Stephen Garratt **Owner** Stephen & Jackie Garratt **Times** 12-1.30/6.30-8.45, Closed 25-26 Dec, Closed Mon (open for group booking of 15 or more), Closed L Sat, Closed D Sun **Prices** Starter £5-£6.75, Main £12-£19, Dessert £4.95, Service optional **Wines** 80 bottles over £20, 20 bottles under £20, 6 by glass **Notes** Vegetarian available, Dress restrictions, Smart casual **Seats** 35 **Children** Min 14 yrs **Parking** 40

The Bear Hotel

◉ Traditional British, European

A 15th-century coaching inn with inspired cuisine and a welcoming atmosphere

☎ 01873 810408
High St NP8 1BW
e-mail: bearhotel@aol.com
dir: Town centre, off A40 (Brecon road). 6m from Abergavenny

Located in the heart of the beautiful Brecon Beacons National Park, this charming coaching inn dates back to 1432. It retains its original character, complete with oak beams, open fires and antique furnishings, and exudes a friendly atmosphere. There is a welcoming bar with cosy areas, and booking a table to eat here is not required. The restaurant and function room offer more formal dining and appealing specials add to the imaginative menu. Fresh local produce and home-grown herbs are skilfully prepared to create top-notch British and European dishes. To start, try lobster, prawn and salmon ravioli with wilted spinach and lemon butter sauce, perhaps followed by roast fillet of Welsh Black beef with dauphinoise potato, spinach, wild mushrooms and garlic and herb butter.

Chef Stephen Hodson, John Ganeiu **Owner** Mrs J Hindmarsh, Stephen Hindmarsh **Times** 12-2/7-9.30, Closed 25 Dec, Closed Mon, Closed L Tue-Sat, Closed D Sun **Prices** Starter £3.75-£7.50, Main £9.95-£18.95, Dessert £5-£5.50, Service optional **Wines** 47 bottles over £20, 22 bottles under £20, 10 by glass **Notes** Vegetarian available, Dress restrictions, Smart casual **Seats** 60, Pr/dining room 30 **Children** Portions, Menu **Parking** 40

see advert opposite

Gliffaes Country House Hotel

◉ Modern British

Traditional country-house setting with innovative, modern dining

☎ 01874 730371
NP8 1RH
e-mail: calls@gliffaeshotel.com
web: www.gliffaeshotel.com
dir: 1m off A40, 2.5m W of Crickhowell

Idyllically situated in 33 acres of gardens and wooded grounds by the River Usk, this impressive Victorian country house in Italianate style has a glorious history of fly fishing. Elegant and generously proportioned public areas include a balcony and conservatory from which to enjoy the stunning views over the valley, and a formal panelled dining room with artwork from Welsh artists adorning the walls. Typical dishes on the modern British menu include starters like crab and smoked salmon roulade with tomato and rosemary coulis, with perhaps a main course of blue cheese and pea risotto flavoured with truffle and rocket. Imaginative desserts feature rosewater and vanilla crème brûlée with shortbread biscuit, or choose from the selection of local Welsh cheeses.

Chef Stephan Trinci **Owner** Mr & Mrs Brabner & Mr & Mrs Suter **Times** 12-2.30/7.30-9.15, Closed 2-31 Jan, Closed L Mon-Sat **Prices** Fixed D 3 course £34, Service included **Wines** 45 bottles over £20, 33 bottles under £20, 8 by glass **Notes** Sunday L, Vegetarian available, Dress restrictions, Smart casual preferred, Civ Wed 40 **Seats** 60, Pr/dining room 18 **Children** Portions, Menu **Parking** 30

Manor Hotel

◉ Traditional, International

Real food from local produce and stunning views

☎ 01873 810212
Brecon Rd NP8 1SE
e-mail: info@manorhotel.co.uk
dir: 0.5m W of Crickhowell on A40, Brecon road

Its bright white exterior in sharp contrast to the lush green hills that surround it, this impressive manor-house hotel sits in one of the most beautiful valleys in the Brecon Beacons National Park overlooking the River Usk. Enjoy a drink in one of its comfortable bars or lounges, and then move through to the restaurant, an informal affair with a bistro feel and stunning views. Local ingredients underpin the wide-ranging menu, including meat and poultry from the family farm in Llangynidr and seafood delivered daily. Start with slow-roast belly pork served with apple sauce, onion rings and jus, and then tuck into Glaisfer Farm chicken with bubble-and-squeak and tarragon sauce.

Chef Mr G Bridgeman **Owner** Mr G Bridgeman **Times** 12-2.30/6.30-9.30 **Prices** Food prices not confirmed for 2009. Please telephone for details. **Wines** 23 bottles over £20, 26 bottles under £20, 8 by glass **Notes** Sunday L, Civ Wed 250 **Seats** 54, Pr/dining room 26 **Children** Portions, Menu

Nantyffin Cider Mill Inn

◉ British, Mediterranean ☻

16th-century setting for well prepared cuisine.

☎ 01873 810775
Brecon Rd NP8 1SG
e-mail: info@cidermill.co.uk
dir: 1.5m W of Crickhowell on A40 at junct with A479

This 16th-century former drover's inn and cider mill, situated on the outskirts of Crickhowell, still houses the cider mill and mill wheel within the old apple store, which is now the dining room. Welcoming log fires, large exposed beams, stone walls and chic décor set the scene and service is supplied by friendly, knowledgeable staff. The menu and specials blackboard provide well-prepared dishes with international influences as well as traditionally British fare, using fresh local ingredients. Try breast of free-range chicken stuffed with mozzarella and tomato served with soft polenta and sage and lemon sauce, followed by home-made glazed lemon tart with strawberry and raspberry sorbet and coulis.

Chef Marius Petre **Owner** Vic & Ann Williams **Times** 12-3/6-11, Closed Mon (Oct-Mar) **Prices** Starter £5-£6.95, Main £15.95, Dessert £4.95-£7.95, Service optional **Wines** 22 bottles over £20, 41 bottles under £20, 9 by glass **Notes** Sunday L, Vegetarian available **Seats** 60 **Children** Portions **Parking** 40

CRICKHOWELL *Continued*

Ty Croeso Hotel & Restaurant

◉ Traditional Welsh V ◔

Relaxed dining with strong Welsh emphasis and stunning views

☎ 01873 810573
The Dardy, Llangattock NP8 1PU
e-mail: tycroeso@gmail.com
dir: Please telephone for directions

Set high on a hillside overlooking the River Usk, this former workhouse infirmary of Victorian origins certainly lives up to its name - Ty Croeso means 'House of Welcome' in Welsh. Served in the relaxed and comfortably refurbished restaurant, or on the flower-filled terrace, the compact carte and excellent value Taste of Wales menus put the emphasis on quality local produce. Simple, accomplished preparation hits the mark. Try the goats' cheese soufflé starter, follow with rack of Welsh lamb with rosemary mash, or Welsh Black sirloin steak with pepper sauce, and finish with roasted fig and almond tart.

Chef Lisa Grenfell **Owner** Linda Jarrett **Times** Closed Sun, Closed L all week ex BH wknds **Prices** Fixed D 3 course £20, Starter £4.50-£5.75, Main £9.50-£19.50, Dessert £5, Service optional, Groups min 12 service 10% **Wines** 1 bottles over £20, 23 bottles under £20, 4 by glass **Notes** Vegetarian menu **Seats** 40 **Children** Portions, Menu **Parking** 16

| HAY-ON-WYE | Map 9 SO24 |

Old Black Lion Inn

◉ Modern British

Simple, honest cooking in Welsh borders setting

☎ 01497 820841
26 Lion St HR3 5AD
e-mail: info@oldblacklion.co.uk
web: www.oldblacklion.co.uk
dir: 1m off A438. From TIC car park turn right along Oxford Rd, pass NatWest Bank, next left (Lion St), hotel 20 yds on right

Located on a main road in the small town of Hay-on-Wye, this historic inn has a whitewashed exterior, and inside is full of original architectural features, charm and character. Well supported by locals and casual diners alike, the smart dining room has a plum-coloured décor and provides access to a patio for alfresco dining in

summer. The bar is also used for dining, with wooden beams, scrubbed tables and rustic wooden seating. Friendly young uniformed staff serve simple starters such as blue cheese and beer soup with croûtons, followed by main courses like herb-crusted local rack of lamb with sweet potato and mint mash, and rosemary and port jus.

Chef Peter Bridges **Owner** Dolan Leighton **Times** 12-2.30/6.30-9.30, Closed 24-26 Dec **Prices** Food prices not confirmed for 2009. Please telephone for details. **Wines** 16 bottles over £20, 23 bottles under £20, 6 by glass **Notes** Vegetarian available **Seats** 60, Pr/dining room 20 **Children** Min 5 yrs **Parking** 20

The Swan-at-Hay Hotel

◉ British, French ▭ ◔

Family-run hotel serving imaginative food

☎ 01497 821188
Church St HR3 5DQ
e-mail: info@theswanathay.co.uk
dir: 100 yds from town centre in the direction of Brecon

This elegant yet relaxed hotel was once a coaching inn and still retains many period features. A popular family-run hotel, it offers a choice of dining venues including a bright bar area and pleasant, more traditional, restaurant with beautiful Georgian windows overlooking tranquil gardens. Service is relaxed and friendly. The menu changes every two weeks, reflecting what is in season locally and demonstrating a Mediterranean influence. Starters might include white bean and lentil soup, or moules marinière made with Welsh mussels in Pernod, cream and parsley sauce. Main courses include confit pork belly made with local pork, and braised Welsh Marches lamb shank with ginger carrots, mange-tout and mint and honey sauce.

Chef Harry Mackintosh, Dan Cross **Owner** Amy & Harry Mackintosh **Times** 12-2/6.30-9 **Prices** Food prices not confirmed for 2009. Please telephone for details. **Wines** 14 bottles over £20, 19 bottles under £20, 7 by glass **Notes** Sunday L, Vegetarian available, Civ Wed 80 **Seats** , Pr/dining room 20 **Children** Portions **Parking** 16

| KNIGHTON | Map 9 SO27 |

Milebrook House

◉◉ Modern, Traditional British ◔

Charming family-run hotel with contemporary food

☎ 01547 528632
Milebrook LD7 1LT
e-mail: hotel@milebrook.kc3ltd.co.uk
dir: 2m E of Knighton on A4113 (Ludlow)

Surrounded by typical wooded rolling Marches landscape, in 3 acres of grounds and gardens in the Teme Valley, this charming mellow stone dower house dates from 1760. The former home of explorer Sir Wilfred Thesiger, it once played host to Emperor Haile Selassie. His imperial majesty would have enjoyed the exquisite formal gardens with its remarkable variety of indigenous and exotic trees and plants. Nowadays the country-house hotel's kitchen

garden provides virtually all the vegetables, herbs and fruits served in the elegant, traditional restaurant, complementing the local produce that makes its way onto the kitchen's imaginative modern British menus. Food is presented with real flair and panache and has high aspirations. Start with grilled, naturally-smoked haddock on tomato salad glazed with Welsh rarebit, and for mains perhaps choose roasted breast of local organic chicken stuffed with port salut cheese, wrapped in Parma ham on olive-infused mash with basil cream sauce. Excellent wine list.

Milebrook House

Chef Christopher Marsden **Owner** Mr & Mrs R T Marsden **Times** 12-2/7-9, Closed Mon, Closed D Sun (open for residents) **Prices** Fixed L 2 course fr £11.95, Fixed D 3 course fr £31.95 **Wines** 30 bottles over £20, 34 bottles under £20, 34 by glass **Notes** Sunday L, Vegetarian available **Seats** 40, Pr/dining room 16 **Children** Min 8 yrs, Portions **Parking** 24

| LLANDRINDOD WELLS | Map 9 SO06 |

The Metropole

◉ Modern British V

Stylish dining room with well-balanced menus

☎ 01597 823700
Temple St LD1 5DY
e-mail: info@metropole.co.uk
dir: In centre of town off A483

This imposing Victorian hotel dominates this famous spa town, and has been run by the same family for over 100 years. The lobby leads to the informal Spencers Bar and Brasserie and an elegant lounge, while the smart dining room exudes style with contemporary leather and suede high-backed chairs complemented by classic ivory and white linen creating a relaxed, upbeat vibe. Modern British dishes with a classical twist include kiln-roasted and poached Welsh salmon with charred ciabatta and chive oil, followed by a main course of roasted fillet of Welsh Black beef with confit tomato, creamed celeriac, woodland mushrooms and port wine reduction.

Chef Nick Edwards **Owner** Justin Baird-Murray **Times** 12.30-1.45/7-9.30 **Prices** Fixed L 2 course £11.50-£15, Fixed D 3 course £26-£30, Service optional **Wines** 24 bottles over £20, 54 bottles under £20, 7 by glass **Notes** Sunday L, Vegetarian menu, Civ Wed 200, Air con **Seats** 200, Pr/dining room 250 **Children** Portions, Menu **Parking** 150

LLANFYLLIN
Map 15 SJ11

Seeds

⚫ Modern British ↓ NOTABLE WINE LIST

Unfussy food in dinner-party setting

☎ 01691 648604
5 Penybryn Cottages, High St SY22 5AP
dir: Village centre, on A490, 15 mins from Welshpool, follow signs to Llanfyllin

Original beams and slate floors combined with curios, maps, books and original works of art provide a truly intriguing setting at Seeds, a low-ceilinged parlour with an intimate dinner-party atmosphere. Jazz music plays in the background and friendly staff provide relaxed service, while the menu offers up unfussy modern British fare. Try mushroom and asparagus risotto or a platter of Italian meats and melon, followed by sautéed chicken breast with port and cream sauce or trio of fish in white wine, cream and cheese sauce. Comforting puddings include lemon posset with mixed berry sauce and treacle tart.

Chef Mark Seager **Owner** Felicity Seager, Mark Seager **Times** 11-2.15/7-8.30, Closed 25 Dec, 2 wks Mar, 1 wk Oct, Closed Mon-Wed, Closed D Sun **Prices** Fixed L 2 course £11.65-£22.90, Fixed D 3 course £25.25-£28.25, Starter £3.70-£6.95, Main £7.95-£15.95, Dessert £4.25-£5.95, Service optional **Wines** 30 bottles over £20, 81 bottles under £20, 3 by glass **Notes** Sunday L, Vegetarian available **Seats** 22 **Children** Portions **Parking** Free car park in town, street parking

LLANGAMMARCH WELLS
Map 9 SN94

Lake Country House Hotel & Spa

⚫⚫ British, European

Fine dining and old-fashioned charm in beautiful surroundings

☎ 01591 620202 & 620474
LD4 4BS
e-mail: info@lakecountryhouse.co.uk
web: www.lakecountryhouse.co.uk
dir: 6m from Builth Wells on A483 from Garth, turn left for Llangammarch Wells & follow signs to hotel

A splendid Victorian country house set in fifty acres of wooded grounds, this imposing hideaway also boasts sweeping lawns, rhododendron-lined paths and riverside walks. In keeping with tradition, afternoon tea is served in the drawing room by the fire, while the spacious dining room is a luxurious affair with white-clothed tables, quality crockery and cutlery, and impeccably directed, old-fashioned service. The kitchen delivers interesting flavour combinations via a sensibly compact, four-course dinner menu, which changes daily and makes good use of locally sourced produce. Try line-caught sea bass, celery, mushrooms, new potatoes, vine tomatoes and tarragon velouté and round things off with fig pannacotta, coffee ice cream and chocolate tuile. Gourmet and vegetarian menus also available, plus an excellent wine list.

Lake Country House Hotel & Spa is AA Hotel of the Year for Wales

Times 12.30-2/7.30-9.15

LLANWDDYN
Map 15 SJ01

Lake Vyrnwy Hotel

⚫ Modern British

Stunning views and beautifully presented food

☎ 01691 870692
Lake Vyrnwy SY10 0LY
e-mail: info@lakevyrnwyhotel.co.uk
web: www.lakevyrnwyhotel.co.uk
dir: Follow tourist signs on A495/B4393, 200 yds past dam at Lake Vyrnwy

The location of this country-house hotel above Lake Vyrnwy is the stuff of dreams. Set in 24,000 acres of woodland and moors, the hotel looks over the lake's famous gothic tower and across the rolling hills all around. The accommodation makes the most of the views, not least the conservatory restaurant where produce from local farms, the lake itself and game shoots, further enhances the connection to the landscape. The food here is attractively presented and the seasons are adhered to. Start with crab, tiger prawn and potato tian before herb-coated loin of Lake Vyrnwy lamb served with a mini shepherd's pie and leek and grain mustard risotto.

Chef David Thompson **Owner** The Bisiker family **Times** 12-2/6.45-9.15 **Wines** 111 bottles over £20, 19 bottles under £20, 9 by glass **Notes** Fixed D 5 courses £33.50-£37.50, Sunday L, Vegetarian available, Dress restrictions, Smart casual preferred, Civ Wed 220 **Seats** 85, Pr/dining room 36 **Children** Portions **Parking** 80

LLANWRTYD WELLS
Map 9 SN84

Carlton Riverside

⚫⚫⚫ – see page 570

Lasswade Country House Restaurant with Rooms

⚫⚫ Modern British ✪

Pro-organic Edwardian country-house dining

☎ 01591 610515
Station Rd LD5 4RW
e-mail: info@lasswadehotel.co.uk
dir: On A483, follow signs for station, opposite Spar shop, adjacent to tourist info office, 400yds on right before station

An idyllic location with wonderful country views, this Edwardian house has a traditional dining room with polished inlaid mahogany tables and elegant chandeliers. There's a great emphasis on organic and quality local produce, like smoked organic salmon (served with watercress pesto) from the Welsh borders, fish fresh from Milford Haven, or Welsh Black beef reared only a quarter of a mile away. Cooking is simple without any pretension, in dishes like roast cannon of Elan Valley mutton with leek soufflé and Madeira jus, or medallion of Welsh Black beef glazed with grain mustard hollandaise and olive mash. Finish with a warm fig and honey tart or a plate of unpasteurised Welsh cheeses.

Chef Roger Stevens **Owner** Roger & Emma Stevens **Times** Closed 25 Dec, Closed L all week **Prices** Fixed D 3 course £28-£40, Service optional **Wines** 9 bottles over £20, 17 bottles under £20, 2 by glass **Notes** Dress restrictions, Smart casual **Seats** 20, Pr/dining room 20 **Children** Min 8 yrs **Parking** 6

Carlton Riverside

LLANWRTYD WELLS　　Map 9 SN84

Modern

Superb honest cooking in delightful family-run riverside restaurant

☎ 01591 610248
Irfon Crescent LD5 4SP
e-mail: info@carltonrestaurant.co.uk
web: www.carltonrestaurant.co.uk
dir: Town Centre beside the bridge

Set beside the river bridge in the centre of town, this small, characterful three-storey restaurant with rooms - a former AA Restaurant of the Year for Wales winner - is home to the friendly and enthusiastic Gilchrists (the husband-and-wife team previously at Carlton House). The stylish, intimate restaurant combines quality contemporary fabrics and furnishings with the charm of the house and river views. It's all very soothing, with comforts provided by high-backed chocolate-brown leather chairs and cream napery, and the diligent and attentive service of Alan Gilchrist. Wife Mary Ann looks after the cooking, her confident, one-woman act undertaken with panache, underlining her obvious passion and talent. Her fixed-price menus (the Chef's Menu is a no-choice affair, while the Irfon Menu offers a compact selection) make a virtue of simplicity, the wonderful straightforward approach driven by stunningly fresh, local seasonal produce. It's honest with no gimmicks, and everything is full of flavour and perfectly timed. Smoked haddock and leek gratin topped with gruyère cheese shows the style, followed by seared fillet of beef with buttered spinach, potatoes Savoyarde, and red wine and mushroom sauce, and to finish warm chocolate fondant with home-made pistachio ice cream.

Chef Mary Ann Gilchrist **Owner** Dr & Mrs Gilchrist
Times 12.30-2.30/7-9, Closed L Mon-Sat, Closed D Sun
Prices Fixed D 3 course £22.50-£25, Starter £5-£9, Main £12-£26, Dessert £5-£9, Service optional **Wines** 60 bottles over £20, 15 bottles under £20, 4 by glass
Notes Sunday L, Vegetarian available **Seats** 20
Children Portions, Menu **Parking** Car park opposite

LLYSWEN　　Map 9 SO13

Llangoed Hall

◉◉ Traditional British V

Fine dining in a magnificent setting

☎ 01874 754525
LD3 0YP
e-mail: enquiries@llangoedhall.co.uk
dir: On A470, 2m from Llyswen towards Builth Wells

Situated in the Wye Valley, against the stunning backdrop of the Black Mountains, this historic country-house hotel is a haven of peace and quiet. The hall sits on a site dating back to 560AD where, it is said, the first Welsh Parliament was held. A noteworthy collection of fine artwork adorns the walls, perfectly complemented by antique furniture and luxurious fabrics. In the restaurant with its blue and white décor, service is friendly and efficient, and the appealing menu offers adventurous and accomplished dishes featuring local ingredients. Expect starters like Gower crab ravioli with shrimp and champagne sauce, followed by duet of Breconshire venison loin with celeriac purée, steamed venison pudding and Calvados sauce. Irresistible desserts may include dark chocolate fondant pudding with pistachio baked Alaska.

Chef Sean Ballington **Owner** Sir Bernard Ashley
Times 12.30-2.30/7-10 **Prices** Fixed L 2 course fr £17.50, Fixed D 3 course fr £37.50, Starter fr £9.50, Main fr £26, Dessert fr £9.50, Service optional **Wines** 110 bottles over £20, 9 bottles under £20, 6 by glass **Notes** Sunday L, Vegetarian menu, Dress restrictions, Jacket at dinner, no denim jeans, Civ Wed 80 **Seats** 50, Pr/dining room 80 **Children** Min 8 yrs, Portions **Parking** 50

MONTGOMERY　　Map 15 SO29

Dragon Hotel

◉ Welsh, International

Historic inn serving accomplished restaurant and bar food

☎ 01686 668359 ＆ 668287
Market Square SY15 6PA
e-mail: reception@dragonhotel.com
dir: Behind the town hall

This fine 17th-century coaching inn stands in the centre of town and is a popular haunt for locals and tourists alike.

Beams and timbers from the nearby castle - which was destroyed by Cromwell - are visible in the lounge and bar. The homely, traditional décor extends to the cosy beamed restaurant, which has a fireplace converted from an old bread oven. A wide choice of soundly prepared, hearty dishes is available in both the restaurant and bar. The Welsh cooking is via wholesome dishes that make sound use of local seasonal produce. Expect starters like tempura freshwater prawns and baby corn with teriyaki dip, followed by local beef fillet with a shallot and Dijon mustard crust, red wine reduction and Pont-Neuf potatoes.

Dragon Hotel

Chef Thomas Fraenzel **Owner** M & S Michaels
Times 12-2/7-9, Closed L all week ex by prior arrangement **Prices** Fixed L course £22.50, Fixed D 3 course £22.50, Starter £3.95-£6.25, Main £10.25-£19.50, Dessert £3.25-£4.50, Service optional **Wines** 7 bottles over £20, 43 bottles under £20, 12 by glass **Notes** Sunday L, Vegetarian available **Seats** 42, Pr/dining room 50 **Children** Portions **Parking** 20

WELSHPOOL   Map 15 SJ20

Royal Oak Hotel

◉ Welsh

Sympathetically refurbished former coaching inn with enjoyable, imaginative food

☎ 01938 552217
The Cross SY21 7DG
e-mail: relax@royaloakhotel.info
web: www.royaloakhotel.info

Dating back over 350 years, this former coaching inn sits in the heart of the small, busy market town of Welshpool. Sympathetically renovated in 2007, its minimalist décor highlights the many retained period features, including exposed beams, polished wood floors and open fires. Whether you choose the red or green dining room, service is friendly, attentive and well informed. Seasonality and freshness of produce is paramount here, with ingredients locally sourced wherever possible. Dishes are accurately cooked, achieving a clarity of flavour, such as the starter of smoked haddock gnocchi, with lemon and dill cream sauce, perhaps followed by pan-fried breast of duck with creamed cabbage and braised potatoes.

Times 6.30-9.30 (Bar 10-9)

RHONDDA CYNON TAFF

MISKIN   Map 9 ST08

Miskin Manor Country Hotel

◉◉ Traditional International **V**

Enjoyable, romantic dining in traditional manor house

☎ 01443 224204
CF72 8ND
e-mail: info@miskin-manor.co.uk
dir: 8m W of Cardiff. M4 junct 34, towards Llantrisant, turn left into private rd before lights

An impressive manor house, steeped in Welsh history and just a stone's throw from the M4, yet secluded in 22 acres of gardens. Original features abound, notably in the oak-panelled restaurant with its grand fireplace and decorative ceiling, which provides a relaxed, romantic setting with lovely garden views. The kitchen steers a traditional line with occasional modern detours and takes great pride in sourcing fresh seasonal quality Welsh produce. Ravioli of crayfish, baby spinach and smoked garlic with truffle emulsion, thyme-roasted rack of Welsh lamb stuffed with apricots and Y Fenni cheese, or red snapper with crab and pea linguine and saffron cream sauce, and Penderyn crème brûlée with fig sorbet are fine examples of the fare.

Chef Mark Beck, Ian Presgrave **Owner** Mr & Mrs Rosenberg **Times** 12-2.30/7-10 **Prices** Food prices not confirmed for 2009. Please telephone for details. **Wines** 13 bottles over £20, 33 bottles under £20, 12 by glass **Notes** Sunday L, Vegetarian menu, Dress restrictions, Smart casual, Civ Wed 100 **Seats** 50, Pr/dining room 20 **Children** Portions **Parking** 200

PONTYCLUN   Map 9 ST08

Brookes Restaurant & Private Dining Room

◉ Modern International

Welcoming restaurant offering innovative cuisine

☎ 01443 239600
79-81 Talbot Rd, Talbot Green CF72 8AE
e-mail: staffbrookes@btconnect.com
dir: M4 junct 34, follow signs for Llantrisant, turn left at 2nd lights

The bright blue frontage makes it hard to miss this buzzy eatery. Bold and contemporary, with its glass block surfaces and whitewashed walls hung with modern art, this chic restaurant offers a selection of innovative dishes. The extensive seasonally-changing menu fuses traditional and modern styles, with a mix of Italian, British, French and even Thai cuisine. Try the home-made mushroom soup served with French bread, followed by fillet of haddock with a parsley, lemon and brioche crumb on a sauté of spinach with sauce vièrge, and perhaps raspberry, vanilla and Grand Marnier crème brûlée with chocolate brownie to finish. The upstairs café bar is popular with shoppers.

Times 12-2.30/7-10.30, Closed 24 Dec, 1 Jan & BHs, Closed Mon, Closed L Sat, Closed D Sun

PONTYPRIDD   Map 9 ST08

Llechwen Hall Hotel

◉ Modern Welsh

Country retreat with imaginative food in relaxed surroundings

☎ 01443 742050 & 743020
Llanfabon CF37 4HP

Set at the top of a hill with a stunning approach, today's country-house hotel has served many prior purposes in its colourful 200-year history, including a private school and magistrates' court. Victorian-styled with deep-red furniture and traditional appointments, its dining-room's well-spaced tables come dressed in their best whites, while service is typically relaxed, friendly and efficient. The kitchen's modern approach takes its cue from fresh, local ingredients, so expect clean, simple, not overworked dishes that allow the main ingredient centre stage. Grilled pork tenderloin served with straw potatoes and sauce béarnaise, and lemon tart with champagne sorbet are fine examples of the fare.

SWANSEA

LLANRHIDIAN   Map 8 SS49

The Welcome to Town

◉◉ British, French

Country inn serving flavoursome local cuisine

☎ 01792 390015
SA3 1EH
web: www.thewelcometotown.co.uk
dir: 8m from Swansea on B4231. M4 junct 47 towards Gowerton. From Gowerton take B4295

Once a court house and jail, this 300-year-old whitewashed coaching inn is set in a rural part of the beautiful Gower peninsula and has a village-pub feel. Traditional period features have been retained: blackened oak beams, simple whitewashed walls, stone fireplace and a central bar, with wooden tables and chairs, and white linen continuing the unpretentious theme. The accomplished, skilful kitchen's modern approach - underpinned by classical roots - uses only the best local produce. Try terrine of ham knuckle with fried quail's egg and pineapple pickle, followed perhaps by fillet of Welsh beef au poivre with buttered spinach and fondant potato. Finish with apple tarte Tatin and clotted cream ice cream. Good vegetarian options are available.

Chef Ian Bennett **Owner** Jay & Ian Bennett **Times** 12-2/7-9.30, Closed 25-26 Dec, 1 Jan, last 2 wks Feb, 1 wk Oct, Closed Mon **Prices** Fixed L 2 course £15.95-£29, Fixed D 3 course £33.50-£43, Service optional **Wines** 18 bottles over £20, 10 bottles under £20, 6 by glass **Notes** Sunday L, Vegetarian available **Seats** 40 **Children** Portions **Parking** 12

REYNOLDSTON   Map 8 SS48

Fairyhill

◉◉ Modern British ▫ ◆ NOTABLE WINE LIST

Enjoyable dining at elegant country-house hotel

☎ 01792 390139
SA3 1BS
e-mail: postbox@fairyhill.net
web: www.fairyhill.net
dir: M4 junct 47, take A483 then A484 to Llanelli, Gower, Gowerton. At Gowerton follow B4295 for approx 10m

This delightful 18th-century house is hidden away on the Gower Peninsula in 24 acres of grounds that include

Continued

REYNOLDSTON *Continued*

mature woodland, a trout stream and a beautiful lake. Sympathetically restored with great care, the house has a welcoming entrance hall leading on to a comfortably furnished lounge and cosy bar, and a dining room that extends through two rooms. The large terrace allows diners to enjoy the mild Gower climate. Service is attentive and friendly, and the accurate and skilful modern British cooking makes the most of locally-sourced, often organic ingredients, some from the kitchen garden. Take a starter of seared scallops with red pepper, mango and coriander salsa and tempura courgette flower, and follow with pan-fried grey mullet with fennel-roasted potatoes, pak choi, sun-dried tomato and herb oil, or perhaps simply grilled Gower lobster with Thai butter and local crab wontons.

Times 12.30-2/7.30-9, Closed 26 Dec, 1-25 Jan, Closed Sun (Nov-Mar)

SWANSEA   Map 9 SS69

Bartrams @ 698

⊛⊛ Modern European **V**

Vibrant, modern venue with views across Swansea Bay

☎ 01792 361616
698 Mumbles Rd SA3 4EH
dir: From Swansea head towards Mumbles, at rdbt head for the pier for 1m, restaurant is on the right

A former fisherman's cottage with exposed brick walls and feature fireplaces, this relaxed restaurant overlooks Swansea Bay. From the groovy typographics of the frontage to the chic, modern interior (high-backed leather chairs, darkwood tables, artfully exposed brick, floor-to-ceiling feature radiators and a glass theatre kitchen), there's a young, funky, happening feel to this contemporary restaurant and coffee shop. Quality, local free-range and organic produce feature where possible; think pan-seared scallops with tempura of cauliflower and sultana dressing, followed by rump of Welsh lamb with minted Puy lentils, ratatouille and lamb jus. Blackboard specials reflect seasonal changes and display the dessert list (a vanilla crème brulée might head-up the list), while diners can bring their own wine for a small corkage charge.

Chef Steven Bartram, Jonathen Monopoli **Owner** Steven & Suzette Bartram **Times** 12-2.30/6-9, Closed 25-26 Dec, Closed Mon, Closed D Sun **Wines** 6 bottles over £20, 27 bottles under £20, 8 by glass **Notes** Seasonal menu 2-3 courses £15.95-£18.95, Sunday L, Vegetarian menu, Dress restrictions, Smart casual **Seats** 40
Children Portions **Parking** On street & car park

The Dragon Hotel

⊛ Modern European

Buzzy city-centre hotel brasserie

☎ 01792 657100 & 0870 4299 848
The Kingsway Circle SA1 5LS
e-mail: enquiries@dragon-hotel.co.uk
dir: M4 junct 42. At lights (after supermarket) turn right. Turn left into Kings Ln. Hotel is straight ahead

This contemporary and stylish hotel in the heart of Swansea boasts two restaurants, the busy ground-floor Dragon Brasserie with open-plan kitchen, and the main restaurant for more formal dining. With its floor-to-ceiling windows to enable you to watch the hustle and bustle of the city, the Brasserie offers both fixed-price and carte modern European menus including a variety of interesting dishes featuring local produce. Try a starter like leek and potato soup with warmed Caerphilly cheese and croûtons, followed by roasted rump of Welsh lamb with ratatouille, dauphinoise potatoes and watercress.

Chef Sam Thomas **Owner** Dragon Hotel Ltd
Times 12-2.30/6-9.30 **Prices** Fixed L 2 course £9.95, Fixed D 3 course £18.95, Starter £4.95-£7.95, Main £9.95-£19.95, Dessert £5.50-£6.95, Service optional **Wines** 5 bottles over £20, 24 bottles under £20, 10 by glass **Notes** Sunday L, Vegetarian available, Civ Wed 220, Air con **Seats** 65, Pr/dining room 80 **Children** Menu **Parking** 30

Hanson at the Chelsea Restaurant

⊛ Modern Welsh, French

Quality cooking in relaxed surroundings

☎ 01792 464068 & 07971 163 148
17 St Mary St SA1 3LH
dir: Situated in Small Ln between St Mary Church & Wine St

This contemporary restaurant is hidden away down a quiet side street in the city centre. Set on two floors, with fireplaces and wood-panelled walls, it is a comfortable, relaxed place renowned for its use of local ingredients. The modern Welsh menu includes a variety of fish dishes, as well as some traditional French dishes, with specials displayed on the chalk board. Choose from chargrilled sea bass, seared scallops and deep-fried spicy seafood parcels on three sauces, thyme-scented chicken supreme with fondant potatoes and sautéed wild mushrooms, or roast skate with mussels and shellfish medley.

Chef Andrew Hanson **Owner** Andrew & Michelle Hanson
Times 12-2.30/7-11.30, Closed 25-26 Dec, BHs, Closed

Sun **Prices** Fixed L 2 course £11.95-£14.95, Starter £4.50-£7.50, Main £9.95-£18.95, Dessert fr £4.95
Wines 20 bottles over £20, 20 bottles under £20, 8 by glass **Notes** Vegetarian available, Dress restrictions, Smart casual **Seats** 50, Pr/dining room 20
Children Portions, Menu

The Restaurant @ Pilot House Wharf

⊛ Modern European

Harbourside restaurant with an emphasis on fresh fish

☎ 01792 466200
Pilot House Wharf, Trawler Rd, Swansea Marina SA1 1UN
e-mail: info@therestaurantswansea.co.uk
dir: Please telephone for directions

Fresh local seafood is the draw at this striking boat-shaped building on the harbourside overlooking the River Tawe. Panoramic views, cream-painted rough-cast plaster walls and modern tables and chairs provide a light, contemporary dining space, reached via a spiral staircase in the tower, where service is relaxed and informal. The location ensures the promise of the freshest fish, displayed on daily chalkboard menus. Expect an uncomplicated, modern approach as in oven-roasted hake with crisp pancetta and prawn velouté, or baked halibut with mussels, clams and cockles. Meat-lovers are not forgotten, with perhaps venison and partridge featuring on the menu.

Chef Rob Wheatley **Owner** Helen Tenant
Times 12-2/6.30-9.30, Closed 25-26 Dec, 1 Jan, BHs, Closed Sun-Mon **Prices** Fixed L 2 course £10.95, Starter £4.45-£7.95, Main £12.95-£19.95, Dessert £5.45, Service optional **Wines** 12 bottles over £20, 20 bottles under £20, 4 by glass **Notes** Vegetarian available **Seats** 46
Children Portions **Parking** 20

VALE OF GLAMORGAN

BARRY   Map 9 ST16

Egerton Grey Country House Hotel

⊛ Modern, Traditional British ❀

True country-house dining in a lovely wooded valley

☎ 01446 711666
Porthkerry, Rhoose CF62 3BZ
e-mail: info@egertongrey.co.uk
dir: M4 junct 33, follow signs for Airport then Porthkerry, then turn left at hotel sign by thatched cottage

Situated in a wooded valley, this Victorian former rectory is a distinguished, grey stone hotel where the 7 acres of beautifully restored gardens are a must-see in summer. The main dining room occupies the former billiard room, panelled in antique Cuban mahogany, where chandeliers, fine bone china, crystal, silverware and candlelight provide a feast for the eye. Modern British fare - underpinned by a classical French influence - is the style; think chicken liver parfait with red onion marmalade, roast rack of Usk Valley lamb with fondant potatoes and garlic and rosemary jus; and a glazed lemon tart with raspberry sorbet to finish.

Chef Andrew Lawrance **Owner** Mr R Morgan-Price & Huw Thomas **Times** 12-2.30/6-9 **Prices** Fixed L 2 course £12, Fixed D 3 course £30.50, Service optional **Wines** 40 bottles over £20, 25 bottles under £20, 6 by glass **Notes** Sunday L, Vegetarian available, Dress restrictions, Smart casual, Civ Wed 40 **Seats** 40, Pr/dining room 16 **Children** Portions **Parking** 60

HENSOL   Map 9 ST07

La Cucina at Vale Hotel Golf & Spa Resort

◉ British Mediterranean

Modern golf restaurant with traditional wood-fired ovens

☎ 01443 667877
CF72 8JY
e-mail: reservations@vale-hotel.com
dir: M4, 3 mins from junct 34, follow signs for Vale Resort

Part of the Hensol Castle estate in a stunning setting, surrounded by 600 acres of beautiful countryside, this restaurant is located above the hotel and golf course in the golf clubhouse. The fresh, polished interior has a vast vaulted wooden ceiling and well-spaced tables. Menus offer a good choice of Mediterranean fare, with the likes of Portuguese sardines roasted in the wood-burning oven, served with lemon oil and Halem Môn sea salt, followed by breast of chicken stuffed with spinach, red pepper and ricotta cheese, wrapped in Parma ham and baked. Alternatively, choose from one of the grills, or go for an authentic pizza from the wood-fired ovens.

Times 12.30-2/6-10, Closed Sun & Winter opening times vary

LLANTWIT MAJOR   Map 9 SS96

Illtud's 216

◉ Modern Welsh

Historic, atmospheric restaurant utilising fresh, locally-sourced produce

☎ 01446 793800
Church St CF61 1FG

This former 16th-century malt house in the town's old quarter is now home to Georg Fuchs (previously at St David's Hotel in Cardiff) and wife Einar's restaurant - Illtud was reputedly a monk who brewed beer on the property. Original features offer a nod to a medieval-style banquet hall, with pitched ceiling, rows of rustic chairs and tables (laid with tall black candle holders), stonewashed walls, long curtains and ceiling canopies draped from one side of the room to the other. Pictures and paintings lend light relief, while the stone floors come scattered with many rugs. Georg's modern Welsh cooking is driven by seasonality and fresh quality ingredients from the abundant local larder; take rib-eye steak with béarnaise sauce, and to finish, perhaps the house speciality apple strudel served with crème anglaise.

Times 12-2.30/7, Closed Mon **Prices** Food prices not confirmed for 2009. Please telephone for details.

LLANARMON DYFFRYN CEIRIOG   Map 15 SJ13

The Hand at Llanarmon

◉ Welsh

Local fresh produce delivered with skill in traditional setting

☎ 01691 600666
LL20 7LD
e-mail: reception@thehandhotel.co.uk

This pastel-painted, 16th-century inn at the heart of a peaceful village - now a small family-run hotel - literally does extend the hand of welcome, with a large namesake wood-carved hand extending friendship at the front entrance. Inside, there's a predictable wealth of charm and character, with rustic furnishings and soft fabrics blending with exposed beams and brasswork throughout the bar and dining areas. The kitchen's crowd-pleasing menus change daily to make the very best of quality fresh produce from the abundant Welsh larder. Dishes come intelligently not over embellished to allow flavours to shine; take grilled whole Ceiriog trout served with lemon, walnut and dill butter, and from homely desserts, perhaps choose between a lemon meringue pie and sticky toffee pudding.

Times 12-2/6.30-8.45

West Arms Hotel

◉◉ British, French

Historic inn with fine food in the beautiful Ceiriog Valley

☎ 01691 600665 & 600612
LL20 7LD
e-mail: gowestarms@aol.com
dir: Exit A483 (A5) at Chirk (mid-way between Oswestry and Llangollen) and follow signs for Ceiriog Valley (B4500) - 11m

Set in the beautiful Ceiriog Valley, this delightful 16th-century drover's inn has a wealth of charm and character with an abundance of exposed beams, flagged floors, polished brass, inglenooks and ornate fireplaces. The traditional bar with its alluring menu is popular with locals, and shooting parties also like the traditional dining here. The restaurant's classic décor continues the

---

theme with tables set with white and burgundy linen and silver cutlery, while the kitchen's classically-inspired and well-executed dishes come with a modern edge and use local and Welsh produce. Grilled fillet of wild sea bass served on prawn risotto with a confit of tomatoes is a fine example of the fare, followed by fillet of Welsh beef wrapped in watercress glazed with stilton, with woodland mushrooms and Burgundy sauce.

Chef Grant Williams **Owner** Mr & Mrs Finch & Mr G Williams **Times** 12-2/7-9, Closed L Mon-Sat **Prices** Fixed D 3 course £32.90, Service added but optional 10% **Wines** 31 bottles over £20, 23 bottles under £20, 11 by glass **Notes** Sunday L, Vegetarian available, Civ Wed 70 **Seats** 34, Pr/dining room 10 **Children** Portions, Menu **Parking** 20

WREXHAM   Map 15 SJ35

Kagan's Brasserie

◉ British

Friendly hotel brasserie in beautiful grounds

☎ 01978 780555
Best Western Cross Lanes Hotel, Cross Lanes, Bangor Road LL13 0TF
e-mail: guestservices@crosslanes.co.uk
dir: On A525, Wrexham to Whitchurch Rd, between Marchwiel and Bangor-on-Dee

Set in 6 acres of beautiful grounds, this hotel was built as a country house in the late 19th century and has been a hotel since 1959. The oak panelling in the front hall is Jacobean and dates back to around 1620. Kagan's is a relaxed and friendly brasserie-style restaurant, with slate and oak floors, rustic tables, log fires in winter and patio dining in summer. The modern British menu draws inspiration from around the globe. Food is simply cooked using fresh local ingredients and might include chicken breast stuffed with mushroom duxelle on braised leeks with tarragon sauce.

Chef Mr Vinnie Williams **Owner** Michael Kagan **Times** 12-3/6.30-9.30, Closed D 25-26 Dec **Prices** Food prices not confirmed for 2009. Please telephone for details. **Wines** 34 bottles over £20, 29 bottles under £20, 20 by glass **Notes** Sunday L, Vegetarian available, Dress restrictions, Smart casual, Civ Wed 140 **Seats** 50, Pr/dining room 60 **Children** Portions, Menu **Parking** 70

Northern Ireland

Mussenden Temple, Downhill

BUSHMILLS   Map 1 C6

The Distillers Arms

⊚ Irish 🕙

Traditional-style inn serving hearty Irish food

☎ 028 2073 1044
140 Main St BT57 8TR
e-mail: simon@distillersarms.com
dir: On main street, 250mtrs from Old Bushmills
Distillery

This inn is one of a number of listed buildings located in
the small town of Bushmills, famous for its whiskey
distillery. Once the home of the distillery owners, it dates
back 250 years and has some interesting features. The
spacious open-plan restaurant is laid out over two levels
and finished with natural stone, a traditional beamed
ceiling and a real fire in winter. Short seasonal modern
Irish menus are strong on local produce, with an
especially good seafood range. Try Old Bushmills
whiskey-cured salmon, or fish pie with scallops.

Chef Dylan Starrs **Owner** Simon Clarke
Times 12.30-3/5.30-9, Closed 25-26 Dec, Closed Mon-
Tue in winter, Closed L Wed-Fri in winter **Prices** Starter
£3.95-£6.95, Main £10.95-£18.95, Dessert £4.95, Service
included **Wines** 10 bottles over £20, 30 bottles under
£20, 4 by glass **Notes** Sunday L, Vegetarian available
Seats 85, Pr/dining room 30 **Children** Portions, Menu
Parking 15

CARNLOUGH   Map 1 D6

Frances Anne Restaurant

⊚ Modern, Traditional 🕙

Fine dining in genteel hotel

☎ 028 2888 5255
Londonderry Arms Hotel, 20 Harbour Rd BT44 0EU
e-mail: ida@glensofantrim.com
dir: 14m N of Larne on the Causeway Coastal route

Set in a pretty fishing village overlooking the glorious
Antrim coast, this historic hotel was built as a coaching
inn in 1848 for Lady Londonderry - whose great grandson,
Sir Winston Churchill, also owned the property at one
time. Oak carvings, antique furniture and driftwood
sculptures comprise the tasteful décor, which combines
with original Georgian fittings. The kitchen's modern
approach contrasts with its traditional surroundings;
expect simple contemporary cooking that makes good use
of quality produce from the local larder, such as pan-
fried supreme of County Down chicken with pancetta.

Chef Manus Jamison **Owner** Frank O'Neill
Times 12.30-2.45/7-8.15, Closed 24-25 Dec, Closed L
Mon-Sat **Prices** Fixed D 3 course fr £20, Starter
£3.95-£5.75, Main £10.95-£15.95, Dessert £3.25-£5.25,
Service optional **Wines** 9 bottles over £20, 21 bottles
under £20, 5 by glass **Notes** Sunday L, Vegetarian
available, Civ Wed 100 **Seats** 80, Pr/dining room 14
Children Portions, Menu **Parking** 30

BELFAST   Map 1 D5

Aldens

⊚ Modern

Stylish restaurant serving imaginative food

☎ 028 9065 0079
229 Upper Newtownards Rd BT4 3JF
e-mail: info@aldensrestaurant.com
dir: At x-rds with Sandown Rd

This striking contemporary restaurant is just a short
distance from the city centre and has a stylish interior,
its large etched-glass screens and matching windows
providing intimate areas, complemented by subtle
lighting and well-appointed tables. The varied modern
menu includes traditional favourites alongside seasonal
and more complex offerings. Heart-warming dishes
include pork and leek sausages with onion gravy, or
salmon fishcakes with rocket and radish salad, while
more adventurous combinations might feature oysters
in tempura batter with soy dipping sauce, or perhaps
roast squab pigeon with soft polenta and truffle jus.
Friendly staff and attentive service ensure a loyal local
following.

Times 12-2.30/6-10, Closed 1 wk Jul, BHs, Closed Sun,
Closed L Sat

Beatrice Kennedy

⊚ Modern International

Imaginative food in listed Victorian building

☎ 028 9020 2290
44 University Rd BT7 1NJ
e-mail: reservations@beatricekennedy.co.uk
dir: Adjacent to Queens University

A short walk from Queens University and situated in a
former townhouse, this intimate restaurant is reminiscent
of a French bistro. Rich, plum-coloured walls, wooden
floors, lazy colonial ceiling fans and the sounds of big-
band jazz give it a 1940s style, with shelves of books
adding to the informal atmosphere. Leather chairs, white
linen tablecloths, candles and chandeliers add to the
intimate mood. Smartly turned-out staff are well
informed and friendly. Expect good value, modern
international cuisine: crispy pancetta with mussels,
white beans and chorizo, followed by Finnebrogue venison
with root vegetable and potato pie and blackberry jus, or

Barbary duck breast with braised red cabbage, fondant
potato and apple purée.

Times 12.30-3/5-10.30, Closed 24-26 Dec, 1 Jan, Etr,
Closed Mon, Closed L Mon-Sat

Cayenne

⊚ Modern International V 🕙

**Globally-influenced food in relaxed, hip and friendly
surroundings**

☎ 028 9033 1532
7 Ascot House, Shaftesbury Square BT2 7DB
e-mail: belinda@rankingroup.co.uk
dir: Top of Great Victoria St

Paul and Jeanne Rankin's flagship restaurant has a vivid
colour scheme and innovative, interactive artworks by
local-born artist Peter Anderson. Graphic art screened
lighting with coordinated music performs alongside
smartly uniformed, well-informed staff. There's a sense
of theatre about the food, too, with its predominantly
oriental influences (plus Pacific, Indian and
Mediterranean touches) applied to well-sourced Irish
ingredients. Imaginative dishes are well presented
without over embellishment. Recommendations include
salt 'n' chilli squid with napa slaw, chilli jam and aioli,
pork pot stickers and tuna au poivre with wasabi potato
salad and crispy shallots.

Chef Paul Rankin **Owner** Paul & Jeanne Rankin
Times 12-2.15/5-late, Closed 25-26 Dec, Etr Mon, May
Day BH, 12-13 Jul, Closed L Sat-Sun **Prices** Fixed L 2
course fr £12, Fixed D 3 course fr £19.50, Starter
£5.75-£9.50, Main £14.50-£23.50, Dessert £5.95-£6.50,
Service optional, Groups min 6 service 10% **Wines** 60
bottles over £20, 20 bottles under £20, 15 by glass
Notes Vegetarian menu, Air con **Seats** 150, Pr/dining
room 16 **Children** Portions **Parking** On street, NCP

The Crescent Townhouse

⊚ Modern European V 🕙

Townhouse brasserie offering creative cuisine

☎ 028 9032 3349
13 Lower Crescent BT7 1NR
e-mail: info@crescenttownhouse.com
dir: Opposite Botanic Railway Station, on corner of Lower
Crescent and Botanic Ave

This stylish, smartly presented Regency townhouse
turned boutique hotel is centrally located near the
Botanic Gardens and railway station. With a striking
19th-century façade, it offers accomplished, creative
cuisine at a wallet-friendly price. Complemented by the
popular colonial-style Bar Twelve on the ground floor, the
buzzy and cosmopolitan Metro Brasserie has a
globetrotting range that sets the best of traditional Irish
cooking alongside more modern European ideas. Take
wok-fried chilli squid with papaya, mango and lime
salad, or perhaps roasted wild sea bass on fennel and
new potatoes with vanilla and olive beurre blanc.
Vegetarians might opt for rosemary dauphinoise with

Continued on page 577

Deanes Restaurant

Modern French, Irish NOTABLE WINE LIST

Exemplary modern cooking from arguably the best restaurant in Northern Ireland

☎ 028 9033 1144
36/40 Howard St BT1 6PF
e-mail: info@michaeldeane.co.uk
dir: Located at rear of City Hall. Howard St on left opposite Spires building

The refurbished Deanes restaurant, now situated in the larger ground floor of the Howard Street building, is firmly established as the stylish and contemporary flagship for the expanding Deanes Restaurant Group. Situated just round the corner from its sibling Vin Café and Bistro in Bedford Street, and just half a mile from the vibrant new Deanes at Queens' bar and grill, it makes it an ideal location for owner Michael Deane to oversee all three city-centre operations. The crisp linen tablecloths and designer setting have proved very popular with the dining elite of Belfast and make early booking advisable. The open kitchen provides diners with the theatre of chefs-on-show, though this is a calm and disciplined brigade, while service is suitably impeccable and knowledgeable but relaxed. High quality, precision cooking, great combinations and clear flavours showcase the best of the province's produce; a modern approach of the most refined and confident order. Consistency is key here, there's nothing too overly faddish either, just quality through and through. Take a saddle of rabbit served with macaroni gratin, chervil root purée, roast cep and a smoked bacon and verjus reduction, or perhaps pan-fried halibut accompanied by a tagliatelle of local squid with sauce of confit tomato and shellfish and parmesan gnocchi. Peripherals like breads and petits fours all hit form too, as might a warm chocolate fondant with stout ice cream and macadamia tuile. An excellent wine list, including a notable list of pudding wines, proves a fitting accompaniment.

Chef Michael Deane, Derek Creagh **Owner** Michael Deane, Derek Creagh **Times** 12-2.30/6-9.30, Closed 25 Dec, BH's, 12-13 Jul, Closed Sun **Prices** Fixed L 2 course £16.50, Starter £7.50-£11, Main £17-£23, Dessert £8-£11, Service added but optional 10% **Wines** 99 bottles over £20, 8 bottles under £20, 9 by glass **Notes** Vegetarian available, Air con **Seats** 70, Pr/dining room 40 **Children** Portions, Menu **Parking** On street (after 6pm), car park Clarence St

BELFAST *Continued*

fennel confit, chargrilled leeks, roasted vegetables and sauce vièrge.

Chef Karl Taylor **Owner** Wine Inns Ltd
Times 12-3/5.45-10, Closed 25-26 Dec, 1 Jan, 11-12 Jul, Closed L Sun **Wines** 11 bottles over £20, 31 bottles under £20, 9 by glass **Notes** Early Bird 2-3 courses £16.95-£19.90, Vegetarian menu, Dress restrictions, Smart casual, Air con **Seats** 72, Pr/dining room 35 **Children** Portions **Parking** Opposite hotel

Deanes Restaurant

◉◉◉◉ – *see opposite*

Green Door Restaurant

◉ Modern European

Fine dining in a stylish city-centre hotel

☎ 028 9038 8000
Malone Lodge Hotel, 60 Eglantine Av, Malone Road BT9 6DY
e-mail: info@malonelodgehotel.com
dir: At hospital rdbt exit towards Bouchar Road. At 1st rdbt, right at lights onto Lisburn Road, 1st left into Eglantine Ave.

This attractive hotel is set in a Victorian terrace in the leafy suburbs of the university area of South Belfast. The unassuming frontage opens into a spacious interior with a smart lounge, bar and stylish, intimate Green Door Restaurant - very atmospheric with its dark-coloured walls and subdued lighting. Quality Irish produce is used in well-presented seasonal dishes, some with unusual flavour combinations. Main dishes might include roasted monkfish with cumin-roasted carrots and spicy carrot sauce, duck breast with Anna potatoes, orange and cardamom glaze, or loin of wild boar, pappardelle pasta and hot mustard relish.

Chef Dean Butler **Owner** Brian & Mary Macklin
Times 12.30-3/6.30-10, Closed D Sun **Prices** Fixed L 2 course £11.50, Fixed D 3 course £18.50-£22.50, Starter £3.95-£5.50, Main £9.95-£15.95, Dessert £4.50-£5.95, Service optional **Wines** 7 bottles over £20, 28 bottles under £20 **Notes** Sunday L, Vegetarian available, Civ Wed 120, Air con **Seats** 60, Pr/dining room 120 **Children** Portions, Menu **Parking** 35

James Street South Restaurant & Bar

◉◉ European

Imaginative cooking in contemporary city-centre restaurant

☎ 028 9043 4310
21 James St BT2 7GA

This intimate modern restaurant - located in the centre of Belfast on a quiet side street close to the main shopping and business district - has quickly attracted a loyal local following. Stark white walls contrast with colourful artwork, together with wooden floors, frosted-glass windows and stylish minimalist design, and there's a small

contemporary bar at the entrance for waiting guests. Good value two- and three-course fixed-price menus are offered for lunch, with a pre-theatre dinner menu available alongside the carte. The well-constructed, imaginative modern menu changes frequently to keep up with the seasons. Quality ingredients are cooked with flair, without the need for over-embellishment, to produce clean flavours and make the most of the high-quality local produce. Roast cod with surf clams, butter-braised leeks and caviar cream makes an interesting main course, with a subtly flavoured orange pannacotta served with rich mocha tart for dessert.

Times 12-2.45/5.45-10.45

Malmaison Belfast

◉ British

Contemporary-style converted seed mill offering satisfying dishes

☎ 028 9022 0200
34 - 38 Victoria St BT1 3GH
e-mail: mdavies@malmaison.com

Ideally located for the city centre, this converted seed mill has a tastefully embellished, ornate exterior which stands out from the crowd. Inside, the hotel exudes quality with a funky style found in fun furnishings and interesting artifacts. The bar, where champagne and cocktails cheerfully flow, is popular in its own right. With plain bistro-style tables, the brasserie delivers simple, enjoyable dishes with friendly service. An important aspect of the Malmaison dining experience is also the 'home-grown and local' menu, featuring the finest local produce. Try carefully prepared meals such as warm salad of Clonakilty pudding, followed by roast loin of Oisín venison, with colcannon mash and Madeira jus.

Times 12-2.30/6-12.30am

Shu

◉◉ Modern Irish V ◐

Fashionable, funky restaurant with modern Irish food

☎ 028 9038 1655
253-255 Lisburn Rd BT9 7EN
e-mail: eat@shu-restaurant.com
dir: From city centre take Lisburn Road lower end. Restaurant in 1m, on the corner of Windsor Ave

Set in a fine Victorian terrace, you would be forgiven for expecting a traditional interior, but Shu was modernized in 2000 by a renowned Belfast architect, and its cool, minimalist, contemporary restaurant is decked out in warm chocolate browns and beige, with swathes of suede and leather seating, polished, well-spaced tables and wooden floors. Smartly turned out, well-informed, confident service and a theatre-style, open kitchen give the fashionable package added edge. Shu's up-to-the-minute, lengthy Irish menu - with French influences - perfectly suits the surroundings. Serious cooking, seasonality and the use of quality local produce are keynote, delivering accurate, carefully presented, eclectic dishes to get the tastebuds tingling. Foie gras and chicken liver parfait, and wild hake, fennel, saffron, new potatoes, baby artichokes and tapenade show the style.

Chef Brian McCann **Owner** Alan Reid
Times 12-2.30/6-10, Closed 25-26 Dec, Closed Sun **Prices** Fixed L 2 course £10, Starter £3.75-£8, Main £10-£19, Dessert £5, Service optional, Groups min 6 service 10% **Wines** 44 bottles over £20, 18 bottles under £20, 17 by glass **Notes** Vegetarian menu, Air con **Seats** 100, Pr/dining room 24 **Children** Portions **Parking** On street

CO DOWN

BANGOR Map 1 D5

Clandeboye Lodge Hotel

◉ Modern

Creative cooking in a contemporary country setting

☎ 028 9185 2500
10 Estate Rd, Clandeboye BT19 1UR
e-mail: info@clandeboyelodge.co.uk
dir: M3 follow signs for A2 (Bangor). Before Bangor turn right at junction signed to Newtownards, Clandeboye Lodge Hotel and Blackwood Golf Course

Just 3 miles west of Bangor, this modern hotel cultivates a country-house ambience and is set beside the 200 acres of woodland, gardens, lawns and lake that make up the Clandeboye Estate. The restaurant is popular for its designer looks - think spiralling chandeliers, wood panelling and marble-topped tables - as well as for its courteous waiting team. A tempting menu features some intriguing combinations: kick off with a carpaccio of pineapple and watermelon with mint and Malibu syrup perhaps, before tucking into calves' liver with pancetta mash and onion marmalade. Presentation is simple and effective.

Times 12/9.30, Closed 25-26 Dec

1614

◉◉ Modern, Traditional British

Flavourful dining in an atmospheric inn

☎ 028 9185 3255
Old Inn, 15 Main St, Crawfordsburn BT19 1JH
e-mail: info@theoldinn.com
web: www.theoldinn.com
dir: Take A2 E from Belfast. 5-6m turn left at Ballyrobert lights, and 400 yds to Crawfordsburn. Inn is on left

The 1614 restaurant is the fine-dining option at the 17th-century Old Inn, owned and run by the Rice family for over 23 years. The interior retains its historic character with

Continued

BANGOR *Continued*

oak panelling, chandeliers and local coats of arms. Good quality soft furnishings, fixtures and fittings complete the picture. Frequently changing and keenly priced menus rely on seasonal ingredients, notably seafood from County Down ports and locally produced beef, lamb, game and vegetables. Typical dishes include seared sea scallops with cauliflower purée, roasted cauliflower and saffron beurre blanc, and local Finnebrogue venison rump with cassis sauce, potato gnocchi and spinach. Food is also served in The Churn Bistro and the Parlour Bar. Committed staff provide friendly and helpful service.

Chef Alex Taylor **Owner** Danny Rice
Times 12.30-2.30/7-9.30, Closed 25 Dec, Closed L Mon-Sat, Closed D Sun **Prices** Food prices not confirmed for 2009. Please telephone for details. **Notes** Dress restrictions, Smart casual, Civ Wed 85 **Seats** 64, Pr/dining room 25 **Children** Portions, Menu **Parking** 100

DUNDRUM   Map 1 D5

Mourne Seafood Bar

☺ Seafood

Vibrant fish restaurant 30 minutes from Belfast

☎ 028 4375 1377
10 Main St BT33 0LU
e-mail: bob@mourneseafood.com
dir: On main road from Belfast to The Mournes, on village main st

As befits a restaurant that owns its own oyster and mussel beds, shellfish is the star of the show at this popular place. Situated in a picturesque village at the foot of the Mourne Mountains, this simply presented restaurant, with wooden seats, wood flooring and basic table settings, has a cracking atmosphere and a preponderance of premium seafood. There's nothing too complicated on the menu - just high-quality ingredients handled with confidence and care. Meat and poultry dishes make a cameo appearance, but fish-lovers won't

want to miss garlic-roasted langoustines or roast skate wing with caper butter sauce.

Chef Neil Auterson **Owner** Bob & Joanne McCoubrey
Times 12/9.30, Closed 25 Dec, Closed Mon-Tue (winter)
Prices Fixed L 2 course £8.95, Fixed D 3 course fr £21.95, Starter £3.95-£7.95, Main £8.95-£18.95, Dessert £4.50-£4.95, Service optional, Groups min 6 service 10%
Wines 18 bottles over £20, 22 bottles under £20, 5 by glass **Notes** Fixed D menu Sat only, Sunday L, Vegetarian available **Seats** 75, Pr/dining room 16 **Children** Portions, Menu **Parking** On street

PORTAVOGIE   Map 1 D5

The Quay's

☺ British, International V

Top-quality seafood dining in quayside location

☎ 028 4277 2225 & 4277 1679
81 New Harbour Rd, Portavogie BT22 1EB
e-mail: quays@info.co.uk
web: www.quaysrestaurant.co.uk
dir: Take Portaferry road out of Newtownards and head towards Greyabbey, through Kircubbin and then Portavogie

A modern building comprising a bar, lounge and split-level restaurant, The Quay's is right on the shore with the sea in front and Portavogie harbour behind. The restaurant, overlooking the harbour, is decorated in uplifting Mediterranean tones and furnished with wooden

tables and comfortable chairs adding to the relaxed atmosphere. Seafood, naturally, is the speciality of the house with top dishes like Portavogie hand-shelled prawns, The Quay's seafood mixed grill, and scallops on Irish black pudding with parsnip purée. There's also plenty for meat-eaters and vegetarians from an extensive menu.

Chef Aaron Hanna, Dean Nickels, James Robinson & Kelly Moffat **Owner** Francis & Diane Adair
Times 12-2.30/5-8.30, Closed 25 Dec, Closed Tue (except BHs) **Prices** Starter £3.95-£5.95, Main £7.95-£25.95, Dessert £3.95, Service optional **Wines** 6 bottles over £20, 23 bottles under £20, 8 by glass **Notes** Sunday L, Vegetarian menu **Seats** 95 **Children** Portions, Menu **Parking** 60

see advert below

CO LONDONDERRY

CASTLEDAWSON   Map 1 C5

The Inn at Castle Dawson

☺ Traditional

Period-house dining with river views

☎ 028 7946 9777
47 Main St BT45 8AA
e-mail: info@theinnatcastledawson.co.uk
dir: Castledawson rdbt, from Belfast take 3rd exit, from Londonderry take 1st exit

Situated at the heart of the village with stunning views over the gardens and river, this large period house has undergone major renovation. The front reception still has the original black-and-white floor tiles, while cosy lounges and a small bar prove ideal for aperitifs. The modern dining room is spacious and comes with contemporary décor and comfortable furnishings, the subdued lighting creating a relaxed ambience. There's also a wall of glass to take in those views, double-height ceilings and a working stove as a focal point. The kitchen deals in quality local produce and mainly classical dishes

with a twist. Take a starter of smoked Lough Neagh eel served with beetroot, soda bread and horseradish, and follow with pan-roast salmon with spinach, white beans and merguez sausage for main course.

Chef Simon Toye **Owner** Simon Toye **Times** 12-2.30/5-10, Closed L Sat **Prices** Fixed D 3 course £22.50, Starter £3.95-£6.50, Main £9.95-£19.50, Dessert £4-£6, Service optional, Groups min 6 service 10% **Wines** 4 bottles over £20, 16 bottles under £20, 4 by glass **Notes** Sunday L, Vegetarian available, Air con **Seats** 90 **Children** Portions, Menu **Parking** 12

LIMAVADY	Map 1 C6

The Lime Tree

◉ Traditional Mediterranean ✆

Reliable neighbourhood restaurant with a welcoming atmosphere

☎ 028 7776 4300
60 Catherine St BT49 9DB
e-mail: info@limetreerest.com
dir: Entering Limavady from the Derry side, the restaurant is on the right on small slip road

Informal and unpretentious, this restaurant has a relaxed, friendly atmosphere and a loyal local following. The classical cooking has a pronounced Mediterranean influence and is strong on fish. Starters, all served with home-made wheaten bread and hand-rolled Irish butter, include crab cakes with Malin Head crabmeat and lemon and olive oil dressing. An all-time favourite main course is seafood thermidor - a selection of fresh fish glazed with a mild cheese and brandy sauce - and for dessert the Lime Tree crème brûlée is recommended.

Chef Stanley Matthews **Owner** Mr & Mrs S Matthews **Times** Closed 25-26 Dec, Closed Sun-Mon, Closed L all week (except by prior arrangement) **Wines** 11 bottles over £20, 31 bottles under £20, 5 by glass **Notes** Early bird menu Tue-Fri 6-7pm 2-3 courses £12.50-£14.95, Vegetarian available **Seats** 30 **Children** Portions, Menu **Parking** 15 **Parking** On street

---

Radisson SAS Roe Park Resort

◉ Modern V ✆

Enjoyable dining alongside a golf course

☎ 028 7772 2222
BT49 9LB
e-mail: reservations@radissonroepark.com
dir: On A6 (Londonderry-Limavady road), 0.5m from Limavady. 8m from Derry airport

This popular and impressive hotel is part of its own golf resort with extensive leisure facilities. Greens Restaurant serves fine local cuisine and a choice of international dishes in modern yet elegant surroundings. To demonstrate the range, some particular favourites are fillet of beef with champ potatoes, crispy parsnips and beef jus and seared scallops on a bed of tomato and saffron orzo, with spring onions and dried pancetta. A less formal, lighter dining experience is available in the

Coach House Brasserie, which overlooks the golf course.

Chef Emma Gormley **Owner** Mr Conn, Mr McKeever, Mr Wilton **Times** 12-3/6.30-10, Closed Tue-Thu in Jan, Closed Mon, Closed L Tue-Sat, Closed D Sun **Prices** Starter £3.95-£6.50, Main £14.25-£19.95, Dessert £6.15, Service optional **Wines** 8 bottles over £20, 23 bottles under £20, 8 by glass **Notes** Sunday L, Vegetarian menu, Dress restrictions, Smart casual, Civ Wed 250, Air con **Seats** 160, Pr/dining room 50 **Children** Portions, Menu **Parking** 250

LONDONDERRY	Map 1 C5

Beech Hill Country House Hotel

◉ Modern Irish ✆

Elegant country house serving stylish food

☎ 028 7134 9279
32 Ardmore Rd BT47 3QP
e-mail: info@beech-hill.com
dir: A6 Londonderry to Belfast road, turn off at Faughan Bridge. 1m further to Ardmore Chapel. Hotel entrance is opposite

Beech Hill was built as a family home in 1739. During World War II it was used as a base by the United States Marines, and a small museum honours this connection. This impressive hotel stands in 32 acres of glorious woodlands and gardens, and the elegant dining room extends into a conservatory to make the most of the lovely view. Skilfully cooked dishes are prepared from carefully sourced Irish ingredients, with a strong emphasis on sustainable and organic produce. Try risotto of Malin Head crabmeat with prawns or Mulroy Bay mussels and chorizo, followed by pan-fried Moss Brook Farm pork belly with caramelised fillet of pork.

Chef Raymond Moran/Paul Curry **Owner** Mr S Donnelly, Mrs P O'Kane **Times** 12-2.30/6-9.45, Closed 24-25 Dec **Prices** Fixed L 2 course £15.95, Fixed D 3 course £29.95, Starter £6.95-£8.95, Main £16.95-£23.95, Dessert £5.95-£6.95, Service optional **Wines** 22 bottles over £20, 46 bottles under £20, 8 by glass **Notes** Sunday L, Vegetarian available, Civ Wed 80 **Seats** 90, Pr/dining room 80 **Children** Portions **Parking** 50

Tower Hotel Derry

◉ Modern

Bistro-style restaurant within the city walls

☎ 028 7137 1000
Off the Diamond, Butcher St BT48 6HL
e-mail: reservations@thd.ie
dir: From Craigavon Ridge to city centre. Take 2nd exit at the end of bridge into Carlisle Road then to Ferryquay St, take 3rd exit on right onto Shipquay Street, turn left at bottom and follow road around to car park on Magazine Street

Right in the centre of the city, the Tower is the only hotel within the historic Derry walls, with fantastic views from the restaurant. The contemporary and stylish bistro is a bright, relaxing space, open-plan with the Lime Tree bar,

which is ideal for pre-dinner drinks, and an increasingly popular venue with the local community, tourists and corporate guests. The modern dishes are a fusion of local and international ideas.

Chef Barry O'Brien **Owner** Smorgs Ltd **Times** 12.30-2.30/6-9.45, Closed Xmas, Closed L (booking required) **Prices** Fixed D 3 course £22-£27, Starter £5-£10, Main £10-£15, Dessert £5-£10, Service included **Wines** 5 bottles over £20, 18 bottles under £20, 8 by glass **Notes** Vegetarian available, Civ Wed 300, Air con **Seats** 100, Pr/dining room 20 **Children** Portions, Menu **Parking** 35

MAGHERA	Map 1 C5

Ardtara Country House

◉◉ Modern International

Modern fusion cuisine in a country-house setting

☎ 028 7964 4490
8 Gorteade Rd BT46 5SA
e-mail: valerie_ferson@ardtara.com
dir: Take A29 to Maghera/Coleraine. Follow B75 (Kilrea) to Upperlands. Past sign for W Clark & Sons, next left

Originally built in 1896 as the Clark Linen Factory, the building was renovated as a family home and now has all the appearances of a traditional country-house hotel. Appearances can be deceptive however, and the classic décor of the dining room conceals some funky modern fusion cooking making an impact on the menu. Dishes might include a starter of cod with spicy ricotta and baby spinach millefeuille and yellow Kashmir curry sauce. A more traditional main course would be roast sirloin of McKees beef served with baked potato, Yorkshire pudding, wild mushrooms and red wine gravy. For an exotic dessert, try Guanaja dark crunchy chocolate with butterscotch sauce and crème Chantilly.

Times 12.30-2.30/6.30-9

Republic of Ireland

Lough Leane

CO CAVAN

CAVAN   Map 1 C4

Cavan Crystal Hotel

◉◉ Modern

Innovative cooking in contemporary hotel

☎ 049 4360600
Dublin Rd
e-mail: info@cavancrystalhotel.com
dir: Approach Cavan on N3, straight over rdbt, hotel immediately on left

Contemporary design, matched by the use of native timber, handcrafted brick and crystal chandeliers, make this a particularly distinctive new hotel. The modern dining room is on the first floor, backed by a friendly team of professionals. There's a health and beauty clinic here, and the Cavan Crystal shop and factory are on the same site. The cuisine is innovative in style and presentation, the cooking confident and using fine-quality local ingredients with integrity and some unusual twists. Accuracy, flavour balance and texture contrast all hit the right note in dishes such as a roulade of chicken with Wensleydale cheese and Parma ham stuffing, or perhaps a lavender and honey parfait served with a berry madeleine and raspberry sorbet.

Times 12.30-3.30/6-10, Closed 24-25 Dec

VIRGINIA   Map 1 C4

The Park Manor House Hotel

◉ European, International

Fresh produce served in a former hunting lodge

☎ 049 8546100
Virginia Park
e-mail: reservations@parkhotelvirginia.com
dir: Follow N3 to Virginia and when in village take first left. Hotel entrance 500 yds on left

The hunting lodge of the Marquis of Headfort from 1750 to 1939, this imposing property enjoys a superb location in 100 acres with mature gardens and woodland. The two restaurants, the Marquis and Marchioness, are renowned for their architectural interest. Here, classic cuisine with a global influence is offered, with the chef making excellent use of local produce, including fruit, vegetables and herbs from the estate's organic gardens. Try seafood chowder with pesto oil, braised shank of Cavan lamb with roast root vegetables and

rosemary, and mixed berry crumble topped with honey oatmeal crumb.

Times 12.30-3.30/6.30-9.30, Closed Jan, Xmas, Closed L Mon-Sat

CO CLARE

BALLYVAUGHAN   Map 1 B3

Gregans Castle

◉◉ Modern French, Irish

Country-house hotel dining with splendid views of The Burren

☎ 065 7077005
e-mail: res@gregans.ie
dir: On N67, 3.5m S of Ballyvaughan

With magnificent mountain views over the unique landscape of The Burren towards Galway Bay, the appropriately austere exterior of this family-run 18th-century country house belies the comfort and style to be found within. Elegant public rooms are furnished with beautiful antiques, and window tables in the restaurant make the most of the view across the bay. Skilful cooking shows enthusiasm and good use of high-quality local and organic produce, notably lamb from the village butcher. A typical meal may feature a main of roast loin of Irish pork with mustard and herb pommade served with ravioli of pork, redcurrant jus and apple crisp. Staff are renowned for their personal service.

Times Closed seasonal, Closed L all week

ENNIS   Map 1 B3

Temple Gate

◉ European

Modern dining in a Gothic-style building

☎ 065 6823300
The Square
e-mail: info@templegatehotel.com
dir: Follow signs for the Tourist Office, hotel is in same square

Built on the site of the former Convent of Mercy, this charming townhouse hotel retains much of its original Gothic style, but in a contemporary context. Refurbished in April 2008, JM's Bistro provides a relaxed, elegant setting, with high ceilings, warm rose-coloured décor, and crisply-clothed tables. A lengthy menu of predominantly traditional Irish dishes with a European twist takes in starters like pan-seared scallops with crispy pancetta, pea and spinach purée and chive velouté, while mains might feature thyme and rosemary braised lamb shank with buttery colcannon and redcurrant and rosemary glaze. The Great Hall, once the 19th-century convent's church, makes a fabulous setting for weddings and banquets.

Chef Paul Shortt **Owner** Paul Madden
Times 12.45-2.30/7-9.45, Closed 25-27 Dec, Closed L request only Mon-Sat **Prices** Fixed L 2 course €17-€20,

Fixed D 3 course €28-€35, Starter €6-€10, Main €18-€27, Dessert €6-€8, Service optional **Wines** 4 bottles over €20, 15 bottles under €20, 4 by glass **Notes** Sunday L, Vegetarian available, Dress restrictions, Smart dress **Seats** 90, Pr/dining room 200 **Children** Portions, Menu **Parking** 100

LISDOONVARNA   Map 1 B3

Sheedy's Country House Hotel

◉◉ Modern Irish

Pleasant country-house cooking of the classic and modern style

☎ 065 7074026
e-mail: info@sheedys.com
dir: 20m from Ennis on N87

Situated on the edge of The Burren, close to Lahinch golf course, Doolin and the Cliffs of Moher, this small family-owned and managed hotel has been in the Sheedy family since the 18th century and is the oldest property in the village. Originally a stone farmhouse, today it's a comfortable base for touring the region and exploring the breathtaking scenery. Food is strong on classic dishes with some modern influences and if some don't feature home-grown vegetables and herbs, you can be sure the produce was locally sourced. You could start with local organic St Tola goat's cheese on a caramelised onion tart with chervil dressed leaves, and follow with baked fillet of hake with sweet parsnip purée and saffron dressing, or seared scallops with coriander and lentil sauce.

Chef John Sheedy **Owner** John & Martina Sheedy **Times** Closed mid Oct-mid Mar, Closed 1 day a week Mar-Apr **Prices** Starter €8-€15, Main €21.50-€29, Dessert €7.85-€9, Service optional **Wines** 11 bottles over €20, 15 bottles under €20, 2 by glass **Notes** Air con **Seats** 28 **Children** Min 8 yrs, Portions **Parking** 25

NEWMARKET-ON-FERGUS   Map 1 B3

Dromoland Castle

◉◉ Traditional Irish, European V

Elegant dining in historic castle

☎ 061 368144
e-mail: sales@dromoland.ie
dir: From Ennis take N18, follow signs for Shannon/Limerick. 7m follow Quin. Newmarket-on-Fergus sign. Hotel 0.5m. From Shannon take N18 towards Ennis

Standing majestically over 410 acres of its own private demesne, this imposing castle turned luxury hotel dates back to the 16th century and is steeped in history. The magnificent public rooms are warmed by log fires, while the atmosphere in the elegant, fine-dining restaurant - with its Venetian silk wall hangings, crystal chandeliers and Irish linen - is enhanced by the soothing chords of the resident harpist. An attentive waiting team ushers guests to their seats and an extensive carte of classic European and traditional Irish cuisine including a dedicated vegetarian menu. Expect ambitious cooking

Continued

NEWMARKET-ON-FERGUS *Continued*

from a skilful kitchen. You might start with smoked pimento tapioca 'sushi' with tomato apple pickle purée and marinated goat's cheese, and follow with a main course of twice-cooked guinea fowl with cider glaze, Puy lentils, cabbage and squash purée in Calvados sauce.

Chef David McCann **Owner** Earl of Thomond **Times** 12.30-1.30/7-10, Closed 24-27 Dec, Closed L Mon-Sat **Prices** Fixed L course €40, Fixed D 4 course €68, Starter €16, Main €32-€35, Dessert €13, Service added 15% **Wines** 10 bottles under €20, 10 by glass **Notes** Sunday L, Vegetarian menu, Dress restrictions, Jacket **Seats** 80, Pr/dining room 40 **Children** Portions, Menu **Parking** 140

SPANISH POINT　　　　　　Map 1 B3

Admiralty Lodge

🏵 European

Modern cooking in peaceful country-house hotel

☎ 065 7085007
e-mail: info@admiralty.ie
dir: Please telephone for directions

Overlooking the picturesque Spanish Point on the west coast of County Clare, this country-house hotel occupies a peaceful and relaxing setting, and its close proximity to two excellent golf courses also makes it a perfect spot for golfers. The well-appointed and elegant Piano Room restaurant offers contemporary cuisine with an emphasis on local produce. Start with Inagh goat's cheese mousse and follow with pan-fried fillet of sea bass in a crispy crust, served with baby spinach and white wine sauce. Round things off with a glazed chocolate marquise.

Chef David Godin **Owner** P & A O'Malley **Times** Closed Jan-Feb, Closed Mon **Prices** Fixed D 3 course €40, Starter €7.95-€10.95, Main €22-€29, Dessert €7.95-€9.95, Service optional **Wines** 25 bottles over €20, 15 bottles under €20, 6 by glass **Notes** Vegetarian available, Dress restrictions, Smart casual, Air con **Seats** 40, Pr/dining room 10 **Children** Min 3 yrs, Portions **Parking** 40

CO CORK

BALLYCOTTON　　　　　　　Map 1 C2

Bayview Hotel

🏵🏵 Modern Irish, French 🍃

Accomplished cuisine in comfortable country house with dramatic views

☎ 021 4646746
e-mail: res@thebayviewhotel.com
web: www.thebayviewhotel.com
dir: At Castlemartyr on N25 (Cork-Waterford road) turn onto R632 to Garryvoe, then follow signs for Shanagarry & Ballycotton

Perched on a hillside overlooking the small, unspoilt fishing harbour of Ballycotton, the Bayview certainly offers breathtaking coastal views. As you'd imagine from the location, local seafood is a speciality here but doesn't monopolise the menu. The kitchen's modern Irish approach is underpinned by classic French themes and international influences, and also makes fine use of local meats and produce, with named suppliers proudly listed on the menu. Skill, creativity, flavour and bold presentation blend on a balanced, well-executed repertoire. Take the pan-seared Castletownbere scallops with pea purée and Fingal Ferguson salami dressing to start, followed by pan-fried fillet of turbot with Jerusalem artichoke purée, salsify sticks and vanilla butter, rounded off with a selection of Cork and Tipperary farmhouse cheeses.

Chef Ciaran Scully **Owner** John & Carmel O'Brian **Times** 1-2/7-9, Closed Nov-Apr, Closed L Mon-Sat **Prices** Starter €10.50-€14.50, Main €28-€35, Dessert €10.50-€15.50, Service optional **Wines** 6 bottles over €20 **Notes** Dress restrictions, Smart casual **Seats** 65, Pr/dining room 30 **Children** Portions **Parking** 40

BALLYLICKEY　　　　　　　Map 1 B2

Sea View House

🏵🏵 Traditional

Impressive Irish cooking in a delightful country house

☎ 027 50073 & 50462
e-mail: info@seaviewhousehotel.com
dir: 3m N of Bantry towards Glengarriff, 70yds off main road, N71

This friendly hotel in a tranquil village close to Ballylickey Bridge enjoys wonderful views of Bantry Bay and the mountains beyond. Secluded in colourful gardens, the immaculately maintained hotel has earned a reputation for consistently high standards over many years. The dining area consists of several rooms, decorated in warm tones of green and elegantly furnished with antiques and fresh flowers, and a delightful garden room. Cooking is country-house style and shows skill, enthusiasm and sound use of top quality local produce to give a modern twist to classic dishes. Fresh fish is a feature on the daily fixed-price dinner menu. Examples include warm light seafood mousseline with crab from nearby Castletownbere, and meatier options such as guinea fowl wrapped in smoked bacon served on a whiskey sauce. Desserts include such treats as strawberries marinated in orange liqueur on a crisp meringue base accompanied by home-made strawberry ice cream.

Times 12.30-1.45/7-9.30, Closed Nov-Mar, Closed L Mon-Sat

BALTIMORE　　　　　　　　Map 1 B1

Baltimore Harbour Hotel

🏵 Classic

Harbourside hotel offering enjoyable food

☎ 028 20361
e-mail: info@bhrhotel.ie

This quaint, very traditional seaside hotel in a pretty fishing village has been a fixture in the area for many years. The views across Baltimore harbour and the coastal islands are magnificent and there can be few better places to have a window table at sunset than the Clipper Restaurant - the adjoining Chartroom Bar is good for a music session, too. The menu features good-quality West Cork produce and locally-landed seafood: crab claw with citrus dressing, followed by seared tuna steak on squid ink tagliatelle.

Times Closed Xmas & wkdays Nov-Mar

Casey's of Baltimore Hotel

◉ Traditional, Seafood

Enjoy fresh fish, coastal views and a warm welcome

☎ 028 20197
e-mail: info@caseysofbaltimore.com
dir: From Cork take N71 to Skibbereen, then take R595.
Hotel is at entrance to village on right

Friendly family-run hotel with a cosy pub that boasts
open fires and traditional music at weekends. The
restaurant's simple décor sees pine furniture teamed
with local art, although the stunning sea views tend to
hold most people's gaze. Given the proximity, it's no
surprise that seafood is the speciality, with the day's
catch often delivered fresh from the proprietor's own
trawler and mussel beds. In addition to this fantastic
sea harvest, ingredients include locally-sourced
vegetables and traceable meats from the farmlands of
West Cork, all served up in a lengthy range of dishes
from a cold or hot seafood platter to prime Irish
Hereford fillet steaks.

Chef Victoria Gilshenan **Owner** Ann & Michael Casey
Times 12.30-2.30/6.30-9, Closed 21-26 Dec **Prices** Fixed
L 3 course fr €30, Fixed D 3 course fr €42, Starter €8-€15,
Main €19-€45, Dessert fr €6, Service optional **Wines** 5
bottles over €20, 15 bottles under €20, 2 by glass
Notes Sunday L, Vegetarian available, Air con **Seats** 100
Children Portions, Menu **Parking** 50

CLONAKILTY Map 1 B2

Inchydoney Island Lodge & Spa

◉◉ Modern French

Fresh West Cork food in a glorious coastal setting

☎ 023 33143
e-mail: reservations@inchydoneyisland.com
dir: From Cork take N71 following West Cork signs.
Through Innishannon, Bandon & Clonakilty, then follow
signs for Inchydoney Island

Situated between two fabulous beaches, this destination
resort hotel enjoys breathtaking panoramic views of the
Atlantic Ocean. There's designer furniture in the
reception, a plethora of paintings for sale, a newly
refurbished lounge for pre- and post-dinner drinks and a
restaurant with a contemporary look and stunning sea
views. French and Mediterranean influences are evident
in the menu, with fresh seafood and local organic
produce used where possible, in dishes of baked local
crabmeat with Coolea cheese crust, celeriac remoulade,
crisp wonton basket and Granny Smith apple salad,
followed by roast fillet of Irish beef in a turmeric and herb
crust. For visitors using the on-site spa, lighter options
are also available, such as salmon carpaccio with chive
blinis, native oysters and marinated cucumber, baby
potato salad and sakura cress.

Chef Adam Medcalf **Owner** Des O'Dowd
Times 12-9/6.30-9.45, Closed 24-26 Dec, Closed L all
week **Prices** Fixed D 4 course €60, Starter €12, Main €35,
Dessert €10, Service included **Wines** 5 by glass

Notes Vegetarian available, Dress restrictions, Smart
casual, Air con **Seats** 90, Pr/dining room 250
Children Portions, Menu **Parking** 250

CORK Map 1 B2

Maryborough Hotel & Spa

◉ Modern International V

Enjoyable dining in a popular hotel restaurant

☎ 021 4365555
Maryborough Hill
e-mail: info@maryborough.ie
dir: Please telephone for directions

Located just outside Cork, this Georgian country house
with a contemporary extension stands in 14 acres of
listed gardens and woodland. The restaurant offers a
wide-ranging modern European menu designed to suit
most tastes and is popular with both locals and business
travellers. The split-level dining room has a contemporary
feel and features its own walk-in wine cellar. Try prawn
and fennel tortellini with shellfish cream sauce to start,
followed by seared duck breast, ravioli with duck leg
confit, Savoy cabbage, golden raisin purée and prune jus,
with iced Baileys and chocolate parfait and caramelised
banana to finish.

Chef Gerry Allen **Owner** Dan O'Sullivan
Times 12.30-2.30/6.30-10, Closed 24-26 Dec
Prices Fixed L 2 course fr €25, Fixed D 3 course fr
€49.50, Starter €6.90-€14, Main €26-€35, Dessert fr
€9.50, Service optional, Groups min 10 service 10%
Wines 44 bottles over €20, 11 bottles under €20, 4 by
glass **Notes** Sunday L, Vegetarian menu, Dress
restrictions, Smart casual, Civ Wed 100, Air con
Seats 120, Pr/dining room 60 **Children** Min 10 yrs D,
Portions, Menu **Parking** 300

Orchid's Restaurant

◉ Modern Irish

Simple modern cuisine in chic surroundings

☎ 021 4845900
Hayfield Manor, Perrott Av, College Road
e-mail: reservations@hayfieldmanor.ie
web: www.hayfieldmanor.ie
dir: From Cork take N22 to Killarney. On Western Rd at
University gates turn left into Donovan's Rd, then right
into College Rd and immediately left into Perrott Ave

An architect-designed property set in its own secluded
grounds, Hayfield Manor retains its original fireplaces,

pillars, high ceilings and cornicing, alongside
contemporary additions. There are two dining options: the
glass-walled Perrotts Garden Bistro serving an informal
menu, and the elegant Orchids Restaurant, with its purple
décor and relaxed atmosphere. Here you will find modern
cuisine with a cosmopolitan feel in a room overlooking
classical gardens. Dishes making the best use of Irish
ingredients include crab and prawn linguine with orange
and tarragon cream, and pan-fried hake with pumpkin and
courgette risotto, baby leeks and truffle velouté.

Chef Graeme Campbell **Owner** Mr J Scally
Times 12.30-2/7-9.30, Closed Sun, Closed L all week
Prices Fixed L 3 course fr €40, Fixed D 4 course fr €69,
Service optional, Groups min 8 service 10% **Wines** 170
bottles over €20, 2 bottles under €20, 14 by glass
Notes Tasting menu available, L served festive season
only, Vegetarian available, Civ Wed 50, Air con **Seats** 80,
Pr/dining room 32 **Children** Portions, Menu **Parking** 100

GARRYVOE Map 1 C2

Garryvoe Hotel

◉ Modern Irish ☺

Sea views and simply-prepared fresh local food

☎ 021 4646718
Ballycotton Bay, Castlemartyr
e-mail: res@garryvoehotel.com
web: www.garryvoehotel.com
dir: From N25 at Castlemartyr (Cork-Rosslare road) take
R632 to Garryvoe

There are great views over Ballycotton Bay and the
beautiful beach from this seaside hotel, where modern
interior design extends into the classic restaurant. There
is a strong emphasis on local produce, especially the
catch from the nearby pier. Straightforward, modern Irish
dishes are the forte, traditionally presented on good
quality china. Start with a nostalgic Ballycotton prawn
cocktail with little gem lettuce, avocado and Marie Rose
sauce, and follow with golden-fried fillets of Ballycotton
plaice with gribiche sauce, then date and pecan pudding
with fudge sauce and vanilla ice cream.

Chef Kevin O'Sullivan **Owner** Carmel & John O'Brien
Times 1-2.30/6.45-8.45, Closed 24-25 Dec, Closed L
Mon-Sat **Prices** Fixed L 3 course €28-€33, Fixed D 3
course €41-€47, Starter €6.50-€9.50, Main €24-€30,
Dessert €6.50-€10.50, Service optional **Wines** 6 by glass
Notes Sunday L, Vegetarian available, Civ Wed 100
Seats 80, Pr/dining room 40 **Children** Portions, Menu
Parking 80

GOUGANE BARRA Map 1 B2

Gougane Barra Hotel

◉ Irish, French ☘

Fresh local produce in a stunning lakeside setting

☎ 026 47069
e-mail: gouganebarrahotel@eircom.net
dir: Located off R584 between N22 at Macroom and N71 at Bantry. Take the Keimaneigh junct for hotel

Set beside a lake in a peaceful valley surrounded by mountains on the edge of the National Park, this hotel makes a handy touring base for West Cork and Kerry or a great spot to simply relax and enjoy the view. Top-notch local ingredients distinguish the cooking at this friendly family-run hotel where seafood is a speciality. A small team do the honours, delivering a tempting menu of dishes, many of which are slow-cooked on an Aga. Start with pan-fried Clonakilty black pudding with apple sauce, mixed leaves and a sprinkle of bacon perhaps, before tucking into the likes of roast sea bass with clams, crystallised lemon and coconut foam, or West Cork lamb cutlets, courgette onion confit and rosemary gravy.

Chef Katy Lucey **Owner** Neil & Katy Lucey
Times 12.30-2.30/5.30-8.45, Closed 18 Oct-10 Apr, Closed L Mon-Sat **Prices** Fixed L 2 course €21, Fixed D 3 course €36.50-€38, Starter €6-€9, Main €18-€26, Dessert €5.50-€7.50, Service optional **Wines** 10 bottles over €20, 44 bottles under €20, 6 by glass **Notes** Sunday L,

Vegetarian available **Seats** 70 **Children** Portions, Menu **Parking** 40

KINSALE Map 1 B2

Actons Hotel

◉ Modern, Traditional European ☘

Waterfront townhouse hotel strong on seafood

☎ 021 4772135
Pier Rd
e-mail: info@actonshotelkinsale.com
dir: From Cork Airport continue to Five Mile Bridge take R600, on arrival into Kinsale take first left onto Emmet St then first left onto Pier Road, Actons Hotel is located on right

An established modern hotel overlooking Kinsale's bustling harbour, Actons occupies several Georgian townhouses on the waterfront. Drinks and light meals are served in the bar, and the adjacent garden in fine weather, while more formal fare is available in the Captain's Table. The restaurant is a bright, contemporary, nautically-themed room with polished tables and crisp white linen. A blend of modern Irish and European cuisine places the emphasis on seafood and healthy options prepared from fresh local produce. Try mussels with smoked salmon and shallots, seafood platter, and traditional Irish home-made apple pie.

Chef Paul McBride **Owner** Candela Ltd
Times 12.30-3/7-9.30, Closed Xmas & Jan, seasonal,

Closed L Mon-Sat **Prices** Fixed L 2 course fr €19.50, Starter €6.50-€15, Main €22.50-€35, Dessert €5.50-€8.50, Service included **Wines** 26 bottles over €20, 34 bottles under €20 **Notes** Sunday L, Air con **Seats** 80 **Children** Portions, Menu **Parking** 60

Pier One

◉ Modern, Traditional European

Waterfront hotel with harbour views

☎ 021 4779300
Trident Hotel, Worlds End
e-mail: info@tridenthotel.com
dir: From Cork take R600 to Kinsale. Hotel at end of Pier Rd

This hotel enjoys a wonderful location on the waterfront of historic Kinsale, affording fabulous views. Pier One, the fine-dining restaurant, is located on the second floor. The interior is bright and modern with large windows, rustic stone walls and artwork by well-known Irish artists. The style of cooking is modern Irish with traditional French and European influences, and the seasonal menu uses the best of local produce from land and sea. Expect the likes of West Cork lamb cutlets with a herb crust served on a rosemary jus, and baked sea bass with a fennel and caper butter.

Chef Denis Galland, Frank O'Reilly **Owner** Trident Dawncross Ltd **Times** 1-2.30/7-9.30, Closed 24-26 Dec, Closed L Mon-Sat **Prices** Fixed L 3 course €25-€27.50, Fixed D 3 course €30-€40, Starter €6-€14, Main €18-€35, Dessert €6-€9, Service optional **Wines** 24 bottles over

---

Longueville House

MALLOW Map 1 B2

Modern French

Classical cooking in splendid Georgian manor house

☎ 022 47156 & 47306
e-mail: info@longuevillehouse.ie
dir: 3m W of Mallow via N72 to Killarney, right at Ballyclough junct, hotel 200 yds on left

This handsome Georgian manor house is magnificently sited in a 500-acre estate in the heart of the Blackwater Valley. The open fires, antique mirrors and glittering chandeliers all evoke a bygone age of gracious living. Diners have a choice: there's the timeless elegance of the Presidents' restaurant under the gaze of former Irish presidents; the renovated Victorian Turner Conservatory, where white drapes and candlelight lend a touch of romance; or The Library. William O'Callaghan, the chef-

proprietor, masterminds the kitchen, his menu reflecting the top quality produce supplied almost entirely by the estate; seasonal vegetables, fruit and herbs from the walled garden, free-range eggs from their own hens and ducks, lamb and pork from the farm, and fish from the river that runs through the estate. The impressive cooking is underpinned by classical French themes, with flavourful dishes displaying high skill, balance, and plenty of enthusiasm. There might be escalope of halibut with rosemary-scented polenta and pearl onion sauce, or wild mallard duck with Jerusalem artichoke mousse and wild sloe sauce, with caramelised apple tarte Tatin and Longueville apple brandy ice cream to finish. Peripherals like canapés, breads and petits fours hold up the style through to the end.

Chef William O'Callaghan **Times** 12.30-5/6.30-9, Closed 8 Jan-17 Mar, Closed Mon-Tue (Nov-early Dec)

€20, 30 bottles under €20, 6 by glass **Notes** Sunday L, Vegetarian available, Dress restrictions, Smart casual **Seats** 90, Pr/dining room 200 **Children** Portions, Menu **Parking** 60

The White House

◉ Traditional, International

Bistro-style menu served in a lively atmosphere

☎ 021 4772125
Pearse St, The Glen
e-mail: whitehse@indigo.ie

Situated in the town centre, this traditional-style family-run restaurant with rooms and bar was established in the 1850s. Adjacent to the bar, the restaurant is rustic in style and there is live music each night. The menu offers traditional Irish cuisine with a bistro twist, using vegetables from their own garden and lots of local fresh fish. Expect starters such as battered king prawns with garlic butter, while main courses might feature roast hake with mussels and prawns and a white wine sauce, served with carrots, cauliflower and cabbage. Finish with apple pie and cream.

Times 12/10, Closed 25 Dec

MACROOM Map 1 B2

Castle Hotel

◉ Modern Mediterranean 🌱

Good food in a friendly, family-run hotel

☎ 026 41074
Main St
e-mail: castlehotel@eircom.net
dir: On N22, midway between Cork and Killarney

Run by the Buckley family for over 50 years, there are three dining options at this popular, long-established hotel - a traditional-style Irish bar (with a good-value carvery lunch every day), a continental café, and B's Restaurant which serves up bistro-style food with a contemporary twist. The split-level main dining room has something of an art deco feel with grey, black and deep red tones and high-backed chairs. Local produce is high on the agenda in dishes such as pan-fried pork steak with pancetta, pear and walnut risotto with Calvados jus, and home-made desserts like warm chocolate and orange zest fondant with chocolate tuile.

Chef Pat Ryan **Owner** The Buckley Family
Times 12-3/6-9.30, Closed 24-28 Dec **Prices** Fixed L 3 course €26.50-€30, Fixed D 3 course €42-€45, Starter €6-€11, Main €15-€28, Dessert €5.95-€7.50, Service included **Wines** 2 bottles over €20, 10 bottles under €20, 3 by glass **Notes** Sunday L, Vegetarian available, Air con **Seats** 50, Pr/dining room 150 **Children** Portions, Menu **Parking** 30

MALLOW Map 1 B2

Longueville House

◉◉◉ – *see opposite*

CO DONEGAL

DONEGAL Map 1 B5

Harvey's Point Country Hotel

◉◉ Modern, Traditional

Accomplished cooking in a tranquil setting

☎ 074 9722208
Lough Eske
e-mail: info@harveyspoint.com
dir: From Donegal 2m towards Lifford, turn left at Harvey's Point sign, continue to follow signs, taking three right turns to Harvey's Point gates

Nestling in trees on the shore of Lough Eske at the foot of the Blue Stack Mountains, this family-run country hotel provides luxurious relaxation in the wilds of Donegal. Service is personal as well as professional. The split-level restaurant offers great views over the lake, while its fixed-price menus take a modern Celtic approach. Ingredients are top quality and the cooking shows flair, skill and technical ability. Starters might include pan-seared scallops served with a nest of squid ink pasta with tomato concasse, and expect mains like breast of guinea fowl wrapped in Parma ham with leg confit stuffed with mushroom and nut accompanied by wild mushrooms in a cream sauce, Parisian roast potatoes and chiffonade of cabbage. For dessert, try lemongrass crème brûlée with raspberry sorbet set on a tuile basket.

Times 12.30-2.30/6.30-9.30

DUNKINEELY Map 1 B5

Castle Murray House Hotel and Restaurant

◉ French

Relaxed waterside dining specialising in seafood

☎ 074 9737022
St Johns Point
e-mail: info@castlemurray.com
dir: Situated on St Johns Point

A beautifully located clifftop hotel on the coast road to St John's Point, with wonderful sea and coastal views across ruined Castle Murray and McSyne's Bay. Watch the sun sink into the sea from the sun lounge and then dine on fresh, locally landed seafood in the traditional and welcoming restaurant, which also makes the most of the sea views. The seasonally-changing, French-inspired carte might take in a crab, tiger prawn and saffron tart, served with a tomato and chilli coulis, followed by pan-fried sea bass with vanilla-infused cream and tempura cauliflower, and banana, chocolate and rum crumble.

Chef Remy Dupuy **Owner** Marguerite Howley
Times 1.30-3.30/6.30-9.30, Closed mid Jan-mid Feb, Closed L Mon-Sat **Prices** Fixed D 4 course €50-€65 **Wines** 24 bottles over €20, 28 bottles under €20, 5 by glass **Notes** Sunday L, Vegetarian available, Civ Wed 30 **Seats** 80 **Children** Portions, Menu **Parking** 25

LAGHY Map 1 B5

Coxtown Manor

◉ European

Comfortable manor house serving seasonal local produce

☎ 074 9734575
e-mail: coxtownmanor@oddpost.com

A manor house situated set in 16 acres amidst the rolling hills of South Donegal, this comfortable hotel has been refurbished to a high standard, with a cosy cocktail bar and dining room complementing the delightful bedrooms. Owner Eduard Dewael cooks dinner using mainly local and organic produce. Lots of local seafood and meat appear on the seasonal menu and everything is made on the premises, including breads, sauces and ice creams. Start, perhaps, with a well-flavoured prawn risotto and move on to a tender and pink rack of lamb served with caramelised chicory and gratin potatoes. Finish with a decadent Belgian hot chocolate fondant.

Times 7.30-9, Closed Mon, Closed L all week

RATHMULLAN Map 1 C6

Fort Royal Hotel

Modern Irish, Seafood

Country-house dining in mature gardens sloping down to the sea

☎ 074 9158100
Fort Royal
e-mail: fortroyal@eircom.net
dir: Telephone for directions

No shortage of ways to raise an appetite at this friendly hotel: take a stroll around the grounds and you'll find a tennis court, a 9-hole pitch and putt course, and private access to a magnificent sandy beach. Set on the shores of Lough Swilly, Fort Royal has been run by the Fletcher family for more than fifty years and offers a high standard of hospitality. Its bright and airy restaurant overlooks the garden, which supplies fresh fruit, vegetables and herbs, while fish and meat comes from award-winning suppliers in the region. Tuck into warm salad of duck with croûtons and Cashel blue cheese; perfectly cooked turbot fillet with a chive hollandaise sauce, and pannacotta with mixed berry compôte.

Times Closed L all week

Rathmullan House

Modern Irish

Quality local and artisan ingredients simply treated with reverence

☎ 074 9158188
e-mail: info@rathmullanhouse.com

Rathmullan dates back to 1760 and its Weeping Elm Restaurant is set in three hexagon-shaped sunrooms (of silk Arabian-tent-like design) overlooking Lough Swilly and the hotel's well-planted gardens. Crisp linen and friendly, informed service set the scene for some highly accomplished cooking. The kitchen - under chef Chris Orr (ex London's famous River Café) - is driven by fresh, quality local ingredients, including organic produce from the walled garden or carefully sourced artisan suppliers. Menus change daily to reflect seasonality and availability, with dishes intelligently simple but executed with flair and skill; take a loin of local lamb served with a crisp tart of red onion marmalade, wilted spinach, purée of creamed shallots and a rosemary jus.

Times 7.30-8.45 **Prices** Food prices not confirmed for 2009. Please telephone for details.

ROSSNOWLAGH Map 1 B5

Sandhouse Hotel

Traditional

Fine food in stunning Donegal Bay location

☎ 071 9851777
e-mail: info@sandhouse-hotel.ie
dir: 10m S of Donegal & 7m from Ballyshannon on coast road

Once a fishing lodge and perched on the shore at Rossnowlagh, this fine hotel overlooks miles of secluded coves and sandy beaches. The recently refurbished, split-level restaurant is formal but very friendly. All residents dine, so booking is required for non-residents. A daily-changing menu offers the finest fresh local produce, including locally-landed seafood and prime beef and lamb. The style has classical roots but acknowledges more modern trends. Expect terrine of Donegal Bay crab in a light crème fraîche served with rocket salad, followed by boned loin of lamb with sage stuffing, with a classic Charlotte russe to finish.

Chef Sid Davis, John McGarrigle **Owner** Brian Britton **Times** 12.30-2.30/7-9.30, Closed Nov-Feb, Closed L Mon-Sat **Prices** Fixed L 2 course €20-€30, Fixed D 3 course €35-€45, Starter €12.50-€17.50, Main €20-€35, Dessert €7.50-€12.50, Service optional **Wines** 30 bottles over €20, 50 bottles under €20, 20 by glass **Notes** Sunday L, Air con **Seats** 80, Pr/dining room 30 **Children** Portions, Menu **Parking** 30

DUBLIN

DUBLIN Map 1 D4

Clarion Hotel Dublin IFSC

Traditional Italian

Sophisticated corporate hotel with Italian cuisine

☎ 01 4338800
I.F.S.C.
e-mail: sinergie@clarionhotelifsc.com
dir: Financial Services Centre

This well-designed, modern hotel is located in the heart of the financial service district. The restaurant offers modern Italian dishes with some innovative ideas like 'make your own bruschetta'. Starters include carpaccio bresaola with rocket salad or one of a good selection of pasta or rice dishes. Main courses include the signature dish of home-made agnolotti with spinach and fresh

ricotta, vine ripe tomatoes and basil sauce; chicken saltimbocca alla Romana or sea bass cartoccio baked in a parcel with cherry tomatoes, olives and white wine. Desserts like pannacotta or tiramisu bring proceedings to a satisfying close. The attentive staff provide a professional service.

Times 12-2.30/6-9.45, Closed 24-26 Dec, BHs, Closed L Sat & Sun

Crowne Plaza Dublin Airport

American, Asian

Popular hotel restaurant with an international feel

☎ 01 8628888
Northwood Park, Santry Demesne, Santry
e-mail: info@crowneplazadublin.ie.
dir: Telephone for directions

This comfortable modern hotel enjoys a peaceful setting in the mature 85-acre woodlands of Northwood Park. Meaning 'east meets west', Touzai is a bright, contemporary restaurant and its style is reflected in both the décor and the seasonal menu, which fuses the techniques and flavours of Asia and California with those of the Pacific Rim. You might start with spicy quail and chickpea fritter with roasted tomato and cumin purée, or tuna and wasabi burgers with red onion and lime salsa, before tucking into pan-fried sea bass with pepper and spices, served on warm lentil salad with anchovy and rosemary sauce.

Times 12-2.30/6-10.30, Closed 25 Dec, Closed L Sat

Finnstown Country House

European, International

Crowd-pleasing country-house cooking

☎ 01 6010700
Newcastle Rd
e-mail: manager@finnstown-hotel.ie
dir: From M1 take 1st exit onto M50 southbound. 1st exit after Toll Bridge. At rdbt take 3rd left (N4 W). Left at lights. Over next 2 rbts, hotel on right

A short drive from central Dublin, this magnificent country house nestles in 45 acres of mature grounds and has a loyal local following. The period detail is impeccable throughout - particularly the dining room, which positively glows with Georgian-style opulence. With its foundation in simple, straightforward cooking, the menu adds influences from around the world with good seasonal awareness. Try a starter of tempura of king prawns with a sweet chilli dressing, followed by a main of grilled salmon, monkfish and sole with buttered spinach and lemon and prawn beurre blanc, and chocolate banoffee pie to finish.

Times 12.30-2.30/7.30-9.30, Closed 24-26 Dec, Closed D Sun

Restaurant Patrick Guilbaud

– *see opposite*

Restaurant Patrick Guilbaud

Modern French 🖵 V

Ireland's finest restaurant

☎ 01 6764192
Merrion Hotel, 21 Upper Merrion St
e-mail: restaurantpatrickguilbaud@
eircom.net
dir: Opposite government buildings,
next to Merrion Hotel

A suitably grand stage for the city's eponymous temple of gastronomy, this generous-sized, contemporary-styled dining room has been given a further modern edge following complete refurbishment in 2007. The impressive collection of modern Irish art blends well with the new vibrant and colourful carpet and the swish Italian leather chairs, while the former inner courtyard garden terrace has been enclosed with a glass roof to create a second lounge for diners, the perfect space for post-dinner drinks. Immaculate napery graces well-spaced tables, while immaculate service - from a veritable brigade of waiting staff - is precise and measured, without losing that friendly touch. Before descending the steps to the dining room, there's also a small - but equally stylish - bar-lounge for aperitifs. And, while the restaurant's location in the opulent Georgian splendour of the Merrion Hotel is equally fitting, it does have its own street entrance as well as access through the hotel lobby itself.

Patrick Guilbaud's modern interpretation of classic French cuisine more than lives up to the billing, and focuses on the very best seasonal Irish produce to grace his intricate cooking, delivered via an impressive array of menu options that includes a good-value fixed-price lunch, extensive and enticing carte (including a vegetarian menu) as well as a tasting offering. Expect plenty of sophisticated flair and innovation, impressive attention to detail, silky technical skills and luxury. Think lobster ravioli - perfectly cooked Clogher Head lobster wrapped in thin egg pasta with a delicately scented, rich and creamy coconut sauce - or Brittany slow-roasted squab pigeon with buttery cabbage, bread mousseline and mead and almond jus, and to finish, perhaps roast figs with red wine, fromage blanc, star anis and almond praline. Ancillaries, like canapés, amuse-bouche, breads, pre-desserts and petits fours also impress and add to the high-end experience factor. Reservations are essential though, as it attracts the rich and famous and the highflying business crowd.

Chef Guillaume Lebrun **Owner** Patrick Guilbaud **Times** 12.30-2.15/7.30-10.15, Closed 25 Dec, 1st wk Jan, Closed Sun-Mon **Prices** Fixed L 2 course fr €38, Tasting menu €180, Starter €25-€58, Main €46-€50, Dessert €20-€25, Service optional **Wines** 1000 bottles over €20, 12 by glass **Notes** Tasting menu 7 courses, Vegetarian menu, Dress restrictions, Smart casual, Air con **Seats** 80, Pr/dining room 25 **Children** Portions **Parking** Parking in square

DUBLIN *Continued*

Stillorgan Park Hotel

◎ Traditional International

Stylish hotel with contemporary international menus

☎ 01 2881621 & 2001800
Stillorgan Rd
e-mail: sales@stillorganpark.com
web: www.stillorganpark.com
dir: Please telephone for directions

This strikingly-designed modern hotel stands next to the national broadcasting institution, RTE (so expect to see some familiar faces). Enjoy a drink in the atmospheric Turf Club Bar before dining in the restaurant, with its rich colours, mosaic tiles, modern artwork and hand-painted frescoes. Quality Irish ingredients are used in a contemporary menu with international influences. Roasted fillet of pork with gremolata crust and apple and black pudding on lemon and sage sauce, or half duckling with celeriac and sweet potato dauphinoise, glazed baby carrots and Kirsch and black cherry jus shows the style.

Chef Enda Dunne **Owner** Des Pettit
Times 12.30-3/5.45-10.15, Closed 25 Dec, Closed L Sat, Closed D Sun **Prices** Fixed L 2 course €22-€25, Fixed D 3 course €43.60-€49.50, Starter €6-€9, Main €22.50-€25, Dessert €6.95, Service included **Wines** 12 bottles over €20, 10 bottles under €20 **Notes** Early bird menu, Sunday L, Vegetarian available, Air con **Seats** 100, Pr/dining room 60 **Children** Portions, Menu **Parking** 300

The Tea Room @ The Clarence

◎◎◎ European, Irish

Designer hotel with distinctive ballroom restaurant

☎ 01 4070800
6-8 Wellington Quay D2
e-mail: reservations@theclarence.ie
web: www.theclarence.ie
dir: From O'Connell Bridge, proceed W along quays, located after Ha'penny Bridge

The Clarence owners, U2's Bono and The Edge, have brought contemporary styling and a 'must-visit' cachet to this classic 19th-century hotel overlooking the River Liffey in the city's Temple Bar district, while successfully retaining its traditional features. The lofty Tea Room restaurant, originally the ballroom, is a perfect example - an elegantly simple setting flooded with light from huge windows. Bustling with diners, it's the perfect place for people watching, as is the hotel's famous Octagonal Bar. The kitchen's modern approach - underpinned by a classical French theme - delivers with style, driven by high quality seasonal Irish produce and intelligent simplicity that allows flavours to shine; take slowly poached and pan-fried breast of squab pigeon served with wild mushroom ravioli and Madeira sauce.

Chef Mathieu Melin **Owner** Bono, The Edge & Quinlan Private **Times** 12.30-2.30/7-10.30, Closed 25-26 Dec, Closed L Sat **Prices** Fixed L 2 course €26, Fixed D 3 course €39, Starter €12-€24, Main €24-€42, Dessert €10-€14, Service optional, Groups min 8 service 12.5% **Wines** 131 bottles over €20, 10 bottles under €20, 17 by glass **Notes** Vegetarian available, Dress restrictions, Smart casual **Seats** 80, Pr/dining room 70 **Children** Portions **Parking** Valet Parking

Chapter One

💻

☎ 01 8732266
18/19 Parnell Square
web: http://www.theaa.com/travel/index.jsp

Modern twists to consistently excellent classic French cooking.

Prices Food prices not confirmed for 2009. Please telephone for details.

Les Frères Jacques

💻

☎ 01 6794555
74 Dame St
web: http://www.theaa.com/travel/index.jsp

French classic cooking with an emphasis on seafood.

Prices Food prices not confirmed for 2009. Please telephone for details.

One Pico

💻

☎ 01 6760300
5-6 Molesworth Place, School House Ln
web: http://www.theaa.com/travel/index.jsp

Sophisticated and ambitious cuisine in stylish surrounds.

Prices Food prices not confirmed for 2009. Please telephone for details.

CO DUBLIN

KILLINEY Map 1 D4

PJ's Restaurant

◎ Traditional, International

Fine dining overlooking Dublin Bay

☎ 01 2305400
Fitzpatrick Castle Hotel
e-mail: reservations@fitzpatricks.com
dir: Please telephone for directions or see website

An 18th-century property, the Fitzpatrick Castle Hotel stands on the brow of Killiney Hill overlooking Dublin Bay, just nine miles from Dublin's centre. The beautiful location alone is worth the drive from the city. PJ's is the elegant fine-dining restaurant, with crystal chandeliers, well spaced tables, crisp linen and good quality glass and silverware. Fresh local produce is a feature of the seasonal menu, which might offer fig and gorgonzola salad with walnuts and herb vinaigrette; fillet of ostrich with sweet potato mash and crème de cassis jus; and individual baked Alaska.

Chef Sean Dempsey, John Bueno **Owner** Eithne Fitzpatrick **Times** 12.30-2.30/6-10, Closed 25 Dec, Mon, Tue, Closed L Wed-Sat, Closed D Sun **Prices** Fixed L course €39, Fixed D 3 course €50, Service added 10% **Wines** 25 bottles over €20, 14 bottles under €20, 2 by glass **Notes** Sunday L, Vegetarian available, Air con **Seats** 65, Pr/dining room 50 **Children** Portions **Parking** 200

PORTMARNOCK   Map 1 D4

Osborne Restaurant

◉◉ Modern, Traditional

Creative cuisine in a superb location

☎ 01 8460611
Portmarnock Hotel & Golf Links, Strand Rd
e-mail: sales@portmarnock.com
dir: Follow N1 towards Drogheda. At junct with R601 turn to Malahide. 2m turn left at T-junct, through Malahide & 2.2m hotel on left. Off M1 take Malahide junct, then onto Portmarnock

Once home to the Jameson family, famous for their Irish whiskey, this imposing 19th-century mansion is perched between the sea and a magnificent 18-hole golf course designed by Bernhard Langer. The sophisticated Osborne Restaurant offers stunning views of the garden, golf course and hills beyond. Innovative, modern dishes are the staple of the menu, conjured from the finest local ingredients, including fresh fish and seafood from Howth. Expect accomplished cooking with plenty of flair, as in house favourites like seared scallops with smoked bacon, cucumber and coconut salad, sea trout, tomato and shaved fennel with lemon dressing, and loin of rabbit with Swiss chard, duxelle of mushroom, pumpkin purée and figs.

Chef Paul Quinn **Owner** Natworth Ltd **Times** 11.30-3/7-10 **Prices** Fixed L 2 course fr €25, Fixed D 3 course fr €30, Tasting menu €70-€150, Starter €5.75-€14, Main €18-€32, Dessert €6, Service optional **Wines** 69 bottles over €20, 16 bottles under €20, 9 by glass **Notes** Tasting menu 8-12 courses, Vegetarian available, Dress restrictions, Smart casual, Air con **Seats** 100, Pr/dining room 20 **Children** Portions **Parking** 100

SKERRIES   Map 1 D4

Redbank House & Restaurant

◉ Modern European 🍷

Reliable cooking in a picturesque village

☎ 01 8491005
5-7 Church St
e-mail: info@redbank.ie
dir: From Dublin, M1 N to Lissenhall interchange, take exit to Skerries

This long-established restaurant, in a fishing village some 18 miles north of Dublin, is housed in a former bank with a well-stocked wine cellar in the vaults. Service is faultless with a warm welcome guaranteed from friendly, accommodating staff. Locally-landed fish and shellfish feature strongly in a range of dishes which take a modern approach. Specialities include whole Dublin Bay prawns cooked in fresh fish stock and served with garlic butter or Balbriggan razor fish cooked in their shells with butter, garlic, parsley and ground almonds, and mains like rack of Black Hills lamb with a gratin of aubergine, courgette and tomato, and a rosemary and garlic jus.

Chef Terry McCoy **Owner** Terry McCoy **Times** 12.30-4/6-10, Closed 24-26 Dec, Closed L Mon-Sat, Closed D Sun **Prices** Fixed L 2 course €33, Fixed D 4 course €50, Starter €10-€19, Main €23-€43, Dessert €10, Service included **Wines** 30 bottles over €20, 25 bottles under €20, 2 by glass **Notes** Sunday L, Vegetarian available, Dress restrictions, Smart casual, Civ Wed 55 **Seats** 60, Pr/dining room 10 **Parking** On street

---

CO GALWAY

CASHEL   Map 1 A4

Cashel House

◉◉ Traditional International **V**

Food without fuss and a wealth of seafood in a heavenly location

☎ 095 31001
e-mail: info@cashel-house-hotel.com
dir: S of N59. 1m W of Recess

Standing at the head of Cashel Bay, this elegant mid-19th-century country-house hotel is surrounded by 50 acres of beautiful, award-winning gardens and woodland walks. Run by the McEvilly family since 1968, it has a thoroughly established feel with assured and friendly service and a genuine sense of comfort. In the conservatory restaurant, the famous Connemara lamb and an abundance of locally-landed seafood grace the French-influenced menu - warm parcel of quail with smoked duck and brandy sauce, for example, to start, and then gratin of cod with bacon, tomato and dill or poached local salmon with creamy mashed potato and sorrel sauce. To finish, warm apple tart with cream or chocolate mousse cake.

Chef Arturo Amit, Arturo Tillo **Owner** Dermot & Kay McEvilly & family **Times** 12.30-2.30/7-8.30, Closed 2 Jan-2 Feb **Prices** Fixed L 3 course €30-€35, Fixed D 4

---

course €60, Service added 12.5% **Wines** 90 bottles over €20, 4 bottles under €20, 5 by glass **Notes** Sunday L, Vegetarian menu, Dress restrictions, Smart casual **Seats** 70, Pr/dining room 10 **Children** Portions, Menu **Parking** 30

Zetland Country House

◉◉ Modern International

Sea views and modern full-flavoured cuisine in refined setting

☎ 095 31111
Cashel Bay
e-mail: info@zetland.com
dir: N59 from Galway towards Clifden, turn right onto R340, after approx 4m turn left onto R341, hotel 1m on right

Standing on the shores of Cashel Bay, this charming country-house hotel is an oasis of gracious living amid a sweeping landscape of mountains, lakes and sandy beaches. Built as a sporting lodge in the early 19th century, much of the original charm has been recreated alongside modern-day sophistication. Turf fires smoulder in the cosy lounges, while comfortable bedrooms have wonderful sea views. The elegant dining room retains a refined air and is the setting for sampling some excellent local produce, including herbs and vegetables from the hotel garden. The kitchen delivers modern, yet simple and earthy cooking, resulting in full-flavoured dishes. The fixed-price, daily-changing concise menu reflects the seasons and may offer casserole of Cashel Bay mussels in white wine cream sauce, followed by rack and loin of local lamb with Lyonnaise potatoes, then brie and pear tart.

Chef Samuel Lecam **Owner** Ruaidhri Prendergast **Times** Closed L all week **Prices** Food prices not confirmed for 2009. Please telephone for details. **Wines** 30 bottles over €20, 8 bottles under €20, 6 by glass **Notes** Fixed D 5 courses **Seats** 75, Pr/dining room 20 **Children** Portions **Parking** 40

CLIFDEN — Map 1 A4

Abbeyglen Castle Hotel

French, International

Elegant restaurant in a hospitable country-house hotel

☎ 095 21201
Sky Rd
e-mail: info@abbeyglen.ie
dir: From Galway take N59 to Clifden. Hotel 1km on the Sky Road

This 19th-century property is set in 12 acres of sheltered parkland and gardens that descend to the sea. Relaxed fine dining with background piano music is provided in the elegant first-floor restaurant. The menu offers country-house cooking of quality local produce, featuring Connemara meat and game and freshly caught seafood, including lobster, crab and oysters from a seawater tank. Typical dishes are baked crab parcels - crêpes filled with fresh flakes of local crab and glazed with a mousseline sauce - or pan-fried supreme of halibut accurately caramelised and garnished with asparagus spears and prawns in a white wine sauce.

Chef Kevin Conroy **Owner** Mr P Hughes **Times** Closed 4-30 Jan, Closed L Mon-Sun **Prices** Fixed D 3 course €42-€48, Starter €6.50-€14, Main €26.95-€39, Dessert €8.50, Service added 12.5% **Wines** 23 bottles over €20, 29 bottles under €20, 8 by glass **Notes** Vegetarian available **Seats** 75 **Children** Min 12 yrs **Parking** 40

Ardagh Hotel & Restaurant

French, Mediterranean

Assured cooking of local produce in a stunning setting

☎ 095 21384
Ballyconneely Rd
e-mail: ardaghhotel@eircom.net
dir: Galway to Clifden on N59. Signed in Clifden, 2m on Ballyconneely road

Hiding behind a modern façade, this quiet family-run hotel is full of traditional charm with turf fires and comfy couches. It stands on the shores of Ardbear Bay so there are wonderful views, particularly at sunset, from its first-floor restaurant, which has a bright Mediterranean feel. As you'd expect given the setting, there is a strong emphasis on carefully cooked seafood and other excellent local produce, with lobsters, oysters and mussels arriving fresh from a seawater tank in the foyer, plus herbs and vegetables from the hotel's garden. Alternatives might include starters like roast quail on salad tiède of cherry

tomatoes, bacon slivers and grilled pepper strips topped with fried quails' eggs, followed by pan-seared scallops with Asian stir-fried vegetables.

Times Closed end Nov-end Mar, Closed L all week

Brown's

Modern Irish, European

Welcoming hotel with a fine reputation for seafood

☎ 095 21206 & 21086
Alcock & Brown Hotel
e-mail: alcockandbrown@eircom.net
dir: From Galway city take N59 to Clifden. Follow one-way system to centre. Hotel in town square

Brown's restaurant is a part of the very friendly, renovated hotel at the top of the town, known as the Alcock & Brown. The dining room has a fresh modern décor, transformed at night by dimmed lights and candles. There's a wide-ranging carte plus daily specials offering fairly straightforward cooking of prime ingredients, starring locally-landed seafood (perhaps grilled fillets of sea bass, or a fresh seafood platter) and Connemara lamb (maybe roast leg with a herb stuffing). Finish with Bailey's cheesecake or sweet cream profiteroles with chocolate sauce.

Times 12.30-2/6-9.30, Closed 22-26 Dec

GALWAY — Map 1 B3/4

Camilaun Restaurant

Modern International

Enjoy dinner overlooking the lovely garden

☎ 091 521433
Ardilaun Hotel & Leisure Club, Taylor's Hill
e-mail: info@theardilaunhotel.ie
dir: 1m from Galway city centre, towards Salthill on the west side of the city, near Galway Bay

The newly renovated Camilaun Restaurant, noted for its sense of occasion, is located in the 19th-century Ardilaun Hotel, overlooking landscaped grounds on the edge of Galway city. It also has a number of lounges and extensive leisure facilities. Internationally-influenced dishes are prepared from high-quality local ingredients, such as lamb cutlets marinated in honey and mustard with coriander-infused couscous and a crispy chilli sauce diablo, or quail breast stuffed with gorgonzola and enveloped in pimento accompanied by poached quail egg and confit salad. A carvery lunch is served on Sundays.

Chef Nigel Murray **Owner** John Ryan
Times 1-2.15/6.30-9.15, Closed 23-27 Dec, Closed L Sat **Prices** Fixed L 2 course €12.75, Fixed D 3 course fr €32, Starter €8.75-€10.50, Main €14.95-€26.50, Dessert €6.75, Service added 10% **Wines** 18 bottles over €20, 27 bottles under €20, 11 by glass **Notes** Vegetarian available, Dress restrictions, Smart dress, Civ Wed, Air con **Seats** 180, Pr/dining room 380 **Children** Portions, Menu **Parking** 300

Galway Bay Hotel

Modern International, Seafood V

Light, contemporary restaurant with sea views and fresh Irish cuisine

☎ 091 520520
The Promenade, Salthill
e-mail: info@galwaybayhotel.com
dir: 2m from Galway city centre

Refurbished in an elegant, contemporary style, with soothing colours, stylish furnishings and high-backed chairs. The Lobster Pot restaurant enjoys magnificent triple-aspect views over Galway Bay. The cuisine style is modern Irish with international influences and there's a strong emphasis on fresh Irish produce, notably fresh fish and seafood, including fresh lobster from the tank. Take blackened fillet of monkfish 'Cajun style' with pink grapefruit and peppercorn sauce, or perhaps lobster grilled or thermidor, while meat options might feature tournedos of Irish beef with a truffle Madeira sauce. Round off with a raspberry mousse gâteau or a plate of Irish cheeses.

Chef Mr Ciaran Gantly **Owner** John O'Sullivan
Times 12.30-2.30/6.30-9.15, Closed 25 Dec (residents only), Closed D Mon-Sat **Prices** Food prices not confirmed for 2009. Please telephone for details. **Wines** 25 bottles over €20, 25 bottles under €20, 10 by glass **Notes** Sunday L, Vegetarian menu, Air con **Seats** 196, Pr/dining room 400 **Children** Portions, Menu **Parking** 350

Park House Hotel & Park Room Restaurant

International

Appealing menu in bustling city-centre hotel

☎ 091 564924
Forster St, Eyre Square
e-mail: parkhousehotel@eircom.net
dir: In city centre, off Eyre Sq

A popular city-centre hotel built around a three-storey former grain store with its impressive, 19th-century stone façade. Paintings of old Galway line the walls of the celebrated Park Restaurant, which bustles with locals at lunchtime and becomes more intimate in the evening with soft lighting and elegant, linen-clothed tables. The cooking has a classical base, offering a wide choice of appealing, accomplished dishes that make good use of fresh ingredients, notably local seafood. Take baked fillets of black sole stuffed with cod, salmon and shrimp mousse accompanied by a spicy provençale and pesto sauce.

Times 12-3/6-10, Closed 24-26 Dec

River Room

◉ Contemporary Irish, International

Modern cuisine in an 18th-century country residence

☎ 091 526666
Glenlo Abbey Hotel, Bushypark
e-mail: info@glenloabbey.ie
dir: Approx 2.5m from centre of Galway on N59 to Clifden/
Connemara

Built in 1740, today this cut-stone abbey sits in a
138-acre lakeside golf estate and has been lovingly
restored to its original glory, featuring sculptured
cornices and fine antique furniture. The classical River
Room Restaurant is an oval affair on two levels, with
high ceilings, well spaced tables, lake views and
professional but relaxed service. The modern Irish cuisine
displays flair and imagination, with the skilful cooking
based on quality local produce, particularly seafood. Try
terrine of Aran Islands smoked salmon in lemon butter
and soft herbs, with tempura of anchovy and shallot
dressing, and for mains, grilled fillet of North Atlantic
halibut with tomato, chargrilled artichoke, and
asparagus and prawn bisque.

Times Closed 24-27 Dec, Closed Mon-Sun

RECESS (SRAITH SALACH)   Map 1 A4

Ballynahinch Castle

◉◉ Modern International

Fine dining in a castle overlooking the river

☎ 095 31006 & 31086
e-mail: bhinch@iol.ie
dir: Take N59 from Galway. Turn right after Recess
towards Roundstone (R331) for 2m

This superb 16th-century castle enjoys one of the best
locations in Connemara: set in 350 acres of woodland
and lakes and overlooking a bend in the Ballynahinch
river. As well as stunning views, visitors can look forward
to log fires, personal service and an air of informal
elegance. The Owenmore restaurant invites with crisp
linen, gleaming silverware, sparkling glassware and
relaxing river views. The fixed-price dinner offers
international cooking based on the freshest local and
seasonal produce, including wild salmon from the river
and locally sourced seafood. Expect the likes of duo of
Connemara cured beef and pork with sweet pepper and
tomato relish and cumin toast to start, with roast
Connemara rack of lamb with potato, celeriac and truffle
gratin dauphinoise, creamed spring cabbage and
rosemary garlic jus to follow.

Chef Xin Sun **Owner** Ballynahinch Castle Hotel Inc
Times Closed 2 wks Xmas, Feb, Closed L all week
Wines 42 bottles over €20, 20 bottles under €20, 5 by
glass **Notes** Fixed D 5 courses €60, Dress restrictions,
Smart casual **Seats** 90 **Parking** 55

Lough Inagh Lodge

◉ Irish, French

Irish country dining with lovely mountain views

☎ 095 34706 & 34694
Inagh Valley
e-mail: inagh@iol.ie
dir: From Galway take N344. After 3.5m hotel on right

Situated on the shores of one of Connemara's most
beautiful lakes, Lough Inagh, this elegant hotel feels
more like a family home, with guests treated to a
particularly high standard of hospitality. With a backdrop
of mountains and spectacular scenery on all sides, this
former 19th-century fishing lodge boasts comfortable
lounges with turf fires, a cosy oak-panelled bar, and an
intimate dining room, where seafood and wild game
dishes are a speciality. Fresh fish is cooked simply and
served with subtle sauces that enhance rather than mask
natural flavour. For a starter, try smoked haddock tartlet,
followed by spiced duck with a Madeira and orange
sauce. Desserts might include saffron-infused plums
with an Amaretto mousse.

Times Closed mid Dec-mid Mar

RENVYLE   Map 1 A4

Renvyle House

◉ Modern

**Country-house dining with a romantic setting and
literary connections**

☎ 095 43511
e-mail: info@renvyle.com
dir: N59 west of Galway towards Clifden, through
Oughterard & Maam Cross. At Recess turn right, Keymore
turn left, Letterfrack turn right, hotel 5m

Destroyed and rebuilt over several centuries, this
attractive country house is located between the
Connemara mountains and the wild Atlantic coast. Yeats
honeymooned here and it was once the home of Buck
Mulligan from James Joyce's Ulysses. Dinner is an
atmospheric occasion with turf fires and soft lighting.
The menu draws on great local produce and cooking is
vibrant, with dishes such as grilled langoustines on a
bed of crisp salad leaves with citrus dressing,
accompanied by chilli jam, or roast orange-glazed
duckling with champ, steamed mange-tout and baby
carrots, followed by crème brûlée with lightly poached
berries in syrup.

Times Closed 4 Jan-14 Feb

ROUNDSTONE   Map 1 A4

Roundstone House Hotel

◉ Modern Irish

Great sea views and cracking seafood

☎ 095 35864
dir: Telephone for directions

This delightful, family-run hotel in a terraced-village
setting enjoys magnificent sea views to the backdrop of
the rugged Connemara Mountains. There are cosy, well-
appointed, linen-dressed tables in Vaughan's Restaurant,
where service is suitably informal and friendly. The
extensive carte comes brimful of quality produce from the
abundant local larder, particularly seafood. Expect dishes
along the lines of lobster salad served with Marie Rose
sauce and a salad, or John Dory with lime, lemon and
orange juices, boiled and gratin potatoes, steamed beans
and carrots. The emphasis here is strictly on freshness,
simplicity and clarity of flavour, allowing the main
ingredients to shine.

Times Closed Nov-Feb

CO KERRY

CAHERDANIEL (CATHAIR DÓNALL)   Map 1 A2

Derrynane Hotel

◉ Irish, European

Enjoyable dining with spectacular Atlantic backdrop

☎ 066 9475136
e-mail: info@derrynane.com

Perched on a spectacular clifftop location on the Ring of
Kerry, this friendly family-run hotel offers guests
stunning ocean views of Kenmare Bay while eating in the
bright, spacious dining room. The small dedicated
kitchen team produces modern Irish dishes with
European influences, using quality and fresh produce. A
bar menu is also available and includes pannini and
ciabatta alongside home-made soup, and scones.

Times Closed Oct-mid Apr

KENMARE   Map 1 B2

*From November 2008 the dialling codes for the
establishments listed under this location are as shown
(i.e. 064 66). Prior to that date use the 064 prefix only.*

Cascade

◉◉ Irish, European V

Romantic waterfall setting for excellent cuisine

☎ 064 6641600
Sheen Falls Lodge
e-mail: info@sheenfallslodge.ie
dir: From Kenmare take N71 to Glengarriff. Take 1st left
after suspension bridge. 1m from Kenmare

On the banks of the Sheen, this former hunting lodge is
set in wonderful grounds. The elegant dining room has

Continued

KENMARE *Continued*

vast windows and well-spaced tables overlooking the dramatic backdrop of a floodlit waterfall. The kitchen delivers a new and extensive menu of accomplished dishes every day, but its attention to the quality of ingredients remains a constant. Excellent local produce is a feature, including fish and meat from the hotel's own smokery. An unfussy and confident approach results in top-notch cooking. Try a carpaccio of cured Irish beef to start served with tomato espuma and red chard leaves, followed by roast loin of Iberico pork with a square of local pork belly confit and caramelised apples and carrots.

Chef Philip Brazil **Owner** Sheen Falls Estate Ltd **Times** Closed 2 Jan-1 Feb, Closed L all week **Prices** Food prices not confirmed for 2009. Please telephone for details. **Wines** 817 bottles over €20, 6 bottles under €20, 6 by glass **Notes** Tasting menu available, Vegetarian menu, Dress restrictions, Smart casual (jacket), No jeans or T-shirts **Seats** 120, Pr/dining room 20 **Children** Portions, Menu **Parking** 75

KILLARNEY	Map 1 B2

From November 2008 the telephone numbers for the establishments listed under this location are as shown (i.e. 064 66). Prior to that date drop the initial double six.

The Brehon Restaurant

◉ Modern International

Modern-hotel dining meets innovative cooking and prime local produce

☎ 064 6630700
The Brehon Hotel, Muckross Rd
e-mail: info@thebrehon.com
dir: Enter Killarney follow signs for Muckross Road (N71). Hotel on left 0.3m from town centre.

The smart dining room of this recently built, modern, design-led hotel is a bright, split-level contemporary space with a classic look and views towards the Killarney National Park. White linen and formal service there may be, but staff are very friendly. The kitchen's modern approach - with nods to the Mediterranean and beyond - suits the surroundings, driven by tip-top, fresh seasonal produce from the abundant local larder. Expect dishes like tournedos of Irish beef fillet wrapped in pancetta and served with pea and parsnip purée and a red wine and shallot jus, or perhaps crispy monkfish tempura accompanied by yakasobi noodles and home-made teriyaki dip.

Chef John Drummond **Owner** O'Donoghue Family **Times** Closed L bookings only **Prices** Fixed L 2 course €22-€32, Fixed D 3 course €35-€60, Starter €8.50-€13.50, Main €22-€32, Dessert €6.50-€8, Service included **Wines** 53 bottles over €20, 23 bottles under €20, 13 by glass **Notes** Pre-show menu available, Sunday L, Vegetarian available, Dress restrictions, Smart casual, Civ Wed 200, Air con **Seats** 120, Pr/dining room 100 **Children** Portions, Menu **Parking** 100

Cahernane House Hotel

◉◉ Modern European, International V

Lakeside manor-house dining

☎ 064 6631895
Muckross Rd
e-mail: cahernane@eircom.net
dir: From Killarney follow signs for Kenmare, then from Muckross Rd over bridge and hotel signed on right. Hotel 1m from town centre

Built in the 17th century as a private residence, the hotel is set in parkland on the shores of Lough Leane, with the Kerry Mountains as a backdrop. The gracious interior retains original features in the old part of the property, adding period furniture and modern pieces to create an inviting ambience. The spacious restaurant is comfortably appointed and the kitchen knows its stuff, making the most of top-notch local ingredients in great combinations that consistently impress. Simply-described dishes on the classic carte might include chicken foie gras terrine, fillet of Irish beef with potato fondant, salsa verde and red wine jus, and warm chocolate fondant with pistachio ice cream.

Chef Maurice Prendiville **Owner** Mr & Mrs J Browne **Times** 12-2.30/7-9.30, Closed Jan, Closed L all week ex by arrangement **Prices** Fixed L 2 course €25, Fixed D 3 course €40-€52, Starter €7-€13, Main €22-€30, Dessert €7-€9, Service optional **Wines** 98 bottles over €20, 22 bottles under €20, 20 by glass **Notes** Tasting menu available, Sunday L, Vegetarian menu, Dress restrictions, Smart casual, no shorts, Civ Wed 60 **Seats** 50, Pr/dining room 18 **Children** Portions, Menu **Parking** 50

Killeen House Hotel

◉ Irish, European

Fine dining in a charming county-house hotel

☎ 064 6631722 & 6631773
Aghadoe, Lakes of Killarney
e-mail: charming@indigo.ie

This charming Victorian country-house hotel located on the edge of town comes set in delightful gardens. Its stylish décor shows in comfortable sitting rooms, a cosy bar and a restaurant spread over two rooms, with lovely table settings and fresh flower displays. The kitchen's country-house cooking suits the surroundings and is driven by prime seasonal local ingredients. Good technical skills and flavour shine in dishes like a rack of Kerry lamb with a rosemary and pine-nut crust served with its pan juices, Tuscan white bean and tomato dressing and garlic potato gratin, and to finish, perhaps a tangy lemon tart with praline mascarpone cream.

The Lake Room Restaurant

◉◉ Modern Irish, European V

Luxury hotel restaurant with stunning views

☎ 064 6631766
Aghadoe Heights Hotel & Spa
e-mail: info@aghadoeheights.com
dir: 2.5m from Killarney, off N22

The glamorous and luxurious Aghadoe Heights Hotel overlooks lakes, mountains and golf courses, and includes a spa among its many attractions. The Lake Room restaurant, not surprisingly, enjoys views over the water and is a stunning setting for some fine food. The room is divided by timber-framed panels with sheer and linen fabric inserts which can create intimate areas or sections for large groups. Another spectacular feature is the glass-walled wine cave in the middle of the room, where diners can actually pick out what they fancy with the help of the sommelier. Minimal touch, maximum flavour is the philosophy behind the food. Menus are seasonal and the dishes traditional with a modern twist, such as a starter of rabbit with black pudding and foie gras and main-course herb-crusted cod with braised fennel and vanilla and thyme hollandaise.

Chef Gavin Gleeson **Owner** Pat & Marie Chawke **Times** 12.30-2/6.30-9.30, Closed 25 Dec (residents only), mid-week Dec-Mar, Closed L all week (occasional Sun open) **Prices** Food prices not confirmed for 2009. Please telephone for details. **Wines** 132 bottles over €20, 11 bottles under €20, 21 by glass **Notes** Vegetarian menu, Dress restrictions, Jacket, smart dress, no jeans or trainers, Civ Wed 150, Air con **Seats** 150, Pr/dining room 80 **Children** Portions, Menu **Parking** 120

The Park Restaurant

◉◉ European

Fine cuisine in elegant hotel restaurant

☎ 064 6635555
Killarney Park Hotel, Kenmare Place
e-mail: info@killarneyparkhotel.ie
dir: From Cork take R22 to Killarney. Take 1st exit for town centre, then at 2nd rdbt take 2nd exit. At 3rd rdbt, take 1st exit. Hotel 2nd entrance on left

Within walking distance of Killarney's winding streets, this attractive modern hotel offers old-fashioned country-house comforts like roaring fires and deep sofas as well as a warm Irish welcome. The elegant, classical Park Restaurant has well-spaced, smartly laid tables and a pianist who plays each evening. It offers fine cuisine, making good use of local seasonal produce from land and sea in its modern dishes - underpinned by classical roots - which display skill and interesting combinations. Starters might include tian of Dingle Bay crabmeat and guacamole, roast scallop, aged balsamic and rocket leaves, followed by roast breast of Skeaghanore duck, cider braised red cabbage, duck foie gras ballotine and raisin sauce, or perhaps a pan-fried fillet of Irish beef, wild mushroom pithivier, red onion marmalade and sauce béarnaise.

Times Closed 25-26 Dec, Closed L all week

KILLORGLIN   Map 1 A2

Carrig House Country House & Restaurant

◉ Modern Irish, European

Fine dining in country house overlooking lake

☎ 066 9769100
Caragh Lake
e-mail: info@carrighouse.com

Overlooking Caragh Lake, this charming Victorian country manor is set in woodland gardens, which contain 935 plant species. Furnished in period style, it has log fires in the public rooms, formal linen tablecloths and delightfully friendly service. The innovative cuisine makes excellent use of seasonal products, cooked with care and with judicious use of herbs and spices. Starters might include local scallops with basil-scented tagliatelle, saffron cream and a concasse of red pepper, and mains such as fillet of John Dory on a julienne of leeks and sweet potato. Finish with cinnamon-marinated pears in a warm parcel of crisp filo pastry served with crème anglaise.

Times 7-9

PARKNASILLA   Map 1 A2

From November 2008 the telephone numbers for the establishments listed under this location are as shown (i.e. 064 66). Prior to that date drop the initial double six.

Parknasilla Hotel

◉ Traditional

Formal dining in a dramatic location

☎ 064 6645122
e-mail: res@parknasilla.gsh.ie
dir: From Killarney take N71 to Kenmare. On entering town pass golf club. Hotel entrance on left at top of town

A Victorian property in an extraordinary location, with stunning Atlantic, woodland and mountain views. A sweeping staircase, stained glass windows and log fires are among the period features, and the Pygmalion Restaurant is suitably grand and elegant. The set-price dinner menu might offer salad of brill scaloppini, and spiced chicken breast with vegetable couscous. Alternatively there's a short carte of classic dishes: foie gras on toasted brioche, and fillet steak of Irish Angus beef. Cocktails are served in the clubby Doolittle Bar. (George Bernard Shaw was a frequent visitor.)

Times Closed Jan-11 Feb, Closed L all week

TRALEE   Map 1 A2

The Walnut Room

◉ Modern, Traditional

Smart, modern hotel restaurant using fresh local produce

☎ 066 7194500 & 066 7194505
Manor West Hotel, Killarney Rd
e-mail: info@manorwesthotel.ie
dir: On the main Killarney Road next to the Manor West Retail Park

This smart modern hotel is part of a large retail park just 5 minutes from the centre of town. After a hard day shopping, relax over a drink in the cocktail lounge - complete with piano - before taking your place for dinner in the fine-dining Walnut Room, a comfortable contemporary restaurant with rich, warm décor. High quality ingredients, cooked with flair and due attention without the need for over-embellishment, feature on the seasonal menu, which includes the freshest of fish from nearby Dingle Bay and a carvery option at lunch. A starter of local crab crème brûlée with sesame seed crust and melba toast might be followed by a duo of pan-seared duck breast with fondant potato, red cabbage, redcurrant reduction and raisin jus.

Chef Bart O'Sullivan **Times** Closed 25 Dec, Closed L all week **Prices** Fixed D 4 course €39.50, Starter €5.50-€9.50, Main €19.50-€27, Dessert €6.50, Service added but optional 10% **Wines** 30 bottles over €20, 20 bottles under €20, 8 by glass **Notes** Vegetarian available, Air con **Seats** 70, Pr/dining room 50 **Children** Portions, Menu **Parking** 150

WATERVILLE   Map 1 A2

Butler Arms Hotel

◉ European, Seafood

Enjoyable cuisine in snug dining room overlooking the ocean

☎ 066 9474144
e-mail: reservations@butlerarms.com
dir: Telephone for directions

Located at the furthest end of the famed Ring of Kerry, this long-established, seasonal seaside hotel has been in the Huggard family for four generations. The restaurant's bright, cosy, sea-facing room comes with formally laid tables and comfortable seating, but service is suitably friendly and attentive. The kitchen deals in prime local ingredients, with menus changing each evening and making excellent use of seafood. The straightforward, light, modern approach delivers well-presented, accurately cooked dishes, such as seared scallops with seasonal leaves and a wasabi and lime dressing, perhaps followed by a rack of lamb with sprouting broccoli and root vegetable purée and an orange and chocolate parfait finish.

Times Closed 31 Oct-4 Apr, Closed L all week

CO KILDARE

LEIXLIP   Map 1 D4

Leixlip House

◉ Modern Irish

Fine dining in charming hotel

☎ 01 6242268
Captains Hill
e-mail: info@leixliphouse.com

Overlooking Leixlip village, just 8 miles from Dublin city centre, this charming 18th-century property retains its elegant period style with antique furniture and classical décor. The Bradaun Restaurant is a bright, airy room where diners are served by friendly, professional staff. The menu makes excellent use of the finest ingredients and harmonious combinations of flavours. Take a starter of twice-baked Gabriel cheese soufflé with wild garlic and Borettana onion purée, tomato fondue and bacon lardons, followed by grouper stuffed with sorrel, smoked haddock and langoustine with cauliflower and parmesan purée, accompanied by baby carrots with honey, fennel seeds, parmesan and sorrel velouté. Booking is essential, especially at weekends.

Times 12.30-4/6.30-9.45, Closed 25-26 Dec, Closed Mon, Closed L Tue-Sat

NAAS   Map 1 D4

Killashee House Hotel & Villa Spa

◉ Irish

Elegant dining in magnificent surroundings

☎ 045 879277
e-mail: sales@killasheehouse.com
dir: 1m from Naas on old Kilcullen road. On left past Garda (police station)

In its former lives this Victorian manor house has been a convent and a preparatory school for boys. How things change: set amid 80 acres of beautifully kept grounds it is now a luxuriously appointed hotel and spa. The restaurant, Turners, is a magnificent room on a grand scale with pillars, chandeliers, intricate plasterwork and gold and scarlet soft furnishings. A harpist plays on Friday and Saturday nights, adding to the sense of occasion. Excellent raw ingredients are used in the preparation of dishes such as warm goat's cheese soufflé with parmesan cream followed by main-course loin of Wicklow lamb with tian of vegetables and café au lait basil sauce.

Chef Paul Murphy **Owner** Mr & Mrs Tierney **Times** 1-2.45/7-9.45, Closed 24-25 Dec, Closed L Sat **Prices** Food prices not confirmed for 2009. Please telephone for details. **Wines** 80 bottles over €20, 24 bottles under €20, 12 by glass **Notes** Vegetarian available, Dress restrictions, Smart casual, no jeans, Air con **Seats** 120, Pr/dining room 650 **Children** Portions, Menu **Parking** 600

NAAS *Continued*

Maudlins House Hotel

◉ Modern Irish, French

☎ 045 996999
Dublin Rd
e-mail: info@maudlinshousehotel.ie

This establishment was awarded its Rosette/s just as we went to press. Therefore we are unable to provide a description - visit www.theaa.com for the most up-to-date information.

Times Closed L Mon-Sat **Prices** Food prices not confirmed for 2009. Please telephone for details.

NEWBRIDGE	Map 1 C3

Keadeen Hotel

◉◉ International

Stylish dining in family-run hotel

☎ 045 431666
e-mail: info@keadeenhotel.ie
dir: N7 from Dublin to Newbridge. Hotel 1m from Curragh racecourse & 0.5m from Newbridge town centre

Kildare's longest established family-owned and run four-star hotel has been welcoming guests for over 37 years. First opened in 1970, it's grown to meet the ever-changing needs and expectations of guests, whilst maintaining its tradition of superior quality and service. The Derby restaurant is a stylish venue for sophisticated country-house style dining. Service is formal but unobtrusive, befitting the elegant décor and fine table settings. The menu makes use of the very best local produce, typically a main course of tender cannon of lamb with dauphinoise and a honey and thyme sauce. The Club Bar is an alternative eating option, and offers a relaxing place to enjoy a drink or meal.

Times 12.30-2.30/6-9.30

STRAFFAN	Map 1 C/D4

Barberstown Castle

◉◉ Irish, French

Fine dining in a 13th-century castle with attractive grounds

☎ 01 6288157
e-mail: barberstowncastle@ireland.com
dir: From Dublin take M50, exit for M4 at rdbt and follow signs for castle

A castle turned country-house hotel, this historic property features Victorian and Elizabethan dining rooms, complete with period furniture, overlooking the gardens. Lunch can be taken in the airy conservatory tearoom, and aperitifs in the elegant drawing room, but dinner is an atmospheric occasion by candlelight. Service is appropriately professional, and the cooking accomplished, making the best of quality produce. Starters might include Irish

smoked salmon and lime crab salad with crispy prawns, curry oil and balsamic reduction, followed by loin of venison with braised cabbage, salsify, pancetta and cranberries. Conclude your meal with dessert - maybe pear and apple tart with almond crust and honey cream - or a selection of Irish farmhouse cheeses.

Times 12.30-2.30/7-9.30, Closed 24-28 Dec, Jan, Closed Mon-Tue, Closed L Wed-Sat

The Byerley Turk

◉◉◉ – *see opposite*

CO KILKENNY	

KILKENNY	Map 1 C3

Kilkenny River Court

◉ International

Dining on a grand scale

☎ 056 7723388
The Bridge, John St
e-mail: reservations@kilrivercourt.com
dir: Telephone for directions

This comfortable riverside hotel boasts an impressive restaurant, designed to reflect the classical beauty of Kilkenny Castle and the surrounding area. Wonderful views of the river are framed by large picture windows and no expense has been spared with the décor, using marble flooring, crystal chandeliers and Georgian furniture. An extensive international menu showcases fresh, seasonal local produce; think beech-smoked trout layered with spinach and fresh salmon wrapped in filo pastry, a cannon of Slaney Valley lamb, Shellumsrath goose, or alternatively, perhaps lemon and coriander sea bass.

Times 12.30-2.30/6-9.30, Closed 24-25 Dec, 25-26 Jan, Closed L Mon-Sat

THOMASTOWN	Map 1 C3

The Lady Helen Restaurant

◉◉ Modern French

Impressive country mansion offering superb fine dining

☎ 056 7773000
Mount Juliet Conrad Hotel
e-mail: info@mountjuliet.ie
dir: Just outside Thomastown heading S on N9

This elegant 18th-century Georgian mansion is a haven of gracious living in a beautiful setting overlooking the River Nore. Standing in 1,500 acres of parkland with its own golf course, the hotel retains many of the mansion's original features. The formal dining restaurant is decorated in grand country-house style and has lovely panoramic views. The cooking is likewise classical, with European influences and modern interpretations. Good use is made of local ingredients, and fresh vegetables and herbs come from the kitchen gardens. Main courses focus on game from the estate in season. Starters might include sweet white Wexford crab mousse with caramelised quince and aspic-

glazed quail's egg, or slow-braised Kilkenny pork belly in cider. Try mains like poached and roasted cannon of Irish lamb with wild mushroom farce and soft herb polenta, steamed vegetable and myrtleberry jus.

Times Closed L all week

CO LEITRIM	

CARRICK-ON-SHANNON	Map 1 C4

The Landmark Hotel

◉ Contemporary ♥

Modern dining in a waterfront setting

☎ 071 962 2222
e-mail: reservations@thelandmarkhotel.com
dir: From Dublin on N4 approaching Carrick-on-Shannon, take 1st exit at rdbt, hotel on right

The Landmark Hotel stands opposite the marina overlooking the River Shannon. CJ's is the fine dining evening restaurant, classical in style with blue and gold décor, well spaced tables and an impressive antique fireplace. The regularly-changing menu offers imaginative modern dishes underpinned by classical French techniques, served by friendly staff. Start with terrine of smoked duck and foie gras with a wonton of duck leg; followed by roast loin of lamb with celeriac purée, red wine jus and a miniature cottage pie. Finish with chocolate assiette, comprising a glass of light chocolate mousse, a warm, crisp-crusted chocolate fondant and white chocolate ice cream.

Chef Eunan Campbell **Owner** Garen & John Kelly **Times** Closed 24-25 Dec, Closed Sun (CJ's only) **Prices** Fixed L 2 course €21, Fixed D 4 course €39-€45, Starter €8-€15, Main €18-€30, Dessert €7, Service optional **Wines** 12 bottles over €20, 24 bottles under €20, 8 by glass **Notes** Sun L served in Broadwalk Cafe, Sunday L, Vegetarian available, Dress restrictions, Smart, Civ Wed 300, Air con **Seats** 80, Pr/dining room 50 **Children** Portions, Menu

MOHILL	Map 1 C4

Lough Rynn Castle

◉ Modern, European

Modern cooking in secluded loughside surroundings

☎ 071 9632700 & 071 9632714
e-mail: enquiries@loughrynn.ie

This newly opened hotel is majestically set in 300 acres of breathtaking scenery on the shores of Lough Rynn. A converted sandstone stable is now the elegant fine-dining restaurant. With great importance placed on the use of good local produce and seasonal ingredients, well-chosen combinations are cooked with great care. Expect dishes like rillette of duck and roast quail set on a bed of wilted spinach with raisin jus, followed by loin of venison with sauce poivrade, Parmentier potatoes and spicy braise of red cabbage, and white chocolate and Cointreau parfait to finish. Take a stroll round the walled gardens and meandering corridors before or after your meal.

Times 12-2.30/7-9.30

The Byerley Turk

Modern, Traditional Irish

Luxurious golfing hotel with an impressive restaurant

☎ 01 6017200
The K Club
e-mail: hotel@kclub.ie
dir: 30 minutes from Dublin. From Dublin Airport follow M4 to Maynooth, turn for Straffan, just after village on right

Set amid 550 acres of County Kildare countryside by the River Liffey, this elegantly restored country-house hotel boasts two championship golf courses and came to global attention when it hosted the Ryder Cup in 2006. The golf pavilion houses two informal eateries - Legends and Monza - but it's the fine-dining option, the gracious Byerley Turk restaurant that's the real drawcard. Dominated by a painting of the thoroughbred racehorse after which it's named, the Byerley Turk boasts high ceilings, ornate chandeliers, lofty windows with lavish drapes, rich brocade wall coverings, marble columns, elegantly dressed tables and views over the gardens. Dress code is formal (strictly jacket and tie), while the silver-and-cloche service is a polished affair, yet friendly to match the tone. The contemporary Irish cuisine - underpinned by a classical French theme - is delivered via an appealing dinner carte and tasting option, built around tip-top fresh seasonal produce from the abundant Irish larder. Clear flavours, technical proficiency and luxury abound in highly accomplished dishes like roasted langoustine tails with tortellini of Jerusalem artichoke. For mains, choose between the likes of tronçon of turbot with sautéed forest mushrooms, caramelised onion and baby potatoes, or An Beef Tuath - the Ryder Cup signature dish of two mignons of Irish beef, shallot and wild mushroom crown, organic carrots with garlic and potato foam and mead sauce.

Chef Finbarr Higgins **Owner** Michael Smurfit **Times** Closed Mon-Tue, Closed L all week **Prices** Food prices not confirmed for 2009. Please telephone for details. **Wines** 600 bottles over €20, 2 bottles under €20, 8 by glass
Notes Sunday L, Vegetarian available, Dress restrictions, Jacket & tie, Air con
Seats 36, Pr/dining room 16
Children Min 3 yrs, Portions
Parking 100

CO LIMERICK

ADARE
Map 1 B3

Dunraven Arms

◉◉ Modern European

Innovative dishes in an atmospheric setting

☎ 061 605900
e-mail: reservations@dunravenhotel.com
dir: Telephone for directions

Situated in one of Ireland's prettiest villages with its thatched-roof cottages, this hotel feels like a country house and offers sophisticated comfort. The smart interior has lovely open fires, while large windows look over the village. The attractive dining room offers modern European cuisine, with extensive use of fresh local produce. Renowned Dunraven beef is always on the menu, carved from the trolley, and fresh fish is delivered daily. Starters might include asparagus wrapped in Parma ham with béarnaise sauce and poached eggs, with mains such as fillet pork with black pudding pithivier served with pickled cabbage, apple and cinnamon butter. Finish with a fruit-filled brandy snap basket, served with raspberry sorbet and lemon tartlet. Bistro-style cuisine is on offer at the Inn Between in one of the thatched cottages.

Times 12.30-2.30/7-9.30, Closed L Mon-Sat

LIMERICK
Map 1 B3

Mc Laughlin's Restaurant

◉ Modern European

Enjoyable dining in pretty Limerick

☎ 061 335566
Castletroy Park Hotel, Dublin Rd
e-mail: sales@castletroy-park.ie
dir: 5 mins from Limerick City, follow signs for University of Limerick, hotel opposite

McLaughlin's is a modern hotel on the outskirts of Limerick with a range of eating options, including a conservatory for snacks and afternoon tea, and a bar for bistro fare. The formal restaurant does a brisk trade with locals and residents alike, conjuring a comprehensive modern menu from quality local ingredients. A single ravioli of lobster and scallop is an impressive starter served in a saffron-scented fish broth with cucumber linguine. Follow with the likes of market-fresh fish, parsley-crusted rack of venison with peppercorn essence, or house-smoked fillet of prime Irish beef with truffle-scented dauphinoise.

Chef Janet McNamara **Owner** Fordmount Developments **Times** 12.30-2.30/5.30-10, Closed L Sun-Fri **Prices** Fixed L 2 course fr €24, Fixed D 3 course fr €45, Starter €7-€11, Main €21-€30, Dessert €6-€7, Service optional **Wines** 25 bottles over €20, 16 bottles under €20, 8 by glass **Notes** Earlybird menu 5.30-7pm, Sunday L, Vegetarian available, Dress restrictions, Smart dress, Air con **Seats** 78, Pr/dining room 14 **Children** Portions, Menu **Parking** 200

River Restaurant

◉ Modern International

Innovative cooking in smart riverside hotel restaurant

☎ 061 421800 & 061 421870
Hilton Limerick, Ennis Rd
e-mail: tom.flavin@hilton.com
dir: Please telephone for directions

The smart, bright-and-airy River Restaurant of this modern Hilton hotel is aptly named, with its outstanding views over the River Shannon. Contemporarily styled, it comes with a warm atmosphere and friendly but professional service, while the kitchen continues the upbeat theme, with its innovative, contemporary twists on classical dishes. Take a seafood bouillabaisse (panache of fish and seafood served with rouille and gruyère and garlic croûtons), and a raspberry pannacotta teamed with fresh fruit minestrone and red berry tuile. Technical skill, seasonality and flavour parade with a light modern touch.

Chef Tom Flavin, Lenaick Cosse **Owner** John Lally, Lalco **Times** 12.3-2.3/5.3-10 **Prices** Fixed L 2 course €20-€25, Fixed D 4 course €35-€45, Starter €5-€12, Main €21-€29, Dessert €6-€9, Service optional **Wines** 25 bottles over €20, 22 bottles under €20, 10 by glass **Notes** Sun brunch inc champagne available, Sunday L, Vegetarian available, Air con **Seats** 80 **Children** Portions, Menu

CO MAYO

BALLINA
Map 1 B4

Mount Falcon Country House Hotel

◉ French V ☺

Country-house cooking with French flavour

☎ 096 74472
Mount Falcon Country House Hotel, Foxford Road
e-mail: info@mountfalcon.com
dir: 3m S of Ballina. Located left side of N26 Foxford to Ballina Road

Set in 100 acres of parkland by the River Moy, Mount Falcon, built in 1876, is a hotel of some character with spa and conference facilities. The décor is smart and contemporary and the restaurant, situated in the original kitchen and store rooms, is stylish and comfortable. Great emphasis is placed on the provenance of the ingredients, which include salmon, trout and eel from the Moy, local organic vegetables and cheeses from Connaught and Munster. The French origins of the chef are evident from the menu and starters like confit of duck, a perfect rendition, served with red cabbage and Madeira jus, showcase his talents. Well presented main-course cod Wellington is filled with a leek and fennel fondue and served glazed in a copper dish. There is a splendid cheese trolley and one with chocolates and petits fours too.

Chef Philip Farineau **Owner** Alan Maloney **Times** 12.3-2/6.3-9.3 **Prices** Fixed L 2 course €15-€30, Fixed D 3 course €40-€52, Starter €8-€12, Main €15-€26, Dessert €7-€12, Service optional, Groups min 10 service

10% **Wines** 140 bottles over €20, 12 by glass **Notes** Sunday L, Vegetarian menu, Civ Wed 200 **Seats** 80, Pr/dining room 14 **Children** Portions, Menu

CONG
Map 1 B4

The Connaught Room

◉◉ Contemporary ☺

Innovative cuisine and sumptuous setting in lough-side castle hotel

☎ 094 9546003
Ashford Castle
e-mail: stefanmatz@ashford.ie
dir: From Galway take N84 through Headford towards Cross. In Cross turn left towards Ashford Castle gates.

Set in over 300 acres of beautiful grounds, this magnificent castle (dating from 1228) turned luxury hotel occupies a stunning position on the edge of Lough Corrib. The dinner-only Connaught Room is the hotel's fine-dining restaurant and the castle's original dining room, dating back to the 1800s when the Guinness family owned the estate. Intimate and luxurious, its hand-carved wood panelling, wooden fireplace, elegant high ceilings and lough views come complete with atmospheric live harp music and attentive, formal service. The ambitious kitchen is renowned for its signature seven-course tasting Menu Dégustation (carte also available) that showcases tip-top regional produce. The modern approach is underpinned by a classical theme, high skill and clear flavours; take a fillet of Irish beef served with braised cheeks and root vegetables.

Chef Stefan Matz **Owner** Ashford Castle Ltd. **Times** Closed Mon-Wed, Closed L all week **Prices** Tasting menu €130-€155, Starter €12-€39, Main €35-€39, Dessert €15-€20, Service added 15% **Wines** 600 bottles over €20, 20 bottles under €20, 20 by glass **Notes** Tasting menu 5-7 courses, Vegetarian available, Dress restrictions, Jacket & Tie **Seats** 30, Pr/dining room 60 **Children** Portions, Menu **Parking** 115

The George V Room

◉ European V ☺

Spectacular castle setting overlooking the Corrib

☎ 094 9546003
Ashford Castle
e-mail: neilgrant@ashford.ie
dir: From Galway take N84 through Headford & Glencorrib towards Cross. Turn left for Cong. Ashford Castle gates in approx 5km

The magical setting of 13th-century Ashford Castle is the location for the George V Room, which was originally created for a royal visit. The luxurious and sophisticated dining room is the perfect setting for refined and enjoyable cuisine, exuding an air of timeless sophistication with its high ornate ceilings, sparkling chandeliers and formal table service. The cooking style reflects its surroundings - classical and elegant and based on classical French cuisine, with food prepared and presented in a light, contemporary style. You might begin with baked gâteau of crab meat and roast vegetables with carrot and ginger jam, and follow with fillet of halibut in prawn bisque sauce, spinach and asparagus, or maybe roast of the day served from the carving trolley.

Chef Stefan Matz **Owner** Ashford Castle Ltd. **Times** 1-2/7-9.30, Closed L Mon-Sat **Prices** Fixed L course €39, Fixed D 4 course €70, Starter €18.50, Main €32-€35, Dessert €15, Service added 15% **Wines** 600 bottles over €20, 20 bottles under €20, 20 by glass **Notes** TDH and Tasting menu available, Sunday L, Vegetarian menu, Dress restrictions, Jacket & Tie, no denim **Seats** 120, Pr/dining room 50 **Children** Portions, Menu **Parking** 115

Lisloughrey Lodge Hotel

◎◎ Modern International ✹

Elegant country-house dining with stunning lake views

☎ 094 9545400
The Quay
e-mail: lodge@lisloughrey.ie
dir: Please telephone for directions

This beautiful lakeside property dates from 1824 and was once part of the Ashford estate. Standing in 10 acres of grounds proudly overlooking Lough Corrib, its spectacular panoramic lake views, mature woodlands and quay make for a truly unique and relaxing setting. The fine-dining Salt Restaurant is located on the first floor and features four intimate rooms in which diners enjoy the modern Irish cuisine. Since the hotel opened its doors in 2007, the chef has made quite a name for himself locally, the intelligent simplicity of his cooking allowing high-quality, locally-sourced produce to speak for itself. A Bluebell Falls soufflé starter served with beetroot three ways shows the style, followed by butter-basted monkfish tail with sautéed Irish lobster, watercress and rhubarb risotto.

Chef Wade Murphy **Times** Closed 24-26 Dec **Prices** Food prices not confirmed for 2009. Please telephone for details. **Wines** 112 bottles over €20, 8 bottles under €20, 8 by glass **Notes** Vegetarian available, Civ Wed 180 **Seats** 56, Pr/dining room 14 **Children** Portions, Menu **Parking** 100

MULRANY Map 1 A4

Nephin Restaurant

◎◎ Modern V ✹

Atlantic views and contemporary cooking

☎ 098 36000
Park Inn Hotel
e-mail: info@parkinnmulranny.ie
dir: From Westport take N59 throught Newport, continue on R311 to Mulrany village, hotel on right

There are splendid views over the Atlantic from this imposing Victorian former railway hotel and, with 42 acres of grounds and leisure and business facilities, there is plenty to occupy all of the senses. The décor is

bright and contemporary and there is seemingly a great view from every window. The menu treads a classical path and cooking displays good technical skill and an eye for presentation. Clare Island scallops with thin slices of chorizo, Jerusalem artichoke purée, basil butter and red pepper espuma is a starter displaying sound control with the balance of flavours, and main-course fillet of lamb is wrapped in a black pudding from the locally renowned Kelly's and paired with a croquette of white pudding and a mint and apricot salsa. Pear tart displays equally impressive skill with a light puff pastry case and a light vanilla mousse and little cubes of jelly.

Chef Seamus Commons **Owner** Tom & Kathleen O'Keeffee **Prices** Fixed L 3 course fr €25.50, Fixed D 4 course fr €49, Starter €9-€30, Main €25-€40, Dessert €8-€15, Service optional **Wines** 100 bottles over €20, 50 bottles under €20, 10 by glass **Notes** Tasting menu available, Sunday L, Vegetarian menu, Air con **Seats** 100, Pr/dining room 50 **Children** Portions, Menu **Parking** 200

WESTPORT Map 1 B4

Bluewave Restaurant

◎ Modern European

West Coast dining with impressive views

☎ 098 29000
Carlton Atlantic Coast Hotel, The Quay
e-mail: info@atlanticcoasthotel.com
dir: From Westport take coast road towards Louisburgh for 1m. Hotel on harbour on left

This bright, modern hotel on Westport Harbour was once a woollen mill, and the façade of the old building has been carefully restored to preserve the original stonework. The Bluewave Restaurant, situated on the fourth floor, commands spectacular views over Clew Bay and has a relaxed, peaceful atmosphere. Good use is made of local ingredients on the daily-changing menu, especially seafood, with dishes such as smoked bacon shank and cabbage terrine, steamed Clew Bay mussels with pear and leek cream, or seared salmon with minted pea and chorizo compôte.

Chef Frank Walsh **Owner** Carlton Hotel Group **Times** Closed 20-27 Dec, Closed L all week **Prices** Fixed L 2 course fr €19.95, Fixed D 4 course fr €39, Service added but optional 12.5% **Wines** 12 bottles over €20, 14 bottles under €20, 1 by glass **Notes** Vegetarian available, Air con **Seats** 85, Pr/dining room 140 **Children** Portions, Menu **Parking** 80

Knockranny House Hotel

◎ Modern French, International

Stunning views from an elegant restaurant

☎ 098 28600
e-mail: info@khh.ie
dir: On N5 (Dublin to Castlebar road), on the left before entering Westport

Clew Bay and Croach Patrick provide the scenic backdrop to this modern hotel. Its impressive, split-level restaurant, La Fougère, has many window tables with wonderful views. Local produce makes a strong showing including smoked products from the hotel's own kiln and herbs from the kitchen garden. The menu offers modern Irish dishes with French influences, such as Clew Bay clam, mussel and tomato broth with Kilkeel crab dumplings, horseradish cream and crispy leek, or slices of roasted pork tenderloin on organic pearl barley, leek and grey chanterelle mushroom ragout with baby carrots and shallot jus.

Chef David O'Donnell **Owner** Adrian & Geraldine Noonan **Times** 1-2.30/6.30-9.30, Closed Xmas **Prices** Fixed D 4 course fr €54, Service optional **Wines** 8 by glass **Notes** Sunday L, Dress restrictions, Smart casual, Air con **Seats** 140, Pr/dining room **Children** Portions, Menu **Parking** 150

CO MEATH

KILMESSAN   Map 1 D5

The Station House Hotel

European, Mediterranean

Country-house cooking in a converted railway station

☎ 046 902 5239 & 902 5586
e-mail: info@thestationhousehotel.com
dir: From Dublin N3 to Dunshaughlin, R125 to Kilmessan

A converted railway station set in 12 acres of grounds, this family-run hotel has bags of charm and a great reputation for family celebrations. The cosy Signal Restaurant delivers country-house cooking with a touch of French flair. Top quality local ingredients are sourced and skilfully treated, and the menus are truly seasonal. Typical dishes are minced lamb and vegetable wonton with mango and red onion chutney, followed by haunch of wild boar with pancetta and cassoulet. Finish with luscious white chocolate cheesecake spiked with pistachio nuts. Bar food is served in the Platform Bar and Lounge.

Chef David Mulvihill **Owner** Chris & Thelma Slattery **Times** 12.30-3/4.30-10.30 **Prices** Fixed D 4 course €25-€49.95, Starter €4.95-€13.95, Main €15.95-€29.95, Dessert €5.95-€8.95, Service optional **Wines** 8 bottles over €20, 29 bottles under €20, 4 by glass **Notes** Fixed L 4 courses, Fixed D 5 courses, Sunday L, Vegetarian available **Seats** 90, Pr/dining room 180 **Children** Portions, Menu **Parking** 200

CO MONAGHAN

CARRICKMACROSS   Map 1 C4

Restaurant at Nuremore

– *see opposite*

CO SLIGO

SLIGO   Map 1 B5

The Glasshouse

Modern

Contemporary cuisine overlooking the Garravogue River

☎ 071 9194300
Swan Point
e-mail: info@theglasshouse.ie

Set along the river boardwalk of the striking Glasshouse Hotel, the bright Kitchen Restaurant is intimate and colourful with a Mediterranean vibe and fantastic views over the river. Contemporary interpretations of classic dishes are on offer, with some unusual but effective combinations. Examples are asparagus wrapped in Parma ham with grilled pineapple and orange brandy dressing to start; and a main course of pan-fried venison medallions on a bed of sauerkraut, grilled apple and wild berry jus. Finish with refreshing Malibu and lemongrass marinated fresh fruit with champagne sorbet. There is also a swish ground-floor bar.

Times 12-5/6.30-9.30

CO TIPPERARY

CASHEL   Map 1 C3

Cashel Palace Hotel

Traditional French

Country-house cuisine set in former ecclesiastical kitchens

☎ 062 62707
e-mail: reception@cashel-palace.ie
dir: On main street in Cashel town centre

Situated in the centre of Cashel, this fine Queen Anne house has been home to archbishops, earls and lords in its time, and is now an elegant and inviting hotel. There is a bar

named after the black stuff and a restaurant, Bishop's Buttery, which occupies the flagstoned basement and boasts vaulted ceilings, open hearths, crisp white linen and friendly, professional service. The cooking leans toward classic French cuisine and makes sound use of local produce, with game in season and fish from the Waterford coast among the specialities. Start with foie gras and spiced apple terrine with caramelised fig compôte and toasted brioche before chargrilled fillet of Tipperary beef with fondant potato, celeriac and truffle purée and sauce béarnaise.

Times 12-2.30/6-9.30, Closed 24-27 Dec, Closed L Sun

CO WATERFORD

WATERFORD   Map 1 C2

Athenaeum House Hotel

Modern European

Innovative fare in a luxury boutique hotel

☎ 051 833999
Christendon, Ferrybank
e-mail: info@athenaeumhousehotel.com
dir: From station on N25 towards Rosslare, through lights, then right and next right

Set in 10 acres of parkland on the banks of the River Suir close to the city, this sympathetically restored Georgian house now operates as a chic boutique hotel offering a high level of comfort. With its friendly and professional service, Zak's is the bright and airy, conservatory-style restaurant (with terrace) where modern artworks sit alongside period pieces and innovative food is served. The modern European cooking has a strong classical basis, with excellent ingredients used in interesting combinations. Take chicken liver parfait with redcurrant jelly, perhaps confit duck legs with Puy lentil casserole, or Irish beef fillet with basil pesto and Merlot jus.

Chef James Crawford **Owner** Stan & Mailo Power **Times** 12.30-3.30/7-9.30, Closed 25-27 Dec **Prices** Fixed L course €23, Fixed D 3 course €23, Starter €5.50-€12, Main €16-€28, Dessert €6-€12, Service optional **Wines** 7 bottles over €20, 9 bottles under €20, 10 by glass **Notes** Sunday L, Vegetarian available, Civ Wed 70, Air con **Seats** 100, Pr/dining room 30 **Children** Portions, Menu **Parking** 40

Faithlegg House Hotel

Modern Irish, European

Country-house cooking in elegant surroundings

☎ 051 382000
Faithlegg
e-mail: reservations@fhh.ie

An 18th-century mansion has been sensitively restored to form the centrepiece of this hotel overlooking the River Suir estuary. It offers both luxurious guestrooms and self-catering accommodation. In the elegant, spacious dining room, with views of the gardens, the service is professional but friendly. The cooking is solid country

Continued on page 600

Restaurant at Nuremore

Modern French **V**

Innovative cuisine with bold combinations at country-house hotel

☎ 042 9661438
e-mail: info@nuremore.com
web: www.nuremore.com
dir: 11m from M1at Ardee turning (N33)

Located in beautiful rolling Monaghan countryside overlooking parkland and the championship golf course, Nuremore is an oasis of country-house calm and tranquillity. The split-level dining room has recently been refurbished with an extension to the conservatory, and has a comfortable, modern feel with pleasant views over gardens and the lake. The imaginative menu more than befits the setting, aptly demonstrating the flair and accomplished technical skill of chef Raymond McArdle's well-motivated brigade and pleasant, attentive front-of-house service. His modern approach, underpinned by a classical French theme, utilises tip-top produce, enhanced by contemporary styling of presentation and ingredient combination. Menu descriptions don't really do justice to the intricate work that graces dishes. Nonetheless, to show the style, take an accomplished starter of Annagassan white crab and lobster cocktail, mango relish and parmesan crisp, or hand-dived Wexford sea scallops, with confit of chicken,

cauliflower purée and Madeira jus. Follow with line-caught wild halibut baked with lemon confit, warm tomato fondue, white beans and black truffle, and to finish, fennel and vanilla parfait with chocolate velouté. Peripherals like breads, amuse-bouche, pre-desserts and petits fours also hold top form through to the end. Lunch offers exceptionally good value.

Chef Raymond McArdle **Owner** Gilhooly family **Times** 12.30-2.30/6.30-9.45, Closed L Sat **Wines** 153 bottles over €20, 37 bottles under €20, 18 by glass **Notes** Prestige menu €80, Sunday L, Vegetarian menu, Civ Wed 200, Air con **Seats** 120, Pr/dining room 50 **Children** Portions, Menu **Parking** 200

WATERFORD *Continued*

house with European influences. Starters might include seafood risotto made with locally landed crab and mussels, topped with shards of crisp parsnip. For mains, try roast leg of lamb from a nearby farm, served on a bed of champ and crushed carrots with wilted spinach and fondant potato. A light mango bavarois with pineapple and champagne sorbet makes the perfect dessert.

Times 6.30-9.30, Closed L Mon-Sat

Waterford Castle

◉◉ Modern, Traditional ☙

Modern interpretations of the classics in romantic castle setting

☎ 051 878203
The Island
e-mail: info@waterfordcastle.com
dir: Please telephone for directions

Set on its own enchanting 310-acre island, with an 18-hole championship golf course, the castle is an impressive 16th-century building. There are views across the surrounding deer park from the Munster Room, an oak-panelled restaurant with ornate ceilings and mullioned windows. The seasonal set menu draws on excellent seafood caught at nearby Dunmore East, well-kept local cheeses and organic vegetables where possible. Try seared scallops with confit garlic mash and oxtail jus, followed by haunch of Wicklow venison marinated in wine and juniper. Round off with poached pear with roasted almond parfait. Saucing is a particular strength, often with an impressive twist, and presentation of dishes is contemporary on unusual shaped plates of glass and slate.

Chef Michael Quinn **Owner** Munster Dining Room **Times** 12.30-1.45/7-9, Closed Xmas, early Jan, Closed L Mon-Sat **Prices** Fixed L 3 course fr €33, Fixed D 4 course fr €65, Starter €14, Main €30, Dessert €12, Service added but optional 10% **Wines** 50+ bottles over €20, 8 by glass **Notes** Dress restrictions, Jacket or shirt required for D **Seats** 50, Pr/dining room 80 **Children** Portions, Menu **Parking** 200

CO WESTMEATH

| ATHLONE | Map 1 C4 |

Hodson Bay

◉ Traditional, International

Smart lakeside hotel with a fine restaurant

☎ 090 6442000
Hodson Bay
e-mail: info@hodsonbayhotel.com
dir: From Athlone follow signs for Roscommon. Approx 2.5m on entering Hodson Bay follow signs for the hotel on right

Renowned Irish hospitality can be found at this rural idyll on the picturesque shores of Lough Ree in the heart of some of the country's most spectacular countryside.

L'Escale restaurant is the showcase for the hotel's fine dining and offers a menu that combines traditional Irish cooking with international influences, producing honest, imaginative dishes with flair. Local seafood is a speciality, delivered fresh every day, with a lobster tank on the premises. A typical starter might be blue cheese risotto with sautéed mushrooms, while mains might include supreme of salmon with creamy wine sauce and a ratatouille of carrot, peppers and onion. For dessert, try lemon flan served with a chocolate cookie parfait with raspberry coulis.

Times 12.30-2.15/7-9.30

Wineport Lodge

◉ Modern, Classical

Wholesome cooking in spectacular setting

☎ 090 6439010
Glasson
e-mail: lodge@wineport.ie

A truly impressive location on the shores of the inner lakes of Lough Ree on the Shannon. Customers can arrive by road or water, and dine on the deck or in the attractive dining room. Spectacular views and friendly service reflect the highest standards of Irish hospitality. Wholesome local produce is served up in generous portions. Try a starter of spiced Thai soup, or goat's cheese and roast beetroot spring roll with thyme and maple drizzle. To follow, maybe monkfish en papillote with sundried tomato, basil, Pernod and lemon, or roast fillet of cod with honey, curry and grain mustard and red onion coriander fritters would appeal. To complement the interesting dishes there's a serious dedication to wine here.

Times 3-10/6-10, Closed 24-26 Dec, Closed L Mon-Sat

CO WEXFORD

| GOREY | Map 1 D3 |

Marlfield House

◉◉ Classic

Elegant restaurant in a country-house setting

☎ 053 9421124
Courtown Rd
e-mail: info@marlfieldhouse.ie
dir: 1m from Gorey on R742 (Courtown road)

A sense of luxury pervades this family-run country-house hotel, from the opulent furnishings to the gracious service. Cocktails are served in the elegant library and coffee and petits fours in the drawing room. The restaurant is in a flower-filled conservatory overlooking beautiful gardens and carefully kept lawns. Vegetables and herbs from the kitchen garden feature among the mainly local ingredients put to good use in the kitchen. Accurately cooked dishes are offered from a succinct four-course menu, and the style is classically based with modern influences. Daube of wild Irish venison with horseradish creamed beans, pancetta and tarragon, and

seared fillet of John Dory with beetroot risotto, fennel, baby asparagus and vinaigrette Parisienne are fine examples of the fare.

Chef Colin Byrne **Owner** The Bowe Family **Times** 12.30-2/7-9, Closed 1 Jan-28 Feb, Closed L Mon-Sat **Prices** Fixed L 3 course €45-€50, Fixed D 4 course €68-€70 **Wines** 100 bottles over €20, 20 bottles under €20, 6 by glass **Notes** Sunday L, Vegetarian available, Dress restrictions, Smart dress, no jeans, Civ Wed 130, Air con **Seats** 70, Pr/dining room 50 **Children** Min 8 yrs D **Parking** 100

The Rowan Tree Restaurant

◉ Modern, International

Enjoyable dining in modern hotel spa

☎ 053 9480500
Ashdown Park Hotel, The Coach Rd
e-mail: info@ashdownparkhotel.com
dir: On approach to Gorey town take N11 from Dublin. Take left signed for Courtown. Hotel on left

Part of a contemporary spa hotel, situated at the edge of the picturesque town of Gorey, this elegant restaurant offers both carte and fixed-price daily-changing menus with efficient, yet relaxed and friendly service. Clever use of fresh local produce means that the simpler dishes are often the most enjoyable. European and international dishes may include fresh fig with mascarpone and Parma ham, followed by pan-fried mullet on citrus-scented couscous with asparagus purée, or braised Wicklow venison shank on leek mash and juniper sauce. Don't forget to leave room for dessert - the rich chocolate marquise is especially good.

Chef David Crossoir **Owner** Pat & Tom Redmond **Times** 12.30-2.30/6-9.30, Closed 24-25 Dec, Closed L Mon-Sat **Wines** 19 bottles over €20, 14 bottles under €20, 10 by glass **Notes** Early bird menu €25, Sunday L, Vegetarian available, Dress restrictions, Neat dress, Air con **Seats** 110, Pr/dining room 90 **Children** Portions, Menu **Parking** 150

ROSSLARE Map 1 D2

Beaches

◉ Traditional European

Classic cuisine in a Victorian seaside hotel

☎ 053 9132114
Kelly's Resort Hotel & Spa
e-mail: kellyhot@iol.ie

Founded in 1895 by William Kelly, by a 5-mile stretch of sandy beach in Rosslare, the hotel is now run by the fourth generation of the family. Beaches Restaurant is traditionally opulent and the ideal home for some of the hotel's famous art collection. Chef Jim Aherne has been pleasing guests with his classic cuisine for over 30 years, and his menus reflect the value placed on fresh local produce. Pride is taken in dishes such as nettle soup, fillet of sole hermitage, and roast goose with chestnut stuffing.

Times 1-2/7.30-9, Closed mid Dec-mid Feb

La Marine Bistro

◉ Modern

Bistro-style cooking at a smart seaside resort hotel

☎ 053 9132114
Kelly's Resort Hotel & Spa
e-mail: kellyhot@iol.ie

The stand-alone restaurant of this resort hotel has a maritime theme to its décor and views of the busy kitchen. The atmosphere is casual and relaxed, and the menu offers uncomplicated cooking of the freshest produce with an emphasis on allowing the natural flavours of the main ingredient to shine through. There's a good choice of seafood, including a starter of salt and pepper squid, presented with a crisp salad and dipping sauce. Follow with fried fillets of ray wing, served with nut butter and caperberries, and pannacotta and fresh strawberries to finish.

WEXFORD Map 1 D3

Newbay Country House & Restaurant

◉ Modern European

Popular country-house dining with excellent, simply-prepared dishes

☎ 053 9142779
Newbay, Carrick
e-mail: newbay@newbayhouse.com
dir: Take Cork road from Wexford, left after Citroen garage, at x-rds turn right, restaurant on right

This elegant late-Georgian house sits in 25 acres of mature gardens and parkland, just a short drive from Wexford town. The Cellar Bistro has an informal atmosphere, with an adjacent bar and outdoor heated terrace. Upstairs is the fine-dining restaurant, where quality ingredients are handled with confident simplicity allowing flavours to shine through. Fish dishes are a speciality, with the fish brought in from the hotel's own

trawler. Your choice might include Thai crab cakes with red onion and chilli marmalade and basil mayonnaise, followed by a starter of pan-fried cannon of monkfish with sweet potato champ, shellfish and chestnut cream. Booking is essential, especially at weekends.

Chef Paul Wildes **Owner** Alec Scallan **Times** 12-3/6-9.30, Closed Xmas, New Year, Closed L Mon-Thu **Prices** Fixed L 2 course €22.95, Starter €5.25-€15.95, Main €23.95-€31.95, Dessert €6.95, Service optional **Wines** 14 bottles over €20, 15 bottles under €20, 6 by glass **Notes** Early bird menu 5 course D available 6-7pm, Sunday L, Vegetarian available **Seats** 75 **Children** Portions, Menu **Parking** 70

Seasons Restaurant

◉ Modern International ✍

A good variety of dishes in a friendly hotel setting

☎ 053 9143444
Whitford House Hotel, New Line road
e-mail: info@whitford.ie
dir: From Rosslare ferry port follow N25. At Duncannon Rd rdbt, turn right onto R733, hotel immediately on left. 1.5m from Wexford town

The Whitford is a long-established family-run hotel and leisure club with a strong local following. Dinner is served in the spacious Seasons Restaurant, to the accompaniment of live classical music at weekends. The simplicity of the international menu descriptions belies the quality of the dishes and the careful attention to detail they represent. Start with three local cheeses deep-fried in three different crumbs or symphony of seafood, followed by Barbary duck breast on celeriac and sweet and sour blueberry jus, with fruit delice - mango mousse with tangy passionfruit layer - for dessert.

Chef Siobhan Devereux **Owner** The Whitty Family **Times** 12.30-3/7-9, Closed 24-27 Dec, Closed L Mon-Sat **Prices** Fixed L 2 course €15.95-€19.95, Fixed D 3 course €24.95-€33.95, Starter €5-€10.50, Main €16-€36, Dessert €7.50-€8.50, Service optional **Wines** 15 bottles over €20, 42 bottles under €20 **Notes** Sunday L, Vegetarian available, Air con **Seats** 100 **Children** Portions, Menu **Parking** 150

CO WICKLOW

MACREDDIN Map 1 D3

The Strawberry Tree Restaurant

◉◉ Modern ✍

Dramatic dining venue specialising in organic and wild food

☎ 0402 36444
Brooklodge Hotel & Wells Spa
e-mail: brooklodge@macreddin.ie
dir: From Dublin take N11, turn off at Rathnew for Rathdrum, then through Aughrim to Macreddin (2m)

Situated in a purpose-built village which boasts a country pub and brewery, café, bakery, smokehouse, equestrian centre, 18-hole golf course and spa, The Strawberry Tree is Ireland's first certified organic restaurant. It is situated in a luxurious country-house hotel and the dining area occupies three grand rooms, each with mirrored ceilings, modern lighting and dark blue décor. Attention to detail is very much in evidence when it comes to the sourcing of ingredients, both organic and wild, and seasonality lies at the heart of everything. Creativity and skill is evident in the output from the kitchen brigade. Start with seared wild scallops, perfectly caramelised, and enhanced by a wild mango salsa, follow on with roast duck with cep sauce (rare breast and confit leg) and end with apple and walnut tartelette.

Brooklodge Hotel & Wells Spa is AA Hotel of the Year for Ireland

Chef Norman Luedke/Evan Doyle **Owner** The Doyle Family **Times** 1-6/7-9.30, Closed L Mon-Sun **Wines** 10 bottles under €20, 10 by glass **Notes** Fixed D 5 courses €65, Vegetarian available, Dress restrictions, Smart casual, Civ Wed 120, Air con **Seats** 142, Pr/dining room 50 **Children** Portions **Parking** 400

RATHNEW   Map 1 D3

Hunter's Hotel

◉ Traditional French

Beautiful views and 300 years of history

☎ 0404 40106
e-mail: reception@hunters.ie
dir: N11 exit at Wicklow/Rathnew junct. Take 1st left,
R761. Restaurant located 0.25m before village

This delightful country house is Ireland's oldest coaching
inn and is set in beautiful gardens on the banks of the
River Varty. It's been in the same family for five
generation since 1820 and has developed a reputation for
friendliness, hospitality and classic country-house
cooking. The attentive staff serve accurately cooked
dishes, utilising first-class local and seasonal produce,
including home-grown fruit and vegetables. Typical
starters include pan-fried scallops served with a garlicky
yogurt sauce, orange-glazed roast duck with redcurrant
jus, sweet red cabbage and herb roasted potatoes,
followed by a pear poached in red wine with a rich
sabayon and cinnamon ice cream for dessert. Afternoon
tea in the garden is a delight.

Times 12.45-3/7.30-9, Closed 3 days Xmas

WOODENBRIDGE   Map 1 D3

Redmond Restaurant

◉ European ✪

Beautiful location and fine cuisine

☎ 0402 35146
Woodenbridge Hotel
e-mail: info@woodenbridgehotel.com
dir: 7km from Arklow

Situated in the green and wooded Vale of Avoca, this
smart establishment is reputedly Ireland's oldest hotel. It
is next to the Woodenbridge Golf Club and offers two
dining options, the informal Il Ruscello Mediterranean
restaurant, and the fine-dining Redmond restaurant.
Take a pre-dinner drink in the cosy bar while you choose
where to dine. Redmond's features plenty of Irish seafood,
including brill, John Dory, salmon and scallops, while
meats are an extensive choice from duck to veal. An
impressive wine cellar stores a good collection of wines
from around the globe.

Chef Roman Sliwa **Owner** Billy & Esther O'Brien
Times 12.30-3/7-9 **Prices** Fixed L course €28, Fixed D 4
course €37, Starter €8.75-€12.50, Main €21-€28, Dessert
€8, Service included **Wines** 10 bottles over €20, 18
bottles under €20, 5 by glass **Notes** Sunday L, Vegetarian
available, Civ Wed 200 **Seats** 80 **Parking** 400

KEY TO ATLAS

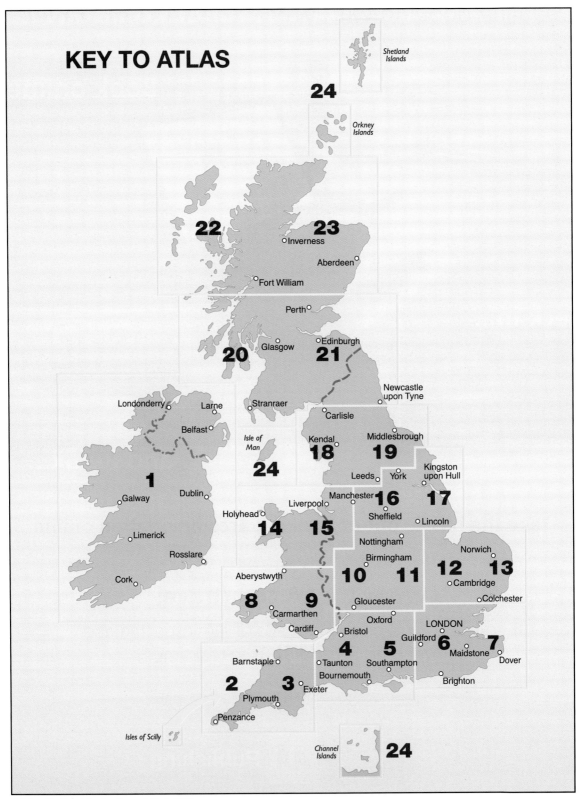

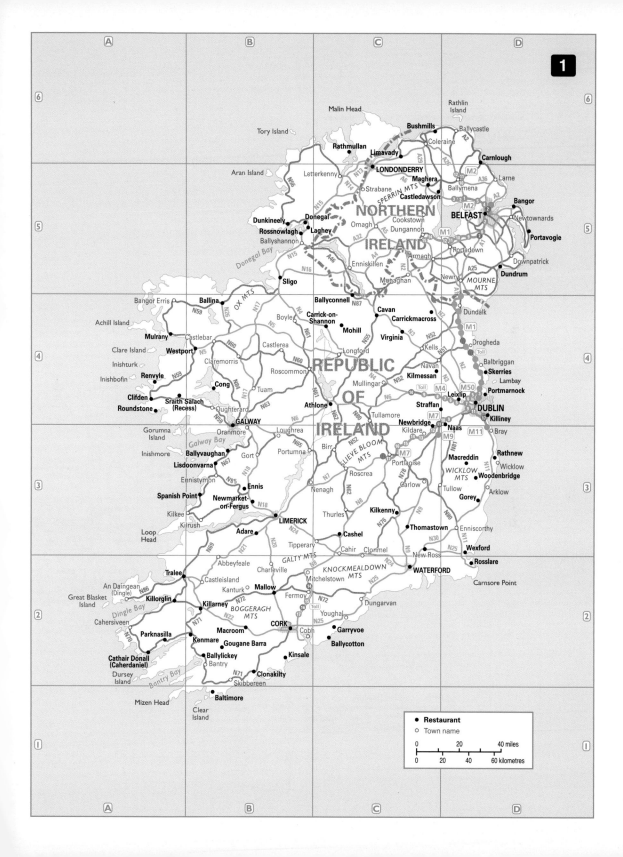

2

For continuation pages refer to numbered arrows

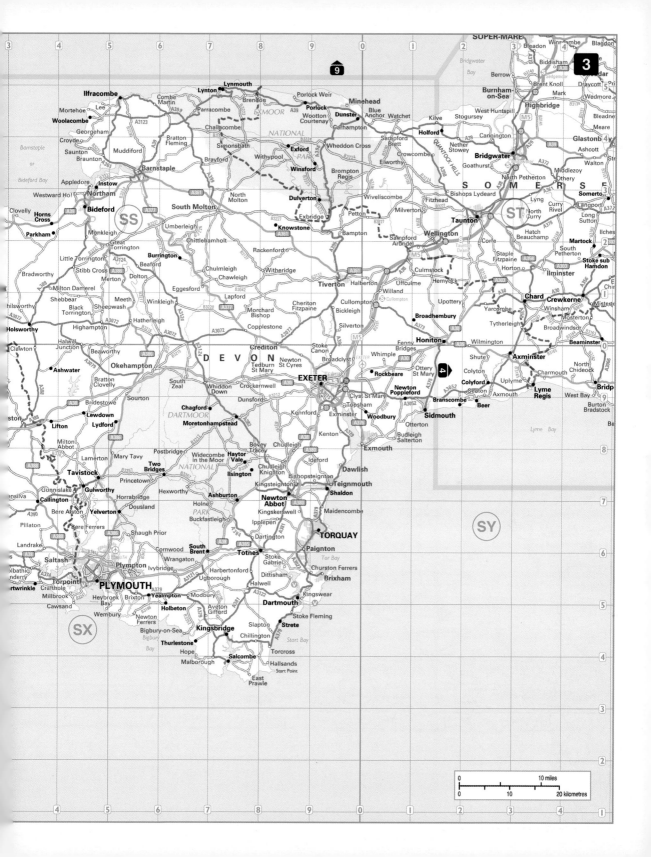

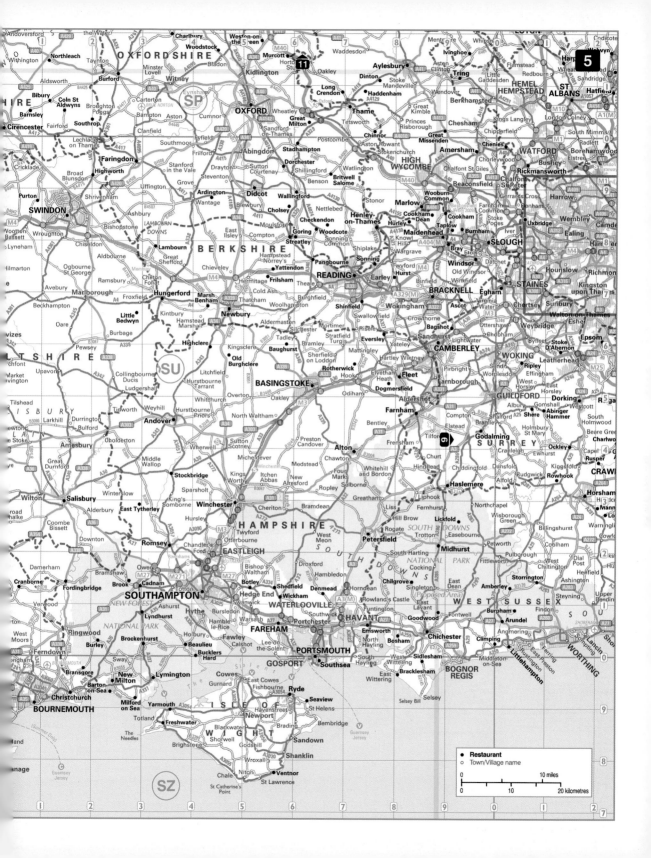

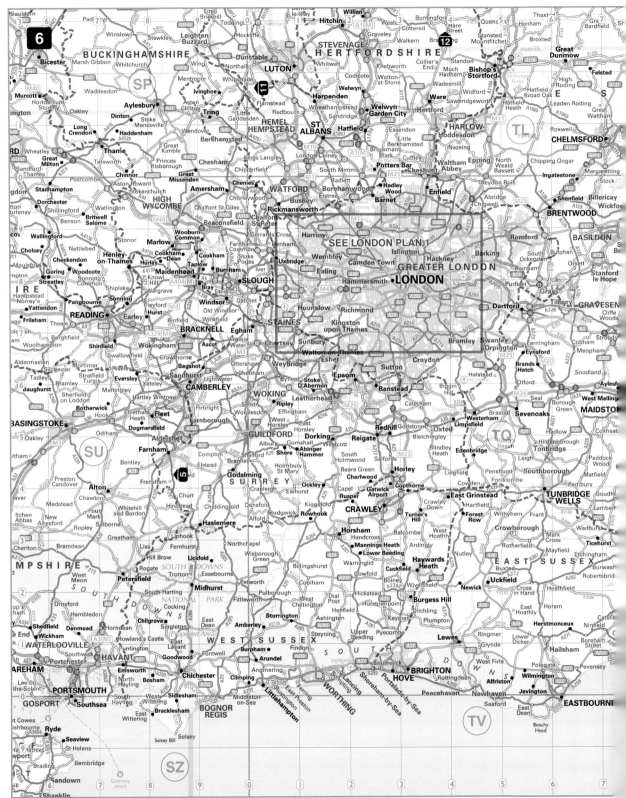

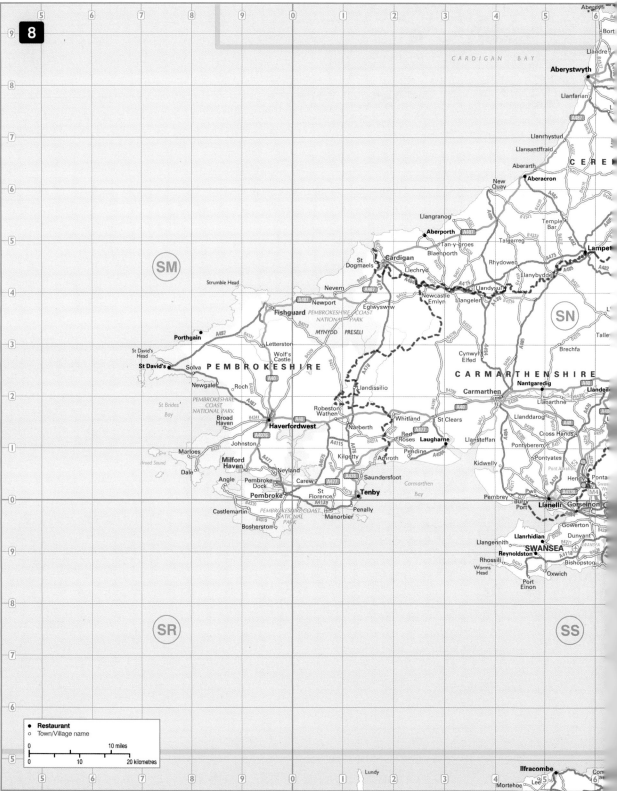

CARDIGAN BAY

Aberdyfi
Bort
Llandre
Aberystwyth

Llanfarian

Llanrhystud
Llansantffraid
Aberarth
Aberaeron
C E R E

New
Quay

Llangranog
Temple
Bar
Aberporth
Talgarreg
Tan-y-groes
Lampet
Blaenporth
St
Dogmaels **Cardigan**
Rhydowen
Llanybydder
Llechryd
Newcastle
Emlyn **Llandysu**
Strumble Head
Nevern
Llangeler
Newport
SN
Eglwyswrw
Fishguard PEMBROKESHIRE COAST
NATIONAL PARK
MYNYDD PRESELI
Brechfa
Letterston
Cynwyl
Elfed
Wolf's
Castle
Porthgain
CARMARTHENSHIRE
St David's
Head
Talle
Carmarthen **Nantgaredig**
Llandeil
Solva
St David's
Newgale
PEMBROKESHIRE
Llandissilio
Llanarthne
Roch
Llanddarog
Newgale
St Brides'
Bay
PEMBROKESHIRE
COAST
NATIONAL PARK
Robeston
Wathen
St Clears
Whitland
Cross Hands
Broad
Haven
Haverfordwest
Narberth
Pontyberem
Red
Roses **Laugharne**
Llansteffan
Johnston
Pontyates
Marloes
Kilgetty
Pendine
Kidwelly
**Milford
Haven**
Amroth
Broad Sound
Carmarthen
Bay
Tenby
Dale
Neyland
Saundersfoot
Llanelli Gorseinon
Angle
Pembroke
Dock Carew
St
Florence
Pembrey
Pembrey
Burry
Port
Pembroke
Penally
Castlemartin
Manorbier
Gowerton
PEMBROKESHIRE COAST
NATIONAL PARK
Dunvant
Bosherston
Llanrhidian
SWANSEA
Llangennith
Reynoldston
Bishopston
Rhossili
Worms
Head
Oxwich
Port
Einon

SM
SR
SS

- ● **Restaurant**
- ○ **Town/Village name**

0   10 miles
0   10   20 kilometres

Lundy

Ilfracombe
Lee
Mortehoe

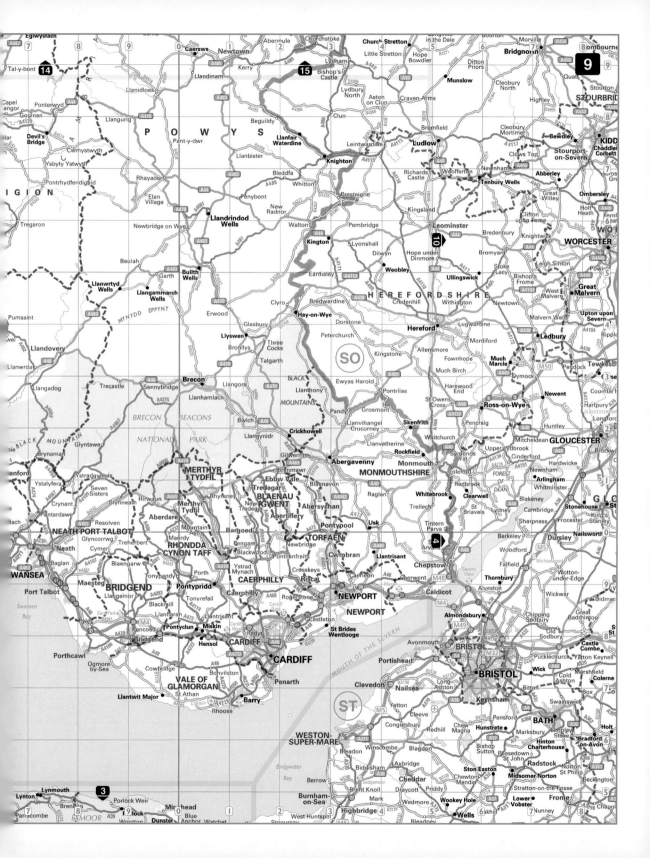

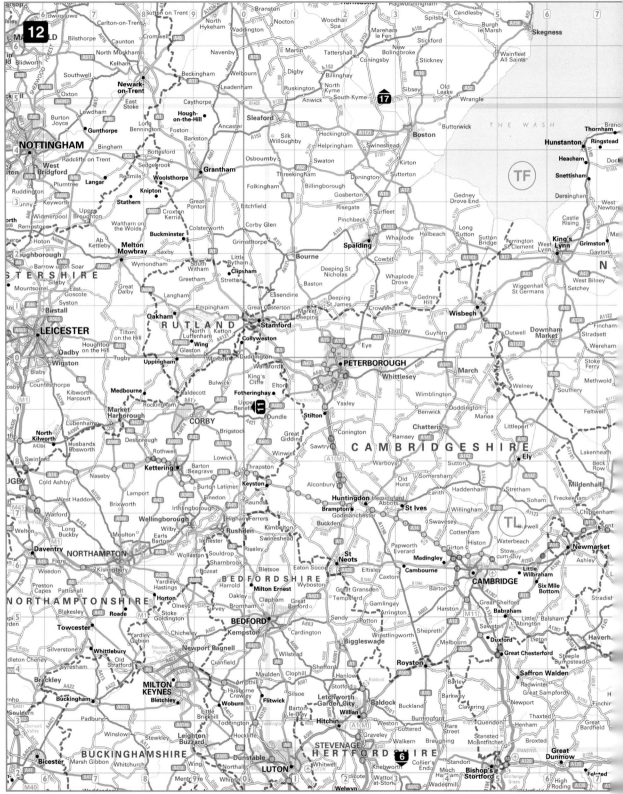

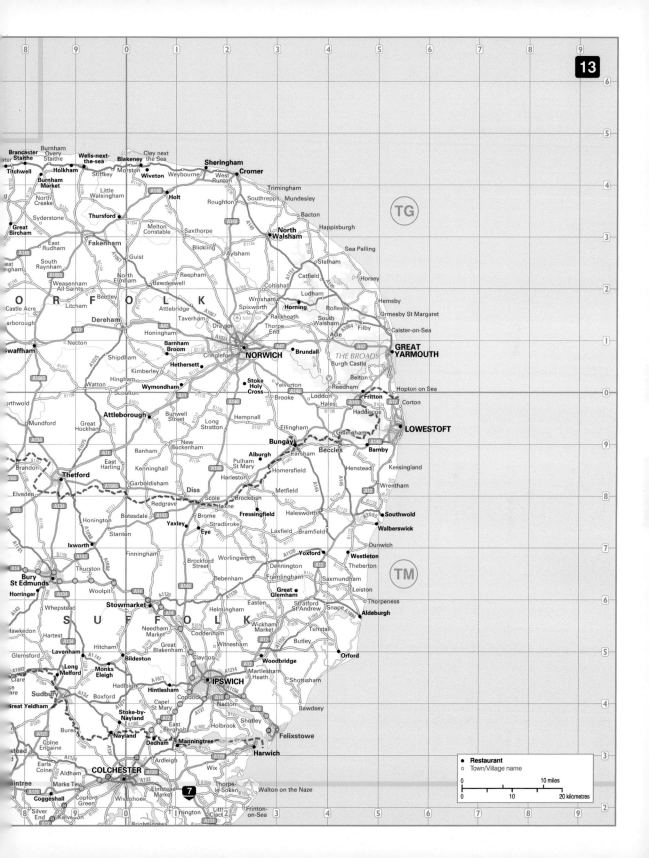

14

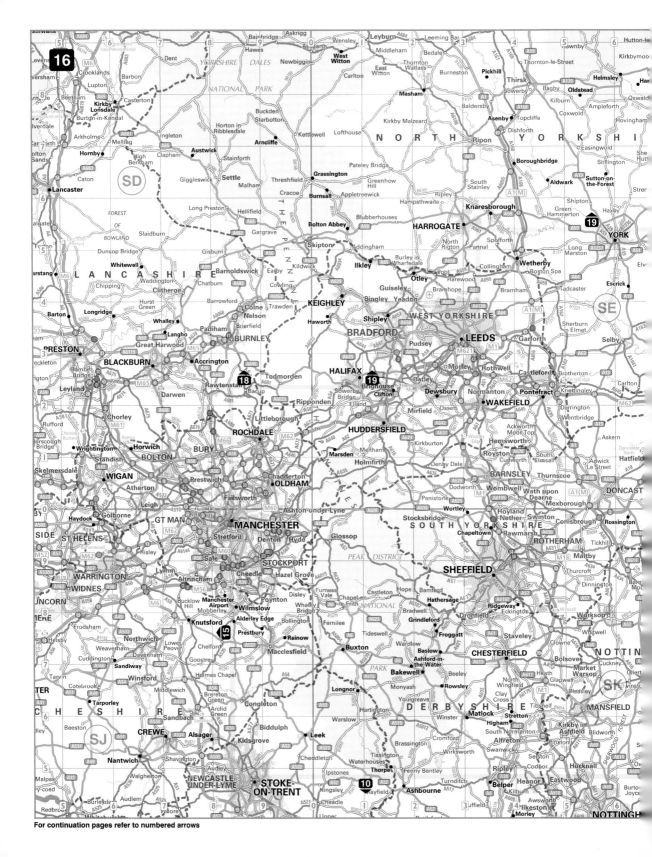

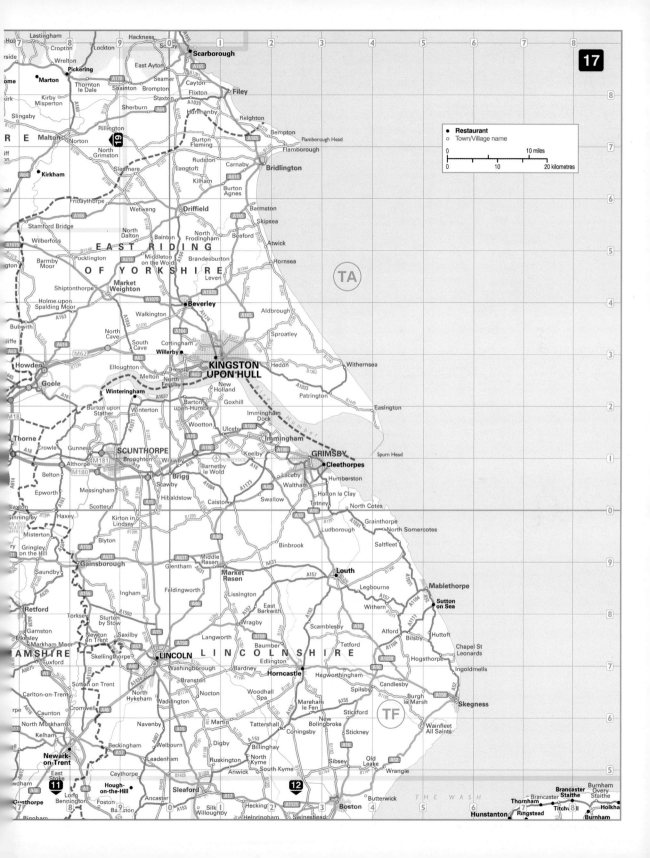

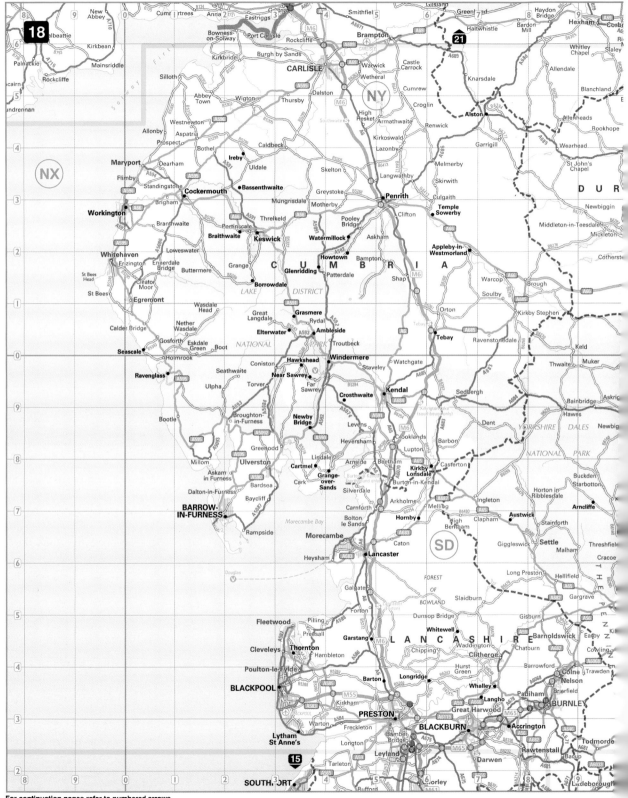

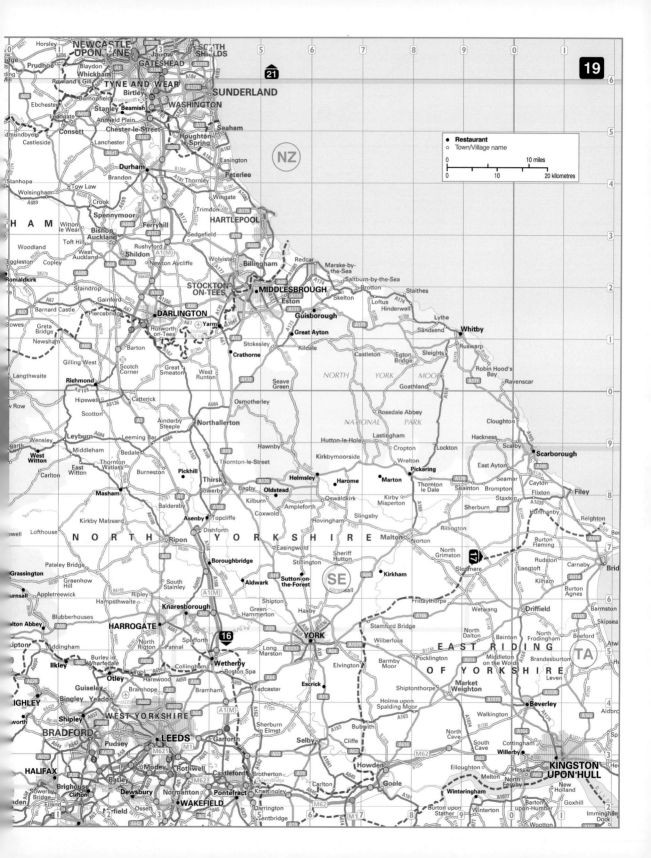

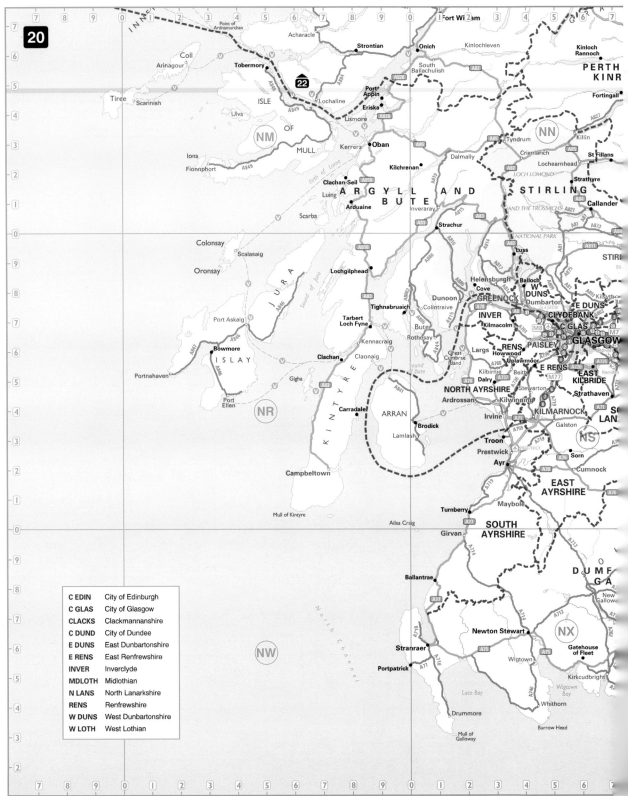

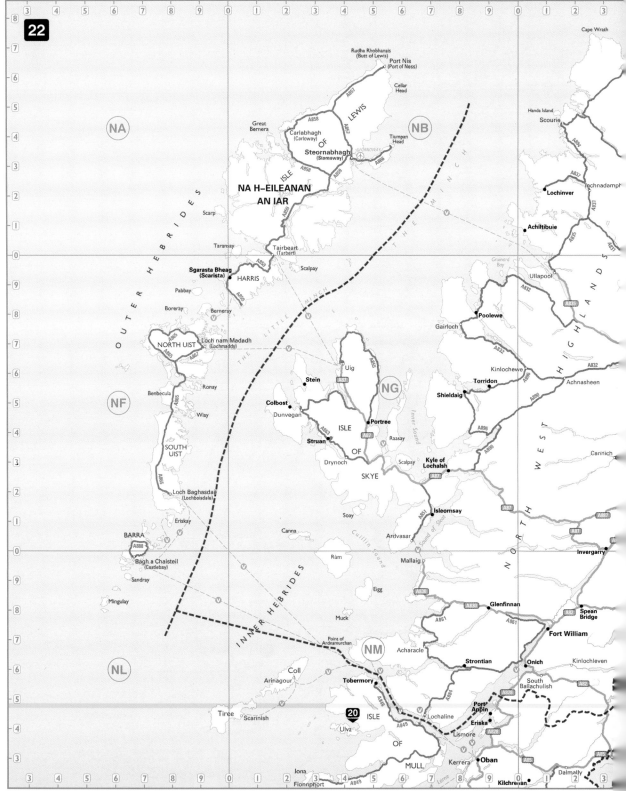

Cape Wrath

Rudha Rhobhanais
(Butt of Lewis)
Port Nis
(Port of Ness)
Cellar
Head

Handa Island
Scourie

A894

LEWIS

A858
Carlabhagh
(Carloway)

Great
Bernera

A857

A857

Steornabhagh
(Stornoway)

A858

NB

Tiumpan
Head

Lochinver

Inchnadamph

A837

A858

A859

STORNOWAY

A856

NA

ISLE

OF

A831

NA H–EILEANAN
AN IAR

Achiltibuie

A859

Scarp

THE MINCH

Taransay

A835

Gruinard
Bay

Ullapool

Tairbeart
(Tarbert)

Scalpay

A832

A835

Sgarasta Bheag
(Scarista)

A859

HARRIS

A860

Pabbay

THE LITTLE MINCH

Poolewe

Boreray

Berneray

Gairloch

A832

A865

A867

Loch nam Madadh
(Lochmaddy)

NORTH UIST

A865

Uig

A87

Kinlochewe

Torridon

A832

Achnasheen

Stein

NG

Benbecula

Ronay

A865

NF

Wiay

Colbost

Shieldaig

A896

Dunvegan

A863

Portree

SOUTH
UIST

A865

ISLE

OF

Struan

Raasay

A87

A896

A890

Drynoch

Cannich

SKYE

Scalpay

Kyle of
Lochalsh

A87

Loch Baghasdail
(Lochboisdale)

Soay

A87

Eriskay

BARRA

A888

Canna

Ardvasar

A851

Isleornsay

Sound of Sleat

NORTH

A887

A87

Invergarry

Bagh a Chaisteil
(Castlebay)

Rùm

Mallaig

Inner Sound

WEST

Sandray

Eigg

A830

Glenfinnan

A82

Spean
Bridge

Mingulay

Muck

A861

A830

A861

Fort William

INNER HEBRIDES

NL

Point of
Ardnamurchan

NM

Acharacle

Kinlochleven

Coll

Arinagour

Strontian

A884

Onich

Tobermory

South
Ballachulish

A82

Tiree

Scarinish

A848

Lochaline

Port
Appin

A828

20 ISLE

A849

Eriska

Ulva

OF

Lismore

A828

Iona

MULL

Kerrera

Oban

A85

Fionnphort

A849

Lorne

Dalmally

Kilchrenan

Kilchrenan

NA H–EILEANAN

Cuillin Sound

OUTER HEBRIDES

HIGHLANDS

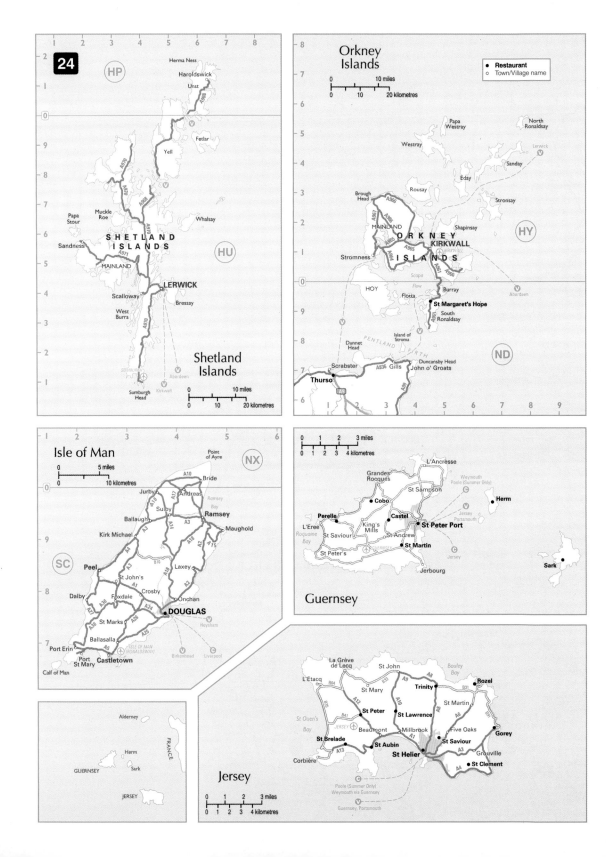

Index of Restaurants

The Automobile Association would like to thank the following photographers and companies for their assistance in the preparation of this book.

Abbreviations for the picture credits are as follows: (t) top; (b) bottom; (l) left; (r) right; (c) centre (AA) AA World Travel Library.

1 Balmer Lawn, Brockenhurst; 4 Photodisc; 16, 17 Novelli Associates Ltd; 18t, 18b AWT Restaurants; 19 The Pot Kiln; 21 Raymond Blanc; 22t Chris Terry/Tom Aikens; 25 Stockbyte; 26 David Loftus/Petersham Nurseries; 27 Philip Hollis/Petersham Nurseries; 28-31 Julian Castaldi/Simon Wright; 36 Photodisc; 38 Photodisc; 39 AA/C.Sawyer; 40/1 AA/M. Kipling; 219 AA/J.A.Tims; 480/1 AA/David W. Robertson; 546/7 AA/W.Voysey; 574 AA/G.Mundy; 580 AA/S.McBride.

All other photographs in the first section of this guide are supplied by the AA World Travel Library.

Every effort has been made to trace the copyright holders, and we apologise in advance for any accidental errors. We would be happy to apply the corrections in the following edition of this publication.

Please send this form to:
    Editor, The Restaurant Guide,
    Lifestyle Guides,
    The Automobile Association,
    13th Floor, Fanum House,
    Basingstoke RG21 4EA

    or fax: 01256 491647
    or e-mail: lifestyleguides@theAA.com

Please use this form to tell us about any restaurant you have visited, whether it is in the guide or not currently listed. Feedback from readers helps us to keep our guide accurate and up to date. Please note, however, that if you have a complaint to make during a visit, we strongly recommend that you discuss the matter with the restaurant management there and then, so that they have a chance to put things right before your visit is spoilt. The AA does not undertake to arbitrate between you and the restaurant management, or to obtain compensation or engage in correspondence.

Date:

Your name (block capitals)

Your address (block capitals)

....

....

....

e-mail address: ....

Restaurant name and address: (If you are recommending a new restaurant please enclose a menu or note the dishes that you ate.)

....

....

....

Comments:...

....

....

(please attach a separate sheet if necessary)　　　　　　　　　　　　　　　　　　　**PTO**

We may use information we hold about you to write, e-mail or telephone you about other products and services offered by us and our carefully selected partners, but we can assure you that we will not disclose it to third parties.

Please tick here if you DO NOT wish to receive details of other products or services from the AA.

Readers' Report Form

YES   NO

Have you bought this guide before? ☐ ☐

Please list any other similar guides that you use regularly...

....

....

What do you find most useful about The AA Restaurant Guide?

....

....

....

....

Please answer these questions to help us make improvements to the guide:

What are your main reasons for visiting restaurants (circle all that apply)

business entertaining   business travel   trying famous restaurants

family celebrations   leisure travel   trying new food

enjoying not having to cook yourself   to eat food you couldn't cook yourself

other ....   because I enjoy eating out regularly

How often do you visit a restaurant for lunch or dinner? (circle one choice)

once a week   once a fortnight   once a month   less than once a month

Do you use the location atlas?...

Do you generally agree with the Rosette ratings at the restaurants you visit in the guide?
(if not please give examples)...

....

Who is your favourite chef? ....

Which is your favourite restaurant? ....

Which type of cuisine is your first choice e.g. French ....

Which of these factors are most important when choosing a restaurant?

Price   Service   Location   Type of food   Awards/ratings

Décor/surroundings   Other (please state):...

Which elements of the guide do you find most useful when choosing a restaurant?

Description   Photo   Rosette rating   Price   Other..